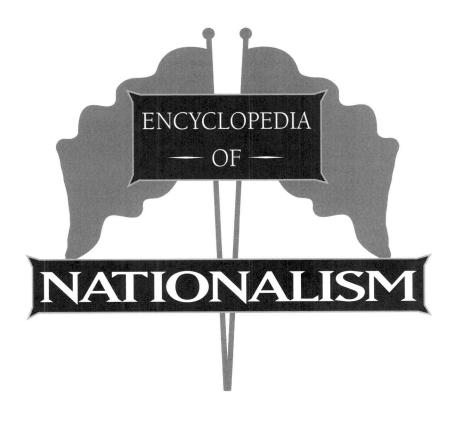

# ENCYCLOPEDIA

## — OF —

# NATIONALISM

LEADERS, MOVEMENTS, AND CONCEPTS

VOLUME 2

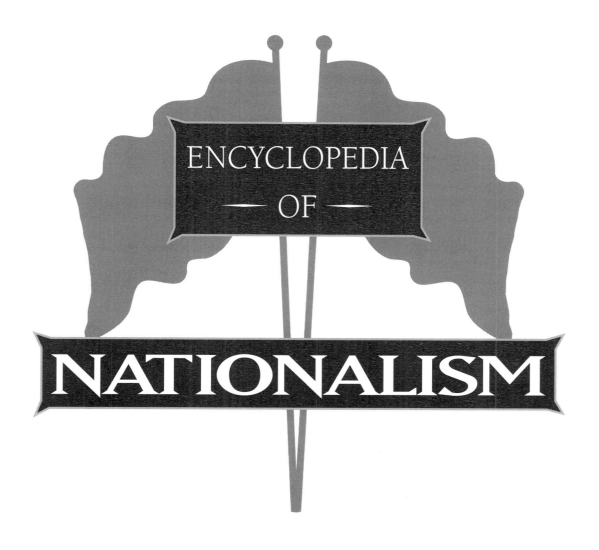

# ENCYCLOPEDIA

## — OF —

# NATIONALISM

LEADERS, MOVEMENTS, AND CONCEPTS

VOLUME 2

**ACADEMIC PRESS**

A Harcourt Science and Technology Company

SAN DIEGO    SAN FRANCISCO    NEW YORK    BOSTON    LONDON    SYDNEY    TOKYO

Academic Press
*A Harcourt Science and Technology Company*
525 B Street, Suite 1900, San Diego, California 92101-4495, USA
http://www.academicpress.com

Academic Press
Harcourt Place, 32 Jamestown Road, London NW1 7BY, UK
http://www.academicpress.com

Library of Congress Catalog Card Number: 00-102545

International Standard Book Number: 0-12-227230-7 (set)
International Standard Book Number: 0-12-227231-5 (volume 1)
International Standard Book Number: 0-12-227232-3 (volume 2)

PRINTED IN THE UNITED STATES OF AMERICA
01  02  03  04  05    EB    9  8  7  6  5  4  3  2

# CONTENTS

# CONTRIBUTORS

RAFIS ABASOV

ALFIA ABAZOVA

THOMAS AMBROSIO

MARCOS ANCELOVICI

FREDERICK F. ANSCOMBE

ALEX J. BELLAMY

MARIT A. BERNTSON

NARAN BILIK

MARK BIONDICH

JULIAN BIRCH

JACK BLOOM

CHARLES W. CAREY, JR.

ERIKA CASAJOANA

KAREN A. CERULO

SUE ELLEN CHARLTON

RICARDO CICERCHIA

JOSEPH CODISPOTI

CHRISTOPHER CONWAY

JOHN F. COPPER

JEFFREY J. CORMIER

SARAH M. CORSE

PHILIPPE COUTON

TOMAS CROWDER-TARABORRELLI

AMANDA DICKINS

WILLIAM J. DUIKER

HOWARD EISSENSTAT

E. C. EJIOGU

LINAS ERIKSONAS

RUSSELL FAEGES

MARKUS FELTEN

HANNA FREIJ

DAVID S. FREY

PETER A. FURIA

JENNIFER GARCIA

JOHN GLENN

MATTHEW M. GOLDSTEIN

JEFF GOODWIN

JENNIFER RAE GREESON

FOREST GRIEVES

ARMAN GRIGORIAN

BAOGANG GUO

MARTINE GUYOT-BENDER

ALEXANDRA HRYCAK

IMELDA HUNT

JAMES JANKOWSKI

KIRK JOHNSON

KIMBERLEY JONES

EZEKIEL KALIPENI

HILAL KHASHAN

KARI KOHL

PHILIP KOHL

CORWIN R. KRUSE

LESTER KURTZ

MARIAM KURTZ

M. BAHATI KUUMBA

SCOTT LEVI

JACOB T. LEVY

PETER H. LOEDEL

VERA LUKOMSKY

ZINE MAGUBANE

KARL MAGYAR

HISAKO MATSUO

C.E. MUDDE

JOANE NAGEL

EMIL M. NAGENGAST

CHRISTIAN NIELSEN

MARC NORDBERG

TASHA OREN

KAREN OSLUND

EDUARDO PALADIN

TIBOR PAPP

HYUN OK PARK

TIIU POHL

STEPHEN POULSON

JAAKKO PUISTO

NGAI PUN

MATTHEW RHODES

JOHN P. RICHARDSON

KEVIN ROBERTS

VICTOR ROUDEMETOF

LAURA E. RUBERTO

JASON A. SCORZA

BRENDA SHAFFER

FERAIDOON SHAMS

WILLIAM P. SIMMONS

LYNETTE P. SPILLMAN

JERRY STUBBEN

WILLIAM J. SWART

JULIET S. THOMPSON

SUSAN L. THOMPSON

WAYNE C. THOMPSON

ROBERT CHR. THOMSEN

GABRIEL TOPOR

DONNA LEE VAN COTT

BRIAN WILLIAMS

KRISTI M. WILSON

JAMES WINGATES

MARK WORRELL

PRISCILLA YAMIN

M. HAKAN YAVUZ

JOHN W. YOUNG

DANIEL ZISENWINE

# A

**ACHEBE, CHINUA** 1930–, Albert Chinualumogu Achebe, Africa's foremost novelist whose first novel, *Things Fall Apart* (1958), set in an Igbo clan at about the close of the 19th century at the time of Europe's "pacification" activities on the continent to make room for the imposition of alien rule, opened a new literary window on Africa and its cultures to the world—the book's worldwide sales figures run into several millions in several languages. In later years Achebe, who is Igbo himself, disclosed that he wrote the book in response to books on Africa by Europeans who relied on prejudices and myths about Africa circulated in Europe by travelers and amateur anthropologists to misportray Africans as savages and to denigrate their cultures. Achebe claims that such books as Joyce Cary's *Mister Johnson* (1951) and Joseph Conrad's *Heart of Darkness* (1903) are narrated in ways that control readers' sympathies and make it impossible for them to take sides with the African characters in the books. His quest to correct such misportrayals of the continent, its peoples, and their cultures has driven all of Achebe's works and has in turn placed him at the center of Africa's cultural nationalism.

Achebe continues to play a frontiers-clearing role in Africa's literary scene. His recognition and utilization of the immense cultural resources that abound on the continent in his art attest to this assertion. Achebe believes that colonialism has placed the burden and role of teacher on African writers, who must educate both their fellow Africans and non-Africans alike about Africa in their art. Achebe's four other novels—*No Longer at Ease* (1960), *Arrow of God* (1964), *A Man of the People* (1966), and *Anthills of the Savannah* (1987)—three children's books, numerous poems and short stories, and three collections of essays equally attest to his role as a consistent African cultural nationalist. Achebe is the founder of *Okike: An African Journal of New Writing* and *African Commentary: A Journal for People of African*

*Descent* (defunct). He was the founding president of the Association of Nigerian Authors.

Achebe argues that African literature does not need to pander to the paradigm of universality in order to be relevant—that its relevance as an art form must begin with the efforts of its creators to understand their society and feel kinship with it rather than be alienated from it in the quest for universal acceptability. He insists that African literature and society must be understood together and the way to do that is to search for beneficial knowledge from works of African literature, i.e., that colonialism left otherwise viable cultures in a state of disorganization and forced the people to embrace views and attitudes that have threatened their survival. Achebe's nationalism is not restricted to the arena of culture and art. In 1967 he suspended his art interests and joined hands with the rest of his people in their quest to secede from Nigeria as the Republic of Biafra on account of the pogrom they suffered at the hands of a rampaging mob in Northern Nigeria. (The social anthropologist Simon Ottenberg, who has written and published extensively on aspects of Igbo culture, once described Achebe as "a writer who moved from being a literary figure to being a political individual.")

Achebe is emeritus professor of literature at the University of Nigeria, Nsukka, where he taught literature for several years.

**ADAMS, GERRY** 1948–, Leader of the Irish political party Sinn Féin. As an elected member of the Northern Ireland Assembly, his supporters have lauded him for his vital contributions to the peace process in Ireland and as a politician of the people. Alternately, his critics have denounced him as a sponsor of terrorism for his links with the Irish Republican Army (IRA).

Gerry Adams was born in West Belfast, Northern Ireland. He was first elected President of Sinn Féin (Irish for "we ourselves" or "ourselves alone") in 1983. Sinn

Féin is an Irish Republican party whose primary goal is unification of the 26-county Republic of Ireland with the six counties which compose Northern Ireland. Those who support the reunification of Ireland, whether Republican or not, are termed Nationalists and are predominantly Catholic. In 1983 Adams was elected as a Member of the Parliament of Great Britain and Northern Ireland. His nationalist beliefs, and those of other Sinn Féin members, led him to refuse to take his seat at Westminster in part because of the required oath of loyalty to the Queen.

In September of 1993 Adams worked with John Hume, leader of the Social Democratic Labor Party (SDLP), toward finding a negotiated settlement for a lasting peace in Northern Ireland. He was later credited with having influenced the IRA leadership in announcing their cessation of military activities. Although this cease-fire was later to be renounced and the IRA's military campaign to resume, Adams continued to seek mechanisms by which a democratic process could lead to peace. These efforts, along with the contributions of many others, led to a public resumption of the cease-fire and the continuation of the peace process in 1996. These combined efforts led to the Good Friday Agreement.

Through his political career, critics of Adams and Sinn Féin have repeatedly sought to link him with the paramilitary activities of the Irish Republican Army. The Irish Republican Army has engaged in a paramilitary campaign to attempt to force the withdrawal of Great Britain from Northern Ireland. Because of these activities many have termed the IRA a terrorist organization. Because of Adams' Republican activities the British interned (imprisonment without trial) him in 1972. As evidence of his stature within the movement, he was subsequently released to engage in negotiations with the British regarding a cessation of violence and, later, a possible British withdrawal.

Gerry Adams was elected as a member of the Northern Ireland Assembly in landmark elections, held in June of 1998, pursuant to the terms of the Good Friday Agreement. Adams, a key participant in negotiating the terms of the Agreement, stated Sinn Féin viewed the Agreement as a steppingstone to a united 32-county Ireland and not the final peace settlement.

Gerry Adams writes a weekly column for an Irish American newspaper, the *Irish Voice,* and is the author of several books. Among his more notable writings are *Falls Memories* (1982), *Cage 11* (1990), and *Free Ireland: Towards a Lasting Peace* (1995). Books about Adams and the Republican struggle include *A Biography of Gerry Adams* by Colm Keena and *The Troubles* by Tim Pat Coogan.

**ADENAUER, KONRAD**   1876–1967, Chancellor of the Federal Republic of Germany (FRG) from 1949 to 1963. He was mayor of Cologne from 1917 to 1933, when he was removed from office by the Nazis. He was arrested in 1934 and 1944. After the Second World War he became a founding member and the first national leader of the Christian Democratic Union (CDU). He played a leading role in drawing up a new constitution for the FRG and was elected the FRG's first chancellor in 1949. He also played an important part in making Bonn, a city close to his home on the Rhine, the capital of the FRG in 1949.

Adenauer's opponent in the 1949 election was Kurt Schumacher, leader of the Social Democratic Party of Germany (SPD). Both proclaimed national reunification to be their highest priority, but Adenauer and Schumacher contrasted sharply in their views of how to achieve this end. Whereas Schumacher advocated a middle path between the Cold War superpowers, Adenauer argued that a policy of strength through integration in the Western camp was the FRG's only realistic path to national reunification. The CDU's electoral victory in 1949 meant that Adenauer's "integration ideology" became the foundation of FRG foreign policy. Under Adenauer the FRG entered NATO and, in partnership with France, became the engine of West European economic integration.

Adenauer was criticized for his autocratic leadership style. Adenauer did not trust the German populace in the realm of foreign policy making and was determined to consolidate power in the office of the chancellor. Adenauer's domestic critics described the FRG in the 1950s as a "Chancellor Democracy." In order to ensure a firm hold on FRG foreign policy, Adenauer served as his own foreign minister until 1955. The success of the FRG economy (the *Wirtschaftswunder*) in the 1950s and the solid anti-communism of the majority of West Germans allowed Adenauer to pursue his Western integrationist priorities free from any serious domestic opposition. In the 1950s the SPD repeatedly condemned Adenauer for his willingness to forego the immediate pursuit of national unity in favor of an anti-Communist devotion to the Western alliance. Kurt Schumacher labeled Adenauer the "Allies' Chancellor."

There has been considerable scholarly debate over Adenauer's true concern for national reunification. It is well known that Adenauer saw Prussia as the primary source of past German militarism and aggressive nationalism. Adenauer was a devoted Rhinelander who saw Germany's proper orientation as toward the West. His contempt for Prussia is captured in his claim that "whenever I cross the Elbe I must draw the curtains [in my train car] to avoid looking at the Asiatic Steppe." Many historians argue that Adenauer actually welcomed the 1945 division of Germany, because it created, in Adenauer's view, a new German state (the FRG) dominated by the Western, liberal, and industrial elements of Germany and free to the Eastern militarism responsible for two world wars.

Adenauer remains one of the most controversial figures of postwar German history. He dominated West German politics from the creation of the FRG until he stepped down in 1963 at the age of 87. He laid the groundwork for the FRG's Cold War pattern of multilateral and antinationalist foreign policy priorities by firmly embedding the FRG in West European and Atlantic organizations. He had priorities of national reconciliation with France and with the Jews through his support of Israel. He was also one of the staunchest European supporters of U.S. anti-Communist foreign policy.

For further reading see Hans-Peter Schwarz's *Konrad Adenauer* (Berghahn, 1995), Terence Prittie's *Adenauer* (Stacey, 1971), and Anthony Glees' *Reinventing Germany* (Berg, 1996).

**AFGHANISTAN, NATIONALISM IN**   The Republic of Afghanistan is a country in Central Asia sharing borders with Pakistan (to the south), Tajikistan, Iran, Turkemistan, Uzbekistan, and the People's Republic of China. Kabul is its capital city and has been the site of considerable violence over a long history stretching from the colonial struggles between Britain and Russia in the 19th century to the Cold War conflicts between the Soviet Union and the United States in the 20th.

Evidence of human habitation in the region dates back as early as 100,000 B.C.E. Today it has been drawn into the international scene lying, as it does, at the crossroads between the Middle East, Central Asia, South Asia, and East Asia. Before the Soviets occupied Afghanistan in 1979 the country was not widely known outside the region; indeed, some Western journalists used to refer to being sent to remote, uninteresting assignments as being "sent to Afghanistan." Since the Soviet invasion, however, Afghanistan has been in the international news frequently, although because of events that have inflicted great suffering on its people.

Early attempts at independence by Afghanistan nationalists involved a revolt in 1709 led by Mir Veys Khan against the Persian ruler of the region. His success in routing the Persians from his part of what became Afghanistan subsequently inspired his son to expand the territory, a move that was unsuccessful.

Modern Afghanistan was allowed some autonomy in the 1880s after 'Abdor Rahman Khan returned from central Asia, where he had been living in exile, proclaiming himself amir of Kabul. Although never completely colonized, Afghanistan was also not completely independent, and served as something of a buffer between British India and Russia.

In the Republic of Afghanistan (1973) Prime Minister Daud Khan initiated a series of reforms and attempted to move away from both the Soviet Union and the United States by weaving bonds with other Muslim countries. The National Assembly approved his new constitution in 1977 but a major leftist opposition movement emerged, angered with the government's corruption and nepotism.

In a successful military coup in 1978, Daud Khan and most of his family were killed, inaugurating the Democratic Republic of Afghanistan on April 27 of that year. The Soviet occupation the following year lasted until the unraveling of its empire began in 1989. However, the Soviet Union had never been successful in subduing opposition movements and guerilla activities, and Afghanistanis taught the Soviets the lesson that the Vietnamese taught the United States: even a well-armed superpower will have difficulty defeating a nationalist movement fighting in its home territory.

**AFRICAN NATIONALISM**   The historical narrative of African nationalism began at the end of 1950s, when the European imperial rule loosened its grip on the continent. The advent of independence in Ghana preceded British Prime Minister Harold Macmillan's prophetic "the wind of change is blowing throughout the continent" speech. It was in the South African Parliament on February 3, 1960, when Macmillan eloquently advocated the cause of liberation for the world's colonized peoples in general and for Africa in particular. The prescience of his metaphor in South Africa was not realized until some three decades later in the 1990s, when Apartheid collapsed. The prime minister also spoke of the "African national consciousness" and reminded his audience that, "whether we like it or not, we must all accept [independence] as a fact and come to terms with it." What followed was a period of tranquility before the storm. The process of decolonization was rather swift in character. It swept across the continent with varying speeds and signaled Africa's entry as an active participant into the international arena and hence the dawning of a new era in world history.

In the following decades of decolonization, African intellectual leaders, more adamantly than ever, rallied under the banner of nationalism. Their ideological stand on Pan-Africanism and African unity was also seen as a supranationalistic manifestation of anticolonialism and Africa for Africans sentiments. For George Padmore, one of the foremost ideologues of Africanism, "Pan Africanism [offered] an ideological alternative to Communism on the one hand, and Tribalism on the other; it [rejected] both white racialism and black chauvinism." To be sure, the African human yearnings for equality, justice, and independence did not operate in a vacuum. They were deeply rooted in the centuries-old European domination of non-European lands, peoples, and cultures.

Prior to independence, African nationalism exemplified itself in many forms. Within and outside the continent, it varied in its intensity from moderate protestation to violent and revolutionary movements against colonialism. In Algeria, Angola, Congo, Djibouti, Egypt, Eritrea, Ethiopia Guinea, Guinea-Bissau, Ghana, Kenya, Morocco, Mozambique, Namibia, Nigeria, Tanzania, Tunisia, Somalia, South Africa, Sudan, and Zimbabwe modernizing nationalism assumed divergent, yet arduous paths. Following independence, however, African nationalism lent itself to what Azikwe depicted as a framework of "mental emancipation" from the grip of colonialism. Above all, it embraced the preservation of African culture, identity, tradition, and distinctiveness.

Negritude, as both a cultural movement and a philosophy of humanism, had its birth in Paris during the 1930s and drew Senghor (future president of Senegal from 1960 to 1980) and the Caribbean intellectuals, notably Aime Cesaire, together. They romanticized the African heritage and offered a rationale for its peculiar characteristics. Senghor defined negritude as "the sum total of cultural values, which characterized black people." In large measure, African nationalism was also a manifesto of revulsion against the evils of imperial domination as expressed in the political and social thought of many Western-educated African elites. For them, the theory of the state and the modernizing nationalism included postulates on Marx and Gandhi as well as other European thinkers. And for many pioneers of independence, the implementation of the democratic single-party system offered an alternative approach to governance. In retrospect, Julius Nyerere, Kwame Nkrumah, Sekou Touré, and even Leopold Sedar Senghor sought to achieve progress and development within the context of African socialism. They advanced various theoretical justifications for the concepts of democracy, freedom, sovereignty, feudalism, federalism, and the responsibilities of the state.

By historical standards, however, the European colonization of Africa and its partition under the provisions of the Berlin Conference in the 1880s was of relatively short duration. One would hardly have expected that the European colonial involvement in Africa would end as it did some eight decades following the partition. But characteristic features of the 19th century were different from those of the 20th. The political tempo of the former was one of relentless domination, and that of the latter was benign liberation. In essence, the 20th century parameters of power witnessed two great world wars and the emergence of East–West polarization. The economic strains of the two world wars were too enormous and left their indelible mark upon the old colonial empires. Moreover, the world division into two hostile ideological camps of the Communist totalitarian East and the capitalist democratic West produced its own discourse on Africa. These forces both hindered and hastened the process of independence and invariably affected the nationalistic sentiments throughout the colonial settings.

The ascendancy of nationalism in Africa before and after independence assumed varying interpretations and analyses. For James S. Coleman, African nationalism was synonymous with anti-colonial movements. It traversed the "traditionalist," "modernist," and "syncretistic" paths. Lord Haily, however, in his seminal work, *African Survey* (1956), coined the term "Africanism" to define African nationalistic aspirations. Thomas Hodgkin, in his *Nationalism in Colonial Africa,* considered African nationalism to function on varied ethnolinguistic, territorial, regional, and ultimately Pan-African strata. At times, the nationalistic movements in lower levels tended to generate conflict with the ideal objectives of the higher or Pan-Africanist level. Finally, for Gabriel Almond and James S. Coleman, in the *Politics of the Developing Areas* (1971), "African nationalism emerged to challenge, compete with, and ultimately displace" the vital colonial socializing structures. These structures included political, educational, religious, and other social organizations. In recent decades, many African countries have undergone the triumph and defeat of nationalistic fervor, changing in the process the loci of the centralizing state power and patrimonial state.

For additional sources see Claude Ake's *Democracy and Development in Africa* (Brookings Institution, 1995); N. Chezan, R. Mortimer, J. Ravenhill, and D. Rothchild's *Politics and Society in Contemporary Africa* (Lynne Rienner, 1993); Basil Davidson's *Black Man's Burden: Africa and the Curse of the Nation-State* (James Currey, 1992); Maxrui Ali's (Ed.) *General History of Africa* (University of California Press, 1993); and Leopold Sedar Senghor's "Negritude: A Humanism of the Twentieth Century" in *The African Reader: Independent Africa* (Vintage Books, 1970).

**AFRIKANER NATIONALISM**  The Afrikaner people in South Africa are made up primarily of Dutch and French Huguenots, although they include other peoples as well. They arrived in the latter part of the 17th and the early part of the 18th centuries. Their emergence as a people was a process that took place in response to conflicts with other groups, notably African tribes, against which they fought as they expanded into the area, and the British Empire, which became hegemonic. When the British gained control of the original Cape Colony at the beginning of the 19th century, they began placing controls on the farmers. The most onerous of these from the point of view of the Boers (the word for farmers in Afrikaans, the language of the Afrikaners, who were, for the most part, a rural people) was the abolition of slavery without fully compensating the slave owners for their losses. The controls also included ordinances that abolished the legal distinctions between Africans and whites, while only English speakers were allowed to fill official posts, including serving on juries. These policies all caused harm to the Afrikaners.

Several thousand of them responded by leaving settled areas and heading north and east into the hinterland in what became known in Afrikaner mythology as the Great Trek. In one case, a large group of settlers came into conflict with the expanding Zulu tribe in the Battle of Blood River in which a relatively small group of Afrikaners fought a huge Zulu war party. They managed to prevail, thanks to the guns they bore. The unexpected victory from this battle became one of the key events to which the Afrikaners looked back and from which they created the mythology of their special place. They compared themselves to the Jews in the Bible, and thought of themselves as a "chosen people," whose sufferings would eventually be redeemed.

The settlers came to see themselves as no longer European, but a legitimate part of the African continent—hence the name "Afrikaners," which, by the end of the 18th century, had become well established. They formed two republics, the Transvaal Republic and the Republic of the Orange Free State, which remained independent until the discovery of gold in 1886. At that point the British poured in, and by 1900 the two states had been declared British territory. A brutal war ensued in which Britain carried out a scorched earth policy and placed tens of thousands of prisoners, including women and children, into concentration camps, where some 26,000 died of the diseases that swept through the camps. Faced with these terrible circumstances, the Afrikaners surrendered, and their republics were incorporated into the Union of South Africa, which was dominated by the British, who gained most of the wealth in the Union even though they remained a minority. This traumatic experience helped deepen the sense of peoplehood that the Afrikaners held of themselves.

Following the war, there was a serious debate among Afrikaners concerning which route to take now: whether they should organize themselves against all others, including the British, or whether they should join with the British. This issue was fought out in elections in 1920 in which Jan Smuts, the leader of the South African Party, which pressed the amalgamationist trend, was victorious over the Afrikaner-based Nationalist Party, which insisted that "by God's honor" it would "never" lose itself. Smuts' support came primarily from the cities, where the Afrikaner population was relatively small.

Now came the period in which these tales of the "holy period" of Afrikanerdom were developed. In 1913, a monument was dedicated to the women and children who died in the concentration camps in the war, and in 1938 a monument to the Great Trek was begun. Both of these became major points of pilgrimages, which were supplemented by gatherings of Afrikaners throughout the country on December 16, the anniversary of the Battle of Blood River, to renew their covenant with God.

One of the key issues around which Afrikaner nationalism was organized was to elevate the status and use of the Afrikaans language, which had not been used by educated Afrikaners, and had not been a language with a literary status. D. F. Malan, one of the leaders of this movement, insisted, "Raise the Afrikaans language to a written language, make it the bearer of our culture, our history, our national ideals, and you will raise the People to a feeling of self-respect and to the calling to take a worthier place in world civilization." Though English was the language of public life, the Afrikaners insisted that Afrikaans be the language for their church services.

Nonetheless, some Afrikaner leaders joined with the British to form a joint, white party: the United Party. Those who refused to take such a step felt that to do so would mean the end of the distinctive Afrikaner identity. They demanded political independence and economic solidarity to close the gap with the British (who enjoyed as much as a three to one advantage in incomes) and a cultural policy that emphasized the use of the Afrikaans language together with separate Afrikaner organizations.

Those pushing for a separate Afrikaner identity organized the idea of a 100-year commemoration of the Great Trek in 1938. For this purpose, replicas of the wagons used a century earlier were created. They traveled from town to town, organizing rallies that stressed the need for Afrikaner unity, with meetings around campfires attended by hundreds and thousands. This movement led people to adopt the dress and styles of their forebears. The journey culminated in a huge rally at the planned site of the monument to the trekkers, where some 100,000 have been estimated to have gathered. While there are differing estimates of how significant an impact these events had on the Afrikaner *Volk*, one prominent historian recalled that "every Afrikaner I interviewed, of whatever political persuasion, recalled the events and activities of the 1938 centenary with deeply personal intensity."

In the 20th century many *Boers* began moving into the cities; whereas in 1910 only 10 percent of Afrikaners were urban, by 1960, 75 percent were. As they started moving in after 1910 and into the 1920s, most of them got jobs on the lowest rungs. This situation put them at odds with the British, who owned and managed the businesses, and forced them to compete with the unskilled black labor force, whose cost was considerably below what they were willing to work for, and from whom they differed mainly in their being white. They increasingly saw their status and living standards degraded. There was some fear that they would develop a class identification and leave behind their ethnic status as central to their lives. Many of them joined the Labor Party, but that affiliation did not last for long, as they soon came to regard the party as an agent of British imperialism.

Their political leaders likened the move to the cities to the Great Trek away from the cities and suggested that now Afrikaners were even more threatened by Africans than they had been a century earlier. They began to build up institutions to improve the situation of their people. Probably the most important of these was the *Broederbond,* which knit together the Afrikaner elite, and which sought to protect the entire Afrikaner nation, including the poor, workers, and businessmen.

The outbreak of World War II, which saw the South African government enter on Britain's side, provoked the formation of a party to unite the Afrikaner people. In 1948, the National Party narrowly won the elections. The result was the transformation of the South African polity, economy, and culture. The party introduced the policy of apartheid, which systematized discrimination against nonwhites. A number of strict laws were passed classifying all citizens by race, prohibiting interracial marriages and interracial sex, segregating a host of facilities, and requiring different racial groups to live in different areas, go to different schools, and prepare for different occupations. Blacks, in particular, were di-

vided into tribal "nations" and were said to be citizens of those nations and not of South Africa, and therefore to have no political or economic rights in South Africa, regardless of the fact that they and their families had lived in the cities for years, or even generations. Territory was set aside that supposedly made noncontiguous pieces of territory separate countries, while reserving the best farmland for the Afrikaners. Blacks were said to be citizens of those "countries," and were only allowed to "visit" South Africa if there were jobs for them.

These laws put nonwhites at a grave disadvantage to whites and reserved special benefits for Afrikaners, especially working- and lower-class Afrikaners. Over the 45 plus years that the policy was in effect, the economic position and status of Afrikaners was extraordinarily improved, with advances in education and entry into managerial, entrepreneurial, and civil service positions. Farmers were guaranteed stable labor supplies from the Africans, while the wages they had to pay were kept low. White workers were provided with job protection from African and "colored" competitors, and they were guaranteed that blacks would not have supervisory positions over them. New businesses were begun by the state, which took an increasing share of the economy, and Afrikaners were put into the upper positions there and in the civil service. Some scholars contend that the improvement in the standard of living of the Afrikaners that these policies produced has been unrivaled in the world.

But as time passed and the position of Afrikaners improved, while that of Africans, coloreds, and Asians worsened, it became increasingly clear that the demographics boded ill for whites, whose percentage of the population grew smaller with every year. This was so despite the government's efforts to attract Europeans from Poland, Portugal, and elsewhere. Moreover, as the educational and material position of Afrikaners improved, there was less fear and defensiveness on their part, while at the same time there was growing international oppositon to the racist government policies. By the 1970s, a split was developing among Afrikaners between those who felt that the apartheid policies had to continue and their opponents, whose sense was that not to make major reforms would provoke an armed uprising which, in the long run, they must lose. The latter argued that democratic reforms were necessary to save the Afrikaner people from the inevitable ruin they were facing.

In 1982, the prime minister, P. W. Botha, announced a new constitution which would establish a presidency and three houses of parliament: one each for whites, coloreds, and Asians, with blacks being left out. The president would create a president's council from the three houses; lest there be unity between the nonwhites and dissident white members of parliament, it was established that the majority party in the white parliament would get all the white seats, and they constituted a majority of the council. Moreover, the white house could override the others. The intent was obvious: to try to get support from the two smaller minority groups and thereby to increase the bargaining power of the whites vis-à-vis the blacks.

The program did not work; it never attained the necessary legitimacy among the nonwhites, most of whom did not participate in the elections. Meanwhile, there was increasing pressure from South Africa's main trading partners to impose sanctions against the apartheid policies. Africans and other races were organizing into the United Democratic Front, which was able to apply increasing pressure on the government. The government responded with a savage crackdown which, however, did not succeed. Meanwhile, the economy was under increasing pressure from international sanctions and a world recession in the early 1980s, which brought with it increasing inflation and decreasing productivity, while investments went elsewhere.

In 1989, Botha was succeeded by F. W. de Klerk, who soon released Nelson Mandela, the leader of the African National Congress (ANC), who had been in prison more than a quarter century; he also repealed most of the apartheid laws. In 1994, new elections were held. The ANC won 63 percent of the vote and Nelson Mandela became the new president of the country.

**AITMATOV, CHINGIZ** 1928–, Kyrgyz writer and politician, born in December 1928 in the Kyrgyz village of Sheker in the Kirov district, then the Kyrgyz Soviet Republic. He was the son of one of the leading Kyrgyz Communists who was repressed during the Stalinist purges of 1937.

In 1942, at the age of 14, he started work in his village. He then studied at the Kyrgyz Agrarian Institute, where he began to write short stories. In 1956–1958 he attended the Gorky Literary Institute (Moscow). In 1959 he joined the Communist Party and worked as a correspondent for the prestigious newspaper *Pravda* in 1959–1989, Aitmatov was the People's Deputy of the Supreme Soviet (Soviet Parliament); he was also a member of the Central Committee of the Communist Party. Since November 1990, he has been ambassador to Luxembourg.

However, it was Aitmatov's literary works that won him the reputation of one of the most distinguished non-Russian authors writing in Russian. His early writings combined the delicate psychological portrait with the magical culture, landscape, and pastoral lifestyle of the traditional Kyrgyz society [*Tales of Mountains and Steppes* (1962, translataed in 1969); *Farewell, Gulsary!* (1966, 1970); and *The White Steamship* (1970, 1972)]. The stories *Dzhamilyia* (1958) and *Pervyi Uchitel* (1962) were screened and became classics of the Kyrgyz cinema.

Aitmatov was the first Kyrgyz author to raise the appreciation of traditional Kyrgyz folklore to the level of philosophical analysis. In his later writings, Aitmatov has remained faithful to his early themes while adding fresh nuances. His writing gravitates toward mystical imagery and philosophical parable. Aitmatov combines the traditional images of Kyrgyz folklore with motives of classical world literature within the context of precipitous social cataclysms [*The Day Lasts More Than a Hundred Years* (1980, 1983); *Plakha* (1986); and *Tavro Kasandry* (1977)]. Most of his novels, which were screened by the Kyrgyz film studio, have had a powerful impact on the formation of the Kyrgyz *Weltanschauung*.

Aitmatov remains one of the most popular writers and politicians in post-Soviet Kyrgyzstan. He was the person who suggested the candidacy of Akayev for the presidency in Kyrgyzstan in October 1990. He also supported the moderate nationalism of Akayev against the extreme nationalists during debates on the Law on Languages and other issues in the 1990s.

In the former Soviet Union and in present-day CIS, Aitmatov is one of the most celebrated non-Russian writers. He has won wide international recognition and his short stories and novels have been published in 130 languages with a total circulation of 40 million copies.

For further reading see *Myth in the Works of Chingiz Aitmatov* by N. Kolesnikoff (University Press of America, 1999) and *Parables from the Past: The Prose Fiction of Chingiz Aitmatov* by P. Joseph Mozur (Pitt Series in Russian and East European Studies, no. 22, 1995).

**AKAYEV, ASKAR** 1944–, Kyrgyz politician and scientist, the first president of the Kyrgyz Republic. Akayev was born in November 1944 in Kyzyl-Bairak in the Kemin District, then the Kyrgyz Soviet Republic. After completing his schooling in his native village he worked at the Frunzemash plant in Frunze (now Bishkek) for a year. He completed his university degree in 1968 and the *Kandidat Nauk* degree in 1972 at the Institute of Precision Engineering and Optics in Leningrad (now St. Petersburg). From 1972 to 1986 he lectured in Leningrad and then in Frunze. He started his political career by joining the ruling Communist Party in 1981. In 1986–1987, he served as head of the Department of

Science and Education of the Kyrgyz Communist Party Central Committee. In 1987 he was elected the vice-president, and in 1989 the president, of the Kyrgyz Academy of Science. He has authored more than 80 publications.

In 1989, Akayev was elected the People's Deputy in the Soviet Parliament, where he was a member of the Council of Nationalities. In October 1990, he was elected the first president of Kyrgyzstan by the Republic's parliament, which was confirmed by a popular vote in 1991. In 1990 and 1991, Akayev was frequently voted by the Soviet newspapers among the top 20 of the most popular politicians in the USSR.

Akayev's views on the political process and national question were formed by his personal experience as a scientist and by his experience as a member of the Soviet Parliament. The interethnic conflict in the southern part of the country in the summer of 1990 also left distinctive marks on his political attitudes. After the disintegration of the USSR, he worked to reform the political system in the republic toward one of the most democratic states in Central Asia and to ease tensions between the Kyrgyz and other ethnic groups. He vetoed a provision of the Law on Land which declared that the country's land resources are the wealth (*dostoyanie*) of the ethnic Kyrgyz. Also he has advocated the liberalization of the Law on Language and introduced Russian language as the official language of the Republic (the Kyrgyz language is the state language). The new constitution, adopted in May 1993, guarantees equal rights to all people of the state and maintains the secular nature of the Republic.

After reelection for a second term in December 1995, President Akayev, facing a growing economic meltdown, took a tougher stand toward the opposition and mass media. He also strengthened his wide-ranging powers through a referendum of 1996. Although the political opposition has often claimed that there were some authoritarian tendencies in Akayev's political attitudes, the president has preserved most of the democratic features of his policy throughout the 1990s. He supports the concept of technocratic modernization as a national unifying idea and as an alternative to extreme nationalism or traditional values.

For further reading see N. Kumar's *President Akayev of Kyrgyzstan* (New Delhi, 1998) and J. Anderson's *Kyrgyzstan* (Harwood Adademic, 1998).

**AKÇURA YUSUF** 1876–1935, One of the earliest of Turkish intellectuals to not only recognize the ideological weakness of the Ottomanism and Islamism of Sultan Abdülhamid II, but to also suggest that nationalism was the logical alternative to these. Although his conception of Turkish nationalism had an important Islamic ingredient, he fully was aware of the constitutive role of ethnicity in the construction of nationalism. Akçura's ideas on nationalism developed in Kazan, the capital of Tataristan in Russia, Istanbul, and Paris. However, his connection with Kazan was the crucial element in the formulation of his thoughts on nationalism and Islam. Akçura benefited from his experience in Kazan, where modernization and identity formation were taking place before such was occurring in the Ottoman Empire.

Akçura was born in Tataristan and moved to Istanbul and visited his country every summer vacation. Sahabeddin Mercani (1818–1889), a leading modernist religious scholar of Kazan, and Ismail Gaspirali played an important role in his understanding of the relationship between Islam and nationalism. Akçura treated Islam as a national force and used it to raise ethnic consciousness. His Russian experience made him very sensitive about the trinity of Islamic identity, Turkish ethnicity, and territoriality. In Istanbul, Akçura studied in the imperial military academy and realized the significance of the state and nationalism. He was exiled to Libya (1897) due to his political activities within the illegal Committee of Union and Progress (CUP). His friends helped him to escape from Libya to Paris. He studied political history at the École Libre and met with Serafettin Magmumi, a leading CUP nationalist theoretician. In Paris, he wrote several essays in *Sura-yi Ummet* and *Mesveret*. His master's thesis focused on the importance of nation rather than state. Akçura argued that nationalism was the only way to preserve the state and Turkish culture.

After receiving his degree at the École Libre in 1904, he went to Kazan where he wrote his most famous article, "Üç Tarz-I Siyaset" (Three Policies). In this article, Akçura examined three questions: Is the creation of an Ottoman civil nation on the basis of liberty and equality possible? Is it possible to create an Islamic state? Under what conditions can an ethnic-based Turkish nationalism emerge and take political form? After examining the weaknesses and strengths of each option, he identified ethnic-based nationalism as the most viable option. Akçura saw Islam and Turkish nationalism as different layers of identity. He, for example, pointed out, "I am an Ottoman Muslim Turk." Nevertheless, he developed two nuanced arguments about the political future of Russian Muslims and the Ottoman Empire. In the Russian Empire he emphasized the role of Islam, whereas in the Ottoman Empire he focused on Turkishness. His views crystallized in his journal *Türk Yurdu*.

In Kazan, he was elected to the First Muslim Congress held at Nizhni Novgorod in 1905. Akçura also served in the Russian Parliament (1906–1907). After the closure of the Duma, he wrote a critical booklet about the political situation in Russia and had to move to the Ottoman Empire.

After the CUP revolution (1908), Akçura was welcomed to Istanbul and he established the Turkish Society and later the Turkish Heart Association, and published *Türk Yurdu* in 1911. He tried to raise national consciousness by educating people in history and geography. He reinterpreted history to serve Turkish nationalism. Akçura had a clearer image of homeland and nation than other Ottoman intellectuals due to his Russian and European experience. History, for Akçura, was a way of thinking and mapping society on the basis of evidence deduced through a process of discovering roots and lineages of diverse pieces of information about past events. Building a nation, for Akçura, involved the manipulation of both time and space to create the frame of reference for the historical imagination.

Akçura's notion of nationalism distinguished itself through two major contributions: his elaboration of the interaction between Islam and nationalism, on the one hand, and of economic conditions and nationalism, on the other. Akçura claimed that the development of nationalism among the Muslim people would lead to consolidation of transnational Islamic solidarity. Akçura argued that national consciousness is produced as a result of profound economic changes.

There are very few studies in Yusuf Akçura. See M. Hakan Yavuz's "Nationalism and Islam: Yusuf Akçura and Üç Tarz-I Siyaset," *Oxford Journal of Islamic Studies* (1995).

## AL-AFGHANI, AS-SAYID JAMAL AL-DIN 1838–1897,

Mystery shrouds the early years of Jamal al-Din al-Afghani's life. Self-account mentions the village of Sa'dabad in Afghanistan as al-Afghani's birthplace, and Kabul as the site of his primary education. According to some Persian historians, however, al-Afghani was born in the village of As'adabad near Hamadan in western Iran. They assert that he wanted to be known as a Sunni, because he did not want to be identified with Shi'ism.

The political views of al-Afghani—self-declared foe of the British empire—and his consistent criticism of British colonial policies made his sojourns in the territories it controlled more frequent than his liking. Al-Afghani made a strong impression on numerous scholars in India and Egypt during his extended visits there. During his turbulent years of exile and acerbic criticism of Muslim incompetence and British selfishness, al-Afghani won for himself the title of a renowned 19th century Muslim reformer.

Al-Afghani was a Salafi Muslim who believed in the brotherhood of all believers, and advocated the establishment of an Islamic League for that purpose. Everywhere he went, he exhorted the faithful to rise, in order to live happily and freely. Al-Afghani condemned the oppressive rulers of the Eastern peoples for their raw exercise of authority, mainly due to ill-upbringing and poor character. He blamed them for abusing and pulverizing the people, and implored all to appreciate the importance of science and inquisitiveness for making a real change in their lives.

Al-Afghani initiated his calls for reform in the East as a Pan-Islamist, but later shifted his advocacy to Pan-Arabism when the latter began to attract attention and support in west Asia. This turnaround brought charges of opportunism against al-Afghani. In fact, his criticism of the British has been the subject of scrutiny. His attacks on the British and advice for them to get rid of their selfishness are sometimes interpreted as expressions of frustration by al-Afghani who, to no avail, counted on the British to secure for him a major political appointment in the East.

## ALEVI ORGANIZATIONS The Alevis, who compose

11 to 30 percent of Turkey's total population and spread out all over Turkey, used to be called Kizilbaş and Bektaşi and are a syncretic Muslim religious group that combines shamanistic, Christian, Shi'ite, and Turkish Sufic elements in their understanding of Islam. Different methods and contexts of Islamization of Turks have created a constant religious cleavage between Orthodox (Sunni) and syncretic (Alevi) Muslims which has traveled beyond the religious realm to the political and cultural spheres. This religious cleavage has regularly been transformed into a pattern of sociopolitical groupings. This religiocultural cleavage is crucial to the patterns of sociopolitical division in Turkish society.

The practices of Alevis are heteroclite and vary from region to region. The Alevis consider a person's inner spiritual being as equal in importance to the Koran. There is no fixed site or place of worship in Alevism because, they argue, there is no single way of reading and disciplining human practices. The Alevis call on members to internalize faith and control their hands, language, and sexuality. One characteristic of Alevi belief is that it is based on oral culture narratives, poems, songs, legends, stories, and popular sayings. Due to state oppression, the Alevi community institutionalized its religious authority through kinship and narrative stories. These narratives, folk songs, and poems articulate a code of ideal Alevi conduct. In daily practice, Turkish Alevi speak Turkish, and Kurdish Alevi usually speak Zaza or Kirmanji (Kurdish dialects), but for both the liturgy is in Turkish. Most Alevis accept heredity as the basis for their identity: one is born an Alevi.

Some symbols of Alevi identity are the *saz* (Anatolian musical instrument), the *cem* (Alevi gathering for religious festivals and conflict resolution), and the *dede* (a spiritual leader). Some Alevis accept the religious authority of the dede—itinerant holy men who control esoteric knowledge. The kin-based religious leadership remained at the center of Alevi practices until print-based culture and universal education became the dominant medium for constructing knowledge.

In the Ottoman Empire, the Alevi community was viewed as a fifth column of Safavid Iran and treated as blasphemers and heretics. The Alevis were targets of frequent massacres by the central government, which forced them to retreat to small communities in the mountainous areas of Turkey. The state persecution compelled the Alevi community to utilize poetry and music more than printed text to maintain their communal faith and identity. The collective identity forged through isolation played a key role in maintaining the boundaries of the community through dissimulation as a way of overcoming Sunni prejudices. Thus, the boundaries of identity were determined by outside threats rather than by a shared code of conduct. This communal experience of oppression at the hands of the Ottoman state made the Alevi community a supporter of Kemalist reforms, which aimed at instituting a more secular policy.

Due to Sunni-based Islamic revival in the late 1950s, the Alevis formed a separate confessional Unity Party of Turkey in 1966. During the 1970s, the left-leaning groups saw the Alevis as a group susceptible to secular-progressive Marxist ideas. The heterodox interpretation of Islam by the Alevis and their collective suffering were articulated in folk music and poetry, which became associated with left-wing ideas. This association of "leftist" ideas with Alevi culture provided an opportunity for conservative Sunni groups to charge that the Alevis were "Communist." Thus, the Alevi community moved in the late 1970s from being the ally of secular forces to being a "Communist threat." This, in turn, made the Alevis a target of communal pogroms in 1978–1979.

The 1980 military coup introduced Sunni Islam-based Turkish nationalism as a new force against Kurdish and Alevi attempts to keep the nation together. This Islamization of Turkish nationalism further alienated the Turkish Alevi community from the state. One of the major impacts of the proliferation of television and radio broadcasts, periodicals, and newspapers in the first half of the 1990s was to provide new political opportunities for Alevi intellectuals to reframe Alevi identity in terms of ethnoreligious identity. In the 1990s there were seven major Alevi magazines and a dozen radio stations seeking to raise Alevi political consciousness. Since the mid-1980s, the Alevi community has been evolving into a separate ethnoreligious community in Turkey.

For further reading see J. K. Birge's *Bektashi Sufi Order of Dervishes* (Luzac Oriental, 1937); K. K.-Bodrogi's (Ed.) *Syncretistic Religious Communities in the Near East* (Leiden, 1997); and Tord Olsson and Elisabeth Özdalga's (Ed.) *Alevi Identity* (Curzon, 1998).

## ALGERIA, NATIONALISM IN

The genesis of Algerian nationalism goes back to World War I when Algerian immigrants in France came into direct contact with democratic values and principles. Certain events coinciding with the inception and conclusion of World War II—such as increased discrimination by the European colonists against Muslims as of 1940, and the killing of thousands of them in the 1945 riots in Setif—served as a spark for the Algerian war of independence (1954–1962), which, ostensibly, brought to fruition the cause of Algerian nationalists.

Algerians' search for identity, which assumed a strong religious character, began in earnest immediately after the French occupation in 1830. Prince 'Abd al-Qadir, while accepting French control of important coastal parts of Algeria, set up an independent state on much of the Algerian soil during the period of 1832–1839. Finally, he surrendered to the French in 1847, who eventually exiled him to Damascus.

Encouraged by the consequences of the Franco–Prussian War of 1870–1871, which eliminated French domination in central Europe, the Berbers of Kabylia unsuccessfully rebelled in 1871 against French occupation. The pacification of Algeria and deliberate attempts by the French to draw a wedge between Arabs and Berbers did not succeed in muting the manifestation of Algerian identity, now finding deep expression in Islam. For example, during the 1930s Shaykh 'Abd al-Hamid Bin Badis, head of the Islamic Reform Movement, strongly argued that his research had led him to conclude the presence of a viable Algerian nation. Even though his argument included valid points, especially with regard to the strength of religious sentiment and opposition to the French, the tribal and regional structure of Algerian society preempted the development of a modern-type nationalism in Algerian society.

Major obstacles stand between the Algerian people and the formation of a genuine nationalism of universalistic appeal. The Berbers who played an instrumental role in achieving independence, one that exceeds their numerical representation in Algeria's population, have not yet won recognition of their own distinctive culture and Amazighe language. The divide between the Francophones and the Arabizing elements in Algeria polarizes the country's fragile politics. The failure of the developmental efforts of the ruling National Liberation Front (FLN) and the challenge presented by the country's myriad religious groups, namely, the Islamic Salvation Front (FIS), further complicate Algeria's social, political, and ethnic dilemma. Not before the antagonistic groups reach agreement on outstanding divisive issues can one talk about a mainstream Algerian nationalism.

**ALIYEV, HEYDAR** 1923–, Azerbaijani statesman, leading political figure in Azerbaijan in the post-World War II period, native of the Nakhichevan region, which has been his primary political base. Heydar Alirza oglu Aliyev has served since October 1993 as the Republic of Azerbaijan's second elected president in the post-Soviet period. In November 1992, Aliyev founded the Yeni (New) Azerbaijan political party.

During the Soviet period, Aliyev held a variety of positions in the party and security apparatus of Azerbaijan, including chief of the KGB in the republic and first secretary of the Communist Party Central committee of Soviet Azerbaijan (1969–1982). Aliyev was the first Azerbaijani to be elected to the Soviet Politburo, where he served as candidate from 1976 and as a full member from 1982 until his removal in 1987 by Mikhail Gorbachev.

Aliyev's role in the contemporary Azerbaijani national movement is subject to controversy. Advocates of Aliyev point to his contribution during the Soviet period in preventing emigration of ethnic Azerbaijanis from the republic by thwarting Moscow's intentions to attract "surplus labor" to Russia, as well as his limited successes in establishing industries in Azerbaijan and the improvements in the economy of the republic that occurred under his reign. Furthermore, defenders cite Aliyev's part in the posthumous rehabilitation of important Azerbaijani cultural figures such as playwright Husein Javid, and his calls for strengthening ties with Azerbaijanis in Iran, such as in 1981 during Soviet Azerbaijan's Seventh Republic Writers' Congress in Baku. In addition, under Aliyev's leadership, the region of Nakhichevan rejected, on the eve of the Soviet breakup, the referendum on the continuation of the union.

In contrast, critics of Aliyev deny that he played an important role in promoting Azerbaijani nationalism, referring to his past as KGB head, his infamous public praises of Leonid Brezhnev and of Moscow's policies while he served as a Communist Party official, and his oppression of Azerbaijani nationalist figures during the Soviet period.

As president of the independent Republic of Azerbaijan since late 1993, Aliyev has strived to strengthen the country's independence and stability and conducted the foreign policy of the state in a manner which prevents reliance on any one of Azerbaijan's neighbors. Aliyev has adopted nationalist rhetoric and is promoting the growth of Azerbaijani culture and language use in the Republic of Azerbaijan.

For further reading see Audry Alstadt's *Azerbaijani Turks* (Hoover Institute, 1992).

**ALLENDE, SALVADOR** 1908–1973, President of Chile from 1970 to 1973. Born in Valparaiso of an affluent family, Allende attended public schools and graduated from the University of Chile with a medical degree in 1932. During his adulthood he became a Mason.

Allende was attracted to socialist doctrine during his youth. He participated in university politics and in 1933 was a founder of the Socialist Party. He was elected to the Chamber of Deputies in 1937, and he served as minister of health (1939–1942) in the Popular Front government of Pedro Aguirre Cerda. As a senator (1945–1969), he gained a reputation as a master in congressional procedure and soared to the presidency of the Senate (1965–1969). Allende served twice as secretary-general for the Socialist Party.

Allende ran for the presidency of Chile four times. In 1952 he garnered only 5.4 percent of the vote. In 1958 and 1964 he ran as the candidate of the Popular Action Front (FRAP), which was founded in 1956 to unite the Communist, Socialist, and smaller leftist parties. With coalition support, Allende received 28.9 percent of the vote in 1958. The radical movement of Chilean politics in the wake of the 1959 Cuban Revolution raised expectations of an Allende victory in the 1964 presidential election. To prevent that possibility, the Reactionary and Liberal parties broke their alliance with the Radical Party and threw their support to the moderate Christian Democrat Eduardo Frei. After an intense campaign featuring CIA financing and scare tactics paralleling Allende with Cuban president Fidel Castro, Frei won a landslide with 55.6 percent of the vote to Allende's 38.6 percent. Throughout the Frei administration, Allende was the most outspoken leftist calling for more social and economic reform.

The 1970 presidential election offered Chileans clear choices. Reacting to Frei's reforms, the conservatives reorganized as the National Party and chose ex-president

Jorge Alessandri as its nominee. The Christian Democrats endorsed the left-winger, Radomiro Tomic. Allende was the candidate of Popular Unity (UP), a new coalition of the Socialists and Communists and four non-Marxist parties, including the historic Radical Party. Allende won by a whisker: he received 36.5 percent of the vote to Alessandri's 35.2 percent and Tomic's 28.0 percent. After two months of U.S.-orchestrated sabotage to block congressional ratification of the popular election and to instigate a military coup, Salvador Allende took office on November 3, 1970.

Allende's election fixed the world's attention on Chile. Allende had promised to move Chile rapidly toward socialism through the acceleration of agrarian reform and extensive nationalization in key economic sectors. His first year in office was highly successful in meeting these objectives and in building popular support. Thereafter, mounting problems began to plague his government, compounding the difficulties imposed by opposition control of Congress and the judiciary. By 1971's end, ballooning inflation, the exhaustion of foreign currency reserves, and boycott of investment in the private sector had emptied out the economy. Meanwhile, the Christian Democrats and the National Party formalized an anti-UP alliance, the Nixon administration stepped up its destablization campaign, and critical divisions within the UP and Allende's own Socialist Party began to surface.

Although the pace of reform rose dramatically under the UP, popular expectations rose faster, resulting in widespread extralegal worker occupations of haciendas and factories. Torn between his legal obligations and his commitment to the *pueblo,* Allende vacillated on the wave of takeovers; he lost crucial middle-class support by appearing soft on the rule of law. The opposition struck a major blow in an October 1972 "bosses' strike." Called by the *gremio* (GUILD) movement, a broad coalition of business and professional groups, the strike paralyzed the economy, revealed the government's vulnerability, and forced Allende to bring military officers into his cabinet. From this point forward, confrontation escalated and much of the opposition embraced the goal of overthrowing the government.

Despite the growing polarization and the rise of violence, Allende attained an impressive record of reform. Under his administration, the traditional rural estate virtually ceased to exist, the state took control of the "commanding heights" of the economy, and progress was made in the redistribution of wealth. The final test of UP popularity was the March 1973 parliamentary election. The UP received 44 percent of the vote, down from the 49.7 percent it had won in the April 1971 municipal elections but still 7.5 percentage points above the 1970 presidential vote total. Nevertheless, the UP's failure to achieve a congressional majority and the opposition's failure to obtain the two-thirds majority necessary to impeach the president signaled three and a half more years of conflict before the 1976 presidential election. A second gremio strike took place in July and August of 1973. With the country in chaos and the government near collapse, the military staged a bloody coup on September 11. Salvador Allende, otherwise known to the indigent population of Chile as *compañero presidente* (companion president), died in the Palacio de la Moneda while it was under military attack. The overthrow and death of Allende marked the end of democratic Chilean tradition and the beginning of a sanguinary military dictatorship that killed over 3000.

**ALSACE, NATIONALISM IN** Administrative region located in northeast France along the Rhine River that borders the present state of Germany. It comprises the two *départements* of Bas-Rhin and Haut-Rhin, with a population of around two million. Strasbourg is the region's administrative capital. Alsace is often considered a religious, linguistic, cultural, and political maze. Its currently used languages include German, French, and several variations of Alsatian dialects such as high and low Alemanic. Religious communities comprise Protestants, Catholics, and Jews. Culturally, Alsace has been strongly influenced by France and by Germany who both directly and indirectly, and politically and culturally, have at one moment or another claimed the region as their own.

Alsace has been at the heart of ongoing controversies between France and Germany that started with the conflicting Roman and Germanic influences at the beginning of the first millennium. The region became a French territory for the first time when Louis XIV took it as a prize at the end of the Thirty Years' War. At that time, it was predominantly Protestant and using Germanic language, although the region's elite soon started to use French as its main language.

Along with the Lorraine département of Moselle, Alsace was annexed by the German Empire at the end of the Prussian War in 1871 as part of the Treaty of Frankfurt. French language was then prohibited, the population was pronounced German in nationality, and the whole administration and education system switched to a Germanic one. Following the annexation, Alsatian disposition toward Germany went from negative because of the destruction of Strasbourg, and especially of its German-built cathedral, by Prussian armies, to neutral during a period popularly called "cemetery peace," and finally to frank anti-Germanism, in spite of the cultural and economical prosperity and relative autonomy it had attained.

In 1918, at the end of World War I, Alsace became once again a French territory. The population took on the French nationality and the official language was once more French. World War II brought more instabilities. The Nazis reclaimed Alsace as German, imposing German as the official language, until 1945 when Alsace was reintegrated into the French territory. Alsace strongly supported the politics of General de Gaulle after the Liberation. In recent years, the extreme right-wing party *Le Front National* has found many supporters among the Alsatian population.

Alsatians' fluctuating relationship and allegiance to one nation-state or the other reflects the complexity of the region's history. French historians commonly emphasize Alsace's positive disposition toward France, a sentiment that is often related to both 1918 and 1945 French victories over Germany and to the myth of France as a united and indivisible nation. French patriotism was, for example, quite blatant in Alsatian children's literature written in the aftermath of the annexation of Alsace by Germany, such as in *La dernière leçon de français* by Alphonse Daudet (1870), *Le Tour de France raconté par deux enfants* by Bruno (1883), and *L'Histoire d'Alsace racontée aux enfants d'Alsace et de France par l'oncle Hansi* by J. J. Waltz (1912).

It is clear that both France and Germany have always had their opponents and partisans in the region. However, dividing the Alsatian population into two separate camps, pro-France or pro-Germany, reflecting the French–German conflicts, would be inadequate. Indeed, such dichotomy along national boundaries ignores the cultural diversity that makes the region's identity so specific. The strengthening of the Economical European Community is currently encouraging economical and cultural cooperation of Alsace with both Germany and France.

For further reading see Bonnie Menes Kahn's *My Father Spoke French. Nationalism and Legitimacy in Alsace* (Garland, 1990); Jean-Claude Richez and Alfred Wahl's *La vie quotidienne en Alsace entre France et Allemagne. 1850–1950* (Hachette, Paris, 1993); and Bernard Vogler's *Histoire politique de l'Alsace* (Editions la Nuée Bleue, Strasbourg, 1995).

**AMBEDKAR, B. R.** 1891–1956, Indian nationalist and spokesman for the rights of untouchables. Born in the Indian state of Madhya Pradesh, Brimrao Ramji Ambedkar studied at Bombay University and received a Ph.D. at Columbia University and a law degree at the University of London. Called to the Bar in London, he later practiced law in the High Court of Bombay (now Mumbai).

Both Ambedkar's father and his grandfather had served in the Indian army, and his family was economically comfortable. When their son was young, the family moved to Bombay from their village in order to enable him to attend better schools. However, despite his family's accomplishments and his own academic achievements, Ambedkar was often subjected to the same kind of discrimination as all untouchables of his generation.

Ambedkar returned from his education in the United States and the UK in 1923 with a commitment to improving the lives of untouchables and a belief that India should develop its own form of parliamentary democracy. As a result of his participation in the 1930–1932 London Round Table Conferences called by the British government to negotiate political reforms in India, Ambedkar emerged as India's acknowledged leader of the untouchables. At the second conference in 1931, he came into conflict with another brilliant, British-educated Indian lawyer—Mohandas K. Gandhi. Ambedkar took the position that untouchables should have separate electorates for their communities, while Gandhi believed that as Hindus, untouchables (whom he called *Harijans,* "children of God") were not entitled to separate representation. The conflict over elections reflected different philosophies of reform, with Gandhi believing that Hinduism could be reformed to eliminate untouchability and the abuses against untouchables, and Ambedkar insisting on the necessity of legal redress of grievances backed by the political power of the aggrieved. Implied also in this conflict was a distinction between Gandhi's conception of the Indian nation which, despite its multiple communities, he claimed to represent, and Ambedkar's belief in the fundamentally divisive nature of caste which called for separate political leaderships and representation.

During his political life, Ambedkar served in the cabinets of both British India and independent India; he founded three political parties, and wrote nearly 20 books and major political tracts. Elected to chair the drafting committee of the Constituent Assembly in 1947, Ambedkar abandoned many of his radical convictions as he steered the Assembly through the process of drafting India's constitution. His contributions can be seen in some of the special constitutional provisions for social equality for the Scheduled Castes (the term for untouchables first used by the British).

In his writings on caste, Ambedkar argued that caste (and hence untouchability) was an integral part of

Hinduism. Toward the end of his life, he became personally more committed to Buddhism and in 1956 led a mass conversion of some 200,000 of his followers to Buddhism.

Despite numerous continuing examples of discrimination and violence against India's lowest castes—now often referred to as *dalits* (the "oppressed" or "downtrodden")—Ambedkar's legacy may be seen in the political mobilization of former untouchables throughout India, and in the election of India's first dalit President in 1997, K. R. Narayanan, as well as a dalit speaker of the Lok Sabha, the lower house of the Indian parliament, in 1998.

There is a prolific literature on Ambedkhar, published notably in India. Among the better contemporary treatments are two studies from Sage, M. S. Gore's *Social Context of an Ideology: Ambedkar's Political and Social Thought* (1993) and Gail Omvedt's *Dalits and the Democratic Revolution: Dr. Ambedkar and the Dalit Movement in Colonial India* (1994). Also see Ambedkar's own writings, such as his 1936 *Annihilation of Caste,* reissued in New Delhi by Arnold (1990), and *The Untouchables,* first published in 1948 (Amrit, New Delhi).

## AMERICA FIRST MOVEMENT

A political movement in the United States in the period between the outbreak of World War II and U.S. entry into the war in December 1941. Formally the America First Committee, the movement had the immediate goal of blocking U.S. aid to the Allies via the Lend-Lease program and other such measures, and had the ultimate goal of maintaining U.S. neutrality in the war.

America First was said to have a membership of 800,000 at the height of its activity, including such prominent Americans as Senator Gerald Nye and General Robert Wood. Its most famous and most controversial participant was the aviator Charles A. Lindbergh, whose views on the European conflict were thought by his critics to be influenced by anti-Semitism and by tolerance for, or even approval of, the Nazi regime in Germany.

America First disbanded after the Japanese attack on Pearl Harbor and the subsequent U.S. declaration of war. The demise of America First certainly did not mark the end of organized movements opposing U.S. involvement in foreign wars, as the antiwar efforts of the Vietnam era demonstrate. However, it can be argued that America First represents the "last gasp" of traditional American isolationism on a large scale, since from Pearl Harbor onward through the Cold War to the present day, no comparable group has emerged on the U.S. scene.

## AMERICAN INDIANS AND NATIONALISM

Pan-Indian, or nationalist, tendencies have provided an overrunning thread in American Indian history from the 17th century to the present. The Iroquois League of the 17th and 18th centuries, the Ghost Dance of the 1880s and 1890s, and the American Indian Movement of the 1960s and 1970s are some examples of American Indian nationalism involving intratribal unity on a large scale.

In the early 17th century, New England tribes formed unofficial unions in defense against Europen colonists' encroachment on their lands. The Pequot War (1636–1637) and King Philip's War (1675–1677) saw several Indian bands fighting together against English colonies. Pueblo Indians revolted against the Spanish in New Mexico in 1680. The Iroquian-speaking peoples in what is now central New York State formed a powerful buffer between imperial ambitions of the British and the French during the 17th century. The five tribal groups—Seneca, Oneida, Onondaga, Mohawk, and Cayuga—formed a confederacy—an Iroquois League—as an adaptive response to a series of cultural ordeals stemming from the colonial invasion. The league had no coercive diplomatic unity nor central political authority, yet it managed to effectively create diplomatic relations with the English and the French. The aim of the confederacy was to keep tribal independence intact. In a 1701 treaty this goal was temporarily achieved. The Tuscaroras joined the league in 1713. The American Revolutionary War of 1775–1783 caused the destruction of the Iroquois League, as the United States treated confederated tribes as enemies.

Pontiac's Rebellion in 1763 was the result of a brief unity around the vision that all land would be returned to the Indians through divine intervention. The Shawnee brothers Tecumseh and Tenskwatawa (the Prophet) were the leaders of another powerful Indian nationalist movement in 1805–1813. Both brothers saw the nature of the threat to the Indian way of life, and tried to prepare people for its defense. The Prophet had a spiritual vision in 1805, in which he saw the white men disappear after Indians had reformed themselves in order to restore harmony and order. His doctrine fits into a general pattern of revitalization movements before and after him. Tecumseh, on the other hand, campaigned to arouse Pan-Indianism in order to lead a military force against the colonists. After the Battle of Prophetstown in 1811, he traveled from what is now Ohio as far as Georgia and Alabama to meet the Creeks and Cherokees. He believed that joining the British in the war of 1812 would help the Indian cause. However, his dreams of Indian sovereignty died with him in the Battle of Thames (Ontario) in October 1813. After this battle, the

Indian movement ended, and the Prophet's spiritual emphasis also lost momentum.

Tecumseh's visit to the Creeks came at an opportune time. The Creeks were just going through a revivalist movement, and responded with religious vision and creativity to colonial invasion. They felt that they could achieve a new collective identity and purge their lands of colonizers. The various Muskogean-speaking groups of Alabama and Georgia linked their towns in a political confederation designed to transcend local autonomy. The Creek Confederacy was born. The confederacy was hardly united, however, and more conservative bands joined General Andrew Jackson in the Battle of Horse-shoe Bend at the Tallapoosa River in 1814 to defeat the revivalist forces.

Like the Creeks, the Cherokees passed a constitution to appear civilized and to maintain independence. Sequoyah also invented the Cherokee alphabet to create literacy. All southeastern tribes went through cultural changes to accommodate white arguments against savages. All these efforts were essentially nationalist, but managed to stave off the white pressure only temporarily. After the removal to the Indian Territory (Oklahoma) in the late 1830s, however, the southeastern tribes kept looking for an Indian commonwealth.

Wovoka, a Nevada Paiute from the Walker River area, had spiritual visions in 1889. He started to preach for the disappearance of the white man, the reappearance of the buffalo, and the return of the hunting lands for the Indians. Wovoka's message spread like a wildfire, as American Indians were at their nadir at this time, forced to suffer in the reservations without adequate rations or means of subsistence. The Ghost Dance was born. Another religious form of Pan-Indianism, it had especially strong followings in the Great Plains. Old Lakota leader Sitting Bull was among the followers of this new spirituality, which helped create fear among the whites and U.S. military of the Indian upsurge. The Ghost Dance ended with the massacre at Wounded Knee in the end of December of 1890, where the U.S. army gunned down hundreds of Sioux men, women, and children.

Pan-Indianism of the early 20th century was deeply concerned with race, ethnicity, and nationality. Reform Pan-Indianism was a part of Progressive Era reforms, arguing for a pride of being an Indian and for common Indian interest and identities. The so-called Red Progressives, a small group of professional middle-class Indians drawn together by boarding-school experiences, formed a Society for American Indians in 1911, campaigning for reform, especially in education. Physicians Charles Eastman, a Dakota, and Carlos Montezuma, a Yavapai, along with Arthur Parker, a Seneca, were some of their leaders. Fraternal Pan-Indianism formed local Indian groups in the cities. Religious Pan-Indianism formed around a peyote cult. It argued for a religious freedom, and formed a Native American Church in 1918, which has remained perhaps the most popular church among Indians throughout the United States, unifying people around tribalism.

The Indian New Deal created a new basis for American Indian nationalism. Tribal groups could now form official tribal governments with constitutions and tribal courts. The National Committee of American Indians was formed in 1944. It emphasized strong tribal identification. World War II experiences, and the postwar difficulties in adapting to modern life, created an upsurge in American Indian nationalist ideas. This revitalization continued when congressional efforts to end federal responsiblity on reservations, so-called "termination," threatened the very existence of tribal groups in the United States. Termination touched a nerve, drawing Indian groups together in a concerted effort to defeat or modify the program. Additionally, increased educational opportunities with college education and urbanization, which brought Indian peoples from various tribes together, fostered intertribal identity.

A Chicago conference in June of 1961 resulted in the founding of the National Indian Youth Council, led by Clyde Warrior, a Ponca, and in the "Declaration of Indian Purpose," which called for Indians to help themselves. The era of "Red Power" started. Indians argued for the right to run their own affairs with security of their lands and rights. Red Power fits into the general pattern of the civil rights struggle of the 1960s. Pyramid Lake Paiutes of Nevada and the Taos Pueblo of New Mexico argued for their rights to water and won. Fishing rights caused a major struggle in Washington state. The American Indian Movement (AIM), founded in 1968 in Minneapolis by Dennis Banks and Clyde and Vernon Bellecourt (Anishinabeg), became a mouthpiece of American Indian nationalism. Indians of all tribes occupied Alcatraz Island in San Francisco Bay in November 1969, claiming the island was Indian land—as the U.S. government no longer needed it—and wanting to establish a permanent Indian cultural and educational center. Occupation lasted until June 1971. AIM organized a Trail of Broken Treaties to Washington, DC, in a serious attempt to reestablish a treaty-making relationship between Indians and the federal government. As the United States refused to negotiate, Indians occupied the Bureau of Indian Affairs headquarters in October 1972 for a week, declaring it "Native American Embassy." As a response to persistent racism and discrimination at the fringes of Indian reservations, AIM occupied the village of Wounded Knee—the site of the 1890 massacre—in Pine Ridge Reservation in South Dakota as a symbolic reminder of U.S. historic treatment of American Indians. They demanded the enforcement of the 1868 treaty between the Sioux and the United States; the refusal to negotiate resulted in a violent standoff, which lasted from February 28 to May 8, 1973.

Today's American Indian nationalism is most visible in tribal attempts to get more financial and juridical freedom. Casinos have become a means to gain economic wealth, which would provide means for sovereignty. At the same time, tribal identities have been strengthened through improved education. Some tribes have threatened to close all federal highways running through their reservations as a reminder of their existence.

For further reading see Hazel Hertzberg's *Search for an American Indian Identity* (Syracuse University Press, 1971); Stephen Cornell's *Return of the Native* (Oxford University Press, 1988); Alvin Josephy's *Red Power* (American Heritage Press, 1985); Paul Chaat Smith and Robert Allen Warrior's *Like A Hurricane: The Indian Movement from Alcatraz to Wounded Knee* (The New Press, 1996); David Edmunds' *Tecumseh and the Quest for Indian Leadership* (Little, Brown, 1984); and Joel Martin's *Sacred Revolt: The Muskogees' Struggle for a New World* (Beacon Press, 1991).

**AMERICAN NATIONALISM, PRE-1914** Following Hans Kohn's definition of nationalism as a feeling of supreme loyalty to the nation-state, American nationalism, then pertains to beliefs regarding loyalty to the United States. Scholars such as Hans Kohn often argue that the U.S. government institutionalized a "civic" nationalism, based on political principles such as legal and rational concepts of citizenship, rather than an "ethnic" nationalism, based on common language and cultural traditions. But clearly, the wave of nativist movements that led efforts to exclude immigrants, African-Americans, and others from political power attested to the growing strength of the resolutely nativist popular American nationalism that gradually undercut federal civic nationalism over the course of the 19th century. Thus prior to 1914, American nationalism most frequently expressed itself through "ethnic" movements to exclude categories of people deemed incapable of renouncing competing loyalties and obligations, and through "civic" movements to include categories of people who had been denied civil rights in the past.

The U.S. founders self-consciously formed the United States as a democracy devoted to liberal individualism rather than ethnic nationalist principles. They based their understanding of American nationality not on common descent or religion, and not on a unique literary or legal tradition (for the United States shared a common intellectual and cultural heritage with England), but rather on beliefs in natural rights, namely, "that all men are created equal, that they are endowed by their Creator with certain inalienable rights, that among these are life, liberty and the pursuit of happiness." Of course, not all members of the American population were granted equal rights.

As a result of widespread beliefs in the innate dependence of certain groups on others, the country's leadership denied full national membership to many groups, categorically excluding children, women, and slaves—and many others perceived as lacking in reason or incapable of exercising independent judgment. Furthermore, since independence, the U.S. government has undergone several major transformations in how it defines eligibility for citizenship. The primary impetus for these shifts has been periodic movements to exclude certain categories of immigrants considered incapable of upholding democracy. Thus, an ethnic nationalist tradition gradually emerged at the grassroots level to challenge federal civic nationalism.

The country's earliest leaders were opposed to immigration. George Washington fervently believed that immigration would have a deleterious effect on the country's national character and should be discouraged because immigrants "retain the language, habits and principles (good or bad) which they bring with them. . . . I want an *American* character, that the powers of Europe may be convinced that we act for *ourselves* and not for others." Similarly, John Adams and Thomas Jefferson both opposed immigration from absolutist monarchies because they argued that such immigrants would bring their antidemocratic beliefs to the United States and undermine the country's government.

Although many of the country's founders believed that immigration should be restricted to foster the conditions necessary for democratic rule, nonetheless, in keeping with their belief in a minimalist constitution, they did not incorporate anti-immigration legislation into the Constitution and, for decades, it remained unclear whether immigration was a federal or state domain. The first federal policy specifically targeting immigrants was the Alien and Sedition Law of June 25, 1798, which gave the president the authority to deport any alien deemed dangerous to the country's safety and peace or suspected of treason. From 1800, when this legislation expired, to 1875, there was no permanent federal legislation restricting the admission of aliens or permitting their deportation. Immigration regulation was an area of unclear jurisdiction and the subject of repeated clashes between federal and state legislators. Indeed, federal policy actively encouraged immigration to settle the country's newly acquired western territories through such legislation as the Homestead Act of 1862.

Federal restrictions on immigration first began to be introduced in the mid-19th century in response to such ethnic nationalist groups as the Native American movement, the Know-Nothing Party, and the American Protection Association. These groups argued that Catholics were a vehicle for foreign political influence because they owed allegiance to the Pope, a foreign sovereign. In several states anti-Catholic groups persuaded local politicians to pass laws barring Catholics from office and excluding unnaturalized immigrants from voting in local elections. At the federal level, pressure from anti-Catholic movements led to the first congressional investigation of immigration. But the resulting legislation excluded vagabonds and paupers deported from other countries (in other words, individuals unlikely to become independent), rather than Catholics. In response to anti-Catholic sentiment, from 1840 to 1856, the Democratic party had a special plank regarding immigration in its platform: "That the liberal principles . . . which make ours the land of liberty, and the asylum of the oppressed of every nation, have ever been cardinal principles in the democratic faith; and every attempt to abridge the present privilege of becoming citizens, and the owners of soil amongst us, ought to be resisted."

Anti-Catholic movements were unsuccessful in overturning federal civic nationalism. Soon, they were overshadowed by a new wave of ethnic nationalist groups that targeted Asian immigrants. Over the course of the 1870s, organized labor and patriotic groups in the South largely prevented freed slaves from exercising their rights, while on the West Coast, they successfully mobilized popular sentiment against Chinese immigration. These ethnic nationalist movements contended that laborers from these racial groups depressed domestic wages, as well as claiming that they carried traits and values that would corrupt the moral character of the nation. By 1879 anti-Chinese groups had achieved many of their political goals: Californian voters had passed a state-level ban on further Chinese immigration; both major national political parties had added anti-Chinese planks to their platforms; and the U.S. Congress had enacted the first act of restrictive immigration legislation—the Act of March 3, 1875—that provided for the deportation of immigrants brought to the country without their consent or for "lewd and immoral purposes." Local ethnic nationalism so fervent that it often led to lynchings gradually led to the passage of state immigration laws excluding the Chinese (and, in the South, spurred Jim Crow laws denying rights to African-Americans as a group).

Civic nationalism continued to be upheld by the federal government, but gradually, the country's leadership began to capitulate to popular anti-immigrant sentiment. Political leaders who in the past often spoke of open immigration as an expression of the country's democratic philosophy began to treat unrestricted immigration as a necessary evil, ultimately beneficial to the economic development of the country. Until 1885, the federal government continued to allow industrialists and entrepreneurs to bring cheap foreign labor to work in a variety of areas of the economy—even domains where they competed against American citizens. That year, however, evidence that foreign contract laborers were forcing down domestic wages at last led Congress to pass the Alien Contract Labor Law. Through this legislation, Congress prohibited migration to the United States under any contract for the performance of labor or services.

Federal immigration restrictions that followed were initially based on considerations of the effect immigration had on the country's economy, but gradually laws became increasingly focused on preserving the country's national character. After 1889, explicitly ethnic nationalist groups became increasingly powerful and politically influential. Pressure from these groups as well as from organized labor slowly began to erode congressional support for open European immigration.

In response to restrictionist groups and the recommendations of congressional investigations, both the Republican and the Democratic parties adopted planks at their 1892 national conventions favoring further immigration restriction. These efforts were unsuccessful until President McKinley's assassination by an eastern European anarchist alarmed leaders of Congress and led them to introduce new restrictions through the Immigration Act of 1903, which excluded the Chinese, individuals afflicted with mental or physical disease, contract laborers, felons, polygamists, prostitutes and "anarchists, or persons who believe in or advocate the overthrow by force or violence of the Government of the United States or of all governments or of all forms of law, or the assassinations of public officials."

In 1907, public pressure on the government led to a congressional investigation of the social effects of immigration from southern and eastern Europe that was designed to put to an empirical test theories that claimed that this "racial stock" was radically different from the "old stock" Americans of northwest European extraction, and hence that the two could not coexist harmoniously. The results of this investigation were interpreted by the public and by influential congressional representatives as an indication that southeastern Europeans indeed posed a threat to the country's "racial balance." Increasing public pressure was placed on Congress until the government agreed to limit further immigration in order to preserve the country's racial composition. But exclusionary movements remained largely unsuccessful in achieving their real objective of categorical restriction of all southeastern immigrants. Instead, restrictions were introduced that limited immigration numerically to preserve the country's 1890 racial composition. This signaled a dramatic reversal of the country's civic nationalist traditions.

Ethnic nationalist movements of 19th century America targeted Catholics, the Chinese, African-Americans, and, finally, southern and eastern European immigrants—newly assertive groups that were challenging the authority of locally dominant groups and possessed innate characteristics that, ostensibly, inclined them toward irrationality, could not be lost through cultural assimilation, and hence prevented members of certain populations from exercising democratic liberties responsibly. Categorical restrictions based on national character were most successful in the case of African-Americans, less successful in the case of the Chinese—who were protected by the Chinese government's threats of diplomatic repercussions—and largely unsuccessful in the case of Catholics, who were becoming increasingly politically powerful in eastern cities and states where the Catholic population was concentrated. Unrestricted immigration therefore remained the federal policy long after the emergence of a variety of anti-immigration groups, even while some groups—notably, African-Americans and women—continued to be denied political rights.

For a discussion of American anti-immigrant movements see Higham's *Strangers in the Land* (Rutgers University Press, 1988). Hans Kohn's *Idea of Nationalism* (Macmillan, 1944) and his *American Nationalism* (Macmillan, 1957) provide a useful overview of how elites in various times and places came to adopt civic as opposed to ethnic nationalism.

**AMERICAN REVOLUTION**  A late 18th century uprising by the 13 British colonies in North America that eventually formed the United States of America. It was one of the earliest and most significant nationalist oppositions to European colonialism.

In addition to the high-minded principles of freedom from tyranny and inalienable rights that inspired many subsequent nationalist struggles, the American Revolution was also about economic pragmatism. The colonists were fighting not only against tyranny but also against British taxes, an effort by Britain to monopolize settlement and trade to the west of the colonies, and the general effort by British authorities to tighten control over its colonies in North America and elsewhere in the latter half of the 18th century.

A series of acts by King George III and the British colonial adminstration angered the colonists. The Proclamation of 1763 forbid English settlement west of the Appalachian Mountains; although it was intended in part to relieve tension with the Native Americans, it provoked the colonists who wished to expand to the west. The Sugar Act of 1764 increased duties on imported sugar, textiles, coffee, wines, and other products to help pay for the French and Indian War and the cost of administering the colonies. At a Boston town meeting that same year James Otis complained of "taxation without representation" and Boston merchants later began a boycott of British luxury goods. The English Parliament countered with the 1765 Stamp Act that imposed the first direct tax on the American colonies with funds going directly to England rather than to their own American legislatures. Benjamin Franklin warned the Parliament that enforcement of the Stamp Act could lead to revolution.

A series of attacks and counterattacks ensued: boycotts of British goods, acts of defiance, and the famous Boston Tea Party (1773) were countered with British warships, the stationing of imperial troops to control the uprising, and the shooting of protesters by British soldiers (the Boston Massacre on March 5, 1770). The conflict escalated into an open rebellion by armed colonists in 1775 and a series of clashes between British and American forces.

On July 4, 1776, the Continental Congress passed a "Declaration of Independence" drafted by Thomas Jefferson. It was not until 1784 that the U.S. Congress ratified the Treaty of Paris and the Revolutionary War officially ended and the building of a new nation began. A constitutional convention was convened in 1787 at Independence Hall in Philadelphia with George Washington as its president and James Madison and Ben Franklin as its central figures (Thomas Jefferson was in France serving as American ambassador).

An innovative form of government was created with a federal system that balanced power in the states with those at the national level. A further division of power was created within the federal govenment among three branches: an executive branch headed by the president of the United States; a legislative branch comprising two houses of Congress, the House and the Senate; and a judicial branch consisting of the Supreme Court and a system of federal courts.

In 1789 the first Congress convened in New York City; George Washington was unanimously elected as president and John Adams was elected vice-president. On December 15, 1791, a Bill of Rights, a series of 10 amendments to the Constitution, were added to protect individual liberties against abuses of state power.

**ANSCHLUSS** Refers to the union of Germany and Austria in 1938. After World War I, the German portion of the collapsed Austro-Hungarian Empire wanted to join Germany. But the victorious Allies in the treaties of Versailles and St. Germain forbade this. There was agitation for unity in Austria during the 1920s, and Germany supported this when an Austrian, Adolf Hitler, became German chancellor in 1933.

In February 1938 Hitler requested a meeting with Austria's Chancellor Kurt von Schuschnigg at Berchtesgaden to demand concessions for Austrian Nazis. When Schuschnigg tried to delay Hitler by a plebiscite to underscore Austrian independence, Hitler issued an ultimatum on March 11, 1938, demanding the resignation of Schuschnigg. The latter was replaced by the Austrian Nazi Arthur Seyss-Inquart, who invited the German army to occupy Austria, which it did on March 12, 1938. Seyss-Inquart declared the union of the two countries the next day. On April 10, the Nazis conducted a plebiscite that showed, according to Nazi figures, 99.75 percent in favor of the union.

**ANTICOMMUNISM** An ideology circulated in the capitalist bloc during the Cold War, but the origin of which dates back to the 1920s and the emergence of Communism around the globe, including Russia. On the one hand, anticommunism was a transnational ideology that supplied a basis for international powers opposing Communism to forge their alliance. For instance, Japan declared in the 1930s that world politics was then characterized by the wars between Communist and anti-Communist blocs. At that time, Japan lumped itself, Germany, and Italy into an anti-Communist bloc, but grouped its enemies, including America, Britain, and France, into a Communist bloc.

On the other hand, anticommunism was also a national ideology. For instance, within Japan and its colony of Korea, anticommunism performed classic roles of nationalism, obliterating the differences in Japanese society, whether they were based on class, gender, or region. In both the metropole and its colony, anticommunism was instrumental in enforcing the notion of a unified Japan, including Korea, to such a degree

that Japan even sought to convert the thoughts of those arrested for activities against the Japanese state or emperor. In Korea, anticommunism served as a colonial ideology—Japan labeled radical resistance groups as Communist and, hence, framed anticolonial and national resistance as class struggles among Koreans.

After World War II, anticommunism thrived as the Cold War principle which secured the United States as a neocolonial power and the future of former colonies of Japan and Europe as liberal capitalist states under U.S. leadership. Anticommunism again performed as a transnational and national ideology that integrated many newly independent nation-states in Southeast Asia. Inter-regional organizations like SEATO (Southeast Asia Treaty Organization, 1954), ASA (Association of Southeast Asia, 1961), and ASEAN (Association of Southeast Asian Nations, 1967) were organized so they could respond to Communist insurgencies in the region after the wave of decolonization. Anticommunism supplied these organizations with an ideology for their gatekeeping of the capitalist economic system. Anticommunism skewed the political and economic development in these areas both nationally and regionally, effacing the previous models of socialist development. Anticommunism performed a similar role in East Asia. For instance, South Korean nationalism was predicated on anticommunism during the Cold War period. Those who challenged the state and its economic program were considered to be Communists who disrupted the social order and undermined the future of the nation.

**ANTI-SEMITISM** Political and social agitation directed against Jews. The term was coined by the German agitator Wilhelm Marr in 1879 in order to support the anti-Jewish movement which was already underway in central Europe at that time. Although anti-Jewish movements have existed for more than 3000 years, the movement became intense in the late 19th century in Europe, creating a large migration of Jews to North and South America. Anti-Semitism hit its peak with the birth of National Socialism (Nazism) under Adolf Hitler in Germany, eventually resulting in the death of six million Jews and more than six million people of other ethnic groups in the Holocaust between 1940 and 1945. Although violent anti-Semitic movements have declined in the world since the end of World War II, there still exists both prejudice and hostility toward Jews.

Because of expulsion and massacre in Egypt, Rome, and other countries, Jews were forced to become sojourners for centuries, without property-ownership rights. The expulsion of Jews from Spain and Portugal in the late 15th century created a large-scale migration of Sephardic Jews to England, Holland, Brazil, and the

Caribbean islands. Pogroms ("destruction" in Yiddish)—violent government-condoned attacks against Jews—in Russia and Eastern Europe and the German Nazi movement also forced Jews to migrate to North America.

Many stereotypical images of Jews, such as that they were inferior, clannish, too intelligent, greedy, and dishonest, were all without foundation, but these stereotypes reflected the reality of prejudice and oppression of Jews. Jews were not allowed to possess and cultivate land in medieval Europe, which forced them to become merchants. While these Jews were positioned in the middle economic status, they received hostility from both the farmers and the rulers. Anti-government sentiments among farmers were frequently directed toward Jews, making Jews buffers between the wealthy and the poor.

Although Jews are a religious group, nationalist and socialist movements in the early 1930s saw Jews as a racial group, creating discrimination and cultural isolation of Orthodox Jews in Germany. The National Socialist German Workers' Party, widely known as the Nazis, seized power and attempted to establish Greater Germany in Central Europe. Nazis claimed the superiority of the German race, and sought annihilation of the Jews by establishing hundreds of concentration camps. During World War II, Eastern European and French Jews were arrested and sent to these camps where they were massacred. This episode, known as the Holocaust, is the largest anti-Semitic movement in history.

After the Russian Revolution of 1917, about two million Jews migrated to the United States. Unlike German Jewish Americans who migrated in the mid-19th century, Eastern European Jews lived in ghettos under severe working conditions, which further fostered a negative image of Jews. Between 1932 and 1941, a number of anti-Semitic organizations grew and attacked Jewish communities and synagogues. Some of these groups were the German-American Bund, the Silver Shirts, the National Union for Social Justice, and the Christian Front. With the revival of the Ku Klux Klan, "skin heads," and other racist groups, there has been an increasing number of incidents of violent attacks on Jews and their property in the United States and Europe since the 1980s.

**ANTONESCU, ION** 1882–1946, Romania's wartime military dictator (September 1940–August 1944), and probably the most controversial political figure in 20th century Romania.

Antonescu was born on June 2, 1882, in the town of Pitesti. He received a stern and disciplined upbringing from his father, uncle, and stepfather, all of whom were army men. A graduate of the Army Cavalry School in 1906, Antonescu's rise to national fame began during the 1907 peasant uprising, when, in the town of Galați, he pacified several thousand rebels with only a handful of men under his command and without firing a shot. He was decorated for his performance during the 1913 Second Balkan War and again after World War I. During the latter, Major Antonescu's greatest accomplishment was stopping the advance of the Central Powers through Romania in a series of heroic battles in the summer of 1917. Two years later, under Lt. Colonel Antonescu's command, Romanian troops entered Budapest and overthrew Bela Kun's Communist regime from power there.

Honest, incorruptible, blunt, and staunchly nationalistic, Antonescu was preoccupied above all with achieving, and then defending, the unification of ethnic Romanians into a single nation-state. He was promoted to the rank of colonel in 1921, headed the Special School of Cavalry Officers between 1920 and 1922, and was military attaché in Paris, London, and Brussels from 1922 to 1926. He briefly served as war minister in the fall of 1928, and again from December 1937 to March 1938. He was promoted to the rank of general in 1931, and was named army chief of staff in December 1933, a post from which he resigned a year later.

Initially suspicious of the Fascist Legionary Movement, also known as the Iron Guard, Antonescu developed a certain affinity for it in the late 1930s. In May 1938 he appeared as a character witness on behalf the movement's leader, Corneliu Codreanu, whom the govenment had controversially charged with treason. In November 1938 Antonescu was relieved of all command duties after criticizing a regime crackdown against the Iron Guard.

In late June 1940, following an ultimatum from Stalin, Romania's King Carol II surrendered Besserabia (today the independent state of Moldova) to the Soviet Union without a fight. In July he had Antonescu arrested in order to prevent the general from riding a wave of national outrage into power. In September 1940, after Germany compelled Carol to surrender two-fifths of Transylvania to Hungary, the disgraced monarch fled the country, whereupon a joint military–Iron Guard dictatorship was established headed by Antonescu. In January 1941, with Hitler's permission, Antonescu destroyed the Iron Guard, whose violent rampage against its former tormentors and political opponents threatened to destabilize Romania on the eve of the Axis attack on the Soviet Union.

Though he readily joined Nazi Germany in that attack, Antonescu vehemently protested the partial loss of Translvania to Hungary, which Hitler intimated that a strong performance in the campaign against the USSR could reverse. His eagerness to fight the Soviets and his stubborn loyalty to the Axis cause even after the disaster at Stalingrad subsequently rendered Antonescu Hitler's most trusted ally.

Antonescu's reluctance to apply the Nazi-mandated Final Solution inside Romania's 1940 borders enabled roughly half of Romania's interwar Jewish population (some 700,000 people) to survive the Holocaust. Nevertheless, under his watch about 350,000 Jews perished in Romanian-held territories, especially in camps in Transnistria, a narrow strip of land located between the Dniester and Bug rivers.

On August 23, 1944, with Soviet armies poised to overrun Romania, Antonescu was overthrown in a coup d'état orchestrated by young King Michael, Carol II's successor to the throne. Following Antonescu's removal from power, Romania joined the Allied side. Upon the war's end, Antonescu was tried for treason by the Soviet-installed Communist authorities. He was executed by a firing squad on June 1, 1946.

**APARTHEID**  The institutionalized system of racial segregation and white supremacy that officially characterized South African governmental policy from 1948 to 1991. This system created a racial hierarchy in all aspects of social life which was particularly disadvantageous toward the African majority population.

Apartheid, an Afrikaans term (the language of the Dutch descendent settlers) for separateness or apartness, refers to the historically developed system of laws and practices that limited the economic, political, and social lives of nonwhites in South Africa. The development of the apartheid system can be charted back to the relations among the African ethnic groups indigenous to the area (e.g., the Khoikhoin, San, Nguni, and Sotho), the European colonial settlers (e.g., the Dutch, English, and French), East Indians immigrants, and a mixed racial group referred to as "Coloureds."

The Dutch East India Company arrived at the Cape of Good Hope in 1652. They were followed by British and French colonists. The steady encroachment further inland and land displacement caused numerous wars between Africans and Europeans, and among the European colonists. The discovery of gold (1886) and then diamonds (1964) increased European business interest and entrenchment in the region. Both the mining industry and Boer farming system depended on cheap African labor and imported Indian labor. This labor was made available through military conquests and legislative enactments which divested Africans of their access to land and created a working class.

A unified state was established in 1910 which gave Europeans a monopoly over the governmental apparatus and denied Africans, Coloureds, and Indians political and civil rights. A series of legislative measures created a homeland system on the basis of ethnicity. The laws that laid the foundation for apartheid included the Land Acts of 1913, 1936, and 1963—which restricted the African majority to 7.3 percent and later 13.0 percent of the total land area—and the Urban Areas Act (1923), which restricted African residence in urban areas. Under the guise of "separate development," legislation, including the Native Administration Act of 1927 and the 1936 Hertzog Bills, relegated Africans to "native reserves" on the basis of their tribal origin. Together, these measures created a migratory labor system whereby Africans had to migrate to the towns for employment.

The system of apartheid began with the rise of the National party in 1948 that represented Afrikaner nationalist and English interests. Major apartheid laws were the Population Registration Act (1949) which provided for the official racial categorization of all persons; the Group Areas Act (1950) where each racial group was assigned to specifically demarcated living areas; the Passes and Consolidation of Documents Act (1952) which created the passbook required for Africans; and the Bantu Education Act (1953) that provided a separate system of education for Africans.

The earliest organization to oppose the development of apartheid was the African National Congress (ANC) formed in 1912. This national liberation organization linked the various African ethnic groups under a national concept of "African-ness." The Pan-Africanist Congress of Azania, which split from the ANC in 1959, went further in its African nationalist approach. Other antiapartheid groups included the South African Indian Congress, the White Congress of Democrats, the Coloured Peoples Organization, the South African Congress of Trade Unions, the Federation of South African Women, and the Black Sash. Many of these organizations unified in 1955 to create the Congress of the People and adopt the Freedom Charter, which articulated the framework for a democratic transition.

The apartheid government reacted strongly to antiapartheid organizations and activities. The most violent confrontations occurred in response to peaceful antiapartheid protests in Sharpesville in 1960 and in Soweto in 1976. In 1960, the nationalist government banned all liberation organizations and harassed and imprisoned their leadership. The liberation organizations went underground and into exile. The national liberation movement transitioned into an armed phase in 1961 when the ANC created an armed wing, Umkhonto We Sizwe (meaning "spear of the nation"). Acts of sabotage and protest against the apartheid regime continued through the 1980s.

Apartheid began to be dismantled in the 1990s. Nelson Mandela, imprisoned ANC leader, was released from prison and the orders banning national liberation movements were lifted. In 1994 democratic elections were held and the Government of National Unity was inaugurated on May 10, 1994, with an ANC majority. While the official apartheid era ended, racial and national inequalities continue to plague the South African society.

**ARAB LEAGUE**   The move to create the Arab League was initiated during World War II. On September 25, 1944, delegates from Egypt, Lebanon, Transjordan, Syria, and Iraq convened in Alexandria to discuss the creation of a body that would facilitate cooperation among Arab states. It was hoped that it would also soften self-defeating nationalist policies directed against other Arab states. Such activities would weaken the Arab influence in the world. The resulting Alexandria Protocol led to the League's creation on March 22, 1945, by Egypt, Iraq, Syria, Transjordan, Lebanon, North Yemen, and Saudi Arabia. The permanent headquarters were to be in Cairo and would contain a council in which each member-state would have an equal vote, specialized committees, a secretariat appointed by the council and endorsed by two-thirds of the states, and a staff. The door was left open to any Arab state, and additional states and the Palestine Liberation Organization (PLO) joined. In the 1990s it had 22 members.

The League has seldom been successful in resolving disputes among its members. It could not stop the fighting in Lebanon in 1975, nor could it prevent Egypt from making peace with Israel in 1979, a move that provoked Egypt's expulsion from the organization and relocation of the headquarters to Tunis. Egypt was readmitted in 1987, and over the opposition of some members, the headquarters were returned to Cairo in 1990 just in time for the next crisis: the Gulf War against Iraq. The League was split over whether to support the international coalition against Saddam Hussein. In the end, a majority voted in favor of multinational action to liberate Kuwait.

**ARAB NATIONALISM**   The idea that peoples of the Middle East should cooperate to achieve major political, economic, or social goals based upon a common Arab identity enjoyed a relatively brief period of dominant influence in the middle of the 20th century. Although Arab nationalism continues to exert an emotional appeal in the region, its power has been sapped by some of the very factors which aided its earlier genesis. Today it is Islamism which seems to enjoy the vigor that once marked Arab nationalism.

The nature of the relationship between Islam and Arab nationalism has been the subject of frequent debate, since nationalists look upon Islam as an "Arab" religion, but at the same time view Islamist groups as potentially dangerous rivals. Early interpretations of Arab nationalism tended to emphasize the divisions between the two over the ties. George Antonius wrote a most influential book, *The Arab Awakening,* in 1938, a time when nationalism was maturing as a mode of opposition to British and French dominance in the Middle East. Antonius, a Christian, tried to show that Arab nationalism had deep historical roots dating back to the first half of the 19th century, and he stressed the writings of Christians educated in Western missionary schools in Syria. Although the picture presented in *The Arab Awakening* still exerts some influence, more recent scholars have shown it to be as much propaganda as history, in part due to its slighting of the role of religion.

In every Middle Eastern state, from the arrival of Islam to the collapse of the Ottoman Empire, religion was crucial to status. Muslims were dominant, but Christians and Jews were granted considerable freedom, as long as they paid a poll tax, *jizya.* In Arabophone societies that blended pre-Islamic Greek, Persian, Kurdish, Berber, and Arab populations, to name but a few, ethnicity could hardly carry the same importance. Indeed, just as a sophisticated resident of Istanbul in the 19th century might feel insulted if called a "Turk," a word which implied an uncultured Anatolian peasant, so a Damascene notable might well object to being called an "Arab," a term more aptly applied to unlettered Bedouin tribesmen. Both men would describe themselves by religion. Arab nationalism had to accommodate to some degree that historical pattern of identification.

The stability of this system was upset by another formative influence on Arab nationalism, the growth of Western dominance in the Middle East. France occupied Egypt from 1798 to 1801 and began to establish dominance in North Africa in 1830. British influence soon followed in other regions. Over the course of the century many in the Middle East sought an explanation for the West's new dominance. This involved scrutiny not just of European learning and technology but also of Middle Eastern society and culture, including religion.

One resulting reform trend tried to revive Islam by

promoting a return to the practices of the early Muslim community, which was ethnically Arab. This was part of a cultural reawakening closely tied to Arabic language and literature. This pride in the common cultural heritage of Arabic speakers could only grow stronger with the collapse of the explicitly Islamic Ottoman Empire. With Turkish nationalism replacing Islam as the motivating force in the Anatolian remnant of the Ottoman Empire after 1918, the many Arabs (both Muslim and Christian) who did not want the imposition of French or British control looked increasingly to nationalism as a rallying force to coordiante resistance. European states succeeded in maintaining or imposing their control in North Africa and the Fertile Crescent, but resentment of that control—and therefore Arab nationalism—did not die.

The European states accelerated their withdrawal from outright occupation of Arab territories after World War II. With territories such as Syria, Lebanon, and Transjordan gaining formal independence, nationalism changed with the times. The relationship between nationalist sentiment and socioeconomic class in the Arab world defies easy definition, but in the independence era it seems that members of the lower and middle classes adopted nationalism as a vehicle for challenging the wealthy elite, who had been the strongest advocates of early nationalism.

The Arab notables had played an important intermediary role between the state and the rest of the population during both the Ottoman and the European periods. With independence they become the ruling class, and often enjoyed strong support from the West. European states retained considerable formal and informal influence, in part through defense pacts. Identification with the West left the elite vulnerable to attack from below on nationalist grounds, and indeed radical Arab nationalism revolts in the 1950s and 1960s were to destroy the notable class. Radical regimes in Egypt, Syria, and Iraq all pushed through land reform programs that broke the power of the notables in the countryside, and at least partially nationalized much of the industrial and services sectors. Such domestic programs distinguished Arab socialism, which was particularly popular from the late 1950s to the late 1960s, and which was led or heavily influenced by Gamal Abdel Nasser of Egypt. The prestige of Nasser and his programs was dented, however, following Egypt's utter defeat by Israel in the 1967 war.

The Palestine–Israel problem has heavily influenced Arab nationalism in the post-World War II period. The defeat of Arab armies in the 1948 war discredited the old regimes and prepared the way for nationalist coups, such as Nasser's in Egypt. Nasser gained popular acclamation as an Arab hero outside of Egypt as a result of the war of 1956, when a British–French–Israeli scheme to seize the Suez Canal and humble Nasser aroused international condemnation and ended in the aggressors' own humiliation. The dispute over control of Palestine arouses such strong emotions among Arabs for many reasons, including abhorrence of the idea of ceding control of Jerusalem, a holy city for Muslims and Christians as well as Jews, to an unfriendly, non-Muslim state. Israel, moreover, is seen as the most lasting relic of Western imperialism in the Middle East.

The Zionist community took root during the British Mandate in Palestine from the end of World War I to 1948. In 1917 the British had promised limited official support for the creation of a "national home for the Jewish people" in Palestine. Many Jews immigrated to Palestine after the Nazi regime came to power in 1933. Arabs thus see Israel as a British solution to a European problem, imposed at the cost of driving hundreds of thousands of Palestinian Arabs from their homeland. Israel's close ties to the United States and other European countries make many Arabs view it today as a vital ally for Western plans to exert influence in the Middle East.

Until there is a reasonable settlement of the Palestine question, Arab nationalism will remain widespread in the Middle East. It does face challenges, however. Repressive regimes espousing Arab nationalism have ruled such countries as Iraq, Syria, Algeria, and Libya since the 1960s, yet in international affairs they have failed in confronting Israel and have had even less success domestically in raising their citizens' standards of living. Islamist groups have gained strength, as they seem to offer more effective programs in both arenas. Local nationalisms—Syrian and Egyptian, for example—are also growing stronger. Borders drawn by European statesmen after 1918 were viewed in the past as the result of outside powers' attempts to keep the Arabs divided and weak, but with time these boundaries have gradually gained greater acceptance. The present practical limitations of Arab nationalism can perhaps be illustrated by the Iraqi invasion of Kuwait in 1990. An Arab nationalist, Saddam Hussein tried to deflect criticism in the Middle East by portraying the conquest as a blow against Israel, promising to use Kuwaiti oil revenues to support the Palestinians. This won him support among Palestinians but few others. He then tried to cloak himself in Islam by, among other things, adding the phrase *Allahu Akbar* (God is Great) to the Iraqi flag. In the end, however, few Arab states were willing to support his unilateral abolition of one of those Western-drawn boundaries.

The best recent book devoted to Arab nationalism is *The Origins of Arab Nationalism* (Columbia University

Press, 1991), edited by Rashid Khalidi et al. A good overview of the subject also can be found in Albert Hourani's *History of the Arab Peoples* (Harvard University Press, 1991).

**ARAFAT, YASSER** 1929–, Palestinian nationalist leader who led the Palestinian Liberation Organization's (PLO) fight for independence from Israel. In 1996 he was elected the first president of the Palestinian Authority that governed Palestinian-controlled areas of the West Bank and the Gaza Strip. After signing a peace accord with the Israelis in 1993 Arafat received the Nobel Peace Prize jointly with Yitzhak Rabin and Shimon Peres in 1994.

As chairman of the PLO after 1968 and commander-in-chief of the Palestinian Revolution Forces (1971), he was a key leader in the armed uprising against Israeli occupation that left many Palestinians living in refugee camps in areas under Israeli control. In 1973 he became head of the PLO's political department, however, and turned his attention to diplomatic efforts and political persuasion. In a historic speech to the UN General Assembly in November of 1974 on behalf of the Palestinian people, he became the first representative of a nongovernmental organization to address a plenary session of that body.

In the late 1980s he was persuaded by Mubarak Awad and others to participate in the largely nonviolent campaign of the *Intifada* that fought for Palestinian autonomy through mass demonstrations and noncooperation with Israeli authorities. In addition to publicizing their opposition to Israeli rule, the Palestinians strove to make the Israeli occupation increasingly ineffective by refusing to cooperate with authorities and setting up parallel structures. Some observers suggest that the shift from terrorist to Gandhian-style nonviolent strategies was crucial in creating a climate for promoting Palestinian interests and soliciting support from the international community in their struggle with Israel.

Arafat was elected president of a hypothetical Palestinian state by the Central Council of the Palestine National Council (the PLO's governing body) in 1989. In 1993 Arafat formally recognized, for the first time, Israel's right to exist as an independent nation, paving the way for negotiations leading to an Israel–PLO accord.

The accord envisioned a phrased five-year withdrawal of Israeli occupation from portions of the West Bank and the Gaza Strip, leading to Palestinian self-rule by the Palestinian Authority in 1994. As the first president of the Palestinian Authority, Arafat presided over the nation-building efforts of Palestinians beginning in Palestinian-controlled areas of the West Bank and the Gaza Strip.

Arafat came from a large family of seven children, the son of a merchant whose wife was related to Amin al-Husayni (d. 1974), an anti-Zionist who served as grand mufti of Jerusalem. Arafat obtained a degree in civil engineering at the University of Cairo where he joined the Muslim Brotherhood and demonstrated his leadership skills as president of the Union of Palestinian Students (1952–1956).

Although he was commissioned into the Egyptian army and served in the Suez campaign in 1956, he moved to Kuwait after the campaign to set up his own contracting firm as an engineer. He continued to struggle for the Palestinian nationalist cause from Kuwait where he founded Fatah, a leading military branch of the PLO.

**ARCHAEOLOGY AND NATIONALISM** The development of archaeology as a scientific discipline took place during the 19th century, essentially coinciding with the period of nation-building in Europe. These processes were not only chronologically coincident, but also causally interrelated. Archaeology was intimately involved in the establishment of national museums and the ordering and classification of visible material remains found throughout the territory claimed by the emergent nation-state. Each state had to construct its own national identity, a process which required the deliberate forgetting, misremembering, inventing, and discovering of the nation's past. Myths of national origin were elaborated from a variety of sources, including the archaeological remains found within the state's demarcated borders.

The association between nation-building and archaeology was so obvious as to remain largely unquestioned throughout the 19th and most of the 20th centuries; the roots of nations were extended back into the mists of the prehistoric past, uncovered by the archaeologist's spade. The relationship between the state and archaeology varied from country to country in part because each nation had its own specific history and time of national consolidation; the nationalist significance accorded to archaeological data also varied according to the availability of historical records, the relative weighting of historical to archaeological sources, and the empirical contents of those records. Moreover, the archaeological materials accorded significance for nationalist purposes did not necessarily have to have been discovered within the state's borders.

Thus, for example, the development of archaeology in Denmark and the establishment of its national museum ordered by the Three Age system of successive Stone, Bronze, and Iron periods in the early 19th century can be contrasted with the development of archaeology in Britain and France. In the former case, archaeological materials found within the territorially reduced borders of Denmark were used to extend the history of the peoples inhabiting Jutland and the surrounding regions beyond the heroic age of the Vikings. Archaeological remains within Britain and France fulfilled a similar purpose, though the recorded history of these areas extended further back into classical times. France and Britain, however, were also growing imperial powers, and archaeologists frequently followed the flags of their respective countries to study the remains of classical antiquity and of the ancient Near East. They even directly competed with each other bringing back—legally or illegally—monumental works of ancient art to fill the display cabinets of the their two national institutions, the Louvre and British Museum.

Germany, an aspirant imperial power after unification, consciously used archaeologists as part of a state-directed *Kulturpolitik*, extending the rigorous and exacting methods of German scholarship abroad, particularly throughout the lands of the Ottoman Empire. Ironically, German prehistory remained relatively underdeveloped until near the end of the 19th century when G. Kossinna and others began to practice a settlement archaeology that identified archaeological remains as ethnically German. The discipline subsequently received its biggest boost when the Nazis came to power in 1933 and promoted the discovery of German-Aryan remains not only within the contemporary homeland, but throughout neighboring regions as well, justifying their expansion into those areas.

The close relationship of archaeology and nationalism can be traced throughout the world, but its exact nature varies tremendously. Thus, nations, such as the United States, Australia, and Argentina, which today are largely composed of relatively recent immigrants distinguish sharply between the prehistoric and historic archaeological record; the prehistory of indigenous peoples is naturalized and interpreted from a universal evolutionary-natural historical perspective, while material remains postdating contact and conquest are viewed in much more specific historical terms, the most famous and best preserved becoming registered as sites of historical significance—part of the national heritage. Mexico and Peru, on the other hand, exhibit a different pattern: their large indigenous populations, as well as their spectacular pre-Columbian remains, effectively ensure that their pre-Columbian heritage is incorporated into their national identity, a process that is continuously stimulated and enriched by archaeological discoveries.

Contemporary Israel, which is also largely composed of recent immigrants, presents a very distinct case pre-cisely because most Israelis view themselves as returning to their ancestral land; national pride is fostered by the state-sponsored excavation of sites dating to biblical times, while remains dating to earlier and later periods are less intensively investigated. The contemporary African state of Zimbabwe was named after an archaeological site which became an exceptionally powerful symbol of colonial misrepentations and native pre-European accomplishments; today, however, it is unclear whether these ruins are going to be identified with the majority Shona people or more broadly interpreted as ancestral also to the minority Ndebele.

A fundamental difficulty of using archaeological data for nationalist purposes is the inherent ambiguity of material remains; archaeological artifacts—pottery styles, house forms, tools, weaponry, etc.—simply cannot be perfectly correlated with specific peoples. Archaeological cultures and ethnic groups are not synonymous, and a purely prehistoric record is one by definition that lacks written sources and, consequently, cannot reliably be "peopled" by reference to later known ethnicities. Moreover, peoples' sense of themselves continuously changes and cannot be held constant over centuries, much less the millennia of the remote past, making even more problematic any attempted nationalist reading of the prehistoric record.

Nevertheless, archaeology will continue to be manipulated for nationalist purposes—in part just because archaeological sites are physical and visible to a nation's citizens who may interact with it, consciously or not, on a daily basis. Archaeological sites become national monuments which now increasingly are transformed into lucrative tourist attractions. Their artifacts are stored and displayed in national museums and constitute an invaluable part of the national patrimony—a heritage which becomes more and more broadly defined. Both sites and artifacts frequently are incorporated into state regalia as symbols appearing on national flags, currency, and stamps, or are memorialized in patriotic songs and national anthems. Maps are compiled showing the distribution of sites identified ethnically and considered to be part of the state's cultural patrimony; not infrequently, such sites are located beyond the state borders, their representation then constituting an implicit ancestral claim on a neighboring state's territories. All such uses demonstrate forcefully how national identity is continuously constructed through the commemoration of the remote, archaeologically ascertainable past.

Finally, nationalism and the practice of archaeology are also inextricably related at the level of state support for research and employment. Archaeologists often work directly for state institutions, such as museums, research institutes, and antiquities services; even in the atypically decentralized context of the United States, most American archaeologists, whether employed by private or state institutions, must still solicit federally financed foundations for funds to support their research. A state needs an educated elite citizenry, and the instillment of national pride in past accomplishments may be appropriate and laudatory.

The inevitable relationship between archaeology and nationalism only becomes problematic when the nationalist agenda is questionable, when it overinterprets the archaeological record, and when it advances the cause of a specific group or nationality at the expense of others, unjustifiably claiming primordial, exclusive rights to a territory or past accomplishment.

Recent critical edited volumes examining the relationship between nationalism and archaeology include M. Diaz-Andreu and T. Champion's *Nationalism and Archaeology in Europe* (Westview, 1996); P. Ucko's *Theory in Archaeology: A World Perspective* (Routledge, 1995); and P. L. Kohl and C. Fawcett's *Nationalism, Politics, and the Practice of Archaeology* (Cambridge, 1995).

**ARENDT, HANNAH** 1906–1975, Hannah Arendt is a well-known political philosopher whose major contributions to political thinking were established in her monumental writing, *Origins of Totalitarianism* (1951). Derived from her writings, two forms of nationalism can be identified. She tried to distinguish the comparatively ideal kind of classic nation-states like France from the "tribal nationalism" in Eastern Europe.

Tribal nationalism, she argued, was akin to racism as it determined an inborn national character and identity, and thus was one of the leading factors contributing to nurturing totalitarianism. For Arendt, nationalism of this kind was very different from the sense of national character of the mature nation-states of Western Europe.

Nation-states were not ethnic states, but were made possible only where the principle of equality and solidarity of all peoples—guaranteed by the idea of humanity—was approved. A genuine nation-state, Arendt insisted, should be an essentially humanist institution—a civilized structure providing a legal order and guaranteeing basic human rights in general and citizenship rights in particular. This humanist creation was a human-made structure in which people could feel at home and responsibly participate in the political sphere.

For Arendt, politics was a highly specific human activity for which a specific realm for the action of human freedom existed. National identity as a marker of distinctiveness was not inborn nor something one could

possess inherently or internally, but had to be acquired through interactions with others in a bounded territory and culture with a specific sense of self and place. The freedoms and possibilities for action that rights created for individuals were products of human activities, not of some innate biological traits like blood ties or races. Arendt believed that the very possibility of selfhood and national identity was based on membership in a human society in which rights and equality could be actualized in the political realm. The decay of this kind of mature nationalism foretells the origins of totalitarianism.

**ARGENTINEAN NATIONALISM** In the late 19th century and as the centennial celebration of independence in 1910 approached, Argentine writers began to eagerly espouse upon the theme of nationalism in terms of both its native roots and new European intellectual currents. Nationalism in Argentina fell into two major categories: (a) Earlier romanticists emphasized the traditional Indian and colonial roots of Argentina's past. (b) "Integral nationalism," characterized by a renewed dedication to the traditional Spanish pattern of loyalty to family, church, and fatherland—influenced by the Spanish Hispanidad movement and often by fascist and Nazi ideologies that developed after World War I—found such advocates as Manuel Galvez and Leopoldo Lugones.

Nationalism, in its different aspects, was taken up by public leaders and in military circles; it was quickly spread throughout the country by newspapers, literary works, a widespread public school system, and compulsory military service. It first became important politically during the radical administration of President Hipólito Irigoyen (1916–1922, 1928–1930). He showed its influence externally in his insistence on Argentine independence by its neutrality in World War I and his actions on behalf of respect for the sovereignty of all nations in early meetings of the League of Nations. Within the republic, his nationalism manifested itself in widespread opportunities for the middle and lower classes to participate in national life.

By 1930 liberal nationalism had become identified with the oligarchy and its neglect of the interests of the masses, as well as its close ties with foreign trade and culture. At the same time, hatred of foreign economic domination had become an increasingly important element in nationalism during the depression of the 1930s. Integral nationalists demanding change, both military and civilian, were largely responsible for the strongly populist trend taken by the GOU (Grupo de Oficiales Unidos) revolt in 1943 and Juan Domingo Perón's later identification of nationalism with social justice, as well as resistance to capitalist imperialism.

Policies of succeeding governments have shown the influence of populist nationalism in the diversification of the economy, efforts in making the nation more self-sufficient, increased participation of Argentina in international affairs on a wider geographic basis, and the trend toward integration of all its citizens into an Argentine society and culture. Largely remaining intact has been its traditional pride in itself and its accomplishments, including new labor and social welfare.

**ARIBAU, CARLES** 1798–1862, Writer, economist, and politician. Arabau combined business savvy with a remarkable literary and journalistic career. Having moved to Madrid in 1826, he started to be active in relation to his native Catalonia's specific problems around 1850, becoming the unofficial lobbyist in chief for Catalan interests in the capital. He held the posts of director of the mint and of the treasury in the Spanish administration.

His claim to posterity comes from his 1833 poem *Oda a la Pàtria* ("Ode to the Fatherland"), the work of a homesick writer that spontaneously uttered his feelings in his mother tongue. This Catalan poem created a breakthrough, marking this language's resurgence as a means of literary expression. By the 19th century, Catalan had all but disappeared in written form, being neither taught in the schools nor used in religious services, although it remained the usual vehicle for oral communication. Even if Aribau produced most of his poetic works in Spanish, and created poetry in Italian and Latin as well, he is revered in Catalonia as the first representative of the movement of cultural revival known as the *Renaixença* ("Renaissance") that created the basis for, and immediately preceded, modern political nationalism. His "Ode to the Fatherland" is considered the starting point of Catalan romanticism, too.

**ARMENIAN NATIONALISM** The first certain historical references to Armenia occur in Persian inscriptions of the 6th century B.C. For a brief period in the 1st century B.C., an Armenian kingdom under Tigran the Great rivaled the Roman and Parthian empires to its west and east. The Armenian state officially adopted Christianity in the early 4th century A.D., and a distinctive Armenian script was developed in the 5th century. Contemporary Armenian nationalism, which began in the 19th century, frequently refers to Armenia's long glorious past and the symbols associated with it, but even more formative for its development has been the demise of independent Armenian polities and the retraction and scattering of Armenian communities from their historic "homeland"—processes associated with successive waves of Turkish invasions into Anatolia from the 11th century onward. By the early 19th century, most Armenians were divided into communities controlled by the Ottoman, Persian (Qajar dynasty), and Russian empires. The long decline and subjugation of Armenian communities meant that there was little cultural, political, or national consciousness among most Armenians, particularly the peasants living in eastern Anatolia, the southern Caucasus, and northwestern Iran. An initial cultural awakening was stimulated by the activities of Armenian diaspora communities, particularly the activities and publications of the Catholic Mekhitarists in Venice beginning in the early 18th century.

The Russian annexation of the Khanate of Erevan in 1828 led to large demographic shifts, with many Armenians moving into those areas controlled by the Christian Russian Tsar. The Russian administration initially provided security, granted tax exemptions, and placed the Armenians under the religious authority of its spiritual leader, the Catholicos of Etchmiadzin. Throughout the first half of the 19th century, the school system expanded and a first generation of Armenian intellectuals wrote in the eastern Armenian vernacular, and some of them, like M. Nalbandian, adopted strong anticlerical positions and spoke of Armenians as a distinct nationality, as opposed to a religious community, adopting the ideas of the Western Enlightenment and those espoused by Russian liberals. Armenian national and revolutionary consciousness grew throughout the 19th century but was accelerated with the Russification policies of Alexander III and the attempted closing of Armenian schools in the early 1880s. Two revolutionary parties, the *Hnchak* ("Bell") and *Dashnaktsutiun* (Armenian Revolutionary Federation), soon formed and were partly inspired by Russian populist and socialist movements, but were more fundamentally directed toward the liberation of the Armenian communities in eastern Anatolia, suffering under Ottoman rule. From their very inception, the Armenian revolutionary parties were much less concerned about social and class divisions than they were with national liberation and the uniting of the disparate, politically fragmented Armenian communities.

As the treatment and status of Armenians within the Ottoman Empire, the so-called Armenian Question, receded in European consciousness at the end of the 19th century, it became the most pressing issue for the dominant *Dashnak* party, a group of whom seized the Imperial Ottoman Bank in Constantinople in 1896. This act was both preceded and followed by bloody Turkish reprisals against Armenians, setting the stage for even more heinous massacres and the Armenian genocide of

1915–1923 when more than a million Armenians were killed or forcibly displaced from eastern Anatolia. Anti-tsarist activities and the growth of the Social Democratic movement in Transcaucasia at the beginning of the century led to increased state repression, including the demand that the Armenian church turn over its estates to the government. The Dashnaks forcibly resisted this decree, and their power grew from 1903 until the outbreak of the revolution and the establishment of an independent Armenian state which they controlled. Pressed by Turkish forces, who briefly occupied Baku in 1918, and burdened by severe economic problems, which were exacerbated by the influx of thousands of refugees, the Dashnaks had no choice and submitted to Bolshevik rule in 1920. This brief period of independence (1918–1920) inspired Armenian nationalists throughout this century, its tricolor flag being adopted as the state flag of the Republic of Armenia in the early 1990s.

Armenian nationalism in the 20th century has to be divided between the activities of diaspora communities, particularly in Lebanon and the United States, and the expressions allowed to take place or suppressed under the vacillating nationalities' policies of the Soviet state. The diaspora communities were sharply divided and fought among themselves over their policy toward Soviet Armenia—acceptance of Soviet rule and general accomodation or liberation and independence, positions which became more entrenched and complicated with the advent of the Cold War. A general hostility toward Turkey and a demand for their official recognition of the genocide and irredentist claims on historic Armenian lands in eastern Anatolia were more commonly shared concerns of the diaspora communities, particularly those of western Armenians who had survived the events of 1915–1923. Overt forms of cultural expression and nationalism were suppressed and several prominent writers, such as E. Charents, were imprisoned or killed during Stalinist times (1928–1953); during the same period Soviet Armenia was transformed from an agrarian state to an industrial one and the capital city of Erevan was transformed into a bustling modern metropolis. Official and even dissident nationalist sentiments increasingly were articulated in post-Stalinist times, culminating in a massive demonstration in central Erevan on April 24, 1965, the 50th anniversary of the outbreak of the Armenian genocide, and a few years later a huge monument with an eternal flame to the victims was built on a hill overlooking Erevan. Other such monuments, commemorating ancient and modern Armenian history, were built during late Soviet times.

By the late 1980s and the advent of Gorbachev's policies of *perestroika* and *glasnost,* the major issue concerning Armenian intellectuals and nationalists concerned the status of Nagorno-Karabagh (or Armenian *Artsakh*), a mountainous region largely inhabited by Armenians which had been established by the Soviet government in 1923 as an autonomous province (*oblast*) within the Soviet Republic of Azerbaijan. Activists, who formed a Karabagh Committee, decided to test Gorbachev's democratic reforms and freedom of political expression and demanded that its status be determined by a popular referendum. This demand was rejected by the Azeris and ultimately by Gorbachev, though there were attempted changes in the status and administration of Karabagh within Azerbaijan. Killings of Azeris and Armenians occurred, the rhetoric on both sides intensified, and Azerbaijan initiated a crippling economic blockade of Armenia. By 1990, a guerilla war had developed between the two republics, engulfing not only Karabagh but adjacent regions of Azerbaijan, and this conflict became one of the most critical issues precipitating the collapse of the Soviet Union in 1991. L. Ter-Petrosian, a member of the Karabagh Committee, was elected chairman of the Armenian parliament, and Armenia declared its desire to become a sovereign, independent state in summer 1990. Ter-Petrosian became its first president, ruling until spring 1998. The war resulted in approximately 20,000 casualties and ended— at least temporarily—in the liberation of Karabagh and the occupation of adjacent regions of Azerbaijan, accounting for about 20 percent of Azeri territory and creating about 1,000,000 internal refugees within Azerbaijan.

Certain fundamental demographic and geographic facts have shaped and will continue to shape Armenian nationalism. Specifically, while Armenia was the most ethnically homogeneous Soviet republic (Armenians now constitute well over 90% of the total population of the Republic of Armenia), it was also the smallest republic (about the size of Belgium), landlocked, and surrounded by its traditional enemies (Turkey, Azerbaijan) and unstable states (Georgia in the early 1990s and Iran). More than one and a half million Armenians are dispersed throughout Russia and other republics of the former Soviet Union, and even more Armenians live in diaspora communities in Europe, the Middle East, and North America. Due to the economic privations of the Karabagh war, the blockade, a devastating earthquake in northwestern Armenia in 1988, and the general economic and political dislocations associated with the transition to independence, many more Armenians (estimates range as high as 30 percent) have emigrated, particularly to California, during the 1990s. Their increased presence will affect these diaspora communities, and the latter, in turn, will continue to influence Armenian politics and its nationalist expressions into the foreseeable future.

The most sophisticated treatment of the development of Armenian nationalism from the 18th century to the outbreak of the Karabagh war appears in a series of essays by R. G. Suny that are collected in *Looking toward Ararat: Armenia in Modern History* (Indiana University Press, 1993).

**ART AND NATIONALISM**  Nationalism as a political ideology requires an actively conscious process of "invented tradition," in which art, both serious and popular, takes an important role. As Hegel argues, "Nations may have had a long history before they finally reach their destination—that of forming themselves into states." Since nation as a natural and inherent political destiny is a myth, this long history of forming nation-states involves intensive interpellation of ideological articulation. Nationalism thus often has to turn to ethnic arts, notably folk music, legend, opera, dance, and museum, in order to articulate a glorifying national story. "It is nationalism," Ernest Gellner said, "which engenders nations, and not the other way round." Dead cultures and authentic arts can be revived, reinvented, and sometimes radically transformed.

For example, the modern concept of "France" or "the French" was novel to many people when it first appeared, and in daily language it was rarely used to identify territory or people in the Middle Ages. Eric Hobsbawn said that nobody would seek to deny that the concept of France and the French was composed of constructed or invented components. The subjective intervention of constructing a national history has consisted of a fair number of symbols and arts. Besides high cultures, which was often viewed as an important element to nationalism, the popular arts, by nature of their popularity and commonality, have been far more significant to the elevation of national sentiments.

The invention of public ceremonies such as Bastille Day, Hobsbawn argues, has been of particular significance since it mixes both official and unofficial demonstrations and popular festivities. Every man and woman can participate in the artistic activities in the carnival; fireworks, singing, and dancing in the street annually rearticulate and reconfirm the entity of France as a nation. Public celebration has effectively provided legitimacy for a coherent nation-state.

Certain kind of artworks, especially public monuments, have also been part of the invented nationalism.

Massive public statuary contains the image and subsequently the specificity of one's national identity. For example, in France famous statues of varied sizes such as bearded civilian figures have signified a sense of French patriotism at a local level. Ranging from the modest busts of Marianne to various allegorical or heroic accessories which were produced for massive consumption, a sense of national belonging has been created and fabricated. Popular artwork helps to promote national aspirations nearly everywhere when the process of nation construction begins.

**ASSIMILATION**  To bring into conformity with the customs, attitudes, etc., of a dominant cultural group of national culture.

Members of a nondominant ethnic or cultural group living in a "foreign" land generally have two choices: they can retain their differences, even celebrate them, or they can assimilate into the larger group. The choice can have enormous implications for a person's employment and educational opportunities, marital possibilities, and even personal safety.

For example, Jewish communities throughout the world have faced this dilemma for centuries. The decision to retain a strong Jewish identity and wear a *yarmulke*, eat only kosher foods, and study in yeshivas or other Jewish schools sets Jews apart from others in the society. While safeguarding their way of life, it has often served to antagonize members of the mainstream society. In the 19th and 20th centuries, frequent pogroms, or attacks on Jewish villages, occurred in Russia and Eastern Europe. The agenda of the Nazi party in Germany in the 1930s and 1940s, which was largely responsible for World War II, involved the destruction and elimination of the Jews. Many of these Jews were completely assimilated into German culture, and failed to flee because they considered themselves Germans first, and thought only nonassimilated Jews would be targeted.

The assimilation dilemma continues to pose problems for people all over the world—from Hispanic and Asian immigrants in the United States to Arab immigrants in Europe and Roma in Eastern and Western Europe. Assimilation often means losing part of one's heritage, but it opens the door to acceptance and political and economic well-being. In nations in transition, where nationalist flames are fanned by rhetoric and public violence, the decision not to assimilate can be very difficult and dangerous. For some groups, however, the loss of identity is too large a price to pay, and efforts to teach the young their own language and culture continue to flourish around the world.

**ATATÜRK, KEMAL** 1881–1938, founder of the Republic of Turkey and its first president (1923–1938). Born an ethnic Macedonian in the Ottoman city of Salonika (modern Thessaloniki in Greece), Mustafa Kemal rose to prominence as an active reformer and leader. Following education at a military high school and the Ottoman War Academy, Kemal served in the Ottoman military. He became a national hero in 1915 as commander of the Ottoman forces that repelled the Allied campaign in the Dardanelles. In response to the Ottoman defeat and occupation after World War I, Kemal formed a liberation army in 1919 and led a war for independence. By September 1922, Kemal had liberated Turkish Anatolia, signed an armistice with its former occupiers, and abolished the Ottoman regime. The Republic of Turkey was proclaimed on October 29, 1923, and Mustafa Kemal was unanimously elected president of the republic. The national parliament granted Kemal the surname Atatürk ("Father of Turks") in 1934.

Atatürk founded the modern Turkish republic as a homogeneous, centralized, secular, and unitary state, as opposed to the multiethnic, theocratic regime of the Ottomans. The guiding light for his dramatic transformation of Turkey was Kemalism, which comprised six principles (or arrows): *nationalism, statism, revolutionism, populism, republicanism,* and *secularism.* The manifestation of his reform effort were national unity and independence, secular education and government, republic principles (based on Western models), an egalitarian social structure, and dramatic modernization. Among Atatürk's profound and lasting contributions to Turkey were the introduction of parliamentary democracy and the transformation of the legal system, both of which were based on European models.

After more than 75 years, Kemalism still enjoys wide popular support, particularly among conservative institutions like the military. However, its relevance in the modern context is being eroded somewhat by Turkey's newly assertive foreign policy, economic liberalization, Kurdish rights question, and Islamic resurgence.

**AUSTRALIAN NATIONALISM** European invasion of the continent occupied by aboriginal peoples began with the British founding of a penal colony around Sydney in 1788. Various British colonies formed during the 19th century and were federated as Australia in 1901. Connections to Britain remained strong through much of the 20th century, but for most of that time Australia has been functionally independent. Constitutional moves to republicanism strengthened from the 1980s. Although Australia's founding was contemporaneous with the beginning of the modern era of nationalism, Australian nationalism demonstrates an unusual disjunction between cultural and political dimensions, which are often considered to be mutually indispensable.

Culturally, a distinctive national identity developed gradually in the course of the 19th century. As early as 1835, a group promoting more liberal policies in colonial government was calling itself the Australian Patriotic Association. Australian "national character" came to be associated with ideas about the country as a comparatively liberal, egalitarian land of opportunity and progress compared to Europe. By 1888, the centenary of European settlement could be celebrated as an Australian event, and the late 19th century was an important period of national symbolic innovation and institutionalization.

The influential "Australian legend," created in the 1890s by members of the first significant generation of Australian-born, nationalist writers and artists, glorified the egalitarian masculine camaraderie of itinerant bush workers and rural pioneers of the outback, although the Australian population was unusually urbanized. In the 20th century, Australians' experience during World War I, especially at Gallipoli, also became a potent source of symbols of national identity, along with sporting heroes and events, the distinctive land, and material prosperity. From the 1970s, a "new nationalism" revised earlier ideas to include feminist and multiculturalist themes and a new emphasis on the arts.

Nationalism as a political project is weaker in Australia. For most of modern Australian history, the recognition of a distinct cultural identity has typically been viewed as consistent with both broader identification with Britain and with narrower colonial (later, state) identities, and nationalist movements have been comparatively insignificant.

The white Australian political experience of imperial administration was quite positive. In the 19th century, "Australian" interests were articulated in contrast to those of the Empire on such issues as the end of convict transportation, self-government of the colonies, imperial policy in the Pacific, and Chinese immigration, but such differences did not create nationalism.

Imperial policy encouraged the federation of Australian colonies to form the Australian nation-state: the first proposal for federation was made by the colonial office in 1847, before Australian colonies were much interested. Federation was on the political agenda again in the 1880s. The discussion mostly took place among established political elites and did not reflect any intensive popular nationalist moblization. Gradually, though, federation became more influential as a middle class movement, especially in the colony of Victoria, where the Australian Natives Association had formed in 1871. Central issues in the process of federation were intercolonial, not anticolonial: Australian colonies shared similar culture and institutions, but they were divided on pragmatic issues such as economic protection.

In the 1890s conventions and referenda were held to develop a constitutional framework for national government. The Australian government was strengthened in relation to state governments in the course of the 20th century. However, some constitutional, legislative, geopolitical, economic, and cultural attachment to Britain continued after federation and only attenuated slowly.

The most explicit political nationalism in Australian history was articulated by a minority in republican labor circles in the late 19th century, and disseminated in publications like the *Bulletin,* which had a significant circulation in the late 1880s. Some of this nationalism was encouraged by anti-British suspicion among Irish immigrants and by significant and intercolonial labor activism, but church and class projects, respectively, reduced somewhat the mass impact of these potentially nationalist energies. Radical working class nationalism at this time was strongly inflected with explicit racism, which was also sustained by the social Darwinism common in late 19th century thought and which influenced the Australian national identity at least until the 1970s. The republicanism also first fully articulated by this minority only became a mainstream issue a century later.

Comprehensive introductions to various dimensions of Australian nationalism can be found in Richard White's *Inventing Australia: Images and Identity 1688–1980* (George Allen and Unwin, 1981); W. G. McMinn's *Nationalism and Federalism in Australia* (Oxford University Press, 1994); and Stephen Alomes and Catherine Jones, (Eds.) *Australian Nationalism: A Documentary History* (Angus and Robertson, Sydney, 1991).

## AUSTRIAN NATIONALISM
For more than a thousand years, Austria has been part of the German *Kulturnation.* German literature contains many works of Austrian authors and the compositions of Haydn, Mozart, Schubert, and Brahms have long been considered products of German culture. For hundreds of years Vienna was one of Germany's preeminent centers of trade and learning; Europe's oldest remaining German-speaking university was founded in Vienna in 1365. But it was not until the mid-19th century that German-speaking Austrians were forced to consider whether a unified German nation-state should include them.

In 1848 Austria had sent representatives to the Frankfurt Assembly, which sought in vain to draft a liberal constitution for all German-speaking people. Austria failed to thwart Otto von Bismarck's subsequent policy to achieve a "small German" unification centered on Prussia and excluding Austria. Politically excluded from the newly unified Germany in 1871, the two German-speaking states became economic, diplomatic, and military partners, with Austria as the junior partner except in the cultural sphere. Multinational Austria-Hungary became increasingly weakened in an age of rising nationalism. It overreacted when Archduke Franz Ferdinand and his wife were murdered in June 1914 by a Bosnian nationalist in Sarajevo, helping to set off a chain reaction which led to World War I.

During the war, Austria-Hungary became bewildered and confused as losses mounted and Germany's military power ebbed. In 1918 many of its non-German nationalities were in open resistance, and an exhausted Austria simply stopped fighting. On November 11, the Austrian kaiser abdicated, and the next day the German-Austrian Republic was proclaimed, comprising the small German remnant of the former empire. For the next two decades Austria was in turmoil.

In desperation, many Austrians demanded to join the newly formed Weimar Republic. The provisional government declared the new country to be a constituent part of Germany, and early in 1919 the German and Austrian foreign ministers signed a protocol paving the way for unification. But the victorious powers vetoed such a combination and even ordered Austria to eliminate the prefix "German" from its name. Nevertheless, *Anschluss* ("joining" with Germany) dominated Austrian debates.

Not until 1937 did Germany—ruled since 1933 by Austrian Adolf Hitler—decide to force an Anschluss; in February a currency union was proclaimed. Under orders from Berlin, the pro-Nazi Austrian interior minister, Arthur von Seyss-Inquart, seized power in 1938 and called upon the German Reich to save Austria from alleged Communist chaos. On March 11, 1938, three days before a scheduled national referendum to determine whether Austria should become an integral part of Germany (which the unifiers were expected to lose), German troops entered Austria. Two days later it became a province (with its designation from a millennium earlier: *Ostmark*) of the Third Reich.

During this seven-year Anschluss, Austrians were both victims of and participants in the Nazi terror. A fourth of all adult Austrian males joined the Nazi party, a higher percentage than in Germany. Also, about a fourth of the convicted Nazi war criminals were Austrian. On the other hand, Austria had been occupied against its people's will in 1938 and had had no alternative to fighting alongside Germany. Hoping to foment an Austrian revolt against Germany, the Allied Powers declared in October 1943 that Germany's annexation of Austria made the latter "the first free country to fall victim to Hitlerite aggression."

After the war, many Austrians gladly embraced this interpretation, along with the collective absolution and release from reparations it offered. At the same time, unpleasant memories of the war experience helped convince most Austrians that their destiny was no longer linked directly to Germany. The Austrian government, media, and schools embarked upon a persistent and successful policy of instilling in their citizens' minds that Austria was a nation separate from Germany. In a 1956 poll, 46 percent of Austrians indicated that they belonged to the German nation, but by 1991 three-fourths said that an Austrian nationality already existed, with only 5 percent rejecting Austrian nationhood.

In 1955 Austria regained its unity and full sovereignty. The Soviet Union agreed to withdraw its troops and hand over the economic assets it had seized on the condition that Austria adhere to a policy of neutrality on the Swiss model. It opened the way for much more extensive and intimate Austro-German relations. Bilateral trade boomed. Germany became Austria's most important trading partner and source of tourist income. By the 1990s, 40 percent of Austria's industry and 70 percent of its daily newspapers were owned or controlled by German investors.

Considering Germany's economic importance for Austria and the fact that two-thirds of Austria's trade is with the European Union, it is understandable that Austria joined the EU in 1995. Austrians have little fear that they will be dominated by Germany although in other EU countries there were unarticulated fears that Austria's entry might increase the weight of a "German bloc" within the EU. Because the appeal of any form of anschluss has disappeared, most Austrians reacted without anxiety to Germany's unification in 1990. It is possible that after melding with a unified Europe, in which borders become blurred, Austria's fragile identity, which has been carefully nurtured to enable Austria to escape the German legacy, could weaken.

The comforting notion that Austria does not share Germany's history and that the experience between 1938 and 1945 was an aberration to be disregarded was seriously jolted in 1986 when Kurt Waldheim was elected federal president. He was haunted by revelations that he had lied about being a member of the Nazi student union and SA and had served in a *Wehrmacht* unit involved in war crimes in the Balkans. This scandal not only placed a straitjacket on Austria's foreign relations

until he stepped down in 1992, but it again brought to light Austria's complicity in Germany's war effort and crimes.

More and more Austrians have come to agree that their country must "come to grips" with its past. Unlike the Germans, the Austrians have never engaged in a cathartic debate about their Nazi past, hiding behind the comfortable official interpretation that they had been Hitler's first victims. However, in 1991, Ex-Chancellor Franz Vranitzky admitted that many Austrians had supported Hitler and had taken a hand in his crimes; he apologized for the atrocities Austrians had committed. In 1993 he became the first chancellor to visit Israel, where he acknowledged that Austrians had been not only victims but also "willing servants of Nazism." Viktor Klima, the first Austrian chancellor born after World War II, emphasized in 1997 that his government was committed to confronting and studying the Nazi past: "it must teach us."

Jörg Haider, leader of the Freedom Party of Austria (FPO), a fiery young (born 1950) orator and a charismatic crowd-pleaser, has called for a more nationalistic policy and denounced the influx of immigrants. The government felt obliged to respond by introducing some of Europe's toughest immigration laws. One of the FPO's election posters read, "Don't Let Vienna Turn Into Chicago!"

For further reading see Basset's *Waldheim and Austria* (Penguin, 1988); William T. Bluhm's *Building an Austrian Nation* (Yale, 1973); Lonnie Johnson's *Introducing Austria. A Short History* (Ariadne, 1992); Richard Mitten's *Politics of Antisemitic Prejudice. The Waldheim Phenomenon in Austria* (Westview, 1992); F. Parkinson's (Ed.) *Conquering the Past: Austrian Nazism Yesterday & Today* (Wayne State, 1989); and Wayne C. Thompson's "Austria" in *Western Europe*, edited by W. C. Thompson (Stryker-Post Publications, annually updated).

## AUSTRO-HUNGARIAN EMPIRE

The Austro-Hungarian Empire, which met is demise in 1918, was a truly multinational entity. There were eleven major national groups in the empire, separated into "historic nations" (Germans, Magyars, Poles, Italians, and Croats) and "nonhistoric nations" (Czechs, Slovaks, Ruthenians, Serbs, Slovenes, and Romanians). With the growth of the European bourgeoisie in the 19th century and the subsequent development of "national reawakenings" across central and eastern Europe, the so-called nationality question came to dwarf all other problems in Austria-Hungary, finally culminating with the dissolution of the empire.

Nationalism in Austria-Hungary can be divided into

three elements: the assimilatory nationalisms of the Germans, Magyars, and Poles; the autonomist and counter-assimilatory nationalisms of the Croats, Czechs, Ruthenians, Romanians, and Slovaks; and the irredentist nationalisms of the Italians and Serbs. What is significant is that prior to World War I only the empire's numerically insignificant Italians and Serbs (and some Romanians) favored irredentism and both of these national groups had nation-states outside of the empire. Most of the national movements within the dual monarchy aimed at achieving autonomy and most were directed against other specific nationalities within the Empire, with only the Magyars and the irredentists directing their nationalism against the monarchy itself.

The Germans were the leading national group within the empire and exercised an influence that was not at all in proportion to their numbers. Throughout the 19th century, German nationalism was aimed at maintaining those privileges, and the practices of Germanization or national assimilation were not as widespread or pernicious as the Magyar attempts at Magyarization. The second largest national group within the Austrian half of the empire were the Czechs. Like the Croats, the Czech nationalists did not seek independent statehood, but instead desired greater autonomy within the monarchy.

In the late 19th century there was a widespread resurgence of nationalist sentiment amongst the Czechs, who demanded that they be given control of the education system and be allowed to use their own language for administrative purposes. This brought the Czechs into direct conflict with the Germans who occupied large parts of the same territory. Both national groups had significant educated middle classes and so they engaged in a protracted struggle for control of resources. In the late 1880s the Young Czechs were founded, but the idea of establishing a separate Czech state did not become widespread until around 1914. The position of the Slovenes was similar to that of the Czechs. With no history of statehood, the Slovene national movement was largely literary and linguistic, and as with the Czechs, this brought the Slovenes into conflict with the Germans who resided in Slovenia.

The position of the Poles within the Austrian half of the monarchy can be more closely likened to the positions of the Germans and Magyars. With a recent history of statehood, the Poles did not share the need of others for a national reawakening. Furthermore, as a geographically remote part of the empire they were accorded almost complete self-rule, and allied themselves with the Austrians as a way of securing a permanent parliamentary majority over the more troublesome

Croats and Czechs. Polish Galicia contained large numbers of the rurally based Ruthenians. Although they began developing a national consciousness during the 19th century, they were subjected to processes of a national assimilation conducted by the Poles that was very much akin to the aggressive Magyarization program.

The sole irrendentists within the Austrian half of the monarchy were the Italians. It is important though that we should not overestimate the strength of Italian nationalism. The unified Italy of 1861 was brought about by the armies of France and not by the armies of Piedmont and Garibaldi; it is worth noting that more Frenchmen than Italians were killed in the battles for Italian unification and that most Italians that were killed were fighting in the Austro-Hungarian army. Following the unification of Italy, Italian communities in Tyrolia, Istria, and Dalmatia desired secession from the empire, though they were not numerically strong enough to do anything about this. As such, the Italian nationalists in Istria and Dalmatia spent most of their energies trying to assert their cultural superiority and disrupting the development of Croatian nationalism.

The Magyars were totally dominant in Hungary, even more so than the Germans in Austria. The famous Magyar nationalist Louis Kossuth instigated a policy of Magyar supremacy which was aimed at the assimilation of non-Magyars. Those who insisted on using vernacular languages, for instance, were repressed. Within Hungary, Magyarization was hugely successful. In 1848, three-quarters of the population of Budapest were German; by 1910, three-quarters were Magyar. Toward the end of the 19th century, Magyarization increased in pace, as Germanization receded in the Austrian half. Although successful in Hungary, Magyarization produced several anti-Magyar nationalist movements, particularly among the Romanians, Slovaks, and Croats.

In Transylvania, Magyarization led to the founding of the Romanian National Party in 1881, which demanded autonomy at first but later came to advocate irredentism after 1906. The Slovaks were the weakest and least privileged group in the Habsburg monarchy. All the Slovaks lived within the territory of the Kingdom of Hungary, and they had enjoyed no previous experience of statehood. However, as a result of Magyar attempts to suppress Slovak culture in the 1870s, a national consciousness emerged, and nationally oriented groups began cooperating with the Czechs, though a joint Czecho–Slovak state was not widely enthused about until after 1914.

The Croats occupied a position similar to the Poles in the Austrian half of the monarchy. As a result of their history of statehood and strong nobility, the Croats were the only south Slavic group to be in contact with the monarchy, and would often be used by the Austrians as a counterbalance against the Magyars, whose Magyarization program infuriated the Croats. In the 1860s, for example, it was a legion of Jelacic's Croats who initially defended Vienna from the insurrectionist Magyars. The Croats hoped that in return for their continued loyalty they would be rewarded with a trialist solution, with the south Slav inhabitants of the empire being united in a Croatian entity which would have an identical position to Hungary within the empire. This idea was gaining in credence in Vienna, and Archduke Franz Ferdinand was widely purported to have been sympathetic until he was murdered by Greater Serbian nationalists.

The final national group were the Serbs, who were in a unique position as they were separated into different jurisdictions within the empire. Having hijacked the Illryianist ideas of Croats, many Serb nationalists argued for an expanded Serbian state that would incorporate Bosnia-Herzegovina, Motenegro, parts of Croatia, and parts of Hungary. It was this extreme irredentism that was finally to result in the collapse of Europe's last multinational empire. Somewhat curiously, after a century of the dominance of the nation-state, revisionist historians remind us that far from being the "prison house of nations," Austria-Hungary was actually supported by more nationalist groups than opposed it.

For further reading see R. Kahn's *Multinational Empire: Nationalism and National Reform in the Habsburg Monarchy 1848–1918* (New York, 1977); J. Mason's *Dissolution of the Austro-Hungarian Empire* (London, 1985); and A. Sked's *Decline and Fall of the Habsburg Empire 1815–1918* (London, 1989).

**AUTHORITARIANISM** A label applied, not always precisely or consistently, to a wide variety of dictatorial political systems ranging from ancient theocracies and tyrannies to 20th century totalitarian regimes. It also denominates a state of mind or a set of attributes said to characterize actual or potential supporters of authoritarian government. As both a form of rule and a state of mind, authoritarianism in modern times is often associated with nationalism.

Authoritarian regimes are distinguished from liberal democracies primarily by their intolerance of political opposition, censorship of mass media, and restrictions on personal freedom, as well as by the concentration of power in the hands of one person or an elite group. Many analysts further distinguish between traditional or premodern forms of authoritarianism—e.g., dynastic regimes like Saudi Arabia's or personal tyrannies like the Duvalier family's presidential dictatorship in

Haiti—and modern forms. The latter include, among others, fascist and Communist regimes and postcolonial "developmental dictatorships" such as Kwame Nkrumah's single-party socialist state in Ghana in the mid-1960s.

In traditional authoritarian societies, the ruling class generally makes no attempt to mobilize broad support for the regime and puts forward no claim to embody the will of all the people, instead resting content with the apathy and passive obedience of its subjects. Modern authoritarian rulers, by contrast, typically stand at the head of a mass-based political party or movement, rely heavily on bureaucracy and a machinery of agitation and propaganda to manufacture consensus, and legitimize their monopoly on power by appealing to nationalistic ideology.

Nationalism, indeed, according to Amos Perlmutter, "is the most powerful instrument of mass authoritarian regimes." To be sure, the leaders of such regimes have a wide variety of motives, both pragmatic and idealistic, for embracing nationalist belief systems and policies. Besides the legitimizing function, nationalist ideology may enable an authoritarian rulership to mobilize the population behind its project of implementing social and economic reform. Thus, as A. James Gregor documents, Mussolini's Fascist Party utilized authoritarian nationalism in an effort to transform popular consciousness, overturn the bourgeois order in Italy, and bring about rapid modernization. Similar motives appear to have animated the Bolshevik Party in Russia, especially under Stalin, who jettisoned the internationalism of classical Marxism in the process of developing "socialism in one country."

Not surprisingly, the social discord and chaos that often result from authoritarian attempts at modernization are used to justify the continuance of authoritarian measures. Moreover, in newly emergent nations, authoritarian governments may combine repression with nationalism in order to counteract tribalist tendencies, as in Africa, or regionalism and parochialism, as in South Asia. On the other hand, as Peter Alter observes, many authoritarian governments invoke antiforeign nationalism simply as a means of diverting attention from problems at home and reducing popular dissatisfaction with the regime.

In any event, authoritarian politics inevitably accompanies what Liah Greenfeld calls "collectivistic-authoritarian" nationalism, an antilibertarian variety—still common in parts of Eastern Europe and the less developed world—which views the nation in "unitary terms." If the nation is regarded as a collective individual with a "single will," Greenfeld notes, then someone with dictatorial authority must interpret that will for the many who are prevented by ignorance or false consciousness from perceiving it correctly.

Beginning in the 1930s, a number of social scientists, inspired in part by Karl Marx and Sigmund Freud, investigated the link between personality and authoritarianism. Erich Fromm's *Escape from Freedom* (1941) argued that the uprootedness and directionless freedom of capitalist society had left modern people's isolated and suffering from an intolerable feeling of "moral aloneness" and powerlessness, a condition from which they sought escape through conformity with mass opinion, as in democratic societies, and submission to authoritarian leadership, as in Nazi Germany. Fromm profiled an "authoritarian character" which he attributed to many in Europe's lower-middle class, a mainstay of Fascist movements. He described this character as sadomasochistic, dualistically reflecting, at least on an unconscious level, and having a sadistic wish to dominate as well as a masochistic wish to surrender individuality and submit to domination. For such a personality, nationalist doctrine and an all-powerful *Führer* promised "relief from uncertainty," eliminating the burden of freedom and creating a new sense of connectedness.

*The Authoritarian Personality* (1950), an empirical study by several German and American scholars known as the Berkeley group, built on the work of Fromm and others. It identified a cluster of personality traits—derived from responses to a set of discreetly worded questionnaire statements called the F scale—that typified potential supporters of fascism. Criticized for methodological shortcomings and for overlooking authoritarian pathologies of the Left, the book nevertheless spawned an immense amount of further research, some of which discovered positive correlations between nationalist attitudes and authoritarianism.

Although somewhat outdated as a textbook, Roy C. Macridis's *Moden Political Regimes: Patterns and Institutions* (Little, Brown and Co., 1986) remains unsurpassed in the clarity of its definitions. Macridis makes a sharp distinction between authoritarian and totalitarian regimes, a distinction not entirely accepted in Amos Perlmutter's *Modern Authoritarianism* (Yale University Press, 1981). A. James Gregor's *The Ideology of Fascism: The Rationale of Totalitarianism* (Free Press, 1969) and *Italian Fascism and Developmental Dictatorship* (Princeton University Press, 1979) explore the relationship between nationalism and authoritarianism in Mussolini's corporate state. Peter Alter's *Nationalism*, translated by Stuart McKinnon-Evans (Edward Arnold, 1989), highlights the importance of nationalism as both an ideology and a political movement in the developing world,

while *Authoritarian Politics in Modern Society* (Basic Books, 1970), a collection of scholarly essays edited by Samuel P. Huntington and Clement H. Moore, stresses the long-term incompatibility of authoritarianism with economic modernization. An important critique of psychosocial studies of authoritarianism is H. D. Forbes's *Nationalism, Ethnocentrism, and Personality* (University of Chicago Press, 1985).

**AUTONOMY** The ability to act independently. Many regard autonomy as the capacity of the state to affect a desired outcome. As such, autonomy is closely related to power. Put simply, greater power leads to greater autonomy.

The autonomy of states is debated at two levels of analysis. First, nation-state autonomy can be characterized by a capacity to act independent from the influence of other states in the world system. Second, the autonomy of state government itself can be debated. The latter often attempts to answer the following: Who has power (the ability to act autonomously) in a state? This simple questuion has generated a lively, often acrimonious, debate among political and social scholars.

Some theorists, such as Theda Skocpol, have assigned nation-state governments a relatively large degree of autonomy with regard to the capacity to enact and enforce law. These theorists usually cite specific examples (often social welfare laws) where policy was enforced by a government against the wishes of business or other elite interests.

Other theorists, often Marxists, argue that elite class interests control the state. For example, these theorists might be interested in describing the military-industrial complex as a coalition of elite business interests who control government decision making. Some advocates of the theory of late capitalism, such as Claus Offe, believe the state acts as a mediator between elite interests and the working class. Both of these ideas assign more power to the elite and refute the idea that the state acts autonomously from class interests.

Class theorists, not always Marxists, believe that a coalition of identifiable elite rule. C. Wright Mills, who coined the term "the power elite," and William Dumhoff have demonstrated elite families had influence (through foundations, personal contacts, and political donations) on the construction of social policy. These studies are often specific to the United States and were conducted primarily to refute both pluralists and state autonomy theorists.

Pluralists are often reluctant to assign autonomy to state government. These theorists often regard the state as an apparatus through which competing interests (labor unions, political parties, and social movements) make policy. In this model, power is dispersed throughout the system. While certain actors are more autonomous than other actors are, the state is regarded as a field where they can exercise their power in forming policy. These theorists tend to regard the state apparatus as a tool, not a source of power. Robert Dahl is foremost among the pluralist thinkers. He has generally argued that the U.S. system of governance has been strong because it has allowed for a plurality of interests to compete within the governing system.

In general, the same characteristics of the autonomy of states debate exists when using the world system as the level of analysis. Marxists and dependency theorists generally assume that a coalition of class interests, within and across state boundaries, have power. These theorists argue that the structural system of global capitalism systematically deprives small developing states from exercising autonomy from the West. While these states may be formally "independent," they are still controlled by elite interests in the West. Immanuel Wallerstein, originator of "World Systems" theory, is an advocate of this general idea. Likewise, many leaders in the developing world, often citing the influence of the World Bank and International Monetary Fund, label economic liberalism as a form of neocolonialism that prevents small states from exercising autonomy.

In contrast to the Marxists, liberal theorists argue that the capitalist system creates greater autonomy for small states. Because these states have the capacity to choose from a number of markets where they can sell their goods, and because they inevitably have a comparative advantage in the production of a good or service, small states can exercise a high degree of autonomy within the system. Liberal theorists most often believe the role of the state is to build infrastructure and provide for a basic education. They generally point to successful developing countries with export-oriented economies, such as the small Asian nations of South Korea, Thailand, and Singapore, as examples of small states that have developed rapidly and exercise a high degree of autonomy in the world system.

For a study of nation-state autonomy in the global economy see Immanuel Wallerstein's *Modern World System: Capitalist Agriculture and the Origins of the European World Economy in the Sixteenth Century* (Academic Press, 1974) and Robert Gilpen's *Political Economy of International Relations* (Princeton University Press, 1987). For an introduction to the debate concerning the autonomy of state government from elite interests see *Bringing the State Back In*, edited by Evans, Rueschemeyer, and Skocpol, and W. Dumhoff's *State Autonomy or Class Dominance?* (Aldine De Gruyter, 1996).

# B

**BACK TO AFRICA MOVEMENT**    The position that nationalist aspirations for black Americans should involve emigration to Africa rather than an effort to achieve mainstream status within U.S. society.

In the specific sense the movement is principally associated with the efforts of Marcus Garvey (1887–1940) the Jamaica-born U.S. leader of the UNIA (Universal Negro Improvement Association). This was the first major black separatist organization in the United States and it advocated the establishment in Africa of a self-governing nation of black citizens.

At its height in 1919–1920 the UNIA claimed a membership in excess of two million, with activities centered in the Harlem section of New York City. In 1920, Garvey presided over an international convention with delegates from 25 countries, but shortly after this his power declined when he was convicted of mail fraud. The UNIA disbanded without ever affecting a significant relocation of black Americans to Africa.

Though the Back to Africa movement did not succeed in its immediate goal, the policies of Garvey and the UNIA had a lasting effect on black nationalism. Garvey's movement set out to establish black capitalism and economic independence, to stress the importance of black pride and individual self-respect, and to build awareness of African history and cultural achievements. All of these are familiar elements of contemporary black nationalist movements in the United States.

**BADEN-POWELL, ROBERT**    1857–1941, Founded the Boy Scout movement in 1908. The professed aims of the organization were to promote the mental, moral, and physical development of young men by stressing outdoor skills and training in citizenship and lifesaving. The impetus for the formation of the Scouts was Baden-Powell's deep and abiding belief in the need to train a cadre of British youth capable of carrying through the mission of British imperial expansion.

The idea for the formation of a club for boys that would instill habits of discipline, bravery, and manliness in young men was first suggested to General Baden-Powell by his experiences as an army general in Africa and Asia. His experiences in southern Africa not only left the deepest impression on him but also, until he founded the Scouts, were the source of his fame in Britain. Powell became well known after he defended the town of Mafekeng from the Boers for 217 straight days in 1900. When news of his exploits reached Britain the celebrations were so intense that from thenceforward aggressive outbursts of jingoistic enthusiasm were termed "mafficking." Once his success began to wane, Powell embarked on the project that was to earn him enduring recognition—the formation of a disciplinary program for young men that would train them to be fit representatives of the British Empire. It was from his corps of boy messengers formed at Mafekeng that his program, the Boy Scouts, took its name. His initials were the inspiration for the Scout's famous motto, "Be Prepared."

As a military man, Powell based his organization on the strict discipline and regimentation that were both characteristic of and necessary for success in the army. Boys were expected to be loyal to God and country, to retain standards of gentlemanly conduct at all times, and to never countenance fear or dishonesty. Fun and games such as campfires and "African chants" tempered the strict discipline and most of the outdoor activities were meant to aid in the acquisition of military skills as the program grew out of Powell's experiences with military reconnaissance. To pass from one level to the next (similar to scaling the ranks in the army) boys were expected to acquire such skills as flying the Union Jack, tracking through forests, and first aid.

The purpose of the Scouts was not simply to train young men to be efficient soldiers, however. Rather, Powell was most concerned to stem the alarming trends toward internal anarchy, class strife, and social decay that he felt were severely threatening the integrity of the British nation. The Boy Scouts, therefore, were his answer to Britain's need for a healthy, vigorous, and, above all, loyal population. Boys who were alert, yet disciplined, would, he and others believed, make efficient citizens. Thus Boy Scouting drew support from the contemporary vogue for British national efficiency as it promised to promote class harmony and improve the masses as it strengthened the British Empire.

## BALAKIREV, MILY ALEKSEYEVICH  1836–1910, A composer, pianist, conductor, and educator; leader of the group *Moguchaia kucka* ("The Mighty Handful").

Highly influenced by Stasov's concept of national Russian art and preoccupied with a search for its practical applications, Balakirev became an embattled symbol of Russian nationalism in music. Developing Glinka's musical tradition, he attempted to invent an original "Russian" harmonic style connected with melodic and modal idiosyncrasies of Russian folk songs. Balakirev's primary source was the 40 folk songs that he collected in his expedition along the Volga in the summer of 1860 and published as an anthology in 1866. Composing piano arrangements of these songs in the spirit of a national style, Balakirev developed new methods of harmonization which were perceived by his contemporaries as distinctively Russian. This harmonic style could be successfully applied to the musical themes outside of folk material, and it was adopted and further developed by Balakirev's friends, composers of "The Mighty Handful."

As part of his concern with Stasov's theory of Russian orientalism, Balakirev made two folk expeditions to the Caucasus in 1862 and 1863. Balakirev's best compositional accomplishments are his "oriental" works: a symphonic poem, *Tamara* (1867–1882), by Lermontov, and the epochal piano fantasy *Islamey* (1869).

An indisputable authority for his friends, Balakirev transmitted to them his nationalist aesthetic views and musical beliefs. His almost unlimited influence on them lasted from 1856 to the beginning of the 1870s, when increasing individualization led to a natural disintegration of the group. But in the beginning of their professional musical careers, Balakirev alone served as a substitute for as yet a nonexistent conservatory, sharing with his friends his extensive knowledge of old and modern music literature, and rigorously advising their compositional projects.

A convinced adherent of the Slavophiles, Balakirev was a principal adversary of academic musical education in Russia as it was proposed by Anton Rubinstein and his party of Germanophiles. Balakirev carried out public polemics in an extremely malicious anti-Semitic tone, since he believed that Rubinstein's interests were inherently German and Jewish, and thus alien to Russian national identity. (It may be that strong anti-Semitism was a common prejudice among Russian nationalist composers, which Balakirev inherited from Blinka and passed on to many of the composers of "The Mighty Handful," especially to Mussorgsky.)

The second field of fervent struggle between Balakirev and Rubinstein was the issue of the "national musical element" versus a cosmopolitan European musical style promoted by the Germanophiles. Balakirev was especially hostile to the genre and technique of "German" symphonies. Within his circles of composers, Balakirev was an advocate of the genre of program symphonic music, which would follow traditions of Glinka's *Kamarinskaya* and two "Spanish" overtures—compositions that Balakirev considered to be the best examples of Russian national style.

Ironically, in his own compositional practice, particularly in the two Overtures on Russian Themes (1859 and 1869—the second was provided with a new title, *1000 Years*, in 1882, and with yet another, *Rus'*, in 1884), Balakirev, while succeeding in a stylistic purification of folk themes, nevertheless adapted "German" form (sonata-allegro) and methods of symphonic development. He was forced to resort to the advanced European technique in order to disprove the constant accusations of dilettantism that came from the party of Germanophiles. Moreover, Balakirev had no compositional alternative, since historically Russia had not developed a native tradition of secular art music, so that both nationalist composers and the Germanophiles were dependent on Western forms and compositional technique. But while the Germanophiles were interested in classical musical forms and composers, the Balakirev circle admired and learned from modern romantic composers, primarily Schumann, Lizst, and Berlioz.

Perhaps the most fundamental difference between Slavophiles and Germanophiles was the issue of musical amateurism of dilettantism versus professionalism. Their confrontation manifested itself as well in the rivalry of their two concert organizations: Balakirev's Free Music School (founded in 1862 together with the outstanding choral conductor Gavriil Lomakin with the aim of providing an elementary musical education to nonprofessional performers) and Rubinstein's Russian Musical Society, affiliated with the Conservatory. In the framework of the struggle between dilettantism and professionalism, there was actually a hidden struggle between modernism (that is, romanticism) and classicism.

While concerts of the Free Music School presented a modern repertoire and compositions of Balakirev's circle, the Russian Musical Society concerts focused on works of Haydn, Mozart, Beethoven, Palestrina, Handel, and Bach.

The first 16 years (1855–1871) of Balakirev's ideological and cultural activities were a "truly heroic epoch" (Asafiev). A mental and spiritual crisis in 1871 turned Balakirev from a freethinker to a fanatic and extremely superstitious Orthodox Christian. After four years of staying away from his friends and musical life, Balakirev resumed his musical activities in 1876, accepting an appointment as the director of the Imperial Court Chapel. His political views progressed in the direction of ultranationalism and xenophobic chauvinism that put a strain on his relations with Stasov and with surviving members of "The Mighty Handful." Estranged from his old friends, in 1890 Balakirev gathered around himself a new group of younger composers, of whom the most distinguished composer and the most orthodox follower was Sergei Lyapunov (1859–1924).

The only complete biography of Balakirev in English is Edward Garden's *Balakirev* (Faber and Faber, 1967). His nationalism and Slavophilism are discussed in Richard Taruskin's *Defining Russia Musically* (Princeton University Press, 1997), especially in the chapter, "How the Acorn Took Root." Issues of Balakirev's modernism and his rivalry with the Germanophiles are discussed in Robert C. Ridenour's *Nationalism, Modernism, and Personal Rivalry in Nineteenth-Century Russian Music* (UMI Press, 1977).

## BALFOUR DECLARATION

In 1917 Britain sought Jewish support in Europe and America for the Allied war effort. This was a time when British troops were undermining the Ottoman Empire's hold over Palestine and other Arab lands in the Middle East. In this setting, the British secretary of state for foreign affairs, Arthur Balfour (1848–1930), sent a letter to a Zionist leader indicating that Britain would support a Jewish homeland in Palestine: "His Majesty's Government view with favour the establishment in Palestine of a national home for the Jewish people, and will use their best endeavours to facilitate the achievement of this object." However, this declaration contained the further irreconcilable pledge that "nothing shall be done which may prejudice the civil and religious rights of the existing non-Jewish communities in Palestine." Such "non-Jewish communities" constituted 90 percent of Palestine's inhabitants.

The British were never able to overcome the contradiction contained in this declaration. Nevertheless, it became official British policy for two decades, and the victorious Allies endorsed the document at the Paris Peace Conference in 1919. This document served for a while as the basis for London's support of Jewish immigration and settlement in Palestine during the interwar years, when Palestine was a British mandate granted by the League of Nations. However, in a bid for Arab support in the coming World War II, Britain ordered a stop to Jewish settlement in 1939, arguing that it had already fulfilled its responsibilities under the Balfour Declaration. This created a bloody conflict with the Jews in Palestine, who regarded the Declaration as granting them a right to establish a sovereign Jewish state. Finally, in 1948, the British, facing armed resistance from both Arabs and Jews, withdrew from Palestine. The state of Israel was declared, and years of warfare between the new state and its Arab neighbors followed.

## BANCROFT, GEORGE

1800–1891, U.S. historian, born in Worcester, Massachusetts. Bancroft served as U.S. minister to Great Britain and Germany and as Secretary of the Navy; although he helped establish the U.S. Naval Academy at Annapolis, Maryland, he is best remembered as the "father of American history." His most important contribution in this regard was his *History of the United States*. This 10-volume work, which was published between 1834 and 1874, marked a new development in the writing of American history. Earlier historians had contented themselves with writing mainly about the war of the American Revolution or about the history of their state or locality. Bancroft offered the first comprehensive view of the evolution of the 13 colonies from the beginning of the colonial period to the creation of the United States via the ratification of the U.S. Constitution.

Bancroft's *History* reflected his personal views and background. He was a staunch antislavery democrat and a great admirer of President Andrew Jackson, whose political ideals celebrated the common man and abhorred elitism (although, in both cases, only among white Americans). Moreover, in 1820 Bancroft had earned his doctorate at Göttingen University in Germany, where he was greatly influenced by nationalists who believed that the unification of the various German principalities into a single German state was inevitable. Not surprisingly, two themes resonate throughout *History*—that the creation of the United States from a group of disparate colonies was bound to occur, and that democratic principles represent the highest ideal to which a people or nation can aspire.

Bancroft viewed the American Revolution as primarily a political and military event. In so doing, he reflected the views of most contemporary Americans, who thought of the struggle with Great Britain as a contest between "good" patriots and "bad" monarchists (or between good egalitarians and bad elitists), with the victory going inevitably to the forces of good. Several critics took him to task for his unabashed approval of Jacksonian democracy, particularly in the first three volumes covering the colonial period from 1607 to 1748 which were published between 1834 and 1840; one even suggested that the first volume practically urged its readers to reelect Jackson to a third term. Later historians, especially those of the Progressive and New Left schools, took him to task for his failure to regard the American Revolution as a socioeconomic phenomenon, insomuch as it also involved a struggle for power between different social classes and was caused in large part by economic considerations involving far more than unjust taxation.

Nevertheless, Bancroft offered his countrymen a version of their early history that celebrated the righteousness of the patriot cause and the dedication of U.S. nationalism to the complete democratization of society.

Biographies of Bancroft include Lilian Handlin's *George Bancroft, the Intellectual as Democrat* (1984), and Marc Antony DeWolfe Howe's *Life and Letters of George Bancroft* (2 vols., 1908). Richard C. Vitzhum's *American Compromise: Theme and Method in the Histories of Bancroft, Parkman, and Adams* (1973) examines Bancroft's contribution to U.S. cultural nationalism.

**BANDERA, STEPAN**  1909–1959, A leader of the Organization of Ukrainian Nationalists and modern symbol of radical Ukrainian nationalism. Stepan Bandera was born in Uhryniv Staryi in Austrian-controlled Galicia (now in western Ukraine), but was ethnically Ukrainian. After World War I Galicia was transferred to the revived Polish state, which began a policy of Polonization of its populace. Growing up in a period of forced assimilation and oppression against Ukrainians led Bandera to accept violence and subversion as means of creating a Ukrainian state.

While in school in L'viv in 1927, Bandera joined the Ukrainian Military Organization (UVO), an organization dedicated to the destabilization of Poland and willing to use terror to this end [the UVO became the Organization of Ukrainian Nationalists (OUN) in 1929]. He quickly rose within the OUN, becoming chief of propaganda in 1931 and head of the OUN in Galicia in June 1933, until arrested in 1934 for masterminding the assassination of the Polish Minister of the Interior, Bronisław Pieracki. For this he was sentenced to life in

prison and spent the next five years in the Bereza Kartuzka concentration camp, until freed by the fall of Poland in September 1939.

After the head of the OUN, Evhen Konovalets, was killed in 1938, Andrii Melnyk was elected to lead the group. Melnyk represented an older generation of Ukrainian nationalists who had been active in 1917–1920 in trying to secure a Ukrainian state. Younger nationalists, those of Bandera's generation who had fought Poland in the 1930s and many of whom had spent time in jail for their cause, opposed Melnyk and wanted to militarize the OUN. On February 10, 1941, Bandera called a conference of radicals in Kraków, Poland. The conference refused to accept Melnyk as leader, and named Bandera head of the OUN. This lead to the split of the OUN in the spring of 1941 into two groups: OUN-B (Banderites), who were more militant, younger, and supported Bandera, and OUN-M (Melnykites), who were generally older, more ideological, and supported Melnyk. These groups were to clash, often violently, for many years, both ideologically and for financial support.

One of the main sources of financial support for the OUN in this period was Germany. In April 1941, 600 Banderites were formed by the Germans into a military force, the Legion of Ukrainian Nationalists. Bandera and his supporters hoped to use this group both to liberate Ukraine and as the nucleus of a future Ukrainian army. The Legion fought against the Soviets in the June 1941 German invasion in two operational groups, Nachtigall and Roland. In addition to the Legion, Bandera sent some 1500 members of the OUN-B into Ukraine behind the advancing German forces. Their mission was to aid with anti-Soviet propaganda and to build an independent Ukrainian administrative system.

On June 30, 1941, Bandera and another OUN-B leader, Iaroslav Stets'ko, declared a sovereign Ukrainian state in L'viv. Bandera hoped that the Germans would accept this as an allied state, but Berlin wanted a subordinate, not a free, Ukraine. A few days later Bandera was arrested and sent to Germany, where he was interred in a concentration camp until September 1944. In addition, the Germans disbanded the Legion, arrested its leaders, and transferred support to the OUN-M. These acts led the Banderites to join the Ukrainian Insurgent Army (UPA) in 1943 to fight both the Soviets and the Germans. By November 1943 Bandera's OUN-B supporters were leading the UPA, which was the main Ukrainian resistance movement and was centered in Galicia, having over 100,000 members (an additional 13,000 Galicians fought against the Soviets in the German Galician Division).

After the war Stepan Bandera remained in Germany where he could direct resistance against the USSR (the UPA continued to fight the Soviets until 1953) and seek support among radical Ukrainian émigrés, displaced persons, and UPA members who fought their way to Germany. In May 1953 Bandera was elected the head of the OUN abroad. He then founded the OUN-R (Revolutionary) to continue the fight for an independent Ukraine from outside the Soviet Union. The OUN-R received much support from displaced Ukrainian workers and peasants (the intelligentsia tended to support Melnyk's OUN-M), many of whom emigrated to Canada and the United Kingdom.

Although Bandera was assassinated by a Soviet agent in Munich, Germany, in 1959, the OUN-R has continued as an influential émigré nationalist group. This organization is well funded and has long supported militant Ukrainian nationalism. In 1991, with Ukraine's declaration of independence, the OUN-R became active in Ukrainian post-Soviet politics. In 1992 the OUN-R helped found, and now provides support for, the Congress of Ukrainian Nationalists (KUN), a strongly nationalist anti-Soviet and anti-Russian political party that supports Ukraine's integration into Europe and is against membership in the Commonwealth of Independent States (CIS). The Congress of Ukrainian Nationalists had 5 members in parliament (out of 450) in 1997.

## BANGLADESHI NATIONALISM

The People's Republic of Bangladesh was established as an independent state in 1972. The region was originally East Pakistan, part of the Muslim homeland created in 1947 at the time of the partition of British India.

During negotiations with the British for India's independence, the All-India Muslim League agitated for a Muslim homeland, breaking with the Indian National Congress and Mohandas Gandhi, who wanted a united India. Those areas with a majority Muslim population were to become Pakistan and those areas with a majority Hindu population would be part of India.

The original Pakistan consisted of two geographically separated sections, West Pakistan in the Indus River Valley and East Pakistan more than 1000 miles to the east in the delta of the Ganges and Jamuna rivers. Although united by law and by the Islamic faith, the two parts of the country were culturally quite different. The proud people of Bengal, with a rich literary and cultural tradition, were increasingly unhappy with a nation ruled from Islamabad.

Tensions between the two regions escalated following the war with India over Kashmir in 1965. A clash occurred between the Awami League, the major political force in East Pakistan, and the central government. The leader of the league, Mujibur Rahman (Sheikh Mujib), was arrested in 1966 and accused of conspiring with India.

When the Pakistani head of state General Mohammad Ayub Khan refused to stand for election in 1970, protests flared throughout the country but especially in Bengal in East Pakistan. He resigned, the elections occurred in December 1970, Sheikh Mujib's Awami League swept the elections, and the sheikh called for independence of East Pakistan except for its foreign policy. Negotiations between East and West Pakistan failed, leading to open warfare between government troops and the Awami League. Millions of East Pakistanis, including Mujib, fled across the border into India to escape the fighting, and in December 1971 India invaded East Pakistan.

The new Bangladesh ("Bengal Land") government was established in January 1972 with Mujib as its first prime minister.

## BARAKA, IMAMU AMIRI (LEROI JONES)

1934–, A community organizer and writer who created a radical black literature through poems, drama, and critical essays. Baraka, in the late 1960s, also became a leading black power spokesman in Newark, New Jersey. He was the head of the Temple of Kawaida, described by Baraka as an "African religious institution—to increase black consciousness." It was under Baraka's leadership that the Temple successfully obtained a $6.4 million mortgage through New Jersey State Finance Agency for the construction of the Kawaida Towers, a 16-story low- and middle-income housing project in the 70 percent white district of Newark's north ward. It was Baraka's battle against Assemblyman Anthony Imperale, head of the white North Ward Citizens Committee, that made black history. Baraka, in a series of political, court, and street protest actions, so successfully used the system to pioneer this project that he turned the tables on his white opponents in Newark by making them feel like the "disgruntled minority."

In March 1971, Baraka achieved national prominence as chairman of the National Black Political Convention in Gary, Indiana, composed of 8000 nationalist and moderate blacks who represented a wide selection of political views. The group approved a political platform called the "Black Agenda," which demanded reparations, proportional congressional representation for blacks, an increase in federal spending to combat crime, and other platform issues that related to black economic and political empowerment, such as a resolution opposing the integration of schools.

As early as the 1970s, Baraka's writings reflected change from an avante garde aesthetic to a black nationalist perspective, and again to his own nationalism, which was a version of Marxist-Leninism. This ideology resulted in the publication of *Motion of History, Six Other Plays* (1978) and *Slave Ship: Selected Plays and Prose of Amiri Baraka/LeRoi Jones* (1979). Although he is not currently a spokesman for any nationalist organization, he is the founder of a Newark jazz organization created for the restoration of Newark's jazz history. His writings on music, his poetry, and his critical essays are a platform for his ideological views on black nationalism. He likewise is a pioneer of many music and writing workshops that seek to maintain and develop a black aesthetic as opposed to a Western ideology.

Baraka is a critic, poet, activist, and playwright recognized as an outspoken critic and advocate for the rights and equality of African-Americans. He tours colleges and university campuses speaking and reading from his varied works.

## BASQUE NATIONALISM

Movement that promotes the recognition of the political personality of the Basque country. It was born during romanticism in the middle of the 19th century. Together with Catalan nationalism, it represents the most important resistance to Spanish centralism. Basques fought two Carlist wars in 1833–1839 and 1872–1876, trying to defend their *fueros* or feudal liberties from the uniformity drives of Spanish nationalism.

The 4000-year-old Basque language (also known as Euskera) is probably Europe's oldest. Today, one-third of the population knows Euskera, although this proportion is growing.

The main founding father of Basque nationalism is Sabino de Arana (1865–1903). He gave the Basque country a unified name—the neologism Euskadi—and a flag, that of the political party he founded in 1895, the Basque Nationalist Party (BNP). To belong to his party one had to trace back four paternal and maternal generations of genuine Basque family names. He believed that immigrants should not be allowed to learn the Basque language because they did not belong to the nation. His political heirs prefer to overlook such embarrassing views and stress instead his vision and his defense of Basque identity.

During the Second Republic (1931–1936) the BNP became the most important party in Euskadi. It attenuated the racist and Catholic fundamentalist legacies of Arana by adopting a Social-Christian ideology. Thanks

to a younger generation of leaders headed by José Antonio Aguirre (1904–1960) and Manuel de Irujo (1891–1981), the BNP realized an impressive ideological turn: from an electoral coalition with Carlist elements in 1931 to the defense of the legitimate republican government during the civil war in 1936. In contrast to Catalan efforts, the BNP's first attempt to get political autonomy, which it regarded only as a first step toward independence or restitution of the fueros, was derailed by the party's alliance with antirepublican forces and the BNP's rejection of the (certainly anticlerical) Republican Constitution of 1931 on religious grounds. In 1936, in alliance with the left-wing government, the BNP obtained a Basque Statute of autonomy, which was about to be approved when the civil war broke out. It was in force in Biscay from October 1936 to the territory's fall in June 1937. The provinces of Alava (Araba) and Navarre (Nafarroa) followed the military subversion.

Franco's authoritarian regime (1936–1975) suppressed Basque cultural and political expressions, but in doing so provoked a reaffirmation of the national conscience. Navarre and Alava, deemed the "loyal" provinces, kept their traditional privileges of financial autonomy. The execution of more than 700 nationalist priests contributed to the alignment of the powerful Basque Catholic Church with the nationalist cause. In Navarre and Alava the church sided with Franco or remained indifferent.

In 1941, Irujo gathered Basque exiles in London to form a military unit—later dissolved by Churchill—and draft a Basque constitution. In 1945, another BNP member, Aguirre, presided over a Basque government in Paris. Aguirre was substituted by Jesús María de Leizaola at his death in 1960. A clandestine BNP completed its ideological evolution by cofounding the European Union of Christian Democrats.

In 1959, part of a more radical generation launched *Euskadi To Askatasuna* (ETA, "Euskadi and Freedom") out of the youth organization of the BNP. ETA created two antagonistic sectors of nationalists divided by the acceptance or not of terrorism as a legitimate means to achieve independence. ETA's most famous action was the killing of Franco's prime minister and heir apparent, Luis Carrero Blanco, in late 1973, cheered by democratic forces.

In 1960, the first *ikastolas*—schools teaching in Basque—reopened. Their multiplication ran parallel to the implementation of a unified, standard Basque language, the *Euskera Batua*, invented in 1968.

After Franco's death in 1975, Basque self-rule did not need to be reestablished because Franco never formally abolished it: all official acts adopted by the Republic after July 18, 1936, were considered nil and void by the insurgents, so Franco had simply ignored the Basque Statute.

In the constituent parliament elected in 1977, the BNP representatives, after failing to pass an amendment by which the Constitution would abolish all laws against the fueros enacted since 1839, held a detached attitude. They obtained a Basque Statute of autonomy in 1979, a law derived from the 1978 constitution, without needing to explicitly recognize its supremacy. The BNP did not approve nor condemn the Constitution, for it introduced them into an acceptable regime of liberties, honored the existence of nationalities, and recognized the existence of historical Basque rights prior to it. The BNP accepts the legitimacy of the present Basque autonomous community of only Biscay, Guipuzcoa, and Alava because the Constitution establishes that Navarre may, by a simple majority decision of its parliament and a referendum, enter it at any moment.

The Basque president, or *lehendakari,* has so far always been a member of the BNP. At present, the party's most important figures are its president, Xabier Arzalluz (b. 1932), and the lehendakari, José Antonio Ardanza (b. 1941).

**BEGIN, MENACHEM** 1913–1992, Leader of Israel's nationalist Heirut (later, Likud) party and prime minister for two consecutive terms. Begin was the first right-wing politician to be elected to lead Israel. Although known for his staunch support for Jewish settlements in the occupied territories and his general opposition to land concession, Begin is also the first Israeli leader to sign a peace treaty with an Arab country. Along with Anwar Sadar of Egypt, he was the recipient of the 1978 Nobel Prize for peace.

Born in 1913 in Brest-Litovsk, Russia, he joined Jabotinsky's Betar—a hard-line Zionist movement, distinguished by its rejection of social ideology—in 1929. While completing his studies at the University of Warsaw, he rose through the ranks of Betar, assuming leadership by 1935, when he received his law degree.

After his parents and brother were killed by the Nazis, Begin joined the Free Polish army and traveled with it to Palestine in 1942. There he assumed command of Irgun (the National Military Organization, also known as Etzel), a military splinter group of the more moderate Haganah (precursor to the Israeli army).

In February 1944, Begin declared an armed revolt against the British Mandatory government in an effort to drive them out of Palestine. In 1946, the Irgun blew up the British headquarters in Jerusalem, housed in the King David Hotel. Begin maintained that Irgun issued a warning about the bombs, yet the blast killed 91 people—British, Arab, and Jewish.

The bombing turned Begin into a pariah among Haganah supporters and most Jewish organizations—with Ben-Gurion urging Jews to turn Irgun members in to the authorities. Disguised as an old rabbi, Begin managed to elude a British manhunt and continued to command Irgun, which committed its most notorious military action in April of 1948, a mere month before the declaration of Israel's creation. In a reprisal against an Arab attack, Irgun forces—together with Lechi, another radical military group led by Yitzhak Shamir—captured the Arab village of Deir Yassin, killing over 200 of its residents. In June of 1948, shortly before the Irgun disbanded, Begin was almost killed when Irgun members, on board a weapons transport ship, exchanged fire with the Israeli army.

In 1948 Begin founded and led the Herut (Freedom) Party on the platform of restoring Israel to its historic borders encompassing both sides of the Jordan River and a procapitalist internal policy. Mapai's most vigorous opponent, Begin's party concentrated on cultivating the support of poor Israelis and those of Eastern descent, who were largely ignored by the Mapai government. In 1951–1952, he led a large-scale opposition to Ben-Gurion's acceptance of the reparations offer from West Germany. In 1967, Begin was named a minister to the unity government but resigned in 1970 in protest of the cabinet's acceptance of the Rogers Plan, a UN peace proposal requiring Israel to withdraw from the 1967 occupied territories.

Moving his party closer to the mainstream, Begin formed the Gachal bloc with the Liberal Party in 1965 and founded the Likud Party in 1973. In the aftermath of the Yom Kippur War and widespread criticism of Golda Meir's government, Likud's popularity rose, winning it 39 seats in the 1973 elections. In 1977, the public's growing discontent with the status quo granted Likud an unexpected victory that signaled a profound tide change in Israeli politics.

As prime minister, Begin initiated a privatization process of government-run agencies, yet loyal to his most dedicated supporters, he made services for the poor a priority, creating policies for affordable education and housing. In his second term, he encouraged Ethiopian Jewish immigration, culminating in the celebrated "Operation Moses," which airlifted thousands of Ethiopian Jews to Israel. He also instituted a policy to encourage settlement building in the occupied territories, becoming the first Israeli leader to refer to them by their biblical names, Judea and Samaria.

After a series of secret negotiations, President Sadat

of Egypt made a historic trip to Jerusalem, leading to the Camp David Accords in September 1978. The Egypt–Israel peace agreement, signed by Begin and Sadat in 1979, provided for Israel's phased withdrawal from the Sinai—completed in April of 1982. Sharply criticized by members of his party for the land concessions, Begin was less compliant regarding the five-year plan for Palestinian autonomy, also part of the Camp David Accords. While disagreements over the term itself accounted for some of the stalling, Begin's continued West Bank settlements policy and his statements regarding the status of East Jerusalem made clear his unwavering refusal to give up land he considered integral to Israel's security and part of its God-given homeland.

Along with Israel's growing economic problems, Begin's second term suffered a decline in public confidence after the 1982 invasion of Lebanon. The Ariel Sharon-led military operation, "Peace for Galilee," was initially planned as a limited campaign to repel attacks from the northern border, where PLO troops had been shelling nearby Israeli towns. As the operation escalated into a full-scale invasion of Lebanon, public opinion turned sharply against it within Israel, as well as internationally. The situation only worsened after the notorious Sabra and Chatila massacres. As an Israeli investigation placed indirect blame on Sharon, forcing his resignation, and censured Begin for showing indifference to the reports, mass demonstrations protested Likud policies and Israel's involvement in Lebanon.

As the Israeli peace movement grew, and public morale plunged over Israeli–Palestinian clashes, an already distraught and ailing Begin suffered another blow with the death of his beloved wife Aliza. On September 19, 1983, Begin resigned from office and went into virtual seclusion. He died of heart failure in March 1992.

## BELARUSIAN NATIONALISM
Belarus is a newly independent nation that declared its independence following the breakup of the Soviet Union in 1991 and soon became, along with Russia and Ukraine, one of the founding members of the Commonwealth of Independent States.

The pro-Russian orientation of the new state took on importance in 1996 when the first president of the Republic of Belarus, strongman Alyaksandr Lukashenka, proposed to reunite Russia, Ukraine, and Belarus into the Union of the Slavic Republics, with Moscow as the capital. In 1996 a bilateral treaty on closer integration was signed by Yeltsin and Lukashenka, thus providing a starting point for a future Russian–Belarusian federation. However, Russia remained a reluctant party in this bargain—the Russian parliament did not ratify the treaty because of economical considerations, while the

Belarusian authorities were eager to speed up the process in hopes of reestablishing a new incarnation of the Soviet Union.

The setback of Belarusian nationalism started in 1995 when an overwhelming majority of the population (about 77 percent) voted in a national referendum for the old flag of the Belarusian Soviet Socialist Republic (SSR). The historical symbol of the state ("The Knight") and the national white–red–white flag, adopted by the Belarusian parliament in 1991, were replaced by the Soviet ones. Thus Belarus became the first nation ever to apply voluntarily for a reunion with its former imperial power.

The Belarusian authorities regarded the dissolution of the Soviet Union and the following declaration of an independent Belarus as a great misfortune. Feeble support for Belarusian statehood can be explained by a weak form of Belarusian nationalism that appeared rather late, similar to Catalonian and Welsh nationalism.

Its modern beginnings date back to the first decade of the 20th century; however, the roots of Belarusian nationalism are indeed of an earlier date. The main obstacle on the rocky road of nationalism in Belarus has been the lack of attributes that could be used for construction of a modern Belarusian identity. There has been a lack of a main nationalist argument, i.e., the absence of Belarusian statehood in the past.

Therefore in their quest for the origins of statehood, Belarusian nationalists have had to redraw the past along nationalist lines to date back traces of Belarusian statehood to as distant a past as possible.

Two Belarusian historians, Vatslau Lastouski before World War I and Usevalad Ihnatouski, president of the Academy of Sciences of the Belarusian SSR, in the 1920s, have attempted to project current nationalism into the distant past. Belarusian nationalists looked for traces of Belarusian autonomy even in the Kievan Rus (10th to 11th centuries). They assumed that the Kievan Rus claimed by Ukrainian nationalists as the precursor of their modern state was not a centralized kingdom and that some of its northern-eastern parts, such as the city-states of Polotsk and Novgorod, were in fact pre-Belarusian states. The Grand Duchy of Lithuania that had enormously expanded eastward in the 13th to 14th centuries into the territory of present Belarus was regarded as a binational Lithuanian-Belarusian state. Belarusian nationalists even claimed that the Lithuanians who had lent the name to the principality were in fact Belarusians, only without naming themselves that way. Eventually everything that was ascribed to the Grand Duchy of Lithuania, due to a fascinating linguistic twist, became at once part of Belarusian national history.

According to such nationalistic interpretation, in

1795 after the third partition of the Polish–Lithuanian Commonwealth, it was not the Duchy but Belarus that was incorporated into the Russian Empire. The only real national statehood that could pass for being Belarusian in letter and in spirit was the Belarusian National Republic (BNR), declared in Minsk on March 25, 1918, by the Council of the BNR under surveillance of the German military authorities. The Council was made up of two representative bodies of Belarusian nationalists from Vilnius and Minsk who disagreed on the future capital of the republic. Belarusians from Vilnius and the nearby area made plans of reestablishing the Grand Duchy of Lithuania as a multinational federation with a Lithuanian, Belarusian, Polish, and Jewish population, while the Minsk-based nationalists attempted to create a national state of Belarusians. The latter were more down-to-earth, being fully aware of the emerging neighboring Lithuanian and Polish national states.

Despite Belarusian efforts to keep the Belarusian state alive, the BNR ceased to exist when the German troops were pushed back by the advancing Red Army at the end of 1918. Yet the 10-month period of unrecognized independence made a valuable contribution to the course of Belarusian nationalism.

During the short existence of the BNR, Belarusian national culture thrived. The first Belarusian grammar was published, over 125 primary schools with Belarusian as the language of instruction were opened, and numerous Belarusian cultural and educational societies started their activities. It came as a surprise to many observers that the Bolsheviks did not subdue Belarusian nationalism but maintained it by employing nationalist rhetoric in the Soviet propaganda against neighboring Poland.

According to the 1921 Riga Peace Treaty between Poland and Soviet Russia, Belarusian ethnic territories were divided among the two neighbors, and so was Belarusian nationalism. During the interwar period (1921–1939) the Polish part of the country was under the permanent influence of the Catholic culture, while the Soviet part of Belarus became the separate Soviet Socialist Republic.

In 1939 Western Belarus was incorporated into the Belarusian SSR, thus reassembling divided Belarusians under Soviet rule. The United Nations granted the Belarusian SSR a seat at its Constituent Assembly in 1945, securing one extra vote for Moscow. Belarusian statehood within the USSR was only a nominal one; it provided Belarusians with at least formal signs of their national otherness, despite the fact that the main official language was Russian. Belarusian language was regarded as a dialect of the noncultured, used mostly by peasants in rural backwaters of the country. In the

1980s in Minsk, the capital, there was not a single Belarusian-language secondary school. To speak Belarusian in public meant to be accused of nationalism.

Thus after more than five decades of Soviet rule in the country, Belarusian nationalism was reduced to a minimum. When perestroika started, only a tiny group of intelligentsia gave their support to the nationalist politics of the Belarusian National Front (BNF) led by Zyanon Paznyak. What made Belarus different from the other Soviet republics was the fact that the Belarusian *nomenklatura* (party hierarchy) neither joined the ranks of nationalists nor showed any interest in their idea, as was the rule elsewhere in the USSR.

The identity of Belarusian Communists was totally uprooted. Even Russian regional Communist leaders sought to distinguish themselves more than their Belarusian counterparts. After the aborted coup in Russia in August 1991, Belarusian nationalists did not succeed in seizing power, and the Communists remained in power under the name of the Party of Communists of Belarus, suppressing the following attempts of the democratic opposition to hold new parliamentary elections. President Lukashenka was elected by direct vote in 1994 and soon dissolved the parliament and introduced a Soviet-style authoritarian dictatorship. Belarusian nationalists were persecuted; the leader of the BNF, Paznyak, had to seek political asylum in the USA. According to the latest reports, Belarusian language has been once again condemned. Those who use it in public are being harassed by Belarusian authorities.

Fur further reading see D. R. Marples' *Belarus: From Soviet Rule to Nuclear Catastrophe* (St. Martin's Press, 1996); slightly pro-Russian Vakar's *Belorussia: The Making of a Nation* (Cambridge, MA, 1956); or the nationalist interpretation of Jan Zaprudnik's *Belarus: At a Crossroads in History* (Westward Press, 1993).

**BELGIAN COLONIES AND NATIONALISM**   The territory of present-day Belgium has its roots in the former Austrian (Catholic) territories in the Low Countries. At the Congress of Vienna (1815) the Protestant part became the Kingdom of the Netherlands. With strong support from France, Belgium proclaimed its independence from the Netherlands in 1830. After a short successful uprising, Leopold became the first king of Belgium. The newly formed state consisted of the coastal cities of Brugge, Ostende, and Antwerp. These trading cities had long played an important role in the overseas affairs of the Flemish trading companies. In the 1720s, for example, the Austrian emperor Charles VI had founded a trading company for Asia, operating out of what is now Belgium, which equipped commercial ships for India. In a very short time, Austria established a lucrative trade with India. However, it lost out to its competitors because of their stronger military power, and it was forced out.

Leopold II, son of the country's first king, had much interest in colonial activity because he compared Belgium with the Netherlands. He thought that with its earlier commercial traditions Belgium could be as successful as the Dutch in their overseas activities. He financed the Association Internationale du Congo (AIC) mostly from his own pocket. In the 1870s and 1880s the entire Congo Basin was still unoccupied by European powers, and a joint Anglo-German attempt in the middle of the 1880s sought to keep the French out. In accordance with Leopold's wishes, the Berlin Conference of 1884 found a solution by forming and legalizing the AIC as an independent state, the Congo Free State, with Leopold as its king.

Because it had started as a private enterprise of the king, less financial and public support came from Belgium itself. Therefore, the king based his project on volunteers and professionals from all over Europe. For example, the U.S. journalist with Welsh origins, Henry Morten Stanley, embarked on an arduous journey to Africa in search of the Scottish missionary, David Livingstone. Stanley negotiated many favorable treaties with local chiefs that resulted in the development and exploration of the Congo Free State.

Conditions were harsh, since Leopold reportedly condoned deplorable labor and torture as instruments to produce wealth. Some say that about eight million Africans lost their lives during the 23 years of Leopold's exploitation. Bowing to strong international pressures after a commission reported that the colony's administration was scandalous, the parliament passed an act in 1908 annexing the Congo Free State of Belgium. But Leopold had already enriched his treasury with the immense copper deposits in Katanga Province (now Shaba) during his years of possession. From 1908 on there was no change in public opinion in favor of colonialism, and this led to a severe shortage in administrators and mercenaries. Liberal trade principles were often weakened by offering trade monopolies. This resulted in large trusts. Later many military officers were engaged in administrative tasks. After World War I, Belgium entered the League of Nations, which awarded it a League mandate over two former German colonies in Africa, now called Rwanda and Burundi. Both were formally independent from the Belgian Congo, but in reality they were ruled together with the Congo.

Following World War II, one of Belgium's most serious and prolonged postwar crisis was the painful decolonization of the Belgian Congo, which was 80 times the size of Belgium with a vastly larger population. Over 100,000 Belgians had settled there. Belgium had developed economic interests in the colony although it had sought to avoid mutual economic dependence. It opened up the Congo to foreign investment and trade.

In the 1950s winds of African nationalism began to reach gale proportions, especially after the new French president, Charles de Gaulle, offered the French colonies in Africa their independence in 1958. Up to that point all attempts to achieve Congolese independence had been unsuccessful and had been ignored by the colonial government. But the negative Belgian reaction to de Gaulle's proclamation made the prospect of independence very popular among most Congolese politicians. A Congolese nationalist, Patrice Lumumba, emerged as a highly visible proponent of a free Africa. On January 4, 1959, riots broke out in the Congo; 42 persons died in events that deeply shocked the Belgians.

The Congolese had not been prepared for freedom. Belgium quickly granted independence on June 30, 1960. Unfortunately, a series of bloodbaths ensued, sparked by greed for power and wealth as well as by tribalism. It was not until seven years later that the Congo (subsequently called Zaire and now the Democratic Republic of Congo) became orderly, in part because of vigorous efforts of the Belgians and of UN troops.

The copper, cobalt, and uranium mines in the southern Shaba Province are still of great interest to Belgium. When this province was invaded from Angola in mid-1978, Belgium and France sent paratroopers to evacuate white families and to secure the area. In 1979 the Belgian government again sent paratroopers to Zaire to join in training exercises near Kinshasa, the capital city. Thus, Belgium retains a great interest in its former African colonies. The bulk of its relatively large development aid (0.06 percent of its GNP) went to the Congo, as well as to Rwanda and Burundi, which had been granted their independence in 1962. The Congo was not always a grateful recipient of such aid, and by the end of the 1980s Belgium's importance as a source of trade and aid had declined. In 1989 Belgium halted all development plans in the Congo in response to former President Mobutu's suspension of payments on Belgian loans. In 1990 it used its diplomatic influence to try to diminish civil unrest in Rwanda, and in 1991 it sent 750 commandos to the Congo to help evacuate Belgian citizens from the riot-torn country.

Public support and manpower had been limited during the first phase of Belgian colonialism. It therefore played a more minor role in the development of Belgian national identity and pride than was the case in some other European countries. But when it appeared that the Congo was going to be lost, many more Belgians seemed to be interested in somehow retaining the colony. However, the government was unable to capitalize on this interest by introducing a timely, enlightened, and mutually beneficial policy. It therefore retreated faster than necessary from its African pursuits.

**BELGIAN NATIONALISM** The development of Belgian nationalism has been impeded by the existence of conflicts originating from linguistic policy, social discrimination, economic dislocation, and, especially, the existence of Flemish and Walloon nationalist movements in the country. Belgium has been a federal state since 1992, with three regions split heavily along linguistic lines—French-speaking Wallonia (32 percent of the population), Flemish-speaking Flanders (58 percent of the population), and bilingual Brussels (10% of the population, in which 80% speak French). This federal system came after decades of institutional reforms designed to produce some element of self-government in each linguistic region.

The Walloons and Flemings lived fairly peacefully together until the early 1800s. The 1815 Congress of Vienna established Belgium as a part of the Kingdom of the Netherlands, under whose reign it remained for only 15 years. Following secession, Belgium made French the official language, which resulted in conflict between the two groups. French was the language of administration, business, and industry, and quickly became the key to upward mobility, whereas Flemish was considered backward—the language of peasants. Flemings resented this domination and pushed for linguistic equality. The 1989 Equalization Bill established Flemish equal to French. Linguistic laws of the 1930s established limited unilingualism in Flanders and Wallonia and bilingualism in Brussels. These laws led to the creation of a Dutch-speaking elite. The 1960s' language laws refined and hardened territorial unilingualism.

Cultural deprivation in Flanders and economic depression in 20th century Wallonia eventually led to the growth of nationalist movements in each country arguing for either autonomy within a Belgian state or complete independence. Although nationalist parties do not dominate politics in either region, they exist side-by-side with both Flemish and Walloon versions of social democratic, liberal, and socialist parties who place leaders in regional governments and the National Parliament. These regional and linguistic differences have hindered the development of Belgian nationalism.

**BENEŠ, EDVARD** 1884–1948, Czech politician, diplomat, and statesman, born in Kožlany, the Czech Republic (then the Austro-Hungarian monarchy). Beneš,

with Tomáš G. Masaryk and Milan R. Štefanik, is recognized as one of the founders of the Czechoslovak Republic. Yet, he is often criticized for the lack of leadership and resolve at critical historical junctures of the Czechoslovak state, including the 1938 Munich Agreement and the 1948 Communist coup d'état.

Beneš studied philosophy in Prague, and sociology and political science in Paris and Dijon, France. He returned to Prague in 1908 and became a lecturer at the Business Academy and the Charles University. After the outbreak of the First World War, Beneš became a liaison between Masaryk and the Czech resistance, the *Maffie*. In 1915 he left Prague and actively participated in the organization of Czech and Slovak emigrants, and in the formation of the first Czechoslovak National Council (*Československa Narodna Rada*, ČSNR) in 1916.

In the 1918 provisional government of the newly created Czechoslovak Republic, Beneš was put in charge of foreign affairs, and he served as the foreign minister until 1935, when he was elected president. During the following years, betrayed by England and France at the Munich Conference in 1938, Beneš presided helplessly over the dismemberment of Czechoslovakia. He spent the six years of the German occupation in exile in London, and was reelected president in 1945 on his return to the liberated Czechoslovakia. Beneš resigned from his post a few months after the 1948 Communist takeover, and died in September of the same year.

Among the most significant works by Edvard Beneš are *Svetova valka a naše revoluce* (*The World War and Our Revolution*) (Praha, 1927); *Pamkěti* (*Memoirs*) (Praha, 1947), published in English (Boston: Houghton, Mifflin, 1954); and *Šest let exilu a druhe světove valky* (*Six Years of Exile and the Second World War*) (Praha, 1946). A short biography can be found in Dana Plickova *et al., Kdo byl kdo v našich dejinach do roku 1918* (*Who was Who in Our History Until 1918*) (Praha: Libri, 1993). Among the more extensive works dealing with Beneš's life and work are Gordon A. Craig and Felix Gibert, eds., *The Diplomats, 1919–1939* (Princeton, NJ: Princeton University Press, 1994); František Havliček, *Edvard Beneš: Člověk, sociolog, politik* (*Edvard Beneš: The Man, the Sociologist, the Politician*) (Prague, Prospektrum, 1991); Vladimir Gonec, ed., *Edvard Beneš a stredoevropska politika* (*Edvard Beneš and Central-European Politics*) (Brno: 1997).

**BEN-GURION, DAVID** 1886–1973, Among the most prominent figures in Israeli national history, Ben-Gurion headed the Zionist worker movement in Palestine and founded what became Israel's Labor Party, which dominated Israeli politics until 1978. It was Ben-Gurion who officially announced the creation of the State of

Israel in 1948, led the transitional government following the State's creation, and served as Israel's first prime minister and defense minister. More than any other leader, Ben-Gurion shaped the structure and style of Israeli politics, and was the architect of many of its fundamental policies.

Born David Gruen in Plonsk, Poland, in 1886, Ben-Gurion was the son of an ardent Zionist who worked to provide his young, intellectually promising child with a Hebrew education. Deeply influenced by his father's views and shaped by extensive private education in Hebrew and Jewish history, Ben-Gurion pursued the Zionist cause from a young age, establishing a Hebrew-speaking Zionist club when he was a teenager, joining the Zionist organization Poalei Zion ("Workers of Zion") in 1903, and immigrating to the Ottoman-governed Palestine in 1906.

Working as a guard and an agricultural worker in Zionist workers' collectives in Galilee, Ben-Gurion further developed his idea that Zionism's primary goal was the resettlement and development of the Jewish homeland, especially the desert. He quickly rose in the ranks of Poalei Zion, was elected to the central committee, and took part in the establishment of a Jewish self-defense group, *Hashomer* ("The Watchman"). Along with other prominent Zionist leaders, Ben-Gurion was exiled by Palestine's governor, Djemal Pasha, in 1915 after protesting anti-Jewish policies. Along with future president Ithak Ben-Zvi, he made his way to New York where the two established the Zionist pioneer organization, *Ha Halutz* ("The Pioneer"), dedicated to preparing young Jews to settle Palestine. Upon his return, Ben-Gurion was among the founders of the national federation of workers, the *Histadrut*, in 1920, and was elected its secretary-general the following year. He formed *Mapai*, the Zionist Labor Party, in the early 1930s, becoming chair of its executive committee in 1935. In this capacity, he effectively oversaw the affairs of the Palestine-based Zionist movement, took a leadership role in the 1942 drawing of the Biltmore Program—proclaiming a Jewish state as the primary goal of the Zionist movement—and, following the British restriction on Jewish immigration in 1939, led the political struggle against the British mandate.

On May 14, 1948, Ben-Gurion officially proclaimed the creation of Israel as an independent state and assumed leadership of the preliminary government. Immediately following his declaration, a coalition of Arab states who rejected the UN partition plan launched a military attack. Having worked to establish a joint Israeli defense army from various military factions within the Jewish Yeshuv (settlement movement), Ben-

Gurion anticipated the attack and oversaw the battle that followed. Following the war (thereafter known as the Israeli War of Independence) and Israel's first democratic election in January of 1949, Ben-Gurion assumed the joint position of prime minister and defense minister after building a government from a coalition of smaller parties.

As prime minister, he oversaw the establishment of most official state institutions, focusing primarily on absorption of large numbers of immigrants (which, in the first three years of statehood, averaged 18,000, and sometimes as many as 30,000, new arrivals each month). Among his most cherished projects was rural development of agricultural settlements, which he continued to regard as the foundation of Zionism.

Known as a tough and stubborn leader, as well as a thoughtful and erudite man, Ben-Gurion often clashed with his coalition partners, particularly in regard to religion and its role in Israeli political life. As a secular leader who had encouraged socialist principles, Ben-Gurion resisted a close association between religious and government law, causing repeated, but not permanent, defections of Orthodox coalition members. In 1951, Ben-Gurion's agreement to accept reparation money from West Germany caused a violent, public demonstration; nevertheless, the agreement was signed in 1952.

After a two-year hiatus spent in Kibbutz Sde Boker, Ben-Gurion returned to politics and was again elected prime minister in 1956. He remained in office until 1963, resigning as a conflict with former Defense Minister Pinchas Lavon escalated into a full-scale scandal and tensions grew within the Mapai Party. Lavon—who charged that Ben-Gurion's associates had fabricated evidence of his culpability for an intelligence failure in Egypt—had become the old leader's chief nemesis. Despite the great admiration he commanded, Ben-Gurion's last years in office were marked by personal conflict, waning public support, and his single-minded preoccupation with what had come to be known as "the Lavon affair." Before he finally retired in 1970, Ben-Gurion would resign from Mapai three times, form two unsuccessful parties, and wage a bitter war against the party he founded.

In 1968, Ben Gurion's new party, *Rafi* ("List of Israeli Workers"), rejoined Mapai and other factions to form the Israel Labor Party. Ben-Gurion would try unsuccessfully to form yet another new party: *Hareshima Hamamlachtit* ("The State List"), which won him a mere four Knesset seats in the 1969 elections. In 1970, Ben-Gurion retired permanently from political life, returning to Sde Boker in the Negev Desert, where he passed away during the Yom Kippur War on December 1, 1973.

**BERLIN, ISAIAH** 1909–1997, One of the leading English political philosophers of the 20th century, and both a leading analyst of the intellectual origins of and a prominent liberal sympathizer with nationalism. The author of such renowned essays as "Two Concepts of Liberty" and "The Hedgehog and the Fox," Berlin eventually abandoned both analytic philosophy and the study of the Enlightenment for interrelated studies in the intellectual history of pluralism, nationalism, and what he termed the "Counter-Enlightenment."

Berlin was born a Russian Jew in Riga, in what is now Latvia. By 1917 his family lived in Petrograd (now St. Petersburg), where he witnessed some of the fighting of the February and October revolutions. The family left Petrograd for Riga, and then for England, where they arrived in 1921. Berlin's memories of the Russian Revolution left a deep impression, and many of his relatives in Riga were later killed by the Nazis; much of his life's work was devoted to trying to understand what he took to be the gross intellectual errors underlying totalitarianism. Berlin was educated at Corpus Christi College, Oxford. He spent three years during World War II in the United States, reporting to the British government on American views about the war. After the war ended, Berlin spent a brief time as a British attache in Moscow; but he was back in Russia for long enough to meet with many of the leading Russian intellectuals and writers, spurring an intense study of 19th and 20th century Russian thought. Other than those two interruptions, Berlin spent his entire adult life at Oxford.

Berlin's most enduring interests were to be found in the 18th and 19th centuries, in the thinkers who reacted against the Enlightenment's faith in reason, progress, and universalism. Berlin was convinced that the ends and goods of human life are plural and irreconcilable, that the quest for unity and perfection in human life was incoherent and all but doomed to result in tyranny. He found, in what he termed the "Counter-Enlightenment thinkers," the roots of this pluralism. In the early nationalists who celebrated their local good lives against French rationalistic universalism, and especially in Herder, Berlin saw his intellectual forebears. His essays on Giambattista Vico, Johann Herder, J. G. Hamman, Joseph de Maistre, the Counter-Enlightenment, and romanticism all express and address humanity's essential pluralism, which was not recognized by Enlightenment rationalists. Berlin grounded his liberalism in this pluralism; toleration and liberty allow many lives to be led, while totalitarianism arose out of the "pursuit of the ideal" using the power of the state.

Berlin's pluralism was also intimately related to his understanding of nationalism, as was made clear not only in his writings on early nationalists like Herder but also in a number of essays specifically on nationalism. Unlike many liberals, Berlin saw no likelihood of nationalism's ever fading away or being transcended; he saw it as too tied up with the variety of human life. Berlin also understood, however, that nationalism can easily turn into a local form of the pursuit of the ideal and of homogeneity, something "ideologically important and dangerous." He characterized nationalist ideology and doctrine—as distinct from simple national sentiments—as including four positions. These are "the belief in the overriding need to belong to a nation; in the organic relationships of all the elements that constitute a nation; in the value of our own simply because it is ours; and finally, faced by rival contenders for authority and loyalty, in the supremacy of their [the nation's] claims."

Berlin's two seminal essays on nationalism, "The Bent Twig: Notes on Nationalism" and "Nationalism: Past Neglect and Present Power," appeared in 1972 and 1978, respectively, a decade and a half before the current revival of interest in nationalism among political scientists and political theorists. (The title of the former essay was drawn from his favorite quote from Kant, which he paraphrased as "Out of the crooked timber of humanity no straight thing was ever made.") They both sharply attacked what Berlin saw as the organic and narcissistic myths of nationalist doctrine while reminding liberals and socialists that nations are an enduring part of the real, pluralistic world.

Berlin was also a lifelong Zionist, arguing that in a world of nations, to be truly safe everyone must have someplace where they belong. Though he was deeply committed to England, Berlin always maintained that as a Jew in England he must be something of an outsider. He and other Jews might be welcome as long as they behaved well, but to have a national homeland was precisely to have a place in which the sense of belonging is unconditional. He thus thought that the status and safety of Jews in the Diaspora were importantly increased by the existence of the state of Israel. Berlin's liberalism and pluralism led him to support territorial compromise with the Palestinians, and he was deeply unsympathetic to the Likud government that assumed office in Israel in 1978; but this did not alter his conviction that the Jews must have a state of their own.

Berlin's most important writings on nationalism are found in *Vico and Herder* (Hogarth Press, 1976), *Against the Current* (Hogarth Press, 1979), *The Crooked Timber of Humanity* (Vintage Books, 1990), and *The Magus of the North: J. G. Hamman and the Origins of Modern Irrationalism* (Farrar, Straus, and Giroux, 1993). His influential writings on Zionism remain mostly uncollected, but "Jewish Slavery and Emancipation" appears in Norman Bentwich, ed., *Hebrew University Garland* (Constellation Books, 1952) and in *Personal Impressions* (Hogarth Press, 1980). Berlin included pieces on Chaim Weizmann and "Einstein and Israel." Books about Berlin include John Gray, *Isaiah Berlin* (Princeton University Press, 1996) and Claude Galipeau, *Isaiah Berlin's Liberalism* (Clarendon Press, 1994).

**BIKO, STEPHEN**    1946–1977, South African national liberation movement leader. He is best known for his participation in the Black Consciousness Movement initiated by South African college students of the 1960s. He died in police custody after being arrested for breaking banning orders.

Biko was born Bantu Stephen Biko in Tarkastad, the Eastern Cape in South Africa. In 1969, as a medical student at the "Non-European" University of Natal, Biko and other African students formed the South African Students' Organization, which was affiliated with the White National Union of South African Students. The SASO advocated the unity of black South Africans and emancipation from the psychological oppression and internalized inferiority that resulted from the apartheid system of racial discrimination and oppression. Their political philosophy was influenced by the writings of Franz Fanon, Paulo Friere, and Malcolm X. Biko's organization became a catalyst for the formation of the Black Peoples Convention, the National Association of Youth Organizations, Black Community Programs, the South African Students Movement, and Black Women's Federation.

Biko received restrictive "banning" orders (1973) and, from that point on, experienced banning, numerous arrests, and police harassment. Through work with affiliated community projects, publications, and youth organizations, the Black Consciousness Movement's ideas spread. They impacted the development of the Soweto uprising against Bantu education and the mandatory learning of Afrikaans in 1976, which was harshly attacked by the South African Defense Force.

Biko was arrested in 1977 for breaking banning orders. Five months after his death, all Black Consciousness Movement organizations were banned. Stephen Biko and the Black Consciousness Movement are the basis for several political organizations that continue to exist in South Africa including the Black Consciousness Movement of Azania and the Azanian People's Organization.

Stephen Biko's biography, written by exiled South African journalist Donald Woods, is titled *Biko* (New York:

Paddington Press, 1978). A collection of his articles is titled *I Write What I Like* (Harmondsworth: Penguin, 1988). For a comprehensive treatment of his life and the Black Consciousness Movement, see *Bounds of Possibility: The Legacy of Steve Biko and Black Consciousness*, edited by N. Barney Pityana, Mamphela Ramphale, Malusi Mpumlwana, and Linda Wilson (London: Zed Books, 1992).

**BISMARCK, OTTO VON**    1815–1898, Chancellor of the second German empire from 1871 to 1890. He is commonly credited with the unification of Germany in 1871. Bismarck was a Prussian Junker who served in various positions in the diplomatic service of the Prussian state from 1851 to 1862. In 1862 King Wilhelm I appointed Bismarck Prussian minister-president and foreign minister. In 1871 he became chancellor of Germany. In 1890 Kaiser Wilhelm II (grandson of Wilhelm I) forced Bismarck to retire from politics.

A staunch conservative, Bismarck resisted the liberal national unification movements of his day and was determined that the Prussian monarchy would be the foundation of German unification. Bismarck held a "kleindeutsch" view of Germany, as opposed to the "grossdeutsch" argument that national unification required inclusion of all German-speaking peoples. His plan for a united Germany excluded the "Germans" in Austria-Hungary and in Switzerland.

He unified the German states under Prussian leadership through a series of masterful diplomatic and military successes. On taking over the Prussian government in 1862 (under King Wilhelm I) he pursued three central policies aimed at unification: the expansion of the military budget, the marginalization of Austria, and the manipulation of France. First, beginning in 1862 Bismarck significantly increased the Prussian military budget. This entailed a difficult struggle against the Prussian liberals who demanded social reforms. Prussia's military successes, beginning with the victory over Denmark in 1864, increasingly muted the liberal opposition to his military spending plans. Bismarck's most famous quote was his 1862 statement to the Prussian parliamentarians that "Germany is not concerned with Prussia's liberalism, but with its power . . . the great questions of our day [such as national unity] will not be decided through speeches and resolutions, that was the mistake of 1848, but through iron and blood."

Second, through a crushing Prussian victory over Austria in 1866, he marginalized Austria and made Prussia the dominant force in the German realm. The victory over Austria made Bismarck into a German hero, even to the point that most of the liberal opposition across Germany became his supporters. After 1866 German liberalism took a back seat to Prussian militarism until 1945. Bismarck demonstrated his diplomatic skills by not humiliating the Austrians after their 1866 defeat so that he would not lose them as a future ally.

Third, he limited French interference with his struggle against Austria and then tricked the French (through his manipulation of the "Ems Telegram") into declaring war on Prussia in 1870. The German states rallied behind Prussia, defeating France in 1871. In January 1871 in the palace of Versailles, the leaders of the German states founded the second German empire with Wilhelm as "German Kaiser" and Bismarck "German Chancellor."

For the remainder of his career as chancellor, Bismarck struggled against liberal and socialist reform movements domestically. In foreign policy he resisted pressure for German expansionism. His highest priority was to forge diplomatic alliances and pacts aimed at preventing France from gaining allies in its future war of revenge against Germany, a war that Bismarck saw as inevitable. Wilhelm II became kaiser in 1888 and came into intense conflict with Bismarck. Wilhelm II was unwilling to tolerate Bismarck's almost total control over German politics and Bismarck was forced to resign in 1890. In retirement Bismarck attacked the new kaiser's foreign policies. His autobiography is one of the most eloquent, but also one of the most subjective, works on German history.

For further reading see Erich Eyck, *Bismarck and the German Empire* (W. W. Norton, 1964), Otto Pflanze, *Bismarck and the Development of Germany* (Princeton University Press, 1990), and Alan Percivale Taylor, *Bismarck, the Man and the Statesman* (Random House, 1975).

**BLACK NATIONALISM** A philosophy of unity of action and common interests among black people formulated in the United States and the Americas during the 1960s. It advocates self-reliance and racial/ethnic pride as solutions to the colonization of and discrimination against people of African descent.

The black nationalist philosophy is one of many that developed during the height of the civil rights/black power movement in the United States and national liberation movements in the Third World. It is very similar to the ideologies that characterized the national liberation movements of the 1950s and 1960s in Africa, Asia, and Latin America. Black nationalism likens the situation of blacks in the Americas to the classic colonial relationship.

Organizations like the Black Panther Party, the Re-

public of New Africa, the Nation of Islam, and the Congress of African People are associated with black nationalism. The different forms of black nationalism include black cultural nationalism, which focuses primarily on validation of African/black culture, and black revolutionary nationalism, a more militant, socialist, and internationalist strain. The objectives of black nationalism range from economic solidarity to territorial separation.

An analysis and collection of primary documents related to black nationalism can be found in *Black Nationalism in America,* edited by John H. Bracey, Jr., August Meier, and Elliott Rudwick.

**BLACK PANTHER PARTY** The Black Panther Party for Self-Defense, later Black Panther Party, was founded by Huey P. Newton and Bobby Seale in October 1966 in Oakland, California. It was a black nationalist political party that proposed a ten-point program which included reparations for past injustices against blacks, release of all black prisoners, and trial by all-black juries. This party was the target of many of the FBI's COINTELPRO activities, led by J. Edgar Hoover, and was considered to be the nation's major domestic threat in the late sixties and early seventies because of its enforcement of the citizens' civil law, which declared that all citizens can bear arms.

Often overlooked was the party's involvement in education and antipoverty programs. Also the Black Panther Party was granted the party status of a liberation movement on September 13, 1970, by the Algerian government during the exile of member Eldridge Cleaver. On July 18, 1977, the Black Panther Party ended its radical posture and became part of Oakland's mainstream political system. The party actively helped to elect John George as Alameda County supervisor and Lionel Wilson as the city's first black major.

In the late 1980s and early 1990s, youth interest in black nationalism, as a result of the hip-hop movement, sparked renewed interest in the Black Panthers and the film *Panther* was released.

**BOER NATIONALISM** The early nationalism of the descendents of Dutch, German, and French settlers who settled in South Africa and are now commonly referred to as Afrikaners, Boer nationalism is an early form of what came to be understood as Afrikaner nationalism and was instrumental in the evolution of racism in South Africa.

The Dutch East India Company administered the Cape between 1652 and 1795. In 1657 they released some of the employees from their contracts and gave them land with the status of "free burghers." The word *Boer* (Dutch for "farmer") first came to be applied to these individuals who migrated beyond the Cape peninsula and its immediate hinterland and became seminomadic pastoral farmers.

Boer nationalism emerged in response to perceived threats from English-speaking people and English institutions on the one hand and indigenous peoples on the other. The earliest expression of this sentiment occurred in the 1830s when many of the frontier Boers left the Cape colony for the interior in response to what they perceived as the dominance of the English in civil and legal affairs. The issue of the status and treatment of African laborers was a particular source of contention as the Boers protested the efforts of the British to regulate relations between masters and servants.

The motivations behind the "Great Trek," as it came to be called, reflect the two main themes in Boer nationalism. The first was a strong feeling of antipathy toward the British, motivated by British imperialism in the subcontinent and by the indignities the Boers suffered at the hands of the British during the Anglo-Boer War (1899–1902). The number of Boer women and children who perished in English concentration camps during and after the fighting and the Anglicization policy that followed provided the key pillars of the anti-British portion of the nationalist mythology. The hallmarks of Boer nationalism are use of and commitment to Afrikaans as a language and Afrikaner culture and a strong sense of having been a victim of oppression.

The second theme in Boer nationalism was racism. The strong adherence of the Boers to Calvinism and the idea that the Boers were God's chosen people blended with their desire to expropriate land from the indigenous people as well as to subject them to forced labor. Thus, the line between Christian and heathen corresponded to that between savage and civilized and white and black. The Calvinist concepts of a national calling and destiny were given immense prestige by one of the founding fathers of Boer nationalism, Paul Kruger, president of the Transvaal Republic. For Krueger, the victory of the Dutch over the Zulu at the Battle of Blood River demonstrated that God endowed the Dutch with the destiny to rule South Africa and civilize its heathen inhabitants.

The core elements of Boer nationalism—antipathy to the English and the Africans, a strong commitment to the church, and an extreme sensitivity to protecting Boer language and culture—provided the roots for and found deeper expression in Afrikaner nationalism and nationalist sentiment in the 20th century.

**BOLÍVAR, CULT OF**    The national cult of Simon Bolívar (see "Bolívar, Simon") is a salient component of popular and elite culture in Venezuela and Colombia, where the hero of independence is seen as the very basis of national identity. This profound, national affection for Bolívar finds expression in intellectual and literary history, political discourse and popular folklore, and religious practices. Bolívar's stature as a national symbol of identity, however, did not spring into being spontaneously during the Wars of Independence, but rather developed slowly during the course of the 19th century.

In 1830, Venezuela withdrew from the Republic of Greater Colombia and rejected its most impassioned defender, the Venezuelan born Simon Bolívar. In his place, Jose Antonio Paez, hero of independence and the military commander of Venezuela, was adopted as titular head and protector of the new nation. Because the participants of the secessionist Congress of Valencia feared that Bolívar would take military action against them, the new Venezuelan nation was born under the sign of an official rejection of the hero of independence. News of Bolívar's death was celebrated, and his mortal remains were neglected in the Colombian town of Santa Marta.

Severe political, social, and economic tensions in Venezuela caused the ruling elite to split into the ruling Conservative Party, associated with laissez-faire policies and anti-Bolívarian sentiment, and the oppositional Liberal Party, which espoused protectionism and the celebration of Bolívar's memory. In 1842, under increasing pressure from the Liberal Party, the Conservatives sponsored an elaborate state funeral for Bolívar, whose remains were ceremoniously transported back to Caracas. From this moment onward, and culminating in the first centenary of the hero's birth in 1883, Bolívar's symbolic stature overcame the partisan divisions of the era of independence and came into focus as a nationalist icon. Bolívarian memoirs, biographies, poems, and historical episodes were published throughout the 19th century, presenting the hero as a messianic, historical agent.

In Colombia, the cult of Bolívar was also born out of a waning of the ideological positions of the era of independence. Unlike Venezuela, which could claim for itself the mantle of Bolívar's homeland with great drama and sentiment, Colombian political culture had to appropriate Bolívar through academic debates about the political arc of a career that had brought him into conflict with Colombian interests during the Greater Colombia experiment of 1821–1830. Colombian Liberals tended to view Bolívar as a despotic soldier, whereas

Conservatives painted a more heroic and democratic image of the man. At century's end, however, Bolívar was being viewed as a powerful, all-inclusive national symbol through a large array of commemorative newspaper articles and literary production.

The iconic Bolívar is quite ubiquitous in present-day Venezuela and Colombia, as evidenced by statues, inscriptions, and other monuments to his memory. Further, a great wealth of historiography, fiction, and poetry has kept Bolívar at the center of nationalist culture. Clearly, Bolívar is at the very heart of Venezuelan and Colombian identity. To speak, write, or represent Bolívar has meant to enter into a conversation about what it means to be a Venezuelan or Colombian.

For the Venezuelan cult of Bolívar, see *El Culto a Bolívar, Esbozo para un Estudio de las Ideas en Venezuela* (Grijalbo, 1989) by German Carrera Damas, and "Monumental Space and Corporeal Memory: *Venezuela Heroica* and the Cult of Bolívar in XIXth Century Venezuela" by Christopher Conway, in *La Chispa '97: Selected Proceedings*. For the Colombian case, see Miguel Americo Bretos's *From Banishment to Sainthood: A Study of the Image of Bolívar in Colombia, 1826–1883* (Ph.D. Dissertation, 1976).

**BOLÍVAR, SIMON** 1783–1830, Simon Bolívar, also known as The Liberator, led the emancipation of present-day Venezuela, Colombia, Ecuador, Peru, and Bolivia from Spanish rule during the Wars of Independence (1810–1825). Born into one of Caracas's wealthiest families, the young Bolívar was sent to Spain to complete his education. After the death of his bride in Venezuela, Bolívar wandered in Europe and made an oath to personally liberate Latin America from Spanish rule.

The Venezuelan independence movement was sparked by the Napoleonic invasion of Spain in 1808 and the installment of Joseph Bonaparte on the Spanish throne. The Creole elite rejected the French king in 1810, but became divided on the issue of self-governance. Bolívar lobbied for independence, while others maintained the authority of the legitimate, Spanish king. In the summer of 1810, while on a diplomatic mission to London to secure English military protection for the budding independence movement, Bolívar convinced Francisco de Miranda, a Venezuelan expatriate and veteran of European wars and revolution, to return to Caracas. Once independence was declared in 1811, Miranda became the political and military leader of the First Republic. Relations between Miranda and Bolívar were strained from the beginning, and worsened after the younger soldier lost the port of Puerto Cabello to the Royalists. When Miranda capitulated in 1812, Bolívar and other patriot officers branded him a traitor and turned him in to the Royalists.

In the summer of 1813, Bolívar secured a small contingent of men and supplies from neighboring New Granada and, in a quick succession of military victories called the "Admirable Campaign," swept into Caracas and founded the Second Republic. He assumed dictatorial powers and attempted to orchestrate the pacification of Venezuela under the patriot banner. In the East, caudillos such as Marino, Arismendi, and Piar maintained patriot control, although their attitude toward Bolívar's calls for unity and support was begrudging at best. This lack of support, in conjunction with the rise of an explosively effective counterrevolutionary force of nomadic *llaneros* (plains men), led to the collapse of the Second Republic in the summer of 1814.

Bolívar wasted no time in attempting to regroup for another expedition to liberate Venezuela, once again from New Granada. The counterattack had to be postponed because Venezuela's independent neighbor was torn by a regionalist civil war between Federalists, Centralists, and competing city-states. Bolívar was mobilized by the Federalists against the Centralists, but his military and diplomatic attempts to unite the separate factions failed in 1815, forcing bolivar into exile in Jamaica. In one of the foundational documents of Latin-American intellectual and political history, the "Carta de Jamaica," Bolívar steered the future destiny of Latin America away from Spain and toward England, outlining a vision of a united, independent continent: "It is a grandiose idea to attempt to form one nation out of the New World" he wrote in his foundational document, "with only one tie to link its parts together and to the whole...."

From Jamaica Bolívar reinitiated a concerted, patriot offensive. By 1817 he had made progress in consolidating his leadership over different patriot factions. While building on his military base from the Venezuelan hinterland of the Orninoco basin, he convened the Congress of Angostura, which declared the Venezuelan Third Republic in 1819. In his speech to the Angostura congress, Bolívar declared the sovereignty of the people, rejected the slave trade, and called for a hereditary senate and a strong executive. Military successes followed, with the liberation of New Granada at the Battle of Boyaca (1821) and the liberation of Venezuela at the Battle of Carabobo (1822). At the Congress of Cucuta (1821), patriot delegates outlined the constitutional foundations of Bolívar's brainchild: the Republic of Greater

Colombia, encompassing the Audiencia of Quito, the Viceroyalty of New Granada, and the Captaincy General of Venezuela.

Bolívar was not content to remain in Bogotá, the capital, in his new role as president, but rather got dispensation from his government to militarily and politically pursue the integration of Quito to Greater Colombia, and to liberate the Viceroyalty of Peru, one of Spain's most culturally entrenched colonies. Between 1822 and 1825, Bolívar succeeded in these designs and effectively ended the Wars of Independence. In 1825, at the pinnacle of his fame and glory, Bolívar could afford great optimism about the future; he planned a loose league of Latin American nations to meet in Panama, as well as a Federated State of the Andes larger than even Greater Colombia. The rumors surrounding these plans alienated Bolívar from Bogotá and Caracas, and exacerbated his already controversial reputation with accusations of monarchical designs. Bolívar rushed back to Bogotá to rein in the increasing tensions.

In Bogotá, Bolívar faced acrimonious challenges to his authority, provoked by his centralist views and political connections to Caracas, which had been in conflict with Colombian lawmakers since the creation of Greater Colombia. As constitutional negotiations between Bolívarians and anti-Bolívarians broke down in Bogotá, Bolívar stepped in and assumed dictatorial powers to save the republic from chaos. It was the beginning of the end, however, and on September 25, 1828, Bolívar narrowly escaped assassination at the hands of his political enemies. Venezuelan separatism took shape shortly afterward, and Bolívar's declining health and public stature quickly dissolved into his retirement from public life. The disillusioned Bolívar died in exile, rejected by both Bogotá and Caracas. The union he so passionately defended broke down with his death, and Ecuador, Colombia, and Venezuela rose out of the ashes of the Greater Colombia experiment.

Simon Bolívar was not a nationalist in a modern and narrow sense of the word, since he gravitated toward broad, Pan-American geopolitical designs that were in direct opposition to historically separate regional cultures and preexisting administrative and political networks of power. Nonetheless, his role in liberating such a vast area of territory from Spanish rule and his constitutional and political initiatives inaugurated the republican era in five nations. In his afterlife, Bolívar has become a powerful national icon in Venezuela and Colombia (see "Bolívar, Cult of") and an enduring symbol of Latin American independence throughout the rest of the continent.

Standard biographies of Bolívar include those by Gerhard Masur, Indalecio Lievano Aguirre, and Tomas Polanco Alcantara.

**BONAPARTISM** A 19th-century French political ideology supportive of Napoleon I (Napoleon Bonaparte) and Napoleon III (Louis Napoleon). Among his supporters, Napoleon I had gained the reputation, partly fashioned by his own propaganda, of a social and political savior. He was credited for restoring political, social, and religious order after the internecine conflicts of the French Revolution, promoting efficient government and defending the liberty of the French people domestically and that of oppressed nationalities outside France's borders. Although there was no organized Bonapartist party during his reign, the idea of an imperial dynasty embodying these political principles was emerging.

After the exile (1815) and death (1832) of Napoleon I, Bonapartists were few and poorly organized. His successor, Napoleon II, was in poor health and had been detained in Austria. In addition, his supporters had to contend with the recent memory of Napoleon I's defeat and the negative social and economic consequences of the Napoleonic wars.

By the 1830s and 1840s a cult that admired Napoleon's political and military genius started to grow, benefiting from a favorable comparison with the perceived mediocrity of Louis Philippe's government. Bonapartism became a significant and organized political movement after the 1848 revolution. Louis Napoleon, the nephew of Napoleon I, playing on the weakness of the republicans after the overthrow of the monarchy, was elected president that same year, seized full power in an 1851 coup, and was voted emperor in 1852.

Although both regimes were imperial and autocratic, Bonapartism under Napoleon III was different from the rule of Napoleon I. With the exception of a few small-scale military campaigns (in Italy, Crimea, and Mexico), the Second Empire was a chiefly civilian, populist, plebiscite-supported government. There were two main Bonapartist factions: a conservative, authoritarian pro-Catholic group, and a more radical republican, democratic group that nonetheless viewed Napoleon III's strong leadership favorably. In effect, Bonapartism during that time was the coalescence of these different political views around the idea of political authority, revolutionary legitimacy, and populist credibility largely inherited from Napoleon I. These divisions were reflected in the evolution of the Second Empire from an authoritarian regime until the mid-1860s, to a quasi-parliamentarian, liberal administration from 1867 until its end in 1870.

Bonapartism continued to exist as a political and electoral force for the next two decades, but disappeared into obsolescence before the strength and stability of the Third Republic.

The importance of Bonapartism for French nationalism is twofold, both in its initial expression as the ideas of Napoleon I and later as an organized political force: First, it provided a unifying political ideology, based on ideologically neutral notions of political authority, administrative efficiency, and geopolitical strength, which ended two revolutionary crises. Second, it fostered France's bureaucratic centralization, with First Empire initiatives like the Civil Code that bears Napoleon's name or the political control of all regions through centrally appointed prefects, and the continued expansion of central power under the Second Empire. This in turn greatly contributed the coalescence of France as a national state.

Bonapartism has also been used, often as a term of abuse, to describe the concentration of power in the hands of a single leader intent on eliminating the political instability caused by antagonistic political factions or classes during revolutionary episodes. Leon Trotsky's analysis of Stalin's regime in *The Workers' State, Thermidor and Bonapartism* is a classic example of the larger conceptual use of the term. It is most often used in Marxist literature, and indeed Marx is credited with first describing Bonapartism as a counterrevolutionary movement in his analysis of the events of 1851 in France. Bonapartist seizures of power are often carried out in the name of "national unity" and may result in domestic nationalistic militarism and countervailing nationalistic responses from threatened states, as during the French First Empire in Europe.

## BORODIN, ALEXANDER

1833–1887, Russian composer and chemist, member of "The Mighty Handful." A full-time professor in the St. Petersburg Medico-Surgical Academy and a scientist who achieved international stature for his contributions to organic chemistry, Borodin became "the only composer who has ever claimed immortality with so slender an offering" (Sir Henry Hadow). His musical output consists of an "opera-farce," *Bogatyri* (*The Valiant Knights*); an unfinished opera, *Prince Igor;* three symphonies (The Third Symphony is also unfinished); a symphonic sketch, *In Central Asia;* several chamber ensembles; and fifteen songs. Upon Borodin's death, his compositions were completed and orchestrated by Rimsky-Korsakov and Glazunov.

In his search for a "national spirit," Borodin followed the two different paths established by Glinka. The patri-

otic nationalism in *Prince Igor,* with its affirmation of a national hero as a protagonist, obviously emanates from Glinka's *Life for the Tsar.* It coexists with the very sympathetic portrayal of Russian antagonists that also continues Glinka's nationalist tradition, but with the difference that Glinka describes enemies from the "West" (the Poles), whereas Borodin portrays enemies from the "East" (the Polovtsy).

The Polovtsian domain of *Prince Igor* originates from the oriental tradition of Glinka's *Ruslan and Lyudmila.* Because the ethnographic data about the ancient Polovtsy was scant, Borodin, who had never been in the East, created his highly original world of exoticism, based in part on his own fantasy, in part on his study of Arabian and Hungarian songs, and in part on impressions drawn from contemporary art music (Glinka and his friends from the Balakirev Circle). Borodin's celebrated orientalism, although not entirely genuine in the strict sense, was nevertheless very faithful, especially according the standards of the 19th century.

Reworking a 12th-century historical chronicle, *Slovo o polku Igorevom* (*The Story of Igor's Campaign*), Borodin succeeded in creating large choral scenes that represented the people of pagan Russia, with their conjoint and joyous mentality. Usually avoiding direct quotations, Borodin created his own themes based on the stylized embodiment of typical features of Russian folk songs (the most celebrated example is the Chorus of Villagers from Act IV). At the same time, Borodin modernized the psychology and behavior of the main characters in the spirit of 19th-century romantic opera. His Igor, whom Russian audiences perceived as "the knight-errant of the Russian national ideal" (Dianin), is given the musical discourse and emotional range of a contemporary hero. Very alien to the canon of medieval Russian epic was Borodin's concept of romantic love as the central psychological motivation and dramatic force of the action (Igor-Yaroslavna and Vladimir-Konchakovna). Even more modern was Borodin's romanticizing of the chivalry, exoticism, and sensuousness of the Orient, which was entirely a concept of the 19th century that developed simultaneously in Russia and Western Europe.

Composers of the Balakirev Circle (*The Mighty Handful*) celebrated Borodin as a creator of Russian national symphonies. Not provided with formal programs (although their main outlines are known through Stasov, with whom Borodin discussed their content), his symphonies are clearly connected to heroic epos of ancient pre-Christian Russia. Suggesting a variety of associations with battles scenes, with games and feasts of Russian knights (*bogatyri*), and with images of wild galloping and spacious landscapes, the symphonies reveal Borodin's admiration of that period in Russian history that resulted in the fortification of the state and the development of the nation. The musical material of the symphonies, as always in Borodin's works, is built on the opposition of Russian and oriental themes, and on the formal level shows a flexible and independent approach to the European symphonic model.

Borodin's only programmatic composition is his orchestral piece *In Central Asia* (1880), commissioned for the official celebration of the Central Asia campaigns waged by Tsar Alexander II. Despite its "militarized" program, describing "a caravan that crosses the vast desert escorted by Russian soldiers," the music offers a peaceful and idyllic juxtaposition of oriental and Russian themes.

Borodin was a composer whom Stasov admired to the highest degree (not less than he worshiped Glinka), since he most completely fulfilled Stasov's theory of Russian national art. However, contemporary Western scholarship (Taruskin) tends to argue that the patriotic nationalism of Borodin was in perfect accord with the expansionist colonial politics that Russia pursued in the 19th century, and which was enthusiastically supported by the majority of leading Russian figures, including Stasov and Borodin himself.

The best biographical source is Serge Dianian's *Borodin,* translated from the Russian by Robert Lord (London, New York, Toronto: Oxford University Press, 1963). An enlightening discussion of Borodin's orientalism is found in the chapter "Entoling the Falkonet" in Richard Taruskin's *Defining Russia Musically* (Princeton, N.J.: Princeton University Press, 1997).

**BOSNIAN NATIONALISM** The formative period of Bosnian history was the era of Ottoman rule (1463–1878), when Bosnia's religious composition underwent significant change. During the period of Bosnian independence (1390–1463), the country was a Christian land with three denominations: Catholic, Orthodox, and Bogomil, the last being a heretical sect, persecuted by the other two churches, but by far the largest of the three. Under the Ottomans, most of the native Bogomil population, which also formed the country's social and political élite, gradually converted to Islam, which became the dominant religion in Bosnia.

When Bosnia was occupied by Austria-Hungary in 1878, nationalism had already started to penetrate the country. Because the three religious communities (Muslim, Orthodox, and Catholic) spoke what was basically the same language, national identity increasingly became tied to religious identity. The Orthodox became

Serbs, the Catholic community Croats, with the Muslims initially without a distinct national identity. Unlike the Serbs and Croats, the Bosnian Muslims did not experience a 19th-century national awakening, largely because they remained culturally and religiously tied to the Ottoman empire. At first some Muslim intellectuals opted either for a Croat or Serb identity, but the vast majority were committed to a Bosnian identity, especially since the Muslims had long formed Bosnia's social and political élite under Ottoman rule. What complicated the predicament of Bosnian nationalism, however, was the fact that Bosnia's Serbs and Croats, who together formed the majority of the population, tended increasingly to look to Serbia and Croatia for national leadership. As nationalism spread among their neighbors, and political pressures arising from those nationalisms grew, Muslim identity and nationalism grew.

The first Austro-Hungarian governor of Bosnia, Benjamin Kállay (1839–1903, governor 1881–1903), promoted a Bosnian identity and Bosnian nationalism that would include Muslims, Serbs, and Croats. The purpose of this policy was to offset the competing claims of Serb and Croat nationalists, but it failed. Bosnian identity and nationalism remained limited to the Bosnian Muslims, who sought to defend Bosnia-Herzegovina's territorial integrity against the competing claims of Serb and Croat nationalism.

The creation of the Kingdom of Serbs, Croats, and Slovenes in December 1918 presented the Bosnian Muslims with much different circumstances. According to the prevailing ideology of Yugoslav unitarism, there was only one Yugoslav nation and it consisted of the Serb, Croat, and Slovene "tribes." The Bosnian Muslims, though speakers of Serbo-Croatian, were not regarded as a distinct nationality. The most important party of the Bosnian Muslims was the Yugoslav Muslim Organization (JMO). Founded in 1919, it had the support of the majority of the Muslim intelligentsia and social élite. The JMO sought to defend Muslim identity, which meant the Muslims' religious, social, and economic rights within Bosnia-Herzegovina, and to safeguard the territorial integrity of the country. It was led by Mehmed Spaho (1883–1939) from 1921 to 1939, and then by Džaferbeg Kulenović (1891–1956) to 1941. To protect Bosnian Muslim interests, the JMO policy was one of tactical maneuvering between the Serb and Croat parties. The JMO spent the 1921–1927 period in opposition, but participated briefly in government in 1928. Once the royal dictatorship was proclaimed in January 1929, it again joined the opposition. Between 1935 and 1938 the JMO participated in government, with the goal of preserving Bosnia's territorial integrity. This policy failed, however. In August 1939, the Belgrade government and the Croat Peasant Party negotiated the *Sporazum* (Agreement), granting Croatia autonomy within Yugoslavia. The autonomous Croatian unit included segments of Croat-populated Bosnia-Herzegovina, especially western Herzegovina and central and northeastern Bosnia.

Bosnian nationalism was delivered another political blow in April 1941, after the Axis invasion of Yugoslavia. An "Independent State of Croatia" was established, which included all of Bosnia-Herzegovina. The policy of the Croatian fascist regime was to regard the Bosnian Muslims as Muslim "Croats," and it suppressed all signs of Bosnian nationalism or identity. By late 1941, much of the Bosnian élite openly criticized the Croatian regime, especially its policy toward its minorities, and called for Bosnian autonomy.

With the creation of communist Yugoslavia in 1945, Bosnia-Herzegovina became one of the six constituent federal republics. Initially the communist authorities did not recognize a Bosnian Muslim nationality. To resolve the vexing Serb-Croat dispute over Bosnia-Herzegovina, however, the Yugoslav government in 1971 conferred recognition on the Bosnian Muslims as a nationality.

More recently, Bosnian nationalism has been closely tied to Alija Izetbegović (b. 1925). Before the war he was best known for his *Islamic Declaration*, which called for Islamic renewal among the Bosnian Muslims. He was accused by the Yugoslav Communist authorities of promoting a purely Muslim Bosnia, and in 1983 was sentenced to fourteen years in prison, of which he served five. In 1990 Izetbegović was one of the founders of the Party of Democratic Action (SDA), the main Bosnian Muslim party, and became the first elected president of Bosnia-Herzegovina.

The recent war in Bosnia-Herzegovina, which began in 1992 after that republic seceded from Yugoslavia, has strengthened Bosnian Muslim identity. In 1993 Bosnian Muslim leaders adopted "Bosniak" to denote the Bosnian Muslim nationality. The central goal of Bosniak nationalism has been, as in the past, to preserve Bosnia's territorial integrity and the Bosniaks' national rights within that state. Since Bosniak nationalism has so recently been forged in conflict against Serb and Croat nationalisms, it does not appear that it will wane any time soon.

## BOUCHARD, LUCIEN  1938– , Lucien Bouchard is an eloquent and passionate speaker in both French and English. Like most Quebequois of his generation, he entered politics as a Liberal, but he was lured into the Progressive Conservative Party (PC) by his ex-friend Brian Mulroney, who sent him to Paris as Canada's ambassador. In 1990 he became the founder and first leader of a new party in the House of Commons, the Bloc Québécois (BQ), composed originally of a breakaway group of nine PC and Liberal members of parliament (MP) from Quebec.

Because of their common goal of Quebec independence, the Parti Québécois (PQ), which only competes in Quebec provincial elections, supported the BQ, which contests only federal parliamentary seats in Quebec, in the 1993 and 1997 Canadian elections. With the PC collapsing, the BQ captured fifty-four of the seventy-five seats in Quebec in 1993 and forty-four in 1997. All but six of the MPs for the neophyte BQ were new to Ottawa. Many spoke no English.

As a group, Bouchard's BQ caucus members had little in common other than their commitment to separate from Canada. They were quick to learn how to operate in parliament. As the second largest party in the House of Commons in 1993, the BQ became the official opposition for four years. But Bouchard signaled the impermanence of his party in Ottawa by refusing to reside in Stornaway, the mansion at the disposal of the opposition leader. "We don't intend to settle in Ottawa. The presence of the Bloc in Ottawa is by definition temporary."

While leader of the opposition, he made official visits to Paris and Washington to explain his party's separatist agenda. These caused outrage in the rest of Canada; the *Edmonton Sun* described his Paris trip as a "one-finger salute to the country." In 1994 he nearly died from a flesh-eating disease that cost him a leg. Rising from doom, he enjoys considerable sympathy for his personal courage and support for his milder form of Quebec separatism, which allows for continued economic ties with Canada.

In the lead-up to the 1995 Quebec provincial referendum on independence, Bouchard had expressed his opinion publicly that the separatist option should include close ties with Canada. He was able to persuade then-PQ leader Jacques Parizeau to agree on a "soft" referendum question that called for negotiating with Ottawa on an economic and political partnership with an independent Quebec.

The referendum results showed that a majority of Quebec francophones support that concept. In the campaign Parizeau stepped aside to allow Bouchard to energize it. A charismatic master of lofty emotion, he became a hero and savior in Quebec, the most popular figure since René Lévesque (see separate entry). His oratorical skill brought separatists within a whisker of victory, winning 49.4 percent of the votes in a huge

94 percent turnout. This was ten percentage points higher than in 1980. As in 1980, the difference was made by anglophones and immigrants, who voted overwhelmingly against independence, while 60 percent of francophones voted "yes." Regarding the outcome in the 1995 Quebec referendum as a moral victory, Bouchard evoked the memory of Lévesque by proclaiming: "Let us keep the faith. The next time will be the right one. And the next time may come sooner than people think."

The day after the failed 1995 referendum on Quebec independence, Jacques Parizeau announced his resignation as premier. A confident Bouchard, who left his post as BQ leader and took over the premiership of Quebec in early 1996, promised a new referendum. He defiantly rejected any option but sovereignty, asserting that "no one is going to get us into sterile discussions we've been having for 30 years. No longer will sovereigntists be begging for anything from the rest of Canada." This attitude guarantees that Quebec will vigorously test Canada's fragile unity for many years. His mother captured the mood of many Quebecois: "I've never met an English-speaking Canadian. But I'm sure they are as nice as any other foreigners."

Approaching the November 1998 Quebec provincial elections, Bouchard's strategy was to say as little about secession as possible while emphasizing the need to shore up Quebec's economy. The results pleased neither him nor hard-line secessionists. Thanks to the single-member constituency electoral system, his PQ won seventy-six seats. The Liberals, led by Jean Charest, former leader of the federal Conservatives, won only forty-eight. But the perfectly bilingual Charest had hammered at the dangers of another referendum and won 43.7 percent of the popular votes, while the PQ won only 42.7 percent. It is the popular vote that counts in refenda. Including the 11.8 percent of voters choosing the Democratic Action of Quebec Party (ADQ), whose leader Mario Dumont called for a decade-long referendum moratorium, a clear majority of Quebequois voted against a referendum soon. Bouchard concluded: "They like what we are doing as a government, but they are not prepared to give us the conditions for a referendum right now." He therefore put the sovereignty issue temporarily on ice.

With the BQ and the Reform Party winning votes by presenting radically conflicting views of Canada, it will be difficult for Prime Minister Jean Chrétien or any other federal politician to develop a national accord on Quebec. The cracks in the Canadian federation are wider than ever.

See Laurence Martin, *The Antagonists: Lucien Bouchard and the Politics of Delusion* (Viking, 1997).

**BOURGUIBA, HABIB** 1903–, Prominent Tunisian nationalist who led his country to independence from French colonial rule in 1956, and president of Tunisia, 1957–1987. Born in Monastir, Tunisia, Bourguiba studied law in France, and began practicing in Tunis. He quickly became involved in Tunisian politics, publishing newspaper articles and participating in the emerging nationalist movement. Bourguiba and others were disappointed by what they perceived as a lack of vigor and determination within the ranks of Tunisia's then main nationalist party the *Destour* (Arabic for "constitution"). He left the party in 1934 and helped establish the Neo-Destour party, which, under his stewardship, became the major political force of Tunisian nationalism in the country's struggle for independence. The party attracted a large following, as Tunisians became increasingly negative in their attitudes toward the French protectorate and its policies.

Many of Bourguiba's ideas charted the course of Tunisian nationalism. In what was to become one of the salient features of his political and cultural platform, he emphasized in his speeches and writings that while Tunisia sought its own independence from France, it did not wish to abandon its cultural and economic ties with the West. Bourguiba was nevertheless frequently arrested and imprisoned by the French colonial authorities during the 1930s in an attempt to curb his strong personal influence, and reduce the Neo-Destour's increasing popularity within Tunisian society.

After World War II, and following renewed French harassment, Bourguiba fled to Cairo, where he continued to advocate Tunisia's independence. France's decision to grant independence to Tunisia brought Bourguiba to the negotiating table. During this period, Bourguiba also managed to contain radical figures within his own party, securing his own unchallenged leadership position. After attaining independence in 1956, Bourguiba formed a government and, with the abolishment of the monarchy in Tunisia in July 1957, became president. He was reelected to this post several times, and was proclaimed president for life in 1975.

Many of Bourguiba's policies left an indelible mark on Tunisia's political landscape. He promoted a moderate, pro-Western foreign policy, and distanced himself from radical ideologies that underpinned several Arab regimes in the 1960s, such as Egypt and Algeria. Domestically, however, Bourguiba differed from his cultivated international liberal image. He maintained a one-party political system, limited dissent, and feared strong aides and associates undermining his position. Alarmed by the rise of Islamic fundamentalism in the 1970s and 1980s, Bourguiba suppressed political Islamist activity in Tunisia, in accordance with his earlier enacted laws which restricted Islamic law and secured the supreme position of the state's secular laws and institutions.

Throughout the 1980s, the aging Bourguiba's behavior became increasingly erratic, as he appeared to be losing his ability to rule. On November 7, 1987, he was declared by physicians as unfit to retain his post, due to poor health and senility, and according to the provisions of the Tunisian constitution, was removed from office and replaced by his prime minister, Zayn al-Abidin Ben ʿAli. Since 1987, Bourguiba has resided in his native Monastir, and seldom appears in public. He is still credited as the father of modern independent Tunisia, and revered as the "Supreme Combatant" who led the nationalist uprising against the French.

## BRAZAUSKAS, ALGIRDAS  1932–, Lithuanian national ex-Communist leader, a construction engineer, minister of Building Materials Industry, deputy chairman of the State Planning Committee, secretary of the Central Committee for Industry and Economy of the Lithuanian Communist Party (LCP), first secretary of the Communist Committee of the LCP, deputy of the Supreme Council of the USSR, deputy of the Supreme Council of the Lithuanian SSR, later the Republic of Lithuania, deputy prime minister, chairman of the Lithuanian Democratic Labor Party (former LCP), chairman of the Seimas (Parliament) of the Republic of Lithuania, and president of the Republic of Lithuania, the only high ranking Communist Lithuanian to transform into a democratic national leader, born in Rokiskis, Lithuania.

Brazauskas's early career was typical of a Lithuanian Communist of the post-Stalinist era, who climbed the career ladder from the ranks of technical intelligentsia to the top of the party due to his organizational skills rather than ideological rhetoric, which used to be common practice. After graduating from the Kaunas Polytechnical Institute in 1956, the year Lithuania broke away from Stalin's cult, Algirdas Brazauskas took up a professional career as a construction engineer. In the late 1950s and early 1960s, he was nominated for a number of leading positions in state-owned construction companies in Lithuania.

He reached the top of the professional ladder in 1964, when he was appointed minister of Building Materials Industry. He subsequently became deputy chairman of the State Planning Committee in 1967. The next promotion led up the political ladder. In 1977, Brazauskas was recruited to the Central Committee (CC) of the Lithuanian Communist Party (LCP). Secretary of the CC of the LCP for almost eleven years (1977–1988), he was responsible for the state-planned economy of

the country. In fact, this post was even more important than that of minister of economy. (Note that these posts were totally dependent on the Moscow-based governing bodies of the USSR.)

With the perestroika movement initiated by Gorbachev in 1985, Brazauskas stepped out from the shadow of the Central Committee. In 1988, he was one of the few members of the CC of the LCP who did not hesitate to take part in the first political rallies organized by the Lithuanian reform movement *Sajudis,* led by Vytautas Landsbergis. Brazauskas soon became associated with the progressive wing within the LCP. His activities leant a lot of credit to the Communist Party and earned him the post of first secretary of the Central Committee of the LCP in 1988.

Being at the top of the country's leadership in 1989, Brazauskas made three unprecedented decisions that secured him entry into Lithuanian history textbooks and later ensured him popular support in presidential elections. First, the Vilnius Cathedral, which was regarded by nationalists as a national shrine and which had been closed by the regime in 1950, was handed back to the Catholic Church. Second, the Lithuanian national flag and anthem, which were banned in 1949, regained their previous status, and, third, the Lithuanian language was declared the only official language of the country.

At the end of 1989, Brazauskas took one more step of the utmost importance: Under his leadership, the Lithuanian Communist Party declared its secession from the Communist Party of the Soviet Union. This very action signaled a breakdown of the party structure, the backbone of the Soviet regime. In protest to this, Russian-speaking members of the LCP left the party and declared their loyalty to the CP of the USSR. The newly formed body was called the Lithuanian Communist Party on the Platform of the Communist Party of the Soviet Union.

During 1988–1990, Brazauskas took a moderate stance in Lithuanian politics. He spoke out for a greater autonomy of the Lithuanian SSR within the Soviet Union and advocated a step-by-step policy regarding a bargain with Moscow.

According to his family, Brazauskas kept celebrating Christmas at home during his term in office as secretary of the CC of the LCP, a religious holiday banned by the Communist authorities. All in all, Brazauskas can be regarded as a follower of the traditions of national Communism set up by the long-lived first secretary of the CC of the LCP, Antanas Sniečkus, in the late 1960s and the early 1970s. He tried to combine the positive aspects of the Communist system and of Lithuanian nationalism in a pragmatic way.

In 1990, Brazauskas became chairman of the Supreme Council of the Lithuanian SSR, which was still under control of the LCP. In March 1990, the first democratic parliamentary elections in Lithuania swept the Communists away from power. The members of *Sajudis,* who won the elections, appointed Brazauskas to the post of deputy prime minister in the first democratic government led by the ex-Communist economist Kazimiera Prunskiene. In 1991, the cabinet was reshuffled leaving Brazauskas out of the government. He joined the parliamentary opposition as chairman of the Lithuanian Democratic Labor Party (LDLP), formerly the LCP.

In the 1992 parliamentary elections, the LDLP led by Brazauskas won the majority of seats. Brazauskas was elected chairman of the Seimas (Parliament) of the Republic of Lithuania. The next year he successfully ran for the presidency in the direct-vote elections and overwhelmingly defeated his rival Stasys Lozoraitis, an American Lithuanian and former Lithuanian ambassador to the United States. In 1997, Brazauskas refused to run for a second term saying that his Communist past could be a burden for Lithuania as it stepped into a new millenium. In 1998, the president handed over his office to Valdas Adamkus, an American Lithuanian and former senior official in the U.S. Environmental Protection Agency.

**BRETON NATIONALISM** The term *Breton* refers to the inhabitants and traditional language of Brittany, a region of western France. Before being incorporated into France in the 16th century, the Brittany peninsula had developed its own culture and language, inherited from Celtic invaders who had colonized the region between the 5th and 7th centuries. The relations between semiautonomous Brittany and the central government were thereafter marked by tensions and occasional uprisings against French authority, the most famous of which remains the bloody counterrevolutionary Chouans revolt that began in 1793.

After the revolution the increasingly centralizing French state attempted to impose French as the national language and sought to eradicate local vernaculars. There was some resistance to this trend, and between the Revolution and the end of World War II, Breton activists remained the most active of all French ethnocultural minorities. The moderate Breton Regionalist Union, the first modern Breton political group, was formed in 1898, followed by the more radical separatist Breton Nationalist Party in 1911.

A small Breton intellectual movement also persisted as peninsular philologists and historians continued to write and publish in their traditional language. The achievements of both political and literary/cultural Breton groups nevertheless remained limited. French linguistic standardization proceeded apace, and by the post-World War II period Breton had nearly disappeared as a living language. A plan by the Parti National Breton to seek independence by negotiating with the Germans during World War II durably tarnished the image of Breton separatism.

Alongside other minority languages and cultures, Breton experienced a revival in the 1960s and 1970s. Festivals, musical groups, and linguistic initiatives emerged to bring back the language and celebrate Breton culture and heritage. Breton language schools, known as *diwan* schools, were created, the Cultural Institute of Brittany was founded, and, more recently, a comprehensive dictionary of the Breton language was published.

More vocal and radical nationalist groups emerged in Brittany during the 1960s, and some engaged in terrorist activities, particularly after 1968, such as bombing French governmental buildings. Violent campaigns continued and intensified until the late 1970s, carried out for the most part by the Front de Libération de la Bretagne. These culminated in the bombing of a wing of the Versailles Palace in 1978.

A large number of small and ideologically diverse nationalist groups emerged during that period. None of these groups has thus far managed to elicit popular support for anything more than cultural preservation. The devolution of some powers by the central state to regions since 1982 may have contributed to the decline of the radical wing of the movement by allowing some regional decision making. The entrenchment of regions as political units and the sympathy of European institutions for infranational minorities may, however, strengthen Breton nationalism in the long run.

The Breton language is presently spoken and written by 100,000 and understood by perhaps 500,000 people.

Suggestion for further reading: Beer, William R., *The Unexpected Rebellion: Ethnic Activism in Contemporary France* (New York: New York University Press, 1980).

**BREZHNEV, LEONID** 1906–1982, General secretary of the Communist Party of the Soviet Union from 1964 to 1982, born in Dneprodzerzhinsk, Ukraine. His parents were Russian, his father having arrived in the town to work at the steel plant that had been constructed in the Dnieper valley by a Franco-Belgian consortium. Brezhnev was eleven at the time of the Soviet revolution and would therefore have lived through those tumultuous times, experiencing the social and economic turmoil that accompanied such a huge political upheaval firsthand. Brezhnev's first formal interaction with the Communist Party was his enrollment in the communist youth league, *Komsomol,* in 1923. In 1931, after being a candidate member for two years, Brezhnev became a member of the Communist Party and eventually worked his way up from being a regional first secretary to chairman of the Presidium of the Supreme Soviet of the USSR. Brezhnev was a key figure in Khrushchev's ouster in 1964 and worked quickly to consolidate his new position as first secretary (later renamed general secretary) of the Communist Party, which he held until his death in November 1982.

Since the early years of the Soviet Union the Communist Party had put forward the argument that national divisions would be overcome through a three-stage evolutionary process of flourishing/rapprochement/merger (*ratsvet/sblizhenie/sliyanie*). The Soviet nationalities policy was therefore said to be based on allowing nationalities a certain degree of cultural autonomy while at the same time promoting the coming together of these nationalities, which would eventually lead to the merging of nationalities and proletarian unity within the Soviet state. Through most of the Brezhnev period this line was followed with the exception of the final term, the "merging" of nations. This was dropped after 1969 and the concept of the emergence of a new historical community of people, the "Soviet people" (*Sovetskii narod*) came into vogue. This became noticeable at the 1971 party congress where Brezhnev reiterated the Khrushchev line of the "flourishing" and "coming together" of the Soviet nationalities, while also asserting that "In the years of socialist construction, a new historical community of people—the Soviet people—arose in our country. New and harmonious relations between classes and social groups, nations and nationalities—relations of friendship and cooperation—were born in joint labor, in the struggle for socialism and in battles for its defense."

This reference to the creation of the "Soviet people" had a dual purpose. First, it fitted in with the new era that was said to exist, that is, the period of "developed socialism," which was said to have superseded Khrushchev's "mature socialism." The Soviet Union could thus be shown to be steadily progressing toward a Communist state. But in conjunction with references to the "Soviet people" there was a noticeable absence of references to the final "merging" of the nations. In this way Brezhnev could proudly point to the success of socialism within the Soviet Union and also point to the problems still to be overcome in the nationality area without contradicting himself. It was therefore wholly consis-

tent to talk of the "Soviet people" and at the same time state that "we don't at all believe that nationality differences are disappearing in the Soviet Union, much less that the merging of nations has occurred."

The Soviet constitution of 1977 revitalized the nationality question with certain factions proposing the removal of the republics' right to secede and thereby making the federation a redundant notion. Brezhnev appears to have advocated that the existing federal structure be retained, which was, in any case, the final outcome. Brezhnev made it evident in his constitution speech that there had been serious discussion of this issue with some comrades coming "to incorrect conclusions" about the nationality question by suggesting the concept of a "unified Soviet nation" via the liquidation of "the Union and autonomous republics."

Although the Brezhnev period continued much of Khrushchev's ideological initiatives on the nationality question, in practice many of the benefits gained by the nationalities during the Khrushchev period were eventually lost under Brezhnev. In 1966 the Sovnarkoz reforms initiated by Khrushchev, which established local economic councils and therefore greater local autonomy, were reversed by the reestablishment of all-union and union republic ministries and the abolition of the Central Committee bureaus for Central Asia and the Transcaucasian republics. The trend toward recentralization was further strengthened by the resolutions of the Central Committee in February 1972. This meeting agreed on an increase in centralization of economic planning with a concomitant increase in territorial specialization, thereby emphasizing a division of labor between the republics. This erosion of local power was worsened by Brezhnev's policy of developing Siberia as the driving force of the Soviet economy's expansion. In real terms this meant that the Russian Soviet Federated Socialist Republic was given economic priority for development over, and at the expense of, the other republics.

**BRITISH COMMONWEALTH** The Commonwealth of Nations (until 1946 the British Commonwealth of Nations) is a loose, voluntary association of the former ruler and the ruled. It grew out of the special status Britain granted in 1931 through the Statute of Westminster to four dependencies (Canada, Australia, New Zealand, and South Africa), which had large European populations and were largely sovereign and self-ruling. When many colonies demanded and won their independence after World War II, those who wanted the benefit of practical cooperation, friendship, trade, and investment with Britain and with each other were invited to join regardless of whether they had republican or nonparliamentary forms of government. Members, who by 2000 numbered fifty-one, are also free to leave the Commonwealth, as the Republic of Ireland did in 1948. South Africa also left in 1961 and Pakistan in 1972 although both rejoined in 1994 and 1989, respectively.

The symbolic head is the British monarch, even though some members are republics. Member states regularly confer at biennial Commonwealth gatherings held in various member countries. There are events such as the Commonwealth Games (a mini-Olympics). Citizens of Commonwealth countries enjoy certain benefits in the United Kingdom, such as lower tuition at British universities. A Commonwealth Secretariat was created in London in 1965 to coordinate the associations' activities. Sometimes Britain must assume responsibilities under the aegis of the Commonwealth, such as in helping to arrange a transition to democracy in the tiny Caribbean island of Grenada after four years of totalitarian rule and an invasion by the United States and six other Caribbean island states.

Today the sun technically does not set on the British empire. Ten dots on the map are still ruled by Britain: Pitcairn in the south Pacific Ocean; Bermuda, British Virgin Islands, Caymans, Leeward Islands, Turks, and Caicos in the Caribbean area; the Falkland Islands and St. Helena in the south Atlantic Ocean; Gibraltar in the Mediterranean; and Diego Garcia in the Indian Ocean. However, because they are not sovereign states, they are not members of the Commonwealth. The same applied to Hong Kong. Painstaking negotiations with the People's Republic of China (PRC) resulted in an agreement that gave the PRC sovereignty over the colony in July 1997. Although China guaranteed Hong Kong's capitalist economy and lifestyle for 50 years, Hong Kong became a part of the PRC. It is thereby ineligible for Commonwealth membership.

Britain faces alone the complicated problems that concern the smaller enclaves it rules. Local inhabitants in these smaller countries fear their larger neighbors and look to Britain for protection. Britain has declared that the principle of self-determination must not be violated and that the subject peoples can be absorbed by a neighboring land only by their consent. The principle is an admirable one, but it has a high cost. The 2100 inhabitants of the Falklands, located off the Argentine coast, called on Britain to defend them from Argentina in 1982. Britain's military victory did not convince Argentina to renounce its claims to the islands. As a deterrent, London stations 2000 troops on the islands. The 31,000 inhabitants of Gibraltar cling to their rock and are largely self-ruling. But they rely on British protection because they are afraid of becoming a part of Spain. In 1985 the border between Gibraltar and Spain was reopened, and discussions over its sovereignty and eventual disposition continue. Finally, Northern Ireland is a part of the United Kingdom and is therefore disqualified from Commonwealth association, except through London.

**BRITISH EMPIRE**   Imperial expansion was critical to the self-definition of the British as a people. In a highly complex discourse that included literature, political tracts, religious ephemera, and fiction, the British propagated the idea that the spread of the British Empire was critical for the spread of civilization throughout the globe. The guiding principle of British expansion was that of bringing "Christianity, Civilization, and Commerce" and was best expressed by the notion of a "White Man's Burden" to bring civilization and enlightenment to the benighted nations around the globe.

The ideology behind the expansion of the British Empire always involved a strong element of racism. The British envisioned a world in which Britain, the white dominions of Australia, Canada, New Zealand, and South Africa, and the United States would in concert undertake to ensure the peace and prosperity of the world under Anglo-Saxon hegemony. The identity of race and language was held as the first principle and race was exalted as the basis of Greater Britain.

The second motivating principle behind the expansion of the British nation was that of commercial gain. The British incorporated large tracts of India, Africa, and Asia into their imperial domain and these areas were critical sites both for the production of raw materials as well as for the export of finished goods. Thus, racial and religious ideologies were marshaled in defense of a British global economic dominance.

British nationalism found expression in a variety of cultural practices such as the Boy Scouts, which purported to train young British lads for a lifetime of service to the Empire; sports and games, which were thought to equip young men for the demands of ruling an empire; and popular literature. Writers such as Rider Haggard, Rudyard Kipling, and John Buchan used the exploits of their fictional heroes to inculcate young readers with a belief in the necessity of empire and certainty in the supremacy of the Anglo-Saxon race.

Key works on the British Empire include those by Lawrence James, *The Rise and Fall of the British Empire* (St. Martin's 1999), and Ronald Human, *Britain's Imperial Century, 1815–1914* (Batsford, 1976).

**BRITISH NATIONALISM**   Britons seldom speak of "British nationalism." Those nations that do normally had to fight for their independence from a foreign ruler.

The British never had to do this, as did the Americans or the Irish. Nor has Britain experienced a political revolution in the modern age that would have caused them to ask themselves such fundamental questions as who they are and what their rights are. The very name of their country, United Kingdom, indicates the joining of various peoples in one political entity. It implies diversity in a state in which one can be English, Scot, Welsh, Northern Irish, or a descendent of one of Britain's former colonial peoples while carrying a British passport and obeying laws and regulations established by supranational institutions of the European Union (EU).

There are occasional displays of overt British pride. An exhilarated population celebrated enthusiastically when victory in Europe was achieved in 1945. In 1952 most British observed with reverence the coronation of Queen Elizabeth II, who succeeded her father, George VI, on the throne. The monarch symbolizes the unity of the country and the continuous thread through a millennium of English history. She is the focus of national pride. Politics touches not only the mind, but also the heart. She helps provide her subjects with an emotional attachment to their country. She is therefore an important cornerstone for the kind of low-keyed, but deeply rooted patriotism that most English share.

In 1982 Argentine troops invaded and captured a small group of offshore islands that had long been settled and ruled by the British. Prime Minister Margaret Thatcher galvanized the nation with her firmness and resolution in organizing the recapture of the Falklands Islands. The British basked again briefly in imperial glory. An overwhelming majority of them applauded their leader for her ability to deal with a crisis and win back control of the islands, albeit at tremendous financial cost. The Falklands War boosted her Conservative Party's popularity. Sensing the political winds blowing briskly at her back, she called an early election and won an astonishing electoral triumph in June 1983. Her leadership image, established in the Falklands War, was an invaluable political asset. In 1991 Britain's participation in the war to drive Iraq out of Kuwait was solidly supported at home. The United Kingdom sent a powerful contingent of land, air, and naval forces to contribute to the stunning victory. The same applied in 1999 to Britain's part in stopping Serb atrocities in Kosovo.

In the 21st century at least three factors soften or complicate feelings of British nationalism: devolution, integration with Europe, and the transformation of Britain into a multicultural and multiracial society. Under Prime Minister Tony Blair, whose New Labour government was elected in 1997, the British government transferred important powers to Northern Ireland, Scotland,

and Wales. By the end of the 20th century all three had their own elected parliaments. The Scots and Welsh have their own languages that are being revived with some success. They have their own brand of nationalism and nationalist parties that do well in elections (see entries on "Welsh Nationalism" and "Scottish Nationalism"). Welsh nationalism is tied to the Welsh language and is alive though not robust. The language motive is weaker in Scotland, and unlike in Northern Ireland, there is no religious motive. Alex Salmond, leader of the Scottish Nationalist Party (SNP), remarked that "we are a mongrel nation." All three peoples have a separate identity that competes with their British one. On top of that they are part of a country that is integrating more and more with Europe; that is an additional identity that challenges their being primarily British.

For centuries Britain was a global power, whose interest in Europe was merely to prevent any one power or combination of powers from upsetting the military balance there and dominating the entire continent. Now its focus is increasingly on Europe. This is true despite the fact that the British are more sensitive and cautious about relinquishing their sovereignty and currency to supranational authorities in Brussels and Frankfurt than are many other EU members. In 1973 the United Kingdom entered the EU, a move that has had a dramatic impact on its economy. The EU now buys 43 percent of British exports, compared to 31 percent in 1972. In practice, British governments have tended to put British interests ahead of European interests. They have been cool on a common EU energy policy, a directly elected European Parliament, and Economic and Monetary Union (EMU). Britain has shown little interest in deepening or expanding European integration. Prime Minister Thatcher successfully reduced the British contribution to the EU budget. She argued that it is no time to create new bureaucracies and weaken national parliaments just when Eastern European nations are digging themselves out from underneath their bureaucracies and breathing new life into their legislatures. At the historic 1991 summit in Maastricht, Britain agreed to greater economic and political union on the condition that the United Kingdom could "opt out" of a single European currency if it chose; "opt outs" are designed to protect a country's sovereignty. After much agony, parliament finally accepted the treaty in 1993. Nevertheless, the Conservative Party's feuding over Europe dragged it down in the polls and was an important reason why it was trounced in the 1997 elections. There is no consensus in Britain on integration with Europe.

The Labour government is more supportive of greater British participation in a more united Europe although Prime Minister Blair promises to put British interests first and to have a referendum before ever scrapping pound sterling and adopting the Euro. He decided that the United Kingdom would not join the first wave of monetary union. One of his first acts was to make the Bank of England more independent of the government. Such independence for central banks is one of the EU's prerequisites for participation in the common currency. His government also made the European Human Rights Charter enforceable in British courts.

The rapidity with which Britain has become a multicultural and multiracial society profoundly affects the way many residents of Great Britain understand who is "British." For 900 years Britain had experienced almost no immigration, except from Ireland. Now it is no longer a racially homogenous society. As a consequence of decolonization, especially since the 1960s, Asians and blacks poured into Britain from India, Pakistan, Africa, and the Caribbean. By the end of the 20th century the population was 7 percent nonwhite (half of them Asians of Indian, Pakistani, and Bangladeshi descent). This percentage is likely to grow because of the declining birth rate of white Britons.

Some whites have reacted negatively to the visibly different newcomers in their midst. Because of complaints that this demographic change was happening too quickly, immigration was restricted by the 1981 British Nationality Act. The number of successful applicants for British citizenship in 1993 was the lowest in more than a decade. Britain is now faced with the difficult problem of integrating large groups of nonwhite minorities, who tend to be concentrated in the decaying inner cities, even though there is less residential segregation by race in Britain than in the United States. Such concentration gives the impression that the minority presence in the United Kingdom is far greater than it actually is. A fifth of London's population belongs to an ethnic minority, and that figure will rise to a third by the year 2010. Having come to the United Kingdom much later than the forebears of African Americans, they often speak little or no English, worship religions that are unfamiliar to most British, and dress or groom themselves in very different fashion from the rest of the population.

British blacks have not penetrated the top levels of business, the professions, judiciary, or the cabinet, as the American black élite has. Only 1 percent of soldiers is from a minority, compared with 5 percent of civil servants. This may change as a result of an increase in nonwhite enrollment at British universities; 12 percent of students are from ethnic minorities, almost double their representation in the overall population.

Some white British became uneasy about being swamped by immigrants, and this strengthened intolerant and exclusive nationalist sentiments. Young white gangs of "skinheads" and the "punk-rock" and "heavy-metal" set derive morbid amusement from "Paki-bashing." Those whites who want to exploit the rising racial tensions, such as the neo-Nazi British National Party, seldom find favor with voters. Violent outbreaks often stem from youth unemployment and disillusionment, poor living conditions, racial discrimination, and inefficient police practices. The unarmed Bobbies, who always seemed to symbolize British tact and tolerance, have been severely criticized for alleged racism, arrogance, and brutality. They are regarded with distrust and suspicion in many nonwhite areas. In an effort to improve their public image, the London Metropolitan Police has begun to recruit more black policemen. Deplorable race riots helped raise the awareness of the extent to which racial problems fester in a society in which many citizens have not yet accepted the fact of a multiracial Britain. There is no consensus among Britons about race relations.

The spread of the kind of electorally significant anti-immigrant sentiment and support for racist right-wing parties seen on the continent has been prevented. This is due to a combination of tough anti-immigration policies, unusually detailed laws against racial discrimination, and the fact that legal immigrants have always been treated not as migrant workers but as permanent settlers, with automatic rights to vote, to run for office, and to claim social security benefits. Three-fourths of blacks are British citizens, and most of the rest are Commonwealth citizens who can vote in Britain. It has been difficult to integrate blacks and Asians into the political process, except in direct defense of their own interests. But there has been progress. Nonwhites have visible positive role models in sports and the arts, and more are succeeding in business and the professions. There are grounds for optimism that the lauded English tolerance and gradualism will lead more British to accept the immigrants and their children as nonwhite Britons.

The election of regional parliaments in Scotland, Wales, and Northern Ireland, the magnetic pull of Europe, and the undigested heterogeneity of British society make it less likely than ever that a demonstrative British nationalism will reemerge in the 21st century.

**BULGARIAN NATIONALISM** Modern Bulgarian nationalism emerged in the 19th century, and was defined initially by its struggle for religious emancipation from the Greek-dominated Ecumenical Patriarchate of the Orthodox Church, based in Constantinople, and Ottoman Turkish political power. The Bulgars were in a less favorable position than most other Balkan nationalities. Politically they were more directly exposed to Ottoman power than other Balkan nations; they were territorially close to Constantinople, the seat of the Ottoman Turkish goverment, and Bulgaria was vital to the Ottomans for strategic purposes. In cultural and religious terms, on the other hand, the Bulgars were under the control of the patriarchate in Constantinople. The Bulgarian Orthodox Church, founded in the 13th century and based in Ohrid (Macedonia), had been subjected to Greek domination soon after the Ottoman conquest and was abolished in 1767.

Bulgarian nationalism, like other East Central European nationalisms, proceeded through a number of stages, the first of which was the literary and cultural awakening of the early and mid-19th century. The small Bulgarian merchant class and nationally conscious Bulgarian Orthodox clergy supported the creation of Bulgarian schools, the first of which were founded in the 1830s. As the educational and cultural awakening developed, Bulgarian nationalism evolved into a struggle for an autocephalous Bulgarian Orthodox Church, led by Bishop Ilarion Makariopolsky. The 1860s was a decade of intense religious struggle between the Bulgar and Greek clergy. In 1870 the Ottoman government, under Russian diplomatic pressure, established the Bulgarian Exarchate, an autonomous ecclesiastical organization that encompassed most Bulgars. By the 1890s the exarchate had, with Ottoman approval, expanded to include most of Macedonia within its jurisdiction.

The political struggle of Bulgarian nationalism for an independent Bulgaria was a much more complicated affair. During the Eastern Crisis of 1875–1878, rebellions against Ottoman Turkish rule broke out in the Balkans, from Bosnia-Herzegovina to Bulgaria. In 1877, Russia went to war against the Ottoman empire, ostensibly to secure the rights of the Bulgarians and other Orthodox Christians. Under Russian pressure, the Ottoman government signed the Treaty of San Stefano (March 3, 1878), which stipulated the creation of a Great Bulgarian state, including present-day Bulgaria, Macedonia, and Dobrudja. Because of Great Power, especially British and Austro-Hungarian pressure, the San Stefano treaty was never implemented.

Under the terms of the Congress of Berlin (June 1878), which superseded San Stefano, Bulgaria was divided into two parts. Bulgaria proper, north of the Balkan mountains and south of the Danube, was given autonomy within the Ottoman empire, paid an annual tribute to the sultan, and received a European prince, Alexander of Battenberg (1878–1885). The other area, Eastern Rumelia, became a semiautonomous unit of the Ottoman empire under European Great Power administration. Bulgarian nationalists resented the terms imposed by the Congress of Berlin, and regarded the San

Stefano frontiers as Bulgaria's legitimate and natural borders. San Stefano had an important impact on the evolution of Bulgarian nationalism, for the goal of all Bulgarian nationalists remained the creation of a San Stefano Great Bulgaria.

In 1885 a revolt broke out in Eastern Rumelia demanding the region's unification with Bulgaria. This in fact occurred, and represented a step toward Bulgarian unification. Bulgaria also obtained a new ruler in Ferdinand of Saxe-Coburg (1887–1918). In September 1908 Bulgaria declared independence from the Ottoman empire, exploiting the chaos in Constantinople that was caused by the Young Turk revolution.

The proclamation of independence did not appease Bulgarian nationalism, for all Bulgarian nationalists aspired to create a Great Bulgarian state, including, above all, Macedonia. Since the late 19th century both the Bulgarian exarchate and autonomous government had been active in promoting Bulgarian propaganda in Macedonia, attempting to convince the Macedonian Slav population that they were in fact Bulgars. But in Macedonia, Bulgarian nationalism ran into not only the native Macedonian nationalist movement, but the competing demands of Greek and Serbian nationalism.

Although Bulgaria, Serbia, and Greece had signed political and military alliances in 1912, aimed against the Ottoman empire, the three powers could not resolve their differences over Macedonia. During the First Balkan War (1912–1913), Bulgaria, Serbia, Greece, and Montenegro succeeded in occupying most of the Ottoman empire's Balkan territories. Bulgaria feared the loss of Macedonia to Greece and Serbia, however, which prompted it to attack its erstwhile allies. This led to the Second Balkan War (1913), which Bulgaria lost. The Second Balkan War was disastrous for Bulgaria; it was forced to cede most of Macedonia to Serbia and Greece, and the southern Dobrudja region to Romania.

A Great Bulgarian state seemed elusive, and Bulgaria emerged from the Balkan Wars as a revisionist power. That explains why, during World War I, Bulgaria joined the Central Powers (Germany, Austria-Hungary, Turkey). In 1915 Bulgaria was promised all of Macedonia for her entry into the war. Once again, however, a Great Bulgarian state proved ephemeral. The Treaty of Neuilly (November 27, 1919) stipulated that Bulgaria pay a war indemnity, return western Thrace to Greece, Dobrudja to Romania, and, most importantly, Macedonia to the new Kingdom of Serbs, Croats and Slovenes ("Yugoslavia").

In the interwar era (1918–1941) Bulgarian nationalism remained a potent political force, nurtured on the losses that the country had experienced in the Balkan Wars and World War I. When the first postwar premier,

Alexander Stamboliski (1919–1923), attempted to pursue a conciliatory foreign policy vis-à-vis the new Yugoslav state, he was assassinated by members of the Internal Macedonian Revolutionary Organization (VMRO), which had the tacit approval of the Bulgarian military. Only in the context of World War II, as an Axis ally, was Bulgaria able again briefly to annex Macedonia (1941–1944). Since 1945 Bulgarian nationalists have largely resigned themselves to the loss of Macedonia, which Bulgaria officially recognized in 1992 as an independent state.

**BUNGE, ALEJANDRO** 1880–1943, Argentine economist. Educated in his native Buenos Aires and in Germany, Bunge was the foremost intellectual representative of the 1920s and 1930s reaction against the open, agrarian, exports-led model of economic development that had spurred Argentina's expansion from the late 19th century on; he favored a more active role for the state in the promotion of local industries. A leader of the Social Catholic movement, he directed the Circulos de Obreros Católicos between 1912 and 1916, confronting both liberals and socialists in numerous debates about labor policies.

Bunge began his career in public administration as director of statistics of the National Department of Labor between 1913 and 1915, later becoming director of the Office of Statistics between 1915 and 1920 and 1923 and 1925. In 1918 he founded the influential Revista de Economía Argentina, a forum for the new economic ideas, which he directed for more than two decades. Bunge also taught economics at the universities of Buenos Aires and La Plata and wrote several books, among which *La Economía Argentina* (1928–1930) and *Una Nueva Argentina* (1940) showed the keenest insight.

**BUTHELEZI, MANGOSUTHU** 1928–, Son of Chief Mathole and Princess Constance Magogo Zulu is the leader of the Inkatha Freedom Party (IFP), a political party that claims to represent the ethnic claims of the Zulu-speaking people of South Africa. Buthelezi and the IFP enjoy their strongest support in the region of the country in which it was formed, Natal. Most of South Africa's Zulu-speaking African population is concentrated in natal (75 percent of the total). And about 90 percent of the Africans resident in the province are Zulu speaking.

Buthelezi has always maintained the legitimacy of his rule based on the fact that he is the great grandson of King Cetshwayo kaMpande and the daughter of a princess. However, his rise to power cannot be understood outside of the rise of bantustan legislative assemblies as part of the administrative machinery of the apartheid state. The Bantu Authorities Act of 1951 reaffirmed and redefined the role of chiefs and the tribe as the base of an administrative pyramid. On September 6, 1957, Buthelezi was officially installed as a chief and thus became an official mouthpiece of the Bantu authorities and began working within the apartheid "separate development" framework.

The Zulu nationalism expounded by Buthelezi and his party cannot be separated from the promotion and defense of free market capitalism and commercial interests. The desire for the African petty bourgeoisie in Natal to defend its interests in the 1920s and 1930s found expression in the promotion of Zulu identity through means of the first Zulu political movement, which bore the name Inkatha. The first Inkatha constitution, written in 1928, was drawn up by a white lawyer, based in Durban, at the instigation of sugar interests in Natal. The document ensured that the interests of the conservative African petty bourgeoisie and tribal élites were firmly entrenched in Inkatha. On March 22, 1975, Inkatha YaKwazulu (Inkatha of the Zulu people) was revived in Natal. By the time the first copies of its constitution were published the name had changed to Inkatha Yesizwe (Inkatha of the Nation). The reformed Inkatha, no less than its predecessor, used appeals to a separate Zulu identity, which excluded others outside of the Zulu nation.

Throughout the apartheid era, the IFP clashed heavily with its main political rival, the African National Congress (ANC). These conflicts were most often portrayed as ethnic or tribal antagonisms between Zulu-speaking people and other ethnic groups. However, the differences between the ANC and the IFP go far beyond issues of ethnic nationalism. The two parties differ fundamentally not only on matters of what role ethnicity should play in national politics, but also on matters of economic ideology. Despite the large numbers of Zulu-speaking workers who are members, the IFP, like the Inkatha of old, represents the interests of capital and espouses a free market ideology.

In the postapartheid era Inkatha has continued to espouse Zulu separatism and has vehemently opposed the policies of its chief rival, the ruling ANC. In the weeks leading up to the election it was feared that Buthelezi and the IFP would boycott the election and, further, would agitate for an independent Zulu state within the union. Since the collapse of apartheid, Buthelezi and his movement have witnessed a steady erosion in their legitimacy as the ANC's ideology of nonracialism and its project of cross-racial nation building have proved to have more popular ideological appeal.

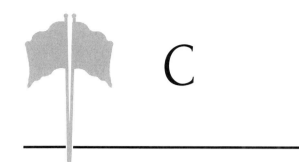

# C

CALHOUN, JOHN C. 1782–1850, U.S. statesman, was born near Abbeville, South Carolina. Calhoun served as U.S. senator, secretary of war, and vice president under presidents John Quincy Adams and Andrew Jackson, but he is best remembered as a leading proponent of states' rights and the author of the doctrine of nullification.

In his early career, Calhoun was a staunch nationalist. As a leader of the "War Hawks," he strongly supported the War of 1812 with Great Britain. After the war's conclusion he became one of the leading advocates of Henry Clay's American System, a form of economic nationalism that sought to promote the commercial interests of the United States by imposing high tariffs on imported foreign manufactures, improving transportation links between the factories of the East and the plantations and farms of the South and West, and reestablishing the Bank of the United States as the cornerstone of a national banking system. As secretary of war from 1817 to 1825, he played a major role in modernizing the nation's armed forces.

Calhoun's retreat from nationalism began after the high tariffs of the 1820s aroused great opposition in South Carolina and other southern states. The tariff bill of 1828 was known throughout the South as the "Tariff of Abominations" because it greatly increased the prices southerners paid for manufactured goods without protecting southern agriculture from foreign competition. Despite his ambition to become president, Calhoun ceased supporting high tariffs and other nationalizing measures and instead sought ways to rid the South of this noxious problem. His solution was nullification, a theory that he began to voice publicly in 1832. He used as a starting point the position espoused in the Virginia and Kentucky Resolutions of 1798, which asserted a state's right to nullify an act of Congress, in this case the Alien and Sedition Acts, thus rendering it null and void

within its borders. Calhoun declared that, although courts could offer their opinions as to the constitutionality of congressional action, the power to nullify such action on the grounds of unconstitutionality lay entirely with the states. He further believed that only a constitutional amendment, which required a two-thirds vote in both the House and Senate and ratification by three-fourths of the states, could force an individual state to abide by an act that it found abhorrent. Although Calhoun's theory of nullification was popular throughout his home state—South Carolina nullified the tariff bill of 1832, which led to the passage of a compromise tariff the next year—no other southern state embraced his doctrine and most rejected it outright.

When slavery became a major political issue after the Mexican War, Calhoun became more and more an advocate of regionalism over nationalism. As one of the leading advocates of the proslavery stand, Calhoun argued that the federal government merely acted as the agent of the several states, particularly in the case of the territories acquired during the war. Instead of conceding to Congress the right to regulate slavery in these lands, he argued that the territories were owned jointly by all the states and that the federal government had no right to prohibit a citizen of any state from carrying his property, including slaves, into any of the territories. As the national debate over the expansion of slavery into the territories became increasingly contentious, he proposed to safeguard the economic interests of the South by abandoning nationalism altogether. Inspired by the precedent set by republican Rome, whose government was headed by two tribunes, Calhoun called for a constitutional amendment creating a dual presidency. The approval of both presidents, one of whom would be elected from the South and the other from the North, would be required to enact a congressional bill.

Calhoun offers an interesting example of a politician

whose views on nationalism evolved during his career. Like many other southerners, Calhoun became increasingly disenchanted with a strong national U.S. government because he perceived that government's policies to be increasingly inimical to the economic interests of his region.

Biographies include those by Irving H. Bartlett, *Calhoun: A Biography* (1993); John Niven, *John C. Calhoun and the Price of Union* (1988); Merrill D. Peterson, *The Great Triumvirate: Webster, Clay, and Calhoun* (1987); and Charles M. Wiltse, *John C. Calhoun* (3 vols., 1944–1951).

## CAMBODIAN NATIONALISM

Cambodia, also known as the Kingdom of Cambodia (1970–76), the Khmer Republic (1976–1979), Democratic Kampuchea (1979–1989), or the People's Republic of Kampuchea, is a country in the southwestern Indochinese peninsula of Southeast Asia with a complicated and violent history in the 20th century. It is still in a state of flux at the time of this writing.

Cambodia, or Khmer, was once a thriving empire that encompassed much of the Indochinese peninsula from the 11th to the 13th centuries including much of present-day Vietnam, Laos, and Thailand, so that its cultural influence over the region was substantial.

In 1954 Prince Sihanouk's government was recognized as the legitimate authority of the nation at a Geneva Conference trying to settle the so-called First Indochina War. The purpose of the decision was to prevent the Viet Minh from gaining power over any sections of Cambodia as they had in Laos.

Sihanouk was not universally liked in his own country, however, where both Democrats and Communists opposed his authoritarianism. He abdicated his throne in March 1955 to his father, Norodom Suramarit, and mobilized a political movement, the Sangkum Reastr Nium ("People's Socialist Community"), drawing people away from the powerful Democrats. Elections took place later in the year, with widely reported abuses by Sihanouk's police. His party won every seat in the National Assembly and he took power and retained it until he was overthrown in 1970.

Worried about both his U.S.-backed neighbors of Thailand and South Vietnam, and the possibility of being overrun by a unified Vietnam under Communist control, he declared neutrality in international affairs. Sihanouk broke off relations with the United States in 1965, however, and concluded secret agreements with the North Vietnamese, allowing them to station troops on Cambodian territory. The agreement resulted in an American invasion and bombing of eastern Cambodia in 1970.

In March 1970 the National Assembly voted to remove Sihanouk from office while he was out of the country visiting the Soviet Union. The ousted leader sought the assistance of the Chinese and allied himself with the Cambodian Communist forces, who had been his bitter enemy just a few days before.

After a devastating civil war Lon Nol's regime in Phnom Penh collapsed despite large quantities of American aid, and the victorious Communist forces ordered the urban inhabitants to leave immediately for the countryside. Many of them died in forced marches, and some of those who survived may have envied the dead.

A long decade of civil war ensued with devastating results, subsiding only toward the end of the 1980s when international pressure was brought to bear. The Vietnamese forces withdrew, the U.S. initiated an economic boycott of the country, and the United Nations moved in to broker a settlement among the various competing factions. Although not entirely successful by any means, some relief was brought by the United Nations actions that included establishing a Supreme National Council that included all four major factions fighting the civil war and the introduction of UN peacekeeping forces.

## CANADIAN NATIONALISM

In many ways the term Canadian nationalism is an oxymoron. The geographical size of Canada and the diversity of its people have conspired to inhibit any strong manifestations of nationalism. The fact that Canada is composed of at least four very different elements—the native peoples (often referred to as First Nations), French-speaking Canadians (those living within the borders of Quebec are most commonly referred to as Quebecois), English-speaking Canadians, and recent immigrants—appears to be one of the major obstacles facing nationalist mobilizers.

In fact, it could be argued that with the possible exception of recent immigrants, who spend much of their time trying to assimilate into either Quebec- or English-speaking Canadian society, each of the other three groups considers itself a distinct nation. It has been observed that in the case of French speakers in Quebec, for example, the Quebecois are a nation without a state, while English-speaking Canadians as a whole, have a state without a nation. For that reason, virtually every discussion of nationalism in Canada is overshadowed by a form of nationalism that is both more prevalent and powerful; that is to say, it is overshadowed by Quebec nationalism.

Yet, there have been some expressions, however faint, of English-speaking Canadian nationalism since the Act of Confederation in 1867. At the turn of the century, for example, while Liberal Prime Minister Wilfred Laurier was in power, a debate began between those who wanted to pursue ever closer ties to Great Britain (often labeled "imperialists") and those who wished to see Canada seek greater political, economic, and cultural autonomy from the British Empire. Both world wars appear to have solved that dispute in favor of the latter, as Britain commenced its decline, and the United States its rise, as a world power. American capital began to flood into Canada in the form of direct investment, and along with it came American cultural influence, almost impossible to stop because the two countries speak the same language. As a result of these two long-term trends—the growing economic dominance of the Canadian economy by Americans and the influx of American cultural products—things came to a head in the 1960s and 1970s, as Canada witnessed its strongest expression of English-speaking Canadian nationalism since Confederation.

Couched in terms of increased economic and cultural independence from the United States, the cultural and economic nationalism of this time was confined to a relatively small group of university professors, publishers, writers, journalists, and artists. On the one hand, Canadian cultural nationalists fretted over the influence that American culture was having on Canadian society (usually accompanied by slogans such as "Yankee Go Home"), and worked to develop and preserve a distinct set of uniquely Canadian social and cultural values. Canadian economic nationalists, on the other hand, concentrated on pushing the federal government to implement polices (including trade tariffs and investment quotas) that would reduce foreign investment in Canada and foster a strong, Canadian-controlled, economy.

Yet in spite of the objections of both cultural and economic nationalists during the time, the mid-1980s saw a marked shift away from protectionism in both economic and cultural matters, toward a more "continentalist" position. In 1987, for example, Conservative Prime Minister Brian Mulroney signed the Free Trade Agreement (FTA) with American President Ronald Reagan. The FTA effectively opened the economic and cultural borders between the two countries, undermining the hopes of nationalists of stemming the tide of American influence.

Canadian nationalism, therefore, especially since the 1960s, has been limited to preserving Canadian economic and cultural identity against the influence of the larger American market. This would explain, as well, the predominantly anti-American tone of much of Canadian nationalism. What has spurred Canadian nationalism more than anything else has been a fear that once cultural and economic sovereignty disappear, political independence will soon follow.

For an overview of the history of the Canadian identity see *The Canadian Identity* by historian W. L. Morton (University of Toronto Press, 1961). In 1965 Canadian philosopher George Grant wrote *Lament for a Nation: The Defeat of Canadian Nationalism* (McClelland & Stewart), considered by many to be the defining text on Canadian nationalism. Historian Ramsay Cook's *Canada, Quebec and the Uses of Nationalism* (second edition, McClelland & Stewart, 1986) is an excellent examination of both Québec and Canadian nationalism. Finally, Jack Granatstein's *Yankee Go Home? Canadians and Anti-Americanism* (HarperCollins, 1996) is a look at the anti-American tendencies in Canadian nationalism.

**CAPITALISM** Capitalism is a social system in which human needs are met through exchanges of commodities within a marketplace. The basic unit of value under capitalism is the commodity—any good or service whose exchange yields its owner a profit. The basic medium of such transactions is money, which becomes the measuring rod by which profit and loss are calculated. The basic source of value under capitalism is human labor. A social system can be described as capitalist if profit-seeking exchanges of goods, money, and human labor become the typical means by which resources are allocated.

The exchange of goods, money, and human labor are elements of capitalism as well as such noncapitalist social systems as feudalism, state socialism, and various forms of patrimonialism. What differentiates capitalism is the primacy of impersonal, rationalized profit seeking over alternative modes of exchange. Comparative historical analyses and social scientific research have produced a rich variety of discussions of how exchanges were conducted in noncapitalist social systems. One classic noncapitalist case is the Kula ring, a closed trade circuit anthropologist Bronislaw Malinowski (1922) observed in the north Melanesian region surrounding the Trobriand Islands. The Kula ring's basic unit of value—and the medium through which many intercommunal transactions were initiated—was polished shell necklaces and bracelets, each of which was given a name, a personality, and a history of its own. These objects were exchanged annually by permanent, life-long trading partners dispersed throughout a vast island archipelago. Bargaining over the number of objects given or received was prohibited, as was removing them from the circuit. The principles of exchange in the Kula trading network serve as a useful contrast to capitalism, where transactions of most resources are profit seeking, impersonal, and mediated by money.

Capitalism first emerged during the early modern period (ca. 1450–1700) in Western Europe, where it fueled the emergence of nation-states as well as nationalist ideologies. However, its relationship to nationalism has been the subject of considerable scholarly debate. In particular, neoclassical economists and Marxists have proposed very different general theories regarding capitalism's effect on political systems.

Neoclassical theory retains (in modified form) many of the assumptions about how governments construct well-run markets that Adam Smith first put forth in 1776 in his *Wealth of Nations*. Smith, arguing against mercantilists and physiocrats, insisted that macroeconomic growth was a by-product of the increasing division of labor, itself a function of self-interest. Within a free market, self-interested exchanges lead individuals to select the course of action that is most socially optimal, because their increased productivity will provide others with scarce and useful goods. Hence, governments should remove barriers to free enterprise in order to raise a country's living standards.

Classical economic theorists argued that governments could use economic analysis in order to help design superior policies that could more efficiently harness human potential and generate sustained economic growth. And, indeed, modern states are indebted to the Neoclassical model and its predictions and assumptions. Quantitative methods of analysis applied to empirical data using Neoclassical assumptions are now central to the decisions of state governments and international agencies regarding macroeconomic stability and growth. Although there is no economic theory of nationalism, Neoclassical economists suggest that nationalism and other forms of protest result when governments fail to use markets effectively. In other words, nationalism results as the consequence of preventable market failures that are in turn caused by government ineffectiveness.

Marxism, by contrast, assumes that free markets are by their nature dehumanizing, and crisis prone, and Marxist approaches to nationalism most typically view it as a response to the inequities that markets invariably produce. According to Karl Marx, economic approaches to human behavior provided a partial and ultimately inaccurate understanding of the state's role in economic development and, as a result, a flawed understanding of the laws and logic of capitalism. While economic laws and predictions hold true in the short term, in the long run states act as agents of the capitalist class, and thus, inevitably, free market enterprise leads to severe class conflict and political upheaval, including nationalism. Such crises will end once private property is abolished and industrial techniques are adapted to serve broader human needs. This should free individuals from the compulsion to work, end class exploitation, and create the possibility for the withering away of the state and hence the establishment of a more rational and truly democratic social order in which nationalism will no longer occur.

Marx's theories have influenced a variety of scholarly treatments of nationalism and related political movements. Marxist scholars of nationalism Eric Hobsbawm and Benedict Anderson consider the spread of capitalism to be a primary cause of the emergence of Western nations and nationalism, but they argue that different kinds of non-Western nationalism occur because of a variety of other factors, chief among them, the nature of state institutions imposed by Western empires on colonial territories, rather than as a result of capitalism alone.

The definitive discussion of the Kula ring as a noncapitalist exchange system is found in Bronislaw Malinowski's *Argonauts of the Western Pacific* (Routledge, 1922). A selection of Karl Marx's most significant writings can be found in *The Marx-Engels Reader,* edited by Robert C. Tucker (Norton, 1978). Joseph Schumpeter's *History of Economic Analysis* (Oxford University Press, 1954) offers a comprehensive survey of economic theory. George Lichtheim's *Marxism* (Routledge and K. Paul, 1964) examines the emergence of this paradigm. Eric Hobsbawm's *Nations and Nationalism Since 1780* (Cambridge University Press, 1990) and Benedict Anderson's *Imagined Communities* (Verso, 1983) represent the most important recent Marxian theories of the relationship between capitalism and nationalism.

**CARIBBEAN NATIONALISM** The Caribbean region is composed of about 1000 separate islands. The Greater Antilles to the north include Cuba, Jamaica, Hispaniola, and Puerto Rico. To the south, the Lesser Antilles are divided into the Windward and the Leeward Islands. On the South American mainland, the nations of Guyana, Suriname, and French Guiana are normally included as members of the Caribbean community.

Caribbean nationalism began in the early 19th century with the independence movement in Haiti, and since then has evolved regionally. Most of the modern nation-states of the Caribbean have been or continue to be controlled by Western imperial powers. Although the ethnic and political backgrounds of each Caribbean country are different, the region's nations have experienced similar obstacles to realizing the dreams of nationalism.

National consciousness in the French and Spanish Caribbean has a distinct origin and trajectory from the British Caribbean. In former colonies of France and Spain, the development of nationalist governments was marred by turmoil and conflict. British protectorates, however, progressed to national consciousness through more incremental means.

The first wave of nationalist movements in the Caribbean was a reaction against colonial rule. In many colonies, the enslavement of Africans produced highly stratified societies with minority whites in control of the black majority. Tension between different ethnic and racial groups fomented the earliest nationalist sentiment in the region.

In the 1790s, African slaves in the French colony of Saint Domingue fought for their freedom. The French National Convention outlawed slavery in the colony in 1794, but the insurgents, led by Toussaint L'Overture, felt threatened by the reinstitution of slavery in Guadeloupe. By winning their struggle for freedom and independence, the former slaves of Haiti established the first republic of former slaves in the region.

Less than two decades after Haiti became the Western Hemisphere's second oldest free nation, its nationalist fervor had not waned: The Haitian government took control of Spanish Santo Domingo and occupied the province until 1844. Weary of Haitian control, however, rebels in the former Spanish colony had sowed their own nationalist sentiments. They declared independence from Haiti and renamed their nation the Dominican Republic.

Nationalism continued to develop during the remainder of the 19th century. Although the last slaves in the region were not emancipated until 1886, most colonies and new republics in the Caribbean were grappling with the legacy of slavery. In nations where a plantation society dominated, slavery itself was the foundation on which the political culture necessary for the development of nationalism originated. Even in nations where nationalist fervor created new governments, most of the changes were political, not social: The majority of people in the Caribbean languished in economic squalor despite the establishment of nationalist governments.

Twentieth-century nationalism in the Caribbean has been marked by efforts to redress these lingering economic ills. The United States, especially after the Span-

ish-American War, began intervening in the region to support these efforts. Akin to the dominance of European colonial powers, however, American political and economic intervention only perpetuated the region's dependence on international assistance. Consequently, many Caribbean nations have used their antipathy toward U.S. intervention to fuel nationalist sentiment.

During the mid-20th century, the worldwide struggle between Communism and capitalism struck the Caribbean, and sparked a wave of nationalist and independence movements. Today, of the sixteen independent Caribbean nations, only three achieved independence before 1960. More than 80 percent of people who live in the Caribbean live in these independent states.

In the last half of the 20th century, Caribbean nationalism has been closely linked to regional and national economic independence. Efforts such as the West Indies Foundation (founded in 1958) and the Caribbean Community (1973) have forged stronger economic bonds among Caribbean nations. Caribbean nation-states have also grappled with the problem of making local consciousness and regional identity coexist. Recently, Caribbean nations have worked to end external influence, whether from a colonial power or a dominant economy.

Helpful studies include Franklin W. Knight's *The Caribbean: The Genesis of a Fragmented Nationalism* (Oxford, 1990) and Eric Williams's *From Columbus to Castro: The History of the Caribbean, 1492–1969* (Harper and Row, 1970).

**CARLYLE, THOMAS** 1795–1881, Historian, critic, and writer; born in Ecclefechan, Scotland. He is best known for his theory on the "rule of all life" which proposed that inequality should be the guiding principle in human relations. Carlyle became renowned in the 1840s for his attacks against Christian philanthropy and his opinions regarding Africans, the Irish, and the West Indian Slaves. Author of an extraordinarily racist article, "Occasional Discourse on the Nigger Question," a response to John Stuart Mill's "The Negro Question," Carlyle strongly opposed the view that it was the duty of the strong to help the weak. Rather, the strong should rule over the weak, the rich over the poor, and the superior over the inferior. He vehemently opposed universal suffrage or any other form of popular participation. Rather, he felt that such matters should be left to the ruling class "hero" or great man of insight with the wisdom and capability to rule over his inferiors. Heroes, according to Carlyle, defined humankind and history was nothing more than biography of the their greatest achievements.

Carlyle was particularly committed to the idea of

"Teutonic Supremacy" or the superiority of the Nordic races. Carlyle felt the English were a chosen people, whose special mission it was to throw open the wastelands of the world. As such, Carlyle was one of the first 19th century writers to view Anglo-Saxon imperial triumphs as being clear products of the racial superiority. John Bull, from a chapter in *Past and Present* (1843), became a national symbol of English strength and character. Carlyle's ideas about the superiority of the Anglo-Saxons and the British nation were later taken up by such devotees of imperialism as J. A. Fronde, Anthony Trollope, Rudyard Kipling, and Cecil John Rhodes.

**CARMICHAEL, STOKELY** 1941–, Born in Trinidad and moved to the United States in the late 1940s. He became a U.S. citizen in 1953, and attended Howard University, where he earned a BA in philosophy in 1964. Carmichael became well known in the 1960s as one of the leaders of the radical student wing of the civil rights movement. Carmichael headed the Student Non-Violent Coordinating Committee (SNCC) from 1966 to 1967, and joined the Black Panther Party in 1967. He popularized the term *Black Power,* which emphasized black community and political and legal representation.

African American students redirected the civil rights movement in the 1960s by emphasizing the importance of grassroots organization. They grew impatient with the NAACP's method of relying solely on legislative means to gain equality. As the leader of the Lowndes County Freedom Organization in Alabama (1964–1966), which had a black panther as its symbol, Carmichael argued that blacks must organize themselves to face continued subjection to the rules of white society. The Freedom Organization focused on community control and self-determination. Carmichael believed that by gaining a better sense of community, and by organizing themselves politically, blacks could take control of their affairs. Registering to vote was a key issue. Recovering cultural roots, African heritage, and a new sense of identity formed initial steps toward building a new social order.

Carmichael's ideas were not new. Neither was the argument for Black Power. Carmichael, however, helped publicize the idea. Black Power called for black people to unite, to recognize their heritage, to build a sense of community, to define their own goals, and to lead and support their own organizations. Carmichael argued that the civil rights movement had only addressed middle-class issues, and ignored the concerns of the poor before students took the lead. He rejected the goal of African American assimilation into middle-class America because class, he said, perpetuated racism. De-

segregation was not enough unless blacks could join white institutions, not vice versa.

Carmichael's militant pronouncements of gaining equality by any means necessary and the SNCC's rejection of white members in 1966 scared many conservative whites and led to a backlash. SNCC folded by 1969, and the FBI increasingly pressured the Black Panther Party. Carmichael went underground. Today he gives public lectures on civil rights issues.

Suggested reading: Stokely Carmichael and Charles Hamilton, *Black Power: The Politics of Liberation in America* (New York: Random House, 1967) and Clayborne Carson, *In Struggle: SNCC and the Black Awakening of the 1960s* (Cambridge: Harvard University Press, 1981).

**CASTRO, FIDEL** 1927–, Born in Mayari, Cuba. Castro has been pesident of Cuba since he established a Communist dictatorship there in 1959. Castro was a member of an antigovernment faction during political turmoil in the 1950s, attempting to overthrow Fulgencio Batista. After the Cuban Revolution, the Castro regime executed thousands of political opponents who were former comrades during the revolution, and established a one-party socialist state, nationalizing many industries. People all over the world have held a negative image of Castro as a Communist dictator.

Cuba has been a politically unstable country since its independence from Spain in 1902. Before Castro established the Communist regime, the country was ruled by Sergeant Fulgencio Batista. Batista's unpopular regime led to the underground movement to overthrow his rule. Castro, then a lawyer, led the movement and gained support from the revolutionary group. After Batista fled the country on January 1, 1959, Castro literally seized power and established the one-party socialist state, nationalizing many industries. Although the United States had a diplomatic relationship with Cuba, offering economic aid, the relationship turned sour when the Castro regime seized oil refineries and sugar mills owned by American businesses. Castro also imposed strict control over private ventures with foreign nations.

After the Cuban Revolution, Castro established a close diplomatic relationship with the USSR, and Cuba became dependent on Communist nations economically. In 1961, the Eisenhower administration imposed a trade embargo, banning political and economic relationships between the United States and Cuba. The Cuban Missile Crisis of 1962 became a basic element of the Cold War, and successive American administrations have seen Castro as a Communist dictator. Attempts were made to overthrow the dictatorial Castro regime, but Castro's political opponents were imprisoned and executed. On September 28, 1965, Castro announced an exile policy that permitted those Cubans who had relatives in the United States to leave the island, designating the small fishing port of Camarioca in the northern part of Cuba as the port of departure. Thousands of Cubans, especially those in the middle and upper-middle classes who saw their wealth, education, and status challenged by the Castro regime, went to Miami in Florida, crossing the Havana Straits. These exiles were welcomed by the U.S. government as political refugees.

Castro has been an isolated political figure amidst the independence movements on the continent of Africa and in Latin America. Although Castro tried to extend his Communist alliance to other nations in Latin America, the Kennedy administration stopped those attempts. Fourteen Latin American countries severed diplomatic relationships with Cuba in 1963, isolating the Castro regime. There were even several CIA plots to assassinate Fidel Castro between 1960 and 1965. Castro was seen as a major figure in the Nonaligned Nations movement. Although Castro is known as a Communist dictator, he tried to change his international image in the 1970s through dialogues with Cuban exiles, which surprised the refugee community in Miami and other capitalist nations.

After the collapse of the USSR and the dissolution of the Community of Economic Cooperation (COMECON) in Eastern Europe in 1989, the Castro regime lost diplomatic contact with the USSR, which damaged the Cuban economy and engendered a 60 percent decline in its gross domestic product.

**CATALONIAN NATIONALISM** Movement that promotes the recognition of the political personality of Catalonia or of the Catalan-speaking area, born during Romanticism in the middle of the 19th century. Together with Basque nationalism, it represents the most important resistance to Spanish centralization and uniformization tendencies of the modern state. Both Catalonian and Basque nationalists drew inspiration from Germany's national feelings before it became a nation-state.

Its immediate antecedent is the *Renaixença*, or Renaissance, a cultural and literary revival started in 1833, when Carles Aribau published *Ode to the Fatherland in Catalan,* a language practically unused in written form at the time. Catalonian nationalism is not based on ethnicity but on language, culture, history, and territory, and it has traditionally been deeply influenced by Catholicism.

Early Catalonian nationalists expressed themselves through different political channels: Carlism, which demanded the restitution of Catalonian liberties abolished in 1716 by Philip V; republican federalism; and demands of decentralization.

Valentí Almirall is considered the founder of Catalonian nationalism. He dominated the Catalan scene from 1879 to 1887, giving the movement a political character. Almirall launched the first, if ephemeral, newspaper in Catalan, and his dream was to implement the model of American federalism in Spain.

With the announcement of the First Spanish Republic in 1873, nationalists tried to declare a Catalan state within it. By the time of the monarchic restoration in 1874, the Barcelona bourgeoisie had sympathies for a pragmatic Catalonian nationalism: cultural, traditionalist, and respectful with the established powers.

In 1885, a Catalonian cultural entity presented King Alphonse XII the "Memoir in Defense of the Moral and Material Interests of Catalonia," signed by intellectuals and some industrialists. Soon thereafter, some of its members founded the first Catalonian openly nationalist party, *Lliga de Catalunya* (League of Catalonia), which was romantic and socially conservative, whose first success was to defend the provenance of Catalan civil law. It inspired the *Bases de Manresa* of 1892, a political reform proposal written by artists, erudites, and liberals that advocated a federal state, the officiality of the Catalan language, and corporatist suffrage. In 1901, it changed its name to Regionalist League. Nationalism had pervaded the broader layers of society and the league was electorally so popular that the traditional conservative-liberal dichotomy of Spanish politics became a regionalist-republican one in Catalonia.

In 1906, the league's leader, Enric Prat de la Riba, published a seminal book, *The Catalan Nationality*. As did most Catalonian nationalists, Prat defended Pan-Iberianism. In 1914, he became the president of a new organism—the *Mancomunitat*—that administratively comprised the four Catalan provinces, the first autonomy accorded in Spain. In 1923, General Primo de Rivera's new dictatorship eliminated it. A radical party of former league members led by Francesc Macià relentlessly opposed Primo de Rivera's dictatorship from exile in France.

In 1930, republicans, socialists, and Catalonian nationalists made the Pact of Saint Sebastian to prepare for the dictatorship's imminent end. Macià headed an alliance of left-wing nationalist parties to form the "Republican Left of Catalonia" (RLC). It would inherit the league's past central role after proclamation of the republic following the municipal elections of 1931.

Catalonia obtained statute of autonomy in 1932, a compromise falling short of the RLC's federalist platform.

Catalonian nationalism was torn during the Civil War (1936–1939). Its most conservative elements, such as the league's leader Francesc Cambó, chose the insurgents' side. The regime of General Franco was centralized and culturally intolerant. Its kidnapping, summary trial on charges of subversion, and execution in 1940 of the Catalonian exiled president Lluís Companys was both a humiliation and a warning to Catalonian nationalists.

Catalonian nationalism publicly resurfaced in the 1970s. The Spanish quasi-federal system of 1978 is a concession to Catalonian and Basque nationalists' involvement in a model transition to democracy. Though imperfect and inconclusive, this regime succeeded in channeling nationalist tensions to civilized political negotiation. Josep Tarradellas, a former secretary of Companys' government, who had been elected president of the exiled *Generalitat,* or Catalonian government, in Mexico in 1954, agreed with the president of the Spanish government Adolfo Suárez, on the reestablishment of a provisory *Generalitat* and his return. When Tarradellas arrived in Barcelona on October 23, 1977, one million people greeted him on the streets.

Catalonia obtained a new statute in 1979. Jordi Pujol, founder and leader of the moderate nationalist party Democratic Convergence of Catalonia (DCC), has won all autonomic elections since 1980. DCC defines itself as a political project willing to govern, central in Catalonain politics and centering in Spanish politics. It requests recognition by Spain of Catalonia's national character and wishes a plurinational state. It also proposes that the Europe Union should respect its cultural diversity and to build itself largely from this diversity, avoiding the historical mistakes of state-building.

## CATHOLIC CHURCH AND NATIONALISM

In 1931, Pope Pius XI denounced nationalism for its "statolatry which is no less in contrast with the natural rights of the family than it is in contradiction to the supernatural rights of the Church." At the time, the Church feared not only the co-optation of the faithful by the modern and often anticlerical state, but found the racist tendencies of totalitarian nationalism an offense against morality. Nevertheless, the Church would come to endorse in varying degrees nearly all of Europe's leading nationalist states through a series of Vatican diplomatic efforts and local political activism. The Church hierarchy's capitulation and even support of fascist nationalism was the unfortunate culmination of a Church policy undertaken against the newly powerful forces of 19th- and 20th-century secularization, which it feared threatened the very existence of the Church. Certainly, nationalism violated the universalistic predilections of the Church, and fascism threatened to challenge the privileged position of the Church in the public sphere. Nevertheless, the superficial conservatism of these newly emergent ideologies was seemingly less anticlerical than either the progressive and anticlerical forces of liberalism, socialism, and the emergent Communist totalitarianism. Rome's support of nationalism may have helped to temper the secular tendencies of liberalism and to prevent the final victory of Communism in Western Europe. However, this contribution came at a terrible price for the moral constitution of the Church. In its quest for survival, the Church implicated itself in the atrocities of the Holocaust even as it struggled against the extermination of the Jews.

Since its inception, the Church has played an active role in the political world, an inevitable consequence of its manifestation as both a spiritual and a temporal institution. Nationalism, as both an ideology predicated on the principle of the right to national self-determination and a political tool for popular mobilization, has roots going back as far as the earliest of Church conflicts with the secular world of politics in Western Europe.

Scholars generally agree that the 11th century concept of dualism marks the first and most important institutionalization of a clear separation of power between secular authority and the ecclesiastical hierarchy. Specifically, dualism reconciled the conflict between the Church and the German states by giving Rome the right to select its own bishops from whom secular rulers could nevertheless demand an oath of loyalty—one that could always be extracted by a force of arms when necessary. Under this new division of power, the Church was generally without means of physical coercion. Hence, in order to exercise and maintain its influence, it had to develop other means. Not only did it accumulate tremendous wealth with which to buy influence, but it also established a virtual monopoly on intellectual capital, including control over education and juridical innovation. But perhaps most significantly, Rome's network of Churches and priests afforded a unique ability to mobilize or quell popular discontent. It could back up the excommunication of a monarch with his repudiation from the pulpit, effectively undermining his capacity to govern.

In fact, it is from some of the early explorations of Church sanctions against secular abuses of power that many of the modern political concepts of sovereignty legitimacy and self-determination were first developed.

While these concepts alone did not necessarily give birth to nationalism, they did confer normative import to the great mass of unmobilized people and conceptually structured the process of harnessing previously nonactualized sources of power in such a way as to encourage both democratic and nationalist movements.

With the invention of the movable type printing press (1455), the Church lost its virtual monopoly on ideas in Western Europe, and as a result confronted one of the first manifestations of nationalism. Protestant leaders and their secular champions were quick to seize on this new technology to challenge the authority of the Church and enhance their own power. They did so by undermining the universalistic absolutism of the Church exemplifed by the Latin mass, favoring both a Bible and Church services in the vernacular. By translating the Bible into the local dialect spoken by the uneducated and educated alike, these early pioneers took the first step toward creating official "national" languages associated with a distinct body of people and a territory. Their political innovation was no less revolutionary. By privileging the individual's direct and personal connection to the Divine, and thus questioning the need for an official Church as intermediary, Protestantism also challenged the Church's monopolistic claim to endow temporal rulers with divinely sanctioned legitimacy. Nevertheless, while sovereignty had been deracinated from Church soil, it remained willed by God and hence was not yet solely dependent on the "will of the people."

At the Council of Trent (1545–1563), the Church responded forcefully with aggressive institutional renewal, establishing the Jesuit order and endowing it with extraordinary powers to innovate both in the field of ecclesiastic education and popular mobilization. The Church reemphasized the pilgrimage, and, availing itself of the recently rediscovered Christian Catacombs (1578), sought to assuage the needs of its flock with a flood of new saints. In some cases it even advocated the use of the vernacular, which facilitated the transformation of local vernaculars into new languages. By 1648, the expansion of Protestantism had been halted by the Church and its Jesuits. Rome could again secure for itself a privileged position in all but northern Europe and, furthermore, go on to establish new footholds throughout the world in this, the age of European exploration and colonization.

However, the French revolution (1789) brought a renewed assault on the Church, only this time according to a more clearly articulated expression of sovereignty connected to the nation, now completely independent of any connection to the Divine. By endowing the people collected in the nation with the sole power to confer legitimacy on the state, the revolutionaries toppled the twin forces of the Crown and the Church in one fell swoop. Nationalism, as an expression of popular sovereignty, assumed many forms. However, rejection of the Church emerged early on as a common denominator. In its liberal manifestation, nationalism rejected the Church for its privilege, conservatism, and ties to absolutism. In its state-sponsored form, as in Germany, nationalism rejected the universalistic aims and institutions of the Church as incompatible with the parochial nature of the nation. This Church crisis reached its apogee by 1870 when the Italian *Risorgimento* appropriated the papal territories as part of the unification of the Italian nation-state, forever destroying the temporal ambitions of the Church.

In this last quarter of the 19th century, the Church responded decisively to this threat. Wherever appropriate, it employed its vast network of schools and churches to embrace the youth through education and mobilization, reinforcing religious identity over the new competing identities of class and devotion to the modern state. To forestall any further defections by the faithful by the anti-Catholic liberal and nationalist causes, the Church sponsored spectacular rallies, promoted new pilgrimages, and created countless regional associations to restore the Church's central position in the daily life of its increasingly urbanized flock. While the Church often challenged the legitimacy of parliamentary politics, even going so far as to threaten Italian voters with excommunication for voting in elections, it nevertheless did eventually endorse the electoral support of pro-Catholic political parties. In fact, in 19th-century Ireland, it proved an innovator both in national and popular party mobilization. In Germany, the *Zentrum* (Center) Party was founded in 1871 in defense of Catholic interests against Bismarck's anti-Catholic *Kulturkampf*. It would become the archetype of Catholic parliamentary effort. While these interests were largely limited to Church property and educational institutions, as well as Church control over the sacred rituals of birth, marriage, and death, the Church did embrace a number of nonspiritual aims by first championing the interests of the rural classes. In 1891 the papacy took a revolutionary step with its encyclical *Rerum Novarum* by establishing the foundations for a distinctly Catholic social vision that rejected modern forms of capitalism, liberal democracy, and socialism.

Immediately following World War I and the Russian Revolution (1917), the Church accelerated its participation in parliamentary politics and popular mobilization. This period between the two world wars was the "golden age" of Catholic associationalism. The Church expanded its efforts to promote distinctly Catholic youth groups, women's organizations, trade unions, and insurance leagues, to name a few. Through these Catholic organizations the Church sought to maintain its influence over the faithful by responding to their changing needs brought on by industrialization, urbanization, and modernization. The Church was not above endorsing the nationalist card, realizing as had the "international" socialists, the power of the exclusionary ideology of nationalism. For example, the new states of Czechoslovakia and Yugoslavia both came under significant attacks from cleric-led Catholic Slovak and Croat nationalisms, respectively.

It is difficult to determine the extent to which the Vatican itself promoted clerical nationalism. Rome had the means of sanctioning political activism by clerics, especially since the first Vatican council, which had renewed and considerably strengthened the authority of the papacy. Nevertheless, the Vatican did not promote clerical nationalism throughout Europe, and did not explicitly integrate nationalism into its general social and political elaboration of *Rerum Novarum* in Pius XI's new encyclical *Quadragesimo Anno* of May 1931.

Nevertheless, by the 1930s, this encyclical had become the intellectual cornerstone of numerous rightwing nationalist movements. It realized its first political expression in Salazar's Portugal (1933) and in the following year again when Dolfus achieved his goal of a "social, Christian, German Austria on a corporative basis and under strong authoritarian leadership." Pius XI declared this "witness to Catholic visions and convictions" and that Austria "now has the government, it deserves." In 1939 and 1941, clerical nationalism facilitated the independence of Slovakia and Croatia, respectively, in both cases, securing for the Church an important position in political and daily life. While Franco's Spain, Vichy France, and Mussolini's Italy had much weaker ties to the Church, they nevertheless found ideological inspiration in *Quadragesimo*'s economic and social blueprint for state-sponsored corporatism.

However, in nearly every case, Catholic moral principles would fall subservient to the logic of fascism. While the Church often assumed a leadership role in its early struggles against secularism and socialism, it increasingly found itself a victim of parliamentary politics, and then fascist scare tactics. Forced to compromise its principles in the name of self-preservation, the Church found itself conferring legitimacy on policies over which it had little if any control.

Already with the Lateran Pacts of 1929, the Church abdicated participation in Italian politics in exchange for official recognition by Mussolini's new fascist government. Increasingly the papacy shifted its efforts from indirect action through the national churches to direct Vatican diplomacy. Yet, by the outbreak of World War II, the Church could do little more than stand back and watch as fascism supplanted loyalty to Church and family with devotion to the state and leader as embodiment of the nation. Even in those cases where the Church had established a dominant position through the efforts of Catholic nationalism, as in the newly formed Slovak state under the leadership of Monsignor Tiso, it found itself polluted by the twin influence of fascism and anti-Semitism.

With the close of World War II, the Church moderated its antiliberal position, embracing democratic reform wherever possible, while persevering in its struggle against communism and anticlericalism. In Western Europe, Christian Democratic parties assumed a central role in postwar reconstruction and democratization. In the East, the Church struggled underground and through diplomacy against the institutionalization of Communist authority. It is now apparent that the Church played a critical role in Poland's revolution against socialism and Soviet oppression, the catalyst for the eventual collapse of the entire Soviet bloc. Cardinal Wyszyński has explained that Church policy was simply to defend the Polish nation. "There have been moments when the state fell silent, and only Christ's Church could speak out in the Polish nation. It never stopped speaking out. . . . We ought to realize this when we speak of establishing correct relations between the Nation and the Church, between the State and the Church in our country." But the Polish nation is not alone in having received support from the Church.

In 1998, Indonesia officially declared its willingness to recognize autonomy for East Timor. For more than twenty years the Church was the sole advocate of the nationalist struggle of the Timorese against Indonesia's 1975 occupation of the Portuguese colony and its ensuing political violence and "creeping Islamisation." In fact, their cause only received widespread international recognition in 1996 when the Nobel Peace Prize was extended to the Catholic Bishop Carlos Belo and his compatriot Jose Ramos-Horta.

While indeed the Church has not abandoned nationalism as a tool of political mobilization in defense of Church interests and continues to challenge unfettered capitalism, it has nevertheless proven to be a staunch advocate of democracy. In 1991, Pope John Paul II chose to celebrate the 100th anniversary of *Rerum Novarum* with a new, yet distinctly Catholic social vision in his *Centesimus Annus*. In defiance of the alleged "end of history," he renounced the validity of any single ide-ology, including nationalism, underscoring the multi-dimensionality of man and the importance of a "uni-versalistic compassion." He also elaborated on these general principles in his October 5, 1995, "Address to the Fiftieth General Assembly of the United Nations," this time with a specific reference to religious national-ism. While the Church continues to champion the rights of nations to self-determination, it now recog-nizes the nation as only one of many expressions of hu-man solidarity.

For further readings on the Church in the age of nationalism, consult Martin Conway, *Catholic Politics in Europe, 1918–1945* (London: Routledge, 1997) and *Catholics, the State, and the European Radical Right, 1919–1945* edited by Richard Wolff and Jürg Hoensch (Boulder, Colo.: Social Science Monographs, 1987). For a more general discussion of religion and politics, see Jose Casanova, *Public Religions in the Modern World* (Chicago: University of Chicago Press, 1994).

**CAVOUR, CONTE** 1810–1861, Camillo Benso di Ca-vour was born in Turin and died in the same city. He was the prime minister of Piedmont from 1852 until his death, and is widely credited with creating the first unified Italian state by bringing together the northern states and ridding them of Austrian rule and then uni-fying them in 1860 with Garibaldi's recently acquired posessions in the south. This despite the fact that in 1838, before his political career began, he described himself first as Piedmontese, second as Western Euro-pean, and only third as an Italian.

In 1830 he joined the Piedmontese army, but left in 1831 feeling disillusioned at the high degree of absolut-ism in his country and proclaiming himself to be a radi-cal liberal. His liberal ideas were bolstered by a tour of England and France in 1835, and he returned duly im-pressed by the industrial might of the English. Between 1835 and 1848, Cavour spent his time running the fam-ily farm at Grinzane where he became noted as a highly successful landowner. In 1848, after the passing of the liberalizing *statuto* by King Charles Albert, Cavour be-came editor of the famously titled *Il Risorgimento* ("the resurrection," a term adopted by many Italian national-ists, such as Mazzini, to describe the national reawaken-ing in Italy) and was elected in a by-election as a deputy for Turin.

Following heavy defeat by the Austrians over Lom-bardy in 1849, the abdication of Charles Albert, his re-placement by Victor Emmanuel II, and controversy over the civil marriages bill, Cavour was appointed prime minister by the king in return for a guarantee that he would not allow the aforementioned bill to pass. This was the last time that the king was to have such an in-fluence in Piedmontese politics. Cavour resolutely be-lieved in the virtues of consitutional monarchies, assert-ing that they were less corrupt and prone to extremism than republics, but learning from de Tocqueville he also believed that it would be impossible to stem the tide of liberal democracy. His ambition was to delay this pro-cess for as long as possible. In the field of domestic poli-tics Cavour achieved note for establishing the authority of parliament over the monarchy and for reordering the public finances, bringing them in line with the modern states of Europe. It was in the field of foreign policy, however, that Cavour achieved historical notoriety.

In the wake of the crushing defeat inflicted on the Piedmontese by the Austrians in 1849, Cavour was keen to avoid conflict until he was sure of receiving outside help. He knew that the Italians could not defeat the Aus-trians alone. As such, when Mazzini led a republican revolution in Milan in 1853, Cavour was almost as vig-orous as the Austrians in attempting to suppress it. Their joint efforts were successful, and Cavour was somewhat embarrassed when the Austrians publicly thanked him for his efforts. The Piedmontese prime minister used the events in Milan to argue that the Aus-trian position in Italy was abnormal, and at this point he set about trying to curry favor among the other great powers for the removal of the Austrians from Italy.

In 1855, Piedmont entered the Crimean War as part of the Anglo-French alliance and this, albeit limited, participation served to place the Italian question on the agenda in the chancellories of Western Europe. In 1858, Cavour traveled to Plombieres in France and concluded a secret treaty with Napoleon III. The king of France agreed that should the Austrians attack Piedmont, the French armies would come to the aid of the small king-dom in return for tracts of land in Savoy, including Nice. This was the opportunity Cavour was waiting for; all he had to do was ensure the rapid deterioration of Austrian–Piedmontese relations. This proved to be none too difficult. In response to the mobilization of the small Piedmontese army, the Austrians issued an ultimatum that Cavour immediately rejected. Austria attacked and a bloody war ensued, in which the French prevailed. Although the Treaty of Villafranca, concluded by France and Austria, was exceptionally reactionary in that it restored the pre-war rulers to the central Italian states, which had undergone revolutions during the fighting, those aspects of the treaty were never imple-mented and Piedmont came to exercise effective control over most of northern Italy (with the exception of Ve-netia), as the Austrians were forced to withdraw.

This was not the end of Cavour's troubles, however. Toward the end of 1860, the impetuous nationalist, Guiseppe Garibaldi, launched his crusade of a thousand men. Landing on the coast of Sicily, this band of men, which was expected by Cavour to be resoundingly defeated, swelled in numbers and conquered not only Sicily but also the southern mainland, in the name a unified republican Italy. Garibaldi threatened to march on the papal states and Rome. This presented a dilemma to Cavour, because the papist Napoleon III had pledged to defend Rome from attack, and so Cavour was faced with the French intervening to crush the Italian nationalists. To resolve the situation, Cavour made his boldest move. With the agreement of Napoleon III and Victor Emmanuel II, Cavour ordered the Piedmontese army to invade the papal sates and claim Rome ahead of the arrival of Garibaldi's revolutionaries. Italy stood at the brink of civil war, as armies representing two different ideas about the meaning of "Italy" (the republicans and the Piedmontese monarchists) faced each other. War was averted when Garibaldi acquiesced to the demands of Cavour and ceded the territories he had gained to Piedmontese jurisdiction.

This first kingdom of Italy was the kind of state desired by Cavour. It was a conservative, constitutional monarchy, far removed from the republicanism espoused by Garibaldi and Mazzini. The precise role of Cavour in establishing that state is still a contested historical issue. We should perhaps note that in the wars of Italian unification, more Italians died while fighting in the Austrian armies than were killed fighting the colonial overlord. Cavour's premature death in 1861 meant that he had no role in shaping the new Italy, but his legacy continued to be of significance until the advent of fascism.

For further reading see H. Hearder, *Cavour* (London, 1972), E. Holt, *Risorgimento: The Making of Italy 1815–1870* (London, 1970), D. Mack Smith, *Cavour* (London, 1985), D. Mack Smith, *Cavour and Garibaldi 1860: A Study in Political Conflict* (Cambridge, 1954), and A. J. Whyte, *The Political Life and Letters of Cavour* (Oxford, 1930).

## CEAUŞESCU, NICOLAE
1918–1989, Romanian Communist leader who combined a nationalistic foreign policy with Communist orthodoxy at home. An activist in the Romanian Communist youth movement in the 1930s, he was arrested and imprisoned in 1936 and again in 1940. It was his fortune to have shared a cell with Gheorghe Gheoghiu-Dej, who would become the country's Communist leader in 1952 and would promote Ceauşescu through the ranks to become his

successor after his death in 1965. Ceauşescu's foreign policy of independence from the Soviet Union was popular both in his own country and in the Western world. He terminated the country's active participation in the Warsaw Pact and forbade the permanent stationing of foreign troops, including those of Warsaw Pact allies, on Romanian soil. He condemned the pact's invasion of Czechoslovakia in 1968 and did not send troops, and he denounced the Soviet Union's war against Afghanistan from 1979 to 1989. He refused to break ties with Israel and to boycott the Olympic games when the Soviet Union demanded that its allies do so.

His nationalist anti-Soviet foreign and defense policy did not mean that he was a tolerant leader at home. He created a cult of personality that fed his own megalomania. His secret police, the Securitate, were brutal and omnipresent. He placed his wife, Elena, and other family into top posts, and his corrupt regime allowed all of them to become rich in a land that became increasingly pauperized. He decided to make his country even less beholden to outside powers by paying off the country's sizable foreign debt. To do so, much of Romania's industrial and agricultural products were exported, thereby depriving the population of basic necessities and reducing the diet practically to a starvation level. He also concocted grandiose schemes, such as razing thousands of villages and moving their inhabitants into city apartments.

Finally, he tightened the repression of the large Hungarian minority. This helped bring about his undoing because it was in the city of Timisoara, located in the region with the heaviest Magyar population, that the first demonstrations against his regime broke out on December 17, 1989. Ceauşescu ordered troops to fire on the demonstrators. The unrest spread to the capital city of Bucharest and forced him and his wife to flee in a military helicopter. They were quickly captured, put through a hurriedly and ill-prepared military trial, and shot on Christmas Day in 1989.

## CENTRAL AMERICAN NATIONALISM
Central America is composed of seven small nations: Belize, Costa Rica, El Salvador, Guatemala, Honduras, Nicaragua, and Panama. The region's geography—the nations are juxtaposed between the Atlantic and Pacific Oceans and North and South America—has molded its history and politics.

Central American nationalism has teetered between the individual identities of the seven nations and the shared consciousness of the region's peoples. Before 1838, six of the nations were colonies of Spain: Panama was part of Colombia, Belize was a British colony, and the other five were part of Mexico. On October 15, 1821, the five Mexican provinces won their independence from Spain. They were annexed to Mexico, but national consciousness quickly ended that union. In July 1823, the provinces declared their independence, and founded the Central American Federation.

The federation was short lived. Almost immediately after its creation, conflicts between liberals and conservatives consumed its government. Ideological dissension was aggravated by discord between local and national governments, and the federation's president, Manuel Jose Arc, could not keep the provinces united. In 1838, the five former colonies each declared their independence.

After the breakup of the Central American Federation, nationalism in the region ebbed. In 1903, however, when Panama declared its independence from Colombia, a new wave of regional identity sparked efforts to reunite the republics. In 1907, the republics formed the Central American Court, which had jurisdiction in conflicts among the region's nations. Although the court dissolved in 1916, every country except Nicaragua and Panama formed a central government called the Republic of Central America. Like its 19th-century forerunner, however, the republic was beset with internal rivalries and was dissolved in less than a year.

Since the 1920s, Central American countries have attempted to maintain strong ties without a formal central government. To that end, the Central American Union was founded in 1923. This alliance has encouraged a shared understanding of each republic's identity and culture. After World War II, the Central American republics forged greater cooperation in the region. The establishment of the Organization of American States in 1948 and the Organization of Central American States in 1965 has aided that goal. The Alliance for Progress, founded in 1961 with major support from the United States, achieved limited accomplishments in social welfare and economic growth.

American intervention has been frequently unpopular, and has fueled nationalist fervor throughout the 20th century. During the last three decades, nationalism in the region has become connected to economic and political independence from the United States. In 1960, the region's countries formed the Central American Common Market, which brought some economic development to the region. The growing middle class—a result of regional economic expansion—clamored for democracy and more efficient government.

Conflicts between military rulers and civilian governments were aggravated by the worldwide struggle between Communism and capitalism. While the 1980s saw this turmoil come to a head, the peace accords of the 1990s, especially in El Salvador, Honduras, and Nicaragua, have restored order to the region.

Helpful studies include George Black's *The Good Neighbor* (Pantheon, 1988) and Clifford Krauss's *Inside Central America* (Summit, 1991).

**CENTRAL ASIAN NATIONALISM** Central Asia is a territory consisting of the five ex-Soviet republics of Uzbekistan, Kazakhstan, Turkmenistan, Kyrgyzstan, and Tajikistan. For much of its history, this region was dominated by nomadic Turkic Muslim groups who identified themselves either on a tribal basis or simply as Muslims. Although prior to the 20th century there was a vague sense of ethnicity among the peoples of Central Asia, Central Asians often defined themselves first and foremost as farmers or nomads. Uzbek farmers, known as Sarts, for example, had little shared sense of identity with nomadic Uzbeks.

Similarly, there was little sense of shared ethnicity among the second largest people in Central Asia, the Turkic Kazakhs, who were divided into hordes that often competed for pastures. The Turkmen, a nomadic Turkic people, were also divided into quarreling clans, such as the Salor and Tekke, and spent much of their time raiding among themselves. The Kyrgyz and Tajiks were also divided into clans or on a regional basis.

With the Russian conquest of Central Asia, which took place from 1730 to 1895, the Muslim peoples of Central Asia became subjects of an empire that did not recognize the ethnicity of its subjects. The Uzbek and Tajik lands of Russian Central Asia were divided into two vassal states known as the Emirate of Bukhara and the Khanate of Khiva, while the territories of the Kazakhs, Kyrgyz, and Turkmen were directly annexed into the Russian Empire. On the eve of the Russian Revolution of 1917, however, a Pan-Turkic intellectual movement began in Central Asia (especially among the Uzbeks) that called for a greater sense of unity among the Turkic peoples. This period also saw the rise of a narrower Kazakh national movement known as *Alash Orda* (Horde of Alash) among the Russified intelligentsia of this people. These nationalist phenomena were, however, largely elite movements and the Central Asian masses in the Russian Empire continued to identify themselves according to their traditionalist tribal/Islamic origins.

With the fall of the Russian Empire an attempt was made to establish an independent Uzbek government in the city of Khokand but this movement was crushed by local Bolshevik forces. Attempts by the Kazakh *Alash Orda* to achieve independence met with a similar failure.

Although Marxist theory predicted that national identities would be replaced by a wider proletarian identity, Soviet leader Vladimir Lenin sought to co-opt nationalisms in the USSR by officially recognizing them. Far from destroying ethno-national identities in the USSR, Lenin recognized national identity in all levels of the Soviet system. In a process that some have seen as an attempt at *divide et impera* designed to break down any sense of greater Turkic or Muslim unity in Central Asia, the region was carved into five ethnically based Soviet Socialist Republics of Kazakhstan, Kyrgyzstan (also known as Kirghizia), Turkmenistan, Uzbekistan, and Tajikistan. An innocuous cultural form of national identity was promoted in these territorial units as the Soviets sought to spread Marxist concepts to even the most out of the way mountain villages via the medium of ethnic groups' national languages and cultures.

Although the territorial administrative borders of the Central Asian republics were rather haphazard (the Tajik-dominated cities of Bukhara and Samarkand were granted to the Uzbek SSR, Uzbek lands in the Ferghana valley were granted to Kyrgyzstan, etc.), they soon took on real meaning to the people circumscribed by them. Clan/regional and Islamic bases for identity were gradually superseded by a wider sense of Uzbekness, Kazakhness, and so on.

Although the Soviet period saw the cementing of national identities in Central Asia, there was little nationalist agitation in the region at this time. While there were sporadic anti-Soviet guerrilla movements among the Central Asians during the 1920s (known as the Basmachi rebellions) in general this region remained calm after the 1930s. Many outsiders who believed Soviet propaganda felt that the Soviet regime was in fact achieving success in its policies of Sovietization (in practice, Russification) in Central Asia.

By the late 1980s, however, nationalist dissent had broken out throughout much of the Soviet Union with the Baltic republics calling for outright independence from the USSR. Central Asia, by contrast, was quiescent and run by loyal Communist Party bosses who owed their positions to Moscow. With the collapse of the Soviet Union in the winter of 1991 these Communist Party bosses (with the exception of president Askar Akayev of Kyrgyzstan, who was not a Communist) found themselves the reluctant "founding fathers" of five Central Asian nations that had inherited borders, capitals, and, to a certain extent, national identities created during the Soviet period.

Since independence the leaders of the Central Asian republics have attempted to further promote patriotic nationalism in their states. In this respect the forging of national identities in states arbitrarily created by an out-side power resembles earlier efforts to create Iraqi or Jordanian national identities in states carved in the Middle East by outside colonial powers. President Islam Karimov of Uzbekistan, for example, has sought to create a secular national identity by stressing such slogans as "Uzbek unity for the future" and by emphasizing the Uzbeks' shared national history. The greatest threat to Karimov's plans for creating a secular national identity in post-Soviet Uzbekistan is actually the rise of fundamentalist Islam in some regions of the republic (most noticeably the Fergana valley).

In Turkmenistan, president Saparmurad Niyazov has created a cult of personality around himself and has linked Turkmen nationalism to his role as *Turkmenbashi* (Leader of the Turkmen). Since 1991 nationalism has also been promoted in Kyrgyzstan and Kazakhstan. *Yurts* (the felt tents of the Eurasian nomads), traditional clothing, and dances are once again appearing in national festivals in these countries and the process of replacing Russians in positions in the government, education, and industry has accelerated. This process is of course resented by local Russians who settled in these lands during the Russian Imperial and Soviet periods. The potential for interethnic conflict is quite real in northern Kazakhstan, which was heavily settled with Russians who aspire to unify northern Kazakhstan with Russia. For the most part the nationalism of the Kazakhs and Kyrgyz is not, however, virulently anti-Russian and Russians continue to live in both these republics in large numbers.

The Turkic republics of Central Asia have, with minor exceptions, avoided national conflict of the sort seen in the Caucasus since 1990, but the non-Turkic republic of Tajikistan has seen almost nonstop violence since 1991. The subnational differences between northern and southern Tajiks as well as differences between Tajiks living in the mountainous Badakshan region and those in the plains have prevented the construction of a strong sense of Tajik national identity in this state and have led to open warfare between regional groupings, which continues in a muted form to this day.

Although created during the Soviet period, the national identities of Central Asian peoples (with the exception of the Tajiks) have proven to be remarkably durable. While there is the possibility that fundamentalist Islam could threaten the secular nationalism promoted by Central Asia's leaders, seventy years of secularization and a decade of post-Soviet national identity construction will likely prove to be a formidable barrier to the spread of fundamentalism in the region.

**CHIANG KAISHEK** 1887–1975, Best known as the president of the Republic of China when the Nationalist

Party or Kuomintang (KMT) ruled China before 1949 and Taiwan after that, Chiang was born in Chekiang Province and was named Jui-yuan by his grandfather and Chung-cheng by his mother. He later took the name Chieh-shih, which is written Kaishek in Cantonese. Chiang Kaishek's father died when he was nine and he was raised by his mother. He received a local, traditional Chinese education, though he went to Japan at the age of nineteen to study for several years.

In 1908, while in Japan, he joined the Tung Meng Hui—a nationalistic, revolutionary organization founded by Sun Yatsen that sought the overthrow of the "foreign" Manchu (or Ch'ing) dynasty that ruled China from 1644 to 1911. Its success, or rather that of Sun's followers in China, in October 1911, prompted Chiang to return to China to assume command of a military unit. Subsequently he joined the Nationalist Party and became a close follower of Sun.

After Sun Yatsen's death in 1925 Chiang struggled with two other Sun followers for control and leadership of the Nationalist Party. He won and became Sun's successor. Chiang, however, was not concerned much about political ideals or even party politics or ideology; he was a military man and felt that China's problems, particularly its disunity, had to be solved by military means. In 1926, after gaining control of the KMT and having built a modern army, Chiang launched the Northern Expedition from his base of operations in South China to expel the warlord government in Beijing and unify the country—a task he accomplished in 1928.

As a military man Chiang's nationalist sentiments were strong. He felt that China had suffered at the hands of foreign imperialism. He thus sought above all else to make China a strong country again. These ideas can be found in his book *China's Destiny*. He made various efforts to promote nationalism and patriotism in China. He advocated democracy and a republican form of government in China, but said he sought to fulfill Sun Yatsen's teachings and ideas about politics rather than alter them. He declared that the most immediate tasks were to unify China and preserve its unity and to stimulate nationalist feelings among the Chinese people. Democracy, he said, had to follow.

Chiang, however, enjoyed only a short respite from military conflict: In 1931 Japan invaded Manchuria and turned it into a puppet state that was made part of the Japanese Empire. In 1937, China and Japan engaged in full-scale war. Chiang fought the Japanese and subsequently the Chinese Communists while at the same time trying to prevent China's disintegration and bring about reform of various kinds. In 1936, he aligned with the Communists in a united front against the Japanese, but this agreement did not last long.

During World War II, Chiang was considered a major player in the war against Japan, although certain American military leaders, especially General Joseph Stilwell, did not feel that Chiang was sincere in fighting the Japanese. Stilwell also doubted his competence and the honesty and ability of his subordinates. Chiang's leadership was also weakened by the fact that he lost most confrontations with the Japanese on the battlefield, while the Communist won smaller guerilla-type engagements and did very well in the propaganda war against Chiang. Chiang and the Nationalist Party also suffered from bearing the responsibility for maintaining the economy and social stability during wartime.

Chiang's forces, though clearly favored over the Communists in 1945 when World War II ended, made some serious logistical mistakes. He and his party also lost the "hearts and minds" of the Chinese people. In 1949, he was defeated by the Communists and resigned from the presidency of the Republic of China.

Chiang and many of his supporters in the Nationalist Party, the Nationalist government, and the military subsequently fled to Taiwan. In March 1950, Chiang returned to power, once again assuming the presidency of the Republic of China, which no longer governed China but only Taiwan, the Pescadores, the Offshore Islands, and some islands in the South China Sea. It was Chiang's dream, using Taiwan as a base of operations, to recover China, or the mainland, from the Communists. The dream, however, faded with time and for a variety of reasons including the strength of Mao's military in the newly formed People's Republic of China and the viability of his government, plus lack of support from the United States. Also, this goal never had much support from the locally born Chinese or Taiwanese. Chiang himself seemed to revise, or perhaps give up, this hope, when in the late 1950s he referred to the goal as "seventy percent political" (rather than a military plan).

In any event, Chiang ordered a cleansing of the Nationalist Party and the government shortly after he settled in Taiwan. He subsequently focused on economic development, arguing that Taiwan would be a showcase and that its economic success would prove the superiority of his capitalist and democratic regime and its ideology over Communism. In 1965, Taiwan began to boom economically and because of the subsequent "Taiwan economic miracle" to a considerable degree Chiang was vindicated. Taiwan's economic success also helped him in his nation-building objectives in Taiwan, though he had to contend with subethnic differences on the island. Chiang oversaw political change and democratization in Taiwan but this was limited in scope and was felt mostly at the local level.

Chiang remained president of the Republic of China and head of the Nationalist Party until his death in April 1975. Though criticized by historians for his misrule of China during the 1940s, his defeat by the Communists, and later his authoritarian-style rule in Taiwan, Chiang is credited with launching and building Taiwan's economic miracle and for starting, though belatedly according to some critics, its political development. He was castigated by leaders in Beijing for many years, but was to a large extent rehabilitated after Mao's death and has since been praised for his leadership and his efforts to build nationalism in China.

Chiang's son by his first marriage, Chiang Ching-kuo, was president of the Republic of China from 1978 to 1988. He allegedly had another son, Chiang Wei-kuo, from a Japanese woman to whom he was not married, who was a military general and head of the National Security Council in Taiwan for some years. Chiang Wei-kuo, however, just before he died said that Chiang Kai-shek was not his father. Madam Chiang Kaishek, who converted him to Christianity and who was well known as Chiang's spokesperson in dealing with the United States and other foreign countries, had no children.

A biography of Chiang is *Chiang Kai-Shek: His Life and Times* by Keiji Furuya (St. John's University Press, 1981).

## CHILEAN NATIONALISM

Chile's constitutional history during the 19th century shows only surface changes. Liberals battled conservatives over such issues as the respective virtues of the parliamentary and the presidential systems, but these struggles were superficial, and underneath the same group continued to rule. Until 1891, Chile preferred the strong president, though never to the point of embracing outright the personal regime of the military caudillos. After 1891 the pendulum swung back to congressional rule. In Chile it was an oligarchy rather than a caudillismo that took over the reins of government, ended the frantic succession of constitutions, and brought the country under the class rule of the criollos, by the criollos, and for the criollos. Between the end of the wars of the Pacific in 1883 and 1891, both the army and the navy became predominantly commanded by men of middle-class origin. This change in the social composition of the armed forces began to show up on the political scene in the 1920s. In Chile's intellectual community a growing concern with social problems and the ordinary people accompanied the changes in the military. Early in the 20th century Chilean literature became oriented to social problems. The exploitation of native workers by the large and mostly foreign mining corporations was a favorite theme. Baldomero Lillo and other figures like Federico Gana and Mariano Latorre probed Chilean nationality through descriptions of the countryside and regional customs.

World War I (1914–1918) provoked several changes in Chile. Sympathies were divided; the upper classes had economic ties with Great Britain and cultural ties with France, but the German immigrants in southern Chile naturally favored Germany, and the army was largely influenced by German experts who had helped to reorganize the military forces.

The end of war brought a decline in the demand for nitrates and plunged the country into an economic crisis that was the first serious challenge to the oligarchy. In 1920, social change was already a burning issue in Chilean politics. Elected to the presidency in 1920, Arturo Alessandri was the first national political figure to attempt to exploit the concern with social change and social justice.

In 1930, when Chile began to articulate in a popular manner some of her revolutionary nationalist demands, 45 percent of the population was urban. In May 22, 1927, General Ibáñez gained the presidency unopposed. With the support of the military, he did much for the masses and appeared to have the potential to lead a populist nationalist movement. Despite the potential for nationalist and populist support for Ibáñez, his movement collided with Chile's growing economic nationalism when he sold many of the national nitrate mines to the Guggenhein interests. For many Chilean nationalists, Ibáñez became the man who ruled the country at a time when U. S. capital seemed to be taking it over. Indeed by 1930, foreign capital investments exceeded those of domestic investments in manufacturing, industry, and mining. Such developments blurred his nationalist-populist image and made him vulnerable when the full effects of the depression were felt in Chile. Between 1929 and 1932 revenue from the sale of nitrates and copper fell from $27 million to $3.5 million. As a result, the country in 1931 could buy only 12 percent of what it had imported in 1929. In the face of this almost complete collapse, Ibáñez resigned in 1931.

After 1931, a group that spoke for Chile's lowest classes, a coalition of Socialists and Communists called Frente de Acción Popular headed by Salvador Allende, increasingly identified with Chile's economic nationalism.

After twenty-seven years, a Socialist president has been elected in Chile. The nationalistic platform has been modified since the election of Salvador Allende in 1970. Nationalism must adapt to the reality that globalization has imposed. New Presidente Ricardo Lagos, a leading dissident during this country's seventeen-year dictatorship and a cabinet minister in subsequent elected governments, defeated rightist J. Lavin on Sunday, January 16, 2000, to became Chile's first Socialist president since the late Salvador Allende was overthrown in a bloody 1973 coup.

**CHINESE NATIONALISM** A multifaceted concept that has been endorsed by the nationalists in the late 19th century, the antitraditionalists and the anti-imperialists during the May Fourth Movement, and the modernists in the late 20th century.

The Chinese were historically complacent and cosmopolitan. Since the beginning of its civilization some 5000 years ago, the Chinese consistently held a China-centric view of the world with China being the supreme center of the world. However, two significant events challenged the universe the Chinese have created for themselves. The first one was the establishment of the Manchu dynasty in the 17th century. Manchu was a relatively small ethnic group whose members lived in the northeastern part of China. It conquered all of China in 1644 and ruled China for the next two and a half centuries. The second event was the First Opium War (1839–1842). Great Britain, frustrated by the rejection of the Chinese imperial court to grant it equal status, determined to open up China by force. China suffered humiliating defeat in the war. In a few decades, China fell into the status of a "hypercolony" where several major imperialist countries competed for spheres of control.

The nationalist movement that emerged in China in the late 19th century was a reaction to these two developments. It had strong anti-Manchu and antiforeign sentiments. Liang Qichao was the first scholar to introduce the Western concept of "nation" (Minzu) to China from his translation of the Japanese word "minzoku." Dr. Sun Yatsen adopted the concept of nationalism ("Minzu Zhuyi") as the first of his Three Principles of the People. Sun's nationalism had a clear ethnic and cultural orientation that endorsed a return to the majority rule of the Han people and the preservation of Han-dominated culture. The Xingzhong Hui (Society to Restore China's Prosperity) founded by Sun in Honolulu in 1894 set out "to drive out the Tatar barbarians [Manchus], restore China and establish a republic." The ethnic element of the restoration nationalism was largely achieved with the downfall of the last Manchu emperor of the Qing dynasty in 1911. But the cultural revival and restoration remained a crucial element of Chinese nationalism since then. Its propagators, such as Sun Yatsen and Chiang Kaishek, shared many similarities with the "father" of cultural nationalism, German thinker Johann Gottfried von Herder. Like Herder, they also emphasized the need to integrate individuals with their nation, and sought various ways to recover China's historical glamor and prosperity. Sun called for the Chinese to restore their "national spirit" and traditional morality, and Chiang launched his New Life Movement in the 1930s trying to restore Confucianism and the traditional system of group responsibility and mutual aid.

Earlier Chinese nationalism also had a strong antiforeign element. Frustrated by the growing Christian influence in China, angry peasants in northern China launched the Boxer Uprising in 1900 aimed at driving foreigners, especially foreign missionaries, out of the country. But the xenophobia only resulted in a joint expedition of eight imperialist powers against China. The anti-Western sentiment reached its peak during the May Fourth Movement in 1919 but soon changed its course. When Western powers at the Versailles conference decided to let Japan take over the Shandong peninsula from defeated Germany instead of returning it to China, student demonstrations broke out in Beijing and quickly became a nationwide patriotic movement. Unlike previous nationalist reactions, this movement manifested strong antitraditionalist and anti-imperialist sentiments. It wanted to recreate China's national grandeur by way of westernization and by adoption of advanced Western science and technology. Many Chinese came to the conclusion that the only way for China to restore its place in the world was to speed up its modernization process and to build a "rich country and strong army."

After World War II and the revolution of 1949, modernization gained momentum. The Communist government launched ambitious plans for industrialization. However, the Cold War environment separated China from the West, which in turn led Communist leaders such as Mao Zedong to take a very strong anti-imperialist and anticapitalist view. China resorted to self-reliance to develop its economy. Due to the lack of experience and the fanatic zest of the Great Leap Forward (1958–1960), a major setback of Chinese economy occurred in 1959–1962 that was followed by another ten years of a man-made disaster, the Cultural Revolution (1966–1976).

After Mao's death, anti-imperialist and anticapitalist nationalism has subsided. Since 1979 modernization has once again become a top priority for the nation. China has opened its door to Western investment and Western technology. In just two decades, China's GDP has quadrupled. With its newly added economic strength, China is becoming increasingly assertive in international affairs. Nationalist feeling is once again on the surge. After a century of national ascendance, China has restored Han Chinese rule, regained its sovereignty, canceled unequal treaties, and restored its territory integrity. With the return of Hong Kong in 1997 and Macao in 1999, colonialism finally came to an end in China.

Will an economically strong China became aggressive and expansionist? This concern of the international community is not totally unfounded. The decline of Communist ideology allowed nationalism to fill the vacuum and became the driving force of China's modernization. Patriotism is portrayed as part of the national soul that reflects state interests and national will. The government has intensified its patriotic education as ways of unifying the thought of its people and promoting political loyalty to the state. However, China at the same time has refused to endorse the concept of "the greater China," which included the Chinese mainland, Taiwan, and Hong Kong, for fear of alarming her neighbors over her intentions. The desires of China to become an equal member of the international community and to integrate its economy into the world economy will make cultural nationalism an unlikely choice for the Chinese. Instead, China has increasingly become a strong voice for the political and rational nationalism that originated during the French Revolution. The core demands of Chinese foreign policy, such as sovereignty, equality, and nonintervention, all have their origin in the Westphalia conference of 1648 that gave rise to the modern nation-state system. Indeed, ethnic nationalism is now a major threat to China's own internal stability. Some extreme minority nationalists in Tibet, Xinjiang, and Inner Mongolia are calling for independence from China. Authorities in Beijing had to impose marshal law in Lhasa in order to stop a Tibetan separatist riot in Tibet in 1989. For this very reason China has carefully avoid using the term *nationalism* all together in its state-controlled media since 1949. Rather than nationalism, the term *patriotism* is used to encourage the loyalty to geographically unified and ethnically diversified China.

Readers may find *The Revival of Chinese Nationalism* by Wang Guangwu (Leiden, The Netherlands: International Institute for Asian Studies, 1996) and *In Search of a Right Place: Chinese Nationalism in the Post−Cold War World* by Zhao Suisheng (Hong Kong: Hong Kong Institute Asia-Pacific Studies, 1997) very useful sources for further inquiry.

**CHIRAC, JACQUES** 1932–, Chirac graduated from the Institut d'Etudes Politiques in 1954. He later studied international relations at Harvard, paying his way by working as a waiter at Howard Johnson's. During the Algerian War he served as an officer in the French Foreign Legion. He completed the prestigious Ecole Nationale d'Administration (ENA) in 1959. His subsequent political rise was meteoric, working, as always, so energetically that Pompidou gave him the nickname "The Bulldozer." From 1974–1976 he served as prime minister under President Valéry Giscard d'Estaing. Believing that he was given too little leeway to pursue his own policies, he became the first prime minister in the Fifth Republic to quit due to disagreements with the president. He reconstructed the Gaullist party, renaming it the Rally for the Republic (RPR), which he dominated for the rest of the century.

The 1986 parliamentary elections produced a slim conservative majority and created something new since the beginning of the Fifth Republic in 1958: a president whose party had a minority of seats in the National Assembly. Therefore, President François Mitterrand, who had defeated both Chirac and Giscard in the 1981 presidential elections, was compelled to appoint Chirac as prime minister. Observers coined the word *cohabitation* to describe the relationship between a strong president and an equally strong prime minister who is not willing merely to execute the will of the president. This showed that the institutions of the Fifth Republic are more adaptable and resilient in democratic politics than even its founder Charles de Gaulle had ever imagined. The experiment proved that two ideologically opposed sides could find common ground and cooperate with each other in the interest of the French nation.

As soon as Mitterrand appointed Chirac, the latter declared that he would play an active role in foreign and defense policy, fields traditionally reserved for the president. In domestic affairs, Chirac moved quickly, with a sharp eye on the 1988 presidential elections. He enacted the largest number of reforms by any French government since 1958. He abolished the proportional representation electoral system, which Mitterrand had intentionally introduced in order to reduce the Communists' parliamentary seats and to prevent any party from winning a majority. This system had enabled the right-wing National Front (FN) to win thirty-five seats and thereby reduced Chirac's usable majority to only two deputies, even though the right, as a whole, had won 55 percent of the vote.

Mitterrand was the first Fifth Republic president to have his wings clipped while still in office. He could not stop a single policy the Chirac government wanted to pursue. However, by knowing how and when to assert his residual authority, he succeeded in preserving his authority, and his popularity soared. By standing above the political fray and focusing on the nation's interests, he let Chirac, who was in the trenches doing day-to-day combat, acquire serious political bruises. Mitterrand thereby enhanced his own chances of reelection and diminished Chirac's chances to win the presidency. The 1988 presidential election led the country into yet another untested experiment: a minority government. It was the least ideological struggle in recent French history. Shouldering the blame for much that displeased voters and unable to unite the conservatives behind him, Chirac garnered only 46 percent of the votes to Mitterrand's 54 percent.

In the 1995 presidential elections Chirac campaigned energetically under the banner "France for All" to try to show that he stood above party politics. He repeated in his standard stump speech that French society "is more divided and dangerous than ever." With a turnout of 80 percent, Chirac won 52.6 percent of the votes, defeating the Socialist Lionel Jospin. Chirac did best among farmers, businesspeople, shopkeepers, artisans, and the professions. For the first time, a conservative candidate won a majority of voters under age thirty-five, as well as more than 40 percent of blue-collar workers and French describing themselves as underprivileged. Because a record 6 percent of blank ballots was cast, he actually won only 49.5 percent of the votes cast, making him the first president to be elected with fewer than half the total votes. His victory left the right in control of the presidency, 80 percent of the seats in the National Assembly and two-thirds in the Senate, twenty of twenty-two regional councils, four-fifths of the departmental councils, and most of the big cities. Never in the history of the Fifth Republic was there such a concentration of power.

On the first day of his presidency Chirac traveled to Colombey-les-Deux-Eglises to emphasize his political roots by laying a wreath at the burial site of his mentor, de Gaulle. On the following day, he lunched with German Chancellor Helmut Kohl in Strasbourg to underscore the importance of France's ties with its powerful neighbor. He promised a less monarchical presidency than that of his predecessor. He ordered that the fleet of military jets and helicopters at the disposal of the president and cabinet be disbanded and that ostentatious signs of power, such as motorcades with screaming sirens and motorcycles racing through the streets, be banned.

During his campaign, Chirac promised "profound change" and an attack on unemployment as his "priority of priorities." It soon became obvious that he could not fulfill his campaign promises of lower taxes and bountiful jobs, and his approval rating plummeted.

Without preparing the public, he suddenly announced an abrupt reversal of his economic policy from creating jobs to cutting the deficit in order to ensure that France would be able to join Europe's monetary union in 1999. The sense of betrayal over the unexpected U-turn from job creation to austerity ignited in 1995–1997 the worst strikes since 1968.

In 1997 he made a fateful decision to call early parliamentary elections. Control of the National Assembly changed hands for the fifth straight parliamentary election in sixteen years. Tired of Chirac's broken promises made only two years earlier to protect the social net and reduce France's 12.8 percent unemployment, while lowering taxes and government spending, voters turned back to the Socialists, led by Jospin, a former diplomat, economics professor, and education minister. President Chirac, who disastrously misread the mood of the French public, was obligated to accept cohabitation for the third time in eleven years.

Chirac maintained control only over foreign and defense policy. The end of Superpower confrontation meant that France had to reexamine the three pillars of its defense policy—its nuclear forces, its draft army, and its operational independence from permanent alliances. Without a Soviet threat, France had problems defining a clear purpose for its atomic *force de frappe*. It became difficult to maintain its expensive triad of forces, which in 1991 consumed a fifth of total defense spending. France's underground nuclear test series in 1995–1996 unleashed a violent world outcry, especially in Asia and the Pacific, where they took place. Taken aback by the worldwide protest, Chirac swore that these tests were needed to perfect computer simulation programs that would make further testing unnecessary.

France continues to maintain the largest and most diversified military capability in Western Europe. Despite the changed security environment in Europe following the end of the Cold War, there was still a consensus to maintain—as the ultimate security guarantee—a minimal nuclear force posture for the purpose of *dissuasion*, the French version of deterrence. A significant change is that these nuclear weapons are to be linked to European security, not just the defense of French territory and interests.

France's traditionally independent stance on defense is being increasingly challenged by the reality of an emerging European Security and Defense Identity (ESDI) within NATO that the French government has come to accept. Under President Chirac, France cooperated more closely with NATO than any time in the previous three decades. He even announced France's intention to rejoin NATO's integrated command structure, from which de Gaulle had withdrawn France in 1967. But Chirac coupled this intent with a demand unacceptable to the United States: that a European head NATO's Regional Command South in Naples, which directs the American Sixth Fleet in the Mediterranean. By the end of the 20th century, France had not found a way to back away gracefully from this demand.

In cultural policy, Chirac, who speaks excellent English, backs France's official effort to protect the French language from English-language encroachment in advertising, education, and the scientific and computer world. He argues that "the stakes are clear. If, in the new media, our language, our programs, our creations are not strongly present, the young generation of our country will be economically and culturally marginalized."

Chirac, whose approval ratings reached 79 percent for his handling of the Kosovo crisis in the spring of 1999 and for his willingness to work constructively with Socialist Prime Minister Jospin, has seen his responsibilities shrink to little more than foreign and defense policy. He spoke in 1997 of the "extreme difficulty of changing anything at all in a profoundly conservative and fossilized country." This is not the first time that France has experienced cohabitation. However, this is the first time that such a divided executive lasted longer than two years. Polls in 1998 indicated that a majority of the French people like such a system of checks and balances that honestly reflects the divisions within the French population.

## CHORNOVIL, VYACHELSLAV   1938–, Literary critic, journalist, dissident and politician, Chornovil was born in the Kyiv region. He graduated in 1960 from Kyiv University and began to work as the editor of Ukrainian Soviet Socialist Republic radio-television broadcasting and for the *Komsomol* (Communist youth organization). He was one of the *shestidesiatniki* (Soviet liberals of the 1960s). In 1967 he was sent to report on the trials of twenty Ukrainian nationalist dissidents for the Soviet press. Instead, he prepared a book sympathetic to the dissidents and highly critical of what he considered to be the arbitrary and illegal manipulation of the Soviet Legal Code and system by authorities. The book, *Lykho z rozumu* (Woe from Wit; published in English as *The Chornovil Papers*), circulated as *samizdat* (literally "self-publishing," a term used to describe the underground press during the Soviet era) in Ukraine. Chornovil was arrested and imprisoned in Siberia from 1967 to 1969 for this work, although in the West it won him the British Tomalin Prize for journalism.

After his release from prison he returned to Ukraine where he edited the samizdat journal *Ukrainskyi visnyk*

(Ukrainian Herald). Under his editorship, the journal reported on human rights violations in Ukraine. After his arrest in 1972, the journal was edited by Stepan Khmara and became much more radical in tone. Chornovil was again exiled to Siberia until 1979. In that year Chornovil became a member of the Ukrainian Helsinki Group (UHG), an organization dedicated to ensuring Soviet compliance to the Helsinki accords on human rights, which it signed in 1975. In 1980 Moscow cracked down on this group, and Chornovil was again sent to Siberia.

With the advent of Mikhail Gorbachev's *perestroika,* Chornovil joined the Ukrainian Helsinki Union (UHU) in 1988. Although the UHU was the descendent of the UHG, it was also tacitly formed as a political alternative to the Communist Party. In 1989 the UHU tried to form a broad democratic coalition in Ukraine, but failed. Such an umbrella organization of all political opposition, named *Rukh* (Ukrainian for "movement," more fully called the All-Ukrainian Movement for *perestroika*), was formed by Ivan Drach and the Writer's Union of Ukraine. *Rukh* worked to promote Ukrainian sovereignty, language, culture, and ecological protection. By its founding congress in September 1989, *Rukh* had 280,000 members.

In March 1990 *Rukh* won 24 percent of the seats in parliamentary elections. Chornovil, leader of the L'viv Oblast Council from 1990 to 1992, won one of these seats from L'viv. In the December 1991 presidential election (held concurrently with a referendum on independence), Chornovil ran as the *Rukh* candidate and took second place to Leonid Kravchuk. Although Chornovil received most of the votes in nationalist western Ukraine, he only received 23.3 percent of the vote for Ukraine as a whole, compared to Kravchuk's 61.6 percent.

As the Communist Party of Ukraine lost support, *Rukh* became more nationalist. Originally dominated by *shestidesiatnik* dissidents like Drach and Chornovil, many younger nationalists soon rose to power. Partially due to this generational change, but also due to disagreement over whether to support Kravchuk's administration, *Rukh* began to disintegrate with liberals and centrists leaving to form new political parties. The UHU formed the Ukrainian Republican Party, which Chornovil quit because he believed it to be overcentralized and too similar to the Bolsheviks in structure. In August 1992 the nationalist rightwing of *Rukh* left to form the Congress of National-Democratic Forces. Chornovil became leader of the remainder of *Rukh* and turned it into a political party with 50,000 members in December 1992. The new *Rukh* remained liberal and anti-

Communist, believing in democracy and a free market. In 1997 *Rukh* was a political faction with twenty-five members and a party with twenty-two members (including Chornovil) in Parliament. Most of *Rukh*'s support comes from western Ukraine.

## CHURCHILL, WINSTON

1874–1965, Seldom in the modern age has the world seen such a versatile man as Churchill. A product of Sandhurst, Britain's Royal Military College (now Academy), he was a courageous and distinguished soldier, with youthful service in India, in the cavalry at Omdurman in the Sudan, in South Africa during the Boer War, and in France during the Great War. He was a gifted writer and journalist with an accurate eye to self-promotion. His penetrating, vivid, and inspiring use of language and his skill as an orator, biographer, and historian would not only provide him with a living between government posts and in retirement, it was used to inform, convince, inspire, and galvanize his nation to rise to its "finest hour" during the Battle of Britain. While he was a man of the world, he was deeply patriotic, with a rock-firm belief in Britain's greatness, its historic responsibility in the world, the beneficial influence the British Empire had throughout the globe, and the value of its principles and ideas for mankind. He despised dictatorship of both the left and right, and he revered democracy, which, he once joked, was the worst form of government except every other type that mankind had ever tried. But it was as a wartime leader that he demonstrated what a giant he really was.

He was a man who did not shy away from controversy, and he often found himself in the midst of it. Before both world wars he warned against the rising military power of Germany and reminded his countrymen and their leaders how crucial Britain's own military preparedness was. As First Lord of the Admiralty after 1911, he successfully advocated the largest naval expenditure in British history and brought the fleet to the peak of readiness. In the wake of the failed Dardanelles and Gallipoli campaigns, he resigned and went to France as a lieutenant-colonel in the 6th Scots Fusiliers. He returned to Parliament in June 1916. The following year he became a very effective and energetic minister of munitions, and in 1919 he was named secretary of war. One of the most contentious issues of that time was home rule for Ireland. He had bitterly opposed this, but he changed his mind and played an important role in the negotiations that culminated in the Irish treaty of 1921.

During a long hiatus from power during the interwar years, he repeatedly and unsuccessfully warned his na-

tion of the growing German menace. As Hitler began to threaten more and more of Europe, Prime Minister Neville Chamberlain practiced a policy of appeasement. This only whetted the German appetite. Churchill described as "a total and unmitigated defeat" the Munich Agreement with Hitler, which gave the Nazis a free hand in Czechoslovakia and which Chamberlain had praised in September 1938 as bringing "peace in our time." After an attack on Poland in September 1939, Britain joined France as allies in World War II, and Churchill was recalled to the Admiralty. When Hitler's forces invaded the Low Countries on May 10, 1940, Chamberlain resigned, and Churchill was appointed prime minister. He later wrote in his memoirs that his entire career before that had been a preparation for the wartime role that was now thrust on him. All his considerable talents and energy were concentrated on saving Britain and the values it stood for.

Serving as his own defense minister, he immersed himself in the conduct of the allied struggle. He elaborated a strategy of victory that regarded Nazi Germany as the primary enemy that had to be defeated. Any country that shared this objective, even the Soviet Union, was suitable as an ally. Britain's "grand alliance" was with the United States, with whom he negotiated a bundle of Anglo-American accords, including the creation of a unified military command in all theaters, a combined chiefs of staff, and the pooling of both partners' military and economic resources. During the Battle of Britain in 1940 he was seen everywhere, visiting military installations, damaged neighborhoods, and factories, giving his people hope and encouragement. His courage and his words epitomized the best of the British spirit and inspired the nation to withstand withering aerial attacks from bombers and rockets. His leadership was crucial in keeping Britain alive. With tremendous assistance from the United States, Britain and its allies were victorious, but prostrated and devastated at the end of the conflict in 1945.

Churchill joined President Truman and Joseph Stalin in Potsdam outside Berlin to decide future policy toward Germany. But on July 5, 1945, before the completion of the Potsdam Conference, voters delivered a dramatic blow to the Tories by electing the first Labour prime minister with a clear majority of 145 seats in the House of Commons, Clement Attlee. Although the British deeply admired Churchill as a great wartime leader, they associated his Conservative Party with the soup lines and unemployment of the prewar depression. Labour had ably guided the home ministries in the national government during the war. It had impressed the British as being the best team for creating full employment, housing, and better social security and health care for a people who had just sacrificed so much in the war effort.

Out of power he delivered an unforgettable speech in Fulton, Missouri, on March 5, 1946, warning of an "iron curtain" that was cutting through the heart of Europe and the need for Great Britain and the United States to remain united as protectors of peace and democracy against Soviet Communism. His fervent, well-articulated anti-Soviet conviction was important in persuading Americans to adopt a Cold War policy.

Churchill also advocated greater European unity. He gave the most important cue to European leaders that the daunting problems they faced could not be solved within the narrow confines of the traditional nation-state. Before the war he had encouraging words, while distancing Britain itself from a united Europe: "We see nothing but good and hope in a richer, freer, more contented European commonality. But we have our own dream and our own task. We are with Europe, but not of it. We are linked, but not compromised. We are interested and associated, but not absorbed."

For decades his countrymen shared his sense of not totally belonging to Europe. He had spoken like an ardent federalist during the war. In March 1943 he had advocated in a radio broadcast a "Council of Europe" that would oversee effective working institutions, including a common military organization. On May 9, 1946, he added: "I see no reason why . . . there should not ultimately arise the United States of Europe, both those of the East and those of the West which will unify this continent in a manner never known since the fall of the Roman Empire, and within which all its peoples may dwell together in prosperity, in justice and in peace."

In a speech delivered at Zürich University on September 19, 1946, he renewed his call for a Council of Europe encompassing at least ten states. Blending idealism with pragmatism, he put his finger on the key: "The first step in the re-creation of the European family must be a partnership between France and Germany. . . . There can be no revival of Europe without a spiritually great France and a spiritually great Germany. . . . If this is their wish, they have only to say so, and means can certainly be found, and machinery erected, to carry that wish into full fruition." This conciliatory view reflected Churchill's motto: "In War: Resolution. In Defeat: Defiance. In Victory: Magnanimity. In Peace: Goodwill."

Under his chairmanship, a United Europe Committee was founded with such luminaries as French Socialist Léon Blum, Italian Prime Minister Alcide de Gasperi, and Belgian Foreign Minister Paul-Henri Spaak as honorary presidents. Their efforts led to a European Movement two years later, one of a proliferation of pro-Europe groupings. In contrast to the post-1918 era, they enjoyed public support and that of many parliamentarians and cabinet members, who had shared common disasters and common fears, and who had common ideals and goals. For them, the European ideal had become a replacement for exaggerated nationalism, which had become discredited. It was seen as an antidote to Communist ideas, which had a strong appeal in Europe immediately after the war. Not only could unity revitalize the economy, but it could do the same for European culture, which many thought was being challenged by powerful influences from America.

At age seventy-seven, Winston Churchill was returned to power in 1951, and his Tories ruled until 1964, the longest period of continuous party government in modern British history. His government returned the iron and steel industries and road transport to private ownership, although iron and steel were renationalized by Labour in 1967. However, accurately sensing the sentiments of the British nation, the Tories did not make a radical U-turn. The party accepted the national welfare and health services, as well as the commitment to full employment. Following a stroke, Churchill was finally persuaded to step down in 1955. His successor was his long-time foreign minister Anthony Eden.

**CINEMA'S ROOTS IN NAITONALISM** Nationalism played a key role in the birth of the cinematic industry. As a new cultural form that emerged at the very end of the 19th century, cinema was highly affected by its national capital and culture. All major industrialized nations of the late 19th century had some claims to the initial invention of "the cinema." The film industry was often considered in terms of national categories, and cinema was perceived as an expression of national cultures, containing elements of larger national histories. The first nationalistic film made in the United States, *The Monroe Doctrine,* was understood as the "favorite dogma of the American people," signifying the coming of the "American century" in the 20th-century film industry.

However, the impact of nationalism on the cinema in the early period was profoundly complicated by the trend of internationalism. Because production costs were too high for a single national market to support, film companies had to look for foreign markets and thus film-making was highly cosmopolitan during its beginnings. For example, in the peep-hole kinetoscope age (1894–1895), the U.S.-based big film company, the Edison Manufacturing Company, shot various European and international stars altogether in one vaudeville program: Eugen Sandow and Louis Attila (Germany), Luis Martinetti (Italy), Juan Caicedo (Colombia), Alcide Capitaine (France), Sheik Tahar (Arabia), and Toyou Kichi (Japan). Different ethnic Americans also appeared. The silent nature of motion pictures effaced the barrier of national language and helped to transgress national identity by producing a shared viewing experience for people all over the world.

National sentiments nevertheless were still deeply rooted in the cinema in the 20th century. Edison was an American symbol of technological sophistication and had become "the father" of new technologies transforming American life. Edison's films made a crucial contribution to America's identity and its sense of national superiority. Cinema, as the dream factory, restates a discourse of "imagined community" for the American culture.

**CIS** The Commonwealth of Independent States (CIS) was established as a loose successor organization to the Soviet Union by the Belovezhky accords signed by Russian President Boris Yeltsin, Ukrainian President Leonid Kravchuk, and executive chairman of the Belarusian Supreme Soviet Stanislav Shushkevich outside of Minsk on December 8, 1991. A follow-up meeting on December 21 added the Central Asian states of Kazakhstan, Kyrgyzstan, Turkmenistan, Tajikistan, and Uzbekistan plus Armenia, Azerbaijan, and Moldova. These last two states subsequently withdrew from or failed to ratify CIS membership, but by 1994 illicit Russian support for internal separatist movements had pressured both, as well as Georgia, back into theCommonwealth, leaving only the three former Baltic republics outside.

Although the CIS went on to develop a broad agenda of activity ranging from trade to border patrol to peacekeeping and to create several institutional structures to carry out its functions, from its inception the CIS has suffered from several interrelated problems.

First, there has been lack of clarity or agreement as to whether the CIS was to function merely as a temporary umbrella facilitating and stabilizing the process of deconstructing the old Soviet Union or as an ongoing framework for the reintegration of the Soviet successor states. The former trend has tended to predominate, as illustrated by the ending of the joint CIS military command and the abandoning of the Russian ruble as a common currency by 1993.

Second, Ukraine and many other members have viewed the CIS as a potential instrument of renewed, neo-imperial domination by Russia over the so-called "near abroad." Accordingly, they have opposed efforts to give the body any effective, supranational powers.

Third, even though approximately 800 agreements (many duplicative) for greater cooperation have been signed among CIS members, the vast majority have remained unratified and/or unimplemented. For example, commitments to create a "common economic space" in the form of a free trade zone or customs union have been signed in almost every year of the CIS's existence.

Fourth, the body has been plagued by "variable geometry," with different members joining a varying patchwork of CIS agreements. For example, only nine signed the CIS Collective Security Treaty, and only five the agreement for a CIS customs union.

Five, the CIS has been steadily undermined as an overarching framework by the proliferation of more manageable subgroupings of its members. These include the would-be Russian-Belarusian Union, the economic and potentially security cooperation of the so-called GUUAM group (Georgia, Ukraine, Uzbekistan, Azerbaijan, and Moldova), and the Central Asian Union.

As the organization's leading backer, Russia has called for thoroughgoing reforms to resolve such problems and revive the CIS. However, the lack of agreement on the desirability or direction of change together with Russia's increasingly evident weakness and other members' growing confidence in their national independence has left the CIS moribund in most areas. Though summits and other meetings continue to take place on a semiregular basis, the CIS may find it difficult to avoid a continued decline in importance in the years ahead.

A concise overview of the development of the CIS is "End of the Line for the Commonwealth of Independent States," by Paul Kubicek, in *Problems of Post-Communism* (March/April 1999), pp. 15–24.

**CITIZENSHIP** The state of being vested with the rights and duties of a citizen. Citizenship is used as a tool by nationalists to draw distinctions between those who are properly part of a nation and those who are not. Citizenship is earned differently in different countries. For example, in the United States, anyone born of at least one American parent, born within the borders of the United States, or inducted a citizen after passing the citizenship examination is considered a citizen. In Japan, on the other hand, a citizen is only someone born of Japanese parentage; no matter how long a person's family has lived in Japan, if the parents are not of Japanese ancestry, the person remains a legal alien. Similarly, in many former Soviet republics, only those whose ancestry is of the majority ethnic group and who speak the national language are generally granted citizenship.

Citizenship can become a divisive tool of nationalist organizations. Citizens are acceptable, while noncitizens, or noncitizen groups, become the object of nationalist propaganda. Gaining citizenship becomes increasingly difficult in times of trouble or as a nationalist movement is growing. Examples of the restricting of citizenship rules are numerous in post-Soviet Europe.

In the Baltic republics, where ethnic Russians tended to have an advantage in education, housing, and job placement during the Soviet era, governments in the early 1990s passed laws declaring a national language and restricting citizenship to those who spoke that language. Thus, the ethnic Russians became resident aliens in a land where they had once had privileged positions. This issue quickly became a source of friction between the Russian federation and most of the former Soviet republics. Russian nationalists have in turn denounced these countries for violating the human rights of "Russians abroad" as interpreted from international human rights declarations such as the Helsinki accords.

Citizenship is used by nationalists to draw exlusive barriers within their countries. People who belong to other ethnic or linguistic groups can be denied the rights and privileges of being a member of the society, leading either to "voluntary" emigration or a loss of voice in the society.

**CITY-STATES**   The term *city-state* originated from its ancient Greek name *polis,* and often referred to the cities of ancient Greece, Phoenicia, and Italy in the classical and medieval periods. In the realms of political thought of the 18th and 19th centuries, city-states were taken less seriously as actual polities with specific boundaries and diverse political experiences than an ideal form of government—the principle of democracy and popular sovereignty. City-states like Athens were often portrayed as the model and exemplar of the civic culture that embraced the elements of autonomy and popular sovereignty—government by people and for people.

Nationalism, as an ideological movement, certainly could not emerge without origins. For many historians millennial Christianity prepared the way for the rise of nationalistic sentiments, whereas for political philosophers it was the ancient polis that laid down the spirit of civic humanism and the principle of democracy and self-government. It seems possible to trace certain main national beliefs back to the classical ideas of ancient Greek and even medieval Italian city-states, notably Bruno Latini and Machiavelli in the 15th and early

16th centuries. Civic duties, popular participation, solidarity, and identification of one's place—the virtues of Greek and Italian forms of polis—became an important component of later civic nationalism. During the French revolutionary period, it became a common belief that people should be active participants in the political power of the nation-state. In the words of Locke, "Wherever any number of men so unite into one society as to quit every one his executive power of the Law of Nature, and to resign it to the public, there and there only is a political or civil society."

The belief that the agreement to establish a common legislature and government and, thus, a state or nation-state, was based on the principle of popular freedom and sovereignty. The perception of government as a manifestation of democratic will and an identification of the state as sovereign of the people were deeply rooted in French revolutionary political thought. People were nothing and ought to be everything; and it was what the revolutionaries meant when they declared, "Sovereignty is one, indivisible, inalienable and imprescriptible: it belongs to the nation." By proclaiming the principle of popular sovereignty, the French revolutionaries fundamentally altered the prevailing conception of the state. Nationalism, for them was, first of all, a doctrine of popular freedom and sovereignty. This stream of civic nationalism differed from cultural nationalism, which stressed ethnic identification of one's tradition and the unlimited surrender of one's love to country, in that it was more rational and cosmopolitan.

**CLASS INTERESTS**   Class, according to Marxism, is the horizontal division of society based on differential access to the means of production. The dominant class exploits other classes and appropriates their surplus through its control of the means of production. The Weberian version of class tends to focus on power and status as well as economic position as markers.

Marx and Engels viewed nationalism as a false consciousness masking class interest, a mystification of the ruling class to blunt class consciousness. The Marxist tradition attempted to reduce ethnic issues to class problems and treat them as residuals of capitalism to be supplanted by proletarian internationalism. They condemned the Slav peoples of the Habsburg Empire, during the revolutions of 1848–49, for standing opposite to German-speaking Austrians and the Magyars, to the advantage of conservatism. But events compelled them to recognize the importance of such issues and that nationalism and tradition were things a proletarian movement could not ignore and could even make use of in a transitional period. Lenin, after the successful October

Revolution, called for a balance between the duty of the socialists in dominant countries to work for the liberation of oppressed nationalities, and that of socialists in dominated countries to oppose narrow-minded nationalism. Stalin wrote a pamphlet titled "Marxism and the National Question" in 1913, and it became the standard formulation of Bolshevik views. Stalin observed that there was danger of local nationalism that could easily infect the workers, and socialists should do their best to resist it. But minority nationalism could only be checked by a socialist pledge of full rights of self-determination. Practicing this Marxist line, James Connolly gave his life in the Dublin rising of 1916 for the sake of fusing socialism with nationalist revolt. However, since the fallout between the USSR and China, the common tie of class became untied and individual patriotism came to the fore. Especially after the demise of the former Soviet bloc, nationalism has been rampant in these countries.

**CLAY, HENRY** 1777–1852, U.S. statesman, was born in Hanover County, Virginia, and eventually settled in Kentucky, then a part of the West. Clay served as speaker of the House of Representatives (1811–1820 and 1823–1825), secretary of state (1825–1829), and U.S. Senator (1831–1842 and 1849–1852), and ran unsuccessfully for president three times. He is best remembered as the chief author of the American System, a form of economic nationalism, and as "The Great Compromiser" for his involvement in three major compromises to preserve the Union.

Clay began articulating the American System in 1810, the year after he was first elected to the U.S. Senate. At the time the West was just beginning to contribute significantly to the U.S. economy by exporting its agricultural surplus to the eastern states, which had always been commercially oriented and were now becoming heavily industrialized as well, in exchange for manufactured goods. Because western roads were few in number and in generally poor condition, most of this surplus made its way east in a roundabout way via the Mississippi River and New Orleans. The American System sought to unite the economic interests of East and West by imposing high tariffs on manufactured goods (thus protecting the commercial interests of the East), using the extra revenue created by these tariffs to improve transportation between East and West by building federally subsidized roads and canals, and re-establishing the Bank of the United States as the cornerstone of a national banking system that would facilitate the collection of taxes and the disbursement of federal expenditures. Although the tariff and bank portions of

Clay's plan became institutionalized in 1816, the necessary federal funding for improving western transportation was never appropriated by Congress, and so this development was left to the individual states. Albeit Clay's American System did much to cement the relationship between East and West, it also helped to alienate the South from the rest of the country because southerners perceived that its economic interests were greatly harmed by the tariffs that Clay's program espoused.

Despite his strong regional self-identification, Clay held strong nationalistic beliefs, which led him to work assiduously on three occasions to affect compromises between the free states of the East and West and the slave states of the South. In 1820, he served as the chief architect of the Missouri Compromise, by which both sides agreed to divide the territory acquired by the Louisiana Purchase in 1807 into free and slave territories. This compromise was so successful that it effectively nullified slavery as a topic of national debate for more than twenty years. In 1833, he helped bring about an end to the nullification crisis, whereby South Carolina had threatened to secede from the Union over the tariffs of 1828 and 1832, by gaining sufficient support from all three regions for a compromise tariff bill. In 1850, following several years of intense bickering over the question of slavery in the territories obtained from Mexico as a result of the Mexican War, he attempted to gain congressional support for several measures known collectively as the Compromise of 1850 by appealing to the nationalistic fervor of all parties.

Clay offers an interesting example of a politician whose nationalism evolved over the course of his career. In 1798, he ardently supported the Kentucky and Virginia Resolutions, which declared that a state had the right to nullify any act of Congress that it believed to be unconstitutional. In 1812, he served as leader of the "War Hawks," a group of mostly western congressmen who advocated war with Great Britain. He did so because he believed such a war would make it impossible for western Indians, who were supported by the British in Canada, to operate as an impediment to western expansion. However, by 1820 Clay's presidential ambitions induced him to take a more nationalist view concerning regional matters, hence his involvement in the three compromises.

A biography is Glyndon G. Van Deusen, *The Life of Henry Clay* (1937, reprint 1967). Clay's role in the development of U.S. nationalism is discussed in Maurice G. Baxter, *Henry Clay and the American System* (1995), Robert V. Remini, *Henry Clay: Statesman for the Union* (1991), and Merrill D. Peterson, *The Great Triumvirate: Webster, Clay, and Calhoun* (1987).

## CODREANU, CORNELIU ZELEA

1899–1938, Founder and leader of the Legion of the Archangel Michael and its paramilitary arm, the Iron Guard. The two became indistinguishable and were commonly known as the Legionary Movement, a Romanian fascist formation active in the 1930s.

Codreanu was born in 1899 near the town of Iași in the province of Moldavia. His father, whose original last name had been Zelinski, was a teacher of Ukrainian or Polish origin. In 1919 Codreanu began studying law and the University of Iași, where his extracurricular activities consisted mostly of anti-Semitic and anti-Communist agitation. In 1922 he attended lectures at the University of Berlin, where he claimed to have personally enlightened several future prominent Nazis. In 1923 he joined the virulently anti-Semitic League of Christian Defense founded by professor Alexandru Cuza. In 1924 Codreanu assassinated the police chief of Iași, who had attempted to curb anti-Semitic activities, but was subsequently acquitted. The same year he broke with Cuza over the latter's unwillingness to abandon parliamentary politics.

In 1927 Codreanu founded the Legion of the Archangel Michael, an organization with anti-Semitism as a core element in its guiding ideology. The legion was also fervently committed to Christian Orthodoxy, anticommunism, and sought to purge Romanian political life of its pervasive corruption. In 1930, Codreanu established the legion's paramilitary arm, the Iron Guard.

In August 1931, having decided to compete in parliamentary elections after all, Codreanu gained a seat in a by-election in his native district of Iași. In December 1933, after a massive wave of repression against the guard, its members retaliated by murdering prime minister Ion Duca, with Codreanu's approval.

In 1934, Codreanu's forces regrouped as a new political party, Everything for the Homeland (*Totul Pentru Țara*). In the rigged elections of 1937, the party officially gained 16 percent of the vote, though its share of the vote was probably higher. In February 1938, in a move designed in part to neutralize the increasingly popular legion, King Carol II declared a royal dictatorship, abolishing the entire parliamentary system along with the constitution and all political parties.

Surprisingly, Codreanu reacted by disbanding the organization, announcing his political retirement, and preparing to go into exile in Italy. In April 1938, before he could do so, he was arrested for slandering historian Nicolae Iorga, Romania's leading intellectual. In May, Codreanu was additionally tried on trumped-up charges of treason and convicted to ten years of hard labor.

On the night of November 29–30, 1938, Codreanu and a dozen of his followers were executed by garroting while being transported to the Jilava prison. The official announcement claimed that they had been shot while trying to escape. In September 1939, the Iron Guard avenged his murder by assassinating prime minister Armand Călinescu, and later Iorga as well.

## COLLINS, MICHAEL

1890–1922, Born in County Cork, Ireland, he is known for his participation in the negotiation of, and agreement to, the Anglo-Irish Treaty of 1921. Collins was a member of the Irish Volunteers (later to become the Irish Republican Army) and led the Irish Republican Brotherhood (IRB). He fought in the Easter Rising in 1916 and became an organizer for the political party Sinn Féin. Collins also became a chairman of the provisional government of Ireland and a minister for finance.

Michael Collin's participation in the armed struggle through the Irish Volunteers and the Irish Republican Brotherhood engendered him great respect from his fellow colleagues. The Easter Rising had been planned by the IRB and sought to establish a free and independent Irish Republic. After the Easter Rising he was taken prisoner by the British and eventually ended up at the Frongoch prison camp in Wales. While imprisoned at Frongoch, Collins improved his command of the Irish language and honed his organizational skills as he worked with an Irish Republican Brotherhood cell.

In furtherance of the cause of Ireland, Collins commanded an elite "hit unit" or assassination group, known as the Squad. Under his command the Squad was responsible for numerous deaths. Collins is also known for his strategic military skills and deft intelligence gathering, and is credited by some with developing a modern approach to paramilitary warfare.

Collins, as a member of a delegation that negotiated the Anglo-Irish Treaty, viewed the treaty, albeit imperfect, as the best possible outcome given the situation at the time. Although the Treaty did not include the entirety of Ireland, he felt they had negotiated a significant steppingstone to a united and free Irish republic; it was "freedom to achieve freedom." Eamon de Valera, president of the Dáil Eireann (the Irish Parliament), had aspired to an agreement of external association without any obligation of members of a future government owing allegiance to a British monarchy. He was presented with a required oath of allegiance and dominion status for Ireland within the British Empire. While the Treaty passed the Dáil Eireann many nationalist Irish men and women felt they had been betrayed. Others felt, for the first time, that there was hope in this limited victory.

The Irish Republican Army split over the Treaty and Collins, along with the responsibilities as chairman of the provisional government and duties related to his job as minister of finance, took on much of the work related to dealing with the IRA. He tried to find balance in gaining military control of the country while at the same time supporting covert military policies aimed at undermining the British authority over the counties of northeastern Ireland.

Collins was assassinated in an ambush in his home county of Cork by former comrades who were presumably unable to come to terms with the treaty, the provisional government spawned by it, and the role of Collins in it all. Irish nationalist perceptions of Collins have ranged from those who think he made the best deal possible in signing the treaty to those who have viewed him as a traitor who betrayed the cause of the united Irish republic.

Among the many works on Collins, those among the most cited are *The Man Who Made Ireland; the Life and Death of Michael Collins* by Tim Pat Coogan, Frank O'Connor's *The Big Fellow*, and T. Ryle Dwyer's *Michael Collins and the Treaty* and *Michael Collins: The Man Who Won the War.*

## COLOMBIAN NATIONALISM
Colombian nationalism is weak relative to other Latin American countries and Colombians lack a strong sense of national identity. Many scholars attribute this to cultural and class cleavages, the capacity of the country's economic elite to dominate politics and to mobilize voters through the Liberal and Conservative Parties without recourse to nationalist or populist appeals, and the failure of the country to achieve social and geographical integration.

The challenge of unifying geographically diverse regions containing rival power centers preoccupied early Colombian governments. Unification of the United Provinces of New Granada, which declared independence from Spain in the 1810s, was impeded by its scattered and isolated population and natural obstacles that impeded the establishment of transportation and communication networks. Venezuela and Ecuador seceded from New Granada (also known as Gran Colombia) in the 1830s, after which fiercely independent local elites established a radically decentralized, loose federal system. An era of chaos and interregional violence did not end until 1886, when Conservatives imposed a highly centralized constitution. National unity continued to be prevented by brutal armed conflict between the country's hegemonic Liberal and Conservative Parties, particularly between 1899 and 1902 and 1948 and 1957, when hundreds of thousands died in interparty blood-

letting. In the 1970s and 1980s, class conflict divided the country. The refusal of the oligarchy to open the political system fueled armed Marxist movements with a presence today in most of the national territory. Indeed, if Colombians share one national characteristic it is the capacity to carry on in the face of extreme levels of violence.

Economic nationalism, which is strong in other South American countries, also is weaker in Colombia. In the 1940s and 1950s, Colombian elites sought to build a national steel industry (now in private hands) and to return foreign petroleum concessions to the state. In the 1960s Colombia sought to decrease economic dependence on the United States by forging closer trading ties with Latin American countries. Following the multinational agreements of the Andean Pact, a 1975 law required all Colombian banks to be 51 percent Colombian owned. But there has never been official hostility to foreign investment and Colombia has remained more hospitable to international investors and firms than neighboring countries. Economic nationalism may be moderated by the fact that, with the exception of petroleum, most land and productive resources have remained in Colombian hands.

Another reason for weak Colombian nationalism is the absence of a unifying culture. A rigid racial hierarchy based in colonial era caste distinctions among whites, slaves, and Indians has prevented the emergence of the *mestizo* (mixed-race) national identity promoted by intellectuals and political elites. Since the mid-19th century, Colombian intellectuals and political polemicists have sought the roots of the country's endemic violence and ungovernability in the poor fit between its geographically dispersed ethnically heterogeneous population and the homogeneous, extremely centralized political institutions imposed by Hispanic elites. Many have sought to achieve national integration by forcibly integrating ethnic enclaves under a unifying Catholic faith. Among the earliest intellectuals focusing on the "problem" of Colombia's ethnic heterogeneity and the preponderance of mestizos are José María Samper and Sergio Arboleda in the 19th century, and Laureano Gómez in the 1920s. Parallel to this intellectual tendency was a politically weaker project that sought a more authentic Colombian identity in the country's indigenous heritage. This affirmation of indigenous heritage, known as *indigenismo,* gained wider adherence in the 1930s and 1940s, when a revival of interest in the position of the Indian swept across Latin America. Colombia's most influential indigenist was socialist intellectual Antonio García.

Although they comprise less than 3 percent of the

population, after two decades of grassroots mobilization beginning in the 1970s, indigenous Colombians—who speak sixty-four distinct languages—became a highly visible and symbolically important political force in the 1990s. Their political zenith converged with a national movement for constitutional reform that enabled them to codify a regime of constitutional rights for Indians and African Colombians that has become a model for other Latin American countries. Their success may be attributed in part to Colombians' historical hunger for national identity and unity: Colombian indigenous organizations presented the recognition of diverse Colombian identities as a means to reconcile past hatreds and transgressions against all types of minorities. The 1991 National Constituent Assembly marks the end of the elite project to force a homogeneous, Hispanicized national identity on a culturally diverse population, and the beginning of the official embrace of the "multiethnic and pluricultural" national identity proposed by the indigenous movement.

No important nationalist movements have taken power in Colombia but several are noteworthy. Former dictator General Rojas Pinilla led a national-populist political party, Alianza Nacional Popular (ANAPO), in the 1960s as an alternative to the bipartisan National Front that governed Colombia between 1958 and 1974. Rojas Pinilla's nationalism was essentially a critique of the oligarchic National Front's degrading dependence on the United States. The movement peaked in 1970 when Rojas Pinilla narrowly lost to the official National Front candidate, who his supporters maintained stole the election. In 1973 the Movimiento 19 de Abril (M-19) used the alleged fraud against ANAPO as a rallying cry, taking its name from the date of Rojas Pinilla's alleged victory. Convinced of the impossibility of social change through elections, the M-19 took up arms against the Colombian government. The M-19's nationalism came in the form of hostility to U.S. economic, military, and political influence. In 1990 the M-19 signed a peace treaty with the government and became a political party (Alianza Democrática M-19).

Anti-U.S. sentiment has fueled Colombian nationalism since 1903, when U.S. intervention secured the secession of the Colombian province of Panama. Since the 1980s it has been manifested mainly as resentment of U.S. influence with respect to its antinarcotics policy. The extradition of Colombian drug traffickers in the late 1980s inflamed Colombian resentment and led (together with brazen attacks by the drug cartels on Colombian public and private institutions) to a constitutional prohibition on extradition in 1991. Colombian indignation was aroused again in 1997, when the United States "decertified" Colombia for its insufficient cooperation in U.S. counternarcotics policies. Under U.S. pressure, Colombia repealed the ban on extradition. Anti-U.S. nationalism is often tinged with class conflict, since the oligarchy maintains close ties to U.S. businesses and educational institutions and relies on U.S. support to maintain its political dominance.

Nationalist sentiments also have been aroused sporadically by border conflicts, particularly with Venezuela. But Colombia has only fought one war with its neighbors—a brief border skirmish with Peru in the 1930s—another possible explanation for the weakness of nationalist sentiment.

COLONIALISM   The search for colonies is one manifestation of imperialism as a society establishes political and economic control over another. Colonialism is the overall policy of establishing and maintaining colonies, which involve territories and peoples held in a dependent and inferior relationship to a parent state.

While there are numerous examples of colonies being established in early world history, the dynamic states developing in Europe as early as the 14th and 15th centuries began to look outward and compete with each other. Aided by developments in shipbuilding and navigation, Spain, Portugal, England, and France moved to explore and then settle the New World in the Western Hemisphere in the 16th and 17th centuries. While religion, avarice, and adventure were important in the European colonization of the Americas, the politico-economic theory of mercantilism was particularly strong. Mercantilism held that national strength and security in a world of competing states were dependent on a favorable balance of trade and the accumulation of gold in the treasury. While the theory was flawed, it nonetheless helped to mold the policies of colonial competition by European powers.

By the late 1800s a second phase of colonialism swept Europe as states competed for the prestige, based on nationalism, of accumulating colonial holdings in Africa and Asia. Much of the impetus came from King Leopold II of Belgium, who took possession of the Congo in 1876, thus stimulating British and French interest in Africa. Portugal, Italy, Spain, and Germany also ended up with colonial holdings there. European colonial interest in Asia has a long history. By the 1580s Russia pushed beyond the Urals and by 1858 had taken control of all territory in eastern Siberia north of the Amur River. Britain was establishing control in India in the late 1700s and in Hong Kong and Burma in the mid- to late 1800s, while the French were establishing a protectorate over Indochina.

The motivating factors behind colonialism are numerous and complex, but they would likely include such features as economic gain, religion, nationalism, and national prestige, a sense of a civilizing mission (perhaps mixed with feelings of cultural or racial superiority) to save "backward" peoples, surplus population, complex economic dynamics such as those suggested by the theories of John Hobson and V. I. Lenin, and social Darwinism, which would link explanations of colonialism to the struggle for dominance, survival of the fittest, and power politics.

Thorough scholarly discussions of the history and dynamics of colonialism are provided by George H. Nadel and Perry Curtis, *Imperialism and Colonialism* (Macmillan, 1964) and David K. Fieldhouse, *The Colonial Empires* (Delacorte, 1966) and *Colonialism, 1870–1914: An Introduction* (St. Martin's Press, 1981).

Adapted from Grieves, Forest, *Conflict and Order: An Introduction to International Relations.* © 1977 by Houghton Mifflin Company. Used with permission.

## COMMUNALISM

The concept of communalism refers to competition between groups based on membership in rival communities. Communities may be distinguished from one another based on one or more of a number of characteristics such as religion, language, or place of origin. For example, speakers of French and of Flemish in Belgium can be thought of as comprising separate communities based on language. Likewise, communal divisions based on religion can be seen between Protestants and Catholics in Northern Ireland or between Hindus and Muslims in India.

It is important to realize that the existence of multiple groups based on such markers does not necessarily foreshadow the rise of communal politics or identities in a society. In Switzerland, for instance, language is not a strong force for partitioning the nation into communities despite the presence of large numbers of French-, German-, or Italian-speaking inhabitants.

For communities to arise, communal identities must be constructed and lines of demarcation between "insiders" and "outsiders" must be imbued with meaning. A sense of belonging must be instilled in members of the group; people must see themselves as part of the "family." History can be mined and interpreted to provide a sense of permanence and naturalness to distinctions. Reference may be made to a "golden age;" myths and memories may become part of the collective conscience.

Competition for scarce resources appears to be a major factor in the genesis of communalism. When groups have little interaction with one another or desired resources are plentiful, there is little need to foster collective identities in opposition to one another. When contact and competition increase so does the strain between groups. This is likely to lead individuals to organize themselves based on perceived similarities and to favor those with whom they feel a communal bond.

The presence of communal friction can have conflicting consequences for nationalist politics. When no group is able to achieve and maintain a distinct position of privilege, turning communal loyalties into nationalism is problematic. It is only when one group is able to gain a sustained political and economic advantage that distinctions between communities can be consistently manipulated to take on a nationalistic tenor. An example can be seen in the changing nature of the religious conflict in Northern Ireland. In the early 1800s Protestants competed with Catholics in Belfast for relatively abundant unskilled jobs in the textile industry. Neither group was able to gain an advantaged position and political leaders were unable to utilize sectarian conflicts for nationalist ends. By the end of the century, however, a shifting economy made it possible for Protestants to secure a privileged place in the Belfast labor market. Disputes became more protracted and began to broaden from quarrels over communal boundaries to clashes over the allocation of resources. Ulster Unionists, for instance, were able to mobilize support from working-class Protestants who did not wish to lose their position of economic dominance. As time passed, religious affiliation became shorthand for one's position on Irish nationalism and the future of Northern Ireland.

Much of the literature on communalism concentrates on the case of India; the discord between Hindus and Muslims is the classic case of communal conflict. An example of this line of research is *Democracy, Nationalism, and Communalism* by Asma Barlas (Westview Press, 1995). For a more general discussion of the concept of communities see *Imagined Communities: Reflections on the Origin and Spread of Nationalism* by Benedict Anderson (Verso, 1991).

## COMMUNISM

A form of societal organization in which all property and production facilities providing the goods for that society are communally owned. It is argued that such a society would be more equitable because, by eliminating private ownership, Communism would eradicate the imbalance of social, economic, and political power arising from the control of the means of production by one particular class. Marx and Engels's brand of Communism was infused with a form of social evolutionism that argued that the social contradictions inherent within the class structure of society led to successive social upheavals in which the old ruling class was replaced by a new one. From their perspective, Communism, with its absence of class structure, represented the final stage of social development and was said to be preceded by progressively less developed stages: socialism; capitalism; feudalism; and slavery. Communism should therefore be regarded as distinct from socialism, a social stage prior to Communism in which the state becomes a significant owner of raw materials, property, and production facilities.

In their analyses of the Irish and Polish independence movements, Marx and Engels had provided an explanation of nationalist movements as a reaction to the oppressive and exploitative behavior of the dominating colonial state. A sociological description of the consolidation of the nation was also forthcoming in the "Communist Manifesto": "The bourgeoisie keeps more and more doing away with the scattered state of the population, of the means of production, and of property. It has agglomerated population, centralised means of production, and has concentrated property in a few hands. The necessary consequence of this was political centralisation. Independent, or but loosely connected provinces, with separate interests, laws, governments and systems of taxation, became lumped together into one nation, with one government, one code of laws, one national class interest, one frontier and one customs tariff." However, just as the consolidation of the nation had been associated by Marx and Engels with the centralization of the means of production under the influence of the dominant capitalist class, the pending dissolution of the nation was also to be explained by the very same processes. It was argued that capitalism had begun to "draw from under the feet of industry the national ground on which it stood."

The prediction of the final dissolution of nations was informed by two historical tendencies, one of which concentrated on the internal processes within each nation; the other process focused on relations at the international level. First, the need of raw materials and the search for new markets was said to lead to ever increasing trade at the global level and therefore to a growing interconnectedness of world society. Marx and Engels argued that this would create a homogenizing tendency because the only way each nation could compete with the deluge of cheap goods from the industrialized countries was to adopt the same mode of production. This, it was argued, would lead to a reduction in national differences. Secondly, with the consolidation of capitalism, a division of labor was taking place on a global scale. The growing cooperation and interdependence initiated under capitalism meant that once Communism had eliminated the antagonistic relations between nations,

true social cooperation on a global scale would take place.

At first sight the attainment of Communism would appear to contain a paradox. The basis of Communism would be communal ownership and yet the nation, one of the strongest forms of community, played no part in the blueprint for such a future society. However, this can be explained by the dissolution of such affective social bonds by the previous stage of development—capitalism. The international relations forged during the capitalist stage of development meant that once Communism had been attained, the global division of labor would entail cooperation on a global scale, which implied the overcoming of particularist outlooks such as nationalism and the establishment of a community of humankind in which social activity would be directed toward the good of all.

## COMMUNIST INTERNATIONAL (COMINTERN) A
supranational federation of national Communist parties active from 1919 to 1939. Though ostensibly an international organization, the Comintern was based in Moscow and was controlled at its upper levels by the Union of Soviet Socialist Republics; thus its policies were tied closely to events internal to the USSR.

Also known as the Third International, the Comintern arose after the socialist Second International splintered over policy on World War I. While many socialist centrists opposed what they saw as a nationalist war and called for peace, Russian Vladimir Lenin advocated turning the war between nations into a worldwide civil war between classes. Lenin carried out this strategy within Russia by leading the Bolshevik revolution in 1917; in 1919 he declared the first congress of the Comintern in Moscow to promote world revolution and to thwart the centrist socialism of the Second International.

In 1920, delegations from 37 nations attended the second congress of the Comintern, where Lenin laid out his "21 Points" defining the mission and membership of the federation. Designed to overhaul the international socialism that had failed to oppose World War I, these conditions required all national parties to adopt centralized structures modeled on the Soviet party, to include the word "Communist" in their names, and to purge moderate socialists from their ranks. Member parties were to be governed by the Comintern, not by rank-and-file constituents in their own nations; between congresses, policy that was binding on all member parties would be set by an executive committee affiliated with the Central Committee of the Soviet Party.

As it became clear that world-class revolution would

not follow WWI, the Comintern at the third congress in 1921 adopted a "united front" policy designed to create a more broadly based working-class movement by joining Communist efforts with socialist and liberal causes. This cooperation with moderate socialism increased after Lenin's death in 1924, as Lenin's successor, Joseph Stalin, purged the left wing from the Soviet party in order to defeat his rival, Leon Trotsky.

In 1928, when Stalin had achieved secure control of the USSR, Comintern policy shifted dramatically at the sixth congress. Following Stalin's dictum of "socialism in one country," all Comintern member parties were instructed to make support of the USSR, the world's only socialist state, their top priority. Further, in a swing back to the left, the "united front" policy was abandoned and moderate socialists and liberals were again declared enemies of the Comintern. This policy, which ignored the rise of fascism and focused opposition on the moderate left, continued into the 1930s; under it, German Communists even went so far as to cooperate with the Nazis in order to bring down the moderate Weimar Social Democrats.

At the seventh and last congress in 1935, the Comintern responded to the increasingly apparent threat of fascism with another policy shift back to the "united front" approach. This congress ordered the creation of "popular fronts" that would align Communists with moderate socialists, trade unionists, and liberals to defeat fascism. Under this policy, the Comintern during the Spanish Civil War recruited and commanded International Brigades of soldiers to fight with the republicans against the fascist nationalists. More than 50,000 volunteers from a dozen nations joined the fight between 1936 and 1938, serving in such forces as the French Commune de Paris Battalion and the American Abraham Lincoln Battalion.

The "popular front" policy of the Comintern continued until 1939, when Stalin joined Hitler in signing the Nazi-Soviet Non-Aggression Pact. Although this move seemingly demonstrated Stalin's greater concern for the national success of the USSR than for the international Communist struggle, the official Comintern line was that fascism had been deemed a lesser threat to Communism than Allied bourgeois nationalism. Member parties were ordered to oppose the Allied war against fascism, until Germany invaded the USSR in 1941.

The influence of the Comintern in Western Europe and North America waned radically after 1939 due both to Stalin's pact with Hitler and to increasing revelations of Stalin's oppressive regime within the USSR. After World War II, Stalin replaced the defunct Comintern with a body called the Cominform; under the stress of conflict between the USSR and China, the international communist movement dissolved entirely by the mid-1950s.

A recent history of the Comintern is McDermott and Agnew, *The Comintern: A History of International Communism from Lenin to Stalin* (1996). A history from the USSR is *Outline History of the Communist International*, trans. Bernard Isaacs (1971). A study of the influence of the Comintern on the United States is Klehr, Haynes, and Anderson, *The Soviet World of American Communism* (1998).

## COMMUNITARIANISM

Communitarianism emerged in the United States at the beginning of the 1980s in reaction to what was described by communitarians as a state of moral decay, radical individualism, and reign of instrumental rationality. However, the catalyst event was the publication in 1971 of *A Theory of Justice,* a work written by John Rawls, which marked a revival of political philosophy and of neo-Kantian contract theories. About ten years later, communitarianism came forth as the most substantive and incisive critique of what came to be known as Rawlsian "procedural liberalism," that is, a liberalism stressing the priority of individual rights and legal procedures and depicting the individual as a rational, autonomous, free subject.

Four thinkers distinguished themselves as the most original and challenging communitarian critics: Alasdair MacIntyre, Michael Sandel, Michael Walzer, and Charles Taylor. Since they disagree in several of their conclusions and usually do not even use the label "communitarianism" to characterize their work, one has to be careful not to conflate their thinking. For example, Taylor is inclined toward German nationalist romanticism as embodied in the work of J. G. Herder, whereas regarding certain issues Walzer is close to the American pluralist and pragmatic tradition as found in the work of John Dewey. Nevertheless, to varying degrees, they all share an inspiration in Aristotle and Hegel. Moreover, MacIntyre and Taylor also share religious commitments. But what brings them together more than anything else is their common opponent, procedural liberalism.

Contrary to liberals who present the self as "unencumbered" by any social attachments and as prior to its aims, communitarians argue that the self is actually defined by the community to which it belongs as well as by its ends. Therefore, the self is not always free to choose its ends and values, as liberals pretend. It is through its belonging to a community rather than by escaping it that it can attain a real and substantive moral autonomy. Since the aims constituting the self are those of its community, the ethical principles peculiar to that community (Hegel's *Sittlichkeit*) are superior to and more genuine than the universal principles upheld by liberals (Hegel's *Moralität*).

Following this rejection of universalism, communitarians attach an intrinsic value to the community and to the social relations constituting it. They are both goods in themselves which must not be assessed on instrumental grounds. The self has thus an obligation to sustain its community, for the disappearance of the latter would jeopardize its autonomy and self-realization. It has to aspire to a politics of the common good. Consequently, the communitarian "community" is more than a mere association of free and equal citizens; in many respects it resembles Ferdinand Tönnies's idealized *Gemeinschaft*.

It has been argued that communitarianism is guilty of moral relativism, conservatism, and antiliberalism (generally equated with antidemocratic positions). All of these accusations are denied by communitarians. They point out (1) that more than their celebration of *Sittlichkeit*, it is liberalism's emphasis on procedures and individual rights at the expense of the common good that fosters moral relativism; (2) that they put forward social demands and egalitarian claims that imply social changes; and (3) that their political ideal is closer to participatory democracy and to ancient or Machiavellian civic republicanism than to an authoritarian or totalitarian regime.

Although not a direct one, the relationship between communitarianism and nationalism is quite obvious. The obligation of the individual to sustain its community becomes the duty of the citizen to sustain or defend its nation. Communal solidarity becomes national solidarity. In both cases, the nature of the entity and of its relationship to the individual dictates a loyalty and duties that outweigh obligations toward outsiders, that is, human beings as such. Thus, when presenting the community as a *polis* and invoking the republican tradition, communitarianism can translate into civic/liberal nationalism or patriotism. Nevertheless, the emphasis on the inescapable social and cultural embeddedness of the self, as found, for example, in the work of Charles Taylor, can also legitimize ethnic and cultural claims put forward by minorities, thereby fostering the development of a logic close to that of ethnic nationalism. Communitarianism is then faced with a paradox: It advocates civic virtue and a republicanism giving priority to the common good over particular interests, but at the same time its understanding of the self and its celebration of *Sittlichkeit* legitimize particularistic claims made in the name of "subnational" cultural or ethnic communities.

**CONFEDERATE NATIONALISM**  The complex of ideologies that enabled citizens of the eleven states that seceded from the United States of America in 1860–1865 to identify themselves as citizens of a new nation, the Confederate States of America (CSA).

Because the CSA was at war with the United States throughout almost its entire existence, Confederate nationalism often is defined more specifically as the morale of the Confederate Army during the American Civil War. Delineating the components of Confederate nationalism then becomes an attempt to identify the emotional attachments and belief systems that united Confederate soldiers from diverse classes and geographical regions and made them willing to die, in unprecedented numbers, for a nation that had been newly created. In this common interpretation, Confederate nationalism is judged "successful" during the early years of the Civil War, when the fighting forces of the CSA were strong, loyal, and victorious in battle; conversely, Confederate nationalism is considered to "fail" in the later years of the war, when troops were plagued by desertion, internal insurrection, and military defeat.

Confederate nationalism is of particular interest to students of nationalism because it was created so quickly and self-consciously under the duress of war. Secession served the interests of only a small class of southerners, the planter elites who believed that their wealth and power, based on slavery, were jeopardized by the election of Abraham Lincoln as U.S. president in 1860. However, the need for more broadly based support of secession among southerners became apparent almost immediately when Lincoln opposed secession with military force. To resist forced reassimilation into the Union, planter elites had to generate a nationalism that would both unite the eleven seceded states in a central military effort, and inspire the white masses of those states to defend secession with their lives.

Constructing such a unifying nationalism was a daunting task, because the eleven southern states that became the CSA lacked many distinguishing features of modern nationhood. Unlike European nationalists fighting for independence, Confederates could not differentiate themselves from their foes on the basis of language, race, or cultural heritage—though some erstwhile propagandists adopted novelist Sir Walter Scott's bifurcation between oppressive Anglo-Saxons (Yankees) and rebellious Norman Scots (Southrons). Additionally, though modern nationalism usually is based in mass print culture, the Confederate states lacked both the popular literacy and the networks of publication and distribution common in more industrialized nations, including the northern United States; instead, Confederate leaders anomalously depended on oral media such as sermons, proclamations, and songs. Finally, the Confederate states possessed no prior historical or even mythic alliance or unity—at most they had become aligned as a political faction in the decades preceding secession.

To justify southern independence and a war to maintain it, as well as to differentiate the CSA from the northern United States, Confederate elites claimed a divinely appointed mission—thus the national motto "Deo vindicus." This mission melded political and moral imperatives: to preserve the economic system of slavery, which ostensibly resolved the conflicts between labor and capital inherent in northern industrial capitalism; and to maintain deferent, hierarchical social relations, which ostensibly reflected the original tenets of American republicanism in contrast to the atheistic democratization of the north. Obviously this reactionary ideology of mission served the interests of the planter elite, but as the war progressed and Confederate leaders became ever more dependent on the white masses for fighting force, more progressive interpretations of national mission battled with this official version, and Confederate nationalism became ever weaker, more contested, and more diffuse.

The ideology of national mission was propagated in the Confederate states through two chief forums: the constitutional convention and the evangelical Christian pulpit. Each forum was a familiar part of U.S. nationalism and had great popular appeal, yet remained largely under elite control at the outset of the war. Soon after secession, conventions in each southern state set out new constitutions declaring allegiance to the preservation of slavery, republicanism, and independence from Yankee perversion of the ideals of the American Revolution. And throughout the war, the southern clergy proved the most influential legitimators of the new nation, developing a "just war" theology that posited the fighting as defensive, necessary to uphold the moral ideals of the nation against evil, even demonic, Yankee invaders. But as the white masses and evangelical clergy became ever more powerful, and especially as the CSA suffered increasing military defeat, the clergy challenged the elite definition of national mission by searching for national sins and proposing reform of wartime profiteering and, most subversively, of slavery. Fundamentally, evangelical Christianity proved a shaky foundation for Confederate nationalism, for the radical egalitarianism of evangelicalism stood in direct ideological opposition to the reactionary hierarchies of the Confederate elite.

Since defeating the CSA in 1865, the U.S. government has vigorously denied that Confederate nationalism ever existed, even naming the "Civil War" to denote an internal uprising rather than a contest between two independent nations. U.S. historians generally have perpetuated this interpretation, considering Confederate nationalism to be simply a spurious extension of sectionalism whose ultimate bankruptcy was proven, in hindsight, by the military defeat of the CSA. The anomalous characteristics of Confederate nationalism, described above, lend some support to this view; yet a more emotional charge is suggested by the vehemence of the denials. Evangelical Christianity and "just war" theology played a central role in U.S. nationalism as well during the Civil War; indeed, Lincoln created the U.S. Thanksgiving holiday to celebrate divine assistance at the battles of Gettysburg and Vicksburg—so proslavery nationalism seems an oxymoron to U.S. national morality. Additionally, the ideology of consensual union is essential to U.S. nationalism, and the imperial conquest and forced assimilation of another nation antithetical to it; thus the belief that a Confederate nation never existed perhaps resolves the challenge to U.S. nationalism posed by the secession conflict.

Despite (or perhaps because of) this denial, symbols of Confederate nationalism have retained potent meaning. The Confederate battle flag, in particular, has become the most infamous icon of racism in the United States; it was adopted by the terrorist Ku Klux Klan during Reconstruction, was raised by the "Dixiecrats" in opposition to racial integration in the South during the 1950s and 1960s, and often is displayed alongside the Nazi swastika by hate groups today. The battle flag also has been displayed internationally to signify rebellion against national governments; sightings have been reported in locations as diverse as Sicily, Catalonia, and postapartheid South Africa. And though Confederate nationalism had such a brief political and military existence, it lives on in U.S. culture today, integrated into the national imagination as the heroic lost cause epitomized by the most successful film in history, *Gone With the Wind* (1939, rereleased 1998).

A concise and elegant study of the subject is Drew Gilpin Faust's *The Creation of Confederate Nationalism* (1988).

**CORSICAN NATIONALISM** Legally part of the republic of France, the island of Corsica lies in the Mediterranean Sea approximately 100 miles (160 km) south of France and 50 miles (80 km) west of Italy. Known to many as the birthplace of Napoleon Bonaparte, emperor of France, Corsica was under the control of the Italian city-state of Genoa for most of the period from the late 13th century to the middle of the 18th century. Spontaneously rebelling against Genoa's corrupt rule in 1729, Corsicans were able to create a nominally independent state from 1752 to 1768 under the leadership of Pasquale Paoli. Paoli was chosen to head the fledgling national government and oversaw the adoption of a constitution proclaiming the sovereignty of the Corsican people in 1755. In 1768, Genoa sold the island to France after the latter, preoccupied with security concerns in the Mediterranean, had its proposal to Paoli for a French protectorate over Corsica rejected. By 1769, French troops had ended Corsican dreams for independence, despite a brief period in the 1790s when, following the turmoil of the French Revolution, Britain endeavored to negotiate its own protectorate over Corsica.

The long history of external intervention and control over Corsica, the rebellion against Genoa's corrupt rule, and the brief period of autonomy marked Corsican nationalism as one of the first rebellions of subject peoples in the modern era. The memory of the 18th-century events subsequently contributed to the growth of contemporary Corsican nationalism, although ironically Napoleon's singular military and political career ultimately contributed more than Pasquale Paoli did to a sense of Corsican identity within the context of French rule. Himself an island emigrant, Napoleon set the pattern for many of Corsica's young men who, in the 19th and 20th centuries, played important roles in the French military and civil services, both on the mainland and in France's colonies. Still, it is Paoli, not Napoleon, who has served as the symbolic father of modern Corsican nationalism.

In addition to the historical claim of independence, however short or precarious the period, Corsican nationalism draws on the distinctive attributes of indigenous Corsican culture: the Corsican dialect (closer to Italian than French), the importance of the extended family and strongly differentiated gender roles in island social life, codes of honor and the vendetta, and occultism. The erosion of cultural distinctiveness by modernization during the past forty years has diminished the basis of a unique Corsican identity underlying nationalist claims, but simultaneously has contributed to resentment over a long history of external domination.

Since the late 1960s, economic grievances have also been an important factor contributing to the rise of several groups demanding greater Corsican autonomy within the French Republic or, in extreme cases, outright independence. By the mid-1970s, twice as many Corsicans lived in mainland France as on the island. Employment opportunities have long been limited because many jobs are seasonal (including those in tourism, an especially important industry) and businesses have been dominated by the mainland French. More-over, the 1960s exodus to Corsica of some 17,000 French-Algerian settlers, the *pieds noirs,* contributed to arguments that Corsica was the victim of economic colonialism. Particularly important in the wine industry, the Algerian French were seen as unwelcome rivals who grew rich at the expense of the traditional Corsican peasantry.

The early 1970s marked the beginning of a continuing history of violent outbreaks, including bomb attacks on government buildings and on other visible signs of the mainland French presence, such as banks, travel agencies, and holiday homes. Tension mounted in 1975 when a small group of armed autonomist militants led by Edmond Simeoni (who later became a mainstream politician) occupied the wine cellar of a *pied noir* who owned almost 3000 acres of land that, the militants argued, should have been distributed to young Corsican farmers. Interpreting the events as an out-and-out insurrection, the government sent in a large contingent of police to rout the protesters and quickly dissolved Simeoni's organization, Action for the Renaissance of Corsica (ARC, Action pour la renaissance de la Corse). During the subsequent two decades, other small, banned autonomist organizations came and went.

In the early 1980s, a newly elected Socialist government in Paris moved to decentralize authority through a series of political reforms. In 1982, special autonomy laws established a directly elected Corsican Assembly, with wide powers in executive decision making for the island in the areas of education, agriculture, transportation, housing policy, and economic development. During the same period, a university named for Pasquale Paoli was established in the town of Corte, and the building that had housed Paoli's original independence government became the home of the Center for Corsican Studies. The center in turn has become part of a wider revival of Corsican language (which is now taught in the schools) and culture, including traditional Corsican music and the restoration of ancient monuments.

Despite this linguistic and cultural revival and the devolution of some political authority, which has pleased most Corsicans, a nationalist movement—albeit divided—persists. Banned groups, such as the Corsican National Liberation Front (FLNC, Front de liberation nationale de la Corse), have continued to take responsibility for the hundreds of bombings each year that in the 1990s targeted symbols of French authority. Although most estimates place the number of terrorists at fewer than 500, their attacks undermined efforts to build a stable economy and increasingly alienated most Corsicans. In response, the French government pursued a strategy of repression of dissident groups combined with massive economic subsidies to Corsica. Nonetheless, several high-profile acts of violence, such as the 1996 bombing of the office of Bordeaux's major, Alain Juppe (at the time also prime minister of France), and the 1998 assassination of the newly arrived prefect for Corsica, Claude Erignac, disrupted efforts to find a permanent resolution to Corsican grievances.

The books of Dorothy Carrington, particularly *Corsica: Portrait of a Granite Island* (John Day, 1974) and *The Dream-Hunters of Corsica* (Weidenfeld & Nicolson, 1995), offer well-researched and gracefully written overviews of Corsican history and the culture that undergird nationalist sentiment.

## ĆOSIĆ, DOBRICA

1921–, Serb author and intellectual, member of Serbian League of Communists Central Committee, 1965–1968; member of Serbian Academy of Arts and Sciences, 1977–; president of the Federal Republic of Yugoslavia (Serbia-Montenegro), June 1992–May 1993. Initially trained in agriculture, Ćosić became a member of a Communist group in Yugoslavia in 1938, and subsequently received political training. In World War II, Ćosić was active as a political commissar with the Communist partisans. During this period he also engaged in political writings.

After World War II, Ćosić remained active in the Yugoslav Communist Party. In the decade following the war, he forged close personal links to students in Belgrade who would later become influential in Serbian and Yugoslav society. Ćosić rose to prominence in Yugoslavia as the author of several controversial novels. These included *Daleko je sunce* (*Distant Is the Sun*, 1951), *Koreni* (*Roots*, 1954), and *Deobe* (*Divisions*, 1961). Increasingly, Ćosić began to challenge the official depiction of the partisans and the Serb royalist *Četnik* movement of World War II through an examination of struggles within Serbian society.

Public statements on politics made by Ćosić provoked a polemical confrontation between Ćosić and a Slovene intellectual, Dušan Pirjevec, in 1961 and 1962. The debate brought into question the postwar Communist slogans of socialist Yugoslavism and national unity, or *bratstvo i jedinstvo* (brotherhood and unity).

In the 1960s and 1970s, the subsequent writings and speeches of Ćosić, and the criticisms thereof, made more apparent a growing divide between Serb intellectuals on the one hand, and Slovene and Croat intellectuals on the other. In particular, Ćosić's assertion that Yugoslavism should transcend all other national identities in Yugoslavia provoked criticism that he was advocating a veiled form of Serbian nationalism at the expense of smaller nations and of the non-Serbian republics in Yugoslavia. Yet this criticism ignored Ćosić's belief that a Serbian-led centralism could only fail in Yugoslavia. In fact, Ćosić's thoughts reflected his perception of a fear of reawakening nationalism in Yugoslavia.

After the purge of Yugoslav Vice President Aleksandar Ranković, a Serb, in 1966, Ćosić was among those Serbs who grew increasingly critical of the Yugoslav League of Communists and the structure of the Yugoslav state. The purge of Ranković marked an attack by the Communists against centralizing pressures in the party leadership. Although the exact reasons behind Ranković's ouster remain obscure, Serbs felt that this attack was unjustified and was, by contrast, a manifestation of regional and even secessionist tendencies. Ćosić's statements during the 1960s and 1970s were often at the margin of what was politically acceptable to the Yugoslav League of Communists. Although Ćosić continued to write prolifically, he did not have ready access to the press. The marginalization of Ćosić was particularly evident in the period from the early 1970s to the death of Tito in 1980.

Recent scholarship has emphasized the gradual nature of Ćosić's growing disenchantment with Yugoslavism and his emergence as the leading intellectual Serb nationalist. The process stretched from the early 1960s to the mid-1980s, a period during which the League of Communists of Yugoslavia criticized Ćosić heavily. Nonetheless, the comparatively liberal political atmosphere in Yugoslavia allowed Ćosić openly and with increasing vigor to deplore the political climate that he felt restricted Serbdom and Serbian identity to Serbia proper. Ćosić felt that Serbdom was under siege everywhere in Yugoslavia, and that Serbs outside of Serbia proper were prevented from enjoying their own identity. During the 1970s, Ćosić also wrote his four-volume *Vreme smrti* (*Time of Death*). This massive work dealt with the catastrophic Serbian losses during the first two years of World War I, a process that Serb historians and intellectuals have called the "Golgotha" of the Serb nation.

In 1986, the Serbian Academy of Arts and Sciences published a memorandum in which Serbia was portrayed as the victim of the development of postwar Yugoslav politics and economics. Ćosić was widely suspected of being one of the main authors of the memorandum. Recent research has demonstrated that there is no evidence to support this allegation.

Ćosić continued to write numerous novels in the 1980s and 1990s. He also spoke publicly. His prominent intellectual role in Serbia since World War II earned him the accolade of "father of the Serb nation." His role in drawing attention to perceived wrongs against Serbia after World War II made him popular with many Serbs. Ćosić endorsed Slobodan Milošević at several points in the late 1980s. Ćosić stated that he admired Milošević for providing political expression for the frustration of the Serb people. Although the endorsement was not completely without reservations, it presented a huge boost to Milošević. Ćosić also had contacts to Radovan Karadžić, the leader of the Bosnian Serb nationalists. Ćosić stated publicly on several occasions in the late 1980s and early 1990s that the collapse of the Yugoslav state was inevitable.

The election of Ćosić as president of the Federal Republic of Yugoslavia in June 1992 was widely supported by the Serb public. In 1993 Ćosić sided with Yugoslav Prime Minister Milan Panić against Serb President Slobodan Milošević. Ćosić's increasing opposition to Milošević led to Ćosić's ouster in May 1993.

## COSMOPOLITANISM

*Cosmopolite* means basically "citizen of the world." It derives its meaning from the ancient Greek *kosmos,* world, and *politês,* citizen. The cosmopolitan individual is characterized by the ability to live equally in all countries, that is, the ability to "be at home in the world." With the advent of the Enlightenment in the 18th century, people started to use *cosmopolitanism* not only to refer to the disposition to live as a cosmopolitan person, but also to refer to the ability of enlarging one's horizons in order to integrate other, foreign perspectives. Cosmopolitanism became associated with a willingness to engage and become involved with otherness, an attraction toward the contrast rather than the same, and ultimately a concern for human kind as a whole.

The cosmopolitan person is thus worldly wise, made of diverse cultural influences and experiences, and open to the world. Similarly, the cosmopolitan city is made out of a multiplicity of peoples and cultures and blossoms at their crossroads. Contrary to multiculturalism, which implies the maintenance of a plurality of distinct cultural groups, cosmopolitanism entails an enlargement, a surpassing, a fusion of horizons. Therefore, the fact of having people from different cultures living in a city is not enough to make that city cosmopolitan, in the same way that visiting many countries does not make a person cosmopolitan. Cosmopolitanism arises out of the uniqueness engendered by the interpretation of cultures. The cosmopolite is not a free-floating individual, completely detached from all particularisms and thereby equally indifferent to all cultures, but rather a person rooted in and nurtured by several memories and histories. He does not aspire to a symbiosis with a supposed "world culture" but rather to the surpassing of *his* culture so as to leave the comfort of the known and identical and thereby put his anchoring points at risk. In this sense, cosmopolitanism is different from universalism. Although they both distrust enclosures and parochialism, the latter aims at the unity of humanity and is not concerned with diversity, while the former relies on diversity. Indeed, without otherness cosmopolitanism loses its *raison d'être.* Paradoxically, at the same time that it fosters crossings and mutual permeation, it needs the subsistence of difference. Thus, it is an ambition or project that cannot, by definition, ever be realized but at the expense of its own dissolution.

Cosmopolitanism has always aroused the suspicion of nationalists, because it favors the development of multiple attachments—"extranational" attachments—at the expense of the monopoly of loyalty demanded by the nation. This suspicion is exacerbated when nationalism is grounded in ethnicity: In addition to not being faithful enough to the nation-state, the cosmopolite jeopardizes the purity of the nation by integrating alien cultural references and preoccupations, and eventually a foreign universe. Moreover, because she had the opportunity to distance herself from her society and culture, the cosmopolite often takes a reflexive and critical stance toward the "national culture," then running the risk of becoming a "traitor" in the eyes of nationalists. Such a hostility can also be nourished by the fact that cosmopolitanism is generally the privilege of a minority, a minority often looked at with *ressentiment* by nationalists.

Nevertheless, in the case of independence movements, cosmopolitanism can be combined with nationalism, or at least with sovereignty, insofar as the creation of a nation-state is seen as a step toward other nations. Along this line of thought, in the same way that one has to learn one's history in order to understand the history of others, one has to create a *polis* so as to accede to the *cosmopolis.* Similarly, during the heydays of the Enlightenment, cosmopolitanism coexisted with patriotism. At the same time that English, French, and American leaders were building or consolidating their nations, they thought of themselves as embracing humanity. The nation was their vehicle, their ship, to reach the cosmopolis. In the same vein, many authors put forward the idea of a "rooted cosmopolitanism" and stress that being open to the world does not necessarily imply ignoring one's obligations as a citizen of a specific country. All the more since, as a vast number of people painfully experience everyday, individuals have political rights only as citizens of particular states. Therefore, the characterization "citizen of the world" must not be understood *stricto sensu*. We are very far from a world citizenship, and yet cosmopolitanism has existed for several centuries.

## COUGHLIN, CHARLES

1891–1971, Roman Catholic priest who was active as a radio commentator, born in Hamilton, Ontario, Canada. Coughlin served as pastor from 1926 to 1966 of the parish of the Shrine of the Little Flower in Royal Oak, Michigan, near Detroit. He began his radio career on Detroit station WJR in 1926. At first his broadcasts were based on his sermons and focused on religious issues, but he soon expanded to political and social commentary. His audience grew as the medium of radio itself expanded. By the mid-1930s his rich, mellow voice (described by the author Wallace Stegner as "a voice made for promises") was heard every Sunday afternoon by a national listenership estimated at more than one-half of the entire U.S. radio audience.

Coughlin was an early supporter of Franklin D. Roosevelt and once said that he was instrumental in Roosevelt's 1932 defeat of Herbert Hoover. However, Coughlin broke with Roosevelt in 1936 over the expansion of the New Deal. An attempt by Roosevelt to heal the breach was unsuccessful, and by the beginning of World War II Coughlin was perhaps the leading critic of FDR's presidency and in particular of interventionist policies such as lend-lease, not only through his radio broadcasts but also through his magazine *Social Justice*.

Coughlin's broadcasts in the early days of World War II, prior to U.S. entry, presented the standard America First view of the conflict as a purely European matter with no appropriate role for the United States. However, Coughlin went even further in his public statements than most isolationists by explicitly describing the conflict as a "Jewish war" in which the lives of American Christians should not be needlessly sacrificed for the benefit of "atheistic Jews who espouse communism."

After the Japanese attack on Pearl Harbor and the subsequent declaration of war by Germany against the United States, Coughlin's extreme isolationism went against the grain of American opinion. In 1942 *Social Justice* was banned for violations of the Espionage Act and Coughlin's church superiors censured him and removed his radio program from the airwaves.

Coughlin then remained largely in obscurity until his death, resurfacing briefly from time to time to express an opinion on issues such as the civil rights movement (which he opposed) and U.S. participation in the Vietnam War (which he favored).

The extent to which Father Coughlin is the symbolic parent of the present wave of populist-conservative radio talk shows (e.g., Rush Limbaugh) has been debated. The association of Coughlin with the current talk-show climate is made by critics of the genre, and denied by its supporters, because Coughlin's virulent anti-Semitism makes him an unsuitable model for any contemporary broadcaster.

A thorough recent biography of Coughlin is *Radio Priest*, by Donald Warren (The Free Press, 1996).

## CRAZY HORSE

1842–1877, Born along Rapid Creek near what is now Rapid City, South Dakota, Crazy Horse was a member of the Hunkpatila band of Oglala Lakota Sioux. Many Lakotas consider him the greatest of their leaders because of his uncompromising resistance to the advancement of white settlement in the Sioux country, and his courageous and masterful leadership in battles such as the so-called Fetterman Massacre in 1866 and the Battle of the Little Big Horn in 1876.

As a young man Crazy Horse was aware of the increasing conflict between the prowhite trading chiefs and the band leaders who feared and hated whites, which they saw as intruders. He was trained to become a warrior and got his name because of his reckless riding habits. He took an antiwhite stand as he realized the extent of U.S. deceit and corruption involved in the terms of the 1851 Fort Laramie Treaty and in the white conduct of trade with the Lakotas. In 1854 Crazy Horse had a vision of a guardian spirit that would make him invulnerable in the battle. This spirit gave him added prestige in a Lakota society where military achievements were highly valued. The Bozeman Trail, leading to the Montana gold fields through Sioux homeland, caused resentment among the Indians, who attacked the forts along the trail. Crazy Horse led the band that destroyed Captain William Fetterman's troops in northern Wyoming in December 1866. The new Fort Laramie Treaty in 1868 ended the warfare temporarily. Crazy Horse did not sign what proved to be a disastrous treaty for the Sioux, as most of their lands were ceded to the United States, and they were assigned to reservations.

The weak peace was shattered in 1874, when gold seekers entered the Black Hills in western South Dakota, a place sacred to the Sioux. The U.S. military protected the whites. The Sioux battled to drive the whites away and to keep enough of the plains country free for themselves and the buffalo on which they depended for survival. The blatant disregard and underestimation of the Sioux strength by Colonel G. A. Custer led to the battle at the Little Big Horn River on June 25, 1876. In this famous battle, Sioux troops led by Crazy Horse and Gall completely annihilated Custer's forces. After the fight, an embarrassed U.S. army relentlessly chased down Lakota military leaders, which forced a band led by Sitting Bull to escape to Canada. Crazy Horse was chased down in May 1877, and was killed by the army resisting imprisonment in September 1877.

Crazy Horse is a less well-known figure than for example Hunkpapa Lakota Sitting Bull or Oglala Lakota Red Cloud (from a different band than Crazy Horse), who were more accommodating to whites. However, he better signifies the Sioux patriotism in his refusal to accept the presence of white traders and military in Sioux homeland. His was a pursuit for lands free from reservation limitations, where the Sioux could live as they always had. He was a big inspiration for the American Indian Movement in the 1960s and 1970s. Crazy Horse on horseback is memorized as a massive sculpture on a Black Hills mountainside in South Dakota.

The most definitive and by far the best biography is Mari Sandoz, *Crazy Horse, the Strange Man of the Oglalas: A Biography* (Lincoln: University of Nebraska Press, 1992), a 50th-anniversary edition, which provides a Sioux perspective. Stephen Ambrose, *Crazy Horse and Custer: The Parallel Lives of Two American Warriors* (Garden City, N.Y.: Doubleday, 1975) has a conventional approach.

**CRNJANSKI, MILOŠ** 1893–1977, Serb diplomat, writer, and intellectual. Crnjanski received his education in Vienna, Rijeka (in present-day Croatia), Timişoara (Romania), and Belgrade. He specialized in the study of philosophy. During World War I, Crnjanski was a soldier in the Austro-Hungarian army. Crnjanski served in the Yugoslav diplomatic corps in the 1930s at posts in Berlin and Rome. Although originally an atheist, Crnjanksi propounded a particularly messianic form of Serbian nationalism during the 1930s. For Crnjanski, the Serbs represented the true faith and the true nation. The Croats and the Slovenes had betrayed the Pan-Slavic cause by joining the Catholic Church. Orthodoxy was the natural faith of all Slavs. Crnjanski fundamentally did not understand why the other South Slavic nationalities refused to perceive that it was in their "objective" interest to amalgamate with the Serb nation. Although Crnjanski regarded Russia as the natural leader of the Orthodox and Pan-Slavic world, he believed that Russia had forfeited its right to leadership due to the rise of Bolshevism. Therefore, Serbia should assume the leadership role among Slavs. During the 1920s and 1930s, Crnjanski also wrote extensively on contemporary political issues facing Yugoslavia. His writings were informed by Serbian nationalism and by strong anti-Communism.

Crnjanski saw a strong continuity in Serb history, beginning with the founding of the Serb Orthodox Church by St. Sava in the 13th century. In Crnjanski's writings, Serbdom appeared as a noumenon which possessed primordial purity and permanence. In his most famous work, *Seobe* (*Migrations*), this noumenon was described as an "endless blue circle." Thus, it could survive for several centuries even in the absence of a state or a church, as happened to a large extent during Ottoman rule. Serbdom was an "endless blue circle," an admittedly irrational and illogical force, but one that was perhaps more powerful than any other. The single, secular, and corporeal life of the individual was therefore itself senseless and vain.

**CROATIAN NATIONALISM**  Croatia was settled by the Slavic-speaking Croats in the 7th century A.D. An independent Croatian kingdom existed from circa 925 to 1102, when it was incorporated into the neighboring kingdom of Hungary. The loss of independence did not necessarily entail the loss of political and social privilege on the part of the Croatian nobility, which remained the bearer of Croatian state right thereafter. In 1527, a year after the battle of Mohacs, in which the Ottoman Turks destroyed much of the Hungarian political elite, the Croatian Estates elected the Habsburg ruler Ferdinand I as the kingdom's monarch. From that point to 1918 Croatia remained part of the Austrian Empire, though between 1868 and 1918 it was part of the Hungarian half of the dual monarchy.

Modern Croatian nationalism emerged in the early 19th century as a response to the political pressures exerted by Magyarization. Two factors have been of immense importance in shaping modern Croatian national identity and nationalism. The first is the concept of historical state right, the belief that the medieval Croatian state never completely lost its independence. The second is various forms of identity associated with other Slavs, especially the Southern Slavs. This was a reflection of the Croats' numerical inferiority vis-à-vis the Habsburg monarchy's ruling German and Magyar elites, the weaknesses arising from the division of the Croat lands, as well as the presence of a significant Serb minority within the Croat lands.

The first stage of Croatian nationalism is associated with the Illyrianist movement (1836–1848), which succeeded in laying the groundwork for a Croatian literary language. Its most important work was in the cultural sphere. In 1842 it formed *Matica Hrvatska* (Croat Literary-Cultural Foundation) to promote the Croatian language, and was also the first Croatian political movement to demand that Croatian ("Illyrian") be adopted as the country's official language. During the revolutions of 1848 the Illyrianists sought to achieve Croatian political autonomy within a federalized Habsburg monarchy.

Illyrianism spawned two Croatian political movements. The first was Ante Starčević's Party of (Croat State) Right, founded in 1861, which argued that Croatia's state right had never been abrogated, and that as such Croatia was an independent state. Starčević regarded the Croatian lands to be not only present-day Croatia, but also Bosnia-Herzegovina and Slovenia, and adopted a political definition of nationhood. All people in this Great Croatian state, whether Catholic, Muslim, or Orthodox Christian, were defined as Croats.

The other movement was Josip Juraj Strossmayer's Yugoslavism. Unlike the Party of Right, Strossmayer and his supporters were prepared to cooperate in politics and cultural life with the other Southern Slavs of the monarchy, the Serbs and Slovenes, in order to achieve the unification of the Croatian lands within a federalized monarchy. Both Starčević and Strossmayer had an important role in shaping Croatian identity, but their influence was limited largely to Croatia's intelligentsia.

Croatian nationalism only attained a mass following under the leadership of Stjepan Radić's Croatian People's Peasant Party, founded in 1904. Radić linked peasant social and economic emancipation to the Croatian national aspirations. His party was inconsequential in the Habsburg period of its existence (1904–1918) because of the highly restrictive electoral franchise in Croatia. With the creation in 1918 of the Kingdom of Serbs, Croats and Slovenes ("Yugoslavia") and the introduction of universal manhood suffrage, Radić's party became the only significant Croatian political party and the second largest in the whole country, which was confirmed in all elections of the 1920s.

As an opponent of Yugoslav unification—he feared the loss of Croatian national rights in a highly centralized state, dominated by the numerically larger Serbs—he was able to organize Croatia's peasant masses behind his party. Since 1918 Croatian nationalism has been defined in opposition to Belgrade, just as before 1918 it was defined by its opposition to Vienna or Budapest, or both.

Between Radić's assassination in 1928 and the outbreak of World War II in 1939, Croatian nationalism was defined above all by its struggle for some form of autonomy, even independence, from Belgrade. In 1939 autonomy was obtained in the form of the *Sporazum* (Agreement) between the Croat Peasant Party, now led by Vladko Maček, and the Belgrade authorities. The *Sporazum* provided Croatia with home rule; internal af-

fairs, economic, social, and cultural policy were autonomous, with defense, fiscal, and foreign policy remaining in Belgrade. The extreme wing of Croatian nationalism, represented by the exiled Ustaša movement of Ante Pavelić, demanded an independent Croatian state. In April 1941 Nazi Germany and fascist Italy attacked Yugoslavia and partitioned the country. Pavelić was installed as the leader of the so-called "Independent State of Croatia" (1941–1945), in reality an Italo-German creation, a regime that perpetrated numerous crimes against its minorities.

In 1945, with the creation of Tito's Communist Yugoslavia, Croatia became one of the six constituent Socialist republics of the country. Croatian nationalism, like the country's other nationalisms, was suppressed by the Communist authorities. Croatian nationalism had not disappeared, however, but simply lay dormant. During the late 1960s, renewed calls were heard in Croatia for greater autonomy for the republics, particularly in economic policy. This movement was suppressed in 1971–1972 by Josip Broz Tito's government as part of a wider campaign against reformist elements in all of Yugoslavia.

Until the late 1980s Croatian nationalism lay dormant. It was revived again mainly in response to the perceived threat posed by the Serbian leader Slobodan Milošević, who championed the cause of a strongly centralized Yugoslav federation. With the declaration of Croatian independence in June 1991 and the war in Croatia (1991–1995), which secured that independence, the aims of Croatian nationalists have seemingly been realized.

## CROMWELL, OLIVER

1599–1658, Unlike the War of the Roses, the English Civil War in the 1640s was not simply a fight over who should occupy the throne, but an ideological struggle to determine the very nature of English government and society. Oliver Cromwell had been born into a wealthy and influential family in Huntingdon, England. He studied in Cambridge although his father's death required him to terminate his studies before receiving a degree. First elected to Parliament in 1628, he became a Puritan in the 1630s. Puritans were Protestants who advocated the people's right to observe simpler modes of church organization and worship, but their religious convictions quickly became political. When a power struggle between Parliament and the king broke out, it sparked the civil war in 1642.

When the new parliamentary army was created in 1644, Cromwell became second in command although he had had no previous military experience. Nevertheless, he proved himself to be a military genius and brilliant cavalry leader. His soldiers, who reportedly entered battle singing religious hymns, were dubbed "the Ironsides" and never lost a battle. They defeated the king's forces at Naseby in 1645 and captured the monarch the following year.

When the victorious parliamentary forces split into Presbyterians, the majority who advocated sharing political power with the king, and Independents, Cromwell supported the latter when the two factions began fighting in 1648. He put down the revolt. His army removed the Presbyterians from parliament, abolished the House of Lords, and seized the king. Cromwell was a key figure in the trial and beheading of Charles I in 1649. This was the only English monarch to die for religious reasons and the last to be killed for political reasons. Englishmen continued to debate whether Charles was a martyr for the causes of royal stability and the Anglican Church or whether he deserved to die for opposing the representatives of the people.

England became a republic, the Commonwealth of England. As first chairman of the Council of State, Cromwell led successful military campaigns against Ireland and Scotland from 1649 to 1650. His troops' brutality and atrocities they perpetrated have never been forgotten in those two lands, which were brought under England's control. He also strengthened the English navy.

Cromwell had hoped to rule in a liberal and democratic way. But continued factionalism, the inability to enact major reforms, and the threatening anarchy in English society caused him to assume absolute power as lord protector in 1653. The commonwealth was ended and replaced by the protectorate. He demanded strict moral behavior, and he limited press and other freedoms. In 1667 Parliament offered him the title of king, but he declined. When Cromwell died in 1658, his son Richard replaced him as lord protector. But he was not a competent ruler and resigned in 1659. In 1660 Parliament restored the monarchy and offered the crown to Charles Stewart, the son of the dead king. Charles II returned from the continent to which he had escaped and was greeted by a joyful people.

**CULTURAL IDENTITY**  Cultural identity can be distinguished from ethnic identity, which implies the existence of a common ancestry, and from national identity, which requires the development of a national consciousness and of a nationalist movement. Cultural identity is not a by-product of blood ties, for blood does not convey any meaning in itself. Cultural identity is essentially a social construction that confers a particular meaning to the attributes of individuality, whether it is

gender, sexual orientation, professional occupation, political convictions, artistic taste, and so on. In this sense, it is a more comprehensive identity. However, it does not necessarily follow that cultural identity *appears* to people as being more important, or more "real" than other forms of identity. Actually, it tends to be more fluid and imponderable than many identies because it relies on neither a delimited territory nor on clear membership criteria such as citizenship or biological/physical features. This being said, its constructed and changeable character does not imply that it is an illusion or that it does not produce real social effects.

Cultural identity can be studied from both an objective and a subjective perspective. These perspectives are more complementary than mutually exclusive. The objective perspective requires the establishment of "objective" identification and membership criteria—such as language, religion, and customs—by an outside observer regardless of the importance individuals attach to them. From this perspective, individuals need not be conscious of their cultural identity. They are guided by internalized principles which they perceive as "natural" and self-evident. These principles, in turn, translate into a certain world view and set of routinized practices. The use of objective criteria allows for the boundaries defining a common or collective cultural identity to be drawn more easily. This is also partly the result of this perspective's need to delimit the object and unit of analysis so as to ensure that it remains "identical" despite changes of content. It thus tends to rely on finite categories rather than continuously changing forms.

The subjective perspective, on the other hand, looks at cultural identity from the standpoint of the involved individuals. Identity thus varies according to the feature individuals decide or happen, for contingent reasons, to emphasize. It is built and defined on the basis of a register of defining characteristics, the goal being to distinguish oneself from other cultural groups and identities. Identities are then constructed, adapted, and reconstructed depending on the situation encountered. They do not exist in isolation from the rest of the world or society. Therefore, the subjective perspective stresses the social process through which individuals become aware of their distinctive features. In this process, they realize that their understanding of the world is not "natural" but rather proper to them and to the group they now see themselves as belonging to. Becoming self-conscious of one's identity requires thus the encounter of otherness. Identity is constructed through a dialogue, possibly conflictive, with the "other." Even if conflictive, this relation can be useful for groups because it allows them to reassert their boundaries and their identity. In this sense, from the subjective perspective, identity can only be grasped within a "relationship to," that is, in a relational dynamic. Hence the importance of webs of relationships and social networks.

Nevertheless, one should not draw the conclusion that identity is constructed from scratch and that one can become whatever one wishes. Some initial "materials" of identity—ascribed characteristics such as, for example, gender or skin pigmentation—are given. What varies is their meaning and significance, thereby bringing about a relatively autonomous cultural identity. Moreover, despite individual variation, it is important not to overlook or downplay the existence of collective cultural identities defined by a common core of values and practices that allow for shared meanings and rules. The fact of being born in the midst of a particular collective cultural identity also influences the scale and nature of choices and possibilities available to us. Some boundaries are thus more difficult to cross than others.

Besides, one of the first objectives of emerging nationalist movements is often to define as much as possible these boundaries and argue that they can only be crossed at the expense of one's authenticity. Indeed, when developed along cultural principles, nationalist movements define the nation as the embodiment of the collective cultural identity—which then becomes the national identity—and of the most essential features of the individual selves that constitute it.

## CULTURAL NATIONALISM

While sometimes conflated with political nationalism, cultural nationalism is a distinct form of nationalism that seeks to celebrate, and glorify, the national culture of a community. An integral part of this national culture is, of course, the language of the community; it manifests itself in the poetry, folklore, myths, legends, epic stories, and music of a distinct linguistic and cultural group. More specifically, cultural nationalists are concerned with the cultural revitalization and moral regeneration of their nation, working through historic and cultural societies to elevate and rejuvenate the submerged moral purity of their nation's past.

The many differences between political and cultural nationalism help to bring more clearly into relief the exact nature of the latter. The major goal of most political nationalists is the creation of an independent state or some more modest form of political autonomy: one nation, one state. Their perception of the nation is usually framed in rational-legal terms; for them the nation is composed of a relatively homogeneous collectivity of educated citizens participating in the *polis*. Political nationalists tend to construct centralized organizations, such as political parties staffed by professional politicians and bureaucrats, to attain their goals.

Cultural nationalists, on the other hand, are less interested in a separate state per se, as much as they are in the protection and preservation of a distinct historical tradition. In a way, cultural nationalism is not constructed from above, as is sometimes the case with political nationalism, but is reanimated from below, often emanating from a grassroots base. As a result, the major work of this brand of nationalism is conducted by historicist intellectuals and academics who set up small-scale decentralized organizations such as historical, cultural, and language societies to study and develop the cultural heritage of the community. With the aid of the disciplines of philology, anthropology, archaeology, folklore, and topology (and in some instances from the genetic sciences), academics, intellectuals, and journalists take on themselves the task of fashioning and diffusing a unique cultural history and identity, from a nation's fragmented past. In many cases these groups are the basis for larger educational movements and cultural revivals that seek to promote a sense of pride in the distinctive cultural heritage of the nation.

Other than academics and intellectuals, artists and musicians often play a critical role in promoting the ideals of cultural nationalism. As Johann Gottfried Herder (1744–1803), one of the first theoreticians of cultural nationalism, once wrote: "a poet is a creator of a people; he gives it a world to contemplate, he holds its soul in his hand." Here one thinks of Jan Kollar, the epic poet of the Slavs, or Elias Lonnöt, the creator of the Finnish epic ballad *Kalevala* (1835), or even the Polish national poet Adam Mickiewicz, author of *The Books of the Polish Nation and of the Polish Pilgrimage* (1832). Such works reconstruct great myths and recount the heroic deeds of courageous ancestors, all in an attempt to instill dignity and pride in a nation's past. Composers like Richard Wagner (1813–1883) and Jean Sibelius (1865–1957) write musical scores and operas, extolling the virtues of the *patrie*, and its ancestors. "A national work of art," said the German social democrat Otto Bauer, "such as Wagner's *Meistersinger*, has a national influence, because it is a part of the nation's history and so teaches us to love the nation itself." Similarly, painters such as the Canadian "Group of Seven" come to shape a nation's consciousness with their depictions of expansive landscapes, instilling a sense of awe and wonder at the natural beauty of the national homeland.

Yet, for all their respective differences, there are instances where it is both theoretically and empirically difficult to disentangle cultural nationalism from political nationalism. The Irish cultural revival fostered by

George Petrie at the beginning of the 19th century, for example, dovetailed with, and at times was indistinguishable from, Daniel O'Connell's brand of political nationalism. The latter's long-term goal was the eventual restoration of an Irish parliament, for the former it was the revival of the ideals of a medieval, Christian Ireland. However, in practice, the various organizations representing these ideals and values often merged, thereby blurring the distinction between the two forms of nationalism.

Some students of nationalism argue that cultural nationalism precedes, and eventually manifests itself as, some form of political nationalism. For others, the eventual end of political nationalism (i.e., a bureaucratic state structure) is a necessary precondition for the attainment of the goals of cultural nationalism. They argue further that the state provides an important instrument with which to enact cultural policies that in turn foster and protect national cultural institutions. Either way, there is a symbiotic relationship between cultural and political nationalism.

John Hutchinson's books, *The Dynamism of Cultural Nationalism* (London, 1987) and *Modern Nationalism* (1993), provide an excellent overview of cultural nationalism. See also Philip E. Rawkins, "Nationalist Movements within the Advanced National State: The Significance of Culture," in *The Canadian Review of Studies of Nationalism* (Fall 1983).

## CYPRIOT NATIONALISM
The island of Cyprus belonged to the Turkish empire from 1571 to 1914. At the onset of World War I, it was taken over by Britain, which protected it since 1878 in accordance with the Cyprus Convention. In 1925 it became a crown colony, but the majority of Greeks on the island demanded a union called *enosis* with Greece. These demands became violent after World War II. In 1960 Turkey, Greece, and Britain agreed to create an independent Cypriot Republic in 1960. The leader of the *enosis* movement, Archbishop Makarios, became president. However, continued violence between Greeks and Turks on the island prompted the United Nations to send peacekeeping forces in 1964.

A failed coup attempt by Greek officers, which forced Makarios to leave the island, provoked Turkey to send its troops to occupy the northern part of the island. All Greeks north of the "green line" were expelled. Even though they will not leave NATO, many Greeks continue to ask: "What good is NATO to us if it cannot prevent the Turks from invading Cyprus or from threatening Greek interests in the Aegean?" At the beginning of the 21st century more than 30,000 Turkish troops still occupy 37 percent of the island although the Turkish minority comprises only 18 percent of the population.

Greece suffered a shocking setback in 1983 when Turkish Cypriots declared an independent "Republic of Northern Cyprus," thereby undercutting UN efforts to find a solution to that conflict. Turkey is the only country in the world to recognize the new republic, while all other nations recognize the Greek-dominated Cypriot government. By the beginning of the 21th century, 1200 UN peacekeepers still patrolled the line that divides the two communities. The Greeks suspect that the Turks might try to seize other Greek islands lying close to the Turkish coast, such as Rhodes.

Such fears may seem ridiculous to the non-Greek. But Greeks are quick to point out that the Turks maintain a 125,000-person Army of the Aegean equipped with 110 landing craft on their southwestern coast, that Turkish politicians have sometimes in the past refused to recognize that the Aegean islands are Greek, and that the Turks actually demonstrated in Cyprus that they are willing to use military means to back up their aspirations in the area. In 1996 U.S. diplomatic intervention was required to defuse a crisis over Turkish occupation of an uninhabited Greek island. Greeks conveniently forget that the Greek majority in Cyprus, particularly under Archbishop Makarios (who returned as president of the Greek part in 1975 but died two years later), sometimes abused the Turkish minority Cypriots.

Greece's position remains unchanged: that Turkish troops and settlers must be withdrawn, and effective guarantees must be given to a Cypriot Republic. In 1997 the EU decided to consider Cyprus's application for membership, but it rejected Turkey's three-decade-old application. Greece rejected any linkage between Greek Cypriot EU entry and a final settlement of the island's division and threatened to veto further EU expansion if such a linkage were made. The EU accepted Greece's position. Turkey strongly objects to any arrangement whereby a Greek Cypriot government might be admitted to the EU, while Turkish Cypriots and Turkey itself are left out. The EU's offer of membership to Greek Cypriots sharpens the divisions on the island. There is no imminent settlement of the thorny issue of Cyprus's division, especially since the 1998 reelection of Glafcos Clerides as Greek Cypriot president. Despite their political differences, Clerides and the leader of Turkish-Cyprus, Rauf Denktash, have been friends since their school days. But this has done little to lessen tensions.

Clerides spurned UN talks on Cyprus and called for firmer support port from Athens. To strengthen his hand, he won Russian agreement to provide 300 sophisticated surface-to-air missles. The Turks said they would destroy them the moment they arrived. Also, a 1993 defense pact with Greece permits continued construction of a military air base at Paphos that could accommodate Greek F-16s deployed there in time of crisis. One American official noted that "these are acid concerns for Turkey—Greek jets and Russian missiles on Cyprus." To prevent military conflict, an American diplomatic mission in 1997 got Clerides to postpone receipt of Greek F-16s. Clerides also announced that the Russian missiles would not be deployed on Cyprus. Instead they were deployed in 1999 on the Greek island of Crete, placing Turkey well outside of the missiles' ninety-mile range.

It will be a long time before four excitable forms of nationalism—Greek mainland, Greek Cypriot, Turkish, and Turkish Cypriot—will cease clashing on and around this beautiful Mediterranean island.

**CZECH NATIONALISM**   The history learned from nation builders and the history of a nation are two distinct yet overlapping narratives. The modern Czech nation and Czech nationalism were born of the late 18th-century space afforded by the Enlightenment-inspired Habsburg policies of Empress Maria-Theresa (1740–1780) and her son Joseph II (1780–1790), codified in the 19th century by Fichte's students of romanticism, and politicized at the close of the 19th century. But the materials for the birth of a nation lay in the imaginations of poets and the minds of scholars who would draw on and claim for themselves a much older history.

Certainly the most influential of the early Czech historians was František Palacký (1798–1876) who, as "Father of the Nation," gave first expression to a linear history of the Czech people defined specifically by Czech–German relations. Significantly, his story imparted to the Czech people a unique culture imbued with the moral elements of Kantian rights-based claims in a teleology of national struggle beginning with the 15th-century Hussite rebellion and culminating in the 19th-century struggle against the Habsburgs. Yet ironically, at least from today's vantage, he published his *History of the Czech Nation in Bohemia and Moravia* not in Czech, but in German. Indicative of the status of literary Czech, most of the original nation-building texts from the first half of the 19th century, whether philological or historical, were written in German, since at the time, literate Czechs, scholars and readers alike, had a far better command of German than Czech.

Most historians of the Czech people have examined the medieval history of the Great Moravian Empire and the early Bohemian Crown in their quest to deepen the roots of the Czech nation. Nearly all agree that the Czech people had their first great mark of distinction with the Hussite Rebellion, and not without reason. In the 14th century Charles IV assumed the throne of the Holy Roman Empire, making Prague the center not only of his empire, but of Central Europe. One of his most significant acts was to establish the first university east of the Rhine. It is in this university that Jan Hus (1369–1415), an advocate of Wyclif's ideas and rector of the University of Prague, allegedly championed the rights of Czechs against the increasingly dominant Germans. There is little doubt that he advocated the interests of Bohemians, and especially of Bohemia's Slavs. Hus augmented Bohemian influence at Prague's university, and as a result also managed to shift the balance of religious power in Prague to the advocates of religious reform. Whether he did so on behalf of Czechs, Bohemians, or religious radicals remains unclear. Nevertheless, the consequences of his mobilization were profound for all concerned. A victory for Czech national development, Hus's legacy was a travesty for Charles University, which lost most of its prized scholars and students to a host of new institutions established to accommodate those fleeing the Prague heresy. It also ended badly for Hus himself who was sentenced to death by the Council of Constance and burned at the stake on July 6, 1415, for his various heresies. His martyrdom fostered a devastating war (1420–1436) from which the Bohemian Czechs won unprecedented ecclesiastical autonomy from Rome including the right to conduct services in Czech. Nearly 100 years later, Martin Luther would declare himself a Hussite as he launched the Protestant Reformation. However, this triumph came at a terrible price as Prague and Bohemia would languish in a state of near economic and political ruin, never again to achieve the status and power it had realized under Charles IV.

Whereas the Hussite Rebellion was used to mark the genesis of the modern Czech nation, the 1620 defeat of the Hussite Behemians at the battle of White Mountain became the "Czech national tragedy." Famous for having triggered the thirty-years war, the so-called "defenestration of Prague" in 1618 was a challenge to the authority of the Habsburgs by the largely Protestant Bohemian Estates who had decided to cast their lot with a Calvinist German Prince rather than the Catholic Habsburgs. The Habsburg representatives thrown from the window in the Prague castle returned to Vienna to report his conspiracy. Vienna responded with swift retribution in the name of Roman Catholicism. The thirty-years war drew in most of the great European powers, dividing them along confessional lines until the French intervened, having realized the expansionist aims of the Habsburgs. While Habsburg defeat led to the separation of the Spanish and Austrian regions, Bohemia's subjugation by the Austrian Habsburgs stood unchallenged.

Hans Kohn, in a sly attack on Palacký's nationalist teleology, argues that the Habsburg defeat of the Bohemian Crown (held by a German at the time) halted the deluge of German Lutherans into Bohemia, hence actually saving the Czech culture from certain assimilation. But this "defense of Czech culture" came at a tremendous price as the Habsburgs wiped out Bohemia's merchant cities and reestablished the great landed seats of the Bohemian nobility in the hands of mercenaries and foreigners, most of them indifferent to everything but the labor of the indigenous Czech and German Bohemians.

For the next century the Czech language lived on only as a peasant vernacular. German, French, and Latin prevailed as the languages of commerce, the aristocracy, and the Church, respectively. However, in 1740 Empress Maria-Theresa assumed the Habsburg throne and implemented an aggressive policy of political centralization. In 1749 she abolished the separate Czech and Austrian court chancelleries, and later imposed German as the official language of the imperial administration. But it must be understood that this was not part of a general policy of nation building. Despite the push to germanize the administration, provincial administrators were expected to have command of the local vernacular. Hence Czech actually became an official language of instruction in the 18th century at not only the Military Academy in Vienna, but also the Vienna Polytechnic and Vienna University. Vienna's purely political aims were equally apparent with Emperor Joseph II (1780–1790) who not only continued his mother's practice of promoting elementary education in the vernacular, but also dismantled some of the more repressive feudal economic practices of the time with his emancipation of the serfs, and challenged the position of the Church with the Toleration Pact of 1781. The hope had been to further weaken the aristocracy by challenging their economic autonomy and their control over the peasantry.

In fact, during Joseph's short reign, more Czech textbooks were published than in the preceding 150 years. Of the many expressions of the new literary Czech receiving competing aristocratic and court sponsorship at the outset of the 19th century, Josef Jungman's (1773–1847) work proved the most lasting. He not only rooted his version in an appealing romantic nationalist ideology, but institutionally linked it to František Palacký's new Czech history through the leading Czech cultural society of the time, *Matice česká,* and Jungman's own schools.

The first hint of a politicized Czech national expression came in the wake of the news of the 1848 revolution in France. Cultural societies throughout the empire became the institutional bases for political revolution as self-professed national spokesmen, not just Czechs, demanded political autonomy and cultural rights. In fact, the Czechs made only the weakest of showing in comparison to the far better organized and integrated German and Hungarian nationalists. Nevertheless, Prussia's rejection of Habsburg Pan-Germanism and Russia's defeat of the very real Hungarian challenge suggested that the time was not ripe for the breakup of the empire.

Industrialization and public education in the vernacular would prove the major allies of Czech nationalists. The industrialization of Bohemia not only reconfigured the urban landscape, but also the ethnic composition of its cities as Czechs flowed in from the countryside to man the new factories. Homogenization of the Czechs into a common Czech culture and language was facilitated by the imperial school system which in a matter of 100 years lifted Bohemian literacy from 20 to 95 percent. By the 1860s, twelve high schools offered instruction in Czech, and students at Charles University could take many of their classes in Czech. By the 1890s, the Czech University had nearly as many faculty as Prague's German University. In fact, the future founder of Czechoslovakia, T. G. Masaryk, began his career at the Czech University where he formulated a number of the principles on which the new Czechoslovak state would be founded.

This new public educated in the Czech language created a growing demand for Czech and Slavic culture. Czech theaters and public buildings were erected, and Czech music and theater commissioned to satisfy and reinforce the increasingly sophisticated national awareness of the Czech public and their fascination with all things Slav.

Political participation in the Vienna Parliament and the Bohemian Diet would also offer Czechs opportunities for national expression through political party formation whether on behalf of an autonomous Bohemia, unity with the Slovaks, or membership in a greater pan-Slav federation. A generation of Czech nationalists emerged in the 1870s, taking advantage of the growing number of political cleavages in the empire to offer their support to the imperial govenment in exchange for cultural concessions, including the recognition of Czech on par with German in the Bohemian administration. However, the still dominant Bohemian German minority defended their prerogatives with a virulent German nationalism, overturning many of the concessions won by the Czechs.

Czech nationalism never attained the feverish pitch of Hungarian, Serbian, and German nationalism—each in its own turn contributing to the downfall of the Habsburg Empire. The legacy of these more virulent nationalisms was a democratic Czechoslovak First Republic, created by the allies to punish and contain German and Hungarian nationalism. Hence, beginning in 1918, the Czech people embarked on a new century of national self-discovery.

As a starting point for further research on the Czech nation and Czech nationalism, consult Derek Sayer's *The Coasts of Bohemia* published in 1998 by Princeton University Press. For an excellent overview of the Czechs under the Habsburgs, consult Robert Kann and Zdenek David's *The Peoples of the Eastern Habsburg Lands, 1526-1918* published by University of Washington in 1984. For a detailed discussion of the Hussites, consult Howard Kaminsky's 1967 book, *A History of the Hussite Revolution*, published by University of California Press.

## CZECH NATIONALISM, POST-1918

On August 26, 1992, the leading Czech and Slovak political parties met in the city of Brno to plan the offical breakup of Czechoslovakia, which on New Year's Day 1993 would give the Czechs a nation-state for the first time in their history. This final conflict between Czechs and Slovaks completed Bohemia's (the historic land of the Czech people) long evolution from one of Europe's most multiethnic historic kingdoms to a nearly homogeneous Czech nation-state. Bohemia's most radical and rapid national transformation occurred during its manifestation as the political center of Czechoslovakia (1918–1939, 1945–1993). During this time the Czech people experimented with a variety of national manifestations, each dictated by the political imperatives of the day. At the outset of the 20th century, pan-Slavism had captured the imaginations of Bohemian Slavs yearning for political autonomy. But with the fall of the Habsburg empire and the Russian revolution, Czechoslovak nationalists took up the banner, advocating the idea of a Czechoslovak nation that would unite the Slovaks of Northern Hungary with the Czechs of Bohemia and the Moravians of Moravia into a single cultural nation. This new Czechoslovak nation was to preside over a territory composed of Germans, Hungarians, Poles, Romanys (Gypsies), Ruthenians, and Jews—the polyglot legacy of the Habsburg Empire.

This new Czechoslovakia emerged from the ashes of the Habsburg empire, fragmented in 1918 by Allied retribution and Wilson's principle of self-determination. To prevent future aggression, the Allied powers created a new Czechoslovak democracy between Austria and Germany with the hope of containing future German nationalist aggression. Remarkably, not ten years earlier, few Czechs so much as dreamed of a sovereign state for themselves. Yet for the duration of the war, the future Czechoslovak presidents, T. G. Masaryk and Edvard Beneš, struggled to convince the Allied powers that Czechoslovakia was not only a viable political unit, but a legitimate one. It would be imprudent to suggest that Masaryk and Beneš were themselves responsible for the creation of Czechoslovakia, largely a product of international diplomacy. Nevertheless their war-time efforts did position them to assume a central role in giving form to the new state.

To this end, Masaryk synthesized both a historic justification for the new state, by underscoring the medieval importance of the Bohemian Crown, and an ethnic imperative for the Czechoslovak nation, which was the "reunification" of the Czechs and Slovaks. Masaryk also used Palacký's history of the Czech Hussite "democratic" struggle against Roman Catholicism and German oppression to emphasize the essential democratic nature of the Czechoslovak nation. This not only reassured the international community of the importance of supporting Masaryk's Czechoslovakia, but also served as useful national teleology with which to mobilize the Czech people to fight for a new democratic government. Never mind that during the war Masaryk himself had seriously contemplated a monarchy for the Czech people with a Romanov on the throne.

Despite its national pretensions, Masaryk's new Czechoslovakia was anything but a nation-state. In 1921, it counted 6.4 million Czechs, 2 million Slovaks, 3.1 million Germans, $3/4$ million Hungarians, and nearly $1/2$ million Ukrainians. Hence, of the total population of 13.4 million, Czechs accounted for 47.8 percent of the population, or less than a majority. Fearing the obstructionist potential of the 3 million ethnic Germans in Bohemia, Masaryk understood the importance of promoting Czechoslovak nationalism, but was overly confident that the cultural proximity and fragmentation of the Slovaks, the former Slavs of Northern Hungary, would make them unconditional allies to the Czech cause.

To ensure their much needed support, Masaryk and the advocates of the new Czechoslovak nationalism undertook the enormous project of expunging 50 years of Hungarian nation building, and a 1000-year history of Magyar rule. The Czechs encouraged an invigorated postarmistice Allied assault on the last vestiges of the

Hungarian army still struggling to hold on to Slovakia, and then implemented an aggressive policy of de-Magyarization. Slovak was officially placed on par with Czech as one of the two official expressions of the Czechoslovak language, and "cooperative" Slovaks were invited from their still war-torn province to Prague to participate in the drafting of a new constitution.

While the new Czechoslovak national idea liberated the Slovak people from Magyarization, it failed to guarantee the Czechs an unconditional domestic political ally. Certainly, many, if not most, Slovaks did not oppose the Czechoslovak idea and would come to find it preferable to a more explicit minority status in Hungary. However, victims of Prague's aggressive secularization and democratization found in exclusively Slovak national idea a useful basis for political mobilization.

Using its organizational advantage, the Catholic Church in Slovakia, under the leadership of Monsignor Andrej Hlinka (1864–1938), promoted a new Slovak nationalism, giving it a distinctly antimodern, anti-progressive, antisecular, antisocialist, and even anti-democratic hue. Throughout the Czechoslovak First Republic (1918–1939), it was able to mobilize a growing number of the discontented to its generally ambiguous "autonomy" platform. While it never won real political autonomy under the auspices of a democratic "Czecho-Slovak" Republic, it did successfully stave off assimilation, aggravated Czech–German tensions, and articulated a political alternative to Czechoslovak democracy.

From the outset of the republic, the German minority was also divided in its support for the new Czechoslovakia. The reversal of the prewar language requirements certainly proved a serious source of opposition from the German minority, which objected to having to learn Czech in order to keep their jobs in the government bureaucracy. Nevertheless by 1926, the two main German parties abandoned their opposition status, agreeing to enter into a Czechoslovak government.

However, the Depression proved a major setback for the Czechoslovak cause. Especially vulnerable to the economic crisis, the German minority suffered a disproportionate level of unemployment. Anti-Czech political mobilization became an increasingly successful political platform for Sudeten politicans, who found they could win not only votes, but also financial backing from Hitler's Germany. Konrad Henlein's Sudeten German Party took only two years to rise to power, winning 60 percent of Czechoslovakia's German votes in the 1935 elections. Despite various efforts to crack down on the Nazi-backed German parties, Prague finally broke down in

1937 and offered to meet virtually all of the Sudeten demands. This caught both the Sudeten Germans and Hitler by surprise. On March 28, 1938, Hitler and Henlein strategized the plan that would become the cornerstone of the Munich Agreement, namely, the dismemberment of Czechoslovakia according to Wilson's principle of national self-determination.

While the Czechoslovak government had secured for itself one of the most powerful militaries in Europe, its domestic political institutions—designed at least in theory to secure minority representation rather than to facilitate unitary response to international crisis—proved ill equipped to handle the threat. Hitler's offer of assistance to Czechoslovakia's aggrieved minorities further weakened the integrity of the government. Whatever will the Beneš government may have still had was broken by the Munich betrayal of Allied military commitments to Czechoslovakia on September 29, 1938.

The occupation of the Sudeten region by the Reich's troops opened up the possibility for further challenges to the integrity of Czechoslovakia. Slovak nationalists seized on this instability to secure Hitler's support for their own challenge to Prague's authority. The ensuing crisis between Prague and Slovakia afforded Hitler the opportunity he needed to take over the rest of Czechoslovakia. On October 6, 1938, in exchange for its role in the final dismemberment of Czechoslovakia, Slovakia was offered political autonomy for the first time in its history under a Nazi allied clerical government. In Bohemia, Nazi "protection" killed 78,154 of Bohemia's 118,310 Jews. The Czech government in exile, frustrated by the relative lack of resistance to Nazi rule, ordered the assassination of Reinhard Heydrich. The Nazis retaliated by having 1381 Czechs executed.

Following the war, the Slovaks were forced back into a union with the Czechs. The first step taken by the Czech government was the expulsion of the Sudeten German minority for its betrayal of Czechoslovakia. Of these, anywhere between 50,000 and 250,000 are said to have died as a direct or indirect consequence of Czechoslovakia's ethnic cleansing. With the loss of Ruthenia, Czechoslovakia now had to contend with only two major ethnic groups and a further diminished Magyar minority. Following the 1948 descent into the Soviet sphere of influence, the Communist Party sought to use economic policy as a means of securing a more powerful union between the Czech and Slovak people. However, economic development failed to weaken the will for self-rule, which expressed itself during the de-Stalinization of the Soviet bloc in the 1960s. Whereas the Czechs protested on behalf of freedom of self-expression and "democracy with a human face," the Slovaks called for autonomy within a Czechoslovak federation. Their demands, unlike those of the Czechs, were not interrupted by the Warsaw Pact invasion on August 20, 1968. The ensuing decentralization of Czechoslovak political institutions did little to promote the cause of Czechoslovak nation building, as some had hoped. Instead, by restructuring the channels of authority along national lines, while preserving a centralized policy-making apparatus, grievances could not be articulated but never satisfied. The new democratic Czechoslovakia inherited a political cleavage between Czechs and Slovaks, still aggravated by the structures of mobilization but no longer forcibly contained by Communism.

The fall of Communism in Czechoslovakia was a relatively non-nationalist affair. Lagging behind the transitions in Poland and Hungary, Czechoslovakia's "velvet revolution" nevertheless surged to the forefront of the Western imagination under the leadership of Václav Havel, the former dissident intellectual, and the decidedly non-nationalist slogan "Back into Europe!" However, the realities of democratic and economic transition dampened the optimistic aspirations of the original revolutionaries, with the Slovak Vladimir Meciar shifting the debate toward increasingly nationalist terms.

A major Slovak critique of the Prague government, a reminder of earlier tensions, centered on the alleged unsuitability of Czechoslovak economic reforms to Slovakia. The Czechs, and the economist Václav Klaus in particular, favored the centralization of economic policy in Prague, while the Slovaks, including Meciar, wanted Bratislava to determine the direction of Slovakia's economy. While at the outset of the debate neither side advocated the actual complete separation of their two nations, their inability to come to a mutually agreeable institutional arrangement for the new Czechoslovakia drove both sides to consider going it alone. One of the most reliable public polls, conducted in August 1991, revealed that of Czechs, only 8 percent favored a split, and of the Slovaks, 16 percent. Nevertheless, the political stalemate convened the leading Czech and Slovak representatives in Brno on August 26, 1992, to draft the dissolution of Czechoslovakia set for New Year's Day 1993.

Normalization of politics in the new Czech Republic has proven remarkably smooth. Nevertheless, the recent attacks on the Romany minority and a resurgence of Czech–German tensions over the expulsion of the Sudeten Germans suggest that the Czechs will have plenty of opportunities to reconsider their history and identity in their quest for inclusion in the European Union.

As a starting point for further research on the Czech nation and Czech nationalism, consult Derek Sayer's *The Coasts of Bohemia* published in 1998 by Princeton University Press. For a less cultural and more political approach, examine anything written by Carol Skalnik Leff, but in particular her *National Conflict in Czechoslovakia*, also published by Princeton. Another interesting source, with contributions by Central European authors, has been edited by Jiří Musil and titled *The End of Czechoslovakia*. It was published by the Central European Press in 1995.

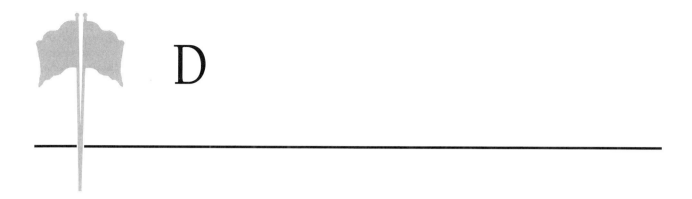

# D

**DALAI LAMA (XIV)** 1935–, Religious and political leader of Tibet now living in exile in northern India, and winner of 1989 Nobel Peace Prize for his role in promoting nonviolent resistance against Chinese rule in Tibet. "Dalai Lama" is a Mongolian word for "Ocean of Wisdom," and is considered a manifestation of the Buddha of Compassion. The given name of the XIV Dalai Lama was Lhamo Thondup; it was later changed to Tenzin Gyatso.

Born to a poor peasant family in Qijiachuan ("Taytser" in Tibetan) in China's Qinghai province, he was chosen at the age of 2 as the reincarnation of the XIII Dalai Lama, a Tibetan Buddhist ritual first established in the 15th century. At the age of sixteen, he assumed the role of a political leader to deal with the challenging task of maintaining Tibet's independence, a status that was self-proclaimed by the 13th Dalai Lama in 1913 in the wake of the nationalist revolution in China. When the Chinese Communists seized power in 1949, they immediately reasserted China's traditional claim of sovereignty over Tibet. After a failed military resistance, the Tibetan government headed by Dalai Lama signed a peace agreement with China in 1951, in which Tibet was given autonomous status.

In 1959, a major Tibetan uprising erupted in Lhasa, but was soon suppressed by the Chinese military. Dalai Lama fled to India, and established a Tibetan government in exile in Dharamsala. His effort to regain Tibetan control over Tibet has attracted worldwide attention and sympathy. His self-made image as a simple, compassionate Buddhist monk has made him a symbol of Tibetan nationalism. In recent years, Dalai Lama has maintained unofficial dialogues with the leaders of the People's Republic of China to seek a peaceful solution to the future status of Tibet. He has indicated his willingness to give up the call for independence in exchange for a high degree of autonomy for Tibet. But the lack of mutual trust between the two sides has rendered no progress so far.

He has many publications. Two of them are his autobiographies: *My Land and My People* (Potala Corp., 1983) and *Freedom in Exile: The Autobiography of the Dalai Lama* (San Francisco: Harper, 1991). A good biography is *The World of the Dalai Lama: An Inside Look at His Life, His People, and His Vision* by Gill Farrer-Halls (Theosophical Publishing House, 1998).

**DANISH NATIONALISM** Denmark is a constitutional monarchy that has been an independent and unified country since the Middle Ages. It was the dominant Scandinavian power from the mid-12th century. The early importance of Denmark in the region was symbolically recognized by the Union of Kalmar treaty of 1397, in which the Danish king, Erik of Pommern, assumed the triple crown of the Scandinavian monarchies. Erik was only seventeen at this time, and power was actually centered in the hands of his great-aunt Margrethe I, who was also the wife of the last Norwegian king and mother of the last Danish king. The Kalmer union broke down several times during the next 200 years and Sweden finally ended their union in 1523, but Norway—along with its hereditary provinces of Iceland, the Faroe Islands, and Greenland—remained part of the Danish kingdom until Norway was lost to Sweden in 1814 after the Napoleonic wars. By the 18th century, Denmark ruled over a large, but scattered empire, including the duchies of Schleswig and Holstein and possessions in India, Africa, and the Caribbean, in addition to the Scandinavian territories. After Sweden's break with Denmark in 1523, the two nations competed for power within the region, fighting eight major wars between 1563 and 1721, resulting in the Danish loss of Scania (Skåne—the southern portion of Sweden) in 1658.

The notion of a Danish national identity has frequently been constructed against the perceived threat of German cultural and political domination. This feeling was strengthened after the 1770s, when a German physician, Struensee, gained control over the government during the reign of an insane king, Christian VII. Although the monarchy was restored and Struensee executed, the notion of the dangers of German influence in Danish political and cultural life had lasting impact. One of the political moments when this concept of "Danishness" emerged was during the conflict over the duchies of Schleswig and Holstein. Holstein was German speaking, whereas Danish was the majority language in Schleswig. In the early 19th century, both duchies had been incorporated into the Danish kingdom, but a German separatist element argued that the two territories were joined and both properly belonged to the German Federation. The "Schleswig-Holsteinists," despite having the historical evidence of the Treaty of Ribe on their side, were overruled in 1846 by Christian VIII's declaration that Holstein must conform with other parts of the monarchy. Following the abolishment of the absolute monarchy in 1848, three years of civil war broke out in the duchies. The unrest was suppressed, but the German-speaking population remained hostile to Danish rule until they were lost to Austria and Prussia in the war of 1864. After this time, considerable anti-German feeling developed in Denmark. The need to strengthen the sense of "Danishness" from within the remaining parts of the kingdom, as a counter against further losses to the south, was an immediate concern after 1864. The rhetoric of this conflict was of course revived during the Nazi occupation of Denmark, when the Danish spirit was represented by a legendary figure, Holger Danske, who was supposed to arise to fight the enemies of Denmark. In the opera by Jens Baggesen (1746–1826), Holger Danske confronts German invaders. Ironically, the libretto for the opera was borrowed from a German poet, Christoph Martin Wieland, and many of the people involved in the production were in fact German immigrants.

The cultural creation of identity for Denmark during the 19th century was carried out to a high degree by patriotic newspapers, hymns, clubs, and in the folk high school movement. The folk high school movement was the creation of a theologian, N. F. S. Grundtvig (1783–1872), who envisioned these courses as the means to promote Danish identity. The courses, which last three or four months and emphasize music, art, Danish history, and literature, are still a prominent feature of Danish cultural life. The philosophical orientation of Grundtvig's philosophy is based on the ideal of education for everyday life rather than book knowledge. However, Grundtvig's own conception of Danish national identity was based largely on his study of old Nordic myths, including the stories of Danish kings in *Saxo Grammaticus* and the *Prose Edda* of the medieval Icelandic poet Snorri Sturluson. These national myths also provided sources of inspiration for poets such as Adam Oehlenschläger and saga scholars and philologists like Thomas Bartholin and Arni Magnússon, who was responsible for collecting and cataloging the saga manuscripts in Iceland in the early 18th century. Interest in Danish folk culture was also expressed in the folktale collections of Evald Tang Kristiansen and by the music of Niels Gade, who composed pieces based on Danish folk songs with Nordic themes. Patriotic literature also advanced the notion of a tradition of Danish heroism reaching back into the medieval past. Ove Malling's *Great and Good Deeds of the Danes, Norwegians, and Slesvig-Holsteiners*, one of the most well-known examples of the genre, is a collection of stories, many from the medieval period, about Danes (including all the members of the joint Dano-Norwegian kingdom) who exemplified moral virtues such as courage or fidelity.

As Denmark lost its former possessions and declined as a major European power in the 19th and 20th centuries, a sense of pride in Denmark's position as a small country began to dominate Danish political life. According to this view, Denmark's position as a minor country protected Danes from the cultural threats posed by modernity and materialism. Danish culture made a virtue out of its own smallness, sense of security, and comfort, themes that still occupy important positions in the Danish worldview. Today, the Danes are among the strongest skeptics of the European Union. The initial vote in 1992 was a narrow rejection, and the subsequent approvals have been strongly contested. In this respect, Denmark retains its sense of national identity and moves only reluctantly toward a postnationalist consciousness.

**DARÍO, RUBÉN**   1867–1916, Born in Metapa, Nicaragua, which was later renamed Ciudad Darío. At 14 years of age he joined the editorial staff of the local daily. In 1883 he traveled to El Salvador, and on his return to Nicaragua in 1884, he worked as a reporter and spent many hours reading at the Biblioteca Nacional. In 1886 he moved to Chile and became an avid reader of French poetry, especially the Parnassians, which is the most notable influence in his *Azul,* one of his most renowned collections of short tales and verse.

Darío returned to Central America in 1889 and worked steadily on his poetry and newspaper articles. In 1890 he married Rafaela Contreras. In 1892 he was appointed secretary of Nicaragua's delegation to Spain's celebration of the fourth centennial of Columbus's voyage of discovery. After his wife's death, he was named Colombias's representative to Buenos Aires. In Paris he met Théodore de Banville, Paul Verlaine, and later, in New York, José Martí. Throughout his stay in Argentina he discharged his consular duties and also managed to write for *La Nación* and others journals, becoming the leader of a group of young and brilliant writers. With one of them, Ricardo Jaime Freyre (from Bolivia), he founded the literary journal *Revista de América*.

At the same time Darío published *Los raros* and *Prosas profanas*. He was recognized as the leader of the Modernist movement. In his work *Prosas,* he deliberately breaks with romanticism. He was sent by *La Nación* to Spain in 1898 to report on the aftermath of the Spanish-American War. The results of these accounts were later collected in *España contemporanea* (1901). During this stay in Madrid he reaffirmed his leadership of modernism and met the younger poets of the time, among them Antonio Machado, Manuel Machado, and Juan Ramón Jiménez. He also met Francisca Sánchez, who became the mother of his son.

In 1900 he chose to reside in Paris, France. In 1905, Darío published *Cantos de vida y esperanza,* in which he introduced a note absent from his earlier poetry: sociopolitical concerns for the future of Latin America and Hispanic culture. The Spanish defeat in 1898 and Theodore Roosevelt's imperialist policies in Central America had awakened Latin Americans to the fact that the United States could no longer be regarded as a trusted neighbor. Instead, it appeared as a menacing force with the ability to absorb the southern half of the continent. *Cantos de vida y esperanza* manifests this new awareness and the new sense of allegiance to Spain as the mother country.

During the following years Darío maintained his residence in Paris, publishing a number of acclaimed books: *El canto errante* (1907), *El viaje a Nicaragua* (1909), and *Poema del ontoño* (1910). In 1911 he joined *Mundial* magazine in Paris. That same year, while in Buenos Aires, he wrote *Autobiografía,* a work serialized in *Caras y Caretas.* He returned to Paris in 1913. When World War I began, Darío was ill and in economic straits, but he accepted another lecture tour throughout the Americas. He spoke at Columbia University in New York, where he contracted pneumonia, and later died in Leon (Nicaragua) on February 6, 1916.

## DAVIS, JEFFERSON

**DAVIS, JEFFERSON** 1808–1889, Only president of the Confederate States of America (CSA) during the American Civil War (1861–1865). Davis presided over a class-riven new nation fighting a war for independence against great material odds, facing disintegration of morale from within and military coercion from without. The shortcomings of his leadership, though perhaps inevitable, were many and are seen as culminating in the defeat of the CSA in 1865.

Like his fellow Confederate leader, General Robert E. Lee, Davis distinguished himself in service to the U.S. government before the southern states seceded in 1860–1861. Like Lee, he was educated at the U.S. Military Academy at West Point and became a national hero for his innovative military command in the Mexican War (1846–1848). Davis also served in both the U.S. Congress and Senate, and as secretary of war under President Franklin Pierce. As the crisis between northern and southern states worsened in the 1850s, Davis opposed secession; however, he maintained the right of individual states to secede from the United States, and more strongly opposed any war to force states to remain in the Union.

When his home state, Mississippi, seceded in January 1861, Davis resigned from the Senate with a plea for peace. In February, he was elected provisional president of the newly formed CSA by the Confederate Convention; as his first presidential act, he sent a peace delegation to Washington, D.C. But President Abraham Lincoln refused to receive Davis's delegation and instead resupplied U.S. troops stationed at Fort Sumter in Charleston, South Carolina. Reluctantly, Davis ordered South Carolina troops to fire on the fort, beginning the Civil War.

Davis faced innumerable problems as leader of the new CSA. On the military front, the southern states were at enormous disadvantage compared to the northern states in terms of both population and manufacturing capacity. Davis created makeshift factories for production of war materials, and sent envoys to Europe both to purchase arms and to seek foreign recognition of and support for the new Confederate government; he also enacted an unpopular conscription law in 1862. Davis made the happy choice of Lee for commander of the Confederate forces on the northern front of the CSA, the Army of Northern Virginia, though both Davis and Lee have been criticized in hindsight for their inordinate focus on defending the northern front and the Confederate capital at Richmond, Virginia, at the expense of other strategic locales.

Even more dire were the conflicts Davis confronted

on the home front. The wealthy landowners of the Confederate states had led their states out of the Union in order to preserve slavery, upon which their power was based; they opposed any attempts of Davis's government to unify the CSA at the expense of their privilege. At the same time, the majority of the white population of the CSA did not stand to benefit from either slavery or secession, but did suffer the brunt of privation caused by the war; however, it was these very common people who Davis needed to staff the armies to repel invading U.S. forces. Caught between these two intransigent classes of citizens in the crucible of war, Davis's government disintegrated from within even before U.S. military forces brought it down from without.

When Lee surrendered at Appomattox without Davis's consent in April 1865, Davis and his cabinet moved south, hoping to continue the war until favorable terms of surrender could be obtained from the United States. He was captured on May 10, 1865, and treated as a major threat to the Union; first imprisoned in leg irons, he was kept under armed guard for two years. Stories that Davis had attempted to flee dressed as a woman circulated wildly in the northern United States, often accompanied by caricatures of the defeated president in a dress. Although Davis pressed the U.S. government to try him for treason, because he believed that the trial might establish the constitutionality of secession, the United States never formally charged Davis with any crime. To the end of his life, Davis refused to apply to the U.S. government for amnesty, instead remaining a defender of southern independence. Perhaps because of this, Davis as a political or military figure was never reassimilated into U.S. national culture, as was Lee—though his birthday was celebrated as a holiday in many southern states into the mid-20th century, his citizenship was not restored until 1978.

The definitive three-volume biography of Davis is Hudson Strode, *Jefferson Davis* (1955–1964). A biography by a contemporary is Frank H. Alfriend, *The Life of Jefferson Davis* (1868); a study of Davis's role as a nationalist leader is Paul D. Escott, *After Secession: Jefferson Davis and the Failure of Confederate Nationalism* (1978).

**DAYAN, MOSHE**    1915–1981, With his distinctive eye patch and the perennially rolled-up sleeves of his plain workman's shirt, Moshe Dayan's image was instantly recognizable around the world. At the height of his popularity, as the leader of Israel's most successful military confrontations—the 1956 Sinai Campaign and the 1967 Six Day War—Dayan epitomized the Israeli image of a plain speaking, kibbutz-born soldier-politician.

Moshe Dayan was born on May 20, 1915, in Deganya near Lake Galilee, the oldest kibbutz in Palestine. As a teenager, he received early military training in the British Police's Jewish Patrol Unit and at the officer school of the Haganah—the Jewish national defense force that would become the Israeli army. After fighting with the British in World War II, he became a Haganah unit commander and a lieutenant colonel in the 1948 War of Independence. At the end of the war, he negotiated the cease-fire agreement with Jordan and took part in the armistice talks.

In 1953, now-General Dayan was appointed army chief of staff. In 1956 he orchestrated and led Operation Kadesh, the invasion of the Sinai Peninsula, defeating Nassar's Egyptian army. While Ben-Gurion negotiated the return of the territory in exchange for a UN presence in the area and free passage in the Strait of Tiran, the military operation did much to establish the Israeli army as a powerful force in the region, and General Dayan as a capable military strategist.

In 1958, Dayan resigned from the army, attended the Hebrew University in Jerusalem, and joined the Mapai Party. In 1959 he was elected to the Knesset and served as the agriculture minister in Ben-Gurion's government. A Ben-Gurion protégé, Dayan quickly became associated with the "young guard" in the Mapai Party. Along with Shimon Perez, Dayan became an outspoken critic of party policies and the all-powerful Histadrut worker's union, arguing for the nationalization of many agencies under its tight control. Ben-Gurion, involved in his own battle with the secretary-general of the Histadrut, Pinchas Lavon, tacitly encouraged these critiques. However, as the "Lavon affair" turned into a political scandal, Ben-Gurion resigned in 1963, stripping the Dayan-led young guard of his powerful patronage.

In 1964, Dayan resigned from the government and, along with his old mentor, Ben-Gurion, and his friend Perez, resigned from Mapai to form Rafi (The List of the Worker's of Israel) in 1965. Running as a modern party and a labor antidote to the old socialist establishment, Rafi failed to defeat Mapai, gaining only ten seats in the Knesset (to Mapai's Forty-Five). However, Dayan himself soon rose to unprecedented fame and popularity. In 1967, as tensions with Egypt grew in the Sinai, Prime Minister Eshkol was widely criticized for failing to act decisively and public pressure mounted to appoint Dayan to the post of defense minister. Following his appointment on June 1, 1967, Dayan expressed reluctance to direct the Israeli army to the Suez Canal and the Golan Heights, warning that the war could go on for years if the army went too far. However, by June 10, when the Six Day War officially ended, Israeli troops had reached the Suez Canal and captured the entire Sinai Peninsula and the Gaza Strip, taken control of the Golan Heights and the West Bank, and captured East Jerusalem. In the euphoric aftermath of the war, Israelis celebrated a unified Jerusalem and Dayan and his troop leaders as national heroes.

As minister of defense, Dayan was the architect of Israeli military presence in the West Bank and Gaza and the military governor of the occupied territories. In this capacity, he instituted a policy of discreet military presence and the elimination of road barriers and travel restrictions between Israel and the occupied territories. While a critic of hard-line policies against Arab residents of the occupied territories, and a supporter of free passage and trade on both sides of the "Green Line," Dayan's policy also aimed to create "facts on the ground." Regarding the territories as necessary for Israeli security at the time, Dayan envisioned the occupation of the territories as permanent.

Although controversial, Dayan remained a highly regarded cabinet member in the Israeli Knesset after Rafi rejoined Mapai in 1968. However, his popularity would wane after the surprise attack by Egypt and Syria in October 1973. Launched on Yom Kippur, the Jewish Day of Atonement, the attack found the army wholly unprepared. Dayan, along with Prime Minister Golda Meir, were widely criticized for breeches in Israeli intelligence and the lack of military preparedness, and many called for Dayan's resignation.

In 1977, Dayan defected from the Labor Party and joined the newly elected cabinet of the Likud, led by the hawkish Menachem Begin. As foreign minister, Dayan began a series of secret talks with Anwar Sadat, helped facilitated Sadat's historic visit to Israel, and played a key role in the Camp David accord between Egypt and Israel on September 17, 1978, and the subsequent peace agreement.

While he shared Begin's opposition to Palestinian statehood, Dayan grew increasingly uneasy with Begin's steadfast opposition to autonomy in the occupied territories—this despite a Camp David provision to begin such negotiations. Believing that some concessions were necessary to the peace process he helped negotiate, Dayan resigned in protest in 1979. He died on October 16, 1981, shortly after attempting a political comeback as an independent.

## DE GAULLE, CHARLES  1890–1970, General Charles de Gaulle gained fame during World War II by refusing to accept German domination over his native France. He fled to Britain in 1940 and organized the Free French movement. He reminded his countrymen by ra-

dio that "France has lost a battle, but not the war." By 1943 he had gathered into his hands command of the entire French resistance movement. His claims to be the legal French government in exile and the sole spokesman for France irritated Winston S. Churchill and Franklin D. Roosevelt, who, for a time, found it politically wise to maintain diplomatic recognition of the Vichy government. His wartime experiences with the British and Americans did not leave him with a strong admiration for the two countries, and his resentment was to disturb these two nations' relations with France even after 1958 when he became France's leader. He was regarded as perhaps the most nationalist leader in the Western world.

Local resistance forces and delegates from de Gaulle's headquarters in London assumed political control in liberated France. On August 25, 1944, de Gaulle arrived in Paris with French troops, and the following day he led a triumphant march down the broad Champs-Élysses.

For the next year and a half, de Gaulle's provisional government exercised unchallenged authority in liberated France. He hoped that the predominantly young, patriotic, idealistic Frenchmen in the resistance movement would provide the spark for national revival and change. His movement also encompassed French Communists. Nevertheless, he was always suspicious that his desired revolution was not the same as theirs; they wanted "to establish their dictatorship by making use of the tragic situation of France." He successfully blocked their efforts to gain a ministry controlling foreign affairs, defense, or the police.

De Gaulle engaged in feverish diplomacy in order to reestablish France's position in world affairs: He helped create the United Nations, fought successfully for a permanent French seat on the Security Council, and secured a French occupation zone in Germany as a victorious power.

De Gaulle preferred a constitution with a strong executive and a weak parliament. "Deliberation is the work of many men. Action, of one alone!" Sensing that his views on the future republic were not gaining support, he resigned as temporary president in January 1946. He expected a wave of popular support to swell in his favor, but such a movement failed to materialize. He withdrew from direct involvement, awaiting a crisis that would direct his countrymen's eyes again on de Gaulle, the savior.

The Algerian rebellion, which began in 1954, shook France and unleashed conspiracies against the government, assassinations, and ill-fated military coups d'état. It ultimately brought de Gaulle out of retirement. Many, especially French generals, believed that only de Gaulle could save Algeria and protect France from civil war.

He said that he would respond to the call only on his own terms: that he be granted unrestricted authority to cope with the crisis. In mid-1958, he was appointed prime minister, and he quickly went to Algeria and gave an enthusiastic French throng the highly ambiguous assurance "I have understood you!" He knew the situation was hopeless. In late 1958 he was indirectly elected president of the republic, spelling the death knell of the Fourth Republic and the birth of the present Fifth Republic.

Always a realist under his mantle of magnificence, de Gaulle was convinced that Algeria could no longer be held by force, but he proceeded very cautiously in seeking a settlement of the crisis. He did not want to provoke a military coup d'état in France itself. He shrewdly allowed all groups to think that he shared all of their own objectives. Sensing that the right time had come, he announced a referendum for early 1961 to decide whether Algeria should be granted self-determination. Fifteen million said yes; only five million said no. He thus had received a free hand to pursue negotiations with the Algerian National Liberation Front (FLN), and he directed Prime Minister Georges Pompidou to lead them. In March 1962 France granted Algeria full sovereignty.

De Gaulle had already offered all other French colonies the option of becoming independent while retaining cultural ties with France. By 1960 all but Guinea had accepted this. By 1962 the French Empire had practically ceased to exist. Far from weakening France, this shedding freed its hand for a more assertive foreign policy, and it eliminated the searing domestic division stemming from unpopular colonial wars. De Gaulle was able to show his countrymen that it was possible to have a measure of grandeur without a colonial empire. He was an agent of modernization and also the guardian of the idea of French mission and grandeur. His task was to change France without discarding her glorious tradition.

With social peace and economic prosperity at home, de Gaulle could turn full attention to his major interest: foreign affairs. He had been displeased with France's position in the world when he came to power. The fate of Europe had been determined by the Soviet Union, the United States, and Britain. After the advent of the Cold War in 1946–1947, French security had fallen almost exclusively into the hands of NATO, commanded by a general from the United States, which in his words, "brings to great affairs elementary feelings and a complicated policy."

De Gaulle and all his successors knew that the Soviet Union posed a threat to Western Europe, which ultimately needed American protection. He also knew that the United States' tolerance level toward its European allies was high. He therefore decided that France could achieve foreign policy independence. He had bitter memories of what he considered a personal snub by Churchill and Roosevelt during the struggles of World War II. His first step was to develop French atomic weapons. When he was informed in 1960 of the successful French explosion in the Sahara, he exclaimed: "Hurray for France!"

Seeking to strengthen the center of Western Europe, he signed a treaty with West Germany in 1963. It basically called for regular consultation and semiannual state visits. A disappointed de Gaulle later referred to this treaty as a "faded rose" because it had failed to persuade the West Germans to loosen their own ties with the United States. Nevertheless, it was an extremely important and imaginative policy observed by all his successors. He boosted a development that few Europeans would have considered possible in 1945: For the first time in European history, the idea of a war between France and Germany was unthinkable. He recognized that French interests were best served in a cooperative, democratic Europe. But he emphasized that it must be a "Europe of Fatherlands," that is, of entirely sovereign nation-states. He insisted on France's veto power within the European Union (EU).

The United States reluctantly honored de Gaulle's demand that American troops (whom he called "good-natured but bad mannered") be withdrawn from French soil, a move that greatly increased NATO's logistical problems. This was a logical step to follow his announcement a year earlier that France would withdraw from NATO's integrated command (although not from NATO itself). He did not oppose the presence of American troops elsewhere in Europe because he did not want to remove France from the NATO shield. He was convinced that in case of war in Europe, Frenchmen would be more willing to fight because they would see their sacrifice as primarily a French defense effort, not an American one. Thus, in his opinion, the Western alliance was strengthened, not weakened, by his move.

The changes were not universally supported in France at the time, but by the early 1970s they had been embraced by all political parties, including the Communists. The basic Gaullist goal to create an independent Europe under French leadership, and thereby to diminish Soviet and U.S. influence, was not accomplished. Nevertheless, his design to create an independent French foreign policy has been followed by his presidential successors, despite some changes in emphasis and style. He gave France a role of which it could be proud, and he ultimately won the world's respect for his country.

The events of May 1968 (an economic and political crisis brought on by student and worker revolts) so shook de Gaulle's grip on power that he decided he needed to restore his authority. He announced a referendum and, as usual, warned that if his recommendations were not accepted, he would resign. The unspoken issue was de Gaulle's popularity and his continued presidency. In April 1969 he was handed the first referendum defeat in French history—a stinging rebuke.

Never tempted by dictatorship over his country, he resigned immediately and returned for the last time to his estate in Colombey-les-deux-églises in eastern France. Even three decades after his death in 1970, de Gaulle's legacy enjoys widespread approval. His predictions came true in the 1990s: the collapse of Communism and the USSR, upheaval in Eastern Europe, the unification of Germany, and an emergence of a more independent Europe. He had spoken of "Europe from the Atlantic to the Urals" long before it became a reality.

The best sources are his own *The War Memoirs of Charles de Gaulle*, 3 vols. (Simon & Schuster, 1960) and *Memoirs of Hope and Endeavor* (Simon & Schuster, 1970). See also Philip H. Gordon, *A Certain Idea of France. French Security Policy and the Gaullist Legacy* (Princeton, 1993) and Nicholas Wahl, ed., *De Gaulle and the United States, 1930–1970* (Berg, 1992).

## DE MIRANDA, FRANCISCO

1750–1816, Pioneer patriot. Born in Caracas, he served as a captain in the Spanish army from 1772 to 1782 in Spain, the United States, and the Bahamas. After being convicted of smuggling, fined, and then deprived of his commission, he escaped banishment by fleeing to the United States, where he tried to persuade Alexander Hamilton and Henry Knox to aid the revolutions in the Spanish colonies. In 1792 he battled as a lieutenant general in the French revolutionary army, but was imprisoned in 1792–1797 on a charge of treason. On February 2, 1806, he secretly organized an expedition to free Venezuela from Spanish control. In August, again aided by a British admiral, Thomas Cochrane, Miranda succeeded in occupying the city of Coro for five days before he pulled out because there was no following. Miranda did not return to Venezuela until December 12, 1810, after the Junta Suprema of Caracas (Suprema Junta Conservadora de los Derechos de Fernando VII) had replaced the captain general following the events of April 19, 1810. Miranda was appointed as the commander of the

patriot forces subsequent to the Declaration of Independence (La Declaracion de la Independencia) on July 5, 1811, but the patriot government was only to last one year. With the independence movement weakened by the earthquake on March 26, 1812, and the successful campaign by the Royalist commander, Domingo de Monteverde, Miranda was given dictatorial powers on April 23, 1812. Miranda, however, effected the end to the First Republic with the signing of the Pact of San Mateo on July 25.

## DE VALERA, ÉAMON

1882–1975, President of the Republic of Ireland and founder of the political party Fianna Fáil. Born in New York, in the United States, to a Spanish father and Irish mother, de Valera was raised in Ireland from a young age. His greatest accomplishments are considered to be his work toward the achievement of political sovereignty for the Republic of Ireland and the founding of Fianna Fáil. Detractors and critical commentators cite his inability to end partition between the six counties of Northern Ireland and the Republic of Ireland as his most significant political failure.

de Valera was active in the armed campaign against Britain through his membership in the Irish Republican Brotherhood (IRB) and the Irish Volunteers (later the Irish Republican Army). As a commandant of the Irish Volunteers he led a battalion in the Easter Rising in 1916. The rising had been planned by the IRB and sought to establish an Irish Republic (which was proclaimed by the Irish Citizen Army). Although more than 1000 Irishmen and women participated in the uprising, seizing several buildings in Dublin, including the general post office, the rebels surrendered after a British army landing. For his part in the rising, de Valera was sentenced to death, a sentence subsequently commuted to life imprisonment. He was released from prison in 1918 and shortly thereafter elected a member of parliament for the area of East Clare.

In October 1917 he was elected president of the political party Sinn Féin. Two days later he was elected president of the Irish Volunteers, two of the most powerful bodies in Ireland. His goal was to unify the efforts of the two organizations to work toward an independent Irish Republic whose citizens would choose their own form of government. Also arising out of this Sinn Féin convention, or Ard Fheis, was that elected Sinn Féin representatives would so constitute a national assembly, the Dáil Eireann. De Valera became president of Dáil Eireann in April 1919.

As the situation between Ireland and Britain deteriorated, and the military campaign against British rule increased, Britain, under the leadership of Lloyd George, decided to enter into negotiations with representatives of de Valera's government. De Valera put together a delegation of men to go to London to enter talks. De Valera himself did not take part in the talks. When the delegation emerged from the negotiations with the Anglo-Irish Treaty, de Valera was incensed. De Valera had envisioned an agreement of external association without any obligation by members of a future government to owe allegiance to a British monarchy. Instead he was presented with a required oath of allegiance and dominion status within the British Empire for what was to the Seorstát Éirann (Irish Free State).

Despite de Valera's strong arguments against the treaty, it was debated and approved by the Dáil in January 1922. Civil war broke out and the Four Courts were seized in Dublin by the Anti-Treatyites. The provisional government responded with force and de Valera and his cabinet resigned. He also resigned his officership with the Irish Volunteers, reenlisted with the Anti-Treatyites, and fought against the provisional government.

Political differences within Sinn Féin ultimately led to a parting of the ways and de Valera's founding of the party Fianna Fáil in 1926. Fiann Fáil's primary objectives were the unification of the Irish nation, an end to partition, and full sovereignty for the twenty-six counties of the Irish Free State. The party also sought to rebuild the national Irish structure with a focus on Irish culture and sound economic policies. Fianna Fáil became a political tour de force and assumed power under de Valera's leadership in 1932. De Valera became taoiseach, or prime minister, of the Irish Free State in 1932 and held that post until 1948. Fianna Fáil lost power and in 1949 the Republic of Ireland was formed. De Valera and Fianna Fáil regained power. In 1959 he resigned as taoiseach and leader of Fianna Fáil. He was elected president of the Republic of Ireland (considered a ceremonial position) in 1959, a post that he held until his retirement in 1973.

Considered an opportunistic nationalist by some and a committed revolutionary nationalist by others, there is little dispute that de Valera established the landscape on which an independent Irish Republic would grow and prosper.

Books on de Valera include *Eamon de Valera*, a thorough biography, as is M. J. McManus's *Eamon de Valera*. Also, John Bowman explore de Valera's attitudes and policies toward Northern Ireland in *De Valera and the Ulster Question 1917–1973*.

**DECLARATION OF INDEPENDENCE** The Continental Congress appointed a committee to draft a statement proclaiming the independence of thirteen British colonies in America and explaining the theoretical grounds for this declaration. Thomas Jefferson was selected to author it although the committee made a few editorial changes. The Continental Congress approved the final document, which was proclaimed on July 4, 1776.

The document commences with a preamble asserting that the thirteen colonies are severing their bonds with Britain. The most important section comes next. Arguing that "a decent respect to the opinions of mankind requires that they [the colonies] declare the causes which impel them to the separation," Jefferson lays the theoretical groundwork for revolution in unforgettable language. He speaks of such self-evident "truths" that *all* people are born equal and have rights, including those of "life, liberty, and the pursuit of happiness." He asserts that just government must be based on the "consent of the governed." When a government dispenses with that consent or fails to recognize the rights of the people, then the people have the "right of revolution," meaning that they can destroy a tyrannical government and create a just one. Government must be limited and must always be answerable to the people, who remain sovereign. His language and argumentation clearly reflect the thinking of Englishman John Locke, as established a century earlier in his monumental political book, *Second Treatise on Government*. Locke argued that revolution must not be resorted to for trivial reasons, but only after "a long train of abuses" that seem to aim toward despotism and after every effort has been made to remedy the wrongs legally and peacefully.

The longest part of the declaration is the bill of particulars against the British king. This is a long list of specific abuses that the British king allegedly performed: failing to assent to the colonial legislature's laws, preventing them from meeting, quartering troops in people's homes, failing to protect the populace from attacks, cutting off trade with the world, and so on. In fact, though, it was usually the British Parliament and the British governors in the colonies that committed the misdeeds listed in the declaration.

The world historical significance of this document is that for the first time in history a revolution was proclaimed on the basis of rights that *all* persons possess, not just Americans. Thus it is a message for all mankind, not just for four million British colonists in North America. The fact that their political order is founded on universally valid principles is crucially important for American nationalism. Because America is a richly pluralistic society, no form of nationalism or patriotism could be based on a single race or ethnic group.

Instead, America's is a "patriotism of values." What it means to belong to the American nation is that one embraces the principles presented in such eloquent, moving language in the Declaration of Independence and the United States Constitution, which was written in 1787. This quality makes American nationalism inclusive, not exclusive.

## DECOLONIZATION

The collapse of colonial expansion, which began with World War I, accelerated following World War II and the establishment of the United Nations.

Many forces contributed to decolonization. Two world wars had not only left the European colonial powers exhausted, with little strength left to control their colonies, but the spectacle of the "parent" nations (which presumed to lead the colonies by example) locked in bitter struggles could only present an unsettling picture to colonial areas that might have seen themselves being exploited to help fight someone else's wars. Further, the defeat of the Russians in the Russo-Japanese war, the successful actions of the Japanese in Southeast Asia prior to and during World War II against the French, British and Dutch, and, finally, the defeat of the French at Dien Bien Phu sent strong messages that superior Western technology could be defeated and inspired growing confidence among colonial peoples.

The transplantation of Western intellectual ideas, born in the Enlightenment, Renaissance, Reformation, and Industrial Revolution, gave native leaders a basis on which to challenge their colonizers. If colonial powers could justify their policies as a civilizing mission, then the policies would seem to have been successful as Western notions of freedom, progress, self-determination, and equality took root, even if sometimes in unique forms.

World opinion regarding colonialism also changed as modern communication and international travel made the unflattering realism of far-off colonies accessible to audiences in the parent countries. Media access also helped native leaders define a sense of national identity to their own publics.

Finally, if theories concerning social Darwinism, nationalism, and power politics have validity in explaining the domination by stronger states of their weaker neighbors, then logically the same arguments could be used to explain decolonization as the colonies became strong enough to resist.

The United Nations charter placed substantial emphasis on nonself-governing territories and the trusteeship system, encouraging dependent states to move toward full and equal participation in the international community. The emergence of new states doubled the membership of the United Nations by the 1960s, providing an important forum for urging further decolonization.

Useful literature on decolonization includes the classic by Rupert Emerson, *From Empire to Nation: The Rise to Self-Assertion of Asian and African Peoples* (Harvard University Press, 1960), as well as John D. Hargreaves, *Decolonization in Africa* (Longman, 1988), Miles Kahler, *Decolonization in Britain and France* (Princeton University Press, 1984), Raymond Betts, *France and Decolonization 1900–1960* (Macmillan, 1991), and Henry S. Wilson, *African Decolonization* (Edward Arnold, 1994).

Adapted from Greives, Forest, *Conflict and Order: An Introduction to International Relations.* Copyright © 1977 by Houghton Mifflin Company. Used with permission.

## DELANEY, MARTIN

1812–1885, First black to rise to the rank of major in the U.S. army, a medical doctor and graduate of Harvard Medical School, and a writer who developed a profound black power ethic. Interested in identity and self-realization, Delaney began the process of blacks recognizing the power of cultural continuity as far back as the antebellum period. His political career during Reconstruction, however, was not very successful. Many of his writings were based on his belief that Africans, pioneers of civilization, were capable of building a future both for themselves and whites, but that, first, blacks must understand their African culture and what was peculiar to them. This was an idea rarely advanced by other blacks at the time. Delaney's black nationalism argued for the positive qualities that blacks possessed and could teach others.

He worked with Frederick Douglass on the staff of the *North Star,* an abolition newspaper. Unlike Douglass, who saw liberation coming through struggle in America, Delaney thought that struggle in America alone could not achieve freedom for blacks in America. Though he agreed that free blacks should never accept racism, freedom was forever beyond their grasp in America unless those of talent emigrated to establish a nation for themselves, in America or in Africa, that would generate so much good that the lot of their people would be enhanced throughout the world.

It was rare for black leaders to address the issue of African ethnicity in print, but Delaney made as much of it as one could expect, given his exceptional grasp of African culture, linking the culture of Africans in New Orleans to that of Africans in Cuba without permitting ethnic consideration to obscure the larger cultural pattern in either location. Ethnicity came before him in an arresting context but did not cause him to break with nationalist traditions in naming his people. Just as activist Henry Highland Garnet saw a Pan-African mix in the African parade on Emancipation Day in New York, Delaney read about one in "a popular American literary periodical" and found its analog among slaves in New Orleans. His knowledge of Africa leaves little doubt that, had he pursued the matter at some length, he might have provided a theory of culture, of the meaning of being African in America, and its significance for nationalism, to parallel his Pan-African political stance, but he did not.

Prior to the outbreak of the Civil War, Delaney led an investigation into the Niger Valley in West Africa, later publishing an official report of his exploration in a study that contained specific recommendations for black reparation. During the war itself, Delaney served as a medical officer.

Retirement enabled him to write *Principles of Ethnology* (1878). His best known work, however, remains a political tract entitled "The Condition, Elevation, Emancipation and Destiny of the Colored People of the United States, Politically Considered" (1852). He also wrote the novel *Blake,* published in 1870, and *Search for a Place* by Delaney and Robert Campbell, published in 1869.

Delaney died in Xenia, Ohio, home of Wilberforce University.

**DEMOCRACY** Rule by the people, summed up by Abraham Lincoln's pithy aphorism "government of the people, by the people, and for the people." The term is derived from the Greek *demos* meaning "the people" and *kratos* meaning "rule." This apparently straightforward idea actually turns out to be far more complicated than it first appears. Although the meaning of democracy is clear, the question of how "the people" are to govern themselves is left entirely open. This gives rise to various conceptions that may be very different from one another. One of the major fault lines that separate these interpretations is the distinction between direct and representative democracy. The former involves the people directly in the process of policy making so that they participate in the decisions that shape their lives. This form of democracy therefore not only entails the people voting on various policy issues but actively engages them in open debate, thereby allowing them to shape and influence the final policy outcome. Representative democracy, on the other hand, refers to a system of government whereby binding rules are made by elected representatives of the community.

In the contemporary period, representative democracy has become the most pervasive. At the same time, representative democracy has often been associated with individual political equality, neatly encapsulated by Bentham's dictum, "each should count as one, none should count for more than one." However, several difficulties arise with this form of democracy, based as it is on the individual, when one considers the multicultural/multinational nature of most societies. If there is an overwhelming cultural majority within a state, then more often than not that particular majority's interests will be represented. Citizens of a representative democracy based on a form of majority voting may have an equal say at the ballot box, but such a system does not guarantee that their interests will be represented. This form of representative democracy does not therefore necessarily prevent a "dictatorship of the cultural majority," whereby representatives of minority cultures either fail to get elected or are too few in number to have any impact within the legislature.

These issues raise the question of what we actually mean when we use the term *representation*. Two principal meanings suggest themselves: the microcosm understanding of representation, and the agent conception of representation. The former interprets representation to mean mirroring the various groups that constitute a particular society; the legislature should thus be an exact portrait, in miniature, of the demographic composition of society. The agent conception, on the other hand, proposes that representatives in the legislature act on behalf of their particular constituents, regardless of the particular background of the elected representative.

Two of the most common solutions to these difficulties are federalism and consociationalism, which entail a mixture of these two forms of representation. Federalism involves the greater devolution of power toward self-government, usually on a territorial basis. Regional autonomy and representation are constitutionally guaranteed and clearly delineated. Central government either does not have the right to amend or redefine these territorial units or there is a legal guarantee that redefinition is carried out through consent. The constitution is indissoluble, unlike confederation, which is a voluntary gathering of various states that can be dissolved at any time. Group liberty is adhered to by the autonomy of such ethno-territorial units, that is, they have the power to pass laws, secure language rights, and promote their forms of education. However, federalism still relies on a degree of centralism, that is, the agreement that all territorial units will abide by basic state laws; for example, the teaching of one main second language.

Consociationalism, on the other hand, is a system of power-sharing among the élites of various social groups (ethnic, religious, etc.) in which each group is guaranteed a place in the cabinet, which therefore becomes a grand coalition. Consociationalism involves accommodative behavior through compromise on the part of ethnic élites who are assumed to represent their group's interests. In this form of governance there is a degree of proportionality in the legislature, government, and bureaucracy. Minority groups have a veto over certain basic issues that affect their vital interests, thus ensuring that no laws will be passed that are contrary to their particular interests. It also entails some form of community autonomy in various state institutions such as education, media, and local self-government. The finances for such activities are also allocated proportionally.

## DENG XIAOPING (TENG HSIAO-P'ING)   1904–1997,
Veteran Chinese Communist who became known as the chief architect of China's breathtaking economic reform in the 1980s and 1990s. He is also described by some as China's Bismarck for his programmatic political style and his tough stance on political reform. His ideas contain elements of Marxism, nationalism, and eclecticism and were canonized officially by the Chinese Communist Party (CCP) as Deng Xiaoping Theory after his death.

Deng was born to a rich peasant family in Guangan, Sichuan. He left China for Paris at the age of sixteen to pursue higher education, but ended up becoming a professional revolutionary in Moscow six years later. Deng's association with the overseas leadership circle of the CCP ensured him rapid advancement within the CCP on his return to China. Together with others, he organized two peasant uprisings in Guanxi province against the nationalist government in late 1929 and early 1930. When these uprisings failed, he went to Shanghai, and worked as the CCP's secretary at its underground party headquarters. One year later he joined Mao Zedong in the Red Army base in Jiangxi province. From this time on, Deng Xiaoping became an ardent supporter of Mao. For that reason, he was removed from power for a while for the first time when Mao himself became a victim of a power struggle within the CCP. In 1934, Deng walked along with defeated Red Army soldiers during the Long March, and was one of the participants of the historical party meeting in Zunyi, in which Mao firmly established his supreme authority over the entire CCP and its army. When the Sino-Japanese war broke out in 1937, the CCP formed a coalition with the nationalist government in Nanjing, and reorganized the Red Army into the Eighth Route Army. Deng became the political commissioner of the 129th Division of the new army. Between 1938 and 1952, Deng fought his way throughout China, and contrib-

uted to the defeat of the Japanese and the eventually the downfall of the nationalist government during the Chinese Civil War (1946–1949).

After the Communists came to power, Deng's political career took off. He was first appointed vice premier of the State Council in 1952. Soon he became a member of the powerful politburo and the general secretary of the Central Committee of the CCP. Through his diligent work, he proved himself to be someone who could get things done efficiently. He was a close associate of President Liu Shaoqi, who became the chief policy maker when Mao retreated to an inactive role after the dismal failure of the Great Leap Forward (1958–1960). However, Mao's obsession with the theory of class struggle led to his decision to launch the Cultural Revolution (1966–1976), another disastrous mass campaign aimed at achieving ideological purity and political correctness. Deng Xiaoping, along with Liu Shaoqi, was removed from power and castigated as China's "people in power taking the capitalist road." Not only did he lose his personal freedom, he was also sent to do physical labor in a machine factory in Jiangxi.

As the Cultural Revolution entered its final years, Deng was recalled to office in 1973 to assist Premier Zhou Enlai in restoring economic and political order that had been torn apart by the mass campaign. However, his liberal reform effort soon encountered strong resistance from the radical group "Gang of Four" headed by Mao's wife Jiang Qing. He was removed from office for the third time in his life in April 1976. But this time things quickly turned in Deng's favor. Mao died in September of that year, and the Gang of Four was arrested in a coup. Deng was once again reinstated a year later.

With all these ups and downs, Deng clearly had achieved his political maturity, and soon established himself as the paramount leader of China. Determined to modernize China with full speed, he laid out a policy of reform and openness. With his unique decisive and authoritarian style, he made great inroads in pushing his reform agenda by undoing the policy and practices of the past and by introducing markets and competition to transform the rigid planned economy. Economically he put eclecticism and pragmatism into full use by experimenting with liberal reform to accelerate China's economic development. But politically, Deng was reluctant to carry out meaningful political reforms. His insistence on maintaining the Communist Party's monopoly of power eventually led to the Tiananmen Square crisis in 1989, in which the army was used to crack down on student demonstrators who demanded more political freedom.

Deng, like many other Communists of his generation,

is first and foremost a nationalist who devoted his entire life to regaining China's sovereignty, striving for China's modernization, and achieving China's unification and integration. He endorsed the policy of "one country, two systems" to be used as a formula for the unification of Hong Kong, Macao, and Taiwan with the Chinese mainland. In the two decades of Deng's reign, China experienced the greatest awakening in history. The country's real GDP increased fourfold, and the economic growth was kept at an average rate of ten percent annually. As a result, China has become one of the largest economies in the world. This unprecedented growth in turn helped millions of Chinese out of poverty. Deng certainly will be remembered for his contribution to the rise of the Chinese nation at the turn of the 21st century.

Deng's writing is officially published in a two-volume collection title *Selected Works of Deng Xiaoping* (Beijing: Foreign Language Press, 1984). One of his daughters, Deng Rong, wrote a biography of him: *Deng Xiaoping: My Father,* Vol. 1 (English translation by Xiao Yang, Basic Books, 1995). Other biographies include *Deng: A Political Biography* by Benjamin Young (M. E. Sharp, 1998) and *Deng Xiaoping: Chronicle of an Emperor* by Ruan Ming (English translation by Wang Liu *et al.*, Westview Press, 1992).

**DEVLIN, BERNADETTE**   1947–, Born in County Tyrone, a leader of the civil rights movement in Northern Ireland and former member of parliament, Devlin has been an unwavering human rights advocate and supporter of reunification of Northern Ireland with the Republic of Ireland.

Although often referred to as an Irish Republican or an Irish nationalist, she has also been a strong proponent of socialism. As such, she was a founding member of the Irish Republican Socialist Party (IRSP). However, she left the organization about a year later because of the organization's militaristic stance.

Devlin was elected to the British Parliament at the age of twenty-one, in April 1969, for the constituency of Mid-Ulster. She won with an overwhelming majority of the Catholic and nationalist vote. At that time she was the youngest woman ever elected to that position. In 1981 she was poised to run again and stated she would only stand down for an H-Block candidate (the H-Blocks are an alternative name for H. M. Prison the Maze, also known as Long Kesh).

Devlin was a member of the National H-Block Committee, which campaigned on behalf of the prisoners. H-Block prisoners were predominantly men imprisoned for their real or perceived activities against the United Kingdom. While the U.K. government has viewed them

as terrorists and paramilitary groups, the prisoners, specifically, the Republican prisoners, view themselves as freedom fighters engaged in a war of national liberation. The Republican H-Block prisoners were involved in a high-profile campaign, including a hunger strike, to draw attention to the deplorable conditions of their incarceration. Ultimately, an H-Block candidate by the name of Bobby Sands did stand and win a seat in Parliament that election. Bobby Sands tragically died soon after while on a hunger strike.

Devlin was herself the target of a murder attempt. After the phone wires to her home had been cut, members of the Ulster Defense Association, a loyalist terror group, entered her home and shot her numerous times. Whereas Devlin lived to tell about it, five other members of the H-Block Committee did not survive murder plots against them.

Devlin's activism publicly developed while a student at Queen's University of Belfast. Her involvement with the People's Democracy and the Civil Rights Association earned her respect among friend and foe. Modeled on the civil rights movement in the United States, the civil rights movement in Northern Ireland was not the exclusive domain of either Catholics or nationalists. It drew support from the trade union movement and Protestants who were neither unionists nor loyalists. Grievances and injustices addressed by the movement included abuses under the Special Powers Act, gross discrimination in public housing allocations, job discrimination, and electoral gerrymandering accompanied by a preference system for loyalists and unionists.

She has come out as a thoughtful critic of the Good Friday Agreement of 1998. Her primary concerns about the agreement are that it offers nationalists a false sense of reality, and is not a real step toward peace, but instead an entrenchment of the British presence in Northern Ireland. Devlin's arguments focus more on the British as an impediment to democratic progress than as an obstacle to a united Ireland.

At a young age she wrote an autobiography, which includes an in-depth look at the civil rights movement in Northern Ireland. The book is titled *The Price of My Soul.*

**DIASPORA NATIONALISM**   Identification with a national origin by members of a national/ethnic group who reside outside of that nation is diaspora nationalism. This form of nationalism and its links to a national identity have been the basis for the creation of organizations, movements, and state structures.

The diaspora concept was originally used to describe the Jewish dispersion throughout the world as a result of persecution. It is also applicable to the condition of numerous national groupings that have experienced geographic dispersal as a result of either voluntary or involuntary migration. Diaspora nationalism forges allegiance to a national identity on the basis of a common historical origin. It often underlies structures of transnational linkage between the global pockets of these national groupings.

In addition to the Jewish diaspora, an African diaspora exists that was caused by the transatlantic slave trade and an Asian diaspora has resulted from labor migrations. Diaspora nationalism can lead to the reconstruction of a national homeland as in the state of Israel for the Jewish diaspora. In some cases, diaspora nationalism transcends the boundaries of a nation-state by promoting international solidarity and exchange as in the Pan-African movement.

**DICTATORSHIP**  As commonly used, the term *dictatorship* embraces an array of governments headed by one person or a small group and distinguished by the arbitrary and unchecked exercise of power and frequent outrages against human rights. Certainly dictators like Hitler, Stalin, and Iraq's Saddam Hussein resemble in many respects the classical portrait of tyrants painted in Plato's *Republic* and Aristotle's *Politics,* to say nothing of such fictional representations as the characters Number One in Arthur Koestler's *Darkness at Noon* and Big Brother in George Orwell's *Nineteen Eighty-Four.* A nuanced understanding of modern dictatorship, however, must take several complicating factors into account, including its sometimes intricate relationship to nationalism.

To begin with, some forms of dictatorship are strictly legal and legitimate. Constitutional dictatorship originated in the ancient Roman Republic, but nearly all modern, democratic political systems also permit the formation of "crisis governments" to deal with emergencies such as war, insurrection, and economic depression—always with the provision that emergency power, usually reposing in the executive branch, will expire when the crisis has passed.

As for extraconstitutional forms of dictatorship, many scholars insist on differentiating between modern dictatorship and earlier types of absolutism and tyranny. The power and reach of traditional despots and divine right monarchs, they argue, were sharply circumscribed by religion, custom, and widespread belief in a divine or natural law superior to human will.

Beginning with the French Revolution and the reign of Napoleon, however, a new and far less limited form of despotism arose, one made possible by the decay of traditional society and beliefs and the rise of the mod-

ern nation-state. Rather than invoking divine right, dictators from Napoleon onward exploited the spirit of nationalism and appealed to the principle of popular sovereignty as justification for authoritarian rule. Claiming to embody the undivided will of the nation and often resorting to plebiscites as a means of legitimating their power, they governed autocratically in the name of the people and *la patrie.* The 20th century brought important innovations that tended to increase the scope and duration of mass-based dictatorial regimes, including tightly disciplined political parties and technologies of mass communication that enabled governments to shape and direct public opinion as never before. Perhaps logically, such developments culminated in the appearance of the totalitarian state in Russia and Germany after World War I. In both the Stalinist and Hitlerite dictatorships, according to Alfred Cobban, nationalist ideologies became the new religion, furnishing an emotional force "which put the cohesion and self-consciousness of the primitive tribe behind the great state of modern times." Nevertheless, as many commentators note, aggressively nationalist ideology endangered the very dictatorships it was designed to buttress by sometimes impelling them—as happened with the fascist regimes—toward disastrous military adventures.

Cobban, writing in the late 1930s, viewed the nonhereditary, personal rule of Hitler, Stalin, and Italy's Benito Mussolini—all of whom gained supposedly unlimited power through a combination of force and consent—as the very epitome of the new-style dictatorship. Other scholars have taken a different view. Paul Brooker, for example, who defines dictatorship rather inclusively as "a regime that is not a democracy nor a monarchy," regards ideological one-party states led by a party committee or a military junta as the most advanced type of 20th-century dictatorship. In his judgment, the personalized dictatorships of Stalin and Hitler, which reduced the mass party to a mere agent of the leader's will, marked a degeneration from the more creative and "modernized" party-led dictatorships.

At any rate, if it is granted that dictatorship need not entail the rule of one person, then it becomes evident that an enormous number and variety of extraconstitutional dictatorships have existed in modern times. Moreover, some types clearly have been more lawless and cruel and more systematic in their attempts at control than others. As Ronald Wintrobe observes, the rulers of so-called "tinpot regimes" seek to govern repressively "only to the extent necessary to stay in office and collect the fruits of monopolizing political power." Unconcerned with rallying their subjects in support of an ideological agenda or great national enterprises, dictators like Haiti's François "Papa Doc" Duvalier and the Philippines' Ferdinand Marcos leave private life largely undisturbed and demand only outward obedience and acquiescence. On the other hand, totalitarian dictatorships such as Hitler's, Stalin's, and Mao Zedong's in China seek to subordinate all spheres of life to their control and to transform society in accordance with a new vision of reality. To that end they wield almost unbounded power with a ruthlessness and thoroughness probably unprecedented in history, relying on pervasive police terror to intimidate real or imagined enemies and on all available means of mass communication to indoctrinate and mobilize the population on behalf of their goals and policies. Between tinpot and totalitarian regimes lies a broad range of dictatorial states, more or less ideological and more or less nationalistic, having leaders who in some cases possess a sense of messianic purpose and in all cases claim to rule in the interest of the masses. President-for-life Akhmed Sukarno's anti-parliamentary "guided democracy" in Indonesia in the early 1960s, Julius Nyerere's single-party presidential government in Tanzania (1964–1985), and Mustapha Kemal's dictatorship of the Republican People's Party in Turkey (1923–1938) fall into this intermediate range of authoritarian dictators whose aspirations generally are neither totalistic nor purely self-aggrandizing.

For many of these regimes as well as for the totalitarian states, dictatorship serves the goals of nation building. As early as 1513, in the impassioned final chapter of *The Prince,* the Florentine political thinker Niccolò Machiavelli advocated the unification of Italy through the strong hand of an authoritarian ruler. Although the experience of England would later prove that nation-states can come into being through more gradual and constitutional processes, many 20th-century nationalists, whose timetable often will not allow for slow evolution, have regarded dictatorship as the preferred route—perhaps the only route—to rapid political and economic modernization. Thus dictators as temperamentally and ideologically diverse as Stalin, Mussolini, and Ghana's Kwame Nkrumah have created "developmental dictatorships" to accelerate economic and social growth. Furthermore, for many emerging nations of Africa and Asia in the postcolonial era, dictatorship accompanied by extreme doses of nationalistic and anti-imperialist ideology seemed to offer the only hope for forging a nation-state amid profound regional, ethnic, or tribal divisions.

To be sure, many dictators—Serbia's Slobodan Milošević is only one of the latest examples—exploit nationalist emotions and ethnic hatreds for largely self-interested reasons. If nothing else, nationalist hysteria may divert attention from unfulfilled promises and languishing economies. Yet under some circumstances the iron-fisted dominion of one or a few is probably the most appropriate form of government for a society—a fact acknowledged by the 19th-century English liberal philosopher John Stuart Mill. Both Mill and certain champions of the 18th-century Enlightenment envisioned reform-minded autocrats ruling backward peoples with the noble intention of civilizing them. In somewhat the same spirit, Kemal's relatively mild rule in Turkey aimed at fashioning the remnant of what had been the Ottoman Empire into a modern, secular state with some measure of democracy and liberalism. In spite of periodic setbacks, by the 1980s Turkey appeared to have evolved a stable multiparty system.

Ronald Wintrobe's *The Political Economy of Dictatorship* (Cambridge University Press, 1998) offers a public choice analysis of the phenomenon, while Paul Brooker's *Twentieth-century Dictatorships* and *Defiant Dictatorships* (New York University Press, 1995 and 1997) emphasize the variety and durability of dictatorships and their likely survival well into the 21st century. Several older but still useful analyses are Alfred Cobban's *Dictatorship: Its History and Theory* (Haskell House, 1939), Hans Kohn's *Revolutions and Dictatorships: Essays in Contemporary History* (Harvard University Press, 1939), and Franz Neumann's *The Democratic and the Authoritarian State* (Free Press, 1957). Hannah Arendt's *The Origins of Totalitarianism* (World, Meridian Books, 1958) remains the best and perhaps most influential study of the totalitarian state, and certainly the most philosophically informed. *Dictatorship and Totalitarianism: Selected Readings*, edited by Betty B. Burch (D. Van Nostrand, 1964), provides a brief and accessible collection of primary documents and interpretive essays.

**DILLEN, KAREL**  1925–, Born in the Flemish city of Antwerp, the heartland of Flemish nationalism, Dillen was strongly influenced by his schoolteachers. Although he joined the nationalist student organization *Ontwikkeling* (Development) and described himself as an "inactive Black shirt," his mother kept him from actively collaborating with the Nazis during World War II. After the war, Dillen worked for a time as a controller for the U.S. army in Antwerp, as an employee in the Antwerp city hall, and as a censor for the English in Bonn. After completing his military service, Dillen returned to Antwerp and participated in almost all of the radical Flemish nationalist organizations, often holding leading positions.

After a brief and unsuccessful period with the Sint-Arnoudsvendel, the first postwar, Flemish nationalist youth movement in Antwerp, Dillen became a staff member of the weekly *Opstanding* (Resurrection). There he honed his polemical style and came into contact with many old radicals of the Flemish movement, including many prominent excollaborators. One of them, the former Eastern Front soldier Toon van Overstraeten, became his mentor and friend, and together they founded the *Jong Nederlandse Gemeenschap* (Young Dutch Community, JNG). During this time Dillen started to speak at Flemish nationalist meetings, rapidly gaining fame for his radical and uncompromising nationalism and his relentless fight for amnesty and rehabilitation of the "victims of post-war repression," including prominent collaborators. In addition, Dillen fought for the return of traditional Flemish events, such as the *Ijzerbedevaart,* into the hands of the radical wing of the Flemish movement.

During the 1950s, Dillen made his first foreign contacts. Most notably, he attended the infamous Malmo International, where right-wing extremists from all over Europe founded the unsuccessful European Social movement. One of the few people he stayed in regular contact with, and who influenced his thinking, was the French revisionist Maurice Bardeche. Dillen translated his book *Nuremberg ou la Terre Promise* (Nuremberg or the Promised Land, 1948) into Dutch, and in 1956 he became the editor of the monthly *Dietsland-Europa,* which emulated the French magazine *Défense de l'Occident* of which Bardeche was editor.

Though mainly active within nonparty political organizations, Dillen eventually also joined the *Volksunie* (People's Union, VU), the first successful Flemish national political party in postwar Belgium. He was immediately appointed head of the youth wing in Antwerp, by far the most influential within the VU. From there he built his position as the most influential radical nationalist within the party. When the VU increasingly headed into a left-wing progressive direction, Dillen fought vehemently to bring the party back to its Flemish nationalist core. Increasingly he worked outside of the party, among others as chairman of the Flemish nationalist "think tank" *Were Di* (1962–1975) and as a columnist of the satirical Antwerp weekly, *'t Pallieterke* (1965–1978), and in 1971 he left the VU.

In 1978 he cofounded the *Vlaams Blok* (Flemish Block, VB), originally an electoral list of two small Flemish nationalist splits, and became its party chairman and parliamentary representative for almost two decades. After having spent almost ten years as the sole VB delegate in the Belgian Parliament, Dillen moved to the Belgian Senate in 1987, and to the European Parliament in 1994. As a result of his increasing age and decreasing health, in 1996 Dillen appointed Frank Vanhecke, his long-time personal secretary and fellow MEP, as his successor as party leader. Dillen still functions as the party's honorary chairman and leader of the party faction in the European Parliament.

Dillen wrote a few booklets, most notably *Wij, marginalen* (Uitgeverij A.M.U., 1987). Also of interest are his two volumes of collected interventions in the European Parliament, entitled *Vlaanderen in Straatsburg* (1991 and 1993). The most authoritative biography on Dillen is by Pieter Jan Vestraete, *Karel Dillen: Portret van een Rebel* (Aksent, 1992).

## DOLLFUSS, ENGELBERT

1892–1934, Dollfuss rose rapidly in Austrian politics after studying economics and law in Vienna and Berlin. Following World War I, Austria was hopelessly divided into two hostile camps, represented politically by socialist democrats, whose strength was in Vienna, and the conservative Christian Social Party, which was strongest in rural areas and to which Dollfuss belonged. These camps not only created social institutions such as sports clubs, reading circles, and youth groups, which isolated their members from those in the other camp, but they also created large and well-armed paramilitary units. The socialists had their *Schutzbund* (Protective League), and the opposing *Heimwehr* (Home Guard) had become so heavily armed by 1933 that it reportedly had tanks and howitzers and enough material to equip 500,000 men for a military campaign of moderate length. In February 1934 paramilitary troops loyal to Dollfuss defeated the socialist democrats in bloody clashes.

Inflation, unemployment, and working class and rural poverty eroded the sympathy and patience for a formally democratic state, which could be kept alive during the 1920s only by loans from the League of Nations. The worldwide economic depression that shook Europe so violently in the early 1930s eliminated whatever shreds of stability were left in Austria and opened the door to political extremism.

Dollfuss, a diminutive man who reportedly liked his nickname of "Mini-Metternich," became chancellor in May 1932. He decided against entering a customs union with Germany, a decision vehemently criticized by many Austrians, nationalist and social democratic alike. He sought to protect his rule by converting Austria into a corporatist state (one in which all citizens belong to highly organized groups that are bound together by the political leaders in order to achieve the state's goals) on the model of fascist Italy.

Italy became his major foreign ally. In 1933 Mussolini agreed in Riccione to guarantee Austrian independence under the condition that Dollfuss abolish all political parties and alter the Austrian constitution according to the Italian fascist model. Hoping to use Mussolini to prevent Austria's incorporation into Hitler's Nazi Germany, Dollfuss complied. He outlawed parties and replaced them with a Fatherland Front. In 1933 he dissolved Parliament, and in early 1934 he ordered the arrest of political opponents, especially socialists, liberals, and trade union leaders. He even ordered that artillery fire be directed against workers' tenements in Vienna and that ruthless methods be used to suppress any resistance within the working class districts.

By May 1934, his regime was a dictatorship. He promulgated a constitution that allowed him to rule Austria as a dictator, but his time was very short. In July the Austrian Nazis, incited by Germany, attempted an unsuccessful coup d'état in Vienna. They were able to seize the chancellery for only a few hours, during which time they murdered Dollfuss. He was replaced by Kurt von Schuschnigg, who until 1938 tried in vain to preserve Austrian independence.

**DOSTOYEVSKY, FYODOR**  1821–1881, Russian novelist, one of the greatest writers of the 19th century. His novels have had a profound impact on the development of modern Russian and Western literature.

Dostoyevsky was born in Moscow on November 11, 1821, into the extremely religious family of a military doctor. Dostoyevsky graduated in 1843 from the St. Petersburg Military Engineering School. However, he found out that government service was not for him and instead turned to writing. His first novel, *Poor People,* was published in 1845.

In the 1840s, Dostoyevsky began to regularly attend meetings of a secret revolutionist society, the members of which were soon arrested and sentenced to death. However, the punishment was later changed to hard labor in Siberia followed by a term as a soldier in the ranks. Four years of hard labor and five years of military service was a brutal experience, which deepened Dostoyevsky's views on human psychology and behavior and, consequently, had a far-reaching impact on his literary works. A genius of psychological analysis, Dostoyevsky was able to portray the world of human suffering and the tragedies of insulted personalities, who realized their indignity and humiliation and made attempts to protest: *Notes from the Underground* (1861), *The Insulted and Injured* (1861), and *Crime and Punishment* (1866). His novels were perfect reflections of the controversial Russian society of the 19th century, when people were

desperate for kind and sincere relations but were disillusioned by the evilness of the reality (*The Idiot,* 1869).

The novel *The Brothers Karamazov* (1879–1880) is a manifestation of Dostoyevsky's talent, which is considered a masterpiece of not only Russian but world literature. The novel is the reflection of the author's philosophical and religious views expressed through a passionate debate among three brothers—metaphysical symbols of body, mind, and spirit. The debate revolved around the eternal struggle between evil and good, the expiation of sin through suffering, the need for a moral force.

Russian literary critiques named Dostoyevsky the founder of the ideological novel, in which the plot's development was dependent mainly on the struggle of ideas, on the confrontation of worldviews that were expressed through different characters. This polyphony of ideas in his novels reflected the polyphony of the Russian social life. His writing had a profound influence on the ideas of messianic nationalism in Russia. Also this polyphony prompted controversial interpretations of his literary heritage and the impact it has made on the 20th-century culture of the world. Dostoyevsky has been named a Christian apologist, a Messianic nationalist, a predecessor of Nietzschean ideas, and a predecessor of modern existentialism. The universal controversy of ideas and worldviews in the literary heritage of the great master of psychological analysis still engages the minds of the people worldwide.

Further readings include Joseph Frank, *Dostoevsky* (Princeton, N.J.: Princeton University Press, 1976); *The Dostoevsky Archive: Firsthand Accounts of the Novelist from Contemporaries' Memoirs and Rare Periodicals, Most Translated into English for the First Time, with a Detailed Lifetime Chronology and Annotated Bibliography,* compiled by Peter Sekirin ( Jefferson, N.C.: McFarland & Co., 1997); and *Letters of Fyodor Michailovitch Dostoevsky to His Family and Friends,* translated by Ethel Colburn Mayne (New York: Horizon Press, 1961). Dostoyevsky's work includes *The Brothers Karamazov,* translated from the Russian by Constance Garnett (London: Heinemann, 1912); *The Idiot,* translated from the Russian by Constance Garnett (London: Heinemann, 1964); and *The Short Novels of Dostoevsky* (New York: Dial Press, 1945).

**DOUGLASS, FREDERICK**  1817–1895, Probably the foremost African-American voice in the abolitionist movement of the 19th century. Escaping to New York disguised as a sailor from Baltimore, he was taken on as an agent by the Massachusetts Anti-Slavery Society where he began his life's great work.

Douglass soon became an increasingly familiar figure to abolitionists throughout the country. In 1845, after publishing his "Narrative of the Life of Frederick Douglass" at great personal risk, he went to England, where he raised enough money, through lectures on slavery and women's rights, to buy his freedom. Upon his return and after a controversial dispute with journalist and abolitionist William Lloyd Garrison, he left the newspaper, *The Liberator,* to begin publishing the *North Star.* Douglass knew that the struggle for liberation could not be won unless blacks took the lead in waging it. It is doubtful any leaders, except for David Walker and Henry Highland Garnet, were more aware than he of the consequences of attempting to fight for abolition while pursuing an independent course. Over most of the 1840s, Douglass was the chief spokesman for an integrationist approach to the race problem in America.

With the outbreak of the Civil War, Douglass met President Lincoln and assisted him in recruiting the celebrated 54th and 55th Massachusetts Negro regiments. In 1871, during the Reconstruction period, he was appointed to the territorial legislature of the District of Columbia; in 1872 he served as one of the presidential electors-at-large for New York and shortly thereafter became secretary of the Santa Domingo Commission. In 1877, after a short term as a police commissioner of the District of Columbia, Douglass was appointed marshal—a post he held until he was named recorder of deeds in 1881.

Eight years later, in return for his support of the presidential campaign of Benjamin Harrison, Douglass was appointed to the most important federal post he was to hold—minister resident and consul general to the Republic of Haiti, and later, chargé d'affaires for Santa Domingo. However, when he saw his efforts being undermined by unscrupulous American businessmen, interested solely in exploiting Haiti, he resigned his post in 1891. Four years later, Douglass died at his home in Washington, D.C.

**DUBČEK, ALEXANDER**  1921–1992, Slovak politician, reformer, and statesman, born in Uhrovec, Slovakia (then Czechoslovakia). Dubček is best known for his leading role in the 1968 Prague Spring, when he attempted to reform the Soviet style of political regime and replace it with the so-called "socialism with a human face."

Dubček spent his childhood and youth in Bishkek, Kyrgyzstan (then the Soviet Union). He finished high school in Gorkii (now Nizhnii Novgorod), and in 1938 returned to Czechoslovakia. In 1940 he became a member of the underground Slovak Communist Party, and

actively participated in the 1944 Slovak national uprising against the German occupation. After the war he worked as a factory manager, and from 1949 on occupied various functions in the Slovak branch of the Czechoslovak Communist Party. In 1960 Dubček finished his studies at the Moscow Political University, and in 1963 he became the first secretary of the Slovak Communist Party's Central Committee.

After the resignation of Antonin Novotný in 1968, Dubček was elected the first secretary of the Czechoslovak Communist Party's Central Committee, and attempted one of the most significant reforms of a Soviet-style Communist regime at the time. The Prague Spring reforms included freedom of speech and religion, the elimination of censorship, and limited forms of private ownership. Dubček's attempt to build socialism with a human face, however, was short lived. The invasion of the Warsaw Pact armies led by the Soviet Union in August 1968 put an abrupt end to the Prague Spring reforms.

Under pressure from Moscow, Dubček resigned from his post in April 1969. For a short time he was the chair of the Federal Assembly and then the Czechoslovak ambassador in Turkey. In the early 1970s, during the period of so-called "normalization," he was expelled from the party and became a clerk in a forest plant. Dubček rose to prominence once again with the fall of Communism in 1989, when he again became the chair of the Federal Assembly. He died unexpectedly after a car accident in November 1992.

Among the most significant works by Alexander Dubček are Alexander Dubček and Andras Sugar, *Dubček Speaks* (London and New York: I. B. Tauris, 1990); *Sovietskoie Vtorzhenie v Czechoslovakiu* (*The Soviet Invasion of Czechoslovakia*) (Moskva, 1991); and *Nadej zomiera posledna* (Bratislava, 1993). For the English translation, see Jiri Hochman, *Hope Dies Last: The Autobiography of Alexander Dubček* (New York: Kodansha International, 1993). The most extensive account of Dubček's role in the Prague Spring reform is given in Peter Ello, *Czechoslovakia's Blueprint for Freedom: Dubček's Unity Socialism and Humanity* (Washington, 1968); Jiri Valenta, *Soviet Intervention in Czechoslovakia, 1968: Anatomy of a Decision* (Baltimore: Johns Hopkins University Press, 1991), and Pavel Tigrid, *Why Dubček Fell* (London: MacDonald and Co., 1971).

**DUBOIS, W. E. B.**  1868–1963, William Edward Burghardt DuBois was born in Massachusetts. He built a long career as a premier African-American scholar, poet, essayist, and philosopher. He had a Ph.D. from Harvard University, and was a resident scholar and teacher at

Atlanta University. He was a cofounder and a leading spokesman for the NAACP, and published and directed dozens of studies on African Americans and race.

DuBois's early career reflected his scholarly interest in the origins and position of blacks in turn-of-the-century United States. His breakthrough study was *Philadelphia Negro* (1900). His *The Souls of Black Folk* (1903) criticized Booker T. Washington (founder of the Tuskegee Institute in Alabama) for being a compromiser, of depreciating institutions of higher learning, and of having too narrow an educational program, which concentrated solely on vocational education for blacks. DuBois argued that Washington ignored the reduction of the political and civil status of the blacks in the South, and that vocational training would not enable blacks to improve their economic position. DuBois claimed that silent submission to civic inferiority would sap the manhood of the race.

DuBois founded the Niagara movement in 1905 calling for freedom of speech and criticism, manhood suffrage for blacks, abolition of all distinctions based on race, the recognition of the basic principles of human brotherhood, and respect for the working person. The movement gained the support of many white organizations with an abolitionist spirit. Many of these organizations soon merged to form the National Association for the Advancement of the Colored People (NAACP) in 1909. DuBois was the only black in the leadership of the organization. Because of his presence, the organization was labeled radical. His responsibility was to edit *The Crisis*, the voice of the organization, which he did for dozens of years. DuBois also was responsible for organizing the Pan-African Congress, the first of which was held in Paris, France, in 1919.

DuBois criticized Marcus Garvey and the United Negro Improvement Association as being bombastic and impractical. On the other hand, he supported the Harlem Renaissance in the 1920s by publishing the works of black writers in *The Crisis*. He also lectured widely. At Atlanta University, he started *Phylon: A Journal of Race and Culture* in 1940, creating a broad medium of articulation for black scholars, directed the Conference on Negro Problems annually from 1896 to 1914, and initiated a number of studies on black culture and history.

Toward the end of his life, DuBois became more interested in his African heritage. He wrote studies on African history and the continent's significance to world history. He also became more disillusioned with the state of blacks in the United States, eventually renouncing his U.S. citizenship and moving to Ghana in 1961.

He died there two years later on the eve of the 1963 March on Washington, D.C.

DuBois has been an inspiration and source for generations of black scholars, although he has become less well known through the years. Malcolm X and Martin Luther King, Jr., both owed much intellectually to him. DuBois signifies the rise of black identity and the struggle for equality.

Works by DuBois include *The Autobiography of W. E. B. DuBois: A Soliloquy on Viewing My Life from the Last Decade of Its First Century* (New York: International Publishers, 1968); *Black Folk, Then and Now* (Millwood, N.Y.: Kraus-Thomson, 1975, orig. 1939); *Black Reconstruction: An Essay Toward a History of the Part Which Black Folk Played in the Attempt to Reconstruct Democracy in America, 1860–1880* (New York: Atheneum, 1972, orig. 1935); and *The Souls of Black Folk* (Boston: Bedford Books, 1997, orig. 1903).

**DURKHEIM, EMILE** 1858–1917, French. Durkheim was the highly influential pioneer of structural-functionalist sociology. While nationalism was a minor theme in Durkheim's own work, his sociology offers a distinct approach to understanding its history and nature. Durkheim identified two basic types of society, based on differing structural-functional principles. One, the segmented type, has parts that are the same in structure and social functions and are bound together by sentiments of similarity. The other, the organized type, has parts that are differentiated in structure and function, allowing division of labor, and are bound together by consciousness of their complementary differences. The volume and density of the segmented type are necessarily low, such that any growth in society requires the development of division of labor—moral as well as economic—as a necessary adaptation. Viewed through these theoretic lenses, national societies appear as a historically recent and probably transitory stage of social development.

The earliest societies, those closest to the segmented model, were organized in clans, based on "blood" relationships (often fictitious). In contrast, village, regional, and national societies form a sequence of larger and more dense societies, organized on a predominantly territorial basis. French national society began to emerge in the 14th century as division of labor began to develop between regions that had hitherto been loosely linked and largely autarchic. At first this process linked regions; as it progressed, it broke through the barriers delineating regions as distinct societies, leading to an organized society on a national scale. As part of this process, local customs "merge into one another and unify, at the same time as dialects and patois dissolve into a single national language." The result, by the late 19th century, was that "[t]he Norman is less different from the Gascon, and the Gascon from the Lorrainer or the Provencal; all share hardly more than the characteristics common to all Frenchmen."

This process, however, does not halt at the national level. Durkheim argued that a European-wide society had already begun to emerge in the early 19th century, parallel with which the differences between national societies were fading, as their institutions and customs converged. Nor could the nations of Europe, any more than the provinces of France, forever contain the developing division of labor.

Durkheim hesitated to predict the development of a single global society. The reason is that, according to his theory, and contrary to conventional wisdom, division of labor does not create societies; it can only develop within an already existing society, however tenuous, and he was uncertain whether the differences existing among societies around the world, ca. 1900, were too great to allow the emergence of a common society. Neither, however, did he rule out this possibility.

The most distinctive feature of this analysis is its reversal of the usual relationship theorized between nations and distinctive group characteristics. Most students of nations and nationalism conceive of them in terms of some such characteristics defining nations. In contrast, while Durkheim did not deny the existence or importance of distinguishing national characteristics, he theorized the emergence of national societies in terms of the fading and increasing diffuseness of group characteristics, which become ever less important in larger and denser societies, relative to division of labor and individualism.

An overview of Durkheim's theory of social development in English is *The Division of Labor in Society* (The Free Press, 1984).

## DUTCH NATIONALISM

The Netherlands is a confident, rich, and tolerant country whose influence in Europe far exceeds its small size and population. Its national consciousness was sharpened by a bloody eighteen-year struggle against Spanish rule that ended in 1581 and by its subsequent determination to defend its sovereignty against foreign incursion, most recently from Nazi Germany. With the highest population density in Europe, it fully utilized its access to the ocean by reclaiming land from the sea, establishing colonies on many continents, and becoming a successful trading na-

tion, with the largest and most active port in Europe, Rotterdam.

The early history of Benelux (Belgium, Netherlands, and Luxembourg) is tightly intertwined. Around 500 A.D. a Germanic tribe, the Franks, invaded the area and established a linguistic frontier that exists today in the middle of what is now Belgium. North of the line, Germanic tongues evolved into the Dutch language and into Flemish, a Dutch dialect spoken in northern Belgium. South of the line people spoke a vulgarized Latin that developed into French.

By 1543 Charles V had unified most of what is now Benelux under Spanish rule. His reign was a time of great economic, artistic, and intellectual advancement. It was the time of the great humanist, Erasmus of Rotterdam; Mercator, the most widely known cartographer in the world; and the painters van Eyck and Pieter Brueghel.

The Reformation, which Martin Luther unleashed in 1519, divided Europe and with it the Low Countries. Charles V abdicated in 1555 in favor of his son, Philip II, who was determined to defend the Catholic faith. He was cruel and inflexible in attempting to suppress Protestantism, which in its Calvinist form was particularly strong in the Netherlands. Because Spain was severely weakened by its continuous struggles against England and France, the Netherlands was able to secure its independence in 1581.

During the 17th century the Dutch were involved in almost constant war. But it was also a time of commercial success, naval supremacy, and cultural flowering. It was the Netherlands' "Golden Age," and Dutch confidence and prosperity were vividly recorded in the paintings of the Dutch masters. Amsterdam became a major point of departure for the entire world. It was also a city that was constantly moving inland as more and more land was reclaimed from the sea. Dutch traders could be found in every corner of the globe, most often representing huge private companies such as the Dutch East and West India Companies. Their activities extended to Central Asia, where they had obtained the first tulip bulbs in the 16th century, India, Ceylon (now Sri Lanka), China, and Indonesia, where they established a colony which they controlled until 1949. In 1652 they established a colony on the southern tip of Africa.

This Cape colony was snatched by the British in 1806, but in 1836–1838 the Dutch descendants moved in a "Great Trek" into the interior of what is now the Republic of South Africa and established the Afrikaaner colonies of Transvaal in 1852 and the Orange Free State in 1854. Speaking a dialect of Dutch called Afrikaans, they became the predominant white group in South Africa. Until well into the 20th century the Dutch retained sympathy for their Afrikaner relatives, who had created an economically prosperous state in an inhospitable land and who had successfully resisted cultural assimilation by the British. However, the Dutch gradually turned against the Afrikaners because of the latter's policy of racial segregation known as *apartheid*. Until majority rule was introduced in 1994, the Dutch were among the South African government's most determined foes.

In 1609 a navigational failure had brought the Dutch to North America. Henry Hudson, an English sea captain in the service of the Dutch, sailed westward in search of a passage to the East Indies and China. He failed in his mission, but he bumped into what is now New York and sailed up a river that now bears his name. His contact with America resulted in the establishment of the Dutch West India Company and in the subsequent settlement of the New World. In 1614, six years before the Pilgrim father landed, the Dutch established Fort Nassau on an island just below the present-day city of Albany, New York, a city that the Dutch incorporated in 1652 as the town of Beverwych. In 1625 an even more important fort and town had been founded on Manhattan Island, and five family farms were established to supply the soldiers and merchants. The name of the town was Nieuw (New) Amsterdam. It was soon to become the most important city in the Dutch North American colony, called New Netherland. Only a year later the Dutch governor made the famous deal with the local Indians, buying the whole of Manhattan Island for 30 guilders' worth of merchandise.

If one looks at a current map of New York City, New Amsterdam's boundaries extended to Pearl Street and to the northern wall, called *de wal*, now Wall Street. The farm on Manhattan Island belonging to the last Dutch governor, Pieter Stuyvesant, is now a rundown area known by its Americanized name—the Bowery, from *Bouwerij*, the Dutch word for farm. New Amsterdam was a very cosmopolitan city in which eighteen languages were spoken. In strict accordance with Dutch West India policy, religious or other discrimination was forbidden. It was therefore both more tolerant than the Massachusetts Bay Colony and more fun. There were many inns for drinking and dancing, and sports were popular. The Dutch continued to found cities in their colony. Among them were what is now the Bronx, Staten Island, Breukelen (Brooklyn), Bergen (now Jersey City), Hackensack, and Ridgewood.

The growth of New Netherland was halted abruptly by one of the three wars Holland fought against England in the 17th century. When British warships sailed into New Amsterdam's harbor in 1664, Stuyvesant saw no alternative to surrender. The Dutch also lost their settlements in Brazil, although they managed to hold on to Dutch Guiana and a handful of Caribbean islands known as the Netherlands Antilles.

The 18th century was for Holland one of political and cultural decline. When the French came again in 1795 the Dutch were unable to offer serious resistance. French occupation brought fundamental changes to the Netherlands, which had been ruled by an enlightened oligarchy, with a high official called a *stadholder* (not a monarch) at the top. Although it was not a modern democracy in that power was not exercised by leaders elected by universal suffrage, the Dutch republic had nevertheless been one of the most democratic countries in Europe with the possible exception of Switzerland. The French introduced the Napoleonic Code and the selection of members of parliament on the basis of limited but free elections. But the Dutch grew restive under French control, especially after Louis Napoleon, the brother of the French Emperor, was made king of Holland in 1806. The Netherlands was annexed directly into the French Empire in 1810. Napoleon's reversals gave the Dutch the chance to reassert their independence. In 1813, after Napoleon's defeat in the Battle of Leipzig, William I of the House of Orange-Nassau was proclaimed king of the Netherlands. For the first time the Netherlands became a monarchy with a Dutch monarch on the throne. Dutch troops took an active part in the final defeat of Napoleon.

When the great powers of Europe met at the Congress of Vienna in 1814–1815, they combined the Netherlands, Belgium, and Luxembourg to form the "Kingdom of the United Netherlands," with William I as king. This union did not last long. In 1830 the sparks of revolution flying from Paris landed in Brussels. The overwhelmingly Catholic Flemings and Walloons (Belgians who speak French) sensed religious discrimination by the predominantly Protestant Calvinist Dutch, despite the tradition of religious tolerance in the Netherlands. Although it was the only thing that drew Flemings and Walloons together, Catholicism was enough to unify them against the Dutch. In 1830, after a brief skirmish in Brussels, Dutch troops withdrew, and a provisional Belgian government proclaimed independence within three months. The Dutch attempted to invade Belgium, but the French and British announced their determination not to allow the Dutch to reassert control. At the London Conference of 1831, a border between the Netherlands and Belgium was drawn. The Treaty of Twenty-Four Articles, signed in London in 1839, granted the Dutch a slice of northern Belgium.

The Dutch continued to rule Luxembourg, which gradually established separate institutions and administrations. Political autonomy was granted in 1839, and in 1848 the country received a liberal constitution similar to that of Belgium. The Dutch became more benevolent rulers and cooperated in Luxembourg's movement toward democracy and independence. Finally, in 1867 the Treaty of London proclaimed Luxembourg an independent and neutral country with the Dutch king as grand duke. In 1890 Adolf of Nassau, whose family was related to the Dutch ruling family, became the grand duke and chose to reside in Luxembourg City. The close historical ties with the Netherlands continue to be symbolized by the fact that the two countries have almost exactly the same flag.

The Dutch tried to keep themselves out of the grips of the major powers through a policy of neutrality. During World War I, they remained neutral and unoccupied. When the German army was hurled westward again in May 1940 the Dutch were unable to remove themselves from the melee. In the first large-scale aerial bombardment of a densely populated city, German dive-bombers destroyed 90 percent of Rotterdam's city center within forty minutes. The German attempt to capture Queen Wilhelmina and the Dutch government by dropping crack paratroop units over the Hague failed, and the queen, Crown Princess Juliana, and the cabinet managed to escape to London, where they worked to bring about a German defeat. Holland fell within five days and was ruled for the remainder of the war by a Nazi-appointed Dutch reich commissioner, an Austrian named Seyss-Inquart. Some Dutch collaborated with the Germans, but thousands were active in the resistance movement. Holland was not liberated until May 1945. When the horror was over, the Netherlands was left with 280,000 civilian dead, vast expanses of flooded areas, wrecked harbors and industries, an economy close to total collapse, and the determination never to allow such a national catastrophe to happen again.

The Dutch set about to mend their physically broken country, a task that they were able to complete surprisingly quickly. All would have gone better if the Netherlands had not been forced to face the same searing problem that was plaguing other European powers at the time: decolonization. The jewel of the colonial empire was Indonesia. In 1619 the Dutch East India Company had created a city it called Batavia (now Jakarta) on the island of Java. From this base the Dutch extended their control over most of the archipelago's 3000 islands. Their policy of drawing a distinct line between themselves and the native population was a major factor that fanned the flames of an independence movement in the 20th century. Indonesia was an attractive target for Japanese expansion after 1940. The Dutch government, which tried to maintain a policy of neutrality in the Pacific war, could not organize a credible defense. Indonesia was captured in February 1942.

When the Dutch returned at the end of the war to reclaim what they believed was theirs, they found that they were not wanted by a native population whose leaders had declared the islands' independence in August 1945 immediately after the Japanese surrender. After four years of tension and military conflict, a settlement was reached that recognized an independent Indonesia within a kind of union which the Dutch equated with the British Commonwealth of Nations. They had insisted on retaining full control of their economic investments, which at the time accounted for almost 15 percent of their national income. Indonesia nationalized all Dutch properties in 1957. Relations also remained sour because of the Dutch retention of West Irian, part of the island of New Guinea. In 1962 West Irian was turned over to the United Nations, which seven months later transferred sovereignty to Indonesia.

After a painfully drawn-out severance from Indonesia, the Netherlands was more cooperative in helping its other colonies gain independence. In 1975 Suriname was freed. More than a quarter of the population fled to Holland in the final days before independence. The Netherlands notified the six islands in the Netherlands Antilles that they must begin preparing for self-rule. They are now organized into four self-governing communities—Aruba, Bonaire, Curaçao, and the Leeward Islands.

Having paid a high price for its failed policy of neutrality in 1940, the Netherlands' defense policy is based on NATO, of which it is a founding member. Entering the 21st century, it has a flexible volunteer army designed for rapid deployment actions and UN peacekeeping. Almost half the army troops are assigned to a joint German–Dutch corps headquartered across the German border in Münster. The command for this joint corps rotates between a German and a Dutch general. Several Dutch naval vessels were sent in 1991 to the Persian Gulf, and missile batteries were deployed to Turkey. As a sign of Dutch national sensitivities, American soldiers of the 32nd Tactical Fighter Squadron in Soesterburg are required to wear patches indicating that they are serving Her Majesty, the Queen of the Netherlands. Dutch soldiers served in Bosnia. In 1999 it deployed one ship, sixteen combat aircraft, and 738 troops in the NATO air war against Yugoslavia to stop ethnic cleansing in Kosovo. Although the Netherlands is one of the most persistent advocates of European integration, its people retain a pride and confidence so solid that their nationalism is low-key, inclusive, and inoffensive.

**DVOŘÁK, ANTONÍN** 1841–1904, Czech composer, born to the family of a butcher, in Nelahozeves, the Czech Republic (then the Habsburg Monarchy). Dvořák, despite his talent, encountered obstacles in his pursuit of a musical career. He gained his father's permission to enter the organ school in Prague only in 1857, where he spent eleven years, some of them playing in the orchestra of the *Prozatimni* (Temporary) Theater.

Dvořák destroyed most of his early works because he found them unsatisfactory. In 1875 he received a stipend that allowed him to devote more time to composition. Dvořák's work from this period was inspired by Czech and Moravian folklore. He composed the *Moravske Dvojspevy* (Moravian Doubles) and the *Slovanske Tance* (Slavic Dances). These works were received favorably by the public, as well by the critics, and Dvořák was awarded a position of a full-time professor at the Prague Conservatory. In 1892, he was appointed the director of the National Conservatory in New York, where he spent nine years.

The main body of Dvořák's work centers around his nine symphonies. The most acclaimed is his *Symfonie z Noveho Sveta* (The Symphony from the New World), which was inspired by his experiences in the United States. In addition, he wrote eleven operas, the most popular ones, *Čert a Kača* (The Devil and Kača) and *Rusalka* (The Nymph), were inspired by Czech folk tales.

A relatively complete account of Dvořák's life and work can be found in Klaus Doge, *Antonin Dvořák: Leben, Werke, Dokumente* (Zurich: Atlantis Musikbuch-Verlag, 1997), and in a collection of essays, Michael Beckerman, ed., *Dvořák and His World* (Princeton, N.J.: Princeton University Press, 1993).

**DZIUBA, IVAN** 1931–, Born in Mykolaivka in Donetsk Oblast, Ukraine. He graduated from the Donetsk Pedagogical Institute in 1953 and attended graduate school before becoming editor of the journal *Dnipro*. Dziuba is a writer and literary critic who became a political activist and dissident during the liberalizing years when Nikita Khrushchev was leader of the USSR.

One of the so-called *shestidesiatniki* ("people of the 1960s," refers to those writers and thinkers in the Soviet Union who stretched the limits of the permissible after Khruschev's denunciation of Joseph Stalin), Dziuba demanded atonement for the brutal excesses of Stalin against Ukraine, such as the Great Famine of 1932–1933 in which some five to seven million Ukrainian peasants were starved to death during collectivization, he also demanded an increase in civil liberties and the right to Ukrainian national development.

As a writer, Dziuba wanted to liberate and revitalize Ukrainian literature, partially through studying it in relation to Western European literature (an important nationalist theme is to link Ukraine with Europe rather than Eurasia and Russia). As a political activist he spoke out against anti-Semitism and the arrest of Ukrainian nationalists. Like the leader of Ukraine at this time, Petro Shelest (first secretary of the Communist Party of Ukraine, 1963–1972), Dziuba was a national Communist—a supporter of Ukrainian nationalism but also a believer in Communism.

In 1965 Dziuba published his most important essay, *Internationalism and Russification,* a work that many consider to be the most influential nationalist text of the era. In this work, Dziuba quoted Karl Marx and Vladimir Lenin to show that the forced Russification of Ukraine was nothing more than colonialism with an ideological facade. He decried this policy as a continuation of Russian imperialist expansion, and called for a return to the more open nationalities policies that Lenin instituted in the 1920s. Dziuba could not get this text published openly, but in 1966 it began to circulate as *samizdat* (literally "self-publication," a term used to describe dissident works clandestinely circulated in the Soviet Union and abroad).

As a result of *Internationalism and Russification,* Dziuba's works ceased being published in 1965. He was arrested in January 1972, and in March was expelled from the Writer's Union. In exchange for writing a public recantation of his political statements, he was released from prison in 1973. In 1978 Dziuba published *Hrani krystala (Facets of a Crystal),* a repudiation of *Internationalism and Russification.* For this act he was readmitted into the Writer's Union. While some look to his work as a dissident for inspiration and believe that his actions were constrained by the political climate of the time, more strident nationalists criticize him heavily for his recantations and for supporting Communism. Even so, Ivan Dziuba is seen as an important advocate for modern Ukraine. He served as Ukraine's minister of culture from 1992 to 1994, when he became the editor of the journal *Suchasnist.*

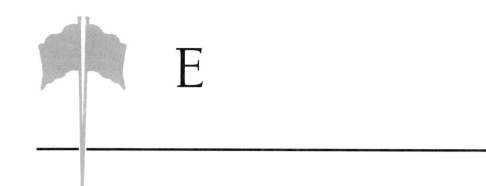

# E

**ECONOMIC NATIONALISM**   This particular brand of nationalism is premised on the belief that the overall success of the nation lies in, or at the very least is intimately connected with, the successful control of the national economy. Friedrich List (1789–1846), one of the most important theoreticians of economic nationalism, expressed the following in his 1856 book *The National System of Political Economy:* "Between the individual and humanity there is the nation . . . it is only through the nation and within the nation that the individual can receive spiritual training, *achieve productive force, security and welfare* . . . (emphasis added) and that "[i]t is the task of national economy to accomplish the economic development of the nation, and to prepare it for admission into the universal society of the future." This understanding of the important relationship between the nation and its productive forces is accompanied by the notion that economic wealth, efficiency, and prosperity might profitably take a back seat to the more pressing goal of economic independence from foreign influence and control.

Although there are rare instances in which economic nationalism is a more or less autonomous grassroots movement, usually arising out of a national minority's struggle for economic independence within a larger political-economic entity (e.g., Czechoslovakia at the end of the 19th century, or Quebec during the 1920s and 1930s), in the vast majority of cases economic nationalism is present only after a degree of political and cultural sovereignty has been realized. The reason for this is that the major instrument used to implement the policies that supporters of economic nationalism push for is the modern bureaucratic state.

Depending, of course, on the specific circumstances in which a state finds itself, its economic policies will take on a variety of shapes. However, the usual cornerstone of economic nationalist policy making is some form of economic protectionism. Protectionist policies encompass everything from tax concessions or subsidies for domestic producers, to high import tariffs and import quotas against foreign competitors. The state may also take an active role in the economy by nationalizing what are often considered strategic areas of the national economy; this may include the steel industry (and other similar heavy industries), national resources, and in some instances agriculture. The goal of such policies is to foster and strengthen the nation's domestic market by protecting it from unwanted foreign competition. As opposed to the free-trade policy recommended by neoclassical economic policies, economic nationalism places a strong emphasis on state intervention and control over the economy, in an attempt to wrestle it from the hands of foreigners (defined as both foreigners residing in other countries with investments in the host country, and as foreign nationals working in the host country in branch plant companies) and put it under the control of nationals. The trilogy of protectionism, etatism, and autarky are the pillars of virtually all economic nationalist policy.

A crucial distinction exists between the economic nationalism of countries with strong states and the economic nationalism of underdeveloped countries. The end of the 19th century witnessed a growth in the former, as European states such as Germany, Britain, and France seemed anxious to implement a variety of protectionist economic policies in their respective bids for imperial supremacy. One of the consequences of such policies was to reinforce and strengthen the development of a growing domestic military-industrial machine. The same situation arose in Germany during the 1930s with the full employment objectives set by the policies of the Nazi minister of economics, Hjalmar Schacht. In both of these instances, economically protectionist measures were used as part of a general push toward militarist and expansionist objectives (and eventually toward war).

The situation was somewhat different from 1950 into the 1970s. Newly created states, emerging from the massive decolonization that followed World War II, struggled to become full-fledged members of the world economic system. However, the relative backwardness of their economies meant that in order to catch up with the already fully industrialized nations, the implementation of protectionist policies was seen as crucial. This perception, reinforced by the rhetoric of anti-imperialism and Marxism, gave rise to a wave of essentially defensive economic nationalisms that occurred during the middle of the 20th century.

Overall then, the major goal of economic nationalism is to place the economy under the control of the nation. The key elements of this control are the encouragement of industrialization, the nationalization of capital, and extensive state intervention in the economy. While there is much debate about the extent to which these goals are attainable with the standard economic nationalist policies already mentioned, nationalists themselves believe that it is only through economic independence that true political and cultural independence can be achieved.

Friedrich List's *The National System of Political Economy* ( J. B. Lippincourt, 1856) is probably the first thoroughgoing theoretical statement of economic nationalism. For economic nationalism during the interwar period, see J. G. Hodgson's, ed., *Economic Nationalism* (New York, 1933). Otto Hieronymi, ed., and his colleagues examine economic nationalism during the 1960s and 1970s in *The New Economic Nationalism* (New York, 1979); and Harry G. Johnson's, ed., *Economic Nationalism in Old and New States* (University of Chicago Press, 1970) is a good comparative work.

## EGYPTIAN NATIONALISM

With its geographical unity created by the Nile River, its lengthy and world-renowned historical heritage, and its relative internal homogeneity, the bases for a distinctive national identity are unusually well defined in Egypt. Yet because the Egyptians also speak the same language (Arabic) and most share the same religion (Islam) as their neighbors simultaneously presents Egyptians with alternative foci for identity and loyalty. The result is that Egyptian nationalism has expressed itself with different emphases in different historical contexts.

The existence of nationalism in premodern Egypt is a contested issue. During the long pharaonic era of antiquity, for much of which Egypt was an independent political unit, Egyptian literary works expressed an awareness of the favorable geographical conditions that advanced the achievements of pharaonic civilization. Even in the subsequent Islamic period, when the Islamic faith and the Arabic language had become dominant in Egypt and made Egypt part of a larger Arab-Muslim universe of discourse, it is possible to identify a sense of regional pride in Egypt as a land of unique fertility and prosperity, historical splendor, and contemporary wisdom. Whether such sentiments merit the appelation "nationalism" is partially a matter of definition.

An unambiguous sense of Egyptian nationalism developed in the 19th century. The existence of a separate political trajectory from the long governorship of Muhammad Ali (1805–1848) onward; Egypt's precocious socioeconomic development, which distinguished it from many of its neighbors over the course of the century; the discoveries of European Egyptologists, which revealed Egypt's unique historical heritage; and the influence of European concepts of nationalism on Egypt's Westernized elite are perhaps the most important factors underlying the emergence of modern nationalism in Egypt. By the 1870s, Egyptian intellectuals were writing about Egypt as a distinct land and people with a history stretching back to the Pharaonic era. The first political manifestation of this nationalism was the Urabi movement of the late 1870s, early 1880s, a movement of protest against both the unrestrained despotism of the Muhammad Ali family and the growth of European economic interference in Egyptian affairs. Its slogan, "Egypt for the Egyptians," expresses the nationalist flavor of the movement.

This early demonstration of Egyptian nationalism was cut short by the British occupation of Egypt in 1882. For the next several decades the primary focus of Egyptian nationalism was on terminating the British occupation. By the first decade of the 20th century several political parties had emerged in Egypt. The best known and probably the most influential was the National (Watani) Party led by Mustafa Kamil, an Egyptian lawyer-ideologue whose nationalist outlook combined a fervent Egyptian patriotism with a largely instrumental attachment to the Ottoman Empire as a potential lever for ousting the British from Egypt. This anticolonial Egyptian nationalism reached its apotheosis in 1919, when wartime deprivations and the post-World War I slogan of self-determination combined to produce a countrywide uprising led by the Wafd Party. Even after British suppression of the "revolution" of 1919, three years of protest and political turmoil ensued. In 1922 Great Britain unilaterally declared Egypt an independent state, although it did reserve several areas of Egyptian affairs for British supervision. A formally independent Egyptian parliamentary monarchy was established in 1922–1923.

For the three decades of the parliamentary monarchy (1922–1952), terminating the lingering British presence continued to be a central concern of Egyptian nationalists. Although an Anglo-Egyptian treaty of alliance in 1936 redefined the basis of the British position, nonetheless Britain retained both military forces and significant influence in Egypt. Internally the dominant outlook within Egyptian nationalism under the parliamentary monarchy remained within the generally liberal framework that it had initially assumed in the 19th century: secular in ethos, viewing representative government as the proper political form for the Egyptian nation-state, laissez-faire in its economic approach. It was also narrowly Egyptian in the sense of seeing Egypt as a unique national community separate from its Arab and Muslim neighbors. Although a broadening of Egyptian nationalist conceptions to emphasize Egypt's links with its Arab and Muslim neighbors began to occur at the popular level from the 1930s onward, the regional policies of successive Egyptian governments pursued Egyptian national interests rather than asserting broader aspirations prior to the Egyptian revolution of 1952.

The revolution of 1952 marked the beginning of a new era for Egyptian nationalism. By 1954 the new regime led by Jamal Abdel Nasser finally negotiated an agreement for British evacuation from Egypt; the last British troops left Egyptian soil in 1956. Simultaneously Nasser broadened Egyptian nationalism by asserting Egypt's Arab character and its leadership of Arab nationalism. The new context of the post-World War II period, in which Egypt and the other newly independent Arab states faced the common problems of how to deal with the remnants of imperialism, the Cold War, and Israel, led Nasser to define Egypt's place in the world in broader terms than his predecessors. First promoting Arab solidarity vis-à-vis the West and Israel, later calling for Arab unity, Nasser undertook a redefinition of the meaning of nationalism in Egypt. The late 1950s and 1960s were the heyday of Arab nationalism in Egypt, the view that Egypt was part and parcel of a larger Arab nation. By 1958 Egypt had united with Syria in the United Arab Republic, a name that Egypt retained for the remainder of the Nasser years in spite of Syria's secession in 1961.

Under Nasser's successors, Anwar Sadat (1970–1981) and Hosni Mubarak (1981–), the nationalist pendulum has swung in the opposite direction. Sadat's reversal of many of Nasser's policies included a deemphasis of Arab nationalism and a reassertion of Egypt's distinctiveness within the Arab world. Politically, his pursuit of rapprochement with the United States and peace with Israel effectively ended Egypt's drive for Arab leadership and resulted in Egypt's temporary isolation within inter-Arab politics. President Mubarak has muted the more acerbic aspects of Sadat's stormy relationship with the Arab world, in the process achieving a partial reintegration of Egypt into the Arab fold since the late 1980s. Nonetheless, Mubarak has not reasserted Nasser's drive for Arab leadership. Although seeking to play a major role in regional politics, the framework within which this is being pursued is one of the acceptance of existing states and the assertion of specifically Egyptian interests in the region. Alternative visions of the proper nature of Egyptian nationalism—Nasserist spokesmen calling for a return to a policy of Arab nationalist leadership and Islamist ideologues maintaining that Egypt must find its national destiny within a larger Muslim community—exist but do not shape state policy at the close of the 20th century.

## EISENSTEIN, SERGEY

1898–1948, Soviet film director, scriptwriter, and theoretician. Eisenstein was born in Riga, Latvia. In 1915 he finished secondary school and continued his studies in the Institute of Civil Engineering in Saint Petersburg. In 1918 he volunteered for the Red Army and participated as an engineer. In the army he became interested in the theater and kept busy in theatrical productions as an actor, artist, and producer. In 1920 Eisenstein left the army and enrolled in Moscow's Proletkult (Proletarian Culture) theater. Later he studied in the School for Stage Direction under Vsevolod Meyerhold, a well-known theatrical producer who taught radical methods. In 1923 Eisenstein published a manifesto called *The Montage of Attraction* in which he opposed the traditional montage with the impact of the percussive attractions, which included methods of circus, show, and art of posters.

In 1925 Eisenstein produced two films: *Stachka* (*The Strike*) and a film dedicated to the 20th anniversary of a Russian revolution in 1905, *Bronenosets Potemkin* (*The Battleship Potemkin*). *The Strike* was intended to be a part of a series of revolutionary films named *Towards Dictatorship;* the series was never completed. Instead of the traditional plot Eisenstein portrayed a sequence of emotional episodes—the indignation of the workers, the expulsion of the masters in the factory, the scatter of the demonstrators, and cossacks' slaughter of unarmed workers. At the same time Eisenstein paid attention to the methods of movie making: to the assembly (montage) of the film, grandiose layout, rhythm, and metaphor. In the other film, *The Battleship Potemkin,* the same methods were used: sequence of episodes, music, and attraction; closeups of the faces of fleeing civilians; slaughter of the workers by the tsarist troops, waves of the sea like the revolutionary wave, a cradle falling from the stairs. Although a black and white movie, the red revolutionary flag was colored pink in the film. Both of these silent movies were like chronicles of the grand revolutionary period of Russian history and promoted patriotic feelings. They concentrated on the revolutionary masses and not so much on the individuals.

In the 1920s Eisenstein visited a number of European and North American countries lecturing on modern art and new methods of filming and studying the new techniques of sound film making. He lectured in Berlin, Zurich, Paris, London, and the United States. In Hollywood he tried to produce a film but found no interest in his ideas. Eventually he obtained modest funds to make an epic film on the 1000 years of Mexican history from ancient Indian cultures to the modern times entitled *Que Viva Mexico!* from an American novelist, Upton Sinclair. The film was, however, never finished and Eisenstein returned to Moscow. He lectured, wrote articles, and tried to make films but was accused by the authorities of not understanding the meaning of propaganda films as Eisenstein concentrated on the antipodes of philosophical tragedy in history. His new sound film, *Alexander Nevsky* (1938), was a success in the Soviet Union. The synthesis of dramatic episodes, music, decorations, and acting presented a heroic picture of Russian history. It was about the medieval prince who defeated Western aggressors, the Teutons (German Crusaders). The film was a combination of two basic ideas: the importance of individuals (Prince Alexander Nevsky) and of the masses (the simple Russian people of the 13th century) in history.

The last film by Eisenstein, *Ivan Grozny* (*Ivan the Terrible;* Part I, 1944; Part II, 1946) was completely different from his previous movies. Instead of the masses, an individual—a Russian tsar who united the small and weak Russian principals into one strong Russian state in the 16th century—was the center of the movie. Ivan Grozny was a character who developed from a progressive statesman into a hesitant, lonely, and cruel dictator. Stalin accused Eisenstein of betraying the official method of art—socialist realism (revolutionary masses, socialist form, and ethnic essence) and an inclination to the extreme individualism that confronted this official method.

Eisenstein's films had an immense influence on Soviet movies even after his death. English-language collections of his writings include *The Film Sense* (1942), *Film Form* (1949), *Notes of a Film Director* (1959), and *Film Essays with a Lecture* (1968).

**EL SALVADOR, NATIONALISM IN**   The Republic of El Salvador, a country in Central America with San Salvador as its capital, is a former Spanish colony that became part of the Federal Republic of Central America (formerly the United Provinces of Central America) in 1824. The name El Salvador was not used until 1841. Its people have been subjected to substantial civil violence and external intervention in recent decades.

An expedition of Spanish conquerors led by Pedro de Alvarado arrived in El Salvador from Guatemala in 1524 and took the area by force despite fierce opposition from the Pipil, a Nahua tribe indigenous to the area. The Spanish settlement of San Salvador was begun in 1525 but was attacked by Pipil warriors and resettled several times until its permanent establishment in 1528.

The indigo farmers initiated the fight for Salvadoran independence. These Spanish settlers who relied on indigenous workers were at first interested in independence from the Guatemalan archbishopric and merchants who controlled the region. Uprisings in 1811 and 1814 were unsuccessful, however, and in 1821 Salvadorans joined the Guatemalan effort to gain independence from Spain. They did not wish to follow Guatemala into the Mexican Empire, however, and sought annexation into the United States.

When the Mexican government collapsed in 1823 the Salvadorans sent a delegation to a Central American constitutional convention in Guatemala City and became part of the Federal Republic of Central America. Salvadoran rebel leader Manuel Jose Arce, who had participated in the 1811 uprising, became the first president of the united republic. Although Arce's presidency collapsed in 1829 following a civil war that began in 1827, the federal capital was transferred to the city of San Salvador until its disintegration.

The new Salvadoran republic was rife with internal and international conflict, perhaps foreshadowing the nation's troubled history. From 1841 until 1863 only one head of state managed to serve two full years. Finally, in 1871, the liberals were able to begin a sixty-year period of rule and the nation's economic center shifted from indigo to coffee. The domestic stability of the nation came at the cost of subjugation to the coffee barons, a closely knit set of families that had established coffee plantations.

A military coup by General Maximiliano Hernandez Martinez in 1931 initiated a series of military governments that ruled through 1979. Harsh rule and human rights abuses led to the formation of an array of opposition movements, including guerilla organizations. The government responded with little change except to escalate the repression until civil war broke out following a 1979 military coup; the struggle continued well into the 1990s.

The Roman Catholic Church in El Salvador, traditionally a supporter of the country's élites but whose cathedrals were filled with the nation's poor, gradually began to take up the cause of the opposition. Archbishop Oscar Arnulfo Romero, a moderate if not a conservative when he took office, moved increasingly toward opposition as his priests and nuns were harassed and tortured. The conflict between the church and state of El Salvador reached its apex when the archbishop was assassinated while offering mass in March 1980.

The administration of U.S. President Ronald Reagan backed the ruling powers in the struggle against the opposition groups, providing it with massive financial and military aid as well as military training, especially for the government of Jose Napoleon Duarte, who became president in 1984.

Efforts to bring about peace in the country met with limited success in the 1990s. The major guerilla organization, the Farabundo Marti National Liberation Front (FMLN), has become a major player in electoral politics. An article in *The Economist* in March 1997 entitled "Take Out Life Insurance Before You Enter" noted that although the guerilla war seemed to have ended, the violence had not.

**EMERSON, RALPH WALDO**  1803–1882, American essayist and critic, born in Boston, Massachusetts. Admired by Nietzsche for the "cheerful transcendency" of his individualistic creed, Emerson was the leading spirit and most well known of the American transcendentalists, an inchoate—but highly influential—intellectual movement active in New England during the 1840s. The most famous expressions of Emerson's transcendentalism are *Nature* (1836), his first short book, and *Essays, First Series* (1841), which includes transcendentalist manifestos such as "Self-Reliance," "The Over-Soul," and "Circles."

Emerson's transcendentalism is committed to individual self-development and self-expression, and to the moral equality and radical possibilities of all human beings. Social organizations and political institutions are defensible, from this perspective, only to the extent that they are consistent with these commitments. Emerson's transcendentalism, therefore, is hostile to virtually every form of collectivism, including liberal utilitarianism, socialism, and nationalism. According to Emerson, collectivism is only legitimate when it is based on the belief that all human beings, regardless of ascriptive traits, participate in a universal spirit or soul. So Emerson writes, "A nation of men will for the first time exist, [when] each believes himself inspired by the Divine Soul which also inspires all men."

Emerson is mainly remembered as the quintessential American man of letters. In "The American Scholar" (1837), an oration before the Phi Beta Kappa Society of Harvard University, Emerson declares intellectual independence from European life and literature as definitively as Thomas Jefferson had declared political independence from England. Emerson heralds a revolution in literature and manners that rejects Europe's reputed taste for aristocratic refinement and embraces, instead, the common and familiar, the rough and democratic. This revolution in literature and manners, Emerson predicts, will be accompanied by an analogous political movement in which new importance would be given to the individual, until "man shall treat with man as a sovereign state with a sovereign state."

Normally reticent about politics, Emerson was, nonetheless, extremely sympathetic to the agenda of America's abolitionist movement and active in their affairs, especially during the 1850s. In numerous speeches and lectures, Emerson declared slavery to be incompatible with the founding principles of the United States and with basic tenets of morality. Idealism, not pragmatism, generally characterizes Emerson's political writings. As the issue of slavery gradually tore his country apart, Emerson argued that war and disunion should not be feared, especially when compared with the devastating moral impact of slavery on American society. Emerson also blasted Daniel Webster for his crucial support of the Compromise of 1850 in his "Fugitive Slave Law" addresses of 1851 and 1854. Once the Civil War began, however, Emerson pledged himself wholeheartedly to the preservation of the Union.

The attractiveness of Emerson's democratic individualism as an alternative to collectivist visions of modern society has been debated. Many critics find Emerson's vision either too religious or too alienating. Even so, his legacy as a founder of a characteristically American literature, and a major influence on writers such as Henry David Thoreau, Walt Whitman, William James, Emily Dickinson, and Robert Frost, cannot be disputed.

The definitive intellectual biography of Emerson is Robert D. Richardson, Jr., *Emerson: The Mind on Fire* (University of California Press, 1995). An excellent study of Emerson's political life is found in Len Gougeon, *Virtue's Hero: Emerson, Antislavery, and Reform* (University of Georgia Press, 1990). The classic study of Emerson in the context of American literature and letters remains F. O. Matthiessen, *American Renaissance* (Oxford University Press, 1941).

## ENAHORO, ANTHONY    1921–, Nigerian nationalist politician who in 1953 moved a motion in the federal legislature calling on Britain to grant political autonomy to Nigeria in 1956. Enahoro was born in Uromi, Benin, in present-day Edo State of Nigeria. Enahoro came of age at the time when the agitation for self-rule was gathering momentum among Nigerians. His love for politics directed him to an initial career in journalism. In 1943 he joined Nnamdi Azikiwe's *West African Pilot,* which at the time was noted for its crusading and anticolonial journalism style, as a reporter. Within two years he had risen to the position of assistant editor at the *Pilot.* Subsequently Enahoro was appointed editor of Azikiwe's *Southern Nigeria Defender* at the tender age of twenty-one, which made him the youngest person ever to edit a major newspaper in Africa. The *Defender's* role was similar to that of the *Pilot* at a time when the press was looked on as a crucial molder of opinion and mobilizer of consciousness in the anticolonial struggle in Nigeria.

Enahoro's crusading journalism earned him jail terms on two separate occasions. He also went to jail two other times for political reasons. He embraced active partisan politics as a member of Obafemi Awolowo's Action Group (AG), and served in various ministerial and legislative capacities on its platform. Enahoro played an active role as a member of the AG during the various constitutional conferences that paved the way for Nigeria's political independence on October 1, 1960. In 1964, Enahoro and the entire AG leadership were charged with treasonable felony. He escaped to England but was returned to Nigeria for trial after a protracted extradition case, which was equally celebrated. Enahoro and his codefenders were tried and convicted but were released in 1967 by General Yakubu Gowon's military government.

In the 1990s Enahoro has rethought nationalism. He believes that the countries of Africa must be seen in terms of the ethnic nationalities residing within their borders. The manner in which these "nations," as he calls them, were forced together to form countries in Africa is at the root of the political instability, economic underdevelopment, and the retardation of cultures that African countries have continued to experience ever since they attained political independence. The reason, he believes, is that each country is governed as a unitary entity in a situation that calls for true federalism. As Enahoro sees it, the recipe for the termination of political despotism and for the revitalization of the continent and its cultures lies in a devolution of political power back to the various nationalities in a way that will allow them to enter true confederal unions with one another within the boundaries of each respective country. Each *federating unit* will then assume the autonomy and right to develop its national language, culture, and local political and economic affairs without interference from the center.

Typical of him, Enahoro has adopted an activist stance on how to realize his new prescription in Nigeria. In 1992 he spearheaded the formation of the Movement for National Reformation (MNR) the platform from which he has sought to mobilize Nigerians for the restructure of the country along ethno-national lines.

Enahoro's new position on nationalism made him an enemy of Nigeria's military government under the late General Sani Abacha, which detained him without trial in 1995 and compelled him to escape to the United States the next year where he has lived in self-exile ever since.

*The Fugitive Offender* (London: Cassel, 1965) is Enahoro's political and prison memoirs.

## ENGELS, FRIEDRICH    1820–1895, German writer, philosopher, and revolutionary. Engels collaborated with Karl Marx and extended Marx's writings after his death. In response to international events, Engels often attempted to clarify Marx's positions on the national question.

According to Marx and Engels, and in line with their theory of historical materialism, the development of the modern nation-state is closely tied to the rise of capitalism. They argue that as the feudal economic system was displaced by the capitalist mode of production, large areas of land were subsumed into the nation-state, a political entity based on a common language. Engels argues that this centralization was necessary for the development of capitalism because it provided large markets with large pools of mobile workers. However, such centralization tends to eliminate local customs and languages.

As a universalizing force, the development of the nation-state is a prerequisite for the inevitable Communist revolution. In the *Communist Manifesto,* Marx and Engels argued that a Communist revolution will not occur until after the proletariat became conscious of the universal suffering of their class within a nation. They write, "the proletariat must first of all acquire political supremacy, must rise to be the leading class of the nation."

However, the proletariat will soon realize that nationalist interests are merely an illusion created by the bourgeoisie to direct the proletariat away from their true, universal class interest. Further, nationalism is used as a tool to turn the proletariat from different nations against each other.

Eventually under Communism, according to Engels (and Marx), nations will wither away just as the state does. The proletariat class would eventually become conscious of the universality of its class interests, and would realize they have more in common with the working classes in other countries than in nationalist interests within their country. Ironically, nations are necessary for the revolution, but superfluous after it.

In their less theoretical works, Engels and Marx judge individual nationalist movements by how well they contribute to the rise of a centralized nation-state. Those movements that successfully form centralized states further the historical destiny of Communism, while those nationalist movements that remain on the periphery get in the way of the eventual Communist revolution. Therefore, Marx and Engels praised nationalist movements such as those in Ireland and Poland, which furthered the efforts of Communism. In fact, Engels was one of the first to call for the "self-determination of nations." Nevertheless, Engels employed harsh, essentially racist, language when denouncing less successful nationalist movements in Wales, Slovakia, Serbia, and elsewhere.

In retrospect, Engels, like Marx, seemed to fail to give due credit to ethno-cultural ties. Historical events have shown that they overemphasized the universal ties of class interests at the expense of nationalism.

An excellent discussion of the place of the nation in Marx and Engels's thought is provided by Ephraim Mimni, "Marx, Engels and the National Question," in *Science & Society* 53(3) (Fall 1989), pp. 297–326. An important book-length work is Roman Rosdolsky, *Engels and the "Nonhistoric" Peoples: The National Question in the Revolution of 1848* (Glasgow: Critique Books, 1986). For Engels's discussion of nationalism see "Decay of Feudalism and Rise of Nation States," in Engels, *The Peasant War in Germany* (Moscow: Progress Publishers), and his essays on Pan-Slavism that appear in Blackstock and Hoselitz, *The Russian Menace.*

## ENGLISH NATIONALISM

Below the cover and rhetoric of unity, signs appeared in the 16th century that pointed toward a growing sense of shared destiny among people who spoke the same language, had a common culture, and believed that they somehow belonged together. Nations and nationalism were slowly forming. Almost nowhere was this more apparent than in England. Norman French (brought to the island by the forces of William the Conquerer in 1066) had been assimilated into its Anglo-Saxon language to form the English language. The English Channel ensured its geographic separation from the European continent. Therefore, its people had developed a common language and culture. They also had an increasingly centralized government under the rule of powerful monarchs.

In 16th-century England, King Henry VIII challenged the authority of an outside authority, the Catholic pope in Rome, over his realm's affairs. When Henry realized that his wife Catherine would not produce a son, and because he was lusting after the attractive, dark-haired Ann Boleyn, he had asked the pope to grant him an annulment from Catherine, claiming that the marriage was illegal in the first place. Unfortunately for Henry, Catherine's uncle, Charles V, of the Holy Roman Empire had his troops in Rome at the time. When the pope refused to grant Henry's request, in an unprecedented move, Henry had himself declared head of the church in England. He had thereby established the principle that his country had the right to make its own decisions, a right that would later be called "national sovereignty."

His daughter Mary succeeded him, but she died after only five years on the throne. Her half-sister, Elizabeth I, became queen, and with her, one of the great ages in English history began, when England's greatness and independence were unquestioned. Because the Catholic Church considered Elizabeth illegitimate, she moved the country back toward Protestantism. It was a moderate Protestant position. The old forms of worship were retained in English, and there was no vigorous attempt to be overly scrupulous in matters of doctrine. As Elizabeth put it, "We shall make no window into any man's soul." At this time, Elizabeth's cousin, Mary Stuart, abdicated the throne of Scotland in favor of her son James and fled to England. For years, Roman Catholic attempts to oust Elizabeth flurried around Mary, who was Catholic. Despite "that divinity that doth hedge a king" (or queen), Elizabeth finally yielded to the advice of her court and had Mary beheaded in 1587.

That same year, Sir Francis Drake, having already stolen Spanish gold from the New World, raided the port of Cadiz. In reprisal, the next year Spain sent a great armada to invade and conquer England. But a "Protestant wind" and English naval tactics carried the day; less than half of the armada managed to limp back to Spain. England had established itself as a ruler of the seas, a position it would continue to enjoy for almost 400 years. It also collectively savored the euphoria of victory, which could only strengthen the idea of English nationhood. National pride was further boosted by the flowering of English culture during the Elizabethan

Age. The brightest blooms were uses of the language that still affect our thought and speech. Although William Shakespeare was the most magnificent of the blossoms, others, such as Spenser, Drayton, Donne, and Marlowe, also flourished.

When Elizabeth died unmarried in 1603, James Stuart, king of Scotland, became James I of England and the whole island was united under one monarch. Wales had already been joined to England. Wales is technically a principality whose titular ruler is the Prince of Wales, who is always the heir apparent to the English throne. But it lost all traces of political identity through the Act of Union with England in 1535. By the 17th century England was at the forefront of a European-wide shift toward the idea that individuals belonged to nations and that those cultural entities had a right to create their own states to protect and promote their interests. Further centuries of imperial greatness, astonishing wealth and global influence, and victories in two world wars in the 20th century solidified the islanders' pride in their country.

However, it is difficult to speak in terms of "English nationalism" after the 17th century because the United Kingdom encompasses more than England. The three large regions on the outer fringe of the United Kingdom comprise less than a fifth of its total population: Wales (2.9 million), Scotland (5.1 million), and Northern Ireland (1.6 million). These populations compare with 48.7 million in England. The combination of the three entities on the largest island constitute "Britain." Until 1999 all three peripheral regions were, in varying degrees, Celtic in background and relatively poor economically. All three were ruled by departments of the central government: the Wales Office, the Scottish Office, and the Northern Ireland Office. The British prime minister in London appointed a secretary of state for each, and these politicians, who never come from the areas they control, sat in the cabinet.

Although these regions' relations with London have rarely been smooth, regionalism was seldom a major factor in British politics after the twenty-six southern counties won their independence from Britain in 1921. All shared in British nationalism. As the largest, richest and most influential nation within the United Kingdom, the English never felt threatened or disadvantaged. They expended very little time and effort in trying to distinguish in their own minds the difference between British and a more restricted English nationalism. For most, they were one and the same. British successes were their own. However, Scots, Welsh, and Northern Irish (themselves divided between Protestants loyal to Britain and Catholics who prefer union with the Irish Republic to the south) retained national identities separate from the English. These identities varied greatly in intensity. Many of the differences were masked by a common language, the facade of unitary government, and economic prosperity.

This changed dramatically in the 1970s. Strapped with a disproportionate number of dying industries and unhappy with the remoteness of central government, nationalist parties in Wales and Scotland grew. At the end of the 20th century Westminster transferred important powers to these regions. "Devolution," which resulted in all three having their own elected parliaments in 1999, represents a historic shift in the way Britain is governed. It also provides the English with more visible reminders of the distinctions between them and the smaller nations that belong to the United Kingdom.

## ENLIGHTENMENT

Often thought of as rationalist secularism, Enlightenment refers to a loosely configured constellation of ideas, including reason, rationality, universality, cosmopolitanism, and independence of individuals from supernatural power. Because it brought about an uneven decline of ontological truth and divine/cosmological power over human beings, the birth of Enlightenment in 18th-century Europe liberated people from their hierarchical relations with the world.

The complex relationship between Enlightenment and nationalism is coupled with that of capitalist development. Benedict Anderson and Michael Mann, two scholars who have contributed to conceptualizations of nationalism, both identify the relationship between nationalism and capitalism as being crucial, yet there are key differences in the way they view capitalism and its relationship to nationalism, as well as the place of the Enlightenment in the formation of nationalism. According to Michael Mann, Enlightenment thoughts supplied the petit bourgeoisie, in the wake of the revolution in France, with the ideology that mobilized various groups of dissent against the Old Regime, including lower lawyers, clerks, officials, and local notables who serviced the regime and were dispersed throughout it. This weakened the moral basis of the Old Regime. As a result, with written language, officials resorted to rhetorical persuasion, instead of factional fights, which contributed to the formation of ideological networking among élites. Furthermore, the Enlightenment, in conjunction with the growth of literacy, brought together the petit bourgeoisie, lower clergy, and upper peasantry (third-estate assemblies) in their Declaration of Rights in 1789 in the National Assembly, when it voted to destroy entirely the feudal regime. It was the Enlightenment ideas with which the revolutionaries postulated the contrast between the old and new regimes, representing the old regime as dynastic particularism and the New Republic as the universal nation for free and independent citizens.

Anderson has brought a Copernican turn to understanding nationalism, since he considers it to be a cultural artifact rather than an ideology invoked by the petit bourgeoisie or state élites to mobilize other classes. For Anderson, the Enlightenment is a cultural root of nationalism that people came to imagine by reading print materials such as newspapers and novels. Once this nationalism emerged in the West, it became a mobile "modular" form that was imitated and consciously exploited in a Machiavellian spirit around the globe.

In the colonial context, the Enlightenment represents itself as the knowledge of progress and civilization. It became a tool for the colonial power to legitimize its exploitation of the colonized in terms of its obligation to enlighten the not-yet-civilized others. The colonial education circulated ideas that identified the West as being different because it embodied reason and rationality, whereas those not in the West belonged to notions of the spirits and nature. By privileging the notion of the Enlightenment as a progressive idea, the West was able to turn to this constructed difference to develop a hierarchy of the West over the non-West. The colonial education endowed national elites of the colonized with a perspective that informed how national elites envisioned their new independent society and their relations with the uneducated masses, whose culture was seen to stand in opposition to the Enlightenment and thus needed to be overcome. Moreover, the elites' appreciation and assessment of their current and a new independent society was shadowed by their images of European civilization. Benedict Anderson terms this bewildering consciousness of these national elites the "specter of comparisons."

Further reading includes Michael Mann, *The Sources of Social Power, Volume II: The Rise of Classes and Nation-States, 1760–1914* (Cambridge University Press, 1993), Benedict Anderson, *Imagined Communities* (London: Verso, 1991), and Benedict Anderson, *Spectre of Comparisons* (London: Verso, 1998).

**ENVER PAŞA**  1881–1922, Turkish general who commanded the Ottoman forces during World War I, and flamboyant military officer and visionary nationalist in the late Ottoman state. With his impassioned commitment to the Ottoman state and wide horizons char-

acterized by his shifting stress on Pan-Islamism and Pan-Turkism, Enver Paşa carved a space in the Turkish collective psyche. He was the only Turkish general who journeyed to what Turkish nationalists viewed as their ancestral home, Turkistan, to defend and raise the political consciousness of the Turkic peoples.

Enver Paşa, whose family moved from Macedonia to Istanbul, was born in 1881 and graduated from the imperial military academy in 1902. His understanding of nationalism was molded during his three-year-long duty in Macedonia, the hotbed of the Balkan nationalist movements against Ottoman rule. Because the ethnic Orthodox churches were the cultural and institutional repository of Balkan nationalist movements, Enver Paşa realized the power of religion in the constitution of nationalism. Due to his political activities within the illegal Committee of Union and Progress (CUP) since 1906, he was recalled and appointed to a new post in Istanbul. Refusing to obey this order, Enver Paşa and his fellow officers and a large number of troops escaped into the Macedonian hills. This challenged the authority of the Istanbul government and initiated the Young Turk revolution in 1908. When the new government was threatened by the cohesive and critical position of these young military officers, Enver Paşa was sent to Berlin as a military attaché in 1909. He briefly returned to Istanbul to join the military against the Istanbul mutiny of April 13, 1909. In 1911, he resigned from his job in Berlin and joined the Turkish forces in Libya. He also played a critical role in the Balkan wars of 1912–1913. When the defeated Ottoman government surrendered Edirne, one of the early capitals of the Ottoman state, to the Bulgarians, Enver Paşa and his allies overthrew the government and installed the CUP in power.

Enver Paşa reorganized the army and recaptured Edirne after the Balkan Christian allies had a falling out, leading to his soaring popularity. The liberation of Edirne helped him to become the leading member of the inner core of the CUP and the minister of war. He remained the leader of the pro-German clique since Germany was in a power struggle against the Ottoman states' main rivals: Britain and Russia. Before entry into the war, Enver Paşa established a secret guerrilla organization, known as *Teskilat-i Mahsusa*, which engaged in clandestine activities in the Balkans and the Caucasus. His impetuous policies and in particular the disastrous winter campaign in Sarikamis, in northeastern Anatolia, in December 1914 helped bring about the defeat of the state. Undeterred, Enver Paşa saw the Russian revolution as an opportunity to form a new empire out of the Turkic peoples of Russia. His ill-conceived offensives resulted in the defeat of Ottoman armies in the Caucasus. When the armistice was signed in October 1918, Enver Paşa and the prominent CUP leaders fled to Germany. He later went on to Turkistan and organized the population under the banner of the Army of Islam against the Bolsheviks. He fought bravely and was killed in battle in Tajikistan in August 1922.

Due to his experience in the Balkans, Enver Paşa realized the power of religion and its centrality to the identity of Muslim populations throughout the region. Unlike the later ideologues of Kemalism, he favored a more considered and judicious mix of cultural-religious identity and Turkish nationalism. Although official Turkish historiography presents Enver Paşa as being solely a Pan-Turkish figure, he was more in favor of a Turkish-Islamic synthesis that was more in accordance with the sentiments of the majority of the population. His personal integrity, undaunted courage, and loyalty to the Turkish-Muslim nation made him a tragic and flawed hero. His struggles in the Balkans and Central Asia highlighted the fact that despite later Kemalist attempts to limit Turkish-Muslim sentiments and identity to the soil of Anatolia, and to a broader ideological construct of being a part of Europe, historic ties to surrounding populations and territory could not be effectively sundered.

On Enver Paşa see, Glen Swanson's "Enver Pasha: The Formative Years," in *Middle East Studies* 16 (1980), pp. 193–199; on Enver's relations with Germany, see Ulrich Trumpener, *Germany and the Ottoman Empire, 1914–1918* (Princeton University Press, 1968); and for his activities in Russia, see Masayuki Yamauchi, *The Green Crescent under the Red Star: Enver Pasha in Soviet Russia, 1919–1922* (Tokyo: Institute for the Study of Languages and Cultures of Asia, 1991).

**EQUALITY** The Italian nationalist leader and thinker Giuseppe Mazzini argued in 1861 that "there is no true Country without a uniform right. There is no true Country where the uniformity of that right is violated by the existence of caste, privilege, and inequality." Nationalism has long been used as a justification for opposing inequalities and ranks within the nation. According to this vision of nationalism, the only distinction of fundamental moral and political importance is between insiders and outsiders, members and nonmembers of the nation. The nationalism of the French Revolution sought to destroy the distinctions between nobles and peasants, clergy and laypeople, Jews and Gentiles, Bretons and Frenchmen. *Fraternité* and *egalité* were closely related; how could the unequal feel like brothers? At least the early stages of a nationalist movement are often democratic and egalitarian in their ide-

ology, demanding both the freedom of a people (from rule by others) and rule by the people (in a democratic nation-state). The late Ernest Gellner argued that nationalism's economic function has been to create internally homogeneous populations that could function as fluid labor pools. The "modular" education Gellner described, which replaces inherited or apprenticed trades with a basic set of skills applicable to any of the jobs available in a complex economy, encourages both assimilation and egalitarianism.

Advocates of social democratic egalitarian politics often argue that nationalism is necessary for such politics to succeed; why would anyone make the sacrifices equality demands if they did not feel that they were helping their brothers? Contemporary theorists including David Miller, Yael Tamir, and Michael Walzer have made this argument forcefully. The argument is sometimes accepted by critics of material egalitarianism as well; the classical liberal F. A. Hayek argued that multinational states would be less likely than nation-states to turn to socialism.

The alleged beneficiaries of such homogenizing egalitarianism are not always grateful for the boon. Advocates of Kurdish independence argue that Turkish nationalism, which is internally egalitarian in this way and insists that there can be no distinctions drawn between Turks and Kurds, has rationalized coercive assimilationist policies against the Kurds. The egalitarian assimilationism of republican France has been opposed by Jews, members of the regional nationalities such as the Bretons, and today by Arab Muslim immigrants. The "melting pot" of American nationalism has met periodic resistance from immigrants and consistent resistance from American Indians.

On the other hand, since the egalitarianism of nationalism stops at the nation's border, minorities have also suffered when defined out of the nation. Here the exclusion of Jews from the German, Polish, and Russian nations is only the most prominent example. The Romany (Gypsies) have been considered aliens by, at one time or another, most of the nations of Europe; they have been subject to deportations, official violence, and a lack of legal protection against private and mob violence. If American Indians suffered coercive assimilationist policies at the hands of those who considered them part of the American nation, they suffered deportation and war at the hands of those who did not. Early American nationalism was democratic and egalitarian among the whites who were considered to make up the nation; black slaves were emphatically not included.

Nationalism is always Janus-faced on the subject of equality. By insisting that the only distinction that matters is that between national and non-national, it is internally egalitarian and externally deeply inegalitarian. In addition to the treatment of local minorities who are considered outside the nation, external inegalitarianism manifests in nationalist resistance to immigration, open trade, and foreign economic assistance. To those who advocate global equalization of wealth, nationalism seems a great barrier to equality. To those concerned with unjust distinctions at home, it seems an ally.

On the other hand, Mazzini and many of his heirs who have advocated liberal nationalism for all nations have thought that equal membership in equal nations was a more secure basis for global equality than was a utopian cosmopolitanism or internationalism. Today, in some respects the formal equality of nation-states is a *sine qua non,* more widely respected than the formal equality of persons within a state. Every nation-state, no matter how large or small, receives one and only one vote in the UN General Assembly. Every sovereign unit is equally formally sovereign, equally legally immune to interference by other states. Further complicating matters, the internal egalitarianism of nationalist theory and rhetoric has often fallen away in nationalist practice. When political leaders could claim that the nation was threatened by false friends at home, alien minorities nearby, or war from abroad, the interests of the nation have been used to justify illiberal, inegalitarian, and undemocratic rule.

## ESTONIAN NATIONALISM

In 1991 Estonians realized a dream they have seldom savored in history: independence. Unfortunately this did not automatically eradicate the legacies of an overbearing Soviet Empire. To maintain control over a sprawling multinational state and promote its own socialist industrialization, the Kremlin had intentionally mixed peoples and changed borders. Estonia must deal with the residual problems.

Estonians constituted 97 percent of the country's population in 1945 (after Russia had incorporated predominantly Russian-speaking areas in the East), 72 percent in 1953, 64.7 percent in 1979, and 61.5 percent in 1989. By 1997 this had risen to 65 percent due to Russian outmigration after independence, leaving an ethnic mix of 28.7 percent Russians, 2.7 percent Ukrainians, 1.5 percent Belarussians, 1 percent Finns, and 1.9 percent other nationalities. Massive inward migration of Russians and outward deportation of Estonians had dramatically changed Estonia's demographic mix and threatened its national survival.

The question of citizenship became vital. Estonians faced the prospect of continued heavy Russian internal influence if all residents were granted automatic or dual citizenship. This is not only a question of control over the two nations' affairs, but a matter of principle: In the Estonian view, the majority of Russians had been permitted to settle in Estonia in order to implement Moscow's policy of occupation after it had forcibly annexed Estonia in 1940. On what basis could occupiers and their descendants expect to be recognized as citizens? The 1949 Geneva Convention declared that the settlement of occupied territory under the aegis of a military occupation regime is impermissible.

Determined to remain masters in their own house, Estonians based their citizenship laws on legal continuity from independence in 1918 to the present. This makes Soviet rule over Estonia from 1940 to 1941 and again from 1944 to 1991 illegal and gives Soviet domination the character of "occupation." Russia rejects this. Estonia granted citizenship automatically to pre-1940 residents and their descendants. In Estonia a sixth of the Russians qualified; subsequent naturalization raised this to over a third by 1998.

Confronting criticism that Russian speakers were being made permanent noncitizens, Estonia offers citizenship to all persons who meet certain criteria, including residency for six years, willingness to take a loyalty oath, and demonstrated competence (though not fluency) in Estonian, a difficult Finno-Ugric language unrelated to Russian. With a copy of the constitution in their hands, applicants must also answer questions in Estonian about the political system.

Few Russians can meet the language requirement without major effort. There was an outcry that the new restrictions were "unfair" and "human rights violations." Russians in Estonia resent both the need to get residency permits and their status as "aliens," with the implicit risk of deportation, even though many of them have lived much or all of their lives in Estonia. Most want to stay.

The rights of those who do not speak Estonian are greater than in some other small nations, like Quebec province in Canada, that fear absorption and destruction of their cultures. Parents are free to send their children to Russian-language schools and face no restrictions on using their language at the workplace. It is an advantage to speak Estonian, and the defense forces and many categories in the civil service are blocked to noncitizens. Article 50 of the constitution states that where more than half of the permanent residents in a locality are members of an ethnic minority, such as in the overwhelmingly Russian-speaking northeastern part of Estonia, they have a right to deal with the state and local authorities in their own language.

Unlike in most democracies, legal resident aliens in Estonia are permitted to vote in local elections. State radio and television are broadcast in Russian. There are Russian-language theaters and a wide variety of Russian newspapers and magazines are available. Many university courses are taught in Russian, and almost all examinations may be written in Russian. Although Russian speakers and Estonians lead largely separate lives in Estonia, they bear little hatred or deep aversion toward each other. Ethnic tensions are not only far below the threshold of violence, they are actually diminishing as non-Estonians are adjusting to the requirements established in the citizenship laws.

The official Estonian view on citizenship is based both on the nation's determination to preserve itself after almost being overwhelmed and absorbed by Russians from 1944 to 1991 and on notions of citizenship widely held in the rest of the world. It does not limit citizenship to ethnic Estonians but offers it to anybody who follows certain procedures, learns Estonian, and demonstrates a basic knowledge of Estonian's political system. Genuine citizenship involves more than merely endowing an individual with certain rights and duties. In the fuller sense, a citizen is a person who feels a moral commitment and loyalty to the state and who is willing to put aside some aspects of self-interest in favor of the community at large.

Estonia wants citizens whose primary loyalty is to Estonia, not to another state, and who recognize the Estonian character of the restored republic. It fears reabsorption by Russia. Thus it feels justified in withholding the franchise in national elections from a fifth of the adult population. It considers the "Russian fact" to be a challenge to the very existence of the Estonian nation, and that justifies a departure from the principle of the near-universal right to vote.

A diminutive nation is much more sensitive about protecting its national identity from extinction than is a large nation like Russia, which is less likely to understand why the smaller nation is so concerned. A small nation is more likely to worry more about a large ethnic minority within its border than is a country like Russia, a fifth of whose population is composed of scores of non-Russian nationalities.

Like Russia, Estonia must also come to grips with its past. It holds Russia responsible for its termination of independence in 1940, for the loss of at least one-fifth of its population to deportation, execution, or exile, for the reminders of Soviet rule in the country, such as gray, unaesthetic buildings and environmental destruction, and for the fact that Estonia fell far behind the other

Nordic countries economically during a half century of subjugation. Estonia is therefore not inclined to show the kind of deference that Russia, which still desires the respect given to a great power, expects from its small neighbors and former dependencies.

Feeling insecure and knowing that no Western power will defend them militarily without a formal guarantee, the Baltic states seek to enter NATO and the EU. Although Russian leaders have expressed no fundamental objection to Baltic membership in the EU, NATO is another matter. A stream of invective that further poisons the atmosphere is directed toward Estonia and the other Baltic states. Moscow rejects assurances from Estonia's capital, Tallinn, that NATO's stance is not directed against Russia.

Russia is displeased that Estonia is the first former colony that stands a good chance of slipping out of Moscow's orbit. Because of its economic progress and democratic political stability, EU leaders invited it in 1997 to begin negotiations toward EU membership. The prospect that it will almost completely free itself from Russia's sphere of influence is very real. Many Russians are not yet ready to tolerate that. For them, alleged mistreatment of the Russian minority in Estonia is not only maddening, but it is a useful tool for applying pressure on Estonia.

Knowing that it must maintain tolerable relations with its powerful neighbor, Estonia tries to apply a policy of "positive engagement" toward Russia, offering cooperation in many areas and an openness to Russian proposals. It successfully negotiated an exit from the "trouble zone" in June 1992, as well as a troop withdrawal agreement that saw the departure of all Soviet troops by August 31, 1994. Although it was often burdened by its citizenship legislation, Estonia did not need to accept any Russian conditions besides allowing retired Russian military personnel to remain.

Estonia must always calculate Russia's response to each law and adjust its policies to those that Russia will tolerate. It wants to settle its border dispute in order to live in peace with Russia and to accelerate its own integration into the Western world. Its need for such security stems not only from a long-standing Russian claim to predominance over the nations along its periphery, but also from the animosity its restrictive citizenship policy creates in Russia. The situation requires continued patience and persistence, qualities Estonians have long demonstrated.

For the Baltics' independence, see Anatol Lieven, *The Baltic Revolution* (Yale, 1993). For general Estonian background, see Rein Taagepera, *Estonia: Return to Inde-*

*pendence* (Westview, 1993) and Toivo U. Raun, *Estonia and the Estonians,* 2nd ed. (Hoover, 1991). For guerrilla resistance, see Mart Laar, *War in the Woods. Estonia's Struggle for Survival 1944–1956* (Compass, 1992).

**ETHIOPIAN NATIONALISM** Ethiopia has a population of about fifty-five million and is located in the Horn of East Africa. It contains a mix of ethnic and linguistic groups that have struggled to reconcile their historical differences. Among the dominant languages are the Semitic languages (Amharic and Tigrinya), the Cushitic languages (Oromo, Afar, and Somali), the Sidama languages, and the Nilotic languages. The Oromo people represent about 40 percent of the population. The Amhara are roughly 30 percent of the population and Amharic is used widely as a second language. The Tigray represent about 15 percent of the population. Other large groups include Somali, Welamo, Awi, Afar, Sidama, and Beja.

The dramatic Central Highlands stand at altitudes between 7800 and 12,000 feet. The Great Rift Valley runs north to south through the Highlands and divides the region. Surrounding the Central Highlands are lowlands, steppes, and deserts. Ethiopia has been landlocked since the Eritrea territory became independent (May 1993) after a prolonged civil conflict. Each region has distinct ethnic and language groups that have experienced relative degrees of power and autonomy as Ethiopia became a modern nation.

The Aksumite Kingdom was predominantly Christian by the 4th century A.D. At its height the kingdom controlled the Highlands, Eritrea, Somalia, and coastal regions in southern Arabia. The expansion of Islam in the 7th century caused the decline of the Aksumite Kingdom and most lowland populations converted to Islam, while the Central Highlands remained predominantly Christian. This isolation preserved the unique Orthodox-Ethiopian Christian tradition. About 50 percent of the population, primarily Amhara and Tigray, are Christian. About 40 percent of the population are Muslim. The remaining population practices a variety of indigenous religions that are often hybrids between animism and other traditions.

Much of the current tension between Ethiopian groups can be traced to rivalries between Christians and Muslims that were superimposed onto traditional divisions based on geographic region (Highland versus Lowland communities), occupation (pastoral versus agricultural), and tribal affiliation. In the 12th and 13th centuries, Christian kingdoms among the Tigray and Amhara, sometimes little more than a confederation of

city-states using the written language of the Aksum, reemerged in the Highlands. A loose confederation of Islamic groups, at different periods, often came close to establishing control over the Highlands. After defeating a Zagwe (Muslim) incursion, the Amhara leaders legitimized their rule by claiming lineage to both the Aksum and King Solomon of Israel. According to this legend the Aksumite kings were descended from a union between Solomon and the Queen of Sheba.

During the 16th century, when confrontation with Islamic groups weakened the Christian kingdom, the Oromo people migrated into the Highlands. They were primarily searching for grazing land and also displaced some Muslim groups in the lowland areas. Some Oromo integrated with existing groups, but most remained a distinct ethnic group.

Three well-known Amhara kings are responsible for the establishment of modern Ethiopia. Emperor Tewodros II of Gondar governed from 1855 to 1868 and consolidated control over the Highland area. Yohannis IV governed from 1869 to 1889 and managed to extend his authority into Eritrea. He died fighting the Sudanese Mahdists. Menelik II (1889–1913) repelled an Italian invasion at Adowa in 1898. While the Italians retained control of the Eritrean coast, the victory ensured Ethiopia of its continued independence from the European powers. Menelik II later cooperated with the British in a series of military engagements that allowed him to gain control of the Ogaden region, which is inhabited primarily by Somali tribes.

Ethiopia, unlike the rest of Africa, was never colonized and was formally admitted to the League of Nations in 1922. Admittance to the league, the defeat of the Italians at Adowa, and the international acclaim later enjoyed by Emperor Haile Selassie greatly enhanced Ethiopia's standing in the developing world for much of the early 20th century.

Within this context, an Ethiopianism movement in southern Africa, the United States, and the Caribbean (Jamaica) was established. The term was generally used to describe breakaway Christian missions throughout southern Africa. In these churches Africans fused Christianity with African traditions. Ethiopianism was also supported by American black churches and radical leaders in the "return to Africa" movement. Many adapted Ethiopianism into the African independence ideology. Ethiopian movements were also evident in the Zulu rebellion of 1906 and in the Nyasaland uprising of 1915.

Another notable event influenced by Ethiopian nationalism was the spontaneous Ras Tafarian social movement in Jamaica. Inspired by the coronation of Ras Tafari (hereafter referred to as Haile Selassie) in 1930, the Ras Tafari movement developed an elaborate social and religious philosophy that portrayed Ethiopia as the symbolic homeland for black Jamaicans.

The Ethiopian's heroic, but doomed, defense against a second Italian invasion, which began on October 3, 1935, also enhanced the country's standing in the world. Emperor Haile Selassie fled the country and later gave a renowned speech to the League of Nations. In his address he cast the Ethiopian invasion as a test case for the league, stating that if the invasion was not repelled the league would have failed to establish collective security in the world.

After the Italians were defeated by the allies in World War II, Haile Selassie undertook a series of constitutional reforms that attempted to modernize the traditional land tenure system. Selassie never managed to consolidate the factions within the kingdom, but did reestablish Ethiopian authority in Eritrea. Factors that undermined Salassie's authority included Eritrean, Oromo, and Tigray separatist movements, the inability to tax traditional nobles, and growing dissatisfaction among young modernizers and the military.

In 1974, following a period of widespread famine, a group of 120 men, most of whom were anonymous, organized the Coordinating Committee of the Armed Forces, Police and Territorial Army. Referred to as the Derg ("committee" in Amharic) they elected Major Mengistu Haile Mariam as chairman and governed over an increasingly chaotic society for thirteen years. The Derg initially maintained the monarchy and tried to build a coalition of reformers and military elite while limiting the power of the traditional nobles. The Derg eventually assumed complete authority over Ethiopia on September 12, 1974, and imprisoned Haile Selassie. Eventually, after suppressing civilian discontent, as well as countercoup attempts, Major Mengistu Haile Mariam emerged as the leader of the Derg.

The Derg adopted a socialist philosophy and eventually aligned itself with the Soviet Union and Cuba when the United States failed to aid them during a military struggle against the ethnic Somalis in the Ogaden who wanted to join Somalia. As a result of this alliance, Somalia moved away from the Soviet Union and established a closer relationship with the United States.

Severe famine (1984–1988) exacerbated by civil conflict prevented the Derg from establishing a stable government. A disastrous relocation policy directed toward famine victims, the withholding of famine relief for military purposes, and the decline of the Soviet Union eventually isolated the Derg and caused a total economic collapse. The Ethiopians People's Revolutionary Democratic Front (EPRDF) deposed the Marxist military government in May 1991. Soon after, the Eritrean separatists (EPLF), after decades of periodic struggle, gained independence and formed the nation-state of Eritrea.

The new Ethiopian government is based on increased regional autonomy and democratic principles with a bicameral legislature, an executive, and an independent judicial system. Currently Prime Minister Meles Zenawi and President Negasso Gidada lead the government. They are considered part of a trend toward the establishment of a new, technocratic African elite. There was optimism that conditions in Ethiopia—which remains one of the poorest countries in the world—might begin to stabilize, but there continue to be problems with unifying the country's diverse ethnic groups. Recent border skirmishes with Eritrea have also diminished expectations.

**ETHNIC CLEANSING**   Ethnic cleansing refers to the mass removal of an ethnic, linguistic, or religious group from a territory by forcible population transfer or genocide. Widespread use of the term, which derives from the Serbo-Croat word *čišćenje*, began during the early 1990s in reference to the wars of Yugoslav succession in which Serbs in Croatia and Bosnia "cleansed" ethnic Croats and Bosnian Muslims from territory they controlled (although all sides eventually adopted this policy to varying degrees).

The primary purpose behind ethnic cleansing is the desire to ensure military and political control over territory through demographic means by removing opposing ethnic groups. This was designed partly so that individuals would never want to return, thus eliminating the possibility of future territorial claims by nations and individuals. The means by which this is done include threats, indiscriminate shelling, sniper fire, beatings, mass murders, systematic rapes, the use of trucks and buses to transport a population, and making the release of prisoners conditional on flight from the area.

Forcible population transfers of any type, including those based on ethnicity, are prohibited under international law by the Hague Conventions (1907), the Nuremberg Principles (1945), and the 1949 Geneva Convention and its additional protocols.

Although the term is relatively new, the phenomenon it describes is not. Possibly the earliest example was carried out by the Assyrians in the eighth-century B.C. Later examples include the expulsion of Jews from various European countries during the Middle Ages, English policy in what is now Northern Ireland, the displacement of the Native Americans by settler populations in the New World, numerous population transfers after World War I, Nazi policies during World War II, the expulsion of some 12 million Germans from Eastern Europe after World War II, mass population exchanges between India and Pakistan upon partition of the Indian subcontinent, and Serbian policy in Kosovo in the late 1990s.

See Andrew Bell-Failkoff, *Ethnic Cleansing* (Macmillan, 1996); John Alego and Adele Algeo, "Among the New Words," in *American Speech* **68**(4) (Winter 1993) pp. 411–412.

## ETHNIC NATIONALISM

This form of nationalism sees the boundary of the nation as circumscribed by the boundary of a particular ethnic group. Ethnic nationalism places the emphasis on an individual's community of birth, thereby making common descent and ancestry the most salient features of the nation. Bismarck's exhortation to the German people to "think with your blood" emphasizes the importance of consanguinity as the basis of the nation. Ethnic nationalism also celebrates vernacular culture, often mobilizing distinct ethnic communities for the purpose of elevating submerged cultural and ethnic values to what their promoters consider their rightful place on the world stage.

In the literature on nationalism a distinction is sometimes made between various manifestations of ethnic nationalism and its polar opposite, most commonly referred to as "civic nationalism." For example, Hans Kohn originally made the differentiation between "Eastern" nationalism (or ethnic nationalism) and "Western" nationalism (or civic nationalism) in 1956, followed by John Plamenatz's similar distinction twenty years later in 1976. Civic or Western nationalism is a form of territorial nationalism that stresses a set of laws and civic political institutions as the only true foundation of membership in a nation. Each member of such a nation is first and foremost a citizen, with equal rights and obligations to fellow citizens, regardless of ethnic group affiliation. On the other hand, non-Western or Eastern ethnic nationalism is based on a community of common descent as opposed to territory, vernacular culture instead of law, and blood ties instead of citizenship. Britain, France, and America are usually cited as examples of civic nationalism, Eastern Europe (i.e., the Balkans), Asia, and Africa are used as an examples of places where ethnic nationalism has played a stronger role.

Roughly speaking, we can identify three major periods of ethnic nationalist unrest. The first period was during the 19th century when several small ethnic communities claimed some form of ethnic self-determination against large imperial centers, such as the Habs-

burg, the Romanov, and the Ottoman Empires. This was followed by the mid-20th-century decolonization that many postcolonial states in Africa, Asia, and the Middle East experienced. The Kurds, the Tamils, the Armenians, and the Moros, to name only a few, are examples of ethnic groups that aim to establish their own ethnic state, either by secession from a colonial state or as a reaction to a majority ethnic group attempting to do the same. Finally, a third wave of ethnic nationalism has manifested itself as a struggle for autonomy and separation. This has happened in parts of Western Europe, as well as in Yugoslavia, Romania, Poland, and in many other states in the wake of the collapse of the former Soviet Union. The disintegration of Yugoslavia, for example, has witnessed some of the worst forms of ethnic nationalism, leading to civil war as well as to brutal acts of ethnic cleansing.

While most forms of nationalism contain both civic and ethnic elements, there is a general concern over the marked tendency of ethnic nationalism to lead to some form of violence. The logical correlate of basing a nation solely on the criteria of ethnicity is that it excludes those not born into that ethnic group from participation in the life of the nation. Unlike civic nationalism, which is based on the legal rights of common citizenship, ethnic nationalism clearly demarcates those eligible for inclusion in the nation from those who are not. This leaves open the possibility that ethnic differences will be exploited by political élites and/or by members of the intelligentsia, who attempt to fan the flames of ancient tribal and ethnic hatreds for political gain.

As a result, the most often asked question when dealing with ethnic nationalism is: What is the best way to contain ethnic differences so that ethnic violence is not the only possible outcome? The answers to this question include everything from federalism to some arrangement of consociational democracy. The hope here is that such arrangements will diminish the likelihood of ethnic nationalist violence by promoting power sharing among ethnic groups.

Anthony Smith has written extensively on the relationship between ethnic identity (and ethnicity) and nationalism. For example, his *National Identity* (Penguin Books, 1991) explores his major contention that an "ethnic core" lies at the heart of all forms of nationalism. Walker Connor is another scholar who believes that nationalism has a basically ethnic core to it. See his *Ethnonationalism: The Quest for Understanding* (Princeton University Press, 1994). Hans Kohn's *The Idea of Nationalism,* 2nd ed. (Collier-Macmillan, 1967) as well as John Plamenatz's "Two types of Nationalism" (in *Nationalism: The Nature and Evolution of an Idea,* Eugene

Kamenka, ed. (Edward Arnold, 1976) look at the distinction between ethnic and civic nationalism.

**ETHNICITY** A categorical identity. Ethnic sentiments are often believed to pose serious threats to international and domestic security and to be the source of violent forms of nationalism. However, ethnicity is rarely itself a source of violent social conflicts. Most commonly, members of ethnic groups are loyal and peaceful and seek acceptance of their culture and greater integration into the society in which they live. There are many more ethnic groups than there are ethnic nationalist movements.

When is ethnic nationalism likely to arise? Modernization theorists treated ethnic separatism as a "disease" of the transition from tradition to modernity triggered by the anomie and rootlessness of modernization. Anthropologist Clifford Geertz is generally regarded as one of the most prominent proponents of this approach.

Yet ethnically based nationalist movements have emerged in the 20th century in many industrial societies that had, according to modernization theories, already overcome earlier phases of ethnic and regional disunity. Theorists have developed two broad theories to explain this phenomenon: one that sees ethnic nationalism as an outcome of uneven development, the other that sees it as a by-product of state rationalization.

Theorists of uneven development assume that industrialization will fail to overcome the pressure of ethnic separatism wherever a "cultural" division of labor develops in which ethnic groups are confined to subordinate positions in the labor market. This is particularly likely in cases where a core region uses raw materials and labor from an ethnically distinct periphery to fuel its own economic development. After its integration into an industrial economy, it is likely that these peripheral areas will fail to develop industrial enterprises, and will act as markets for industrial goods produced in the core. The populations of such regions will become proletarianized and prone to revolt, particularly during periods of economic turmoil.

An alternative theory of ethnic nationalism views it as an outcome of state-building projects. Modernizing governments—with increasing revenue requirements—need civil servants capable of managing military and police operations, collecting domestic taxes, maintaining domestic order, and transmitting necessary skills through schools. Such civil servants often become powerful intermediaries between their government and the ethnic groups they administer, gradually developing autonomous interests as well as the skill necessary to mobilize ethnic nationalism.

Each of these theories seems to work for some cases but not for others. The uneven development approach predicts that ethnic separatism will occur in economically exploited regions. With qualifications, this explains ethnic separatism in Great Britain as well as Asian colonies. However, it is a poor explanation for the breakup of state socialist countries, where the strongest nationalist movements had their social base in regions that were more prosperous than their country's respective core. Similarly, stronger separatist movements in Canada have developed among French Canadians than among the indigenous peoples who live in outlying areas exploited primarily for their natural resources.

State-centered theories offer a better explanation of the breakup of Yugoslavia, the USSR, and of ethnic nationalism in other federally structured countries. State-led modernization in federal states created the cultural, economic, and political institutions through which ethnic elites and ethnic constituencies gradually consolidated power. When the central state began to decentralize, ethnic elites began to assert greater control over federal units. This explains why, in former state socialist countries as well as Quebec, ethnic nationalism typically found the strongest support among relatively privileged white-collar workers and intellectuals rather than among blue-collar workers.

Two prominent applications of the uneven development approach to ethnic nationalism have been developed to account for ethnic mobilization in the case of Great Britain, Tom Nairn's *The Break-Up of Britain* and Michael Hechter's *Internal Colonialism*. Ernest Gellner's *Nations and Nationalism* utilizes a version of this approach as the basis for a general theory of nationalism. The state rationalization approach to ethnic separatism has been adopted in a number of works, chief among them Benedict Anderson's *Imagined Communities* (Verso, 1983), John Breuilly's *Nationalism and the State* (St. Martin's Press, 1982), and Eric Hobsbawm's *Nations and Nationalism Since 1780* (Cambridge University Press, 1990).

**ETHNOCENTRISM** Ethnocentrism was introduced to the social sciences by the American sociologist William G. Sumner, who defined it in his 1906 *Folkways* as putting the values and norms of the own culture central in the judgment of others. Implicitly, this also meant that one's own culture is held as superior to all others. The concept was integrated into mainstream social science, however, as a consequence of the classic study on *The Authoritarian Personality* by T. W. Adorno and his colleagues. Since then ethnocentrism has gotten a second meaning, that is, an ethnic or cultural interpretation of the more general process of "ingroup–outgroup differentiation." Ethnocentrism combines a positive attitude toward one's own ethnic/cultural group (the ingroup) with a negative attitude toward the other ethnic/cultural groups (the outgroup). These interlinked attitudes are the result of two mechanisms: social identification and social counteridentification.

The operationalization of the positive identification with the ingroup comes close to certain definitions of nationalism (e.g., by Hans Kohn); that is, stressing national pride, the importance of national symbols, and so on. Some scholars consider ethnocentrism and nationalism to be inseparable, whereas others argue that nationalism and chauvinism are just forms of ethnocentrism. The negative identification toward the outgroup(s), on the other hand, resembles phenomena generally termed as prejudice, stereotyping, or xenophobia. In fact, ethnocentrism is often used interchangeably with these terms; some authors define ethnocentrism as collective xenophobia.

Since the 1950s, and influenced by the work of Adorno and by the behavioralist revolution within the social sciences, hundreds of empirical studies using some type of ethnocentrism scale have been executed worldwide. They showed that ethnocentrism is closely linked to authoritarianism, conservatism, and nationalism. Though criticism has come up over the Western bias of the operationalization of the concept, most scholars believe that ethnocentrism is a universal phenomenon. Various scholars even go so far as to argue that it is an intrinsic characteristic of all humans. Although this view has been taboo for a long time, the recent popularity of sociobiology has brought it back in the academic debate. However, other scholars, mainly those working within the sociopsychological research tradition, consider ethnocentrism to be either a character feature of certain individuals or a product of a specific socialization process (within the family or within the larger society). They point to the strong correlations between high levels of ethnocentrism and low levels of education and income found in empirical studies throughout the world.

Many commentators have interpreted nationalism as an ethnocentric reaction to mass immigration or ethnic minorities. Both the recent rise of extreme right parties in Western Europe and the alleged widespread of nationalism in Eastern Europe is considered in terms of an "ethnocentric backlash." The existence of multiethnic societies and the ongoing discussions about the building of multicultural societies would have encouraged less-educated Europeans to adopt their intolerant stand toward "the others." What is new, however, is that these processes have also brought an ethnocentric reaction from an unexpected corner, including notable philosophers such as the American postmodernist Richard Rorty. While rejecting intolerant ethnocentrism and nationalism, they claim to defend the "tolerant us" against the "intolerant them."

Among the classic works on ethnocentrism are William G. Sumner, *Folkways* (Ginn & Company, 1906); T. W. Adorno, Else Frenkel-Brunswik, Daniel J. Levinson, and R. Nevitt Sanford, *The Authoritarian Personality* (Harper, 1950); Gordon W. Allport, *The Nature of Prejudice* (Addison Wesley, 1954), Robert A. LeVine and Donald T. Campbell, *Ethnocentrism. Theories of Conflict, Ethnic Attitudes and Group Behavior* (John Wiley, 1972); and Henri Tajfel, *Human Groups and Social Categories* (Cambridge University Press, 1981).

**ETHNOGENESIS** Ethnogenesis or the formation of a people (*ethnos*) became a major research goal for Soviet historical sciences—history, archaeology, historical linguistics, folklore studies, and so on—from the middle 1930s on. The question for study was the origins of a people: the origins of the early Slavs and Russians in particular, but also the beginnings of all the Turkic-speaking peoples, Caucasians, Siberians, and other non-Russians that constituted roughly half the population of the Soviet Union. Other countries, which were influenced by Soviet historical studies, such as in Eastern Europe and China, also addressed to varying degrees this same research problem: the determination of when a certain collective group—an ethnos or a nationality—first came into being. Ethnogenetic studies still flourish today throughout the former Soviet bloc and have become ever increasingly popular in many of the new independent states or upgraded ethno-administrative territories that formed after the collapse of the USSR.

Theoretically, ethnogenesis appears to be a legitimate subject for research; the search for origins seems even to demystify chauvinistic and incredible accounts of a people's past. The assumption is that ethnoses (and, correspondingly, nationalities) have a determinable historical origin: None have been divinely ordained or existed since time immemorial. In practice, however, ethnogenetic studies have often hindered substantive historical scholarship and been manipulated by nationalist ideologues and unscrupulous politicians for the purpose of proving the chronological priority of one's own group over others, a determination that often entails territorial claims to lands deemed ancestral. Part of the difficulty relates to the quality of the sources: The linguistic and archaeological data for which ethnic attributions are made are inherently ambiguous and the historical sources are typically sparse and inadequate for determining a people's origins. As practiced, most ethnogenetic studies have assumed a primordialist perspective on ethnicity: Groups not only have an ascertainable beginning, but once formed, they assume all their objective characteristics (speech, clothing, food practices, house forms, religion, customs, etc.) which supposedly still define them today. Ethnoses are thought to have origins, but they are conceived as crystallized essences, little perfectly formed homunculi, at birth exhibiting all their distinguishing characteristics. The assumption, of course, simplifies the problem of inadequate sources, but the result is pseudo-history.

For a discussion of the emergence of ethnogenetic studies in the Soviet Union see V. Shnirelman's article "From Internationalism to Nationalism; Forgotten Pages of Soviet Archaeology in the 1930s and 1940s," in *Nationalism, Politics, and the Practice of Archaeology*, P. L. Kohl and C. Fawcett, eds. (Cambridge, 1995). A fascinating example of the political manipulation of ethnogenetic research is provided by Shnirelman's study of the conflicting claims over their origins between the Chuvash and Tatars of the middle Volga: *Who Gets the Past? Competition for Ancestors Among Non-Russian Intellectuals in Russia* (Woodrow Wilson Center, 1996).

**EUGENICS**     Eugenics is the effort to promote in human beings the inheritance of ostensibly desirable traits and suppress in them the inheritance of qualities deemed undesirable through the scientific regulation of procreation. It is based on the belief that man's character and mental capacities, as well as his physical traits, are shaped mainly by heredity and, therefore, can be improved in subsequent generations through selective breeding.

Although eugenics proposals can be traced back to antiquity, the late 19th and early 20th centuries witnessed an explosion of interest in eugenics, both in the United States and in Europe. During this period, eugenicists argued that criminality, mental illness, feeblemindedness, and poverty are at least partially biologically determined and, therefore, could be eliminated by promoting the procreation of superior types (positive eugenics) and preventing the procreation of inferior types (negative eugenics). Like the social Darwinists, the eugenicists attempted to apply the Darwinian theory of evolution to human beings. However, unlike most social Darwinists, many eugenicists believed that they could improve on nature by regulating human reproduction. Therefore, although their views are often characterized as merely conservative or reactionary,

they shared with Progressive social theorists the belief that even the most intractable social problems could be solved by the application of human reason and ingenuity.

The term *eugenics* was coined in 1883 by Sir Francis Galton (1822–1911), who was the grandson of Erasmus Darwin and the cousin of Charles Darwin. Galton, an accomplished English statistician and scientist, believed that mental capacity is both hereditary and quantifiable. In his major works, *Hereditary Genius* (1869), *Inquires into Human Faculty* (1883), and *Natural Inheritance* (1889), Galton argued that science could increase the proportion of persons with higher mental capacities through the selective breeding of exceptional men and women. Galton studied the pedigrees of particularly prominent and gifted men in an effort to prove that nature, not nurture, was the primary determinant of human intelligence and character. Karl Pearson (1857–1936), Galton's biographer and most prominent English disciple, shared his mentor's view that social class is largely determined by biology. He also shared Galton's view that heredity, not education or environment, is the main factor in determining mental characteristics. Believing that human progress is only possible through the domination of lesser races and classes by superior races and classes, it was Pearson who would put an explicitly reactionary and nationalist stamp on the eugenics movement.

Eugenics soon became popular in the United States, due to the efforts of Charles B. Davenport (1866–1944), the founder of the Eugenics Record Office and outspoken promoter of eugenics, and Henry H. Goddard (1866–1957), author of *The Kallikak Family* (1912), an infamous book on hereditary criminality and imbecility. Many American eugenicists, including Davenport and Goddard, had nativist inclinations and advocated strict restrictions on immigration in order to minimize the pollution of America's racial stock. A major success was scored with the passage of the Immigration Act of 1924, which established strict quotas for immigrants of suspect nationalities. The American eugenicists also supported the involuntary sterilization of habitual criminals, the insane, epileptics, and the so-called "feebleminded" (a category that, according to some intelligence tests, encompassed as much as 40 percent of the population). Unlike Galton, who was primarily interested in fostering population growth at the upper end of the intelligence distribution, American eugenicists were more concerned with decreasing the size of the population at the lower end. Founded in 1922, the American Eugenics Society took a leading role in promoting the eugenics viewpoint, and was instrumental in the passage of sterilization laws in twenty-seven states, under which thousands of citizens were surgically rendered incapable of reproduction. American eugenics thought also had a strong racist element. Some racial groups, most notably blacks but also Jews and most "non-Nordic" whites, were believed to be naturally inferior to "Nordic" or "Aryan" whites. Since interbreeding between races would tend to dilute the superior racial stocks, the eugenicists lent scientific support to already existing antimiscegenation laws.

Although eugenics is more closely associated with German nationalism than it is with American nativism, some leading German eugenicists actually looked to America for legitimization of their own racial hygiene programs. The main purpose of the Nazi regime was to promote the racial purity of German people and create a racially based national community (*Volksgemeinschaft*). Eugenics was used by the Nazi regime to lend scientific respectability to its 1933 plan to sterilize more than two million undesirables, to the anti-Semitic Nürnberg Laws (1935), which deprived Jews of citizenship and forbade intermarriage and sexual relations between Jews and Germans, and to the vicious persecution and mass extermination of approximately six million Jews.

After the heyday of the eugenics movement in the United States and Europe, and until the emergence of the discipline of sociobiology, there was a virtual taboo on serious discussion of hereditarian theories of human intelligence and personality. Due to the frightful authoritarian legacy of Nazism, these theories continue to be viewed with suspicion, as are eugenics practices such as genetic screening to avoid the perpetuation of hereditary diseases, the termination of pregnancies when genetic defects are discovered, and the creation of special sperm banks for genetically "superior" donors. Efforts by some developing nations of Africa, Latin America, and Asia to control population growth through a combination of family planning, contraception, and abortion also remain controversial, as do laws in China that critics contend condone the forced sterilization of persons with serious genetic conditions.

Fine accounts of the eugenics movement in the United States are Mark H. Haller, *Eugenics: Hereditarian Attitudes in American Thought,* rev. ed. (Rutgers University Press, 1984) and Carl N. Degler, *In Search of Human Nature: The Decline and Revival of Darwinism in American Social Thought* (Oxford University Press, 1991). Discussions of eugenics in both England and the United States include Daniel J. Kevles, *In the Name of Eugenics: Genetics and the Uses of Human Heredity* (University of California, 1986) and Elazar Barkan, *Retreat of Scientific*

*Racism: Changing Concepts of Race in Britain and the United States between the World Wars* (Cambridge University Press, 1992). For a discussion of eugenics in Nazi Germany, with an emphasis on the relationship between American and Nazi eugenics movements, see Stefan Kühl, *The Nazi Connection: Eugenics, American Racism, and German National Socialism* (Oxford University Press, 1994).

**EUROPEAN ECONOMIC COMMUNITY** The European Economic Community (EEC or Common Market) was a forerunner of the present European Union. Following the entry of the European Coal and Steel Community (ECSC) in 1952, which joined France, Germany, Italy, and the Benelux countries in a common effort to manage their coal and steel resources, the same countries signed the Rome Treaties in 1957, creating the European Economic Community and the European Atomic Energy Community (EURATOM), which went into effect in 1958. The creation of the EEC was one of many post-World War II efforts to organize the shattered European economies into a regional structure that would attempt to manage the rebuilding following the war and ensure that nationalism and state conflict would find new avenues for expression.

The EEC created a customs union, requiring the gradual elimination of and an end to customs duties within the community and a common external tariff. Further, membership in the EEC meant a commitment to the free movement of capital and labor, a common investment policy, and a coordination of goals in such areas as social welfare, agriculture, transport, and foreign trade. These measures had impressive results; trade both within the community and with the rest of the world increased substantially. Many member EEC states envisaged an evolution from an economic community to a political union. The institutions of the EEC included an EEC Commission, responsible for the implementation of the EEC Treaty, a Council of Ministers, representing the national governments, a European Parliament, initially consultative, but since 1979 directly elected and increasingly a part of the decision-making process of the emerging European Union, and a Court of Justice, with important supranational powers regarding community law and treaty interpretation. The institutions of the EEC were merged with those of the ECSC and EURATOM in 1967. The resulting European Community (EC) became the European Union (EU) in 1993.

As the EEC developed, the founding countries signed a convention with their former African colonies (Yaoundé I, 1963) that led to a host of subsequent agreements linked with Yaoundé and Lomé which covered some seventy African, Caribbean, and Pacific countries, making the successor European Union a prominent contributor to economic development. Further, by 1975, both a customs union and a common agricultural policy (CAP) had been put into place within the EEC.

While important supranational evolution was apparent in the institutions of the EEC, even its ultimate successor, the EU, particularly with qualified majority voting in the council and the binding decisions of the Court of Justice, finds that the member states still figure prominently in the decision-making process within the organization. Nonetheless, the EEC's history remains an impressive departure from past European state relations.

Interesting contemporary literature on the European Economic Community that captures the politics and aspirations of the time period includes the work of Ernst Haas, *The Uniting of Europe* (Stanford University Press, 1961), Emile Benoit, *Europe at Sixes and Sevens* (Columbia University Press, 1961), Walter Hallstein (first president of the EEC Commission) *United Europe: Challenge and Opportunity* (Harvard University Press, 1962), Richard Mayne, *The Community of Europe: Past, Present and Future* (W. W. Norton, 1963), and Werner Feld, *The European Common Market and the World* (Prentice-Hall, 1967).

Adapted from Grieves, Forest, *Conflict and Order: An Introduction to International Relations,* © 1977 by Houghton Mifflin Company. Used with permission.

**EUROPEAN UNION**   The European Union (EU) represents both a determined effort to move European states beyond the disastrous and bloody history of competing nationalism and state conflict and an important experiment in supranationalism and transnational cooperation.

From before the Holy Roman Empire to modern times, European unity has been a recurring theme—unfortunately all too often involving military means. As ideas on liberalism and democracy developed, such figures as the English Quaker William Penn suggested in 1693 the idea of a European Parliament. Later the French philosopher Jean-Jacques Rousseau suggested a European federation. In the 1920s Austrian Count Richard Coudenhove-Kalergi published *Paneuropa* (1923) and founded the Pan-European Union, which in addition to arguing for European federation, counted among its members important European figures (e.g., Edvard Beneš, Aristide Briand, Edouard Herriot, Georges Pompidou, Carlos Sforza, and Konrad Adenauer), some of whom had prominent roles in European integration following World War II.

World War II left both victors and vanquished in Europe exhausted, with their economies in shambles. The reconstruction of Europe spawned a number of political and military regional organizations such as the Council of Europe and the North Atlantic Treaty Organization (NATO). Because France and Germany had fought each other in three horrendous wars in less than a century, perhaps it was fitting that Franco-German rapprochement became a key to launching the organizational structure and commitment that ultimately produced the European Union.

An important step came on May 9, 1950, when French Foreign Minister Robert Schuman proposed a pooling of French and German coal and steel production under a common authority in an organization open to all the countries of Europe. This revolutionary Schuman Plan resulted in the establishment of the European Coal and Steel Community (ECSC). The ECSC Treaty, which went into effect in 1952 under the bold leadership of Jean Monnet, joined France, Germany, Italy, and the three Benelux countries in a common European authority able to make some decisions independent of the various member governments. Robert Schuman saw in the ECSC institutions the seeds of supranationalism, in which the participating countries would agree to a partial abandonment of sovereignty.

In the same spirit, in 1957 the six members of the ECSC signed two additional treaties in Rome, which went into effect in 1958, establishing the European Economic Community (EEC or Common Market) and the European Atomic Energy Community (EURATOM). The EEC created a customs union among the members dedicated toward economic union and ultimately political union. EURATOM was designed to meet the growing need for new sources of power and enable the members to coordinate nuclear energy resources and research.

Progress toward what would become the European Union has not been without controversy and conflicting visions of the goal. Picking up on the theme sounded in Winston Churchill's famous 1946 speech in Zurich calling for a "United States of Europe," some have called for a Europe based on federalism, along the lines of versions that would be familiar to observers of the American model. Others have pushed notions of functionalism or transnationalism, which assume that the path to international unity lies not in the head-on confrontation of national sovereignties typical of intergovernmental organizations, but rather in the quiet transnational organization of social functions. According to this kind of scenario, states standardize transnationally step-by-step simple functional areas such as railroad gauges, purity of pig-iron, and the ingredient labels on canned produce. At some point states have everything in common and little that separates them.

On the other hand there are those more in the tradition of Charles de Gaulle's call for "l'Europe des États"—a Europe that cooperates within the more traditional intergovernmental framework that favors national sovereignty over supranational institutions. The "Euroskepticism" expressed by such leaders as Charles de Gaulle and Margaret Thatcher would be bolstered by public referenda, parliamentary debates, and court review articulating criticism and public distrust during the 1990s in such countries as Denmark, France, the United Kingdom, and Germany—suggesting that some governments might be more "European" than their constituent publics.

In spite of the controversies, progress toward European unity has been impressive. In 1967 the ECSC, the EEC, and EURATOM merged their institutional structures. The resulting European Community (EC) has been enlarged several times, with Denmark, Ireland, and the United Kingdom joining in 1973. Greece, Spain, and Portugal were admitted in the 1980s, along with Austria, Finland, and Sweden in the 1990s. In 1979, direct elections to the European Parliament were held. In 1986, the signing of the Single European Act established a full internal market and extended the practice of majority voting within the community institutions.

On November 1, 1993, the Treaty on European Union previously signed in Maastricht on February 7, 1992, came into force. The European Community, which was primarily economic in focus, was transformed into a European Union resting on three "pillars." The first pillar concerns the traditional institutional procedures and operations of the Commission, European Parliament, Council, and Court of Justice—institutions of the European Union continued from its predecessors (ECSC, EEC, EURATOM) in which increasing supra-nationalism intermingles with increasing democratic control via elections to the European Parliament. The other two pillars involve matters over which national governments previously had sole power—foreign and security policy on the one hand and domestic affairs (e.g., immigration, asylum, police, and justice issues) on the other. The most visible aspect of the Maastricht treaty for average citizens surely relates to the introduction of a common currency (the "euro") on January 1, 1999.

Whatever the ultimate configuration of the European Union, it must be regarded as an extraordinary experiment in the effort to channel the dynamic forces of nationalism and sovereignty into creative international cooperation.

Very useful examinations of the European Union can be found in Derek W. Urwin, *The Community of Europe: A History of European Integration Since 1945* (Longman, 1995), Stephen George, *Politics and Policy in the European Community* (Oxford University Press, 1991), Clive Archer and Fiona Butler, *The European Community: Structure and Process* (St. Martin's Press, 1992), John Pinder, *European Community: The Building of a Union* (Oxford University Press, 1995), and David Wood and Birol Yeşilada, *The Emerging European Union* (Longman, 1996).

Adapted from Grieves, Forest, *Conflict and Order: An Introduction to International Relations.* © 1977 by Houghton Mifflin Company. Used with permission.

**EXPLORATION**    The development in Europe of power-conscious national states, with standing armies, professional officers, and engineers, stimulated an outburst of topographic activity in the 18th century, reinforced to some extent by increasing civil needs for basic data. Many countries of Europe began to undertake the systematic topographic mapping of their territories. Such surveys required facilities and capabilities far beyond the means of private cartographers who had prior to this time provided for most map needs. Originally exclusively military, national survey organizations gradually became civilian in character. The Ordinance Survey of Britain, the Institut Géographique National of France, and the Landestopographie of Switzerland are examples of this process.

Elaborate national surveys were undertaken only in certain countries. The rest of the world remained largely unmapped until World War II. In some instances colonial areas were mapped by military forces, but with the exception of the British survey of India, such efforts usually provided piecemeal coverage or generalized and sketchy data.

The explorations of the 16th century by Spain, the first modern empire, incorporated the New World into the global scene. In the 19th century countries such as Britain, France, Austria, and the United States made exploration a money-making venture. The 19th-century explorations helped to consolidate the supposed superiority of the European nations.

Exploration, colonization, and national consolidation of the European states, the main motivation for imperial expansion, existed from the 18th century until well into the 20th century.

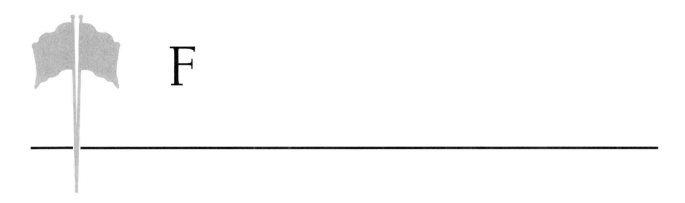

# F

**FANON, FRANTZ** 1925–1961, World War II veteran, physician, psychiatrist, journalist, writer, and revolutionary activist, born in Martinique (French) of black middle-class parents. Fanon was a brilliant writer whose works present the most eloquent view of colonialism, its psychological and material costs to colonized individuals, and the dynamics of the processes that will bring relevant social change. His four books—*Black Skin, White Masks; A Dying Colonialism; The Wretched of the Earth;* and *Toward the African Revolution*—influenced generations of activists in the Third World and even in the West whose civilization he relentlessly attacked. American black nationalists of the defunct radical Black Panther Party who associated the condition of American blacks with that of the rest of the Third World adopted Fanon's *The Wretched of the Earth* (in the 1960s *Time* magazine called it one of the five most important books of the preceding ten years) as "a kind of revolutionary bible."

Fanon's exposure to French racism as a child in Martinique and while in school in France made him decide, upon certification to practice psychiatry, to flee as far away as possible from the West and its racism to anywhere he could focus on the practice and research of the branch of psychiatry he calls *communal therapy*. When Fanon finally found his way to Algeria, North Africa, in 1953 he witnessed the violent and repressive side of French colonial racism. French colonial violence in Algeria was cause for Fanon to rethink violence as a weapon of oppression in the hands of colonizers against the colonized. Also, he felt convinced that victims of colonial oppression could appropriate violence as a weapon in their struggle for political liberation. Fanon has been called the apostle of political violence, and rightly so. He conceived violence in the context of liberation politics. Fanon's emphases on how the colonized peoples of the Third World must channel violence toward constructive political goals set him apart from

Georges Sorel whose later writings tend to portray raw violence devoid of political goals as healthy in itself.

Fanon was strongly influenced by the ideas and lives of Carl Jung, Nietzsche, and Aime Cesaire (the poet/political activist, his fellow black Martinican, and teacher). Fanon lived his belief that theories and ideas must stem from action. Hence, upon his expulsion from Algeria by the French colonial authorities on suspicion of aiding the Algerian militants of the *Front de Liberation Nationale* (FLN) in their armed campaign to end colonial rule in Algeria, Fanon joined forces with the FLN as a full-time partisan.

Fanon was an effective spokesman for the Algerian nationalists, and when the provisional government of Algeria was formed in 1958 he was appointed its ambassador to Ghana from where he canvassed his advocacy of Pan-Africanism and economic nationalism all over Africa and in the rest of the Third World.

For Fanon, the political liberation of the new nations of the Third World from colonial rule through consciously created and properly managed violent revolutionary upheavals was not to be an end in itself. It was only a first step toward the economic warfare that needed to be waged against Western nations for their century-long plunder of Third World resources. This would force them to make reparations to the Third World. Fanon believed that the only way such a war could be won was for Third World nations to unite in the boycott of Western goods and capital and to play the East and West blocs against one another in their Cold War. Thus, Fanon's ideas were forerunners of both the Organization of African Unity, (OAU) and the Non-Aligned movement. Fanon died December 6, 1961, of leukemia.

**FASCISM** Though the claim that there is no general consensus on a definition is made with respect to many, if not most, concepts in the social sciences, nowhere is it so appropriate as with the concept of fascism. The actual writing of the term is even disputed. Several scholars make a distinction between "Fascism," denoting only the Italian interwar phenomenon, and "fascism," describing the generic phenomenon. Other major debates involve such questions as whether fascism is an ideology or not, whether it denotes one single phenomenon or a multitude of phenomena, whether it existed in just one "epoch" or is of a generic nature. One of the few points on which a consensus does exist is that Mussolini's prewar movement in Italy was fascist (or Fascist), yet debates have arisen over the question of whether the same can be said of his regime. In addition, although just a minority of scholars reserve the term exclusively for Mussolini's movement, which other movements or regimes are to be labeled fascist is again highly debated. Some include virtually all right-wing authoritarian regimes, including postwar dictatorships such as Franco's Spain and Pinochet's Chile, while others are very selective and exclude even Hitler's Nazi Germany.

Of course, at the heart of these debates lie definitional questions. Hundreds, if not thousands, of definitions of fascism have been put forward since the 1920s, linking it to almost every other phenomenon, sometimes in a positive though most often in a negative (i.e., anti-) way. Most authors would agree that fascism is a phenomenon of the 20th century. But there the consensus again stops. For example, fascism has been called reactionary, conservative, progressive, and revolutionary. It has been termed both right wing and left wing, secular and (pseudo-)religious, capitalist and socialist, irrational and rational, modern and backward, and so on.

Far from being generally accepted, the definition of Stanley G. Payne does hold the status of *primus inter pares* within the field. Most elements of his three-tier definition can be found in almost all other definitions of fascism. The first tier denotes the ideology and goals of fascism (e.g., nationalism, authoritarianism, modernism, secularism, militarism, expansionism). The second lists the "fascist negations" (i.e., anti-Communism, anti-liberalism, anti-conservatism). The third tier entails both the style (masculine, youthful, military, mystical) and the organization (mass party, militia, leadership principle) of fascism. A more parsimonious, but also more contested, definition is provided by Roger Griffin, who even more clearly links fascism to nationalism: "Fascism is a genus of political ideology whose mythic core in its various permutations is a palingenetic form of populist ultra-nationalism."

In addition to definitions, a plethora of theories of fascism exist. Most can be divided very roughly into three major schools. The Marxist school considers fascism as the violent agent of bourgeois capitalism. The totalitarianism school, in sharp contrast, considers fascism to be the right-wing variant of extremism, the antithesis of democracy. Within this school, many see fascism as a reaction to Communism, that is, the left-wing variant of extremism. Finally, the modernization school sees fascism, and nationalism more generally, as a reaction to rapid processes of social and economic modernization. All three schools can also be found in the study of neofascism or right-wing extremism.

Among the classic texts on fascism are Stanley G. Payne, *A History of Fascism, 1914–1945* (The University of Wisconsin Press, 1995); Walter Laqueur, ed., *Fascism: A Reader's Guide* (University of California Press, 1976); and the more controversial Ernst Nolte, *Three Faces of Fascism* (Holt, Rinehart and Winston, 1966); Zeev Sternhell, *Neither Right nor Left* (Princeton University Press, 1996); and Roger Griffin, *The Nature of Fascism* (Pinter, 1991). A good textbook overview of generic fascism is provided by Roger Eatwell, *Fascism: A History* (Viking Penguin, 1996); while an invaluable reader of classic texts of both fascists themselves and their scholars is provided by Roger Griffin, ed., *Fascism* (Oxford University Press, 1995).

**FEMINISM AND NATIONALISM** Feminism, broadly defined, is the struggle against the oppression of women and for women's political, social, and economic equal rights with men. Thus, feminist academics and activists examine the role of gender in constructing states and societies and place women at the center of political analysis.

Feminism has had a complex dynamic with nationalist movements, including anticolonial struggles, national reform movements, and religious or cultural nationalist revivals. The role of women in nationalist struggles and in states has been debated in almost every nationalist movement. It is difficult to draw generalizations about the relationship between feminism and nationalism because women's issues and national movements vary by country.

With regard to the relationship between women and nationalism, feminists have struggled to make women's experiences and issues of the home and of the private sphere central to the understanding of nations and nationalist movements. It has been argued in feminist studies that "nations" and nationalism are gendered, such as common references to countries as the "motherlands." It has also been shown that women's physical bodies and behavior are usually viewed as either strengthening or betraying the nation. Moreover, it has been illustrated that citizenship rights are different for women and men, and that women's interests are marginalized in the construction of nations.

Feminists in nationalist movements struggle over how to reconcile their national identity with their political identity as women. Nationalist movements are sometimes credited with politicizing women, bringing them into the political arena and offering them a means to critique existing power relations. For example, in Northern Ireland during the 1970s, women became more involved in the political organization Sinn Fein. At the same time, as in the case of the American and French Revolutions, relations between men and women were transformed due to the necessities of war, but did not survive once the new nation-states were established.

Another tension in the relationship between feminism and nationalism is that a critique of patriarchal attitudes and practices in nations and nationalist struggles is sometimes lost in nationalist claims. Many nationalist movements regard women's inequality to be a consequence of colonialism and neocolonialism, and see restoring the precolonial society as a way of ensuring women's equality and freedom.

Despite tensions, there are some feminist nationalist movements. In a feminist nationalist movement, women struggle for their rights as women and rights as nationalists in a variety of contexts. The issue is conjoining the two in societies that deny women's rights. Palestine and South Africa are considered fairly successful examples of places where feminist and nationalist politics come together.

Feminists who struggle both against colonialism and for women's rights look to the possibilities of working toward an international feminist movement. The United Nations' 1993 *Human Development Report* and 1995 *Report on the Fourth World Conference on Women* show that women internationally continue to be unequal with men. However, developing feminist alliances with women from formerly colonialist societies is difficult, and feminist attempts at such alliances are open to critique from actors in nationalist movements.

There is a growing body of work on this topic. For more on the relation between women, gender, and nationalism, see Partha Chatterjee, *The Nation and Its Fragments: Colonial and Postcolonial Histories* (Princeton University Press, 1993) and Nira Yuval-Davis and Floya Anthias, eds., *Women-Nation-State* (St. Martin's Press, 1989). For a discussion about feminism and nationalism see Cynthia Enloe's *Bananas, Beaches, and Bases: Making Feminist Sense of International Politics* (University of California Press, 1990) and Lois West, ed., *Feminist Nationalism* (Routledge, 1997).

## FICHTE, JOHANN GOTTLIEB VON   1762–1814, German philosopher and one of the early proponents of German nationalism. Fichte's prodigious intellect allowed him to overcome his lower class family background and rise to prominence as one of the leading intellectuals in Germany. He attended the Universities of Jena, Wittenberg, and Leipzig as a theology student. In 1792 Fichte published a Kantian analysis of religion, *A Critique of All Revelation,* which established him as one of the foremost minds in all of Germany. Fichte then held teaching posts at Jena and Erlangen. From 1810 to 1814, Fichte served first as dean, then as rector, at the newly instituted University of Berlin. He died in 1814 from typhus.

Fichte's early philosophy expanded Kant's idealistic philosophy. Kant had bifurcated reality into things as they appear, the phenomenal world, and "things in themselves," the noumenal world. For Kant, the free will was only able to transcend the empirical world when it dealt with the ethical realm of *a priori* principles; that is, when it considered questions of "ought," not questions of what is. For Kant, the moral will must be allowed to be free to transcend the phenomenal world. Fichte embraced Kant's moral philosophy based on *a priori* principles and also stressed the necessary freedom of the ego. For Fichte, however, the ego is not only able to perceive the ethical, noumenal world, but is also the creator of the phenomenal world in that its perceptions alter the reality of the world. Therefore, Fichte's philosophy, even more so than Kant's, stresses the freedom of the ego.

The ego achieves its necessary freedom in history, which is the unfolding of reason in five distinct stages. Fichte argued that Europe, in his time, was mired in an age of "completed sinfulness" because it embraced reason as the freedom of the will for its own sake. Thus, society becomes the clash of rational wills that seek no higher moral purpose beyond their own ends. However, Fichte believed this stage would soon be replaced by a fourth, and higher stage, where reason would be used to achieve both freedom and morality. In this stage, individual interests would be equivalent to the common good.

Fichte explains in great detail the path to this fourth stage in his most famous work, *The Addresses to the German Nation. The Addresses* was written in response to the Prussian defeat and occupation by Napoleon and delivered in French-occupied Berlin during the winter of 1807–1808. These addresses, intended for a mass audience, exhorted the German people to unite and resist French occupation just as their ancestors had resisted the Romans. Fichte argues that the Germans had to prevail in order to realize their destiny as world leaders in culture.

Like the German romanticists of the period, Fichte embraced the unification of Germany through its culture, namely, its literature. German literature is exceptional because it is expressed in the German language. He argues that the most characteristic part of a nation is its language. And of the major modern European nations, the Germans alone spoke a primordial language, that is, a language that had been preserved basically intact through the centuries. Thus, Germans needed to purge French cultural influences as well as the French army.

According to Fichte, language and culture can only be disseminated through state-controlled education. This education is not concerned with the interests of the individual student, but with the common interest. Properly implemented, education will do no less than create perfect human beings fit for inaugurating a new epoch of history. Those who resisted education, who resisted the greatness of the German culture, had to be compelled to obey. After all, the state, because it is based on the common good, retains absolute power.

Moreover, in this fourth epoch of history, the state will establish a socialized economy, in particular, a "closed commercial state." Fichte calls for restricting trade with foreign countries. With a solely internal economy, the state could more readily regulate the economy, which it must do almost completely. The resources of the economy must be mobilized for the ultimate purpose, the inculcation of virtue into the masses.

It must be stressed that Fichte was advocating an idealized Germany, one that did not yet exist. It was up to the German people and government to create and nourish such a state.

Although *The Addresses* was mostly ignored during Fichte's lifetime, it became the blueprint for future German nationalists. Despite Fichte's denunciation of despotism and his embrace of liberalism, his views had a profound influence on later Germans including Kaiser Wilhelm and Adolf Hitler.

Fichte's classic statements on nationalism are contained within *The Addresses to the German Nation* (New York: Harper & Row). For Fichte's socialism, see *Closed Commercial State*. Many excellent secondary sources, while dated, are available including Eugene Newton Anderson's *Nationalism and the Cultural Crisis in Prussia, 1806–1815* (New York: Farrar & Rinehart) and *Johann Gottlieb Fichte: A Study of His Political Writings with Special Reference to His Nationalism* by H. C. Engelbrecht (New York: Columbia University Press).

**FILIPINO NATIONALISM**     The Republic of the Philippines, an island state in Southeast Asia that became an independent state in 1946, witnessed a series of nationalist struggles during the 19th and 20th centuries. The independent republic still retains the name of the 16th-century Spanish King Philip II who controlled the colony.

At the end of the 19th century the Filipino nationalist struggle against Spanish colonial rule ended after 333 years with the transfer of Philippine sovereignty from Spain to the United States by the Treaty of Paris (1898). Filipino leaders refused to accept the transfer, however, and their troops controlled the entire country except for the capital city of Manila until 1902, when the Americans finally subdued most of the resistance. Some guerillas continued to fight until as late as 1906.

Neither of the two major goals of the revolutionary nationalist movement had been met. They were not independent because the United States had simply replaced Spain as a foreign authority governing the islands, and the social change they attempted to bring about was prevented by powerful economic institutions. Nevertheless, the Filipinos had the distinction of being the first Asian nation to try to rid themselves of European colonial control.

In the 1960s a new Filipino identity emerged out of an increasing Asian identity and a rejection of the nation's role as a sort of outpost of Christianity. A nationalist influence on culture and the arts emphasized the Filipino language, although English remained the primary language of commerce and government, as well as the major medium of instruction in the universities. This cultural renaissance laid the groundwork for a new vision of a country less dependent on the United States.

The movement was marred in the eyes of many by the increasing repression of the Filipino dictator, U.S.-backed Ferdinand E. Marcos, who declared martial law in 1972, arresting opposition politicians, cracking down on violent crime, and attempting to suppress Communist insurgency. An opposition movement grew in response to Marcos's repression under the leadership of Benigno S. Aquino, Jr., who was assassinated as he returned from exile in 1983. His widow Corazon C. Aquino and his brother Butz Aquino took up the opposition banner.

A strong populist movement grew into the Philippine "people power" revolution, a nonviolent uprising that inspired subsequent nonviolent nationalist movements around the world. Over a period of several years a solid base of grassroots organizing occurred, primarily in the churches (especially in the Christian Base Communities). People systematically trained volunteers in the strategies and tactics of nonviolent action with the help of outside experts such as Hildegard Goss-Mayr and Richard Deats from the International Fellowship of Reconciliation. A Philippine chapter of the Fellowship of Reconciliation known as the Aksyon Para sa Kapayapaan at Katarungan (AKKAPKA) organized more than forty seminars on active nonviolence in thirty provinces. The core of the movement was a vast network of decentralized popular organizations leading to parallel institutions and mass demonstrations.

When Marcos allegedly rigged the presidential elections in 1986 and declared victory, a mass mobilization occurred on behalf of Cory Aquino, the opposition candidate. Every effort by Marcos to repress the opposition was thwarted. When he ordered the print and broadcast media to clear their stories with the information ministry, they ignored the order. The Catholic Church appealed to sympathizers to bring supplies to the protestors; by the second day the crowd had swelled to 40,000 including 7,000 nuns and 5,000 priests and seminarians.

Marcos ordered General Fabian Ver to clear the protest area. Marines ordered to fire into the crowd took aim and broke into tears, refusing to fire. Marcos sent in the air force to attack; the jets circled eight times but never opened fire. Startled troops were met with gestures of friendship and gifts from the protestors and the invasion was stopped in its tracks. Four days after the uprising had begun there were more than 250,000 demonstrators in the streets and Marcos and his entourage fled the country.

**FINNISH NATIONALISM**   The history of Finland, today a representative democracy, has been a struggle against domination by Sweden on one side and by Russia on the other. For more than six centuries, until it was ceded to Russia by the Peace of Hamina in 1809, Finland was part of the Kingdom of Sweden. The economic, political, and cultural life of the country was controlled by Swedish, Danish, and German nobility, with a few Finnish nobles in lesser positions such as bailiffs or magistrates. The official language of the kingdom was Swedish, and Finnish (which is not linguistically related to any other Scandinavian language) was used only as the oral vernacular. With the Reformation, sermons began to be delivered in Finnish, and the first Finnish books appeared in the mid-1500s. Mikael Agricola's translation of the New Testament appeared in 1548, but it took almost another 100 years for a complete translation of the Bible into Finnish to appear. Most of the leading men of the country saw no need for Finnish books; however, a few nobles, such as Per Brahe and Duke John of Finland, encouraged the study of Finnish because they saw the opportunity to establish an independent kingdom with themselves as the rulers.

Other Swedish officials, however, tried to discourage the use of Finnish as "backwards," and the social differences between Finns and Swedes widened during the 16th and 17th centuries.

During the 18th century the study of Finnish dialects was taken up at Turku University, which moved to Helsinki in 1828 because the capital moved there in 1812. The first Finnish language chair was established at about that time. Juhana Vilhelm Snellman (1806–1881), a philosopher and statesman, pushed for Finnish as the first language of the country, as summed up in his famous statement, "Swedes we are not, Russians we can never be, therefore let us be Finns." The importance of other literary symbols of national pride also became apparent at this time: The Finnish Literary Society was founded in Helsinki in 1831 with the goals of collecting Finnish mythology and translating the *Kalevala* into Swedish or German. The *Kalevala*, Finland's national epic, was compiled by Elias Lönnrot in 1835, based on lines of poetry about Finnish gods and heroes collected in the Russian region of Karelia. As evidence of a Viking-age culture of sophisticated literary achievement, the *Kalevala* played a similar role in the Finnish nationalist movement as the medieval sagas did in Iceland. Other collections of folktales, poetry, and sayings were also undertaken during the 18th and 19th centuries by scholars such as Henrik Gabriel Porthan (1739–1804), and these inspired Finland's national composer, Jean Sibelius (1865–1957), to write music based on these folk songs and epic stories, including the *Kullervo*, an opera based on the *Kalevala.*

While Finland was part of Sweden, it was the battleground for numerous wars between Sweden and Russia, which destroyed many Finnish towns. In a peace treaty in 1721, Sweden was forced to surrender the Karelia region, later considered to be the most culturally "Finnish" of the provinces, to Russia. Following the Napoleonic wars in 1809, Russia was granted all of Finland by the Peace of Hamina. By this time, Tsar Alexander I realized that the Finnish nationalist and anti-Swedish feelings that were growing in the country could be advantageous to Russian interests and did not try to suppress them. Instead, he granted Finland semi-autonomous status as a Russian grand duchy. The Russian policy toward Finland was not assimilationist; the country was held primarily as a buffer zone protecting St. Petersburg against Sweden. Tsar Alexander II reaffirmed the autonomous status of the region by giving Finnish equal status to Swedish as an official language in 1863. His successors, however, took a different attitude and tried to bring Finland more closely under direct Russian control. Under Nicholas II, Russian was made a compulsory language in many schools, and, by the 1899 February Manifesto, the Finnish Senate was deprived of most of its powers.

These acts were met by student resistance and petitioning of the tsar, who refused to meet with the protesters. The repression of Finland intensified following these acts of resistance: top officials were dismissed or exiled, freedom of the press was suppressed, and the Finnish army was disbanded. In 1904, the governor-general Nikolas Bobrikov was shot by a government official. After a general strike in 1905, the Finns gained some concessions, but decrees in 1909 and 1910 put an end to all Finnish autonomy. The country suffered further during World War I due to a commercial blockade, food rationing, and unemployment.

After the Russian coup d'état, the provisional government declared all the measures of the tsarist rule illegal and imprisoned the Russian governor-general. On December 4, 1917, Pehr Evind Svinhufvud, a Finnish patriot who had been exiled in Siberia under tsarist rule, submitted a proposal for a constitution for the Republic of Finland and delivered a speech for Finnish independence. On December 6, his measure was adopted and this date is celebrated as Finnish Independence Day.

The Russian Red Guards attempted to establish a socialist republic and a year of civil war followed, during which Sibelius was arrested. With the help of German troops, Finland was liberated in 1918. On December 12, Baron Mannerheim was elected regent.

Independent Finland continued to feel pressure from Sweden and Russia. Sweden claimed the Åland Islands, which were awarded to Finland by the League of Nations in 1921. Disputes with Russia continued to center on the Karelian region. In 1939, Russian troops invaded Finland, beginning the Winter War, which ended with Finland's loss of southern Karelia. Although World War II, during which Finland again served as battleground between larger powers, effectively ended foreign encroachments on Finland, memory of the occupations remains strong. Today, Finnish recollection of the nationalist struggle remains centered around the primary cultural figures—Lönnrot, Sibelius, and Snellman. In the postwar period, Finland has sought closer relations and cooperation with its Scandinavian neighbors through the Nordic Union and entered the European Union in 1994 together with Sweden after a period of "Finlandization" during the Cold War.

**FLAGS** Officially designated representations of a nation. Adopted by every nation within the world community, these symbols convey important information regarding a nation's history, its affiliations, and its future aspirations and goals. Further, national flags codify the subjective nature of the nation; they objectify a nation's identity. In this way, national flags concretize the highly abstract notion of the nation. They make tangible that which might otherwise be impossible to meaningfully apprehend. By blending subjective and objective in this way, national flags move beyond simple representations of the nation. In a very real sense, they become the nation.

National flags constitute a recent chapter in the long history of collective symbolization. Well before the emergence of nations, primitive tribes and clans searched for distinguishing, novel signs that would characterize each group exclusively. These symbols, often referred to as *totems,* served as visible, material markers of a group's personality. Totems signified all that was part of a clan: its possessions, sacred areas, and people. For primitive tribes, totems personified the clan itself. Thus, these symbols were viewed as communal possessions.

The royal families and ruling houses of the ancient, classic, and medieval periods practiced collective symbolization as well. However, unlike the communally oriented totems of the primitives, the banners and standards of these later eras became the logos of the powerful. Specifically, banners and standards of postprimitive periods allowed rulers to impose their identity on those they controlled. For example, ancient Egyptian leaders regularly imposed insignia of the pharaohs on the subjects they hoped to rally. Similarly, ancient Roman rulers maintained sole control over the civilization's glittering standards, symbols considered so sacred that they were guarded in temples when not in use. Rulers used these standards to stimulate awe and terror, especially in those the Romans set out to conquer and amalgamate. During the medieval period, banners were so closely associated with a ruler's legitimacy that to capture the banner of an army or noble house was equated with stripping the ruler of his power. Captured banners were commonly displayed on the tombs of victorious generals or in the homes of those who had won them. These banners served as cues of the victor's dominion. The practices described here stand in stark contrast to the symbolization practices of the primitives. Indeed the rulers of the ancient, classic, and medieval periods installed a tenure of élitism in the history of collective symbolization.

The birth of organized nations signified a new phrase in collective symbolization. During the nationalist period (initiated during the 18th century), every national government adopted its own special set of symbols, with national flags being the most prominent in the array. But from the onset, national flags presented a synthesis of the collective symbols that preceded them. For while national flags were inevitably linked to a nation's leaders, such symbols also remained the property of the nation's citizens. Then and now, national flags typically are designed to reflect the general ideals of a people rather than to trace the lineage of a monarch or a regime.

Many scholars argue that the American flag was responsible for bringing national flags back to the people. Rather than representing a monarch, the American flag was consciously designed as a graphic manifestation of a new political program. Born of the American Revolution (1775–1783), the flag outlined the new structure of the government—stripes and stars representing the distinctiveness, yet unity of the states. All citizens were encouraged to display the American flag. This strategy created a living symbol of the masses as opposed to a relic of rulers.

Following the precedent set by the Americans, many nations constructed flags that mapped desired sociopolitical relations. In Ireland, for example, the national flag was designed to symbolically merge the country's religious factions. National leaders included a green panel in the flag to represent the nation's Catholics; the flag's orange panel signified the nation's Protestants; leaders included a white panel in the center of the flag representing hopes for peaceful coexistence. Venezuela's national flag also appealed to the shared ideals of its citizens. The flag's design connects seven white stars symbolizing the unity of the nation's original provinces. It also presents four different colors chosen to signify four coexisting races.

To ensure that national flags remain live and vibrant symbols, national leaders strive to give flags frequent public exposure. Governments typically equip official institutions and many public spaces with national flags. Students are taught to pledge the flag in the primary grades, and the schools of many nations sustain this practice through the secondary grades. National flags sometimes enter citizens' leisure settings as well. In many nations, citizens salute or pledge the flag at the onset of concerts, sporting events, and other public assemblies. Television stations often end their daily broadcasts with an image of the flag. These images of the flag continually remind a nation's citizens of their cultural autonomy. As such, the flag becomes the basis of a unique conceptual community.

Relations within the nation represent only one of the factors that influence those who construct and adopt national flags. A nation's socioeconomic position within the world community, its lineage, its regional neighbors, and those nations formed during the same historical era are all factors that serve as information centers for emerging nations. For example, research shows that rich and powerful nations tend to adopt flags with simple, basic graphic designs. In contrast, nations furthest from international centers of power tend to adopt highly detailed and embellished flag designs. It is also true that regional neighbors tend to adopt flags with similar designs. Thus while national flags reflect much that is unique about a nation, extranational referents also represent vital stops for national leaders on the road to constructing and projecting their nation's identity.

*Flags through the Ages and Across the World* by Whitney Smith (New York: McGraw Hill, 1975) provides a thorough history of national flags designed prior to 1975. Information on post-1975 flags can be obtained in Deni Brown's *Ultimate Pocket Flags of the World* (New York/London: DK Publ., 1997). In *Identity Designs: The Sights and Sounds of a Nation* (ASA Rose Book Series, New Brunswick, N.J.: Rutgers University Press, 1995), Karen A. Cerulo explores both the intranational and international dimensions considered by national leaders as they choose flag designs that they feel appropriately represent their nations.

## FLEMISH NATIONALISM

Flemish nationalism emerged as a reaction to social and economic discrimination resulting from linguistic policies in 19th- and early 20th-century Belgium. Flanders contains about 58 percent of Belgium's population, and about 55 percent of all Belgians consider Flemish (or Dutch) their native language. However, the historically French-speaking Belgian elite considered Flanders backwards. For close to two centuries, Flanders has fought for Flemish's equal standing alongside French, respect for its culture and history, economic growth, and political power and autonomy.

Flemish national parties like the Flemish National Union (Vlaams Nationaal Verbond) began to emerge after World War I, around the time when Belgium established Flemish as the official language of Flanders. During World War II, Flemish nationalist parties collaborated with the Germans, which resulted in repression in the postwar period of extreme right-wing ideologies. Yet, the second generation of nationalist parties—claiming themselves democratic—took hold in the 1950s, with the main party being the Volksunie (VU). The VU promoted a federal system in Belgium (the Egmont Pact), which angered some of its more virulent nationalists.

The Vlaams Blok (VB) was a nationalist movement

formed in 1978 out of two breakaway movements—the Flemish National Party (Vlaams-Nationale Partij) and the Flemish People's Party (Vlaamse Volkspartij). Its leaders, Karel Dillen and Lode Claes, considered the Egmont Pact a betrayal of Flemish nationalist aspirations and called for a Flemish state within a confederation, rather than a Flemish region in a federal Belgium.

From 1978 to 1987, the VB performed poorly in elections, never gaining more than 2 percent of the vote. It was not until 1988 that the VB became a major force in Flanders. In the 1988 municipal elections, the VB got 17.7 percent of the vote in Antwerp, the region's largest city, which resulted in ten city council seats. A year later the VB sent Dillen to the European Parliament with 20.8 percent of the vote, almost tripling its 1984 results (6.6 percent). In 1991, the VB got 6.6 percent of the national vote and 10.3 percent of the Flemish vote, surpassing the Volksunie, with 25 percent in Antwerp, 10 percent in Ghent, 6 percent in Louvain, and 5 percent in Bruges. In 1994 and as a testament to its organization, the VB presented 1400 candidates in 140 communes in Flanders and Brussels in the cantonal elections. A year later, it got 12.5 percent of the legislative vote in Flanders, the same year that Dillen resigned and appointed Frank Vanhecke as his successor. In the 1999 European elections, the VB sent both Dillen and Vanhecke to the European Parliament.

The VB's success in the late 1980s and beyond is largely attributed to the organizational skills of the young Filip Dewinter, an admirer of France's Jean-Marie Le Pen (Front National). Dewinter moved the VB away from a simple Flemish nationalism to a more xenophobic nationalist populism, drawing from the French Front National's successful ideological package of immigration, crime, and unemployment. Although these themes have taken on greater importance because of the threat they purportedly pose to Flemish identity, Flemish independence still remains the VB's primary goal. Nevertheless, among the Western European extreme-right parties, many consider the VB the most blatantly racist and xenophobic.

See Theo Hermans, ed., and Louis Vos and Lode Wils, co-eds. *The Flemish Movement: A Documentary History, 1780–1990* (London: The Athlone Press, 1992), John Ishiyama, *Ethnopolitics in the New Europe* (Boulder, Colo.: Lynne Rienner Publishers, 1998), Manu Ruys, *The Flemings: A People on the Move, a Nation in Being,* 2nd ed., translated by Henri Schoup (Tielt: Lannoo, 1981), Marc Swyngedouw, "The Extreme Right in Belgium: Of a Non-existent Front National and an Omnipresent Vlaams Blok," in Hans-Georg Betz and Stefan Immerfall, eds., *The New Politics of the Right: Neo-*

*Populist Parties and Movements in Established Democracies* (New York: St. Martin's Press, 1998), and Lode Wils, *Histoire des nations belges. Belgique, Flandre, Wallonie: quinze siècles de passé commun,* translated by Chantal Kesteloot (Ottignies: Quorum, 1996).

**FOLK** In the most basic sense, the folk is the rural, common people of a society; however, this concept of the folk derives meaning only through juxtaposition with an elite, cosmopolitan ruling class. Thus, although the folk often is posited as a mythic, timeless, and unchanging entity, the concept itself is an historically specific ideological construct.

The folk was discovered in Europe during the late 18th and early 19th centuries, as part of the intellectual and artistic movements of romanticism and cultural nationalism. In an era marked by democratic revolution, industrialization, and the rise of the middle classes, the notion that national culture was the property of the metropolitan ruling class was seriously challenged by philosophers, scholars, and artists, who looked instead to the common people as the source of national power. In Germany and England, in particular, intellectuals for the first time turned their attention to lowly popular cultural forms—oral ballads, fairy tales, superstitions, and songs. Through the work of such figures as ethno-linguist Johann Gottfried von Herder, philologists Jakob and Wilhelm Grimm, and poet-dramatist Friedrich Schiller, the folk (*das Volk*) increasingly was proposed to be both the repository of national spirit and the producer of all that made a national culture distinctive.

The concept of the folk is always oppositional and nostalgic, with the folk posited as a premodern antidote to the ills of modernity. The folk is defined as rural and agrarian instead of urban and industrial; attached to the land instead of migrating; rooted, communal, and traditional rather than alienated, isolated, and fragmented. Folk culture is imagined to be oral, organic, and spontaneously occurring, versus the learned artificiality of literate élite culture. The ethos of the folk is cited as the cultural unconscious of an entire society, the true national character often repressed by the cosmopolitan élite.

It is no accident that the construct of the folk arose with modern European nationalism, for that construct has been extremely useful for nationalist claims. A national focus on the folk naturalizes territorial claims, because of the ostensibly intimate connection of folk and land. The invocation of folk culture legitimizes and authenticates a modern nation by implying its timeless, premodern, preliterate history and tradition. And the concept of the folk mythologizes both the communal past of a people and its distinctive, long-evolving collective (racial or national) spirit.

The concept of the folk remained influential in Western nationalism well into the 20th century. In the United States, the greatest focus on national folk forms took place during the decades between the world wars; the USSR also sponsored great folklore scholarship at this time. But following World War II, the association of the folk with explicit nationalist ideology was somewhat discredited, due to the central role it had played in European fascism. Today, the term *folk* is most often used in a more purely cultural sense to denote cultural works produced by unschooled, nonélite artists.

Classic works in the field of national folklore include Jakob Grimm, *Teutonic Mythology*, 4 vols., translated by James Steven Stallybrass (1882–1888); Francis James Child, *The English and Scottish Popular Ballads*, 5 vols. (1882–1898); and Y. M. Sokolov, *Russian Folklore*, translated by Catherine Ruth Smith (1950).

**FORD, HENRY** 1863–1947, Automotive industrialist and entrepreneur. Ford is best known for the technological achievements and business acumen that led to the development of the Ford Motor Company. Ford was also known for his progressive labor policies. Ford was active in politics from 1916 to 1926, when he campaigned for Woodrow Wilson's reelection, ran unsuccessfully for the Senate in 1918, and tackled social, economic, and political issues in his newspaper, the Dearborn *Independent*. However, Ford had more of an international than national vision. Ford was most passionate about his peace work and although he was not a nationalist, he was an anti-Semite who once stated that Jews manipulated the world's money systems, promoted war for financial advantage, and were plotting to destroy Christian civilization.

The Dearborn *Independent* was a weekly newspaper published by the Ford Motor Company from 1918 to 1927. Ford pressured dealerships to distribute the *Independent*, which was the paper's main distribution outlet. Ford purchased the small Dearborn *Independent*, whose circulation was about 1200 at the time, because of his dissatisfaction with the media in general, which he claimed had treated him unfairly and were responsible for his failed Senate bid in 1918. The Dearborn *Independent* covered many of Ford's personal concerns and interests, such as poverty, war, education, labor, employment, morality, and internationalism. However, Ford's Dearborn *Independent* is most remembered for a series of anti-Semitic articles that ran in 1920–1921 and in 1924. The earlier articles dealt with "The Jewish

Question" and were compiled between 1920 and 1922 into four volumes under the general titles *The International Jew: The World's Foremost Problem* (I, 1920), *Jewish Activities in the United States* (II, 1921), *Jewish Influence in American Life* (III, 1921), and *Aspects of Jewish Power in the United States* (IV, 1922). A series of articles in 1924 detailing the Jewish exploitation of farmer organizations in the United States was highly criticized for their anti-Semitic content. The target of the articles, Aaron Sapiro, sued Ford for libel and Ford was forced to apologize publicly and retract his statements. This brought to an end the Dearborn *Independent*.

Ford later denounced the articles, but still found himself dealing with their consequences. *The International Jew* became a bestseller in Germany and was later translated by the Nazis into several languages and distributed worldwide. Hitler praised Ford in *Mein Kampf* and once displayed a photo of Ford in his office. Anti-Semitic and racist groups like the Ku Klux Klan have published *The International Jew*, despite Ford's opposition, and made money off of it for their own organization.

A general reference on Ford is Allan Nevin's *Ford: The Times, the Man, the Company* (New York: Charles Scribner's Sons, 1954). References that deal with Ford's politics include Ford R. Bryan's *Beyond the Model T: The Other Ventures of Henry Ford*, rev. ed. (Detroit: Wayne State University Press, 1997), Allan Nevin and Frank Ernest Hill's *Ford: Expansion and Challenge, 1915–1933* (New York: Charles Scribner's Sons, 1957), and Carol Gelderman's *Henry Ford: A Biography. The Wayward Capitalist* (New York: St. Martin's Press, 1981).

**FRANCO, FRANCISCO** 1892–1975, Spanish general and nationalist dictator (1936–1975), born in La Coruña province. Franco graduated from Toledo military academy in 1910, and in 1926 became, at age thirty-three, Europe's youngest general after combat experience in Morocco, then a bellicose Spanish colony. During the Second Republic (1931–1936), he gained political profile by leading a bloody repression of a miners' revolt in the left-leaning province of Asturias (1934), and by serving as military chief of staff in 1935. He disapproved of the republic's anticlerical and antimilitary positions, and was particularly alarmed by the concession of political autonomy to Catalonia (1932), which he saw as the harbinger of the dissolution of the sacred national unity. Aware of his extreme-right leanings, the Popular Front government created after the February 1936 elections sent him to an outpost on the Canary Islands. This only increased his resentment against the republican regime, and he became one of the leaders of the military coup d'état of July 17–18, 1936. The not-quite-successful coup resulted in a three-year Civil War (1936–1939) and around a million deaths. Franco, who had become generalísimo of the rebel forces in October 1936, in principle faced an uphill battle against the legitimate government, which controlled most of the territory and the biggest cities. But the nationalist forces counted on vital fascist help from Hitler and Mussolini, while democracies mistrusted the republic's ties to Stalin's Soviet Union and did not intervene.

At the end of the war in April 1939, Franco refused to reinstall the monarchy, establishing instead an authoritarian rule that lasted as long as his life. The basis of the new regime were law and order, stability, preeminence of the Catholic Church, and central authority in the hands of the *Caudillo* (chief), responsible for guarding Spain's essences. Franco's concept of Spain absolutely excluded non-Castilian elements, and he tried to eliminate them accordingly. The most tragic legacy of the Civil War was the lasting division of Spain in two halves—the victors and the vanquished—which Franco never pardoned. A brutal postwar repression was carried out as a revenge for the casualties on the nationalist side.

During World War II, Franco initially stood close to Germany and Italy without entering the war directly. From 1943, he gradually distanced himself from a receding Axis. The Allies tolerated Franco's dictatorship after 1945 mainly because the West feared Communism more than a relic of fascism. Ultimately, Franco's staunch anti-Communism allowed him to be accepted by the West in the Cold War dominated 1950s.

Although Franco borrowed the aesthetics and iconography of coetaneous fascism, he never structured power through the only party. Since 1937 he was the head of the compulsorily merged lines of far-right parties, Falange Española y de las JONS, relabeled as El Movimiento (the Movement), to make believe that his effective one-man regime had a sort of political articulation. But the fascist revolution never happened. In Nazi Germany the head of the party took over the head of the state; in Spain it was the opposite.

Franco's political discourse and legitimacy did not vary at all in almost forty years. His speeches reiteratively alluded to the Civil War (which he dubbed "the Crusade"), the Communist menace, the separatists, and the Free Masons. Yet the regime showed a remarkable ability to adapt to changing situations. It provided itself with fundamental laws, among which the most important was the "organic law" (1967). It formed a consti-

tution, completed by the Law of Succession in 1969, which designated Prince Juan Carlos, grandson of Spain's last ruling king Alphonse XIII, as Franco's successor as the head of state, but not as prime minister, head of the armed forces, or chief of the Movement. Francoism only completed itself institutionally upon the dictator's physical decay. In June 1973 he for the first time nominated a prime minister, Luis Carrero Blanco, who the democratic opposition feared could replace the ailing autocrat. In its most spectacular action, the Basque terrorist organization ETA killed Carrero in December 1973. Contrary to Franco's designs, Spain became a democracy after his death in 1975.

**FRANZ JOSEPH** 1830–1916, Given the repression of individual freedoms and of the right of national minorities to manage a part of their own affairs, it is not surprising that the wave of revolution in 1848 shook the Austrian state. A Hungarian nationalist, Louis Kossuth, and others demanded constitutional government for Hungary. But Kossuth admitted that this would be impossible as long as "a corrupting puff of wind that benumbs our senses and paralyzes the flight of our spirit comes to us from the charnel house of the cabinet of Vienna." Fighting soon broke out in Vienna, where a flabbergasted kaiser asked, when told that rebels were taking to the streets, "But are they allowed to do that?" The rebels had momentary success until the revolutionaries themselves became hopelessly disunited over what objectives should be sought.

The Habsburgs were forced to dismiss Metternich, and the incompetent kaiser abdicated in favor of his eighteen-year-old nephew, Franz Joseph, a serious and hard-working monarch who ascended the throne with the words "Farewell youth!" and who ruled for the next sixty-eight years. A constitution, albeit authoritarian in character, was accepted, and Austria sent representatives to the Frankfurt Assembly, which sought unsuccessfully to draft a liberal constitution for all German-speaking people. Ultimately the revolution failed in Austria, as it did almost everywhere else in Europe. Nevertheless, it had badly shaken the empire and revealed deep dissatisfaction with a form of government that was not democratic and did not recognize the rights of subject nationalities. Yet, once the revolutionary storm had blown over, the new ruler showed how little he had learned by enforcing a policy characterized by absolutism and tight centralization.

In 1866 Austria suffered a crushing defeat at the hands of the Prussian army at the battle of Königgrätz. With new breech-loading rifles, which had been used so successfully in the American Civil War, and the capacity to move their troops to the battlefield on new railroads, the Prussians were far better prepared than the Austrians, whose wealth had been spent to construct the stately Ringstrasse in the center of Vienna rather than to modernize their army. This defeat finally wiped away any Austrian dreams of dominating or sharing power over all of Germany and cleared the way for a "small German" unification clustered around Prussia and excluding Austria.

The new German Empire, which was proclaimed in the Hall of Mirrors at the Palace of Versailles in January 1871, had in Austria-Hungary an ally that would become increasingly weakened by its nationalities problem. The 19th century saw the birth of nationalist movements all over Europe. A multinational state like Austria had to swim against the current of the age and could survive only by introducing timely reforms to satisfy the aspirations of national minorities. Austria was never able to do this. Franz Joseph, who reputedly learned to speak every language in his polyglot empire, remained popular, as did his fabled wife, the eccentric Elizabeth (Sissi) of Bavaria, who was assassinated in 1898 by an Italian anarchist in Geneva.

The German-speaking minority of the Austro-Hungarian Empire was able to reach a compromise with the Hungarians in 1867 as a direct consequence of the defeat at Königgrätz. The Habsburg Empire was converted into a dual monarchy, composed of two independent and equal states, with the Austrian emperor serving also as the Hungarian king. Military, diplomatic, and imperial financial affairs were handled in Vienna, but Hungary had its own parliament, cabinet, civil service, and administrative system. While this settlement did increase the efficiency of governmental operations within the empire, it stimulated yearnings for independence or autonomy on the part of the empire's other nationalities, especially the Czechs. From time to time there was talk in the empire of federal reforms that might extend the same privileges to all subject peoples, but these always foundered on the rocks of Hungarian and Austrian intransigence.

Despite a short-lived liberal era in the late 1860s and 1870s, the last decades before World War I displayed growing tension within and along the borders of the Austro-Hungarian Empire. The steady collapse of the Ottoman Empire and growing Russian interest in Balkan affairs (clothed in idealistic terms of Pan-Slavism) seriously threatened the very existence of Austria-Hungary, which sought to preserve the status quo at all costs. In 1912 the Balkan states had fought against Turkey in or-

der to enlarge themselves at Turkey's expense. In 1913 the same Balkan states fought each other over the booty. To Austria's chagrin, the chief winner in both was the rising and highly ambitious Serbia, which began to serve as an attractive model for the Southern Slavs within the Austro-Hungarian Empire. Also, in 1913 a high military official, Col. Alfred Redl, was revealed to have been a spy for the Russians for over ten years. This shocking revelation shook Austrians' confidence in their own governmental structure and weakened its international reputation.

Thus, the Austrians tended to overreact when one of the most important events in world history occurred on June 28, 1914, a Serbian holiday commemorating the assassination of the Turkish sultan in 1389 by a Serbian patriot. Austrian Archduke Franz Ferdinand and his wife were murdered in Sarajevo (Bosnia's capital) by a nationalist Bosnian student, Garrilo Princip. The archduke had become successor to the throne after the kaiser's only son, Rudolf, had become entangled in an extramarital love affair and finally killed himself and his mistress in 1889. The shots of Sarajevo sounded the end of an almost fifty-year absence of major wars among European great powers. Austria held Serbia responsible for this act and, backed by Germany, made unacceptable demands on Serbia. All over Europe, alliances were invoked, threats were made, and "blank checks" and ultimatums were issued. In the end, all major powers had painted themselves into a corner with their many commitments and could not get out. By the first week of August Europe was locked into a war that lasted four long years and far exceeded all previous wars in terms of casualties and destruction.

During World War I Austria-Hungary primarily sought to retain some control over the Balkans. As Germany's military power ebbed, Austria became increasingly bewildered and confused. Proportionately, Austria-Hungary's losses of men were greater than those of Germany: 1.2 million killed and 3.6 million wounded. In 1916 Franz Joseph died and was replaced on the throne by his nephew Karl I.

## FRENCH COLONIES AND NATIONALISM  During the 18th and 19th centuries, France used its military force to expand to various places of the world including Africa, Asia, Antarctica, and the North Atlantic, Pacific, and Indian Oceans. The first step of this extensive colonialist enterprise was to secure a series of outposts in order to support commerce with foreign places. Later, France claimed larger overseas territories as its own and engaged in considerable efforts to develop some of them

according to Western principles. Expansionist arguments for colonialism responded to three main goals best articulated by politician Jules Ferry: (1) expanding foreign markets to support France's rapid industrial growth; (2) responding to European political and economical rivalries, especially those of England; and (3) supporting a so-called humanitarian and civilizing mission that assumed the superiority of European cultures and religions over those in other areas. Opponents of the idea of a French Empire raised the question of the inevitable cultural and economic inequalities between colonial forces and indigenous populations, which they saw as a blatant contradiction to the principles of the revolution and to the republic. Some adversaries to national expansion that involved imperialist strategies denounced the easy temptation to compensate for the loss of Alsace in 1871 to Germany by invading foreign lands. The economic success of the colonies was evident in the Union Coloniale Française, which regrouped over 400 French commercial companies located in the overseas territories. However, the Ministère des Colonies, whose mission was to support the colonial cultural and economic enterprises, never became a strong political force within metropolitan France.

Supporters of the colonies emphasized the economic and nationalistic benefits that could be drawn from overseas territories. Colonies were to serve France at the least possible cost. They were also seen as an easy way to increase French prestige in Europe, help solve its problems at home, and revive national pride and unity. In times of war, France called on volunteers from overseas, recruiting soldiers from several of its colonies (black Africa and Madagascar, Indochina, the Pacific possessions, and the Maghreb) during World War I. After the war, French colonists tried to impose French values and willfully used rivalries between local ethnic groups in order to diminish resistance to the colonial governments. Social policies of assimilation that included services such as health care and education modeled on metropolitan France were intended to pacify the population and entice them into wholeheartedly accepting of the French as "humane" rulers. The anticolonialist movement accompanied the colonialist ambitions all along. Anticolonialist speeches were given by Jean Jaurès and George Clémenceau who both argued that civilization did exist overseas before French arrival, and that problems in France could not be solved with overseas expansion. The socialists especially pointed to the fact that the increasing budget going to support the colonies did not benefit the indigenous people, but a rather small group of French colonial bureaucrats, businesspeople, and their families. In the 1930s, Leon Blum and the left forces of the Popular Front envisioned a radical change of policies that would benefit only the indigenous overseas populations.

Algeria, first invaded in 1830, held a special place among the colonies because it was included as part of official French territory. It was divided into three administrative branches modeled on the French structure. Algeria regained independence in 1962 after a bloody war, called the "Revolution in Algeria" and the "Algerian War" in France during which de Gaulle, the French president, tried to emphasize the notion of *l'Algérie française.*

Local nationalism developed in most colonies in the early to mid-20th century, resulting in independence for most of them. Some territories however are still attached to France, among which are Guadeloupe and Martinique.

For further reading, see Robert Aldrich, *Greater France. History of French Overseas Expansion* (New York: St. Martin's Press, 1996).

**FRENCH NATIONALISM** France, it has often been said, is "weighed down by history." The French have a long memory for their own past, although they do not always agree about its high and low points. Yet, far from being a country exclusively living in the past, contemporary France is a highly dynamic and forward-looking nation. It is among the wealthiest, most technologically advanced and influential countries in the world. Clearly, France has a future, but the French would say that they have a *destiny.* From the time of the Crusades, the first of which was practically an entirely French affair, to the present day, the French have felt a sense of mission to civilize the world.

Perhaps no one expressed this mission better than the great realist Charles de Gaulle, who opened his war memoirs with the following words: "All my life I have had a certain idea of France. This is inspired by sentiment as much as by reason. The emotional side of me tends to imagine France, like the princess in the fairy stories or the Madonna in the frescoes, as dedicated to an exalted and exceptional destiny. Instinctively I have the feeling that Providence has created her either for complete successes or for exemplary misfortunes. . . . But the positive side of my mind also assures me that France is not really herself unless in the front rank; that only vast enterprises are capable of counterbalancing the ferments of dispersal which are inherent in her people; that our country, as it is, surrounded by the others, as they are, must aim high and hold itself straight, on pain of mortal danger. In short, to my mind, France cannot be France without greatness."

The general, who once admitted that he preferred *France* to *Frenchmen,* disdained the petty squabbling of everyday politics. He denied that the essential France was to be found in the yawning provincial bureaucrat, the scandalous French president (Felix Faure) who died in the presidential palace while making love to his mistress, or the impetuous Parisian pamphleteer who plots to bring down the regime. He believed that one must inhale the heady air of the mountain peaks in order to see the true France: "Viewed from the heights, France is beautiful."

Joan of Arc is to many French the ideal symbol of patriotism: a pure lady warrior with a sense of mission who placed God solidly on the side of the French. Whenever she addressed the crowds as "Frenchmen," the response indicated that a new nationalism mingled with a divine mission was emerging. Even for centuries afterward there was no consensus in France concerning the legacy she had left. A monarchical France before 1789 had little use for saviors from the masses, and her mystical, religious aura made her out of place in an enlightened, revolutionary France.

Nevertheless, Napoleon had a beautiful statue of her erected in Orléans in 1803, and the process to have her made a saint was initiated in 1869. Not until the humiliating defeat of France at the hands of the Prussians in 1870 was she embraced as a symbol of vengeance toward an outside power that had taken her native Lorraine. She was finally canonized in 1920. She is undoubtedly the Madonna in de Gaulle's memoirs who incorporated France, since the great French leader also adopted the cross of Lorraine as his own symbol. His stubborn, righteous defense of France's destiny moved an exasperated Englishman, Sir Winston Churchill, to remark that "of all the crosses I have had to bear, the heaviest was the Cross of Lorraine."

The 17th century became "the French century" in all of continental Europe. This was a period when forceful French kings and brilliant royal advisers succeeded in reducing much of the French nobility's powers and in establishing the present borders of France. The glitter of the royal court soon dazzled Europe. When in 1624 Louis XIII chose an ambitious cardinal to be his chief adviser, he gained at his side a tireless servant of the French crown and the French state. Cardinal Richelieu was not a man given to courtly debauchery, theological hairsplitting, or listening for voices from God. "Reason must be the standard for everything," he said, and "the public interest ought to be the sole objective of the prince and his counselors." *Raison d'état* ("reason of state"), the interests of the community, became for him the overriding concerns.

Few leaders embodied France's ideals and pride as much as Napoleon Bonaparte. He was a legendary conqueror who sought to establish a form of European unity based on the ideas of the French Revolution and on the bayonets of France's Grand Army. Europeans viewed Napoleon as the very embodiment of the revolution, and he carried its ideals to every corner of Europe. The principles of "liberty, equality, fraternity" were among his most effective weapons. He was a great military leader who in a series of campaigns sought to pacify Europe under French leadership. By 1806 French domination extended from Holland and the German North Sea coast to the Illyrian Provinces along the east coast of the Adriatic Sea. Italy was completely under French control, and some territories, including Rome itself, were annexed to France.

Napoleon's very successes helped bring about his downfall. French preeminence showed the strength of the modern nation, and Napoleon's invasions stimulated nationalism outside France. Other governments felt compelled to imitate France by introducing popular reforms and raising citizen armies. Soon Napoleon faced opposition, not just from hostile governments and ruling groups, but from entire nations in Europe.

After his fall in 1815, nationalist self-interest and ambitions continued to flourish. The Prussian philosopher Friedrich Hegel and many romantics viewed the nation-state as the best instrument for developing a people's genius. European liberals regarded a powerful centralized state as the best tool against the conservative ideas of ruling princes. Most socialists worked within national movements and pursued national goals, even though Karl Marx had argued that working-class solidarity sprang over national borders and made the nation-states irrelevant. Italy and Germany became unified in 1861 and 1871, respectively, and a restless Germany began seeking its "place in the sun." Nationalism weakened beyond salvation the polyglot Ottoman and Habsburg Empires. Thus, the 19th century left a legacy of assertive nationalism, exaggerated patriotism, and military force to achieve political goals. By the outbreak of World War I in 1914, the triumph of the nation-state was complete.

France suffered frightful losses in World War I, which was largely fought on its soil. In World War II it fared even worse. It was defeated and occupied by Germany. The French nation, shorn of most of its colonial empire, desperately needed to resurrect its pride and its status in the world. After the tumult of the French Fourth Republic, de Gaulle was able to restore social peace and economic prosperity at home. He could then turn full attention to his major interest: foreign affairs. He had been greatly displeased with France's position in the world when he came to power. Colonial wars had sapped almost all of France's attention and military strength. What was worse, the fate of Europe had been determined by the Soviet Union, the United States, and Britain. After the advent of the Cold War in 1946–1947, French security had fallen almost exclusively into the hands of NATO, with an American general in command. That is, France's security was ultimately in the hands of the United States, a friendly, but *foreign* country, which in his words, "brings to great affairs elementary feelings and a complicated policy."

De Gaulle and all his successors knew that the Soviet Union posed a threat to Western Europe, which ultimately needed American protection. He also knew that the United States' tolerance level toward its European allies was high. He therefore decided that France needed and could achieve foreign policy independence. He also had bitter memories of what he considered a personal snub by Churchill and Roosevelt during the struggles of World War II. His first step was to develop French atomic weapons. When he was informed in 1960 of the successful French explosion in the Sahara, he exclaimed: "Hurray for France!"

The basic Gaullist goal was to create an independent Europe under French leadership. In doing this, France could resurrect French preeminence in Europe and restore its status as a world power. The attempt to diminish Soviet and U.S. influence in Eastern and Western Europe, respectively, was not accomplished. Nevertheless, his ambition to create an independent French foreign policy was followed by his presidential successors, despite some changes in emphasis and style. Also at the end of the 20th century France's effort to deepen the European Union (EU) and to intensify European efforts to create a stronger "European pillar" of defense both inside and outside of NATO are motivated in large part by the desire to restore French leadership in Europe.

De Gaulle gave France a role of which it could be proud, and he ultimately won the world's respect for his country. Henry Kissinger recalled that the general "exuded authority" and told of de Gaulle's attendance at a reception given by former President Richard Nixon on the occasion of General Eisenhower's funeral in Washington: "His presence . . . was so overwhelming that he was the center of attention wherever he stood. Other heads of government and many senators who usually proclaimed their antipathy to authoritarian generals crowded around him and treated him like some strange species. One had the sense that if he moved to a window, the center of gravity might shift and the whole room might tilt everybody into the garden."

After World War II, France regarded European integration and a strong EU as a vehicle for its resurrection as a leader that could supplant the U.S. predominance in Europe. One Frenchman needed no prodding. Jean Monnet wrote in May 1950 that "at the present moment, Europe can be brought to birth only by France. Only France is in a position to speak and act." In April he and his colleagues at the Planning Commission had produced a bombshell proposal to place Germany's and France's coal and steel industries under international control. Wise to the sinkholes in any bureaucracy, Monnet made an end run around the "normal channels" and placed the proposal directly into the hands of his friend, Foreign Minister Robert Schuman, as the latter was leaving by train for a weekend in his native Lorraine.

Born in Luxembourg and educated in Germany, Schuman would not turn a deaf ear to any realistic recommendation for securing peace through Franco-German rapprochement. When he returned from the weekend, he announced to Monnet: "I've read the proposal. I'll use it." On the morning of May 9, 1950, Schuman stepped into a press conference in the Salon de l'Horlage at the Quai d'Orsay, France's foreign ministry, and delivered his electrifying message: "It is no longer a time for vain words, but for a bold, constructive act. France has acted, and the consequences of her action may be immense. . . . She has acted essentially in the cause of peace. For peace to have a real chance, there must first be a Europe. . . . France is taking the first decisive step to rebuild Europe and is inviting Germany to play its part. This will transform the situation in Europe. This will open the door to other joint activities inconceivable hitherto. Europe will emerge from all this . . . firmly united and solidly built."

The heart of the proposal was Franco-German reconciliation. Without it, there could be no progress toward European unity. In Schuman's words, the European Coal and Steel Community (ECSC) was designed "to end Franco-German hostility once and for all." His message was directed at a generation of European leaders who had experienced two world wars and the tumult of the interwar years. "Because Europe was not united, we have had war." The pernicious Franco-German rivalry had helped cause three wars in less than a century, and the solution was to link the two peoples so closely economically that they could never fight again. In Monnet's words, the new partnership would make war "not only unthinkable, but materially impossible."

As a signatory to the Treaty of Rome in 1957 France was a founding member of the organization that developed into the EU. Along with the Federal Republic of

Germany (FRG), it has been the chief engine of European integration. However, France clung the hardest to the notion of national sovereignty and was not always an easy partner. In 1965 President de Gaulle refused to send a French representative to the European Council for seven months when the other five declined to accept his demands concerning the Common Agriculture Program (CAP). The real issue was not CAP, but de Gaulle's vision of Europe as an *Europe des Patries,* a league of "fatherlands," which would reserve ultimate sovereignty for themselves. That is why he had opposed the ECSC and the European Defense Community (EDC). France had proposed the latter, an integrated European army, in 1950. However, in 1954 the National Assembly, not wanting French troops to be under supranational control, rejected the proposal. After the vote the Gaullist and Communist deputies stood up and sang the *Marseillaise.* France remained in NATO, which had been formed in 1949.

Monnet recalled the fundamental difference between his and the general's views: "De Gaulle's whole argument was based on the premise that nothing European could be undertaken so long as Europe was not a political reality. But at the same time he affirmed that the only political reality was the nation-state." This nationalist view, which was popular with the British, contrasted sharply with the integrationist approach of Monnet and Schuman and was expressed in de Gaulle's frontal attack on the way the EU operated: "We know—and heaven knows how well we know it—that there is a different conception of a European federation in which, according to the dreams of those who have conceived it, the member countries would lose their national identities, and which . . . would be ruled by some technocratic body of elders, stateless and irresponsible."

The "Luxembourg Compromise" pushed the controversy underground again and enabled the EU to survive. This was an agreement to disagree: "The six delegations note that there is a divergence of views on what should be done in the event of a failure to reach complete agreement." It stipulated that the European Commission consult the individual states before advancing important proposals and that the European Council could not overrule any member nation. In other words, although the partners would try to reach a consensus "within a reasonable time," all votes on matters of vital interest must be unanimous, and each member had veto power. This was a grave setback for the supranational conception of Europe, which was still not acceptable to all members. France had defended the overriding importance of national sovereignty.

**FRENCH REVOLUTION**   On June 17, 1789, the bourgeois element (the "Third Estate") in France decided to declare itself the "National Assembly." When the king panicked and closed the hall in which the Third Estate met, the latter moved to a nearby indoor tennis court and proclaimed in the "Oath of the Tennis Court" that it was the true representative of the people and that it would not disband until it had produced a constitution for France. This was a revolutionary step, unleashing explosive events that an irresolute king could not control. It was the first act in the French Revolution, which went through many stages and lasted ten years. Neither France nor the world would thereafter be the same.

The events at the Versailles meetings stirred up crowds in Paris, which began to look for weapons in arsenals and public buildings. On July 14, 1789, a crowd went to the Bastille, which like the Tower of London was a stronghold built during the Middle Ages to overawe the city and to provide a place of detention for influential prisoners. When the official in charge of the stronghold refused to distribute any weapons, the crowd successfully stormed it. The mob, infuriated that almost a hundred persons had been killed, slaughtered the guards who had surrendered. They then beheaded the commanding officials with knives and paraded around Paris with the heads of their victims on spikes.

The unrest and violence spread to the countryside as manorial lords saw their properties sacked and burned by bitter peasants. The more fortunate escaped with their lives, but royal power vanished quickly. The Marquis de Lafayette, a revolutionary-minded aristocrat who had served on George Washington's staff during the American War of Independence, was given command over the guard in Paris. He designed a flag for the new France to replace the blue and white *fleur de lis* ("lily flag"). He combined the colors of the city of Paris, red and blue, with the white of the House of Bourbon. Thus the tricolor, which is France's flag today, represented a fusion of the new and old regimes.

The sudden acts of violence had frightened the ruling group into granting important concessions. On August 4, 1789, the nobles relinquished their feudal rights, and on August 27 the National Assembly promptly proclaimed the Declaration of the Rights of Man, one of history's most eloquent assertions of equality before the law, the opening of public service to all classes and freedom as an unalienable individual right, limited only by the freedom of others. An enlightened constitutional monarchy was established. The king was forced to return to the Tuileries palace in Paris. There he was under the watchful eye of France's new, moderate regime, guided by the Count de Mirabeau, who like many aristocrats, had concluded that the future lay with the Third Estate.

It is always a great misfortune when moderate and democratic revolutionaries cannot control the beast of revolution once it has been uncaged. As in Russia a century and a quarter later, a more radical "second revolution" often overtakes the first one, wiping away many of the democratic gains in the process. This misfortune befell the French Revolution.

The first signal for change came on the night of June 21, 1791, when the king and his family attempted to escape to Germany. Caught two days later at Varennes, close to the border, they were ingloriously brought back to the Tuileries and locked up in their palace. After this clumsy move, the king's commitment to the new order was no longer credible, and the people's loyalty to him, which had already been eroded, disappeared entirely.

This new situation greatly angered the other monarchies of Europe, especially those of Prussia and Austria. The moderate "Girondists," members of a revolutionary club whose name derived from the department (state) of Gironde and who had gained a majority in the National Assembly in 1792, responded to what they saw as a clear external threat to the revolution. They declared war on Austria. It went badly for France, but it quickly added a new element to the revolution. Seeing the "fatherland in danger," the citizens took up arms, and patriotism rose to fever pitch. Nationalism and revolution joined hands as the French national anthem, the *Marseillaise,* indicates.

Once unleashed, the popular tide became difficult to control. The Tuileries was stormed by a mob that forced a humiliated king to wear a red hat of the revolution and to drink with them from a common bottle. The constitutional monarchy was overthrown, and in September 1792 suspected royalists were hunted down and massacred in prisons, monasteries, and elsewhere. In December the king was tried and convicted of conspiring with the enemy (a charge that was no doubt true), and he was beheaded one month later. Scarcely had the king's head fallen before France found itself at war with all the major monarchies of Europe.

Faced with a frenzied, imperiled nation, the moderates were pushed aside by the radical Jacobins, a revolutionary club that had met regularly since 1789 in the Jacobin Convent in the Rue Honore. It was led by the fanatical Robespierre. A Committee of Public Safety was formed to cope with enemies abroad and at home. On October 10, 1793, the new revolutionary leadership declared that the government of France must remain "revolutionary until the peace." In clear text, this meant a "reign of terror," and political "trials" were begun at once.

On October 16 Queen Marie Antoinette was beheaded, followed by all the Girondists who could be arrested. For the next nine months the guillotine would never cease doing its grisly work. Until Robespierre and his followers' own execution in July 1794, France was subjected to a dictatorship in the hands of fanatically self-righteous people who asserted that "terror is nothing else than swift, severe, indomitable justice; it then flows from virtue."

Enlightened democrats make no claims to know absolute truth and therefore tolerate other men's views and weaknesses. By contrast, the ideologues who controlled France in those bloody days had such an abstract conception of liberty that they lost sight of man. Out of love for humanity and the truth, they would have eradicated the human race. Noted French author George Sand wrote that "during the terror, the men who spilled the most blood were those who had the strongest desire to lead their fellow men to the dreamed-of golden age, and who had the greatest sympathy for human misery . . . the greater their thirst for universal happiness, the more relentless they became." Charles Dickens's description of the revolution in the opening sentence of his *Tale of Two Cities* is memorable: "It was the best of times, it was the worst of times, it was the age of reason, it was the age of foolishness. . . ." The world witnessed the worst and best in man.

Although the French today tend to remember the noblest aspects of the revolution, the terror made it difficult then and now for persons outside of France to have a unified opinion of this first great European revolution. No doubt, many of the 17,000 victims of the terror were in fact enemies of the new republic. Only 15 percent of the executions took place in Paris, and more than half took place in western France, where the resistance to the new order was the greatest. Only 15 percent of the victims were aristocrats or clergymen. However, the number of innocent persons killed was so great that the new republic disgusted respected friends abroad. Also, although France's foreign enemies were ultimately defeated, the French Revolution was knocked off its democratic path. It was almost a century before France was able to return to relatively stable, republican government.

Napoleon Bonaparte seized power in 1799, and for the next fifteen years, France followed this soldier. He clearly preferred order to liberty, and he quickly moved to establish order. Despite his authoritarian style of rule, he was an immensely popular leader who quickly showed that he was a child of the revolution. Other

Europeans saw him as the very embodiment of the revolution who carried its ideals to every part of Europe. These principles were always among his most effective weapons. He promulgated a new constitution and a civil code that reflected the major accomplishments of the revolution: popular sovereignty, underscored by Napoleon's practice of submitting every constitutional change to a plebiscite; trial by jury and equality before the law; a citizens' army; office holding based on competence; abolition of feudal privileges; and freedom of religion and of speech and press (at least in theory). Other governments of Europe felt compelled to imitate France by making popular reforms and raising citizens' armies.

Napoleon remained a great military leader who sought both to secure France's "natural borders" and to pacify Europe under French leadership. This was essentially accomplished by 1802. However, his ambition was to be more than a peacemaker, and his lack of moderation not only sapped his own country's vigor, it ultimately doomed him to defeat. In May 1803 he began an endless series of wars aiming far beyond the mere protection of France's frontiers. Due to stunning victories, French domination by 1806 extended from Holland and the German North Sea coast to the Illyrian Provinces along the east coast of the Adriatic Sea. Italy was completely under French control, and some territories (including Rome itself) were annexed to France. But his very successes helped to bring about his downfall.

His invasions stimulated nationalism outside France. The French occupation of Germany spawned nationalism there, enabling persons in all parts of Germany to put aside some of their local patriotism and to struggle side by side to rid Germany of a foreign power. Because no unified German state yet existed, German nationalism took on an idealistic and romantic character. It was born in reaction to a conqueror who seemed to understand how to achieve French national interests under the cover of high-sounding calls for "liberty, equality, and fraternity." German nationalism and the struggle against alien rule therefore became linked in the minds of far too many Germans with resistance against the ideals of the French Revolution, known in Germany as the "ideas of 1789."

# G

**GAJ, LJUDEVIT**   1809–1872, Croat politician, born in Krapina (Croatia). Gaj is best known as the founder and leader of the Illyrianist movement (1836–1848), the first stage of the Croat national awakening. Gaj studied at the University of Graz, where he became acquainted with students from other Slavic lands and the works of contemporary Slavists, and in 1834 he obtained a doctorate in philosophy from the University of Leipzig.

In the late 1820s he began work on the standardization of the Croatian literary language. In 1834 he founded first the literary journal *Danicza Horvatzka, Slavonzka y Dalmatinzka* (Croatian, Slavonian and Dalmatian Dawn), and then the *Novine Horvatzke* (Croatian News), which was more political in nature.

Gaj attracted a small following of young Croat writers, and together they began work on standardizing the Croatian language, thus laying the foundations of the modern Croatian literary language. The significance of their enterprise lay in the fact that they rejected the kajkavian dialect of Croatian, spoken only in Zagreb and its environs, in favor of the štokavian dialect, which they referred to as *Illyrian*, spoken by the majority of Croats and virtually all Serbs. In December 1835 Gaj formally adopted the štokavian (Illyrian) dialect in his papers, which were renamed *Ilirske Narodne Novine* (Illyrian National News) and *Danica Ilirska* (Illyrian Dawn). The work of Gaj and the Illyrianists, taken together with the endeavors of the Serbian linguistic reformer Vuk Stefanović Karadžić, laid the basis for what later became known as Serbo–Croatian.

Gaj's most important work was certainly in the cultural field, but in 1840 he entered politics. Fearing the threat posed by Magyarization, one of the central demands that his movement articulated was the introduction of Illyrian as Croatia's official language. The Austrian authorities had become sufficiently alarmed by the Illyrianist movement that in 1843 they banned the use of the Illyrian name. Gaj was temporarily forced to leave the

Croatian political scene, only to reappear during the revolutions of 1848. Gaj was opposed to the policy of Magyarization, as articulated by the Magyar revolutionaries led by Lajos Kossuth. During the revolution Gaj participated in a triumvirate that assisted Croatia's military governor, Josip Jelačić, in governing Croatia. By October 1848, however, Jelačić forced Gaj out of the triumvirate because of the latter's receipt of financial aid from the Serbian ruler Miloš Obrenović. From that point on, Gaj's political influence and fortunes waned. Although in 1849 he placed his newspapers in the service of the Austrian government, in 1853 he was briefly detained by the authorities because of his ties to the Serbian government. He attempted to stage a political comeback in the 1860s, but was regarded by many in Croatia as untrustworthy because of his collaboration with the Austrian authorities and the Serbian principality.

Despite the decline of his personal political fortunes, Gaj's importance lies in the fact that he exerted considerable influence on the formation of early Croatian nationalism, especially in the cultural, linguistic, and literary realms.

**GALTIERI, LEOPOLDO**   1926– , Dictator of Argentina (1981–1982). Born in Caseros, province of Buenos Aires, Galtieri graduated in 1945 from the Military Academy (Colegio Militar), where he studied military engineering. In 1949 he attended the U.S. Basic Engineering Course in the Panama Canal Zone, and in 1958 he became a professor at the Senior War College. The following year Galtieri was in charge of the advanced engineering course at the engineering school, and in 1960 he took an advanced engineering course in the United States.

On December 28, 1979, Galtieri became the commander in chief of the Argentine army. When General Roberto Viola fell ill, Galtieri had the military junta declare him president de facto on December 29, 1981.

In 1982 Galtieri approved the plan to recapture the Malvinas (Falkland) Islands from the United Kingdom, last occupied by the Argentines in the early 1830s. The war, which raged from early April to mid–June 1982, was disastrous for Argentina, and Galtieri was forced to step down on June 17.

In 1985, General Galtieri was tried for human rights violations during the dictatorship and incompetent handling of the war against Britain. Galtieri was sentenced to twelve years imprisonment. In December 1990 he was released under a general amnesty.

## GANDHI, INDIRA  1917–1984, Born the daughter of Jawaharlal Nehru, Gandhi entered politics at an early age and participated in the Indian independence movement under her father and Mohandas Gandhi (no relation). After independence she assumed the presidency of the Congress Party from 1959 to 1960, and in 1966, two years after her father's death, she became prime minister until 1977. Her tenure was very controversial, especially her introduction of emergency rule from 1975 to 1977. During this time she introduced a forced sterilization program that was so brutal in its execution that it alienated Moslems and Hindus alike, sparked protests all over the country and abroad, and engendered determined resistance to family planning that persists to this day. In foreign policy she entered into a friendship treaty with the Soviet Union in 1971, and Indian–American relations were strained during her tenure. In December of the same year she ordered an attack against Pakistan that resulted in the breakaway and independence of Bangladesh from West Pakistan. She continued her father's foreign policy of nonalignment, and in 1982 she was named chair of the Non-aligned movement.

Following her extremely unpopular state of emergency in 1975, Congress was voted out of power in 1977. To win back its lost votes and regain power, she intensified her populist political style. She sought to mine votes in Hindu revival circles, using Hindu rituals and symbols and exhorting Hindu nationalism. Moslems and Sikhs were offended. Congress also lent its support occasionally to Moslem and Sikh causes in order to attract votes. She returned to power in 1980. But her personalistic style of leadership adversely affected India's democratic regime by centralizing decision making to such an extent that party and state institutions were bypassed. This weakened both her own party and the central government's Parliament and federal system.

Indira Gandhi's departure from secular politics not only fostered an upswing of communal violence in the 1980s, but it also brought about her own assassination in 1984 at the hand of one of her Sikh bodyguards. In

this decade, the most significant issue in communal politics became Punjab, where a rise in terrorist violence claimed mainly Sikh, but also many Hindu, lives. Meddling in Punjabi state politics in order to increase her own power and influence, Gandhi helped bring down the elected state government. She then sided with the armed supporters of a Sikh priest named Bhindranwale, who occupied the Sikhs' sacred Golden Temple, declared that any non-Sikh must leave Punjab, intimidated many to do just that, beat up Sikhs who protested against him, and generally turned Punjab into an armed camp. As a result, Sikhs living outside Punjab began to be terrorized. Gandhi's shortsighted policy had created hatred between Hindus and Sikhs for the first time in Indian history. She tried to control the monster she had helped create by assuming control of the Punjab and sending in the army to dislodge the priest. In the process the great library of the Golden Temple was destroyed.

In Delhi her assassination unleashed a massive reprisal against Sikhs in which squads of thugs mobilized by Hindu groups murdered thousands. The new prime minister, Indira's son Rajiv (1944–1991), kept the Indian army, which could have prevented much of the killing, in the barracks. His government strengthened the trend toward communalizing politics by refusing to challenge the increasingly belligerent Hindu right, which was calling for *Hindutva* (a nonsecular state that reflects Hindu predominance). At the same time he polarized the situation by supporting the efforts of conservative Moslem groups to increase their influence within the broader Indian Moslem community. He also sent Indian troops to Sri Lanka, thereby offending many Tamils. Like his mother, he too paid the highest price for meddling in communal politics when a female Tamil guerrilla with a bomb strapped to her body blew him up. The ultimate effect of their efforts to restore their Congress Party's dominance by trying to manipulate communal conflicts in their favor was the opposite of what they intended. Congress lost rather than won communal support, and the party continued to decline.

## GANDHI, MOHANDAS  1869–1948, Leader of the Indian freedom movement and a populist opponent of colonialism and racism, Mohandas Karamchand Gandhi had an arguably larger impact on nationalist causes than anyone else in the 20th century. His contribution lies not only in the success of the Indians in shaking off British rule and in inspiring anticolonial movements elsewhere as well, but in his challenge of oppressive social structures in general and his fashioning of nonviolent methods to overthrow them.

Born to a high-level civil servant in Gujarat on the

western coast of colonial India, Gandhi was first educated in Indian schools and then went to London (over the objections of some of his family members) to study law. He was admitted to the bar but also acquired an education about the nature of the British Empire, its life, and culture. Relatively unsuccessful as a young barrister in his home country, Gandhi accepted an offer to aid Indian merchants in South Africa in 1893. There he conducted his first "experiments with truth," that is, nonviolent civil resistance, fighting the laws of a racist regime that discriminated against Indians as well as black Africans.

He experienced the brutality of the South African regime shortly after his arrival. After refusing to shift from the first-class compartment for which he had a ticket, he was physically removed from the train and left to spend a cold night in the dark waiting room of the isolated Maritzburg station. Having not experienced that kind of personal discrimination in England, he at first thought that the British Empire would come to the defense of Indians who were economically, socially, and politically oppressed in South Africa. He soon learned that the empire was part of the problem rather than the solution.

Gandhi soon mounted a campaign of nonviolent resistance to the South African regime. He drew first of all on his own Hindu religious education, which was highly influenced by the nonviolent Jains in his hometown of Porbander, and his understanding of Jesus's Sermon on the Mount. He was also profoundly affected by the writings of Henry David Thoreau and Leo Tolstoy. He mobilized Hindus and Muslims alike for the campaign and experimented with a multiracial, interfaith commune that would represent the kind of society that would replace the one they were fighting.

After considerable success in fighting aspects of the South African regime, Gandhi returned to India as something of a national hero. The leaders of the Indian National Congress promptly attempted to enlist him in their struggle for home rule, a cause that Gandhi supported. After a year of "discovering India" in which he traveled around the country by third class railway, he not only participated but also essentially took over the movement. Sometimes his leadership dismayed the existing Congress leadership, which he challenged for being elitist and misguided in their tactics. Before long, however, he was such a powerful force for independence that even terrorists began to jump on the nonviolence bandwagon.

After a successful local campaign against British administrators in Champaran, and a brutal massacre of demonstrators by British troops at Amritsar, Gandhi decided that the British government's rule needed to end

immediately and that the only way to accomplish that goal was with massive nonviolent civil disobedience. Using the tools of nonviolent direct action developed in South Africa, dubbed *Satyagraha* (Truth Force), Gandhi poured all of his energies into the nationalist movement.

Gandhi fashioned two major campaigns, a boycott of British textiles and the famous Salt Satyagraha. In 1921 he led the campaign for a complete boycott of British cloth, calling on Indians to throw their imported clothing on huge bonfires throughout the country and to take up the spinning and weaving of their own clothes. In doing so he not only went straight to the heart of the British colonial rule in India, which was so closely linked to the textile industry, but he also provided millions of Indians with concrete means for participating in a mass movement while also building a grassroots economic infrastructure.

In 1930 Gandhi conducted his famous Salt March to the seacoast on the Indian Ocean in deliberate defiance of the British Salt Laws. He arrived on the anniversary of the massacre of Amritsar. All over India people were arrested for making and selling salt in protest of British rule. The movement not only swept India but captured the attention of broad sectors of the British population as well, who were beginning to question the British raj.

Enormously popular with the Indian people and convinced that India's freedom had essentially been won, Gandhi turned some of his energies toward problems of Indian society itself, notably the plight of the "untouchables" (or "Children of God" as Gandhi called them) and of women. Some leaders of the Freedom movement criticized him for being diverted from the nationalist cause, but Gandhi insisted that India could not be truly free until all of its people were free.

Gandhi's nationalism contained both an internal as well as an external criticism. It was also free of exclusivism and ethnocentrism. "My . . . idea of nationalism," he contended, "is that my country may become free, that if need be the whole of the country may die, so that the human race may live." Moreover, he contended that Indian nationalism should "be no peril to other nations in as much as we will exploit none, just as we will allow none to exploit us."

## GARAŠANIN, ILIJA
1812–1874, Serb statesman, interior minister of Serbia, prime minister and foreign minister of Serbia, 1861–1867. Garašanin began his political career in the 1830s as an opponent of the autocratic rule of Prince Miloš Obrenović of Serbia. Garašanin served in the government of Aleksandar Karađorđević from 1842 to 1853.

In 1844, during his tenure in government, Garašanin

composed the *Načertanije* (Proposal). Historians continue to debate the degree to which Garašanin was individually and intellectually responsible for the *Načertanije*. In particular, debate revolves around the question of how much Garašanin changed from draft plans for Serbia made by a Polish émigré prince, and a Moravian Pan-Slavist, František Zach. However, it is clear that Garašanin replaced the Pan-Slavic and Illyrian portions of the draft plans with passages about Serbs and Serbdom.

The *Načertanije* contained a dual focus on the borders of the Serbian state and on the relationship between the Serbs and other South Slavs. The key legacy of the *Načertanije* was the idea that the borders of the Serbian state should encompass all those areas inhabited by Serbs. Garašanin accepted Vuk Karadžić's linguistic and assimilatory definition of Serbian identity.

Garašanin clearly had in mind the restoration of the greatness of the medieval Serbian state, to which he believed Serbia retained a historical right. In seeking to fulfill this goal, Serbia would of necessity encounter substantial opposition from the Ottoman and Habsburg Empires, and measured friendship from the Russian Empire. Yet Garašanin did not have in mind the restoration of the exact borders of the medieval state. His focus was predominantly toward an expansion of the Serbian state into Montenegro, Bosnia-Herzegovina, and ultimately Vojvodina, rather than toward the location of the medieval Serbian state in parts of present-day southern Serbia, Kosovo, and Macedonia. Economic concerns about the viability of the Serbian state played a key role in the formulation of Garašanin's nationalism.

Although Garašanin strove for a reconciliation of the Orthodox and Catholic inhabitants of a future state, he saw the inhabitants of these areas as being Serbs nationally, irrespective of their religious identity. Neither Garašanin nor his disciples paid much heed to a distinct identity among Muslim South Slavs. Garašanin's ideas thus provided an important early expression of state-advocated Greater Serbian nationalism.

## GARIBALDI, GIUSEPPE

1807–1882, Italian nationalist revolutionary leader and arguably the most venerated mythical figure of Italy's unification. Garibaldi was born a French citizen in Nice. He died at his family home in Caprera. After joining Mazzini's "Young Italy" revolutionary movement, he volunteered for the Royal Piedmontese Navy in order to train to fight in the revolutionary war, whenever it should come. Garibaldi's rather uncomplicated political philosophy told him that he should fight for republicanism wherever he should find it, unless a king was willing to aid him in his fight for Italy.

Garibaldi was a participant in the failed Mazzinian revolution in Genoa, and for his efforts he was sentenced to death. He escaped aboard ship to Rio de Janiero where he assisted Brazilian and Uruguayan rebels and married his true love and sister-in-arms, Anna Maria Ribeiro de Silva (or Anita). During the siege of Montevideo, Garibaldi formed the Italian Legion among the sizable number of émigrés that were in that city. In 1848, he returned to Italy with his legion to assist the Piedmontese in their struggle against the Austrians. His forces were made to feel less than welcome by Piedmont and after periods fighting in Venetia and Tuscany, the Garibaldini found themselves marching into Rome to defend Mazzini's recently declared Roman republic. This brought Garibaldi into conflict with the French, who wanted to preserve the power and autonomy of the papacy, and following a siege the short-lived republic was crushed and its leaders fled.

Having been made effectively a *persona non grata* in Piedmont, Garibaldi engaged in various trips to England, New York, and Canton, courting support for his ambitions and learning more about the intricacies of republicanism and constitutional monarchy. In 1856 he met Cavour in Turin for the first time, and although the two only exchanged pleasantries on this occasion they formed a closer working relationship. Cavour later informed Garibaldi about the secret treaty of Plombieres, in which the French under Napoleon III promised to assist Piedmont if it were attacked by Austria. The purpose of this information was that Garibaldi was to train his men in preparation for a great war of liberation against the Austrians.

When that war came, in 1860, it became clear that Cavour was not interested in the vision of an Italian republic directed from Rome, dreamed of by Garibaldi. After the disappointment of the treaty of Villafranca, which made no concessions to republicanism and unified less than half of Italy under the flag of the Piedmontese Monarchy, Garibaldi decided to embark on his final revolutionary odyssey. He gathered 1000 volunteers in Piedmont and proceeded to sail to Sicily in order to defeat the Neapolitans, march on Rome, and finally unify Italy. Cavour and many close to Garibaldi courted against this plan, but nevertheless toward the end of 1860 Garibaldi's ships set sail for Sicily.

The odyssey enjoyed phenomenal success. The reactionary armies of Sicily and Naples were crushed and thousands of volunteers flocked to join the Garibaldini on their march for Rome. Upon reaching the papal states, Garibaldi found that the Piedmontese army had reached Rome before his. Recalling that in his youth he had stated that while a republican, he would accept the help of an enlightened monarch, and not wishing to plunge Italy into a bloody civil war, Garibaldi ceded all his gains to the Piedmontese monarch and withdrew from politics, his primary mission accomplished. His last years were spent in Caprera reflecting on his achievements and writing his memoirs. He became greatly disillusioned as to the lack of republicanism, and died in 1882. Along with Mazzini, Garibaldi is the most venerated of Italian nationalists, though his specific role in Italy's unification is hotly contested.

For sympathetic accounts see C. Hibbert, *Garibaldi and His Enemies* (London, 1965) and J. Ridley, *Garibaldi* (London, 1974). For insight into the controversies of Garibaldi's role see D. Mack Smith, *Cavour and Garibaldi 1860: A Study in Political Conflict* (Cambridge, 1954).

## GARNET, HENRY HIGHLAND

1815–1882, Like Frederick Douglass, Garnet achieved fame as an antislavery crusader and in his later years served his country in appointed offices.

Garnet was born a slave in Maryland, escaped with his parents to Pennsylvania when he was nine, and graduated from Oneida Institute in 1840. His eloquent antislavery oratory soon gained him a following. In 1843, he made his famous speech at the Free Colored People Convention in Buffalo, in which he called for a general strike and armed rebellion. The speech was too rousing even for Douglass, who recessed the meeting to let the assemblage cool down. But Garnet, a pastor as well as a political activist, continued to advocate violence to end slavery, if peaceful methods failed.

Nationalism for Garnet, and for those in his tradition, was not an end in itself. He saw nationalism as a means of achieving freedom in the United States, and a means by which Africans might be liberated in a world prejudiced against them. Because nationalism was at least in part a response to racial prejudice, he argued that, under appropriate circumstances, he would be prepared to accept a new order in which blacks would have less than complete autonomy. In this context, he declared, much like activist David Walker, that when slavery and prejudice were uprooted and color was no longer important to white people, black people "should lay aside all distinctive labor [separation] and come together as men and women, members of the great American family." But since it would take a long time after slavery for many whites to give up their belief in African inferiority, the struggle for the liberation of Africans everywhere would require, for him as for Walker, distinctive labor from blacks after emancipation. This was in direct opposition to Frederick Douglass's form of nationalism and labor distribution, which implied an appropriation of a European work ethic for blacks.

Garnet argued that the absence of racial prejudice would not immediately—or even over generations—fundamentally change the conditions of the freed masses without a revolution in land ownership. The thrust of his position, on the question of nationalism as on others, was the premise on which he rested his case for revolt among the oppressed, which was that it was their responsibility to liberate themselves. Because almost all blacks following slavery would be oppressed unless there was a distribution of land among them, action by this exploited class would be required for a change of significance to occur. He argued that no real hope for freedom was otherwise possible.

After the Civil War, Garnet was a pastor in Washington and New York, president of Avery College in Pittsburgh, and U.S. Minister of Liberia.

## GARVEY, MARCUS

1887–1940, Founder and leader of the Universal Negro Improvement Association (UNIA), born in St. Ann's Parish, Jamaica, British West Indies. The UNIA attracted an enormous following among working-class African Americans in New York City and other major urban centers in the United States, and is often considered to be the first black nationalist organization in the United States.

Garvey founded the UNIA in Jamaica in 1914 after traveling to England and Central America and becoming convinced that no race of people could prosper in a nation controlled by another race. Instead of striving for advancement of people of African descent within white-dominated societies that oppressed them, Garvey proposed that black people throughout the world should emigrate to Africa and construct an empire on par with the great nations of the world.

His ideas had little impact in Jamaica, but Garvey found an enthusiastic audience among working-class African Americans when he immigrated to New York City's Harlem in 1916. He bought the newspaper *Negro World* and transformed it into a mouthpiece for his message "Africa for the Africans"; he also established branches of the organization in other major urban centers and purchased the cavernous Liberty Hall in Harlem for mass meetings. Exact membership figures for the UNIA at its height in the early 1920s are not known, though Garvey claimed doubtful figures as high as 4.5 million; UNIA parades attracted up to 50,000 marchers in Harlem.

Garvey's UNIA combined elements of nationalism and entrepreneurship. He declared an Empire of Africa and appointed himself provisional president, adopted red, black, and green as the colors for the movement's banners and militaristic uniforms, bestowed medals and titles on his followers, and paraded to martial music. At the same time, he established entrepreneurial ventures including the Negro Factories Corporation, laundries, and, most famously, the Black Star Line, a proposed shipping line that would transport blacks from the United States and Caribbean to the African Empire. A 1919 assassination attempt only increased his fame, and African Americans across the nation raised over half a million dollars to purchase shares of stock in the Black Star Line. He reached the height of his power in 1920–1921, when he held two UNIA International Conventions in Liberty Hall that drew delegates from states and cities throughout the United States and from four other continents.

Garvey's immense cult of personality among urban African Americans drew the suspicion of the U.S. government, but he found his most vehement critics among middle-class African Americans, such as leaders of the National Association for the Advancement of Colored People (NAACP). These well-educated race leaders, working for egalitarian integration of African Americans into U.S. life, heartily opposed Garvey's advocacy of racial segregation and African colonization; indeed, Garvey even expressed support for white supremacist congressmen and the Ku Klux Klan because they opposed racial mixing. Garvey found few prominent defenders, then, when he was indicted for fraud in the handling of Black Star Line funds and sentenced to prison in 1923; President Calvin Coolidge pardoned him in 1927 but immediately deported him as an undesirable alien. The UNIA dissolved without his leadership.

Garvey's advocacy of racial separatism, black pride, and Afrocentrism have caused many to identify him as the "father of black nationalism" and to see his ideas as ahead of their time in the United States, where they resurfaced after World War II. However, more recently Garvey has been seen as a postcolonial transnationalist, like many 20th-century Caribbean intellectuals and leaders; this interpretation is perhaps more true to Garvey's ambition for a supranational bond uniting all people of African descent, expressed by UNIA slogans such as "Africa a Nation, One and Indivisible."

A classic study of Garvey and the UNIA is David Cronon, *Black Moses* (1955, reprinted 1969). Garvey's own assessment of his career is *Philosophy and Opinions of Marcus Garvey* (1923, reissued 1969, 1992); a more recent study taking into account Garvey's Caribbean roots is Rupert Lewis, *Marcus Garvey: Anti-Colonial Champion* (1988).

**GENDER AND NATIONALISM**   A relatively recent introduction to the study of nationalism. Although early feminists such as Wolstenhume, Ogden, and Florence raised the question of the relationship between gender and nationalism, the first systematic attempts to do this within the field did not emerge until the late 1980s. This perspective is interested in the ways in which nationalism is mediated through gender relations and gendered understandings of the nation. This work has been attempted by writers such as Jayawardena, Kandiyoti, Walby, Enloe, Yuval-Davis, and Anthias. These writers seek to expose the ways in which the politics of patriarchy underlie the politics of nationalism, and how subjective understandings of nation differ according to gendered perspectives. For example, Kandiyoti examines the extent to which elements of national identity and cultural difference are articulated as forms of control over women. In doing this, she notes the differing impact of national movements on the lives of women. These can at times be genuinely emancipatory or alternatively can be a mere instrumental masquerade aimed at further empowering patriarchal modes of domination.

One of the first attempts to address the gender/nation nexus was Cynthia Enloe's *Bananas, Beaches and Bases*. Here, Enloe suggests that nationalist movements are often predicated on notions of masculinity. Such movements have achieved revolutionary changes in the social order without tackling the vestiges of patriarchy that underpinned the prenational society and continues to underpin the national society. In her analysis Enloe raises five key areas in which gender and nationalism interact. First is the issue of the use of women as symbols of the nation. Second, Enloe highlights the exclusion of women's experiences from national mythology. Third, the biological role of women in perpetuating and educating nations is discussed. Fourth, Enloe draws attention to the activities of women within nationalist movements before, fifth, highlighting the ways in which national emancipation and feminist emancipation are often in conflict. Several of these themes have been adapted and extended by other feminist writers.

Nira Yuval-Davis has contributed a great deal of work on these issues in recent years. Her work commences with an articulation of the masculine bias within the study of nationalism. She goes on to contend that the national imagination is built on representations of masculinity and femininity in which women take on the role of symbolic border guards, defining the national motherland as separate from Others. Further, Yuval-Davis expands on the theme of the biological role of women in the national movement. She argues that the position of women in national movements is determined by patriarchal pressure on the biological role of women as child bearers. Thus three discourses are at play. The first is that more is better, so that women are encouraged or forced by the nationalists to have lots of children. The second is the precise opposite, the Malthusian imperative. The final pressure is the eugenicist discourse, which puts emphasis on the national purity of the fetus, a discourse often seen manifested in the war in Bosnia-Herzegovina.

In another important study, Sarah Radcliffe and Sally Westwood reveal the ways in which the nation is constantly reproduced through the day-to-day acts of people. Hence, the mundane tasks often carried out by women are seen in this light as the reforming of national meanings. One particular task carried out by women is the education of the young, and thus women take on a vital role as the purveyors of national knowledge and therefore need to be controlled.

One work that offers a different perspective on this is Jayawardena's analysis of gender, nationalism, and the Third World. This work recalls Chatterjee's interjection that our understandings of nationalism are ethnocentric, and offers some interesting empirical and theoretical insights. For Jayawardena, nationalist movements are not always oppressive for women, as implied by Enloe. Instead, the interjection of Western ideas about self-determination and liberty can often create a space for women's emancipation from prenational patriarchal societies. Furthermore, contrary to Enloe, Jayawardena highlights the cases of the Vietnamese and Chinese national movements and argues that nationalist movements often rely on the activities of women's groups, and that in times of national liberation women are given greater freedom to organize themselves.

Although still in its formative phase, the study of gender and nationalism offers several interesting avenues. First, it draws our attention to the complexity and multifarious nature of the nationalist movement. Second, we are called to look at social practices that have so far been eschewed from the research agendas of studies on nationalism. Third, it brings our attention to the different ways in which nationalism manifests itself. Finally, it points toward a different approach to carrying out empirical work on nationalism. Rather than grand theories of primordialism or modernism, many feminist writers offer "bottom-up" insights into the practices of nationalism, which had hitherto gone unseen. Other than a generally approving piece by Anthony Smith, there has been little engagement between these new writers and the mainstream of writers on nationalism, though there is an interesting debate developing within feminist writings on the subject that could serve to inform other writings.

Important works that address the issues of gender and nationalism are C. Enloe, *Bananas, Beaches and Bases: Making Feminist Sense of International Politics* (Los Angeles, 1989), K. Jayawardena, *Feminism and Nationalism in the Third World* (London, 1986), D. Kandiyoti, "Identity and Its Discontents: Women and the Nation," in *Millennium: Journal of International Affairs* 20(3) (1991), S. Radcliffe and S. Westwood, *Remaking the Nation: Place, Identity and Politics in Latin America* (London, 1996), and N. Yuval-Davis, *Gender & Nation* (London, 1997).

**GENOCIDE** Genocide, the dark side of extreme nationalism, refers to the systematic annihilation of one racial or ethnic group by another. Examples of this are littered throughout human history. The European invasion of the Americas in the 16th century resulted in the decimation of most of the original inhabitants of North and South America. Some groups were intentionally targeted, whereas others suffered the indirect causes of disease brought by the invaders. The 20th century offers numerous cases of nationalistic and ethnic conflict that have resulted in genocide. The conflict in this century of nation-states, empires, and groups—often divided along ethnic lines—has resulted in the greatest number of deaths in human history.

Acts of genocide are often linked to motivations arising from ethnic, religious, economic, or cultural factors that are linked to a differentiation of power. Research provides both uni- and multidimensional models in the analysis of motivational forces behind such acts. Both highlight the important role of grievances in motivating people to engage in such conflict. A group that feels it has been denied a due share of economic, social, and/or political power can be said to perceive a grievance. Once such a grievance is articulated and used to rally a population, the result can often lead to forms of genocide.

The 20th century is characterized by four "tidal waves" of national and ethnic conflicts that resulted in a variety of forms of genocide. These "waves were punctuated by the first and second world wars and by the postcolonial and post-Communist eras." With the crumbling of the Ottoman Empire during World War I, the Armenian minority suffered great atrocities. At the same time the "German and Austro-Hungarian empires [witnessed such] nationalist and fascist movements that repressed minorities and precipitated World War II." The attempted annihilation of the Jewish people and Gypsies as well as other peoples was the outcome. Referred to as the Holocaust, it was a period in history that will live in the collective minds of people of this planet for centuries to come. Following World War II and the exodus of European colonial powers from Africa and Asia, many fragile Third World governments were faced with ruling a diverse and plural population that resulted in an imposition of the hegemony of the ruling ethnic elite over the others. This often spurred the rebellion of minority groups that sought autonomy and self-determination. In a number of countries this rebellion led to genocide in such places as East Timor, Sri Lanka, Pakistan, Iraq, Nigeria, Ethiopia, Sudan, Burundi, and Rwanda to name just a few. The legacy of this genocide still drags on today with groups still vying for control of power and resources. The final wave of genocide in the 20th century resulting from nationalist and ethnic conflict is the recent collapse of the Communist regimes of the old Soviet bloc including the dismantling of the former Yugoslavia. The cases of Slovenia, Croatia, Bosnia-Herzegovina, and more recently Kosovo have turned the world's attention to such questions as the role and responsibility of the international community in addressing internal conflicts when reports of genocide are involved.

It is this most recent wave that has contributed to terms such as *ethnic cleansing* being added to the vocabulary that surrounds this field of inquiry. Genocide can take on many forms, from actual or attempted annihilation of a people to a more subtle form, which is that of cultural genocide. Assimilation, a term not generally associated with genocide, refers to the absorption of one group or culture into another. In the process of this absorption, one group loses its identity and distinctiveness in favor of the other. Numerous governments all over the world have adopted assimilation as their official policy in the hope that it will contribute to the stability and cohesiveness of its plural and diverse populations. However, this cultural aspect of genocide remains problematic.

A number of theoretical paradigms attempt to explain the realities of genocide in the modern world. It is first necessary to understand that conflict between groups is often exacerbated by ethnic and religious cleavages. Although ethnicity and religion play an important role in people's consciousness and in the rise of nationalism, some argue "the conflict in question is primarily political and ideological." Whatever the arguments, the most fundamental cause of genocide is a conflict over the means of production, that is, the ownership of resources and power. Most debates, moral or otherwise, that attempt to understand genocide speak to issues of land, territory, and ownership of property. These cleavages are further deepened when such variables as religion, ethnicity, and language are introduced.

Contrary to the belief that nationalism is beneficial due to the fact that it promotes patriotism and group integration through ethnic pride in the group's history and cultural traditions, the historical evidence overwhelmingly suggests that "nationalism has too frequently degenerated into xenophobia, exclusivism, hegemony, oppression, and in the extreme, genocide." According to Irving Zeitlin, nationalism "compel[s] men to kill one another en masse as their patriotic duty."

Some suggested bibliographic references include Donald Horowitz's *Ethnic Groups in Conflict* (University of California Press, 1985) and Frank Chalk and Kurt Jonassohn's *The History and Sociology of Genocide* (Yale University Press, 1990).

**GEOGRAPHY AND NATIONALISM**   Geography is first and foremost the identification of boundaries—whether economic, natural, cultural or political. In its modern form, it emerged with the 19th century largely as part of an effort by the state to classify, catalog, and discipline the physical and human world for exploitation. Geography's relationship to the nation and nationalism has always been difficult, serving variously to legitimate and deconstruct invented and fictional nations. To bring clarity to this problem, one must first consider how the boundary—geography's primary object of study—helped invent the nation, and then how the value of the nation promoted the development and evolution of the discipline of geography as a tool of nationalists in search of new nations.

Nationalism is understood here to be a political theory of legitimacy predicated on the shift of sovereignty from crown to nation. The structural preconditions for the rise of the nation can be traced to the Peace of Westphalia (1648), which is identified here not as the definitive conclusion to religious war in Europe, but rather as a confirmation of the superiority of the centralized bureaucratic state over the extended imperial model of rule. The nation was itself to be born of this political centralization that had brought the French to a resounding victory.

The most significant of the early state centralizations was begun during the reign of Louis XIII by Cardinal Richelieu and was accelerated in the aftermath of Westphalia. His successor, Louis XIV, not only brought the subject aristocracy to Versailles, uniting and distracting them under a common French court culture, but also charted the precise territorial limits of royal authority and disciplined the bureaucratic apparatus of state. The rigid institutionalization of both the political boundary and tax collection laid the foundation for a new boundary that was to overlap almost exactly that of the political—the boundary retaining the French nation. Assimilation through conscription and integrative education in a national language proved the most effective means of reinforcing political boundaries, once only vaguely suggested by a river, a mountain range, stone marker, or fortification. What had been established by the state in the 17th and 18th centuries was completed in the 19th with the full expression of a national economy.

The resulting nation transgressed traditional physical space by allowing the capital and the state apparatus to penetrate every village and household, alienating all powers beyond the boundary, regardless of physical or historic proximity. A homogeneous population not only facilitated economic development by lowering transaction costs for market exchange and the movement of labor, but also facilitated the mobilization of people in times of war. The nation, as a culturally homogeneous population within a bounded space, was thus first conceived from the will to discipline the polity and economy. The net result was not only to catapult the bureaucratic centralized state to the status of an ideal political form, but also to make a model of the nation and capitalism.

Nationalism, the rejection of status quo authority *and* the quest for political autonomy on behalf of a nation, was also the product of bureaucratic centralization. In France, discontent with the unresponsive regime of Louis XVI provided the spark to ignite the tinder of popular mobilization, which took form according to patterns of interaction that had emerged under the bureaucratic centralized state. Revolutionaries rejected the traditional celestial or hereditary bases of legitimacy, turning instead to the very instruments of their new power, the people whom they dubbed "the nation." However, it took a Napoleon Bonaparte to demonstrate the potential strength of the nation. His display was noticed by revolutionaries and reactionaries alike.

The suggested power of the nation prompted a frenzy of exploration by poets, political entrepreneurs for "lost" or suppressed nations. A few prescient regimes also undertook measures to mount counterrevolutionary national awakenings, as in the case of Germany under Bismarck. Under a strong state, the nation could in fact be created by harmonizing economic, linguistic, and cultural boundaries with the political boundary.

However, for most revolutionaries, a common language or religion was recognized as a favorable condition, but not the sole basis for national identity. In the quest for viable boundaries, geography was enlisted to join in the cataloging and mapping of the full range of human difference. Working with anthropologists, phrenologists, and a host of new scientific disciplines, these early pioneers went far beyond suggesting linguistic and religious boundaries, searching for new ones based on physiological and morphological characteristics. To understand geography as a resource for nationalists, one must consider the evolution of the discipline and its place in the university.

Alexander von Humboldt is often credited by geographers with having established the modern discipline at the outset of the 19th century. Cartography, the drawing of maps, dates back to the ancient world, and examples of demography can be found as early as William the Conqueror's Doomsday book. However, Humboldt allegedly adopted new precise methods of observation and measurement and professionalized the discipline beyond its immediate utility to navigation and property rights. While the objective was to catalog and represent visually the known human and physical worlds, the genesis of the discipline lay in service of the modern state in its quest for not only the mastery of its own subjects, but imperialist expansion.

Both the nationalizing state and nationalists in pursuit of their own polity found value in new methods of categorizing and classifying people according to physical and cultural attributes. As a scientific enterprise, these efforts served to establish not only boundaries between people, but allegedly causal relationships from the physical and natural world to the cultural. At the hands of geographers, this began with the leap from anthropoclimatology to anthropometric cartography, which is to say the racial mapping of people according to the principle that climate determines race. The next step was to relate race, geography, and culture. A classic example of this was Friedrich Ratzel's *Anthropogeographie* published in 1882 and 1891. Efforts to demonstrate scientifically the connections between race and culture, while bogged down in the quagmire of misconstrued categories and inherently suspect "scientific" theories, flourished in this naïve age, receiving considerable political support from those in pursuit of new and seemingly more concrete methods for defining the nation. The institutionalization of many of these principles in Nazi ideology and the Holocaust has done much to discredit the practice, though not completely.

This turn to more "scientific" methods of human classification coincided with the rise of the modern census and modern survey techniques. The 19th-century census, unlike the traditional demographic data found in church and tax records, sought to systematically count and, more importantly, classify the totality of a subject population according to at least sex, age, occupation, language, religion, and nationality. In a few cases the census served to not only represent, but reinforce the notion of national unity. However, with the Habsburgs, the turn to the census was in fact part of a counternational effort, because they sought to demonstrate through geographic representations of census data the cultural heterogeneity of Central and Eastern Europe, and thus the unsuitability of the nation-state model. Nevertheless, the very act of mapping cultural differences suggested the possibility of boundaries where none had existed before.

By the end of the 19th century, the seemingly primordial universality of the nation had taken full shape based not on ethnographic or anthropological evidence, but rather on its utility to the dominant world powers of the age. Collectively, these dominant states strove to transport the nation-state from a regional ideal to a universal principle, embodying it in international law with the Wilsonian principle of a nation's right to self-determination.

The nation-state continues to live on in the international political imagination and serves as the normative basis for new nationalist struggles. Yet, with the seemingly unchecked global influence of the United States, the transnational forces of a global economy are challenging national sovereignty as never before. On the scholarly front, new technologies of statistical analysis and mapping, especially GIS (Geographical Information Systems), are adding ammunition to the already well-developed theoretical campaign to demote the nation from a primordial manifestation of human society to, at best, a construction of the modern state or an imperative of capitalism. Nevertheless, boundaries, whether the product of social evolution, human design, or mere human imagination, continue to shape all aspects of human interaction. While the new tools of scholarship and the forces of a technologically driven global economy may help to bring down the old national boundaries, new boundaries are sure to spring forth bringing with them not only new injustices and prejudices, but also new communities and channels of communication.

For an excellent discussion and starting point for future reflection on the relationship of the boundary and geography to politics and national identity, please consult Peter Sahlins' *Boundaries: The Making of France and Spain in the Pyrenees* (University of California Press,

1989). Gearóid Tuathail's *Critical Geopolitics: The Politics of Writing Global Space* (University of Minnesota Press, 1996) is a good critical overview of geography—heavily informed by poststructuralist critical theory. Finally, for a history of maps, see Jeremy Black's *Maps and History: Constructing Images of the Past* (Yale University Press, 1997).

**GEORGIAN NATIONALISM** Throughout a recorded history which extends back to the Late Iron Age, Georgians' sense of themselves as a distinct people has been shaped by their relations—sometimes peaceful but often politically, economically, and militarily confrontational—with neighboring peoples, such as the Greeks, Persians, Turks, Armenians, and Russians. Modern Georgian nationalism developed in the second half of the 19th century as the result of a complex process associated initially with their annexation into the Russian Empire in 1801 and the subordination of Georgian culture, such as their Orthodox Church and language instruction, to Russian institutions; the emancipation of the serfs and the concomitant social and economic decline of the Georgian landed nobility; the political and economic dominance of the Armenian bourgeoisie in the ancient Georgian capital of Tiflis (Tbilisi); and the incipient industrialization of the economy and the movement of Georgians from the countryside to the cities and the development of a Georgian working class by the end of the century. Stimulated and overwhelmed by Russian rule, Georgian intellectuals began to study their history and distinct culture by the 1840s. Many prominent Georgians, such as I. Chavchavadze, completed their studies in St. Petersburg and returned to the Caucasus to promote the use of the Georgian vernacular and defend their culture against Russian assimilation. With developing capitalism, the decline of the nobility, and the rise of the Armenians, these intellectuals turned nationalists and idealized the Georgian past as harmonious and unified—nobility and peasants peacefully tilling the land for the benefit of all. Other groups criticized this vision and identified themselves with populist movements in Russia and social protest. By the beginning of the 20th century, Marxists, such as N. Zhordania and F. Makharadze, dominated Georgian political life and viewed the Russian autocracy and the Armenian bourgeoisie as enemies of the Georgian people. After 1905 these Mensheviks controlled local political institutions. In 1918 they asserted their independence from the Bolsheviks and for three years (1918–1921) ruled their own state until it was forcibly incorporated into the nascent Soviet Union under policies enacted by the ethnic Georgian Bolshevik leaders Stalin and Ordzhonikidze.

This first independent modern Georgian state faced serious internal and external problems associated with continued fighting against the Turks, subversion by the Bolsheviks, economic blockade by the Allied powers, and general economic chaos. The Georgian socialists became nationalists and suppressed revolts within the country against nonethnic Georgians, such as Ossetians, Abkhazians, and Armenians, who numbered about 30 percent of the total population and who were seeking greater autonomy or freedom for themselves. With the advent of Soviet power, some of these ethnic groups received special political administrative status within Georgia; for example, the South Ossetian Autonomous Region was established in 1922 and the Abkhazian Autonomous Republic in 1931. Throughout the Soviet period, these ethnically consolidated territories within Georgia resisted Georgian hegemony and tried to maintain control over their own institutions and use of their own language and culture. The Abkhazians, in particular, resisted what they considered to be a deliberate policy of Georgification and in the late 1970s won a series of concessions granting them more autonomy and representation within their autonomous republic.

Contemporary Georgian nationalism began to express itself in the late 1980s with the advent of Gorbachev's policies of *perestroika* and *glasnost*. In April 1989 a peaceful demonstration of Georgians in front of the government building in Tbilisi was forcibly dispersed, and twenty Georgians were killed, mainly women and children. The country was shocked, and Georgian nationalism, seeking immediate independence from Moscow, quickly developed. Gamsakhurdia's coalition rose to power in fall 1990, and Gamsakhurdia was elected president of Georgia in May 1991, roughly six months before the dissolution of the Soviet Union. Nonethnic minorities in Georgia feared the rise of Georgian nationalism and the loss of their relative autonomy. The situation quickly deteriorated as Gamsakhurdia abolished the South Ossetian autonomous region in December 1990 and adopted a policy of "Georgia for the Georgians." Mass baptisms to Georgian Orthodoxy were forcibly imposed on Georgian Muslims in Adzharia and adjacent regions, and fierce fighting soon broke out in Abkhazia where nationalist leader Ardzinba sought independence and/or union with Russia rather than continued humiliation and subordination within Georgia. A civil war developed between pro- and anti-Gamsakhurdia factions and Gamsakhur-

dia was forced to leave the country in January 1992 and committed suicide or was killed two years later in western Georgia. The fighting in Abkhazia and Ossetia left tens of thousands of displaced refugees within Georgia who have yet to be resettled or repatriated; the status of these regions and their relation to the Republic of Georgia remain unresolved, politically volatile issues.

The reemergence of an independent Georgia in 1991 was achieved at a terribly high price: ethnic conflicts and civil war. Such an outcome was by no means inevitable. Rather, it was a contingent process in which tragic mistakes were made, passions inflamed, and violence engendered more violence. The desire to shake the Russian yoke was broadly felt by most Georgians, but they did not realize that non-Georgian ethnic minorities also expressed the same desire in relation to Georgia. Georgians now face the challenge of developing a civic, not ethnically based nationalism in which all of its citizens—Georgian and non-Georgian alike—can participate equally.

For the history of Georgian nationalism, see R. G. Suny, "The Emergence of Political Society in Georgia," pp. 109–140 in *Transcaucasia: Nationalism and Social Change,* R. G. Suny, ed. (Ann Arbor, Mich.: The Wilson Center, Kennan Institute for Advanced Russian Studies, 1983) and his *The Making of the Georgian Nation* (Indiana University Press, 1988). For developments after the collapse of the Soviet Union, see Stephen Jones, "Georgia: the Trauma of Statehood," pp. 505–543 in *New States, New Politics: Building the Post-Soviet Nations,* I. Bremmer and R. Taras, eds. (Cambridge University Press, 1997).

**GERMAN COLONIES AND NATIONALISM** German colonial activity began two centuries before Germany became a unified nation-state in 1871; thus it predated German nationalism. Frederick William III, the "Great Elector" of Brandenburg-Prussia from 1640 to 1688, had seen the advantages of global commerce during a short stay in the Netherlands and sought to establish colonial footholds in Africa and the Caribbean. The port of Emden, controlled by Prussia since 1682 and located at the estuary of the Ems River and the North Sea, was his staging area. There he founded the African Commercial Company in 1682 and the East Asia Company a short time later. In 1683 Gross-Friedrichsburg was proclaimed on the Gold Coast of Africa. With the help of the Danes he acquired a part of the Caribbean island of St. Thomas in 1685. A year later he claimed the Arguin Island off the west coast of what is today Mauritania. In 1721 Prussia's King Frederick William I sold these possessions to the Dutch. The German states had still not recovered from the devastating Thirty Years War (1618–1648). Prussia had to concentrate on creating powerful military forces to compete with other European powers that were struggling for continental supremacy. It was simply too weak militarily and economically to hold onto overseas colonies. However, the memories of this first attempt at colonialism became an inspiration for German nationalists in the following century.

Beginning in the 1820s, while Germany was still disunited and weak, German eyes were cast abroad. Explorers like Heinrich Barth, Gustav Nachtigall, and Hermann von Wissmann explored Africa's interior and wrote about their adventures. Scientists like Robert Koch studied the world's great diseases. The Baseler Mission, the Barmen Rhine Mission, and others sent missionaries to convert non-Christians. The creation of the Customs Union by all German states except Austria in 1834 opened Germany up to world trade. Old Hansa cities on the coast founded enterprises, such as Woermann and Godeffroy, outside of Europe. Many new companies profited.

All of these activities paved the way for a variety of publicists who advocated a common national program based in part on colonialism. Germany's first chancellor, Otto von Bismarck, regarded the consolidation of Germany in the heart of Europe as more important after 1871 than gaining overseas possessions. However, in 1884 he gave in to intense public pressure that the growing power of unified Germany should be expressed through overseas engagement. His principle was that "the flag follows trade." Therefore he normally gave governmental charters to existing possessions established by German traders although he sometimes hoisted the flag before granting a charter. In 1884, Germany acquired German Southwest Africa, Togo, Cameroon, and German East Africa. In Asia, he claimed German New Guinea in 1884, and in the Pacific, the Marshall Islands in 1885, the Northern Solomon Islands in 1886, and Nauru in 1888.

These colonies were created in accordance with the principle of nongovernmental support, except in determining their boundaries. It was left to private enterprises to open up a new territory, and they were limited to coastal areas. They enjoyed no military or administrative support because the land area and number of inhabitants were too small to justify a bureaucracy. This system collapsed in the late 1880s because the private enterprises were unable to administer and finance the growing land area and populations. When Kaiser William II ascended the throne in 1888 and dismissed Bismarck in 1890, Germany adopted a *Weltpolitik* (world policy) that focused on overseas activity and led to enhanced nationalistic fervor. The first result was a completely restructured and massively strengthened navy. The second put colonial dreamers in command and made them responsible for colonial policy. This "phase of consolidation" lasted until 1907. Germany tried to occupy all available territories, such as Tsingtao on the northeast coast of China in 1897, the Palau, Caroline, and Northern Mariana Islands (all three purchased from Spain in 1898), and Western Samoa in 1900.

Under William II the German government replaced the private enterprises in governing the colonies, and it established a limited colonial administration. It created strong bases on the coasts, protected by rapidly deployable military forces. It dispatched exploratory expeditions into the interior supported by the military and founded military outposts to control entire colonies. The consequences were the Arab uprising in German East Africa in 1889, the Boxer rebellion in China in 1899–1900, the Herero and Hottentot uprisings in German Southwest Africa from 1905 to 1907, and the Maji-Maji rebellion in German East Africa from 1906 to 1907. All were suppressed. But the growing strength of the local populations, combined with the increased military power of the colonial governments, resulted in rising losses on both sides. This raised the costs for the government.

The government's problem was that the Reichstag (parliament) had to approve the colonial budget. Whenever domestic spending needs were urgent, demands for more money to the colonies had to give way. In general, colonial efforts were politically significant in Germany whenever public opinion was focused on foreign affairs. When the public was primarily interested in social or domestic priorities, colonial efforts and needs fell in importance.

This situation resulted in a colonial reform. Administration was changed in that the colonial office became independent of the foreign office. Until World War I, the colonial office had three secretaries who possessed considerable colonial, economic, and financial experience: Werner Dernburg (1907–1910), Friedrich Lindequist (1910–1911), and Wilhelm Solf (1911–1918). Their emphasis was economic development rather than military occupation. They promoted private investment and attempted to establish a kind of national heritage fund to invest in the colonies, lured by tax breaks. They lent special support to projects that would positively affect future economic development since such investments would help restructure the colonial economies and give them a new base from which the inhabitants could profit. Many German enterprises responded.

With much energy, they transformed the administration from an inflexible governmental office to an efficient body. This reform was necessary for consolidating the colonial budget at a lower level. They sought to develop the colonies by building up an infrastructure of roads, railways, telegraph lines, hospitals, schools, and port facilities. These reforms were successfully implemented in a very short time. They were given a boost by the 1907–1908 Reichstag elections, which the procolonialist parties won. After these elections, opposition to colonial development largely disappeared. Colonies got efficient administration that could provide the basic needs of the inhabitants, who were given good prospects for the future. But the aim of creating financially independent colonies was never achieved. Investments were halted by the onset of World War I in 1914, and they were ultimately expropriated by the Entente powers after the war.

Germany's imperialist era ended with the loss of its colonies during World War I. Only a few of them were able to defend themselves in a global war. All minor Pacific islands were lost to Japanese, Australian, and New Zealand forces without resistance. After skirmishes, Togo and German New Guinea were lost on August 27 and September 21, 1914. Tsingtao surrendered to the Japanese after a three-month siege on November 7, 1914. German Southwest Africa gave up on July 9, 1915, and Cameroon on February 6, 1916. Only German East Africa, led by forces under the command of General Paul von Lettow-Vorbeck, remained in the war until November 14, 1918, when they laid down their arms after the armistice. But German colonies had been important in contributing to a common German national feeling in the 19th century and in providing its new world policy with some coherence and justification after 1890.

## GERMAN NATIONALISM

Perhaps no branch of nationalism has been more debated, studied, and evaluated than that of the German people. German nationalism describes the attachment of the German people to the idea that the German nation should have its own state. A nation refers to the characteristics of a people sharing a common history and heritage, a common language and customs. It is this belief that propelled the formation of a unified Germany in 1871.

German nationalism should therefore be seen in the context of German history and the protracted process of nation building. It is only through this context that one can begin to understand German nationalism—a feeling that showed much promise in a more benign and traditional form before spiraling downward under Imperial Germany and the fanaticism of Nazi Germany. Today, German nationalism remains an intensely debated concept within the context of the reunified nation. What is often labeled the "German Problem" refers to Germany's ongoing struggle to define what it means to be German, to confront the negative manifestations of German nationalism, and to find balance as a German nation-state locked in the center of Europe.

An understanding of German nationalism requires thinking in terms of three distinct historical periods: the rise of German nationalism that culminated in the emergence of the first unified German nation in 1871 under Prussian leadership; the development of Adolf Hitler's extreme and virulent form of nationalism under the guise of National Socialism (Nazism); and the post-World War II struggle within the Federal Republic of Germany over the very nature of German nationalism and German identity. Each historical epoch is linked by a common thread—the struggle to define once and for all who and what the Germans are.

The geographic territory in Central Europe traditionally holding the German people was, up until the 19th century, politically and economically fragmented as a result of occupation by foreign powers, regional and economic cleavages, and religious and political infighting brought about by the Thirty Years War. A common Germanic language and literature—spread in part through the reformation and Martin Luther's writings (Luther's translation of the Bible, in particular)—and a developing cultural tradition did provide a context for emerging feelings of a German identity. But "Germany," unlike Britain or France, remained backward and divided, lacking a strong central state with established administrative, legislative, and legal institutions. While the process of building a unified nation-state continued in Britain and France, the German people remained deeply divided. Even as late as the mid-18th century, Germany was still a collection of dozens of autonomous political units.

It was not until the emergence of Prussia as a leading European actor in the 18th century and the threat of outside interference in German affairs in the 19th century, especially Napoleon's invasion eastward, that the forces advocating a German nation find support across the political, economic, and regional cleavages of the German territories. Perhaps best expressed in the works of Johann Gottfried von Herder (*Another Philosophy of History,* 1774, and *Reflections on the Philosophy of the*

*History of Mankind,* 1776–1803), emerging German nationalists were advocating the idea of belonging to a nation. Herder defined nationalism in terms of kinship, history, social solidarity, and cultural affinity, all shaped by geography, climate, education, and relations with neighbors. Building on these ideas, Johann G. Fichte (*The Addresses to the German Nation,* 1807–1808) and Georg Friedrich Hegel developed the idea of the state, the embodiment of collective life. According to this view, people having commonalities owe their allegiance to the nation, and its legal representative, the state. The state could therefore give expression to the ideas of the nation and feelings of German identity. It was upon these ideas that the Second Reich was created in 1871 by Bismarck's diplomacy and Prussia's military power.

Bismarck's Second Reich sought to control German nationalism by giving it an expression through the state. Although the state retained elements of democratic institutions (direct representation through the lower house of parliament, the Reichstag), Bismarck and the Prussian monarchs were more concerned with preserving and defending the traditional political order. Liberal tendencies in the populace were stifled; conservative, nationalistic, and reactionary forces proved dominant. Furthermore, the Second Reich launched an ambitious national effort to promote Germany's economic and military power, all directed toward catching up with Great Britain and France. The state had become a powerful engine fueling German nationalism. Through a complex and intertwined series of events, conflict arose in 1914 leading to the onset of World War I. It was German government propaganda that further promoted the view that Germany had to fight for its own national defense and for the German people and nation.

Germany emerged from its loss in World War I a dissatisfied nation and people. Weighed down by war reparations, hyperinflation, economic insecurity, territorial losses, and constitutional weaknesses, the Weimar Republic, as the new German institutions of the state were titled, faced a difficult task of mobilizing the masses in support of its policies. Once again fragmented along economic, political, and social cleavages, the Weimar Republic collapsed under such pressures and the political maneuvering of leading German officials. It was German nationalism that would eventually unite the German people in the 1930s under the leadership of Adolf Hitler's National Socialist Party (Nazis).

Hitler's form of fascism, Nazism, uniquely mobilized the masses—largely from the disenchanted and economically weak groups in society—in support of the state and the German nation. In this way, Hitler was able to draw on a common German historical thread—mobilization against outside forces—as a way of diverting attention from internal problems. An extreme form of nationalism, Nazism served to unite Germans of all classes against a foreign enemy and defend the "fatherland" against liberal impulses from the West. Hitler promised the confused Germans a renewed pride in the nation following the economic, social, and political chaos of the 1920s and early 1930s.

Nazism's more extreme nationalistic tendencies were drawn from the belief that certain racial groups—the German people (*das Volk*) and German civilization based on the Aryan race—were superior. Racial mythology thus became an integral part of the nationalistic ideology of Nazism. In the words of Adolf Hitler (*Mein Kampf*), the state had to place race at the center of existence and care for keeping the Aryan race pure. The connection between Aryan race mythology and Germany as a nation was thus strongly developed. It is from these ideas that Hitler's plans for securing *Lebensraum* (living space) for the German people in Europe and his goal of exterminating the Jewish people (the Holocaust) were derived. The all-powerful, authoritarian state (manifested in the Nazi Party and Adolf Hitler as *der Führer*) was the embodiment of the German nation and people. German nationalism as an expression of the German nation in the Nazi state was now complete.

After Germany's defeat in World War II, the German nation was divided and occupied. German nationalism had all but expired on the frozen plains of the east and in the destroyed industrial centers of the west. The Federal Republic of Germany (West Germany), a product of the Cold War, actively downplayed most aspects of nationalism. Nonetheless, an internal struggle over Germany's nationalistic past dominated the intellectual, social, and political debates. Leading intellectual and literary scholars, such as Heinrich Böll and Günter Grass, sought to expose the German people to the negative manifestations of German nationalism. Younger generations (the 68ers) of Germans protested what they perceived to be conservative and nationalistic institutions of higher education, business, banking, and politics.

In the early 1980s, Chancellor Helmut Kohl sought to "normalize" German national identity by employing formerly discredited terms, for example, *das Volk* and *Vaterland,* which had been so closely linked to Nazi terminology. This attempt at a reconciliation of national-historical symbols became part of a process of coming to terms with Germany's nationalistic past, known in German as *Vergangenheitsbewältigung.* This search for "normality" dominated political discourse. The *Historikerstreit* of the mid-1980s, a serious, occasionally misguided effort to assess the import of the Nazi period and Germany's nationalistic past, exposed Germans once again to the difficulty of defining German identity.

The unification of Germany in 1990 gave rise to new concern about German nationalism. The rise of violent neo-Nazi groups, debates on Germany's blood-oriented citizenship laws, and a more assertive German foreign policy (the recognition of Croatia, for example) fueled such concerns. Moreover, the fact that East Germany had not, during the Cold War, gone through a similar process of national soul searching as West Germany suggested to some analysts that the eastern half of a re-unified Germany maintained latent authoritarian and nationalistic attitudes.

However, Germany maintains a stable, peaceful, and generally prosperous anchor in the center of Europe. A more "normal" Germany, with its historic capital of Berlin restored, may have finally found a safe outlet for feelings of German pride and identity. Moreover, German nationalism in some ways may be subsumed by the process of European integration (the Deutsche mark sacrificed for the euro) and globalization. Nonetheless, one suspects that the questions of who and what the Germans are is likely to continue to frame debates about the past, the present, and the future of Germany.

**GIAP, VO NGUYEN** 1910–, Senior general in the People's Army of Vietnam and a veteran member of the Vietnamese revolutionary movement. Giap was one of five children born in a poor family in Quang Binh province, along the central coast of Vietnam. Although his mother and father were peasants, the family had a long tradition of scholarship, and a maternal grandfather had led local resistance against the French conquest at the end of the 19th century. In 1924, young Giap was accepted into the National Academy in Huê, an institute established by the imperial court to train future bureaucrats in Western knowledge. From his childhood years, he had absorbed an intense sense of patriotism, and he was soon expelled from school for taking part in anti-French protests.

During the next few years, Giap became involved in anticolonial activities and eventually joined the Indochinese Communist Party (ICP), which had been created by the veteran revolutionary Ho Chi Minh in 1930. To support himself, Giap earned a law degree from the University of Hanoi and taught history at a lycée in Hanoi. At the beginning of World War II, however, he abandoned his teaching career and became a professional revolutionary. After meeting Ho Chi Minh in South China in the spring of 1940, Giap became actively engaged in the task of building up the party's

guerrilla forces for an eventual attack on the French colonial regime. His wife, the sister of one of the leading members of the ICP, was arrested in Hanoi and later died in prison. In 1944, Giap was appointed commander of the first Armed Propaganda Brigades, which were soon integrated with other guerrilla units and transformed into the Vietnamese Liberation Army (VLA) in May 1945.

After World War II, Giap emerged as the most influential military strategist in the party and a vigorous advocate of the technique of "people's war," adapted from a concept originally drawn up by the Communist leader Mao Zedong in China. In 1951, Giap commanded VLA forces in a major offensive against French positions in the Red River delta in North Vietnam. When that campaign was rebuffed with heavy losses, Giap's forces retreated into the mountains, but reemerged in the spring of 1954 with a successful attack on the French outpost at Dien Bien Phu, near the Laotian border. The fall of Dien Bien Phu contributed to the decision by the French government to accept a cease-fire at the Geneva Conference in July. Vietnam was temporarily divided into two separate countries, with a non-Communist government in the South, and Ho Chi Minh's Democratic Republic of Vietnam (DRV) in the North.

During the next few years Giap was appointed to the rank of senior general in the army and simultaneously served as minister of national defense. He was widely viewed abroad as Ho Chi Minh's chief war strategist during the Vietnam War, but in actuality the leading role was played by his rival Nguyen Chi Thanh, of whose aggressive tactics Giap did not fully approve. After the end of the Vietnam War in 1975, he was dismissed from the politburo (the chief decision-making body of the Communist Party) as a result of policy differences with Ho Chi Minh's successor Le Duan and today lives in semiretirement. He is revered by many Vietnamese, however, who view him as an advocate of moderate policies designed to improve the standard of living and grant greater freedom of popular expression in Vietnam.

**GLIGOROV, KIRO** 1917–, Member of the presidency of the socialist Federal Republic of Yugoslavia, 1974–1978; president of the former Yugoslav Republic of Macedonia, 1991–1999. Gligorov graduated from the University of Belgrade in 1938. He started his career as an attorney in Skopje. In 1944, Gligorov became a leading member of the Anti-Fascist Assembly of the National Liberation Movement of Macedonia and of the AntiFascist Council for the People's Liberation of Yugoslavia. In the decades following World War II, Gligorov worked in Belgrade, where he held various positions in the League of Communists. As a leading liberal Communist in the 1960s, Gligorov put forth an economic reform plan. However, the market-oriented reforms in the plan were considered too liberal by Tito, and the plan was thus discarded. After a stint in the rotating Yugoslav presidency, Gligorov withdrew from politics. In 1989, Gligorov reemerged politically in the government of Yugoslav Prime Minister Ante Marković. Gligorov became president of Macedonia in January 1991.

Macedonia did not consider seceding from Yugoslavia until very late. In June 1991, Gligorov and Bosnian Muslim politician Alija Izetbegović crafted a proposal for a constitutional reform of Yugoslavia. Gligorov and Izetbegović, as leaders of the most volatile and multiethnic republics in Yugoslavia, found common cause. Their plan proposed an "asymmetrical federation" with differing levels of constitutional autonomy for the republics in Yugoslavia. The vague plan was shelved after Slovenia announced its unambiguous intention for full independence. Macedonia proclaimed its independence in September 1991. Since then, Gligorov has tried to steer a path acceptable to both the Macedonian majority and the substantial Albanian minority in Macedonia. His task has been complicated by the ascendancy of both Macedonian and Albanian nationalists in Macedonia. On October 3, 1995, Gligorov was seriously injured in an assassination attempt in Skopje. The identity of the assailants remains unclear. On the international stage, Macedonia's integration into international organizations has encountered strong opposition from Greece, which objects to the new state's use of the name "Macedonia."

**GLOBALIZATION**   During the 1990s, *globalization* has become one of the most popular terms in the literatures of economics and the social sciences. The term occurred more frequently than any other among the abstracts of papers presented at the 1998 World Congress of Sociology. There are, however, difficulties with the conceptual clarity of the term. Malcolm Waters' definition of globalization as "a process in which the constraints of geography on social and cultural arrangements recede and in which people become increasingly aware that they are receding" (*Globalization*, London: Routledge, 1995, 3) provides a starting point for a consideration of the interplay between this social process and nationalism.

One of the most popular interpretations of globalization considers it a relatively recent social process via which transnational and multinational corporations expand around the world, bringing with them the threat of social and cultural standardization. In such a conceptualization, the homogenizing tendencies of "McWorld" are seen as set against the inevitable reaction of social groups (religions and nations) to the Goliath of market-driven uniformity. Nationalism is one of the prime examples of local peoples' struggles against such global forces in order to protect their own distinctiveness and way of life. Benjamin Barber's bestseller *Jihad vs. McWorld* (New York: Ballantine, 1995) captures this line of thinking and makes the argument in graphic detail.

The spectrum of cultural uniformity makes such discussions of globalization part of the broader and ongoing debate on *cultural imperialism,* a highly problematic term used to signify the export of the Western lifestyle into other regions of the globe. This term, although a popular one, suffers from important conceptual contradictions, brilliantly discussed by John Tomlinson in his *Cultural Imperialism: A Critical Introduction* (Baltimore: Johns Hopkins University Press, 1991). A different approach to issues of cultural contact has been adapted by Samuel P. Huntington in his *Clash of Civilizations and the Remaking of the World Order* (New York: Simon and Schuster, 1996). In this reformulation, cross-cultural contact leads to increased conflict between civilizations; the triumph of Western culture is by no means certain, and the West has to develop strategies that recognize and accommodate the incommensurability of cultural values.

All of the aforementioned works engage in discussions of globalization, but generally fail to address the issue head on and lack sufficient clarity. This leads to important theoretical contradictions and gaps. In contrast, more nuanced approaches suggest that the very universality of the nation-state as a cultural form necessitates the development of a more complex view of the connection between nationalism and globalization. From this point of view, the development of the nation-state has been part and parcel of the globalization process since the 16th century. The articulation of the national idea took advantage of the technological and other developments in Western Europe; yet the shaping of the meaning of "nation" has been determined by international currents and cross-national emulation. Consequently, the articulation of nationalism as a global phenomenon cannot be considered simply as a by-product of global economic expansion. Rather, an adequate understanding of the forces that have shaped nationalism requires an understanding of the cross-national and cross-cultural dynamics of the modern world since the 16th century.

For a theoretical discussion along these lines, see Roland Robertson, *Globalization: Social Theory and Global*

*Culture* (London: Sage, 1992), and for more empirically grounded discussions, Benedict Anderson's *Imagined Communities* (London: Verso, 1991) and Liah Greenfeld's *Nationalism: Five Roads to Modernity* (Cambridge: Harvard University Press, 1992). It is inevitable that future research will discuss these themes at greater length and in more depth, and will lead to more sophisticated accounts of the relationship between nationalism and globalization.

## GOEBBELS, PAUL JOSEPH

1897–1945, National Socialist politician and propagandist, born in Rheydt, Germany. As chief propagandist for the National Socialist German Workers Party, Joseph Goebbels was one of the first public figures to appreciate and fully exploit the potential of radio, sound recording, and film for promoting nationalist causes. He excelled at using the new technologies to mobilize mass opinion in support of Nazism and to foster mythical belief in its principal exponent, Adolf Hitler.

Goebbels joined the Nazi movement in 1924, three years after completing doctoral studies in history and literature at the University of Heidelberg. Already inclined toward an almost mystical nationalism and an increasingly bitter anti-Semitism, his views initially found expression in the *Völkische Freiheit* (*People's Freedom*), a nationalist organ for which he briefly worked as managing editor. In March 1925 he became business manager of the central office of the Nazi party's Rhineland North Gau (administrative district) in Elberfeld, where he soon won repute as a dynamic speaker and resourceful sloganeer. In the conflict between Hitler and Goebbels's associate Gregor Strasser—representing respectively the party's nationalist and socialist-revolutionary wings—Goebbels at first backed Strasser's position. By the summer of 1926 he switched sides, having persuaded himself that Hitler was a new Messiah who would lead a death struggle against "Marxism and the stock exchange." Rewarded with the post of Gauleiter (district leader) of Berlin-Brandenburg, he proceeded to revive the party's flagging fortunes in the Reich capital, earning notoriety as an agitator and character assassin amid libel suits, police bans, and street battles between Brownshirts and Communists. He also proved himself a master mythmaker, transfiguring the murdered Nazi street-brawler, Horst Wessel, into a party martyr and national hero. Election to the Reichstag in May 1928 did not prevent Goebbels from using his combative weekly newspaper, *Der Angriff* (*The Attack*), as a vehicle for denouncing the Weimar "system" as well as the Jewish "demon of decay" allegedly responsible for Germany's postwar distresses.

In Hitler's unsuccessful campaign for the presidency in 1932, Goebbels—now carrying additional responsibilities as the party's director of propaganda—innovatively employed mass media to sell his candidate and the National Socialist message. On becoming chancellor the following year, Hitler turned to Goebbels as the logical choice for heading the Reich Ministry for Public Enlightenment and Propaganda. With departments devoted to propaganda, press, broadcasting, film, theater, fine arts, music, and literature, the new agency became the main instrument for totalitarian *Gleichschaltung* (synchronization) of Germany's intellectual and cultural life. Liberal and "Jewish" influences were ruthlessly eliminated. Combining ideological appeals and pecuniary incentives with legal sanctions and coercive terror, Goebbels induced German writers, artists, actors, and filmmakers to serve his avowed purpose of forging a "national community" in harmony with the Nazi worldview. The German people, he declared, must begin "to think uniformly, to react uniformly and to place themselves body and soul at the disposal of the government." Jurisdictional disputes with other ministries and rivalries with party notables such as Herman Göring and Alfred Rosenberg hampered his efforts to exercise complete control over official propaganda. Yet Goebbels's power to mold public thought and opinion, if not unchallenged within party and government, was certainly unequaled. As propaganda minister and director of the Reich Chamber of Culture, he used a wide variety of means—ubiquitous slogans, daily directives to the muzzled press, loudspeaker columns placed in streets and squares, weekly newsreels, mass rallies, and elaborately staged public rituals—to break down mental resistance to the Nazi dictatorship and produce a mindless readiness for action and sacrifice on its behalf.

Goebbels's ideas on propaganda were less than original: In stressing simplicity and repetition, he merely followed Hitler, the Italian fascists, V. I. Lenin and the Bolsheviks, and American advertising. Still, he was a superb practitioner of his craft who possessed an extraordinary ability to sense the public mood and fine-tune his message accordingly. Despite the excesses of his own demagogic rhetoric—typically an incongruous mixture of romantic idealism, pseudo-religious sentimentality, technological jargon, sports metaphors, and vitriolic invective against opponents—he understood that propaganda must bear some correspondence to observable facts or lose credibility with its mass audience. At the same time, he refused to make either truth or morality the standard by which to judge propaganda. The sole criterion, he insisted, must be success: "If it attains its goal, it's good; if it doesn't, it's bad." But the goal was set by the demands of expansionist nationalism and power politics, and Goebbels, ever faithful to Hitler, labored indefatigably to further it. It was he who conducted the great propaganda campaigns that accompanied Hitler's successive territorial demands in Europe in the 1930s, portraying Germany as an aggrieved "have-not" nation whose leader, a man of peace and vision, sought nothing more than what belonged by right to his people. Above all, it was Goebbels who, even before the Nazi takeover, originated the sustaining myth of the regime, the myth of Hitler as the infallible *Führer* and inspired genius who embodied the will of the German nation. As if creating a nationalistic pseudo-religion, he exalted the Nazi dictator as "savior of the fatherland," an "instrument of divine will" whose hypnotic oratory, heard nationwide through the unifying medium of radio, transformed Germany "into one big church embracing all classes and creeds." Spellbound by Goebbels's propaganda, many Germans who detested the Nazi party embraced Hitler with enthusiasm and followed him to the end.

Goebbels's biographers tend to characterize him as a man who lacked core convictions, an opportunist and cynic whose misanthropic outlook stemmed from his physical deformity and self-loathing. It was Goebbels the opportunist, they note, who suppressed his early social-revolutionary views for the sake of advancement in the party. It was Goebbels the cynic, deeply contemptuous of the masses, who matter-of-factly stated that propaganda must appeal to primitive instincts rather than intellect. Yet as Reuth and others point out, the Goebbels who abandoned his petit-bourgeois parents' Catholicism was not wholly devoid of belief. Perhaps from a desperate need to break his fall into the abyss of nihilism, he deceived himself into believing his own myth of Hitler as the "tool of Providence" for saving Europe from a Jewish world conspiracy.

Indeed, Goebbels from the beginning was one of the Third Reich's most energetic proponents of anti-Jewish measures. During World War II he stood at the forefront of those urging Hitler to carry out his intention of exterminating Europe's Jews and the Slavic "subhumanity" to the east. His increasingly strident anti-Semitic propaganda, manifest not only in speeches and articles but in films like *Jud Süss* and *Der Ewige Jude* (*Jew Süss* and *The Eternal Jew*, both 1940), was designed to make Germans more receptive to the "final solution." Adopting a propaganda rule set forth in Hitler's *Mein Kampf*, he merged the enemies of Nazidom into a single demonizing category: Winston Churchill, Franklin Roosevelt, Joseph Stalin, and Marshal Tito, among many others, were all part or pawns of "international Jewry." After the epic defeat of the German Sixth Army at Stalingrad in

February 1943, for example, Goebbels blamed the outcome on the "satanic" forces of world Jewry and called on the German *Volk* to wage "total war" in defense of Western civilization against the Bolshevik-led "hordes from the steppe."

As the Wehrmacht retreated on all fronts, Goebbels held out the prospect of a "super-Versailles" if Germany capitulated. Hitler, he assured his countrymen, could still work another "miracle" and pull off "final victory." He interpreted the failure of the coup attempt of July 20, 1944—thwarted by Goebbels's own coolheaded action—as a providential sign. In its aftermath, Hitler appointed him General Plenipotentiary for Total War with sweeping powers to organize the civilian sector of the home front. Unfortunately for Goebbels, it came too late to reverse the tide of war or the diminishing impact of his propaganda. Euphemistic language and repeated appeals to the example of Frederick the Great could not mask the reality of military defeat or the failure of reprisal weapons like the V-2 rocket to meet the expectations Goebbels had created. His anti-Soviet atrocity propaganda helped to harden German resistance but also precipitated civilian panic as Russian armies advanced in eastern Germany.

Goebbels spent the last days of his life in Hitler's bunker beneath the Reich Chancellery in besieged Berlin, envisioning—between intervals of despair and delusions of an impending split in the Allied camp—a Wagnerian *Götterdämmerung* in which Hitler would die fighting for the fatherland. It would be a final propaganda triumph, securing the Hitler myth in the German consciousness and preparing the way for yet another national "resurrection." The end, however, was more ignominious than glorious. The day after Hitler's suicide on April 30, 1945, Goebbels and his wife Magda—after poisoning their six children—put an end to their own lives.

Although less than perfectly reliable as history, Goebbels's extensive but incompletely preserved diaries are an indispensable source of information on one of the most important figures of the Third Reich. Available English translations include *The Early Goebbels Diaries, 1925–1926*, edited by Helmut Heiber and translated by Oliver Watson (Praeger, 1963); *My Part in Germany's Fight* (Hurst and Blackett, 1938); *The Goebbels Diaries, 1939–1941*, edited and translated by Fred Taylor (Putnam, 1983); *The Goebbels Diaries, 1942–1943*, edited and translated by Louis P. Lochner (Doubleday, 1948); and *Final Entries, 1945: The Diaries of Joseph Goebbels*, edited by Hugh Trevor-Roper and translated by Richard Barry (Putnam, 1978). *The Secret Conferences of Dr. Goebbels: The Nazi Propaganda War, 1939–43*, selected and edited by Willi A. Boelcke and translated by

Ewald Osers (Dutton, 1970), reproduces minutes from Goebbels's daily staff meetings during World War II and shows him at his most Machiavellian. Ralf Georg Reuth's *Goebbels,* translated by Krishna Winston (Harcourt Brace, Harvest Books, 1994), offers an outstanding character study that draws extensively on newly available documents. Also excellent are Helmut Heiber's *Goebbels,* translated by John K. Dickinson (Hawthorn Books, 1972), and Ernest K. Bramsted's *Goebbels and National Socialist Propaganda* (Michigan State University Press, 1965), which combines biography with a thorough analysis of Goebbels's propaganda methods.

## GOETHE, JOHANN WOLFGANG VON  1749–1832,

This genius and universal man has the distinction of being the only German after whom an entire epoch has been named. Born in Frankfurt, the son of a patrician, he was influenced by an artistic but serious father and an imaginative, lively mother. As a student of law in Strasbourg, his poetic talent began to unfold. Of all lyric poets, his work is the most powerful and original. His literary diversity over an eighty-two-year period ranges from the turbulent *Sturm und Drang* to the enlightened classicism to the romantic. Known mainly as a man of letters, Goethe was a scientist, theater director, administrator in Weimar, and artist. He was interested in mining, economics, architecture, horticulture, and landscape gardening. He was inspired by the many women in his life and by his surroundings. A two-year stay in Italy affected him profoundly. His works include lyric, epic, and ballad poetry, drama, novels, and autobiographical writings. His *Faust,* a two-volume tragedy written in verse, best symbolizes the German penchant to overcome the limits of human knowledge while striving for perfection.

Goethe's mind soared well above the minuscule principality where he lived most of his adult life and the confines of the German nation, which in his day was little more than a cultural concept. His advice to those seeking wisdom was: "Read Shakespeare, read Molière. But above all read the Greeks, ever and always the Greeks." The ancient Greeks to whom he was referring had never possessed a concept of "the nation" and knew no nationalism. Because of his eminent cosmopolitanism, the centers sponsored by the Federal Republic of Germany to promote German language and culture throughout the world are called "Goethe Institutes."

## GÖKALP, ZIYA  1876–1924, Leading theorist of Turkish nationalism. His *The Principles of Turkism* (1920) became the manifesto of Turkish nationalism for the reformist Turkish Republic. Gökalp, born in Diyarbakır into a prominent mixed Turkish-Kurdish family,

planted the seeds of the modern Turkish nationalism. His informal education, which was more relevant to his later activities than his formal veterinary training, shaped his understanding of Ottoman society and his political consciousness. Since his father was the editor of a local newspaper, *Diyarbakır Salnamesi,* Gökalp was cognizant of the significance of the print media in the formation of public opinion and nationalism. Moreover, his father's position allowed him to have access to major European works on sociology and nationalism.

In Diyarbakır, he was exposed to the concept of nationalism by reading the works of Ahmet Vefik Paşa (1823–1891), who stressed the significance of Turkish language and history to raise the political consciousness of the Turks. Moreover, due to his family's eminence in the city, Gökalp met frequently with visiting bureaucrats and scholars. For example, he met with Abdullah Cevdet, a leading atheist nationalist thinker, in 1894 and was inspired by his materialist thought. In Diyarbakır, Gökalp also met with Yorgi Efendi, an Orthodox Greek, who lectured on history at the city high school. Cevdet introduced him to the works of French sociologist Emile Durkheim and to Leon Cahun, who wrote the romantic general history of the Turks. Yorgi Efendi constantly stressed the transformative power of nationalism to create a modern secular state. In this period, Gökalp was taken over by deism and a mechanistic understanding of the world.

When Gökalp went to Istanbul to study at the Veterinary College, Cevdet and Efendi convinced him to join the Committee of Union and Progress (CUP) in 1897. Due to his involvement in CUP activities, he was arrested, expelled from the school, and forced to settle in his native town, Diyarbakır. During his years in Diyarbakır, Gökalp carried out several ethnographic fieldwork expeditions among the Kurdish and Turkish tribes. After the Young Turk revolution in 1908, Gökalp formed the local branch of the CUP and participated in an important CUP meeting in Thessaloniki where he was elected to the Central Committee of the CUP (1909–1918).

The cosmopolitan environment and heated debates among Balkan nationalists helped Gökalp formulate Turkish nationalism and publish many essays advocating it in the nationalist literary journal *Genç Kalemler* (1911). After the Balkan War (1912), he moved to Istanbul and continued to publish in *Türk Yurdu, Halka Doğru, Islam Mecmuası,* and *Yeni Mecmua.* In Istanbul, he met with a group of Pan-Turkish émigré intellectuals from the Russian Empire who sought to form a pan-Turkish unity. Gökalp endorsed this view and wrote: "The country of the Turks is neither only Turkey nor Turkistan. The country is a vast and eternal land: Turan."

He served in the Ottoman Parliament and taught sociology at Istanbul University (1913–1919). British troops arrested and tried Gökalp after World War I and exiled him to the island of Malta. He subsequently returned to Diyarbakır. He published his journal *Küçük Mecmuası* (1922–1923). In August 1923, Gökalp was elected as parliamentarian from Diyarbakır and died in 1924. During his period in Ankara, Gökalp wrote *The Principles of Turkism*. In this book, Gökalp argues that "social solidarity rests on cultural unity, which is transmitted by means of education and therefore has no relationship with consanguinity . . . a nation is not a racial or ethnic or geographic or political or volitional group but one composed of individuals who share a common language, religion, morality or aesthetics, that is to say, who have received the same education." In the formation of Turkish consciousness, he stressed the roles of education and the legal system in creating new norms and identities.

Gökalp's utopic conceptualization of Turkish nationalism as a part of greater Pan-Turkish nationalism came to an end with the establishment of the Turkish Republic in 1923, and he then adopted more territorially based nationalism. He developed two key concepts of "civilization" and "culture" to articulate his conception of Turkish nationalism. Culture, for him, was the differentiating feature of a nation and a source of nationalism. Because civilization was a collective product of all nations, Gökalp argued for the adaptation of European civilization through reinterpretation of culture.

His nationalism did not treat Islam and Turkish nationalism as contradictory but rather as mutually reinforcing forces. Although Gökalp was a secular intellectual, he argued that religion leaves profound traces in the constitution of personality. Being aware of the role of religion in the constitution of Muslim personality and communal interactions, Gökalp fused Turkish nationalism and Islam. According to Gökalp, religious community created a state and this, in turn, led to the formation of a nation (*Makaleler VIII*). By utilizing the Turkish-Islamic tradition, Gökalp concluded that the state is an outcome of religious solidarity and that the state is an instrument for nation building.

Gökalp treated oral culture and music as sources of molding a collective consciousness in the Turks. No writer stressed the formative significance of literature and media as much as Gökalp. Gökalp used folk stories and poetry to raise the national consciousness of the Turks (*Yeni Hayat*). He did not conceptualize the nation as a given to be weakened, but rather as a constructed identity and a feeling that could be realized through education. Gökalp considered the role of Islam in the construction of Ottoman state building and defined the connection between Islam, Turkish nationalism, and modernization. He openly defended vernacularization of religious rituals, practices, and liturgy.

For further reading, see Taha Parla, *The Social and Political Thought of Ziya Gökalp, 1876–1924* (E. J. Brill, 1985); Ziya Gökalp, *The Principles of Turkish Nationalism*, translated by Robert Devereux (E. J. Brill, 1968); and Niyazi Berkes, *Turkish Nationalism and Western Civilization: Selected Essays of Ziya Gökalp* (Allen and Unwin, 1959).

## GOMUŁKA, WŁADYSŁAW

1905–1982, Joined the Communist movement in his youth and became an organizer of labor and of youth and a party leader. In the thirties, he was imprisoned, then studied at the Lenin School in Moscow, and later returned to Poland, where he was again imprisoned. Gomułka thus survived while Stalin liquidated the Polish party and murdered most of its leadership. Gomułka remained in Poland, played an active role in the war against Germany, and rose to become party secretary, a position he also filled soon after a Soviet-sponsored government was established.

In the postwar period, Gomułka ruthlessly attacked the party's opponents: He led the struggle against the Peasant Party, which probably would have won a fair election, and he was among those who insisted on forcing the Polish Socialist Party—which had a much longer tradition and much greater support among the workers than the Communist Party—to merge into the Polish United Workers' Party. It was a "merger" that left the Communists in control, with their major competitor for legitimacy nonexistent.

Gomułka openly opposed Stalin's policy of forced collectivization of the peasantry, and he spoke independently on other issues. As a result, he was accused of "nationalist deviationism," expelled from the party, and arrested, all of which won him support among Poles, who were traditionally anti-Russian. But, unlike leaders in the other Soviet bloc states in Eastern Europe, Gomułka was not put on trial, and after Stalin's death, he was released.

A huge demonstration in 1956 that became an attack on the party and state institutions in the city of Poznan, including an assault on the prison and a shooting battle between regime opponents and the secret police in that city, shook up Poland's entire political structure. By the fall, Gomułka had been rehabilitated and returned to the party leadership. When Khrushchev and other Soviet politburo members descended on Warsaw, angry for not having been consulted, they threatened military intervention and actually had Soviet troops that were quartered in Poland begin marching toward Warsaw. In response, Gomułka called out Polish troops, who surrounded the city, and he promised military resistance, while also pledging loyalty to the Soviets. Mollified, Khrushchev left, soon followed by the Soviet officials who had been put into place to ensure that Poland followed the Soviet line. Gomułka swiftly abandoned the hated policy of forced collectivization of the land, reined in the secret police, freed many political prisoners, and came to an understanding with the Church.

It all made Gomułka very popular among Poles, who happily bid the Soviets farewell. Alicja Matuszewska, a Solidarity leader in 1980–1981, recalled that "Gomułka said that the nation's treasury was empty, so people donated their wedding rings and other jewelry." But the wave of elation was based on the faulty premise that Gomułka would further challenge Soviet domination. He did not; in his view, with Poland sandwiched in between Germany and the Soviet Union, the best guarantee of Poland's continuing existence was fealty to the Soviet Union. It was a policy that was continued by all his successors. Gomułka did not even take advantage of Khrushchev's opening in the 1960s to modify Soviet-style policies. Alojzy Szablewski, who led the Solidarity union in the Gdansk shipyard in 1980–1981 and during a strike in 1988, spoke for many: "Since 1960, people said that Gomułka came to unloosen the screw, to oil it and to screw it down once more."

Throughout the 1960s, Gomułka's rule grew increasingly harsh. In the mid-1960s, he launched an attack on the Church for a letter the hierarchy produced granting forgiveness to the Germans for their role in World War II, and requesting that they forgive the Poles. In 1968, students who protested censorship were arrested, beaten, and expelled from their schools. Gomułka also tolerated a major anti-Semitic campaign that blamed the unrest on the children of leading Jewish Communists; most of the rest of the Jews who remained after the Holocaust left the country. And Gomułka was among the Soviet bloc leaders who urged that the Prague Spring of reform be ended by an invasion by the surrounding states. Moreover, he actually sent Polish tanks in, to the great shame and horror of a great many people. Then, in December 1970, worker riots were met with military force, with several people killed—the actual number is still a hotly debated issue—and probably thousands, even tens of thousands, injured. Within days, Gomułka was finished as a political leader.

The result of this record was the loss to the regime of the fealty of much of the younger generation; it was never recovered.

Two good books with differing points of view on Solidarity are *Breaking the Barrier* by Lawrence Goodwyn (Oxford University, 1991) and *The Polish Revolution* by Timothy Garton Ash (Vintage Book, 1985).

**GORBACHEV, MIKHAIL** 1931–, The Soviet Union's last leader, born in Privol'noye, in the Stavropol' region of southern Russia. One of the most outstanding political leaders of the 20th century, Gorbachev became secretary general of the CPSU (1985) and head of the USSR in 1985 (president, in 1988). He was relatively young for the Soviet leadership—fifty-four years old.

Between 1985 and 1990 he launched three successive reform policies: *uskorenye, glasnost,* and *perestroika.* The last of the policies has also become a synonym for all of Gorbachev's reforms at the end of the 1980s in the Soviet Union. However, *uskorenye* ("acceleration") was the first of Gorbachev's attempts to reform the USSR and was aimed at the recovery and improvement of the rapidly declining Soviet economy. Soon after realizing the difficulties of the task he introduced another initiative, *glasnost* ("openness") to let the mass media (newspapers, magazines, television, and radio) publish materials until then strictly closed to the greater public. Gorbachev was interested in changing Soviet society through publishing the archive materials of the Communist past and in starting the national debate over the political and economic future of the USSR and Communism.

*Perestroika* (sometimes called "restructuring") was actually the last, the most important, and the most well-known phase of the reforms in the USSR under Gorbachev. *Perestroika* proposed two basic restructuring accomplishments. First, it designed the transfer of economic responsibilities from the CPSU to the respective administration subdivisions. Second, it meant the transfer of power from CPSU to the popularly elected legislators in the republics. Within the *perestroika* design Gorbachev introduced local (republican and other regional) initiatives to improve the disastrous Soviet economy through changes in the political system by loosening the strict center-periphery connections until then mostly under the rigid rule of Moscow. Various levels of regional authorities were granted more rights than ever before to make their own political and economic decisions on a local scale. In 1988, however, some Soviet Union republics started secessionist movements, which eventually led to the breakup of the USSR in 1991.

In international affairs, under Gorbachev the Soviet troops were withdrawn from Afghanistan in 1988, USSR–China and USSR–U.S. relations improved, and two superpowers—the USSR and the United States—signed a series of arms control agreements. In 1990–1991, during the Persian Gulf War Gorbachev cooperated with the United States. He rejected the Brezhnev Doctrine and gave up the idea of intervention in the Eastern bloc countries as part of his fundamental change in the system. Gorbachev's policy of nonintervention was repeatedly expressed during his meetings and speeches abroad and eventually served as a sanction to the eventual breakdown of the Communist system in Eastern Europe at the end of the 1980s. In October 1990 he was granted the Nobel Peace Prize.

Gorbachev, however, never planned deliberately for the breakup of the USSR and thus the whole Soviet bloc. He intended to carry out the economic and political reforms of the multinational USSR within the limits of the Communist principles, to give Soviet socialism "a human face." However, in 1990 the union republics, based on ethnic divisions, continued to demand more territorial and ethnic rights and enforced the secessionist policies. By the end of 1991 the domestic conflict between the nationalist secessionists and orthodox Communists in the USSR had increased and developed from an ideological conflict into violent clashes that were suppressed by the authorities. By that time Gorbachev realized perhaps the consequences of the *perestroika* policies and the threat to the Soviet system and became inclined toward the orthodox Communists in 1990–1991. In 1991 Gorbachev tried to maintain the Soviet system by establishing a new system of Soviet republics via a voluntary agreement that was to be signed in August. The power conflict and the threat of the breakup of the USSR according to the model, however, provoked an attempted coup d'état by the orthodox Communists, which was followed by the official expiration of the USSR on December 31, 1991. As a result of the collapse of the Soviet Union the newly independent states, based mainly on ethnic divisions, were established. In December 1991 the newly independent states formed an organization called the Commonwealth of Independent States (CIS).

Gorbachev became the chairman of the Socio-political Studies Foundation (The Gorbachev Foundation) in 1992. In 1996 he unsuccessfully ran for the presidency of the Russian Federation. He received less than 1 percent of the votes, which eliminated him from the competition for presidency. At the end of the 1990s various polls in Russia showed Gorbachev to be one of the most unpopular leaders of the USSR among the Russian people.

Further reading: M. Gorbachev, *Gorbachev: On My Country and the World* (Columbia University Press, 1999) and A. Brown, *The Gorbachev Factor* (Oxford University Press, 1996).

**GRAMSCI, ANTONIO** 1891–1937, Marxist theorist who helped found the Italian Communist Party; born in Ales, Sardinia, Italy. As a university student in Turin, Gramsci became an active member of the Italian Social-

ist Party (PSI) and began a career as a journalist. In 1915 he withdrew from the university where he studied linguistics, and began writing regularly for two of the leading socialist papers, *Avanti!* (*Forward!*) and *Il Grido del Popolo* (*The Cry of the People*).

His editorials included an attack on Benito Mussolini, then editor of *Avanti!*, who thought that World War I was necessary. Gramsci argued that the PSI should oppose the war because the class struggle needed to develop unhindered. In 1919 he helped launch *L'Ordine nuovo* (*The New Order*), a weekly cultural journal of the PSI.

In January 1921, Gramsci was among the PSI delegates who split to form the Italian Communist Party (PCI) and, subsequently, *L'Unità*, a daily newspaper connected to the PCI and still published today. (In 1919 Mussolini had helped form another PSI splinter party that would become the Fascist Party.) From 1922 to 1923 Gramsci lived in Moscow as the Italian representative to the Comintern. In Moscow he met Julia Schucht who would later become his wife.

To capitalize on the minimal freedoms fascist law allowed opposing party officials, the PCI named Gramsci party secretary in 1924. During this time Gramsci began writing one of his most famous articles, "A Few Notes on the Southern Question" (published first in France). In it he argued that the Italian Risorgimento was sustained by a kind of colonialism of the southern regions that continued to cause a division between the north and the south. In addition, Gramsci argued that a successful revolution against the capitalist system that kept this north–south divide in place and hindered the progress of the poorer classes required among other things an alliance between southern peasants and northern workers.

In 1925–1926 Mussolini outlawed other political parties and suppressed all opposing organizations; Gramsci was arrested in Rome (November 1926) and incarcerated until his death. While in prison Gramsci kept up a correspondence, rigorously censored by the fascists, with his friends and relatives, often writing to his Communist comrades through letters to his sister-in-law, Tatiana Schucht. Under such a controlled system he laid out his ideas for a class-based nationalism, founded on the everyday cultural practices and regional dialects of a nation's people; such a concept of nation building was in direct contrast to the kind of reestablishment of the Roman Empire that fascism's brand of nationalism dictated.

When Gramsci died, his notes for future projects and his letters were preserved by Tatiana Schucht and later published. Together his preprison writings, prison notebooks, and letters from prison form an incomplete materialist theory. Gramsci takes up a number of issues, including Italian popular culture and folklore as an expression of national identity; the Italian nationalist movement as a kind of failed class revolution; the need for alliances across different groups in order for a successful class revolution; the importance of "organic intellectuals," leaders who come from the masses but can bridge the gap between them and the dominant culture; and industrialization, fascism, and "passive revolution." His work on nationalism and the production of culture has influenced and continues to influence many left-wing intellectuals (such as those from the Subaltern Studies Group and the Birmingham School) and political leaders in Italy and elsewhere.

Two important biographies are *Per Gramsci* by Antonietta Macciocchi and *Antonio Gramsci: Towards an Intellectual Biography* by Alastair Davidson. In English Gramsci's work has only been published incompletely; however, Columbia University Press has begun a long-term project to publish the entire *Prison Notebooks* in English. See also http://www.soc.qc.edu/gramsci/, a web site that lists all available Gramsci resources, including links to the International Gramsci Society and the Fondazione Istituto Gramsci.

## GREEK CIVILIZATION AND NATIONALISM

Greece's mountainous terrain, with small river valleys and almost no large plains except in the north, favored the formation of a kind of small political organization known as a *polis,* a city-state. Its limited size later made possible the unprecedented development of democracy in some Greek cities, especially Athens. The small scale of political units helped perpetuate the never-ending and exhausting conflicts among the various city-states. These conflicts prevented the integration of settlements into a larger political order, such as a nation-state. Citizens viewed the world strictly on the basis of their narrow local patriotism and never developed a sense of Greek national identity. The poetry of Homer, with its portrayal of the Olympian world of the gods, became standard references for all Greeks. The periodic gathering of Greeks for the Olympic Games, first organized in 776 B.C. at the city of Olympia in the western Peloponnisos, and thereafter held every four years, brought Greeks together and showed them some common ideals. But these games never succeeded in creating peace or political unity in the Hellenic world.

Those Greek cities that had only small agricultural hinterlands could relieve the pressures of rapidly growing populations by founding colonies overseas. Between 750 and 550 B.C. such colonies were created along the coasts and on the islands of the entire Mediterranean and Black Sea, including one at Byzantium (now Istanbul, Turkey). Greek colonies sprang up from the eastern coast of Spain to the mouth of the Dnieper River in what is now Ukraine and from what is presently the French Riviera and Sicily (where Syracuse was built) to the toe of Italy, which, along with Sicily, became known as "Greater Greece." The philosopher Plato coined the expression that the Greeks sat around the Mediterranean like frogs around a pond. The Greeks showed themselves to be daring seafarers, traveling as far as Britain. It was the Greeks who gave meaning to the saying that "oceans are bridges."

Through their colonies, the Greek language, culture, and influence were extended over much of the known world. Almost all quickly broke their umbilical cords that tied them to their mother cities and became politically independent. There was no all-powerful overlord to subordinate them. They continued to share sentimental ties and similar viewpoints on ruling, culture, and religion. Their trade with the older Greek cities was the foundation for an enormous growth of wealth in the entire Greek world.

Political developments came to be dominated by the rivalry between the land power, Sparta, and the sea power, Athens. Sparta's expansion had always been of a military rather than of an economic nature. Athens developed a new kind of political order: democracy. The most significant organ in its political system was the Assembly, in which all citizens (who had to be male and not slaves) could attend and vote. This had important drawbacks. The changeability of the majority within the Assembly meant that policy could switch suddenly, and yesterday's powerful and honored leaders could be disgraced and dismissed the very next day. This led to political instability and to a form of permanently latent revolution. This is one reason why such profound political thinkers as Socrates, Plato, and Aristotle condemned democracy as an inferior type of political organization. Only the most competent politicians, who could persuade the masses at any moment, could conduct a coherent and consistent policy. These leadership qualities were best reflected by Pericles, who from 461 to 428 B.C. was able to guide the city to the summit of its power, glory, prosperity, and architectural achievements. Despite all its shortcomings, Athens extended wealth, luxury, leisure, and political power more broadly among its citizens than did any other city.

Athens existed under conditions of almost permanent mobilization and imperialism, maintained by sea power and the exploitation of allies. It was able to survive a grave external threat to Greece in the first decades of the 5th century B.C., namely that of the mighty

Persian empire, whose power by the middle of the 6th century B.C. already extended to the Greek cities along what is today the western (Ionian) coast of Turkey.

Under the Great King Darius, Persia attacked the Greek mainland in 492 B.C. and conquered Macedonia and Thrace. Two years later, he was defeated by a far smaller force of Athenian citizen soldiers on the Plain of Marathon. A messenger ran as fast as he could for 26 miles (42 kilometers) in order to bring the news of victory to Athens, where he reportedly died upon arrival.

After Darius's death his crown prince, Xerxes, laid careful plans for a final blow. The Greeks displayed little solidarity and fraternity with each other in the face of the Persian threat. Nationalism was still unknown. In 480 B.C. his numerically superior Persian units confronted the Greeks' first line of defense at Thermopoly, where in a legendary effort, a Greek force of 7000 courageous soldiers held back the entire Persian army for a week before withdrawing. The enemy was then able to occupy and completely destroy Athens, which had been evacuated just in the nick of time. However, Athens decimated the Persian fleet and defeated its land force at Plateaea in 479 B.C., demonstrating the superiority of well-trained and motivated citizen soldiers over a huge immobile army, composed of diverse peoples who had been involuntarily drafted into service and left on the Greek mainland without logistical support. For the next 280 years the Greek world was spared any serious external threat until the Roman Empire absorbed all of it in 190 B.C.

Athens' victory secured for it enormous prestige in all of Greece, and it ushered in the "Golden Age," when its power and cultural achievements were at their peak. Having carried the main burden of the Persian War, it took quick advantage of its undisputed mastery at sea by constructing a widely spun web of alliances, which extended throughout the entire Aegean area. In 478–477 B.C. it organized the Delian League, which maintained a common treasury on the island of Delos. As the largest contributor, Athens was ensured political and military predominance. Soon, its allies discovered that they were subjects, especially after 454 B.C., when the treasury was transferred to Athens and meetings of the council were terminated.

Athens had wealth and a democratic order that inspired both loyalty on the part of its own citizens, as well as admiration and support on the part of the lower classes in the other Greek cities. Under Pericles Athens launched a major policy of colonization and built its grandiose structures on the Acropolis. Art, science, and philosophy flourished.

The enormous growth of Athens' power and its imperialist foreign policy led to a collision with Sparta. The Peloponnesian War lasted from 431 to 404 B.C. and ended in Athens' defeat and ruin. Because of the alliance systems Sparta and Athens had constructed, almost every city in Greece was ultimately drawn into the conflict.

Based on what he witnessed in this war, Thucydides, a former Athenian general who had been exiled from Athens early in the war for failing to save Amphipolis from the Spartans, developed his pessimistic view that man's insatiable striving for power was the sole motor of history. In his classic book, *History of the Peloponnesian War,* he described the restless and unlimited political passion that was a basic characteristic of the Greeks, along with their yearning for perfection and order in art and philosophy. While they left timeless works, the Greeks were politically volatile and unreliable. In describing Athens' mistreatment of the island of Melos, Thucydides demonstrates that military power and the willingness to use it are significant factors in international politics. Small cities must adjust to this reality or suffer the consequences. There was no international law to protect them.

Athens was so ridden by party squabbles that it could not conduct a successful war. Demagogues in Athens persuaded the volatile majority to execute most of the successful commanders, and its last fleet was destroyed in 405 B.C. In 404 it surrendered to the Spartans, and Athenian greatness came to an end. The Athenian empire had existed for a shorter period of time than had any of the famous empires of antiquity; it had risen and fallen in three-quarters of a century. It was also the smallest of the great empires, with a maximum citizen population of about 60,000.

The mainland of Greece fell into such political chaos that it was left to the mercy of Philip II of Macedon, a wild kingdom of a half-Greek population in the north (now the Republic of Macedonia). Macedon was culturally attracted to Greece, and Philip brought to his court outstanding Greek artists, writers, and scholars, including Aristotle, who tutored the monarch's son, Alexander. A large kingdom, it was a different kind of political entity than the city-states of Greece. Philip could take advantage of the web of rivalries among the Greek cities to the south so that he brought one city after the other under his influence. His victory in 338 B.C. signaled the end of the cities' freedom. He proclaimed a general peace and organized the Greek cities in a league under his control.

Philip had already begun preparations for war against Persia when he was assassinated in 336. His son, Alexander, later known as "Alexander the Great" (356–323

B.C.), who had just turned twenty when he became king, turned a new page in the book of world history. After a breath-taking nine-year 12,000-mile (20,000-kilometer) campaign, the young commander ruled over an empire that stretched from Greece over Asia Minor, the Phoenician coast, Egypt, Mesopotamia, Babylon, Persia, and beyond to the Indus Valley. Bitter internal struggles demanded his entire strategic genius. His army had to engage in constant and exhausting individual combat with wild mountain men, face inconceivable perils in the extensive deserts and dry highlands, and master difficult technical challenges, such as the siege of the sea fortress at Tyre in Palestine.

Genius, energy, ambition, and charismatic leadership so united in the person of Alexander the Great that he could inspire thousands to perform the most incredible feats, and he was honored as a demigod during his own lifetime. His campaigns of conquest were not like the maraudings of Mongols, who left nothing but devastation and terror in their wake. He placed the stamp of Greek civilization on the entire Near and Middle East, not simply by forcing the Greek culture on conquered peoples, but by attempting to foster a synthesis of the Greek and Oriental cultures.

When Alexander died on June 13, 323 B.C., at the age of only thirty-three, his gigantic empire fell into three large parts, which ultimately developed into a relatively consolidated system of states: the kingdoms of Egypt, Macedonia, and Seleucid (most of the former Persian Empire). Minor states, such as Pergamum, Rhodes, and Syracuse, also emerged. The thread of Hellenistic culture ran through all of them. The century following Alexander's death witnessed constant border wars caused by the conflicting interests of the three major kingdoms. A new rising power, Rome, conquered all of the Greek cities in Italy by 270 B.C. These conquests enhanced the influence of Greek culture on Rome itself. Much of the Roman Empire retained Greek culture and usages. The Greek heritage was preserved in great libraries in Alexandria (a Greek city and capital of Egypt at the time) and Pergamum (now in Turkey), where scholars carefully collected, classified, evaluated, and edited classical texts and theories. The classical Greek language gradually gave way to dialects and became a learned language of scholarship. A more simplified Greek facilitated communication among many different peoples. Greek remained the international language of administration, diplomacy, business, teaching, and theology. Greek knowledge, customs, and administrative talents migrated to Rome as Greeks were taken as slaves by the Romans, who often used them as teachers and civil servants.

## GREEK NATIONALISM

Greece is both a very old and a very new country. Not until 1829 were Greeks able to end four centuries of Turkish domination and to create an independent nation-state. That state and the country's contemporary society and culture bear little resemblance to the ancient Greece that so many people have admired throughout the centuries. The large body of Greek classical literature and the many magnificent ruins reflect the grandeur of the ancient past. But the modern Greek's approach to life and his understanding of himself have been shaped far more significantly by the Byzantine past (324 A.D. to 1453), the Orthodox Church, and four centuries of Turkish domination than by the Greece of antiquity.

Greece lived under the sign of the Islamic half-moon for almost 400 years until it won its independence in 1829. But it was Byzantine in tradition, embodied and preserved by the Orthodox Church, which provided the strength of survival and the sense of cultural independence. The Church kept Greek identity alive, operated underground schools, guarded Greek literature and culture, fought any attempt to diminish the use of the Greek language, and, with the approval of the Turkish masters, took responsibility for such acts as baptism, marriage, burial, and most legal and civil administration over Orthodox Christians. Such intense Orthodox political involvement in, and control over, political, social, and religious affairs created in Greece a close union between Church and nation that was almost unique in the world. That union is only now breaking down, as the Greeks are becoming increasingly secular, and as the Church's political and social influence is being strongly challenged. Nevertheless, much of the prestige the Church still enjoys stems from the Greeks' awareness that the Orthodox Church kept the Hellenic flame burning during four centuries of Turkish domination and that, as the chief patron of Greek nationalism, the Church was at the forefront of the struggle for Greek independence in the 1820s.

The war of independence almost totally removed any visible traces of Turkish rule. But the Turks left their traces in everyday Greek life: the warm hospitality and generosity, the food and the manner in which coffee is prepared and drunk, the men's habit of sitting around cafes in midday, while the women are at home working, the music, the distinctly Balkan folklore, the peasant dress, and the reels of red tape and almost impenetrable bureaucracy. On the other hand, the unpleasant memory of long Turkish subjugation, the bloody and emotional struggle with the Turks to regain Greek independence in the 1820s, and the continuing effort to extend Greece's borders to include all Greek-speaking peoples have combined to create a distrust of Turkey that always plays a prominent role in Greek politics.

Exasperated by Turkish maladministration and inspired by the ideals of liberty ignited in Europe by the French Revolution, the Greeks revolted against the Turks in 1821. This struggle immediately stimulated sympathy in all of Western Europe, where the love for Greek antiquity was great. Only a few years earlier the young British poet Lord Byron had written of Greece in *Childe Harold's Pilgrimage*: "Trembling beneath the scourge of Turkish hand, From birth to death enslaved; in work, in deed, unmann'd." Byron even went to Greece to fight for its independence, and his death as a result of fever at Missolonghi on April 19, 1824, lent the struggle an almost divine consecration in the eyes of many Western Europeans.

As so often in 19th- and 20th-century Greek history, foreigners' admiration for Greek antiquity helped focus attention on modern Greece's problems. Foreign observers were apt to show disgust at Turkish atrocities in this brutal struggle and to overlook such behavior when the Greeks committed them. For instance, there was hardly a reaction to the Greeks' hanging, impaling, and roasting alive of 12,000 Turkish prisoners who had surrendered at Tripolitsa. But the outcry was deafening when the Turkish governor later systematically executed 30,000 Greek survivors at Chios and sold another 46,000 into slavery. The atrocities committed by both sides did not hinder the French, British, and Russians from joining the struggle against the Turks in 1827. By 1829 Turkey had to sue for peace.

Chronic instability left the Greek political landscape littered with the wreckage of two dynasties. Absence of political stability ultimately resulted in five removals of kings from power (1862, 1917, 1922, 1941, and 1967), seven changes of constitution, three republics, seven military dictatorships, fifteen revolutions and coups (of which ten succeeded), 155 governments (43 since 1945), twelve wars, and a bitter five-year civil war. Thus, in certain ways, modern Greek politics until 1973 was like a pendulum swinging constantly between the extreme democracy of Athens and the iron military sentiments of Sparta.

About the only thing the Greeks could agree on was that their borders had to be extended until all Greeks were citizens of the Greek state (the "Great Idea"). Thus, where domestic politics divided them, intense nationalism, which can bubble to the surface of any Greek almost instantly, united them. The settlement of 1832 had not created a natural and mutually acceptable frontier between Greece and Turkey, and every Greek government pursued an ingathering policy of some kind to

rectify this. This meant constant friction and occasional war with Turkey, which greatly nourished the hatred that Greeks seem almost always to bear toward their neighbor to the east. It took time, but the Greeks have, with the notable exception of Cyprus and small pockets of Greeks in southern Albania, accomplished their "Great Idea." In 1864 the British turned over to them the Ionian islands, including especially Corfu. In 1881 Greece received a third of Epirus and the bulk of Thessaly. But when it conducted naval actions against the Turks in Crete and the rest of Thessaly a few years later, the Turks declared war on Greece in 1897. They routed the Greek army and even threatened to take Athens—a humiliating defeat for Greece.

The emergence before World War I of one of Greece's greatest 20th-century political leaders, Eleutherios Venizelos, brought Greece many benefits. He introduced important reforms to establish a modern state. An admirer of Western European democracy, he created the foundations of a state of law. He was also able to utilize his international prestige and diplomatic skill to win for his country a handsome chunk of the spoils from the Balkan Wars against Turkey in 1912 and 1913. Greece received a part of Macedonia, the island of Crete, and the Aegean Islands. These additions enlarged the Greek land area by 75 percent and its population by 70 percent.

In World War I Greece declared war on Germany and its allies. Its reward from its new allies was western Thrace, which it received in 1918, and a British promise of a part of Turkey around Smyrna (now Izmir). On May 15, 1919, British ships transported Greek troops to Smyrna in order to collect its booty, but this adventure ended in a catastrophe. American President Woodrow Wilson opposed any carving up of Turkey in spite of its support of Germany in the war. Further, the greatest political leader in Turkish history, General Kemal Atatürk, who created the modern Turkish state, revived his exhausted and humiliated countrymen and organized a heroic defense of Smyrna.

After the British stopped supporting the Greek expeditionary force, the Turks delivered a devastating and fatal blow. The Turkish sword swung freely, and practically the entire Greek population was either killed or driven out of the area around the western coast of Asia Minor where Greeks had lived for 3000 years. The French and British declared themselves to be neutral in the face of this massacre. They refused to take Greek refugees on board their ships although it had been British promises to the Greeks that had unleashed this tragic adventure in the first place. In the end, 600,000 Greeks perished, and almost a million and a half were forced out of Turkey. In return, Turkey agreed to the repatriation of about 400,000 Moslems living in Greece. The one positive thing this unfortunate conflict produced was clearly defined borders between Greeks and Turks (except in Cyprus), with only negligible minorities on the wrong side of the lines.

Greece entered World War II on the side of Britain and France. On October 28, 1940, the Greek government rejected a host of unacceptable demands made by the impetuous Italian dictator Benito Mussolini, who boasted of a "promenade to Athens." Italian troops entered Greece from Albania. Although the British hurriedly sent a limited number of troops to Greece from North Africa, the Greeks themselves were able to drive Mussolini's poor-quality forces back into Albania.

Hitler had already decided that Greece, the "Achilles heel of Europe," should not be allowed to fall into enemy hands. His numerical superior forces broke the Greek resistance on April 6, 1941. The Germans divided Greece into occupation zones, awarding the lion's share to the defeated Italy. The suffering and humiliation of occupation created both Communist and non-Communist resistance organizations in Greece. When the Italian fascist regime collapsed in 1943, its occupation forces left Greece after selling a large part of their weapons to the Greek partisans. The Germans responded to the resistance activity in Greece by shooting hostages and devastating entire villages. These measures hardened nationalist fervor and drove countless young peasants into the arms of the communists.

From March 1944 on, the Soviets, later joined by Yugoslavia and Bulgaria, supported their Greek comrades, and for the next five years a bitter civil war ensued. The United States provided economic and military support to the Greek government as a consequence of the "Truman Doctrine," which promised aid against Communist threats to Greece and Turkey. After breaking with the Soviet Union in 1948, Tito's Yugoslavia closed the Yugoslav–Greek border, thereby preventing needed supplies from being shipped to the Greek Communist rebels. These actions persuaded the Communists to give up the struggle, which had cost them about 80,000 casualties and the government forces about 50,000. This tragic conflict polarized Greek politics for years, sapped Greece's economic resources, and caused considerable destruction in the country.

After joining NATO in 1952, Greece has clashed repeatedly with Turkey over Cyprus and continues to pursue the goal (called *Enosis*) of bringing the island's residents under Greek authority. This became especially urgent when Turkish troops occupied the northern 37 percent of the island, inhabited by Turkish Cypriots,

who constitute only 18 percent of the island's population. In 1983 they declared the "Republic of Northern Cyprus." This, along with disputes over air-traffic lanes, territorial waters, and offshore oil and mineral rights, remain chronic irritants in the relations between the two NATO allies and ready tinder for explosive Greek nationalist sentiments.

Any government in Athens formulating Greece's foreign policy finds a complicated web of problems. They include popular opposition to U.S. military bases in Greece, concern for the Greek minority in southern Albania, and how to deal with an independent Macedonia to the North. The Greeks fear that Macedonia could make irredentist claims on their province with the same name. This prompted Athens in 1992 to oppose Macedonia's right to use that ancient Hellenic name. To soothe Greek national sentiments, allies must use the clumsy temporary name of "Former Yugoslav Republic of Macedonia (FYROM)." Greece ultimately agreed to recognize Macedonia as a sovereign and independent state and lift its trade blockade. In return, Macedonia agreed to redesign its flag and change two articles in its constitution eliminating any hint of a claim on the Greek province of Macedonia.

**GREEK NATION-STATE** In 1832, the Greek nation-state, carved out of the Southern Balkans by the "Great Powers," became a kingdom. The process of transforming a marginal region of the Balkans into a new national center was slow and contested, and continued throughout the 19th century. The first great motivating force for Greek nationalism was known as the "Great Idea." In 1844 the Epirote politician Ioannis Kolletis argued that citizenship should not be limited to those indigenous to the new state; such demarcations were arbitrary since "the battle for independence did not start in 1821 [the Greek revolution] but in 1453 [when the Ottomans captured Constantinople]." Consequently, all those who took part in the effort to overthrow the Ottoman Empire ought to be considered Greeks. This idea caught on, and became a somewhat nebulous principle for conducting Greek foreign policy.

Despite the rhetoric, however, the kingdom of Greece could by no means afford any kind of offensive against the Ottoman Empire. Territorial expansion was initially based on peaceful acquisitions of the Ionian islands (1864) and of Thessaly (1878). The island of Crete, with its repeated revolts over the 19th century, was the principal object of Greek claims. After 1878, Macedonia also became a more concrete irredenta. The promotion of irredentism greatly polarized the Greek electorate. In the 1880s, two main political factions emerged. The modernists (led by I. Trikoupis) advocated modernization of the state before territorial expansion, while the nationalists (led by Th. Deligiannis) argued for the immediate pursuit of nationalist aspirations.

In 1896 Crete revolted once again—this time with grave consequences. The newly formed National Society of Athens, a Greek nationalist association with some 3000 members, convinced the government to go to war against the Ottoman Empire. It led to the worst military defeat in Greek history. In the aftermath of this failure, there was a new round of cultural and paramilitary mobilization. From 1903, military officers became involved in paramilitary warfare in Ottoman-held Macedonia, in what Greek history refers to as the "Macedonian struggle" (1903–1908). In the aftermath of the 1908 Young Turk revolution, it seemed that the main reason for their activities had been eclipsed. Frustrated officers descended on Athens, and in 1909 they carried out a coup that overthrew the government. The officers called on the Cretan Eleutherios Venizelos to assume leadership of their movement.

In 1910, Venizelos formed the Liberal Party. He won the next elections, amended the constitution, and led the country in the Balkan Wars of 1912–1913, which led to the enlargement of the Greek nation-state to include most of southern Macedonia, Epirus, Crete, and other Aegean islands. Between 1914 and 1915 Venizelos was embroiled in a bitter dispute with King Constantine, known as the "National Schism." In 1916, following a military coup in Thessaloniki, Venizelos assumed command of Macedonia, Crete, and most of the Aegean islands. Greece was split into two states: the state of Athens and the state of Thessaloniki. In 1917, after Allied intervention, Venizelos took power in Athens and governed in an essentially authoritarian fashion until 1920. Under his leadership Greece entered World War I on the side of the Allies. In the Sèvres Treaty (1920), Venizelos's diplomatic skills won for Greece control over a portion of Asia Minor. However, an exhausted public voted Venizelos out of office, and King Constantine soon returned to Greece. The new, anti-Venizelist government continued to pursue Greek nationalist aspirations in Asia Minor, leading to the 1922 Asia Minor debacle.

The collapse of the Greek army led to a hasty retreat. Hundreds of thousands of Greek Orthodox Christians fled their homes. In the Lausanne Treaty (1923), once again negotiated by Venizelos, Greece and Turkey reached an agreement involving the "voluntary" exchange of Muslim and Orthodox populations, with the exceptions only of the Muslims of western Thrace and the Greeks of Constantinople (Istanbul). The treaty effectively signaled the end of the Great Idea. For almost

three decades, the Greek nation-state had to deal with the problem of acculturating the 1.2 million refugees who had fled Asia Minor. It was a monumental task that led to national homogeneity. During this period (1928–1932), Venizelos's administration took critical steps toward a Greek–Turkish rapprochement. Greece also participated in the formation of the "Little Entente," uniting Yugoslavia, Greece, and Romania against Bulgaria—the state that had harbored revisionist desires during the interwar period.

World War II led to a new round of nationalist rivalry as Bulgaria occupied and then annexed eastern Macedonia and western Thrace, and carried out a fierce acculturation campaign. In the Greek countryside, a Communist-led guerrilla movement emerged—while the Allied-backed Greek government resided in Cairo. The failure of nationalists and Communists to reach an understanding led to the Greek Civil War (1944–1949). Most of the military action took place in the mountains, especially in Greek western Macedonia, where the Communists supported the Macedonian Slavic population's desire for autonomy, in exchange for their military support. Thousands fled to Eastern Europe, their property confiscated.

After 1922, Greece's territorial ambitions practically came to a halt. The end of the Great Idea meant that modernization took over as the main driving force in Greek politics. Greece's final territorial expansion was the Dodecanese islands, ceded from Italy in 1947. The main focus of post-1945 Greek nationalism has been Cyprus. For almost three decades Greece and Turkey quarreled over the island, eventually leading to the Turkish invasion of 1974 and the effective partitioning of the island into a Turkish-held territory and a Greek Cypriot part. Resolution of this dispute remains an elusive object of Greek–Turkish relations. The Cyprus issue impacted the Greek minority of Istanbul, as repeated riots and state-sponsored persecution during the 1950s forced them to flee into Greece.

**GREEK ORTHODOXY AND NATIONALISM** The Catholic–Orthodox Schism of 1054 divided Christianity into a Greek Orthodox "East" and a Latin Catholic "West." With the conquest of Constantinople by the Ottomans in 1453, the Russian Orthodox Church became the only Orthodox Church associated with an Orthodox secular ruler. The Eastern or "Greek" Orthodox peoples of the Mediterranean basin came under the authority of the Ecumenical Patriarchate of Constantinople. After 1453, the Ecumenical Patriarchate evolved into the prime authority for all Eastern Orthodox peoples under Ottoman rule.

Although some Balkan national histories assert that

this authority stood for Greek national interest, this is not true. The patriarchate considered its foremost obligation to safeguard Orthodox religion from Catholic missionaries. Its operation was a facet of the Ottoman system of religious association (known as the *millet system*) according to which peoples of the same faith were governed by the same religious leadership.

During the Ottoman period, the social division of labor implied a cultural division of labor. Consequently, ethnic labels (such as "Greek") were frequently employed to signify the urban or commercial strata regardless of their actual ethnicity. Although patriarchal authority aided the promotion of Grecophone literature in the Balkans, the central focus of local identities remained a religious ("Greek-Orthodox") one. This system was predicated on negating the political significance of criteria other than the religious.

The collapse of this "Greek Orthodox Commonwealth" began in the second half of the 18th century and intensified in the 19th century. In the 1750–1820 period, secular Greek Orthodox intellectuals (such as Adamantios Korais and Rigas Velestinlis) challenged patriarchal authority by reconceptualizing the meaning of the term "Greek," which up to that point had meant "Greek-Orthodox." In so doing, they provided for the formation of modern Greek national identity, but, simultaneously, they delegitimized the religious worldview that provided the very backbone of Greek Orthodoxy at the time.

In the 19th century, the formation of national churches signified the collapse of this worldview. In Greece and Serbia (both in 1833), secular leaders proceeded to organize national churches, thus curtailing the reach of patriarchal authority. In the 1860s, the Romanian state took similar action, and in 1870, the Ottomans recognized the Bulgarian Exarchate, thus further diminishing the extent of patriarchal authority. Although practically confined to a majority of Greek speakers in the late 19th century, the patriarchate still held on to an ecumenical viewpoint. The 1923 Asia Minor debacle and the departure of the majority of the Greek Orthodox population from Anatolia signified a turning point for the patriarchate. After 1923, its material decline was furthered by the physical decline of the Greek minority of Istanbul, leaving the patriarchate with a community of 3000 by the late 1980s. Following the collapse of the Communist regimes in the 1990s, the patriarchate is attempting to become once again a transnational religious authority, by renewing spiritual and material ties with the rest of the Greek Orthodox churches.

For a general discussion on Greek Orthodoxy and its intertwining with nationalism, see the collected essays of Paschalis Kitromilides in *Enlightenment, Nationalism, Orthodoxy* (London: Valorium, 1994) and Victor Roudometof, "From *Rum Millet* to Greek Nation: Enlightenment, Secularization, and National Identity in Ottoman Balkan Society, 1453–1821," in *Journal of Modern Greek Studies* 16 (1998), pp. 11–48, where the relevant literature is cited.

**GRIEG, EDVARD** 1843–1907, Norwegian composer, born in Bergen. Grieg was a well-known Norwegian composer in the romantic style. His formative years were the decades immediately following the Norwegian independence from Denmark in 1814 (after over 400 years of political and cultural domination), a period when artists made strong efforts to establish what they considered a uniquely Norwegian style. Musicians such as the violinist Ole Bull (1810–1880) and the vocal composers Halfdan Kjerdan (1815–1867) and Rikard Nordraak (1842–1866) drew on the old Norwegian folk melodies, as they were collected by Ludvig M. Lindeman in his *Older and Newer Norwegian Mountain Melodies* (1853–1867) to create a self-consciously national style. Grieg, like other Norwegian composers, incorporated elements of folk music and dances—strong rhythm and melodies that changed abruptly from carefree to melancholy—in his pieces for the piano and violin. One of Grieg's biographers comments that "To make use of native material as the basis for art music became the vital aim of the country's composers from the middle of the nineteenth century on."

Grieg studied in Leipzig as a young man, and then went to Copenhagen, where he associated with many of the leading musical figures of the day, including Niels Gade, who was also his teacher. However, Grieg was dissatisfied with the German romanticism that dominated Leipzig and Gade had already turned away from the notion of a "national style." Grieg felt that the heavy philosophical reasoning that characterized German romanticism was harmful to the imaginative art of music because music had to be felt with the heart. He first showed his longing for the north by setting some of Hans Christian Anderssen's poems to music. Themes of Norwegian nature and folk customs remained prominent in Grieg's work. He collaborated with the playwright Henrik Ibsen on the music for Ibsen's play, *Peer Gynt*, and composed an opera, *Olav Tryvason*, based on the life of the 10th-century Norwegian proselytizing monarch. His *Slaater* are violin arrangements based on three styles of Norwegian folk dances, and were originally meant for the Hardanger fiddle, a violin from Telemark, in southwestern Norway. The *Ballade* are based on a folk song from the Valdres area of Norway called *Den Nordlandske Bondestand* (The Norwegian Farmers).

During his lifetime, Grieg's music was criticized as derivative. His writings reflect his frustration with the inability of his countrymen to interpret his compositions according to the aesthetic standards that he set for them. Nevertheless, he was quite international in his outlook. He traveled a great deal, achieved fame outside Scandinavia, and studied with major composers such as Franz Liszt. After his death he was widely recognized, in Norway and abroad, as a true spokesman for Norwegian national sentiment. His own vision of his music, however, was larger than that, as he wrote in 1881, "As a modern artist, what I am striving for is that which is universal—or, more correctly, that which is individual. If the result is national, it is because the individual is national."

## GRIMM BROTHERS

Jacob (1785–1863) and Wilhelm (1786–1859) Grimm, brothers from Hanau, Germany, studied in Marburg to be librarians and went on to the University of Göttingen together where they wrote their famous book of fairy tales and another on sagas. Although Jacob, as the more original and scholarly of the two, took the lead in the project, Wilhelm was more poetic and a better storyteller. The brothers moved to Berlin where Wilhelm assisted Jacob in writing two volumes of *The History of the German Language* and the greatest contribution to German, the *Deutsches Wörterbuch*, the German equivalent of *The Oxford English Dictionary*. Only four volumes were completed in their lifetime. By recording scores of folktales loved and known by all Germans before there was a unified German state and by contributing to the standardization of a shared language, the Grimm brothers helped strengthen the sense of a common past and future. They therefore reinforced an emerging German nationalism.

## GUATEMALAN NATIONALISM

Since the 19th century, social and economic problems have plagued the young and harassed countries in Central America. The probing historian will find it difficult, if not impossible, to see traces of nationalism in political bodies so often convulsed to the point of disruption.

In Guatemala, President Juan Jose Arevalo (1945–1950) attempted to introduce into his own country some of the innovations of the Mexican revolution. Under his successor, Jacobo Arbenz Guzman, his policy was continued, but with a definite veering to the left. It became a focal point for Communist agitation, leading to a barely camouflaged intervention on the part of the United States and to a return of the military rule. Arevalo has not abandoned hope of being returned to the presidency. In 1963 he once more outlined his pro-

gram in a document called "Letter to the People of Guatemala." He says, "we are nationalist in theory and practice. We want to rule Guatemala without anybody daring to give us advice from the outside. Ours is a defensive and sentimental nationalism, not a narrow, closed and aggressive one. We do not share the opinion of those who think nationalism is a bad word. . . . Our nationalism is a brotherly nationalism which operates on the basis of dignity."

The attitudes of Guatemalans toward political institutions and toward society are affected by the Hispanic antecedents of most of the *ladinos'* population. Values have spread down through most of the society, but not to the lowest parts. There has been a growing flow of values from the middle class. Nationalism and national pride are issues on which all *ladinos* can unite. These feelings have been created by years of paternalistic authority and domination of a large segment of the economy by foreigners. On the other hand, the Indian's culture is incompatible with that of the *ladinos* and he does not experience feelings of nationalism. His attachments are more local and regional. And we can conclude that nationalism is particularly strong only among the 34 percent of the population that is considered to be urban.

## GUEVARA, CHE

1928–1967, Revolutionary leader, born in Rosario, Argentina. Afflicted with asthma, the young Guevara was often confined to bed for days, during which time he developed a passion for reading and playing chess. Although his infirmity kept him from attending school until he was nine years old, once he did enroll he was considered bright by his classmates and instructors. Perhaps as an attempt to compensate for his asthma, Che developed a competitive streak; he did not want to be seen as less able than others. This desire would stay with him for the rest of his life.

In 1939, an influx of Spanish expatriates fleeing the fascists began arriving in Argentina. Surrounded by these refugees, Guevara became quite interested in the conflict. Despite this, as an adolescent, he remained by and large apolitical. It was not until his time as a medical student at the University of Buenos Aires that a political consciousness began to develop.

Like many others in Argentina, Guevara was drawn to the populist message of Juan Perón. Given his own nationalist leanings, he found Perón's call for political and economic self-determination appealing. Che developed a strong resentment toward what he saw as an emerging neocolonial domination of Argentina by American interests. Eventually he laid the blame for much of the poverty, exploitation, and marginalization of the developing world at the feet of the United States.

Guevara came to despise the power of monopolistic corporations such as the United Fruit Company, calling them "kings without crowns." For him, economic liberation was as important as political liberation. "[N]ational sovereignty means . . . the right of a people to choose whatever form of government and way of life suits it. . . . But all these concepts of political sovereignty . . . are fictitious if there is no economic independence to go along with them. . . . If a country does not have its own economy . . . then it cannot be free from the tutelage of the country it is dependent upon."

While in Guatemala in 1954 Guevara became acquainted with several Cuban expatriates: veterans of Fidel Castro's early campaigns against the Batista regime. After the fall of the Arbenz government in a CIA-sponsored coup, Che traveled to Mexico, his revolutionary resolve steeled by what he had witnessed in Guatemala. Here, in the summer of 1955, he met Castro, a kindred anti-imperialist spirit. Together they worked on plans to overthrow the Cuban government.

In November 1956, Guevara, Castro, and eighty others set sail for Cuba. The landing did not go well; many of the men were killed or captured. Guevara and Castro escaped to the mountains and worked to build a network of peasant supporters. On December 31, 1958, Fulgencio Batista fled to the Dominican Republic. Three days later a victorious Che arrived in Havana.

Guevara suggested that Cuba should be an example for all Latin American revolutionaries. By 1962, largely through his efforts, Cuba was backing guerrilla activity throughout the region. Revolutionary organizations in Peru, Nicaragua, Guatemala, and Venezuela were all receiving Cuban assistance.

By 1965, concluding that Cuba's long-term independence depended on successful revolutions elsewhere, Guevara decided to return to the battlefield. His interest by this time had shifted to Africa and in April he left for the Congo. The campaign was a disaster. Infighting and undisciplined forces doomed the endeavor and in November Che and his men withdrew.

Guevara's focus now returned to Latin America. After spending some time in Prague, he went to Bolivia in 1966. Che had considered other locations but settled on Bolivia because of its location in the heart of South America, porous borders, and proximity to his ultimate goal, Argentina.

The Bolivian campaign was no more successful than the Congolese one had been. The Bolivian army soon captured deserters who alerted them to the Cuban presence. Pursued by the military, Che's small group was forced to stay on the run. Having failed to get the support of the Bolivian Communist Party, they were cut off from outside assistance.

On October 8, 1967, Guevara was captured by Bolivian army troops. He was executed the next day in the presence of CIA operative Felix Rodríguez in La Higuera, Bolivia. On October 11, his body was buried in a secret grave.

Guevara's dream of widespread Communist revolution in the industrializing world has not come to pass. In death, however, "Che" has become a revolutionary martyr and remains a recognizable figure worldwide. As a symbol of anti-imperialist defiance he may have as much influence as when he was alive.

An excellent comprehensive biography is *Che Guevara: A Revolutionary Life* by Jon Lee Anderson (Grove Press, 1997). Examples of Guevara's political and military thought can be found in *Che Guevara and the Cuban Revolution: The Writings and Speeches of Ernesto Che Guevara* (Pathfinder/Pacific & Asia, 1987), *Che Guevara Speaks* (Pathfinder/José Martí, 1988), and *Guerrilla Warfare* (University of Nebraska Press, 1985).

# H

HAMILTON, ALEXANDER    1757–1804, U.S. states-man, born on the island of Nevis in the British West Indies and emigrated to New York City in 1772. Hamilton contributed to the rise of U.S. nationalism as an officer in the Continental Army during the American Revolution and as a delegate to the Constitutional Convention in 1787, but he made his most important contributions in this regard as secretary of the treasury from 1789 to 1795.

In 1790 Hamilton submitted to Congress a proposal to redeem the debt incurred during the American Revolution by the Second Continental Congress and by the various states. His plan called for the federal government to assume all outstanding war debts, which it would pay for by issuing bonds. Hamilton had several reasons for increasing and funding the national debt on a long-term basis, an idea that appalled many of his contemporaries. He was very much aware that many leaders of the American Revolution were members of the wealthy class, and he hoped to secure the loyalty of that class by offering it a lucrative stake in the federal government. As informal leader of the Federalist Party, he espoused a strong central government, and he believed that by assuming the states' debts the fledgling federal government would enhance its authority over the states. He also intended that the bonds would serve as a medium of financial exchange by circulating in much the same way as did specie, which was in very short supply after the war, and paper money, whose popularity had suffered severely following the demise of the Continental dollar during the war. Although Hamilton never intended that the national debt reach such astronomical heights as it did in the late 20th century, he did believe that a well-managed public debt would create confidence in and loyalty toward the national government as it had done for many years previously in Great Britain. In this manner he hoped to employ the national debt as a nationalizing force in the United States.

The success of Hamilton's proposal depended on the federal government's ability to raise and manage revenue. To this end, in 1791 Hamilton proposed the implementation of several taxes, the most important one being a tariff on imported manufactured goods. Again, Hamilton had more than one motive; in addition to providing the federal government with much-needed income, he also intended that the tariff protect nascent American manufacturers from foreign, especially British, competition. In this manner he hoped to make the United States into a world-class industrial and mercantile nation along the lines of Great Britain. He also proposed the creation of the Bank of the United States, a national financial institution modeled in part on the Bank of England, whose purpose would be to lend stability to the still-developing American banking system while playing a leading role in the collection and expenditure of federal income throughout the new nation.

All of these measures were enacted by Congress between 1791 and 1792, thus ensuring the realization of the federalist vision of U.S. nationalism. Rather than remain an agrarian nation centered around the yeoman farmer under a relatively inactive central government, as the Jeffersonian republicans preferred, Hamilton's financial program contributed in large part to the evolution of the United States into a nation devoted to mercantile and industrial pursuits under the governance of a strong central authority.

Biographies are Jacob Ernest Cooke, *Alexander Hamilton* (1982) and Forrest McDonald, *Alexander Hamilton: A Biography* (1979, reissued 1982). John Steele Gordon, *Hamilton's Blessing: The Extraordinary Life and Times of Our National Debt* (1997) and Peter McNamara, *Political Economy and Statesmanship: Smith, Hamilton, and the Foundation of the Commercial Republic* (1998) discuss Hamilton's contributions to U.S. economic nationalism.

## HEGEL, GEORG W. F.

1770–1831, German "Idealist" philosopher. Georg W. F. Hegel has been and continues to be both exalted and vilified for his political theory and conception of the nation-state. While some people see in his philosophy of freedom a progressive moment in Western political thought, others view his conceptualization of the state as terminating in nothing less than fascism. Hence, it is not uncommon to find Hegel characterized as a nationalist, authoritarian apologist, and a believer that history culminated, intellectually, in his own imagination and, politically, in the Prussian state. This opinion is incorrect.

Regarding nationalism, Hegel's thought is incomprehensible outside the concept of the nation-state (*das Volk als Staat*). In his *Philosophy of Right,* he confronts the problem of German nationalism directly. Hegel stated that the nation-state is spirit "in its substantial rationality and immediate actuality and is therefore the absolute power on *earth*. . . ." Each state has the right to be autonomous in the eyes of other states and there exists a necessity for each independent state to be recognized by others. Hegel does not suggest, however, the inherent superiority of one nation-state over and against another or that history terminates in any existing political configuration.

Hegel's whole political thought resists a nationalist "reading" as long as one bothers to consider the historical context and the nuance of his philosophy. Historically, Hegel was situated on the cuff of an epochal rupture. At the turn of the 19th century, Germany consisted of a bewildering number of fragmented principalities; industrial capitalism and the ethos of utilitarianism was gaining the upper hand in Europe; and older, feudal forms of social organization, politics, and ethical conduct were struggling against new modern forms. From Hegel's view, a new concept of freedom and human existence had been posited and was being worked out. Even though the family continued to represent a fundamental element in the education and preservation of ethical conduct, the nation or nation-state had emerged as the principal social unit tasked with preserving the legal and ethical life of a particular society; it represented spirit's highest manifestation but not necessarily its end point.

Especially important is the emphasis that Hegel placed on the formality of forced reconciliation embedded in the program of German nationalism and the quality of a state's "being in and for itself." A nation-state, by virtue of actually existing, is "rational" insofar as it exists for some reason—that is, one can retroactively trace a path of development attributing causality to some factors over others; this is not to say that it conforms to the idea of nation-state or reason itself. The nation-state may, therefore, remain in itself or undeveloped while, simultaneously, representing the decisive social power. This is why Hegel qualifies his stance regarding the necessity of national recognition by pointing out that if a nation-state is constitutionally and conditionally undeveloped or one sided, then the demand for recognition is purely "formal."

In his *Lectures on the Philosophy of Religion,* Hegel conceived national spirit as the inescapable "substantial foundation" of a people. This "substantial foundation" was a precondition for education, the further development of consciousness and reflexivity, and the articulation of objective spirit. However, national forms of consciousness and identity were by no means ends in themselves. There is no teleology here and Hegel never implied that the Prussian state marks the final consummation of political history. In fact, Hegel held a contrary and pessimistic position by 1820: that spirit had failed to actualize itself in Germany and that the leading edge of spirit's development lies beyond Europe.

Hegel saw that national spirit constituted a developmental point in the life and history of humanity: It was something to be transcended at some point like other communal beliefs, opinions, matters of faith, and organizations arising from earlier periods. Hegel ridiculed German nationalists for not comprehending that unification of any state that did not flow from the will and dispositions of its people would be only a formal and coercive act of reconciliation. Thus, Hegel wrote in his *Philosophy of Right* regarding the prospects of German unity that "Those who speak of the wishes of a totality [*Gesamtheit*] which constitutes a more or less independent state with its own centre to abandon this focal point and its own independence in order to form a whole with another state know little of the nature of a totality and of the self-awareness which an autonomous nation possesses."

## HENLEIN, KONRAD

1898–1945, Leader of the Sudeten German nationalist movement in Czechoslovakia. Henlein was born to a German father and Czech mother on May 6, 1898, in Maffersdorf bei Reichenberg, then a city in the Bohemian region of Austria-Hungary. During World War I he served in the Austro-Hungarian Imperial Army on the Italian front, was captured in 1918 and released in 1919. Having left as a member of the privileged German minority in the imperial Austrian lands, he returned home a German minority and citizen of the democratic Czechoslovak Republic. He began his adult life as a bank clerk in Gablonz in 1925, also working as a gymnastics instructor in the *Deutsche Turnerver-*

*band*—a Pan-German gymnastics movement with nationalist leanings dating back to the Napoleonic invasions. One of a number of institutions embraced by Sudeten Germans to defend their interests against the newly empowered Czech majority, the gymnastic organization was reconstituted around the Catholic nationalist principles of the Austrian Othmar Spann.

Henlein proved a capable leader, and by 1931 assumed control of the large but still politically weak gymnastics movement. However, in 1933, the more powerful and radical Sudeten National Socialists were barred from parliamentary politics for having conspired with Hitler's National Socialists against Czechoslovakia. The fact that few Germans in Czechoslovakia had mastery of the Czech language, a prerequisite for most administrative positions, served as one rallying point. Another was the allegation that depression era hardships were disproportionately felt by the German minority. Henlein's movement was called on to fill the institutional void and articulate these grievances in parliament. With support from former National Socialists, he founded the *Sudetendeutsche Heimatfront* (Sudeten German Home Front), later renamed the *Sudetendeutsche Partei* (Sudeten German Party). In the 1935 elections, his party was backed by nearly 60 percent of the German-speaking population, winning 44 of 300 seats in the Czechoslovak parliament. Despite government concessions to the German minority in 1937, Hitler's tremendous influence and financial support shifted the party's goals from German autonomy within Czechoslovakia to German secession from Czechoslovakia. On March 28, 1938, Hitler and Henlein strategized the plan that would become the cornerstone of the Munich Agreement, namely, the dismemberment of Czechoslovakia according to the principle of national self-determination. In 1939, following the Munich Agreement and the subjugation of Bohemia and Moravia to direct Nazi control, Henlein was promoted first *Gauleiter* and then *Reichstatthalter* (Reich governor). However, his influence was eclipsed by Karl Hermann Frank who proved a more ruthless administrator. Henlein committed suicide on May 10, 1945, in a POW camp in Plzeň, Czechoslovakia.

For further discussion of Henlein and the Sudeten problem, consult Ronald M. Smelser, *The Sudeten Problem, 1933–1938—Volkstumspolitik and the Formulation of Nazi Foreign Policy* (Middletown, Conn: Wesleyan University Press, 1975).

**HENRY, PATRICK** 1736–1799, U.S. statesman. Born in Studley, Hanover County, Virginia, Henry is best remembered for his brilliant speeches favoring American independence from Great Britain, but he also played an important role as a proponent of national unity both before and after the American Revolution.

In 1765 Henry, a member of the Virginia House of Burgesses, proposed the adoption of seven resolutions related to the repeal of the Stamp Act, a parliamentary bill that outraged colonists from New Hampshire to Georgia. Only five of the resolutions were passed, and those in modified form; nevertheless, all seven were reported to the other colonial assemblies as having been passed as proposed, thus emboldening radicals throughout the colonies but especially in the Massachusetts assembly.

In 1774, following the dissolution of the House of Burgesses by the British royal governor, Henry chaired a meeting of disgruntled delegates that issued a call for what became the First Continental Congress. In 1775, as a delegate to that congress, he pleaded for colonial unity in the face of the British threat by imploring the other delegates to think of themselves as Americans rather than as residents of a particular colony. On his return to Virginia later that same year, he delivered a passionate call for raising a militia to defend the colony from the British army should the need arise. In 1776 he played a prominent role in securing passage of the House of Burgesses' resolution to its delegates to the Second Continental Congress to press for a declaration of American independence from Britain; he also served as governor of Virginia from 1776 to 1779.

Although Henry was a strong supporter of American nationalism, initially he opposed the creation of a strong central government because he feared that it would be as tyrannical as the British monarchy had been. In 1788 he vociferously opposed Virginia's ratification of the U.S. Constitution because he believed that it invested the federal government with too much power and the states with too little, and that it did little to protect the individual rights of citizens. However, once the Constitution was amended in 1791 by the addition of the Bill of Rights, which was influenced largely by the Virginia Bill of Rights of 1776, which Henry helped compose, he became a staunch supporter of American federalism over states' rights. His last public speeches argued against the Virginia and Kentucky Resolutions, which declared that the individual states possessed the power to nullify acts of Congress, in this case the Alien and Sedition Acts, which violated the Constitution.

Henry is occasionally portrayed as a "rabble rouser" who backed away from the institutionalization of American nationalism because he despised strong government, whether American or British, on general principle. It is true that Henry, like many of the early patriots, believed that American nationalism was not necessarily an unmitigated good because of the potential for abuse via the actions of a too-powerful central government. However, once that government guaranteed individual rights, thus making its interests secondary to those of its citizens, Henry did his utmost to promote the advancement of nationalism in the United States.

Biographies are Henry Mayer, *A Son of Thunder: Patrick Henry and the American Republic* (1986) and Richard R. Beeman, *Patrick Henry: A Biography* (1974).

## HERDER, JOHANN GOTTFRIED VON   1744–1803,
Philosopher and literary critic, born East Prussia. Herder is considered by many to be *the* philosophical father of nationalism. He coined the term *Nationalismus* in German, and was enormously influential in his own time. Among English speakers today, however, Herder is read rather sparingly. We often learn of his ideas in contradistinction to those of Kant (his one-time teacher) and Goethe (his informal student). This is frequently attributed to the fact that Herder produced no single masterwork, though it may also stem from uneasiness about his writings on German identity: To some, Herder is the precursor of a tolerant cultural relativism, but to others, he is the thinker with whom a formerly civic patriotism first takes a xenophobic turn.

These interpretive differences are understandable given Herder's moody if not inconsistent presentation of his core ideas. For example, Herder always describes nationality in organic terms, yet alternately compares foreign nations to flowers and invading insects. Indeed, for many, Herder's belief in nations as "natural" entities is controversial in itself. Whereas Rousseau had hypothesized that nations originate in natural communities, the Genevan placed political ends above cultural purity. By contrast, Herder makes cultural preservation his primary goal and discusses politics much less frequently.

It is important to remember that throughout Herder's lifetime, Germany was not a political entity at all. Rather, most German-speaking peoples were ruled by decaying principalities of the Holy Roman Empire or, as was the young Herder himself, by the militarist Prussian state. Though he long feared being called back into military service, a run of good fortune allowed the humbly born Herder to escape Prussia and pursue a career as a scholar and Lutheran minister. Early on in his adulthood, Herder traveled throughout the moribund empire, and was consistently struck by the lack of national feeling among its inhabitants. Particularly among the upper classes, Herder noticed, this was manifested

in a studied avoidance of the German language. Nearly all literature and scholarship was in French and Latin, with artists more generally striving for a universal, neoclassical style.

It is in this environment that Herder called for an authentic German art and culture, first gaining fame with his *Fragments on Recent German Literature*. Specifically, Herder argued that a backward Germany must emulate rather than imitate the greatness of other nations. Throughout his life, he held that each country has its own literary and artistic genius, but that this genius must remain unadulterated in order to flourish. Herder viewed artifice, cosmopolitanism, and elitism as synonymous, and celebrated the folk traditions of multiple nations in his *Voices of the People in Song*. He believed that the heart of a nation rests with its spoken rather than its written language.

Herder's intellectual interests were nothing if not wide ranging, extending to anthropology and natural science as well as to literature and philosophy. In his ironically titled *Yet Another Philosophy of History* he disputed that one could use universal standards to render *any* judgment (moral, aesthetic, or otherwise) on a foreign nation or bygone era. He expanded on these themes in his enormous but unfinished *Ideas for a Philosophy of the History of Mankind*, in which he celebrated nations as a source of *diversity* on the one hand and of *fraternity* on the other.

Notably, Herder's denunciation of European conceit extends to a profound and unwavering condemnation of slavery and imperialism. In this respect Herder is unequaled by other European thinkers (a tribute to his ability to practice the "sympathetic" history that he preached for others). As contemporary as he seems in regard to some topics, however, Herder is typical of his age in his generalizations about "national character." Not least striking are his characterizations of Germany itself, which he consistently depicts as "bold" and "martial." Although Herder himself was pacific and intellectual then, he welcomed the chance for "men of action" to band together for national liberation and defense.

Yet if Herder's pacifism is often exaggerated, he is falsely blamed for the transformation of civic patriotism into a nationalism of birth and blood: In his essay, "Do We Still Have the Fatherland of Yore?," for example, Herder suggests that "the stranger, laboring as a patriot . . . can gain through merit a fatherland other than that of [his] birth," and chides "the simpleton [acting] on the strength of his birth alone." Nor is Herder antidemocratic. He instead suggests, not unreasonably, that he feared persecution for his "republican" views: "Were the tone of our books more republican, I should be able to state many a thing more clearly which I now perhaps speak of darkly or bravely in parables." Such fears notwithstanding, few authors prior to Herder spoke with as much concern for the "poor and hungry" or as much contempt for the "rich and great." As Isaiah Berlin suggests, Herder's truest political descendants may be anarchists and Christian socialists.

One may likewise note Herder's influence on leaders of national liberation movements throughout Europe, including Kollar, Brodzinski, and Mazzini. Herder is of course best known for inspiring subsequent German nationalists, in particular, figures such as Fichte, Jahn, and Stein. Whether Herder would have forgiven the chauvinism of these 19th-century Germans is debatable. He would certainly have deemed Hitler's aping of Napoleonic conquest a supreme betrayal of the national spirit.

While most of Herder's writing is collected only in his *Saṁtliche Werke* (Bernhard Suphan, ed., Berlin, 1877–1913), English collections include F. M. Barnard's *J. G. Herder on Social and Political Culture* (New York: Cambridge, 1969) and Ernest Menze's *Johann Gottfried Herder: Selected Early Works* (University Park: Penn State, 1992). More obscure passages of interest are translated in Robert Ergang's excellent *Herder and the Foundations of German Nationalism* (New York: Columbia, 1931).

Intellectual biographies of Herder include Robert Clark's *Herder: His Life and Thought* (Berkeley: California, 1955) and Wulf Koepke's *Johann Gottfried Herder* (Boston: Hall, 1987). The most famous treatment of Herder's thought in English is Isaiah Berlin's *Vico and Herder: Two Studies in the History of Ideas* (London: Hogarth, 1976).

**HERZL, THEODOR** 1860–1904, Theodor Binyamin Ze'ev Herzl, writer, journalist, playwright, and activist, is known as the father of modern Zionism and founder of the World Zionist Organization. His vision of a political, nationalist Zionism and a secular, socialist Jewish homeland served as a foundation for the Jewish pioneer movement from the turn of the century until the creation of the state of Israel in 1948.

Born in Budapest in 1860, Herzl received a secular education and earned a law degree from the University of Vienna in 1884. He soon abandoned the legal profession in favor of writing and journalism. A prolific playwright, Herzl was also the Paris correspondent of a Vienna newspaper and covered the Dreyfus court-martial in 1894. Although Herzl was preoccupied with anti-Semitism and the assimilation question prior to the Dreyfus Affair, the event profoundly influenced his subsequent thinking and writing on Jewish identity. In

the aftermath of the Dreyfus scandal, Herzl had come to think of anti-Semitism as a fixture in Jewish life that can only be overcome through political means: the creation of a sovereign Jewish state. In 1896 he elaborated on this notion in his famous pamphlet *Der Judenstaat* (The Jewish State). Borrowing from European nationalist thought, Herzl posited Jewish identity as a national collective and argued that Jews could only achieve equality through national status and internationally recognized political independence.

In 1897, he published and edited a weekly paper devoted to nationalist Zionism. In the first issue, he called for an international meeting of Jews (a Jewish Congress) in support of the nationalist cause. The first Zionist Congress met in Basle, Switzerland, in August of the same year and the three-day, international Jewish gathering marked the first official step in the formation of organized political Zionism. During the assembly meetings the Zionist Organization was formed, Herzl elected as its president, and a declaration (known as the "Basle Program") calling for the establishment of a national Jewish homeland was officially adopted as its guiding objective. As the organization's leader, Herzl set about to pursue the plan and seek political and financial support for a Jewish resettlement. By the second congress meeting in 1898, he announced the founding of Zionist Bank, a central financial institution for the collection of resettlement funds and the financing of land negotiations with the Turkish government.

Herzl's vision was greeted with enthusiasm by younger activists, but rejected by many key figures and leading thinkers within the Jewish community. To his great disappointment, Herzl had largely failed to win financial backing from Jewish philanthropists, though he had gained some interest from Great Britain and temporary support from Kaiser William II of Germany. Herzl traveled to Constantinople and other parts of the Ottoman Empire several times, meeting with the German kaiser and the Turkish sultan. In 1902, his negotiations with the Ottoman Empire came to a dead-end and Herzl turned to the british Empire, which controlled the Sinai Peninsula and the island of Cyprus. That same year, he published his novel, *Altneuland* (Old New Land), in which he envisioned a pluralist Jewish state as a socialist utopia. In *Altneuland*, he also coined the often quoted phrase, "If you wish it, it is no fairytale," which became the slogan for the modern Zionist movement.

In the summer of 1902, he was invited to testify before the British Royal Commission on Alien Immigration and later met with British colonial authorities. While Cyprus was quickly rejected as a potential Jewish settlement, the Sinai Peninsula was favorably regarded as a possibility by the British until the Egyptian government rejected water supply negotiations. Following this setback, the British proposed Uganda, in East Africa.

By 1903, Herzl's continuous efforts to make a homeland possible in biblical "Eretz Israel" (the land of Israel) had not advanced, while growing anti-Jewish violence, especially the news of pogroms in Russia, made a solution to the homeland problem appear more pressing. Herzl submitted the Uganda proposal to a vote in the Sixth Zionist Congress and despite great opposition that threatened to split the Zionist Organization, a vote tentatively approved further exploration of the plan.

Between 1903 and 1904, Herzl resumed negotiations with the Turkish government, traveled extensively in his quest to find support, and met with the Russian minister of the interior, the king of Italy, and the pope among others. At the same time, the continuous controversy over the Uganda plan and growing pressures to renounce it from within the Zionist Organization were threatening Herzl's leadership. In a final meeting in April 1904, Herzl managed to reunite the organization with assurances that he still held Palestine ("Eretz Israel") as the ultimate home for the Jewish people and Uganda as only a temporary refuge for Russian Jews. Already suffering from heart disease, Herzl died of pneumonia three months later.

In the following year, the Seventh Zionist Congress voted down the Uganda plan, as the plans to resettle the ancient land of Israel took shape and young European Zionists began emigrating to agricultural cooperatives in Palestine. As the British assumed control of the region, the Zionist Organization Herzl founded relocated to Jerusalem. The independent state of Israel was declared in 1948 and in 1949, Herzl's remains were brought to Israel. He is buried on Mount Herzl in Jerusalem.

## HIDALGO, MIGUEL 1753–1811, Father of Mexican independence. He was the first Mexican leader to challenge Spanish rule of his homeland. Hidalgo, a Roman Catholic priest, left academe in the early 1790s to serve as pastor of several parishes in central Mexico. To promote Mexican and Creole cultures, Hidalgo established his parishes as hubs of rich cultural life and entrepreneurial activity. Hidalgo's efforts and championing of liberal thought drew criticism from the Spanish government.

Spanish control of Mexico hinged on refusing rights to some ethnic groups. For nearly 300 years, the Spanish denied power to Mexican Creoles, and kept Indians and mestizos impoverished and uneducated. By the early 19th century, these oppressed groups were ripe for social upheaval.

Hidalgo sparked the long struggle for Mexican independence on September 15, 1810. As a pastor in Dolores (now Dolores Hidalgo), Hidalgo summoned his parishioners—many of them mestizos and Indians—to church. He proclaimed the "Grito de Dolores" (Cry of Dolores), in which he demanded that the Spanish yoke be broken.

Hidalgo wanted to incite all economic classes to revolt, but peons, or workers, offered the most assistance. The support of the working class was instrumental in Hidalgo's military victories, but it caused the wealthy to distrust the premise of independence. The lack of support from the upper class left Hidalgo's movement imperiled, and he was defeated at the Bridge of Calderon on January 17, 1811. Following the defeat, Hidalgo was captured by Spanish forces, and executed on July 30, 1811.

Despite Hidalgo's execution a decade before Mexico realized its independence, his role in fostering Mexican nationalism is unequaled. To this day, the president of Mexico begins the celebration of the country's Independence Day, September 16, with a reissuing of the "Grito" during the late evening of September 15. Also, nearly every town in Mexico has a Hidalgo monument and a Sixteenth of September street.

Authoritative works include John Anthony Caruso's *The Liberators of Mexico* (P. Smith Publishers, 1954, 1967) and Hugh M. Hamill, Jr.'s *The Hidalgo Revolt* (University of Florida, 1966).

## HIROHITO 1901–1989, Emperor during the Showa era in Japan. Hirohito was born as the first prince of the Taisho Emperor on April 29, 1901. Hirohito was called Michinomiya until he was named the crown prince in 1916. Hirohito traveled to Europe for study and became the regent in 1921. He married Queen Nagako Kuninomiya in 1924 and succeeded to the throne after the Taisho Emperor passed away on December 25, 1926. The Emperor Hirohito is also known as the Showa Emperor because the era between December 25, 1926, and January 7, 1989 (until his death) is designated as Showa. (The era name changes in Japan whenever a new Emperor succeeds to the throne. After the Emperor Hirohito passed away in 1989, Prince Akihito became Japanese emperor and the era name was changed to Heisei.)

During his reign, the Emperor Hirohito faced many changes in the social and diplomatic climate of Japan. Following the dropping of atomic bombs on Hiroshima and Nagasaki in August 1945, Hirohito aired "Gyokuon Hoso" on radio, announcing Japan's defeat by the Allied forces and the end of World War II. Although previous emperors had been recognized as sacred, Hirohito denied this theory, declaring himself as human emperor in 1946. The constitution of Japan, adopted in 1947, states that "the Emperor shall be the symbol of the State and of the unity of the people, deriving his position from the will of the people with whom resides sovereign power."

The name Hirohito has been almost synonymous with emperor to foreign nations. The emperor and empress traveled to many countries in order to establish friendly diplomatic relationships between Japan and these nations. Hirohito was very knowledgeable in biology, publishing great amounts of scholarly work in this field. Much of his work has also been translated into foreign languages. Hirohito promoted arts and sciences among the Japanese people, inviting prominent artists and scientists to an awards ceremony every year. His recognition of and love for these fields has been deeply appreciated by the Japanese.

Although Emperor Hirohito denied his sacredness, many Japanese, especially older generations, still respect the emperor as the highest power of the nation. Particularly some members of the right wing advocate the restoration of Imperial rule in politics, claiming that the emperor should be the highest organ of state power. The notion of imperial rule is also related with the division of the Japanese people into various social classes, such as the nobility, the commoners, and the humble people, providing the nobility with many privileges. The Emperor Hirohito and the present Emperor Akihito have been opposed to such propaganda.

Although the Emperor Hirohito was not given political power, he appointed the prime minister and the chief judge of the Supreme Court as designated by the cabinet. The emperor also performed many ceremonial functions with the advice and approval of the cabinet. Hirohito passed away on January 7th, 1989, ending the Showa era. Hirohito's funeral, which followed the imperial traditions of ancient Japan, was televised all over the world.

**HITLER, ADOLF** 1889–1945, Nazi Party leader and Reich chancellor (1933–1945). Born in Austria, Hitler lived from 1909 to 1913 in Vienna, where he absorbed anti-Semitic prejudices while trying to make a living as an artist. When World War I broke out, he went to Bavaria and enlisted in the infantry. He rose to the rank of corporal, was twice awarded the Iron Cross, and was wounded. He began to emerge from the political shadows shortly after the end of World War I, and he drew around himself a growing circle of enthusiastic admirers. In September 1919, he joined a tiny nationalist group that grew into the energetic, antidemocratic Nazi Party.

Although he had little formal education, Hitler was a fiery speaker, capable of stirring his listeners with haranguing, emotional tirades. Paranoid, continuously tense, and expectant, he was sensitive and suspicious. He had no close relationship with anyone, not even with his mistress, Eva Braun, whom he finally married moments before committing suicide. Untrusting, he always felt that his failures resulted from the enmity or failure of others, even those close to him. He was able, however, to maintain his conduct within nominally acceptable bounds, and some persons considered him to be no more than a "crank." Yet his brand of nationalism was hierarchical (with the German nation far superior to all others), exclusive, intolerant, and brutal. The excesses of his national hubris brought unspeakable suffering to the other nations of Europe.

**HLINKA, ANDREJ** 1864–1938, Roman Catholic priest, politician, a leading advocate of Slovak autonomy, born in Ružomberok, Slovakia (then Černova, the Habsburg Monarchy). Hlinka was known for his radical views on social justice, and on the subordinate position of Slovaks to the Hungarians, and later, after the creation of the Czechoslovak Republic in 1918, to the Czechs. His tall, ascetic stature, personal charisma, and rhetorical skills made him an excellent public speaker, and the biblical analogies used to frame Hlinka's speeches attracted the attention of the Slovak inhabitants of the Austro-Hungarian Monarchy.

Hlinka became politically active in the mid-1890s, as one of the editors of *L'udove Noviny* (People's News), and an adherent of the Catholic People's Party (CPP). His early political essays and fiery speeches were highly critical of the social and national policies of the Austro-Hungarian monarchy. In 1905, along with some Slovak members of the CPP, Hlinka attempted to found the *Slovenska L'udova Strana* (Slovak People's Party) (SPP), which was declared a political party, but never functioned as one.

For his unconstrained political radicalism, Hlinka was imprisoned first in 1907 and then again in 1908. At the same time, Bishop Parvy revoked his statute as a member of the Catholic clergy and banned Hlinka from the Ružomberok (Černova) parish. The *People's News* periodical was also outlawed by the Catholic Church. A major turning point in his life came after the 1907 massacre of fifteen Slovaks in Černova, when the local parishioners demanded Hlinka's presence at the consecration of the new church building. Hlinka spoke out against the Černova massacre, and raised the public awareness regarding the event in the Austro-Hungarian Empire as well as abroad. The repressive action taken by the police was condemned all over Europe, including the Vatican. The Pope formally recognized Hlinka's innocence, and demanded his full rehabilitation.

The tragic events in Černova and the imprisonment somewhat moderated Hlinka's radical views, and following the intervention from the Vatican he was allowed to return to Ružomberok. By 1913, the formerly radical SPP adapted a more conservative orientation that was shared by conservative Catholic political parties. Hlinka's relations with the Czech national revivalists also improved and, inspired by the concept of Slovak autonomy in the independent Czechoslovakia, he became a strong supporter of Czechoslovak national unity.

Yet, the conditions in the newly created Czechoslovakia fell short of Hlinka's expectation. He was dissatisfied with the fact that the Slovaks failed to gain the degree of autonomy agreed on in the "Pittsburgh Agreement," secretly left the country, and presented the demands of Slovaks at the Peace Conference in Paris. For this act he was briefly imprisoned by the Czechoslovak authorities. Consequently, Hlinka reaffirmed his position on the right of the Slovaks for self-determination, and rejected Masaryk's doctrine of Czechoslovakism, according to which Czechs and Slovaks were members of a single, Czechoslovak nation.

In 1925 the SPP was renamed after Hlinka (*Hlinkova Slovenska L'udova Strana,* HSPP) and, with the exception of the 1927–1929 coalition government, it remained in a parliamentary opposition. Although Hlinka is often associated with the rise of the Slovak state in 1939, he never lived to see the independent Slovakia. After the collapse of Communism in 1989, Hlinka's contributions to the Slovak national revival were officially recognized, and with L'udovit Štur and M. R. Štefanik, he remains the most significant figure of modern Slovak history. The 1000 Slovak Crown banknote bears Hlinka's portrait.

Several biographies of Andrej Hlinka have been published. The most extensive is J. M. Kirschbaum and F. Fuga, *Andrej Hlinka v slove a obraze* (*Andrej Hlinka in Words and Pictures,* Toronto–Ružomberok: 1991). A comprehensive study, *Andrej Hlinka a jeho miesto v Slovenskych dejinach* (*Andrej Hlinka and His Place in the History of Slovakia*), was edited by F. Bielik and Š. Borovsky (Bratislava, 1991). For other accounts see Scotus Viator, *The Racial Problems in Hungary* (London: 1908); A. Kolisek, *O Andrejovi Hlinkovi* (Vienna: 1907); and K. Sidor, *Andrej Hlinka* (Bratislava: 1934). On Hlinka's role in Czechoslovak and Slovak politics, see James R. Felak, *At the Price of the Republic* (Pittsburgh: University of Pittsburgh Press, 1994).

**HO CHI MINH**  1890–1969, Founder of the Indochinese Communist Party, later president of the Democratic Republic of Vietnam. Ho Chi Minh was born in 1890 in a small village in central Vietnam, the son of an impoverished Confucian scholar who served as a minor official at the imperial court in Huê. In 1907, Ho (then identified by his real name of Nguyen Tat Thanh) was accepted into the prestigious National Academy (Quoc Hoc) for training in the French language and Western learning. But he soon took part in peasant demonstrations against official corruption and high taxes, and was forced to abandon his studies. In 1911 he left for France to seek the means to liberate his country from the clutches of French colonialism.

In Paris, young Thanh changed his name to Nguyen Ai Quoc (Nguyen the Patriot), and in 1919 he appealed publicly to the leaders of the victorious Allied powers attending the Versailles Peace Conference to grant self-determination to all colonial peoples. Rebuffed, he joined the French Communist Party (FCP) and in 1923 left for Moscow to be trained as a Communist agent. In December 1924 he arrived in Canton, in South China, where he created an embryonic revolutionary party known as the Vietnamese Revolutionary Youth League. The goals of the organization were national independence and world revolution, but Communism was rarely mentioned. In 1930, the league was transformed into a formal Indochinese Communist Party (ICP). A year later, Ho was arrested by Hong Kong authorities as a suspected Communist agent. After his release, he left for the Soviet Union to seek treatment for tuberculosis. But he was also under suspicion by Soviet authorities for his allegedly "nationalist" tendencies in placing Vietnamese independence at a higher level of priority than the issue of class struggle.

In 1941, Ho returned to Vietnam to organize his followers for a future uprising against the French colonial regime, which had been compelled to accept Japanese military occupation of northern parts of Indochina the previous fall. Adopting the pseudonym Ho Chi Minh (Ho who enlightens), he created a broad-based patriotic organization known as the League for Independence of Vietnam (Vietminh Front) to seek independence at the close of the Pacific War. Designed to appeal to a wide stratum of the Vietnamese population, the front was secretly led by the ICP. In August 1945, Vietminh forces launched a successful uprising to seize power in Hanoi at the moment of Japanese surrender to the Allies. In early September, Ho announced the formation of a new Democratic Republic of Vietnam (DRV), with himself as provisional president.

France, however, refused to recognize Vietnamese

independence, and after several months of abortive negotiations, the Franco–Vietminh War broke out in December 1946. For eight years, Ho led a guerilla-based struggle against French colonial troops and the Associated State of Vietnam, a non-Communist puppet government set up by the French in 1949. In 1954, the exhausted French agreed to divide the country at the 17th parallel, with Ho's DRV in the north and a non-Communist government in the south. Elections were scheduled to reunify the country in 1956.

For the remaining fifteen years of his life, Ho Chi Minh served as president of the DRV, while seeking to reunify the two zones and build a socialist society according to the Marxist-Leninist model. Revered by many Vietnamese because of his leading role in the long struggle for national independence, Ho was successful in mobilizing broad support in both zones for a struggle to reunify the country under his leadership. But the sometimes brutal efforts of his regime in Hanoi to create a socialist society in the north antagonized many and led to the charge that his pose as a patriot was a ruse to hide his commitment to the objectives of world Communism. The charge had some basis in fact, for there is substantial evidence that to the end of his life he was a firm believer in the superiority of the socialist system as practiced in Moscow and Beijing. At the same time, however, he was a fervent patriot, and devoted a lifetime to supporting the liberation of oppressed peoples around the world from the yoke of global imperialism.

In 1969, Ho Chi Minh died of heart failure. During the final years of his life, his health had been increasingly fragile, and he played only a marginal role in formulating strategy in the war against the United States. At his death, he was revered by millions of Vietnamese as "Uncle Ho," and after the unification of the country in 1976, a mausoleum was erected in his honor in the center of the capital of Hanoi.

**HOMELAND**   One of the distinguishing features of the modern world is that it has been completely parceled out into individual units or nation-states with carefully demarcated borders, set one against the other. The notion of territory is integral to the concept of nationality. All nations have territories, and sometimes nations or aspirant nationalities fight over territories that they believe to be theirs, to which they often lay some ancestral claim. The concept of a *homeland* is a romantic extension of this sense of territory. The homeland is more than just the physical space over which the nationality exercises or wants to exercise political control. It is always also a home, a place of origin and integrity; its members are imagined as sharing this home, as being part of the same family. Conversely, foreigners are not at home here; they are alien outsiders (*Ausländer* in German) or, at best, guests, tolerated or excluded at the whim of their hosts. Often images of maternity and paternity are linked to the homeland, as in the metaphors of a fatherland or motherland; the homeland is something to which one is primordially attached and rooted, bonded by blood to its soil (*Blut und Boden*), and it may even be God-given as in a promised or holy land.

Typically, a real or imaginary past, conjured up from incomplete historical or ambiguous archaeological sources, is associated with the homeland; the *Heimat* becomes an *Urheimat*, an ancestral homeland from which the nationality claiming it originally sprang. The Serbs maintain a deep primordial attachment to Kosovo, likening it to their Jerusalem, because they believe that they became a people after their defeat by the Turks on the field of blackbirds in Kosovo in 1389 A.D. Another common association is the identification of the homeland with the maximum territorial extent over which a people once exercised or is thought to have exercised political control. Thus, Armenian nationalists claim eastern Anatolia as part of the Armenian homeland not just because Armenians lived there earlier this century before being killed and driven away by the Turks, but also because this land, stretching from the Mediterranean to the Black and Caspian Seas, had been unified under Tigran the Great in the 1st century B.C. when his Armenian kingdom briefly rivaled those of Rome and Parthia. Typically, this association is maximalist and anachronistic. Tigran's reign did not extend over all the areas claimed for it and it only lasted a few decades at most; his kingdom was not exclusively Armenian but multiethnic in composition, contrary to the assertions of modern nationalists. While a homeland is generally accorded a hoary antiquity, this need not be the case. America, the land of the free and the home of the brave, is defined by the political borders of the United States, a territory that has only relatively recently been annexed or conquered by the people who now consider it home. The concept here perhaps seems less mystical and less obscured by the mists of a remote past but it still evokes powerful sentiments and emotions for which Americans are willing to fight and die.

The concept of a homeland thus constitutes one of the fundamental or primordial attributes of a people. The basic difficulties with this concept are its exclusionary character and the fact that often the same land is considered home to more than one people. Germany for the Germans, Russia for the Russians, Georgia for the Georgians are dangerous political slogans, incitements to violence that are meant to cleanse the homeland of the undesirable aliens within it. Eretz Israel is the sacred homeland of the Israelis, but the same territory also represents the lost land of Palestine to the Palestinians. Kosovo is claimed by the Serbs and Albanians; Bosnia by the Serbs, Croats, and "Bosnians" themselves. The list could be extended almost indefinitely. If a home is a place of peace and harmony, a homeland frequently is not. E. Reitz's film *Heimat* (Homeland), which initially appeared as a serial on German television in the early 1980s, represents a classic example of a complex, romantically conceived homeland that still politically echoes or reverberates throughout Europe.

See also A Kaes's *From Hitler to Heimat: The Return of History as Film* (Harvard University Press, 1989).

## HRUSHEVSKY, MYKHAILO

1866–1934, Renowned Ukrainian historian and president of the Central Rada (Council) of the Ukrainian People's Republic (UNR), an independent Ukrainian government that lasted from March 1917 until February 1918. Hrushevsky was born in Kholm (now Chełm in Poland), but was raised in the Russian Caucasus near Tiflis. He moved to Kyiv for his studies, graduating from the Historical-Philological Faculty of Kyiv University in 1890 and earning a master's degree in history in 1894. During his studies at Kyiv University he was heavily influenced by Volodymyr Antonovych (1834–1908), the first historian of modern Ukraine.

In 1894 he was appointed professor to a newly created chair of Ukrainian history at L'viv University. In L'viv he was extremely active in promoting the study of Ukrainian history and culture, as well as publishing prolifically on this topic. In 1898 he cofounded the journal *Literaturno-naukovyi visnyk* (*Literary-Scientific Bulletin*), the most important forum of its time for the discussion of Ukrainian literature and politics. In 1898 he also published the first volume of his monumental *Istoriia Ukrainy-Rusy* (*History of Ukrainian-Rus*, the first volume of which was published in English in 1997). The ten volumes of this series published between 1898 and 1937 covered the history of Ukraine until 1658. This history is important in that it was the first major work of Ukrainian history, was written in Ukrainian, and was written with the purpose of providing a historical pretext for the establishment of a Ukrainian state and nation.

Hrushevsky's main argument from the history was first presented in his article "*Zvychaina skhema 'ruskoi' istorii i sprava ratsional 'noho ukladu istorii skhidn'oho slov'ianstva*" ("The Traditional Scheme of 'Russian' History and the Problem of a Rational Ordering of the His-

tory of the Eastern Slavs," published in Volume 1 of the Russian Imperial Academy of Science's *Sbornik statei po slavianovedeniia*). In this article, he traced the history of Ukraine back to Kyivan Rus (a major trading state from the 10th to 13th centuries), claimed that Ukraine is the modern descendent of Kyivan Rus (through the principalities of Galicia and Volhynia, and the Grand Duchy of Lithuania), and that Russia was simply an outpost of Kyivan Rus (much as Gaul was an outpost of Rome). Hrushevsky's claim challenged the predominant history of the time that said Russia was the descendent of Kyivan Rus. This issue is important because it provided historical legitimacy both for the Ukrainian state and the Ukrainian nation and is so politically charged that Russia and Ukraine continued to argue about the heritage of Kyivan Rus well into the 1990s.

In addition to his many writings on history and politics, Hrushevsky was also active politically. In 1899 he helped to found the National Democratic Party, whose long-term goal was the establishment of a Ukrainian state (he later joined the Ukrainian Party of Social Revolutionaries), and from 1897 to 1913 he built and led the Shevchenko Scientific Society, which was a virtual academy of sciences for Ukraine. This was the first openly pro-Ukrainian scientific society. After the Russian revolution of 1905, Hrushevsky became even more active in politics; for a period he worked with other Ukrainian nationalists in St. Petersburg. By 1908 he was the leader of the Ukrainian movement, and responsible for such acts as founding the popular Ukrainian newspaper, *Selo*, designed to appeal to the peasantry—it was closed two years later by the Russian authorities. Hrushevsky was arrested in 1914, exiled briefly to Siberia, and then allowed to live under surveillance in Moscow.

After the February 1917 Russian revolution, he was freed and returned to Kyiv. On March 17 he was elected chairman of the Central Rada. The original goal of the Central Rada was to gain autonomy for Ukraine in a democratic Russia, but as it met with widespread support and as the Russian Empire collapsed, the Rada declared independence on January 22, 1918. At this time Hrushevsky became president of Ukraine. The Central Rada remained the ruling government until April, despite Kyiv being captured by the Soviets in February 1918.

With the aid of Ukraine's new ally, Germany, the Soviets were quickly driven from Kyiv. However, the Central Rada was deposed on April 28, 1918, by the Germans for failure to provide the German army with food, and replaced by the pro-Central Power Hetmanate government of Pavlo Skoropadskyi (*hetman* is a traditional Ukrainian cossack term meaning "leader"). The hetmanate lasted until December 1918, when it was overthrown by the directory of the UNR of Symon Petliura.

After the fall of the UNR, Hrushevsky withdrew from politics and emigrated to Western Europe where he continued to seek support for Ukraine and advocate an independent Ukraine in his publications. In 1923 he was elected a full member of the All-Ukraine Academy of Sciences (VUAN). He returned to Kyiv in 1924 to become chair of modern Ukrainian history for the VUAN. Under Lenin's relatively liberal nationalities policy, Hrushevsky continued his historical work on the foundations and precedents for Ukrainian independence. By the end of the decade the political climate had changed; Stalin was not as accommodating toward the non-Russian nations as Lenin had been. Hrushevsky was increasingly criticized for promoting bourgeois Ukrainian nationalism and for not accepting official Soviet Marxist historiography. In 1929 he was forced out of the VUAN, and in March 1931 his historical section of the VUAN was closed and his students and co-workers arrested and deported. Hrushevsky was deported to Russia, where he died in 1934.

Hrushevsky's works profoundly affected Ukrainian national development. His writings on history, literature, and culture provided inspiration to all subsequent Ukrainian nationalists, and his history of Ukraine was officially adopted by the Ukrainian politburo in 1990. Because of the links Hrushevsky provided to the heritage of Kyivan Rus, after declaring independence in 1991 Ukraine adopted the Kyivan Rus symbol of the *tryzub* (trident), and in 1996 it introduced a currency named after that of Kyivan Rus, the *hryvnia*.

## HUMAN RIGHTS
The current human rights debate has its origins in a philosophical discussion (John Locke and Thomas Hobbes) concerning the existence of "rights" for individuals in society. One primary idea was that humans, because of their unique ability to reason, were born with "natural rights" meant to ensure their dignity. The concept of natural law as an extension of natural rights was criticized by both liberal and conservative philosophers in the 18th century. Many assumed that rights were constructed by men and women in a societal compact. Some conservative philosophers argued that to maintain order rights could only be granted as an extension of a sovereign state's authority. Nonetheless, arguments in favor of the "natural rights" of men were guiding principles in revolutionary movements in the United States, France, and Britain.

The dominant philosophical argument at the end of the 19th century was that men and women were not born with universal rights, and any rights they enjoyed was the result of historical acts applicable only to their community. But advocates for universal rights continued to use the concept of natural rights to agitate against national policy that discriminated against segments of the population. Examples of movements that embraced a natural rights argument include the women's suffrage movements and antislavery movements in both Europe and the United States. In effect, advocates of these movements argued that there was a "higher" law (often religious principle) than that enacted by national government.

An impassioned argument for universal rights followed World War II when people became aware of the crimes committed by Nazi Germany during the Holocaust. Faced with a state that had enacted laws to facilitate the extinction of the Jews and other ethnic groups as a German moral imperative, many responded that German state policy had to be regarded as an affront to universal norms and therefore a "crime against humanity." Even theorists who were critical of the concept of universal rights generally accepted that the collective establishment of "human rights" in the international system could be useful for preventing human suffering.

The debate over human rights has consequences with regard to nationalism in that proponents of these rights argue that their protection overrides national sovereignty when these rights are violated. Many leaders in the developing world object to human rights legislation sponsored by Western nations because they regard these acts as a potential threat to their national sovereignty. In general, these leaders argue that the use of human rights by Western leaders is a means by which the West could expand its authority in the developing world. Furthermore, many leaders in the developing world argue that if a standard of human rights is adopted worldwide it also has to incorporate retribution for past colonial practices and ensure greater equality in the current world system.

Many advocates of universal human rights stand in direct opposition to those who believe the absolute sovereignty of nation states is necessary to preserve global stability. Advocates of absolute sovereignty argue that establishing a transnational legal authority that could intervene in the affairs of sovereign states due to human rights violations is either impossible or dangerous. Those who regard the establishment of such an authority as impossible believe powerful states would dominate the process and essentially establish their standard of rights worldwide. Others believe the establishment of a transnational authority used to enforce rights is dangerous because nations would fight rather than accept the authority of an international organization.

Other critics of human rights contend that it is the role of national government to define the "rights" of individuals because rights vary according to cultural norms in each state. Therefore, any characterization of human rights as "universal" is false. Furthermore, advocates of absolute sovereignty argue that intervention in the affairs of a nation-state using a standard of human rights will, as a practical matter, only create greater instability and perhaps exacerbate ill treatment of citizens.

Despite these criticisms, the establishment of universal human rights as a standard of international behavior has become an accepted international norm. Throughout the 1990s there were a series of military interventions, sanctioned by the United Nations, into civil conflicts where human rights were being violated. In the past these actions would have been regarded as a violation of nation-state sovereignty. The United Nations (led primarily by the United States) intervened in Somalia with the goal of providing famine relief that had resulted from a prolonged civil war. This was the first time such an intervention had occurred where the parties to a conflict had not explicitly asked the UN to mediate between the parties. In 1999, NATO undertook a military campaign against Serbia to prevent the forced expulsion of the Albanian population from Kosovo. Most recently, an Australian-led international force intervened in the former Indonesian province of East Timor after the Timorese voted for formal independence under a UN-sponsored initiative.

Most human rights legislation and covenants have been negotiated in the United Nations. The primary document used to set a broad standard for international human rights is the Universal Declaration of Human Rights established by the United Nations in 1948. The declaration was not meant to be a binding treaty, but many regard the declaration as a legal standard. Some believe that it is enforceable as state law. It has also become more common for states and international organizations to link foreign policy aid and other enticements to the observation of human rights, but for the most part the protection of human rights at the national level depends on a commitment to enforcement by the individual states.

The application of international human rights law in domestic national courts is an ongoing process. One closely watched, ongoing case involves the extradition of General Augusto Pinochet to Spain from Great Britain. A Spanish court charged Pinochet, former leader of Chile, with involvement in the deaths of Spanish nationals in Chile. While the aging ex-dictator was visiting Britain, a Spanish court requested that he be extradited to stand trial in Spain. Pinochet and the Chilean government fought this extradition, and seventeen months after his arrest, he was freed. He returned to Chile on March 3, 2000. While international jurists have worked to expand the legal standing of international human rights legislation, few violations (usually war crimes) are actually tried in the international courts.

Overall, broad coalitions of groups support human rights worldwide. Many nations and international organizations now regard human rights as being increasingly important in international affairs. And some of the most effective human rights organizations have been international nongovernmental organizations (NGOs), which use publicity as a means of effecting national policy. One very effective NGO is Amnesty International, which uses the UN Declaration of Human Rights as its standard for intervention. Amnesty now conducts a wide range of activities, but is known for identifying people who have been imprisoned because of their political or religious beliefs and conducting letter writing campaigns on their behalf.

For further study the United Nations produces an annual handbook, *Yearbook on Human Rights*, which chronicles human rights violations.

**HUMANISM**   Since every Renaissance art aimed for a dominion or conquest, it was completely appropriate that science should leave its previously contemplative role and focus on the conquest of nature. Humanistic realism bespoke a comprehensively critical attitude. Indeed, the productions of early humanism constituted a manifesto of independence, at least in the secular world, from all preconceptions and all inherited programs.

Attitudes such as the significance of the individual and the idea of the dignity of man took shape in concord with a sense of personal autonomy that first was evident in Petrarch and later came to characterize humanism as a whole. An intelligence capable of critical scrutiny and self-inquiry was by definition a free intelligence; the intellectual virtue that could analyze experience was an integral part of that more extensive virtue that could, according to many humanists, go far in conquering fortune.

Intellectual individualism, which has never been popular in any church, put particular stress on a religion that encouraged simple faith and alleged universal authority. Finally, humanism repeatedly fostered the impulse of religious reform.

Petrarch and Alberti were alert to the sense of estrangement that accompanies intellectual and moral autonomy, while Niccolò Machiavelli (1469–1527) would depict, in *The Prince*, a grim world in which the individual must exploit the weakness of the crowd or fall victim to its indignities. For Machiavelli, who avowed to treat men as they were and not as they ought to be, history would become the basis of a new political science.

Finally, humanism of the Renaissance period would have two fundamental currents: one led by erudites who searched for the ideal of their times in the classics; and the second who searched for the new man by attacking medieval values.

**HUNGARIAN NATIONALISM**   Linguistic analysis indicates that the Hungarian people (or Magyars as they call themselves) can be traced to about 3500 B.C. when the Ugric tribes separated from the Finno-Ugric peoples. In 895 A.D., Magyar tribes pushed into the Carpathian Basin. The Hungarian Kingdom was founded with official papal blessing by Stephen I (István I), later the patron saint of Hungary, in 1000. While ethnic differences mattered little during the Middle Ages, the Magyars were very different from the surrounding Slavs, Germans, Romanians, and others, and this uniqueness would be critical for the development and character of Hungarian national identity. The prediction made by the father of romantic folk nationalism, Johann Gottfried von Herder, that the Magyars would eventually be absorbed by their neighbors and disappear had a harrowing effect on Hungarian nationalists who became obsessed with the possibility of national extinction. This fear largely explains the policy of "Magyarization" in the latter half of the 19th century, aimed at forcibly assimilating non-Magyars.

Austria's "liberation" of Hungary from the control of the Ottoman Empire in the late 17th century meant that the country fell under the control of the Habsburg Monarchy. While the privileges and institutions of the Hungarian nobles were largely maintained under Habsburg rule, foreign, military, and financial matters were decided in Vienna. Ottoman occupation and subsequent Austrian control had a profound impact on Hungarian culture and demographics. Although its Catholicism linked Hungary to the West, external domination during the 16th and 17th centuries in effect froze the feudal structure of Hungarian society, thus reinforcing Hungary's conservative political culture. As a result of population losses due to warfare against the Ottoman Turks, mass deportations, and an influx of non-Magyar people, the Magyars became a minority in historic Hungary (the Crownlands of St. Stephen).

During the late 1790s, Hungarian nobles overwhelmingly supported Vienna's war with the French Republic because of the danger posed to them by the potential spread of France's social revolution to Hungary. Nevertheless, nationalist ideology was introduced into Hungarian intellectual circles by the early 19th century and fundamentally transformed the concept of the *natio Hungarica* (or *populus Hungaricus*). Like other feudal societies based on the idea of "aristocratic nationalism," the upper class, regardless of ethnic affiliation, originally constituted the Hungarian nation. However, with the influx of nationalist concepts, nearly the entire bourgeoisie (largely German or Jewish), half of the aristocracy, and 20 percent of the common nobility were to be excluded from membership in the *natio Hungarica*. More threatening to the Magyar nobility was the fact that according to nationalist precepts, political rights should be extended to all Magyars, including the lower classes.

Nationalism eventually overwhelmed the resistance of the nobility and led to the war of Hungarian independence of 1848–1849, which was crushed by the Austrians, with the help of the Russian tsar. A compromise to establish the Dual Monarchy was arrived at in 1867. This divided the Habsburg empire into two legally equal parts, which possessed sovereignty over internal affairs and allowed Budapest to formulate a nationalities policy without the interference of Vienna. Although there were strong civic undertones in the 1848 rebellion and non-Magyars were promised autonomy and legal guarantees, the passage of the 1868 Nationalities Act introduced a period of Magyarization that eventually involved forced linguistic and ethnic assimilation of minority populations, though there was significant voluntary assimilation in the urban areas.

The defeat of Austria-Hungary in World War I led to the traumatic partitioning of historic Hungary and the rise of aggressive Hungarian nationalism. Under the terms of the Treaty of Trianon (June 4, 1920), the new Hungarian state constituted only 32.7 percent of the territory of historic Hungary and lost 58.4 percent of its total population to annexation by its neighbors. More than 3.2 million Hungarians, one-third of all Magyars, resided outside of Hungary under oppressive conditions, with the largest number living in Romania (1.66 million). Reuniting the Magyars of East Central Europe overwhelmed Hungary's body politic and no interwar

Hungarian government could survive without seeking justice for Hungary. In an effort to regain some of its lost territories, Hungary sided with the rising powers of fascist Italy and Nazi Germany.

Admiral Miklos Horthy, regent of Hungary, was not particularly enamored with fascism or Hitler's Nazism. Consequently, Hungary's initial involvement in World War II was cautious. By 1940, Hungary was able to acquire much of the land it had lost, but at the price of fully aligning with the Axis powers. Despite attempts to extricate itself from its German alliance during the war, Hungary was returned to its Trianon borders by the victorious Allies following World War II.

The Communist takeover of Hungary in 1949 imposed a Stalinist regime that suppressed national sentiments and prohibited discussion of the status of Magyars outside of the country. Among the major demands of the 1956 revolt against Soviet rule were the restoration of Hungarian national pride and sovereignty, and an accounting of the treatment of the Magyar diaspora. Hungarian nationalism was once again stifled after the Soviet invasion by the János Kádár regime.

The peaceful transition from Communist rule in 1989 and the election of a center-right Hungarian Democratic Forum (MDF) government in spring 1990 restored Hungarian nationalist feelings. Though not aggressive, as had been the case during the interwar period, this increase in Hungarian national pride and interest in the five million Hungarians outside of Hungary provoked concern among Hungary's neighbors; especially when Hungarian Prime Minister József Antall remarked that although he was legally the prime minister of the ten million Hungarians in Hungary, he was the prime minister of fifteen million Hungarians in feeling and spirit. Many in Hungary were afraid that the Antall government's advocacy of Hungarian national pride and the Hungarian diaspora would damage the country's chances of integration into Western political, military, and economic institutions. As a result, the MDF lost to the reformed Communists (Hungarian Socialist Party) in the 1994 parliamentary elections. The new government, headed by former foreign minister Gyula Horn, promoted a "historic reconciliation" with Hungary's neighbors based on the Trianon borders.

The future of Hungarian nationalism will likely be tied to Western integration and the growing sense of a civic and cosmopolitan conception of the nation on the European continent. Hungary's ascension into NATO and ongoing negotiations with the European Union place Hungary in the middle of these trends.

For further reading, see *Hungarians and Their Neighbors in Modern Times, 1867–1950*, Ferenc Glatz, ed.

(East European Monographs, 1995); *A History of Hungary*, Peter F. Sugar, ed. (Indiana University Press, 1990); and Jörg K. Hoensch, *A History of Modern Hungary* (Longman, 1995).

**HUSÁK, GUSTAV**  1913–1991, Lawyer, politician, statesman, president of the Czechoslovak Socialist Republic, born in Dubravka (today a part of Bratislava), Slovakia (then Austria-Hungary). Husák, a firm believer in the ideas of Communism, was best known for his leading role in the process of so-called "normalization," aimed at the consolidation of the Czechoslovak Communist Party after the 1968 Prague Spring reform.

Husák rose to prominence during World War II, when he took an active role in the 1944 Slovak national uprising. After the war, he became the chairman of the Committee of Delegates of the Slovak Government and a department head at the Central Committee of the Slovak Communist Party. During the 1954 show trials, Husák was accused of bourgeois nationalism and was imprisoned for life. In 1963 he was partly rehabilitated, and during the 1968 reforms he was appointed a deputy chairman of the government. In 1969 Husák became the first secretary of the Communist Party's Central Committee, and from 1975 until the 1989 Velvet Revolution, he was the president of Czechoslovakia.

On the whole, the role of Gustav Husák in Slovak history is controversial. Although, according to some historians, he played a positive role during World War II and in the 1960s, as the president of Czechoslovakia Husák organized crackdowns on dissidents and was instrumental in the reintegration of Czechoslovakia into the Soviet bloc. Moreover, Slovaks often complain that under his presidency Prague blossomed at the expense of Bratislava, and that he spoke Czech instead of his native Slovak language.

Among Husák's best known publications are *Zapas o zajtrašok* (*A Struggle for Tomorrow*, Bratislava: 1949), *Svedectvo o Slovenskom Narodnom Povstani* (*An Account of the Slovak National Uprising*, Bratislava: 1964), *Z bojov o dnešok: 1945–1950* (*From the Struggles for the Present: 1945–1950*, Bratislava: 1973), and *V bratskej jednote* (*In Brotherly Unity*, Bratislava: 1979). Husák's most recent biography was written by Vladimir Plevza, *Vzostupy a pady: Gustav Husak prehovoril* (*Rises and Falls: Gustav Husak Has Spoken*, Bratislava: 1991).

**HUSAYN, SHARIF**  ca. 1854–1931, Amir of Mecca, 1908–1916, king of the Hijaz, 1916–1924. Sharif Husayn gained a prominent place in the history of Arab nationalism by proclaiming the Arab revolt against the Ottoman Empire in 1916, fighting to win an independent Arab state in the Middle East. He launched the revolt after receiving what he took to be a British promise to support him as caliph of an Arab state to be established after the war in most of Ottoman Iraq, greater Syria, and Arabia. Britain's failure to do so has since been regarded by Arab nationalists as an outrageous betrayal.

It is ironic that Sharif Husayn should be so closely identified with Arab nationalism, because he showed little inclination toward it until World War I. Husayn's prestige was religious, deriving from his descent from the Prophet Muhammad. The Ottoman sultan named him amir of Mecca, in part because he had seemed reliable during his long residence in Istanbul. As amir, Husayn enjoyed some degree of autonomy, but he had to share influence in the Hijaz with a governor appointed from Istanbul. The balance of authority between amir and governor was precarious, and after 1908 Husayn campaigned vigorously against extension of the Ottoman Hijaz railway to Mecca, since it would bolster the governor's (and Istanbul's) power. In this he was successful, but Husayn could not feel secure, given the strong centralizing policies of the Young Turk government in Istanbul. Through one of his sons he asked for British support to counter pressure from Istanbul early in 1914, but even after the outbreak of war he hesitated to break with the Ottomans. A British blockade in the Red Sea, which threatened to cut off vital food and other supplies, as well as hindering Muslim pilgrims' access to Mecca and Medina, finally pushed Husayn to side with Britain. In proclaiming his revolt, he cited not Arab nationalism as the justification but rather the irreligion of the Young Turks. This was not surprising, given Husayn's previous lack of interest in Arab nationalism, and especially in light of the ethnic makeup of the Hijaz's population. It was overwhelmingly Muslim but multiethnic, including many Indians, Africans, Turks, and Berbers.

Although the evidence for considering Husayn a nationalist is thin—as it is also for deeming the Arab revolt of much importance to the defeat of the Ottoman Empire—his place in the history of Arab nationalism is secured by events both before and after his rebellion. In an exchange of letters in 1915 preparatory to the revolt, the British high commissioner in Egypt, Sir Henry McMahon, agreed to support an independent Arab caliphate covering all of the Middle East south of Anatolia and west of Iran, but excluding in effect coastal Syria, part of the Persian Gulf littoral, and wherever Britain could not act "without detriment to her Ally, France." One month after McMahon's letter, Britain and France began negotiating the secret Sykes-Picot agreement to divide Ottoman territories after the war. Sykes-Picot allowed for no completely independent Arab state outside of the Arabian peninsula. After the war Britain did not fulfill completely either Sykes-Picot or the conditions set out by McMahon, but the former took precedence over the latter. Britain agreed to the League of Nations assigning France mandates to rule Syria and Lebanon, and itself accepted similar mandates for Iraq, Palestine, and Transjordan. Although the British later made Husayn's son Faysal king of Iraq and another son, 'Abdallah, amir of Transjordan, many Arabs continue to view Britain's dealings with Husayn as duplicitous.

Sharif Husayn certainly felt the same way. He refused to accept the legitimacy of the Anglo-French domination of Iraq and greater Syria, and he broke off his alliance with Britain. Whereas 'Abdallah and Faysal became tainted by their close relationship with the British, Husayn thus secured a sounder reputation among later Arab nationalists.

Several good articles on Sharif Husayn and Arab nationalism, by William Ochsenwald and Mary Wilson, appear in *The Origins of Arab Nationalism* (Columbia University Press, 1991), edited by Rashid Khalidi. Hasan Kayali's *Arabs and Young Turks* (University of California Press, 1997) also has much information on Sharif Husayn.

## HUSSEIN, KING OF JORDAN

1935–1999, Hussein ibn Talal ibn Abdullah Al-Hashimi was born in Amman in 1935. His grandfather was the British installed king of Transjordan, which after the establishment of the state of Israel absorbed the West Bank and the Eastern Sector of Jerusalem with the holy places. King 'Abdullah was assassinated in 1951 outside of Al-Aqsa Mosque in Jerusalem by a Palestinian nationalist who, like many Palestinians, viewed King 'Abdullah as a British accessory in the loss of Palestine and the displacement of her population. King Hussein assumed the reigns of power after his mentally ill father was forced to abdicate in 1952. Hussein was sworn in as king in 1953 at the age of eighteen. He had been educated at Victoria College in Alexandria, Egypt, then at Harrow and Sandhurst in England. On assuming the mantle of leadership Hussein faced the dilemma of building a state that had survived on British financial aid, while dealing with the rise of Arab nationalism, represented at the time by the figure of Jamal Abd al-Nasser, then the embodiment of Arab nationalism for the large Palestinian population that composed the majority of the Kingdom of Jordan.

Hussein needed to survive within a domestic and regionally turbulent environment, while seeking to appease Britain and the United States at the height of the

Cold War. To appease his domestic constituency, Hussein fired the British army chief in charge of the Jordanian army in 1956 and allowed free elections to be held based on the liberal constitution established during his father's brief reign. The result returned Arab nationalist forces led by Suleyman Al-Nabulsi who in 1957 negated the Anglo-Jordanian Treaty. However, when the Nabulsi government sought to establish strong ties with the USSR and released Communist Party members from jail, Hussein dismissed the government and sought help from the United States through the Eisenhower Doctrine in 1958. This began a strong and lifelong alliance between the king and the United States. During this period of challenge by the nationalists and local Communist forces, Hussein formed an alliance with the Muslim Brotherhood against the aforementioned forces. With American and British help earlier, King Hussein was able to use the traditional bedouin tribe in the East Bank to form the core of the Jordanian army and the bulk of the public sector in Jordan. Palestinians were given free reign to work and vitalize the private sector.

The next real test for King Hussein came in June 1967 when he joined the Nasser-Syria campaign after Israel started the Six Day War. The Israeli had asked King Hussein to stay out of the conflict, but he could not for he definitely would have been branded an anti-Arab nationalist, at the cost of saving the West Bank and East Jerusalem. Hussein's own sense of Arab solidarity compelled him to join the war and in spite of losing the West Bank and East Jerusalem, he was able to survive. To ensure his continued claim over the lost areas, he embarked on a domestic and propaganda campaign for the "Unified Kingdom" to offset any challenge from the now rising tide of Palestinian nationalism embodied by the Palestine Liberation Organization (PLO), which had set up shop in Jordan's now bulging Palestinian refugee camps. King Hussein sought to appease the guerrillas by allowing them to recruit in the camps but not to launch operations against Israel from across the Jordan River. This delicate balance was not to last long. In September 1970 a civil war erupted that culminated in the expulsion of the PLO to Syria and Lebanon. From 1973 to 1983 Jordan enjoyed a period of prosperity as a result of the rise in oil prices and the Lebanese civil war, which started in 1976, ushering in an era of investments in the kingdom. Moreover, Jordanian labor was in demand in the Gulf region as a result of the oil boom.

After Egypt had signed a peace treaty with Israel at Camp David in 1979, the Reagan administration in 1982 approached Hussein to be the Palestinian representative in a similar peace treaty with Israel, to the exclusion of the PLO who had been defeated and expelled from Lebanon, in what was then known as the Jordanian option. During this period, King Hussein sought to mold some form of a national consensus about Jordanian national identity that was to be composed of East Bank Jordanians and the Palestinians who became refugees after the wars of 1948 and 1967. However, his attempts to build this consensus were dashed when the Palestinian uprising, known as the *intifada,* started in the West Bank, Gaza Strip, and East Jerusalem in December 1987. This clear manifestation of Palestinian nationalism forced King Hussein to cut his legal and administrative ties with the West Bank, even though he never submitted this measure to Parliament for ratification. This has left the door open for him and his successors to continue to play a role in shaping the fate of the Palestinian-Israeli Peace Process and especially control over the Muslim holy places of the Noble Sanctuary and Al-Aqsa Mosque. More importantly, King Hussein also sought to dispel right-wing Israeli assertions that "Jordan is Palestine." But his attempts to foster Jordanian nationalism among the East Bank Jordanians faced a severe test in April 1989.

As the 1980s were coming to an end, Jordan faced an increasing economic and fiscal crisis, and under pressure from the IMF and the World Bank was forced to engage in budget cuts especially in the public sector, where many East Bank Jordanians are employed. As the government decided to raise the price of fuel, cigarettes, and other basic commodities, riots broke out in Ma'an in the southern part of Jordan, which had traditionally been a stronghold of the monarchy. Facing a serious challenge to the legitimacy of his government, since he was popular with the mass public as the father of the nation, King Hussein declared that Jordan would have free elections in November of that year. The result of the first elections was a strong showing for the Muslim Brotherhood who had used their charitable organizational structure over the years to build a base of support among both Palestinian refugees and East Bank Jordanians on the basis of an Islamic identity. With the Jordanian public feeling the vigor of their first free elections since 1957, the Jordanian street was swept by the euphoria of Arab nationalism when Saddam Hussein invaded and occupied Kuwait and then demanded linkage between his withdrawal from Kuwait and the Palestinian–Israeli conflict. Riding the wave of public support for Saddam, King Hussein sought to find an Arab solution to the crisis but was vehemently opposed by the Bush administration and labeled as pro-Saddam. This further hurt Jordan's relations with the Gulf Arab states, particularly Kuwait and Saudi Arabia. However, his estrangement from the United States would not last long given his vital role in any peace process. When the Madrid peace process was initiated by the United States to find a solution for the Palestinian–Israeli dispute, Jordan and the Palestinians formed a symbolic joint delegation. But once Yasser Arafat had his Oslo Accord with the Israelis, King Hussein quickly followed suit and signed a peace agreement with Israel in 1994. Later King Hussein sought warm relations with the Jewish state to the public opposition of his constituency, which were against any normalization with Israel. It was revealed that King Hussein has had secret dealings with the Israelis during his tenure in office. One of his final acts was to help the Clinton administration at the Wye Accords in 1998. While he was receiving chemotherapy treatment for his leukemia, he helped to strike a deal between Yasser Arafat and the Likudist Prime Minister Benjamin Netanyahu. King Hussein died on February 7, 1999, in Amman, and his funeral was attended by close to fifty heads of states including President Clinton.

## HUSSEIN, SADDAM

1937–, President of Iraq. Hussein was born on April 28, 1937, in Takrit, a Sunni small town on the Tigris River. His family consisted of landless peasants who did not care much to have Saddam educated, especially since his natural father had died prior to Saddam's birth. His stepfather, an abusive and illiterate man, al-Haj Ibrahim al-Hassan, forced the young Saddam to steal livestock and chickens from their neighbors. Disappointed with his inability to get an education, Saddam decided to slip away and move in with his uncle Khairallah Talfah, who had been involved in the Rashid Ali uprising against British colonial rule in Iraq in 1941. As a result, Khairallah was dismissed from the army and imprisoned, which embittered him against the British and the British-sponsored Hashemite Monarchy. Saddam learned his extreme nationalism from his ultranationalist uncle, making the young Saddam predisposed to becoming involved in the turbulent politics of Iraq during his high school education in Baghdad. Saddam was unable to finish his high school education in Iraq as a result of involvement in a failed assassination attempt against the then Iraqi President Abdul Karim Qassem who had overthrown the monarchy in 1958, being allied with the Ba'th Party in which Saddam was now a member. Having escaped capture by Qassem's security and finding refuge in Syria, Saddam moved to Cairo, where he finished his high school education at the age of twenty-four. In Cairo, Saddam admired and absorbed Nasser's nationalist ideology and its anti-Western, anti-Israeli rhetoric.

In 1963, Ba'th Party military officers overthrew and executed Qassem. Saddam was by now a militant activist on behalf of the party. When the Iraqi president, Abd Al-Salam Aref, decided to end his alliance with the Ba'th Party, Aref dismissed the Ba'thi members from

within the government and the leadership structure, and imprisoned many of them including Saddam Hussein. During his two-year imprisonment, Saddam resumed the law studies he had started in Cairo. He managed to escape from jail in 1966 and went underground and worked to reorganize the Ba'th Party in a highly secretive and tightly knit revolutionary organization. During these underground years Saddam also laid down the ideas for the various secret security services and militia that were to become the hallmark of his power structure down the line. Moreover, a fellow Takriti high-ranking military officer, Ahmad Hassan al-Bakr, took Saddam under his wing. When al-Bakr overthrew the Aref regime in 1968, he declared himself as president, prime minister, and commander in chief of the Iraqi armed forces. In 1969, al-Bakr appointed Saddam his vice-president and deputy chairman of the Revolutionary Command Council (RCC), the actual ruling body in Iraq from then on. During the 1970s, Saddam organized and made operative his plans for the various security services to consolidate Ba'thi rule in Iraq, while fighting an American/Iranian-backed Kurdish insurgency in northern Iraq, led by Mulla Mustafa Barzani. Saddam used the revenue from the nationalized Iraqi oil company and the subsequent increase in oil prices from 1973 to purchase weapons from the USSR and France to put down the insurgency. The Kurdish revolt was put down brutally and without any mercy for the Kurdish population, after which Saddam reached an agreement in 1975 to divide Shatt Al-Arab Waterway between the two countries, in return for the shah of Iran ending his support for the Kurdish revolt.

In 1979, Saddam was opposed to a union that al-Bakr had instigated with Syria in 1978, so he ushered al-Bakr out of power under the pretext of ill health and old age. When Saddam took over all of al-Bakr titles, he carried out a purge similar to that of Stalin in which he executed all high-ranking members of the Ba'th Party he distrusted or perceived to be allied with Syria. He proceeded to establish himself as the undisputed leader of Iraq with total control over the military and every aspect of Iraqi life. Saddam used his Takriti family ties to consolidate his control further within the RCC and the military establishment.

After the shah was overthrown by the Islamic Revolution led by Ayatollah Khomeini in Iran in 1979, Saddam was denounced as an infidel and an agent of Western imperialism. Saddam used the threat of a Shi'ite inspired revolt among Iraq's Shia majority population to first execute the leading Shia cleric in Iraq and his sister and then invaded Iran in September 1980. Saddam presented himself as the heroic Arab leader standing up to the Persians in defense of the Arab Gulf monarchies. He also used the Iran–Iraq War as a mechanism to initiate Iraqi nationalism by manipulating the symbols from Iraq's ancient past and the Mesopotamian, Assyrian, and Arab past and to legitimize his autocratic rule. When the First Gulf War ended in a draw, Saddam declared it a victory for Iraq and built an "arch of victory" modeled after his own arms and hands. In spite of Iraq's huge financial and human losses, Saddam by the end of the war had amassed a large well-trained army and highly sophisticated military industrial research program. Yet he needed more funds to finance what he perceived to be Iraq's natural role of leadership and dominance in the Gulf region and the Arab East after the decline of the former Soviet Union.

When the price of oil plummeted to $11 dollars per barrel due to Kuwait and the United Arab Emirates extending their OPEC quota, Saddam used the loss of revenue to invade and occupy Kuwait on August 2, 1990. The United States led an international coalition and drove the Iraqi forces out of Kuwait, but President George Bush stopped short of overthrowing Saddam Hussein. The United Nations imposed economic and other sanctions on Iraq as a result of its invasion and subsequent to its defeat after the war. When the shia and then the Kurds revolted against Saddam's rule, Bush failed to rally to their support and Saddam used his Republican Guard and helicopters to suppress the uprising. He remains in power in spite of the crippling sanctions that have devastated the Iraqi economy and caused inhuman and endless suffering for the Iraqi population.

**HYPERNATIONALISM**   As a term coined by John J. Mearsheimer in the article "Why We Will Soon Miss the Cold War" (1990), *hypernationalism* refers to a belief "that other nations or nation-states are both inferior and threatening" when compared to one's own nation. It is a form of extreme nationalism that will bring out destructive results and is perhaps the single greatest threat to peace, according to Mearsheimer. Nationalism can be taken as a synonym for "love of country." But hypernationalism nurtures extremist feeling of one's own country by viewing other nations or nation-states as rivals or enemies. It is a construction of "unreal communities" that nation-states compete with each other and one's survival depends on the defeat of others.

Hypernationalism found its fertile soil in the European states since most of them were nation-states composed of people from a single ethnic group who might imagine their nation to be under constant threat from other states. In a world of no peace, other ethnicities or nationalities were not supplementary cultures or traditions forming a neighborhood, but instead the bedrock for rivalry. The teaching of self-exculpating or self-glorifying history was a force of trouble to articulate hypernationalism. However, hypernationalism can only be sustained under a military system of mass armies. To mobilize mass participation, nation-states had to appeal to extreme nationalist sentiments that created senses of self-sacrifice for "love, and then defense of the country." Hypernationalism declined drastically in Europe after 1945 when the armed race was over and the world order entered the new era of the Cold War.

# I

**ICELANDIC NATIONALISM**  The Republic of Iceland has been an independent country since 1944 and was formerly part of the Kingdom of Denmark. Unlike the nationalist struggles of many other nations, Icelandic independence was achieved in a series of constitutional arrangements and without violent confrontations. The rhetorical strength of the Icelandic nationalist movement of the 19th century was largely based on the glorification of Iceland's period of medieval independence, from its settlement by Norsemen in the early 10th century until union with Norway in 1262–1264. When Norway was incorporated with Denmark under the Union of Kalmar treaty, the Norwegian territories of Iceland, the Faroe Islands, and Greenland became *de jure* Danish provinces in 1397. Although the Danish-Norwegian union was dissolved in 1814, the former Norwegian territories remained under Danish sovereignty.

After union with Norway, Iceland retained its medieval law code and substantial authority over its internal affairs. Gradually, however, the center of power shifted to Copenhagen, especially during the 17th century, after the establishment of the absolute monarchy in 1660 and the introduction of Danish monopoly trade in 1602. The latter act was a particular point of criticism for leaders of the Icelandic nationalist movement, such as Jón Sigurðsson and Tómas Sæmundsson, who drew on classical liberal notions of free trade to argue that the nation's poverty could be blamed on its exploitation by foreign merchants. The monopoly was partially lifted in 1787 and fully in 1854, but trade remained dominated by Danes until the latter half of the 19th century.

From the beginning, Icelandic nationalism was heavily influenced by liberal developments in Copenhagen and by Johann Herder's theory of a national spirit, particularly as it was studied by Icelandic university students in Copenhagen including Sigurðsson and Sæmundsson. In the 1830's, when consultative assemblies for various parts of the Danish Kingdom were convened, Icelandic nationalists successfully lobbied King Christian VIII: for reestablishment of the medieval Althing as the representative assembly. In 1848, following the revolutionary developments elsewhere in Europe, the absolutist monarchy was abandoned and Iceland was promised a constitution. A period of complex legal negotiations followed, resulting in the enactment of the Status Law of 1871 and a new constitution in 1874, at the celebration of the 1000-year anniversary of Icelandic settlement. The constitution, however, was deeply unsatisfactory to Icelandic nationalists, because it defined Iceland as an inseparable part of the Danish realm and the newly established ministry for Iceland was in fact held by the Danish minster for justice as a sideline. Although legislation could not be enforced in Iceland without the agreement of the Althing, the situation appeared to nationalists as though Icelandic affairs were still directed from Copenhagen.

Home rule was granted in 1903–1904, and the Icelandic minister for domestic affairs, appointed by the Althing, resided in Reykjavík. In the meantime, other developments in Denmark paved the way for full Icelandic independence. After the defeat of Germany in World War I, the Danes made a claim for the return of the Danish-speaking territories in Schleswig. Icelandic nationalists were quick to apply Danish arguments about the identity of language, spirit, and people to their own nation, and the Copenhagen government was in no position to dispute them. In 1918 a treaty made Iceland a separate state in a personal union with the Danish Kingdom, giving the citizens of each country equal rights. This treaty could be terminated by either country after twenty-five years, and effectively ended the nationalist struggle, since most people simply waited for the treaty to expire before establishing a republic in 1944.

Simply because the Icelandic nationalist struggle was conducted peaceably and resolved by legalistic solutions, one should not reach the conclusion that feelings of hostility and oppression were not strong among Icelanders. Sigurdsson and the other nationalists accused the Danes of oppression and exploitation of their country, pointing to the poverty of Iceland as compared to Denmark and the other parts of the kingdom as evidence of Danish profiteering at their expense. When Iceland was free, in its period of medieval independence, the population had been more numerous and the country richer. Evidence of this state was preserved in the Icelandic medieval texts, especially in the family sagas, which portrayed a prosperous country where the Icelandic heroes gave elaborate feasts, owned expensive weapons and clothing, and were received with honor at the courts of kings. Although such pictures are hardly an accurate picture of everyday life in 10th-century Iceland, they were widely believed in the 19th century. Nationalists compared these accounts with the impoverished state of Iceland as it was represented in the reports of the Danish land commissions of the late 18th century, when the combined effects of volcanic eruptions, harsh winters, famine, and technological underdevelopment drove the population down to levels below those of the settlement period. To blame this condition purely on Danish management was certainly unfair, but it was rhetorically powerful at its time.

As this reasoning suggests, a major weapon of the Icelandic nationalists was the argument for Icelandic cultural uniqueness. Only Iceland had produced the cultural treasure of the family sagas, they argued, and thus the Danish possession of all the manuscripts at the Royal Library in Copenhagen was a sore point of Danish–Icelandic relations. After full independence was achieved, Icelandic academics began lobbying for the return of the manuscripts. This claim caused heated debate, and when the Danish Parliament agreed to authorize the transfer in 1965, the decision was greeted by Danish student protests and the flag at the Royal Library being flown at half-mast. Thirty-two years later, when the transfer was finally completed, however, it was noted with little fanfare and the issue had long since become moot. Similarly, while it was possible to read Icelandic children's textbooks in the decades after World War II about the centuries of Danish oppression, today most Icelandic historians agree that it is unlikely that Iceland was any worse off economically under Danish rule than it would have been otherwise. The Icelandic nationalist struggle, although lengthy and passionately fought, is no longer politically relevant to the Icelandic relationship with its former colonial ruler.

**IDENTITY** Identity refers to an individual's location in the social world. It involves ideas about who we are and how we relate to others. We can distinguish between two broad categories of identity: individual and collective. The former refers to our sense of that which makes each of us unique; it involves a perception of "I." The latter pertains to our identification with others; it implies a sense of "we." Although they are interrelated, it is the notion of collective identity that is most pertinent with respect to nationalism. A "nation" can be thought of as a sense of peoplehood: an "us" that stands in opposition to other nations. As such it is a type of collective identity. To be part of a nation implies notions of unity and common interest.

We must note that identities are not simply given, rather they are continually constructed and reconstructed through interaction with others. We may think of identity as a process that evolves and changes over time. My identity as a sociologist does not mean the same thing today as it did two years ago nor will it carry the same connotations two years in the future. Likewise, an ethnic or national identity such as Frisian, Pakistani, Croat, or Tutsi is mutable and changes with time and place. To be Somali in Italy may be a far different thing than to be Somali in Somalia; to be German in 1999 may be quite unlike being German in 1939.

Identities cannot be defined in isolation. They only have meaning in comparison to other identities. In essence, they are defined as much by what they are not as by what they are. The creation of an identity implies a sense of separateness as well as a sense of unity. To hold a collective identity requires both an "us" and a "them." The notion of an "other" is imperative. Forming a collective identity necessitates the construction of boundaries as well as membership. The individual must develop both a sense of sameness (to those who share the identity) and difference (from those who do not). For example, the concept of aboriginal nationality among Inuit groups in Canada requires not just a recognition of ethnic commonality but also a shared sense of opposition to and difference from an "English Canadian" or "Quebecois" identity.

In a related vein, recognition by others is an important element of identity. Power and autonomy may rest, at least in part, on the legitimacy conferred by others. "Identity politics" are therefore necessarily social phenomena. The ability of the Ojibwe or the Lakota to sue the U.S. government over breaches of treaty rights relies on the recognition of Native American identities by the courts. Similarly the gay rights movement is predicated on the public recognition of "homosexual" as an identity. Without such recognition, actions have no political meaning.

Identity should be conceptualized as multilayered. Each of us embraces a number of identities, the salience of which changes with the situations in which we find ourselves. A person living in the United States may hold an American identity when discussing international politics, think of herself as Catholic on Sunday morning, and identify with her Dutch ancestry while watching the World Cup. Sometimes these identities may coexist quietly, at other times they may compete with one another. As an example, an Indian Muslim might find his national and communal identities at odds with one another during a period of strife between Pakistan and India.

Excellent discussions of the importance of identity on politics can be found in *Social Theory and the Politics of Identity,* edited by Craig Calhoun (Blackwell, 1994). Identity plays a key role in many types of social movements, from those promoting feminism to those proclaiming nationalist sentiments. For quality overviews of the role of identity in movements see *New Social Movements: From Ideology to Identity,* edited by Enrique Laraña, Hank Johnston, and Joseph Gusfield (Temple University Press, 1994) or *Social Movements and Culture,* edited by Hank Johnston and Bert Klandermans (University of Minnesota Press, 1995).

## IMPERIALISM

The stage of capitalism characterized by accumulation on a world scale and the acquisition of colonies under a centralized imperial ruling nation, country, or group is described as imperialism. This system creates inequalities and power differences between nations and national groupings within societies.

The theory of imperialism was initially articulated by V. I. Lenin in the Marxist conception of periodized capitalism. Lenin outlined the five main characteristics of 20th century imperialism as (1) the export of capital, (2) centralized production, (3) merged banking and industrial capital, (4) division of the world into spheres of influence, and (5) capitalist redivision of the world. He predicted that imperialism was the highest and last stage of capitalism.

Twentieth-century imperialist penetration of less powerful countries and regions by more powerful, industrial nations has occurred through the process of colonization. The colonial relationship is usually initiated by the forced entry of an imperialist power into a nation. The imperialist power uses military, economic, political, and cultural means to arrest the independent development of the colonized country and produce dependent and subordinate relations. This process results in the division of the world into spheres of influence and differential levels of power, resources, and prestige on a global scale. There is a fundamental contradiction between the imperialist interests and those of the colonized nation.

Anti-imperialist movements and revolutions reached their height in the mid-20th century. Their efforts have been focused on achieving national liberation and political independence from the colonizing country. This is usually followed by attempts at economic independence, self-sufficiency, and, in many cases, the development of socialist economic relations.

## INDIAN NATIONALISM

In the post-Cold War world, ethnic violence is an ominous specter. Talk of an end to nationalism is now almost forgotten, as brutal intercommunal warfare broke out in the disintegrating Yugoslavia, in the collapsed Soviet Empire, and in Africa and Asia. As central governments in many countries become weakened or nonexistent, and as political leaders or parties see benefit in fueling or exploiting ethnic unrest, groups in many countries are more willing to use force to achieve political objectives. In India, this has prevented the emergence of a unified Indian nation since 1947. It has also distracted its leaders and made it more difficult for the world's second most populous country to have the kind of influence that would befit a land of almost a billion inhabitants.

Nationalism in a large nation like India is insufficiently strong to prevent communal violence. When ethnic or communal tensions within a multinational state become violent, it is primarily because political leaders or organizations have chosen to exploit them for their own purposes. There are innumerable causes for such tensions: the will to unify separated ethnic groups, to undo forced deportation or the effects of migration into one's territory, territorial claims, linguistic disputes, conflicting religious and ideological beliefs, discrimination, and many more.

The motives for political actors to manipulate these problems also vary. They include their own material interests, the usefulness of scapegoats to explain policy failures, strong ideological or religious convictions, or simply the desire to maximize their votes in elections. Animosity can be intensified by ethnic stereotyping, which attributes special traits of intelligence, character, and personality to members of ethnic groups. Communities can feel that their physical safety, language, or culture is threatened or that they suffer from widespread and persistent discrimination. Enhanced political mobilization, the process by which individuals become players in the political arena, creates conditions for groups to organize more effectively along communal lines. This process is facilitated by improvements in mass communications and transportation.

The possibility that demands would lead to violent conflict is especially great in polyethnic societies such as India. Because a huge heterogeneous state like India lacks adequate institutional means for expressing ethnic grievances effectively, groups are more likely to resort to force to express their demands. In response, governments tend to adopt coercive strategies that prove to be counterproductive.

While all of the above play a role in creating the conditions for conflicts, political leaders' decisions to exploit them are almost always a prerequisite for transforming them into actual violence. Arguments based on "ancient hatreds" since "time immemorial" absolve leaders, governments, and political organizations from responsibility for atrocities and at the same time assign blame to enflamed, emotional masses. They assume that history is more than a mere context for human actions and actually has some kind of volition of its own. They also ignore significant historical facts, such as peaceful Hindu and Moslem interaction in India for centuries and their common cause during the nationalist struggle against British rule.

An examination of the ethnic or communal tensions in India reveals the lack of an overarching Indian national identity. It also elucidates some of the causes of conflict and especially the effect that political leadership can have on either preventing serious disagreements from ending in violence or in fanning the tensions in such an irresponsible way that bloodshed is likely. It is a relatively new independent state in its present form: India gained its independence from Britain in 1947. Long rule by outsiders left a legacy of resentment. Tension exists between the majority group and minority groups (Moslems) with family and cultural ties to a powerful neighboring country (Pakistan) that takes a keen interest in the treatment of this minority. This means that the loyalty of those minorities to India remains suspect in some people's minds. Finally, the leaders of the various communities have considerable influence on their constituencies. Community leaders in India are increasingly inclined to exploit communal hatreds for political gain.

India is a huge country with 960 million people and twenty-five states so large and different that they could be big countries in their own right. The population mix is complex, with about 85 percent Hindu, 12 percent Moslem, 2 percent Sikh, and 2 percent Christian. There are flash points at all extremities, with important external linkages: in Kashmir in the north, among Tamils in the south, and among Mongoloid peoples in the northeast. Scores of different languages are spoken, seventeen of which are declared "official" and one of which—English—is an indispensable *lingua franca*.

The world's largest democracy, India offers political avenues for groups to voice their grievances. This expansion of democracy is difficult to manage in such a large complicated country. Not only religious-oriented communities, but also groups representing the interests of untouchables (now called "Dalits") and backward castes (all of which enjoy official privileges in university placement and state employment) and upper-caste Indians who resent those privileges have become more assertive in the political process. The multilayered caste system of class and occupation has become somewhat less rigid and relevant in urban areas, where only 30 percent of the population lives. But it is still strong in rural India and significantly defines the country's mainly Hindu society. Half the population is illiterate, and many Indians have little formal education despite the legal requirement to go to school.

Despite Mahatma Gandhi's example of nonviolence, India has experienced much bloodshed in recent decades. Its independence in 1947 was the result of a long national struggle against British rule. Freedom was followed by partition, massive dislocation of people, and as many as two million deaths. A half-century later India is wracked by small wars, from caste conflict in Bihar and tribal insurgencies in the northeast to periodic fighting with Pakistani soldiers or guerrillas in Kashmir. All this diminishes any coherent all-Indian national identity. India has failed to create this although there is no dispute over who is an Indian citizen. Because both India and Pakistan entered the ranks of the nuclear powers in May 1998, an impressive achievement applauded by nationalists and ordinary citizens in both countries, their warfare against each other is of graver international concern. Except in Kashmir, there is no significant foreign pressure on Indians to accommodate various groups' aspirations peacefully.

Conflicts in India often involve religious beliefs. When morality is inserted into a controversy, participants tend to be less compromising and tolerant. Deep religious differences also create international friction between India and Pakistan. They thereby contribute to India's most dangerous security threat, made worse by the mutual acquisition of nuclear weapons in 1998. The word "ethnic" is seldom used. In India frictions are labeled "communal" because they involve communities identified by religious differences. Most Hindus, Moslems, Sikhs, Christians, and members of other communities in India are of the same race. Strictly speaking, it would be misleading to call their conflicts "ethnic." The term "communal conflict" came from British colonial analyses of religious conflicts. It has been broadened to describe any violent conflict or repression that is aimed at communities on the basis of ethnic, racial, or language issues, not just religion.

Although the Indian subcontinent has known much violence during the past few millennia, only in the past 100 years or so have differences between Hindus and Moslems dominated public life. Since the 1970s, diverse conflicts between Hindus and Sikhs have also crystallized into a communal struggle. Most Sikhs had not demanded a separate homeland in 1947 and now form the majority in the state of Punjab. Hindu extremists increasingly target Christians, whose proselytizing they resent.

The British share responsibility for the hardening of communal lines. In precolonial times caste, occupational, and locality differences were of much greater importance in Indian minds than their identities as either Hindu or Muslim. That changed somewhat after the British came. For census and official record-keeping purposes, they categorized various groups in religious terms. When they sought in 1909 to mollify nationalist demands, they introduced a limited franchise to Indians. But because Indians were required to vote within their Muslim or non-Muslim communities in order to acquire some political representation, these community distinctions were hardened, and their sense of a common Indian identity weakened.

British colonial politics after the 1920s established communal quotas, representation, and electorates in a kind of communally structured federal system. Artificially created, these distinctions derived strength from a divergence of social habits and widened to become the basis of communalism. Over time dangerous communal ideologies and perceptions took shape.

The Congress movement had understood itself to be secular and open to all religious groups, but it was supported mainly by Hindus. When the dialogue between it and the Muslim League broke down completely in the final years of British rule, partition into the two states of Pakistan and India seemed in 1947 to be the only solution. The worst killing frenzy and population shifts known to the Indian subcontinent in modern times were the consequences. They left bitter memories in the minds of Hindus and Moslems. Novelist Gita Mehta lamented: "Non-violence may have expelled the British from India, but our first lesson in freedom was the violence of Partition."

Muslims were reduced from one-fourth to one-sixth of India's population, and many Hindus regarded them as aliens loyal to a foreign enemy. This attitude hardened in the wake of an Indian–Pakistani war in 1965, India's involvement in the Bangladesh breakaway from Pakistan in 1971, and an interminable dispute with Pakistan over Kashmir. Hindu revivalism's tendency to dress itself up as Indian nationalism does not help the situation.

After independence India's new leaders in the Congress Party, above all Jawaharlal Nehru, tried to build a single nation. They went about that task by attempting to separate religion from public life and to guarantee minorities that their religious faith would have no relevance to their rights as citizens. They attempted to contain Hindu communal assertiveness and to guide it into nation-building activity. They hoped that this secularism would hold a very heterogeneous Indian society together. That attempt succeeded for several decades.

Free India created a regime committed to secularism and democracy and adopted a constitution that promised everybody equal treatment before the law, regardless of caste or community. The Congress Party, which ruled India most of the time for over four decades, initially supported these principles. Until the death of Prime Minister Nehru in 1964, India remained largely free of major communal riots. But conservative religious organizations persisted in giving a communal twist to political discussions, and rioting flared up again in the late 1960s. During the 1970s, communally oriented politics got a boost from the electoral decline of the Congress Party.

The destruction of the 16th-century Babur Mosque in the city of Ayodhya in 1992 demonstrated most tragically the inclination of central and district governments and of armed forces and police to show partisanship in communal conflicts, either by meddling or by failing to protect victims. For more than a century some Hindus had claimed that this holy site, located in the midst of a cluster of Hindu temples, had been built on the birthplace of the god-king Rama. To avoid religious clashes, it had been padlocked for a half century. But fishing for votes, Prime Minister Rajiv Gandhi went to the site and promised to bless India with a Rama government. Hindu revivalist parties, such as the Bharatiya Janata Party (BJP) and the more radical Shiv Sena party (whose name refers to the sword of a 17th-century Hindu warrior who defeated Moslem armies) in the state of Maharashtra, made the temple the central election issue. On December 6, 1992, they organized the "spontaneous" destruction of the temple by a mob of 300,000 Hindu extremists (called *kar sevaks*). The police force looked on passively. The next day, while Ayodhya's Moslem community was being systematically attacked by Hindu mobs, the BJP member of parliament from Ayodhya stated: "We thank the state and district administration, the Uttar Pradesh Police and the PAC for giving us all the help we needed to complete our mission."

The destruction of the temple and the violence that followed in a number of Indian cities touched off the worst unrest that Bombay (renamed Mumbai) had experienced since partition. When outraged Muslims and proponents of a secular India demonstrated in the streets, they were met by determined police and Hindu counterattacks. For a week, the city was shut down in fear, as police and Muslims battled. A month later it was again rocked by a series of bombings and mob violence that killed more than 1000 persons, most of them Muslims. The police did not impede Hindus.

The violence after Ayodhya changed the daily life of communities in many parts of India for the worst and helped raise communal conflict to unprecedented levels in the 1990s. Effective international pressure on Indian governments at various levels to observe human rights is largely absent. Improved communications can turn local disputes (which are always involved in Indian riots) into national ones. Weakened central governments of wobbly coalitions cannot protect victims. The splintering of Indian politics makes control over police forces, local administrations, and militant allies more difficult.

No one party dominates political life any longer. Only Congress and the BJP are national parties. Decentralization reflects the fact that India has become more democratic. An increasing number of Indians participate in the political process. Small parties that are based on regional, religious, or lower caste interests are crucial for forging a coalition in New Delhi. For example, the BJP government reelected in October 1999 was a shaky coalition of twenty-four parties Almost all parties, except Congress and the Communists, would now accept it as an ally in New Dehli.

Nehru's attempt to build a single nation has failed in recent years. With the political center in New Delhi becoming weaker and the party system more fractured, political groups have claimed religious sanction for their aggressive actions in a rough-and-tumble electoral environment.

In conclusion, India's founders and the Congress Party intended to create a secular Indian nation under a rule of law. However, religion and politics have not remained separate, and a sturdy Indian national identification that can overcome community differences has not been developed. As politics has become more fragmented and decentralized, political leaders have in-

creasingly entered the volatile arena of community conflicts in order shore up or enlarge their support. World public opinion does not provide an effective check on the treatment of minorities in India. There is small wonder that a saddened Gita Mehta asked in 1997: "Whatever happened to India's proud pluralism? Whatever happened to non-violence?"

**INDONESIAN NATIONALISM**  The Republic of Indonesia (Republica Indonesia) is the largest and most populous country in Southeast Asia and consists of a long archipelago of islands at the juncture between Asia and Oceana. It was colonized by the Netherlands and known as the Dutch East Indies. After a brief period of Japanese occupation (1942–1945), Indonesia proclaimed its independence, although it was not actually achieved until 1949.

Sporadic uprisings against foreign rule prior to the 20th century were unsuccessful (e.g., the Padri War and the Java War) and 20th-century nationalism began as more of a cultural than a political movement. In 1908 a retired Javanese doctor named Wahidin Sudirohusodo founded a society he called *Budi Utomo* ("High Endeavor"). The purpose of the organization was not to foment a populist rebellion but to create an élitist cultural movement that would accommodate traditional culture and the modern world. A popular movement called the *Sarekat Islam* ("Islamic Association") was created in 1912 and grew rapidly under the charismatic leadership of Said Tjokroaminoto.

By the end of World War I a variety of nationalist organizations existed and the colonial government responded to growing unrest by creating a People's Council (*Volksraad*) composed of appointed and elected representatives of the three racial divisions acknowledged by the government: Dutch, Indonesian, and "foreign Asiatic." The council was more of a debating society than an actual government, however, and some nationalist leaders refused to participate in it.

Internal conflict among the nationalists peaked when the Sarekat Islam expelled its Communist members and an independent Indonesian Communist Party (Partai Komunis Indonesia, or PKI) intensified its opposition to colonial rule. Its campaign culminated in unsuccessful revolts in Java in 1926 and western Sumatra in 1927.

The Indonesian Nationalist Association, later the Indonesian Nationalist Party (Partai Nasional Indonesia, PNI), was formed under the leadership of Sukarno, who was arrested in 1929. The PNI dissolved and reformed as Partindo, which tried to mobilize a mass movement less dependent on a leadership constantly subject to arrest. The nationalist movement encountered a foreign power again in the 1940s, this time not the Dutch colonialists but the Japanese.

Rather than confront the new power, nationalist leader Sukarno chose accommodation and welcomed the Japanese as an Asian power that would counter the European colonialists. The Japanese made him their chief adviser and co-opted him for their own purposes as much as possible. After the Japanese defeat and withdrawal, as well as unsuccessful attempts by the Dutch to regain their former colony, the Indonesians finally obtained their independence on December 27, 1949.

The Indonesians had traded a foreign despot for a local one, however, and Sukarno moved to dismantle the democratic process by implementing what he called "Guided Democracy," which sometimes pitted the military and the PKI against each other to his advantage. He engaged in various flamboyant policies and personal practices, identified Indonesia's future with hostility to the West, and was deposed in a bloody coup in 1965. Suharto, head of the army, who banned the PKI and kept Sukarno under house arrest until his death in 1970, replaced him.

Suharto's regime moved quickly to rebuild bridges burned by Sukarto. Ending a serious confrontation with Malaysia and rejoining the United Nations, Indonesia also became a major leader in the Association of Southeast Asian Nations (ASEAN). Although very successful economically, the Suharto government had to deal with widespread social changes that destabilized the country's social order and gave rise to new nationalist groups within the nations borders, for example, among the Chinese, and to some opposition from Islamic groups.

Perhaps the most difficult trial resulted from Indonesia's 1975 military occupation of the territory of neighboring East Timor with its own nationalist movement. The leaders of the movement, José Ramos-Horta and Bishop Carlos Belo, received the Nobel Peace Prize in 1996 for their efforts, which began to bear fruit for the East Timor nationalists as the region appeared to move toward autonomy in 1999.

Suharto himself became increasingly unpopular among the Indonesian populace and was removed from office by a popular uprising in 1998.

**INDUSTRIAL REVOLUTION**   The introduction of new production techniques led to the Industrial Revolution, which began in Great Britain during the second half of the 18th century and spread throughout much of Europe and the United States during the following decades. Developments in metallurgy, textile production,

and steam technology resulted in great socioeconomic changes. The mechanization and concentration of weaving and spinning in large urban mills, for instance, provided new employment opportunities for people in overpopulated rural areas that that led to the migration of workers and their families to fast-growing cities.

This first phase of industrialization was followed during the late 19th and early 20th centuries by what is often referred to as the Second Industrial Revolution. The increasing use of electricity, the development of steel, and the emergence of mass production along Taylorist and Fordist lines marked this second phase.

These two overlapping historical-economic developments had a dramatic impact on the formation of clearly demarcated nation-states. First, the advent of industrialism meant that societies affected by this phenomenon were becoming more homogeneous, due to the development of transport infrastructures, rapid urbanization, and the spread of mass-produced commercial and cultural commodities.

More importantly, states were becoming increasingly interested in controlling and fostering industrial output, in large part to improve their military power and hence their geopolitical standing. This was particularly the case for late-developing countries. Whereas the Industrial Revolution in Britain and the United States occurred with little state intervention, industrialization in Germany and Japan was largely state driven. This increasing involvement of states in social affairs led to the regulation and standardization of production and commerce, expanded central bureaucracies, and the relative homogenization of languages and cultures along national lines, in part through mass education.

There is some disagreement, however, about the influence of the Industrial Revolution on nation formation and nationalism. For some major theorists like Ernest Gellner, the link is self-evident: Nation-states emerged as unified political actors after the Industrial Revolution, and many smaller scale nationalist movements can be explained in terms of the uneven spread of the Industrial Revolution and the inequalities this engendered.

Others point to the fact that Britain and France were, among others, exhibiting signs of nationalism well before the mid-1700s. Explanations for preindustrial political nationalism usually point to the emergence in Europe of a competitive multistate system. Military and to a lesser extent diplomatic and commercial competition between states led to the large-scale mobilization of human and material resources within states and consequent nationalist expressions of support by significant parts of subject populations before the first Industrial Revolution.

Contemporary separatist nationalist movements, in Ireland, Quebec, or East Timor, for instance, have seemingly little to do with the onset of industrial production. A variety of causes independent of the timing and spread of the Industrial Revolution, including cultural, sociostructural, and political factors, have been advanced to explain their emergence.

It is generally agreed, however, that the diffusion of widespread cultural nationalism was a by-product, if not the direct result in many instances, of the Industrial Revolution. Even the seemingly rural regions where separatist movements have emerged in recent decades may be affected by the delayed effects of urbanization and the aftermath of mechanized production.

Debates have emerged in recent years about the effect of the Third Industrial Revolution. This latest phase, currently taking place, is characterized by the spread of computers, automation, and information technology. Its effect on nationalism is generally thought to be the inverse of the earlier phases of industrialization. Quick transfers of information and funds have led to the formation of transnational networks and institutions, the globalization of trade and culture, and the declining importance of strictly national boundaries.

Although the evidence that nation-states are declining is inconclusive, it is clear that this latest phase of industrialism is encouraging the formation of social forces that challenge the political and cultural supremacy of nation-states.

It has also been pointed out that the emergence of transnational political and economic structures, facilitated by globalizing economic forces, may actually encourage regionalism and the political assertiveness of subnational minorities. Scotland and Quebec are examples of cases where nationalist leaders have expressed wishes to remain part of larger transnational institutions (the European Union and North American Free Trade Agreement, respectively) in the event of independence. These latest technological, economic, and political changes may therefore have a double-edged effect: the erosion of existing national units and the reinforcement of smaller cultural subunits.

**INDUSTRIALIZATION** Ernest Gellner (1925–1995) is the theoretician of nationalism for whom the connection between industrialization and nationalism is most crucial: "The roots of nationalism," he once said, "in the distinctive structural requirements of industrial society are very deep indeed." In fact, the process of industrialization plays a fundamental role in the whole of Gell-

ner's social and political philosophy: The great transformation from agrarian to industrial society, according to him, provides the social mooring for much of the modern world. In the case of nationalism, the transformation to a modern industrial society is a necessary—although not sufficient—cause of modern nationalism.

On Gellner's model, an important distinction needs to be made between agrarian and industrial social structures. Agrarian society is characterized by diverse cultural pockets of hermetically isolated groups. Here culture and social status is all pervasive and extremely resistant to change. Culture (language, ritual, etc.) is predominantly defined as *in situ* local culture, homogeneous within groups, and exhibiting great diversity between groups. While the mass of the population is engaged in the daily routine of physically demanding manual labor, a small group of clerics is occupied with developing a literate high culture. However, the vernacular low culture of the peasant seldom confronts, in any meaningful way, the high literate culture of the clerics.

The advent of industrialization radically changes the social structure of agrarian societies. Industrial society is characterized by a sustained, exponential rate of economic growth. The stability of the agrarian division of labor is replaced with a highly mobile, complex division of labor that is in constant flux. Instead of the manipulation of things being the major preoccupation of work, the movement of people and meanings now takes primacy. In this new world, messages and meanings need to move effortlessly between distant anonymous interlocutors. The medium of communication must, therefore, be universal, context free, homogeneous, and standardized.

This new form of standardized context-free communication is, in Gellner's view, a *functional requirement* of a modern industrialized society. The institution best suited by far to impart this new form of communication is the educational system—and the institution best able to support such a standardized mass form of education is the modern state. In a sense, the imposition of a high literate homogeneous culture on the mass of the population ushers in the age of nationalism.

However, there is an even more compelling way in which industrialization plays an instrumental role in the formation of nationalism. As important as the transition to industrial society is for the formation of nationalism in a general sense, *the uneven diffusion of industrialization* is even more critical. Early industrializers reap the benefits of industrialization far sooner than late industrializers. If these two groups happen to be in close and constant contact with each other, and if such differences are accentuated by ethnic or linguistic differences, then inevitably some resentment on the part of the latter group develops. Those of the disadvantaged group who participate in some way in the culture of the advantaged group will feel this tension even more acutely and will, as a result, be provoked to take steps to move their own indigenous group to "catch up" with the dominant group. The attainment of a national state is, in most cases, perceived to be the best way to obtain such a goal.

Contrary to this view, several arguments question the supposed link between nationalism and industrialization. The first is the fact that the period of rapid industrialization in Europe and America (roughly between 1815 and 1914) was accompanied by a time of relative peace and contained conflicts that had very little to do with nationalism. The second is the fact that signs of nationalist sentiment were manifest during and directly after the French Revolution, a time before industrialism had fully developed. Still, while the exact weight that should be assigned to industrialization as a cause of nationalism is under dispute, that it is an important factor to be considered is not.

See Gellner's chapter "Nationalism" in his *Thought and Change* (University of Chicago Press, 1964), as well as his *Nations and Nationalism* (Cornell, 1983) and *Nationalism* (Weidenfeld & Nicolson, 1997) on the relationship between nationalism and industrialization. For criticism of the link between industrialism and nationalism, see John Breuilly "Reflections on Nationalism" in *Philosophy of the Social Sciences* **15** (1985).

**INTERNATIONAL COMMUNITY** The term *international community* is ambiguous. It may be used to refer to an international society of states or to the concept of a global society composed of individuals. As a result of this ambiguity, the international community may be depicted as either a complement or a challenge to the nation-state. The concrete manifestation of international community, in the form of international organization, has increasingly been called on to intervene in nationalist conflicts.

International community is most commonly used to refer to an international society composed primarily of states, rather than individuals. According to the "English school" of international relations, this society of states moderates the virulence of international conflict and anarchy. It facilitates communication and reconciles expectations through the reciprocal recognition of legal doctrines and diplomatic conventions, such as sovereignty and diplomatic immunity. Recognition by the international community provides the formal legitimization of new nation-states. Thus, in this form, the international community may be understood as encompassing, framing, and supporting the nation-state.

International community is also used to refer to the concept of a global society or a society of humankind. These supranationalist conceptions are descendants of the "natural law" tradition, which envisions an international community of mankind. They depict international community as moderating, containing, or even superseding the nation-state as a form of political organization. In this sense they represent a critique of or a challenge to the concept of the nation-state.

However, the existence of international community, in either form, is controversial. It suggests a level of social cohesion in a world that is characterized by anarchy and conflict at the international level, leading some scholars to deny the possibility of its existence altogether. Another critique is that the "international" community is too Western or Eurocentric in its orientation, not truly international at all. Early Western thinking about international community was often marked by the Christian origins of the natural law tradition, and limited the scope of the community to "Christendom" or the Western world.

Despite the difficulties, a number of nationalist thinkers have suggested that international community complements, or at least does not contradict, nationalism. There was no contradiction for early 19th-century thinkers such as Herder or Mazzini, whose pronationalist thinking embraced a polycentric conception of value rather than a hierarchy and consequent international struggle. International politics could accommodate both the diversity of nations and the unity of a loose form of international community. Indeed the satisfaction of national demands for recognition would create peace that could create or strengthen such a community.

The idea that international community could enable the peaceful coexistence of nation-states by moderating interstate conflict also has a long tradition. Early examples include the Abbé de Saint-Pierre's project for perpetual peace (as interpreted by Jean-Jacques Rousseau) and Immanuel Kant's idea of a "pacific union" of republics. Both authors advocate a form of confederation or alliance that would ensure peace while simultaneously maintaining the sovereignty and independence of its members.

In the 1950s and 1960s the idea that international community was a necessary precursor to peace led political scientists such as Karl Deutsch to try to quantify the level of international community and measure its development over time. More recently, international relations scholar Michael Doyle revived interest in the

Kantian concept of a pacific union when he noted the relative absence of violent conflict between liberal democratic states. This work led Michael Walzer to advocate, as a complement to the "completion" of an international system of nation-states, the "complication" of the international system in which free alliances build peace and stability.

Concrete attempts to organize the international community mushroomed in the 20th century. The League of Nations and its successor the United Nations have been the broadest in scope, both of membership and function. However, there are also a host of other international bodies defined along more specialized functional or regional lines, such as the World Trade Organization or the European Union. The expanding scope of membership in these organizations demonstrates how the conception of international community has broadened over time.

This expansion is largely the result of movements of national liberation and decolonization. However, the international community has manifested an ambivalent attitude to the principle of self-determination, fearing its potential to incite conflict at home and abroad. Even the newest members of the international community have proved reluctant to recognize and hence confer legitimacy on any reorganization of international borders. Acceptance of the territorial status quo was a central tenet for the Organization of African Unity at its inception in 1963, despite the arbitrary nature of the colonial borders inherited by the new states. More recently the international community was hesitant to admit the successor states of the former Yugoslavia.

The international community's scope of responsibility has also expanded over time. The original framework of international community was noninterventionist, but this has changed. The international community has taken direct action, not only imposing arms embargoes and other forms of sanctions but even sending international peacekeeping forces to areas that are torn by nationalist conflict. This aspect of the international community has come to the fore since the end of the Cold War, an event which freed the United Nations from the constraints imposed by the stalemate between Western bloc and Eastern bloc interests. The end of the Cold War also resulted in a rise in nationalist conflict, ensuring increased demand for action by the international community, despite the difficulties and controversies such action entails.

## IRAN, NATIONALISM IN

Iran is a multiethnic society with approximately 50 percent of its citizens of non-Persian origin. The largest minority group in Iran is the Azerbaijanis, and other major groups include the Kurds, Baluchis, Arabs, and Turkmen. Figures on the ethnic groups are estimates because Tehran has not openly conducted and published statistics on the ethnic breakdown in Iran. The approximate figures are Azerbaijanis and Turkic tribal groups, 25–30 percent; Kurds, 9 percent; Baluchis, 3 percent; Arabs, 2.5 percent; Turkmen, 2 percent; and small numbers of Armenians, Jews, and Assyrians. Religious and ethnic divisions do not correspond: The Persians and Azerbaijanis are both Shi'ite, whereas the Baluchis, Turkmen, and the majority of the Kurds are Sunni. The ethnic minorities form the majority of the population in Iran's border areas, whereas the Persians dominate in the center of the country.

The Pahlavi regime implemented a policy of fostering Iranian nationalism based on the idea of identifying the Iranian state and nation with the Persian people and the Persian language. As part of this policy, the regime attempted to forcibly assimilate the various ethnic groups in Iran and Persianize them. Ethnic minorities were not recognized by the Pahlavi regime, referring to them, if at all, as "tribal" groups and their separate culture and languages as "local," and no collective rights were granted by the Pahlavi regime to the non-Persian ethnic groups. Religious minorities were recognized and granted limited cultural autonomy and, in contrast to the ethnic minorities, received permission to operate schools in their native languages. The regime classified groups, such as the Armenians and Jews, as religious groups, notwithstanding the fact that many members of these identified ethnically.

Each time in the 20th century that there has been major erosion in the central power in Iran, many of the ethnic groups and periphery regions have seized the opportunity and asserted ethnic-based demands and raised calls for self-rule of different forms. For example, toward the fall of the Qajar dynasty, revolts based in Gilan, Khorasan, and Iranian Azerbaijan took place. In addition, in October 1945, protected from Tehran by the Soviet troops that occupied northern Iran, Azerbaijani activists carried out a revolt for control of the province of Azerbaijan. A similar revolt followed in January 1946 led by Kurdish activists who established a provincial government in Mahabad. Most Western accounts of the revolts in Azerbaijan and Kurdistan and the short-lived provincial governments there in 1945–1946 tend to present them as Soviet puppet-states, and not as a local-based phenomena. Although Soviet support was clearly essential in providing opportunity and tools, most of the goals and demands that the provincial governments addressed were local based, such as the right to native language use. During its short year of existence, the provincial government in Azerbaijan established the first provincial university in Tabriz and lessons were conducted in the Azerbaijani language, which was also used in government offices, the school system, publishing, and radio, and similar measures were adopted in the Kurdish republic. An additional Kurdish uprising took place in Iran in 1967–1968, which had been affected by the Kurdish autonomy movement in neighboring Iraq.

Ethnic minorities played an especially important role in the Islamic revolution because the ethnic groups had compounded grievances toward the Pahlavi regime due to its policy of suppressing their ethnic culture and giving preferential treatment in the economic sphere to the Persian-dominated center. Moreover, many Azerbaijani and Kurdish families had relatives who had been killed or exiled by the regime after the fall of the provincial governments in 1946. In addition, ethnic minorities possessed special networks of connections among themselves in different locations throughout Iran, making them a force that was relatively easily mobilized for the antiregime activity of the revolution. Many activists from the ethnic minorities anticipated that the revolution would create opportunity for autonomy. In the initial period after the Islamic revolution in 1979 there was an outburst of publications in the minority languages, chiefly Azerbaijani, Kurdish, and Armenian, and many members of the various ethnic groups in Iran were actively involved in ensuring language rights for the ethnic minorities in the new constitution of the Islamic Republic and in public bodies. Article Fifteen of the constitution states that the Islamic Republic of Iran will officially permit the use of the "local and nationality languages" in their press and mass media and allow the teaching "of their literature" in schools. Though the implementation of these clauses was prohibited, they later served as important bases of claims by ethnic activists struggling in Iran for the right to use their language. Paradoxically, the Islamic Revolution itself unintentionally inspired the ethnic minorities to aspire toward cultural freedom and expression. Its slogans of equality between all the ethnic groups and its stress on the universalism of Islam led many members of the ethnic minorities to believe that in the new regime they could be on equal footing with the Persians. The shah's regime was associated with Persian-centered policies and severe suppression of the various ethnic minorities. Based on the new regime's declared hatred of the Pahlavi policies, many members of the ethnic minorities were led to believe that it would eliminate all of those policies associated with the past regime, and when their expectations were not met, many members of the ethnic minorities rebelled against Khomeini's attempts to impose absolute rule on the provinces. Within months of the es-

tablishment of the Islamic Republic in February 1979, Khomeini's regime was engaged in an outright military confrontation with the Kurds, which lasted from March until the late fall, and the regime encountered in December 1979 a rebellion in the Azerbaijani provinces, centered in Tabriz.

Despite the fact that the policies of the Islamic Republic did not meet the expectations of many of the ethnic activists, the regime has conducted a much more lenient policy than the shah toward the languages and cultures of the non-Persian groups in Iran. Publications in these languages have increased dramatically in Iran, and a large number of clerical elite are themselves non-Persians, such as Ayatollah Khamene'i. Some speak the minority languages publicly, augmenting the legitimacy of their use.

In the 1990s unprecedented events took place in Iran in the sphere of ethnic identity and relations. For example, in the 1997 presidential elections in Iran, supporters of Mohammad Khatami distributed election materials in the Azerbaijani and Kurdish languages, exemplifying his recognition of the multiethnic composition of Iran and the importance the non-Persian groups attach to the status of their mother tongues. Khatami's leading role in the holding of the 1999 elections to local government exemplifies his desire to tap into the ethnic minority groups and Iran's periphery as part of his struggle with the ruling elite in Iran.

Iran's ethnic groups are particularly vulnerable to external manipulation and considerably subject to influence by events taking place outside its borders, since most of the non-Persians are concentrated in the frontier areas and have ties to co-ethnics in adjoining states, such as Azerbaijan, Turkmenistan, Pakistan, and Iraq. The situation of Iran's ethnic minorities, first and foremost the Azerbaijanis, has been particularly influenced by the Soviet breakup. The establishment of the Republic of Azerbaijan challenged the national identity of co-ethnics beyond the borders of the new state and served as a stimulant for many Azerbaijanis in Iran to identify with the Azerbaijani ethnic group.

For additional reading, see Erhard Franz, *Minderheiten in Iran* (Hamburg: German Orient Institute, Middle East Documentation, 1981), and Shahrzad Mojab and Amir Hassanpour, "The Politics of Nationality and Ethnic Diversity," in Saeed Rahnema and Sorab Behdad, eds. *Iran after the Revolution: Crises of an Islamic State* (London: I. B. Tauris and Co. Ltd, 1996).

**IRANIAN NATIONALISM** Contemporary Iranian nationalism developed on two planes: state sponsored and intellectual led. In view of the fact that Iran's population is multiethnic and multilingual, adherents of Iranian nationalism have attempted to foster the idea of common origin of the peoples in Iran, and stressed the importance of a common historical experience and attachment to the Persian language as a component of collective Iranian identity. This stress on unity propagated by Iranian nationalists created many common goals with Iranian modernizers.

With his rise to power (1921) and the establishment of the Pahlavi dynasty (1926), Reza Shah (formerly Reza Khan) set out to create a modern, unified, and centralized state and saw the fostering of one nation and one language as fundamental to achieving this aim. Reza Shah implemented a state policy of fostering Iranian nationalism based on the idea of identifying the Iranian state and nation with the Persian people and the Persian language. In this manner, Reza Shah merged state identity with the identity of the largest ethnic group in Iran. The regime cultivated the idea that the Iranian nation shared a common racial "Aryan" descent, collectively possessing a 2500-year-old civilization, and propagated it through the state-controlled media and schools. The regime glorified Iran's pre-Islamic past and its Zoroastrian religion. The periods of non-Persian (Turkish and Arab) rule over Iran were considered the chief impediments in the past to the development of Persia's grandeur. The state-sponsored ideology denied the linguistic, cultural, and social diversity of Iran. Non-Persians, such as the Azerbaijani and tribal Turks, were related to as ethnic Persians who had only been linguistically "Turkified" by Turkish "occupiers" of Iran. The regime attempted to assimilate the various ethnic groups in Iran and Persianize them. This policy included closing minority-language schools and publications. During the Pahlavi period, the regime propagated the theme of the greatness of the Iranian Persian nation, the magnificence of Persian literature and language, and the exalted level of Persian culture. Non-Persian cultures in Iran, in contrast, were generally treated by the regime as primitive, uncivilized, and underdeveloped. Many non-Persians internalized these messages and viewed their own ethnic culture through the prism of the regime and attempted to assimilate into Persian identity. Yet for others, this policy, in contrast to the goal of program, spurred the development of ethnic-based nationalism.

The Pahlavi state-sponsored nationalism was proceeded by espousals of the Iranian national idea by intellectuals, beginning in the mid-19th century. Prominent among the Iranian intellectuals who affected the development of the Iranian national idea were Mirza Fath 'Ali Akhundzade (1812–1878), 'Abdul al-Rahim Talebzade (1834–1909), and Ahmad Kasravi (1890–

1946). Many of the early Iranian nationalists viewed factionalism in Iranian society as the major obstacle to its modernization and empowerment and, consequently, to its ability to rid itself of dependence on foreign elements. Thus, many of them advocated unifying Iran under the Persian language and culture; however, their approach to Persianization was predominantly utilitarian. In fact, the majority of the early Iranian nationalist thinkers were not even Persians.

Many Iranian intellectual nationalists active in the first half of the 20th century shared Reza Shah's belief in the importance of a unified Iran for its development and modernization. Many were pleased by the shah's state-sponsored glorification of the Iranian nation and Persian language and culture, and his tenacity in repelling attempts by non-Persians in Iran at cultural or political autonomy. Conversely, though, many intellectual nationalists rejected the role of foreign forces in Reza Shah's rise to power in Iran as well as their decisive part in preserving that of his son, Mohammed Shah, as well as his authoritarianism, and these factors led to an irresolute relationship between Reza Shah's program and many of the leading intellectuals of the period.

Elimination of foreign dominance in the Iranian economy and control of national resources has served as an important rallying point of the contemporary Iranian national movement, yet the fact that in the modern era Iran did not experience extended periods of foreign occupation in vast areas of its territory greatly affected the extent of national cohesion among various forces in Iran and subsequently the timing and growth of the national movement in Iran. Principal events in the contemporary Iranian national movement were the Tobacco Protest (1891–1892), the Constitutional Revolution (1906–1908), the period of the first National Front (1949–1953), and the 1963 revolt. The National Front period was the most notable of all. Under the leadership of Mohammed Mossadeq, a broad coalition of forces strove to demand of the nationalization of Iran's oil industry. In May 1951, Mossadeq became prime minister of Iran, and in this role personified Iran's movement toward democracy and cessation of Iran's dependence on foreign powers. However, the National Front movement was plagued with the internal fragmentation inherent in such a large coalition. More importantly, Anglo-American intervention to topple the nationalist government and reinstall the shah determined the fate of the Mossadeq-led national movement in Iran, bequeathing anti-American sentiments to the national movement in Iran and consequently creating a persisting uneasy relationship in Iran between nationalism and Western liberalism. The resentment toward Western liberalism is embodied in the 1962 publication of Jalal Al-e Ahmed's *Gharbzadegi* (Westoxication), which gave birth to a discourse of the same name centering on the importance of native ideological sources for the Iranian national movement.

Iranian nationalists succeeded at critical junctures in history to recruit the merchant class (*bazari*) and the clerics (*ulama*) to support their aims. The bazari were especially attracted to the nationalist idea due to their objection to the concessions granted by the successive shahs to foreign business elements.

A notable theme in the contemporary history of Iran is the consistent uneasiness between Iran's Muslim identity and its pre-Islamic Iranian national identity. Defeat of the National Front movement in 1953 helped pave the way for the rise of political Islam in Iran. Many of the forces competing with political Islam had been delegitimized: the liberal national option had failed with the downfall of the National Front, Communism was seen as a foreign tool, and reactionary nationalism was associated with the Pahlavi monarchy. In the 1960s, many Iranian intellectuals looked to Islam for solutions to Iran's national question. Ali Shari'ati was the most important thinker in this field. Some Iranian ideologists, such as Mehdi Bazargan, attempted to form a synthesis between Islam and Iranian nationalism. But the uneasy relationship between the universally oriented and antidivisional nature of Islam and Iranian nationalism endured. The centrality of the Arabs and Arabic to Islam contributed to the troubled relationship between Islamic and Iranian identity. Some have interpreted the fortification of Shi'ite identity in Iran since its adoption as its state religion in the beginning of the 16th century as an attempt by the Iranians to distinguish themselves from the rest of the Islamic world and retain their particular identity and institutions within Islam.

The quandary of the relationship between Islam and Iranian identity has not been solved, but rather exasperated by the establishment of the Islamic Republic in Iran. The revolution was carried out by a wide coalition, including both Islamic-oriented and Iranian nationalist forces. Khomeini and many of his successors emphasized the Islamic identity of the Iranians and the Islamic *umma* instead of Iran, and have subordinated Iranian identity to a wider Islamic identification. This subjugation of Iranian national identity has served as a major source of discontent with the regime and opponents often express their dissatisfaction with the clerical regime through assertion of Iranian nationalism. Khomeini adherents assert that their ideology represents true native-based nationalism, and not an ideology that is a product of European and American culture. In fact, Khomeini's

dictate of "neither West nor East" and policy and rhetoric of emphasizing Iran's independence and rejection of foreign influence contain many elements common with Iran's modern national movement. Moreover, the leaders of the Islamic Republic have understood the holding power of Iranian nationalism, and have resisted, for instance, Muslim reconciliation attempts to rename the Persian Gulf the "Islamic Gulf" and have tenaciously guarded the superior status of the Persian language in Iran under their reign and rejected ethnic-minority requests for autonomy.

See Ervand Abrahamian, *Iran Between Two Revolutions* (Princeton: Princeton University Press, 1982); James A. Bill and Wm. Roger Louis, eds., *Musaddiq, Iranian Nationalism and Oil* (London: Tauris, 1988); and Sussan Siavoshi, *Liberal Nationalism in Iran: The Failure of a Movement* (Boulder, Colo.: Westview Press, 1990).

**IRAQI NATIONALISM**  Consider the assumption that for nationalism to exist members of the nation need to internalize and endeavor to maintain and protect their identity, which is a process of national formation that is both psychological and physiological. Furthermore, for a group to actually become a nation, the members must incorporate within themselves the symbols of a nation and seek either to enhance or protect their identity community. Iraq as a political entity in the modern sense of a state did not come into political existence until 1921 when the British mandate power at the time brought together three distinct groups, the Sunni Arabs of central and northern Iraq, the Shi'ites of the south and the marsh lands, and the Kurds of the northern and eastern parts of the country. There was no real political bond between these three groups except that they were part of the Ottoman Empire and the Sunni Arabs were the political administrators for the empire. Moreover, the new political entity had within its borders Jews, Yazidis, and Chaldenian and Assyrian Christians. It is noteworthy to point out that the first king of Iraq, Faisal I, noted that, "There is still—and I say this with a heart full of sorrow—no Iraqi people but unimaginable masses of human beings, devoid of any patriotic idea, imbued with religious traditions and absurdities, connected by no common tie . . . prone to anarchy, and perpetually ready to rise against any government whatever" (Hanna Batatu, p. 25). Hence, it was the task of any modern ruler of Iraq to seek to mold a sense of national identity from this mass of humanity inhabiting the new state of Iraq.

From the outset of the Iraqi state there was tension between those who were proponents of Arab nationalism, especially within the military and the high levels of the bureaucracy, given that they were Sunni Muslims to whom Arab nationalism was a salient identity community with which they could easily identify. On the other hand, there were those who sought to establish a sense of an identification with Iraq proper, and thus include within it the various ethnic and religious communities within the state. Both tasks were monumental, and the fact was that the monarchist rule, orchestrated by then Prime Minister Nouri al-Said, a Sunni Muslim, was most interested in the survival of the Hashemite rule in Iraq, with British patronage.

The monarchy was overthrown by a violent coup in July 1958, led by Abd Al-Karim Qassem, who was reported to have a Shi'ite parent. The Ba'th Party advanced the idea of unity with Syria and Egypt, but Qassem was opposed to the idea and suppressed those forces who sought unity with Syria and Egypt. The Iraqi Communist Party, whose rank and file included many non-Sunni Iraqi, supported Qassem's policies, which advocated a local Iraqi identity, that is, Iraqi patriotism (al-Wataniyah al-Iraqiyah).

After the overthrow of Qassem in 1963, Abdel Salam Aref, who was of a conservative bent and religious, held sectarian allegiance and was not interested in party politics. His personal secretary indicated that while he was willing to ride the Ara nationalist wave, in reality he was neither a unionist nor a nationalist (Ali Ghayoun, p. 224). But Aref was fully aware of the divisions within Iraq and the struggle within the Ba'th Party itself, between its military and civilian ranks for control over the state. When Abdel Salam Aref was killed in an airplane crash, his brother, Abdel Al-Rahaman Aref, became the compromise between the various factions competing for power. The second Aref was equally cognizant of the conflicts, even though he and his foreign minister Abd al-Rahman Al-Bazzaz sought to pursue a policy that articulated Arab nationalist slogans while trying to seek compromises with the various ethnic and religious factions within Iraq.

When the Ba'th Party came to power in July 1968, it argued that al-Bazzaz's approach was void of any identity principles that had been sought in the coup of 1963. Hence, the Ba'th sought to articulate an Arab nationalist identity community in all of its slogans, especially when dealing with monarchist regimes in the region and in the context of the Arab–Israeli conflict. Yet in spite of this rhetoric the Ba'th Party did not take real tangible steps to achieve the dream of the Arab nation.

What actually happened was the focus turned toward Iraqi patriotism as illustrated by Mesopotamian identity as argued by Amatzia Baram (pp. 426–456). According to Baram Iraqis were encouraged to perceive themselves as the cultural and civilizational heirs to Mesopotamian and Medieval-Islamic identity (p. 30). This process of manipulating identity symbols was significant, particularly during the war with Iran. The Iraqi regime sought to achieve two objectives during this period. One was to create and manipulate symbols that are salient not only to Sunni Arabs, but also to the Shi'ite Arabs—who could easily identify with their coreligious Shi'ites in Iran—and to a very limited extent the Kurds. The second objective was to link the persona of Saddam Hussein after 1979 with that of the undisputed leaders of neo-Mesopotamian Iraqi nation, such as Nebuchadnezzar or Hammurabi (see Baram, p. 31). These attempts of national symbol manipulation were an admission on the part of the Ba'thi leader that Iraq needed an identity of its own separate from the rest of the Arab nation and one that he could capitalize on to legitimize his personal rule. Moreover, Saddam's symbolic manipulation did not end with the Iran–Iraq War of 1989, but took on Arabist and Islamic tones after he ordered the invasion of Kuwait in August 1990. Here the audience was not only the Iraqi public but also the Arab masses whom he believed would rise against their rulers and endorse his occupation and annexation of Kuwait.

It can be argued that Iraqi national identity did manifest itself to a certain extent during the Iran–Iraq War when many Shi'ites did not support the Iranian regime call to overthrow Saddam or to defect to the Iranian side. However, it is difficult to fully predict that such an identity is the most salient among the Sunni, Shi'ite, and Assyrian Christian Arabs in modern Iraq. There is no doubt that if Kurds were given the international support to secede from Iraq they would take advantage of the opportunity. Moreover, the Iraqi regime is by far the most authoritarian in the region and highly personalized, making the assessment of actual saliency and commitment to an Iraqi national identity among these various sectarian and ethnic groups very hard to predict.

See Ali Ghayoun, *The Revolution of February 8, 1963 in Iraq, the Conflicts and Changes,* "Thawrat 8 Shobat 1963 fi Al-Irak, al-Sira'at wa al-Tahawolat," (Baghdad, Iraq: Dar Al-Shoon Al-Thakafiya Al-A'ma, 1990) (in Arabic); 'Abd al-Rahman al-Bazzaz, "This is Our Nationalism," in Jacob Landau, ed. *Man, State, and Society in the Contemporary Middle East* (New York: Praeger, 1972), pp. 22–37; Amatzia Baram, "Re-Inventing Nationalism in Ba'thi Iraq 1968–1994: Supra-Territorial and Territorial Identities and What Lies Below," in William Harris *et al., Challenges to Democracy in the Middle East* (Princeton, N.J.: Markus Wiener Publishers, 1997), pp. 29–56; idem, *Culture, History and Ideology in the Formation of Ba'thist Iraq, 1968–89* (New York: St.

Martin's Press, 1991); and Hanna Batatu, *The Old Social Classes and the Revolutionary Movements of Iraq* (Princeton: Princeton University Press, 1978).

## IRISH NATIONALISM

As D. George Boyce claims in his *Nationalism in Ireland,* deciding when to start a history of Irish nationalism is like starting a game of rugby football: Both begin when someone picks up the ball and runs with it. Most historians trace the roots of Irish nationalism to 1171, when King Henry II established an English presence in Ireland in order to protect England's western shores from a potential Norman threat. Between the 12th and 17th centuries, English concern over the mixing of Anglo and Gaelic cultures led to the development of a system of penal laws limiting the interaction between Anglo and Gael. The result was the slow development of an English administrative, governmental, and legal system in Ireland.

Irish nationalism can be divided into two phases, before and after 1921, when Ireland was partitioned into the twenty-six-county Free State (which later became the Republic of Ireland) and the six-county British statelet of Northern Ireland. From the late 18th century to 1921, Irish nationalists mobilized a variety of reactions against English political, civil, and cultural hegemony in Ireland. There is a tendency to understand these reactions as fundamentally anti-Protestant. However, although religious differences played an important role in Irish nationalism, what remained historically consistent about Irish nationalism was its critique of English political control in Ireland, no matter what the religious affiliation of the nationalists. In addition, while the recent history of Irish nationalism has been marked by military conflict, the bulk of Irish nationalism, especially prior to 1921, was carried forward through British parliamentary debate rather than paramilitary activity.

Irish Presbyterians were the first to mobilize against the injustices of the penal law system and promote the need for Catholic inclusion in the Irish Parliament. In response to their failed rebellion in 1798, the British government enacted the Act of Union (1801), which unseated the Irish Parliament and incorporated Ireland within the British Empire. Following the Act of Union, however, Irish Catholics remained disenfranchised. As a result, they mobilized under Daniel O'Connell to fight for emancipation. Their agitation led to the Emancipation Act of 1829, which allowed propertied Catholics to become members of the British Parliament and removed other restrictions of the penal system. Following emancipation, Irish nationalists, both Catholic and Protestant, turned their attention toward the repeal of the Act of Union.

Subsequent failures of the potato crop between 1845 and 1849 fueled the anti-English sentiment of Irish nationalists. The lack of support from England during the famine, and thus the mass starvation and disease that followed, were considered the direct result of English political mismanagement of Ireland. In reaction, Irish nationalists mounted a two-pronged movement against the English presence in Ireland. The Irish Republican Brotherhood, founded by James Stephens in 1858, mobilized a revolutionary force in Ireland to pursue Irish independence through physical force. The IRB drew substantial support, both ideological and monetary, from the famine diaspora in the United States. In addition, the more benign Home Rule movement, under the leadership of Isaac Butt and Charles Steward Parnell, pursued the creation of a limited Irish Parliament through political agitation in the British Parliament. Legislation for Irish home rule was placed before the British Parliament on four different occasions between 1887 and 1914. While the last Home Rule provision, which excluded six Ulster counties in the north of Ireland in order to appease Protestant threats of civil war, passed the House of Commons in 1914, it was nevertheless tabled by the onset of World War I.

Reacting to the postponed vote on home rule, and in an attempt to force a political solution forward while England was preoccupied with World War I, members of the Irish Republican Brotherhood launched a rebellion on Easter 1916. Seizing the general post office and other strategic buildings, they raised the Irish tricolor and proclaimed Ireland an independent republic. The Rising lasted only a week, and although it was a complete military failure, it was an important symbolic victory for Irish nationalists. The harsh reaction by the British military transformed the Irish rebels into national heroes. In the aftermath of the Rising, the Irish population flocked to support the Sinn Féin party, which had emerged in 1905 to aid the pursuit of an independent Irish Republic. After winning the majority of parliamentary seats in the general election of 1918, members of Sinn Féin walked out of the Westminster Parliament and enacted their own Irish Parliament, the Dàil Eireann, in January 1919. Meanwhile, the Irish Republican Brotherhood, renamed by Michael Collins and Harry Boland as the Irish Republican Army, launched a guerilla war to support and protect the newly created Dàil.

In response to the public popularity of Sinn Féin and the paramilitary activity of the IRA, the British government negotiated and finally ratified the Anglo-Irish Treaty in December 1921. The treaty created an Irish Free State that excluded six of the Ulster counties with strong unionist sentiment. The Dàil accepted the treaty under the threat of war with England, and although many nationalists were angered over the separation of the six counties, members of the Dàil touted the treaty as a "stepping stone" to a future and complete Irish Republic.

In many ways, Irish nationalism after 1921 can be better described as an irridentist movement, because its primary goal was to rejoin Northern Ireland with the Irish Republic rather than create an Irish state. Between 1923 and 1962, the IRA launched a series of paramilitary campaigns in an attempt to cripple the British infrastructure in Northern Ireland and thus undo the partition. During the 1960s, growing resentment of the social, political, and educational inequalities for Northern Irish Catholics fueled civil rights protests. Between 1972 and 1988, these demonstrations degenerated into paramilitary activity. Commonly referred to as "The Troubles," aggression between the IRA, loyalist paramilitary organizations, and the British military during this period claimed more than 3000 lives.

Between 1988 and 1993, secret talks between Gerry Adams, president of Sinn Féin, and John Hume, president of the Social Democratic Labor Party, and joint efforts between England, Northern Ireland, the Irish Republic, and the international community resulted in the Downing Street Declaration. The declaration proposed all-party talks in an effort to bring a peaceful settlement to the Northern Irish conflict. In response, the IRA announced a cease-fire in 1994, and many unionist groups followed suit. Multiparty talks produced the Good Friday Agreement in 1998, which argued for the creation of a Northern Ireland Assembly, representative of all parties, to take executive and legislative authority in Northern Ireland. This agreement was voted into policy by the people of Northern Ireland and the Irish Republic on May 22, 1998.

The future of Irish nationalism, despite the agreement, remains tenuous. Although the agreement creates the potential for political settlement in Northern Ireland, it does not propose the inclusion of Northern Ireland in the republic, contrary to the desires of most nationalists. In addition, recent quarreling over disarmament has led to threats that some groups, nationalist and unionist, may be excluded from the assembly. Finally, inequality and sectarianism at the community level are still in need of conciliation. Thus, while the agreement has created a political settlement in Northern Ireland, the future of Irish nationalism remains uncertain.

**IRISH REPUBLICAN ARMY** In 1912, after severely limiting the power of the House of Lords, the House of Commons finally passed a Home Rule Bill for Ireland, but by that time the Protestants in Ulster were afraid of being controlled by a Catholic majority. Sir Edward Casson organized the Ulster Volunteers, a military group armed with German guns to oppose the move. The next year the Irish Volunteers were formed by the Irish Republican Brotherhood and the Sinn Féin (pronounced "Shin Fane," meaning "We Ourselves" or "Ourselves Alone") to oppose the Ulster Volunteers. Sinn Féin is the political arm of the Irish Republican Army (IRA) that grew out of the Brotherhood. Sinn Féin refuses to take any seat in the British Parliament, whose authority it does not recognize. In the 1997 elections it won an all-time high of 16 percent of the votes in Northern Ireland. Two of its candidates, Gerry Adams and Martin McGuinness (an IRA leader who has served jail sentences), won seats, which remained vacant. Sinn Féin does occupy seats in local councils on both sides of the Irish border, though.

In the 1997 Irish elections, Sinn Féin won a paltry 2.5 percent of the votes. The result underscores two facts: Although polls indicate that two-thirds of Eire's population believe ideally that Ireland should one day be a unified nation, the overwhelming majority abhors the violent attempt to unify Ireland by bullets and bombs. It is precisely to try to overcome its isolation that leader Gerry Adams ended the party's boycott of the Irish (though not of the British) Parliament. As he stated: "We've lost touch with the people for the simple reason that we have not been able to represent them in the only political forum they know. To break out into the broad stream of people's consciousness, we have to approach them at their own level." To many traditionalists, this approach smacked of betrayal. As one die-hard remarked, "when you lie down with the dogs, you get up with the fleas."

Because it also seeks the overthrow of the Dublin government, the IRA has been banned in the south since 1936. Government raids and arrests provide frequent reminders that the IRA can expect no tolerance within the republic. In 1982 a Dublin court convicted an Irishman for possessing explosives, even though the crime was committed in Britain. This was the first application of a 1976 law that was part of Irish-British cooperation against terrorism in both countries. In 1981 a U.S. court convicted the Irish Northern Aid (NORAID) committee for failing to list the IRA as its principal foreign agent. The Irish government ordered its diplomatic representatives in the United States to boycott the 1983 annual St. Patrick's Day parade in New York City because the organizers of the parade had chosen an IRA supporter as grand marshal. In explaining its decision, the Irish government noted that the IRA's actions, which included collecting money from unsuspecting Irish-Americans to finance violent operations in Northern Ireland, "have deepened the wounds of our troubled history and continue to postpone the day of Irish unity and reconciliation." Dublin frequently appealed to Americans not to support violence in Ireland. Funds from NORAID declined, and the IRA sought to fill its coffers by means of extortion and racketeering in Northern Ireland.

In 1969 the IRA sprang to life again in Ulster (Ireland's northern six counties) and launched a modern terrorist campaign to remove the British from the territory and reunify the entire island. It has received money and arms from overseas sources ranging from Gadhafi in Libya to NORAID. The IRA murdered Lord Mountbatten in 1979, and in 1984 it launched a grisly bombing of the hotel in Brighton where British Prime Minister Margaret Thatcher was staying. She narrowly escaped death, and several Tory leaders were killed or wounded.

The IRA is a dedicated and ruthless band of 400 to 500 paramilitaries operating in small cells called "active service units." It is divided into two groups: The "official" IRA was formerly Marxist, but now it seeks power through elections; the "provisional" IRA (Provos) was strictly nationalist, but it shifted to armed struggle to convert Ireland into a Marxist state. This shift was one reason why Irish-Americans became less generous toward the IRA. Both these wings face some competition from the smaller, but more radical Irish National Liberation Army (INLA), the paramilitary wing of the Marxist Irish Republican Worker's Party.

From 1976 to 1982 the IRA campaigned for special treatment as "political prisoners." After the failure of tactics such as refusing to wear prison garb and smearing the walls of the cells with their own excrement, they resorted to hunger strikes. The deaths of ten IRA hunger strikers in Maze Prison in 1981 sparked renewed militant Catholic nationalism. Shortly before his death, one of the hunger strikers, Bobby Sands, even managed to win a seat in the House of Commons while he was still in prison.

The most effective antiterrorist measure undertaken by the British government in 1983 was the granting of pardon or lenience to one-time terrorists if they would tip off the police (in Northern Irish slang, "to grass") on the whereabouts of active terrorists. The testimony of such "supergrasses" led to a dramatic number of arrests in *both* the IRA and Protestant Ulster Volunteer Force. These organizations were so paralyzed that terrorist deaths in Northern Ireland dropped by half in one year,

from ninety-seven in 1982 to about fifty in 1983. IRA terrorists did give British Christmas shoppers a grisly sign of life in 1983, however. They exploded a bomb outside of the bustling Harrods Department Store in London, claiming still more innocent lives (including an American teenager, a fact that understandably hurt IRA fund-raising in the United States) in their ruthless struggle.

The Brighton bombing of 1984 was another grim reminder of the IRA's intent to wreak as much havoc as possible, this time by assailing the highest levels of British government itself. Having organized into "cells," the IRA became more difficult for police to combat. The violence prompted the Irish Republic to ratify the European convention on terrorism, which requires the extradition of terrorists.

By the end of the century, the death toll stood at 3600 since 1969. In doing its bloody work, the IRA had the tactical advantage over the 30,000 security forces, which were kept on the defensive by the IRA's meticulous planning and constant shifting of tactics. To minimize its own losses, it increasingly struck at "soft targets," such as bands, military hospitals, off-duty RUC officers, and civilian firms that supply goods and services to the security forces. It also acquired state-of-the-art equipment; for example, it possessed surface-to-air missiles to use against army helicopters.

In 1993 optimism was ignited by a joint declaration by the British and Irish prime ministers offering Sinn Féin a seat at the bargaining table to discuss Northern Ireland's future if the IRA renounced violence. Former Prime Minister John Major, who admitted that his government had conducted secret meetings with the IRA, promised that Britain would not stand in the way of a united Ireland if a majority of Northern Ireland residents supported such a step. His Irish counterpart pledged that there would be no change in the six counties' status without majority consent.

The following year President Bill Clinton, betting that the IRA wanted peace in Northern Ireland, made a risky decision to grant a visa to Sinn Féin leader Gerry Adams to come to the United States. Although the British government criticized him for this, it triggered a series of historic events. On August 31, 1994, the IRA declared a cease-fire, which prompted the Irish government to begin meeting with Sinn Féin leaders. Six weeks later Protestant loyalists also declared a truce. While paramilitaries on both sides continued to terrorize their own communities, intersectarian violence and IRA attacks on British forces stopped. As a result, the British government relaxed its security measures in Northern Ireland and began drawing down its 18,000 troops. In December, London opened direct talks with Sinn Féin and, later, with the Protestant paramilitaries. In February 1995 the British and Irish governments issued a "Framework for Agreement," outlining their proposals for Northern Ireland's future.

The U.S. government did its part to keep the momentum going by permitting Sinn Féin to open an office near Dupont Circle in Washington in 1995 and to raise money legally in the United States. Much to London's displeasure, Clinton invited Gerry Adams to a St. Patrick's Day party in the White House honoring Ireland's *Taoiseach* (prime minister). In May, the United States also organized a Northern Ireland Investment Conference in Washington that brought together more people from more different Northern Irish parties under one roof than ever before. It was also attended by top government officials from the United Kingdom and Ireland and was the venue for the first meeting between Gerry Adams and Britain's ex-secretary of state for Northern Ireland Patrick Mayhew. This was the highest level meeting between British and IRA leaders in seventy-five years and a giant step toward Adams's goal of receiving the same recognition and treatment accorded to Northern Ireland's other political leaders.

In February 1996, the IRA ended an eighteen-month cease-fire and launched a bombing campaign in Britain and Northern Ireland. Tony Blair's Labour government, which for the first time appointed a woman—Marjorie "Mo" Mowlam—as secretary of state for Northern Ireland, departed from the previous government's policy of not admitting Sinn Féin to multiparty talks until the IRA ends its violence campaign. Sinn Féin insisted that there could be no preconditions to its participation in negotiations, which resumed in June 1997.

A couple of weeks after becoming prime minister, Blair lifted the ban on official contacts with Sinn Féin in order to explain London's position and to assess whether the IRA was really prepared to renounce violence. Gerry Adams accepted the offer. Blair dropped London's insistence that terrorists disarm before joining peace talks. He visited Northern Ireland on May 16, 1997, in order to demonstrate that he is willing to take risks for peace in the six counties.

To continue the negotiation process, he invited Gerry Adams to a meeting in Downing Street in December. This was the first visit by an Irish Republican leader to the prime minister's private residence in seventy-six years. It was a richly symbolic encounter, with the meeting over tea held in the cabinet room, the target of an IRA mortar attack only six years earlier. A month later, in January 1998, Adams returned to Downing Street to hear from the prime minister that the peace process is an "absolute priority" and that "the status quo

is not an option." To balance his gesture to Sinn Féin, Blair told Protestants that "none of us . . . even the youngest, is likely to see Northern Ireland as anything but a part of the United Kingdom."

On December 1, 1999, a new coalition government in Ulster was formed that shares power devolved from Westminster in London. It included both hard-line Protestant Rev. Ian Paisley and former IRA commander Martin McGuinnes, as minister of education.

**IRON GUARD**  Fascist movement in 1930s Romania. The Iron Guard was founded in 1930 as the paramilitary wing of, but practically indistinguishable from, the Legion of the Archangel Michael, an organization established in 1927 by Corneliu Z. Codreanu. Its members were commonly known as "Legionaries" and the group itself as the Legionary movement.

The Legionary movement is best defined by what it reviled, namely, Jews, Communism, industrialism/commercialism, and parliamentary democracy, each of which was deemed to be an affront to the supposedly Christian Orthodox, honest, and just spirit of the Romanian nation. That spirit, thought Codreanu and his followers, was embodied by the peasant and his simple village lifestyle close to the ancestral soil.

The Iron Guard's violent anti-Semitism, anticommunism, anticapitalism, and authoritarianism were attributes that it shared with other contemporary fascist movements. Setting it apart from other European radical rightists, however, were the legion's strong commitment to the Orthodox religion, its morbid cult of death, and its agrarian primitivism. A mystical organization stressing patriotism, work, piety, dignity, and justice, the Iron Guard was primarily dedicated to eradicating the rampant corruption that indeed pervaded Romanian political life in the interwar period. As such, the legion was the sworn enemy of Romania's ruling elite, including King Carol II and most political parties, whom Codreanu sought to replace with a dictatorship of new and "virtuous" men.

In the fight to rid Romania of corruption, the legion did not espouse a precise political program, focusing instead on liquidating its alleged sources, above all, Jews, Bolshevism, and "Judeo-Communist" exploiters of the Romanian peasantry. Though certainly an extreme nationalist movement committed to the defense of Greater Romania's borders, the Iron Guard devoted little attention to Romania's non-Jewish minorities, such as the 1.5 million Hungarians who accounted for 8 percent of the country's population.

The legion was structured into small groups or "nests" and its members all bore a fanatical devotion to Codreanu, their "captain." Its most ardent supporters and loyal members were found among idealistic students, unemployed intellectuals, disgruntled civil servants, poor peasants, underpaid soldiers, and the usual hooligans and thugs who routinely find a home in such violent movements of rage.

The Iron Guard failed to win parliamentary representation after competing in the June 1931 rigged elections. In the July 1932 elections the Guard won five seats, and by December 1933 its increasing popularity invited a massive government crackdown. The Guard retaliated by assassinating Prime Minister Ion Duca on December 29, 1933.

In 1934 Codreanu recast the legion as a political party, *Totul Pentru Tara* (Everything for the Homeland). In the yet again rigged election of December 1937 it officially received over 16 percent of the vote, though the legion's level of popular support was undoubtedly higher and steadily rising. In February 1938, partly in reaction to the threat posed by the Iron Guard, the king abolished parliamentary democracy and declared a royal dictatorship.

Astonishingly, Codreanu meekly complied with the new order by dissolving his organization. In April Codreanu was arrested and in late November 1938 he was murdered by the police. The Iron Guard avenged their captain by assassinating prime minister Armand Calinescu in September 1939. Violent reprisals by the state followed but were ended in January 1940 in deference to Hitler.

In September 1940, after Axis pressure forced King Carol to relinquish two-fifths of Transylvania to Hungary without a fight, the monarch fled the country in disgrace. On September 14 a "National Legionary State" was established as a joint Iron Guard–army dictatorship, with general Ion Antonescu as head of state. The legion subsequently unleashed an orgy of killings against Jews, political opponents, and former tormentors in the state apparatus. Nicolae Iorga, Romania's foremost intellectual, was its most famous victim.

An unstable Romania torn by terror and bloodshed was not, however, in Hitler's interest. Hitler expected his oil-rich Balkan ally to reliably commit considerable military and economic resources to the war against the Soviet Union. He therefore allowed Antonescu and the army to destroy the Iron Guard in early 1941. Horia Sima, Codreanu's successor, was granted asylum in Germany, but the legion, after several days of vicious street battles beginning on January 21, 1941, was permanently eliminated from the Romanian political scene.

**IROQUOIS CONFEDERACY** Scholars have theorized that American Indian society and government influenced the formation of certain key aspects of American,

and perhaps European, democratic thought and institutions. This is not a new theory but one that has resurfaced both academically and politically in recent times due to multicultural and revisionist pressures. Professor Donald Grinde explains the central tendency of the debate in that "when people begin to talk about the roots of the Constitution, and they talk about ancient Greece and Rome and John Locke and Rousseau and the Enlightenment, I want them also to have to deal with Indian ideas and specifically, the Iroquois."

The U.S. Senate supported this theory by acknowledging "the contribution of the Iroquois Confederacy of Nations to the development of the United States Constitution . . ." through the following resolution: "That (1) the Congress, on occasion of the two hundredth anniversary of the signing of the United States Constitution, acknowledges the historical debt which this Republic of the United States of America owes to the Iroquois Confederacy and other Indian nations for their demonstration of enlightened, democratic principles of Government and their example of a free association of independent Indian nations" (S. Con. Res. 76, 9-16-87 : 111–112).

The Iroquois Confederacy, which dates to 1142 A.D., is ranked with the government of Iceland and the Swiss cantons as the oldest continuously functioning democracy on earth. The five initial member nations of the confederacy were the Senecas, Onondagas, Oneidas, Mohawks, and Cayugas. The legislative body was called the Council of Sachems or Grand Council made up of 50 sachems or lords, as called by the British in reference to their own House of Lords. The sachems were all male but were chosen and removed by the female head of each clan. All citizens of the Iroquois Nation had the right to be heard and were encouraged to introduce their opinions to the councils, either through their own oratory or depending on the situation through a member of the council. Unlike the U.S. Congress, the decisions reached by the Grand Council had to be unanimous, similar to the United Nations Security Council. Judicial review among the Iroquois operated within the Council of Women in conjunction with the Council of Men, with the war chiefs carrying out their decisions. The combined council, much like the U.S. Supreme Court, could overrule an act of the Grand Council. Several of the founding fathers wrote about and utilized the Iroquois Confederacy and other Native American governments as models during the founding of the U.S. government.

Benjamin Franklin, who began his distinguished diplomatic career by representing Pennsylvania in treaty councils with the Iroquois and their allies and published Indian treaty accounts on a regular basis from 1736 until the early 1760s, utilized the Iroquois Confederacy as a model for the Albany Plan and the Articles of Confederation. John Adams in *A Defence of the Constitutions of Government of the United States of America*, a critical survey of world governments, included a description of the Iroquois and other Native American polities. In his preface, Adams mentioned the Inca, Manco Capac, and the political structure "of the Peruvians." Adams believed that American Indian governments collected their authority in one center (a simple or unicameral model), and he also observed that in American Indian governments "the people" believed that "all depended on them."

Thomas Jefferson saw American Indians and their societies as conceptions of life, liberty, and happiness, a phase he authored in the Declaration of Independence. Writing to James Madison on January 30, 1787, from Paris, Jefferson examined three forms of societies: (1) Without government, as among our Indians. (2) Under governments wherein the will of every one has a just influence, as is the case in England in a slight degree, and in our states in great one. (3) Under governments of force, as is the case in all other monarchies and in most of the other republics. Jefferson wrote further that, "It is a problem, not clear in my mind, that the 1st condition [the Indian way] is not the best. But I believe it to be inconsistent with any great degree of population. The only condition on earth to be compared with ours, in my opinion, is that of the Indian, where they have still less law than we." In *Notes on Virginia*, Jefferson provided a description of Indian governance, which in some respects resembled the one the United States was erecting in his time, the pattern of states within a state which the founders called federalism.

Sixteenth- through 18th-century European political philosophers, early colonialists, and the founding fathers identify that American Indian society did influence European and colonial American democratic theories and institutions. In terms of the political philosophers, American Indians offered a distinct comparison to European society that did not previously exist. The colonists and founding fathers utilized American Indian society as both a counter to English society and in forging a unique American Democratic identity.

*Exemplar of Liberty: Native America and the Evolution of Democracy* (UCLA Press, 1991) by Donald A. Grinde, Jr., and Bruce E. Johansen, and *Exiled in the Land of the Free: Democracy, Indian Nations and the U.S. Constitution* (Clear House Publishers, 1992) edited by Oren R. Lyons and John C. Mohawk are the premier texts on the influence theory.

**IRREDENTISM, CONCEPT OF**   The term *irredentism* is derived from the Italian word *irredenta*, meaning "un-

redeemed." It originally referred to the political movement during the latter half of the 19th century to detach Italian speakers from Swiss and Austro-Hungarian control and bring them into the newly formed Italian state. Modern usage denotes territorial expansion by an existing state based on an ethnic, national, or historical rationale. Irredentism is different from secession in the sense that irredentism means the subtraction of territory from one state and adding it to another; secession refers to subtraction alone.

Exactly what qualifies as a case of irredentism is a matter of dispute in modern scholarship, with some arguing for a broad definition and others restricting it to attempts by existing states to annex only those territories of another state where their conationals live. During the 1990s, the most notable cases of irredentism were the Serbian irredentist projects in Croatia and Bosnia; Croatian designs on Bosnia; and Armenia's involvement in the Nagorno-Karabakh region of Azerbaijan. Some additional examples of potential or actual irredenta under the narrower definition include German designs on Polish and Czechoslovak territory in the 1930s; Greeks in Turkey and Albania; Albanians in Kosovo (Yugoslavia) and Macedonia; Somalis in Ethiopia and Kenya; Hungarians in Slovakia, Vojvodina (Yugoslavia), and Romania; Russians in Ukraine, the Baltic states, and Kazakhstan; and numerous cases in Africa.

Some scholars working with a broader definition of irredentism have applied the term to cases in which a state attempts to annex territories for purely historical reasons, even though there are no conationals residing there (e.g., Argentina's invasion of the Falkland Islands/Islas Maldives); when a stateless ethnic group aims to secede and set up its own state from the territory of a number of neighboring states (e.g., Kurds in Iraq, Iran, Turkey, and Syria); and when a state seeks to establish demographic dominance over territory already possessed by the state (e.g., the importation of Han Chinese into Tibet, Israeli settlement projects in the West Bank, and Serbian ethnic cleansing in Kosovo).

See *Irredentism and International Politics*, Naomi Chazan, ed. (Lynne Reinner, 1991); Myron Weiner, "The Macedonian Syndrome: A Historical Model of International Relations and Political Development," in *World Politics* 23 (July 1971), pp. 665–668; and Donald L. Horowitz, "Irredentas and Secessions: Adjacent Phenomena, Neglected Connections," *International Journal of Comparative Sociology* 33 (1–2) (1992), pp. 118–130.

**IRREDENTISM, HISTORY OF**   Irredentism is the advocacy of the acquisition of a region in another country by reason of historical, political, or ethnic ties. It therefore has a natural tie to nationalism, and nationalist groups often call for the transfer, or return, of such regions as a primary component of their political platforms.

The Helsinki Final Act of 1975 guaranteed national borders as they existed at the time, unless changes were agreed to by all parties involved, through negotiation, not war. This has not stopped nationalist groups from making irredentist claims on other lands.

One prominent example of irredentism is post-Soviet Moldova. The lands of Romania, Moldova, and Transylvania have all been a part of Greater Romania at various times during the last few centuries. A majority of people in these lands speak the same language, Romanian, and are affiliated with the Eastern Orthodox church. Romania has successfully acquired Transylvania, and many in Romania aspire to reintegrate Moldova into Greater Romania. During the breakup of the Soviet Union in the early 1990s, nationalist groups in Moldova called for union with Romania. In the years since, however, public opinion and nationalist sentiment have turned in favor of independence.

Another prominent example of irredentism is the issue of China and Taiwan. In 1949, when Communists won control of China, a small band of Chinese nationalists fled to Formosa, now Taiwan. While Taiwan has never declared itself independent from China, it has functioned as an independent state since 1949. China actively seeks the reintegration of Taiwan, and insists that its foreign partners recognize only one China. The Asian nation uses its size, the threat of military power, the lure of huge markets, and its seat on the UN Security Council, among other tools, to enforce compliance.

Irredentism poses unique problems for the international community because of the adjoined issue of redrawing of national boundaries. Irredentist politicians and leaders must use their nationalist rhetoric to convince citizens of the desired territory to wish to join them, or give up hope of uniting.

**ITALIAN NATIONALISM**  Italian nationalism cannot be traced directly from ancient Rome because the concept of "the nation" was completely unknown in that time. Nationalist ideas were spawned by the French Revolution and Italians' reactions to French occupation. After Napoleon's hold on Italy was broken in 1815, the Congress of Vienna reestablished Austrian domination in northern and central Italy. The Pope was granted the Vatican's pre-Napoleonic holdings again and the Bourbon king, Ferdinand I of the Two Sicilies, again became ruler of southern Italy. But the spark of the Enlightenment, Italian nationalism, and the right of Italians to establish a democratic state continued to ferment within a few secret societies of bourgeois intellectuals.

Prince Metternich of Austria stated correctly in 1815 that Italy was not a nation, but rather a "geographic concept." The only state within Italy that played an active role in Europe was Piedmont-Savoy, where the unification movement originated. The parochialism that had its roots in Italian history also resisted the few who dreamed of national unification. Numerous uprisings from 1820 to 1831 were all crushed. The revolutionary movement relied on the efforts of Giuseppe Mazzini, Count Camillo di Cavour, and Giuseppe Garibaldi. They made up the triple constellation of the "Resurgence," the name they gave to Italian political unification in 1861.

After most of northern and central Italy unified in 1860, thanks to the efforts of Piedmont-Savoy, the cauldron of unification began to bubble in the south. In the spring of 1860 revolts broke out in Sicily, which gave a highly talented military adventurer his chance to reenter the center stage in Italy—Garibaldi. A former member of Mazzini's "Young Italy" movement, he had spent thirteen years as a soldier of fortune in Latin America, where he became a master in the leadership of irregular forces and guerrilla warfare. He had raced back to Italy in 1848 when he heard of the revolutionary activity there. He formed military forces first in Lombardy, then in Venice and finally in Rome, where he served under Mazzini to defend the Roman Republic, which had just been created. From April to the end of June 1849, Garibaldi's legion, clad in red shirts and Calabrian hats, had defended the "Eternal City" valiantly against French troops protecting the Pope. Prolonged resistance had proved to be impossible, so Garibaldi fled with his troops to the tiny independent republic of San Marino, where he disbanded his army and went into exile.

Revolts in Sicily in 1860 again drew Garibaldi into southern Italy. In May he packed his 1000 irregulars, mostly students, poets, and soldiers of fortune, into rickety steamers and set a course directly to Sicily. When he arrived at Marsala, he declared himself dictator of Sicily and proceeded to defeat piecemeal the confused and divided Neapolitan troops defending the island. By mid-July he poised for his strike against the Bourbon Kingdom of the Two Sicilies with its capital in Naples. Riding a tide of popular enthusiasm, Garibaldi's army, which had swollen to 10,000 men, crossed the Strait of Messina in mid-1860, and his units produced panic among the Neapolitan troops whenever they appeared. On September 7, a jubilant Garibaldi entered the city of Naples in advance of his troops. In less than five months he had conquered the Kingdom of the Two Sicilies, a country of 11 million inhabitants.

On September 18 Piedmontese troops crushed the Pope's forces at Castelfidardo and then defeated a remaining Neapolitan army at Capua. These successes prompted the Piedmontese Parliament to annex southern Italy. Overwhelming popular support for union with Piedmont was expressed in plebiscites. In February 1861 Victor Emmanuel II was proclaimed king of Italy, and a new Italian parliament representing the entire peninsula except Rome and the province of Venetia assembled. Florence became Italy's capital until 1870.

The historical differences between northern and southern Italy were not overcome through the unification and establishment of a monarchy. Despite the initial enthusiasm in southern Italy for joining the newly unified state, northern rulers considered the south to be a conquered province of the north. They displayed little respect for traditional practices in the south, regarded the people as backward and rural, and included it in a highly centralized governmental administration that was imposed on all of Italy. Therefore, the Italian king's popularity in the south disappeared almost overnight, and southerners again began to look northward with distrust and resentment that survives to this day. The new national leaders next turned to the province of Venetia, which was still in the clutches of the Austrian Empire. When the latter entered a war in 1866 against Prussia, however, Italy immediately sided with the victorious Prussians, who granted their allies the prize Italians had wanted.

Only Rome remained outside the new Italy. The Vatican resented the reduction of its secular power in unified Italy. It was taboo even to speak of Piedmont and that part of Italy ruled by it. But when France became locked in war against Prussia in 1870, French troops could no longer defend Rome against the rest of Italy. Hence, in September royal Italian troops marched into Rome unchallenged, and the national capital was transferred to the city without delay.

In an unsuccessful attempt to divert attention from domestic political paralysis and tensions, Italy embarked on a colonial policy that was not only unprofitable, but it also robbed Italy of its strength. After a casualty-ridden expedition into the East African coast of Eritrea, Italy temporarily conquered this area in 1889–1890. A subsequent campaign in Ethiopia ended in catastrophe soon thereafter, costing the lives of 15,000 poorly equipped soldiers when the Ethiopians drove them out. Italy took Libya and the southeastern Greek islands (Dodecanese) from Turkey, which was in the process of disintegration. Rebellions, violent protests, assassinations, and bloody reactions against

the forces of order became so commonplace by the turn of the century that many observers believed that the young kingdom could not survive.

Sick and tired of these internal conflicts, a movement of bourgeois intellectuals under the leadership of the poet Gabriele D'Annunzio and the political thinkers Gaetano Mosca and Vilfredo Pareto gained respect. They practically declared war on the parliamentary system. D'Annunzio called on young Italians to seek fulfillment in violent action that would put an end to the parliamentary maneuvering, general mediocrity, and dullness that characterized public life. A jingoist National Party was created in 1910 under the leadership of Enrico Corradini. He never tired of painting an attractive picture of martial heroism, of total sacrifice of individualism and equality to one's nation, of the need for reestablishing discipline and obedience, of the grandeur and power of ancient Rome, and of the personal gratification that comes with living dangerously. Its extremist appeals were heard enthusiastically by many Italians, who needed only the travails of a long and disappointing war to make a dangerous leap toward fascism.

Although Italy had allied itself with Germany and Austria-Hungary in 1882, it declared its neutrality at the outbreak of World War I in 1914 on the grounds that its allies were waging an aggressive war. In 1915 it entered the war on the side of the French and British. It lost 600,000 men in battle, and the Italian economy was wrecked. To make things worse, the aftermath of the Paris peace settlement following the war never fulfilled Italy's high expectations. Trentino and the city of Trieste did become part of the country, as did the Istrian Peninsula and the German-speaking part of South Tirol, which even today remains a bone of contention between Austria and Italy.

Desperate economic and social conditions enabled Benito Mussolini to seize power in 1922. He tried to unify the Italian nation by outlawing all opposition and emulating the heroic epoch of ancient Roman conquerors. Like Hitler, he sent troops to fight on Franco's side in the Spanish civil war, and he joined the Axis powers in World War II. An active Italian resistance was militarily significant. Regular troops and partisan units fought against the Germans ever since the fall of Mussolini in mid-1943. After the war that resistance remained a symbol of wartime solidarity, but it did not lead Italians to put aside their many regional, political, and social differences, as many had hoped.

After the war, Italy found itself again in the strange position of being both the conquered and conqueror in that it had led attacks against Albania, Yugoslavia, and Greece and the conquered. In contrast to Germany, Italy was able to preserve its national unity. The peace treaty required Italy to renounce all claims on Ethiopia and Greece and to cede the Dodecanese Islands back to Greece and five small Alpine areas to France. In addition, the Istrian Peninsula (including Fiume and Pola) was awarded to Yugoslavia. The Trieste area west of the new Yugoslav territory was made a free city until 1954, when it and a 90-square-mile (135-square-kilometer) zone were divided between Italy and Yugoslavia.

Italy joined the United Nations in 1955, but the two main pillars of its foreign policy are the European Union (EU) and NATO, of which it was a founding member. In 1991 it sent ten Tornado aircraft and five naval vessels to the Persian Gulf to support its allies' war effort against Iraq. In 1993 Italy was one of the first countries to send troops on the UN humanitarian mission to Somalia, part of which had been ruled by Italy until 1960. When NATO launched an air war against Serbia in 1999 to try to stop ethnic cleansing in Kosovo, Italy stood by the alliance. Although its own aircraft were not involved, it sent 2000 troops to Albania to administer humanitarian aid, and it permitted NATO pilots to use fourteen bases in Italy, including especially Aviano in the northeast. Although some parties, such as the separatist Northern League and the United Communists, opposed the air strikes, Prime Minister Massimo D'Alema, a former Communist, declared that "we'll be loyal to the end."

A thorny problem that has enflamed Italian right-wing parties and nationalist groups is immigration. Italy is a natural bridge between the burgeoning populations of Africa and the rich nations of Europe. By 1999 legal immigrants living there numbered around one million. About 800,000 illegals had slipped in, and loopholes in the law make it difficult to deport them. Many Italians dislike the fact that some of them are involved in prostitution and drug rings in the major cities. Other European countries fear that Italy could be a gateway into the EU after becoming a member of the EU's Schengen group, which lifts border controls for those persons already inside an EU country. To the east, the collapsing Communist regimes in Albania and Yugoslavia present threats to Italy. In 1997, for the first time since World War II, Italy led a multinational force, including 6000 of its own soldiers, into Albania to restore order.

Perhaps the greatest threat to Italian national unity in the 21st century is the Northern League, an assortment of groups seeking regional autonomy and independence in the north. The most successful is the Lombard League, led by Umberto Bossi. The Northern League captures a fifth of northerners' votes in national elections. As the largest party north of the River Po, it wins up to 40 percent of the votes in some northern regions. In 1994 it temporarily entered the ruling coalition in Rome.

The league stands for federalism and devolution of power to the regions. It capitalizes on local dissatisfaction against what is seen as misrule by Rome, which does not seem to act vigorously to stem the wave of immigrants and to reverse Northern Italy's subsidizing of the south. It charges, with considerable justification, that too much of those funds ends up in the pockets of Mafia contractors. A clean-government party, it benefited from the country's campaign against corruption. Its spokesman, Roberto Maroni, announced that "our purpose of breaking up Italy is not linked to ethnic or religious identities, but to economic issues."

Emboldened by its strong election showing in 1996, the league proclaimed northern Italy an "independent and sovereign" republic called "Padania" (for the River Po) and called on the United Nations to recognize its right of self-determination. Unlike the Basque country in Spain and France, Padania has never existed before. Nevertheless, its supporters are playing government. They moved their fifteen "ministers" into a Renaissance building in Venice and swore in a self-nominated "parliament" in their "capital city" of Mantua. In 1997 they held unofficial parliamentary elections and charged the assembly with writing a new constitution that would make Padania either independent or loosely confederated with Italy. Advocates wave their own flag, wear green shirts, and call themselves "citizens of the North." They call on northerners to refuse to pay their taxes to Rome. Despite these trappings, opinion polls suggest that most northerners oppose secession although many agree with some of the league's criticisms. Bossi did not help his cause in 1997 by referring to the Pope as a "foreigner" and saying that the Italian flag belongs in the toilet. This remark brought a million Italians into the streets in Milan and Venice to demonstrate for national unity.

**ITO, HIROBUMI** 1841–1909, Born in Choshu-han, in the southern part of Japan. Ito became an active politician during the Meiji era (1868–1912). He studied politics under Shoin Yoshida, who was against the government's diplomacy, which had created social, economic, and political problems after the opening of the country in 1854. While studying under Yoshida, Ito met other political activists who were against the diplomatic policy and opposed trading with Western nations. Ito traveled to England in 1863 with his comrades in order to study politics.

Although Ito was originally against the diplomatic policy, he participated in signing the treaty with England, France, America, and Holland after Choshu-han was attacked by the naval forces of these four nations. After this incident, some political activists in Choshu-han became more or less conservative, including Ito. He was assigned many diplomatic tasks by the Meiji government. Between 1871 and 1882, Ito traveled to America and Europe to study the political systems and constitutions of various nations. Ito developed a proposal for the Meiji Constitution, which was greatly influenced by the German Constitution. The Meiji Constitution, designated by the Meiji Emperor, stated that the emperor held the primary right in politics, making Japan the first constitutional monarchy in Asia. Ito also established the cabinet system and became the first prime minister in 1885.

Ito was active in expanding Japan's commodity market abroad, especially to Korea. After defeating China in the Sino-Japanese war of 1895, Ito signed the Shimonoseki Treaty with China, and gained additional access to several Chinese ports. Ito also signed a treaty with Korea, declaring himself as superintendent of that country. After this, resistance emerged among Koreans to Japanese rule over Korea, which led to Ito's assassination by a Korean political activist in 1909.

## IZETBEGOVIĆ, ALIJA  1925–, President of Bosnia-Herzegovina, 1990–.

Izetbegović was trained as a lawyer and was involved in Muslim intellectual circles in Bosnia-Herzegovina in the 1970s and 1980s. He had earlier been a member of the Islamic, anticommunist organization *Mladi muslimani* (Young Muslims), and had been imprisoned by the Yugoslav government after World War II. In 1983, Izetbegović was tried and sentenced to fourteen years in prison for writing the *Islamic Declaration* (published ten years earlier, in 1973), in which he allegedly proposed to overthrow the Yugoslav state and establish an Islamic republic. Serb nationalists in Bosnia-Herzegovina have cited the *Islamic Declaration* as evidence for Izetbegović's alleged desire to create an Islamic fundamentalist state in Bosnia-Herzegovina. Although the *Declaration* does indeed contain substantial praise of Islamic values, the Serb nationalists' reading of it is misconstrued. In 1984, a book by Izetbegović entitled *Islam between East and West* was published in the United States. In the book, Izetbegović called for a compromise between Western materialism and Islamic values. Izetbegović was released from prison in November 1988.

In May 1990, Izetbegović founded and became the head of the Party of Democratic Action (Stranka Demokratske Akcije, or SDA), a predominantly Muslim party. In late February and early March 1992, a referendum on the independence of Bosnia-Herzegovina received the overwhelming support of the Muslim and Croat population, but the Bosnian Serbs boycotted the vote. On March 3, 1992, Izetbegović declared the independence of Bosnia-Herzegovina. Fighting in Sarajevo began two days later. Izetbegović traveled to North Africa and the Middle East in March and July 1991, lending fuel to the claims of Serb nationalists that he was pursuing an Islamic political agenda. In June 1991, Izetbegović and Macedonian President Kiro Gligorov proposed a constitutional reform of Yugoslavia. Gligorov and Izetbegović, as leaders of the most volatile and multiethnic republics in Yugoslavia, found common cause. The plan, which proposed an "asymmetrical federation" with differing levels of constitutional autonomy for the republics in Yugoslavia, was discarded after Slovenia announced its unambiguous intention for full independence.

During the war in Bosnia-Herzegovina, Izetbegović charged that Serbia, in cooperation with the Bosnian Serbs, was prosecuting genocide against the Muslim population of Bosnia-Herzegovina. Izetbegović frequently accused Europe and the United States of hypocrisy for refusing to lift the arms embargo, and he claimed that the West's reluctance to intervene betrayed a general antipathy toward Islam. Western negotiators viewed Izetbegović as an uncooperative and idealistic leader. Under heavy pressure from the United States, Izetbegović signed the Vance-Owen Plan, which proposed an ethnic cantonal structure for Bosnia-Herzegovina, in March 1993. Due to opposition from the Bosnian Serbs, the plan was never realized. In March 1994, Izetbegović signed the Washington Framework Agreement, which envisaged a Muslim-Croat federation between Bosnia-Herzegovina and Croatia. Although minor progress was made toward this goal, the Herzegovinian Croats successfully resisted any serious attempts to realize the plan. In November 1995, Izetbegović signed the Dayton Accords, which ended the war in Bosnia-Herzegovina. Since then, Izetbegović and the SDA have exhibited increased reluctance to allow the return of Serbs and Croats to areas now controlled by the Bosnian government.

# J

**JAPANESE NATIONALISM**   Japanese nationalism was commonly known as fascism between the mid-1930s and the end of World War II, when the military officials seized control of Japanese politics. The term is also used to refer to the right-wing movement that seeks the restoration of the emperor as the highest power in the nation. Another interpretation of Japanese nationalism is the belief that Japanese are pure "Yamato Minzoku" ( Japanese race) and superior to other races. Purity of the race is also related to the geographical isolation of the country and the government's seclusion policy from the rest of the world between the 17th and the mid-19th century.

Although Japan had diplomatic relationships with foreign nations for many centuries in spite of its geographical isolation, the first three generations of Tokugawa shoguns tried to close the country through the prohibition of Christianity and trade control. Christianity, which teaches equality among people before God, was not compatible with the feudal system, which separated the Japanese into four different social classes, creating a caste system. "Sakoku" (seclusion policy) was completed in 1639, allowing only Dutch and Chinese traders to visit the port of Nagasaki in the southern part of Japan. Although Sakoku contributed to the development of unique Japanese culture and traditions for almost 200 years, the absence of diplomatic relationships drove many Japanese to adopt Western culture when Sakoku ended in 1853.

Near the end of Sakoku and collapse of the Shogunal government due to frequent visits of foreign traders and diplomats to Japan, there emerged a movement to restore Shintoism and the emperor system. The movement, which emphasized nationalism, was very popular among the lower class warriors and wealthy farmers, and became the "Sonno Joi" movement. The Sonno Joi movement in the early 1800s promoted respect for the emperor and the abolition of the shogun government.

After the Meiji Revolution in the 1860s, Japan established the Meiji Constitution which abolished many previous restrictions, such as the land owning system and the class system, providing equality among the Japanese. To catch up with the industrial development of the Western nations, Japan also welcomed Western cultural influence on Japanese traditions, in the areas of industry, politics, arts, food, clothing, and so forth. At the same time, there emerged the civil rights movement, which further promoted democracy and westernization. However, there were many Japanese, especially previous warriors, who were against the new Meiji government and the philosophy of equality among people. This was the origin of the right-wing group, which criticized westernization, supported nationalism, and sought the revival of the emperor system. During the Sino-Japanese war (1894–1895) and the Russo-Japanese war (1904–1905), the government emphasized militaristic nationalism, colonizing several parts of Korea and China. These incidents partly contributed to nationalism in a negative way, nurturing the ideology that Japanese were superior to people of other nations.

Imperialism supported by fascist government grew in Europe as well as in Asia in the early 20th century, which led to World Wars I and II. In Japan military officials, led by Lieutenant General Hideki Tojo, literally seized control of Japanese politics for ten years from the mid-1930s. The fascist government prohibited freedom of speech, Christianity (which taught love to people regardless of race), proletarian literature, and Marxism. The government also established "Kokumin Gakko" (National Elementary School) in 1940, where students were socialized into Japanese nationalism and patriotic devotion to the country. Fascism and nationalism were popular themes in arts and literature during this period.

After Japan was defeated in World War II, the Allied Force General Headquarters eradicated Japanese fascism and promoted democracy in politics. The Japanese Constitution, which became effective in 1947, stipulates that the Japanese people desire peace for all time and renounce war forever as a sovereign right of the nation. However the right-wing group continues to exist, supporting fascism and claiming the emperor as the highest political organ of the nation. Some members of the group are strong supporters of Japanese nationalism. They believe that the Japanese are a pure race, and resist westernization of Japanese traditions and values. Their ideology is occasionally regarded as discriminatory against minority groups in Japan and against guest workers from other countries. Verbal attacks against these minority groups in quest of purity of the Japanese race are frequently written on walls in public.

## JARUZELSKI, WOJCIECH

1923–, One of the most controversial figures in modern Polish history. During World War II, he and his family were deported to Siberia by Soviet forces, where his parents perished. Nonetheless, although the Soviets tightly controlled the Polish army assembled in the Soviet Union, he joined it. After the war, he joined the Polish Communist Party and rose steadily through the ranks of both the military and the party. He became minister of defense in 1968 and continued in that position throughout most of the 1980s. In 1981, he became prime minister of Poland, and later that year, general secretary of the party. Jaruzelski was thus in a central position of authority during most of the Polish Republic's periodic postwar upheavals.

In December 1970, a workers' uprising on the Baltic coast, especially in the port cities of Gdansk, Gdynia, and Szczecin, was met with massive military force that included tanks and soldiers firing live bullets at workers. The government claimed that there were forty-three dead, while many witnesses from that period allege many more dead and thousands injured. Jaruzelski claimed that he played no role in the decision to send in the military, nor in the orders to shoot. Doubts about that claim remain, and in 1997, there was an attempt to put him on trial for his role in those events, but eventually the government dropped the charges.

In February 1981, as the government became increasingly unable to impose peace, Jaruzelski was elevated to the position of prime minister, while retaining his control over the military. Because the army was one of the few institutions that still had some popular respect, there was hope that he would be able to calm the situation. But, within weeks, an apparent provocation against Soli-

darity leaders in the north central city of Bydgoszcz brought tensions in the country to a new height.

In the fall, an extraordinary party congress, the elections for which were quite democratic in the big factories and the larger cities, nonetheless left Jaruzelski and his allies in control. Jaruzelski's government sent troops into 2000 villages, and later into Poland's main cities under the pretexts of creating order and doing inventories to determine what supplies the country had. This and other measures were a prelude to what was effectively a military coup, in which some 10,000 Solidarity activists and leaders were interned, mostly on the night of December 12–13, 1981.

Jaruzelski has consistently maintained that he was acting in good faith, protecting Poland against the worse spectacle of a Soviet invasion, and he has been supported in that view by Adam Michnik, a leading intellectual opponent of the Communist regime. But many in the opposition felt that a military invasion was improbable, given the immensity of the economic, political, and military burden it would impose on the Soviets, who were already bogged down in Afghanistan. The work of several scholars seems to support the opposition's view.

After several years of stalemate, Jaruzelski offered to negotiate with the opposition about the future shape of Poland. The result was semi-free elections in which Solidarity won every seat but one of those it was allowed to contest. Within a year, Lech Walesa, the Solidarity leader, demanded and got free elections for the presidency—Jaruzelski stepped aside. Poles are deeply split regarding how to judge Jaruzelski: patriot or traitor?

Two good books with differing points of view on Solidarity are *Breaking the Barrier* by Lawrence Goodwyn (Oxford University, 1991) and *The Polish Revolution* by Timothy Garton Ash (Vintage Book, 1985)

## JEFFERSON, THOMAS

1743–1826, Third president of the United States of America and the principal author of its Declaration of Independence from the British Empire. Jefferson's erudition and eloquent pen thrust him into a leadership position at the earliest stages of American nationalism and resulted in his inspiring nationalist movements around the world for the centuries that followed.

At the age of thirty-one he penned his first well-known anticolonialist essay, "A Summary View of the Rights of British America," which served as the instructions for the Virginia delegation to the Continental Congress. It attracted widespread attention among colonists growing restless with British rule, although it was far too radical at the time for many members of the Congress. In it he contended that the colonial legislatures were subject only to the king, and not to the British Parliament. The concept was ahead of its time, but not as far ahead as some thought, because the conflicts between the colonies and the British regime were escalating more rapidly than most expected. "The God who gave us life gave us liberty at the same time," Jefferson insisted. "The hand of force may destroy, but cannot disjoin them."

In 1776 Jefferson was placed on the committee with Benjamin Franklin and John Adams to draft a statement explaining the reasons for the imminent decision by the colonists to break with the British. The young Jefferson's skills at writing were so respected even by such eminent statesmen that the task of first drafting the document was given to him. In the words of that document, which became the Declaration of Independence, Jefferson penned a rationale for revolution that still inspires would-be nationalists.

Jefferson stood above even his remarkable contemporaries in eloquence with the pen, but he himself knew that he was not an orator. Although chosen to be the third president of the new nation, his accomplishments as head of state never surpassed his contribution to the philosophical foundations of American nationalism.

Jefferson was able to strike a conciliatory tone in the midst of considerable controversy surrounding federalist policies, and despite the radicalism of his rhetoric as a young revolutionary, he attempted to build some consensus among conflicting sides in the new nation. Moreover, he was able to bring about a number of remarkable changes during his two terms in office, notably the Louisiana Purchase, the acquisition of the entire western Mississippi River Basin from Napoleon that nearly doubled the size of the country.

Rather than seek a third term in office, Jefferson chose to follow Washington's lead of voluntarily limiting his tenure to two terms and returned to Virginia. In his home state his last great contribution to his new nation was the creation of the University of Virginia; he not only designed the buildings and supervised their construction but also recruited faculty and worked with them to design a curriculum.

## JEMILEV, MUSTAFA 1944–, Most outstanding nationalist leader in the Crimean Tatar nationalist movement, born in the village of Ay-Serez in the Sudak region of the Crimean peninsula. On May 18, 1944, the seven-month-old Jemilev (often Dzhemilev) was deported from his homeland along with the rest of the Crimean Tatar nation of nearly 200,000 (a Turkic-Muslim ethnic group indigenous to the Crimean peninsula) to

Central Asia (primarily to Uzbekistan). All Crimean Tatars, including women and children such as Jemilev, were spuriously charged with "mass treason" against the Soviet homeland during the Nazi invasion of the USSR and ethnically cleansed from their ancient homeland.

Jemilev's family was exiled to a special settlement camp in the town of Gulistan (Uzbekistan) and it was only in 1956 that they, like the rest of the Crimean Tatar nation, were released from the camps. Although released from the camps, the Crimean Tatars were forbidden to return to their homeland, which had become part of Ukraine in the Crimean Tatars' absence. At this time many Crimean Tatars began to agitate for the right to return to their natal territory.

In the 1960s Jemilev, who worked in an aviation factory in the Uzbek capital of Tashkent, joined the Crimean Tatar national movement and soon distinguished himself as a bold voice of resistance to the Soviet regime. Jemilev was part of a young faction of the Crimean Tatar national movement that called for directly challenging the Soviet government's policy of forbidding the Crimean Tatars from returning to their cherished homeland. Rather than continuing a passive policy of sending petitions to Moscow requesting the right to return to the Crimea, Jemilev and the younger guard sought to link their struggle to the wider dissident movement in the USSR.

For his "anti-Soviet" activities Jemilev was imprisoned six times (the first sentencing took place in 1969) and he used the occasion of his sentencings to deliver fiery speeches calling for the right of his people to return to their native land. From the time of his first arrest at twenty-three until the age of forty-three Jemilev spent only seven years unincarcerated. Jemilev's case was publicized to the world by Soviet dissidents, such as Andrei Sakharov, and he soon achieved a Mandela-like status among his people.

By the late 1980s the political scene in the USSR had begun to change under the influence of Soviet president Mikhail Gorbachev's policy of openness, and Jemilev was released from prison. By 1989 the Soviet government also gave into the pressure from Crimean Tatar nationalists and granted the exiled Crimean Tatars the right to return to their homeland.

By 1991 the informal Crimean Tatar "initiative groups" (dissident cells) had been replaced by two nationalist parties, known as the National Movement of the Crimean Tatars (Russian, the NMKT) and the Organization of the Crimean Tatar National Movement (OKND). Jemilev was chosen to lead the more radical of the two parties, the OKND, which was uncompromising in its calls for the total repatriation of the

Crimean Tatar people to the Crimea. In June 1991, the Crimean Tatars held a historic *Kurultay* (Congress) in Simferopol, the capital of the Crimean Republic, and elected Jemilev (who was given the honorific name Kirimoglu, i.e., "Son of the Crimea") head of a permanent Crimean Tatar parallel government known as the *Mejlis* (Parliament).

Much of Mustafa Jemilev-Kirimoglu's work in the subsequent years has been focused on gaining Ukrainian citizenship and greater rights for tens of thousands of Crimean Tatars who have since 1989 immigrated to the Crimea from Central Asia (approximately half of the former Soviet Union's 500,000 Crimean Tatars have returned to the Crimea). While the returning Crimean Tatars, who are extremely nationalistic, have clashed with local Slavic populations on several occasions, Jemilev has largely been seen as a voice of moderation. While firmly demanding the right of his people to the Crimean homeland, Jemilev's tactics have tended to be nonviolent.

In 1998, Jemilev was elected to the Ukrainian *Verkhovna Rada* (Parliament) as a candidate for the Rukh party (a nationalist Ukrainian party that sympathizes with the Crimean Tatar cause). Jemilev, the tireless scourge of the governmental system that has oppressed his people, is now working within the system to improve the lot of impoverished people as they attempt to rebuild their lives in a post-Soviet Crimea dominated by local Russians.

For the definitive history of the Crimean Tatars, see Alan Fisher's *The Crimean Tatars* (Stanford, Hoover Press 1979), Edward Allworth's *The Crimean Tatars. Return to the Homeland* (Durham; Duke University Press, 1998) deals with more contemporary issues. See Brian Glyn Williams, "The Crimean Tatar Exile in Central Asia. A Case Study in Group Destruction" in *Central Asian Survey* 2 (June 1998) for an analysis of the contemporary struggle of Crimean Tatars.

## JINNAH, MOHAMMED ALI

1876–1948, First governor-general (1947–1948) and founder of the Muslim state of Pakistan, also known as A'id-e Azam, Arabic for "The Great Leader." An English-educated lawyer in British India, Jinnah became a major figure in the Indian independence movement and a collaborator with Gandhi. In the end, however, he insisted on the formation of a separate Muslim state, claiming that Muslims would be maltreated in a Hindu-dominated India.

The eldest of seven children, he suffered the loss of his mother and wife while studying law in London. At the age of nineteen he was called to the bar in London where the liberal Prime Minister William E. Gladstone influenced him. He also joined the campaign of a leading Indian nationalist, Dadabhai Naoroji, when he ran successfully for the English Parliament.

After his return to India he became involved with the nationalist cause and the Indian Nationalist Party in which he provided key leadership. At first he refused to join the All-India Muslim League when it was formed in 1906 and was known as the "Ambassador of Hindu-Muslim unity." He finally joined the Muslim nationalist cause and in the end broke with Congress and insisted on a partition of British India into two states, one a Muslim homeland and the other predominantly Hindu.

Upon independence from Britain Jinnah became the first Pakistani head of state and was considered the father of the nation. Soon after taking office, however, his health began to fail and he died a year later in 1848.

## JOAN OF ARC

1412/13?–1431, Both a historical and mythical figure, Joan of Arc ( Jeanne d'Arc, also known as *Jeanne la pucelle*) was a peasant maid who guided the weak and contested dauphin Charles, son of Charles VI who submitted to English rule in France, into regaining the French crown and territory during the Hundred Years War between France and England (approximate dates, 1337–1457).

Joan of Arc was born in Domrémy in the French province of Lorraine. She presumably heard the voice of God through saints summoning her to assist the dauphin in reclaiming the French crown and ousting the English. Her legendary itinerary started in early 1429 at Vaucouleurs when she raised her first troops in support of Charles. Later that year, in the castle of Chinon, she convinced the dauphin to accept her help to go into battle against the English. In May, her troops liberated Orléans forcing into retreat the English who had besieged the city since 1428. She was instrumental in the coronation of the dauphin as Charles VII, the king of France, on July 17 in Reims in 1429. On September 8, however, she failed to liberate Paris and, on May 23, 1430, was captured in Compiègne probably with the help of a French faction allied to the English. Her subsequent trial led by the bishop of the town of Beauvais, Cauchon, and supported by the University of Paris, lasted from February through May 30, 1430, when she was publicly burnt as a heretic on the main square of Rouen. The principal grounds of accusation were her refusal to deny the divine sources of the "voices" that ordered her to take up the arms against the English and her insistence on wearing men's clothes. A three-year-long trial (1452–1455) annulled the first one. She was proposed for canonization in 1869 and officially canonized in 1920.

Joan of Arc has captured the public's imagination for over four centuries. Her native village of Domrémy, in the department of the Meuse, has been a common tourist attraction since the 16th century. She has been the focus of continuous, if shifting and sometimes paradoxical, national and religious cults, especially in the 19th and 20th centuries. She is commonly associated with French singular and courageous heroism in the face of foreign invasion.

Napoleon in particular restored her cult by authorizing the celebration of the Orléans victory on May 8. At the end of the 19th century, she became the symbol of both Dreyfus's supporters, who claimed she, like the Jewish colonel, was an outsider victim of an unfair trial, and of Dreyfus's opponents who saw in her the image of a true French identity. In the early 1900s, she became the symbol of the reactionary movement and newspaper, *Action Française,* which espoused a political program that included the restoration of a militaristic monarchy. Later, she embodied French national unity that could transcend differences; during the Nazi occupation of France, she symbolized the Vichy government's *Révolution Nationale* led by Philippe Pétain. More recently, feminist theorists have seen her as a female symbol of strength and political power.

Joan of Arc's fate has been the object of countless literary, musical, and visual representations that span across the four and a half centuries since her death in Rouen. They include Voltaire's parody *La pucelle d'Orléans* (1730), a critique of the French royal house; Bernard Shaw's theatrical piece *Saint Joan* (1923); and composer Arthur Honegger's opera *Jeanne au bûcher* on Paul Claudel's text (1938). Cinematographic representations include Carl Theodore Dreyer's famous *La passion de Jeanne d'Arc* (1928), Robert Bresson's *Le procès de Jeanne d'Arc* (1962), and, more recently, *Jeanne la pucelle* by Jacques Rivette (1993). The numerous statues and paintings representing her usually focus on either her political or her religious symbolism.

For critical work examining Joan of Arc's symbolism, see Marina Warner's landmark *Joan of Arc. The Image of Female Heroism* (New York, Knopf 1981); J. van Herwaarden, ed., *Joan of Arc. Reality and Myth* (Rotterdam, Hilverum, 1994); and Susan Crane "Clothing and Gender Definition: Joan of Arc" in *Journal of Medieval and Early Modern Studies* **28** (1996), pp. 297–320.

**JOHNSON, LYNDON B.** 1908–1973, Born in Texas into a political family, Johnson was elected to the House of Representatives in 1937. He returned to Congress after serving as a naval lieutenant commander in the Pacific War from December 1941 until 1942, when the president called members of Congress back to Washington. After eleven years in the house, he was elected to the Senate in 1948. There he shared some of the responsibility for maintaining the bipartisan support for Dwight D. Eisenhower's foreign policy. He became an acknowledged expert in legislative rules and tactics and rose to majority leader. He was John F. Kennedy's vice president from 1961 until Kennedy's assassination in Dallas in November 1963.

As president, Johnson was an activist in implementing civil rights legislation and other aspects of his "Great Society" program. In foreign policy he sent American troops to intervene in the Dominican Republic in 1965. This use of American forces was criticized both in Congress and in the rest of Latin America. But he faced his most intractable challenge in Indochina.

He inherited his predecessor's commitment to prevent South Vietnam from falling to the Communists. Congress initially gave him a largely free hand through the Tonkin Bay Resolution, which was granted after a dubious incident involving an American warship off the Vietnamese shore. This resolution reflected widespread American support for Johnson's cautious support of South Vietnam. This policy helped him win the 1964 election. In fact, despite the United States' inability to defeat the Vietcong and North Vietnamese forces in Indochina and despite growing protests on American streets against America's involvement, especially after the 1968 Tet offensive, the majority of Americans continued to support their government's Vietnam policy. There was also a broad consensus among the foreign policy elite and his own advisors throughout his presidency that the United States had to persist in its policy. Nevertheless, frustrated by his inability to improve the prospects for victory, and challenged by leaders in his own party, especially Robert Kennedy and Eugene McCarthy, he decided not to seek reelection in 1968. During Johnson's presidency, America lost much of its hubris about the rightness of its role in the world and the desirability of global military and political involvement. It gained stark recognition about the limits of American power.

**JORDAN, JUNE** 1936–, American poet, writer, activist, and educator, born in Harlem, New York City. Jordan writes in a number of different genres for a variety of audiences from children to adults, but she is best known as a poet. She is noted for bringing art and politics together to aid others in understanding the black experience in America. While neither a black nationalist nor an American nationalist, she writes at the intersection of both, exploring the relationship between identity and the American nation.

In her political essays she is both critical and optimistic about America. She examines the relationship between the myth of the American dream, American social and economic inequalities, and the experience of being inside and outside of the nation. In doing so, she discusses the heterogeneous nature of American national identity as the new "we." She exposes the powerful role of whiteness in maintaining inequality and "white supremacy as our national bottom line." In addition, she looks at the relationship between gender and sexual identity and America. Throughout her essays she illustrates tensions and contradictions in American politics and society and encourages her readers to change and take action against the status quo.

Many themes in her work focus on maintaining and developing black self-determination against a hostile American society. In a biographical work, *Civil Wars,* written in 1981, she addresses flaws in white interpretations of black life and urges blacks to formulate their own self-image. She also sees violence as a permissible means of black struggle. Her books for children are written in "black English" and reflect her dedication to the survival of the black community.

Jordan's collections of political essays are *Affirmative Acts* (Anchor Books, 1998) and *Technical Difficulties: African American Notes on the State of the Union* (Pantheon Books, 1992).

**JOSEPH (CHIEF)** 1840–1904, Chief Joseph became nationally famous as a military genius in 1877 as he led the Nez Perces through Idaho and Montana in an attempt to allow his people to be left alone and free in their homeland. His band avoided General O. O. Howard's troops, but due to exhaustion were forced to surrender to General Nelson Miles's numerically superior forces. Joseph's attempt to find peace for his people, the so-called Nez Perce War, was one of the last episodes in the struggle that the United States carried out to dispossess the Indians of their lands. Joseph gained national sympathy among whites, but this did not help his people to retain their lands.

Joseph was born in the Grande Ronde River valley in northeastern Oregon, and lived his young life in the nearby Wallowa River valley. Little is known of his early life. Joseph's band of Nez Perces called this region their home. The other major band of Nez Perces lived in the Lapwai region of western Idaho. The 1855 treaty between the two bands and the United States called for two different reservations. The U.S. Congress, however, negated the treaty and in 1863 a new treaty was imposed on unsuspecting Nez Perces, who were assigned to a single reservation in Lapwai. As most people in Joseph's band, which was led by his father Old Joseph until 1873, did not know about the treaty, and none of them had signed it, they refused to move to the assigned reservation.

The 1863 treaty gave white cattlemen and gold-seekers an excuse to encroach on Nez Perce lands. This led to confrontations between the whites and the Indians. The United States backed up the whites and put pressure on Joseph to move his people to the reservation by 1877. Trying to avoid a war, Joseph reluctantly agreed, but many others refused to give up their homeland. Joseph listened to his people and war ensued, resulting in a heroic struggle during which Joseph led a band of Nez Perce warriors, women, and children, skillfully maneuvering through Idaho, Yellowstone National Park, and Montana in an attempt to reach Canada. Eventually the Nez Perces, exhausted by the escape effort and fierce winter, were overpowered in north-central Montana by Miles's forces. Joseph and his band were imprisoned, and eventually relocated to the Colville Reservation in northeastern Washington State. Joseph was never allowed to return to his beloved Wallowa Valley.

Chief Joseph signifies an attempt by a Native American leader to keep the homeland of his people secure and intact. The Nez Perces were a people who had pride in their high level of independence and low level of intermixing and contact with whites. This may have led to white misconceptions about Nez Perce culture and made them appear hostile. Joseph, as a perceptive leader, became a key to the Nez Perce struggle against forceful removal to a reservation and to an assertion of inalienable rights to their home, which they had never relinquished in fraudulent treaties.

Chester Anders Fee's *Chief Joseph: The Biography of a Great Indian* (New York: Wilson-Ericson, 1936) is old, but still the only biography of Chief Joseph. Also see Merrill D. Beal's *"I Will Fight No More Forever": Chief Joseph and the Nez Perce War* (Seattle: University of Washington Press, 1984), and the brief *Chief Joseph's Own Story* (Fairfield, Wash.: Ye Galleon Press, 1981).

**JOVANOVIĆ, SLOBODAN** 1869–1959, Serb jurist, historian, and politician. Jovanović was the son of Vladimir Jovanović, a well-known Serb politician and jurist. Slobodan Jovanović received his primary and secondary education in Belgrade. He then studied in Zurich, Munich, and Geneva, receiving a law degree in 1890. He held a number of posts in the Serbian bureaucracy and foreign service. From 1894 to 1897 Jovanović worked with the Serbian Ministry of Foreign Affairs to disseminate government propaganda in areas outside Serbia populated by Serbs and other South Slavs. He became a professor of law in Belgrade in 1897. This marked the beginning of a prolific career in commentary on jurisprudence, history, politics, and literature. He became a full member of the Serbian Academy of Arts and Sciences in 1908. In the years before and during World War I, Jovanović served as a public relations officer for the Serb army.

During World War I, Jovanović came into personal contact with Colonel Dragutin Dimitrijević-Apis, a leader of the Black Hand, a conspiratorial nationalist organization. After World War I, Jovanović devoted his time to academics, although he also remained active in politics. He also functioned as an adviser to King Aleksandar Karađorđević on constitutional questions. Jovanović argued that the Serb nation's devotion to a state-building project and its long 19th-century struggle for liberation from the Ottoman Empire predisposed it to the construction of a centralist Yugoslav state.

In 1937, Jovanović became president of the newly founded *Srpski kulturni klub* (SKK, Serb Cultural Club). Jovanović, although more moderate than the SKK vice-president, Dragiša Vasić, argued that a Yugoslav identity had only existed to the extent that the government forced it on the population of Yugoslavia in the 1920s. Furthermore, Jovanović believed that the personal dictatorship of the regime had been camouflaged during the first decade of the Yugoslav state, only to reveal its true face in 1929. Jovanović claimed that the mistakes of the first ten years of Yugoslavia had come about due to misguided unitarist policies, rather than from Serbian nationalist policies. Jovanović never articulated how Serbdom could coexist with Yugoslavism, nor could he explain how a robust Serbdom could avoid attacking Croatdom. The SKK subsequently rejected the 1939 compromise agreement (*Sporazum*) granting wide autonomy to Croatia within Yugoslavia.

In 1941, Jovanović lent his support to the coup against the signers of the treaty with Nazi Germany. As Germany invaded Yugoslavia in April 1941, Jovanović fled into exile with the Yugoslav government. From January 1942 until June 1943 he served as the prime minister of the government-in-exile. After World War II, the People's Courts of Yugoslavia tried Jovanović *in absentia* and sentenced him to twenty years in prison. The Communist government in Yugoslavia banned the publication of Jovanović's prodigious and diverse writings. Jovanović never returned to Yugoslavia and died in exile in 1959.

## JUÁREZ, BENITO   1806–1872, Born in the village of San Pablo Guelatao, Oaxaca. His parents were Zapotec

Indian peasants who died when he was a three-year-old toddler. At the age of twelve he moved to the city of Oaxaca in an attempt to receive an education. Later, he was taken in by Antonio Salanueva, a Franciscan monk who encouraged Juárez to attend the seminary for his education. He rejected an ecclesiastical career in order to study law at the newly founded Institute of Sciences and Arts, where he received his degree in 1834. In 1831, even before Benito Juárez received his law degree, his political career began with his election to the city council of Oaxaca. In 1833, he was elected to the state legislature, and in 1841 he was appointed civil judge. In 1843, he married Margarita Maza. In 1845, Juárez was named by liberal forces to the executive committee for the state, after the legislative body was dissolved in a revolt led by General Mariano Paredes.

In 1846, elected to the national congress, Juárez supported President Valentín Gómez Farías in his attempt to use church property to pay for a costly war with the United States. The Rebellion of the Polkos, in 1847, brought Antonio López de Santa Anna to the presidency, and forced Juárez to return to Oaxaca. From 1847 to 1852 he was governor of Oaxaca, and in these last years he became director of the Institute of Sciences and Arts. When Santa Anna returned to the presidency in 1853, Juárez fled.

Juárez and his allies provided the political platform for the liberals' Revolution of Ayutla in 1854. President Álvarez named Juárez titular of the secretariat of justice and ecclesiastical affairs. Juárez wrote the *Ley Juárez*, which eliminated the right of ecclesiastical and military courts to preside over civil cases, and President Álvarez ratified it in November 1855. Juárez resigned the following month, returning to Oaxaca, where he took office as governor in January 1856 and served for nearly two years. Juárez supported and swore to uphold the Constitution of 1857. President Ignacio Comonfort selected Juárez minister of government in November 1857. Elected president of the Supreme Court, Comonfort signed a decree to shut down Congress and have Juárez incarcerated. Juárez was freed in January 1858 and escaped from the capital, just before conservative militarists ousted Comonfort and declared Félix Zuloaga president. The coup notwithstanding, in accordance with the Constitution of 1857, Juárez succeeded Comonfort in the presidency, taking the oath of office on January 19, 1858 in Guanajuato, hence leaving Mexico with dual presidents and civil conflict.

During the "War of the Reform" (1858–1860), Juárez escaped to Guadalajara, where he was captured and nearly executed by conservative forces. Later he made his way to Colima, then Manzanillo, and via Panama,

Havana, and New Orleans to Veracruz, where the liberal governor, Manuel Gutiérrez Zamora, allowed Juárez to establish his government. With the support of radical liberals like Miguel Lerdo de Tejada and Melchor Ocampo, Juarez issued reform laws separating the church and state, establishing civil marriage, and civil registration of births and deaths, secularizing the cemeteries, and expropriating the property of the church. The reactionary forces held most of central Mexico but were unable to dislodge the Juárez government from Veracruz. Perennially lacking funds to pay the improvised forces that fought the conservatives, the liberal government expropriated and sold church property.

During the war, Juárez authorized arrangements with the United States. The McLane-Ocampo Treaty, which Juárez's secretary of foreign relations Melchor Ocampo negotiated with the U.S. diplomat Robert M. McLane in 1859, allowed U.S. protection of transit over routes across Mexican territory in exchange for several million dollars. By the end of Comonfort's term in 1861, there were new elections, with Juárez winning a majority. His government's suspension of payments on the foreign debt led to the intervention of Spain, France, and Great Britain. Spanish and British forces soon withdrew, but French forces stayed, supporting the estab-lishment of a Mexican Empire. The French Intervention (1862–1867) provides conflicting images of Juárez. A bold Juárez led the republican forces that tenaciously defended Mexico and its republican constitution during years of struggle against foreign and imperial armies. But Juárez's critics charge that he illegally extended his presidency when his constitutional term ended in 1865 and that he arbitrarily ordered the arrest and jailing of Jesús Gonzalez Ortega, who ought to have replaced him in the presidency.

The rise and ebb of the imperial armies sparked a moment of unity for Mexican liberals, but Juárez's attempt to defy the Constitution and strengthen the presidency by referendum again led critics to charge him with dictatorial methods. Juárez garnered sufficient support to win the presidential elections of December 1867. By the time of the 1871 elections, Juárez could no longer count on a majority of votes, and the election passed to Congress, which elected him to another term. Porfirio Díaz resorted to rebellion, but Juárez was able to defeat him, again with an extension of extraordinary powers. Juárez died July 18, 1872, becoming, after his death, a preeminent symbol of Mexican nationalism and resistance to foreign intervention.

# K

**KÁDÁR, JÁNOS** 1912–1989, Born of proletarian parents, Kádár's tenure as first (general) secretary of the Central Committee of the Hungarian Socialist Workers Party, from October 1956 through May 1988, made him the longest serving of Hungary's Communist leaders. Kádár joined the Socialist Workers Party in 1930 and became general secretary of the Communist Young Workers movement and a member of the then-illegal Communist Party one year later. Between 1931 and 1937, the Horthy government occasionally incarcerated him for his political activities. From May 1942 on, Kádár was a member of the Communist Party's Central Committee and led the small Communist underground in Hungary. Arrested again in 1944, he escaped from prison that same year, but in the interim lost his top leadership position to Moscow's preferred man, Mátyás Rákosi. From May 1945 to August 1948, Kádár was the secretary of the Budapest branch of the Communist Party, played a substantial role in the affairs of the police and security forces, served on the party's Central Committee, and was the head of the party's Central Cadre Division. In 1948 he rose to secretary of the interior and was a key organizer of the show trial of László Rajk.

Kádár too fell prey to the purges, accused by his own associates of a Titoist antistate conspiracy and jailed from 1951 to 1954. This period of internment was crucial to establishing his credentials not necessarily as a reformer, but as a victim of the excesses of Hungary's Stalinist period. Rehabilitated in 1954, he began working his way back up the bureaucracy. He reached the pinnacle of power in the revolutionary days of October 1956. First, the Hungarian Workers Party, with the Kremlin's consent, named him party first secretary. Second, having been persecuted by Hungary's Stalinists and enjoying some good graces in Moscow, Kádár was an acceptable choice for both the Nagy government and the Kremlin to serve as the minister of state. These two appointments gave Kádár the power base that allowed him to remain the key figure in Hungarian politics for the next thirty years.

The most crucial factor in Kádár's rise, however, was Kremlin support. At the height of the revolution on November 2–3, he negotiated with Nikita Khrushchev, agreeing to cooperate with Soviet forces and suppress the revolution. On November 4, 1956, Kádár proclaimed the formation of a new Revolutionary Worker-Peasant government. He shocked Hungarians by admitting that the policies enacted by the Rákosi government were responsible for worker discontent, but did so just as Soviet tanks embarked to crush the revolution. Although he brought about many of the reforms he promised, including reform of the party, higher living standards, more housing, less bureaucracy, and more worker control of production, these carrots were complemented by severe repression of all revolutionary activity. Martial law, summary judgment, and secret trials resulted in the execution of more than 2000 participants in the 1956 revolution, including Imre Nagy himself. A large portion of Hungary's intellectual élite was among the tens of thousands who fled Hungary during Kádár's first months in office.

However, Kádár soon introduced a more consistent rule of law. In 1961 he began to release participants in the 1956 uprising and initiated a gradual relaxation of restraints on cultural freedom, travel, and some forms of political expression. He coupled legal reform with economic reform, allowing decentralization, some forms of private ownership and private production, as well as revision of hated collectivization and industrialization policies. These policies, culminating with the New Economic Mechanism of 1968, produced significant improvements in Hungarian standards of living.

Kádár's collective reforms produced a distinctive brand of Hungarian Communism that, ironically, was premised on the measured sacrifice of some of Hungary's national sovereignty. In exchange for leeway to determine domestic policy, Kádár purposely allowed the Soviet Union to determine Hungary's foreign policy. Deemed "Goulash Communism" by contemporaries and some academics, Kádár's policies, shored up by Western loans, produced a sense of well-being over the course of the 1960s and 1970s and gained Hungary the reputation of being "the happiest barrack in the bloc."

However, pressures to privatize and democratize continued to mount, especially in the late 1970s, in light of changing economic conditions, Hungary's signing of the Helsinki Accords, and the persistence of one-party rule. Through the 1980s, the unofficial black market economy expanded, while the official economy stagnated. This promoted the development of a reform movement within and without the Workers Party that Kádár was unable to control. After 1985, his hold over both the party and society diminished, and in May 1988, the party named Károly Grósz to replace the partially senile Kádár as its general secretary.

Kádár died on July 6, 1989, and thus did not live to see the total disintegration of the Hungarian Communist project. He did, however, suffer the humiliation of the ceremonial rehabilitation and reburial of Imre Nagy, endorsed by his own party. Further English analyses of Kádár's career can be found in Andrew Felkay's *Hungary and the USSR 1956–88. Kádár's Political Leadership* (Greenwood Press, 1989), Bennett Kovrig's *Communism in Hungary from Kun to Kádár* (Hoover Institute Press, 1979), and Charles Gati's *Hungary and the Soviet Bloc* (Duke University Press, 1986).

## KANT, IMMANUEL

**KANT, IMMANUEL** 1724–1804, One of the world's philosophical giants. He was of Scotch and German ancestry and lived his entire life in Königsberg (in former East Prussia), from where he never traveled farther than a few miles. Nevertheless, he was widely read and cosmopolitan. He was an eccentric bachelor his entire life. He was said to have been so punctual that housewives could set their clocks when he passed on the way to his lectures. A professor of philosophy at the University of Königsberg from 1755 to 1797, he also worked in astronomy.

His early education emphasized Leibniz's teachings, but he claimed that the works of David Hume jolted him out of his dogmatic slumber. He decided that Leibniz's thought placed too much confidence in human reason and led to dogmatism. By contrast, Hume engendered too little confidence in reason and led to skepticism. Thus, a careful study of the presuppositions, capacities, and limits of human reason was essential. He first proposed this in his 1770 doctoral dissertation, *On the Forms and Principles of the Sensible and Intelligible World,* and brought his analysis to completion in the *Critique of Pure Reason* (1781).

He dealt with the ethical question of what a person ought to do in his *Foundations of the Metaphysics of Morals* (1785) and *Critique of Practical Reason* (1788). He argued that morality consists of actions in accordance with consistent, necessary, and universal principles, which are categorical, not conditional. He formulated his "categorical imperative": "Act in such a way that the maxim of your actions can be elevated to a universal law." In other words, one should follow a rule that every other person can also follow, and one should ask for no special privileges. Any double standard is wrong. One should claim no rights that he is not willing to grant to others. This is practical or moral reason.

Because man is the rational animal on earth, he must unconditionally respect the humanity of every individual. One should never regard a person as a means to something else, but always as an end in itself. His focus on what is common among all human beings—their dignity and capacity for reason—prevented him from attributing much importance to the narrower concept of "nation," which hardly entered Germans' discussions until the French Revolution. At first he greeted this Europe-shaking event, which promised liberty, equality, and fraternity, with open arms. But the ferocity of the reign of terror inclined him and other contemporary German intellectuals, such as Goethe and Schiller, to change their minds. Kant's cosmopolitanism was revealed most clearly in a famous essay, *Perpetual Peace.*

## KARAĐORĐEVIĆ, ALEKSANDAR

**KARAĐORĐEVIĆ, ALEKSANDAR** 1888–1934, Prince of Serbia, 1888–1909; prince regent of Serbia, 1909–1920; king of the Kingdom of Serbs, Croats, and Slovenes, 1921–1929; king of Yugoslavia, 1929–1934. Born as the second son of King Petar of Serbia, Aleksandar was educated in Switzerland and Russia as a child. After the overthrow of the Obrenović dynasty by the military in 1903, Aleksandar's father returned to Serbia and assumed the throne. The crown prince, Đorđe, was plagued by emotional and mental instability and abdicated in favor of Aleksandar in 1909, who returned to Serbia from Russia. Relations between the two brothers remained tense, because Đorđe on at least one occasion tried to reclaim his former title as heir to the throne.

As a member of the royal family, Aleksandar had held different ranks in the Serb military since his 15th birthday in 1903. Aleksandar convincingly demonstrated the results of his military training through his command of an army in the Balkan Wars. However, Aleksandar's relations with the military were initially problematic. In particular, Aleksandar encountered opposition from Dragutin Dimitirijević-Apis, and his conspiratorial group of officers *Ujedinjenje ili smrt* (Union or Death, also known as *Crna ruka,* or the Black Hand), who openly admired the Prussian model of a nation-state led by a strong military. When King Petar, only days before the assassination of Archduke Franz Ferdinand in June 1914, named Aleksandar as prince regent of Serbia (an abdication in all but name), a clash between Aleksandar and *Crna ruka* seemed likely. At this time, Aleksandar began to gather Serb army officers loyal to him in a group known as the *Bela ruka,* or White Hand.

However, these problems were pressed into the background after the outbreak of World War I in 1914. Aleksandar, who refused to be evacuated to a safe haven outside Serbia, joined his soldiers on the long march to the Adriatic Sea in 1915. Aleksandar's participation in this arduous and disastrous retreat of the Serb army greatly enhanced his legitimacy in the eyes of the Serb nation. In addition, Aleksandar performed ably as a military commander. By the time Belgrade was liberated in 1918, Aleksandar had solidified his reputation as the leader of the Serb nation.

Of major significance to the later evolution of Aleksandar was the trial, in Thessaloniki in 1917, of Dragutin Dimitrijević-Apis and other members of *Crna ruka.* Accused of plotting to overthrow the civilian government of Serbia and of attempting to assassinate Aleksandar, Apis and several other conspirators were sentenced to death and executed. Although the trial allowed Aleksandar, *Bela ruka,* and Serb Prime Minister Nikola Pašić to fortify their positions as the leaders of Serbia, lack of substantial evidence for the charges, the partiality of the court, and the brutality of the punishments meted out combined to make the victory a Pyrrhic one for Aleksandar.

Aleksandar endorsed Serb politicians' plans for a strongly centralist Kingdom of Serbs, Croats, and Slovenes after World War I, despite the desires of non-Serbs for a federal or confederal state structure. The creation of the new state affected the extrapolation of the Serb Karađorđević dynasty onto the new kingdom, without concessions to distinct traditions among non-Serbs. On the day of the promulgation of the new constitution, St. Vitus Day (June 28), 1921, Aleksandar survived an assassination attempt. With the death of Petar, Aleksandar became king in August 1921. The following year he married Marie, the daughter of King Ferdinand of Romania.

Throughout the 1920s Aleksandar demonstrated a general disregard for parliamentary democracy and frequently injected himself vigorously into domestic political debates. Aleksandar's active involvement in politics contributed to the tumultuous nature of parliamentary politics in the new state.

In 1928, the fragile political system of Yugoslavia received a severe blow when Stjepan Radić, leader of the Croat Peasant Party, was shot on the floor of the Yugoslav Parliament along with several other members of his party. When Radić succumbed to his wounds several weeks later, the country was thrust into a dramatic political crisis. Several months passed without a resolution of the situation, which grew worse with the advent of violent riots in Croatia in December 1928.

On January 6, 1929, King Aleksandar proclaimed a "personal dictatorship," in effect suspending the Parliament and the constitution of Yugoslavia. He announced that the political parties had failed Yugoslavia and had proven unable to transcend "tribalism," that is, Serb, Croat, and Slovene identities. Aleksandar declared that he would henceforth ban all political parties and entities bearing "tribal" (*plemenski*) names in an effort to reach out to the "Yugoslav people." Accordingly, Aleksandar officially renamed the country the "Kingdom of Yugoslavia" on October 3, 1929.

Ideologists of the 6th of January dictatorship viewed Aleksandar's resort to autocratic rule as a necessary decision if Yugoslavia were to survive. Although they identified parliamentary democracy as the main culprit of the failed policies of the 1920s, the ideologists also stated that Serb nationalists had, at times, proved arrogant and inconsiderate in their relations with non-Serbs. Aleksandar stated that his regime would promote a "unitarist" ideology known as the *jugoslovenska misao* (Yugoslav thought), which would create a Yugoslav nation able to transcend the previous "tribal" identities of the region.

Aleksandar's ideology was also characterized by a strong anti-Communist element. However, by relying heavily on Serb politicians and military officers to implement the centralist policies of his government, Aleksandar alienated the non-Serbs in Yugoslavia. Aleksandar also failed to reach any compromise with Vladko Maček, the successor to Radić as the head of the Croat Peasant Party. Despite the claims of the regime's ideologues, the dictatorship's policies failed to garner legitimacy among non-Serbs. The extensive use of police terror by Aleksandar's government made it increasingly unpopular. Even Serbs living outside Serbia proper voiced complaints about the strong centralist features of the dictatorship. Non-Serbs therefore regarded the ideology of Aleksandar's dictatorship as de facto Serbian nationalism rather than as a truly Yugoslav nationalism.

In 1931, under pressure from the French government, Aleksandar issued a new constitution that in effect institutionalized and legalized the dictatorship. Some minor movements were made in the direction of parliamentary politics. However, this did not lead to any fundamental change in the attitude of the unitarists toward non-Serbs. Moreover, the period since 1929 had witnessed a growing gap between the regime and more traditional Serb nationalists such as Slobodan Jovanović and Dragiša Vasić. Many Serb nationalist intellectuals were upset with the regime's preoccupation with unitarist ideology and felt that this led to a neglect of the Serb nation's interests. In this sense, therefore, Aleksandar's conception of nationalism alienated the Serbs who should have been his most natural supporters, and simultaneously failed to attract a significant following for his ideology outside the Serb nation.

During the early 1930s, Aleksandar's government tried with some success to improve relations with its neighbors, especially Bulgaria. Yugoslavia's strongest international ties, however, remained to France. On October 9, 1934, while on a state visit to France, Aleksandar was assassinated in a joint attack by terrorists from the fascist Croat Ustaša movement and the Internal Macedonian Revolutionary Organization (VMRO).

## KARADŽIĆ, RADOVAN

1945–, Born in Montenegro, president of self-proclaimed Bosnian Serb Republic, 1992–1996. Karadžić is a trained psychiatrist and amateur poet, who has published several volumes of poetry. Before the dissolution of Yugoslavia, he practiced psychiatry in Sarajevo. In 1985 he was imprisoned by Yugoslav authorities for fraud. Although Karadžić entered politics through an ecological party in Bosnia-Herzegovina, he quickly switched to nationalist politics and founded the Serb Democratic Party (*Srpska demokratska stranka,* or SDS) in 1990. The reasons for this political shift remain unclear. At this time, Karadžić became the leader of the newly founded SDS after several other candidates turned down the position. Karadžić claimed that the Bosnian Muslims, led by Aliya Izetbegović, were attempting to establish an Islamic republic that would threaten the rights of Bosnian Serbs. Karadžić advocated the establishment of an independent Serbian republic in Bosnia-Herzegovina, or preferably the expansion of the Serbian state to include all areas of Serbian settlement in Croatia and Bosnia-Herzegovina.

In April 1992, Karadžić proclaimed the founding of the Serbian Republic of Bosnia-Herzegovina (*Srpska Republika Bosne i Hercegovine*). From 1992 to 1995, Karadžić and the commanding general of the Bosnian Serb army, Ratko Mladić, were the leading architects of

the policy of ethnic cleansing in Bosnia-Herzegovina. This policy involved using terror, including killings, rape, and torture, to force the displacement of Croats and Muslims in an effort to construct an ethnically homogeneous Serbian state. During the early stages of the war, Karadžić also met several times with nationalist Croats to discuss a possible partitioning of Bosnia-Herzegovina. In May 1993, Karadžić accepted and signed the plan of David Owen and Cyrus Vance for a Bosnian state based on ethnic cantons. At the same time, however, Karadžić orchestrated the rejection of the plan by the self-styled Bosnian Serb parliament. This initiated a substantial deterioration of Karadžić's relationship with the president of Serbia, Slobodan Milošević. Until January 1994, Milošević provided material and ideological support for Karadžić's prosecution of the war in Bosnia-Herzegovina. Yet Milošević applied increasing pressure on Karadžić to accept a peace agreement that would include a loosening of international sanctions on Serbia and Montenegro, which by January 1994 had precipitated hyperinflation. Karadžić accused Milošević of abandoning the Bosnian Serbs in order to get international sanctions on the Federal Republic of Yugoslavia lifted. Milošević prevailed and forced the Bosnian Serbs to agree to the Dayton Accords, which ended the war in the former Yugoslavia in November 1995.

The accords stipulated Karadžić's resignation from the presidency of the Serbian Republic and required him to refrain from political activity. However, despite intense international pressure, Karadžić continued to appear and speak in public, and the SDS refused to elect another president. Repeated violations of this agreement caused international intervention to force his removal from public life in July 1996. Since 1995 the International Criminal Tribunal for the Former Yugoslavia has issued multiple indictments against Karadžić for war crimes and crimes against humanity. However, Karadžić remains free and continues to retain substantial political and economic power in the Serbian Republic. During the war, Karadžić, along with other SDS members, profited considerably from organized crime and smuggling operations. This led to considerable resentment in the population of the Serbian Republic, but Karadžić remained very popular due to his image as a savior of the Serb nation. In 1997, Karadžić's supporters, led by Momčilo Krajišnik, struggled for power in the Serbian Republic against Biljana Plavšić, who initiated a campaign against corruption and organized crime.

## KARADŽIĆ, VUK

1787–1864, Serb linguist, ethnographer, and reformer of Serbian language. A peasant by birth, Karadžić received training from the Slovene linguist Jernej Kopitar, who in turn was influenced by Johann Gottfried von Herder. Karadžić fought a campaign against the Serb Orthodox Church to modernize the Serbian language. He sought to find a suitable replacement for the mixture of dialects and Old Church Slavonic that existed in Serbia in the early 19th century. Karadžić chose the eastern Herzegovinian Ijekavian subdialect of the widely spoken Štokavian dialect as the foundation for the modern Serbian language. He also designed and pushed through a modernization of the Cyrillic script for the Serbian language. This provided the language with a firm and dynamic base among the Serb peasantry. Karadžić's reforms and his published collection of Serbian folksongs won him great celebrity among contemporary intellectuals throughout East Central Europe and Germany. Many other Slavic nationalist intellectuals, similarly engaged in struggles against archaic liturgical languages, were influenced by Karadžić's construction of a modern secular language based on the vernacular.

Karadžić, borrowing from the theories of a German historian, August L. von Schlözer, defined any speaker of the Štokavian dialect as a Serb, whether Orthodox, Muslim, or Catholic. Karadžić's inclusive views of Serbdom laid the foundation for an assimilative approach toward Croat and Muslim Štokavian speakers. In Serbia, Karadžić's ideas were adopted by Ilija Garašanin, another leading Serb nationalist, who sought to extend the borders of the Serbian state to encompass all "linguistic" Serbs. Some Serbs in Serbia proper, who spoke Ekavian, resented Karadžić's emphasis on Ijekavian. Karadžić's linguistic nationalism also encountered some opposition among Croat intellectuals. Although many Croats spoke Štokavian, substantial numbers spoke two other dialects, Kajkavian and Čakavian. Furthermore, only a minority of Croat Štokavian speakers spoke the Ijekavian variant. Ljudevit Gaj was among many prominent Croat opponents of Karadžić's reforms who resented what they saw as the marginalization of Croatian identity by Karadžić. However, Croat Illyrianists supported the shift to Štokavian. By the 1890s, a younger generation of Croat intellectuals espoused Karadžić's program. Karadžić's linguistic understanding of Serbdom remained axiomatic to most Serb nationalists throughout the late 19th and 20th centuries and laid the grammatical foundations for the modern Croatian and Serbian languages.

**KARIMOV, ISLAM** 1938–, Born in Samarkand, Uzbekistan to an Uzbek father and a Tajik mother, both of whom died while he was still young, leaving him to be raised in an orphanage. Despite this, Karimov was a dedicated student. He earned a degree in mechanical engineering from the Central Asian Polytechnical Institute and spent the early part of his adult career working as an engineer at an aircraft factory in Tashkent. From 1966 on, however, Karimov focused his career on government service. In that year, Karimov was hired to work for the State Planning Committee of Uzbekistan, eventually rising to the position of first vice-chairman. He earned a doctorate from the Tashkent Institute of National Economics and his government career began to accelerate, especially following his 1983 appointment to the position of Minister of Finance of the Soviet Republic of Uzbekistan. Three years later, in 1986, he was appointed chairman of the State Planning Committee, vice-chairman of the Council of Ministers, and Deputy Head of the Government of Uzbekistan. In June 1989, Karimov assumed executive control of the Soviet Republic of Uzbekistan as the first secretary of the Central Committee of the Uzbekistan Communist Party. On March 24, 1990, he was formally elected president of Uzbekistan by the Supreme Council of the Uzbek Soviet Socialist Republic.

On August 31, 1991, under Karimov's leadership, the Republic of Uzbekistan announced its independence from the collapsing Soviet Union (the state's Independence Day is formally celebrated on September 1). The newly-founded Republic of Uzbekistan became at once the most populous nation, and arguably the most influential political, economic, and social power in post-Soviet Central Asia. Just a few weeks later, in November 1991, Karimov supervised the transformation of the Uzbekistan Communist Party to the People's Democratic Party. Shortly thereafter, on December 29, 1991, he won the independent Republic of Uzbekistan's first national elections and was elected to the presidency with an overwhelming 86 percent of the vote. On March 26, 1995, a referendum was passed (with 99.6 percent of the vote) extending Karimov's first term as president until the year 2000. Thus far, his highly centralized administration has maintained a relatively stable social climate and slow, cautious economic reforms and privatization. While acting cautiously in his relationships with his neighboring states, Karimov has on occasion exerted his country's influence in an effort to contain the civil wars of Uzbekistan's neighbors, Afghanistan and Tajikistan.

Note that, although according to the laws of Uzbekistan rival political parties are not illegal, they have not been encouraged under the Karimov regime. The Erk ("Freedom") Democratic Party, for example, was banned on December 9, 1992, and its chairman,

Muhammad Solih (who won 12 percent of the vote in the December 29, 1991, election), now lives in exile. Abdul Rahim Pulatov, the chairman of the Birlik ("Unity") People's Movement, has suffered a similar fate. In recent years Karimov, himself a Muslim who has traveled to the Islamic holy city of Mecca and who took the oath to office with one hand on the Koran, has been hardest on Islamic political groups. In 1992–1993 President Karimov banned the young Islamic political parties Adolat ("Justice") and the Wahhabi-funded Islamic Renaissance Party. Since the mid-1990s, Karimov's government has acted to further suppress the activities of Islamic organizations, especially in Uzbekistan's Ferghana Valley. His harsh policies have recently evoked an angry response and, on February 16, 1999, President Karimov narrowly escaped an assassination attempt as a number of car bombs detonated outside of his office in Tashkent, Uzbekistan's capital, where he was due to be arriving at the time of the explosions. According to the official account, the individuals responsible were Islamic radicals from the Ferghana Valley and they have since been apprehended and sentenced to death.

**KEDOURIE, ELIE**  1926–1992, British academic and intellectual historian, born in Baghdad, died in Washington. Kedourie's primary field of research was the history of the Middle East since the late 19th century, but he also wrote several very influential works on the development of nationalism both in Europe and in regions outside the European-Christian cultural area. His impact in all of these fields derived from his ability to mount strong challenges to accepted wisdom, challenges which he supported with clear, solidly structured arguments. His flavorful essays still not only educate but also entertain readers.

Kedourie began to study the phenomenon of nationalism as an assistant lecturer at the London School of Economics in the 1950s; his book *Nationalism* (1960; fourth edition, 1993) was the result. As a historian of ideas, Kedourie was interested in the philosophical underpinning for the ideology of nationalism, rather than in building a model relating the development of nationalism to modernization in politics, economics, or culture. He saw nationalism, like socialism, as an artificial means to fill the spiritual void created by the great impersonal forces of the modern world. Modern ethnic nationalism grew out of Kant's idea of morality, which the individual saw as a law, formulated by reason and emanating from within the self, rather than imposed by another. This need for individual self-determination was reinterpreted by followers of Kant. Just as the individual's consciousness determines his existence, the

world must be the product of a universal consciousness. True freedom comes from loss of individuality and absorption into that universal consciousness. Some sociolinguistic groups are capable of making more rapid progress toward that goal than others. For such a post-Kantian as Fichte, an early proponent of corporatist ethnic nationalism, German speakers were just such a group. Fichte was motivated largely by pique over French dominance in the public life of many German states. Given the turmoil in Europe unleashed by the French Revolution and Napoleon, Fichtean ideas of national destiny came to be adopted by many.

Kedourie believed that the newly dominant European idea of nationalism was introduced to other areas by Europe's growing imperial reach. As he wrote in his introduction to *Nationalism in Asia and Africa* (1970), the conquering European nations abroad at first attracted men who emulated the West, notably in education, before repelling them as members of a subordinate nation. The alienated then adopted the ideas of nationalism as a new means to power—not unlike the case of Fichte and his turn to German nationalism—and used Western techniques and technology of mass media to spread the new ideology among a steadily more literate population. Gandhi, for example, fit this pattern. Even in his ultimate rejection of the British nation, Gandhi adopted a Western-style, romanticized vision of India as his "true" civilization.

Kedourie saw something similar in the development of nationalism in the Middle East. The early adherents of Arab nationalism, such as 'Abd al-Rahman al-Kawakibi, adopted the ideology out of ulterior personal motives. In the case of Kawakibi, who put forth a case for an Arab caliphate, Kedourie detected manipulation of a poor Syrian émigré by the Khedive of Egypt, who saw himself as the best candidate for the position (although, ironically, the Khedive's claim to be "Arab" was not utterly convincing, being a descendant of the Albanian Muhammad Ali and not speaking Arabic as his first language). Britain encouraged Arab nationalism during World War I, hoping to split the Muslim community that might otherwise rally in support of the Ottoman sultan. Arab nationalism grew rapidly after the war, but in Kedourie's view it never really displaced the traditional mode of identification in the Middle East, religion. Kedourie believed that Islam, as the religion of the Arabs, and nationalism have never been in opposition, and indeed that Islam is the soul of Arabism. The struggle against the Jews of Israel after World War II replaced the age-old struggle against the Christians of Europe, who had finally been driven back. This element of Kedourie's writings on Arab nationalism has drawn sharp criticism—it does not adequately explain tension between nationalists and Islamists, such as the Muslim Brethren, for example, nor does it address the powerful appeal of Arabism among many non-Sunni Muslims in Syria and Palestine. Yet his points are argued with sufficient force that they continue to influence debate on Arab nationalism today.

## KENNEDY, JOHN F.

1917–1963, The youngest person to be elected president of the United States, Kennedy conspicuously and energetically asserted American power and influence in the world. His presidency uncritically embraced U.S. globalism. His charisma, good looks, and youthful vigor, despite serious health problems, made him popular both in the United States and in the world at large. He was the son of Joseph P. Kennedy, a wealthy Boston businessman who had been Franklin D. Roosevelt's ambassador to the United Kingdom in the interwar years. John Kennedy served as a naval officer in World War II, a conflict that claimed the life of his older brother, Joe Jr. He was elected to the House of Representatives in 1946 and the U.S. Senate in 1952. But his principal political efforts were directed toward being elected president, a goal he achieved in 1960 when he defeated Richard Nixon.

Kennedy came to power determined to be an activist president, and his foreign and defense policies manifested this. He claimed in 1961 that the Cold War had entered a critical stage. As he argued in his first State of the Union speech, "each day we draw nearer the hour of maximum danger" stemming from a progressively more aggressive USSR. He articulated very well the American consensus on the nature of the Cold War and the global danger to the Free World stemming from Communism. He demanded of Congress the largest arms buildup in American peacetime history in order to meet the growing Soviet threat, and he got what he asked for.

His administration began with a foreign political fiasco in the Bay of Pigs invasion of Cuba by Cuban exiles. Judging the new president to be weak, Soviet leader Nikita Khrushchev tried in 1961 to force a settlement in Berlin that would favor the USSR. However, Kennedy responded decisively by mobilizing the support of Americans. He called for higher defense spending, and he threatened the Soviet Union militarily. By the time the Berlin Wall had been constructed in August 1961, Americans had the feeling that they had narrowly escaped war. This idea was strengthened the following year when President Kennedy resolutely opposed the Soviet deployment of missiles in Cuba capable of reaching targets in the United States. Khrushchev backed down, but the Cuban Missile Crisis is now regarded as the closest the two superpowers ever came to nuclear war. To reduce that danger, Kennedy had a "hot line" to the Kremlin installed, persuaded the Soviet Union to sign a limited Test Ban Treaty in 1963, and introduced a policy of limited détente.

To deal with the threat of Communist insurgency in the Third World, Kennedy created American counterinsurgency forces that could be inserted into crises areas if American efforts at nation building did not succeed. His administration sought to promote democracy, tried to change relations with Latin America through the Alliance for Progress, and created the Peace Corps to help countries develop their infrastructure. If these peaceful measures failed, Kennedy was willing to send American troops, as he did in Vietnam. During his presidency, he increased the number of American military advisors from 500 to 16,500 and approved of a coup that involved the assassination of South Vietnam's leader, Diem. It remains a subject of scholarly debate whether he would have pursued the same Vietnam policy as Lyndon B. Johnson, his successor to the presidency in November 1963 following Kennedy's tragic assassination in Dallas. Not until after the United States became embroiled in a seemingly endless and unwinnable war in Vietnam did Kennedy's countrymen begin asking seriously about the limits to American power that Kennedy had not seen.

## KENYAN NATIONALISM

Kenya became a British colony in the mid-1890s. Prior to becoming an official colony, the first Europeans to penetrate the interior were German and British missionaries. In 1895, the coastal area leased from the sultan of Zanzibar was established as a British protectorate under the name of the East African Protectorate. It came under the administration of the British Colonial Office in 1905, and in the next few years many British and South African farmers settled on the temperate and fertile plateau known as the "White Highlands," obtaining grants of land from the Kikuyu. The Kikuyu regarded the transaction as a lease, while the Europeans considered it a freehold sale, which soon caused extreme bitterness and resentment on the part of the Africans who now found themselves landless. In 1920 the protectorate was united with the protectorate of Zanzibar, renamed Kenya, and made a crown colony.

Kenyan nationalism can be traced to the end of World War I. Beginning from the 1920s there were signs of an embryonic African nationalism, led principally by a minority of educated Kikuyu, who resented the white occupation of their traditional lands and the political and social supremacy of the European settlers, which was confirmed in 1923 by the Devonshire White Paper. Interestingly, however, the Devonshire White Paper also declared that Kenya was primarily an African country, and that African interests must be paramount in case of conflict.

Although African pressure groups began to form in the 1920s and 1930s, it was not until 1944 that the nationalist movement came to take center stage with the formation of the Kenya African Union (KAU). Soon after World War II, KAU began to gain mass support in bitter opposition to the increased influx of European settlers from the newly independent India and Pakistan. In 1947 Jomo Kenyatta, a member of the Kikuyu ethnic group who had campaigned vigorously against European occupation of Kenya during his fifteen-year stay in England, assumed the presidency of this nationalist organization. Furthermore, many of the African soldiers returning at the end of World War II were soon disillusioned by their ill treatment at the hands of the colonial government, which refused to recognize and compensate them. In 1946 a group of ex-army Kikuyus formed a secret society that came to be known as the Mau Mau. The group had similar aims as those of Kenyatta's KAU—to end British colonial rule—but sought to achieve them by violent means. Mau Mau launched a campaign of guerilla warfare against the white settlers. A state of emergency was declared and Kenyatta, who was regarded by many as the leader of the Mau Mau movement, was arrested, tried, and found guilty of managing Mau Mau and sentenced to life imprisonment in 1953. During the Mau Mau uprising and the imposition of the state of emergency between 1952 and 1956 colonial government forces had killed more than 11,000 Kenyans, most Kikuyu, while only a handful of Europeans were killed by the Mau Mau.

The British government, which was in the process of granting independence to other African and Asian territories, acknowledged the African desire for a self-governing Kenya, with African majority rule. In 1957 Britain entered into informal talks on Kenya's future with African leaders. In elections held in 1961 the Kenya African National Union (KANU, the successor of KAU), whose acknowledged leader was Kenyatta, won handsomely and was recognized as the biggest single party in the country. In August 1961 Kenyatta was freed and allowed to attend constitutional talks in London in 1962. The constitutional talks paved the way for self-government. In the general elections held in May 1963 KANU (predominantly Kikuyu) scored an overwhelming victory over its rival, the Kenya African Democratic Union (KADU), an amalgamation of other ethnic groups fearful of Kikuyu political domination.

Kenya became independent on December 12, 1963, with Kenyatta as the first prime minister. In December 1964 it became a republic within the Commonwealth, with Kenyatta as its first president. During Kenyatta's rule, opposition was not tolerated and in certain cases was ruthlessly suppressed.

In short, Kenyan independence involved some of the most characteristic elements of the African liberation movements: settler occupation, resistance to settler occupation, a wavering colonial policy, and a charismatic black leader, Jomo Kenyatta. When Kenyatta died in 1978 he was succeeded by Vice President Daniel arap Moi, who built on Kenyatta's achievements, but at the expense of democratic freedoms. During his tenure there have been political detentions, press censorship, and Kenya was declared a one party-state in 1983. By the late 1980s Moi's rule became increasingly autocratic, and calls for multiparty politics grew. In December 1991, in response to increasing domestic and international pressure for political reform, President Moi announced the introduction of multiparty politics. In spite of these political reforms, it has been alleged that Moi continues to manipulate the system in order to cling to power.

For further reading, see M. Azevedo, ed., *Kenya: The Land, the People, and the Nation* (Durham, N.C.: Carolina Academic Press, 1999); Marshall S. Clough, *Mau Mau Memoirs: History, Memory, and Politics* (Boulder, Colo.: Lynne Rienner, 1998); Keith Kyle, *The Politics of the Independence of Kenya* (New York: St. Martin's Press, 1999); W. R. Ochieng', *A Modern History of Kenya, 1895–1980* (London: Evans Brothers, 1989); and B. A. Ogot and W. R. Ochieng', *Decolonization & Independence in Kenya, 1940–93* (London: James Currey, 1995).

**KENYATTA, JOMO** 1891–1978, Distinguished Kenyan statesman and politician who led the struggle for Kenyan independence from Great Britain and was instrumental in the creation of modern Kenya. He struggled for more than half a century to free his country from colonial rule, a cause for which he was vilified and imprisoned by the British colonial administration. He was born sometime between 1891 and 1895 at Ngenda village near Nairobi in Kiambu District. His name at birth was Kamau wa Muigai, which was changed to Johnstone Kamau after he attended Dagoretti Scottish Mission School and subsequently converted to Christianity. After graduating from the mission school he joined the colonial government to work as a clerk and meter-reader for Nairobi Municipality from 1921 to 1926. Sometime in the late 1930s he adopted a new name, calling himself Jomo Kenyatta (Jomo means "burning spear" and Kenyatta refers to the beaded belt, or kinyata, that he habitually wore).

He began his political career in 1924 when he joined the Kikuyu Central Association (KCA), an organization formed by concerned Kenyans who wanted to politely pressure the British colonial government to change its land and racist policies. He soon rose in the ranks of this organization and served it in various capacities as translater, communications officer, general secretary, and editor of *Mwigwithania*, a Kikuyu political journal between 1924 and 29. In February 1929 he went to England to lobby for African rights in Kenya. He lectured and pleaded the African cause to the British public at public places such as Trafalgar Square in London. He urged the British government to abolish its imperialist and racist policies and allow Africans to establish their own schools. While in London he joined the League Against Imperialism. In 1930, after being branded as a troublemaker by the British government, he returned to Kenya and established the first of many African independent schools and colleges, an activity that the British colonial government openly opposed.

Kenyatta returned to England in 1931 and enrolled to further his education at the Quaker College of Woodbrooke at Selly Oak in Birmingham. Between 1932 and 1933 he spent a year in Russia studying at a Communist international institute. He also traveled extensively elsewhere in Europe. He later enrolled to study anthropology under the world-famous Professor Malinowski at the London School of Economics where his major sociological work, *Facing Mount Kenya: An Anthropological Study of the Kikuyu*, was published in 1938. While studying in London he continued his activism and political campaigns against British colonialism and racial excesses in Africa. In May 1942 Kenyatta married an English woman, Edna Clarke, at Storrington, West Sussex, where he had moved from London after the outbreak of World War II. Edna was his second wife, the first was Ngina, whom he had married in Kenya many years earlier.

He was among the organizers of the Fifth Pan-African Congress, which was held in Manchester, England, in October 1945. In 1946 he departed England for his homeland, Kenya, where he continued his political activities. In addition to political activism, he became a teacher at the Independent Teachers College in Githunguri, rising to become principal of the college in 1947 as well as president of the Kenya African Union, which later became the Kenya African National Union (KANU), a political party that has been in power since independence.

KANU soon developed into a formidable African political party that challenged European occupation of Kenya and boldly demanded independence. The colonial government took immediate military action by declaring a state of emergency in October 1951. Kenyatta was arrested on charges of managing an illegal organization, the Mau Mau, a secret association that had been formed to oppose colonial policies. After an unfair trial, he was convicted and jailed for seven years in a remote colonial outpost in northern Kenya. Kenyatta's Mau Mau guerrilla movement fought hard against the brutal onslaught of British forces. By 1957 the British were forced to make concessions to the Africans and Kenyatta was finally released in 1961. Upon his release he was appointed minister of state for constitutional affairs and economic planning in a transitional government. He was a key figure in the negotiations at Lancaster House for a new constitution that led to the granting of independence in 1963 when he became prime minister. The following year, in December 1964, Kenya attained the status of a republic and Jomo Kenyatta became the first president of modern Kenya.

Although revered by many Kenyans, Kenyatta ruled the country with a strong hand. The Lancaster Constitution dictated a multiparty system of government, but under Kenyatta's rule from 1963 to the time of his death in 1978, Kenya was governed as a single-party state, with the ruling KANU as the only political party allowed to function. Political dissension was dealt with ruthlessly and several political opponents were either jailed without charge or trial under the Preventive Detention Act, and others such as Tom Mboya and Kariuki were assassinated under mysterious circumstances. In spite of his strong-fisted rule, many agree that Kenya under Kenyatta was not a strongly repressive state when compared to other African countries and many Kenyans continue to adore the *Mzee*, as he was popularly called. Furthermore, under Kenyatta's rule during the Cold War, Kenya aligned itself with the West, particularly Britain and the United States. In return, the West was also very generous in pouring development resources into Kenya's infrastructure in support of Kenyatta's pro-Western policies.

Kenyatta died of a heart attack on August 22, 1978 at Mombasa, Kenya's major port. At the time of his death, he was survived by several sons and daughters from both his first (Kenyan) wife and his second (British) wife. His fame still lives on throughout Africa and the world—a legacy of his role in the nationalist struggle and nation building, his campaigns for the African cause during his stay in Europe, his role in the Pan-Africanist movement, and, more importantly, his astute statesmanship.

Many works have been written about the life and achievements of Jomo Kenyatta. The most prominent of these works include *Mzee Jomo Kenyatta: A Photobiography*, compiled by Mohamed Amin and Peter Moll and published in 1978 by Marketing & Pub. Ltd in Nairobi; *Jomo Kenyatta*, written by Dennis Wepman and published in 1988 by Burke in London; *Jomo Kenyatta: A Biography*, written by Eric M. Aseka and published by East African Educational Publishers in Nairobi in 1992; and an insightful comparative analysis of African political leadership by A. B. Assensoh titled *African Political Leadership: Jomo Kenyatta, Kwame Nkrumah, and Julius K. Nyerere*, published in 1998 by Krieger Pub. Co. in Malabar, Florida.

**KHACHATURIAN, ARAM**  1903–1978, Soviet Armenian composer. Deeply rooted in Trans-Caucasian musical folklore, Khachaturian's music made a substantial contribution to the Russian tradition of orientalism, which was recognized in the 19th century as an essential component of Russian nationalist musical style.

In the Soviet Union, where all the main points of Stasov's aesthetic theory were preserved (including musical realism, folklorism, a prioritizing of opera and program music, and a hatred for formalism), the requirement for orientalism was not relevant. Instead, it was replaced by a requirement for the development of national compositional schools in each republic. In the music of non-Russian Soviet composers, Trans-Caucasian, Middle-Asian, or Baltic musical folklore served as a local "national" element, bringing at the same time a color of "exoticism" that had been historically associated with Russian music. According to Soviet cultural policy, local folk elements were expected to merge with Russian national style, which, in its turn, was always in a controversial juxtaposition to Western style.

However, in the case of Khachaturian, orientalism was a major nationalist element of his individual compositional style. Strongly resembling the sensuous style of Borodin's imaginary East, but based on actual folklore, Khachaturian's orientalism fused with the style of so-called Russian academism, which was developed in the late 19th century by Rimsky-Korsakov and his students, composers of the *Beliaev Circle*. Khachaturian acquired this tradition in the Moscow Conservatory, where he studied composition under Nikolai Myaskovsky, former pupil of Rimsky-Korsakov.

Khachaturian's style is based on Armenian, Georgian, and Azerbaijan folk music and is best represented by his *Piano Concerto* (1936) and *Violin Concerto* (1940). Without quoting folk tunes, the composer adopted their melodic, rhythmic, and modal characteristics, as well as various improvisational styles and traditions of folk performers (*ashugs*, *khanandes*, and *sazandars*).

Khachaturian's *First Symphony* (1934), devoted to the 15th anniversary of the founding of Soviet Armenia, presents dramatic episodes of Armenian history, images of a native nature, and scenes of people's festivities. Written in the tradition of Borodin's epic symphonies, this work was celebrated by its contemporaries as the first "Armenian" symphony.

Khachaturian's *Second Symphony* (also known as *The Bell Symphony*, 1943) is a patriotic composition, belonging, together with Shostakovich's *Seventh* and *Eighth*, and Prokofiev's *Fifth* and *Sixth*, to a group of Soviet antiwar symphonies. The third movement of this symphony is intended as a requiem in memory of the soldiers who laid down their lives for their country. The main theme of this movement, Armenian song lament *Vorskan Akhper* (*Brother Hunter*), depicts an image of a mother weeping over her dead son.

The most popular works were Khachaturian's two ballets, *Gayane* (1942; rev. 1957) and *Spartak* (1954; rev. 1968.) The subject of the first ballet is the patriotism of Armenian peasants and their happy prewar life in Soviet Armenia. The protagonist, Gayane, a woman of high ethical ideals, struggles with her husband, a traitor, for the sake of her native village. (Plots treating the theme of traitors and political wreckers were quite popular in the Soviet literature in the period of Stalin's rule.) However, Khachaturian's music, based on both actual and stylized folk tunes and dances, was much more successful than the ballet scenario, which in the future underwent numerous changes. The ballet was enthusiastically received. The bellicose "Sabre Dance," characterizing Armenian Kurds, became Khachaturian's undisputable "hit." For the wartime Soviet audience, this dance was charged with a feeling of victorious patriotism.

The second ballet, *Spartak*, depicts a slave rebellion in ancient Rome. Its plot obviously served political purposes: Soviet historians and ideologists presented a slave rebellion as a precursor to the Russian Revolution of 1917, adopting Karl Marx's opinion that Spartak "was the true representative of a proletariat of antiquity." A change of entourage did not affect Khachaturian's musical style: Ancient Rome is shown by means of colorful Armenian-style music. As Boris Schwarz noted wittily, the Roman "Sword Dance" is a twin to the Armenian "Sabre Dance" from *Gayane*.

Throughout his career Khachaturian wrote popular songs, hoping that they would be "heard on the streets."

Some of them, such as the "Armenian Drinking Song" and "Song of Erevan," became popular in Armenia. He was commissioned to compose the music for the national anthem of the Soviet Armenian Republic.

Despite his efforts to compose following the ideological and stylistic requirements of socialist realism, Khachaturian became one of the victims in the Stalin and Zhdanov campaign against the formalism in music. His composition written for the celebration of the 30th anniversary of the October Socialist Revolution, a *Symphony-Poem* for orchestra, organ, and fifteen trumpets (1947), became an object of severe official criticism. In the Communist Party's Decree of 1948, Khachaturian, together with Shostakovich, Prokofiev, and several other composers, was accused of "formalistic distortions and anti-democratic tendencies which are alien to the Soviet people and its artistic taste." After Stalin's death, Khachaturian was the first of the Soviet composers to begin a struggle for liberation of art from the party's ideological guardianship.

There are two Khachaturian's biographies, both titled *Aram Khachaturian,* and available in English translation. One is written by Grigory Schneerson (Moscow: Foreign Languages Publishing House, 1959), the other by Victor Yuzefovich (New York: Sphinx Press, Inc., 1985). Khachaturian's aesthetic views, as related to the ideological requirements of the Stalinist and post-Stalinist Soviet Union, are presented in Boris Schwarz's *Music and Musical Life in Soviet Russia, 1917–1970* (New York: W. W. Norton & Company, 1972). Khachaturian's approach to Armenian folklore is discussed in James Bakst's *History of Russian-Soviet Music* (New York: Dodd, Mead & Company, 1962).

**KHOMEINI, AYATOLLAH**  1900–1989, Primary religious leader of the Iranian Revolution (1979). The revolution was initially composed of many ideological factions (religious, socialists, Communists, and liberal-democrats), but Khomeini and his followers emerged as the most powerful group in the country.

Saayid Ruholla Mussaui Khomeini was born 180 miles south of the Iranian capital of Tehran in the town of Khomein. One of six children in a religious family, his father was killed when Khomeini was young. Khomeini's grandfather, father, and father-in-law all attained the rank of Ayatollah, the highest level of standing in the Shi'ite Islamic tradition.

As a young religious scholar in Qom he broke with traditional Shi'ite thought and exhorted the religious leadership to take more activist positions concerning political and social problems. Many traditional Shi'ite scholars argued that connections made between the

ethereal aspects of Islam and the mundane aspects of daily life (politics) would lower Islam to the level of the mundane. Khomeini rejected this position and argued that Islamic values should be used as a means of fighting unjust governance and to establish a just society. Khomeini was often viewed in the West as a traditional member of the Shi'ite religious establishment, but this perspective failed to recognize that he had challenged the conservative religious leadership in Iran. In this respect, Khomeini's assertion that active religious guidance was necessary for governing legitimacy represents a break from traditional Shi'ite religious thought.

Khomeini's first published treatise, *Unveiling the Secrets* (1941), condemned the increasing secularization of Iranian society and criticized Reza Khan Shah for increased dependence on the West. In 1961 Khomeini led a series of demonstrations against legislation that allowed women and non-Muslims to run for public office. In 1963 Khomeini published a series of articles denouncing the "White Paper" reforms instituted by the shah. As a result of his activism Khomeini was arrested and jailed briefly in 1963, but following his release he led a series of antigovernment demonstrations throughout 1963–1964. He was then exiled by the shah to Turkey in 1964, but emigrated to the Najaf region of Iraq. From here Khomeini produced *Guardianship of the Islamic Jurists* (1970). This text formalized his ideas concerning the right of religious authorities to act as an oversight to governance.

Khomeini was expelled from Iraq in 1977. He emigrated to Paris, made contact with other Iranian exiles in France, and continued to produce articles and audiotapes that were smuggled into Iran. These tapes and written exhortations greatly contributed to the destabilization of the shah's regime. A series of widespread demonstrations against the Mohammed Reza Shah throughout 1978 forced the shah to leave the country.

Khomeini returned to Iran in January 1979 and his followers formally strengthened their control of the Iranian government by establishing legal standing for the religious élite in the new Iranian Constitution. They then moved to eliminate factions who opposed them. During this period of Iranian political instability Saddam Hussein, president of Iraq, launched an invasion of Iran in an attempt to reestablish control over the Shatt-al-Arab. Hussein had reluctantly ceded this territory to Iran in a 1975 treaty.

Previously, a group of radical Iranian students had stormed the American Embassy in Tehran on November 4, 1979, and subsequently held fifty-two American embassy personnel hostage for 444 days. Khomeini did not order this action but later supported the embassy takeover. This was countered with economic sanctions by America and its allies. The United States also attempted a military rescue of the hostages, which was aborted, but resulted in the deaths of American servicemen.

In his writings and speeches Khomeini's philosophy was consistently against the concept of the nation-state. Khomeini often stated that the concept was Western and used to divide and conquer the Middle East. Khomeini generally referred to the Islamic "nation" as the entire Muslim world, and this concept of Islamic nationalism is codified in the Iranian Constitution. As such, Khomeini regarded the Iranian Revolution as a vanguard movement that would act as a catalyst to other religious movements in the Middle East. Another Khomeini position was that Islamic governance was incompatible with the institution of monarchy. This was first used to combat the monarchal philosophy of the shah, and then used to condemn the legitimacy of the monarchies in the Gulf region. In particular, Khomeini attacked the monarchy of Saudi Arabia that also tied its governing legitimacy to Islamic (Sunni) religious principle. In this respect, Khomeini and many of his followers were internationalists and actively supported both Shi'ite and Sunni Islamic movements throughout the Middle East. In particular, the Shi'ite movement (Hezbollah) in Lebanon was given financial and military support during the Lebanese civil war.

Despite the fact that Khomeini's stated philosophy is against the formation of states in the Muslim world, his followers did have to reorganize the apparatus of the Iranian state. Following the Iranian Revolution governance was established in accordance with Shi'ite Muslim religious traditions. Because most other countries in the Middle East do not have a majority shi'ite population they would not adopt the same governing system that was established in Iran even if they were inclined toward establishing an Islamic state.

Khomeini established the Velayat-i-Faqih (guardians of Islamic jurists) and exercised oversight to ensure that the laws of the state were in accordance with Shi'ite tradition. Khomeini offered guidance in his Friday prayers, or issued religious fatwas that outlined his general positions. It was then left to the Majles-al Shura (the elected assembly) and Guardian Council to interpret these guidelines into practical policy. Often, as debate continued, groups would ask Khomeini for further "guidance" if they could not resolve a dispute. On several occasions Khomeini did interject himself into specific political debates and sided with different factions on different issues. Khomeini also reversed positions that he had previously directed the Majles to adopt. The

most dramatic reversal of policy was his sudden acceptance of UN Resolution 598, which ended an eight-year war with Iraq.

Just before Khomeini's death in 1989 he issued an unambiguous fatwa (religious finding of law) that condemned Salman Rushdie to death for authoring a fictional text, *Satanic Verses*. While the text was considered blasphemous toward the prophet Muhammad throughout the Islamic world, the fatwa was regarded as a clear violation of international law by most countries.

That Khomeini led a movement that consolidated control over the Iranian revolution while fighting a war with Iraq and enduring severe economic sanctions is a remarkable accomplishment. While this success came at a high cost in terms of loss of Iranian life (nearly a half million) and tremendous damage to the Iranian economy, Khomeini's general ideology of Islamic governance set a powerful example for other religious movements in the region. Currently, the power of the Velayat-i-Faqih, which Khomeini institutionalized into the Iranian constitution, is being challenged by elected officials in the executive branch of Iranian governance.

A good translation of Khomeini's writings is *Islam and Revolution,* translated by Hamid Alger (Mizan Press, 1981). For an excellent description of the Iranian Constitution, how it was established, and the specific powers of the Velayat-i-Faqih, read *The Constitution of Iran: Politics and the State in the Islamic Republic* by Asghar Schirazi (I. B. Tauris Publishers, 1998).

**KHRUSHCHEV, NIKITA** 1894–1971, Born into a peasant and coal mining family in Kalinovka in the southwest part of Russia, Khrushchev joined the Bolshevik movement in 1918 and moved rapidly up the party ranks. By 1939 he had acquired a seat in the politburo. He concentrated his work on Ukraine during World War II, organizing military units and then guiding the efforts to get the Ukrainian economy and infrastructure up and running after the conflict. In 1955 he became premier of the Soviet Union. His first dramatic surprise was his secret speech at the 20th party congress in February 1956 revealing and condemning Stalin's crimes and terror against the Soviet people. The resulting destalinization and feeling that the regime would be significantly liberalized was widely accepted. However, they also sparked a renewal of nationalist fervor throughout the Soviet Empire and encouraged Hungarians and Poles to rebel against Soviet domination of their countries. Khrushchev suppressed these expressions of anti-Soviet and pronationalist sentiments by ordering Soviet tanks and troops to crush the rebellions. Even though he continued to rule in a dictatorial way, he nevertheless did reduce the intrusiveness of the secret police (KGB) and the application of terror against his own people.

As a statesman, Khrushchev blended bluster and threats with more peaceful gestures. He authorized heavy spending on the military and space programs. In 1957 the USSR launched the first satellite to circle the earth, *Sputnik I,* and in 1961 Yuri Gagarin became the first human to orbit the earth. Such space activity proved that the Soviet Union had a high science base and possessed adequate missile technology to threaten the United States with intercontinental ballistic missiles (ICBM). This spurred the arms race between his country and the United States. From 1958 to 1961 he threatened West Berlin, insisting that it become a "free city" with no official ties to West Germany. In 1960 he failed to prevent a monumental split between the People's Republic of China (PRC) and the Soviet Union. In 1962 he threatened to deploy missiles in Cuba that could reach targets in the United States. A resolute President John F. Kennedy forced him to back down. The humiliation of these failures brought about Khrushchev's forced retirement as party and government chief in 1964. He spent the rest of days writing his memoirs, *Khrushchev Remembers,* published in English in 1970.

**KIM IL SUNG**  1912–1994, Ruler of North Korea from 1948 to 1994. Kim Il Sung rose to power in North Korea immediately after he returned to Korea in 1945 from northeast China (Manchuria), where he had engaged in anti-Japanese partisan struggles. Kim Il Sung served as the leader of the Provisional People's Committees, which implemented, under the auspices of the Soviet Union, the two primary issues of the time: land reform and the purge of those who collaborated with the colonial power during the Japanese occupation (1910–1945). Land reform in 1946 confiscated without compensation land owned by Japanese and Korean landlords and distributed it free of charge to the landless instead of adopting the Soviet model of collectivization. This land reform, which included the purge of the collaborators, brought popular support and power to the Communist leaders. Completed within a month, this land reform stood in dramatic contrast to the program in the south. There, land reform was not announced until 1950 and was implemented so slowly that landlords had enough time to sell their lands. Consequently, this left only small pieces for sale to peasants at prices set by the land reform laws in South Korea.

Kim Il Sung and those of his comrades who returned from Manchuria gradually gained control over other Communist groups, the Korean People's Army, and the Korean Workers Party by the mid-1950s. His four-decade rule was marked by sporadic, nevertheless significant, tensions with both China and the Soviet Union, tensions signifying that North Korea was making some efforts to carve its own autonomy within the socialist bloc. The basis of North Korea's proclaimed autonomy from foreign pressures—in principle, if not always possible—was the Juche ideology. While unsympathetic historians regard it as almost a myth invented in the 1970s to form a basis for a cult of believers following Kim Il Sung, the Juche ideology, according to North Korea, originated in the experience of the struggles between the peasants and colonizers in Manchuria during the 1930s. This ideology does embody the idealization of the anticolonial struggles by Kim Il Sung and his associates, but the drive for nationalism forms its centerpiece, or crux. The term *Juche* refers to the principle of self-reliance, the reliance on one's power, and the spirit of self-sufficiency. Stories of the experiences of Kim Il Sung and his partisan armies were circulated in various publications of the North Korean government, several of which continued to circulate after the 1960s. These books are not read simply as history books but as political textbooks for state institutions, political meetings, and study groups in factories, schools, and villages. These textbooks are used as ways of instructing Korean citizens on how to practice and achieve self-reliance by using as examples the revolutionary acts of Kim Il Sung and his armies. The Juche ideology buttressed North Korea's economic programs. For instance, under the slogan of "Produce and Study Following the Examples of the Anti-Japanese Partisan Army," the revolutionary consciousness and experience of Kim Il Sung and his comrades in their anti-Japanese revolutionary struggles in Manchuria was elevated as the only way to overcome shortages of foreign aid and natural resources, to invent new technology collectively, and to achieve the maximum productivity of work. In other words, this version of a nationalism based on the idealized memories of the anticolonial struggles in Manchuria furnished the basis of the power of Kim Il Sung and political and economic policies in North Korea.

**KING, MACKENZIE**  1874–1950, Canadian prime minister. The 1921 election ushered in a long era of Liberal Party domination in Canadian federal politics, first under the leadership of William Lyon Mackenzie King, who ruled Canada for most of the rest of his life, until his death in 1950. He had received a Ph.D. from Harvard and had served for years as an industrial relations consultant for the Rockefellers in the United

States. He remained a bachelor all his life, and is widely regarded as the strangest (but largely respected) politician in Canadian history. He was deeply immersed in spiritualism and had a kind of psychopathic devotion to his deceased mother. However, despite all his personal quirks, he was responsible for making the Liberal Party an effective and attractive "all-things-to-all-people" grouping that could unite Canadians of many different persuasions.

When he became prime minister, there was much disagreement within Canada about how quickly the country should move toward autonomy from Britain. While the debate was going on, the government took several concrete steps. In 1922 Prime Minister King indicated to Britain that Canada could no longer be committed in advance to military actions on the basis of its association with the British Empire. In 1923 it assumed the right to negotiate and sign treaties and to make its own foreign policy. It did promise Britain the courtesy of keeping it informed about what Canada was doing. In 1927 Canada sent its first ambassador to the United States.

Unlike in 1914, when Canada had become automatically involved in World War I on Britain's entry, in September 1939 the Canadian government and Parliament deliberated for a week after fighting had commenced in World War II before declaring war on Britain's side. He realized that Britain could no longer be the primary provider for Canadian defense. Therefore, his government negotiated a defense agreement with the United States at Ogdensburg in 1940. In August 1940 he and President Franklin D. Roosevelt agreed to a Permanent Joint Board on Defense, which could design defense arrangements for the North American continent. In 1941 these two leaders also penned the Hyde Park Declaration, which provided for the sharing of defense production and for increased trade in defense equipment. These were measures that deepened the meshing of the two countries' economies. These agreements were a clear indication that Canadian defense was no longer linked exclusively with that of the British Empire.

World War II created a potentially dangerous domestic political situation for Canadians and threatened to open up the terrible wounds of 1914–1918. Parliament adopted the declaration of war almost unanimously, but support from French-speaking Canadians stemmed largely from the King government's promise not to draft Canadians into the armed forces for service abroad. Prime Minister King unmistakably sensed the danger, and he resisted sending conscripts to war zones until November 1944, when he finally ordered 16,000 draftees overseas. Angry riots broke out in Quebec province,

and some Quebecois came close to mutiny at some military bases. However, victory in Europe in May 1945 fortunately defused this gathering domestic political storm, and a relieved Canada proceeded to demobilize its draftees as quickly as possible.

In 1997 a panel of twenty-five scholars of Canadian history evaluated and ranked Canada's twenty prime ministers. They especially valued a leader's coherent vision of the country and well-articulated goals in domestic and foreign policy. In their opinion, William Lyon Mackenzie King was the best. They were impressed by his great political skills, his devotion to unity, his establishment of Canada's international identity, his steps toward establishing the social welfare safety net, and the brilliant way he ran Canada's enormous war effort.

See Henry Ferns and Bernard Ostry, *The Age of Mackenzie King* (James Lorimer, 1976) and H. B. Neatby, *William Lyon Mackenzie King*, 3 vols. (Toronto, 1963, 1976).

**KING, JR., MARTIN LUTHER**   1929–1968, Premier figure of the civil rights movement and the most prominent black leader in the United States. He was thrust, almost by accident, into a position of leadership after Rosa Parks was arrested in Montgomery, Alabama, for refusing to give up her seat so a white man would not have to be seated in a row in which a black was also seated. In response, leaders of the black community moved to organize a boycott of the buses and sought someone to head the movement.

King was chosen because he was a good speaker and, having been in town for a short time, had made few enemies. But his talents and dedication enabled him to transcend the leadership of the bus boycott to become a major national civil rights leader. He soon launched the Southern Christian Leadership Conference (SCLC), the first new civil rights organization in decades, in order to spread the new militancy that was evidenced in Montgomery. He maintained a firm commitment to nonviolent direct action, which in his view did not involve compromising basic principles, but was a moral commitment that enabled him to appeal to a broad spectrum of whites, as well as blacks, even while he demanded change NOW, as he put it. King came purposely to confront white power and authority, bringing out into "the light of day" the brutality that had traditionally been visited on blacks by whites, and thereby subjecting it to national scrutiny. This approach was consistent with King's overall strategy: to keep his eye on the goal, to forge the broadest coalitions possible to make social changes.

As King's stature grew with his victories, he transcended his relationship to the African American community and became increasingly the conscience of the nation, speaking up against American participation in the war in Vietnam, calling for the national spotlight to turn not only on issues of race, but also on the downtrodden of the nation and of the world. His evolving views led him to undertake a program to combat poverty in America. He led the SCLC to organize unions, especially in the South. He was supporting unionized garbage workers who were striking for better conditions in Memphis, Tennessee, when he was assassinated in that city by a gunman or men about whose identity there remain many questions. At that time, he was preparing for the "Poor People's March on Washington," an effort to refocus the nation's attention on the poor. He intended a substantial assault on the market as the only means of distributing the nation's jobs and valued goods.

King sought to speak for the downtrodden, black or white. His importance in this regard is evidenced by the fact that no one was able to take his place after he was murdered. Though King has been pictured as a "moderate" leader, in comparison with Malcolm X, who had severely criticized King for his prointegrationist policies, it was Malcolm who changed his course and began to seek to join the movement that King led. Moreover, King's words and actions became increasingly confrontational vis-à-vis American policies, as he assaulted the war while he prepared for the Poor People's March, which he envisioned as "dislocative and disruptive."

Two excellent political biographies of King are Taylor Branch's three volumes, of which two have so far been published: *Parting the Waters* (Simon and Schuster, 1988) and *Pillar of Fire* (Simon and Schuster, 1998).

## KIPLING, RUDYARD

1865–1936, Born in Bombay, India, Kipling spent much of his childhood with foster parents in Southsea and went to school in Westward Ho! before returning to India to become a journalist. He permanently emigrated to England in 1889. His books were first made available to the English public in 1890 and by the end of the century it could be fairly said that no other writer of his time had so profoundly swayed the English populace in favor of imperialism. Popularly known as the "bard of empire," he was one of the most prolific and popular writers of his day, author of such well-known children's tales as *The Jungle Book* (1894) and *Kim* (1901). It is to Kipling that we owe the phrase "White Man's Burden," which he first penned in a poem by that same name in 1899. Kipling's essays, novels, poems, and tales were some of the most effective cultural instruments for the promotion of British jingoism. He, more than any other writer, reflected the diverse ideas that went under the general term *imperialism*. His poems reminded his countrymen that they ruled over an empire in which the sun never set.

Kipling provided Victorian England with an elaborate rationalization for Anglo-Saxon supremacy. He was a firm believer that English-speaking peoples should be united and urged that this vision of imperial unity include not only Britons but British settlers in the white dominions of Australia, Canada, New Zealand, South Africa, and the United States. He also felt the ideal of Anglo-Saxon supremacy could serve as a source of unity between the British aristocracy and working classes. His poetry was part of a general attempt to promote the idea of the unity of English-speaking people throughout the British Empire.

The main thrust of Kipling's work was to show that other races and nations were both different from and inferior to the Anglo-Saxons. Therefore, it was the responsibility of the Anglo-Saxon to provide guidance and tutelage to them through their incorporation into the British Empire. In turn, the inferior races and nations owed ultimate allegiance to the Anglo-Saxons, becoming minor wards of the empire, rather than citizens. Kipling's writings did much to justify the spread of British imperial rule, and it is for this reason that he quickly gained the devotion of such noted British imperialists as Cecil John Rhodes, who built a small cottage for Kipling on the grounds of his estate in Cape Town.

Biographies of Kipling include Martin Symour-Smith's *Kipling: A Biography* (St. Martin's Press, 1999) and Philip Mason's *Kipling: The Glass, the Shadow, and the Fire* (Harper and Row, 1975).

## KLAUS, VACLAV

1949–, Czech economist, politician, and statesman; prime minister of the Czech Republic, 1993–1997. Born in Prague, Czechoslovakia, Klaus rose to prominence after the 1989 Velvet Revolution, and is known for his leading role in the transition from a command to a market economy.

Like a few other Czech scholars under Communism, Klaus had the opportunity to study economics at Cornell University, where he was first introduced to Milton Friedman's and Friedrich Hayek's neoclassical economic school of thought, which influenced his future economic practices and policies. In 1970 Klaus became a staff member at the Czechoslovak State Bank, and in 1987 he joined a group of Czech economists sponsored by SBCS and the Czechoslovak Academy of Sciences. The group's main objective was to develop alternative models that could function more effectively within the framework of the socialist economic system.

Klaus, during his professional career, was never involved in politics, and his role in the 1989 Velvet Revolution was marginal. In the aftermath of the revolution Klaus gained recognition with his advocacy of a rapid economic reform. He was appointed the first minister of finance in post-Communist Czechoslovakia. In October 1990 he was elected chairman of the *Občanske Forum* (OF, Civic Forum).

In 1991 it became clear the OF would not be able to accommodate diverse political and economic interests and Klaus formed the *Občanska Demokraticka Strana* (ODS, Civic Democratic Party). At the founding congress in April 1991 he was elected a party chairman. Klaus's ascendancy to leadership was completed in June 1992, when the ODS won a plurality of seats in the Czech National Assembly, and Klaus became the prime minister of the Czech Federal Republic.

After the June 1992 elections, Klaus negotiated a peaceful dissolution of the Czech and Slovak Federation with his Slovak counterpart, Vladimir Mečiar, and on January 1, 1993, he became the prime minister of the newly independent Czech Republic. He was forced to resign when a series of financial scandals tied to the ODS became public in November 1997. Besides Václav Havel, Klaus is the best known figure of the post-Communist Czech politics.

Among the most acclaimed works by Vaclav Klaus are *Renaissance: The Rebirth of Liberty in the Heart of Europe* (Washington, D.C.: Cato Institute, 1997); *Ekonomicka teoria a realita transformačnich procesu* (*Economic Theory and the Reality of Transformation Processes*) (Prague: Management Press, 1995); and *Česka cesta* (*The Czech Way*) (Prague: Profile, 1994). A biographical essay about Vaclav Klaus was written by Karel Hviždala, *Prvni zprava: Rozhovor s Vaclavem Klausem* (*The First from the Right: Discourses with Vaclav Klaus*) (Prague: Nakladatelsvy Cartoonia, 1992).

## KOHL, HELMUT

1930 – , Chancellor of the Federal Republic of Germany from 1982 to 1998. In 1969 he was elected minister president of the state of Rhineland-Palatinate. In 1976 he ran unsuccessfully as the chancellor candidate of the Christian Democratic Union (CDU). Helmut Kohl became chancellor in 1982 when the Free Democratic Party (FDP) abandoned Chancellor Helmut Schmidt and the Social Democrats (SPD) to form a ruling coalition with the conservative CDU.

As chancellor, Kohl made European integration and the Franco-German partnership his highest foreign policy priorities. He viewed this partnership with France as symbolic of the FRG's policy of reconciliation for the pre-1945 pattern of aggressive German foreign policies. He developed a close personal relationship with French President François Mitterrand. Kohl also saw Franco-German cooperation as the engine of European integration. Throughout his sixteen years as chancellor, he was one of Europe's strongest advocates of European political and economic union. He played an instrumental role in the movement toward the European Monetary Union (EMU) in the 1990s.

Kohl (the "Unification Chancellor") oversaw the unification of the FRG with the former German Democratic Republic (GDR) in 1990. He provoked international controversy by issuing an aggressive "ten point plan for national reunification" in December 1989, when the fate of the GDR was still uncertain. During the following months, however, Kohl's government resolved all the diplomatic obstacles to national unity. The most significant of these issues were the status of the Polish–German border, the removal of Soviet troops from East Germany, and the termination of all allied occupation rights in Germany. After the euphoria over national unification in October 1990, Kohl's popularity declined when he was unable to deliver on his campaign promise of "blooming landscapes" in East Germany. He was defeated in 1998 by a SPD/Green Party coalition led by Gerhard Schroeder (SPD). Helmut Kohl held the office of German chancellor longer than anyone aside from Otto von Bismarck.

For further reading, see Clay Clemens, ed., *The Kohl Chancellorship* (Frank Cass & Co., 1998) and Karl Hugo Pruys, ed., *Kohl: Genius of the Present* (Edition Q, 1996).

## KONOVALETS, EVHEN

1891–1938, Served in the military of the short-lived Ukranian People's Republic and led the Organization of Ukrainian Nationalists (OUN) for many years. Born in Zashkiv, L'viv Oblast in then-Austrian-controlled Galicia, he studied law at L'viv University before joining the Austrian army during World War I. Captured by the Russians as a 2nd lieutenant in 1915, he shortly escaped with other Galician officers and formed the Galician-Bukovinian Battalion of Sich Riflemen in November 1917. (Andrii Melnyk, later head of the OUN, was his second in command.)

Konovalets led the Sich Riflemen as a colonel in the army of the Ukrainian People's Republic (which lasted from January to April 1918 and December 1918 to October 1920). The battalion saw combat in early 1918 against a Bolshevik uprising and a Soviet invasion of Kyiv (the city fell on February 9), and in the retaking of Kyiv with German assistance in March. Konovalets and others refused to recognize the pro-German Hetmanate government that was established, so the Sich Battalion was disbanded and disarmed. It was revived that fall, fought against the Ukrainian Hetmanate, and helped to capture Kyiv for the Ukrainian People's Republic in November–December 1918. The Sich Battalion (which had grown to corps size) was disbanded by the Poles in December 1919 and Konovalets was arrested and briefly interred in a Polish prisoner of war camp.

In 1920 the Ukrainian Military Organization (UVO) was formed with some 2000 members. Konovalets was elected to head the UVO in 1921, and in the next two years led an underground war against Poland, including assassinations, attacks on government buildings, railroads, and Polish estates, and a failed assassination attempt against Polish leader Marshal Józef Piłsudski in L'viv in 1921. In addition to violent struggle, the UVO under Konovalets established foreign language press centers and publishing houses to gain international support, formed Ukrainian veterans groups abroad, and brought the issue of Ukrainian independence to the League of Nations. By 1923 the UVO was losing popular support because many Ukrainians were beginning to accept Polish rule.

UVO activities continued sporadically throughout the 1920s, during which time Konovalets lived in Western Europe and sought aid for the group—mostly from Germany. By 1927 the UVO began to recruit university students in an attempt to rejuvenate the movement. One of these was Stepan Bandera. At a conference in Vienna in 1929, Konovalets turned the UVO into the Organization of Ukrainian Nationalists (OUN). Consisting of veterans of the 1917–1921 struggle (like Konovalets and Melnyk) and younger nationalists (Bandera), the OUN was based in Galicia, Bukovina, and Transcarpathia.

The OUN advocated armed struggle against socialism, capitalism, liberalism, and democracy, and wanted to build a one-party state under a strong leader for Ukraine. The OUN used terror and assassination in an attempt to destabilize the Polish government, and fought to a lesser extent against Romania and the Soviet Union. Funded largely by Germany, the OUN gained mass support among Ukraine's youth in the 1930s. Konovalets remained the group's leader until he was assassinated by a Soviet agent in 1938 in Rotterdam. His death led to the splitting of the group between those loyal to Melnyk and those who supported Bandera. The main legacy of Konovalets's leadership of the OUN was the establishment of pro-OUN groups in all centers of Ukrainian émigrés abroad.

## KOREAN NATIONALISM

In the 20th century, Koreans have radically recreated versions of their nationalism at least three times, experiencing a major rupture almost every forty years. From 1910 to 1945, there was the colonization and the formation of the Korean diaspora; then, from 1945 to 1980, the national division of Korea during the Cold War period; and, finally, during the 1990s, the formation of a transnational Korea, which comprises both the two Koreas and the Korean diaspora. Colonialism and South Korean's recent globalization are considered two major mechanisms underlying the transformation of these three nationalisms.

The first rupture is marked by the colonization of Korean by Japan after centuries of independence in 1910. Many studies of nationalism during this colonial period tend to focus on the forms and characteristics of the changing independent struggles led by various groups, including intellectuals and peasants during various periods. For instance, the nationwide demonstration in 1919 was considered to be the largest popular protest. Intellectuals in the 1920s engaged in the production of journals, newspapers, literature, and other print materials in their efforts to educate themselves as well as the public, a step that they considered crucial in working toward independence. This cultural nationalism was succeeded by radical peasant movements in the 1930s, when Japan geared for the mass mobilization of labor power of Koreans and economic resources for the Pacific war during the 1930s. In addition to these nationalist struggles, a factor still not fully recognized in the study of nationalism under colonial rule is the impact resulting from the formation of the Korean diaspora, another crucial effect of colonialism.

Current estimates indicate that about 15 percent of the total Korean population of 20 million has immigrated to the United States, Japan, and its other colonies, including Manchuria (northeast China) and Sakhalin. This dynamic has extended the Korean identity beyond the Korean peninsula. This formation of the Korean diaspora suggests the need to expand the definition of Korean nationalism beyond the one used during this period, which took the narrow view of confining the Korean nation to only those living on the Korean peninsula, and to conduct more studies on the diasporic identities of Koreans.

Following World War II, the liberated Korea was divided into South and North in 1948. Each Korea became the other's primary enemy, building armies to defend each from the other, inventing one Korea as a model of authoritarian capitalism and the other as a model of authoritarian socialism. The character of each Korean state reflected both colonial legacies and Superpower tendencies during the Cold War period. South Korea's nationalism was built on two fundamental characteristics: the restoration of colonial institutions and the fusion of anticommunism with anti-North Korean nationalism. The postliberation regimes reinstated many Koreans who had collaborated with the Japanese, an action thus negating the very meaning of liberation. The colonial legacy was especially visible in South Korea's armies and police forces. Park Chung Hee's regime from 1961 to 1979 consolidated the colonial basis of the state, binding it with the economic development program. Under Park's regime, the state achieved a good deal of legitimacy through economic development, largely obscuring its contested origin. Anticommunism and anti-North Korean nationalism constituted a major political ideology set above the constitutional rights of individuals. Challenges to the state were contained on the grounds that they violated the social contract needed to build a stronger nation and to defend the nation from North Korea. Anti-North Korean nationalism of the state also figured into the democracy movement in the 1980s, led by students, workers, and clergymen who contended that democracy in South Korea would not be possible without reconciling with North Korea.

The nationalism of the North Korean state also stemmed from Korea's colonial legacy, especially the anticolonial revolutionary struggle in Manchuria (northeast China). Kim Il Sung and his partisan comrades had operated the independent struggle close to, or within, Korea by establishing resistance networks between northern Korea and Manchuria. From 1946 until Kim Il Sung's death in 1994, they dominated top political leadership. Their anti-Japanese struggle in Manchuria became the basis for the legitimacy of their power and the crux of North Korean nationalism, the self-reliant ( *Juche* in Korean) ideology.

In recent years, the contrast between the two Koreas could not have appeared more striking: While severe famine and increasing defections undermined the North's claims on self-reliance, the South's developmental success was phenomenal and has resulted in a rapid recovery from the financial crisis in the late 1990s. In drawing this stark contrast, however, it is easy for commentators to miss a third rupture since the late 1980s, which is the emergence of a new integrated Korea that comprises not just the two Koreas but also the Korean diaspora. South Korea and North Korea have expanded economic cooperation through trade and through the South's investment in the North. Korean Chinese and Korean Americans have not only mediated these economic exchanges between the two Koreas but also directly participated in the two Korea's economies as laborers and investors. This new integration of Koreans is

shaped under South Korea's leadership and its policy of globalization. The South Korean globalization in the 1990s evoked strong national sentiment, calling for national unity in order to help Korea survive and gain leadership in the international community under the sea of change after the Cold War. At first glance, South Korean globalization seems very inclusive, reaching out to embrace the entire dimension of the Korean diaspora. Yet, an emerging characteristic of the transnational Korean community is hierarchy. South Korea represents itself as the authentic embodiment of the Korean nation, presenting its own usage of Korean language and culture as the genuine rendition of national tradition and spirit. It considers the cultural practices of other Koreans to be deformed by the influence of North Korea and its socialist ideology. The formation of this new Korean nationalism and the impact of the threads of new relations among Koreans across borders remain to be seen and the significance interpreted.

**KOROŠEC, ANTON** 1872–1940, Leader of the Slovene People's Party (*Slovenska ljudska stranka* or SLS), 1918–1940. A Catholic priest, Korošec was one of the leaders of the Slovene Catholic nationalist movement during the Austro-Hungarian period. He later steered it toward association with Croat and Serb movements. Korošec proved instrumental in building the SLS into an organized and dominant political force in Slovenia. During World War I, Korošec increasingly directed the SLS away from the Habsburg state. In May 1917, Korošec, along with fellow Slovene nationalist leaders Janez Krek and Ivan Šušteršić, signed a declaration with the South Slavic Club in Vienna calling for unification of the Austro-Hungarian lands inhabited by the Catholic South Slavs. In August 1918, Korošec coordinated the establishment of a national council in Ljubljana that sought to coordinate Yugoslav integration. In October 1918, Korošec became president of the National Council of the Slovenes, Croats, and Serbs, which decided on October 31 to amalgamate with Serbia and Montenegro to form a state of the South Slavs. In his role as president of the National Council of the Slovenes, Croats, and Serbs, Korošec entered into disputes with Nikola Pašić, the Serb Radical Party leader, over the future structure of the Yugoslav state. In 1919, Korošec expanded SLS activities to Croatia. This resulted in the formation of the clericalist Croat People's Party (*Hrvatska pučka stranka* or HPS).

In his long political career in Yugoslavia, Korošec proved adept at exploiting the constant conflict between Serb and Croat politicians to the favor of the

Slovenes. His skill in maneuvering won him the distrust of both Serb and Croat politicians. Although aware that the existence of the Yugoslav state was to the advantage of the small Slovene nation, Korošec consistently militated against excessive unitarist centralism. Korošec sought selective support from the Yugoslav government, for example, in seeking to extend the borders of the Yugoslav state to include those Slovenes residing in Austria and Italy. In the period of uncertainty between the assassination of Croat Peasant Party leader Stjepan Radić in 1928 and the proclamation of King Aleksandar's dictatorship in January 1929, Korošec became the Yugoslav prime minister. He was the only non-Serb to hold this post in Yugoslavia between 1918 and 1941. After 1929, Korošec was the only non-Serb in the cabinet of the royal dictatorship. He resigned in March 1930. In 1933, Korošec was arrested along with Vladko Maček and Ante Trumbić. Korošec was released after the assassination of King Aleksandar in October 1934. He served in the cabinet of Prime Minister Stojadinović after 1935, and joined the new government party, the Yugoslav Radical Union (Jugoslovenska Radikalna Zajednica, or JRZ). Korošec officially changed the name of the SLS to JRZ.

**KOSSUTH, LAJOS** 1802–1894, Born of a noble but landless family in what is today northeast Hungary, Kossuth can be seen as a prototypical representative of the enlightened, gentry-led, liberal nationalism that developed in Hungary in the post-Napoleon period. Educated as a lawyer, Kossuth was an inflammatory writer and talented speaker who soon became an influential politician and journalist. He first gained renown during the 1832–1936 "Reform Diet," when he edited partisan synopses of the parliamentary debates. Habsburg authorities tolerated his writings and political activities until 1837, when they charged Kossuth with disloyalty and sedition. Jailed until May 1840, Kossuth founded *Pesti Hirlap* soon after his release, establishing it as the leading voice for abolition of serfdom and noble tax exemption and promulgation of civil rights and administrative independence for Hungary.

Through this journal, Kossuth agitated for greater, though not total separation from Austria. Austrian Chancellor Metternich gradually lost patience with Kossuth and in 1844 orchestrated Kossuth's dismissal from *Pesti Hirlap*. Popular, fiery, and self-confident, Kossuth returned to politics, triumphing in an 1847 parliamentary election. In Parliament, he became the central figure in the liberal Party of United Opposition. With the moderating aid of Ferenc Deák, Kossuth crafted the party's program, providing Hungary with a blueprint for the revolution of 1848–1849.

Under Kossuth's leadership, Hungary won incredible concessions from Vienna in the heady revolutionary days of March and April 1848. The Habsburg court consented to the "April Laws," including the abolition of feudalism; independent economic, military, and political administration of Hungary; Hungary's right to unite with Transylvania; equality before the law for all; expanded suffrage; tax reform; and numerous other political, legal, and economic changes. During this first phase of the revolution, Kossuth served as finance minister in the Batthyány government, the government Vienna recognized as legitimate. One of his crucial decisions was to fund and recruit a 200,000-man-strong domestic defense force. This decision had two major effects. First, it necessitated the printing of Hungarian money, to which the Viennese court objected. Second, it created an army that became the core of Hungary's miliary resistance to Vienna.

When war broke out in September 1848 against Habsburg troops led by the Ban of Croatia Josip Jelačić, the Hungarian Parliament adopted emergency measures, permitting Kossuth near-dictatorial powers. Initial results were positive. Hungary's ragtag army stopped Jelačić, helping incite the September 1848 Revolution in Vienna. Events soon turned and by October, the Habsburgs counterattacked. Faced with military defeat and forced to relocate the government several times, Kossuth kept the Hungarian government functioning and feverishly recruited men of all nationalities to supplement the Hungarian National Guard, while his clever general Görgey continued the fight. Only in April 1849 did Kossuth opt for complete independence from Austria. At his behest, the Debrecen Parliament adopted a declaration of independence, the revolution's climax. Within two months, the Hungarian army suffered losses that inexorably led to the revolution's end. Defeat was sealed in May when Russian Tsar Nicholas I sent an army to aid Vienna against the Hungarian revolutionaries.

Like many of Europe's liberals, Kossuth's liberalism was paternalistic and frequently clashed with his nationalism. In principle, Kossuth desired legal equality, but he was not a radical democrat. Despite emancipating Hungary's serfs, for which he earned the admiration of Hungary's poorer classes and the moniker "the Great Liberator," he did not afford the masses an immediate role in politics. Instead, he favored restricting the power to vote and govern to a select élite.

Kossuth's liberalism was based on individual rights. Therefore, it is no surprise that his policies toward

Hungary's numerous nationalities before, during, and after the revolution were inconsistent and sometimes contradictory. The crux of the problem was that Kossuth failed to recognize the desire of ethno-national groups for collective rights. Well before 1848, Kossuth championed making Hungarian the national language, spoken by all in public and in schools. He fundamentally believed in the superiority of the Hungarian people and culture and that eventually the non-Hungarian minorities would realize that progress could only be achieved if they were to assimilate or "Magyarize," that is, become linguistically and culturally Hungarian. Thus, Hungary's famous April Laws contained no consideration of collective rights for Hungary's non-Hungarian minorities. At the outset of the revolution, Kossuth was willing to grant concessions such as political self-governance to "historic" people in Hungary, such as the Croats, but he was unwilling to give "nonhistoric" people, such as the Slovaks, similar rights.

In a series of measures that emerged from the twin needs of dealing seriously with the nationalities question and salvaging Hungary's anti-Habsburg struggle, Kossuth appeared to revise his stance on ethno-national autonomy. On July 14, 1849, he signed an agreement with Romanian leaders granting cultural rights to ethnic Romanians. On July 28, prompted by Kossuth, the Hungarian Parliament granted broad ethnic rights to all minorities, made Judaism a recognized religion, and made Jews full citizens. Though the sincerity of Kossuth's transformation on the nationalities question has been the subject of intense academic debate, later in life Kossuth did devise several plans for federation or confederation of the Danubian nationalities, recognizing that liberal principles could not survive among competing nationalisms.

Kossuth fled Hungary amid controversy in August 1849, escaping through Turkey. The question of his extradition nearly resulted in war between Turkey and England, on the one hand, and Austria and Russia on the other. He had wildly popular tours of the United States and England, where he was greeted as a hero. He lived much of the remainder of his life as a pauper in Italy, where he attempted to convince Italian, French, German, and British leaders to help provoke a second revolution in Hungary. He mixed with other émigré revolutionary circles and several times tried and failed to foment revolution in Hungary. He opposed the Compromise of 1867 with the Habsburgs, which granted Hungary many of the rights it had won in 1848 and lost in 1849 but stopped short of Hungarian independence. From Turin, Italy, he served as head of the Kossuth Party and remained active in Hungarian politics until his death in 1894. Amid great fanfare, his body was buried in Budapest.

István Deák's *The Lawful Revolution: Louis Kossuth and the Hungarians, 1848–49,* published in 1979 by the Columbia University Press, while not a biography, is the authoritative English language text on Kossuth.

**KRAMÁŘ, KAREL**  1860–1937, One of the founders of Czechoslovakia and a leading conservative politician. Kramář was born December 27, 1860, in Hochstadt, then in the Bohemian lands of the Habsburg Empire. The son of a successful master builder, he studied in Prague, Strasbourg, Berlin, and Paris, finally receiving his doctorate of law in 1884. He became active in politics shortly after, briefly allying himself with T. G. Masaryk, the "father of Czechoslovakia." He was elected to the Reichsrat in 1890 and then to the Bohemian Landtag three years later. In 1895 he and his "Young Czechs" political party agreed to join the government of Count Casimir Badeni in exchange for a new law that would place the Czech language on equal footing with German in Bohemia and Moravia. However, the ensuing German nationalist reaction forced the government to rescind this legislation, a serious blow to Kramář and the Young Czechs. The subsequent extension of the suffrage proved an even greater defeat, shifting the political cleavages from national to class lines. However, World War I brought new opportunities to Kramář.

As one of the leaders of the secret secessionist movement, the *Maffie,* he was tried and sentenced to death for treason. The publicity surrounding the trial restored his fortunes and those of the nationalist movement. Locked up in jail, he set the agenda for the future constitution of Bohemia, which he saw as best served under a Romanov wearing the Bohemian crown in alliance with a "Slav imperium." He even briefly influenced Masaryk in this regard. However, the Russian Revolution dashed his hopes but also eased Austrian fears of a Czech nationalist uprising. The new emperor Charles gave amnesty to Kramář in hopes of securing order within the empire. Kramář quickly joined Beneš in Paris where he took an active role in the peace process on behalf of an autonomous Czechoslovakia.

As head of the National Democratic Party, arguably the oldest Czech political party, Kramář was declared prime minister in 1919. He set about implementing a policy designed to secure the new boundaries of state, and establishing social peace and economic stability, both at the cost of the working classes. Furthermore, his anti-German and anticlerical policies both stimulated the formation of anti-Czechoslovak political movements in the Sudeten and Slovak regions of the new state. His government was replaced after the first elections, largely because of the social discontent spawned by his conservative policies. Kramář remained a moderately prominent political figure in Czechoslovak politics, supported by the powerful conservative industrialists. He emerged again briefly at the forefront of national politics on two occasions. In 1926 he lent his support to the dictatorial ambitions of a small right-wing nationalist movement, which was deftly broken apart by Masaryk and Beneš. However, he only moved into the opposition in 1934 when he formed the electorally unsuccessful Czech fascist "National Unification" block, continuing to play a minor role in Czechoslovak politics. He died in 1937, the same year as his chief political rival and superior, the nationally beloved T. G. Masaryk.

For further references on Kramář, please consult David Kelly's *The Czech Fascist Movement* (Boulder, Colo.: East European Monographs, 1995).

## KYRGYZSTANI NATIONALISM

Kyrgyzstan is a small Central Asian nation of 4.7 million people. It achieved independence after the Soviet disintegration in 1991, an event that allowed the Kyrgyzstani people to establish their own nation-state for the first time in their history.

The rise of Kyrgyzstani nationalism can be traced in three stages. During the first stage, from medieval times to the 19th century, the Kyrgyz tribes, who populated the mountain areas of Tian Shan and Pamiro-Alai, formed their own distinct language, culture, and identities. Throughout this period, these Turkic-speaking nomads interacted with their settled neighbors and gradually embraced Islam, with a strong influence from Sufi mysticism, while preserving some features of their shamanic past. A strong oral tradition of literature and poetry, which featured the use of the traditional musical instrument, the *Komuz,* produced one of the most comprehensive tales among Central Asians, *The Manas. The Manas,* a story about a legendary hero of the Kyrgyz people, became an encyclopedia of the Kyrgyz history and traditions that reflected a distinct national culture.

The second stage is associated with Russian/Soviet dominance in Central Asia. This stage began in the middle of the 19th century with the incorporation of most of the Kyrgyz tribes into the Russian Empire. The turning point of this period was the defeat of the Kokand Khanate by the Russian army and the establishment of the Turkestan Governor-Generalship in 1867. The incorporation of the Kyrgyzstani territory into the Russian Empire brought a number of changes, including modernization of the economy, education, and political systems. After the Russian Revolution of 1917, it took almost ten years for the Bolsheviks to establish firm control over the territory of present-day Kyrgyzstan and to suppress local resistance (also known as the *Basmachi* movement). In 1924, the Kara-Kyrgyz Autonomous Oblast (part of the Russian Federation) was created. In 1936, the republic received a new name and a new status as the Kyrgyz Soviet Socialist Republic. The Soviet regime brought with it secularism, persecution of the Islamic clergy, and closure of mosques. The Soviets also introduced the Latin and later the Cyrillic alphabet, raised literacy levels, and brought modern industries to the area. However, Soviet modernization was introduced at a severe price, as thousands perished during the Stalin's purges and as development was achieved through harsh economic measures. Gradually, with the emergence of mass literacy and the new intelligentsia and the relaxation of repression in the 1960s, modern Kyrgyzstani nationalism began to emerge.

The third stage began after the Soviet disintegration in 1991. Unlike the Baltic republics of Azerbaijan, Gorbachev's policy of *perestroika* did not provide the catalyst for a national liberation movement or mass political participation in Kyrgyzstan. The road to Kyrgyzstani independence in 1991 was without large-scale national-liberation wars and conflicts. The process was on the whole peaceful with the exception of the interethnic conflicts that occurred in June 1990 in southern Kyrgyzstan. Although in the early 1990s the radical nationalist groups were strong and cogent, by the middle of the 1990s the government adopted the policy of moderate nationalism. According to the 1990 Kyrgyzstani Law on Languages, the Kyrgyz language replaced Russian as the official language, although the implementation of the law has never been rigidly enforced and the Cyrillic alphabet is still used. The Republic experienced large-scale mass emigration of people in 1989–1996 (almost 15 percent of the population, mainly Russians and Russian-speaking population, left the country). The Kyrgyzstani leader, Askar Akayev, turned to moderate nationalism, revival of national symbols (such as *The Manas*), and the idea of technocratic modernization of the country. He vetoed a provision of the Law on Land, which declared that the country's land resources are the wealth (*dostoyanie*) of the ethnic Kyrgyzs. Akayev has also advocated the liberalization of the Law on Language and he proposed to the legislature that the Russian language become the official language of the republic (while the Kyrgyz language is the state language). The new constitution, adopted in May 1993, guarantees equal rights to all people of the state and it has maintained the secular nature of the Republic.

For further reading, see J. Anderson, *Kyrgyzstan: Central Asian Land of Democracy?* (Harwood Academic Publishers, 1998); Jo-Ann Gross, ed., *Muslims in Central Asia: Expressions of Identity and Change* (Durham, 1992); R. Szporluk, ed., *National Identity and Ethnicity in Russia and the New States of Eurasia* (Armonk, 1994); and *Central Asia: 130 Years of Russian Dominance, a Historical Overview,* Edward Allworth, ed. (Duke University Press, 1994).

# L

LANDSBERGIS, VYTAUTAS  1932–, Lithuanian nationalist leader, professor of music and pianist; chairman of the Homeland Union (Lithuanian Conservatives); chairman of the Seimas (Parliament) of the Republic of Lithuania; former chairman of the council of the reform Lithuanian nationalist movement *Sajudis;* former deputy of the Supreme Council of the USSR; former chairman of the Supreme Council of the Lithuanian SSR, later the Republic of Lithuania; referred to as "a hero of Lithuanian independence" by the Western media, born in Kaunas, the interim capital of interwar Lithuania.

Nationalism has a long-standing tradition in the Landsbergis family. Vytautas's grandfather, Gabrielius Landsbergis, a playwrite, was a prominent Lithuanian nationalist before World War I, and his father, Vytautas Zemkalnis-Landsbergis, a well-known architect, was an ardent advocate of Lithuanian independence during World War II.

Vytautas Landsbergis has made a major contribution to his family tradition and to maintenance of nationalist ideas under the Soviet regime by investigating the unique of works of M. K. Ciurlionis, fin de siècle artist and composer. It was important for Lithuanian nationalism surviving under the cover of the official culture of Soviet Lithuania to present itself to the world with such a striking figure as was Ciurlionis. By praising the high standards of the composer, Landsbergis was at the same time speaking for the Lithuanian national cause.

Having graduated from the Lithuanian Music Academy in 1955, Vytautas Landsbergis took up an academic career and spent the following forty years teaching music at Lithuanian music schools and the Lithuanian Music Academy, where he finally became a professor. He has established himself as a musician, a pianist in particular, and a historian of art and culture.

The politics of *perestroika* proclaimed by Gorbachev in 1985 came into effect in Lithuania in three years. In 1988 the Lithuanian nationalist movement, namely, the Lithuanian Reform Movement, known as *Sajudis* ("The Movement"), was started by a group of Lithuanian academics and intellectuals. Professor Landsbergis was at the very forefront of this first independent civic initiative. Achievement of a greater sovereignty of Lithuania was declared as a short-term goal of Sajudis. Restoration of Lithuanian independence, a long-term goal, was at that time only supported by a minority of the Sajudis.

In 1989, at the Constituent Congress of Sajudis, Landsbergis was elected member of the Council of Sajudis and later became its chairman. In the same year, he was elected deputy of the Supreme Council of the USSR, where he met Gorbachev among other Soviet communist leaders and held a number of heated discussions on sensitive issues such as the Molotov-Ribentrop Pact, civic human rights, and a nation's right for self-determination. Since then Landsbergis has been a professional politician instead of a professor of music, and nationalism and radicalism have become a part of his rhetoric.

Soviet propaganda has at different times portrayed Landsbergis as an ardent nationalist, a fascist, and an enemy of Russia and the Russian-speaking minority in Lithuania. On March 11, 1990, Landsbergis was elected deputy and subsequently chairman of the first independent Lithuanian Parliament. On the same day, the Parliament under his leadership declared Lithuania's independence. Although the office of the president was not introduced until two years later, Landsbergis served as head of state and was repeatedly referred to by the Western media as the Lithuanian president.

In 1990 Landsbergis was awarded the Norwegian People's Peace Prize, for which funds were specifically raised to highlight the distinction between Landsbergis and the 1990 Nobel Peace Prize winner, Gorbachev, who unsuccessfully attempted to bridle Lithuanian nationalism by introducing economical blockades in Lithuania in 1990. The blockade was doomed to fail because the Soviet state-planned economy was too centralized. In fact, the blockade helped the nationalists to mobilize the nation against the "common enemy," the Soviet Union.

The 1992 parliamentary elections brought the rule of the Sajudis to an end, since nationalists were not capable of sustaining economical advances and were still haunted by the past. Landsbergis, regarded by the West as "a hero of Lithuanian independence," waited until the next elections to make his political comeback with the Homeland Union (Lithuanian Conservatives), the party that evolved from the right-wing part of the outlived Sajudis. At the end of 1997 Landsbergis ran for the presidency but was voted out in the first round. He still remains chairman of the Sejm, a post to which he was elected in 1996, though his image has been significantly tarnished.

## LANGUAGE, NATIONALISM AND

Language is a crucial element of culture because it is part of it at the same time that it is endowed with the ability of naming it. Language is indeed closely interwoven with the way we perceive and experience the world. For example, the range and structure of the vocabulary available to us determine our capacity to characterize our experiences. Moreover, this vocabulary derives its meaning from a semantic community, a web of interlocutions that we enter as we learn to speak. In this sense, the meaning of words is necessarily holistic, it relies on a community. According to 18th-century early German romantic J. G. von Herder, that community is necessarily a national one.

Herder argued that each nation is endowed with a particular language that binds the souls of the members of the nation and allows their communion. Rather than being a mere instrument of communication that can be mastered, as for example Hobbes and Locke had argued, language is for Herder the embodiment of the collective experience of the nation. It registers the sentiments, the emotions, the sorrows, the rage, and the joys of the nation's history. It expresses and allows a way of realizing our humanity that is proper to our nation. Following the idea of authenticity dear to romantics, Herder claimed that only our native language or "mother tongue" can express the originality of the self. Those who try to express themselves in a language that is not theirs have to submit themselves to a foreign spirit that they will never properly understand and that will actu-

ally prevent them from realizing themselves and being authentic, that is, true to themselves. For that reason, the national language ought to be worshipped and preserved from foreign contamination. Linguistic borrowings or imitations will necessarily be phony and betray the spirit of the nation or the "national genius," the *Volksgeist*. According to Herder, the latter is the privilege of those born in the midst of the nation. It will always be closed and inaccessible to foreigners. Thus, language has a crucial role in the transmission of national identity. It is through it, and only through it, that the younger generations can accede to the *Volksgeist*. In this sense, acting as a terrible metaphor of the organic unity of the nation, language is depicted as the umbilical cord relating the nation to its sons and daughters.

Although the original purity of language and the existence of a *Volksgeist* were questioned in Herder's lifetime and ultimately invalidated, they turned out to be incredibly attractive and useful for nationalists. For example, they worked as a mobilizing tool for nations without states and allowed established nation-states to deny that immigrants could ever be assimilated or become "authentic" nationals even by learning the national language. Similarly, they gave to philosophers and even more to poets cultivating the complexities and beauties of the national language and spirit the very prestigious and desirable status of keepers of the national identity.

Nevertheless, despite Herder's excess, the idea that language is interwoven with the way we perceive reality remains a fruitful and important one, as was shown by the 1960s controversy surrounding Lee Whorf's study or as illustrated by the political implications of talking about a "peace process" to label the situation in Israel and the Middle East or of calling certain kinds of nationalist movements civic rather than ethnic. Moreover, every language is composed of some elements that cannot be translated. It is precisely within these elements that the original and unique perspective on reality is carried by each language. And it is for that reason that the disappearance of a language necessarily implies the loss of a certain interpretation of reality even though its most representative works may have been translated.

## LANGUEDOC NATIONALISM

Languedoc is a historical, linguistic, and cultural region that comprises a large part of southern France centering on the cities of Toulouse, Montpellier, and Nîmes. Once a province of Old Regime France, it is now divided into a number of smaller administrative subsections. The name *Languedoc* refers to the language traditionally spoken in the south of France, and in particular the word *oc* meaning yes, in contrast to the *oï* or *oui* of northern France (hence, the term *langue d'oc*). Languedoc nationalism is therefore often referred to as Occitan nationalism, although the region where variants of Occitan are spoken is much larger and diverse than historical Languedoc proper, and includes parts of Spain and Italy.

The 12th century saw a flowering of Occitan culture, disseminated in particular by the troubadours, whose songs and poetry were expressed in the *langue d'oc*. Until the French Revolution (1789), Languedoc benefited from a large measure of political autonomy, bolstered by its cultural, linguistic, and to some extent religious (as a center of Protestantism) distinctiveness. During the French Revolution, the defeat of the federalist Girondins, originally representatives of the Occitan (in the broader sense) department of Gironde, marked the end of any possibility of continued regional self-governance.

The increasing political and cultural centralization of the French state, from the early 19th century onward, led to a decline of regional languages including Occitan. Around the mid-19th century Occitan writers such as Frédéric Mistral briefly benefited from the popularity of romanticism and attendant interest in local cultures. But during the last third of the century increasing French nationalism, due in part to geopolitical tensions within Europe, particularly with Prussia and later unified Germany, resulted in the decline of regionalism throughout France well into the 20th century. Efforts were made during that period by individuals and groups to promote linguistic and cultural survival, but remained for the most part apolitical, often attempting to show the contribution of Languedoc culture to French national identity.

By the 1960s, however, Occitan nationalism had reemerged, spurred in part by the well-publicized success of overseas liberation movements, particularly Algeria's, and worldwide decolonization. The intellectuals who formed the bulk of this small-scale movement saw similarities between their own struggle for cultural survival and that of other minorities and oppressed peoples. Despite its organizational and ideological fragmentation, the movement experienced some measure of success in defending Occitan language and culture. The struggle was encouraged by the success of post-Franco neighboring Catalonia in reasserting its cultural and linguistic distinctiveness, in addition to the support of European institutions for minorities.

The movement became more radical after 1968, with the creation of numerous new small parties blending anticapitalism, regionalism, and cultural claims with ethno-nationalism. The trend has abated since the mid-1970s, but a significant, albeit politically weak, cultural Occitan movement persists.

Although limited by its lack of a clear geographic and demographic foundation (unlike comparable movements in Brittany and Corsica), Languedoc nationalism may benefit in the future from the trend toward the devolution of political and economic power of European national states both upward to EU institutions and downward to subnational regions. Estimates about the number of people who speak some version of Occitan vary between half a million and two million, with around ten million having some knowledge of the language.

## LATIN AMERICAN INDIGENOUS MOVEMENTS

Indigenous peoples—the descendants of the native population of Latin America prior to colonization—are the only ethnic group in Latin America whose claims challenge the territoriality of states. They constitute 10 percent of the total population of the region, or an estimated 40 million persons belonging to approximately 400 distinct groups, and are concentrated in southern Mexico, Central America, and the central Andes. In these states, they comprise between 10 and 70 percent of the population. Some individual language groups have more than one million members. A dozen groups have more than a quarter million members that together constitute 73 percent of the total indigenous population of the region. At the other end of the spectrum, roughly 200 groups have fewer than 1000 members.

In the 1970s, Amerindian populations throughout Latin America began to mobilize politically in unprecedented ways to protect their lands and cultures from increasing incursions by multinational companies, colonists, the state, and other intruders. In the 1980s, the social movement organizations they formed placed a greater emphasis on the recuperation of ethnic identities and the construction of a pan-indigenous cultural identity to unite diverse indigenous peoples within each state and in the burgeoning transnational indigenous movement. The construction of distinct indigenous identities and the mobilization on behalf of indigenous cultures represents a rejection of the efforts of white and mestizo (mixed white and Amerindian) elites to assimilate distinct native groups into the national society while continuing to dominate darker skinned groups politically and economically. In ways that vary throughout the region, Latin American indigenous peoples share the common goal of ending ethnic discrimination and the assimilationist policies of Latin American governments.

Contemporary Latin American indigenous organizations seek equal and legitimate status for their cultures, forms of social organization and laws, and the means to facilitate and control their economic development. This goes beyond the right to practice their culture, which many states protected constitutionally in the 1960s and 1970s. The ultimate goal is the transformation of what they view to be a discriminatory, homogeneous state into a "plurinational state," a state whose institutions reflect the cultural diversity of society. In the 1990s, seven Latin American states—Bolivia, Colombia, Ecuador, Mexico, Nicaragua, Peru, and Paraguay—recognized a milder version of this claim, declaring their societies "pluricultural and multiethnic." This terminology rejects the claim of many indigenous organizations that indigenous ethnic groups have the status of peoples or nations, as that term is understood in international law.

Latin American indigenous organizations joined native movements elsewhere in the world in the 1980s to assert a claim to self-determination as peoples or nations that is derived from their interpretation of international human rights conventions. Unlike such movements elsewhere in the world, they almost never threaten secession, or "external self-determination," although there are exceptions, such as the Miskitu in Nicaragua. Most organizations express a claim to "internal self-determination" along with increased, preferential access to the political system at all levels.

The main component of indigenous nationalism is the struggle for autonomy, which has territorial, political, economic, and cultural dimensions. Until 1987, only the Kuna of Panama enjoyed what could be described as territorial and political autonomy, which they won through armed struggle with the Panamanian state in 1932. In 1987, the Nicaraguan government established two multiethnic autonomous regions to accommodate claims of the Miskitu and other smaller groups, who had joined the anti-Sandinista counter-revolutionary guerrilla movement supported by the United States (the "Contras"). Although the regions were largely a failure in terms of indigenous peoples' aspirations, their establishment inspired indigenous organizations throughout Latin America to make similar claims.

Only Colombia's indigenous population can be said to have achieved politico-territorial autonomy. The 1991 Colombian Constitution elevated indigenous reserves (resguardos) to the status of municipal governments, recognized indigenous traditional leaders as public authorities and indigenous customary law as public and binding, with some restrictions, and provided guaranteed representation in the national senate. The governments of Bolivia, Ecuador, Guatemala, and Mexico are currently negotiating some type of politico-territorial autonomy arrangements pursuant to constitutional reforms or peace agreements with armed groups concluded in the 1990s.

An introduction to this topic may be found in Hector Diaz Polanco, *Indigenous Peoples in Latin America: The Quest for Self-Determination* (Westview Press, 1997), and Donna Lee Van Cott, ed., *Indigenous Peoples and Democracy in Latin America* (St. Martin's Press, 1995).

## LATIN AMERICAN NATIONALISM

By the early 20th century, nationalism emerged as a major force with the potential to reshape Latin America. Combining the power of pride with a sense of mission, nationalism exerted a formidable influence on politics, culture, and economics. Despite its significance, nationalism as a concept defies easy definition. Clearly, it embodies an emotional identification of the individual citizen with the nation-state. By varying means, that identification forges a group consciousness that attributes great value to the nation-state and thereby elicits unswerving devotion to it. In short, citizens feel their well-being is intertwined with and depends on that of the nation-state. The Brazilian scholar Júlio Barbuda reduced the complexities of nationalism into a pithy observation: "Nationalism is the emotional synthesis of the fatherland" (*Literatura Brasileira,* 1916).

The roots of nationalism derive from the long colonial past. Already in the 16th century, Iberians born in the New World identified with their locality. That identification accompanied by a sense of pride constituted nativism, a kind of precursor to nationalism. Bernardo de Balbuena expressed such nativism in his book *Grandeza mexicana* in 1604. He praised all things Mexican and concluded that Mexico equaled—even surpassed—Spain. In 1618, Ambrósio Fernandes Brandao interpreted Brazil in a similar fashion in *Diálogos das grandezas do Brasil.* Perhaps he even foretold of future economic nationalism by criticizing those Portuguese who arrived in Brazil to exploit its riches and return wealthy to Europe. In his studies of the colonial past, the Peruvian historian Jorge Basadre spoke of the "self-consciousness" exhibited by the Europeans born in the Americas and by their mestizo and mulatto descendants. That characteristic increasingly separated them from the Iberians.

During the course of more than three centuries of colonial governance, the psychology of the Latin Americans, particularly the elite, changed from a feeling of inferiority before the Iberian-born to one of equality and then to superiority. They reflected the symbolic observation about the importance of the New World made by the Brazilian intellectual Sebastiao de Rocha Pita: "The sun now rises in the West." The Americans thus challenged Europe.

The struggles for independence began in Haiti in 1791 and ended in Peru in 1824. In Haiti, Mexico, and northwestern South America these wars were lengthy, and in general they aroused the basic emotion that gives rise to nationalism—hatred of the outsider. They forced many Latin Americans to explain why they believed they should be free of European governance and what they expected from their own constitutions, governments, and societies. Incipient political nationalism accompanied the emergence of the new nations.

After independence began the difficult task of creating nation-states, a challenge that lasted through much of the 19th century. The elites sought to maintain the unity, independence, and sovereignty of the nation-states they governed. They imposed the symbols of nationality—flags, anthems, and heroes—and developed a rhetoric of nationalism. Wars, boundary disputes, and foreign threats imposed an "us versus them" mentality on much of the citizenry, thereby intensifying political nationalism. From 1829 to 1854, for example, Juan Manuel de Rosas ably manipulated the Argentine distrust of foreigners to weld diverse and querulous regions into a national union. Mexico suffered disastrous invasions of the French in 1838, the United States from 1846 to 1848, and again the French from 1862 to 1866. Memories of these events aroused a combination of resentment of foreign intrusion and pride in local resistance, basic ingredients of political nationalism.

With sufficient political control and growing economic prosperity, the elites, in the names of the nations they governed, pursued certain broad, common goals during the last half of the 19th century. They wanted to modernize and chose Western Europe, whose technology, prosperity, and lifestyles they admired, as their model. Some aspects of modernization contributed to both nation building and nationalism. Improvements in communication and transportation, notably after 1860, better unified the nations, thereby enhancing a greater sense of nationality. To the degree that the elites achieved some of their goals, they felt a pride and satisfaction akin to nationalism.

The high rate of miscegenation among Indians, Africans, and Europeans also contributed to nationalism, although it took the elite a long time to accept the connection. The accelerating rate of mixture obscured both racial and ethnic origins to create a more homogeneous mestizo population. Some racial combinations were even unique to specific countries. While becoming more conscious of the traits of their distinctive populations, the citizens of diverse nations developed a stronger sensibility about national identity. Defending racial mixing against the poisonous North Atlantic doctrines of racial hierarchy that glorified the Caucasian, intellectuals at the close of the century further honed nationalism. As a positive contribution, nationalism eventually defended racial equality, at least in theory. Otherwise, the Latin Americans would be accepting an inferior status. In turn, attention to racial contributions to nationality focused attention on cultural diversity.

With its emphasis on the Indian past, the Mexican Revolution promoted cultural nationalism. Indeed, the revolution marked the rise of the mestizo to political power. In the 1920s the intellectual José Vasconcelos celebrated the triumph of the new mestizo "race" (*La raza cósmica*) characterized by beauty, spirituality, and harmony. He declared Mexico's cultural independence: "Tired, disgusted of all this copied civilization, we wish to cease being Europe's spiritual colony." As minister of education, he commissioned Diego Rivera, José Clemente Orozco, and other young visionary artists to paint monumental murals glorifying the Indian past. Musicians and writers further developed those themes. Mexican genius flowered and cultural nationalism soared.

Simultaneously, young Brazilian intellectuals declared their nation's cultural independence. A new generation announced its intentions clearly during Modern Art Week in 1922: "We are the sons of the hills and forests. Stop thinking of Europe. Think of America," exhorted Ronald de Carvalho. Art, music, and literature of a distinctive indigenous flavor flourished, an outpouring exemplified by the painting and murals of Candido Portinari, the compositions of Heitor Villa-Lobos, and the prose and poetry of Mário de Andrade. The intellectuals left the coastal cities, at least temporarily, to explore the countryside and interior, enriching the arts with hearty injections of folklore, in an effort to draw inspiration from ordinary people and folk culture rather than exclusively from Europe. Similar movements sprouted elsewhere in Latin America. The original contours of Latin American literature excited international acclaim. In 1945, Gabriela Mistral of Chile was the first Latin American to receive the Nobel Prize for literature. In the following half-century, four more won the accolade: Miguel Angel Asturias, Pablo Neruda, Gabriel García Márquez, and Octavio Paz.

The financial failure of the Western world in 1929 and the consequent depression shook the always fragile, monocultural, export economies of Latin America. Their collapse ignited the smoldering fires of economic nationalism. They inspired hopes of decreasing dependency by initiating economic development. Nationalists looked to the governments for plans to diversify the economy, making it less dependent on the gyrations of the international market. They urged greater industrialization, a goal appealing to both pride and common sense that promised to broaden the economy as well as keep foreign exchange from being spent to import what could be manufactured at home. The nationalists also called for the recovery of Latin American natural resources held and exploited by foreigners. They regarded those resources as too fundamental to local economic well-being to remain outside of national control. Bolivia's nationalization of the foreign-owned petroleum industry in 1937 and Mexico's similar action in 1938 initiated a process recovery characteristic of economic nationalism for the remainder of the century.

The goals of economic nationalism required governments to play a more active role. They introduced long-range planning. Wider governmental participation shifted the leadership of nationalism from the intellectuals to the governments themselves, which understood the power it conferred. At the same time, the support for nationalism widened to include the middle class and the urban working class. Sensing that trend, astute leaders such as Getúlio Vargas of Brazil, Lázaro Cárdenas of Mexico, and Juan Domingo Perón of Argentina combined nationalism with populism to gain wide support for programs to nationalize foreign-owned property, to increase government planning and participation in the economy, to industrialize, and to institute social welfare programs.

During the last half of the 20th century, the most salient characteristics of nationalism were four. First, populists or the Left dominated the leadership. The military and the elites, groups that once had played vital roles as nationalists, became more closely identified with foreign interests. They seemed more inclined to preserve the institutions of the past and less interested in pursuing economic development that would benefit larger numbers of the population. Second, criticism of foreign economic penetration dominated, intensified by the debt crises of the final quarter of the century. Despite the poverty of a majority of its inhabitants, Latin America exported capital. For example, the UN Economic Commission reported in 1988 that fully $147 billion flowed from Latin America to "developed countries" between 1982 and 1988 as a "net transfer of resources." That flow from poorer to richer nations outraged the nationalists. Third, criticism of the United States mounted because it was the metropolis and the largest single investor and creditor. Fourth, questions of

economic development absorbed the lion's share of attention. The nationalists showed a greater impatience with the ideologies of the past and more interest in experimenting with new ones. In the late 1960s, the secretary-general of the Organization of American States (OAS), Galo Plaza, concluded, "One of the most powerful forces in Latin America today, and one of the least understood outside the region, is the upsurge of economic nationalism."

During the course of a century, the thrust of nationalism altered. While nationalists once contented themselves with tracing the historical roots of their nationality and in glorifying the potential wealth and natural beauty of their land, their focus has shifted to the future. They take seriously the advice José Martí proffered at the end of the 19th century: "A people economically enslaved but politically free will end by losing all freedom, but a people economically free can go on to win its political independence."

**LATVIAN NATIONALISM** Latvian nationalism has been shaped by the desire to be liberated from foreign domination and to protect the small nation's language and culture from absorption. The Baltic states have experienced a succession of foreign masters—Danes, Germans, Swedes, Poles, and Russians. During the Great Northern War, which began in 1700, Russian Tsar Peter the Great conquered Riga and what is now Estonia in 1710. Estonia and Livonia (a state consisting of what is now southern Estonia and northern Latvia) officially became a part of the Russian empire in the 1721 Treaty of Nystad and remained so for more than two centuries.

Latvians had passed down innumerable folk songs, legends, and fairytales. Many were recorded in written form in the 19th century, when the consciousness of Latvian nationhood solidified. The concept of the Latvian nation sprang not from the reality of an independent political state, but from its national culture. There were Latvian fraternities and student organizations at the Universities of Tartu (in Estonia) and Saint Petersburg. Toward the end of the century a national organization, *Jauna strava*, thrived; one of its later members was Janis Rainis, Latvia's most famous poet.

For most of this time, the tsars supported those reforms that enabled Balts to develop their national culture. This ended in 1881, when Alexander III came to power. Sensing a danger from their national revival, he tried to stop it. He ordered a policy of Russification. Russian was declared the official language and the medium of instruction, and the Russian Orthodox religion was imposed. This strict Russification program was terminated after the 1905 Russian Revolution. This was a great emotional event for Latvians, who began struggling against German landlords and the Russian police. Their nationalism grew progressively stronger in the 20th century.

World War I created the conditions for Latvian independence; it was the first time the Latvian national flag was raised. Latvian rifle regiments were formed to fight against the Germans, and many were killed in 1915 when the front line ran right through Latvia. When the Bolshevik Revolution occurred in 1917, many Latvians supported the new Soviet government, hoping thereby to win their freedom. On November 18, 1918, Latvia declared its independence, but it had to continue to fight against German troops and the Red Army in order to secure it. Russia signed a treaty recognizing it on August 11, 1920. However, this recognition lasted only two decades.

The next decade and a half witnessed political instability, as many different political parties and such extreme nationalist organizations as *Perkonkrusts* (outlawed by the government) struggled for control. The inability to reach consensus was made worse by the world economic depression in the early 1930s. In 1934 Prime Minister Karlis Ulmanis, supported by the army and the paramilitary organization *Aizargi,* dissolved Parliament and ruled without it.

Following the German-Soviet Non-Aggression Pact in August 1939, the Soviet Union tightened the noose around the Baltic states' necks. In September 1939 Latvia was forced to accept Soviet troops in Liepaja and Ventspils that numbered more than Latvia's own army. On June 16, 1940, the Soviet Union ordered it to change its government, and it annexed Latvia and the two other Baltic states in August 1940. Russia continues to insist that all three had voluntarily joined the USSR. During the German occupation from 1941 to 1944, Latvians fought on both sides.

The Baltic states spent the next half century as disgruntled but relatively prosperous republics of the Soviet Union. Encouraged by Mikhail Gorbachev's reform proposals, which permitted more free discussion and toleration than ever in Soviet history, Latvians seized the opportunity first to enlarge their self-determination within the Soviet Union and then to gain complete independence. In 1988 a "people's front," composed of both Gorbachev Communists and non-Communist democrats and nationalists, was formed. In the late 1980s nationalist fervor was fanned by the conference of Latvian writers. On August 23, 1989, two million Estonians, Latvians, and Lithuanians formed a human chain from Tallinn to Vilnius to dramatize their demand for freedom.

With large and articulate exile groups, especially in the United States, Latvia and the other two Baltic nations were able to mobilize considerable international sympathy and diplomatic support for their aspirations. This was especially facilitated by the fact that all Western democracies, except Sweden and briefly Australia, had refused to recognize the Soviet Union's annexation of the Baltics in 1940. Latvia declared its independence on May 5, 1990, following a referendum in March. On May 12 the heads of all three Baltic countries signed the Declaration of Concord and Cooperation reestablishing the 1934 Council of the Baltic States.

Gorbachev indignantly rejected these demands for independence and even ordered that Special Force Units of the USSR Ministry of Interior (OMON) use force against dissidents in the streets of Vilnius, Lithuania, on January 13, 1991, killing fifteen. Latvians from all over the country came to the capital to defend their democratically elected Parliament. Nevertheless, on January 21, 1991, OMON troops killed six persons in Riga. The threat of violence also hung over Estonia.

Russian President Boris Yeltsin supported the Balts' call for freedom. Gorbachev ultimately joined him in agreeing to sign a new union treaty on August 19, 1991. This treaty, along with the prospects of Baltic independence, precipitated the Moscow coup attempt against Gorbachev on that day. The insurrection's failure after only three days prompted most countries in the world to recognize the Baltic states' independence. The Nordic countries and the European Community (EC, after 1994 called the European Union—EU) were first, followed by the United States on September 2 and the post-coup Soviet government on September 6, 1991. On September 17, 1991, the Baltic states, which had belonged to the League of Nations, were admitted to the United Nations.

Numerous exiles returned to play important political, military, and economic roles, although Latvians who had lived in comfortable Western exile during the Soviet times sometimes experience resentment among certain segments of the population. They must learn to be tactful in offering more efficient foreign ways of doing things. The United States' first ambassador to Latvia was of Latvian heritage. Gunars Meierovics was a leader in one of the country's most successful parties, "Latvia's Way."

In August 1999, parliament elected President Vaira Vike-Freiberga, who at age seven had fled Latvia before the advancing Red Army and became a psychology professor at Montreal University. While in exile she had lobbied the Canadian government never to recognize the Soviet annexation of the Baltic states and had organized the émigré effort to scan thousands of Latvian folk songs into a computer database. One of her first acts as president was to send back to Parliament a new language law she deemed too harsh because it would have required that private commercial transactions be in Latvian. Although she speaks five languages, Russian was not one of them. Therefore, she immediately began to learn it, as "a challenge to those who have spent 50 years not learning Latvian."

Latvia has a small population: 2.5 million, 790,608 of whom live in Riga. In 1934, ethnic Latvians constituted 75.5 percent of the country's population. Russians were the largest minority in Latvia (12 percent), and they enjoyed citizenship, language guarantees, their own schools, and cultural autonomy. After being bullied into the Soviet Union in 1940, Latvia's demography changed. Indeed, when Soviet rule ended in 1991, 2.3 million Russians were left behind in all the Baltic states, with the lion's share in Latvia.

Russians living in Latvia demanded automatic citizenship ("zero option," adopted by most former Soviet republics). In Latvia the non-Latvian population had reached almost half by 1991 and an astonishing 63 percent in the capital city of Riga (and a majority in the six next largest cities). By 1996 only 56.7 percent of the country's residents were Latvian, 30.3 percent Russian, 4.3 percent Belarusian, 2.7 percent Ukrainian, and 2.6 percent Polish. Massive inward migration of Russians and outward deportation of native Latvians had dramatically changed the demographic mix and threatened its national survival.

Although Russian speakers lead largely separate lives in Latvia, they bear little hatred or deep aversion toward Baltic nationals. According to a 1995 poll, two-thirds (63 percent) of Russians living in Latvia found relations with the majority nationality to be good; only 43 percent found that minorities were being "badly treated." Clearly ethnic tensions are not only far below the threshold of violence, but they are diminishing as non-Latvians are adjusting to the eased requirements established in the citizenship laws.

Devising citizenship policies that are both acceptable to Latvians and tolerable for Russians is the most persistent political problem in relations with Russia and the one that elicits the most visceral resistance from Moscow. For Latvia the question of citizenship was of vital importance. With a large Russian-speaking minority, it faced the prospect of continued heavy Russian influence on most aspects of policy if all residents were granted either automatic or dual citizenship. It therefore rejected these options. This was not only a question of control over the nation's affairs, but a matter of principle: In the Latvian view, the majority of Russians had

been permitted to settle in Latvia in order to implement Moscow's policy of occupation after it had forcibly annexed it in 1940. On what basis could occupiers and their descendants expect to be recognized as citizens?

Determined to remain masters in their own houses, Latvians based their citizenship laws on the notion of legal continuity of its prewar republic. They imposed severe restrictions, granting citizenship automatically to pre-1940 residents and their descendants. Confronting criticism that Russian speakers were being made permanent noncitizens, Latvia opened citizenship to all persons who met certain criteria, including residency for sixteen years in Latvia (extending back into the Soviet era except for ex-Soviet military and security personnel and their families stationed in Latvia) and the willingness to take a loyalty oath. Applicants must demonstrate competence (though not fluency) in Latvian, a difficult language unrelated grammatically to Russian. They must answer basic questions in Latvian about the country's history.

Few Russians can meet the language requirements without major effort. In 1989, only 22 percent of Russians in Latvia had a good command of Latvian. The others had seen no need to learn it because Balts were expected to speak Russian well, and most did so. There was an outcry after independence in 1991 that the new language restrictions were "unfair" and "human rights violations." Latvia's citizenship laws do not discriminate on formal ethnic grounds. It offers citizenship to anybody who follows certain procedures and learns the local language and demonstrates a basic knowledge of the political system. As a result of naturalization, 40 percent of all Russians in Latvia possessed Latvian citizenship by 1998. But since the laws' immediate effect was the disenfranchisement of most ethnic Russian residents, many saw it as discriminatory.

The rights of those who do not speak the local language are greater than in some other small nations, like Quebec province in Canada, that fear absorption and destruction of their cultures. Parents are free to send their children to Russian-language schools although a 1998 law in Latvia calls for the phasing in over a decade of Latvian as the sole language of instruction in public schools. Russians face no restrictions on using their language at the workplace. State radio and television are broadcast in Russian. There are Russian-language theaters and a wide variety of Russian newspapers and magazines available. Many university courses are taught in Russian. It is an advantage to speak Latvian, and the defense forces and many categories in the civil service are blocked to noncitizens.

The Latvian position on citizenship is grounded in

notions of citizenship widely held in the rest of the world. Like most countries, they chose *jus sanguinis* as the principle for conferring citizenship; descent from an individual of a particular nationality. Every child with at least one parent who is a Latvian citizen has the right, by birth, to citizenship.

Latvia feels international pressure to loosen its citizenship laws in order not to antagonize Russia. In October 1998, 53 percent of Latvian voters in a referendum approved of giving automatic citizenship to all children born in Latvia since 1991. Adopted by elected parliaments, the laws appear reasonable by Western standards. Their policies toward minorities have been more successful in easing ethnic tensions than in most former Communist states. International organizations, such as the UN and Council of Europe, have also generally accepted the laws despite Russia's energetic efforts to have Latvia condemned for human rights violations.

Feeling insecure and knowing that no Western power would defend them militarily without a formal guarantee, Latvia and the other Baltic states have made it known that they wish to enter the EU and NATO. Latvia's trade has shifted from about 80 percent to the other Soviet republics to 80 percent toward the West. Latvians regard NATO as the only alliance capable of thwarting any future Russian expansionist temptations or attempts to restore "spheres of influence." With strong Western support, all three Baltic states negotiated the withdrawal of Soviet troops from their territories. Since August 1994 Latvians have been the undisputed guardians of their own nation.

**LAURIER, WILFRID** 1841–1919, In 1896 Sir Wilfrid Laurier led the Liberal Party to victory in the federal elections and launched practically a century of almost continuous Liberal Party rule in Canada. Laurier was a tall, handsome, urbane, superbly educated man, with a courtly air and a cordial manner. He was equally articulate and elegant in both his native French and in English, which he spoke with an appealing French touch. He helped to unify both French and English concerns and to give his party something of a basic philosophy. He believed that his party was heir to British, not continental European, liberalism; therefore cultural toleration should be a guiding rule. He persuaded many of his fellow Quebecois to accept British ideas of freedom and justice.

Laurier was a great admirer of many things British, and he accepted a knighthood. Nevertheless, he, like many Canadians, feared a more active British imperial policy in the world. He had staunchly opposed the creation of a permanent Imperial Council, which could

have imposed tariff and military measures on all the colonies. Even before the end of the 19th century, the Canadian government had secured the right to negotiate, though not sign, treaties. His tenure as prime minister was characterized by extensive and rapid expansion, especially in the Canadian West. It was a sign of Canadian confidence in his day that Laurier could announce: "The nineteenth century was the century of the United States; the twentieth century will be the century of Canada."

Foreign policy disputes had created a rather strong anti-American sentiment in Canada, which boiled to the surface in the federal elections of 1911. Voters rejected the aging Laurier because he had dared to negotiate tariff reductions with Washington. While prime minister his basic nationalist sentiments were Canadian, not Quebecois, and he did much to develop a nationalist viewpoint in Canadian foreign policy. Over time his friendliness toward Britain began to irritate Quebec nationalists, and many of them deserted him in the 1911 elections. However, during World War I he, as the most prominent French Canadian politician, led Quebec's vigorous opposition to conscription although he continued to support the war effort.

See J. Schull, *Laurier: The First Canadian* (Toronto, 1966).

**LAURISTIN, MARJU** 1940–, Outstanding Estonian sociologist and politician, born in Tallinn, Estonia. In 1966 Lauristin finished Tartu University in Estonia, specializing in journalism. Lauristin worked as an editor for Estonian radio and she was involved in the first Soviet sociological research studies carried out in Estonia. In 1976 she defended her candidate thesis in journalism. In the 1970s and 1980s she taught sociology and journalism (theories of journalism) at Tartu university.

At the end of 1980s she became publicly active in the Estonian politics. In 1988 she organized and participated at the Plenum of the Creative Unions, at which Estonian intellectuals publicly presented the idea of defending the rights of the Estonians. Prior to that some Estonian intellectuals, including Lauristin, had come to the conclusion that the Baltic states, although having the status of Soviet republics, would, however follow the path of the East European countries and, in fact, the model of Hungary—an independent existence outside the USSR, albeit as members of the Soviet bloc. The status of the former Eastern Communist countries would gradually transform into the democratic Western model states.

As one of the intellectual leaders, Lauristin belonged

to the political institutions of the Soviet Estonia—to the Estonian Supreme Soviet (Parliament) where she was the deputy chairman in 1990–1992 and to the Congress of the Peoples' Deputies of the USSR in 1989–1990. At the beginning of the 1990s politically active intellectuals and a wider circle of people started discussions on the Estonian citizenship issue. Three arguments dominated: First, Estonia could declare all non-Estonian to be illegal immigrants; second, Estonia could follow the Lithuanian variant, the zero option, by giving everyone (including the Estonians and non-Estonians) citizenship; and the third, Estonia could give citizenship to some non-Estonians. Lauristin advocated the third interpretation according to which, in addition to Estonians, the most loyal non-Estonians should be granted citizenship through uncomplicated mechanisms. The compromise was achieved by the solution of adopting the prewar citizenship law. In all those discussions, however, all parties maintained the importance of the Estonian language being designated the only official language for Estonia.

Since the establishment of Estonia's independence Lauristin has been a member of the Constitutional Assembly. In 1992–1994 Lauristin was the Estonian minister of social affairs, and in 1995–1999, a professor of social policy at Tartu University. Since March 1999 she has been a member of the Estonian Parliament, Riigikogu. She changed her party membership from CPSU to the Social Democratic Party in 1990. Later the social democrats merged with the moderates. As for the ethnic policy she has maintained the idea of integration of the Russian-speaking population into Estonian society. She is a member of various local and international sociological organizations. Lauristin has participated in various ethnic integration projects of which the most well known is the Vera project. She has also published the following books: *Our Changing Lifestyle* (co-author, 1985), *The Freedom Winds of Estonia* (co-author, 1989), and *Return to the Western World* (co-author, 1997).

## LAW AND NATIONALISM

Law is a body of rules in organized society that is enforced by the threat of punishment. Thus, through law, membership in a nation or sovereign state is institutionalized. In the modern era, nations are the dominant type of group in which people live and to which they give their loyalty. The existence of nation-states necessitates cohesion and order gained through nationalist sentiment, a legal structure, and formal institutions.

One influential political theorist of both law and nationalism, Charles-Louis de Secondat Montesquieu (1689–1755), considered in *The Spirit of the Laws* (1748) what ought to be the nature of national government. He argued that the laws of a nation should be fitted to the physical conditions of a country, to its climate, to the nature of the soil, to its situation among nations, and to the way of life of its people.

Later, during the 19th century ideas like Montesquieu's were concretized in a general trend toward the secularization of notions of the state and society from the belief that God's will determined the origin and nature of nations. In legal terms this meant the demise of natural law and the theological conception of the legal order, and the growth of the secular tradition of positive law. Following the Napoleonic Code of 1804, the legal systems of Europe were transformed into national codes. Law was to represent the spirit of the people in written form and would be used to enforce the will of the people.

According to Anthony D. Smith, a number of elements are crucial to the existence of the Western conception of the nation. One important element is patria. A nation requires some common regulating institutions that give expression to common political sentiments and purposes. This commonality is sometimes represented through highly centralized laws and institutions, or a federal system might be used in which unions of separate colonies, provinces, or city-states are governed by institutions and laws designed to protect local liberties and express a common will and common political sentiments, as in the case of the United States or United Provinces of the Netherlands. Another element concurrent with the growth of a sense of legal and political community is a sense of legal equality among members of a community. The legal equality of members of a political community through, for example, citizenship laws, comes from shared values and traditions among the population. Nationalism grows from members having reciprocal legal rights and duties under a common legal system.

In Western, constitutional nations, law can also embody or come to symbolize and express a national collective identity. The setting up of legal systems such as a constitution is an effort to represent what *the people* are. The constitution represents or symbolizes one clear vision of a nation of people and recognizes their authority. In this sense, the law reaches beyond the legal structure and creates or substantiates the national identity of a people.

According to Smith, another model, sometimes called the "ethnic" conception of the nation, was developed outside the West, notably in Eastern Europe and Asia. Historically this model challenges the dominance of the Western model. This ethnic model focuses on birth and native culture as grounds for nationalism. In these societies, language and custom augment the place of law.

Most contemporary nations have elements from both models. Scholars comparing legal systems suggest that nearly all contemporary legal systems are externally imposed through the process of colonialization. Legal systems, such as many in Africa, are partly the outgrowth of colonial experiences. Multiethnic and multinational states have used the law to prevent the development of nationalist movements. Some states such as the former Soviet Union and People's Republic of China adopted population redistribution policies that served to lessen the relationship of ethnicity with territory.

Some states have multidimensional systems that adopt the laws of another nation as the basic framework for substantial parts of their own legal system. For example, for commercial law, Turkey follows the Swiss Code and Japan the German. Some states that borrow legal codes for parts of their systems but retain the existing law for other areas have what are called *dual legal systems.*

The creation of a transnational or multinational legal arrangements is developing and has led to two different trends. One trend is toward national legal compliance with international codes to participate in the global market, which limits the expression of national difference through law. This process means harmonizing laws, ranging from corporate and human rights law. In the case of Europe and the EEC this means the homogenization of European law. Islamic law, for instance, has created some legal devices to avoid direct conflict with Koranic dictum. The creation of legal global communities suggests the possible homogenization of nations through the imposition of laws. This has incited some resistance to a transnational legal order largely based on Western legal concepts and practices. The other trend has been toward the encouragement of national cultures. United Nations charters have declared the right of internal colonies and protectorates to cultural self-determination and to identify as a nation.

Nationalist movements vary in aims and strategies but irrespective of the grounds from which a nationalist movement forms the goal is the right to self-determination. This is the aim to secede and form one's own sovereign state, with little or no connection with the former rulers. Other options include developing different degrees of autonomy through a federal system where national groups have legal control over community affairs, or some form of cultural or political autonomy.

For more information see Anthony D. Smith's *Nationalist Movements* (Macmillan, 1976) and *National Identity* (University of Nevada Press, 1991). For discussions on constitutions see Bruce Ackerman's *We the People: Foundations* (Harvard University Press, 1991) and Anne Norton, *Republic of Signs* (University of Chicago Press, 1993). On international law see *Basic Documents in International Law,* Ian Brownlie, ed. (Clarendon Press, 1983).

## LAWRENCE, T. E.

1888–1935, Thomas Edward Lawrence, "Lawrence of Arabia," was born in 1888 in Tremadoc, Wales, and died in 1935 at Clouds Hill, England. In turn an archaeologist, an army officer, a litterateur, and an enlisted man in the British military, Lawrence cut an intriguing figure of romance that has lodged in public memory because of his association with Sharif Husayn's Arab revolt in World War I. Through the revolt against the Ottoman Empire and in its aftermath, Lawrence exercised a significant influence on the postwar shaping of today's Middle East.

Lawrence's personality and accomplishments have caused much debate, and his wartime activities have been the subject of some of the most intense scrutiny. Controversy continues because Lawrence himself—alternating self-promotion with self-negation in his literary works—is the main source of information about his war service. For two years, beginning in late 1916, Lawrence served as liaison between the Arab Bureau in British-occupied Cairo and Faysal, one of the sons of Sharif Hussain of the Hijaz. Faysal acted as field commander of the sharif's bedouin supporters north of Medina. Faysal's forces harried the Ottoman railway line to the Hijaz and enjoyed some famous successes, notably the capture of the port of Aqaba in 1917. Lawrence acted as an adviser and demolitions expert. As British confidence in Lawrence and the revolt increased, Cairo began to supply Faysal with more significant amounts of money and materiel, which were crucial to the revolt's continuation. The activities of the Arab forces were only a minor factor, however, in the eventual outcome of the Anglo-Ottoman struggle in the Middle East. Nevertheless, Lawrence soon achieved a glowing reputation through the publicizing lectures of the American journalist Lowell Thomas and through publication of Lawrence's own literary masterpiece, *Seven Pillars of Wisdom.*

Lawrence's status as a war hero did help to determine the eventual disposition of former Ottoman territory in the Arab Middle East. In January 1916 Britain and France concluded the Sykes-Picot Agreement, a plan to divide between themselves most of the Ottoman Arab territories as protectorates or zones of influence after the war. According to Sykes-Picot, France would dominate Syria and northern Iraq. The Arab forces' exploits, culminating in their entry into Damascus after Ottoman troops left the city in 1918, made many British officials uncomfortable with giving Syria to the French rather than to Faysal. Lawrence pushed Faysal's case at the Versailles peace conference, but in vain. He was closely involved in the Cairo conference of 1921, however, in which the British decided the fate of other territories. In the aftermath of anti-British unrest in Iraq, the Cairo conferees chose to install Faysal as the new king of Iraq. The dynasty founded with Faysal ruled Iraq until a bloody coup in 1958. Another decision of the Cairo conference led to Faysal's brother 'Abdallah being appointed amir of Transjordan. 'Abdallah's grandson, King Hussein, ruled Jordan from 1953 to 1999.

The great tide of writings on Lawrence continues to surge today. Jeremy Wilson's authorized biography, *Lawrence of Arabia,* appeared in 1990. Lawrence James published a critical reassessment of Lawrence and the Arab revolt, *The Golden Warrior,* in 1993.

## LE PEN, JEAN-MARIE   1928–, French political leader, head of extreme right party, the National Front.

Le Pen first became politically active and used his already formidable debating skills as a law student and member of various right-wing student groups in late 1940s Paris. After a brief military service spent in Indochina during France's attempt at forcefully keeping the colony, he returned to France and joined Pierre Poujade's short-lived grassroots, nationalistic, antitax party and quickly made a name for himself. He was elected to the National Assembly in January 1956.

After enlisting again in the paratroops, and participating in the Algerian war, where he was suspected of torturing prisoners, Le Pen returned to France and became a harsh critic of the decolonization of Algeria. But the extreme right was losing popular support, largely because of its violent rhetoric and actions. Le Pen lost his seat in the National Assembly in 1962.

During the 1965 presidential elections, Le Pen actively participated in a failed attempt to unite the extreme right under a more moderate agenda, represented by presidential candidate Jean-Louis Tixier-Vignancour. The latter's dismal electoral results marked the end of the extreme right as a significant political force for the next fifteen years.

After a few years away from politics, Le Pen created the National Front (NF) in 1972 with the leaders of other extreme right groups, and he was elected its president that same year. The new party quickly embraced a populist, anti-immigration, anticommunist platform blended with economic ideas fluctuating between liberalism and statism. But the NF only managed to win support and votes from a tiny fraction of the population. By the 1981 presidential election, the party was not even able to field a candidate, and a disgruntled

Le Pen, unwilling to support any other party, called for the election of Joan of Arc. That same year marked a triumph for the French left, with the election of François Mitterrand as president confirmed by another socialist victory at the legislative election a few months later.

The combination of economic stagnation, the failed policies of the new socialist governments, and growing concerns over immigrant populations, in particular those coming from North Africa, gave Le Pen's party a new impetus. The National Front registered its first electoral success at municipal elections in 1983. Thanks to newly introduced proportional representation, the National Front won thirty-five seats at the national assembly in 1986, with 9.8 percent of the vote, giving the extreme right a nationwide forum for the first time since World War II. But in the next legislative election two years later, proportional representation was rescinded and Le Pen's party only managed to win a single seat, with the same share of votes.

The National Front nevertheless continued to be successful at the polls, both locally and nationally, during the next few years. The nationalistic, anti-immigration, often anti-Semitic ideas were reaching a wider audience and causing tensions within mainstream political parties. Despite the durability of Le Pen's party, the mainstream right generally refused any alliance, yet was forced to echo some of his ideas on restricting immigration and citizenship laws. In 1995 Le Pen won the support of 15 percent of the electorate at the presidential election. This may, however, have been a high-water mark. The schism led by Bruno Mégret in 1999 seems to have damaged the credibility and popularity of the National Front, now split in two rival factions. The popularity of the extreme right sunk later that year to its lowest level since 1983.

The rise of Jean-Marie Le Pen and his National Front to such a high level of popularity had been unparalleled in Europe until the rise of similar movements chiefly in Austria and Italy at the end of the 1990s. In France, this phenomenon has been attributed to a number of causes, including urban decay, sluggish economic performance, the aftermath of a difficult decolonization, the threat posed to national political institutions by supranational forces such as European integration and cultural globalization, as well as by the perceived inefficacy and discredit of mainstream parties, resulting in voter disenchantment with the mainstream right. The high level of immigration in post-decolonization France has proved an easy target as the supposed cause of these ills.

Le Pen is also the inheritor of a longer tradition of xenophobic, and largely marginal ultranationalism, tracing its roots to late 19th century militarist anti-Semitism, through Poujade's postwar populism. The conjunction of this legacy with Le Pen's vituperative charisma, the National Front's ability to carefully blend latent antiparliamentarism with electioneering, and the propitious social and economic difficulties of the 1980s and 1990s have led to the ascendancy of the NF as France's third major political force. Although Le Pen is still a significant political contender, there is little evidence that his popularity will increase beyond already attained levels.

Suggestions for further reading include Harvey G. Simmons, *The French National Front* (Boulder, Colo.: Westview, 1996); and Jack Veugelers, "A Challenge for Political Sociology: The Rise of Far-Right in Contemporary Western Europe," in *Current Sociology* 47(4) (1999), pp. 78–107.

## LEAGUE OF NATIONS

The first formal attempt at international cooperation occurred with the formation of the League of Nations. This international organization, established in 1919 by the Paris Peace Conference as part of the Treaty of Versailles, had its roots in a number of international forces. These included diplomatic, religious, social, and economic developments that resulted in such international organizations as the Red Cross, the Universal Postal Service, and the International Telegraphic Union during the latter decades of the 19th century. A variety of conferences precipitated the formation of the league and were important stepping stones toward its eventual fruition. Such figures as Jan Smuts, Lord Robert Cecil, Leon Bourgeois, and U.S. President Woodrow Wilson were instrumental in calling for international peace and justice at the end of World War I.

The League of Nations was founded on a covenant, which included twenty-six articles. These articles covered a number of topics from internal organizational matters, to disarmament, from territorial and political independence to the formation of an international tribunal for arbitration and conciliation. The establishment of the League of Nations provided the "first opportunity for a sustained effort for both development and codification of international law." The league was a multipurpose organization with an agenda that addressed such important topics as "territorial waters, nationality, [and] the responsibility of states for damage to the persons and property of aliens."

The original membership of the league was composed of the victorious allies of World War I and most neutral nations. Though President Wilson was a key figure in the establishment of the league, the U.S. Congress failed to ratify the treaty, which prevented the United States from becoming a member. Soon after its establishment the league quickly proved its value by interceding in the Swedish–Finnish conflict over the Aland Islands (1921) and preventing war in the Balkans between Greece and Bulgaria (1925). The league was influential in other matters of international importance from health to aid to refuges.

The seeds of the inevitable destruction of the League of Nations were found in the fragile and volatile idea of national sovereignty. The early refusal of several of the powerful member nations to give heed to the warnings and counsels of the league was evident through the French occupation of the Ruhr (1923), Italy's occupation of Kerkira (1923), Japan's invasion of Manchuria (1931), and the inability of the league to stop the Chaco war between Bolivia and Paraguay (1932–1935). Both Japan's and Germany's withdrawal from the league in 1933 and Hitler's denouncement of the Treaty of Versailles contributed to the downfall of this first and courageous attempt at ensuring peace and cooperation in the world.

In 1938 "faced by threats to international peace from all sides—the Spanish civil war, Japan's resumption of war against China and the appeasement of Hitler at Munich—the League collapsed." The most valuable contribution this international effort made was to pave the way for the formation of the United Nations a few years later. The United Nations has faced problems similar to those the League of Nations had to deal with throughout its tenure. An important issue that both bodies have had to continually address is the question of national sovereignty. For a sovereign nation to be part of something larger than itself intrinsically means that it must give up a certain part of its independence and its sovereignty for the greater good. This is a problematic question that plagued the league more than 70 years ago and continues to be a hurdle with many of the issues that face the United Nations today.

Some bibliographic references include F. P. Walter's *A History of the League of Nations* (1960), George Scott's *The Rise and Fall of the League of Nations* (1974), F. S. Northedge's *The League of Nations* (1986), and Herbert Margulies' *The Mild Reservationists and the League of Nations* (1989).

## LEBANESE NATIONALISM

The proponents of Lebanese nationalism, mostly Maronite Christians, normally identify Prince Fakhr al-Din, who ruled from 1593 until 1633 and whose control included, in addition to modern-day Lebanon, central syria and northern Palestine, as the father of modern Lebanese nationalism. The roots of Lebanese nationalism usually go back to the days of the early Phoenicians some 5000 years ago. Michel Shiha, the 20th-century ideologue of Lebanese nationalism, considered Lebanon—much envied by its neighbors, thanks to its strategic geographical location and civilizational richness—as a distinguished worldly entity. Lebanese nationalists describe their compatriots as determined, efficient, intelligent, and always living in danger.

Shiha considered Lebanon as a special country endowed with a humanistic heritage and incredible human resources. This Mediterranean-looking nationalism thrives between a thin coast to the west and rugged mountains to the east, with the first representing Lebanon's openness to Europe, and the second forming a citadel in steadfast defiance against untoward incursions from the hinterland. Even though Lebanese nationalists see themselves as a link between East and West, they emphasize that the Mediterranean basis represents their vital sphere of attachment, and the world at large as their field of operation. They attribute superior qualities to unique Lebanon, the product of great historical and social interactions involving a plethora of migrating and invading peoples. These qualities include openness, dynamism, deep respect for man, spiritual vision, and fidelity to authenticity.

Lebanese nationalism is a highly controversial concept which, instead of uniting the Lebanese, further sets them apart. Generally unacceptable to Lebanese Muslims who vacillate between Pan-Arabism and Pan-Islamism, Lebanese nationalism does not seem to enjoy strong support within the country's Greek Orthodox community, the second largest Christian group in Lebanon. In a country where the material resources of the political system are allocated on a confessional basis, the sect remains the most important source of identification for the vast majority of the Lebanese, whether by choice or necessity.

**LEE, ROBERT E.** 1807–1870, Confederate general during the American Civil War (1861–1865), born in Westmoreland County, Virginia. Lee served as commander of the Army of Northern Virginia, the preeminent fighting force of the Confederate States of America (CSA), from 1862 to 1865, and as commander of all Confederate armies in 1865. Achieving much military success against staggering odds in the middle years of the war, Lee became the most universally admired hero of the Confederacy and inspired intense devotion in his troops. His leadership was so essential to the CSA that the Civil War is widely considered to have ended with his surrender at Appomattox on April 9, 1865, although battles continued to be fought and the Confederate government continued to function after that date.

Before the secession of the southern states from the union, Lee seemed the person least likely to lead a military rebellion against the U.S. army. He was the son of Colonel Light-Horse Harry (Henry) Lee, a hero of the American Revolution; he was educated at the United States Military Academy at West Point; and his brilliance as a field commander in the Mexican War (1846–1848) brought him national fame. As sectional conflict between northern and southern states grew more heated in the late 1850s, Lee opposed both slavery and secession. But when the states of the Deep South seceded from the United States in the winter of 1860–1861, and President Abraham Lincoln ordered the creation of an army to force them back into the union, Lee chose allegiance to Virginia over allegiance to the United States. He declined command of the army that would be turned against the southern states, and instead took command of Virginia's troops when his state seceded in the spring of 1861.

Always certain that the Confederacy could never overpower the much larger and better equipped U.S. army, Lee aimed instead to keep U.S. troops out of Richmond, the capital of the Confederacy and its major producer of munitions, and to make the war so costly for his enemy that the United States would abandon the fight. Always at a material disadvantage on the battlefield, Lee relied on strategic surprise and disruption of enemy maneuvers to win a number of legendary victories, including two total expulsions of Union troops from Virginia, the decimation of Union forces at the Second Battle of Bull Run, and especially his daring gambit at the Battle of Chancellorsville (1863), where, outnumbered two to one, he split his troops to surround the enemy. But while Lee staved off the Union troops on the northern front, his troops and supplies dwindled and U.S. forces made major inroads into other parts of the southern states. In May 1864 the U.S. sent an enormous, well-trained and -outfitted army under command of General Ulysses S. Grant to break through Lee's tattered ranks; though Lee eventually succumbed to Grant's huge advantages in numbers and supplies, he ingeniously outmaneuvered Grant and inflicted heavy losses on his troops for almost eleven months, even in desperation designing a new type of fortification outside Petersburg that was the first use of trench warfare.

Lee's place in U.S. national culture has evolved over time. As the leading hero of the CSA after the Civil War, he was worshipped by defeated southerners and reviled by the U.S. government, which literally placed the Union war dead at his front door by erecting Arlington National Cemetery on his wife's confiscated plantation. But Lee's many attractive traits seem to have won over his former enemies; the combination of his heroism in the face of terrible odds, his strategic brilliance on the battlefield, and his fatalistic sense of duty made him a popularly admired figure throughout the United States by the post–World War I era, when his statue was placed in the U.S. capitol. Today, Lee's private admiration for the United States and hatred of slavery, secession, and war are as much emphasized by historians as his public military campaign to ensure the success of Virginia's secession from the Union; in this way, he has become an icon of the very nation he strove to defeat.

The definitive, four-volume biography of Lee is Douglas Southall Freeman's *R. E. Lee* (1934–1935). A biography by a contemporary is J. William Jones, *Personal Reminiscences of General Robert E. Lee* (1874; reprinted 1989).

**LENIN, V. I.** 1870–1924, "Lenin" was one of numerous noms de guerre he adopted during his revolutionary career. Born into a middle-class family in the Volga River city of Simbirsk, Russia, Lenin plunged into a life of revolution as a result of his brother Aleksandr's execution in 1887 after being implicated in a plot to assassinate the tsar. He embraced Marxism in 1889, but he would alter it to fit unique circumstances in Russia and the power needs of his Bolshevik Party. The result was what became known as Marxism-Leninism.

He completed law studies in St. Petersburg in 1891, but he never practiced. In fact, he rejected the rule of law in favor of dialectical materialism and a notion of absolute truth understood correctly only by himself and the party that he dominated. He was arrested in 1895, charged with subversion, and exiled in Siberia. From 1900 to 1917 he lived in exile in Munich, Paris, Geneva, Kraków, and Zurich. Trapped in Switzerland when World War I broke out, he accepted Germany's offer of transportation back to Russia, where he and his followers planned and carried out the October Revolution in St. Petersburg. The Bolsheviks then defended and consolidated their rule by accepting a Carthaginian peace imposed by the Germans at Brest-Litovsk in 1918 and winning a bloody civil war within Russia that lasted from 1918 to 1920.

Lenin's genius lay in action, not thought. He was a master of revolutionary strategy, had a superb sense of timing, was decisive and daring, and was fiercely protective of his own absolute power. However, he was able to adapt his Marxist convictions to circumstances unique to his native Russia. Marx had predicted that revolution would occur only in countries that had reached the "highest stage of capitalism" and would be spearheaded by the industrial proletariat rising spontaneously against their oppressors. Realizing that Russia was an overwhelmingly peasant country, Lenin countered that the revolution would happen in the "weakest link" of capitalism.

Nevertheless, his writings and theories were quite influential during much of the 20th century. His chief theoretical contribution was the Communist Party's role as "vanguard of the proletariat," made up of highly disciplined professional revolutionaries and intellectuals, not of the workers, who lacked "revolutionary consciousness." As he wrote in *What Is to Be Done?* (1902), this "party of a new type" would plan and organize the revolution, not wait for such a cataclysm to erupt spontaneously, as Marx had incorrectly predicted. Absolute obedience to the party's unelected leaders would be maintained through "democratic centralism." In the name of the working class, the party would continue to exercise absolute power after the revolution through the "dictatorship of the proletariat."

After the outbreak of World War I, Lenin demanded: "Transform the imperialist war into civil war!" In his tract, *Imperialism, the Highest Stage of Capitalism* (1917), his hatred of nationalism and patriotism was expressed. It is not patriotic sentiments and love of one's nation that prompts individuals to defend their country. Wars, he argued, break out because of the expansionist, insatiable nature of imperialism, which he terms "the highest state of capitalism." Imperialism itself springs from monopoly finance capitalism. A few banks control the world directly or indirectly. With the "surplus capital" that they accumulate, they can gain "super profits" in colonies. This intensifies imperialist rivalry among the great powers, which launch wars in order to get a larger share of the world's wealth. Socialist and trade union leaders, who form a better paid "labor aristocracy," seek a share of the super profits. They are therefore duped into supporting the imperialist wars the capitalists launch, thereby betraying the interests of the exploited workers at home and in the colonies. There will always be wars as long as capitalism and imperialism exist. Peace can come only when the capitalists and their exploitative order are overthrown.

Lenin created a Soviet Union that was isolated in the world. To escape from this dangerous encirclement, he called on revolutionaries throughout the world to break away from socialist movements and to create Communist Parties that would join the Third International founded by the Bolsheviks in March 1919. Instead of serving the interests of their constituencies in their various nation-states, these Communist Parties would accept as binding all decisions made by Russia's Communist Party, which Lenin presented as the only true model for other countries. Out of this Third International grew the Comintern, which maintained links with all Communist Parties throughout the world and became a parallel arm of Soviet foreign policy. Soviet party and state interests were well served by this creation. But there was no room in Lenin's theory for nationalism, which he sought to destroy in all its forms.

**LÉVESQUE, RENÉ** 1922–1987, Born the son of a Quebecois country lawyer in New Carlisle, an anglophone town of 1000 inhabitants surrounded by the French-speaking world of Quebec's Gaspé Peninsula, René Lévesque grew up bilingual. Speaking perfect English, he personally suffered no discrimination for being a francophone. Nevertheless, he remembers the taunts exchanged by bands of French and English Canadians: "They used to call us 'pea-soupers'; we called them 'craw-fish.'" His Quebec nationalism flowered early; while a student in the Jesuit-run Garnier College prep school, he wrote in one of his papers: "Never forget that you are French Canadians, that your own people have been stagnating for generations, and that if they, the people, your people do not act, they are lost!"

During the war, he faced the threat of being drafted. His response was vintage Quebecois: "Though I was willing to go overseas, I was not willing to go in the uniform of His Majesty." He went to New York in 1943 and was appointed war correspondent in the American Seventh Army. At the age of twenty-one, he edited and announced messages to occupied France, and in February 1945 he was attached to the Sixth Army and moved with this unit and the First French Army eastward through France into Germany and Austria. He covered the battle of Nuremberg and was among the first to discover the horrors of the Dachau concentration camp outside of Munich. He witnessed Mussolini's mutilated body and saw Hermann Goering a few minutes after his surrender.

After the war he became a political journalist, which took him across Canada and the United States, to Korea, and back to Europe. He became one of Canada's first TV journalists. His popular program, *Point de Mire* ("Focal Point") made his diminutive figure, his gravelly voice, and his well-informed opinions familiar to millions of Canadians.

He served in the Liberal Party cabinet of Jean Lesage for six years and came to incorporate the aspirations of the Quiet Revolution. He grew impatient with the liberal provincial government, which did not press vigorously enough for an independent Quebec. He was unable to persuade his Liberal party to adopt a manifesto he had published calling for Quebec sovereignty within a common market association with Canada. Therefore, he and a group of disgruntled liberals left the party in 1967 and formed the Movement for Sovereignty-Association (MSA). A year later it merged with a couple of other smaller separatist parties to form the Parti Quebecois (PQ).

The PQ became a basket for a diverse collection of Quebecois who wanted to see the Quiet Revolution carried on with greater energy although they disagreed on how radical the political and economic changes should be. They wanted some kind of sovereign Quebec, but did not agree on just how sovereign. Only Lévesque had the necessary charisma, political skill, and patience to hold the movement together. He was a cautious leader who insisted that the party be democratic and respectable.

His notion of sovereignty-association was a compromise around which party members could unify. Although he was always careful not to define this notion too concretely, he said that "we do not want to end, but rather to radically transform, our union with the rest of Canada, so that, in the future, our relations will be based on full and complete equality." Quebec was only a "half-fledged state" in conflict with the rest of Canada; "in order to end once and for all the struggle of wills, the costly dividing up of energies and resources, the system must be replaced."

Sovereignty-association meant "a sovereign State of Quebec which will accept, or rather offer in advance, new links of interdependence with Canada, but links which will this time be negotiated between equal peoples, as a function of their geographic and other unquestionable common interest." Although the "obsolete constitutional links" would have to be cut, there would still be ties of free trade and travel without passports between Quebec and Canada, a common currency, a joint administration of the St. Lawrence Seaway, and a military alliance with Canada, the United States, and NATO.

He sought the right moment to fulfill a promise he had made during the 1976 election: to conduct a referendum in order to establish Quebec as a sovereign state. This finally happened in May 1980. Lévesque and his party stressed the peaceful and democratic nature of their cause. He wanted nothing to do with undemocratic firebrands.

Lévesque knew how sensitive the question of Quebec independence had always been. He was aware that while many Quebecers were dissatisfied with the federal structure as it existed, they were not in favor of complete independence. He therefore was ambivalent and hesitating. He preferred to proceed toward his goal in stages, thereby reaping scorn from those separatists who wanted immediate and decisive action.

The very wording of the referendum revealed

Lévesque's sensitivity to a wavering francophone attitude about independence: "The Government of Quebec has made public its proposal to negotiate a new agreement with the rest of Canada, based on the equality of nations; this agreement would enable Quebec to acquire the exclusive powers to make its laws, levy its taxes and establish relations abroad—in other words, sovereignty—and at the same time, to maintain with Canada an economic association including a common currency; no change in political status resulting from these negotiations will be effected without approval from the people through another referendum; on these terms, do you give the Government of Quebec the mandate to negotiate the proposed agreement between Quebec and Canada?" He feared a "once and for all" vote to secede and merely asked for the right to talk to Ottawa about a new arrangement. By diminishing the gravity of the choice, he hoped to gather in as large a flock of Quebecois as possible. The PQ narrowly lost the vote.

In 1982 the government in Ottawa produced a new constitution for Canada that spells out provincial rights more accurately than had the British North America Act (BNA). It contains a bill of rights that can be invoked by those who perceive language discrimination anywhere in Canada. Lévesque felt that he had been outmaneuvered in the negotiations leading up to the new constitution and refused to sign it. However, he indicated in 1984 that he would not demand a Quebec veto over future amendments. His willingness to cooperate with Ottawa was not only because the air had gone out of the separatist balloon. He was now dealing with a prime minister in Ottawa, Brian Mulroney, who was from Quebec, and whom Lévesque found much more congenial and sympathetic than he had found Pierre Elliott Trudeau. Quebec's history teaches that Quebec nationalism never dies; it just dies down temporarily. Lévesque decided that the time was not ripe for independence. In 1984, after a bitter intraparty debate that had raged since 1981, he declared that in the next provincial election "sovereignty must not be at stake, neither wholly nor in parts that are more or less disguised." This prompted the resignation of seven PQ cabinet members, and his party's majority in the National Assembly shrunk from 80 to 65. In an extraordinary PQ convention held in 1985, a majority of delegates (869 to 453) voted to shelve the issue of Quebec sovereignty. This caused such an intraparty uproar that Lévesque announced his resignation in June 1985.

See Graham Fraser's *PQ: René Lévesque and the Parti Québécois;* and René Lévesque's *My Quebec* (Totem Books, 1979) and *Memoirs* (Cross Canada Books, 1986).

**LIBERALISM** For much of the 20th century, it has been thought that liberalism and nationalism—whether as ideologies, principles, or political movements—must be in conflict with one another. Liberalism is individualistic, nationalism values an organic community. Liberals have historically supported free trade and free migration, while many nationalists have valued economic autarky and viewed immigration as polluting the nation, emigration as dispersing it. Liberalism is pacific and nationalism warlike—or at least so many liberals have thought.

It was not always so. The freedom of the individual from state oppression and the freedom of the nation from foreign oppression were once widely thought to be allied and related goals. The Declaration of the Rights of Man and Citizen spoke of both the rights of individuals and the nation as the fundamental political unit. For much of the 19th century, liberals, democrats, and nationalists were allied in their criticism of and work against first Napoleonic rule and then the old multinational imperial regimes of Europe. Giuseppe Mazzini, the Italian advocate of the Riorgimento, was perhaps the era's most prominent liberal nationalist leader; Theodor Herzl, the founder of Zionism, also articulated a liberal vision of nationalism.

The English liberal philosopher John Stuart Mill offered a strong endorsement of nationalism and national self-determination. "One hardly knows what any division of the human race should be free to do," he argued, "if not to determine, with which of the various collective bodies of human beings they choose to associate themselves." Suggesting the link between nationalism and democracy, Mill observed that "this is merely saying that the question of government ought to be decided by the governed." Moreover, Mill thought that "free institutions are next to impossible in a country made up of different nationalities," so liberals and democrats should view nationalism as instrumentally valuable. He suggested that members of different nationalities would lack both the mutual sympathy and the mutual comprehension necessary for representative government; they could be too easily set against each other by manipulative governments rather than monitoring and checking those governments. Mill's progressivism led him to suggest that national self-determination was for advanced nations; for backwards nations, the best they could hope for was either enlightened colonial rule by an advanced nation until they had moved forward, or "blending" with a more advanced nation. It is better for the Basque, the Breton, the Scottish Highlander, or the Welshman to assimilate into the French or British nation than "to sulk on his own rocks, the half-savage relic of past times, revolving in his own mental orbit, without participation or interest in the general movement of the world."

The liberal historian Lord Acton issued a striking rejoinder that put the liberal case against nationalism. Nationalism suppresses local minorities; it aims at a final settlement that can never be achieved because there will always be another nation to secede; it places country above moral principles and duties; and, most importantly, by unifying the state and the nation nationalism is likely to create a dangerous attachment to the state. "The presence of different nations under the same sovereignty is similar in its effects to the independence of the Church in the State. It provides against the servility that flourishes under the shadow of a single authority, by balancing interests, multiplying associations . . . [and] affording a great source and centre of political sentiments . . . not derived from the sovereign will."

Both Mill and Acton recognized the enduring force of national attachments; they differed over how best to marshal that force in the defense of freedom. In this they differed from those liberals and socialists who foresaw the withering away of national identity in an internationalist or cosmopolitan moral order. (They shared with those thinkers, and with each other, the idea that there are backward nations that ought to be blended with more advanced ones. Unlike Engels, they did not look forward to the minor nations perishing in a revolutionary holocaust, but Marxists and liberals alike shared the Whiggish, progressive, teleological notions of history that were almost universal in 19th century European thought.)

The Millian vision reached its zenith in Woodrow Wilson's post-World War I insistence on national self-determination and the breakup of the old empires. If the onset of World War I shattered the old liberal internationalist dream of peace through free trade, the aftermath of the war did much the same to the liberal nationalist dream of a Europe of peacefully coexisting democratic nations. By 1927, the Austrian liberal economist Ludwig von Mises could write of rising nationalist tension and conflict, which he thought unavoidable in illiberal interventionist states. The expulsions and persecutions of minorities, irredentism, and finally the rise in Germany and Italy of what seemed to be the apotheosis of nationalism, fascism and Nazism—discredited nationalism among Western liberal intellectuals. While postwar liberals, especially in the United States, were often sympathetic to anticolonial nationalist struggles in Africa and Asia, they thought that nationalism in the West was a retrograde force that must be and would be transcended. For some time the Ox-

ford political theorist Isaiah Berlin was almost alone among liberal philosophers in insisting that nationalism would endure because it responded to genuine human needs and desires.

In the 1980s this began to change, in part due to Berlin's own influence. Liberal thinkers including Joseph Raz, Michael Walzer, and Yael Tamir began articulating liberal defenses of nationalism, more in von Herder's terms than in Mill's but echoing the latter's idea that liberal institutions have to be situated in nation-states. The Canadian philosopher Charles Taylor and the British theorist David Miller also argued that a humane, democratic nationalism was possible and valuable, though neither could straightforwardly be called a liberal. Events in Central and Eastern Europe briefly resurrected the old anti-imperial alliance of liberals, democrats, and nationalists. On the other hand, self-described liberals and nationalists frequently fought in post-Communist democracies; deeply illiberal nationalisms took hold in the warring republics of Yugoslavia; and many liberal thinkers (typically inspired by Kant rather than by Acton) continued to reject the moral claims of nationalism and to ally liberalism with cosmopolitanism or, simply, with individualism.

Mill's defense of nationalism can be found in his *Considerations on Representative Government* (1861), Acton's critique in the essay "Nationality" (1862). The postwar liberal rejection of nationalism is discussed in Will Kymlicka, *Liberalism, Community, and Culture* (Oxford University Press, 1989). Berlin's most important essays on nationalism are found in *Against the Current* (Hogarth Press, 1979) and *The Crooked Timber of Humanity* (Vintage Books, 1990). Yael Tamir, in *Liberal Nationalism* (Princeton University Press, 1993), defends that combination of doctrines, while Thomas Pogge, *Realizing Rawls* (Cornell University Press, 1989), and F. A. Hayek, *The Fatal Conceit* (University of Chicago Press, 1989), criticize nationalism from competing liberal perspectives.

**LIBYAN NATIONALISM**   Libya is a North African nation. It is predominantly desert with arable land along the Mediterranean coast. The majority of its population is Arab (95 percent) but there are significant Berber and Tuareg communities. Other groups include Greeks, Maltese, and black Africans.

Islam was introduced in the 7th century during the expansion of the Ummayad Empire, but most Libyans claim descent from the Arab bedouin tribes of the Bana Hilal and Banu Sulaym who were dispatched by the Fatimid caliph (in Egypt) in the 11th century to put down a Berber rebellion. The origins of the Berbers are unknown, but they predate the Phoenicians, Romans, and Arabs in their occupation of North Africa. Most have assimilated into the larger Arab society, but a few traditional communities continue to exist.

The Mamluks and Ottomans later influenced the region. North African ports functioned as trading areas for these empires and a trans-Saharan trade between Morocco and Egypt was important to the local economy. The trade of Sudanese slaves was prominent and piracy along the coast became infamous. The Ottomans often stationed military personnel (Janissaries) in North Africa, but because the region was far from the Ottoman power center local leaders exercised considerable authority. Many Turkish Jannissaries married Arab women and openly sided with Arab interests. Their offspring, the khouloughlis, were often administrators.

In 1711 Ahmed Karamanli, a khouloughli, seized Tripoli and established a hereditary monarchy. The Karamanli Monarchy, while formally accepting the authority of the Ottoman sultan, reigned almost continuously from 1711 to 1835. When the European powers stopped the coastal piracy, the strength of the Karamanli Monarchy declined and the Ottoman sultan reestablished authority in the region.

An important development in the area of nationalism occurred with the rise of the Sanusi religious orders. Sayyid Muhammad ibn Ali as Sanusi (1787–1859) was a traveling spiritual leader (marabat) who studied throughout North Africa and Arabia. In 1830, while passing through Tripolitania and Fazzan, he was recognized as the Grand Sanusi. He established his first order near Mecca, but was forced by local authorities to return to North Africa and he settled in Cyrenaica. Sayyid Muhammad blended North African Sufism with the asceticism of Orthodox Islam. Not inclined toward dance or other ecstatic religious acts, Sanusi spiritualism centered on contemplation and rationale thought. Sayyid Muhammad insisted that his followers work in a profession and engage in the daily mechanisms of the world. This message resonated with the bedouin tribes of North Africa who were already living an austere existence.

Soon the Grand Sanusi had established orders throughout North Africa, Sudan, and along the pilgrimage route to Mecca. The larger orders functioned as schools, courts, commercial, and cultural centers. The Grand Sanusi's son, Sayyid al-Mahdi, increased the reach of the Sanusi orders and also declared jihad (holy war) against the French. Ahmed ash Sharif succeeded al-Mahdi (1902), but governed in the name of Muhammad Idris who later became the king of Libya.

Italy, scrambling for colonial possessions in Africa, manufactured a conflict with the Ottomans to justify moving troops into the region in October 1911. In the Treaty of Lausanne (October 1912) the Turks recognized the independence of Tripolitania and Cyrenaica and Italy annexed the territories.

The Sanusiyyah maintained authority in Cyrenaica and the Italians were confined to coastal enclaves and Northern Tripolitania. Ahmed ash Sharif sided with the Ottomans and Germans in World War I after the Italians sided with the Allied powers. He was defeated, along with the Ottomans, in Egypt. Idris then assumed leadership of the Sanusiyyah and negotiated with the British for an independent Cyrenaica. In the interwar period, the Italians retained control of Tripolitania and negotiated with Idris concerning the Fazzan and coastal Cyrenaica. The regions were treated as separate entities by the Italians, with some local autonomy given to the elite in Tripolitania and Idris's authority as amir recognized in Cyrenaica and Fazzan.

The nationalists in Tripolitania were not unified and divided among traditional tribal interests, but in 1922 a coalition of Tripolitania nationalist met with Idris and offered to accept his authority. Idris was asked to assume the leadership as a matter of expediency, but he nonetheless accepted and open warfare between the Italians and Sanusiyyah erupted once again. Tripolitanian nationalists, who never really accepted Idris, were easily subdued. The Sanusiyyah in the Fazzan and Cyrenaica were effective fighters, but major resistance ended in 1931 when military commander Umar al Mukkhtar was captured and hanged.

Under Italian authority the region was divided into four administrative sections—Tripoli, Misratah, Benghazi, and Darnah—and formally named Libya. The Italians did introduce a modern infrastructure that was designed to attract Italian immigrants to the "Fourth Shore." Close to 110,000 Italians did immigrate and the best agricultural land was taken from the Arabs and given to the new Italian settlers.

Idris had fled to Egypt to avoid capture and backed the British during World War II. After the Italians and Germans were defeated, the nationalists in Tripoli reluctantly joined forces with the Cyrenaicans and supported Idris. There was an attempt in the United Nations to divide Libya into three spheres administered by the Italians, French, and British, but this plan was narrowly rejected and the entire colonial territory of "Libya" became an independent state with Idris as king of a constitutional monarchy. Governing primarily through personal influence and oriented toward the Western powers, Idris attempted to create a Libyan nation centered on monarchal governance. The country was desperately poor, but oil was discovered in the late 1950s and economic conditions gradually improved. Throughout the 1950s there was a steady rise in Arab nationalism throughout North Africa.

The charismatic leadership of Gamal Abdel Nasser in Egypt was the primary inspiration for the young Libyan officers who overthrew Idris in 1969 in a bloodless coup. Captain Muammar Qaddafi was named the commander of the armed forces and chair of the Revolutionary Command Council and he quickly forced the British and Americans, stationed at two bases inside Libya, to leave the country. Qaddafi was also the first Arab leader to force Mobil Oil into concession arrangements that led to the eventual nationalization of the oil industry in the country. He was consistently a price hawk during the rise of the Organization of Petroleum Producers (OPEC).

A young, charismatic Qaddafi had considerable influence in the Middle East during the 1970s. Inspired by Nasser's attempts at regional unity he tried to unify Libya with surrounding Arab and African states. His attempts at forming governing coalitions led directly to his sponsorship of coup attempts in Egypt and the Sudan. Libyan troops consistently intervened in the civil war in Chad where Qaddafi has a territorial dispute. Increasingly, Qaddafi backed a variety of nationalist organizations (the Black Panthers, the Irish Republican Army, the Nation of Islam and Palestinian factions), which brought him into conflict with the West. In April 1986 the United States bombed sites in Libya, directly targeted Qaddafi, and killed several of his family members.

Qaddafi's socialist-Islamic philosophy is articulated in a two-volume *Green Book*. The government is ostensibly controlled by the People's Congresses. These congresses are organized into twenty-five municipal regions and then divided further down to the level of small communities where people meet periodically to voice their opinions on a range of issues (both scheduled and unscheduled). These small groups then feed into larger committees up to the national level. Theoretically, Qaddafi is no longer officially the general secretary of the People's Congress, but he retains authority in the country. People who visit and live in Libya generally think that these congresses do have an effect on government policy, and that they operate in a democratic fashion. But Libya is also described as an austere and stark society without teeming bazaars and material goods, undoubtedly due to a prolonged embargo enforced by some countries in the West. Qaddafi has recently made overtures to the West and his neighbors, such as extraditing two suspects implicated in the bombing of a Pan American flight.

## LINCOLN, ABRAHAM

1809–1865, American politician and 16th president of the United States, born near Hodgenville, Kentucky. Known as the Great Emancipator, Abraham Lincoln presided over the victory of the North over the South during the American Civil War and, through this victory, was instrumental in the abolition of slavery and the development of a stronger national state in the United States.

From the very beginning of his political career, Lincoln idolized nationalists such as Daniel Webster and Henry Clay, who advocated the use of government power to promote economic development, especially in the West. As a member of the Whig Party, Lincoln served four terms in the Illinois State Legislature (1834–1840), where he proposed numerous internal improvements, including public roads, railroads, and canals. As Lincoln would later write, "The legitimate object of government, is to do for a community of people, whatever they need to have done, but cannot do, *at all,* or cannot, *so well do,* for themselves—in their separate, and individual capacities." In 1846, Lincoln was elected to Congress, where he served one term as the lone Whig in the Illinois delegation. Once in Congress, Lincoln condemned the ongoing war with Mexico as unnecessary and unconstitutional, a position that proved unpopular with his constituents.

Lincoln joined the fledgling Republican Party in 1856. Two years later, he ran against Stephen A. Douglas for the U.S. Senate. On accepting his party's nomination ( June 16, 1858), Lincoln emphasized the dangerous divisiveness of the slavery issue, declaring, "'A house divided against itself cannot stand.' I believe this government cannot endure, permanently half *slave* and half *free.*" During the 1858 campaign, the two candidates met seven times for joint debates. In these debates, Douglas defended the principle of popular sovereignty, arguing that territories and new states should decide for themselves whether to permit slavery, while Lincoln insisted that slavery must not under any circumstances be allowed to spread. Although Lincoln did not consider himself to be an abolitionist, he found slavery morally repugnant and feared that its expansion into territories and new states would cripple economic growth and thwart America's national mission of geographic continuity. Lincoln lost the election to Douglas, but gained valuable national exposure, emerging as one of the principal leaders of the Republican Party.

When Lincoln ran for president in 1860, as the candidate of the Republican Party, he faced a deeply divided Democratic Party. Due to these divisions, Lincoln won a large majority in the Electoral College, but received barely 40 percent of the popular vote, with practically no support in the South. As a result of Lincoln's election and the failure in Congress of the Crittenden Compromise, a set of constitutional amendments favoring proslavery interests, seven southern states led by South Carolina seceded and formed the Confederate States of America, with Jefferson Davis as their new president. Lincoln, in his First Inaugural Address (March 4, 1861), attempted to assuage the apprehensions of the South, promising that no action would be taken to interfere with slavery in states where it already existed. At the same time, Lincoln committed himself to the principle that "the Union of these states is perpetual" and inviolable by individual states by any lawful means. In other words, none of the several states had a right to secede and, as such, could be forced back into the Union by the federal government. When Confederate troops fired on Ft. Sumter at dawn on April 12, 1861, the debate over the legality of secession became moot. The United States awoke to find itself at war with itself, and four more southern states, including Virginia, defied Lincoln's authority and joined the Confederacy.

As president, Lincoln believed that he had a constitutional duty to preserve the Union at any cost. At the same time, he remained morally opposed to slavery. Committed both to Union and to liberty, Lincoln faced a grim paradox. How could the Union be preserved without compromising on the slavery issue? How could slavery be eliminated without tearing the Union apart? Lincoln decided that his constitutional duty must come first, even if this duty sometimes warred with his personal moral beliefs. In an August 1862 letter to *New York Tribune* publisher Horace Greeley, who had viciously attacked Lincoln for failing to adopt a stronger antislavery policy, Lincoln explained his position, "If I could save the Union without freeing *any* slaves I would do it, and if I could save it by freeing *all* the slaves I would do it; and if I could save it by freeing some and leaving others alone I would also do that. What I do about slavery, and the colored race, I do because I believe it helps to save the Union; and what I forbear, I forbear because I do *not* believe it would help to save the Union." But he added, "I have here stated my purpose according to my view of *official* duty; and I intend no modification of my oft-expressed *personal* wish that all men every where could be free."

During the war, Lincoln was a moderate and pragmatic leader of an internally divided Republican Party. Whereas conservative Republicans called for gradual, voluntary elimination of slavery, and radical Republicans demanded immediate abolition, moderates like Lincoln were interested in expediting the eradication of slavery but were fearful of possible consequences, such as race wars and unnecessary conflicts with border states, such as Maryland and Missouri. In 1862, Lincoln angered radical republicans by overruling decisions by his field commanders to emancipate slaves from territories occupied by federal forces. Biding his time until Union forces had scored significant victories over the Confederate rebels, Lincoln issued a preliminary Emancipation Proclamation on September 22, 1862. Applying only to those slaves living under Confederate rule, not those living in border states or territories already occupied by federal troops, Lincoln's act was largely symbolic. Indeed, fewer than 200,000 slaves (out of approximately 4 million) were actually emancipated during the war as a direct or indirect result of Lincoln's final, official proclamation (January 1, 1863).

Lincoln's moderation and pragmatism extended to his vision for postwar reconstruction. In his Proclamation of Amnesty and Reconstruction (December 8, 1863), Lincoln endorsed easy terms for the reestablishment of loyal governments in the Confederacy, and promised amnesty for all but a handful of officers and agents of the Confederate government. In his Second Inaugural Address, Lincoln called for national healing, declaring, "With malice toward none; with charity for all; with firmness in the right, as God gives us to see the right, let us strive on to finish the work we are in; to bind up the nation's wounds . . . to do all which may achieve and cherish a just, and a lasting peace, among ourselves, and with all nations." Although Lincoln's moderate position was unpopular among radical members of his own party, who desired much sterner measures and more inflexible requirements to be imposed against the seceded states, he reiterated his commitment to a moderate reconstruction on April 11, 1865, in what proved to be his last public address.

Lincoln was shot by John Wilkes Booth on April 14, 1865, in Ford's Theatre in Washington, D.C. He died the next morning. Although he did not live to see his reconstruction scheme come to fruition, its spirit was preserved in the reconstruction policies of President Andrew Johnson, Lincoln's vice president and successor. And although he did not live to witness the passage of the constitutional amendment abolishing slavery, the ratification of the Thirteenth Amendment in December 1865 guaranteed Lincoln's place in history as the Great Emancipator.

After his death, essayist Ralph Waldo Emerson called Lincoln "the true representative of this continent; an entirely public man; father of his country, the pulse of twenty millions throbbing in his heart, the thought of their minds articulated by his tongue. . . ." Poet Walt

Whitman wrote, "This dust was once the man, / Gentle, plain, just and resolute, under whose cautious hand, / Against the foulest crime in history known in any land or age, / Was saved the Union of these States." And Karl Marx remembered Lincoln as "the single-minded son of the working class" who led his "country through the matchless struggle for the rescue of the enchained race and the reconstruction of a social world."

A good one-volume biography of Lincoln is Stephen B. Oates, *With Malice Toward None: The Life of Abraham Lincoln,* 1977, reprint edition (Harperperenial Library, 1994). A more exhaustive scholarly study is James G. Randall, *Lincoln the President,* 1945–55, reprint edition, 2 vols. (Da Capo Press, 1997). For an analysis of Lincoln's role in the revolutionary transformation of American society see James M. McPherson, *Abraham Lincoln and the Second American Revolution* (Oxford University Press, 1990). A fine interpretation of Lincoln's political thought is Mark E. Neely, Jr., *The Last Best Hope of Earth: Abraham Lincoln and the Promise of America* (Harvard University Press, 1993).

## LITERATURE AND NATIONALISM

In the modern world, the relationship between literature and the nation is so obvious as to be assumed. Educated people are expected to be conversant with the national literature of their own countries and with the most prominent literary figures and works from related countries. Literature is both interpreted and taught within national units. Course catalogs and anthologies feature such categorizations as "Nineteenth-Century American Literature," "The Rise of the Russian Novel," and "Spanish Literature and the Civil War." These are accepted and familiar literary categories for modern readers and they demonstrate our acceptance of the seemingly natural link between nations and literatures. The seemingly primal connection of literature and the nation is in reality, however, a modern historical phenomena stemming from rising cultural and political nationalism in early 19th-century Europe.

National literatures are far from a natural phenomenon. The idea that literature and nationalism should be allied originated with late 18th-century and early 19th-century theorists of nationalism. These theorists, exemplified by Mme. de Staël (*De la littérature considérée dans ses rapports avec les institutions sociales,* 1800) and other romantic nationalists, first advanced the now accepted idea that literature should embody the unique characteristics of a nation by capturing the national zeitgeist. The underlying assumptions of the literary nationalists were that humanity is naturally divided into homogeneous but distinctive groups, that these groups are marked by a unique set of values and concerns, and that this produces a distinctive national character. German romanticism was one of the strongest proponents of the arguments linking the nation and its cultural products. Early German ideas of nationhood were identified with a specifically literary national spirit, *Nationalgeist,* which portrayed the nation as an organic entity marked by a distinctive *Volksgeist.* Nationalist sentiment and literary theory stemming from this perspective presumes the state to be coterminous with "the people" and their culture. Culture, in this view, then functions to express the uniqueness of the people. Numerous scholarly works stemming from this historical tradition, especially in the fields of literary criticism and area studies, argue for and detail the thematic uniqueness of specific national literatures.

Prior to the nationalist outbursts in the late 18th century, literature was not evaluated in national categories, but was valued in large part for its ability to transcend such categories by speaking across time and place. The "classics," in fact, held their exalted status because of their ability to transcend such parochial constraints as language or nationality to speak to all people, or more accurately, all people of a particular cultural tradition. These texts were held to be superior because they embodied the "best of human thought." Indeed, this assumption that the best literature embodies universal human truths continues to endure in tandem with more nationalist understandings of literature.

In contrast to romantic and nationalist theorists of past centuries, recent theorists of the nation have amply demonstrated the socially constructed nature of nations. Rather than being organic entities slumbering until their awakening, scholars such as Benedict Anderson, Ernest Gellner, and Eric Hobsbawm have shown that nations are "imagined communities" built as much in the minds of their citizens as in military exercises.

Similar to nations, national literatures themselves are created by the cultural work of specific peoples engaged in an identifiable set of activities. The nation and its cultural expression in literature underlies, unifies, and makes meaningful the political formation of the state. Literature helps to sustain the nation-state through its evocation and indeed *creation* of the unifying, emotionally powerful image of the nation and the national identity. National literatures are one method of fostering the emotion that binds the nation and its population. Literary expression helps to construct common images of the nation and the generally available understandings of the relationship between the people and "their" nation.

National literatures also serve as an arena for contesting and revising national identities through the incorporation of new groups and new ideas.

In the modern world, people are part of large collectivities from which they derive important aspects of their identities, but these collectivities are sustained in the abstract, not by the face-to-face interactions of earlier societies. Because of this lack of direct relationships, the ability of media such as literature to envision and widely distribute images of those common identities becomes increasingly powerful. Nation-states are rooted in the fact that although most citizens will never meet, the citizenry as a whole nonetheless shares an image of themselves as a whole. One central task of a national literature is to invent an image of the nation and a concomitant national identity that is capable of mobilizing loyalty and inspiring commitment from citizens. Nation building requires explicit campaigns to create an overarching identity that subsumes subsidiary differences and competing loyalties, such as ethnic or religious ties, that may divide and polarize national populations.

In addition to the internal work of nation building and national identity formation, national literatures perform an important function in the international community. National literatures have become identified as an essential characteristic of modern nation-states. The possession of a national culture has become one of the standard marks of nationhood within the world system. Once national literatures became understood as a basic requirement of a full-fledged nation-state, new nations had to have their own national literature or risk losing their status as a fully formed and independent nation-state within the global community.

Suggested readings on the topic include Wendy Griswold's studies in the *American Journal of Sociology* (1981, 1987) and *American Sociological Review* (1992), and *Nationalism and Literature* by Sarah M. Corse (Cambridge University Press, 1997).

## LITHUANIAN NATIONALISM

Lithuania is an independent nation bordering Latvia, Belarus, Poland, and Russia's Kaliningrad region (formerly East Prussia). According to the preamble of the 1992 Constitution of the Republic of Lithuania, Lithuania reestablished the Lithuanian state in 1918, lost its independence in 1940, and restored independence in 1990. The Republic of Lithuania first appeared after World War I but the present Lithuanian state as well as the Belarusian one (until 1995) claims as its predecessor the Grand Duchy of Lithuania that ceased to exist in 1795 after the Third Partition of Polish-Lithuanian Commonwealth.

Lithuanian nationalism became known worldwide in the late 1980s when the Lithuanian nationalist movement *Sajudis* led by professor Vytautas Landsbergis succeeded in mobilizing in a short time significant support for nationalist politics from the Lithuanian population. It took less than two years (1988–1990) for the Sajudis to come to power in Lithuania through the first reasonably free parliamentary elections in the country since 1926 held at the beginning of 1990. On March 11, 1990, the Supreme Council of the Lithuanian SSR, led by Landsbergis, fulfilled a long-term goal of the nationalist program by declaring the restoration of Lithuanian independence.

Compared to the other East and Central European nations, Lithuanians arrived at their version of nationalism with significant delay but not as late as did the neighboring Belarusians. The 1930s and 1940s featured the early period of Lithuanian nationalism. At that time nationalism was restricted mostly to a tiny academic circle of Samogitians, who came from the historic part of western Lithuania named Samogitia to pursue their academic studies at Vilnius University. They were of low-noble (gentry) origin and, therefore, had more in common with the Lithuanian-speaking peasants than Polish-speaking Lithuanian noble elite. Samogitian gentry widely used the Samogitian drawl of the Lithuanian language, while the majority of the Lithuanian nobles from the other parts of the country preferred Polish, which had been the official language of the Polish-Lithuanian Commonwealth since the union of both nations in Lublin (Poland) in 1569.

Nevertheless, the contribution of Samogitians to Lithuanian nationalism complicated the case. Instead of a common Lithuanian national identity, they promoted a triple identity of Samogitians (by region), Lithuanians (by historical nation), and Polish (by state) that delayed amalgamation of the transregional identity of the encompassed Lithuanian nation for at least two decades.

In the middle of the 19th century Lithuanian identity was still closely connected to the historical traditions of the Grand Duchy of Lithuania. Lithuanian nobles identified themselves as *gentes Lituanus, nationes Polonus* ("Lithuanian of origin, Polish by nationality"). Lithuanian nationalism could successfully evolve only when the Lithuanian identity was separated from its Polish twin. The rise of the Lithuanian-Russian national antagonism contributed significantly to the process.

Favorable conditions for the development of Lithuanian nationalism occurred after the unsuccessful Polish-Lithuanian uprising against Russia in 1864. The Russian authorities banned the use of the Latin alphabet for Lithuanian print; the use of Lithuanian in public was prohibited as well. At the same time Russification was launched on a full scale throughout the former Grand Duchy of Lithuania in an attempt to substitute the Polish cultural influence with the Russian one. Russian colonists were settled in Lithuania, and Lithuanian Catholics were urged to convert to Orthodox faith.

Faced with increasing Russification, the Lithuanian Catholic Church soon found itself on the side of nationalists. A strong impetus for nationalism came from Motiejus Valancius, bishop of Samogitia, who provided accommodation and financial support to a number of prominent nationalists at his residency in Varniai. The first Lithuanian historian Simonas Daukantas was on his payroll as well.

In the 1880s, Lithuanian nationalism was still in its infancy. The first Lithuanian-language magazine *Ausra* ("The Dawn") was begun only in 1883. The magazine gathered all nationalist ideas that had been generated up to date into an ideological program, based on which Lithuanian nation was to be built. Its editor-in-chief Jonas Basanavicius, a physician, worked in Bulgaria for twenty-five years and participated in Bulgarian political life, supporting the idea of Bulgarian independence.

The main contribution of the *Ausra* to the course of Lithuanian nationalism was the idea, spoken publicly for the first time, that a Lithuanian is one who speaks Lithuanian. A clear distinction drawn between historical Lithuanians and modern ones provided nationalists with a starting point for the foundations of a modern Lithuanian state. This approach was adopted by the first Lithuanian political magazine *Varpas* ("The Bell") edited by Vincas Kudirka, the prominent nationalist leader, a speaker on Lithuanian modern nationalism, and author of the Lithuanian anthem.

In 1896 the first Lithuanian political party, the Lithuanian Social Democratic Party, was formed. Lithuanian social democrats supported nationalism, declaring as their chief political aim the achievement of sovereignty of Lithuania within the Russian confederation.

The moderate nationalism of *Varpas* manifested itself in the Lithuanian Democratic Party (LDP), which was founded in 1902 in Vilnius. The LDP's short-term goal was to achieve autonomy within the Russian Empire. According to the democrats, Lithuania had to comprise all of the historic ethnographic Lithuanian lands. The long-term goal projected by LDP was Lithuanian independence. In 1905, Russian authorities lifted the ban on the Lithuanian press, and the first national Lithuanian-language newspapers were started and allow to openly promote Lithuanian national identity.

Lithuanian nationalism took its final shape during World War I. In 1915, after the German occupation, the question of Lithuanian independence became a hot issue. In 1917 the German authorities permitted Lithuanian nationalists to set up an independent advisory body called the Lithuanian Council. At this time the final decision was made concerning the very concept of the reemerging Lithuanian state. The Lithuanian nationalists supported by the German authorities rejected the idea of reestablishing the historical Grand Duchy of Lithuania, which was more common to Belarusians and Polish in Lithuania, and decided to build a new Lithuanian state based on ethnic affiliation.

However, Lithuanian nationalists toyed with the idea of making Lithuania a constitutional monarchy under the patronage of the German Reich. The Count of Württemberg, Wilhelm von Urach, was suggested as King Mindaugas II of Lithuania. In December 1917 the council issued a declaration of Lithuanian sovereignty under surveillance of the German Reich. On February 16, 1918, the same declaration was repeated only without references to special bounds with Germany. The declaration is regarded by the present Lithuanian republic as the act of reestablishing Lithuanian independence. The date of the declaration has been celebrated as the day of Lithuanian independence.

The Lithuanian state was ruined in 1940 after the invasion of Soviet troops. Formally Lithuanian statehood did not cease to exist but was integrated into the USSR in the form of the Lithuanian Soviet Socialist Republic only with formal attributes of a sovereignty. The United States never accepted the annexation and occupation of Lithuania or the other Baltic countries. Prewar Lithuanian embassies in Washington, D.C., and the Vatican survived during the Soviet era. The awareness of the continuity of the once-independent state made Lithuanian nationalism more immune to the unleashed Sovietization. On March 11, 1990, the Supreme Council of the Lithuanian SSR, dominated by the nationalist movement Sajudis, issued the declaration of Lithuanian independence and restored the validity of the 1938 Constitution of the Lithuanian republic, thus linking the reestablished state to its historical predecessor.

The best introduction to Lithuanian nationalism is *The Baltic Revolution: Estonia, Latvia, Lithuania and the Path to Independence* by Anatol Lieven (Yale University Press, 1993) coupled with Alfred Senn's *The Emergence of Modern Lithuania* (New York, 1959). For more up-to-date information see V. Stanley Vardys and Judith Sedaitis, *Lithuania: The Rebel Nation* (Westview Press, 1998). For comparison with other Baltic nations, use *The Baltic States: Years of Dependence, 1940–1980* by Romuald J. Misiunas and Rein Taagepera (Berkeley, 1983).

**LIU SHAO-CHI** 1898–1969, Former president of the People's Republic of China (PRC) from 1959 to 1968, and a pioneer revolutionary who devoted his entire life to the Chinese nationalist and Communist movement, only to find himself a tragic victim of the state that he helped create.

Born in Ningxiang County in Hunan, Liu lived not very far from Mao Zedong's hometown of Shaoshan. Mao subsequently became the number one leader of the PRC and Liu became the number two. Liu studied at Moscow Oriental University in 1921 and became a member of the newly founded Chinese Communist Party. In Spring 1922, Liu went back to China and organized railroad and coal mine workers in Hunan. Liu and Mao collaborated for the first time in organizing a labor strike in the Anyuan coal mine. Between 1925 and 1931, Liu held various positions in the Chinese Federation of Trade Unions and Central Committee of the Chinese Communist Party (CCP). In 1932, Liu joined Mao at the Red Army base in Jianxi province, and marched along with the Red Army during the Long March in 1934–1935. Liu was known to be the first person to propose the concept of Mao Zedong Thought, which eventually became the official ideology of the CCP.

After the founding of the People's Republic of China, Liu first became vice chairman of the CCP, then chairman of the Standing Committee of the People's Congress, and later president of the PRC in 1959. His rapid advancement within the CCP's leadership circle soon made him second only to Mao. However, differences between the two quickly emerged. Whereas Liu advocated an incremental and practical approach toward socialist transformation, Mao wanted a radical one. It was Mao's decision to launch the Great Leap Forward (1958–1960), which brought disastrous consequences and major setbacks for China in the early 1960s. After mild self-criticism, Mao retreated to the back seat and let Liu resume the leading role in the day-to-day operation of the government. Liu took this opportunity to undo many of Mao's radical policies, but nothing was intended to challenge Mao's ultimate authority. Nevertheless, Mao apparently was alarmed by the liberal reforms Liu had carried out. He soon accused Liu of being a revisionist and a "capitalist roader." In the name of preventing revisionism and ideology purity, Mao waged relentless political campaigns against the party liberals, which eventually culminated into the Cultural Revolution (1966–1976). Liu, together with Deng Xiaoping and many others, were stripped from power in 1968 without any due process. Liu was jailed and died in prison one year later. He was not formally reprimanded until 1980, four years after Mao's death.

Liu's official biography is *Liu Shaoqi Zhuan* (China Central Documentary Publisher, 1998). A collection of his work is *Selected Works of Liu Shaoqi* (China Central Documentary Publishing, 1984).

**LOCKE, JOHN** 1632–1704, English philosopher and exponent of rational liberalism. Locke spent a number of years in exile in Holland in an atmosphere of freedom not found in England. One of his important legacies was the publication of *Two Treatises of Government* (1690), which was widely seen as a justification for the Glorious Revolution of 1688 in England, and which explains the formation of the state by a social contract based on the consent of the governed. In contradistinction to an earlier English social contract theorist, Thomas Hobbes, who portrayed in his *Leviathan* (1651) a gloomy human condition in which people are driven by the struggle for human survival and constant war to form a state under the rule of an all-powerful sovereign who could maintain social order by force, and under which people were obliged to support their sovereign because the only alternative was the violence that drove them to create the state in the first place, Locke offers the basis for a democratic state and liberal nationalism.

Locke believed that rational people formed the state through a social contract that also obligated the government to its citizens. The government provided the mechanisms for rational conflict management through legislative, executive, and judicial functions. Should government cease to be responsive to its citizens, Locke argued the people could simply break the contract with government. They did not return to a state of human warfare; they merely concluded a new contract with a new government.

Lockean theory provided a powerful intellectual tool for emerging American nationalism as the founding fathers considered the creation of a new state and government. His ideas form an important part of Thomas Jefferson's Declaration of Independence (1776).

An excellent biography of John Locke is Maurice Cranston's *John Locke: A Biography* (Macmillan, 1957). A standard version of Locke's prominent work is John Locke, *Treatise of Civil Government and a Letter Concerning Toleration,* edited with an introduction by Charles L. Sherman (Appleton-Century-Crofts, 1937), and sound discussions of his ideas can be found in John W. Gough, *John Locke's Political Philosophy: Eight Studies* (Clarendon Press, 1950), and in *Political Writings of John Locke,* edited with an introduction by David Wootten (Mentor, 1993).

Adapted from Grieves, Forest, Conflict and Order: An Introduction to International Relations. © 1977 by Houghton Mifflin Company. Used with permission.

**LUMUMBA, PATRICE**  1925–1961, Nationalist leader and first prime minister of the independent West African nation of the Congo. Patrice Lumumba was involved in the national liberation movement in the Belgian Congo and served as prime minister of the Congo from 1960 to 1961.

Patrice Lumumba was born in the Belgian Congo in 1925. This colony of Belgium was rich in copper, germanium, and uranium, and was, as a result, strongly invested in by multinational mining companies. Lumumba began his political career as president of the African Staff Association. He later founded the Mouvement National Congolais (MNC), which countered the tribal politics of Joseph Kasavubu's Abako Party and Moise Tshombe's Conakat Party. Lumumba became the first prime minister of the independent Congo in June 1960.

Lumumba's government was threatened by a military coup within a week of independence and a secessionist movement in the Katanga province of the Congo led by the Tshombe regime. The secessionist movement had the support of Belgium, the United Nations, the United States, and the multinational mining corporations. Lumumba's government had the support of Africa's Pan-African leaders and presidents. President Sekou Touré of Guinea, aligned with the Casablanca bloc of African leaders who favored African independence and political unity, supported the Lumumba government by sending in troops. The United Nations forces succeeded in overthrowing Lumumba and installing Tshombe.

The Congo situation helped crystalize the oppositional political tendencies among African leaders. At the Brazzaville and Casablanca conferences of 1961, the issue helped to distinguish the Brazzaville bloc, which had been anti-Lumumba and supported continued relations with their former colonizing countries, from the Casablanca group, which sought decolonization and political unity among African countries.

Lumumba was arrested and held in UN custody and eventually captured and killed by Tshombe soldiers in 1961. He remains a martyr for the Pan-African movement. In the resolutions adopted by the All-African Peoples Conference held in 1961 in Cairo, Lumumba was proclaimed a "hero of Africa."

**LUTHER, MARTIN**  1483–1586, Few individuals have influenced the formation of modern Europe as much as Martin Luther. He was the son of a clergyman from Thuringia who was able to save enough money to send his gifted but brooding son to the University of Erfurt to study law. Luther was reportedly shocked by a sudden flash of light and decided instead to become a monk, pastor, and professor in Wittenberg. In 1511 he left for a long-awaited voyage to Rome as a firm believer, but he returned to Germany with his faith in the Church badly shaken. His anger and frustration built up as the Roman pontificate devised a method for raising its own revenues by selling to Catholics forgiveness from their sins.

In countries with strong central rulers, such papal financial maneuvers could be resisted, but until 1517 the Church's agents needed not fear resistance in the weak and fragmented Germany. When one day a papal representative knocked on Martin Luther's door to present the scheme, the simmering kettle boiled over. On October 31, 1517, he published his "95 Theses" branding the Catholic Church an insult to God and challenging it to an open debate over fundamental theological issues. It is not certain that he actually tacked this highly explosive writing on the cathedral door at Wittenberg. What is certain, however, is that the Vatican was never the same after this angry monk rolled his weighty stone in its direction.

The Church decided to enter into a three-year debate with Luther, but this merely stimulated the interest that curious and critical Europeans paid to the stream of speeches and writings that poured from Luther's mouth and hand. When the Pope finally decided to silence this troublesome monk, it was too late. Luther merely burned the Papal Bull (writing) in public and defiantly proceeded to the Reichstag in Worms. There he presented his views on April 18, 1521, to Emperor Charles V and to the leading German nobles, clergy, and bourgeoisie. Luther held firmly to his views and asserted that "as long as I am not contradicted by the Holy Scripture or by clear reasoning, I will recant nothing since it is difficult and dangerous to act against one's conscience."

To protect this renegade with an enormous following in Germany, sympathizers captured him during his journey back to Wittenberg and took him to the Wartburg fortress outside of Eisenach. Under the assumed name of "Junker Jörg," he lived there for a year far away from the furious controversies of the day. In 1522, he completed a German translation of the New Testament. This was not the first German translation of the Bible. More than 170 handwritten ones had appeared in the Middle Ages, and since the invention of the movable type printing press there had been fourteen previous High German (common to southern Germany, Austria, and Switzerland) and three Low German (northern Germany) translations. But Luther, the scholar, was able to penetrate deeply into the Greek and "Vulgata" texts to produce a translation, which, as he himself said, forced the prophets and apostles to speak a comprehensible German. Only such a text could enable the Christian to read and understand the Bible on his own, without the guidance or interpretation of the Church. In 1534, he published his final translations of both the New and Old Testaments, which found their way into enthusiastic hands all over Germany. In this way, Luther's German became the standardized High German that is spoken by the educated in every corner of Germany. Although many dialects continue to be spoken in Germany, Luther gave a fractured land a common language, which is essential for any collection of people who hope to be called a nation.

His call for liberation from the theological confines of Rome unleashed demands for change and other forms of liberation that seriously shook the social structure of Germany. In all of these conflicts, the ultimate visitors were the German princes. Some rebellious Germans found in Luther's words about the "freedom of a Christian man" a divine justification for their goals and actions. Initially, Luther sympathized with peasants' demands and encouraged the lords to take their pleas seriously. But when bands of rebels began to attack fortresses and churches and to dispatch with bloody swiftness those who wielded earthly authority, he became furious and lashed out against those whom he accused of turning Germany into a battlefield.

When it came to "things belonging to Caesar," Luther did not hesitate to decide in favor of order and princely authority. His reaction to this social revolution and its ultimate cruel suppression had serious consequences for Germany. Peasants remained poor, despised, unfree, and without political influence for almost 300 years, until reforms in the wake of the French Revolution finally eliminated the formal chains that had been placed on them. Perhaps more important, Luther's stand left a legacy of freedom in Germany that was interpreted only as inner, purely mental freedom, but not political freedom. Thus, this man who had led the charge against the limits placed on man through Catholic theology actually justified external obedience to the princes and thereby strengthened the hierarchical political order within Germany. This helped to retard the victory of democracy in Germany until the middle of the 20th century. It even allowed some Germans who strongly disapproved of National Socialism after 1933 to remain within a brutal dictatorship, but nevertheless to persuade themselves that they could embark on an "internal emigration."

**LUXEMBURG, ROSA** 1870–1919, Cosmopolitan, charismatic, and articulate Marxist activist for whom nationalism was a gigantic impediment to peace and progress. She was born in the Russian part of Poland and became a German citizen in 1895 by marrying a German worker. A brilliant, independent-minded revolutionary, she participated in the failed 1905 revolution in Russia. Returning to Germany, she joined Karl Liebknecht to found the Spartacus League. Because of her vocal opposition to the German war effort, she was imprisoned for the duration of World War I. But she reentered German politics as soon as the empire fell in November 1918. Although she was damned in the right-wing press as an agent of Moscow, her "Spartacus Program" differed essentially from Lenin's Bolshevik theory in that it advocated a more democratic Communism. She proclaimed that "freedom only for the supporters of the government and for members of a single party" is no freedom at all. Her assertion that "freedom is the freedom of those who think differently" was displayed by dissidents in the former German Democratic Republic (GDR) on January 17, 1988, much to the embarrassment of the ruling Socialist Unity Party of Germany (SED), which had always glorified Luxemburg in its propaganda.

She and Liebknecht were cofounders of the Communist Party of German (KPD) on January 1, 1919. They led the bloody Spartacist uprising that month, in which they were both captured by Free Corps troops and brutally murdered. This act caused the Social Democratic Party of Germany (SPD) government, which had ordered the troops to suppress the uprising, to be severely criticized by parts of the working class and served to deepen the gulf between the SPD and the KPD.

# M

**MACEDONIAN NATIONALISM** Macedonia was settled by Slavic-speaking peoples in the 7th century A.D. Macedonia was ruled by various empires, including Byzantium, Bulgaria, and Serbia, until the 1390s, when it was conquered by the Ottoman Turks. It remained an Ottoman province until the Balkan wars of 1912–1913.

Macedonian nationalism first emerged in the 1860s as a cultural movement asserting the existence of a Macedonian nationality. Led by a small group of intellectuals, Macedonian nationalism faced a number of political and cultural obstacles. Macedonia was among the most contested regions in the Balkans, as well as the last major Ottoman possession in Europe. The Macedonian Slavs possessed a majority in the region, but there were Greek, Albanian, Turkish, and other minorities as well. Macedonian nationalism was therefore confronted politically by numerous obstacles: on the one hand, a Turkish government that opposed all nationalisms as a threat to its empire, and, on the other, by Greek, Bulgarian, and later Serbian claims that the Macedonians were not a nationality. Because the Greek-dominated patriarchate of the Orthodox Church, based in Constantinople, opposed the use of the native language in Macedonia, the Macedonian national movement also had to emancipate itself culturally from Greek control.

Macedonian nationalism became politically organized with the creation of the Internal Macedonian Revolutionary Organization (VMRO), formed in 1894. Its goal was to achieve an autonomous Macedonia by employing revolutionary methods, on the model of the Serbian and Greek revolts of the early 19th century. This autonomous Macedonia might then join a wider Balkan federation. VMRO was challenged, however, by the Bulgarian-supported Supreme Macedonian Committee. The Supreme Committee, whose followers were known as Vrhovists, became an instrument of the Bulgarian government, which hoped to annex Macedonia. By the 1890s the Macedonians became the object of competing propagandas, intended primarily to convince them that they were really Greeks, Bulgars, or Serbs.

The most important undertaking of VMRO was the Ilinden uprising. Beginning on August 2, 1903, the uprising spread to many parts of Macedonia. Although it was crushed over a three-month period by the Ottoman authorities, the scale of the uprising and harsh Ottoman reprisals prompted the Great Powers to intervene. On September 20, 1903, Russia and Austria-Hungary, supported by the other Great Powers, issued the so-called Mürzsteg reforms. The reform program obligated the Ottoman authorities to allow the Great Powers to supervise the Ottoman administration and police in Macedonia.

These reforms were never implemented. After the Ilinden uprising, Macedonian nationalists pinned their hopes on the Young Turks, a reform-minded movement in the Ottoman Empire. The Young Turks pledged to offer the Macedonians religious freedom and other concessions. Their hopes were misplaced. After the 1908 Young Turkish revolution in Constantinople, Macedonia experienced no reform. Macedonian nationalism received its greatest setback, however, during the Balkan wars (1912–1913). Greece, Serbia, and Bulgaria, supported by Montenegro, succeeded in ousting the Ottoman Empire from its last European possessions, and Macedonia was partitioned. The lion's share went to Serbia and Greece, and the smallest portion to Bulgaria.

From the Balkan wars to the end of World War II, Macedonian nationalists had to deal with a tripartite partition of Macedonia, and the fact that none of the partitioning powers recognized a Macedonian nationality. During World War I, the largest part of Macedonia, held by Serbia, was annexed by Bulgaria. After the war, it was returned to the new Kingdom of Serbs, Croats and Slovenes ("Yugoslavia"). VMRO, which had originally struggled for a territorially united and autonomous Macedonia, increasingly became allied to

Bulgaria, since Bulgaria alone of the three partitioning powers aspired to incorporate all of Macedonia. From 1918 to 1934, led first by Todor Alexandrov and then Vanča Mihailov, VMRO operated from Bulgaria as a revolutionary organization employing political terror, directed mainly at the Yugoslav government. In 1934 VMRO was suppressed in Bulgaria by the military, and from then until 1941 VMRO was compromised by its association with the European revisionist states, especially fascist Italy and Hungary.

During World War II, when most of Macedonia was again under Bulgarian occupation, many Macedonians were lured to Tito's Partisan movement, especially since the Yugoslav Communists recognized a Macedonian nationality. In 1945, with the creation of Josip Broz Tito's Communist Yugoslavia, Macedonia became one of the six constituent federal republics. Since 1945 Macedonian identity has been greatly strengthened within Yugoslav Macedonia.

In 1992 Macedonia declared its independence from Yugoslavia, and has since then been an independent state. Macedonian nationalism has achieved its main goal, namely, an independent Macedonian state, but it remains in a precarious position. Although both Bulgaria and Yugoslavia (Serbia-Montenegro) have recognized Macedonia, Macedonia's relations with Greece remain strained, as do relations between Macedonians and the country's large Albanian minority. As long as Macedonians feel that their security remains imperiled by their neighbors, Macedonian nationalism is likely to remain a potent force in the country.

## MACEDONIAN QUESTION, THE

The Macedonian question pertains to the national identity of the people inhabiting the territory of Macedonia. The issue has long been one of the most controversial topics in Balkan politics, of at least equal importance to Bosnia and Kosovo. Its origins—and for that matter, the very definition of "Macedonia" itself—are linked to the proliferation of nationalism in the Balkans during the late 19th century.

From around 1860, Bulgarian nationalists claimed that all regions of the Balkans where "Bulgarian" speakers endorsed the Bulgarian Orthodox Church (also known as the Bulgarian Exarchate) ought to be part of the Bulgarian nation-state. However, in the central Balkans, the mixture of different peoples made it very difficult to clearly demarcate boundaries separating Bulgarians from non-Bulgarians. The creation of the Bulgarian state (1878) provided an opportunity to do so. The San Stefano Treaty included Thrace and Macedonia within the Bulgarian state, but this was drastically re-

vised later the same year by the Berlin Treaty. The longing for the San Stefano Bulgaria became a determining factor in Bulgarian nationalism until at least the mid-20th century.

Post-1878, intense nationalist conflicts occurred in the three counties (vilayets) of the Ottoman Balkans (Monastir, Salonica, Kosovo) among Greeks, Serbs, and Bulgarians. The conflicts centered on the church affiliation of the Orthodox population, with each side trying to win support for their respective national churches. From the 1890s, this conflict assumed violent means: The Internal Macedonian Revolutionary Organization (VMRO) was formed, promoting violence as a means of gaining independence for Ottoman-held Macedonia. VMRO's most well-known act was the ill-fated Ilinden uprising of 1903. In the years after this failed revolt, Greek and Bulgarian bandits battled for the local population's endorsement.

Until the 1912–1913 Balkan wars, the population of the region had included a tapestry of ethnic groups (Vlachs, Greeks, Bulgarians, Serbs, Turks, Cirgasians, Albanians, Pomaci), languages and dialects (Turkish, Bulgarian, Greek, Romanian, Albanian, Serb, and a host of others), and faiths (Catholic, Orthodox of various national churches, and Muslim). The gradual "unmixing" of the peoples took place in the aftermath of World War I, with population exchanges aiming to bring ethnic homogeneity to the region, now divided among Greece, Bulgaria, and the Kingdom of Serbs, Croats, and Slovenes. The most dramatic changes were the departure of the Muslim population from Greek Macedonia and their replacement by Greek Orthodox refugees from Turkey. During the interwar period, there was also strong state intervention by the Greek and Serb authorities to acculturate the Slavic-speaking population into their respective nations. Defeated Bulgaria viewed such attempts as thinly veiled efforts to "denationalize" the Bulgarians of these territories. During World War II, Bulgaria once again occupied large parts of Macedonia and promptly annexed them. Originally met with enthusiasm, the Bulgarian authorities soon discovered that their heavy-handed rule was resented.

By 1943, most of the countryside had fallen into a state of quasi-anarchy, thus greatly facilitating the formation of a Communist guerrilla movement. The movement capitalized on "Macedonian separatism," a viewpoint advocated at the beginning of the century by some VMRO revolutionaries. This move was also consistent with the incipient sense of ethnic difference among Macedonian Slavs, and had already gained popularity among Communist circles during the interwar period. The entire region of Macedonia was soon caught in the flux of the Greek civil war (1944–1949). Greek communists enlisted Macedonian Slavs to their cause and this led to even harsher measures by their right-wing adversaries.

In 1943, the (Slavic) Macedonian Communists issued a declaration of independence for the Yugoslav-held territory of Macedonia. For a brief period after this, Yugoslavs and Bulgarians contemplated forming a broader South Slav federation, which would include the entire geographical Macedonia as a separate republic—that is, the Bulgarian and Greek parts of the territory, in addition to the Yugoslav part. By 1948, the Tito–Stalin rift had ended all such plans. The inhabitants of Bulgarian-held Macedonia (also known as Pirin Macedonia), who had been classified and treated as Macedonians, were once again classified as Bulgarians. In Greece, the victory of the right-wing forces forced the majority of local Macedonian Slavs to flee into Yugoslavia and other Eastern European countries.

After 1945, the Communists greatly promoted nation building in Yugoslav Macedonia, organized as the People's Republic of Macedonia. Through war and forced emigration, as well as state intervention, the majority of the population in Yugoslav Macedonia formed the Macedonian nation. According to the post-1945 state-sponsored perspective, the (Slavic) Macedonians are "indigenous people" victimized by the nationalism of their neighbors. Macedonia (frequently conceived as the entire region and not just the People's Republic) is said to be their homeland. Ever since the late 1950s, this viewpoint has met the consistent opposition of Greece and Bulgaria, for whom such a perspective is a threat to their territorial integrity.

The collapse of Yugoslavia in the early 1990s led to the People's Republic of Macedonia declaring its independence and peacefully disassociating itself from the federation. International recognition was hard won because Greece was opposed to the state's use of the name "Macedonia"—claiming that "Macedonia" belongs to the Greek historical legacy. Additionally, within the new state, relations between the (Slavic) Macedonian majority and the Albanian minority have remained unstable and tense. The ongoing problem of Kosovo deeply affects majority–minority relations in the new state, and the potential for conflict in the region is considered to be a major problem for regional stability.

A plethora of sources on Macedonia is readily available in libraries. Most sources are partisan and reflect the different stages of conflicts over the region. For a general review and further bibliography, see Victor Roudometof, "Nationalism and Identity Politics in the Balkans: Greece and the Macedonian Question," in *Jour-nal of Modern Greek Studies* 14(1996) pp. 253–301; and Victor Roudometof, ed., *The Macedonian Question: Culture, Historiography, Politics* (Boulder, Colo.: East European Monographs, 1999).

**MACHEL, SAMORA** 1933–1986, Nurse, soldier, military strategist, revolutionary politician, and statesman. Machel was a nationalist leader who emerged from a tradition of resistance against Portuguese colonial rule in Mozambique. Machel's grandfather took part in the war against the Portuguese to prevent the imposition of colonial rule. Machel's commitment against colonial oppression was made quite early in his life when he chose to forfeit his exams and leave school rather than undergo a Roman Catholic baptism as Portuguese colonial state policy stipulated for its colonial subjects. The same rebellious stubbornness accounted for his entry into the nursing profession. A fourth-grade education was the highest that an African was allowed to attain after which he had to either enter the Catholic seminary and train to become a priest or join the labor force. Machel refused to accept either and chose to undergo nursing training when the Portuguese administrator in his village was instructed to block his efforts to acquire secondary school education. His nursing training further exposed him to Portugal's inhumane colonial policies—Africans were used as guinea pigs in hospitals for new drugs and certain operations. Machel was attracted to the nationalist ideas of Dr. Eduardo Chivambo Mondlane, who played a major role in the formation of the *Frente de Libertaçao de Moçambique* or FRELIMO, the liberation movement on whose platform the people of Mozambique successfully waged a ten-year war of national liberation against Portuguese colonialism.

Together with Mondlane, whom he succeeded as the leader of FRELIMO a year after he was assassinated in 1969, Machel and others built FRELIMO into a Marxist-Leninist Vanguard Party. Upon independence in 1975 FRELIMO under Machel guided the Mozambican people on the path of socialist reconstruction of their society.

Like other African leaders who led their countries in anticolonial struggles, Machel was Pan-Africanist in his thoughts and anticolonial political involvement. He tied Mozambique's liberation from colonial rule to the liberation of neighboring Zimbabwe and South Africa. Machel became president of Mozambique when Portugal was compelled to hand over power to FRELIMO in 1975. As president, Machel continued to champion the cause of African freedom and unity until his death in 1986 in a mysterious plane crash inside South African territory.

*Samora Machel: A Biography,* by Iain Christie (PANAF Zed Press, 1989) is a good biography of Machel.

## MACHIAVELLI, NICCOLÒ  1469–1527, Italian statesman and man of letters, born in Florence. Machiavelli is best known for his short work *The Prince,* written in 1512 as an advice book for the Medici Dynasty on their restoration to power in his native city. Responding to other classical and contemporary princely advice books, which had argued that rulers should consistently place morality above political expediency, *The Prince* instead advocated the use of cruelty, terror, and treachery in defense of expedient political goals. As such, *The Prince* is to this day viewed as "the Bible of *Realpolitik.*"

Machiavelli's motivation in writing *The Prince,* however, has proven to be one of the most enduring puzzles in the history of political theory. Machiavelli served as diplomat and military adviser for the Florentine Republic from 1498 to 1512, and his other political works, including the *Discourses on the First Ten Books of Titus Livy,* suggest that he preferred popular republican government to autocratic princely rule. It is therefore striking that Machiavelli dedicates *The Prince* to the very Medici family that dissolved the republic (albeit after Florence had proven unable to defend its territories against Spanish attack). Indeed, not only did the Medici restoration lead to Machiavelli's removal from his government post, but also to his imprisonment, torture, and eventual exile (to a small estate outside of the city). These facts have led many to wonder whether *The Prince* might have been written with a secret, conspiratorial, or otherwise "Machiavellian" intent, even though in a letter to his friend Francesco Vettori, Machiavelli suggests that it was not.

Closely related to questions about Machiavelli's motivation in writing *The Prince* are questions about the nature and scope of his patriotic loyalties. It has sometimes been argued that Machiavelli's primary loyalties lie with Italy as a whole, and that he is the first theorist of the national state on a truly modern scale. This view is perhaps most strongly represented in *The Prince*'s concluding chapter, the "Exhortation to liberate Italy from the barbarians," in which Machiavelli argues that Italy's disparate city-states must unite under a single ruler in order to defend themselves against larger and better organized countries (such as Spain and France). Moreover, as Machiavelli argues in *The Discourses,* the mere defense of a nation's borders will prove insufficient in ensuring its freedom. Rather, "Rome became a great city by ruining the cities round about her," overwhelming its neighbors with strength (but then ensuring their continued submission by ruling them justly). There-

fore, although Machiavelli does consider the possibility of a state's less violent "expansion" through clever alliances, it is his account of the great state as an organism, necessarily feeding on weaker states in order to survive, that captured the imagination of subsequent (and particularly 19th-century German) nationalist thinkers, including Fichte, Ranke, and Treitschke. All stripes of nationalist leaders have likewise been influenced by Machiavelli including, most notoriously in the 20th century, Mussolini and Hitler. Mussolini, for his part, wrote an introduction to an edition of *The Prince* and Hitler is believed to have kept a copy of the work at his bedside table.

If this is Machiavelli's undeniable historical legacy, however, a considerably kinder view of the author has recently come to hold sway. Machiavelli's contemporary defenders have argued that his primary loyalties lay not with a unified and expansionist Italy, but with the small and highly cultured (if politically unfortunate) Florentine Republic, whose troubles Machiavelli recounts in his *The Florentine Histories.* These defenders likewise stress Machiavelli's populism, his recognition of the importance of class conflict for political affairs, and his distinction between personal and public morality as important milestones in the history of political theory. Some have gone so far as to prefer Machiavelli's small and vigorous civic republics to the impersonal and individualistic democracies of our own time.

Taking Machiavelli's literary as well as political works into account then, he can at a minimum be cleared from the charge of a clearly articulated racialism or "race-thinking." That said, the author's fascination with war and his romance of the man of action who seeks to "beat and subdue" a world become feminine are likewise constant themes, equally present in his plays *The Mandragola* and *The Clizia* as in his political treatises. While we may thus continue to value Machiavelli for his keen insight and clever prose, his canonical account of nationalism may hold less appeal than do other accounts for those wishing to reinvigorate the doctrine today.

A comprehensive source for Machiavelli's writings is *Machiavelli: The Chief Works and Others, Vols. I–III,* by Allan Gilbert (Durham, N.C.: Duke University Press, 1965). Good introductory essays on *The Prince* and *The Discourses* are found in Quentin Skinner, *The Prince* (Cambridge: Cambridge University Press, 1988); Bernard Crick, *The Discourses* (London: Penguin, 1983); and Max Lerner, *The Prince and The Discourses* (New York: Modern Library, 1950). A good political biography of Machiavelli is J. R. Hale, *Machiavelli and Renaissance Italy* (London: Hutchinson, 1961).

**MALAYSIAN NATIONALISM** Malaya is a former British colony, which achieved independence in 1957, and from 1957 until 1963 it existed as the Federation of Malaya. The Malaysian Federation was formed on September 16, 1963, comprising the Federation of Malaya and three states: Sabah, Sarawak, and Singapore. Singapore left the federation in 1965 due to political and economic disagreements.

The formation of the Malaysian nation and Malaysian nationalism were complicated by the past colonial experience and deep communal differences between the three major ethnic groups of present-day Malaysia: Malays, Chinese and Indians. Malay sultanates, which emerged in peninsular Malaya in the 15th and 16th centuries, actively interacted with Chinese, Siamese, and Indian states that enriched local traditions and customs. By the 15th century the local rulers had embraced Islam and worked toward the creation of centralized states. However, in 1511 one of the most powerful Malay kingdoms, Malacca, was conquered by the Portuguese under Afonso de Albuquerque. In the 18th century, the British Empire slowly but firmly established its control over the territory of present Malaysia. To exploit the local resources, especially in tin mining and rubber, the colonial administration encouraged Chinese and Indian immigration. By the 1940s, the population of West Malaysia (peninsular Malaya) constituted 50 percent Malays, 37 percent Chinese, and 12 percent Indians. This proportion remains almost unchanged to current times.

The Japanese occupation of Malaysia, Sarawak, and North Borneo (present Sabah) induced popular resistance to the occupation, which, after the Japanese defeat in 1945, gave rise to the movement for independence. In this environment, the emerging Malay nationalism was reinforced by the struggle for independence. In 1946, various Malay political groups formed the United Malays National Organization (UMNO), which started pressing the colonial administration for independence. In early 1950s, to overcome the communal differences, the leaders of the three ethnic groups united into the *Barisan National* (National Front). The Front won the first preindependence elections in 1955, and it devised the postindependence constitution in partnership with the British. The constitution has given citizenship to most non-Malays and established the system of special protection for Malays (Bumiputra). Although Malaya achieved its independence peacefully, its troubles with the Malay Communist Party forced a confrontation with Indonesia over eastern Malaysia (Sabah and Sarawak) and communal unrest in 1969. It was believed that the social inequality and poverty among Malays and concentration of economic wealth among Chinese widely contributed to political and social unrest in the country. Facing growing unrest in domestic affairs, the government introduced a security law, which, among other things restricted discussions on sensitive inter-ethnic issues. In 1971, Prime-Minister Tun Abdul Razak introduced the New Economic Policy (NEP), which aimed to reduce poverty and improve the well-being of Malays.

A new era for Malaysian politics started in 1981, when Dr. Mahathir bin Muhammad came to power as prime minister. Dr. Mahathir envisioned formation of *Malay Baru* (New Malays), a better educated, politically and socially active people, strengthened by the moral power of moderate Islamic creed and able to live in peace with other communities. This became a centerpiece of the Malaysian government national idea. Dr. Mahathir, who has remained in power for almost twenty years with the support of *Barisan National,* was able to unite the nation in realization of his technocratic vision Malaysia 2020, putting aside communal and social tensions, although he and his policy were frequently criticized by the opposition for authoritarianism and lack of democracy.

Mahathir bin Muhammad's *The Malay Dilemma* (Singapore: D. Moore for Asia Pacific Press, 1970) gives the best account of the Mahathir's thinking. See also William R. Roff, *The Origins of Malay Nationalism,* 2nd ed. (Kuala Lumpur: Penerbit Universiti Malaya, 1974); Brian Kennedy, *Malaysia, a Multi-Racial Society* (Melbourne: Longman Cheshire, 1982); and Amarjit Kaur and Ian Metcalfe, eds., *The Shaping of Malaysia* (New York: St. Martin's Press, 1999).

**MALCOLM X** 1925–1965, Born Malcolm Little in Omaha, Nebraska, he dropped out of the eighth grade and was given a ten-year prison sentence in 1946 for burglary and larceny. In prison he was introduced to the Lost-Found Nation of Islam (Black Muslims). This changed his life, and he dropped his last name and added an X in order to symbolize his transformation. Paroled in 1952, he joined the Nation of Islam and embraced its ideology that God was about to destroy the white race and that Elijah Muhammad would protect the black race and would found a separate black state. Through their common suffering, black Americans formed a nation of their own, separate and superior to that larger American nation dominated by whites, whom he called "devils." He admitted to taking satisfaction in cases of white suffering.

Malcolm X argued that American blacks should give their loyalty to the black nation and should not seek integration through nonviolent means into white America, as Martin Luther King, Jr., advocated. He despised

King, the civil rights movement, and other black leaders as "mealymouthed." Because of their continuing oppression, blacks had a legitimate right to react violently against racial prejudice. Malcolm X emerged as one of the Nation of Islam's most prominent leaders. He was elevated to national spokesman because of his skill as a provocative, apocalyptic, and fiery speaker, who attracted both black and white audiences.

In 1963 he broke with Elijah Muhammad and quit the Nation of Islam a year later. He created his own organizations, such as Muslim Mosque, Inc. He also drifted away from the narrow African-American conception of Islam as being too restricted. He participated in the annual haj (pilgrimage) to Mecca and journeyed to other Middle Eastern and African countries. He converted to the faith of Islam, changing his name again to El-Hajj Malik El Shabazz. In March 1965, shortly after founding the Organization of Afro-American Unity, he was assassinated by three Black Muslims. One testified a decade later that his murder had been ordered by the Nation of Islam, but this is denied by the Nation itself. His life and black nationalist ideas, espoused by the Black Panther movement, were popularized by his *Autobiography of Malcolm X,* written by Alex Haley in collaboration with Malcolm.

## MALTESE NATIONALISM

Malta is a small but historically and strategically important group of five islands (two of which are uninhabited) in the central Mediterranean Sea 60 miles (96 kilometers) south of Sicily and 180 miles (290 kilometers) north of Libya. For centuries Malta, with its well-sheltered anchorage, has been squarely in the middle of the many struggles to control the Mediterranean Sea and, with that, the traffic between Europe, Africa, and the Middle East. Because of its strategic importance and small size, Malta has always been dependent on exterior powers. This dependence has sharpened the Maltese national identity.

Its people and culture today clearly reflect the influence of the many conquerors who have dominated the islands. Ethnically, the Maltese people are predominantly of Carthaginian and Phoenician origin. The Maltese culture is a mixture of Italian and Arabic traditions. Maltese, which arose from the mixture of Arabic and Sicilian Italian, is the only Semitic language that is written in Latin script. To the stranger it sounds like Arabic. The official language since 1934, Maltese is the most widely used medium of communication. Scholars disagree whether the European or the Arabic component dominates in the Maltese character and nature, but they do agree that the Maltese have a distinct culture and identity of their own.

Until the 16th century the islands were ruled successively by Arabs, who came in 870 A.D. and placed their indelible stamp on the Maltese; by Normans, who displaced the Arabs in 1000 A.D. and who improved Maltese political and legal structures; and later by other European nations. In 1520 Malta came under the control of the Order of the Hospital of St. John of Jerusalem (otherwise known as the Knights Hospitalers or the Maltese Knights), a Roman Catholic religious order. It had been founded in Jerusalem before the Crusades in order to protect Christian pilgrims. Its military mission was to keep the Turks out of the western Mediterranean and to clear the southern Mediterranean of pirates. Their raids on the immense Ottoman Empire so enraged the Turkish sultan that he sent a huge army of 40,000 men and a navy of 200 ships against the heavily fortified islands. The four-month Turkish siege was one of the bloodiest in history, and of 9000 Maltese Knights and soldiers, fewer than 1000 survived unwounded. But their valor, under Grand Master Jean de La Valette, a shrewd military tactician after whom Malta's present capital city was named, forced the Turks to withdraw in 1565. Never again did the Turks attempt to penetrate the western Mediterranean.

Napoleon Bonaparte seized the islands in 1798. Realizing that he would be unable to defend the islands against the British navy, he returned them to the Knights soon thereafter. Not wishing to be subjected again to the Knights' rule, many Maltese rebelled and demanded to be placed under British sovereignty. Britain gladly accepted in 1800. The Treaty of Paris confirmed British sovereignty over Malta in 1814.

Throughout the 19th century, a British governor ruled Malta, whose economy grew almost entirely dependent on the proceeds from British military facilities on the islands. Immediately following World War I the British granted internal autonomy to the Maltese. The experiment failed, and in 1933 Malta reverted to its status of a crown colony. During World War II, this "unsinkable aircraft carrier," as Winston S. Churchill called it, heroically resisted brutal German bombing and refused to surrender even though the islands were frequently cut off from supplies for months at a time. Malta played an extremely significant role in the successful Allied efforts in North Africa, Sicily, and southern Europe. In 1947 the islands were again granted self-government, but a British-appointed governor maintained control over foreign affairs, defense, and currency.

In 1955 Malta's Labour Party won a parliamentary majority and made a radical proposal for full integration of Malta into the United Kingdom. This proposal, which now appears highly surprising in view of the party's later stand on independence, received the support of three-fourths of the voters in a referendum in 1956. However, negotiations to work out such integration broke down two years later. By 1960 the Maltese support for the tie had disappeared. Independence, not integration, became the new goal. This was achieved in 1964 by the Nationalist Party (NP), which had won the parliamentary elections that year.

Malta had difficulty solving its major long-standing economic and foreign policy problem: how to survive economically without the rental fees paid by Britain for use of Maltese defense facilities. In 1971 the strong-willed Labour Party leader, Dom Mintoff, abrogated the Mutual Defense and Assistance Agreement of 1964. After months of difficult negotiations a new seven-year agreement was reached tripling the rental fees Britain was required to pay. He again demanded an increase in 1973. Britain finally decided it could live without Malta's base facilities and withdrew from the island in 1979, after 179 years of military presence there. Mintoff hailed this as "the day of light, freedom day, the day of the new Malta." The economic problems caused by the loss of more than $70 million in revenue were not solved by that freedom. Mintoff's attempts to obtain a quadripartite guarantee of Maltese neutrality and a five-year budgetary subsidy (financial gift with no strings attached) from France, Italy, Algeria, and Libya were rejected. He ridiculed Italy's offer of a loan amounting roughly to $5 million at low interest as "crumbs which no government can accept that wants to be taken seriously." Nor was Britain inclined to help him.

The People's Republic of China gave Malta a modest amount of development assistance after 1971 to construct a dry dock to handle tankers. But that was much too small to solve Malta's problems. Therefore, Mintoff turned to that oil-rich state to the south, whose ruler had shown himself willing to support practically any state or group whose policies were directed against the industrialized West: Libya. Mintoff announced in 1979 that "Europe showed us the cold shoulder, but Libya heartily and spontaneously accepted our suggestions for collaboration." Libya's flamboyant and erratic leader, Muammar Qaddafi, took a 500-man delegation to the ceremony in Malta marking the British withdrawal, and promised the country unlimited aid.

Qaddafi delivered oil and gasoline to Malta almost without charge. The Maltese government was able to derive even greater profit from this gift by imposing a stiff local consumption tax on the petroleum. Libya also invested approximately $150 million in the islands, entered into a defense pact with Malta, and provided helicopters and coastal patrol boats. Qaddafi proudly proclaimed Malta as the "northern outpost of the Arabic world" and even aspired to introduce pure Arabic as Malta's official language. Such pronouncements merely aggravated many Maltese, who from the beginning had misgivings toward this strange marriage of convenience. NP leaders called the ties to Libya an exchange of "one type of colonialism for another."

The marriage was scarcely a year old when a disagreement erupted. Both governments claimed oil rights in the waters between the two states. An angry Mintoff declared Libya "a danger to peace in the Mediterranean" and expelled as "security risks" fifty Libyan military personnel who had been sent to train Maltese helicopter pilots.

Under Mintoff's successor, Fenech Adami, Malta steered a more pro-Western course. In 1981 Malta, which for five years had maintained a consultative arrangement with NATO, received military guarantees from Italy. In exchange, Malta formally declared neutrality and promised not to allow any foreign military bases on its soil. In that same year Malta signed an agreement with the Soviet Union, which pledged to respect Malta's neutrality in return for the right to store up to 300,000 tons of oil on the islands. Malta's differences with Libya were settled in 1984. Both countries agreed to submit their dispute over oil rights in the sea to the International Court of Justice, which rendered a decision satisfactory to both parties. They signed a military cooperation treaty under which Libya would train and supply the Maltese forces and help to protect Malta "in case of threats or acts of aggression." In 1987 the Maltese Constitution was changed in order to entrench both nonalignment and neutrality and to forbid foreign military bases.

In 1986 Mintoff admitted having tipped off Qaddafi minutes before the American bombing raid on Libya, thereby possibly saving the Libyan leader's life. Such "even-handedness" was not shown by the NP government. Malta maintained economic ties with Libya and renegotiated its friendship treaty with it. But Fenech Adami emphasized that he had widened the political distance with Qaddafi and had eliminated the military clauses that had obligated Malta to warn Libya of American air strikes. Fenech Adami's government severed air links with Libya and honored the UN embargo imposed after Libya's complicity in the bombing of a Pan Am plane over Lockerbie appeared obvious.

The Labour Party came back to power in 1996. The new prime minister, Alfred Sant, informed Brussels that he had put Malta's 1990 application for EU membership on hold saying: "The Maltese people voted for a vision of Malta as an open European country which wants its own space." In one of his first acts, Sant formally withdrew Malta from NATO's Partnership for Peace program "because it contradicts our constitutional neutrality. . . . We do not agree that in our case, with the end of the Superpower confrontation, neutrality is no longer relevant." Although Malta allots about 3.5 percent ($10 million) of its budget to the maintenance of its small army and navy, it could never defend itself alone.

After Labour lost power in 1998, the NP government renewed the country's application to the EU, to which it sends two-thirds of its exports and from which it buys three-fourths of its imports. Prime Minister Fenech Adami announced that "Malta is a European country. To us, this will be a homecoming." Nevertheless, it can be expected in the 21st century that Maltese national pride will continue to pull this tiny crossroads nation away from any foreign entanglements that threaten excessively to limit its freedom of action.

## MALTHUS, THOMAS 1766–1834, English economist. His *Essay on the Principles of Population* proposed that human population will naturally grow faster than food production unless significantly checked by large-scale calamities such as wars, famines, or epidemic diseases, or by other universal measures. The inevitable result of this expanding population will be widespread poverty and degradation. Modern advocates of population limits often cite Malthus as the first authority to recognize the threat of global overpopulation.

The predictions of Malthus about population trends were not borne out by the events of the 19th century, since population continued to increase without producing the hardships Malthus envisioned. However, his premise of population tending naturally to exceed available resources influenced Darwin's thinking on evolution, in particular the concept that in a competition of various organisms for limited resources, only the fittest will survive.

The effect of this Malthusian/Darwinian school of thought can be seen in an expansionist view of nationhood; that is, the idea that various nations are in competition for limited resources and therefore a "fit" nation must extend its territory sufficiently to ensure the survival of its own population.

## MANCHURIAN NATIONALISM The term *Manchuria* can have two meanings. As a minority nationality in China it refers to a population of 9,846,776 (1990) spread across Liaoning, Jilin, Heilongjiang, Beijing, and so on. As a geographical term, it refers to Liaoning, Jilin, Heilongjiang, and Jehol, where a large number of Mongols and Han Chinese live. In 1644 the Manchus conquered the whole of China, initiating nearly 300 years of Manchu rule throughout the country. Manchurian nationalism was imagined and created by the invasion of the Eight Power Leagues in the Opium Wars. The ruling Manchus faced both internal Han Chinese rebellions and external warfare. The most influential revolutionary leader, Sun Yatsen, at an earlier stage advocated for the expulsion of the Manchus and restoration of the *zhonghua* (Han Chinese). In the discourse of "race" in modern China, the han regarded themselves as a different "race" from the Manchus, who were supposed to be of barbarous origin.

The fall of the Manchurian Empire in 1911 shattered its dream of an across-nationality central kingdom. The last chance for the Manchurian upper class to recover its past history was the founding of the *Manchukuo*, dramatized and materialized by Japan in 1931. However, the effort was of short duration and ended in 1945. From then on there was no more impressive Manchurian nationalism in China. Actually, Manchurian nationalism has been always a weak, passive movement initiated by internal and external forces. It has to stand in opposition to Western nationalism, Japanese nationalism, Han nationalism, Mongolian nationalism, and the like. In geographical terms, Manchuria has always been a strategic area for nation-states such as Japan and Russia and many wars broke out between the two over this land. Now the Manchus are one of the fifty-six officially recognized "nationalities" in China, though they lost their language and many cultural features.

## MANDELA, NELSON 1918–, First democratically elected president of South Africa. Nelson Mandela is best known for his participation in the African National Congress, the leading national liberation movement organization of the antiapartheid movement in South Africa.

Nelson Mandela was born in 1918 to a royal family in the Transkei region of south Africa. He was the eldest son of a Tembu chief. After running away from home to avoid an arranged marriage, Mandela went to Johannesburg where he studied through correspondence to acquire an arts degree and received a law degree from the University of the Witwatersrand.

Mandela joined the African National Congress (ANC) in 1944. The ANC was formed in 1912 and was the leading organization in the movement against the racially oppressive apartheid government. Its objectives were to achieve full political rights for African people and to establish a nonracial democracy. Mandela was instrumental in the formation of the ANC Youth League in 1946 and placed in charge of volunteers during the Defiance Campaign of the 1950s.

In 1956, Mandela was arrested as one of the 156 political leaders of races arrested on the charges of high treason under the Suppression of Communism Act. The infamous Treason Trial lasted from 1956 to 1960. Mandela headed the defense and succeeded in being acquitted, along with the others, of all charges in 1960. The trial had been successful in destabilizing the movement efforts, however.

In that same year, the ANC and all other liberation organizations were banned. The ANC was forced to operate underground. In 1961, the ANC adopted a strategy of sabotage and armed struggle. Mandela participated in forming the ANC's military wing, Umkhonto We Sizwe ("spear of the nation"). Mandela, along with others, went abroad for military training.

In 1962, after returning from the Addis Ababa conference of the Pan-African Freedom Movement of East and Central Africa, Mandela was arrested on the charge of leaving South Africa without a valid permit and inciting a strike. While serving his five-year sentence, Mandela was charged and made to stand trial for the additional charge of sabotage and conspiracy to overthrow the government. He and nine other men were sentenced to life imprisonment on Robbin Island, a maximum security penal island. In 1982, he was transferred to Cape Town.

Following the escalation of the liberation movement, the bans on the liberation organizations were lifted and Mandela was released from imprisonment in 1990. In 1994, South Africa held its first democratic election. The African National Congress gained the majority in Parliament and Nelson Mandela became president.

His autobiography is *Nelson Mandela: No Easy Walk to Freedom* (1965).

## MANIFEST DESTINY

An ideology advocated by some Americans throughout the nation's history that supports nationalist expansionism, especially in North America.

John L. O'Sullivan first used the phrase in his *United States Magazine and Democratic Review* in 1845 predicting "the fulfillment of our manifest destiny to overspread the continent allotted by Providence. . . . " The concept was quickly incorporated by members of the U.S. Congress into debates regarding territorial issues in 1845 and 1846. Of particular importance were the annexation of Texas, the occupation (with England) of the Oregon Territory, and a war with Mexico (1846–1848).

Prior to the Revolutionary War the British had forbidden settlement west of the Appalachians, a decision enforced by British troops and one of the many issues provoking the fight for independence. After victory over the British in 1783 the Americans sought and obtained an agreement that extended the new nation's borders west to the Mississippi with the exception of Canada (the Treaty of Paris, 1783). Twenty years later the United States nearly doubled the size of its territory with the Louisiana Purchase in which France gave up its control of the western half of the Mississippi River Basin.

By the mid-19th century, U.S. expansionism meant not only war with the Native Americans, who were in most cases unable to offer any successful resistance to the overwhelming military power of the U.S. government, but also war with Mexico. The annexation of Texas was part of the national debate from 1836 when citizens of the Republic of Texas voted in favor of annexation by the United States, a move opposed by both the Jackson and Van Buren administrations. The British supported Texas independence, in part to mitigate U.S. expansion to the west, but Texas was finally annexed in 1846, angering the Mexican government and leading to a dispute about the border.

The idea of manifest destiny was used to justify a U.S. invasion of Mexico, resulting in the capture of Mexico City by Winfield Scott's troops in 1847. In February of the following year, in the Treaty of Guadalupe Hildago, Mexico ceded its claims to Texas and also to land later comprising New Mexico, Utah, Nevada, Arizona, California, and western Colorado. President James K. Polk's military adventures, which were not universally accepted, were widely supported by a sort of missionary zeal summarized in the concept of manifest destiny. Similarly, the idea helped to rally support for expansion into the Oregon Territory, which was a major component of Polk's presidential campaign.

Often supported by references to biblical prophesies and the Christian missionary movements of the 19th and 20th centuries, the concept of manifest destiny was seldom invoked explicitly in the largely secularized political rhetoric at the turn of the 21st century. Its implications for the global role of the United States and its military have persisted as an integral part of American nationalism.

## MANNERHEIM, CARL

1867–1951, Carl Gustaf Emil Mannerheim led Finnish armed forces in three wars, the Civil War of 1918, the Winter War of 1939–1940, and the Continuation War of 1941–1944. Each time the nation's independence was on the line and, therefore, he became a national hero in Finland. Still, he did not consider himself a nationalist, but a cosmopolite and a conservative aristocrat. His politics aimed to secure and save Finnish independence amid the Soviet Union's power politics without particularly emphasizing Finnish nationalism.

Mannerheim was born in 1867 to a Swedish-speaking aristocrat family of nobility on the southwestern coast of Finland. The family had close ties to Sweden, and Mannerheim did not even learn Finnish until he was fifty years old. He chose a military career serving imperial Russia (of which Finland was a part from 1809 to 1917) from 1887 to 1917. He participated as an officer both in the Russo-Japanese War of 1904–1905 and in World War I from 1914 to 1917. Only after the 1917 Bolshevik Revolution did he move back to Finland.

Finland became independent at the end of 1917, fulfilling Mannerheim's dream. In January 1918, a civil war started, and Mannerheim took command of government forces. His army in effect defeated the socialist insurgent forces before the German intervention in May 1918, therefore securing Finnish independence free from foreign influence. After a misjudged attempt to select a Hohenzollern prince for the Finnish throne, Mannerheim served as Finland's first head of state as a regent from December 1918 until the first president was elected in July 1919. Then he resumed his cosmopolitan lifestyle, living mostly in Western Europe. Mannerheim was appointed chairman of the Finnish Defense Council in 1931.

In 1939, as the Soviet Union threatened to invade, Mannerheim was appointed commander-in-chief of the Finnish armed forces. While Mannerheim urged for modest concessions to avoid the invasion, civilian politicians refused to recognize Soviet demands for security. The Winter War of 1939–1940 showed the resiliency of Finnish forces against all odds, and made Mannerheim's reputation as a military genius. In the Continuation War of 1941–1944, Finland fought alongside Germany against the common enemy, the Soviet Union. Mannerheim's personal contacts in Western Europe saved Finland from being considered an Axis country. In 1942, Mannerheim was decorated as the only marshall Finland has ever had. Finland sought peace with the Soviet Union as early as 1943, but German military influence prolonged the war until 1944. Before the end of the war Mannerheim reluctantly accepted the office of president.

Perhaps Mannerheim's greatest achievement was to lead Finland out of the war relatively intact, and to lead the way toward reconciliation with its powerful neighbor, the Soviet Union. His personal character and contacts were a key to his success. His health, however, suffered, due to his advanced age, and he resigned in the spring of 1946. Mannerheim retired in Switzerland, where he died in 1951.

Even if Mannerheim was one of the leading figures in the first decades of Finnish independence, he did not consider himself a nationalist. Speaking Finnish poorly, he still managed to urge moderation in linguistic struggles between Swedish- and Finnish-speaking Finns. His political views were flexible, which helped Finland greatly, especially after World War II. His military career was exceptional, as he served two countries, each for decades, and stayed loyal to both. As a cosmopolitan, he loved the old Russian Empire, but after its disappearance he passionately defended and worked for Finnish independence, for which he is recognized as one of the most beloved national figures in Finland today.

The most important sources available in English are *Memoirs*, translated by Count Eric Lewenhaupt (New York: Dutton, 1954), and *Mannerheim: Marshal of Finland*, by Stig A. F. Jägerskiöld (Minneapolis: University of Minnesota Press, 1986).

## MANZONI, ALESSANDRO

1785–1873, Italian novelist, poet, and dramatist, whose *I promessi sposi* (*The Betrothed*) is often considered the greatest Italian novel; born in Milan, Italy. *The Betrothed* was published in 1827; it was written in the Florentine dialect, and had an immediate patriotic appeal for those interested in the Risorgimento. Manzoni was part of the growing unification movement in Italy, and the language of the novel helped establish the Florentine dialect as the model for standard Italian.

Manzoni's work is pivotal in the so-called *Questione della lingua* (Question of Language), a series of problems and discussions surrounding the formation and use of the Italian language. The Question of Language can be said to have begun with Dante, who often wrote in the Florentine vernacular, instead of Latin, thus creating a new written language. During the Romantic Period, Manzoni became a central figure in the Question of Language, when he chose to write in the spoken Florentine dialect of his day. He wrote various essays considering the problem of the lack of a unified Italian language, but his *The Betrothed*, where he laid down his theory in practice, did more for creating a standard written Italian than any other single text of the Risorgimento. So dedicated was Manzoni to the formation of standard Italian that he published three versions of *The Betrothed* before he was satisfied that its language and syntax were exemplary.

Set in 17th-century rural Lombardy this historical novel tells the story of Lucia and Renzo, two peasants whose attempts to be married are thwarted by the evil and powerful Don Rodrigo. In the end, divine providence wins, and Lucia and Renzo marry. Manzoni's stated purpose for the novel was to represent how divine providence works in the formation of history, and in particular how God's ways are central to the lives of humble peasants. In its day, the novel was thought to be both celebratory of the Catholic Church and blasphemous. That the papal powers in Rome thought the novel was too critical of the Vatican should not be taken to mean that Manzoni was not a devout Catholic. In fact, while he supported national unity, he was opposed to out and out revolution, because of his conservative religious beliefs.

His two tragedies, *Il Conte di Carmagnola* (*The Count of Carmagnola*) (1820) and *Adelchi* (1821), are both remembered for their powerful commentaries on Italian national unity and their anti-Aristotelian stylistic structure. Toward the end of his life, at Cavour's urging, Manzoni became a senator; up until that moment he had stayed out of politics, in an electoral sense. The composer Giuseppe Verdi wrote his *Requiem* (1874) in honor of Manzoni.

*The Betrothed* quickly became a model for Italian novels, and continues to be held up as an exemplary 19th-century novel within the canon of Western literature. Today literary critics, while continuing to praise his writing for its stylistic and historical merit, are quick to point out Manzoni's political leaning vis-à-vis unification. Some critics have attacked Manzoni for his part in linguistically unifying Italy by imposing the northern dialect on all its citizens. For these critics, Italy's nationalist project was built on an imperialist mission that sought to rule over the southern regions. The critics argue further that imposing a northern dialect as the standard language was only one of many affronts to southerners of this nationalist mission.

See also Manzoni's five hymn-poems (*Inni Sacri, Sacred Hymns*). A noteworthy biography is *Alessandro Manzoni* by Enrico Ghidetti.

## MAO ZEDONG 1893–1976,

The worldly known leader of the Chinese Communist Party and one of the founding fathers of the People's Republic of China. Born to a peasant family, Mao associated himself closely with the Chinese peasantry class and eventually turned it into a pivotal force in the Communist movement. He succeeded in organizing a peasant-based revolution to achieve his nationalistic goals of independence and unity. Nevertheless, he failed to build a modern Chinese society that was free from the influence of peasantry utopianism. For the reason, Mao will probably be remembered most as a heroic nation builder and unifier, but not a great modernizer.

Mao grew up in a turbulent era of Chinese history. The most significant event that took place in his youth was the downfall of the Qing Dynasty in 1911 as a result of the nationalist revolution led by Dr. Sun Yatsen. Mao joined the rebellious army for a short period of time, but he soon quit the military and enrolled in a teacher's school in Changsha. Upon his graduation in 1918, he went to Beijing where he worked as a library assistant at Beijing University. It was here that Mao received influence from some of the progressive professors like Li Dazhao, which turned him into a lifelong believer of Marxism. When he returned to Changsha, Mao published the Marxist journal *Xiangjiang Pinglun*, and organized study groups on Marxism and the Russian Revolution. He was one of the twelve participants of a secret meeting in Shanghai in 1921 at which the Chinese Communist Party (CCP) was founded.

The focus of the CCP between 1921 and 1925 was primarily on organizing a labor movement and establishing a united front with the Chinese Nationalist Party (CNP). Mao was a member of the Central Executive Committee of the CCP and an alternate member of the Central Executive Committee of the CNP. From 1926 on, Mao shifted his focus from the labor movement to the peasant movement. He headed Peasant Movement Institutes in Guangzhou and Wuhan. After an investigative study of the peasant movement in Hunan, Mao advocated a workers' alliance with the peasant and considered the peasant to be a pivotal force in Communist revolution in China. In 1927, General Chiang Kaishek broke CNP's alliance with the CCP and purged communists from the nationalist army. In a CCP emergency meeting held in Hankou, Mao supported an armed rebellion against the CNP and suggested that "political power grows out of the barrel of a gun." Mao organized the Autumn Uprising in Hunan, and later joined the remaining forces of Zhu De who organized another failed uprising in Nanchang. They retreated together into mountain areas and started rural-based guerilla warfare in the border region of the Jiangxi and Hunan Provinces. By 1931, Mao had established the Chinese Soviet Republic in Jiangxi, and became president of the provisional central government and political commissioner of the 1st Red Army. Mao's rank within the CCP also rose quickly. He first became vice chairman of the Central Military Committee of the CCP, then in 1933, he was elected a member of the politburo of the CCP. But Mao soon lost his control over military affairs after the CCP moved its headquarters to the Jiangxi Soviet region. The Red Army, now under advice of Li De, a German military adviser sent by Comintern, abandoned Mao's guerilla war strategy. This was quickly proven to be disastrous to the Red Army. By October 1934, the CCP and the Red Army were forced to abandon their Jiangxi Soviet base and took an unprecedented long march toward China's inland. Mao's control over the military was eventually restored at the Zunyi meeting held in the middle of the Long March. From 1935 until his death, Mao never gave up his personal control over the military.

After reaching Yan'an, Mao regrouped with the remaining Red Army forces and sought to form the second united front with the nationalist government to jointly resist Japanese aggression against China. The civil war came to an abrupt end after the Xi'an incident, in which General Chiang Kaishek was kidnapped by two of his generals and agreed to the proposal offered to him by Zhou Enlai, the head of a Communist delegation sent from Yan'an to resolve the crisis. Mao resorted to his guerilla tactics again in Japanese-occupied areas, and quickly extended the Communist-controlled area in northern China. In 1943, Mao was elected chairman of the politburo as well as chairman of the Central Military Committee of the CCP. His ideas were soon canonized as Mao Zedong Thought.

When the war with Japan was over, the CCP and its newly renamed People's Liberation Army took three years to overthrow the increasingly corrupt and unpopular nationalist government, and founded the People's Republic of China in 1949. Mao was elected the first president of the new republic. He promoted land reform and distributed land to millions of landless peasants; he dispatched the Chinese volunteer army to fight with Americans in the Korean conflict; and he also negotiated a friendship treaty with the Soviet Union and invited Soviet experts to help China's economic and military development. However, Mao became increasingly impatient over the progress the new country was making. He believed that his military campaign tactics could be used to accelerate China's economic development. The Great Leap Forward and collectivization movement were launched in 1958, in the hopes of catching up with the industrialized nations and building socialism in a peasant-based society. But Mao failed badly and the entire country suffered three years of economic hardship.

Consequently, Mao stepped back to "the second front," and let Liu Shao-chi and Deng Xiaoping take charge of "the first front."

But Mao's retreat was only temporary. By 1966, Mao again went to the forefront to launch yet another disastrous political campaign, the Cultural Revolution (1966–1976). Mao's motives for waging this massive campaign were complicated. But one of the interpretations was that Mao had increasingly become suspicious of Liu and Deng's policy, and believed they were "capitalist roaders." His obsession with the theory of class struggle led to the construction of the so-called Theory of Continued Revolution under the Proletarian Dictatorship, which focused on the prevention of revisionists from seizing power inside the Communist Party. Liu and Deng were deprived of all powers. The entire bureaucratic structure was paralyzed, and national chaos prevailed.

In Mao's late years, he began to restore public order and amended china's relations with the outside world. He normalized China's relations with the United States, a move that was considered a critical step toward ending China's isolation. He chose Lin Biao, then minister of defense, as his successor. But to his disappointment, Lin plotted to overthrow Mao in 1971. When the coup failed, Lin fled the country and vanished in the Mongolian desert. After this incident, Mao's health declined rapidly, and he died in 1976. Although most of his radical policies have been denounced by his successor Deng Xiaoping, people in China today still show tremendous respect for this extraordinary historical figure. His body is preserved in Mao's Mausoleum in Tiananmen Square in Beijing.

There are many Mao biographies. Mao's doctor Li Zhisui wrote *The Private Life of Chairman Mao: The Memoirs of Mao's Personal Physician* (Random House, 1996). Other biographies include *Mao Zedong: A Bibliography* by Alan Lawrence (Greenwood Publishing Group, 1991), and *Red Star over China* by Edgar Snow (Grove Press, 1973). His writing has been officially compiled into four volumes titled *Selected Works of Mao Tse-tung* (Pergamon Press, 1977).

**MARSHALL PLAN** Europeans paid a heavy price for their inability to join hands and find a common way out of the corner into which they had painted themselves in the 1930s. They experienced Hitler's "New Order," the last futile attempt of a single nation to subordinate by force this diverse continent to the interests of one country. So traumatic was that experience that many victims pondered different forms of unity that would make a repetition of such criminal conquest impossible. Jean

Monnet asserted during World War II that "if the states were reconstructed on a basis of national sovereignty involving, as it would, policies of prestige and economic protection . . . peace will be illusory."

By the time Europeans climbed out of the rubble of World War II, their industrial production stood at only one-third and agriculture at half the 1938 level. International trade and payments had been completely disrupted. U.S. exports to Europe were three times higher than in 1938, and a "dollar gap," which would plague Europe for years, had opened up. During World War I, the primary damage had been done only to battlefields in northern France and Belgium. The air war in World War II had devastated Europe's cities as well. Nearly a fifth of France's houses, two-thirds of its railway stock, and half its livestock had been destroyed. Two million French had been transported to Germany. A fifth of the Dutch were homeless, and much of their valuable reclaimed land was under water.

Not since the Thirty Years War from 1618 to 1648 had the Germans suffered so much destruction and loss of life. Over two million soldiers had been killed, two and a half million had been taken prisoner, more than a million and a half were missing, and at least an equal number had been crippled. Civilian deaths and injury were in the hundreds of thousands, and far more than a million German children had been orphaned. Two-fifths of the buildings in the fifty largest cities had been demolished, and one-fifth of the nation's housing was destroyed. Shocked and hungry Germans without shelter were cramped in the homes of others, in hotels, in makeshift structures, or even in former bomb shelters. Bridges, viaducts, water mains, and power lines were cut. All bridges over the Rhine, Weser, and Main Rivers had been destroyed, and these three key waterways were closed to shipping. Power facilities, even if operable, were often unable to function for lack of coal. Often the only warmth the Germans could get was at warming stations in certain places in the city, where they could go for a few minutes a day. What little food, housing, and work there was also had to serve the flood of refugees who poured in from the Eastern Europe.

The Western allies' assumption that the wartime coalition with the Soviet Union would continue soon proved to be in error. Moscow's treatment of Eastern European nations was not democratic, as the Allies had agreed in the conferences at Yalta and Potsdam in 1945. Talks involving the political and economic future of Germany bogged down. Eyeing a growing Soviet threat to the rest of Europe and fearing that the Soviet Union would take advantage of economic chaos on the continent, American leaders became convinced that U.S. pol-

icy should shed its punitive aspects and shift toward whole-hearted support of Germany's democratic potential. On September 6, 1946, Secretary of State James Byrnes announced a significant change in policy. In Stuttgart's opera house he attempted to quiet Germans' fears by ensuring them that "as long as an occupation force is required in Germany, the army of the United States will be part of that occupation force." A British observer commented on the dramatic effect of this speech: "At the time they were spoken these were bold words, and they came to the millions of Germans who had heard or read them as the first glimmer of dawn after a long, dark night. Their moral impact was incalculable." The Cold War, fear of Soviet power, and American concern that a place be made for Germany in a democratic and peaceful Europe became consistent motives for American encouragement of a unified Europe.

The United States was a recent convert to the cause of European unity. Although there had been proponents during the war, President Roosevelt had not shown any sympathy for it until January 1945. There was fear that any united Europe would be dominated by Germany and that it could possibly be an obstacle to the construction of an open, nondiscriminatory, universalist world, centered around the United Nations, which Secretary of State Cordell Hull and his advisers favored. Hull feared that a unified Europe could "degenerate into a closed commercial bloc" and produce "interregional economic conflicts with dangerous political repercussions." Throughout 1946 the opinion had taken root in the State Department that a common effort by the European peoples would be necessary in order to accomplish the task of rebuilding. In March 1947 the House of Representatives passed a resolution calling for the "creation of a United States of Europe within the framework of the United Nations."

U.S. leaders had hoped that the Soviet Union would agree to an undivided Europe, but the Iron Curtain made this original American vision unrealistic. On March 12, 1947, the U.S. president proclaimed the Truman Doctrine, pledging assistance against the spread of international Communism. American skepticism about achieving anything from further direct negotiations with the Soviets was confirmed when the foreign ministers' conference in Moscow broke down on April 24, 1947, over the question of how to solve the German problem.

So much thinking had already been done in the United States about helping Europe to help itself that the American public was not taken by surprise when Secretary of State George C. Marshall delivered a historic speech at the Harvard University commencement on June 5, 1947. He spoke of the terrible visible destruction in Europe, but this "was probably less serious than the dislocation of the entire fabric of European economy." He proposed European Recovery Program (ERP, better known as the "Marshall Plan"), whose purpose "should be the revival of a working economy in the world so as to permit the emergence of political and social conditions in which free institutions can exist." This was very much in America's own interest: "It is logical that the United States should do whatever it is able to do to assist in the return of normal economic health in the world, without which there can be no political stability and no assured peace." Such generosity could not only help stabilize democracy in Europe and peace in the world, but all trading nations, including the United States, would obviously benefit economically as well.

The scope was to be broad: "Our policy is directed not against any country or doctrine but against hunger, poverty, desperation, and chaos." Thus, the offer was extended also to the Soviet Union and Eastern Europe. It was based on a grand design: "Such assistance . . . must not be on a piecemeal basis as various crises develop. Any assistance that this Government may render in the future should provide a cure rather than a mere palliative." The United States had doled out almost $15 billion in stop-gap aid since the end of the war, but this was not the kind of help that allowed Europeans to plan their own recovery.

Most important of all, although the Americans could provide a spark, the initiative and the responsibility for the recovery had to come from the Europeans themselves. Marshall recognized that the United States was a power in Europe, but it was not a European nation and could never be a European power. It could not lead the move toward European integration, but only encourage and help it. Thus, Marshall said nothing about the form European cooperation should take. The only condition for aid was that European nations had to work together, a crucial point for Congress, which had to approve the funds. The impression in Europe had already taken hold by the summer of 1947 that progress toward a more unified Europe was a key for congressional generosity.

Monnet, who since January 1946 had headed the French Planning Commission, recognized the enormous opportunity that had been offered to Europe: "To tackle the present situation, to face the dangers that threaten us, and to match the American effort, the countries of Western Europe must turn their national efforts into a truly European effort. This will be possible only through a federation of the West." His fellow Europeans jumped at the offer. Meeting in Paris only three weeks after Marshall's speech, representatives of sixteen countries began translating the idea into action.

They declared that "the German economy should be integrated into the economy of Europe in such a way as to contribute to a raising of the general standard of living." They clearly sought to ensure through economic measures that Germany could not become an aggressive enemy again. This was precisely in harmony with U.S. leaders, who were concerned about the economic recovery in the western zones of Germany, for which the Americans were primarily responsible. They did not believe that European economic health could be restored if Germany's economy were permanently shackled. On July 11, 1947, a Joint Chiefs of Staff communiqué stated: "An orderly and prosperous Europe requires the economic contribution of a productive and stable Germany."

The problem was that the rest of Europe was still afraid of Germany. The only way to appease these fears was to create a unified Europe within which opposing interests could be reconciled. It took years for all Europeans to accept this, and it required a great deal of practice, but their leaders were ready in July 1947. In the next few years, West Germans received almost $4 billion in money and supplies through the Marshall Plan. For four years a total of $14 billion ($80 billion in 1990 dollars) in aid flowed to Europe after the U.S. Congress passed the Economic Cooperation Act of 1948.

On April 16, 1948, without the direct participation of the United States, Europeans created the Organization for European Economic Cooperation (OEEC). The basic job of the OEEC was to coordinate the distribution of Marshall Plan money. The State Department was divided over whether it would be good to include the Soviet Union and its new satellites or satellites-to-be in Eastern Europe. The offer had been made to all of them, but Soviet Foreign Minister Vyacheslav Molotov made the debate moot when he rejected it in Paris on July 2, 1947. Sensing that the Marshall Plan and talk of European unity was aimed at undermining the prospects for Communism in Europe and for direct Soviet domination of Eastern Europe, Stalin forbade all Eastern European countries from taking part, even though some had expressed great interest in doing so.

In banding together in the OEEC, Europeans had acknowledged that they were economically dependent on each other and that it was in their joint interest to trade freely, establish a multilateral clearing system, and ultimately create a European Payments Union (EPU), which they did in 1950. They also began to see the positive results of their cooperation: Between 1948 and 1955 trade doubled across Western European borders. Many proponents of European federation, such as Monnet, were disappointed that the OEEC did not develop supranational powers; Britain and the Scandinavian countries were unwilling to relinquish even a morsel of sovereignty. Thus, the OEEC was never more than an instrument for nation-states to serve their own interest. But it gave them much practice in solving important problems together, convinced many doubters that one can work constructively with former enemies, and helped break down the resistance to European integration.

## MARTÍ, JOSÉ   1853–1895, Born in Havana, Martí was a poet and journalist, and a revolutionary and a politician, and the orchestrater of Cuba's war (1895–1898) against Spanish colonialism. For this reason he is best known as the father of Cuba's independence.

Martí was still in school when the first Cuban war of independence, the Ten Years' War, broke out in 1868. In January 1869, aged sixteen, he founded his first newspaper, which he appropriately named *La Patria Libre*. Shortly afterward he was arrested and sentenced to six years of hard labor in a rock quarry. Martí's sentence was commuted to banishment to Spain, where he arrived early in 1871. Martí revisited Cuba, after his first exile, only twice: in 1877 and again from August 1878 to September 1879. During his years in exile he worked as a journalist in Mexico, the United States, and Venezuela, and as a professor in Guatemala.

Martí received recognition throughout the hemisphere, partly as chronicler of life in the United States. He was a privileged observer of the United States during the Gilded Age, and he reported what he saw in his columns for the *Opinión Nacional* of Caracas, *La Nación* of Buenos Aires, and at least twenty other Spanish American newspapers. In 1884 Martí was appointed vice-consul of Uruguay in New York. By this time he had become one of the forerunners of literary modernism in Spanish with the publication of *Ismaelillo* in 1882. In 1889 he published a magazine for children, *Edad de Oro,* written entirely by him, and in 1891 he published his *Versos sencillos,* which marks the ebbing of his poetic career.

Martí spent many of his years in exile organizing the independence of Cuba. He had to hold in check those who favored the autonomy of the island under Spain or who endorsed its annexation to the United States. Martí maintained that in order to avoid these pitfalls, Cuba's struggle for sovereignty would have to be brief and operated with "republican method and spirit." In 1887 he concluded that he would have to assume political leadership if these ends were to be attained. Hence, in 1892

Martí formed the Cuban Revolutionary Party. For more than three years, he worked untiringly until, by early 1895, he was ready to conduct a new and more formidable revolt on the island. At the last minute, however, U.S. authorities seized the boats and the war materials that Martí had secretly procured. Once in Cuba, the generals challenged the principle of civil supremacy so dear to him, and he began to think of returning to the United States in order to cope with the threat of military authoritarianism that he had long feared. He was killed on May 19, 1895.

Martí was a die-hard nationalist; when he worried about expansionists he was thinking not only about Cuba, but of Spanish America as well. He foresaw Spanish America as forming, from the Rio Grande to Patagonia, one single, colossal nation, which he called "our America."

## MARX, KARL   1818–1883, Marx was born in Trier, the son of a German-Jewish bourgeois family that had accepted Christianity. He married a woman of minor nobility. He was forced to flee Germany in 1843 because of the biting social and political criticism that he wrote in his Cologne newspaper, *Rheinische Zeitung.* As a student of classical philosophy in Berlin and Bonn, he had been attracted to the thinking of the Prussian nationalist, Friedrich Hegel, who developed a doctrine called the *dialectic.* This involved the clash of opposites and the development of something entirely new and better. Hegel meant the clash of ideas, but Marx converted this concept of clashing ideas into one of clashing economic forces.

The explosive implications of this theory soon became clear. In his London exile he wrote in 1848 the *Communist Manifesto,* which predicted a violent revolution as a result of which the working (proletarian) class would replace the capitalist overlords who owned the land and factories. This powerful tract ended with the words: "Proletarians of the world, rise up; you have nothing to lose but your chains!" Marx argued that a person's class was far more important than was his nation and that the working classes throughout the world had more in common with each other than with the capitalists in their own lands. Nationalism, he believed, was nothing but a tool concocted by the *bourgeoisie* (the property-owning class) to manipulate, exploit, and control the proletariat in all countries. Wars resulted not from the clash of nations, but from the efforts of the bourgeoisie in various countries to enlarge their profits and secure their sources of raw materials. When the Communist stage is reached, nations would disappear from the world. Such a class rising never came in

England or in Germany. Nevertheless, Marxism became and remains a far more significant intellectual and political doctrine in Europe and the Third World than in the United States.

During the 1848 revolution he returned to Cologne, but he fled back to London in 1849 because he faced treason charges. There he spent the rest of his life. He lived some years as a correspondent of a New York newspaper, but he devoted most of his time to doing research in the British Museum. In 1864, he collaborated in the founding of the International Workingmen's Association, which collapsed in 1876 because of fractious quarrels. His greatest work was *Das Kapital,* the first volume of which was published in 1867, and the final two, thanks to Friedrich Engels, after his death in 1885 and 1895.

**MASARYK, JAN**   1886–1948, Foreign minister of the Republic of Czechoslovakia (1941–1948), and son of the founder and president of the Czechoslovak state, Tomáš Masaryk. Born in Prague, and died in mysterious circumstances during the night of March 9–10, 1948; his body was found in the courtyard of the Ministry of Foreign Affairs in Prague.

Jan was the most lively, talkative, and musically gifted of Tomáš Masaryk's children, but underperformed in intellectual study and took no interest in politics, causing friction between father and son. In 1904 the restless Jan Masaryk sailed to the United States, where he spent ten years traveling and seeking casual employment, while learning to speak English, French, German, and most Slavic languages. He retained a sentimental affection for his homeland and returned shortly prior to the outbreak of World War I. Like members of most national groups residing under the jurisdiction of the Habsburg Dynasty, Masaryk fought in the defeated Austro-Hungarian army.

After the war and the creation of the new Czechoslovakia under the presidency of his father, Masaryk was offered a position within Beneš' new foreign ministry, where his language skills would serve him in good stead. In 1920, he was dispatched to Washington as the chargé d'affaires before moving to London where he worked as counselor of the Czechoslovak legation until 1922. He returned to Prague in 1923 and acted as a link between the diplomatic corps and the government, still headed by his father. After marrying Francis Crane Leatherbee, a union that lasted only five years, Masaryk was appointed as minister to the Court of James in London in 1925, a position he retained until the Munich crisis. In this position Masaryk earned a reputation as

a showman and a playboy, becoming hugely popular in diplomatic circles. Many commentators have argued that Masaryk did much to raise the profile of Czechoslovakia, and he himself claimed to have been successful in making it known that "it [Czechoslovakia] is a country and not a contagious disease."

Although Masaryk did not join in the condemnation of Munich, believing Hitler to be no worse than their other option, Stalin, the Munich crisis, the death of his father, and the abdication of the new President Beneš had a profound effect. Masaryk became interested in politics, not just the niceties of diplomatic life. During World War II, Masaryk transmitted bulletins to occupied areas through the BBC. These broadcasts were simple and direct and proved to be hugely popular, increasing his status and confidence. When, in 1947, the broadcasts were published all copies of the edition were sold in weeks.

After he was appointed minister of foreign affairs of the government-in-exile, Masaryk became more closely involved with the Soviets. His father had taught him that Russia was an imperialist power, a view that Jan held about the Soviets. Masaryk saw the Soviet Union as "a semi-Asian country . . . its state politics being different from the European conception." Despite these views, Masaryk maintained a pledge of loyalty to Beneš, which he had made to his father, despite the president's more sympathetic approach to the Soviets. As such, in 1944 he articulated Beneš' vision of Czechoslovakia as a bridge between East and West, but later clarified this by stating that "bridges get walked on and that would not be convenient for us." The effects of Masaryk's skepticism toward the Soviet Union were duly noted by the Slovak intellectual and politician, Nemec, who asserted that "for these reasons Soviet authorities are taking a tougher line towards us than towards the other nations being liberated."

Toward the end of the war, and afterward, Masaryk was involved in the negotiations with Stalin regarding the future of Czechoslovakia. After an initial lack of success at Yalta, Masaryk secured an agreement for the Communists and non-Communists to share ministerial positions. In the immediate postwar world Masaryk became a leading spokesman for peace, articulating a vision of world politics conducted by disarmed states. However, after recommending that the Czechoslovaks consider accepting the Marshall Plan aid, he was summoned to Moscow for an audience with Stalin. Masaryk later famously commented that "I went to Moscow as a foreign minister of an independent sovereign state, I returned as a lackey of the Soviet government."

When the Communists prevailed in the 1948 elections, Masaryk effectively conceded defeat. Although still head of foreign affairs, he found that the chancelleries of the West were no longer interested in what he had to say. They had, he lamented, given up on Czechoslovakia. Jan Masaryk died three days after the anniversary of his father's death. It is still not known whether he committed suicide or was murdered, though many think that the former is more likely as this weak and ill man posed no threat to anybody.

For an impressive biography of Masaryk, see R. W. B. Lockhart, *Jan Masaryk* (London, 1960), and for Jan's place in the Masaryk dynasty, see Z. Zemun, *The Masaryks: The Making of Czechoslovakia* (London, 1976). On Masaryk in wartime see Z. Zemun and A. Klimek, *The Life of Edvard Beneš 1884–1948* (Oxford, 1997), and on Masaryk and the Communist takeover see J. Korbel, *The Communist Subversion of Czechoslovakia* (New York, 1959).

## MASARYK, THOMÁŠ

1850–1937, Philosopher, pedagogue, publicist, statesman, the founder and first president of the Czechoslovak Republic, born in Hodonin, the Czech Republic (then, the Habsburg Monarchy). Masaryk is considered to be the founder of Czech political realism, a school of thought that transformed the 19th-century romanticized Czech national revival into a pragmatic form of nationalism. He is recognized as the father (*Tatiček*) of the modern Czech state, and the nature of Masaryk's presidency, in which he was the highest moral arbiter, remains an enduring feature of Czech politics.

Masaryk's attitudes about the national revival and politics were initially purely academic. Consequently, determined to voice his opinion on the issues of the time, Masaryk set himself into sharp contrast with the conservative environment of Prague's intellectual community. In 1883, he challenged the authenticity of the Zelenohorsky and Kralovodvorsky manuscripts (*Rukopisy Zelenohorske a Kralovodvorske*), the sacred cornerstones of national continuity. Even though Masaryk's arguments during the so-called "manuscript struggles" turned some of the leading national revivalists against him, the ensuing controversy was instrumental for his entrance into active politics.

In 1891–1893 Masaryk became a representative of the Young Czechs (*Mladočesi*) movement in the Austrian Reichsrat, and he published several works dealing with national and political issues. In 1895 he wrote the seminal "The Czech Question" (*Česka otazka*), as well as the "Our Present Crisis" (*Naše ninejši krize*), a couple of philosophical essays dealing with the lives of Jan Hus and Karel Havliček Borovsky, and in the late 1890s two books, *The Modern Man and Religion* (*Moderni člověk a naboženstvi*) and *The Social Question* (*Otazka socialni.*)

After he became a professor at the Charles' University, in 1899, Masaryk initiated the revision of the "Hilsner Affair," in which a Jew was sentenced for an alleged ritualistic sacrifice of a Czech girl. Consequently, Masaryk became the target of an anti-Semitic campaign. During these turbulent times, Masaryk launched the Czech People's Party (*Česka Strana Lidova*), which in 1905 had been renamed the Czech Progressive Party (*Česka Strana Pokrokova*). In 1907–1914 he represented this party in the Reichsrat.

At the outbreak of the Great War in 1914, Masaryk organized the Czech resistance against the Austro-Hungarian Monarchy, and with Beneš and Štefanik he assembled the Czechoslovak Legions in France. At the same time Masaryk continued to seek the support of France, Great Britain, Italy, Russia, and the United States for an independent Czechoslovak state. In 1918 he was instrumental in the signing of the Pittsburgh Agreement with the Slovak representation in the United States, and of the so-called Washington Declaration, which was a declaration of an independent Czecho-Slovak state. These documents legitimized Masaryk's idea of Czechoslovakism, according to which Czechs and Slovaks would constitute one nation with two, legally equal languages, and formalized the union of the two nations in the newly established state.

Between 1918 and 1920, Masaryk played a crucial role in the drafting of the Czechoslovak Constitution, and in the building of the interwar Czechoslovak democracy. He was elected president four times and left behind a legacy of political consensus and democracy. Despite the efforts of the Communist regime to erase his legacy from the national memory, Masaryk remains an inspiration for Czechs as well as Slovaks. Main streets and squares were renamed after him in most Czech and Slovak cities after the 1989 Velvet Revolution, and his portrait is featured on the Czech currency.

The most significant works by Tomáš G. Masaryk are *Světova revoluce* (*The Making of a State*) New York: Frederick A. Strokes Co., 1937) and *The Meaning of Czech History* (Chapel Hill: University of North Carolina Press, 1973). His most comprehensive bibliography was written by Karel Čapek, *Hovory s Masarykem* (*Discourses with Masaryk*) Prague: Orbis, 1937).

## MASCULINISM AND NATIONALISM

Scholars of masculinity have noted a number of links between manhood and nationhood: similarities in the content of masculinist and nationalist ideologies, a dominance of men and masculinist culture in the governments that administer nationalism, and separate, gendered places for men and women in the nation and the state. Because, by definition, nationalism is political and closely linked to the state and its institutions, such as the military, and because most state institutions have been historically and still remain controlled by men, it is therefore no surprise that the culture and ideology of masculinity go hand in hand with the culture and ideology of nationalism. Masculinity and nationalism articulate well with one another, and the modern form of Western masculinity emerged at about the same time and place as modern nationalism. Contemporary nationalism as a movement and a method for organizing the world's land and peoples began and evolved parallel to modern masculinity in the West during the 20th century. Masculinism can be seen as a centerpiece of all varieties of nationalist movements—fascist, socialist, colonial, imperial, and even anticolonial.

For instance, recent historical studies of the United States argue that contemporary patterns of U.S. middle-class masculinity arose out of a renaissance of manliness in the late 19th and early 20th centuries. A resurgent preoccupation with masculine ideals of physique and behavior around the turn of the century became institutionalized into such organizations and institutions as the modern Olympic movement, which began in 1896; Theodore Roosevelt's "Rough Riders" unit, which fought in the Spanish American War in 1898; a variety of boys' and men's lodges and fraternal organizations, such as the Knights of Columbus and the Improved Order of Red Men, which were established or expanded in the late 19th century; and the Boy Scouts of America, which were founded in 1910 two years after the publication of R. S. S. Baden-Powell's influential *Scouting for Boys*. These organizations embodied U.S. and European male codes of honor, which stressed a number of "manly virtues" described by scholars as "normative" or "hegemonic" masculinity, and which included willpower, honor, courage, discipline, competitiveness, quiet strength, stoicism, sangfroid, persistence, adventurousness, independence, sexual virility tempered with restraint, and dignity, and which reflected masculine ideals such as liberty, equality, and fraternity.

Such catalogs of masculine ideals as the historical and cross-cultural undertakings listed above are "essentialist" definitions of masculinity that stress particular characteristics that are limited by their cultural, historical, and value assumptions, and by their emphasis on ideal types that exclude many men; that is, many (most)

men do not behave according to a "John Wayne" or "Rambo" model of manhood. Nonetheless, whatever the historical or comparative limits of these various definitions and depictions of masculinity, scholars argue that at any time, in any place, there is an identifiable "normative" or "hegemonic" masculinity that sets the standards for male demeanor, thinking, and action. Hegemonic masculinity is more than an "ideal," it is assumptive, widely held, and has the quality of appearing to be "natural." Whether current U.S. hegemonic masculinity is derived from a 19th-century renaissance of manliness and/or is rooted in earlier historical cultural conceptions of manhood, it is certainly identifiable as the dominant form among several racial, sexual, and class-based masculinities in contemporary U.S. society. The same can be said for other countries as well—in Europe, Latin America, Africa, Asia, or the Middle East—and the links between localized varieties of masculinism and nationalism can be found in all of these national settings.

Because of the parallels between masculinism and nationalism, nationalist politics is a major venue for "accomplishing" masculinity for several reasons, all of which tend to maintain the intimate link between masculinism and nationalism. First, the national state is essentially a masculine institution. Feminist scholars point out its hierarchical authority structure, the male domination of decision-making positions, the male superordinate/female subordinate internal division of labor, and the male legal regulation of female rights, labor, and sexuality. Second, the culture of nationalism is constructed to emphasize and resonate with masculine cultural themes. Terms like honor, patriotism, cowardice, bravery, and duty are hard to distinguish as either nationalistic or masculine since they seem so thoroughly tied both to the nation and to manhood. Finally, women occupy a distinct, symbolic role in nationalist culture, discourse, and collective action. This restriction of women to a more "private" sphere of action in nationalist arenas reflects a gender division of nationalism that parallels the gender division of labor in the larger society.

The link between masculinism and nationalism is useful in understanding some events and trends in contemporary politics. In most countries around the world the institutions of government most closely linked to nationalism (the military, defense, foreign affairs) historically have been run by men and often prove resistant to gender integration. For instance, the controversy over the inclusion of women in U.S. military academies, institutions, and in combat roles in the armed services reflects, at least in part, concerns that the presence of women will challenge masculine dominance in these highly valued nationalist institutions. Another feature of contemporary politics that the masculinism/nationalism connection helps to explain is the so-called "gender gap" between men and women in patterns of voting and survey results reflecting a "guns versus butter" gender division. Men tend to be much more likely to support military spending and interventions, whereas women are more likely to support spending and programs that favor domestic issues such as education, support for social programs, and the environment.

Three excellent surveys of contemporary thinking on masculinities are by Robert Connell, *Masculinities* (University of California Press, 1995), George L. Mosse, *The Image of Man: The Creation of Modern Masculinity* (Oxford University Press, 1996), and Anthony Rotundo, *American Manhood: Transformations in Masculinity from the Revolution to the Modern Era* (Basic Books, 1993). For discussions of masculinity and nationalism, see Cynthia Enloe's "Nationalism and Masculinity," in Enloe's *Bananas, Beaches, and Bases: Making Feminist Sense of International Politics* (University of California Press, 1990) and Joane Nagel's "Masculinity and Nationalism," in *Ethnic and Racial Studies* **21** (1998).

**MASS MEDIA** Various definitions of nationalism exist, but they all center on the intensification of feelings about primary allegiance to the national society. Much like other words that end in "ism" (like Communism or capitalism), nationalism implies a set of beliefs, convictions, and a worldview pertaining to the defense and advocacy of the nation contained within a political jurisdiction and "the making of claims in the name, or on behalf, of the nation." It is crucial to point out, however, as Michael Mann so poignantly does, that nationalism, given its political dimensions, "is an ideology which asserts the moral, cultural and political primacy of an ethnic group" over another. This "primacy" has been accomplished to a large extent through the use of the mass media in the latter half of the 20th century. It was the radio that allowed Hitler to mobilize support and articulate to millions the notion of the "primacy" of the Aryan race over the other.

Great technological advances throughout the 20th century have provided a radically different world for the first generation of the new millennium. From the microchip to transportation systems, this century has witnessed such transforming developments that the world will never be the same. It is, however, advances in communication technologies that have had the greatest social and cultural impact. These technologies have facilitated the process of an awareness of shared and common interests and cultural affinities among larger and more diverse groups of people. With the invention of the telegraph in 1844 to the Internet of the 1990s, communication technologies have fundamentally altered the face of nationalism the world over. The creation of the "mass society," first through radio and more particularly through television, allowed the forces of nationalism to expand to encompass larger and more diverse peoples. Today, television reaches out and touches the most remote and underdeveloped corners of the planet. Marshall McLuhan, referring to the communications revolution, wrote of the move toward a "global village." A farmer in India can sit down in his hut after a hard day of work in the rice paddies and watch the evening soap operas, the latest developments on local and national elections, and world headlines. According to B. S. Baviskar, a leading Indian sociologist, the mass media and particularly television has been an instrumental variable in explaining the rise of nationalist sentiments throughout the subcontinent in recent years. "The recent Indo-Pak conflict in the Kargil sector of the Indian state of Jammu and Kashmir brought out the powerful role played by the electronic media in informing and actively involving a large section of the population throughout the country. Unlike earlier wars (of 1947, 1962, 1965, and 1971) when the spread of television was limited . . . this time television channels enabled viewers to see Indians . . . in action . . . and the great sacrifices they made. This coverage generated an unprecedented wave of sympathy and support. . . ."

There are compelling arguments on both sides of this debate. On the one hand, it is argued that mass media have contributed to a lessening of nationalist movements throughout the world. Through an awareness of the history of the "other," empathy grows and it is then easier to identify with people from diverse cultural and ethnic backgrounds. Exposure, in a sense, lessens prejudice and increases understanding and appreciation of the struggles and life circumstances of people from far off lands. The mass media have in large part contributed to a growing sense of global interdependence, not only financially, but also socially, culturally, and politically.

On the other hand, mass media have allowed the sentiments and grievances of the group to be shared instantaneously, which creates nationalist sentimentalities and promotes nationalist movements. As in the case of India, through the images on television, millions became aware of the conflict but also the sacrifices of their fellow Indians, thus creating support and a heightened allegiance to the "nation." In 1962 during the India China war only 22 percent of the Indian population (which remains primarily rural) had any knowledge of the war.

The central question relating mass media to nationalism lies in the problem of nationalism itself. According to Breuilly, "Nationalism is, above and beyond all else, about politics and politics is about power. Power in the modern world is primarily about control of the state. The central question, therefore, should be to relate nationalism to the objective of obtaining and using state power." The renowned author and activist Noam Chomsky speaks to the issue of how states use the media to wield that power. Political leaders also use the media to articulate to millions the nationalist sentiments of their political agendas. Many nation-states have intentionally used the media to create and maintain a nationalist spirit among diverse peoples that have been artificially brought together through state boundaries. Through propaganda in a variety of forms, leaders have persuaded the masses to support their cause. A number of nation-states have instituted official policies to employ national broadcasting to support nationalism. A Canadian prime minister once wrote that "one way of offsetting the appeal of separatism is by investing tremendous amounts of time, energy, and money in nationalism at the federal level. Resources must be diverted into such things as national flags, anthems, education, arts councils, broadcasting corporations, film boards. . . . In short, the whole of the citizenry must be made to feel that it is only within the framework of the federal state that their language, culture, institutions, sacred traditions, and standard of living can be protected from external attack and internal strife." In sum, a central component of nationalism in modern society is the mass media and its use in articulating the ideology and philosophy to the average citizen.

Some bibliographic references include Karl Deutsch's *Nationalism and Social Communication: An Inquiry into the Foundations of Nationalism* (The MIT Press, 1966); Katz and Szecsko's *Mass Media and Social Change* (Sage, 1981); and Jowett and O'Donnell's *Propaganda and Persuasion* (Sage, 1992).

**MAU MAU**   Movement in Kenya of the late 1940s and 1950s, during the period of British colonial rule. Also the name for members of the secret society that fostered the movement. Its intent was initially to bring about new government policies that would improve conditions for Africans in Kenya, and ultimately to end British colonial rule in the country. Jomo Kenyatta, the first president of Kenya, was convicted of being the leader of the Mau Mau and was imprisoned in a remote area of Kenya from 1953 to 1961.

The Mau Mau movement is thought to have evolved out of the Kenya African Union (KAU), a political party composed mainly of Kikuyu and other Kenyan peoples. Mau Mau participants were said to be Kikuyu rebels from impoverished urban areas, though the group became feared for sudden night attacks in rural areas.

After a series of murders of white settlers, the Mau Mau were characterized as African terrorists making war on Europeans, and the British launched a massive campaign to eradicate the movement. Fighting lasted from 1952 until 1956, and although the British won an ostensible military victory, the Mau Mau conflict had set in motion a nationalist wave that could not be checked. Kenya achieved independence seven years later.

Though the term *Mau Mau* became embedded in Western consciousness as a notorious example of violence by blacks against whites, the retaliation against the movement proved to be far more devastating than the movement itself. In fact an official study of the conflict lists 95 Europeans killed, as against more than 11,000 on the rebel side.

**MAZZINI, GIUSEPPE**  1805–1872, Revolutionary Italian republican; founder of Young Italy, a secret revolutionary society (1832); promoter of the Risorgimento, the Italian drive for nationalist unification; born in Genova, Italy.

Described variously as a journalist, professional revolutionary, and statesman, Mazzini is regarded as one of the founders of the modern Italian nation. Mazzini's tireless involvement in political intrigues, many of which were carried out from exile, helped produce the ideological and political conditions that led to the republican reorganization of the kingdoms of Italy into a unified state.

At sixteen, Mazzini, son of the rising European middle class, turned republican activist. Mazzini took a degree in law in 1827, and began representing the poor and publishing articles in progressive journals. His interest in radical politics led him to join a secret revolutionary society, the Carbonari ("charcoal burners"), an offshoot of the anticlerical, antiroyalist Freemasons. Mazzini's involvement with the Carbonari influenced his creation, in 1832, of Giovane Italia ("Young Italy"), another clandestine political organization dedicated to the establishment of a new Italian republic.

Exiled from the Kingdom of Piedmont in 1831 for his revolutionary activities, Mazzini took up residence in Marseilles. From France, Mazzini wrote a widely published and circulated open letter to Charles Albert, the Piedmontese monarch; the letter asked the king to give the Piedmont a constitutional government and to free surrounding kingdoms from Austrian rule. It was in France that Mazzini launched Young Italy. Young

Italy supported democratic political change, but forswore violence; although bourgeois in origin, it held that real democratic reform required the involvement of all classes. Although anticlerical, Young Italy did not reject the existence of God—Mazzini, although critical of organized religion, believed in a divine entity.

Young Italy achieved widespread popularity in its first two years, its membership growing to an estimated 60,000 by 1833. The rapid development of Mazzini's organization, however, did not lead immediately to revolution: An 1833 uprising in Piedmont was put down before it had begun, and led to the executions of a dozen members of Young Italy and an in absentia death sentence for Mazzini. A failed invasion of Savoy a few months later spelled the end of Young Italy as an organization. Mazzini turned to internationalist agitation, helping create Young Europe, Young Switzerland, Young Poland, and Young Germany. In 1837, he settled in London.

In London, Mazzini opened a school and began a newspaper, *Apostolato popolare,* that continued his Italian nationalist project. He founded the People's International League in 1847, and continued to work for revolution across the continent. In 1848, Mazzini returned to Italy to help Milan in its war with Austria, but he soon broke with the Milanese rebels over the issue of Lombard independence. In 1849, he again returned to Italy, this time to Rome, where he joined efforts to expel the Pope. Mazzini was elected "triumvir of the people" in the newly founded Roman state, but the state was soon destroyed by a French army called down by the Pope. Mazzini returned to London, where he established another organization committed to Italian republican unification, the Friends of Italy.

Mazzini returned to Italy to assess the situation under Garibaldi's leadership of the southern part of the country, but he was back in London in 1861 when the Italian republic was officially proclaimed. He participated in the First International, but his religious views made him an anomaly among its more radical participants. He died in Pisa in 1872.

For further reading, see E. E. Y. Hale's *Mazzini and the Secret Societies* and Denis Mack Smith's *Mazzini.*

**MBOYA, THOMAS**   1930–1969, Kenyan labor leader and politician who cofounded the Kenya African National Union in 1960, which helped Kenya achieve its independence in 1963. He was born on August 15, 1930 at Kilima Mbogo near Nairobi to parents of the Luo ethnic group. His parents, who worked on a sisal (rope fiber) plantation, were devout but poor Catholics. They sent him to the local Roman Catholic schools for his early education. After attending mission schools he became involved in the trade union movement and held the key position of general secretary of the Kenya Federation of Labor from 1953 to 1963. As the workers' candidate, Mboya was elected to the Kenya Legislative Council in 1957. He served in the government as minister of labor (1962), justice (1963), and economic planning (1964–1969).

After passing the common entrance examination in 1942 he was admitted to St. Mary's School at Yala about 200 miles from his home in Kilima Mbogo. Coming from a poor background, his parents were unable to pay the required school fees. He was forced to work part time on odd jobs to earn money for the school fees and his upkeep. In 1945 he was admitted to the Holy Ghost College at Mang'u after doing well on the Kenya African preliminary examination which won him an African District Council bursary. After completing the course at Holy Ghost College, he passed his African secondary school examination in 1947. Between 1948 and 1950 he studied at Kabete Sanitary Inspectors' School near Nairobi. With his excellent leadership qualities, he was soon elected student leader, bringing him in direct contact with the colonial school authorities. Conflicts often arose between him and the school authorities.

After completing his studies at the Kabete Sanitary Inspectors' School, he found a job with the Nairobi City Council in 1951 as a sanitary inspector. His energy, courage, and dedication to the African cause in an era of settler colonialism, exploitation, discrimination, and conflict saw him embark on a new mission, that of labor organization. He was soon elected secretary of the African Staff Association, the trade union that represented African workers of the Nairobi City Council. In 1952 he founded the Kenya Local Government Workers' Union and served as its national secretary-general between 1953 and 1957. About the same time he took over the running of the Kenya Federation of Labor following the detention of its leaders soon after the declaration of a state of emergency by colonial authorities. He became director of information and acting treasurer of the Kenya African Union, which later graduated into Kenya African National Union (KANU), the party that has ruled Kenya since independence in 1963.

His dream of further education, which had been stifled by the lack of funding, became a reality in 1955 when he was admitted to Ruskin College, Oxford, after winning a scholarship. From 1955 to 1956 he studied industrial management at Ruskin College. Upon completion of his studies at Oxford, he returned to a turbulent Kenya that was poised for independence. It was an era in which Kenyan nationalism was being expressed overtly. When the colonial authorities lifted the state of emergency in the late 1950s and jailed

African leaders such as Jomo Kenyatta were released from prison, Africans began to overtly organize political parties. Mboya's leadership qualities brought him in direct confrontation with the colonial government. He campaigned vigorously to replace the Lyttleton Constitution with the Lennox-Boyd Constitution, which gave Africans increased participation in the Legislative Council. He traveled to Europe and the United States to lobby for the end of colonial rule. He founded the Nairobi People's Convention Party in 1957 and was elected member of the Legislative Council.

His political and trade union activities were not restricted to Kenya. He embraced Pan-Africanism, which was being championed by African giants such as Kwame Nkrumah. He attended major Pan-Africanist conferences in England and in Ghana. He became a formidable force in his own right on the African scene. He was chosen treasurer of the Pan-African Freedom Movement for East and Central Africa (PAFMECA) and in 1958 he was elected chairman of a committee of the International Confederation of Free Trade Unions (ICFTU). On December 6, 1958, he chaired the first all Africa Peoples Conference (AAPC) in Ghana, a precursor organization to the present-day Organization of African Unity. At the conference, Mboya was elected a member of the AAPC executive council. As testament to his dynamic leadership in the liberation of the continent from the shackles of colonialism, he was awarded an honorary degree of doctor of laws in 1959 by Howard University in Washington, D.C.

While applying his abilities to the fullest on the international scene, he also worked aggressively to advance Kenya's independence. In 1961 he was one of the founding members of the Kenya African National Union (KANU), a party that has ruled Kenya since independence. In 1962 he was appointed minister of labor in the coalition government formed with the opposition Kenya African Democratic Union (KADU). In the pre-independence elections of 1963 he was elected member of Parliament for the Nairobi constituency of Kamukunji and was appointed minister of justice and constitutional affairs. He was elected KANU's secretary-general at the party's national congress in March 1966. He was serving in these and many other capacities when he was assassinated on July 5, 1969, while shopping in Nairobi. His Luo community accused the government of then President Jomo Kenyatta, and by extension his Kikuyu ethnic group, of the murder. This led to a month of street clashes in major towns and cities.

A definitive biography is *Tom Mboya, The Man Kenya Wanted to Forget,* by David Goldsworthy, published by Heinemann in 1982. Another important work on Tom Mboya is *Thomas Joseph Mboya: A Biography* by Edwin Gimode, published by East African Educational Publishers in 1996.

**McCARTHY, JOSEPH R.** 1908–1957, A Republican senator from Wisconsin, McCarthy was the extreme form of the American patriot who saw grave Communist danger to the United States in every corner. Not only were they seen to be infiltrating the U.S. government and its elite associations, but they had seized power in China in 1949, exploded a nuclear bomb in the Soviet Union the same year, and launched an attack on Korea in 1950. America had to resist these things, but it was having difficulty doing so successfully. These were trying times in an America anxious to return to normalcy and prosperity after the Depression and World War II. McCarthy was able to capitalize on many of his countrymen's search for a scapegoat to blame for these adverse developments.

In 1952–1953 McCarthy used his position in the Senate to conduct a slander campaign that reached the point of national hysteria. In this "Red Scare" (a forerunner of which America experienced after the Bolshevik Revolution in 1917–1918), diplomats, scholars, film personalities, and many other Americans were accused of treason, conspiracy, and espionage against the United States. In the absence of hard evidence, McCarthy resorted to innuendo and association to assert people's guilt. So effective was he in whipping up public emotions and paralyzing his victims that most of the nation's elite was afraid for a while to stand up to him. Even Presidents Truman and Eisenhower were afraid to cross swords with him, and they kept the requirements for "loyalty oaths" in place. McCarthy failed to prove the existence of a single Communist agent in the U.S. government. Eventually the Senate censured him for his witch-hunt tactics, but the wreckage of many careers and reputations was left behind.

**MEČÍAR, VLADIMIR** 1942–, Political leader who is to a considerable extent the father of modern Slovak independence. As a young man Mečíar became an official of the Communist youth organization but was expelled for giving a pro-reform speech in 1969, the year after a Soviet-led invasion crushed the Prague Spring movement in Czechoslovakia. He went on to earn a law degree and work as a lawyer for a state bottling plant until 1989. Joining the Public Against Violence (PAV), the umbrella opposition movement in Slovakia that arose during the Velvet Revolution in 1989, he became interior minister in the transitional Slovak republic government through the first half of 1990 and then Slovak republic premier after Czechoslovakia's free June 1990 elections. Though initially critical of more nationalist politicians' calls for greater Slovak autonomy or independence, their success in local elections in November 1990 led Mečíar to embrace much of their positions and rhetoric. Together with indications Mečíar had been a secret police informer during the Communist era, this led PAV leaders to orchestrate Mečíar's ouster from office in April 1991. Accusing his detractors of being stooges of the Czechs, Mečíar founded a new party, the Movement for a Democratic Slovakia (MDS), which quickly became the most popular in Slovakia and finished first in the republic with a third of the vote in Czechoslovakia's June 1992 elections. When Mečíar failed to persuade the new Czech leader, Vaclav Klaus, to accept confederal relations, the two men agreed their respective republics would become independent in 1993.

As prime minister until March 1994 and again from November 1994 to September 1998, Mečíar led his young state into international isolation. His controversial political style blended cronyism in economic policy and in appointments to all levels of state positions, the pursuit of sometimes violent vendettas against political opponents and the independent media, and populist appeals to Slovak nationalism against Hungarians, Czechs, and the West. In perhaps the most dramatic example, Mečíar apparently ordered or encouraged the Slovak secret service to kidnap the son of then-President Michal Kovak in August 1995. Such actions drew pointed criticism from the West, and Slovakia was dropped from the ranks of frontrunners being considered for membership in NATO and the European Union.

Though Mečíar's MDS again finished first in Slovakia's September 1998 elections, his government was replaced by a newly unified grand coalition of opposition political forces. These parties were also able to unite around a joint candidate, former Kosice mayor Robert Schuster, to defeat Mečíar's comeback bid in presidential elections held May 1999.

A good overview of Mečíar's political career is presented in *Slovakia Since Independence: The Struggle for Democracy*, by Minton Goldman (Praeger, 1999).

**MEDIEVAL NATIONALISM**  The medieval mind did not think in terms of the *nation* and *nationalism*. In the writings of St. Augustine (5th century) and St. Thomas Aquinas (13th century), politics was a normative enterprise revolving around doing God's work. In the view of these influential philosophers, earthly kings were agents of God (the "king of kings") and were placed on thrones to serve the interests of the ruled and to elevate their subjects morally from something lower to something higher. Even though there was a wide gap between ideal and actuality, the idea of the unity of all mankind organized to serve goals transcending what later became known as *nations* dominated medieval rhetoric and political writing.

The idea of European unity is more than 2000 years old. Julius Caesar's invasions and conquests of France, southwestern Germany, the Lowlands, and England extended Roman rule beyond southern Europe. During four centuries most of Europe lived within the political, legal, and economic framework of the Roman Empire, which finally collapsed in 476 A.D.

Charlemagne retrieved the banner of universality. In 768 he ascended to the throne of a far-flung Frankish Empire, extending from northwestern Europe south to Rome and from Hungary to northern Spain. He was a leader of extraordinary qualities who spent half his time in the saddle holding his vast territory together. It survived only a few years after his death in 814 and was divided in 817. After bitter and complicated inheritance quarrels, two realms faced each other along roughly the same line as the present border between Germany and France.

The symbolism of European unity was preserved in the eastern Franconian realm, which became the German Empire in 911. In this case, the term *Empire* is misleading because it connotes a centralized unified power. Many heads of local states and independent cities actually ruled. By the 11th century they had collectively become the most powerful in Europe and claimed the title "Roman Empire." In the 13th century this was dignified to "Holy Roman Empire," and in the 15th century "Holy Roman Empire of the German Nation." The reach and power of this multinational empire expanded and contracted, and there was no capital city. The emperor was elected by the highest nobility, and the major and minor nobility met infrequently in an imperial diet, the Reichstag, to which the emperor had to turn if he wanted to conduct a war or increase his revenues.

The emperors focused their attention far beyond what is now the German-speaking world, particularly on Italy. In 962 the Pope crowned the Saxon King Otto I emperor in St. Peter's Cathedral in Rome, a tradition that lasted more than 500 years. This unique privilege, which was bestowed on no other ruler, gave the German Empire a universalistic claim to rule over the entire Western world as the protector of Christianity. This claim never became reality. The emperors' attention became so fixed on Italy that the last Staufen emperor, Friedrich II, tried to rule his enormous realm from Sicily. But within a few years after his death in 1250, the emperors could no longer pretend to control large areas outside Germany. They had lost much of their power and influence within Germany as well. From the 13th century on, the parts of the empire predominated over the whole. After 1438 the imperial crown practically became the sole possession of the Austrian House of Habsburg.

For centuries Europe was fragmented. Only the Roman Catholic Church served as a unifying force, providing one religion, one language (Latin), and a common civilization over most of the continent. It preserved a common body of knowledge and way of looking at the world, and it sought to mediate political disputes. It organized a series of Crusades against the threat of Islam emanating from the Middle East. The first book on European federation, *On the Reconquest of the Holy Land,* published in 1306 by Pierre Dubois, advocated making the French king chairman of a permanent council of princes, which would appoint a supreme court to mediate conflicts in Europe. This book inspired the king of Bohemia, George of Podebrady, to call for European integration to stem the Turkish invasions.

Idealistic plans to replace conflict with cooperation among states resurfaced periodically. Most were inspired by Christian beliefs, such as the Duc de Sully's "Grand Design" for a "most Christian Council" in Europe, proposed during the reign of Henri IV in France. This council was to be supported by a European peace-keeping army. Later, in 1712, the Catholic Abbé de Saint Pierre called on European rulers to establish a European senate in which decisions would be made by majority vote. In 1794, during the aftermath of the French Revolution, German philosopher Immanuel Kant argued in *Perpetual Peace* that the establishment of republican government throughout Europe would create homogeneity and the best balance of peace and stability in the system of states. A few years later, the Englishman Edmund Burke pointed in his *Letters on a Regicide Peace* to the obvious cultural similarities in Europe that could be the basis for political, economic, and cultural integration.

Below the cover and rhetoric of unity, signs appeared that pointed toward a growing sense of shared destiny among people who spoke the same language, had a common culture, and believed that they somehow belonged together. Nations and nationalism were slowly forming.

During the 14th and 15th centuries, French kings waged a "Hundred Years War" to drive the English out of what is now France. In the midst of this struggle, a female savior emerged from the small village of Domremy in Lorraine. At the age of sixteen, Joan of Arc, the daughter of a French shepherd, claimed to have heard the voice of God commanding her to free the besieged city of Orléans and to have the French king crowned in Reims. Having persuaded a French captain to give her a horse and an armed guard, and flying a white flag, she set off to find the king. She told a distrustful Charles VII that she would drive the English out of France and be "the lieutenant of the king of heaven who is king of France." Dressed in a man's armor, and displaying remarkable skill in improving offensive military operations, she liberated Orléans, defeated the enemy forces at Patay and Troyes, and amidst enthusiastic crowds, proceeded to Reims to have the twenty-six-year-old Charles VII crowned on July 17, 1429, in the way traditionally prescribed for French kings. Whenever she addressed the crowds as "Frenchmen," the response indicated that a new nationalism mingled with a divine mission was emerging.

Elsewhere in Europe ideas about man and his state were changing dramatically. In the 14th and 15th centuries northern Italy was the cradle of an intellectual and cultural rebirth known as the *Renaissance.* This reawakening was indirectly stimulated by Venice's refusal to support Constantinople when that city was subjected to a determined Ottoman Turkish attack. When that last remnant of the Roman Empire finally fell in 1453, many highly cultured Greeks emigrated to Italy from Constantinople and gave the Renaissance movement a significant boost. They helped to reawaken Italian interest in the Greek classical authors.

In the depths of the foaming cauldron of bickering Italian city-states a fundamentally new approach to life was born. Man was no longer the *viator mundi* (pilgrim seeking heavenly salvation) of the Middle Ages, concerned with the universal principle of salvation. He became the *Faber mundi* (the creator and master of the world), who shaped his own destiny. Self-assured individualism and rational thought were reflected in the Renaissance conception of the state. Autonomous states were directed by paid public officials according to the guidelines of "reason of state." Carefully calculated business considerations determined politics and administration. The Florentine Niccolò Machiavelli developed the theory of politics that was divorced from religious or other ethical principles. His book, *The Prince,* pointed toward a unified Italian state that was created four centuries later, in 1861.

The end of the 15th century in Spain completed a long struggle to free the Iberian Peninsula of a Moorish presence. Moors from North Africa had begun crossing the Strait of Gibraltar in 711 A.D. Within a very short time they controlled virtually all the Roman cities in the South and East of the peninsula. Spaniards ensconced in strongholds in northwestern Spain hammered away at the Moslem realm in Iberia, which had already been weakened by quarrels and intrigues among the Moslem rulers themselves. Their grip on the peninsula loosened steadily. The military prowess of the newly emerging Kingdom of Castile is symbolized by its hero *El Cid*. Together with the Kingdom of Aragon, which in 1137 had become linked with Catalonia, they slowly but steadily pushed back the Moslems. Moslem rule in most of the peninsula had been broken by the mid-13th century, although a small Moslem kingdom hung on in Granada until 1492. The final defeat of the Moors restored a measure of national homogeneity to Spain. It was a precondition for an increasingly assertive Spanish nation to expand its rule and influence in Europe and to establish a colonial empire abroad.

In 1587, Sir Francis Drake, having already stolen Spanish gold from the New World, raided the port of Cadiz. In reprisal, the next year Spain sent a Great Armada to invade and conquer England. But a "Protestant wind" and English naval tactics carried the day; less than half of the Armada managed to limp back to Spain. England had established itself as a ruler of the seas, a position it would continue to enjoy for almost 400 years. It also collectively savored the euphoria of victory, which could only strengthen the idea of English nationhood. National pride was further boosted by the flowering of English culture during the Elizabethan Age. The brightest blooms were uses of the language that still affect our thought and speech. Although William Shakespeare was the most magnificent of the blossoms, others, such as Spenser, Drayton, Donne, and Marlowe, bloomed in the sunshine. When Elizabeth died unmarried in 1603, James Stuart, King of Scotland, became James I of England and the whole island was united under one monarch.

By the 17th century Europeans had come a long way toward the idea that they belonged to nations and that those cultural entities had a right to their own states to protect and promote their interests.

## MEIJI EMPEROR

1852–1912, The 122nd emperor of Japan, reigned during 1867–1912. He was known for his symbolic role in Meiji Revolution, an era of successful Japanese transition into a modern nation.

Meiji's personal name was Mutsuhito. He succeeded to the throne at the age of fourteen. One year after his enthronement as a powerless monarch, a group of reform-minded *summaries* (warriors) from Satsuma and Choshu overthrew the Tokugawa shogunate government that had controlled the imperial court for more than two centuries, and restored the emperor as the sole legitimate supreme authority. He adopted "Meiji" ("enlightened ruler" in Japanese) as his new reign name, and moved the imperial capital from Kyoto to the modern-day capital city of Tokyo.

Ironically, a full restoration of imperial power was never intended or materialized. The dual system of government was being replaced with a centralized one with Meiji Emperor as the head, but the real power was exercised by a small group of oligarchs from Satsuma and Choshu throughout the Meiji era. Under their auspices, an ambitious modernization program was carried out with a goal of creating "a Rich Country and a Strong Military." Political reform was carried out in 1889 when the Meiji Constitution was promulgated, and a semi-parliamentary system was established. The Constitution was presented as the gift of the emperor, who reserved all sovereignty and the right of amendment. By declaring the emperor to be "sacred and inviolable," it furthered the traditional personality cult of the emperor.

Meiji spent most of his time touring the country and performing his ceremonial duties. But to most Japanese he remained a remote yet revered God. They never heard his voice or had any direct contact with him. He died on July 30, 1912, and was buried in the Momoyama Mausoleum in Fushimi, Kyoto. The Meiji Shrine in Tokyo commemorates him.

A brief biography of Meiji is *Meiji Tenn* by Ki Kimura (Tokyo: Shibundo, 1966).

## MEIR, GOLDA

1898–1978, Israel's first woman prime minister. Born Golda Mabovitch in Kyiv in 1898, as a child, she and her family emigrated to Milwaukee, where she worked as a schoolteacher and became active in the Zionist movement. As a young woman, she served as the Milwaukee chapter leader of Poalei Zion (Workers of Zion), and in 1921 came to Palestine to settle in Kibbutz Merhavya. She moved to Tel Aviv in 1924 and became active in the Histadrut, Israel's national labor union, leading the Women's Labor Council from 1928 to 1934. In the early 1930s she joined Mapai, Ben-Gurion's Zionist labor party, and was promoted to membership in the executive committee of the Histadrut in 1938. During World War II, Meir served on the British War Economic Advisory Council and in 1946 became the acting director of the political bureau of the Jewish Agency for Palestine. In this capacity, she served as the Jewish liaison with the British and developed detailed knowledge of Arab politics.

Disguised as a peasant woman, Meir made several clandestine border-crossings into Jordan in 1947 to meet with King Abdullah, who tried unsuccessfully to persuade the Jews to delay declaring statehood. In 1948 she was a signer of the state of Israel's declaration of independence and an ambassador to the Soviet Union. In 1949, Meir was elected to the first Knesset, serving as the minister of labor until 1956, when she was appointed foreign affairs minister. With Moshe Dayan, she negotiated an arms deal with the French government, but was best known for her commitment to friendly relations with America, and Latin American and African states. Traveling frequently to Africa, she stressed the parallels between the newly independent Israel and African emergence from colonial rule. Her efforts were widely successful, facilitating many exchange programs and cooperation between Israel and Kenya, Tanzania, Burundi, Ethiopia, and Ghana, among other nations.

In 1966, Meir became secretary general of the Mapai Party and, along with Prime Minister Eshkol, negotiated the merger of several factions to create the Labor Party. Following Eshkol's death in 1969, the seventy-one-year-old grandmother became prime minister of Israel. While maintaining the support of moderates within the Labor Party, Meir did not share their views on the possible return of the occupied territories or Palestinian autonomy, and encouraged Jewish settlements in the West Bank, Gaza, and the Golan Heights.

As a prime minister, Meir enjoyed great public support and was admired for her plain-speaking and decisive style, yet her administration was thrown into crisis in the aftermath of the Yom Kippur War. On October 6, 1973, joint Egyptian and Syrian forces attacked Israel. Unprepared, the army suffered considerable casualties and critics charged a failure in intelligence and lax army standards. Although the Israeli army eventually prevailed, Meir and Defense Minister Moshe Dayan were criticized for Israel's lack of preparedness and the prime minister's reported unwillingness to order a preemptive strike. As a special investigation was started over the allegations (it would later clear Meir from direct charges of negligence), calls for Meir's resignation only increased, as did tensions within the party. In April 1947 Golda Meir resigned from office, making way for her successor, Yitzhak Rabin. She died in Jerusalem on December 8, 1978.

**MERCANTILISM** Mercantilism is a school of thought emphasizing the importance of the economic and political interests of the nation as opposed to the economic and political interests of the individual (liberalism). In this regard, *mercantilism* is often used interchangeably with the term *economic nationalism*. Mercantilism can be used to describe a period of history, a philosophical outlook about the state's role in the economy, and the state's use of a number of economic and political instruments to promote the nation's industries and to defend the nation from outside influence, threat, or attack. In all of these three uses, the emphasis of mercantilists is on the promotion of the security, power, and interests of the nation as a whole.

Mercantilism dominated the philosophical outlook of nations during the period from the 16th through the mid-20th century—a period corresponding to the rise of nation-states as the leading actors in the international system. Competition for political and economic power dominated in particular the European landscape. Due to this sense of competition, nation-states were primarily concerned with political, economic, and military development through the accumulation of trade surpluses, the colonization of most of Africa, Asia, and the Middle East, and the amassing of gold and silver. Such policies enhanced the ability of nation-states to develop powerful military capabilities to further the process of state development and to provide security. Not surprisingly, mercantilist philosophies sharpened the nature of competition between nations, especially between Germany, Great Britain, and France, leading to repeated conflict that culminated in World War I.

Mercantilists, best represented in the older historical school and writings of Alexander Hamilton (*Report on Manufacturers*) and the German Friedrich List (*The National System of Political Economy*), emphasize the importance of wealth creation and how wealth creation enhances the power of the nation-state. Economic wealth and power can thus enhance the independence and security of the nation-state. The main objective of mercantilism was thus strategic and material well-being. Nations either ended up being independent or dependent based on their ability to make things for themselves. Ultimately, a nation was worth as much as it could make, not as much as it could buy. Moreover, a zero-sum mentality prevailed—some nations would succeed (and survive through the accumulation of wealth and power), others would fail (and be dominated by great powers).

All of these goals—wealth creation, independence, security, and power—are secured through an active and direct role of the state in promoting the nation's economic interests. In other words, the state must be concerned with both the process and the result of the economic affairs of the nation. Such a role involved, among others, policies designed to protect domestic industries from foreign competition, policies intended to promote domestic industry for export, and policies calculated to enhance the productive and "mercantile" interests of the nation. The final measure of an economic system was what it did for producers—manufacturers and other producer interests—rather than the immediate effect on consumers.

Following World War II, leading U.S. and British officials sought to limit the ability of nation-states to pursue mercantilist policies. Mercantilist policies were blamed in part for the onset of the Great Depression and the downward spiral of trade protectionism and currency devaluations that led to the financial panics and bank closures of the early 1930s. The more malevolent form of mercantilism—as espoused by Nazi Germany and by imperial Japan—was thought to have further led to economic warfare and expansionary economic and military policies. As a result and under U.S. leadership, liberalism—with its emphasis on the free market, the individual, and a minimal role for the state in the economy— emerged as the dominant economic philosophy of the latter half of the 20th century. Liberal global norms and regimes such as those codified in the rules of the General Agreement on Tariffs and Trade (GATT) and the International Monetary Fund (IMF) prevailed under U.S. global economic and political leadership.

Nevertheless, states still sought to minimize their dependence on others while fostering conditions that made others dependent on them. Mercantilism still held sway in the minds of some leading members of the international community. Japan, France, and other developing nations in East Asia (most notably South Korea, Taiwan, and China) and Latin America (Mexico, Brazil) pursued various forms of mercantilism. These nations continued to employ a diversity of instruments to limit their dependency on other nations while promoting favorable trade balances and adding to their power capabilities. While tariffs and currency controls slowly disappeared under pressure from the United States and the global market, nations employed neo-mercantilist strategies such as quotas, voluntary export restraints, export subsidies, nontariff barriers (NTBs), investment promotions, and other forms of special, targeted industry investments. The relative success of many of these nations in promoting rapid economic and political development in the post-World War II period suggested an alternative "mercantilist" model of development, as compared to the free market liberal approach.

Even in the United States in the 1980s and 1990s, occasional economic downturns and a growing sense of competition from abroad led some to argue for a return to more direct forms of state involvement. Neo-mercantilist views could be found in the writings of U.S. public officials such as Ross Perot and Pat Buchanan (*The Great Betrayal*), academics like Lester Thurow (*Head to Head*), and the journalist James Fallows (*Looking at the Sun*). Their influence found its way into some of the policies of the United States—from the development of strategic trade practices and defensive forms of mercantilism as found in a variety of trade legislation (the Omnibus Trade Act of 1988, for example).

In the age of globalization and further global movement toward liberalism, mercantilists argue that states are still the final source of political authority (sovereignty). As long as this basic principle holds true and as long as the effects of the economy and the markets on society are still strongly felt by people and politicians, states will likely still intervene in the economy so as to create the means to generate future wealth and to secure power. Mercantilism will therefore continue to influence policy makers and the international system as some nation-states resist the onset of global commerce, communication, and technology.

**MERI, LENNART** 1929–, The only Estonian president in the 1990s, Meri is the son of a prewar diplomat. He and his family had been deported to Siberia from 1941 to 1946, an experience that dissuaded him from ever joining the Soviet Communist Party. He is a multilingual specialist in Finno-Ugric languages and Baltic prehistory. He made many films and wrote a number of books that have been translated into a dozen languages. He became Estonian foreign minister in 1990 and ambassador to Finland in 1992. He was sworn in as president on October 6, 1992, and was reelected in 1996. His prestige is so great that the office of the presidency gained a level of importance and authority that the drafters of the Estonian constitution had not intended.

Although he is an extremely soft-spoken and dignified man, he is unusually blunt when speaking to international leaders about the dangers of another security vacuum in the Baltic states as was the case in the 1930s. He does not hesitate to lecture his listeners about the precarious nature of Baltic security following independence in 1990 and about the absolute necessity that Estonia become a member of the premier Western organizations—the European Union and NATO. He is equally frank when speaking his mind to Russians. He once said in a gathering of Russian dignitaries: "I hate Russia." After a pause and universal gasps from his listeners, he continued: "The Russia of Lenin. I love the Russia of Pushkin," Russia's most beloved poet.

**MESSIANIC NATIONALISM** Millenarianism connects religion and politics. Operating in nations or in strata completely dominated by religious beliefs, both messianic and national aspirations together organize its political message in the familiar and powerful language and images of traditional values, reemploying and invigorating its age-old symbols. This political phenomenon of nativism or revivalism is called *messianic nationalism*.

The revolutionary nature of messianic nationalism makes it a very powerful agent of social and national change. It demands a fundamental transformation and not just for improvement and reform. The radical version of messianic nationalism inflames followers to active anticipation of the advent and even to push revolt or warfare. Their struggle is presented as a final cosmic tragedy of their identity as nation. Every miniature achievement is viewed as proof of invincibility and as a promise of future victories. On some level it is possible to consider messianic nationalism to be an integrative energy. Adherents are ensured of being in on the history of the nation. The movement fosters a new national collective identity and stimulates a feeling of belonging and a sense of reason; the undoubted idea of working on the winning side.

The conclusion of any messianic nationalism depends on the historical process, on the form of society, and on the nature of the leadership. Every contemporary revolutionary movement against colonialism and imperialism had cultured part of this ideology. It combines diverse components, which are seemingly mutually exclusive: It is historical as well as mythical; it is future oriented as well as tradition oriented.

## METTERNICH, COUNT

1773–1859, Austrian foreign minister, 1809–1848, and house, court, and state chancellor, 1821–1848. Klemens Metternich was born into high German nobility, and in 1801 joined the Habsburg diplomatic corps. After spending time in Paris as an Austrian legation, he was appointed foreign minister. Throughout his political career his foreign and domestic policies were driven by an unswerving aversion to revolutionary, nationalist, or liberalist movements and by a desire to preserve monarchical and aristocratic rule.

Between 1809 and 1815 his main achievement was the preservation of a weakened empire and the securing of a peace settlement at Vienna that actually enhanced the status of the Habsburgs, this despite forming an alliance with Napoleonic France in 1810, a decision that was reversed in 1812 when it became clear to Metternich that France would lose. Metternich is often described as the architect of the post-1815 European states system. Realizing that Austria was not strong enough to police the new order itself, he devised the Quadruple Alliance of great powers and the so-called "congress system" to facilitate the management of the new system. In 1820, the alliance intervened to suppress uprisings in Italy and restore the absolutist monarch, but in doing so was rebuked by the more liberal minded Britain, sounding the death knell for the system. After 1822, Metternich did not attend any more congresses.

Metternich viewed the retention of Habsburg control over Germany as essential and in 1815 was successful in securing the establishment of thirty-nine statelets in Germany, over which Austria could assert its hegemony. However, these statelets were restive and liberal nationalist movements became more widespread. In response, Metternich issued the Karlsbad decree (1819) and infamous "Six Acts" (1832), which gave him sweeping powers to intimidate and persecute agitators.

The decline of Metternich's international system began in 1830, when a revolution in France sparked similar revolts in Germany and Italy. Although the Austrians successfully suppressed the uprisings in Germany and Italy, Metternich wanted to invade France and defeat the insurrectionists. However, his military leaders informed him that the empire did not have the military capacity to launch such an assault. Disheartened, Metternich described this information as the "beginning of the end for the old Europe."

In his domestic policy, Metternich did everything he could to disrupt nationalists and liberals. He did everything in his power to thwart Magyar and Italian nationalism in particular, and was largely successful in engineering divisions within their ranks through the extensive use of *agents provocateurs*. Many argue that Metternich established a police state in Austria. A large network of spies and control of printing presses and the postal system meant that the authorities were quick to respond to the existence of any subversive movement, and they enjoyed wide powers of action. However, a series of bad harvests and the nationalist and liberalist tensions that had developed during this period combined to produce revolution in Vienna in 1848. Thousands took to the street demanding the removal of Metternich, who they saw as synonymous with the government. The situation worsened when guardsmen fired into a crowd, and support for Metternich suddenly eroded. Faced with chaos and a shortage of policemen, the imperial family withdrew its support from Metternich, forcing him to resign.

Metternich withdrew from public life, and traveled to England where he began theorizing about socioeconomic problems and the eternal wisdom of his own principles. He later returned to Vienna, and shortly before his death was again looked on by the monarchy as a source of knowledge and advice.

On Metternich, see A. Herman, *Metternich* (1932, London); N. Pelling, *The Habsburg Empire 1815–1918* (London, 1996); and A. Sked, *The Decline & Fall of the Habsburg Monarchy* (London, 1989).

## MEXICAN NATIONALISM

Between 1910 and 1940 the Mexican Revolution destroyed the sources of power of the traditional Porfirian society and created the bases of a new social order, but in 1940 the revolution reached its Thermidor. Since then, Mexico's rulers have worked to perfect their technique of simultaneously satisfying mass aspirations and economic growth. The goal of reconciling the demands of social justice with economic expansion is thrashed out in a well-organized political party that has a discreet leftist philosophy toward social justice and encourages private enterprise draped in economic nationalism. So far this amalgamation has been Mexico's dominant type of nationalist expression since 1940.

There is not, however, a complete consensus on nationalism in Mexico today. The dominant nationalism in Mexico has been introverted, progressive, and restrained.

The political conflicts between two major political groups, the conservatives and the liberals, agitated the Mexican scene during the 19th century and were only interrupted by abrasive clashes with foreign powers.

Two of these clashes gave particular impetus to the ever-growing self-identity of Mexico. One, the Mexican-American War, and the other, the short-lived domination of the country by the French puppet Maximilian, turned the federalist leader who successfully spearheaded the Mexican resistance into a national symbol. This leader, Benito Juárez, became the symbol not only of resistance to foreign domination but of economic and social reform, as well. Many of the values that Juárez supported were, for the most part, betrayed under the subsequent dictatorship of Porfirio Díaz.

During Díaz rule, over half of Mexico's oil and nearly three-quarters of her mineral wealth fell into American hands alone. In 1910, as estimated by the National Financiera, Americans controlled nearly half of the entire net worth of the Mexican economy. Francisco Madero's opposition to Díaz began slowly and on the local level. He attempted to win elections in his home of San Pedro de Las Colonias, and, as early as 1904, he formed a political club. He also attempted to diffuse his moderate political ideas through two newspapers. Quickly he learned that Díaz could mobilize too much force against him, so he decided that the best way to overcome this opposition was to organize his protest movement throughout the country.

A convention was called in April 1910, at which the clubs were welded into the Partido Nacionalista Antireeleccionista, with Madero as its presidential candidate. Madero's movement was primarily based on the widely held liberal principles of correct political behavior, the traditional anticlerical bias of reformers, and the support of the commercial middle-class mestizos who resented the foreign economic domination of Mexico.

In 1911 the aging Díaz was ousted and Madero became president. What chances he might have had to mount reform were cut short by his murder in February 1913.

But the revolution continued. The rural workers were promised land reform and the mestizo mine and factory laborers were promised social and economic legislation. With this sudden broadening of its goals, the revolution became a popular irresistible force with Emiliano Zapata and Pancho Villa as leaders.

The benchmark of this renovating nationalist drive was the Constitution of 1917, which soon demonstrated just how national the revolution was. The Constitution was a substantive document of Mexico's nationalist ideology. Article 123 in the Constitution of 1917 encouraged the growth of the emergent labor movement. Shortly after 1917, the idea of forming a national labor organization was drawn up and named the Regional Confederation of Mexican Labor (CROM). Obviously the nationalist ideology as expressed in the Constitution drew popular support. This change signified the growth of nationalism among the workers, since anarcho-syndicalism was antinational. Also, more specifically, it signified the increasing growth of populist nationalism.

In March 1929, the National Revolutionary Party was created. Mexico's new revolutionary ruling class took its first step toward establishing internal stability and regularity by conciliating the social forces that had shown the greatest capability for organized violence. These groups had been the military, labor, and peasants. The interests they represented were given group or "sector" representation in the new national party; Mexico had started the formal organization of its popular and renovating nationalist movement.

When Lázaro Cárdenas was elected president the government again became exceedingly active in reform. Cárdenas had absorbed completely the nationalist spirit of the revolution. His nationalist program was, as he said, "not to Indianize Mexico, but to Mexicanize the Indian." He accomplished this Mexicanization by distributing land. The distribution under Cárdenas, coupled with that under the earlier leaders, meant the end of the hacienda system as the dominant economic and political institution of the country. His rule marked the high point of the agrarian emphasis of the Mexican revolution and the final destruction of the semifeudal and semislave economic system of the hacienda. In July 1935, Cárdenas issued a decree, which organized the members of the "ejidos" (communal farms in Mexico) into a national union. This organization was incorporated into the PNR under the name of the National

Peasant Confederation as the peasant sector. It was kept separate from the labor sector and represented only the rural base of the nationalist party and movement.

Most of these attacks on Cárdenas and the revolution had two chief features: defense of the Church and defense of private property. The seriousness of the attack was lessened, however, because the expropriation of the foreign oil companies identified Cárdenas with the kind of economic nationalism that had the widest appeal in Mexico.

By 1940, Mexico's complex nationalist movement had as its mass base two nationally organized groups of workers, one rural and the other urban. Both groups were officially incorporated into the movement. The ideology that sustained the movement during these years was completely nationalistic. It preached an independent nation based on a constructed image of Mexican society, which, while it drew on the past, demanded a new internal identity based on popular sovereignty, social equality, and economic justice.

## MIHAJLOVIĆ, DRAGOLJUB

1893–1946, Yugoslav officer and commander of the Serb Royalist *Četnik* forces in World War II. Mihajlović was born into a middle-class Serb family with strong ties to the Serbian state, bureaucracy, and military. Mihajlović pursued a career in the military, attending the Serbian Military Academy and fighting in the Balkan wars of 1912–1913 and in World War I. He was commissioned as a first lieutenant in 1913 and received military decorations in the latter war. After World War I, Mihajlović returned to the Serbian Military Academy. In 1926, he was assigned to the general staff. In the following years he became a commander of the Royal Guards. From June 1935 to April 1936, he served as Yugoslav military attaché in Sofia. During this time, he was promoted to colonel. Mihajlović was censured in 1939 for proposing a reorganization of the Yugoslav military along national lines. However, Mihajlović continued to advance through several leading positions in the Yugoslav military until the German attack on Yugoslavia in 1941. According to Jozo Tomasevich, Mihajlović developed an interest in guerrilla warfare in the years preceding the war.

Mihajlović was posted to Mostar in March 1941 and sympathized with the anti-German coup of March 27, 1941. Mihajlović planned to organize an uprising against German occupation by royalist *Četnik* (derived from *četa*, armed band) forces in order to restore a royalist and Greater Serbian state. The main ideologues of the *Četnik* forces were Dragiša Vasić, Stevan Moljević, and Mladen Žujović. However, Mihajlović did not seek a direct confrontation with German forces, and several other, unrelated uprisings threw his plans into temporary disarray. Nonetheless, by autumn 1941, Mihajlović emerged as the leader of the *Četnik* movement and was promoted to general by the Yugoslav government-in-exile. In December 1941, Mihajlović received an additional promotion to war minister. Although Mihajlović initially cooperated with Tito's partisans, the two groups fell out in November 1941. This led to the first armed conflict between the two groups. At the same time, Mihajlović sought, but failed to achieve, an antipartisan pact with the German forces. During the course of 1942 and 1943, *Četnik* forces led by Mihajlović reached tacit agreements on coexistence with Italian, Croatian, and German forces. Mihajlović's forces were accused of and undeniably perpetrated atrocities against Muslim and Croat populations. In the course of the war, personal rivalries emerged within the *Četnik* forces, weakening Mihajlović's command. Although the *Četnik* forces stepped up their resistance activities in 1943, the disappointed British government formally shifted their support from Mihajlović to Tito in December 1943. In May 1944, the Yugoslav government-in-exile abandoned its support for Mihajlović. After a failed offensive that ended in October 1944, Mihajlović and the remnants of the *Četnik* forces withdrew to Bosnia-Herzegovina. Mihajlović did not return to Serbia until April 1945, at which time he shifted to entirely anti-Communist resistance. After nearly a year of chaotic guerrilla fighting, the security forces of the Communist Yugoslav government captured Mihajlović in March 1946. He was tried before a "people's court" and executed in July 1946.

## MILL, JOHN STUART

1806–1873, Mill was born in London the eldest of six children of the utilitarian philosopher and political economist James Mill (1773–1836). He was home schooled in a way that can either be admired or rejected: He was taught Greek at age three, Latin at eight, and read six Platonic dialogues before reaching the age of ten. Logic and chemistry came before age twelve. German and French followed. It should not be surprising that he suffered a long-lasting nervous breakdown in 1826.

His father provided the young boy with such a rigorous education to further James's philosophy that the worth or value of a thing is determined exclusively by its utility and that the purpose of all human actions should be to bring about the greatest happiness or good for the greatest number. Son John worked in the India House, served in the House of Commons for the Liberal Party, and devoted his time and energy to causes like universal male suffrage, parliamentary reform, feminism, and birth control.

He wrote important works, such as the essay "On Liberty." In this work he presented a utilitarian argument for freedom. For example, free speech is useful because it prompts us to examine our beliefs and pit them against opposing beliefs. The result is that we understand our own convictions more completely, and they mean more for us because they do not decay into mere dogma and ritual. The same applies to national ideals and nationalism. If we are intolerant narrow-minded jingoists who refuse to listen to or grapple with criticism against our nation or our own patriotic sentiments and instincts, then we will not fully understand our own patriotism. Over time it will become hollow and irrelevant to our lives. We will cease understanding why we love our nation and why we should sacrifice for it.

John Stuart Mill was always deeply concerned with national character. He intensely disliked what he saw as a money-grubbing materialistic quality in the American and English cultures. His disdain extended to most conservatives in his day. He argued that the national sentiments of a people should rest on strong authority and noble ideas.

## MILOŠEVIĆ, SLOBODAN

1941–, President of Serbia, 1989–1997, president of the Federal Republic of Yugoslavia (Serbia and Montenegro), 1997–. Milošević's parents were Montenegrins, both of whom committed suicide. Milošević received a law degree from the University of Belgrade. Thereafter Milošević worked for a state gas company and then a Belgrade bank, Beobanka. He became the president of both. The then president of the Serbian League of Communists (*Savez Komunista Srbije,* or SKS), Ivan Stambolić, picked Milošević as his protégé. With Stambolić's assistance, Milošević became the head of the SKS Central Committee in 1986. In April 1987, the SKS dispatched Milošević to Kosovo to diffuse tensions there between Serbs and Albanians. While there, Milošević was impressed by the rhetoric of the Kosovo Serbs, and he issued a televised oral statement that no one would be allowed to beat the Kosovo Serbs. Most observers of Yugoslavia regard this as a turning point in Milošević's career, because this remark catapulted him to political fame. A public endorsement of Milošević by Dobrica Ćosić, the leading Serb nationalist intellectual, also proved extremely useful to Milošević.

After his visit to Kosovo, Milošević increasingly adopted a nationalistic rhetoric. At the eighth session of the SKS in September 1987, Milošević joined forces with the nationalist wing and forced the ouster of Stambolić and the remaining liberal Serb Communists. Over the next few years, Milošević employed similar tactics to topple a variety of regional and republican governments within the area that now constitutes the Federal Republic of Yugoslavia. Milošević and his allies employed the euphemism "antibureaucratic revolution" to describe what in effect amounted to a grab for total power. As part of this campaign, he revoked the autonomy of Vojvodina and Kosovo in 1989, and installed a trusted deputy, Momir Bulatović, as the president of Montenegro. In both Croatia and Slovenia, politicians viewed these developments with great anxiety, anticipating that Serbia would also try to restrict their power in Yugoslavia. In July 1990, Milošević founded the Socialist Party of Serbia (*Socijalistička Partija Srbije,* or SPS), the successor to the SKS. Although Milošević did manipulate the electoral system, the December 1990 elections demonstrated that he did enjoy substantial popular support in Serbia. In 1990 and 1991, Milošević met on several occasions with Croat President Franjo Tudjman. Tudjman has since acknowledged that their meetings included discussions of partitioning Bosnia-Herzegovina.

After the collapse of Yugoslavia began, Milošević solidified his hold on power in Serbia and Montenegro. The Yugoslav presidency became politically subordinated to the Serb presidency. Milošević, with the support of the Yugoslav People's Army, adeptly positioned himself as the patron of Serb nationalists in Bosnia-Herzegovina and Croatia. During the war in Croatia and Bosnia-Herzegovina, the Serbian government lent substantial material and ideological support to the self-proclaimed Serb entities and their military formations. However, by 1994 Milošević began to apply pressure on the Bosnian and Croatian Serbs to find a settlement. Milošević found it difficult to restrain the leaderships of the Serb entities, and eventually threatened to cease all support to them unless they proved willing to negotiate. Milošević is widely believed to have at least tacitly supported the Croatian offensives against the Croatian Serb statelet in May and August 1995. By the end of the war in Bosnia-Herzegovina, at the latest, it became clear that nationalists regarded Milošević as an unreformed socialist. Milošević is heavily influenced by his wife, Mirjana (Mira) Marković, who leads a neo-Communist Party in Serbia. Milošević is widely recognized, by political allies and adversaries alike, as an adept tactician and skillful employer of mass media. In particular, his tactics, including control of the media, military, and academia, and periodic purges of his associates, have contributed to the absence of a strong and united political opposition movement in Serbia. He has shown himself capable of surviving two rounds of mass demonstrations (in March 1991 and winter 1996–1997) and international political and economic pressure. Since the spring of 1998, Milošević has defied Western protests while conducting a low-intensity war against ethnic Albanian rebel forces in Kosovo.

## MINDSZENTY, CARDINAL

1892–1975, Born József Pehm, Mindszenty Hungarianized his name in the late 1930s, taking the name of the town of his birth. He became bishop of Veszprém in 1944 and then in 1945, bishop of Esztergom. Criticized by some for his connections to the right but also an opponent of the far-right Arrow Cross regime, he became one of the most visible and outspoken of Hungary's anticommunists in the immediate postwar period. In 1948, after the elimination of Hungary's political parties, through the so-called "salami" tactics, which combined division, co-option, persecution, bribes, and terror to destroy all opposition, Hungary's Stalinists turned their attention toward the remaining resistance, led by Church leaders, particularly Mindszenty. The regime, headed by the ruling "Quadriga" of Mátyás Rákosi, Ernő Gerő, József Révai, and Mihály Farkas, charged Mindszenty with espionage and currency manipulation, convicting him in an infamous February 1949 show trial.

Now a cardinal, Mindszenty remained under house arrest until revolutionary troops liberated him on October 30, 1956. His return to Budapest became one of the major events of the 1956 revolution, and it coincided with the reemergence of all of the political parties that had existed between 1945 and 1947. Later Communist writings claimed with characteristic hyperbole that Mindszenty became the center of an attempt by fascists, large landowners, and plutocrats to wrest control of Hungary. While it is unclear precisely what sort of political role the cardinal saw himself playing, he undoubtedly favored a radical change in government. This staunch opposition to Communism set him at odds with the majority of the key figures in the 1956 events, in particular, Imre Nagy.

When the revolution failed, Mindszenty fled to the U.S. Embassy, where he remained a guest of the American government until 1971. During this period, Mindszenty became the object of partisan literature and became a classic martyr figure for many expatriate Hungarians and anticommunists worldwide. After fleeing Hungary in 1971, Mindszenty settled in Vienna, where he remained an outspoken and uncompromising opponent of the Kádár regime until his death in 1975. The Vatican's attempts to broaden its contacts within the Soviet bloc resulted in Pope Paul VI's politically controversial 1973 decision to name a new Bishop of Esztergom. This act filled the administrative seat left vacant since

Mindszenty's flight to the American Embassy, much to the chagrin of the cardinal.

Mindszenty's brand of Hungarian nationalism was fundamentally populist and corporatist, similar to that ascribed to by many Hungarian Catholic thinkers of the late 1930s. It combined a belief in a traditional, structured, organic society based on religious faith with a fierce conviction that an independent hungary must be strong, reliant on neither Germany nor the Soviet Union. Mindszenty also favored social reform guided by Catholic ethics. While not outwardly anti-Semitic, at least after the close of World War II, he favored an exclusive, rather than a broad definition of whom was Hungarian.

Mindszenty's *Memoirs* was published in English by Macmillan in 1974.

## MINORITY GROUPS

Sociologist Louis Wirth in 1954 defined a minority group as people who are singled out for unequal treatment and who regard themselves as objects of collective discrimination. Minority groups are often subgroups within a society that are distinguishable based on visible and identifying characteristics. These members are not only differentiated based on physical or cultural attributes, but others then evaluate these attributes as having positive or negative characteristics. These values are then internalized by the dominant group, which often results in this differentiation becoming institutionalized. The dominant group, consciously or unconsciously, excludes members of minority groups from full participation in society; they are often denied equal access to positions of power, property, and prestige. A minority group does not necessarily mean a minority in terms of population size. The central concern is with the unequal access to resources. Therefore, women are considered a minority group even though they are often the majority in terms of the total percentage of the population.

Minority groups can be differentiated based on a number of characteristics including caste, class, religion, language, culture, and gender. However, the characteristic that is often most tied to nationalism is ethnicity. An ethnic minority refers to a group of people who are either physically (racial) or culturally (ethnic) distinct from the dominant group. This distinction is based on a shared cultural heritage that is unique and different from the dominant group. Ethnic minorities often share a distinct language, religion, dietary customs, artistic expressions, and national origin. And it is these differences that create and sustain conflict between the dominant group and the minority group.

In all societies that contain minority groups, basic

patterns of interactions develop between minorities and the dominant group. These patterns have occurred all over the world, and some societies, like the United States, have experienced each one of them at some time during its historical evolution. These patterns can best be understood when visualized along a continuum from most humane types of interaction to the most inhumane. The humanity of these interactions can also be correlated with the levels of nationalistic sentiments within a population.

*Pluralism or multiculturalism:* This occurs when the dominant group encourages racial and ethnic variation. The cultural differentiation of the minority group is encouraged and society is organized and structured to maintain minority identities yet participate fully in the society's social institutions and politics. Switzerland is an example of multiculturalism. The French, Italians, and Germans have maintained their cultures including their language, which is reflected in the country's official languages. In this case, the coexistence of these groups has been so successful that the "minority group" status would be hard to justify since each has similar access to power, property, and prestige. Nationalism in this case is almost nonexistent.

*Assimilation:* This is an umbrella term that refers to the process whereby a minority group becomes part of the dominant culture. There are different levels of assimilation from forced, which is the most extreme, to melting pot. In the most extreme case, the dominant culture refuses to allow the minority group to maintain its cultural heritage. Here the minority group is unable to practice its religion, speak its language, or engage in other cultural traditions. For example, when the Japanese invaded the Mariana Islands of the Pacific during World Wars I and II the use of the local language was outlawed. Now some fifty years later, some of the older Chamorro people still speak Japanese. On the other hand, assimilation can also refer to the process in which two minority groups come together and share aspects of their cultures with each other, thus forming a new culture. In Brazil, for example, interracial and inter-ethnic marriages are officially encouraged in the hope of producing a uniquely Brazilian ethnicity.

*Segregation:* Groups are formally separated based on their racial or ethnic identity. The dominant group structures societal institutions in order to maintain as little contact with the minority group as possible while at the same time exploiting their labor. An example of this was the United States prior to the social revolutions of the 1960s.

*Internal colonialism:* The term *colonialism* refers to the process by which industrialized nations exploit less

industrialized nations. Conflict theorists argue that internal colonialism refers to the exploitation of minority groups within a country by the dominant elite. This occurs through the use of institutional arrangements and laws that prevent minorities from gaining equal access to resources and benefits. Examples of this can be found in the Appalachian region of North America where the labor of local residents was used in the mining of their own land for coal. The wealth was extracted to benefit outside investors.

*Population transfer:* This can occur in two ways. A minority group can be indirectly transferred because life becomes unbearable. These groups then leave "voluntarily" as was the case for the Jews under tsarist Russia. Direct transfer occurs when a minority group is expelled, as was the case of the Native Americans and Japanese Americans who were relocated to reservations and concentration camps, respectively.

*Genocide:* The most extreme consequence of nationalism is systematic destruction or annihilation of the minority group. Examples include the Holocaust in Germany where millions of Jews were murdered by Hitler's regime and more recently the atrocities in Cambodia, Bosnia, and East Timor.

It is important to note that all of these forms of intergroup relations occur due to varying levels of nationalistic sentiments. Ethnic conflict like that in Rwanda in the summer of 1994 is an extreme example of the atrocities afflicted on a minority group. In less than 100 days, between 800,000 and 1 million people were slaughtered, mostly by machete. The Hutus outnumbered the Tutsis six to one. After the Hutu president was assassinated, the Hutu extremists rallied their followers to avenge this crime on all Tutsis. Radio announcers urged their listeners to disembowel pregnant women and local officials opened stadiums and churches to the fleeing Tutsi minority. According to Mongolia, a Tutsi who is now the vice-president of the National Assembly, "One expected to die. Not by machete, one hoped, but with a bullet. If you were willing to pay for it, you could ask for a bullet. Death was more or less normal, a resignation. You lose the will to fight."

Bibliographic sources include Pierre van den Berghe's *The Ethnic Phenomenon* (Elsevier, 1981), Anthony Smith's *The Ethnic Origins of Nations* (Oxford University Press, 1986), Donald Horowitz's *Ethnic Groups in Conflict* (University of California Press, 1985), and Milton Esman's *Ethnic Conflict in the Western World* (Cornell University Press, 1977).

## MISHIMA, YUKIO    1925–1970, Born in Tokyo; graduate of the law school at the University of Tokyo. After

serving as a government official for a few years, Mishima devoted himself to writing novels. Mishima made his first debut in the literary world by publishing a long novel, *Mask*, which was well received not only in Japan but also abroad. His other words, such as *The Temple of the Golden Pavilion, Kokoro,* and *Thirst for Love,* have been translated into various languages.

Yukio Mishima's work is unique in that he beautified what the society saw as immoral and destructive, using elegant writing styles and sentence structures. His later works, such as *Sword* and *The Sea of Fertility* (the latter work was never completed due to his ritual suicide), concerned the decline of traditional Japanese values amidst the industrial development and modernization of Japan. Mishima organized the Tatenokai (Association of the Shield) in 1968, which stressed physical fitness and martial arts, claiming the necessity of constitutional revision and a revival of the emperor system.

Mishima and his followers of Tatenokai attacked the Office of the Superintendent General of the Self Defense Force in Tokyo on November 25, 1970, in order to proclaim their beliefs of fascism and Japan's military superiority over other nations. Mishima performed *seppuku,* ritual suicide used by warriors in medieval Japan, demonstrating his unfaltering nationalism and patriotism to Japan. Mishima's seppuku was honorable and altruistic suicide, which was different from the suicide of alienation. His suicide was regarded as his final protest against Japan's Westernization.

**MOLDAVIAN NATIONALISM** Throughout the 18th century and into the 19th, Moldavia was a principality governed by local Hospodars but ruled in turns by Russia and the Ottoman Empire. The principalities of Moldavia and Wallachia were united in 1858, and declared independence in 1877. In 1878, the new Romania was recognized as a fully independent state by the Treaty of Berlin. However, Bessarabia, which is part of present-day Moldova, was seized by Russia. At the time of the Bolshevik Revolution, Bessarabia changed hands several more times, going from an autonomous constituent republic of the Federation of Russian Republics, to an independent republic, to union with Romania. The Treaty of Paris recognized Bessarabia's merger with Romania in 1920. The Soviet Union annexed Moldova in 1940 after the signing of the Ribbentrop-Molotov Pact. In 1942, Romania regained the territory after fighting the Soviet Union for it, but lost it again after the Soviet army invaded in 1944. It formally ceded the territory in 1947 as part of the peace treaty following World War II.

Under Gorbachev's programs of *glasnost* and *perestroika,* the Popular Front of Moldavia, a nationalist movement, arose and gained prominence. Its foremost goal was the union of Moldavia and Romania. In 1989, the first secretary of the Moldavian Communist Party, Mircea Snegur, was elected president of the Presidium of the Supreme Soviet. He represented the democratic-nationalist faction of the party. In that same year, the legislature abolished the use of Cyrillic and restored the use of Roman letters in writing Moldavian, a language nearly identical to Romanian.

In 1990, Moldavia declared its sovereignty within the Soviet Union and changed its name to Moldova. In 1991, Moldova refused to take part in a referendum on the continuation of the Soviet Union. In August, Moldova was rocked by incidents similar to the coup in Moscow. Demonstrators came out against the attempted military takeover, and as the coup in Russia collapsed, Moldova declared its independence and formally outlawed the Communist Party.

At that time, approximately 13 percent of Moldova was ethnic Russian, 64 percent were ethnic Romanian/Moldovan, and 14 percent Ukrainian, and small numbers of Gagauz, Bulgarians, and Jews also lived in Moldova. Moldovan nationalists' main goal remained union with Romania. Ethnic Russians in Trans-Dniester and Gagauz in the southwestern tip of Moldova refused to recognize the new regime, and declared independence themselves. This was largely because they feared that Moldova would unite with Romania, and that their rights and culture would be lost in the new state. The ensuing struggle between the Moldovan government in Chisinau and the Trans-Dniestrian Russians turned to civil war in 1992. The Russian 14th army, led by General Alexander Lebed, actively supported the rebels in this skirmish. In July 1992, a bilateral agreement for peace was signed between Moldova and the Dniester Moldovan Republic, guaranteeing the independence of Moldova and granting Trans-Dniester special status within Moldova.

In 1990, Mircea Snegur publicly broke with the leaders of the Popular Front of Moldova, citing his desire for an independent Moldova, rather than union with "another state," as his main reason. In 1991, elections were held, and Mircea Snegur ran unopposed. The Popular Front, unable to nominate a candidate, called for the boycott of elections. The 83 percent of voters who came out in support of President Snegur's reelection, however, offer vital proof that nationalism in Moldova, as well as popular sentiment, now had Moldovan independence as its primary goal. In 1994, the Agrarian Democratic Party, which favored Moldovan independence, won a majority of the vote in parliamentary elections. In a referendum on union with Romania following elections, an overwhelming majority voted against union.

Following these elections, Moldova, Russia, and Ukraine made progress in dealing with the Trans-Dniester issue. Though the problem has not been resolved entirely, the Trans-Dnietrian leadership and the Moldovan government agreed to have Trans-Dniester be an autonomous region within Moldova, with its own Parliament. Trans-Dniester agreed to remain within the economic and defense order of Moldova. One important point in the negotiations was that Trans-Dniester retained the right to opt out completely should union with Romania become a serious consideration for Moldova.

Moldovan nationalism expresses itself in two manifestations now that this crisis has been averted. Some Moldovans believe the republic cannot stand on its own, and in order to remain strong and independent, must reunite—or at least create strong ties with—Romania. Others believe Moldova can survive on its own in today's international order without fearing threat from Russia. In fact, they believe Moldova should foster stronger ties with Russia.

Those in the "Romanian" camp emphasize the history, language, and ethnicity but Moldovans and Romanians share. They believe Moldova can profit from being more closely connected to Romania's economy, and therefore be more likely to be accepted into the "club" of Western European states.

The "independent" nationalists, on the other hand, emphasize the changes that have occurred in the years during which the two nations were separated, and contend that Moldova was never treated as an equal even when it was part of greater Romania. They see Moldovan as a discrete language, and Moldovan culture as distinct from Romanian. This dispute remains at the top of the political agenda in Moldova.

## MONGOLIAN NATIONALISM

There are two versions of Mongolian nationalism: one is in Inner Mongolia, where the old nationalism took shape, developed, and eclipsed in the early half of the century; another is in the Mongolian People's Republic, the new nationalism that arose after the demise of the Soviet bloc in late 1980s.

In the early 13th century, the Mongols became masters of an enormous empire of China. Inner Mongolia was important for its relation to Manchuria and North China. "Out of Mongolia" has fewer direct affiliations with any of the empires founded by Chinghis Khan but occupies the original center of dispersion and remains the core of the Mongolian people.

By the end of the 19th century, China had become subject to pressure from the Western nations. Modern rifles, industries, and railways began to emerge in Mongol-populated regions that soon became the focus of political, economic, and military maneuvering between tsarist Russia, Japan, and China. Large numbers of the Han population poured in and cultivated the land for agricultural use. Mongolian herdsmen were the losers of the "big game." Such warlords as Zhang Zuolin of Manchuria and Yan Xishan of Shanxi victimized the Mongols in many ways, and the Mongols were ruthlessly exploited. Social and economic changes brought in a new structure of interest in which the relation of princes to tribal territories acted as an obstacle to Mongolian unity. The Chinese government guaranteed their vested interest while the rest of the upper classes lost privileges and turned nationalistic. A radical wing of nationalism was recruited largely from young aristocrats and educated youths, without concerted mass support. A pseudo-nationalism surfaced after an "autonomous" province of Hsingan was granted to the Mongols under Manchukuo, a Japanese conspiracy in Manchuria, which restored the Manchu monarchy.

In the 1930s and 1940s there was an autonomy movement in the Western part of Inner Mongolia that was led by Prince Demchukdongrob (Te Wang), designed both to claim that the Mongols were more than "colonial" subjects of China and to align them with China against the further extension of Japanese control. However, this movement was under Japanese control from the very beginning and led to the establishment of the Mongolian Frontier Government, which lasted only six years (1939–1945). The imagined possibility of a Mongolian nationalist movement in alliance with Japan, spreading from Manchuria and the rest of Inner Mongolia to "Outer Mongolia," has since then died. In 1947, the Inner Mongolia Autonomous Region was established under Communism leadership. It was the first of five minority autonomous regions in China. The Inner Mongolian population has integrated well into the "configuration of plurality and unity of the Chinese nation" as Professor Fei Xiaotong would have it.

Following the Revolution of 1911 in China, "Outer Mongolia" began to emphasize the differences between itself and China. The course of the "Outer Mongolian Revolution" was influenced by tsarist Russia. It was in the interest of tsarist Russia to segregate "Outer Mongolia" as its sphere of influence but to avoid challenging protest from other foreign powers that were interested in Asia. After the October Revolution the Soviet Union continued to recognize Chinese sovereignty over what is now called the Mongol People's Republic, but the Mongols there continue to claim independence. Armed with Bolshevik thinking, the leaders of the new revolution took control of "Outer Mongolia." They were not interested in political nationalism but devoted to economic and social revolution. The worship of Chinghis Khan was prohibited and lamaseries were destroyed. However, a new picture of nationalism began to form at the end of the 1980s when the Soviet bloc tore apart both within and without. The nation-state builders are trying their best to create ethnicity and nationalism by inventing at the same time new oppositional "Otherness." The image of Chinghis Khan has again captured public awareness and lamas are high in social position. On January 10, 1992, the Congress reached a decision that the five-pointed star on top of the traditional emblem the *soyombo* be removed from the old flag.

Though some nationalists are advocating for Pan-Mongolianism trying to unite Mongolians in Mongolia, China, and Russian Buriatya, there is no general response. Social and economic issues are more important to most Mongolians at this point than nationalism.

**MONROE DOCTRINE** Milestone declaration by President James Monroe in his annual message to Congress on December 2, 1823, that had a long-lasting impact on U.S. foreign policy. Monroe, expressing the nationalism of a relatively new United States of America, declared the Americas off limits to new colonial adventures. Monroe insisted that the so-called "Old World" and "New World" contained different systems that require a policy of noninterference.

Monroe outlined four principles in his speech. First, that the United States would not interfere in European affairs, either internal conflicts or wars between the European states. Second, the United States would not interfere with existing colonial arrangements in the Western hemisphere. Third, no outside powers would be allowed to develop future colonies in the Americas. Finally, any efforts by European states to suppress or control Western hemisphere nations would be viewed as a hostile act against the United States itself. "We owe it to candor" Monroe proclaimed, "and to the amicable relations existing between the United States and those powers, to declare that we should consider any attempt on their part to extend their system to any portion of this hemisphere as dangerous to our peace and safety."

Although the doctrine originally addressed concerns about potential efforts by continental powers to regain its former colonies in Latin America, it was broadened in scope throughout the history of U.S. policy and involved at various times in the nation's history. The United States did not actually have the military power

to enforce the doctrine in 1823, but the European powers did not have serious intentions of recolonizing the Americas so they did not test it. Moreover, it seemed to have served British interests as much as American, so it had the backing of the dominant naval power at the time, the British navy.

The Spanish Empire had broken up in the years following the end of the Napoleonic wars in 1915. New republics in the hemisphere wished to have recognition from the United States, which gladly endorsed them. The doctrine followed in the wake of U.S. recognition of Argentina, Chile, Peru, Colombia, and Mexico in 1822. It was directed primarily at the continental nations; even the British, interested in expanding trade in the Americas, became concerned when there was talk of France and Spain declaring war on the Latin American republics with the aid of the "Holy Alliance" of Russia, Prussia, and Austria. When the British occupied the Falkland Islands ten years later the United States neither opposed the action nor invoked the doctrine.

Although John Quincy Adams, Monroe's secretary of state, was the outspoken public advocate of the Monroe principles, it was apparently the president himself who decided to make them a matter of public policy rather than an informal behind-the-scenes set of guidelines for U.S. policy.

U.S. President James Polk reminded Britain and Spain of the Monroe Doctrine in 1845 and 1848, warning them not to interfere in Oregon, California, and Mexico. In 1867 the United States objected to France's interference in Mexico's governance and amassed troops on the U.S.-Mexican border.

In the late 19th and early 20th centuries the United States routinely intervened militarily in Latin American countries as an emerging world power, often calling on the Monroe Doctrine to justify its actions. President Theodore Roosevelt added the so-called "Roosevelt Corollary" to the doctrine in 1904 claiming that the United States would be justified in intervening whenever a Latin American nation's government was engaged in flagrant and chronic wrongdoing. The Monroe Doctrine's principle of Latin America as a natural part of the United States' sphere of influence was thus enforced by Roosevelt's self-proclaimed policy to "speak softly and carry a big stick." Although the big stick is not used as frequently at the turn of the 21st century, aspects of the Monroe Doctrine continue to guide U.S. policies in the region.

**MONROE, JAMES** 1758–1831, Few American statesmen have been entrusted with so many high political offices as James Monroe, a slave-owning Virginia planter, who lived only a few miles from Thomas Jefferson's Monticello. He agreed with Jefferson that slavery could not endure in America and that freed slaves should be returned to Africa. He therefore facilitated a resettlement in what would become Liberia, whose capital, Monrovia, bears witness to his involvement.

He served as secretary of war from 1814 to 1815, during which time he improved coastal fortifications and enlarged the army. He was secretary of state from 1811 to 1817 and president from 1817 to 1825. He is best known for his policies to secure not only America's borders after the British invasion during the War of 1812, but also to prevent a resumption of European colonial activities in the Western hemisphere. He firmly believed that America had to expand. It was during his administration that the Floridas were acquired.

On December 2, 1823, he proclaimed the "Monroe Doctrine," drafted by his secretary of state, John Quincy Adams, and supported by Britain. This declared that the Western Hemisphere was henceforth off limits to any form of European colonialism. He added: "We should consider any attempt on their part to extend their system to any portion of this hemisphere as dangerous to our peace and security." He feared a Spanish attempt to restore its monarchical control over the newly independent Latin American republics and a Russian temptation to expand its claims in northern California. For years the British navy enforced this doctrine. It survived into the 20th century, when it was strengthened by the Roosevelt and Lodge Corollaries, authorizing unilateral use of force by the United States and extending its validity to non-European powers, especially Japan. It was recognized in the Treaty of Versailles.

After World War II, Latin American nations increasingly regarded this doctrine as offensive and anachronistic because it authorized North American intervention and meddling in their national affairs. The U.S. government no longer invokes it to justify any of its action in Latin America. Nevertheless, by putting the world on notice that the United States was a strong, expansive, and self-confident nation that would not tolerate outside challenges to its growth and security, Monroe made an important contribution to the evolution of American nationalism.

**MONTENEGRIN NATIONALISM** Modern Montenegro emerged as an independent state in 1878, although parts of it had been practically independent since the early 18th century. The Montenegrin state emerged out of a clan-based society in which Ottoman rule had en-

countered fierce resistance. The Ottoman Empire never succeeded in fully imposing its will on Montenegro, which thus enjoyed a more autonomous existence than Serbia.

Although the Montenegrin clans were members of a common council, or *zbor*, they continuously engaged in intergroup feuds. The clans recognized an Orthodox metropolitan as an adjudicator, thus making Montenegro an ecclesiastical state until the 19th century. In the first half of the 17th century, Metropolitan Danilo organized the persecution of the Muslim population, thus providing the basis for a religious definition of Montenegrin identity. Metropolitan Petar II (Njegoš), who wrote the Montenegrin epic *The Mountain Wreath*, viewed Danilo's rule as crucial to the founding of the Montenegrin nation. Njegoš's writings advocated the physical extermination of Muslims in Montenegro.

From the beginning of the 18th century, Montenegro's population was torn between variants of Montenegrin and Serbian nationalism. Indeed, Montenegro's leaders attempted several times to mobilize nationalism in southern Serbia. Prince Danilo (r. 1851–1860), the first secular Montenegrin ruler, greatly expanded the territory of Montenegro, and asserted his rule at the expense of the individual clans. Succeeding Prince Danilo, Prince Nikola Petrović-Njegoš continued to strengthen Montenegrin nationhood at the expense of the traditional clans. Montenegrin territory continued to expand, and at its apex, after the Balkan wars of 1912–1913, Montenegro included substantial portions of today's Herzegovina, Serbia, and Albania.

Beginning in the 1880s, the ambitions of Prince Nikola collided with the plans of first the Serb Obrenović dynasty and, after 1903, with those of the Karađorđević dynasty. Neither Serb dynasty wished to recognize Montenegro's rival claims for leadership of the Serbs. After the turn of the century, the large number of young Montenegrins living in Serbia proper contributed to the strength of Serb nationalism, and Montenegrin nationalism suffered from an image of backwardness. Nikola attempted to co-opt the young Montenegrins by including them in his governments, but this ultimately proved unsuccessful in preventing the encroachment of the Serbian state and Serbian nationalism. Likewise, the proclamation of the Kingdom of Montenegro only provoked Serb nationalists into further action against Prince Nikola.

The Serb military and political leadership used the exigencies of World War I to further marginalize Nikola. The Serbs accused the Montenegrin nationalists of endangering the military cause by seeking unilaterally to expand further Montenegrin territory. In December 1915, in the midst of military chaos, Nikola went into exile in France. His attempts to stage a comeback throughout the remainder of the war were resolutely opposed by the Serb Regent Aleksandar and his government, and Nikola's efforts proved futile.

After World War I, elections were held in November 1918 for a Great National Assembly in Montenegro. With Nikola still in exile, the Serb government and military manipulated the election, which was won by pro-Serbian forces over the pro-Montenegrin side. Owing to the use of colored ballots, the former thenceforth became known as the "Whites," while the latter adopted the name "Greens." A Green rebellion in January 1919 was put down, but Montenegrin nationalists continued to resist Serb rule until the middle of the 1920s. Nikola's request for Italian patronage for the Montenegrin nationalist cause weakened his standing even among the Greens, and he died in exile in 1921. The labels "Whites" and "Greens" continue to bear significance in Montenegro today.

In 1925 Sekula Drljević picked up the Green cause and formed a Montenegrin federalist party that sought increased autonomy for Montenegro within Yugoslavia. Drljević, who continued to elaborate the differences between Serbs and Montenegrins during the interwar period, did not achieve any political success.

Montenegrin nationalism was next recognized by the Yugoslav Communists. The Communists, who found a solid base in Montenegro during World War II, recognized the existence of a separate Montenegrin nationality. After World War II, Montenegro became one of the six constituent republics of Yugoslavia. It remained allied with Serbia on most issues of policy throughout the postwar period. Montenegro's republican leadership was one of the more conservative in Yugoslavia. Montenegrins, including Milovan Djilas, were prominently represented in the ranks of the Yugoslav Communist Party, but also suffered disproportionately in the purges following the Tito–Stalin split. In the late 1960s and 1970s, some Montenegrin intellectuals pursued anew the question of whether Montenegrin national identity was distinct from Serbian national identity, and demands were issued for the establishment of an autocephalous Montenegrin Orthodox Church.

In 1988, Serbia's president, Slobodan Milošević, toppled the leadership of Montenegro and installed Momir Bulatović, a close and subservient ally, as the president. Bulatović continued to follow Milošević's instructions after 1991, and Montenegro remained as the only republic besides Serbia in Yugoslavia. However, since 1991, Bulatović's main domestic opponent, Montenegrin Prime Minister Milo Đukanović, has capitalized on economic and political dissent among younger Montenegrins. Đukanović and his allies have issued increasingly vocal demands for autonomy from Serbia and have not supported Serbia's military campaign in Kosovo.

## MOROCCAN NATIONALISM

Morocco's existence as an independent North African political entity began more than 900 years ago. A monarch (sultan), whose political authority and power was often challenged, ruled over Morocco. Common religious features loosely united its inhabitants, but traditional gaps between urban centers and the outer periphery limited national cohesion. Morocco remained relatively isolated from the outside world until the mid-19th century, when deteriorating finances and growing colonial European activity in North Africa imposed a greater degree of foreign involvement in its affairs. Morocco's independence was severely compromised with the establishment of the French protectorate in 1912, which theoretically retained the kingdom's institutions intact, but in reality transferred temporal powers to the French governor and his associates. Later that year, Spain attained control of areas in southern Morocco and along the northern coast, as part of a convention reached with France. Spanish rule in these areas derived from France, which enhanced France's status as the major colonial power in Morocco. The French "pacification" policy pursued during the protectorate's early years brought the entire country under almost unprecedented central authority by 1934. This territorial unity, combined with growing resentment of French colonial policies and the advent of a young monarch (Muhammad V) keenly interested in local affairs, altered the political landscape. Social, economic, and demographic changes that occurred during this period raised new issues and ideas within Moroccan society. It was against this backdrop that Moroccan nationalism emerged. Its main tenets included regaining independence under the leadership of a revitalized monarchy and a revival of the country's politics and culture.

Moroccan nationalism was initially promoted by a small group of urban intellectuals. Two questions were of particular importance to the nascent movement: the dispute over its political aims (instituting reforms within the existing framework of the protectorate or complete independence from France) and its attitude toward the monarchy. Nationalist demands focused on reforming the protectorate government, but later called for full-fledged independence. The nationalists also strengthened their ties with the royal palace, embracing

Muhammad V as a political symbol and as an effective leader in the struggle for independence.

An important early ideological foundation of Moroccan nationalism was the Islamic religious movement known as the *Salafiyya,* which sought to rid Islam of practices and ideas it deemed alien to original Islamic conceptions, such as superstitious rituals. The movement gained popularity in Morocco, as part of attempts to revive political and religious life. Its Moroccan adherents attributed their country's ailments to its rule by France "infidels" and denounced the corruptive nature of popular religious superstitious practices in Morocco. The promulgation of the "Berber *Dahir*" (decree) on May 16, 1930, proved to be the catalyst that transformed the small nationalist group into a wider political movement. This French-initiated decree attempted to place Morocco's indigenous Berber tribes under separate jurisdiction, which the nationalists viewed as a step toward converting them to Christianity. This action provoked violent protests among Moroccans, underscoring the degree of discontent from the country's political reality. In the aftermath of the 1930 events, a larger nationalist movement was established. The group, known as the *Comité d'Action Marocaine,* demanded reforms in the policies and composition of the protectorate government.

Nationalist demonstrators often clashed with security forces throughout the 1930s. By 1937, nationalist activity was forbidden, and its leaders were arrested or exiled. World War II and its aftermath renewed efforts to regain independence. A new party, *Istiqlal* (Independence), was founded in late 1943 and quickly emerged as the main national party. It demanded complete independence and the establishment of a constitutional monarchy. Earlier ideas about reviving local culture were marginalized by the emphasis placed on securing independence, which became the central cause championed by the *Istiqlal.* Party ties with the sultan grew during the 1940s, as the monarch became more outspoken in his support of the nationalist cause. By the early 1950s, the Moroccan struggle became more violent, and deteriorated to the point that France exiled the sultan in 1953, naming another member of the ruling family as monarch in his stead. The sultan's exile was a futile attempt to quell nationalist agitation, and ultimately enhanced Muhammad V's position as the symbol of Moroccan nationalists, who demanded his return. French policy changed in 1954, with the rise of a socialist government less intent on maintaining the protectorate. Muhammad V was recognized again as the legitimate monarch, and negotiated Morocco's independence from France, secured in March 1956. This effectively realized the most important goal of Moroccan nationalism. Spain agreed a month later to end its rule over most of its territories in Morocco, except for several areas (Ceuta, Melilla, and the Spanish Sahara region) that remained under Spanish authority.

In the postindependence period, Moroccan nationalism as an ideology was sidelined, and efforts focused on state building and economic development. However, nationalist slogans were later invoked by the government as part of efforts to extend Moroccan rule over the western Sahara region in the mid-1970s. These slogans of national unity and Morocco's political history still command a high degree of public support and recognition of an ideological, political, and social force that helped regain independence and revitalize this historical North African kingdom.

**MORRISON, TONI** 1931–, American writer, born in Lorraine, Ohio. Morrison is one of America's most significant national writers of the 20th century. She is best known for her novels that deal with African-American culture, the legacy of slavery, and the role of race and racism in the lives of African Americans and in American society. Her works include *The Bluest Eye, Sula, Song of Solomon, Tar Baby, Beloved, Jazz,* and *Paradise.* She was awarded the Pulitzer Prize for *Beloved* and has won numerous other honors for her fiction including the National Book Award.

Morrison is also known for her literary criticism through which she explores themes of national identity. In *Playing in the Dark: Whiteness and the Literary Imagination,* she argues that the metaphorical and metaphysical uses of race occupy definitive places in American literature, in the "national" character, and ought to be a major concern of the literary scholarship. Morrison analyzes the works of canonical, quintessentially American authors such as Poe, Melville, Hemingway, and Twain, and shows how their themes of freedom, individualism, innocence, and manhood depended on the existence of an enslaved black population. This "Africanist" presence in American literature embodies and harbors the fears and desires of white authors and white America. Africanism denotes the literary process through which American culture cohered. It was this Africanism, deployed by rawness and savagery, that provided the staging ground and arena for the elaboration of the quintessential American identity. Race functions as a metaphor crucial to understanding the meaning of Americanness.

For examples of Morrison's social and literary criticism, see Toni Morrison, *Playing in the Dark: Whiteness and the Literary Imagination* (Vintage Books, 1992);

Toni Morrison introduction and edited, *Race-ing Justice, En-gendering Power* (Pantheon Books, 1992); and Toni Morrison introduction and edited with Claudia Brodsky Lacour, *Birth of a Nation'hood,* (Pantheon Books, 1997).

**MOSSADEQ, MOHAMMAD**   1882–1967, When this former aristocrat became prime minister in 1951 he embodied and symbolized the nationalist aspiration of the Iranian populace to seek true dignity and sovereignty for their country from foreign forces, mainly British and Russian. Mossadeq was born in Tehran on June 16, 1882, to Mirza Hedayat Ashtiani, the minister of budget and finance in the Qajar Dynasty. His mother was Makeltadj Firouz who was related to the Qajar ruling family. According to one biographer, Farhad Diba, Mossadeq's mother played an important part in his life, and one of Mossadeq guiding principles in politics and life was his mother's advice, who stated, "The importance of an individual in society is equivalent to the hardship he or she suffers on behalf of the people." Mossadeq liberal beliefs were also inherited from his mother as well as his sympathy for the common man. His interest in politics also came at an early age when he used to accompany his father to the Qajar court and observe the royal ceremonies and the discussions that took place there. His formal education took place initially in Iran, then in Paris, France, but due to an illness he returned to Iran. The second time around he went to Switzerland to the University of Neuchâtel, where he obtained a doctorate in law, entering the service of the Qajar court in 1915. During his early political career the young Mossadeq was a cabinet minister and a provincial governor of Fars, where he conducted the affairs of the people in a similar fashion to a federal judge in a Swiss canton. Later on, as governor of Azerbaijan he stood up to the Russian counsel and argued that the capitulation policies ended with the 1921 agreement. He was elected deputy from Isfahan, then of Tehran. During his tenure as a deputy he sought to return Iran to the Constitution of 1906 where the Majless was supposed to reflect the will of the people and the nationalist interests of the Iranian state. During his early political career, he was known for his integrity and unblemished honesty and strong opposition to the authoritarian policies of Reza Shah. In 1936, after campaigning against the authoritarianism of Reza Shah, he landed in internal exile and was later arrested without charges ever being brought against him.

Early on, Mossadeq accurately saw the British government's attempts to control Iran through the Anglo-Iranian Oil Company (AIOC) in which the British government was the primary shareholder. British control was also carried out through the British embassy in Teh-

ran. When he returned to politics after the abdication of Reza Shah he campaigned as a nationalist using his oratory skills and his charisma and winning a seat in the Majless in 1944. In December 1944, he supported a law that sought to prevent foreign control and exploitation of Iranian oil. After World War II, when the former Soviet Union occupied parts of Iran in 1946, the Soviet Union extracted an oil extraction agreement from Iran. Mossadeq opposed it as much as he opposed British oil exploitation and worked to have the Majless annul it in 1947 soon after Soviet withdrawal.

By this time, Mossadeq had cemented his reputation as the prime nationalist politician in Iran, who could rally and generate support from almost all segments of the Iranian populace, from the traditional land-owning elites, to the merchants, the religious establishment, and from among the secular middle class. Moreover, he was the only political figure in Iran who could challenge the authority of Mohammad Reza Shah, who like his father before him sought to cooperate with British interests at the expense of his own country's sovereign interests. Hence in 1949, Mossadeq formed the National Front, a political grouping that included elements from the left and the traditional elites whose most salient goal was to challenge and end the stranglehold of Britain and the AIOC on Iranian oil resources and political dynamics. The AIOC was acting as an independent government within Iran, by providing its own municipal services, including an airport, and ensured security by negotiating protection agreements with the local Arab tribes. However, the AIOC deducted the cost of repairs from Iran's share of revenue if the pipelines were damaged by tribal raids in order for the latter to increase their revenue.

In 1951, the Majlis, riding a wave of anti-British sentiment, initially demanded the cancellation of the concession treaty signed by Reza Shah, but then changed its mind and nationalized the AIOC and asked Mossadeq to become prime minister When Mossadeq took over as prime minister in 1951 he not only had to tackle the British government's campaign to boycott Iranian oil but also to hold onto his multidimensional coalition, which was held together by the single issue of nationalizing the oil company, an issue that represented Iranian sovereignty and control over her own affairs. In 1952, the United States feared Mossadeq was a Soviet ally, especially after the Iranian Communist party (*Tudeh,* i.e., Masses) became the most organized political party in the country. It rose to prominence after the various factions within the National Front began to defect as a result of the loss of revenue and the reform that Mossadeq carried out, which some members of the coalition deemed against their interests. With the country in semichaos and no revenue, a number of unhappy military officers along with the British MI6 and the CIA carried out "Operation AJAX." The aim of the coup was to remove Mossadeq from power and replace him with the Shah, who was in exile at the time. The coup on August 19, 1953, which ended the nationalist rule of Mossadeq, succeeded because, according to Richard Cottam, the court, the army, businessmen, the clergy, and landowners united against him, while the intellectual and liberal segments of the population failed to rally to Mossadeq's cause.

See Richard W. Cottam, *Nationalism in Iran, Updated Through 1978* (Pittsburgh, Penn.: Pittsburgh University Press, 1979); and Farhad Diba, *Mohamad Mossadegh: A Political Biography* (Croom Helm, 1986).

## MUHAMMAD AHMAD

1844–1885, Founder of the religious-political movement that brought the Sudan a period of independence in the 1880s. Although Muhammad Ahmad ibn 'Abdallah died just several months after his followers captured Khartoum, he and his successor, 'Abdallahi, were able to break down many of the long-standing internal divisions in society that hindered the formation of a Sudanese nation.

Sudan in the 19th century was a land of competing groups, both tribes and popular Islamic brotherhoods, or sufi *tariqas.* Egypt established control over Sudan in 1820 and by vigorous rule had been able to reduce the power and independence of many of these groups. The Egyptian government's moves against tribal and sufi authority aroused resentment, as did heavy taxation, the regime's reliance on European and Coptic Christian officials, and its attacks on the slave trade, an important sector of the Sudanese economy. When a vacuum of authority developed suddenly in 1879, as first the Egyptian Khedive Ismail was deposed and then his energetic governor-general in Sudan, Charles Gordon, resigned, unrest in Sudan increased. Muhammad Ahmad made himself the focus of that unrest in 1881, when he declared himself to be the Mahdi, the Divinely Guided One, sent by God to destroy the old and establish a new, purely Islamic order.

Muhammad Ahmad's claim won quick acceptance. In part, this was due to widespread expectations of the appearance of the Mahdi in Sudan at the time, and his religious reputation as a strict sufi ascetic made him a plausible candidate. His similarity of name to the prophet Muhammad ibn 'Abdallah (a parallel that he consciously promoted in his construction of the Mahdist movement) and his victory in an initial clash with a better armed Egyptian force strengthened his claim to

be truly divinely guided and divinely protected. Muhammad Ahmad was a member of the Danaqla tribe, which had been heavily involved in the slave trade, and many of his early followers were from similar tribes settled along the Nile. His chief lieutenant, 'Abdallahi al-Ta'ayshi, came from the Baqqara of the west, and these nomads also gave him crucial shelter and military support in 1881–1882 after that initial fight. With each victory of the Mahdists over badly organized Egyptian expeditions in the western desert, more volunteers joined Muhammad Ahmad's following. Uprisings began along the Nile and, as of 1883, in the east. By January 1885, when Khartoum's Egyptian garrison under British General Gordon fell to the Mahdists, Muhammad Ahmad controlled all of Sudan, except for the extremes of north and south and the port of Suakin. Sudan was united against Egypt under a native leader.

Muhammad Ahmad and, from 1885 to 1898, his successor, 'Abdallahi, weakened the independence of both the tribes and the sufi brotherhoods. Although himself a sufi, whose government bore strong similarities to a sufi *tariqa,* Muhammad Ahmad acted to weaken the influence of Sudan's other brotherhoods. He compelled other sufi leaders to submit to his authority and banned the veneration of sufi saints. 'Abdallahi also repressed any sufi drift away from the Mahdist camp. He acted even more ruthlessly to break the power of tribes that might rival his Baqqara supporters. This naturally alienated many Sudanese, but 'Abdallahi could still muster a formidable force to oppose the British expedition under Kitchener, which succeeded in retaking Khartoum in 1898.

Muhammad Ahmad still exerts an influence on Sudanese national affairs today. He is known as "Abu'l-Istiqlal," the "father of independence." His son, Sayyid 'Abd al-Rahman al-Mahdi, founded the Umma Party in 1945, which campaigned for complete Sudanese independence rather than union with Egypt after Britain's expected withdrawal. Sadiq al-Mahdi, a great-grandson of Muhammad Ahmad, served twice as prime minister of Sudan, most recently from 1986 to 1989.

There is no good biography of Muhammad Ahmad available in English. A good account of the Mahdist period, however, can be found in Peter Holt's *The Mahdist State in the Sudan, 1881–1898* (Oxford University Press, 1958).

## MUHAMMAD ALI

1769–1849, Ottoman soldier, governor of Egypt from 1805 to 1848. Muhammad (Arabic) or Mehmed (Turkish) Ali was born in Kavalla, Macedonia. After acquiring military experience with Ottoman irregular forces in the Balkans, in 1808 he was selected as second-in-command of an Albanian contingent being sent to Egypt to fight the French. Outmaneuvering rivals in 1805 he was appointed governor of Egypt. He held the post until 1848.

Muhammad Ali is often called "the founder of modern Egypt." He inaugurated many of the reforms responsible for Egypt's precocious modernization in the 19th century—Western-style technical education for his bureaucrats and military, major projects of land reclamation, the raising of long-staple cotton for export to Europe, and a program of forced industrialization that ultimately failed. Externally his European-style military began Egyptian conquest of the Sudan and briefly occupied parts of the Arabian peninsula as well as much of coastal Syria before being ousted from Ottoman Asia by an international coalition in 1839–1841. Eventually recognized as the hereditary governor of Egypt by the Ottoman government, his family ruled Egypt until the revolution of 1952.

A military adventurer whose aim was to establish the position of his family and household, Muhammad Ali was not a self-conscious Egyptian nationalist. Power in Egypt in the early 19th century was in the hands of an alien Turkish-speaking military class, with rigid barriers separating this ruling elite from the native Egyptian population. Muhammad Ali's Egypt was certainly not a "nation" in the sense of a unified political community possessing a shared identity and purpose. Nonetheless, his measures of administrative centralization, miliary expansion, and economic development laid the foundations for an Egyptian state distinct from the rest of the Middle East. Muhammad Ali created the state that subsequently became the focus of Egyptian national loyalties.

An older biography of Muhammad Ali is that of Henry Dodwell, *The Founder of Modern Egypt: A Study of Muhammad Ali* (1931). Two recent studies with different perspectives on his "national" achievements are Afaf Lutfi al-Sayyid Marsot, *Egypt in the Reign of Muhammad Ali* (1848), and Khaled Fahmy, *All the Pasha's Men: Mehmed Ali, His Army, and the Making of Modern Egypt* (1997).

## MULTICULTURALISM

The idea that minority cultural communities are deserving of respect and recognition within their host nation provides the foundation for much of the ideology—and in some instances even the policy—of multiculturalism. The whole issue of multiculturalism has become acutely felt in democratic, multiparty, capitalistic states, which perceive themselves as possessing some form of "national culture." More specifically, with regards to nationalism, many of these states hope that multiculturalism will act to dampen or even eliminate secessionist aspirations within their territories.

The large-scale migration that took place to countries in Western Europe and North America, especially after World War II, placed certain strains on relations between minority and majority cultures. On the one hand, members of the majority culture were forced to ask themselves to what degree they were willing to accept various forms of cultural distinctiveness, while at the same time granting the privileges of citizenship. On the other hand, members of minority cultures were faced with the issue of the degree to which they were willing to assimilate into the host country—thereby receiving the economic advantages that went along with such assimilation—while maintaining the cultural and religious traditions of their countries of origin.

Supporters of multiculturalism believe its major promise lies in an enriched civil society, because individual citizens have an opportunity to participate in more diverse cultural traditions, ultimately rendering communication between different groups at the political level much easier. The cosmopolitan aspiration of an enlarged cultural horizon in which citizens might actively participate is also an important component of the multicultural promise. Also, certain conditions of equality are satisfied because disadvantaged groups are given a better chance to compete with those of the dominant culture through government policies aimed at delivering much needed resources. In general, multiculturalism and multicultural policies would reduce, its supporters argue, ethnic and cultural (even perhaps "national") conflict within multicultural states, by leveling the playing field where diverse cultural groups struggle for equality.

Whereas the supporters of multiculturalism tend to be liberal pluralists, the many detractors of multiculturalism come from both the left and the right of the political spectrum. Left leaning critics, for example, worry that the ideology and policies of multiculturalism invariably further ghettoize cultural groups in the very process of marking them off as in need of special treatment. They also point out that multiculturalism serves only to mask real, deep-seated economic and social inequalities, with its emphasis on what they see as the more superficial aesthetic cultural characteristics like food, dance, and music. Critics from the right argue that multiculturalism is a deeply divisive ideology (and policy) that serves to reinforce the differences that exist between groups within a nation, instead of emphasizing the many commonalities. For these critics, multiculturalism is a powerfully disunifying ideology that fragments, divides, and weakens otherwise strong nations.

Without question, the actual diversity of the issues surrounding multiculturalism is as great as that of the various groups pushing for such policies. For example, in Western Europe, where countries such as England and France have had to deal with an influx of immigrants from former colonies, the issue of multiculturalism has centered around matters of race, and the efforts to strike a balance between multiculturalism and equality. Attempts have been made, with varying degrees of success, to reduce racial discrimination at the institutional level while at the same time providing equality for all citizens.

In the United States, the issues are only slightly different. While the overarching concern within the U.S. context is also one of race, it manifests itself in a different way. During the late 1980s there was a general disillusion among many black intellectuals over the shortcomings of the civil rights movement. Many of these intellectuals argued that the movement had failed to address the real problems of inequality between blacks and whites in American society. The result was the development of a form of multiculturalism that manifested itself in affirmative action programs aimed at giving black Americans the needed boost to participate more fully in American society. By the 1990s the issue shifted to one of self-esteem, as some black leaders began to realize that the educational system was, in part, to blame for the poor performance of blacks. This led to a debate over university course curricula and eventually to a flourishing of black and African studies programs with the eventual suggestion in the mid-1990s that black children be taught Ebonics, thought to be a distinctly black American language.

Canada, on the other hand, is one of the few countries with an official multicultural policy. Originally announced in 1971 by then prime Minister Pierre Trudeau, the Canadian Multicultural Act was eventually ratified in 1988. The Canadian situation differs somewhat from the American and Western European cases mainly because the largest minority group is not a racial but a linguistic one. In their struggle to form a separate state, many francophones living in the province of Quebec have come to see multiculturalism as a threat to their already minority status within the Canadian confederation. Being treated as simply another ethnic or cultural group has come to mean an erosion of their power as one of the foundation nations of Canada. In

this way Canada's policy of official bilingualism, which tends to promote the French language, comes into conflict with its policy of multiculturalism (which promotes all cultures and languages equally).

Despite these many differences and difficulties, multiculturalism continues to be a strong ideological and policy program pursued by multinational and multiethnic states. Much of the debate about multiculturalism hinges on a crucial distinction between public and private spheres. In most cases multiculturalism is confined to the latter, permitting private citizens to freely express their unique religious, linguistic, and moral proclivities without undue interference. In fact, in some instances, government funds are made available to encourage the development of these various cultural expressions. However, much of the debate about multiculturalism is over who is to have control of the public sphere, a domain that includes such public institutions as education, law, and politics. Should the Lord's Prayer be broadcast over the P.A. system at the beginning of the school day? Should young Islamic girls be permitted to wear veils to their public school? And should Sikhs be permitted to wear turbans while on duty for the Royal Mounted Canadian Police? Indeed, it is in the public domain where the debate about multiculturalism has been and continues to be the most controversial.

The literature on multiculturalism is enormous. However, John Rex has written extensively on multiculturalism and his "Multiculturalism in Europe and America" in *Nations and Nationalism* 1(2) (1995) is an excellent comparative overview of the issues and is therefore a good place to start.

**MUSIC AND NATIONALISM** Nationalism as a political ideology reached its peak at the end of the 19th century when many new nation-stats emerged and many mature nation-states started imperial expansion. The nationalistic movement eventually came to affect music development in various European countries in the same period. Inspired by national elements like folk songs, folk dances, and various kind of folklore, classical composers strived for incorporating their homeland traditions into the appropriate forms, rhythms, or themes of music. Famous exemplars were the Finnish composer Sibelius's *Finlandia*, Opus 26 (1899), Russian composer Glinka's *A Life for the Tsar* (1836), and Italian composer Verdi's *Va, pensiero* (Chorus of the Hebrew Slaves) from *Nabucco* (1842).

These pieces of music sought to exalt national emotion and identity and thus contributed to an awareness of national consciousness. This form of nationalism, often termed *cultural nationalism,* could enrich the languages of music (presumably a universal style), but could also fall into danger when converted to a form of *triumphal nationalism.* Triumphal nationalist music was a dominant characteristic of glorifying one's national gods, land, and people and its superiority over other nations and cultures. The typical ones were Verdi's *Triumphal March* (1871) and Elgar's *Pomp and Circumstance March No. 1* (1902).

In the early 20th century, the most eloquent English exponent of music in nationalism was Vaughan Williams (1872–1958), whose writings and lectures were published in 1934 as *National Music.* His famous saying is: "My advice to young composers is—learn your own language first, find out your own traditions, discover what you want to do."

But not all kinds of folk music or music with national elements are identified as nationalistic. Nationalistic sentiments can only be nurtured and promoted through a process of negotiation among three parties: composers, performers, and listeners. Nationalism is by and large an ideology that requires intensive articulation and receptive response rather than a purely musical style in technical terms. For example, Chopin's piano music may be considered to have a strong national character, but be less nationalistic. By contrast, Richard Wagner was a nationalist listener and composer who might detect music with national or folk elements in Albert Lortzing.

## MUSSOLINI, BENITO

1883–1945, Born the son of a blacksmith and a schoolteacher, Mussolini had been educated in a seminary, but had been expelled because he reportedly stabbed another student. After teaching school for a few years, he fled to Switzerland in order to avoid military service. He grew tired of exile after a couple of years and returned to Italy to become an effective journalist. This helped launch a meteoric career in socialist politics. In 1911 he was jailed briefly for his inflammatory articles against Italy's colonial war in Libya, and in 1912 he was named editor-in-chief of the major Socialist Party newspaper, *Avanti!* (Forward!) of Milan. His writings and speeches sometimes took excursions into anarchism, and they were always radical. He vehemently rejected moderation and insisted that socialism must destroy the "bourgeois experiment" of democracy.

He never veered from his bitter opposition to liberal democracy. But after the outbreak of World War I, he revealed how fluid his political convictions really were. Unlike his former socialist comrades, he turned nationalist and strongly supported Italy's involvement in the war. He served in the army, rising like Hitler to the rank of corporal. He maintained that it was one of the country's finest hours and that the young heroes had been betrayed by conniving, greedy politicians at home. Italy emerged from the war as a society badly off balance. Lawlessness in the countryside and towns, strikes in the cities, and sharp and often violent domestic disagreements polarized the political scene. The war had brought revolution in Russia. That revolution caused radically revolutionary Communists to break away from more moderate socialist parties in Italy and elsewhere. The establishment of the Communist Party of Italy (PCI) scared many anti-Marxist Italians, who became sympathetic to the idea of a strong leader who could protect Italy from the Communist revolution. This included many wealthy landowners and industrialists.

The war had frustrated the dreams of many Italian nationalists, who had believed that Italy should become a major Mediterranean and Balkan power. Millions of returning veterans were bitter about the fact that their country seemed to show no appreciation for the suffering and sacrifice they had endured. The traditional Italian parties and elites were incapable of coping with the domestic political situation. Therefore, a vacuum and a constituency had been created for a charismatic opportunist and showman with flexible principles, the appearance of raw manliness, and an emotionally appealing, but intellectually fraudulent, political theory that was virulently nationalist.

Mussolini appealed to the lost, the frightened, and the bored. They flocked to the many loosely knit groups that sprang into existence in imitation of the *Fascio di combattimento* (fighting group), which he had founded in Milan in 1919. It took a couple of years for him to gain full control of the fascist movement, named after the Latin word *fasces,* a bundle of sticks around an ax, an ancient Roman symbol of state authority. In 1921 the Fascist party was formally created.

Mussolini quickly saw that the government's inability or unwillingness to bring the rural and industrial violence under control offered a welcome opportunity for the fascists to present themselves as the protectors of life, property, law, and order. His *Squadristi* (blackshirted bully squads) roamed the streets unimpeded, intimidated voters and opponents, and sacked or smashed trade union or Socialist Party headquarters and presses all over Italy, including those of *Avanti!* These brazen, but unopposed acts were merely the prelude to a fascist coup d'etat that had been long planned.

Mussolini mobilized his Black Shirts for a "march on Rome" on October 22, 1922. He showed that he was not entirely confident such a seizure of power would succeed by remaining close to the Swiss border in order to be able to escape into exile in case it failed. King Victor Emmanuel III allowed them into Rome and appointed Mussolini prime minister. Rome fell to the fascists without a shot being fired.

Step by step, Mussolini (who named himself *Il Duce*, "The Leader") transformed Italy into the first European dictatorship outside of Russia. The fascist ideology Mussolini had helped to concoct was superbly compatible with his concept of nationalism. Freedom had allegedly been created through authoritarianism, and nobility and heroism had been established through discipline and sacrifice. The state was glorified, and liberalism, democracy, and socialism were condemned. He combined workers, employers, and other groups into organizations called corporations and abolished trade unions, strikes, and opposition parties and news media. He created a youth movement led by the state and a feared secret police (OVRA). The slogan, *credere, obbedire, combattere* ("believe, obey, fight") reflected the new ideal. The king remained on the throne and the bicameral parliament was permitted to go through the motions as if it were functioning. But all power by 1925 rested with Mussolini and his Fascist party, whose organization reached from 10,000 *Fasci* (local) party groups all the way up to a Fascist Grand Council of about twenty men.

Mussolini's ambition to restore ancient greatness through imperialism and aggressive Italian nationalism was thwarted. Italy was ill prepared for his wars, fought at first on a small scale against Ethiopia in 1935 and then later against Germany's enemies in World War II. After his attempts to conquer Albania and Greece in 1941 had failed, Italy and *Il Duce* became more dependent on Hitler than the Italians had intended. Their initial enthusiasm about the adventure of war soon turned to resignation and disappointment. After capturing Sicily in mid-1943, the allies began bombing Rome on July 19.

The sober reality of war right in the city of Rome brought the downfall of Mussolini. The Fascist Grand Council, formerly a malleable tool in Mussolini's hands that had not met since 1939, demanded his resignation, which the king ordered the next day. Mussolini was arrested as he left the royal palace, but was rescued later by a daring, precision operation by German paratroopers. Totally at the mercy of the Germans, Mussolini eked out a temporary existence as head of a puppet fascist state in German-occupied northern Italy until April 28, 1945, when Communist partisans murdered him and publicly hanged him and his mistress upside down in Milan.

**MUSSORGSKY, MODEST PETROVICH** 1839–1881, Russian composer, member of the group "The Mighty Handful." Inspired in part by Nikolai Chernyshevsky's influential essay "The Aesthetic Relation of Art to Reality" (1855), Mussorgsky believed that music must be socially engaged, stating that art is "a means of communicating with people, not a goal itself." Primarily interested in vocal genres, Mussorgsky searched for a scientific musical equivalent of colloquial Russian speech, aiming to typify human emotions together with the peculiar speech characteristics of different social groups. His point of departure became a theory of accent or stress (*Betonung*) by the German aesthetician Georg Gervinus (1805–1871), who argued that human speech is governed by musical laws. Mussorgsky first experiment was his unfinished opera *Marriage* (1868), a musical setting for the prose text of Gogol's comedy. Following further the path explored by the revolutionary opera *The Stone Guest* by Alexander Dargomyzhsky, who created a distinctively Russian operatic recitative based on the prosody of Pushkin's verse, Mussorgsky tried to develop a completely new melodic discourse that would be derived from the musical embodiment of Russian speech and be partially based on the material of reworked folk songs. Mussorgsky viewed such a melodic discourse as a national alternative to European classical melody, which, in his opinion, had lost its connection with actual human speech and become mere musical artifice.

Deeply interested in the history of Russia and its projection into the present, Mussorgsky took the plots for both of his major operas, *Boris Godunov* and *Khovanshchina*, from Russian history. As a historian, Mussorgsky strove to be as trustworthy as possible in the restoration and recreation of events and in the psychological characterization of personages, taking into account the works of leading contemporary historiographers such as Vladimir Nikolsky and the populist (*narodnik*) Nikolai Kostomarov, while adapting or reconceptualizing the historical approach of Pushkin and Nikolai Karamzin. Despite Mussorgsky's intention to show the people (*narod*) as "a great personality animated by a unified idea," the people in his operas are not presented as a united moving force of a tragedy. Instead, Mussorgsky portrays the crowd more in the terms of a Bakhtinian polyphony of discourses, powerfully presenting different groups and colorful characters.

In his numerous songs and song cycles, Mussorgsky continued his exploration of Russian musical discourse. In accord with a populist (*narodnicheskie*) tendency in contemporary literature and art (led by Nikolai Nekrasov and the artists' group *peredvizhniki*), Mussorgsky's protagonists are often suffering and humiliated types from "the people," such as a peasant woman ("Hopak," "Lullaby to Eremushka"), child-beggar ("An Orphan"), and village idiot ("Darling Savishna"). His cycle "Songs and Dances of Death" is a Russian version of a *dance macabre,* employing national characters and genres, such as a drunken peasant in a snowstorm ("Trepak"). Some of the songs reflect the polemics that Mussorgsky, together with Stasov and Balakirev, led against Rubinstein and the Germanophiles (musical pamphlets "The Classicist" and "The Peepshow" [*Rayok*]).

Despite the fact that in his last years Mussorgsky rejected the possibility of an association of his music and aesthetic views with any existing group of musicians ("Autobiographical Note," 1880), he was undoubtedly a "highly brilliant, stubborn, and enthusiastic exponent of the ideas that matured in the Balakirev Circle" (Asafiev).

The important primary source of Mussorgsky's views and aesthetic is *The Mussorgsky Reader: A Life of M. P. Mussorgsky in Letters and Documents,* Jay Leida and Sergei Bertensson, eds. (New York: W. W. Norton, 1947; revised in 1970). Contemporary Western scholarship on Mussorgsky is best represented in Richard Taruskin's *Mussorgsky: Eight Essays and an Epilogue* (Princeton, N.J.: Chichester, West Sussex, United Kingdom: Princeton University Press, 1993) and in Caryl Emerson's *Boris Godunov: Transpositions of a Russian Theme* (Bloomington, Ind.: Indiana University Press, 1986).

# N

**NAGY, IMRE** 1896–1958, Nagy, best known for his leadership of the Revolution of 1956, became a Communist while a war prisoner in Russia during World War I. He fought in the Russian Civil War, and returned to Hungary in 1921. A member of the Social Democratic Party until he was expelled in 1925, he then joined the Hungarian Socialist Workers Party and was arrested numerous times during the Regency of Miklós Horthy (1920–1944). He fled to the Soviet Union in 1929, where he remained until 1944, when he returned to Hungary as part of the Communist delegation that constituted the core of the Debrecen provisional government.

From late 1944 on, Nagy was a member of numerous high party councils and held various government positions. His primary governmental role was as minister of agriculture, but he also briefly held the position of minister of interior before surrendering it to László Rajk in 1946. In 1949 he was kicked out of all his positions because he adopted "opportunistic" populist views during the socialist agricultural transition period. In other words, he was less than enthusiastic about his task of collectivizing Hungary's agriculture. He submitted a formal self-criticism in 1951 and rejoined the political committee that year.

It was only in 1953 that Nagy gained great political significance. In June 1953, with Soviet permission, he replaced Mátyás Rákosi as premier and verbally attacked Rákosi's politics and methods. He proclaimed a "New Course" in Hungarian domestic affairs, including most notably an end to police terror, forced collectivization, and overindustrialization. This began a three-year power struggle within the Hungarian Workers Party that echoed the struggle in Moscow between hardliners and reformers. Due to the Kremlin's fear that Hungary might collapse into chaos if Rákosi were completely removed, Rákosi and his cohorts maintained key positions in the party, thus ensuring that

the party, by and large, opposed Nagy's reforms. In 1954, it appeared as if Nagy, whose base of support included Hungary's intellectuals, writers, and an older group of Communists who had not been trained in Russia, had won the fight to determine Hungary's future. A combination of political events and heart problems forced him from premiership in 1955, and Rákosi regained control.

Nagy again found himself ousted from the party. This ouster, however, was even shorter lived than his first purge. In March 1956, after the circulation of Nikita Khrushchev's "secret speech" denouncing Stalin's excesses, Hungary's anti-Stalinists were rejuvenated. With the blessing of Moscow's reformist clique, Rákosi saw much of his power eroded by the summer of 1956.

Nagy did not immediately become premier. Rather he was propelled to power by the revolutionary swell that engulfed Hungary in October 1956. Interim Premier Ernö Gerö readmitted Nagy to the party in mid-October in an attempt to reduce revolutionary pressures. This failed, and on October 24, 1956, Nagy reluctantly returned to the premiership, which he occupied until November 4.

At first, Nagy condemned the revolutionary actions of the students and workers councils. Only on October 28th did he actively assume the leadership of the revolution. With Nagy as premier and János Kádár as head of the party, a new Hungarian government instituted a series of reforms. It began reform of the Communist Party and abolished the secret police. It allowed the reconstitution of other political parties, effectively ending the one-party system, and halted collectivization. On October 30 it endorsed a program calling for a free, democratic, independent, and neutral Hungary and renewed negotiations with the Soviets for the removal of the Red Army from Hungarian soil. These negotiations continued and an agreement was signed, even as Soviet tanks moved to crush the revolution.

The nature of the 1956 revolt and Nagy's involvement have been hotly debated. Writers have argued over whether Nagy advocated a form of national Communism or rather an early form of Eurocommunism based on greater ties with the West. Intrinsic to this debate is the degree of Nagy's nationalism. Some authors regard Nagy's plans for a Danubian union, first proferred in 1955, as internationalist and reminiscent of Kossuth's Danubian Confederation. Others, in contrast, stress that Nagy saw union in nationalist terms, as the only means available for the Danubian states to retain national integrity in the face of Soviet and German might. Other scholars interested in questions of nationalism have focused on the political differences between Poland and Hungary in 1956 that permitted Poland to escape radical upheaval and invasion. Some older texts blame Nagy's assertions of Hungarian sovereignty, including his declaration of neutrality and withdrawal from the Warsaw Pact, for forcing the Soviet Union's hand and making invasion inevitable. The more recent consensus, however, is that Moscow chose to invade before Hungary declared neutrality. Newer texts claim that Moscow was simply unwilling to let Hungary escape its orbit, motivated by a combination of political intrigue within the Kremlin; opposition to political pluralism in Hungary; the need for Hungarian missile bases; and the need for order in Europe as Moscow competed with China for converts to Communism in the developing world. Finally, the issue of whether Nagy really led the revolution or whether pressures exerted by true mass upheaval forced him to take the stances he did has also provoked scholarly debate.

When military defeat became inescapable, Nagy sought asylum in the Yugoslav embassy. Yugoslavia's Marshal Tito instead betrayed Nagy, sacrificing him as a gesture of goodwill to Khrushchev. Eventually turned over to Hungarian authorities, Nagy languished in jail, unrepentant. Tried secretly in June 1958, a tribunal of the Hungarian People's Republic sentenced him to death. Along with two other key figures, Nagy was hanged soon after the completion of his trial.

The most complete biography of Nagy, suffused with many of his writings, is János M. Rainer's *Nagy Imre: Politikai Életrajz, Volume 1–1896-1953,* published by the 1956 Institute in Budapest, 1996. The most recent and comprehensive study of the buildup to 1956 and repression of the revolt is titled *The Hungarian Revolt of 1956: Reform, Revolt and Repression 1953–63,* published by Longman in 1996 and edited by György Litván. Bill Lomax's *Hungary 1956,* published by Allen and Busby in 1976, also contains a good analysis of Nagy's policies.

**NAMIBIAN NATIONALISM** Namibia (South West Africa, SWA) has a peculiar colonial history. German colonial control was established in the 1880s following the Berlin Conference. In fact, the area otherwise called South West Africa (both Namibia and South West Africa were recognized by the Windhoek Post Office) became Germany's share from the partition of Africa. At the turn of the century, Namibia witnessed an influx of white settlers from South Africa who were looking for cattle, land, and minerals. Prior to that German missionaries, who participated actively in the establishment of a violent heritage in SWA under the auspices of the Rhemish Mission Society (RMS), and traders arrived before the white settlers from South Africa. De facto German colonial control was followed by the genocidal extermination of mostly the Nama and the Herero, two of the several indigenous groups (others include the Ovambo, the Damara, the Kavango, the San, the Kaoko, the Rehoboth) in the region between 1904 and 1908. The rest of the Herero, Nama, and other indigenous populations who survived this genocide were herded off the fertile sections of the land to the arid sections that the settlers designated "communal lands." Expectedly, the communal lands subsequently became overcrowded. Like South Africa, Namibia became a settler colony. Namibia's colonial history is, therefore, characterized by a lot of settler violence that gave vent to a prolonged and bloody nationalist struggle.

Germany's defeat in World War I by Allied forces ended her occupation of Namibia. In 1920, South Africa received a League of Nations mandate to administer the territory under the league's trusteeship. Thus began the next phase in the painful history of the indigenous peoples of South West Africa. The departure of German settlers was followed by the influx of Afrikaner settlers, who then sustained the cruel eviction of Namibians from the fertile highlands. When apartheid became a state policy in South Africa in 1940, its enforcement was extended to Namibia where Bantustan-style entities were established and called "second-tier authorities" to function like the homeland governments in South Africa itself.

In 1960, following the Sharpeville massacre of protesting youths by the South African security forces, it became obvious to the Namibia peoples that the occupation of their land by the apartheid state was likely to be prolonged. The search for a more coherent platform of resistance against South Africa's occupation compelled the ethnically based Ovambo People's Organization (OPO) to transform itself into a national umbrella of resistance under the name of South West Africa

People's Organization (SWAPO), with Sam Nujoma as president. The backdrop to this was the massacre at Old Location the previous year of Namibians who were protesting their forced relocation to a new apartheid-style township. SWAPO's choice of armed struggle as a principal aspect of its anticolonial campaign won it the recognition of the OAU in 1965 and that of the United Nations General Assembly in 1973 when it was declared "an authentic representative of the Namibian people." The outcome of that choice was that SWAPO began to receive material support from both China and the Soviet bloc. But it wasn't until August 26, 1966, that the South African Police had their first contact with the People's Liberation Army of Namibia (PLAN), SWAPO's armed wing, when it attacked their camp at Omgulumbashe. This was in the wake of a rejection of a case brought by Liberia and Ethiopia on behalf of the Namibian people before the International Court of Justice at The Hague in which they challenged the legality of South Africa's mandate over Namibia. That rejection was on the grounds that both countries lacked the right to bring the case.

Namibia's liberation struggle was initially couched in terms similar to South Africa's at the time. In the mid-1970s, stepped up repression from the South African Defense Forces (SADF) led to the exodus of young people from Namibia into exile where they enlisted as PLAN cadres. Internal pressure from this younger generation of fighters and the need to retain the vital material support from China and the Eastern bloc, compelled the SWAPO leadership to adopt a leftist political program that saddled the movement with the obligation to build "a classless, non-exploitative society based on the ideals and principles of scientific socialism." That adoption placed SWAPO in the same ideological category as FRELIMO in Mozambique and MPLA in Angola as opposed to the ANC, which simply favored the reform of the status quo in a nonracial South Africa. Perhaps this egalitarian socialist vision influenced SWAPO's unequivocal resolve to embark on a gender integration of the PLAN that was well received by the female PLAN recruits.

SWAPO gave the Namibian nationalist struggle a much needed political visibility within Namibia and abroad and helped to achieve political independence for Namibia in 1992 with Sam Nujoma as president.

**NAPOLEON BONAPARTE** 1769–1821, French military leader and emperor. Born in Corsica, shortly after the island became French, Napoleon was educated in mainland France, and began his military career as an officer in 1785. During the French Revolution he was an active member and supporter of the Jacobins, a radical revolutionary group. In 1793 his military abilities became clear as he successfully defeated British forces during the siege of Toulon. That same year, at the age of twenty-four, he was promoted to the rank of general. He then successfully defeated counterrevolutionary forces and won a spectacular series of victories as commander in chief of the army of Italy. He subsequently took an active role in the political organization of Italy along republican lines.

After the disastrous campaign of Egypt, in which much of the French navy was destroyed by Admiral Nelson, Napoleon returned to Paris in 1799. Fearing counterrevolutionary forces within France and military threat from neighboring states, he seized power in a coup later that year. He gave himself full executive powers by drawing up a new constitution that was approved with a large majority in an 1800 plebiscite.

A decisive victory in Marengo against Austria, and the coming of peace in Europe in 1801, increased Napoleon's popularity to its highest level yet. His expansionary ambitions persisted. Alarmed at the danger France represented as a continental power, the British declared war in 1803. Intent on getting rid of Napoleon, they supported the royalist attempt at regaining power. To minimize threats on his life, Napoleon resolved to transform his regime into a hereditary empire. The Imperial Regime, proclaimed in 1804, became increasingly dictatorial and restored some of the traditions of the Old Regime.

The British threat was still pressing and any hope of invading the British isles vanished when Nelson destroyed the French and Spanish fleets off Cape Trafalgar on October 21, 1805. But Napoleon remained dominant on the continent, winning decisive battles at Austerlitz and Jena-Auerstädt. By 1810, despite setbacks in Spain and Portugal, Napoleon's triumph was complete. His empire included much of Italy, Germany, and all of Holland, and most of the states surrounding France had become its vassals.

As the head of state, Napoleon embarked on a series of bold administrative reforms that were to have a lasting effect on French society. One of his most significant achievements was the codification of civil law. The Napoleonic Code blended the legacy of the revolution with clauses protecting private property and economic freedom.

Military triumph, however, was short lived. Napoleon finally and irrevocably overextended his forces in Russia where his *grand armée* self-destructed in a catastrophic retreat during the onset of winter. The news of Napoleon's defeat caused uprisings throughout many of the territories occupied by France. The nationalist fervor unleashed by French troops during the revolutionary wars was now backfiring as Napoleon's defeated enemies sought revenge for similarly nationalistic reasons. By 1814 France was being attacked on all borders.

Napoleon's influence on the course of nationalism in Europe was enormous. The diffusion of the institutions and ideals created in revolutionary France by his victorious armies, the consolidation of states through war during his reign, and the very fear created by an apparently unstoppable French military power did much to stir durable national feelings throughout the continent. Napoleon's conquests, for instance, paved the way for the future unification of Germany and Italy, and resistance to French troops in Spain stirred lasting nationalism.

Domestically, Napoleon's legacy lived on as a myth of national greatness and continental domination. His nephew, Napoleon III, came to power in 1848 largely on the shoulders of that legacy. The institutions Napoleon created or reinforced also greatly contributed to the administrative and political consolidation of France as a unitary nation-state.

## NASSER, GAMAL ABDEL

1918–1970, Army officer, leader of the Free Officers movement, president of Egypt (1956–1958) and the United Arab Republic (1958–1970).

Nasser was born in Alexandria on January 15, 1918. His father's assignments within the postal service resulted in a peripatetic childhood; Nasser had several homes when young, attending primary school in Cairo and secondary schools in Alexandria and Cairo. He entered the Royal Military Academy in 1937 and received his commission in 1938. Nasser's military career included service in the Sudan and combat experience in the Palestine War in 1948–1949.

Subsequent to that conflict, Nasser and other officers disillusioned with the corruption and failures of the existing parliamentary monarchy formed the Free Officers, a secret organization within the Egyptian military. After building up their support within the military, they seized power on July 23, 1952. The king was immediately exiled; in June 1953 Egypt was declared a republic. As the Free Officers cohort consolidated their power in 1952–1954, Nasser also established his personal ascendency within the new regime. Prime minister by 1954, in 1956 he was elected president. Nasser remained president of Egypt, and later of the United Arab Republic, until his death on September 28, 1970.

The Nasser period marked a revolution in both Egyptian domestic and foreign policy. Internally, the new regime undertook a major restructuring of the economy. A sweeping program of land redistribution was inaugurated in 1952. In the early 1960s "Arab Socialism," a collage of policies relying on the nationalization of much large-scale industry and commerce and the development of the state-owned public sector as the engine of economic growth, was implemented. Arab Socialism also involved an effort at leveling class differences and extending the benefits of modern society (formal education, health care, social security programs) to the mass of the population. While the "socialist" thrust of the Nasser era has largely been reversed by Nasser's successors, his legacy lives on in the huge state sector of the economy as well as in many of the social service programs established in the 1950s and 1960s.

Nasser is equally significant in the history of modern Egyptian as well as Arab nationalism. The initial thrust of the new regime was on terminating the lingering British occupation of the Nile Valley. An agreement with Great Britain providing for self-determination for the Sudan was successfully negotiated in 1952–1953. The Sudan agreement was followed by Anglo-Egyptian negotiations for British withdrawal from Egypt proper. These were amicably concluded in late 1954; the last British troops left Egyptian soil in 1956. The early Nasser years thus witnessed the end of the British occupation of Egypt that had begun in 1882.

The Nasser period eventually saw much deeper Egyptian involvement in Arab nationalism than had been the case under previous regimes. Nasser was not an ideological Arab nationalist, at least at the start; he was drawn into promoting Egyptian leadership of the Arab nationalist movement by his concern for achieving the complete independence of Egypt from foreign influence. In the early and mid-1950s, the Western powers were floating various schemes for linking the newly independent states of the Arab world into an alliance with the West. Viewing such projects as the perpetuation of Western imperialism, Nasser's preference was Arab solidarity and defense cooperation organized within the framework of the League of Arab States. When in 1955 the Western-linked Baghdad Pact took shape, Egypt vehemently opposed its extension elsewhere in the Arab world besides Iraq. Nasser's ability to serve as an alternative pole to Western alliance in the eyes of Arabs was enormously reinforced by his international initiatives of 1955–1956: an arms agreement with the Soviet Union in 1955, nationalization of the Suez Canal, and successful resistance to combined British-French-Israeli attack in the Suez Crisis of 1956. After Suez Nasser was the dominant figure in inter-Arab politics, the focus of Arab nationalist hopes throughout the Arab world. "Nasserists" were to be found in many Arab countries, advocating close cooperation and sometimes union with Egypt and through their activities pulling Egypt into the internal politics of such states as Jordan, Lebanon, and Syria. It was his attraction as an Arab nationalist leader that in early 1958 prompted Syrian politicians and soldiers to advocate Syrian union with Egypt in the United Arab Republic (UAR).

Nasser remained the dominant figure in Arab nationalism through the 1960s. Even after the secession of Syria from the UAR in September 1961, his partisans outside Egypt continued to promote union under Nasser's leadership. Abortive unity talks were conducted with Syria and Iraq in 1963–1964, failing over the issue of the allocation of power. Nasser's advocacy of closer Arab cooperation and the adoption of socialism in the 1960s were viewed as a threat by existing Arab monarchies, generating an Arab cold war between self-proclaimed revolutionary and conservative Arab regimes that lasted for much of the decade. It was partially Nasser's desire to gain advantage in this inter-Arab competition that in 1967 led him to imprudent initiatives vis-à-vis Israel when tensions between the latter and Syria threatened regional peace; the result was the war of June 1967 in which Egypt lost the Sinai Peninsula to Israel. Although Nasser's appeal as the focus of Arab nationalist aspirations was much diminished by military defeat in 1967, nonetheless he remained the arbiter of inter-Arab politics. His death of a heart attack in September 1970 occurred at the conclusion of his strenuous efforts to negotiate a ceasefire in a Jordanian–Palestinian civil war in Jordan. For many Arab nationalists Nasser remains the preeminent Arab nationalist leader of the 20th century, a symbol of an era of Arab liberation and solidarity when the goal of Arab unity appeared a realistic prospect.

First-generation biographies of Nasser include Robert Stephens, *Nasser: A Political Biography* (1971), and Anthony Nutting, *Nasser* (1972). A more recent biography is that of Peter Woodward, *Nasser* (1992). Nasser's (ghostwritten) musings about the revolution of July 1952 are available in Gamal Abdel Nasser, *The Philosophy of the Revolution* (1954).

**NATIONAL ANTHEMS** Official patriotic symbols, national athems represent the musical equivalent of a nation's motto, crest, or flag. These songs embody a nation's character; they convey a nation's moods, desires, and goals. Thus anthems, like other national symbols,

become a nation's "calling card." They serve as modern totems—signs by which nations distinguish themselves and reaffirm their identity boundaries.

Every nation adopts a national anthem. The phenomenon is rooted in the signification practices of primitive tribes and clans and, later, the symbolization practices of ancient, classic, and medieval rulers. The earliest national anthems emerged in Central Europe and South America during the late 18th- and 19th-century nationalist movements. In the 20th century, Eastern countries and new independent nations in Africa and elsewhere followed suit.

Generally, national anthems are widely inclusive. In this way, they represent one of the more democratic chapters within the history of symbolization. As opposed to being the sole property of governing elites, these songs function as symbols of the people. Indeed, national anthems are often written or officially adopted because of their ability to capture and inspire the hearts of citizens. The history of specific national anthems aptly illustrates this point. Consider, for example, the German national anthem, *Einigkeit und Recht und Freiheit* or *Unity and Right and Freedom*. Franz Joseph Hadyn composed this anthem following a visit to England. Reportedly, Hadyn was so interested in the effects that *God Save the King* had on the English that he resolved to present his own countrymen/women with a similar composition. Unlike many of his other works, Hadyn viewed this anthem as a "popular" song, one that would move *all* of his fellow citizens. Similar sentiments guided the composition of Malta's national anthem. In bringing words to Robert Sammut's music, lyricist Dun Karm Psaila created a prayer for Malta, an anthem he hoped would unite *all* of the nation's parties and citizens in strong ties of religion and love of country. Finally, consider the national anthem of Vietnam, *Thanh Nien Hanh Khuc* or *Call to to the Youth*. Composer Luu Huu Phuoc created this song during Vietnam's struggle for independence. This music's haunting patriotic rhythms are said to have mesmerized the nation's youth. Before long, young people's enthusiasm for the song spread to the country at large. Thus the song came to embody a collective surge toward freedom. Upon the signing of the 1954 Geneva Accord, *Call to the Youth's* widespread popularity resulted in the immediate designation of the song as Vietnam's official anthem. The anthem was renamed *Call to the Citizens*.

The power of national anthems is aided by the efforts of national leaders who aggressively diffuse these symbols to the broader population. Leaders strive to keep national anthems before the public, thus ensuring universal knowledge of, exposure to, and familiarity with such symbols. Anthems are taught in schools; they are used at state occasions; they serve as a backdrop for public ceremonies and celebrations. In this way, leaders confer legitimacy on the anthem, legitimacy that may be lacking in other patriotic or folk songs.

Because of their special status, national anthems serve several important social functions within a nation. These symbols *crystallize the national identity,* announcing both to citizens and to a nation's neighbors "who" the nation is, where it has been, and where it is going. National anthems also *create and maintain bonds between citizens;* with every performance, anthems contribute to the formation of a collective body. National anthems establish a rallying center for the national collective; in this way they *motivate patriotic action.* Often national anthems function to *honor the efforts of citizens;* linking citizen to symbol creates a symbiotic relationship between the living nation and the symbolic nation. National anthems also serve as a *means for legitimizing authority;* authority figures attempt to merge their goals and desires with these symbols' sacred aura. Finally, national anthems often function as *tools of popular political protest;* when anthems function in this way, the public takes command of them, using the symbols to convey their discontent with the national leadership.

While the function of national anthems is highly similar across nations, the musical design of such symbols is not. When one reviews the more than 180 anthems currently in existence, such differences become strikingly clear. It is useful to think of these variations in the musical structure of anthems as different communication strategies. Depending on the circumstances surrounding an anthem's creation and adoption, composers and national leaders choose different strategies with which to represent the nation. One might be tempted to locate these communication choices in the indigenous characteristics of each nation. Similarly, one might be tempted to explain such choices by referring to certain unique sociopolitical events that surround an anthem's creation or adoption. However, research reveals that differences in the musical structure of national anthems are generated by forces that transcend the peculiarities of any one nation. While the lyrics of an anthem stand as a unique referent to each nation, musical designs of national anthems are systematically linked to the broader social conditions from which an anthem emerges. These conditions include a nation's economic position within the world arena, its political system (authoritarian versus democratic), its regional location, and the cohesiveness of its population. As such, a nation's musical representation of self is largely a product of circumstances beyond the nation. Composers and adopters locate their nations within certain spatial, economical, political, and cultural maps. They then structure their musical statement with reference to those who share a similar location in these domains.

For a comprehensive collection of current national anthems, consult W. L. Reed and M. J. Bristow's *National Anthems of the World,* 9th ed. (London: Blanford Publ., 1997). In *Identity Designs: The Sights and Sounds of a Nation* (ASA Rose Book Series, New Brunswick, N.J.: Rutgers University Press, 1995), Karen A. Cerulo explores the musical design of national anthems. The author charts variations in the musical structure of 180 national anthems, and she explores the link between certain structural designs and extranational social conditions.

**NATIONAL IDENTITY** National identity is a modern phenomenon that presupposes the existence of a nationalist movement and of a national consciousness. It has to be distinguished from having a sense of uniqueness, for the expression of the latter does not require the existence of a nation. Before the emergence of nationalism, some ethnic groups and cultural communities had a sense of their uniqueness without referring to any national identity. Collective cultural identities have "always" existed, but it is only with the emergence of nationalism that they came to be defined in national terms. Thus, for a national identity to exist it is essential that members of the nation see themselves as forming a nation and as thereby sharing an identity.

National identity can be defined on the basis of a common territory, a common language or culture, a common religion, a common history, a common will (Ernest Renan's famous "everyday plebiscite"), and shared political and legal principles. However, none of these characteristics is indispensable to the existence of a national identity, as bespeak the national identities of multicultural societies or of stateless and diaspora nations. Similarly, these defining characteristics can be organized and given significance in very different ways. Therefore, national identity is a polymorphous phenomenon. Moreover, it can be defined in either civic or ethnic terms. When membership criteria are civic, nationality is equated with citizenship and is essentially political and legal. A national identity defined in civic terms can accommodate and integrate new members from distinct cultural or ethnic backgrounds. One can thus *become* American, French, or English; the boundaries of national identity are relatively open and one has the possibility, in principle, to choose one's nationality. On the contrary, when membership criteria are ethnic, nationality is exclusively a privilege of birth that can be neither chosen nor changed. It is neither an issue of speaking the "national" language nor of holding the proper citizenship. All individuals constituting the nation are then said to derive their most *essential* identity from this membership.

One should nevertheless bear in mind that the distinction between civic and ethnic national identities is a conceptual one that applies primarily to membership criteria. In practice, there are many gray areas. For example, even the universalist political principles of civic national identity have to be embodied in cultural and historical practices and rituals so as to be rendered meaningful and to arouse identification and adhesion. In the same way, most residents of civic nations are citizens simply because they were born on the right side of the border. For them, choice is generally not an issue. Moreover, nationalist movements can be more or less civic or ethnic depending on which sector or faction as well as historical era one studies. Finally, national identity is not a fixed phenomenon. A civic national identity can become ethnic and, theoretically, vice versa.

But whether defined on civic or ethnic grounds, national identity is depicted by nationalists as fundamentally homogeneous and as transcending other "subnational" identities based on class, gender, local customs, and so on. In this sense, it expresses the indivisibility of the nation. It draws its attractive power from the equality implied by its principles: All those who share this identity have equal rights and obligations, and are endowed with the same qualities. Claiming a national identity is thus a way of claiming a particular status. Moreover, it provides a powerful prism that allows the individual to situate himself or herself in relation to his or her fellow citizens and to other nations in the world.

To the discussion about the civic or ethnic nature of national identity is added the problem of the origin of national identity. On that subject, there is strong debate in the literature on nationalism between the "constructivist" or "instrumentalist" approach and the "primordialist" approach. The latter is critical of the civic/ethnic distinction and argues that national identity is always built on the basis of primordial relationships such as ethnicity or kinship, that is, relationships that appear to people as "given" and "natural." Consequently, national identities are described as being fundamentally "extensions" of ethnic groups. On the other hand, the "constructivist"/"instrumentalist" approach stresses the mutable and changing character of identity and membership in order to show that national identity is an "invention" of specific groups that use it in a self-interested manner. This approach points out that national cultures are usually not mere by-products of primordial cultures, and that the presence of ethnic groups does not in itself explain the emergence and importance of national membership.

But despite different arguments, both approaches recognize national identity as being distinct from other collective identities. Whether constructed or derived from primordial relationships, national identity cannot be simply boiled down to an ethnic, cultural, political, or territorial identity, and its effect on people remains real and powerful regardless of the explanation put forward.

**NATIONAL MINORITIES** This politically charged term is often used to describe a minority population that inhabits state A, yet its own real or alleged allegiance is to state B. When politicians, journalists, and others from state B refer to such a group as a "national minority," they inevitably raise the issue of state B having a say in its welfare. Such an argument is in violation of state A's sovereignty, and for that reason, in almost all cases, state A will strongly object to the use of the term. Moreover, state A may consider such a designation to be the first step toward its losing control over the territory inhabited by the minority population, and argue that it is a thinly veiled pretext to justify state B's territorial claims.

Although the above description is an abstract one, it has found, and no doubt will continue to find, numerous applications in interstate conflict. The term came gradually into use in the 19th century to describe European populations who were left outside a nation-state's boundaries. East of the Rhine, where the Habsburg, Ottoman, and Romanov Empires reigned supreme, ethnic groups had been scattered among diverse territories and their transformation into nations raised the issue of their statehood. To have a state meant that precise boundaries had to be drawn, and it was impossible to do this without leaving some prospective nationals outside those state boundaries. The problem reached monumental proportions after World War I as the empire of the past were replaced by new nation-states. The drawing of boundaries in some cases (such as Yugoslavia) was a painstaking and complicated affair that involved many countries, and delicate interplay between international and domestic politics.

For committed nationalists, those left outside the nation-state were national minorities. Poland, Germany, Hungary, Romania, Serbia, Bulgaria, and Greece are among the Eastern European countries that have claimed this to be the case. In Germany, the issue was skillfully exploited by the Right, and Hitler was the ultimate beneficiary of the "double standard" imposed by the World War I settlement. It was not, however, the only case. Because the post-World War I arrangements were essentially imposed by the winners, "loser" countries such as Bulgaria inevitably considered that they lacked international legitimacy. Such issues were greatly involved in the local dynamics of many Eastern European countries during World War II. To cite one example, purification of a territory so as to "cleanse" it of the undesirable national minorities was the goal of Croat Ustaša.

With the conclusion of World War II, grave changes took place. In some cases, such as in Poland and Czechoslovakia, the war offered the opportunity to "cleanse" the national territory, in effect solving the problem. In other countries, the war brought new Communist regimes that attempted to handle such issues by developing new organizational structures (for example, Tito's Yugoslavia, or Moldova). In the international arena, the rise of the East versus West antagonism, but also the strong desire to exorcise the Nazi ghost, led to the establishment of the United Nations and a decisive shift from questions of ethnicity and minority toward ideologically based dividing lines. For almost forty years, these broad guidelines remained stable, until the 1989 collapse of Communism in Eastern Europe, and the dissolution of the Soviet Union. The 1990s have witnessed the return of these issues to the international arena, as the wars of Yugoslavia, the breakup of Czechoslovakia, the Hungarian–Romanian dispute over Transylvania, and other less publicized affairs have become once again part of East European politics.

Of course, the application of the term and its surrounding conceptual and political disputes have not remained confined to East Europe. National minorities can be said to include the Kurds, Tibetans, Muslims (in India), and Tamil (in Sri Lanka), and, of course, an entire array of African peoples. It is a foregone conclusion that the migration of the term to other parts of the world will color various international disputes during the next century.

For a discussion of these issues, see Rogers Brubaker, *Nationalism Reframed* (Cambridge: Cambridge University Press, 1996), in which an abundance of secondary literature on individual cases is cited. For the Balkans, see the useful introduction by Hugh Poulton, *The Balkans: Minorities and States in Conflict* (London: Minority Rights Group, 1991). The journal *Nations and Nationalism* often addresses these issues as well, and provides detailed discussions of individual cases.

## NATIONALISM, DEVELOPMENT OF

Liah Greenfeld defines nationalism as the "location of the source of in-

dividual identity with a 'people,' which is seen as the bearer of sovereignty, the central object of loyalty, and the basis of collective solidarity." Therefore, nationalism can be seen as the central link that brings together the concept of state, nation, and nation-state, which enables a people to gain a sense of national identification and thus be motivated to work for their own development and prosperity. Jawaharlal Nehru's comments shortly after India's independence from the British testifies to the role of nationalism in national development: "Any other force [such as communism], any other activity that may seek to function, must define itself in terms of . . . nationalism. No argument in any country of Asia is going to have weight if it goes counter to the nationalist spirit of the country. . . ." Any analysis of the history of nation building in the 20th century illustrates the important role that nationalism has played in the development and establishment of nation-states around the world. The Indian polity, for example, like so many other newly formed nation-states after World War II, demonstrates how people from diverse religious, ethnic, class, and caste backgrounds can share, through nationalism, a sense of identity and belonging.

Nationalism can then be seen as a positive force, which offers diverse peoples a point of common and shared togetherness. It offers them a chance at loyalty to something bigger than themselves and their group. It provides them a point of historical reference and enables people to recognize their similarities through culture, ancestry, or history. This nationalism can occur on several levels. An African can share a sense of loyalty to Africa while also holding certain loyalties to a particular state like Kenya and therefore be called a Kenyan nationalist. But this individual can also have very strong loyalties to his own group, the Kikuyu, in a way that is not distinguishable from nationalism. There are obvious advantages to this communal sense of identity as Africans or Kenyans, but it also poses numerous problems of conflict among groups with strong loyalties within nation-states.

Nationalism encourages democracy through the idea that the state belongs to its citizens and that power should ultimately rest in the hands of the people and that politicians are only instruments and truly public servants. In addition, nationalism encourages self-determination. Perhaps the most striking political developments of this century have been the emergence of new nations across the planet. And as we enter the 21st century this is still the case. Whether democratic or authoritarian, populist, socialist, or Communist, the nationalist revolutions of this century were primarily revolutions of peoples whose aim was and still is to throw off colonial or imperialist rule and influence in the courageous attempt at attaining freer, richer, happier lives. While the motivations and intentions of these revolutionary movements were to give back to the people what they rightfully deserved, many failed to achieve a better standard of living for the masses. Nevertheless, these nationalist movements sought to take back what was rightfully theirs, to establish *their* own national governments, to have these governments act in *their* interests and fulfill *their* ideals. The result is that the nationalist spirit, which discourages imperialism, strengthens these newly formed governments.

Nationalism can both be a product and a facilitator of development and modernization. Many scholars believe that nationalist movements can often encourage economic development. Especially that form of nationalism that places its loyalty to the nation-state can facilitate and provide ample motivation for raising the standard of living of the masses. Finally, nationalism is a positive force for development in that it allows for and encourages political, economic, and social experimentation. Democracy, for example, was an experiment in 1776 in the New World that may have never occurred if not for nationalism among a people. In the age of globalization when Western influence is so evident in all areas of life through media, consumer products, and satellite television, many people are concerned that their cultural heritage and future as unique people is threatened. Nationalism can act as a motivating force that provides new ways of looking at age-old traditions that are threatened from the outside. Nationalism has been the key to the survival of the French language and thus the culture among Canada's Quebecois.

On the other hand, nationalism can and does often lead the process of national development into stagnation. This is the dark side of nationalism—when national divisions are so divisive that modernization and economic development are not only halted but begin to disintegrate. At the recent 50th anniversary celebrations of the United Nations, Pope John Paul II reiterated the sentiments and pleas of both his successors by pointing to the destructive force of nationalism. In denouncing nationalism he drew a clear distinction between patriotism and nationalism. The 20th century will be most remembered on the one hand for the misery and horror caused in many cases by nationalist sentiments and movements, whereas on the other, it will also be remembered for the great obstacles and bridges that have been built to unite peoples and nations that have contributed directly to the most rapid material development our world has ever witnessed.

As our world entered the new millennium, one could not help but wonder with awe at the incredible contradictions of the past 100 years. The global economic and material development and progress of the 20th century outweighs any of the previous 1000 years. It is also within the 20th century that we saw an increase in the number of newly formed independent nation-states. With the dismantling of the colonial powers in Asia and Africa and the Pacific and the crumbling of the former USSR, a large number of nations have found independence and self-determination. Yet, the dark side of this past 100 years has witnessed more destruction and devastation than all of human history combined. Most of this destruction and loss of life is a direct result of nationalism.

The definitive bibliographic source is Karl Deutsch and Richard Merritt's *Nationalism and National Development: An Interdisciplinary Bibliography* (The MIT Press, 1970). Other classic works on development include Barrington Moore's *Social Origins of Dictatorship and Democracy* (Beacon Press, 1966), Immanuel Wallerstein's *The Modern World System I & II* (Academic Press, 1974 & 1980), and W. Rostow's *The Stages of Economic Growth: A Non-Communist Manifesto* (Cambridge University Press, 1964).

**NATIONALITY, CONCEPT OF** It is difficult to give an authoritative definition of nationality. Most people would agree, however, that it has much to do with the Western version of nations and nation-states since the 18th century. Nationality can have three varieties, depending on its usage. The first refers to the state or quality of belonging to a nation. The second denotes an aggregate of people sharing a distinguishing racial, linguistic, and culture and forming one constituent element of a larger group (nation). The third stands for nationalism itself. There is no denying that the concept of nationality differs in both history and cultures. Its core usage, however, is largely rooted in the West.

Europe in the 19th and 20th centuries has been seized with nationalism. The unification of Germany and Italy, and the breakup of the Habsburg and Ottoman Empires, brought about the reorganization of Europe. Nationalism has inspired the political awakening of Asia and Africa. As John Stuart Mill would have it, "the boundaries of governments should coincide in the main with those of nationalities."

By international law, nationality is commonly regarded as an inalienable right of every human being and the UN Universal Declaration of Human Rights (1948) states that "everyone has the right to a nationality" and that "no one shall be arbitrarily deprived of his nationality."

In the first half of the 19th century Mazzini, who played an indispensable part in the making of modern Italy, interpreted the principle of nationality by advocating that the individual nations, as subdivisions of a larger world society, should peacefully coexist.

Marxists were at first not interested in the theme of nationality and looked forward to its speedy demise. They expected that many nationalities would soon fade out and had no regret for the diminishing fate of the Welsh and smaller Slav peoples. In their view, all civilized countries would merge into a single economic whole and the working class would lose their national feelings. The realization of supranational socialism is unavoidable. Due to practical politics they had to take nationality issues more seriously and later tried to integrate them to the cause of proletarian revolution. Stalin believed that nationality is not a racial or tribal phenomenon. It has five essential features: a stable and continuing community, a common language, a distinctive territory, economic cohesion, and a collective psychological makeup. However, all Marxist theorists before the Sino–Soviet split would emphasize the need that nationality issues should give priority to socialist cause and the class struggle against the bourgeoisie. Under Stalin, the autonomous republics of the Soviet Union were "nationalities" but they were not held to imply an individual's relationship to the state.

The quarrel between the USSR and China has strengthened the nationalist tendency of each party. In China the identification of the fifty-six nationalities, modeled on their Soviet counterpart, is based on the principle of equality and unity rather than social evolution. The Soviet model of *natsional'nost'* (nationality) was much moderated. According to the Marxist interpretation of history, all human societies pass through five social formations: primitive Communism, slave ownership, feudalism, capitalism, and finally Communism. In correspondence with this five-stage social evolution model, peoples are also hierarchically categorized into tribes, nationalities, and nations. Despite this, China still treated her fifty-six types of peoples as equals ignoring the particular social stages they found themselves in. They are all *minzu*, which has been translated as "nationality" in English and is now termed "ethnic group" in official discourse, to avoid the possible confusion of statehood with the identified peoples as its constituent parts.

With the increasing power of print and the electronic revolution, which coincided with huge migrations from excolonial states to the rich capitalist centers and the end of the Cold War following the collapse of the former Soviet Union and its allies, great social and economic transformations have taken place. On one hand citizenship began to challenge the old semantics of nationality; the century-long dream of "one nation one state" has run aground on the other. A new school of thinkers has added other issues to the concept of nationality: environmental problems, epidemics, social genders, orientalism, and so on.

In most parts of the world the concept of nationality seems quite outmoded when it is used to refer to minority groups in a nation-state. It denotes more than ever the individual affiliation to the nation-state as is the case in international law.

## NAZARBAYEV, NURSULTAN 1940–, President of the Republic of Kazakhstan, born in the village of Chemolgan in the Kaskelen District southwest of the capital of Kazakhstan, Almaty. Nazarbayev began employment in 1960 as a smelter worker at the Karaganda metallurgical plant after studying metallurgy at Dneprodzerzhinsk in the Ukraine. In 1969 Nazarbayev became involved in Communist Party activities, becoming the secretary of the Communist Party Committee at the Karaganda iron and steel plant in 1972. After this appointment Nazarbayev's political career took hold and, in a relatively short space of time, he became chairman of the Council of Ministers of the Kazakh SSR (1984–1989). It was during this period that Genadii Kolbin, a Russian, became first secretary of the Kazakh Communist Party, a controversial appointment that resulted in protest riots in Almaty in December 1986. Despite the unpopularity of such a move, Kolbin remained first secretary until June 1989 when Nazarbayev replaced him. Nazarbayev became president of the Republic of Kazakhstan in April 1990 and has retained the post ever since. He has thus resided over the transition of the country's status from a Soviet Republic, its declaration of sovereignty, through to its recognition as a fully independent state.

After Kazakhstan's declaration of independence in December 1991 following the failure of the August coup, President Nazarbayev would have had little doubt that the ethnic question would be one of the key issues that would dominate the post-Soviet political landscape. The contemporary demography of Kazakhstan is difficult to ascertain, but the 1989 census indicated that Kazakhs constituted almost 40 percent of the population, Russians almost 38 percent, Germans almost 6 percent, and Ukrainians about 5 percent. The Russian and Kazakh population are therefore present in equal numbers, with the Russians predominating in the north and the Kazakhs predominating in the south. Given the dramatic decline of the economy since the disintegration of the Soviet Union this ethnic composition of the country has confronted Nazarbayev with the worrying possibility of ethnic discord and geographic fragmentation. Since the Almaty riots of 1986 Kazakh–Russian relations have not been marred by large-scale violence. However, there have been large-scale protests in the north, especially in the East-Kazakhstan Oblast, and ethnic tensions remain high over such issues as language rights and economic redistribution.

Faced with the pressures of a resurgent Kazakh identity and the fears of the other ethnic groups arising from this resurgence, Nazarbayev has implemented a dual policy of "Kazakhization" and a state-building project of "harmonization" (garmonizatsiia). The policy of "Kazakhization" has involved the "parachuting" in of Kazakhs into key regional administrative posts that were occupied by non-Kazakhs during the Soviet period. The government has also established the Kazakh Tili (Kazakh Language) organization with the purpose of promoting the Kazakh language and Kazakh culture in the north of the country where the population has become more Russified. The government has also endeavored to revive a greater interest in Islam by sending several imams to the north of the country to redress the religious imbalance between the north and the south. This "Kazakhization" process would appear to include the encouragement of Kazakhs to return to Kazakhstan and the housing of such Kazakh immigrants primarily in the north, possibly to balance the predominant Russian presence in the northern oblasts.

At the same time, these policies that seek to promote Kazakh culture and representation throughout the state are supposed to be balanced by a policy of "harmonization." Essentially this involves a process of state-building that aims to ameliorate the interethnic and intraethnic tensions that have become apparent since independence. This policy of harmonization has included the banning of associations seeking to promote social, racial, national, religious, class, or tribal discord. Organizations that wish to be registered by the state must therefore be ethnically neutral in character. At the same time, although Russian dissension remains over the unequal status of the Russian language, Nazarbayev, in an effort to assuage Russian fears, has endeavored to dilute the recent language law passed by parliament that makes a knowledge of Kazakh compulsory by claiming that it is unconstitutional.

Much hinges on how well Nazarbayev balances the understandable resurgence of Kazakh culture and representation with a policy of harmonization that seeks to balance this resurgence with the rights of all citizens to equal representation. How Nazarbayev's terms of office as president of independent Kazakstan will be judged historically depends, to a large extent, on whether he successfully achieves a balance between the interests and concerns of the Kazakhs on the one hand and the Russians on the other.

**NAZISM** There is perhaps no better example of the kind of nationalism that is exclusive, belligerent, expansive, and threatening to outsiders than National Socialism. Devotion to the nation, defined in racial terms and rigidly directed by the leader of a nondemocratic and monopolistic party, was everything.

On January 30, 1933, Adolf Hitler became chancellor of a country traumatized by the aftermath of a lost war and by a devastating economic depression. Some observers argued that he ascended to the chancellorship legally because his Nazi Party had done well in the 1932 elections. On March 5, 1933, he called for new elections, and his party won 44 percent of the popular votes. Although he used manipulation, he nevertheless got a parliamentary majority on March 23, 1933, to support his Enabling Act, which suspended the Reichstag's power and made him the sole leader of Germany. Also he submitted some of his changes to plebiscites so that he could claim that the people had accepted them. He went to considerable effort to make his accumulation of full power in his own hands seem legal.

That argument is mistaken. When the critical elections came in the years 1930–1933, he unleashed his two private armies, the Sturmabteilung (Storm Divisions, SA) and Schutzstaffel (Protective Troops, SS), to break up other parties' rallies and meetings, to beat up opponents in the streets, to terrorize those who manifested an inclination to vote for another party, and to take other kinds of unnerving actions, such as throwing up blockades around Berlin at election time. No person with democratic convictions and a rudimentary knowledge of the Weimar Constitution could call such tactics "legal." However, after the economic disasters of 1929 and 1930, more and more Germans began to look to the former corporal from Austria, who had gained German citizenship only shortly before becoming chancellor in 1933. As the novelist Erich Kästner wrote: "People ran after the pied pipers down into the abyss."

His Nazi Party enforced a so-called Gleichschaltung, an untranslatable German word meaning the "synchronization" or "coordination" of all independent groups or institutions so that none could exist without supporting Nazi rule. In March and April 1933 he abolished the federal organization of Germany, and for the first time in its history, Germany became entirely centralized, with governors (Reichsstatthalter) carrying out Hitler's policy in the various regions. By June all independent labor unions had been outlawed, and a Labor Front was created with the task of keeping labor under firm control. By July all political parties except the Nazi Party had been abolished, and concentration camps were established, where alleged enemies of the state could be "concentrated" and controlled.

By October all communications media, including film, were brought under Nazi control. All newspapers editors were required to be Aryans (non-Jewish members of an ancient race to which Germans belonged, according to Nazi doctrine). They could not even be married to Jews. This initiated a steadily growing number of measures directed against Jews within Germany, who, according to Nazi ideology, were social parasites who weakened the German nation, of which they were not a part, no matter what service they might have previously performed for Germany. Many Jews, including brilliant intellectuals and scientists, such as Albert Einstein, fled Germany.

In the dark hours of June 30, 1934, known as the "night of the long knives," Hitler had hundreds of potential challengers to his authority within his own party murdered, especially the SA leadership. While his assassination squads were at work, he also eliminated many prominent non-Nazis, as well as leading authors, lawyers, civil servants, Catholic politicians, military leaders such as General Kurt von Schleicher, and harmless citizens who at some time had caused irritation to one or the other Nazi bosses. Former Chancellors Von Papen and Heinrich Brüning escaped by the skin of their teeth. These cold-blooded acts were enough to intimidate most resistance to Hitler inside or outside the Nazi party until his death in 1945.

A senile President Paul von Hindenburg died August 2, 1934, and Hitler simply combined the offices of president and chancellor and declared himself the absolute leader (Führer) of party and state. He required that the nation give retroactive approval of this unconstitutional act in a plebiscite, a favorite maneuver of dictators whereby one may vote "yes" or "no" under the watchful eyes of party henchmen. Despite intimidation measures, five million Germans voted "no" to this act.

With parliament, elections, and state governments eliminated, a single party ruled Germany. Hitler divided all of Germany into districts, each called a Gau and led by a hard-core Nazi called a Gauleiter. These districts were subdivided into circles (each called a Kreis) and groups. Such units were also created for Austria, Danzig, the Saarland, and the Sudetenland. At the top of this party organization was the Führer, Hitler himself. Such rule from the top was called the "leadership principle." The Nazis' policies and rhetoric were expressed not only in party rallies, but in the party's newspaper, the Völkischer Beobachter (People's Observer). It is inconceivable that the party would have been so successful in winning and maintaining power without Hitler's strong will and his ability to coordinate a diverse collection of ambitious Nazis.

Hitler required all officers and soldiers to take an oath of allegiance, not to the constitution of Germany or the German nation, but to him alone. Many German officers had grave misgivings about this. But Hitler's shrewd treatment of the army gradually eliminated the military as an immediate threat to his power, although high-ranking officers would later prove to be his most daring, though ill-fated, foes.

By fall 1934, Hitler had become the undisputed leader of a dictatorial state he called the "Third Reich." This name was used to remind Germans that he had created a new Germany worthy of the two earlier German Empires: the one created by Charlemagne in 800 and the one formed by Otto van Bismarck in 1871. His path to power had been washed by blood and strewn with corpses. Many of his subjects had been driven through fear to passivity.

Nevertheless, Hitler could claim by 1939 with justification that he ruled a people that generally supported him. How was this possible? In the first half of his twelve-year rule he was able to achieve certain things that many Germans and non-Germans alike regarded as little less than miraculous. His accomplishments confused and disarmed his opponents, who in 1933 were still the majority within Germany. But their numbers had dwindled considerably by 1938, even if most of them did not actually become Nazis.

Before 1933, Hitler had shown himself to be an unparalleled organizer and hypnotic speaker. But few Germans expected him actually to succeed in conducting the complex affairs of state. Before he came to power, he remained largely in the realm of fuzzy generalities. For example, he made no concrete suggestions on how to combat the problem of unemployment. After coming to power, he quickly inflicted a heavy dose of terror on the German people. That his rule always rested in part on terror indicated that the whole German people never entirely embraced National Socialism. But terror gradually declined and remained at a level just sufficient to keep the population in a state of fear without driving them into desperate resistance. His orchestration of terror within Germany and his skillful use of his own undeniable charisma were psychological masterpieces from which all would-be dictators could learn.

After 1941 Hitler withdrew more and more from public view and spent most of his time in military headquarters. Since his first goal—to dominate Europe—was slipping out of reach, he turned toward a second goal—the eradication of the Jews. His crimes went far beyond what the world had hitherto known and would only be fully discovered at the end of the war. Earlier and contemporary dictators or would-be world conquerors such as Alexander the Great, Napoleon, and Stalin caused many thousands or millions of deaths. But whether one agreed with them or not, they usually had political or military motives for their brutality. Hitler had none beyond the ethnic cleansing of Jews from Europe. His murder campaign of the Jews worked against his political and military objectives. It diverted troops and transport facilities from the military effort, and it sacrificed a talented and educated part of the German citizenry who had fought for Germany in World War I. This campaign was not only morally repugnant; it sapped the strength of a weakening Germany.

Hitler spared the Jews no misery, but he was careful not to allow most Germans to know for sure what was happening to these victims. The exterminations were conducted mostly in Eastern Europe, outside Germany. Careful precautions were taken to prevent unauthorized persons from witnessing what was happening within the camps. He even took the special measure, whenever possible, of sending German Jews first to large ghettos such as Theresienstadt in Bohemia, where they were able to write postcards back to Germany before being transported to death camps.

Of course, rumors about what was really happening filtered into Germany. But there was no freedom of speech or press. Thus the inability to confirm rumors meant that anyone could reject them or choose to remain in doubt. Most Germans did just that, as did most non-Germans in the areas occupied by German troops. In Germany and in the occupied countries there were persons who took risks by hiding or helping Jews. But nowhere was there the kind of mass uprising that would have been necessary to put an end to that shameful policy. Only the German military was capable of overthrowing Hitler, and the most dangerous plots against Hitler were hatched within the armed forces. In the end, only the military power of Hitler's enemies brought the Third Reich to its knees.

Hitler's policy of liquidating people whom he considered to be racially inferior or *Untermensch* ("subhuman") and "un-German" was not restricted to the Jews. Only about a fifth of the 25,000 Gypsies living in Germany in 1939 survived by 1945, and estimates of the total number of European Gypsies murdered at Hitler's order range up to a half million. In October 1939, German leaders began a five-year campaign to destroy the entire Polish elite and culture. Polish priests, professors, journalists, businessmen, and earlier political leaders were systematically liquidated. When one considers that the Soviet Union conducted a similar policy against the Poles in those areas under its domination—most dramatically in the Katyn Forest in 1939, where Soviet forces murdered 10,000 Polish officers and élites and dumped them into mass graves—it is almost miraculous that Poland was able to survive as a nation. In the end, Poland lost about six million countrymen, about half of whom were Jews and not more than 300,000 of whom had fallen in battle.

The treatment of the Russians and of subject peoples under Russian rule was even worse. German policy in the Soviet Union revealed the extent to which Hitler's racial theories, which posited a hierarchy of races in which the Germans were on top, thwarted Germany's national interests. Many peripheral peoples who had never joined the Soviet Union voluntarily greeted invading German soldiers more like liberators than conquerors. A far-sighted German policy to transform these people into allies might have succeeded. Instead, Russians and non-Russians were treated with the same brutality. Unlike in Poland, the German army was involved in the actions directed against the civilian population in the Soviet Union. Germans especially mistreated Soviet prisoners of war. According to German military records, by May 1, 1944, they had captured more than five million Soviet soldiers, mostly in 1941. However, fewer than two million remained alive. Almost a half million had been executed, 67,000 had fled, and almost three million had died in the camps, mostly of hunger. German mistreatment of the Soviet population helped Stalin unify his people in the war effort against the Germans.

**NEHRU, JAWAHARLAL** 1889–1964, Nehru was born into a prominent Kashmiri Brahman family, the son of one of Mohandas Gandhi's top lieutenants, Motilal Nehru. He was educated in England at Harrow and Trinity College, Cambridge. Although he studied natural sciences and law, his life would be devoted to Indian nationalist politics. His only child, Indira Gandhi (1917–1984), would follow in his political footsteps. Although from his young years he desired India's independence from Britain, not until he met Gandhi in 1916 did he begin to develop a clear idea about how to achieve it. He was impressed by Gandhi's activist approach to struggling for freedom without either hating or fearing Great Britain. Nehru became a top leader in Congress after the tragic Amritsar massacre in 1919, when a local British military commander gave his troops the order to open fire on a crowd of unarmed Indians who had gathered for a meeting, killing 379 and wounding 1200.

In 1929 he was elected for the first time as president of the Congress Party because of the way he attracted the admiration of young and intellectual Indians. That same year he presided over the session in Lahore that announced that India's political goal would be complete independence from Britain, not merely dominion status within the British Empire. For this commitment, Nehru would spend more than nine years in jail during a total of nine imprisonments, ending in June 1945.

While he resolutely sought to break India's ties with Britain, he was appalled by fascism in Europe. When World War II broke out in 1939, the British viceroy in India, Lord Linlithgow, committed India to the war effort without even consulting with India's autonomous provincial ministries. Congress rejected this presumption and withdrew its provincial ministries. Nehru sympathized with the Allied war effort against fascism, but he argued that only a free India could actively support Britain. When Congress adopted the Quit India resolution on August 8, 1942, all of Congress's leaders, including Nehru and Gandhi, were arrested and thrown into jail.

The war saw an intensification of the conflict between the Congress and the Muslim League, led by Mohammed Ali Jinnah, who was later to become the founder of Pakistan. This made unity of action afterward impossible. After the war it became obvious to everybody, including the British, that India was to be independent. However, there was intense disagreement whether there should be one united India that would include both Hindus and Muslims, or two or more separate independent states. Gandhi pleaded for unity, while Nehru reluctantly agreed to partition on August 15, 1947, a decision that he would later regret. The result was a bloodbath as Hindus sought to purge India of Moslems, and Pakistan attempted to drive Hindus out of East and West Pakistan.

Nehru became India's first prime minister in 1947 and remained in that office until his death in 1964. After independence India's new leaders in the Congress Party, above all the popular Nehru, tried to build a single Indian nation. They went about that task by attempting to separate religion from public life and to guarantee minorities that their religious faith would have no relevance to their rights as citizens. Nehru himself claimed to be neither a Hindu nor a Moslem, but an agnostic. They attempted to contain Hindu communal assertiveness and to guide it into nation-building activity. They hoped that this secularism would hold a very heterogeneous Indian society together. That attempt succeeded for several decades.

Free India created a regime committed to secularism and democracy and adopted a constitution that promised everybody equal treatment before the law, regardless of caste or community. The Congress Party, which ruled India most of the time for over four decades, initially supported these principles. Until Nehru's death, India remained largely free of major communal riots. But conservative religious organizations persisted in giving a communal twist to political discussions. There always remained an insurmountable gulf between Nehru's tolerance and secular ideas and the cultural and religious convictions and attitudes of the groups upon whose support he and his party depended. Rioting flared up again in the late 1960s.

Nehru served as foreign minister in his own government, and his three basic planks were economic planning, social reform, and a nonaligned foreign policy. His economic ideas were Marxist, but he could adjust this approach to fit India's unique circumstances. He founded the worldwide Nonaligned Movement. His nonalignment was sometimes questioned. For example, India was the only nonaligned country to vote in the United Nations for the Soviet Union's invasion of Hungary in 1956. Also when the Chinese threatened to occupy the Bramahputra River valley in a bitter border dispute, Nehru turned to the West for aid, thereby inducing China to withdraw. He did not hesitate to use military force to achieve Indian objectives. He led India through the first war against Pakistan, and he sent troops into Portuguese Goa, the last remaining colony on the Indian subcontinent. In 1971 the Portuguese finally withdrew. He failed to solve the dispute over Kashmir, still an intractable problem in the 21st century.

Nehru's attempt to build a single nation had failed as the 20th century came to a close. With the political center in New Delhi becoming weaker and the party system more fractured, political groups have claimed religious sanction for their aggressive actions in a rough-and-tumble electoral environment. Nehru and the Congress Party had intended to create a secular Indian nation under a rule of law. However, religion and politics have not remained separate, and a sturdy Indian national identification that can overcome community differences has not been developed.

**NETANYAHU, BENJAMIN** 1949–, Benjamin ("Bibi") Netanyahu became, in 1996, the first individually elected prime minister under new reforms to Israel's electoral law—defeating Labor's Shimon Perez by a slim margin. Charismatic and persuasive, the new prime minister was nonetheless plagued by scandal and overshadowed at his election by the assassination of Yitzhak Rabin. Rabin had been shot at a 1995 Labor peace rally by a right-wing extremist bent on stopping Israeli–Palestinian peace negotiations and Israeli withdrawal from the West Bank. Identifying himself as a Begin disciple, Netanyahu has been widely criticized for failing to discourage such radicalism and for courting extreme factions within the Israeli religious right.

Benjamin Netanyahu was born on October 21, 1949, in Tel Aviv, the son of a prominent Israeli academic. He spent the last year of his army service as a commander in an élite army unit, then attended the Massachusetts Institute of Technology and received his M.A. in business administration in 1976. That same year, his older brother, Jonathan, was killed while commanding the Air France hostage rescue in Entebbe, Uganda, becoming a national hero and a symbol for Israel's struggle against terrorism. In 1980, Benjamin Netanyahu founded an antiterrorism institute, which he named after his brother.

The author of several books on terrorism, Netanyahu began his political career as the Israeli consul general in Washington, D.C., becoming Israel's ambassador to the United Nations in 1984. During the Gulf War and Iraq's missile attacks on Israel, Netanyahu appeared frequently on American television, coming to prominence as an articulate and charismatic speaker. In 1988 he returned to Israel, to become a Knesset (Israeli Parliament) member and a rapidly rising star in the Likud Party. In 1990, he was appointed deputy minister to Prime Minister's Yitzhak Shamir's office and assumed the party's leadership in 1993, as Shamir retired.

Approaching the election in 1995, polls indicated a close race between Netanyahu and Rabin. Yet, in the aftermath of the Rabin assassination and the outpouring of public grief and outrage, the Likud Party was widely criticized for fostering the unprecedented polarization within Israeli society over the peace process and many predicted a landslide for Shimon Perez. However, suicide bomb attacks in Ashkelon, Jerusalem, and Tel Aviv in February and March appeared to change public opinion. The attacks, said to have been in retaliation for the Israeli assassination of Hamas mastermind-bomber Yahya Ayyash (known as "the Engineer"), claimed the lives of more than fifty Israelis and gave new reasonance to Natanyahu's tough antiterrorist stance and warnings of compromised Israeli security.

On May 29, 1996, Netanyahu won the election by a little under 1 percent of the vote. After a period of uncertainty, Netanyahu and Palestinian President Yasser Arafat finally met in September and publicly confirmed a mutual commitment to the peace process and the interim agreement. For the next three years, negotiations continued in fits and starts, stalled intermittently by terrorist attacks, settlement expansions, and mutual hostilities. By 1997, Arab–Israeli relations in general worsened after several Hamas bombings, an escalating military conflict between Israel and the Hezbollah in Southern Lebanon, and a botched Mossad (Israeli intelligence) assassination attempt on Jordanian soil that severely strained Israel's relations with Jordan. Domestically, Netanyahu's government was charged with corruption and beset by opposition within his own conservative coalition to the terms of the peace negotiations. Generally regarded as a conciliatory figure, not an ideologue like his predecessors Menachem Begin and Yitzhak Shamir, Netanyahu was perceived as precariously poised between his commitments to his conservative coalition and international pressures to see the peace process through to completion. With only marginal public approval, he relied in 1998 on Labor opposition support to pass a new redeployment agreement with the Palestinian Authority. He was replaced as Prime Minister in 1999 by Ehud Barak of the Labor Party.

**NEW ZEALAND, NATIONALISM IN** New Zealand is a Pacific island nation off the coast of Australia first settled by Polynesians in the 1st century B.C.E. and then by Europeans beginning in the 17th and 18th centuries. Any indigenous nationlist movements were overwhelmed by military force before becoming a serious threat to colonial interests. European settlers there never mounted a concerted effort for independence from Britain so nationalist movements have not played a major role in New Zealand's history. National pride, however, has been a significant part of New Zealand's culture in recent decades.

The first European to arrive in what is now New Zealand was Abel Janszoon Tasman who in 1642 was repelled by its inhabitants who managed to kill several of his men before the explorers retreated. For some time, therefore, New Zealand was little more than a line on European maps until the arrival of James Cook's expedition, which circumnavigated and charted the two major islands in 1769–1770. Cook reported that the natives were intelligent and recommended their colonization.

At first New Zealand was primarily an appendix to Australia's whaling industries and a stopping off point for traders. Gradually the indigenous Maori became involved and believed initially that they were benefiting from European trade, exchanging provisions for products they did not have. By the middle of the 19th century most of them had converted to Christianity as part of an energetic missionary movement mounted by the Anglicans, Methodists, and Roman Catholics.

In 1838 New Zealand was annexed by Britain as part of New South Wales and became a separate crown colony in 1841. The New Zealand Association, a commercial enterprise, quickly moved into the colony, "purchasing" huge tracts of land from the Maori through misrepresentation, trickery, and brute force. Eventually the Maori became alarmed at the flood of Europeans but indigenous uprisings were quickly suppressed.

By the late 19th century many Europeans living in New Zealand began to regard themselves as a separate nation; an entire generation born there had no memory of Britain and in the 1890s they formed New Zealand Natives Associations. Their primary national pride was not in military supremacy, however, but in sports, especially rugby football. In World War I New Zealand soldiers marched off proudly to war but suffered a horrible price in the loss of men and thus national leadership. Nearly one in three of the troops between the ages of twenty and forty were killed or wounded.

After the war New Zealand gained political autonomy from Britain as part of the Commonwealth and developed close relationships with the United States as well. The process did not involve any flamboyant nationalist movements or widespread demonstrations, but a gradual transfer of power.

**NGO DINH DIEM** 1901–1963, Veteran nationalist politician and president of the Republic of Vietnam from 1956 until 1963. Diem was born in the Vietnamese capital of Huê, the son of a senior official in the imperial court. He attended the National Academy (Quoc Hoc), a secondary school established by the court in 1896 to train functionaries in Western learning, and then earned a law degree at the University of Hanoi. After graduation, he accepted employment as an official in the court of Emperor Khai Dinh, and in 1933 he was named minister of the interior under Khai Dinh's successor, Emperor Bao Dai. But Diem soon resigned as a protest against interference in imperial affairs on the part of the French colonial regime in Indochina.

For the next several years, Ngo Dinh Diem was not directly involved in politics. In 1945, he refused an offer by Ho Chi Minh, leader of the Indochinese Communist Party, to collaborate with the latter's new Democratic Republic of Vietnam, which had just seized power in Hanoi. A devout Catholic, Diem was opposed to Communism as well as to French colonialism, and in the late 1940s he emigrated to the United States, where he

sought U.S. support for the building of a future non-Communist Vietnam after the departure of the French. U.S. officials respected his strong anticommunist credentials, but many doubted his political capacities, describing him in reports as an unpractical visionary. Nevertheless, in June 1954 Bao Dai, now chief of state, appointed him prime minister of his Associated State of Vietnam, which was collaborating with the French against Ho Chi Minh's DRV, in the hope that Diem would win Washington's support for his own government.

One month later, peace talks in Geneva resulted in an agreement to divide Vietnam temporarily into two zones, with Ho Chi Minh's DRV in the North, and Bao Dai's government in the South. As prime minister in Saigon, Diem quickly eliminated all opposition to his rule, and in 1955 he organized a referendum that resulted in Bao Dai's resignation as chief of state. The following year, Diem was elected president of a newly established Republic of Vietnam (RVN). Although some U.S. officials continued to doubt his political acumen, Diem was viewed as the only political figure capable of resisting a Communist takeover of the entire country, and eventually the Eisenhower administration gave him its full support.

Unfortunately, Diem's authoritarian instincts and his lack of sensitivity to the political and economic aspirations of the Vietnamese people soon led to growing discontent. By the end of the decade, an insurgent movement actively supported by the DRV in the North was posing a severe challenge to his regime. Despite some reservations, President John F. Kennedy affirmed U.S. support for the RVN on the condition that Diem introduce reforms to win greater popular support. Diem actively resisted Communist-led forces in the South (popularly known as the Viet Cong), but resisted U.S. suggestions for political and economic changes. Many perceived that Diem favored Vietnamese Catholics at the expense of the Buddhist majority in the country, and in the spring and summer of 1963, Buddhist demonstrations erupted to protest restrictions placed on their religious activities. In early November, a military coup—with tacit approval from Washington—overthrew President Diem and established a new military regime. Diem was assassinated by his captors the following day. Kennedy's decision to approve the deposition of Ngo Dinh Diem became a major source of controversy in the United States, as his successors showed little capacity to stem the tide of Communist expansion in Vietnam, which culminated in a takeover of the south in April 1975.

# NICARAGUAN NATIONALISM

NICARAGUAN NATIONALISM Nicaragua (Republica de Nicaragua) is a Central American country that achieved independence from Spain in 1821, becoming first a part of the Mexican Empire, then a member of the United Provinces of Central America and finally an independent state. Nationalism in the country's postcolonial history often evolved around two poles: an effort to gain or maintain some independence from the United States, on the one hand, and clashes between polarized domestic factions, on the other, sometimes leading to violence.

As part of a wave of anticolonial struggles in Central America in the early 19th century, Nicaraguan revolutionaries temporarily deposed the Spanish government. Shortly thereafter one part of the country, Leon, chose to rejoin Spain and the rebel Granada region was severely punished for its rebellion. The clash between these two regional factions persisted well into the next century, with Leon usually identified with the Liberal Party and Granada the Conservative Party.

Both Leon and Granada accepted union with Mexico (1822–1823) but could not accept each other. They continued to fight until Nicaragua joined the United Provinces of Central America in 1826. Nicaragua left the federation, however, in 1838.

Once the Spanish were gone in the 1820s, the British and then the Americans moved in to fill the power vacuum and quickly became major players in Nicaraguan politics. The British government, for example, developed alliances with local powers on Nicaragua's eastern Mosquito Coast and seized the port of San Juan del Norte, subsequently renamed Greytown, in 1848. In 1856 an American, William Walker, actually managed to become president of the country. He was thrown from office a year later, however, by efforts of the United Provinces in cooperation with a powerful American enterprise. The Accessory Transit Company was Cornelius Vanderbilt's steamship and carriage operation created to operate between Greytown and the Pacific to take advantage of the California Gold Rush.

In the early 20th century conflicts over a potential canal across the country from the Atlantic to the Pacific ended when the United States sent in the marines, a practice that had become as commonplace as clashes between the liberals and the conservatives. The United States intervened militarily in Nicaragua in 1894, 1896, 1898, 1899, 1907, and 1910. When they did so again in 1912 they seemed there to stay. The U.S. marines withdrew only after U.S.-backed Juan Bautista Sacasa was elected president almost twelve years later in 1933 and the nationalist rebel leader Augusto Cesar

Sandino submitted to the new government. The U.S.-trained Nicaraguan National Guard, led by General Anastasio Somoza Garcia, assassinated the popular Sandino the following year. Somoza then deposed President Sacasa and became president in a fraudulent election in 1937.

Somoza and his family ruled the country for the ensuing decades, maintaining power through repression at home and an alliance with the United States abroad. Somoza's son, Luis Somoza Debayle, followed his father in office in 1957 after the president was assassinated only to be succeeded by two puppet presidents (Rene Shick Gutierrez and Lorenzo Guerrero Gutierrez) and his brother Anastasio Somoza Debayle.

Throughout the Somoza regimes an opposition movement grew in the face of grinding poverty, political repression, and growing inequality. In 1961 the Somoza regime aided the United States in the unsuccessful Bay of Pigs invasion aimed at overthrowing Fidel Castro's Communist government in Cuba. That same year Marxist opponents of the Somoza regime founded the Sandinista National Liberation Front (Frente Sandinista de Liberacion Nacional, FSLN) named after slain nationalist leader Sandino. The Sandinista Revolution that followed mobilized widespread support in the country, including the support of many grassroots groups within the Catholic Church (the Base Communities) that had traditionally supported the ruling élites.

In 1974, following a devastating earthquake in the capital city of Managua that killed 6000 and left 300,000 homeless, the Sandinistas moved against the government, successfully kidnapping a group of Somoza's élites. The government responded with a brutal counterinsurgency that resulted in the deaths of thousands of peasant civilians and widespread sympathy for the Sandinista rebellion. The Sandinistas occupied the national palace in 1978 and the following year captured city after city until Somoza resigned and fled the country on July 17, 1979.

The Sandinistas found it difficult to govern because of the devastated economy, on the one hand, and U.S. opposition to the regime on the other. U.S. President Ronald Reagan, determined not to allow a Communist government to thrive at its doorstep, took stern measures to protect its interests and to undermine the new government's. The Sandinistas nationalized local banks and insurance companies as well as natural resources. They established Statutes on Rights and Guarantees to protect individual rights and freedoms, and established close relations with Cuba and other socialist bloc nations.

The Reagan administration recruited, trained, and armed counterrevolutionaries, the Contras. A U.S. trade embargo in 1985 was followed by a denial by the World Bank and the Inter-American Development Bank of most Nicaraguan requests for loans. With spiraling inflation and a plummeting economy, on the one hand, and a military confrontation with the Contras on the other, the Sandinista government found it difficult to maintain power. In 1987 the U.S. Congress voted against further military aid to the Contras and the Reagan administration turned its attention to the political sphere. In 1990 National Opposition Union candidate Violeta Barrios de Chamorro, whose campaign was financed by the United States, won the presidential elections and the Sandinistas were defeated at the ballot box.

## NIETZSCHE, FRIEDRICH

1844–1900, Nietzsche was regarded in his day as a destructive thinker who despised nationalism, Christianity, humanitarianism, and liberalism. He was an individualist who had no German nationalist sentiments and who regarded the Germans as weak and the Jews as strong. In 1888 he said: "German spirit: for the past eighteen years a contradiction in terms." Born in Saxony, he studied classical philology in Bonn and Leipzig. He had a professorial chair in Basel, Switzerland.

He was more a poetic than a systematic philosopher. Because he suffered from frequent migraine headaches, he wrote aphorisms; his insights are flashes of intuition expressed in short, pithy, and poignant form. He saw life in terms of a biological urge, which he called the "will to power." Life is a never-ceasing effort to give form to this inner impulse. He was deeply struck by the ancient Greek's distinction between the "Dionysian" (spontaneous, frenzied) view of life and the "Apollonian" view, which stressed the measured and the orderly. In his opinion, the former was superior to the latter, as he presented in *Thus Spake Zarathustra*. Although he admired Schopenhauer, Nietzsche was basically an optimist who had hope in a more glorious future. He advocated a liberation of moral standards, which he believed were derived from individuals' will to power. They had to be freed from the leveling tendencies of such morality as Christianity, which favors the "slave morality," the weakest people, the "last man." Heroic persons, not the average, should establish life's values. Knowledge is an instrument of survival and should contribute to the power of such heroic people ("Supermen"), who should be able to rule without moral restraints, that is, *Beyond Good and Evil*, as his

1886 work was entitled. Through conflict, the weak should be weeded out or subjugated. To him, ethical systems or ideas are only "horizons" of the philosopher. They are a result of the will to self-realization.

In 1889 he went mad and spent the final decade of his life staring at the ceiling in Weimar. After his death his sister, Elisabeth Förster, edited his writings in such a way, adding her own views, that Pan-German nationalists and Nazis could invoke his quotable formulations about the "will to power" or superior and inferior human beings to support their causes. It is for that reason that this brilliant thinker, who despised the concept of "the nation," is often mistakenly considered a prophet of nationalism. The misuse of his work is also an example of how it is impossible for a philosopher to maintain control over his or her daring thoughts once ideologues adopt them in selective and simplified form and reshape and apply them according to their own political needs.

## NIGERIAN NATIONALISM

The Federal Republic of Nigeria, located on the western coast of Africa has the largest population of any African nation. It became independent on October 1, 1960, and adopted a republican constitution in 1963. Nigeria is a member of the British Commonwealth with English as its official language among the more than 200 spoken within its territory.

Because the nation of Nigeria is, like many postcolonial states, a construction of European maps and geopolitical decisions, it is an amalgamation of ethnic and tribal groups whose very diversity makes building a unified nation difficult it not impossible. The years following independence produced a series of efforts to create a government and a successful undermining of those actions at every turn.

A group of army officers failed in a coup attempt in 1965; Prime Minister Balewa and two regional premiers were murdered. Major General Johnson Aguiyi-Ironsi stepped in to set up a military government, restore order, and unify the regions, and met with anti-Igbo riots, a collapse of order in the west in January 1966, and his own assassination in July of that year. Lieutenant Colonel (later General) Yakubu Gowon established the next government and tried to convene a constitutional convention but was met with ethnic massacres.

As if that were not enough, the three eastern states of the country seceded on May 30, 1967, proclaiming themselves the Republic of Biafra. Soon the region was the scene of a bloody civil war that lasted until a Biafran delegation surrendered in Lagos on January 11, 1970.

Civilians as well as soldiers paid a very high toll. The civil war was over, but military coups followed military coups.

One ray of hope in a depressing story of unsuccessful nationalist struggles to build a nation is the nonviolent struggle for human rights and a civil society by the Ogoni in the Niger River Delta. The most celebrated member of that community is noted author and activist Kenule Beeson Saro-Wiwa.

Living in the densely populated, economically poor, and environmentally polluted region of Nigeria the 500,000 indigenous Ogoni have been struggling for their ethnic identity at least since the time of the 19th-century British colonialism. They have suffered much from their rulers, both foreign and domestic, but they have never given up hope.

Many of the Ogoni's problems stem from the fact that their region is home to more than 90 percent of Nigeria's oil exports revenues, which in turn comprise over 90 percent of the country's overall export earnings. In struggling to survive, the Ogoni not only encountered resistance from the Shell and Chevron oil companies that operate in the region, but also against the political elite of their own country who benefit from those revenues.

When Ken Saro-Wiwa first began seeking aid for the Ogoni in the international community he was met with deaf ears. Then he found the United Nations Working Group on Indigenous Populations and the Subcommission on the Prevention of Discrimination and Protection of Minorities. Sara-Wiwa met extensively with the Unrepresented Nations and Peoples Organization (UNPO), which helped provide resources and advice for indigenous nations that were willing to commit themselves to nonviolent struggle.

Although the Ogoni nationalists movement has not achieved its goals, and the Nigerian government indeed hanged Saro-Wiwa and eight other activists, their voice is now being heard in the international community. Human rights groups launched an international boycott campaign against Shell and Chevron, and partial sanctions were imposed by the British Commonwealth and other countries against Nigeria.

During the last days before his execution, Ken Saro-Wiwa declared "I'll tell you this, I may be dead, but my ideas will not die."

**NIXON, RICHARD M.** 1913–1994, After serving as a naval officer during World War II, two terms in the House of Representatives, and two years in the Senate until 1952, Nixon was tapped by Dwight D. Eisenhower to be his vice presidential candidate. Nixon was seen to have been a smart choice because of his anticommunist reputation at a time when McCarthyism was still a potent political force. He served as vice president from 1953 to 1961, when John F. Kennedy narrowly defeated him for the presidency. He spent the rest of the decade in the political wilderness until the unpopularity of the Vietnam War brought down President Lyndon B. Johnson and fatally divided the Democratic Party. This reopened the door for Nixon, who was elected president in 1968.

Nixon was a foreign policy president who was determined to get American policy back on the right track after the tragedy of Vietnam, from which he extracted the United States after four more difficult years of fighting and negotiation. He enunciated a "Nixon Doctrine," which called for a retrenchment from many of the global security commitments, including the "containment" of Communism by military means, that America had previously assumed. The policy called for U.S. involvement only when America's national interests are unmistakably at stake. If that is the case, then the United States would support regional powers that would do the fighting, but the United States would not become militarily involved itself. Because some small states might have to be sacrificed, this doctrine spelled the end of the "domino theory," according to which every Communist aggression had to be opposed lest one non-Communist state after the other begin to fall like dominoes.

Despite his earlier reputation as a fervent anticommunist, Nixon did not approach foreign affairs from an ideological perspective. He admired realists like French President Charles de Gaulle, who seemed to be able to divorce sentiments from the sober pursuit of the nation's interests. This enabled Nixon to pursue a policy of détente with the Soviet Union and the People's Republic of China (PRC). He normalized America's relationship with the PRC after twenty-one years of estrangement and made a historic visit to that country in February 1972. He then visited Moscow in May of that year, becoming the first president to travel to the Soviet Union since World War II. The harvest was a series of arms control agreements that placed some limits on the nuclear arms race.

Nixon's second term was demolished by his involvement in the Watergate scandal. In 1974, as impeachment hearings were about to open in the House of Representatives, he became the first president to resign from office. He spent the rest of his life gaining some rehabilitation by writing his memoirs (*RN*) and several respected books on international affairs. He also lent his support to the unpopular reversion of the Panama Canal to Panama and to assistance for Russia and the other Soviet republics after the collapse of the Soviet Union in 1991.

**NIYAZOV, SAPARMURAD** 1940–, Turkmenistani politician; the first president of the Republic of Turkmenistan; born in February 1940 in the capital city of Ashkhabad (now Ashgabad) then the Turkmen Soviet Republic. Niyazov started his career at the local branch of trade unions in 1950. He joined the ruling Communist Party in 1962. He completed his first degree in 1967 at the Leningrad Polytechnic Institute in Leningrad (now St. Petersburg). During the 1970s he rose steadily through the ranks as he was appointed to the Turkmenistan Communist Party apparatus. In 1984–1985 he served on the Communist Party Central Committee in Moscow. In March 1985 he was appointed the chairman of the cabinet of ministers in Turkmenistan and in December 1985 the first secretary of the Turkmenistan Communist Party. In 1989, Niyazov was elected a people's deputy in the Soviet Parliament. In October 1990 he was elected the first president of Turkmenistan by popular vote. In January 1994 the popular referendum extended his presidency until 2002.

Despite Niyazov's typical Soviet nomenclature biography, he introduced one of the most extravagant political regimes in the former USSR. Niyazov's national policy is represented by the slogan *"Khalq, Vatan, Turkmenbashy!"* (People, Fatherland, Turkmenbashy), and combines extreme forms of etatism, egalitarism, and authoritarianism. The president himself insists on his desire to create a "democratic, secular Turkmenistan considering the very specific nature of the Turkmen society" and using the "experience of Turkey, Egypt and western countries."

Soon after his election as the president of this gas and oil rich state, Niyazov accepted the title of *Turkmenbashy* (head of the Turkmens). In this and in his other actions he has often copied the policy of the Turkish leader Kemal Atatürk (1881–1938) and the Soviet leader Joseph Stalin. His cult of personality manifested itself in renaming streets, squares, schools, army units, and public utilities in Turkmenistan after his title *Turkmenbashy* and ensuring his portraits in every corner of the republic. Niyazov has granted free access to water, electricity, and gas for all citizens of the republic, but established tough authoritarian control over political life. Although the country has *Mejilis* (the Parliament) and regular elections take place (the latest parliamentary elections were held in December 1999), the

*Mejilis* does not play any significant role in political life. Niyazov introduced the traditional institutions of the Turkmen society into the political process, such as the Council of Elderly and the Khalq Maslehaty (the National Assembly, which was designed to "represent all Turkmenistanis" and consists of MPs, government officials, and representatives of all regions of the country).

In his ethnic policy, Niyazov has presented himself as the core of the society, the leader who has united all Turkmen tribes and all ethnic groups living in the republic. Turkmenistan is the only country in Central Asia that has granted double citizenship to its Russian-speaking population. The cornerstones of the national revival are the ideas of the national liberation struggle against Russian colonialism, the moral power of Islam and Niyazov's personality. Official Islam receives considerable support from the state, including lavish spending on the building and restoration of mosques and madresehs, but it remains under strict state control.

For further reading, see N. Kumar, *President Saparmurat Niyazov of Turkmenistan: A Political Biography* (New Delhi, 1999) which presents a semiofficial biography of the Turkmenistani leader. S. Akbarzadeh's "National Identity and Political Legitimacy in Turkmenistan" in *Nationalities Papers* 27(2) (1999) assesses some features of the post-Soviet national development.

**NKRUMAH, KWAME** 1909–1972, Nationalist leader and first president of the independent West African nation of Ghana. Kwame Nkrumah, born in the village of Nkroful in present-day Ghana, West Africa, was a Pan-African leader and first president of independent Ghana. Nkrumah was a leader in the national liberation movement proponent of the Pan-African ideology and practice in Africa.

Kwame Nkrumah was educated in Ghana, the United States, and London. He received a bachelor's degree in economics from Lincoln University and graduate degrees in philosophy and education from the University of Pennsylvania. During his time in the United States, he was exposed to the nationalist ideas of Marcus Garvey and the Pan-African views of W. E. B. Dubois. As a student he was active in the African Students' Association in the United States and the West African Student's Union in London. In 1945, Nkrumah assisted in organizing the fifth Pan-African Congress in Manchester, England.

Two years later, Nkrumah returned to the Gold Coast and joined the national liberation movement. In 1948, Kwame Nkrumah was asked to serve as secretary-general of the United Gold Coast Convention (UGCC), a party established to gradually work toward independence from Britain. As a result of Nkrumah's belief in more immediate and radical change, he broke away from the UGCC to form the Convention People's Party (CPP) in 1949. The CPP was voted into power in 1951 and Nkrumah became prime minister of the Gold Coast in 1953.

In 1957, Ghana became independent from Britain with Kwame Nkrumah as the first president. Nkrumah called for a conference of independent African states to discuss the common problems of African nations. The first Conference of Independent African States (CIAS) met in Accra in 1958 at which eight independent African states met. The conference formally declared Pan-Africanism and the commonwealth of the independent nations of Africa as an objective.

Nkrumah continued toward the objective of Pan-Africanism by signing a pact with President Sekou Touré of the newly independent nation of Guinea. The Ghana-Guinea Union of 1959, referred to as the Conakry Declaration, unified these newly independent countries. In 1960, Nkrumah and Touré joined with President Modibo Keita of Mali to form a union between the three African nations. Their hopes were for these efforts to lead toward a United States of Africa. Nkrumah was also instrumental in the summit conference of the Organization of African Unity (OAU) in Addis Ababa in 1963.

In 1966, while on a diplomatic trip to Hanoi, Nkrumah was overthrown by a coup d'état. He was invited by Sekou Touré to become co-president of Guinea. From Guinea, Nkrumah continued to write on the need for a Pan-African socialist revolution and established the PANAF publishing house in 1968.

Kwame Nkrumah's publications include *Toward Colonial Freedom* (1962), *Africa Must Unite* (1964), *Consciencism* (1964), *Dark Days in Ghana* (1968), *Neo-Colonialism: The Last Stage of Imperialism* (1965), *Class Struggle in Africa* (1970), *I Speak of Freedom* (1961), *The Handbook of Revolutionary Warfare,* and *Voice from Conakry* (1967), *Challenge of the Congo* (1967), and *Autobiography of Kwame Nkrumah* (1957).

## NONALIGNMENT

The policy of nonalignment was adopted by formerly colonized nations during the Cold War period as a strategy to avoid the effects of international power blocs and rivalries.

During the Cold War period, the opposing East/Communist and West/capitalist blocks exerted control over the newly independent nations. At the Bandung Conference of 1955, representatives from African and Asian countries met and declared their solidarity, support for national liberation struggles, and desire for independence from foreign domination. They proposed a stance of "positive neutrality" or political nonalignment in which their foreign relations would be dictated by their own interests as opposed to those of the bloc associated with their excolonial powers. This approach emphasized the need for newly independent nations to develop self-sufficiency and avoid manipulations.

This initial conference was followed by the Belgrade Non-Aligned Conference in August 1961 and Cairo Conference of 1964. Participant nations agreed to avoid alliance with a major power and not house foreign bases.

## NORTHERN IRELAND, NATIONALISM IN

The United Kingdom's most serious regional problem by far is Northern Ireland. The Irish island can be said to be England's oldest colony, having been invaded by the English in the 12th century and ruled as a colony until 1800, when it received its own Parliament. Ireland remained legally a part of the United Kingdom until 1922, when the twenty-six predominantly Catholic southern countries formed what is now the Republic of Ireland. The Protestant majority in the six northern countries considers itself to be neither a nation in itself nor a part of the Irish nation that was demanding a severance of all ties with the United Kingdom. They therefore rejected home rule (independence from Britain). The British at the time pledged that no change in the link between Northern Ireland and the United Kingdom would occur without the consent of the majority of the people. Every subsequent British government has held firmly to this commitment.

The largely Presbyterian and Church of Ireland Protestants are descendants of Scottish immigrants who began arriving in the 17th century. Their loyalty to the English crown is based on the monarch's historical status set forth in the 1689 Bill of Rights, as "the glorious instrument of delivering this kingdome from Popery and arbitrary power." It is not surprising that this historical attitude, along with the Protestant's rejection of unification of the two parts of Ireland, has always antagonized the Catholic minority in Northern Ireland (who comprise 42 percent of the population of 1.5 million). Although Northern Ireland is officially a secular state, in actual practice the friction between Catholics and Protestants dominates politics there.

Nationalism takes an unusual appearance in Northern Ireland. The term is applied only to an active element of the Catholic minority, which seeks to terminate British sovereignty over the six northern countries. Because they desire to become a part of the Irish Republic, they also are referred to as "republicans." The majority of Protestants call themselves "loyalists." They do not claim to be a separate nation, but rather to be a part of the United Kingdom. No overarching Northern Irish nationalism exists that could help hold these disparate groups together and strengthen a sense of shared purpose.

Northern Ireland has been in turmoil since 1968, when a Catholic civil rights movement organized internationally publicized street demonstrations to object to Protestant discrimination in housing, jobs, and electoral representation. British government pressure on the Northern Irish Parliament to meet many of the Catholic demands created a Protestant backlash. Peaceful street demonstrations in 1969 gave way to open violence, and British troops were sent to reestablish order.

In retaliation against Irish Republican Army (IRA) violence, some Protestants in the North organzied illegal forces. The best known illegal Protestant paramilitary group, known for its violence, is the Ulster Volunteer Force (UVF). This illegal unit should not be confused with the Ulster Defence Regiment (UDR)—the British army in Northern Ireland), the Royal Ulster Constabulary (RUC—the mainly Protestant police force), and the Ulster Defence Association (UDA—a moderate and legal Protestant paramilitary group). In 1993 Protestant gunmen murdered more people than did the IRA.

The British disbanded Stormont (Northern Irish Parliament) in 1972 and resorted to the unpleasant task of ruling the region directly, through a secretary of state for Northern Ireland. Successive British governments have sought earnestly for ways to devolve government power to the Northern Irish themselves. The problem has always been how to protect the Catholic minority's interests against a perpetual Protestant majority. British governments sought some form of "power-sharing" arrangement that would guarantee the minority Catholic parties a place in any Northern Irish executive. This idea infuriated the two Protestant political parties, the Ulster Unionists and the Democratic Unionists.

The British government tried to restore order. In 1975 it ended the detention of both Catholic and Protestant terrorist suspects without trial, and it has refused to declare martial law in the violence-torn area. Because of the risk of intimidation against jurors, nonjury courts (known as "Diplock Courts") were created for those persons accused of terrorist-related offenses. The British have always contended that the fundamental principles of British justice—a fair trial, the onus on the prosecution to prove guilt, the right to be represented by a lawyer, the right of appeal if convicted—are still maintained for all.

U.S. President Bill Clinton gave a boost to the peace process in November 1995 by paying the first visit to Belfast ever made by an American president. It was a triumph. The very approach of his historic visit helped dissolve a stalemate in the talks and revitalized cooperation. Hours before his arrival the Irish and British prime ministers met and agreed to a breakthrough: preliminary all-party talks, led by former U.S. Senator George Mitchell, would be held. An international "decommissioning commission," led by former Canadian chief of staff and ambassador to Washington, General John De Chastelain, sought a way around the weapons impasse.

John Major admitted that Clinton's coming helped "concentrate the mind." Greeted everywhere in Belfast by cheering crowds waving American flags, Clinton addressed over 100,000 people, the largest throng to gather in the square of Belfast City Hall. He appealed to everyone to put aside "old habits and hard grudges" and seek peace. One witness said: "I've never seen anything like this before. Everybody's come together." His American optimism reportedly made a deep impression. He met with all major leaders in the conflict and invited them to a reception at Queen's University; most came, which would have been unthinkable earlier. It was a very different Belfast that he saw: Gone were the soldiers on the hunt, the countless roadblocks, and the barbed wire. Although the ugly wall topped with razor wire separating Protestants and Catholics, called the "peace line," still stands, most of the blockaded streets have been reopened in Belfast.

There is very little support in Northern Ireland or elsewhere for immediate reunification of Ireland. But not since 1969 have there been so many grounds for optimism that "the Troubles" can end and that the Northern Irish can discuss their future peacefully. As a symbol of returning normalcy with Britain in 1995, Prince Charles became the first member of the royal family to make an official visit to the Irish Republic since 1922. Also in 1995, David Trimble, leader of the Ulster Unionist Party, the main Protestant group, traveled to Dublin and met with the Irish *Taoiseach*. This was the first time since 1922 that a Unionist leader was received in Dublin.

Talks, involving eight Northern Ireland parties and the British and Irish governments, continued, despite the outbreak of renewed violence following the assassination of a Protestant terrorist, Billy Wright, in Maze prison just after Christmas. American George Mitchell emphasized the importance of the negotiations: "We're talking about, literally, people's lives, the possibility of the resumption of the terrible conflict that enveloped this society with fear and anxiety. So, frustrating and tedious as it seems—and it is—you have to be patient and recognize how tough it is for them to move."

In the early morning hours of Good Friday in 1998, after a series of marathon sessions, *all* parties at the table reached a historic agreement: A new 108-member Northern Ireland Assembly would be elected using the Irish Republic's system of proportional representation with the transferable vote. To protect Catholics from being permanently outvoted on sensitive "cross-community" issues and to necessitate consensus, a majority of both Catholic and Protestant blocs or an overall "weighted majority" of 60 percent would be required for decisions. The cabinet would consist of 10 seats distributed proportionally to the four largest parties. The assembly would share power with a new North-South Ministerial Council, composed of ministers from the republic and Northern Ireland. This gives the Irish Republic its first formal role in Northern Ireland's affairs. In return, Ireland's leaders agreed to give up the republic's claim to the North. All parties pledged to use their influence to persuade armed groups to turn in their weapons within two years, and imprisoned members of those armed groups would be released within two years as well.

On May 22, 1998, referenda were held on both sides of the border, and 71 percent of Northern Irish and 94.4 percent in the republic approved of the Good Friday settlement. The following month, the first elections to the new assembly were held, and David Trimble's UUP came out on top with twenty-eight seats. John Hume's SDLP was second, with twenty-four seats. For their indispensable role in the entire peace process, Trimble and Hume shared the 1998 Nobel Prize for Peace. Hume had declared that "we finally decided that agreement for the whole community is more important than victory for one side." Other seats went to Ian Paisely's DUP (twenty), Sinn Féin (eighteen), the Alliance (six), the UKUP (five), Independent Unionist (three), and the Women's Coalition and PUP two each. The great number of parties winning seats demonstrated the effect of the proportional representation electoral system. Trimble became first minister, and the body met for the first time in the traditional Stormont building on July 4.

This being Ireland, an island with so much history and so many memories, things were not destined to go smoothly. In August 1998 a fringe Catholic organization calling itself the "Real IRA" exploded a car bomb in the Northern Irish city of Omagh, killing twenty-eight people. The public was so repelled by this grisly act that

the "Real IRA" apologized and announced a permanent cease-fire on September 12. To maintain his credibility in the Protestant community, Trimble called for a beginning of "decommissioning" (turning in) of weapons even before the creation of a Northern Ireland cabinet. Noting that this precondition had not been in the agreement, Sinn Féin balked at completing the peace process. Endless haggling over paramilitary groups' laying down their arms threatened the peace deal. However, both sides began taking cautious steps to implement the agreement. On December 1, 1999, a new coalition government in Ulster was formed that shares power devolved from Westminster in London. It included representation from both the party of hard-line Protestants, Rev. Ian Paisley, and former IRA commander Martin McGuinnes, as minister of education.

**NORWEGIAN NATIONALISM** Norway is a constitutional monarchy, formerly in union with Denmark until 1814, and then administrated by Sweden until 1905. Owing to the practices of royal intermarriage, the same king reigned over Sweden and Denmark in 1319, and in 1380 all the Scandinavian kingdoms had the same monarch. The countries were formally unified under the terms of the Kalmar Union in 1397. Sweden broke this union in 1523, but the entity legally known as the "Dano-Norwegian Kingdom" lasted until 1814, when Denmark was forced to give up Norway to Sweden following its defeat in the Napoleonic wars. Sweden's break with Denmark also had serious consequences for Norway; Christian III took this opportunity to bring Norway further under Danish control. He had the Norwegian bishops arrested, instituted the Reformation in 1539, and declared that the country "is and should be hereafter, like the lands Jutland (Jylland), Funen (Fyn), Zealand (Sjælland), and Scania (Skåne), part of the Danish Kingdom and under Danish crown forever." Following this edict, Norway was politically and culturally dominated by Denmark after 1523. This period is generally viewed as a time of economic decline and decreasing population in Norway, which was invaded by Swedes during the wars between Denmark and Sweden. In 1642, under the governance of Hannibal Sehested, Norway gained greater control over its own revenues, but formal control remained in the hands of Copenhagen.

This tendency was strengthened in principle when absolutist monarchy was declared in the kingdom in 1660. At the end of the Great Northern War between Denmark and Sweden in 1720, the economic conditions in Norway improved during a period of peace, although public unrest broke out in Christiania (Oslo) at the end of the 18th century due to unemployment and inflation. Later Norwegian nationalists often made their arguments against Danish rule based on economic calculations of Norwegian exports and imports during this period of Danish monopoly trade; however, it is unclear to what extent Norway suffered economically under Danish rule. It would probably be reasonable to characterize Danish rule over Norway as being neglectful rather than tyrannical. While Norwegians might have suffered as a result of being far from the centers of power, they also might have benefited in some ways as well—for example, peasants in Norway were generally under freer conditions than in Denmark.

Culturally, it was clearly a different story, one of Danish domination in artistic and literary spheres until the 19th century. During that period, ideas of nationalism and romanticism flourished in Norway, as elsewhere in Europe. As part of this movement, artists and other cultural figures set out to create self-conscious expressions of Norwegian cultural identity. Among these representations were the music of Edvard Grieg, who drew on old Norwegian folk melodies, and the collections of folktales by P. C. Asbjørnsen and Jørgen Moe (1841). Norwegian literary societies were founded in a patriotic spirit, and the images of the Norwegian farmer and farming culture were glorified.

Especially important to the struggle for a distinctly Norwegian cultural identity was the issue of language and language reform. The Norwegian language, as distinct from the Danish that was the language of political and cultural discussions, had fallen into disuse during the period of Dano-Norwegian unity. Beginning in the early 19th century, efforts were made to "rediscover" the old Norwegian tongue. Debates over language reform were extremely lengthy, complex, and fought over with a passion that often appears absurd in retrospect. Essentially, the goal was to create a language based on a reconstructed "old Norwegian," one that was sufficiently sophisticated for the demands of modern discourse, and was also perceived as fundamentally "not Danish." This was a difficult endeavor, and the result of much negotiation is that Norway today has two official languages—Nynorsk (called Landsmål before 1929), modeled on the dialects of the more rural western Norway, and Bokmål (the older term is Riksmål), on those of the urban and politically influential eastern Norway. Of the two, Bokmål is perceived as both more prestigious and more "Danish"—an indication perhaps that Norway has still not entirely escaped its feelings of cultural inferiority.

In 1814, the year of its union with Sweden, Norway received a constitution, and the parliamentary system was introduced in 1884. Some members of the state bureaucracy wished to continue the tradition of cooperation with Denmark. Among these was the poet Johan S. C. Welhaven (1807–1873) who satirized the over-romanticization of Norwegian cultural identity. He was opposed by poets and artists who rediscovered Norwegian cultural heritage, such as Henrik Arnold Wergeland (1808–1845). After a political struggle the union with Sweden was dissolved in 1905 and Prince Carl of Denmark was elected king of Norway and crowned Haakon VII. During German occupation during World War II, the royal family fled to England and maintained a government-in-exile. The feats of extremely active Norwegian resistance became a source of great national pride; one of their most renowned acts was the destruction of the German heavy-water plant, which thwarted the Nazi hopes of building an atomic bomb.

After the war, Norway joined the European Free Trade Association in 1960, but has been generally reluctant to forge closer ties with other European countries out of concern for maintaining local control over fishing and oil resources. Discussions of Norwegian membership in the European Economic Community went on during the 1960s, leading up to the referendum of 1972, when membership was rejected. In 1994, a second referendum was held about joining the European Union, but this was also rejected. In this same year, the Winter Olympics were held in Lillehammer. This event was seen as an opportunity to promote a tourist image of Norway's special qualities—pure, unspoiled nature, healthy lifestyles, stability, and hospitality.

As expressed to the international community at this meeting, the Norwegian attitude is generally protective of its sovereignty and resources, proud of its national accomplishments and assets, and generally skeptical about further unions with other countries, inside and outside Scandinavia.

**NYERERE, JULIUS** 1922–1999, Tanzania's founding president; set apart from all generations of African leaders by his political philosophy and style of leadership by example. Nyerere was born in the village of Butiama, near Musoma by Lake Victoria, son of a traditional chief. He started life as a mission teacher in the then trust territory of Tanganyika. Nyerere's planned career in teaching was disrupted for good in 1955, a year after he became a founding member of the Tanganyika African National Union (TANU), the nationalist party he represented when he became president. Nyerere accepted a second nomination to the Tanganyika Legislative Council in 1957 only to resign in protest after five months.

Nyerere addressed the Trusteeship Council of the United Nations in New York in 1955 and 1957 as well as the UN Fourth Committee in 1956. In 1958, Nyerere was elected to Parliament in Tanganyika's first election and was returned unopposed two years later in the second general election. By virtue of this second election he was invited by the British colonial governor to form Tanganyika's first Council of Ministers with an elected majority, and he became the first chief minister. Nyerere was sworn in as prime minister in 1961 after the Constitutional Conference. Under him Tanganyika became independent in December 1961 and he was elected president under TANU when the country became a republic the following year. In 1964 when Tanganyika entered a union with the island of Zanzibar, Nyerere became the president of the new union that became Tanzania.

Much of Nyerere's political philosophy and style of political leadership stem from his traditional African roots and Western education under the Roman Catholic mission. Nyerere argued that the basis of an ideal society is "human egality and a combination of freedom and unity of its members." That argument encapsulates the kind of society that he wanted to create in Tanzania—a socialist and democratic nation, free under African conditions and devoid of antagonistic classes. His *Arusha Declaration on Socialism and Self-Reliance* is seen as a charter of that African socialist-style democracy under a nonélite, one-party political system robust with popular participation that he labored to create in Tanzania.

The cardinal feature of Nyerere's vision of African socialism in his country is the *ujamaa* (togetherness) villagization program under which about 12 million Tanzanians were relocated to more than 7000 new villages.

Nyerere believed strongly in African decolonization, unity, and cooperation. He played crucial roles in both the decolonization struggles in Angola, Mozambique, Zimbabwe, and even South Africa and the formation of the OAU and the SADCC. Nyerere was a leader who never hesitated to go against the grains of the way poli-

tics is practiced in Africa, especially when issues call for integrity and moral leadership. In 1977, against the OAU charter of noninterference in the internal affairs of other African countries, he sent 45,000 Tanzanian troops into Uganda to oust General Ida Amin's brutal dictatorship.

Nyerere's understanding of the Cold War between the Eastern and Western bloc of nations made him an advocate of a national development strategy hinging on self-reliance for Third World nations, to help them to avoid being caught in the cross fire of the Cold War. To a good measure, that advocacy manifested in the formation of the Non-Aligned movement and the appointment of the South Commission in 1987 with him as chairman. The commission's report released in 1990 under the title of *The Challenge to the South* was described by one-time Commonwealth Secretary General Mr. Shradrack Ramphel as future development strategies for the Third World.

While Nyerere governed Tanzania as a one-party state, he never ruled out the emergence of multiple political parties in Tanzania. But the emergence of such parties he claimed will indicate the failure of the *Chama Cha Mapinduzi* (CCC), Tanzania's single nationalist party. And indeed, upon his retirement from the presidency and while he was still chairman of CCM he rethought his views on a one-party political system in Tanzania. That rethinking took place at a time when the Cold War was winding down, the Soviet Union was about to wither, and he had the chance to observe and interact with ordinary Tanzanians, which enabled him to discern that the CCM had failed to oversee the running of the economy. Nyerere guided both the debate on and the legislation of a multiparty system that eventually came into effect in 1992 in Tanzania.

Nyerere's views on African socialism, unity, and development are contained in several collections of his speeches and writings. He died in a London hospital in October 1999 of causes related to leukemia.

# O

**O'CONNELL, DANIEL** 1775–1847, Leader of the struggle for Catholic emancipation and Irish national consciousness in Ireland. Born in County Kerry, Ireland, to well-to-do landowners, O'Connell was a lawyer who defended indigent Irish Catholics against perceived injustices, which won him tremendous notoriety. He was a Catholic who strongly believed in the separation of church and state, religious freedom, and nonviolent reform. In 1828 O'Connell won a seat in the British Parliament and used his political power to engage in the Repeal movement which sought to abrogate the Act of Union (which abolished the Irish Parliament) between Great Britain and Ireland.

O'Connell's work on emancipation was primarily undertaken through his membership in the Catholic Committee and, in 1823, as founder of the Catholic Association of Ireland. Notably, he was also elected as a member of Parliament in 1828 as a representative for Clare. The Catholic Association, a broad-based democratic group, was instrumental in improving the standing of tenants in relation to landlords. Moreover the association successfully worked, through the ongoing efforts of O'Connell and others, toward a Catholic Emancipation Bill, which finally came in the form of an act with royal assent in April 1829.

O'Connell's work with the Repeal Association, founded in 1840, engendered the support of the masses and the wrath of the government. At what was to be a great gathering at Clontarf in October 1843, Daniel O'Connell, submitting to the British prohibition of the meeting, directed the crowd to disperse. He was later prosecuted by the government for conspiracy along with five others. The verdict, rendered by a Protestant jury in Dublin, was subsequently reversed by the House of Lords. This incident, along with the inability of the Repeal Association to achieve its goal, in combination with the onset of *an Gorta Mor,* or the Great Hunger, led to O'Connell's decline as a leader. In a time of failing health, on doctors orders he was en route to the warmer climate of the Mediterranean in Italy when he died of natural causes. As was his wish, his heart was buried in Rome and his body in Ireland.

O'Connell sought to transform the early agitation for Catholic civil and political rights into Irish nationalist opinion. He believed Catholics and Protestants could together comprise one Irish community. He viewed the nation as a collective unit and condemned sectarianism. Additionally, O'Connell's view of the future of the Irish nation was not a vision of a sovereign Irish state. While he sought freedom and independence for the Irish nation he did not feel such aspirations should be reached at the cost of the shedding of Irish blood, nor an alienation from the crown.

Books about Daniel O'Connell include *Catholic Emancipation: Daniel O'Connell and the Birth of Irish Democracy, 1820–1830,* by Fergus O'Ferrall; Denis Gwynn's biography, *Daniel O'Connell;* and *Daniel O'Connell, Nationalism without Violence: An Essay,* by Raymond Moley.

**O'HIGGINS, BERNARDO** 1778–1842, Liberator and patriot of Chile. Born at Chillán, he was the natural son of a Chilean mother, Isabel Riquelme, and an Irish father, Ambrose Higgins (later O'Higgins, 1720–1801), a colonial official who later became governor of Chile and viceroy of Peru. It is unclear if O'Higgins saw his father more than once, and he was separated from his mother at ten, when he was taken to Lima to begin his education. In 1795 he was sent to England, where he continued his studies under tutors at Richmond-on-Thames. A decisive influence on the young Creole's life was his meeting, in London, with Francisco de Miranda (1750–1816), from whom he eagerly imbibed insurgent ideas of independence. In 1802 he returned to Chile and inherited Las Canteras, his father's large estate near the Araucanian frontier. He petitioned to be allowed to assume his father's surname and titles of nobility; the surname was allowed, the titles were not.

An active and enterprising "hacendado" (landowner), O'Higgins became friendly with the handful of separatists in the south of Chile. The crisis of the Spanish Empire and the installation of a patriot government in Santiago (September 1810) gave him a chance to broaden his ideals. As a representative of the radical minority, he was elected to the first national congress (1811), but José Miguel Carrera's (1785–1821) seizure of power in November 1811 soon drew him to return to Las Canteras.

The outbreak of the Wars of Independence in 1813 drew O'Higgins into action at the head of militia forces he himself organized. He distinguished himself in a number of battles, including that at El Roble on October 17, 1813, in which he was wounded. When Carrera was dismissed as commander in chief early in 1814, O'Higgins assumed his role. Carrera seized power in Chile once again ( July 23, 1814), but O'Higgins refused to recognize the new regime. Civil war would have broken out had not a new royalist expedition launched a strong offensive. O'Higgins chose to make his stand at the town of Rancagua (October 1–2, 1814), where his forces were totally overwhelmed. Patriot Chile collapsed.

O'Higgins himself fled the carnage and took refuge across the Andes in Argentina. There he became a close associate of José de San Martín (1771–1850), who selected him for a key role in the liberation of Chile. When San Martín's Army of the Andes undertook its epic crossing of the Cordillera, O'Higgins was a divisional commander. His audacious cavalry charge secured victory at Chacabuco on February 12, 1817. In Santiago, four days later, he was appointed supreme director of Chile.

O'Higgins's first three years in power were eclipsed by the need to prosecute the war on independence. Only after the decisive battle of Maipú (April 5, 1818) was Chile finally secure from the royalists. However, the struggle for independence was not over yet. Great efforts had to be made to create a navy and to mount the expedition San Martín was to lead to the viceroyalty of Peru. With Argentina descending into chaos, most of the burden of organizing and financing the expedition fell on O'Higgins's government. The expedition's departure in August 1820 was probably his supreme personal moment.

O'Higgins's government restored the patriot institutions annuled during the Spanish reconquest, such as the Instituto Nacional and the National Library. It abolished the public display of coats of arms and noble titles. It made plans to convert a sheep track running down one side of the city into a tree-lined avenue—today the Avenida Bernardo O'Higgins. O'Higgins also launched a number of diplomatic missions, though his envoy in London failed to secure British recognition of Chile's independence. (The United States extended recognition in 1822.)

As scandal broke loose, the supreme director was suspected of being under excessive Argentine influence. His support for the execution of the three Carrera brothers alienated a powerful faction. Some of his ecclesiastical measures (prohibition of burial in church, temporary banishment of the bishop of Santiago, approval of a protestant cemetery) aroused clerical hostility. His appointment of José Antonio Rodríguez Aldea (1779–1841) as finance minister in 1820 also incurred disapproval from those who distrusted this slippery ex-royalist.

O'Higgins's first constitution (1818) was minimal, and allowed no element of popular election, even though its nominated senate was by no means a subservient body. Pressure for political reform eventually compelled O'Higgins to summon a constitutional convention. This body produced his second constitution (October 1822), which provided a parliament and elections. It also included a clause that would have enabled O'Higgins to remain in office for another ten years, a prospect most Creoles found unacceptable. The final blow to the regime came from the war-ravaged south, where a desperate economic situation breeding frustration and resentment toward the capital prompted General Ramón Freire (1787–1851), intendant of Concepción, to launch a rebellion against O'Higgins. The northern province of Coquimbo followed suit. In Santiago, leading Creoles conspired against the dictator. On January 28, 1823, in a scene of high drama, he was persuaded to abdicate. Six months later he was finally permitted to leave the country, never to return.

Abandoning a plan to visit Ireland, O'Higgins settled in Peru. In 1824 he accompanied Simón Bolívar (1783–1830) during part of the final patriot campaign in the highlands. The Peruvian government had awarded O'Higgins a couple of haciendas in the fertile Cañete Valley, to the south of Lima. Here and in Lima the exiled liberator lived out his final years in peace and harmony, enjoying the company of his mother (until she died in April 1840), his half-sister Rosa, and his own natural son Pedro Demetrio, the fruit of a brief love affair that took place during the patriot campaigns of 1817.

O'Higgins fostered few hopes of restoration to power. In 1826 he gave halfhearted support to a military insurrection in Chiloé, an ill-advised gesture that led the Chilean congress to strip him of his rank. In 1830 the successful conservative rebellion led by his old protégé Joaquín Prieto (1786–1854) may have briefly rekindled his aspirations. He was touched by the attentions of Chilean soldiers occupying Lima during the war between Chile and the Peru-Bolivia Confederation. In 1824 the Manuel Bulnes government (1841–1851) restored his rank and emoluments, news of which reached O'Higgins shortly before his death. He was buried in Lima, and in January 1869 his remains were repatriated to Chile. Just over three years later, in May 1872, an equestrian statue of the hero was inaugurated in Santiago. Appropriately, it shows him in action at the battle of Rancagua.

**OIL AND NATIONALISM** The discovery of oil and its subsequent use by Britain and the United States as the fuel of choice by these naval powers in the late 19th century made the control and access to oil resources a primary motive for imperial control. The British who sought control of Iran managed to get concessions to explore for oil and the rights to export it. They had competition from the Russians and later on from the Americans. After World War I, the British government secured control over oil in Iraq and in many parts of the Arabian peninsula. By controlling the exploration, marketing, and all other technical aspects, the imperial power denied the local nations the benefits of their natural resource as well as the know-how to explore for it themselves. In the Middle East and Latin America, foreign oil companies acted like foreign governments within the local states and were in many ways above local laws. As the nationalist wave started to take hold in post-World War I, the control over the oil became symbolic of national legitimacy and power. For example, in Iraq, when the Ba'th Party took power in 1968, they initially sought to nationalize the Iraq Petroleum Company (IPC) in order to demonstrate their independence from the foreign forces represented by the oil companies in the Gulf region. The Iraqi leadership had an uneasy relationship with the IPC. The Iraqis claimed that during the winter of 1972 the IPC kept turning the taps on and off in order to subjugate the Iraqi economy to a series of financial crises aimed at undermining the regime's ability to secure resources for its development programs. By nationalizing the oil company the Ba'th were able to differentiate themselves from the Qassem regime who refused to nationalize the oil company due to lack of local expertise to run the company. Moreover, in nationalizing the IPC, the Ba'th

Party did set in motion a radical change in the relationship between oil companies and oil-producing states in the region. The oil companies feared that the situation would lead to a tidal wave response among these states, with each trying to demonstrate its independence from the oil companies and attempting to appear more nationalist than the other. OPEC supported such moves, which were likely to weaken the bargaining power of the Western-controlled oil companies and threatened an oil embargo against the Western nations.

IPC nationalization was manipulated by the Ba'th Party as a symbol of nationalism and independence in order to legitimize their regime. Soon after the nationalization the Ba'th lifted austerity measures that were imposed prior to 1973. But more importantly, the Iraqi public rallied behind the Ba'th Party as on no previous occasion since the coup of 1958. Hence control over oil represented not only access to resources but also independence and a powerful symbol of national self-determination, i.e., nationalism.

**OKINAWAN NATIONALISM** Okinawa is the name variously used for the northern Pacific islands constituting part of the Ryukyu archipelago, for Okinawa Prefecture (which is an integral part of Japan and groups the Ryukyus), and also for the island of Okinawa, the largest island in the prefecture.

Okinawan nationalism may best be characterized as a diffuse sentiment, rather than a cohesive, organized movement. The sentiment is rooted in an early history of relative geographical isolation, along with a distinct Okinawan dialect and cultural traditions. Contemporary nationalist arguments reflect Okinawa's tragic role during World War II and the prefecture's subsequent status as a major staging area for U.S. military forces.

From the 15th to the 19th centuries, a Ryukyu Kingdom maintained a large degree of internal autonomy. However, the emergence of an independent nation-state was compromised by two factors. One was the custom of sending tribute missions to the Chinese court, which began in the 14th century and ended only in the 19th century. More importantly, the islands were conquered in the early 17th century by Japan's southernmost feudal realm, the Satsuma *daimyo*. The Ryukyu king agreed to a treaty in 1611 that preserved the kingdom's independence, but placed it under Satsuma's overlordship. This overlordship later established the basis for Japan's incorporation of the Ryukyus as the Okinawa Prefecture when, after the Meiji Restoration of 1868, Japan's new rulers abolished feudal domains, including that of Satsuma. The Meiji introduction of public schooling, along with Japanese administration, led to the steady decline of the Okinawan dialects, as well as many regional customs that were seen as signs of backwardness, such as long hair on men.

Okinawa's strategic location meant that it bore an enormous burden during the Allied ground assault on Japan that began in April 1945. For American troops, the Ryukyus were the prelude to an assault on Japan's mainland; for the imperial forces, the islands were a sacrifice to forestall the primary assault. The battle for Okinawa lasted almost three months and was among the most vicious of the war. Part of the devastation was wrought by Japanese troops who forced civilians from places of hiding, took their food, and often simply murdered noncombatants. By August 1945, when the Ryukyu Islands were placed under U.S. military governance, 250,000 Japanese, including nearly 150,000 civilians on the islands, were dead, along with some 12,500 Americans who were killed. Cities were devastated; industry and agriculture were largely nonexistent. The events of 1945 have become central to understanding Okinawan politics of subsequent decades, particularly the ambivalence—if not hostility—of many Okinawans toward Japan, along with the resentment of the prefecture's militarization that lies at the core of nationalist feelings.

The hostility toward Japan was best expressed in an incident that occured in 1987, when an Okinawan grocer, Shoichi Chibana, burned the national flag (the "Hinomaru") at an athletic meet, claiming the flag symbolized Japan's World War II atrocities. Although Chibana argued that his action was covered by the constitutional right of freedom of expression, he was sentenced to a year's suspended prison sentence. He went on to play an active role as an antiwar landowner, protesting the central government's policy of forcing landowners to lease land to the U.S. military.

Militarization of the prefecture has been the consequence of the occupation of the Ryukyus by the United States after World War II and the subsequent U.S.-Japanese security arrangements prolonging the use of the islands for U.S. military installations. Okinawa was under American military rule from 1945 until 1972, when it reverted to full Japanese sovereignty. Both during this period and after, Okinawans have protested the impact of U.S. rule—particularly the destruction of homes and farmland to expand military facilities. Although Okinawa Prefecture accounts for less than 1 percent of Japan's total land area, it provides 75 percent of the land occupied by U.S. military facilities in the country.

U.S. rights to occupy Okinawan land date from the postwar occupation period. Leases concluded with local landowners have been periodically renewed, often over protests from the original owners who have felt that the central government in Tokyo has done too little to negotiate a reduction in the American military presence. In 1995, the bases controversy exploded when three U.S. military men were arrested for abducting and raping a twelve-year-old Japanese girl.

The primary spokesman for Okinawan grievances against both Tokyo and the United States during the 1990s was the prefectural governor, Masahide Ota, whose stated goal was to remove all U.S. military presence from Okinawa by 2015. As early as 1991, he threatened to withhold his signature from documents forcing local landowners to continue leasing land to the United States; in 1995, confronted with a central government unwilling (or unable) to negotiate base reductions with the United States, Ota refused outright to sign the requisite documents. Ultimately, after pursuing his case through the courts and losing before Japan's Supreme Court, the governor signed the documents— although the circumstances that had led to the conflict remained unresolved.

The future of Okinawan nationalism, such as it exists, is uncertain. In 1998, Ota lost his bid for a third gubanatorial term to a wealthy businessman backed by Japan's long-ruling Liberal Democratic Party. The election results were likely grounded more in economic realism than diminished resentment of the military presence. An economic stimulus package promised by the central government to Okinawa in 1996 had been frozen in response to the refusal of the Ota government to cooperate with Tokyo over the bases issue. In the context of the 1998 Asian economic downturn and Okinawa's dependent economy, acquiescence with a Tokyo-backed candidate may have seemed the wisest course, at least in the short term.

On balance, Okinawan nationalism, unlike nationalist sentiment in many places, has not focused on independence or even a demand for devolution of authority. Nor has it been rooted in a major linguistic or cultural revival. Rather, the dominant sentiment has been pacifism, and the key issues—inextricably interrelated— have been opposition to an excessive U.S. military presence and resentment over the perceived refusal of the central government to respond to Okinawan concerns and interests—a resentment that can be traced to the long history of the islands existing on the fringes of Japanese culture and political authority.

For insights into the tenor of the grievances about the bases question and the sporadic nature of nationalist protests, readers are encouraged to check the numerous web sites maintained by small groups in Okinawa, as well as the prefecture's own web site.

## ONE WORLD MOVEMENT

Reports of murder, war, and violence often spurred by nationalist sentiments whether it is in Kosovo, East Timor, Kashmir, Sierra Leone, or Sudan are what make the headlines around the world. And it is often these headlines that are so loud that they overshadow the polar end of these conflicts. More people are waging peace and cooperation today than ever before. Despite war and misery around the world, millions of people in over 20,000 civilian organizations (up from 985 in 1956) are working everyday to counter war with peace, violence with hope, and genocide with humanitarian relief. In the words of Margaret Mead, "Never doubt that a small group of thoughtful, committed citizens can change the world. Indeed, it's the only thing that ever has." These words ring true to the thousands who recently met to commemorate the centennial of The Hague in the Netherlands. Over 10,000 participants including nobel laureates, religious leaders, and the U.N. secretary-general gathered in the hope of contributing in a very real way to the establishment of a "culture of peace" in the world.

The 20th century has been a century of great progress in international cooperation in all areas of life. The One World movement is a loosely connected structure of a variety of groups and organizations both formal and informal that have worked over the years with different agendas and ideologies but share a common goal, that of one world, one humanity working together for the peace and progress of all. This idea of one world has its roots in the numerous conferences held during the latter half of the 19th century. These initiatives at international cooperation were formalized in the establishment of the Universal Postal Service, the Red Cross, and the International Telegraphic Union. The invention and first use of the atom bomb during World War II gave new impetus to the movement that espoused international cooperation. However, according to the author Boyd Shaffer, "The bomb did not deter nationalism or reduce its intensity and spread, despite the fact that if the great powers should conflict they might eliminate nations and produce one world—a cemetery." The critics and skeptics of the One World movement agree with Shaffer in that "the world is one planet, but there has not been [nor will there ever be]—not in the minds of men—one humanity."

Some argue that the One World movement is a good idea but that international or world organizations, whether political, social, or economic, can lead to an amalgamation of cultures, which can result in the suppression of cultural uniqueness of the weak by the strong. Scholars of globalization argue that the Western cultures, especially the United States of America, are so dominant and powerful that one world simply means a world that reflects the ideologies, values, and ways of life of the West. One world does not mean a world made up of a variety of cultures and peoples with an equal voice. Nationalism and its rise in recent decades is a reflection of that inequality on the world stage.

The Iranian revolution for example in 1979 can be seen in part as a revolution against the "imperialism of the West." The revolutionaries more than twenty years ago wanted their voice to be heard, wanted to dictate the course of their own lives without the powerful influence from outsiders. They wanted their own religion to make sense in the rapidly changing modern world, and nationalism gave many that identity and sense of collective and shared togetherness.

## ORGANIZATION OF AFRICAN UNITY

Established in Addis Ababa in 1963, the Organization of African Unity (OAU) is a vehicle for collaboration and unity among African nations.

Thirty-two independent African states attended its inaugural meeting. The conference adopted a charter of African unity, which struck a compromise between the two main conflicting groups of African nations. The Brazzaville group, former French colonies, held a moderate gradualist position on African independence, whereas the Casablanca group proposed immediate independence from the colonial powers and unity among the African nations.

The conference declared a commitment to decolonization, nonalignment, and disarmament. Its main resolutions were the rejection of minority settle rule, coordination of African liberation movements, noninterference in the internal affairs of African nations, and cooperation between the African states. Membership in the OAU was open to all African states and surrounding islands.

The OAU had some success in influencing the United Nations on matters related to Africa and in mediating several disputes among African states. The Organization of African Unity's powers are limited as a result of its position of noninterference and the volatile nature of African politics.

## ORGANIZATION OF AMERICAN STATES

The OAS, founded in 1948, is a major source of nationalism in the Western hemisphere. Thirty-five member nations from Latin America, the Caribbean, and North America comprise the OAS.

The origins of the organization can be traced to 1889–1890, when the First International Conference of American States was held in Washington, D.C. A product of that meeting, the International Union of American Republics, became the Pan-American Union in 1910.

The maintenance of peace in the Western hemisphere is the traditional goal of the alliance. During the 1960s, the OAS played an important role in Pan-American relations with Cuba. The United States used the organization as a means to alienate Fidel Castro, but other nations later resumed trade with his government. By keeping each country equal in its operations, the OAS has helped to allay the antipathy among some member nations toward intervention in the region by the United States.

Since the 1960s, economic cooperation and development have been the primary goals of the Organization of American States. By working toward economic independence for Latin American and Caribbean nations, the OAS has fostered national identity and cultural consciousness across the Americas.

Helpful works include A. Glenn Mower's *Regional Human Rights* (Greenwood, 1991) and O. C. Stoetzer's *The Organization of American States* (Praeger, 1993).

**ORTEGA, DANIEL** 1945–, Nicaraguan revolutionary leader, born in La Libertad, Chontales, Nicaragua. Ortega emerged as the "first among equals" within the collective leadership of the Sandinista National Liberation Front (FSLN), which led the insurrection that overthrew the dictatorship of Anastasio Somoza Debayle in 1979 and which then ruled Nicaragua until 1990. Many observers believe that Ortega's low-key style and lack of charisma were an asset within a party that feared the type of "cult of personality" associated with so many 20th-century revolutionary leaders.

Ortega was born to a middle-class family and was quite religious as a youth. His father fought with Augusto César Sandino, and both parents were jailed for political activities against the Somoza dictatorship. Ortega joined the Sandinista Front as a student in the early 1960s and was arrested in 1967. He and other Sandinista prisoners were freed in December 1974 in exchange for hostages seized during a daring Sandinista raid on a Christmas party at the U.S. ambassador's residence. After receiving military training in Cuba, Daniel and his brother Humberto emerged as leaders of the so-called Insurrectionist or Tercerista ("Third Way") faction within the Sandinista Front, which argued that military actions could spark a broad national insurrection against Somoza with popular, middle-class, and even upper-class support. The other two factions in the party viewed the peasantry and working class, respectively, as the key force behind any possible revolution. The Terceristas were generally viewed as the most moderate and pragmatic faction within the Sandinista Front, one willing to make strategic compromises in order to attract the support of anti-Somoza business leaders. The insurrection of 1978–1979 seemed to confirm the wisdom of the Tercerista strategy, and Ortega became a member of the nine-member National Directorate of the Sandinista Front, which was created in March 1979.

Ortega was also appointed to the five-member Junta of the Government of National Reconstruction (1979–1984) that nominally ruled Nicaragua following the overthrow of Somoza in July 1979, although the Sandinistas' National Directorate was the real power center in the country. Daniel's brother Humberto became minister of defense. (Another brother, Camilo, was killed in the insurrection.) Ortega became president of Nicaragua (1985–1990) after winning 67 percent of the vote in the November 1984 election, one boycotted by several opposition parties. By the late 1980s Nicaragua's economy was devastated by years of war against U.S.-backed counterrevolutionaries, or Contras, and by U.S. economic sanctions. In the presidential election of 1990, Ortega was defeated by Violeta Barrios de Chamorro, who had resigned from the governing junta in 1980 and became a leading critic of the Sandinista regime. Chamorro won 55 percent of the vote to Ortega's 41 percent.

Despite this defeat, Ortega remained the most powerful figure within the Sandinista Front through the 1990s, surviving factional fights, defections of leading Sandinistas (including Ortega's former vice president, Sergio Ramírez), another defeat in the presidential election of 1996 (Ortega won only 38 percent of the vote to rightist Arnoldo Alemán's 51 percent), and highly publicized charges by his adopted stepdaughter that Ortega had sexually abused her over the course of twenty years.

There is no standard biography of Ortega, though good discussions of the Sandinista movement may be found in John Booth's *The End and the Beginning: The Nicaraguan Revolution* (Westview, 1985) and Dennis Gilbert's *Sandinistas: The Party and the Revolution* (Blackwell, 1988).

**ORWELL, GEORGE** 1903–1950, English novelist, journalist, and essayist, born Eric Arthur Blair in Motihari, Bengal, India. Best remembered for his twin satires on totalitarianism, *Animal Farm* (1945) and *Nineteen Eighty-Four* (1949), Orwell was also a major participant in the British socialist movement at midcentury.

Although championing a radical politics of collective ownership, he extolled tradition and love of country while drawing a sharp distinction between patriotism and nationalism.

Soon after completing his schooling at Eton in 1921, Orwell joined the Indian Imperial Police in Burma. By the end of 1927 he resigned, renouncing imperialism less out of sympathy with the nationalist aspirations of subject peoples than from a sense of guilt over his country's role as their oppressor. Now resolved to become a writer, he endured, by his own account, several years of "poverty and the sense of failure." Most of his early works, such as *Down and Out in Paris and London* (1933) and *A Clergyman's Daughter* (1935), borrowed heavily from his experiences to explore the themes of poverty and exploitation.

Yet is was not until 1937, in *The Road to Wigan Pier,* that Orwell declared himself a socialist. A study of conditions among the working-class poor in northern England, the book included a blistering attack on fellow socialists for uncritically embracing material and technological progress and doctrinaire Marxism. At its core, Orwell insisted, socialism meant justice and liberty, not "machine-worship and the stupid cult of Russia." His subsequent involvement in the Spanish Civil War as a volunteer militiaman on the republican side, movingly described in *Homage to Catalonia* (1938), solidified and deepened his commitment to egalitarian socialism and hatred of Stalinism.

Briefly flirting with antiwar politics in the late 1930s, Orwell warned that the impending conflict with Nazi Germany could result in strengthening British and French imperialism. His position abruptly changed, however, with the outbreak of war. In *The Lion and the Unicorn* (1941), he celebrated English tradition and character and denounced pacifists who saw no moral difference between Western democracy and totalitarianism. Characteristically, he contrasted the decency and patriotism of ordinary Englishmen with an alienated intelligentsia who, he claimed, "take their cookery from Paris and their opinions from Moscow." Arguing that the war was unwinnable without transforming it into a revolution, he called for a socialist movement that appealed to middle-class patriotism "instead of merely insulting it."

Orwell probably never lost faith in the decency of the English people, but he became increasingly concerned about the spread of "nationalist"—as opposed to patriotic—thinking among the intellectual class. He discussed the problem at length in the essay "Notes on Nationalism," written near the end of World War II. Here he repeated his praise of patriotism, defined as "devotion to a particular place and a particular way of life, which one believes to be the best in the world but has no wish to force upon other people." Nationalism, on the other hand, is an aggressive propensity to worship power, to identify "with a single nation or other unit, placing it beyond good and evil and recognising no other duty than that of advancing its interests." The key phrase is "other unit"; according to Orwell, "nationalist" emotions can attach themselves as firmly to a religious group or a political ideology as to a nation. They can even be transferred to a country other than one's own, as Orwell alleged many left-wing intellectuals—disaffected from religion and homeland but still needing something to believe in—had transferred their loyalty from England to the Soviet Union.

A chief characteristic of the nationalist mentality, Orwell observed, is its indifference to objective truth and selective perception of reality. Thus nationalists often suppress or alter the historical record when to do so will serve their cause. Anti-Semites deny the Holocaust, for example, and English Communists deny the existence of forced-labor camps in the Soviet Union. Such dismissal of historical truth amounts to more than simple dishonesty, for the nationalist distorters of history "probably believe with part of their minds that they are actually thrusting facts into the past."

Critics such as the otherwise admiring George Woodcock have faulted Orwell for the lack of conceptual tightness in his treatment of nationalism. Perhaps the real significance of his views on the subject lies in their relationship to *Nineteen Eighty-Four.* Heavily influenced by James Burnham's *The Managerial Revolution* (1941), Orwell as early as 1944 voiced his fear that the major nationalist movements were leading to a world dominated by several unconquerable superstates with centralized economies but no civil liberties. *Nineteen Eighty-Four* presents a detailed picture of such a world, whose politics is predicated on the same denial of reality—now called double-think—that exemplified nationalist thought in the 1940s. In Orwell's dystopian vision of the future, the nationalists of his day have evolved into party functionaries engaged in up-to-the-minute rewriting of history and systematic corruption of language. Like the earlier apologists for Stalin and Hitler, they have placed themselves in the service of total power, embodied in the symbolic figure of Big Brother.

Virtually everything Orwell ever wrote, including much previously unpublished material, appears in the twenty-volume *Complete Works of George Orwell*, edited by Peter Davison (Secker and Warburg, 1998). This authoritative edition supplants the less complete but more manageable *Collected Essays, Journalism, and Letters of George Orwell,* four volumes, edited by Sonia Orwell and Ian Angus (Harcourt, Brace and World, 1968). Two excellent biographies are Bernard Crick's *George Orwell: A Life* (Little, Brown, 1980) and Michael Shelden's *George Orwell: The Authorized Biography* (Harper-Collins, 1991). George Woodcock's *The Crystal Spirit* (Little, Brown, 1966) remains the best critical study, while Stephen Ingle's *George Orwell: A Political Life* (Saint Martin's Press, 1993) and William Steinhoff's *George Orwell and the Origins of "1984"* (University of Michigan Press, 1975) contribute much to an understanding of Orwell's political thought.

**OTTOMAN EMPIRE**   Originally founded ca. 1300, the Ottoman state expanded rapidly and came to rule territories spreading over virtually all of the Middle East west of Iran, the Balkans, and parts of Central Europe and the Caucasus. From their palace in Istanbul (the Ottoman capital after its conquest in 1453), the Ottoman sultans ruled over a populace notable for its diversity of languages, customs, and religions.

For most of its existence, Ottoman rule was fairly unintrusive in the daily lives of the populace, which relied primarily on local or religious leaders, fraternal organizations, and guilds for social services. In particular, religious affiliations, institutionalized in the form of *millets,* formed the basis of group identity and provided most of the administrative and judicial functions for Ottoman subjects. Due to its relatively unintrusive style of government and its co-optation of local and religious leadership into the Ottoman system, the Ottoman state was able to rule over a diverse population with relatively few internal threats to its legitimacy.

By the 18th century, however, expanding European economic penetration was undermining the financial basis of the Ottoman state, which was increasingly unable to compete with its European competitors technologically or militarily. By the beginning of the 19th century, some groups, particularly Christian groups in the European provinces, began to develop new secular élites with economic and intellectual ties to Western Europe. It is among these groups that nationalist sentiment first appeared. As provinces became increasingly integrated into world trade systems and as local élites gained increasing control over regional political and economic structures, ties between the provinces and the central government weakened.

Throughout the 19th century, the Ottoman government attempted to address these threats through a process of centralization and modernization, most famously through the Tanzimat, or "restructuring," pro-

gram. One aspect of these reforms was the attempt to inculcate a sense of Ottoman identity, of Ottoman citizenship, among the various peoples of the empire. This concept, which came to be termed *Osmanlılık,* or Ottomanism, had several incarnations but can basically be seen as an attempt to create a civic nationalism for the Ottoman state. Early formulations of this program are to be found in the liberal Gülhane Rescript (1839) and the Imperial Rescript of 1856, and this trend found its clearest voice in the Constitution of 1876. This attempt at creating a new "social contract" was combined with major reforms in almost every aspect of life as the Ottoman ruling élite attempted to save their empire. While the results of these efforts were mixed in the empire overall, they were a total failure in the European provinces.

Although the importance of Ottomanism should not be underestimated, its effects among the Christian subjects who it was most clearly meant to integrate was precisely the opposite of what was hoped. Even though Ottomanism certainly appealed to some Christian subjects of the empire, it estranged the most important group, the religious leaders of the old *millet* system. Divested of much of the power they enjoyed under the old system, these religious leaders no longer had an interest in supporting the Ottoman state and threw their considerable political and moral weight behind the cause of national liberation. External support for these national movements was provided by one or another European state, either for geopolitical reasons or out of sympathy for the cause of a Christian people under Muslim rule.

A Greek state won independence in 1830, after years of bloody conflict. Significant Greek populations remained under Ottoman rule long after this date, however, and the birth of an independent Greek homeland only increased their desire for independence. In the decades that followed, outside pressure from the Great Powers along with internal agitation and an almost unbroken chain of revolts forced the Ottomans to grant greater and greater autonomy to their European provinces. In the aftermath of a disastrous war with Russia, the Ottoman Empire agreed, at the Congress of Berlin in 1878, to relinquish control over some two-fifths of its territory and one-fifth of its population. Bulgaria, Romania, Serbia, and Montenegro were now, for all intents and purposes, independent states.

The struggle of nationalist groups to gain independence and the attempts by the Ottoman state to prevent the breakup of its territories were marked by particularly brutal intercommunal warfare and state-supported massacres. When possible, armies engaged in "ethnic cleansing" of the sort now associated with the breakup of Yugoslavia. The results of this were twofold. First, the new states were far more homogeneous than they had been under Ottoman rule. Second, because of a massive influx of Muslim refugees from the Balkans (and from the expanding Russian Empire) along with the loss of many of its Christian subjects, the Ottoman state was considerably more Muslim than it had been before and Islamic legitimacy took on increased value as a means of creating loyalty to the Ottoman state.

In 1908, the Committee for Union and Progress, the so-called "Young Turks," staged a coup against the sultan, Abdülhamid II. Reinstituting the Constitution of 1876, the new regime seemed ready to fulfill the promise of a new, liberal Ottomanism that would provide equality to all. The fall of the old regime did not mean the end of nationalist agitation, however. Revolt in Albania, which won independence in 1912, marked the first time that significant numbers of Muslims rebelled against Ottoman rule. In addition, the first and second Balkan wars (1912–1913 and 1913–1914, respectively), in which the new Balkan states legally declared independence and tried to obtain their unfulfilled territorial aspirations, put additional pressure on the new regime. Note that, while there were certainly intellectuals sympathetic to Turkish, Arab, or Kurdish nationalism during this period, popular loyalty among these groups was, right up through the end of World War I, directed almost entirely toward the Ottoman sultan.

World War I spelled the end of both the Ottoman Empire and the triumph of nationalism. With the presence of Armenians on both sides of the Ottoman border and the existence of Armenian volunteer units in the Russian army, the Ottomans feared an Armenian "fifth column." Massacres and deportations effectively eradicated the Armenian presence in Anatolia. An attempt to expand Greek control into western Anatolia was defeated by a Turkish nationlist army under the leadership of Mustafa Kemal (Atatürk) in 1922 and most Anatolian Greeks moved to Greece during the Turkish-Greek population transfers agreed to in the Treaty of Lausanne (1923). Among Arabs and Turks as well, national movements took on new legitimacy and, while support for the sultan was no doubt still evident among the popular classes, the sultan's collaboration with the victorious Entente powers meant the end of even a truncated Ottoman Empire. Nationalism became the primary form of legitimacy for the new states of the Middle East.

# P

PACIFISM   Early pacifism was established as a religious prohibition against killing humans. This principle provided a moral justification for individuals to ignore national law that sanctioned war. Nearly all religious doctrines have a basis for pacifist thought. In particular, the eastern religions of Confucianism, Taoism, Hinduism, and Buddhism often extol the virtue of being sensitive to the plight of all humanity.

The earliest form of modern pacifism in the West was based on a Christian reform movement that rejected the nation's right to conscript individuals into military service. Furthermore, attempts by the state to expropriate religious principle for causes that sanctioned killing (the concept of just war) were often regarded as blasphemy. These views placed the Mennonites, Quakers, and Church of the Brethren communities into conflict with the official religious authorities and governments in their respective nations. Both the state and the church persecuted religious pacifists causing many to leave Europe and established communities in America.

The strategy of early pacifists was to establish communities separate from the apparatus of the nation state. Pacifism was primarily a policy of withdrawal from society, not an attempt to actively change nation-state policy. In modern times the traditional "peace churches" have reversed this stance and endorse actively challenging state policy that causes *inequality*.

Pacifists in the United States during the 18th century espoused a doctrine of civil disobedience to protest state action. For example, William Loyd Garrison's Society for the Promotion of Peace and other antislavery groups expanded Quaker principles to include active civil disobedience. Author Henry David Thoreau was jailed for the nonpayment of taxes due to his refusal to support the Spanish-American War and the institution of slavery.

Leo Tolstoy (1828–1910) transformed pacifist ideas into a philosophy that made a moral argument against the practices of nation-states. Tolstoy, who had read Thoreau's *Civil Disobedience* and corresponded with antislavery leaders in America, has been called a "pacifist anarchist." Unlike the Americans, Tolstoy thought the nation-state system should be completely dismantled through individual civil disobedience. Tolstoy made his appeal using a Christian philosophy but was extremely critical of the established Orthodox Church. Tolstoy also argued that state policy was formulated only to enhance a ruler's power and was directly contrary to the well-being of citizens. In particular, national patriotism was used by rulers to control the ruled. In Tolstoy's words, "Patriotism is slavery."

During World War I new patterns of pacifist thought emerged. In Britain, the Socialist Party was unambiguously pacifist, but their ideology was based on economic principle rather than religious principle. This line of reasoning argued for actively working to affect social change as opposed to withdrawal from society. Bertrand Russell, a British socialist philosopher, was among the first to develop an idea of collective security based on civil disobedience. This philosophy was utilitarian in nature and often advocated widespread disobedience by the citizenry of a country that was faced with invasion. This policy was considered both practical and morally superior to war fighting.

The Mennonites and Quakers had the largest number of conscientious objectors during this war but many who objected were still coerced into serving in the military. Many did not object to serving as noncombatants. Conscientious objection on religious principle became established in the United States and Britain during this period, but objection based on political grounds was not tolerated. As such, socialist internationalists in Britain and the United States were rarely granted conscientious objector status. And among religious groups, Jehovah's Witnesses and other Pentecostals who steadfastly refused to serve in any capacity were jailed.

During the interwar years, pacifism gained greater acceptance as a social philosophy that could transform world society. Thinkers as diverse as Albert Einstein and Aldous Huxley formulated ideas based on passive nonresistance. But as pacificism moved from an individual decision of conscience to an activist philosophy, fissures appeared in the movement. Pacifists who supported the movement due to religious principle were more likely to be "absolute pacifists" who rejected all war as immoral. In contrast, pacifism based on utility or socialist internationalism often advocated collective action as a mean of abolishing all nation-states.

Some pacifists argued for a more relativist position. For example, many supported the idea of a collective security arrangement among states despite the fact that this endorsed selective military intervention as a means of ensuring the general peace. As such, organizations that attempted to prevent war, such as the League of Nations, were often supported by pacifist organizations. Events in the interwar years (the ascension of Hitler and the Spanish Civil War) caused many to move toward a position of relative pacifism that sanctioned aid to countries fighting a defensive war.

In contrast to internationalist pacifism, Mohandas Gandhi applied pacifist principles to a nationalist objective. Gandhi was deeply impressed with Tolstoy's *Kingdom of God Is Within You* (1894), but did not share Tolstoy's cosmopolitan worldview. Gandhi also used the Hindu tradition of *ahisma* (noninjury to living creatures) and *satya* (the search for truth) to fashion a unique version of Indian pacifism. The philosophy of *Satyagraha* endorsed specific forms of action as a means of exposing "truth." Gandhi distinguished between noncooperation and civil disobedience and both were employed in the Indian campaign. As such, Gandhi's pacifism is actually quite active in challenging governing authority.

Gandhi's nationalist followers often regarded the strategies of *Satyagraha* as the most practical means of expelling the British, not as a moral sanction against war. And while Gandhi did argue that pacifism could cause greater world peace, particularly after the invention of the atom bomb, he also took positions that sanctioned the use of military force.

Gandhi's primary contribution to pacifism was the demonstration that nonobedience is a practical strategy that could be employed by a movement in a position of weakness. Until the Indian movement, one criticism of pacifism among nationalists and realist thinkers was that collective civil disobedience was impractical in the face of overwhelming force.

A group that subsequently used passive resistance to affect a change in their treatment within a nation-state was the black civil rights movement in the United States. In this movement, Dr. Martin Luther King fused the traditional Christian doctrine of moral pacifism with the practical strategies used by the Indian nationalists. Like Gandhi, King searched for the means to symbolically demonstrate that racial segregation was an anathema to the universal principles of human dignity.

All the variants of pacifist thought remain relevant today. For instance, nationalist organizations such as the Tibetan Freedom movement employ a pacifist ideology because it corresponds with the teachings of the Dalai Lama. The Palestinian Intifada employed some pacifist tactics (collective action by citizens) because the movement was in a position of weakness. Furthermore, passive resistance has become so pervasive that even extremely isolated groups are aware of pacifist tactics. For instance, a premodern tribe of hunter-gatherers, the Penan, is currently using passive disobedience to protest the deforestation of their habitat in Sarawak.

At the local level, pacifists continue to protest specific aspects of national policy, such as the death penalty. And other individuals continue to use the tactics of pacifism, such as boycotting products produced in inhumane working conditions, in an attempt to affect change in the international economy. Most importantly, in almost all cases the general goal of pacifism has shifted from the prevention of murder to a broader goal concerning the establishment of universal human rights.

Recommendations for further reading include Peter Brock and Nigel Young, *Pacifism in the Twentieth Century* (Syracuse University Press, 1999); Leo Tolstoy, *Writings on Civil Disobedience and Nonviolence* (New Society Publishers, 1987); Bart de Ligt, *The Conquest of Violence: An Essay on War and Revolution* (Pluto Press, 1989); and Ronald Duncan, ed., *Selected Writings of Mahatma Gandhi* (Faber and Faber, 1951).

**PAINE, THOMAS** 1737–1809, U.S. political journalist, was born in Thetford, England, and emigrated to Philadelphia, Pennsylvania, in 1774. Paine wrote on a broad range of topics including abolition, women's rights, and workingmen's rights, but he is best remembered for his pamphlets espousing American independence from Great Britain and the establishment of a strong federal union in the United States.

Paine's most important pamphlet was *Common Sense*. Published anonymously in January 1776, it appeared at a time when many future patriots were still debating the wisdom of breaking away from Great Britain. Although the vast majority of Americans rejected parliamentary claims to sovereignty over the colonial assemblies, most Americans still considered themselves to be Englishmen and felt a great sense of loyalty toward King George III. *Common Sense* disabused them of the notion that the king was the special friend of American colonists while his ministers sought to bring about their financial ruin via taxation without representation; according to Paine, it was the king himself who directed his ministers to burden the American colonies with unjust taxes. More importantly, Paine called for Americans to see their struggle with Great Britain in a totally different light. Rather than work to remove what they considered to be encroachments on the prerogatives of the colonial assemblies, he urged the colonists to declare their independence from Britain. For him, it was "common sense" and only a matter of time that a land as large as the thirteen colonies become independent from an island nation thousands of miles away whose government was completely out of touch with the realities of life in the New World. Furthermore, he urged the American colonies not only to disassociate themselves from Britain but also to band together in a strong federal union. *Common Sense* was a tremendously influential pamphlet; it sold approximately 150,000 copies by the end of the year, an astronomical number for its day, and helped many Americans overcome their misgivings about revolting against the Crown. The basic strategy it employed, that of personally attacking the king, was adopted by Thomas Jefferson in the Declaration of Independence, which was written six months later.

Just as Paine's pen had roused Americans to declare independence, it also roused them to continue fighting for it during the darkest days of the American Revolution. In December 1776, following the Continental army's loss of southern New York and northern New Jersey and its ignominious retreat across the Delaware River, Paine published the first of a total of eighteen pamphlets and articles in the *Pennsylvania Gazette* under the collective title *The Crisis*. These essays urged Americans to put aside state and regional differences and petty jealousies and instead work together in a more federal fashion to address the problems brought on by the war. *The Crisis*, which last appeared in 1783, did much to sustain patriot morale during the war.

Paine addressed the necessity of a strong federal union more specifically in 1780 in the pamphlet *Public Good*. He denounced the inadequacies of the as-yet-unratified Articles of Confederation, which failed to give the central government sufficient power to subordinate the interests of the various states and regions to common national goals. He also issued one of the first calls for a national convention to replace the articles with a "continental constitution," a call that was eventually heeded seven years later in the form of the Constitutional Convention of 1787.

Biographies are Alfred J. Ayer, *Thomas Paine* (1988) and Jack Fruchtman, Jr., *Thomas Paine: Apostle of Freedom* (1994). Paine's thoughts concerning U.S. nationalism are addressed in A. Owen Aldridge, *Thomas Paine's American Ideology* (1984), and Gregory Claeys, *The Political Thought of Thomas Paine* (1989).

**PAISLEY, IAN** 1926–, Minister of the Free Presbyterian Church of Ulster and leader of the Democratic Unionist Party (DUP). He was born in Armagh City, County Armagh, Northern Ireland, to the Reverend and Mrs. J. Kyle Paisley. Reverend Paisley is known for his vitriolic and impertinent comments regarding Irish Catholics and the cause of Irish nationalism.

Holding a degree from the Bob Jones University in South Carolina in the United States, Paisley is famous for his public condemnation of the Roman Catholic Church and the papacy in defense of Ulster. He has used his political positions as a member of parliament, member of the European Parliament, and member of the Northern Ireland Assembly to allege Catholic conspiracies to undermine the union of Great Britain and Northern Ireland. He utilizes Biblical scripture to ground his allegations and further his vision of the Protestant faith.

Paisley's political beliefs concerning Northern Ireland focus on the necessity of the continued unity of Northern Ireland and Great Britain and perpetuating the dominance of the Protestant population. Toward that end he was instrumental in creating the Ulster Protestant Action organization, which sought to maintain preferences for Protestant workers over Catholics. He and his followers, known as Paisleyites, have played a key role in organizing counterdemonstrations in response to civil rights marches and gatherings, often resulting in violent confrontations between civil rights activists and Northern Ireland police.

Reverend Paisley was also a founding member of the Democratic Unionist Party in 1971. His fear of anything that might threaten the union, including efforts toward peaceful negotiation and settlement, led him to call a gathering of loyalist supporters in the wake of the Anglo-Irish Agreement. Five hundred loyalists were gathered in military-style formation and waved firearm certificates as an indication of the repercussions the Thatcher government would face if it continued down the path of perceived conciliation toward the Irish Catholic community.

Books on the Reverend Paisley include *Persecuting Zeal: A Portrait of Ian Paisely* by Dennis Cooke, Clifford Smyth's *Ian Paisley: Voice of Protestant Ulster*, and *Ian Paisley, My Father*, by Rhonda Paisley (his daughter).

## PAKISTANI NATIONALISM

The Islamic Republic of Pakistan is a country in South Asia with Islamabad as its capital. It was created by partition of British India at the time of independence at the insistence of Muslim nationalists who were convinced that a Hindu-dominated India would not be just to Muslims.

Under the leadership of Mohammed Ali Jinnah the All-India Muslim League agitated for a Muslim homeland during negotiations with the British, breaking with the Indian National Congress and Mohandas Gandhi, who wanted a united India. In the end the British granted the Muslim League's demands; those areas with a majority Muslim population were to become Pakistan and those areas with a majority Hindu population would be part of India.

The original Pakistan consisted of two geographically separated sections, West Pakistan in the Indus River Valley and East Pakistan more than 1000 miles to the East in the Ganges River delta. Although united by law and by the Islamic faith, the two parts of the country were culturally quite different. Conflicts emerged immediately between East and West Pakistan and in 1971 the former became the country of Bangladesh.

Muslim poet and philosopher Muhammad Iqbal first proposed a Muslim state in India in 1930 and the name Pakistan ("Land of the Pure") was coined by a Cambridge student, Choudhary Rahmat Ali, in 1933.

The utopian dreams of Pakistan's founders were not realized with independence, however. The country's founding father, Jinnah, died a few months later, and the nation became embroiled in armed conflict with India over the status of territory of Jammu and Kashmir (in 1948–1949, 1965, and 1971). Whereas Kashmir's population was overwhelmingly Muslim, the ruling raj was Hindu and chose to join with India. The ensuing conflicts not only resulted in period war but also a militarization of the region and a draining of precious resources from economic development and social services into the military, which has ruled the country during much of its existence.

## PALESTINIAN NATIONALISM

Palestine is a small but geopolitically significant region in the Middle East with shifting and imprecise boundaries comprising parts of Israel and Jordan and containing both Arab and Jewish nationalists whose conflicting interests have led to widespread conflict and violence in recent decades. Palestinian nationalism is a movement for autonomy and possible statehood by the Palestinians living in the Middle East. The signing of a peace accord with Israel in 1993 led to the creation of a Palestinian Authority and a phased withdrawal of Israeli troops from the occupied territories.

Palestinian nationalism reached a critical point with the establishment of an independent state of Israel in 1948, which forced many Palestinians into a sustained exile and the creation of widespread refugee camps in which families have lived for more than a generation.

Palestine had not been a distinct political entity in recent centuries until the British Mandate enacted by the Council of the League of Nations in 1922. The creation of a British-ruled Palestine was not for the Palestinians, however, but for the express purpose of creating the "political, administrative and economic conditions as will secure the establishment of the Jewish national Home . . . and the development of self-governing institutions."

Palestine has been significant both culturally and politically for millennia. In addition to being considered a Holy Land by Jews, Christians, and Muslims, it lies at the intersection of central routes from the Mediterranean to the East and from Egypt north. Since the creation of the Israeli state, hundreds of thousands of Jews have immigrated to the area until they now comprise four-fifths of the region's population. About 14 percent of the Israeli population are Muslim Arab and another 3 percent Christian Arab.

Estimates of the number of Palestinians living in refugee camps range from 500,000 to 1,000,000, with others fleeing to Lebanon, Jordan, Syria, Egypt, and Iraq. A Palestinian consciousness emerged in the refugee camps, especially in the schools created by the United Nations Relief and Works Agency (UNRWA). Later leadership emerged with the creation of a Palestinian middle class and a significant number of Palestinians educated in universities in Egypt, Syria, Lebanon, Western Europe, and the United States.

The next stage in Palestinian nationalism was the formation of the Palestine Liberation Organization—the PLO—out of an Arab summit in Cairo in 1964. The PLO called for the creation of an independent Palestinian state and the destruction of the state of Israel. The PLO also engaged in guerilla raids into Israel along with the Palestine National Liberation Movement (Harakat at-Tahrir al-Watani al-Filastini), known from a reversal of its Arabic initials as Fatah. Other guerrilla groups joined them, often with different goals, but all of them united in their determination to refuse any political settlement and to accept nothing less than the elimination of Israel and the creation of a Palestinian state. The PLO emerged as the leading nationalist group with Yasser Arafat as its charismatic leader.

The Palestinian opposition had little success, however, in moving toward the creation of any independent political entity until the launching of the largely nonviolent *Intifada* ("shaking off"). Arafat denounced terrorism and most of the PLO leadership followed him, engaging in massive direct action, civil resistance demonstrations, most of it nonviolent. They also created a series of parallel institutions, economic, governmental, educational, and so on that made the Israeli occupation forces increasingly irrelevant.

Although some groups such as *Hamas* (an acronym for the Islamic Resistance Movement) challenged Arafat's authority and their accommodation with the state of Israel, the PLO was successful in signing a peace treaty with Israel. The accord envisioned a phased five-year withdrawal of Israeli occupation from portions of the West Bank and the Gaza Strip leading to Palestinian self-rule by the Palestinian Authority in 1994.

**PAN-AFRICANISM**    Pan-Africanism is the 20th-century composite of organizations, congresses and conferences, and political-cultural activities that share a view of the fundamental commonalities in the history, conditions, and destiny of African people worldwide. The objectives of Pan-Africanism are continental unity among African nations in political, economic, and social realms, as well as international cooperation among people of African descent.

Pan-Africanism is global African nationalism. It focuses on the liberation of Africa and African descendents from the vestiges of European colonialism and imperialist relations. From a Pan-Africanist perspective, African nations are viewed as derivative of the European "scramble for" and Balkanization of Africa. The ultimate objective is independence and the creation of continental unity among the independent African nation-states in the form of a United States of Africa. Racial/national equality and unity among people of African descent globally are additional objectives. Ideologically, these aims are viewed as prerequisites for the liberation of any specific sector of the African population, for example, women, youth, and workers.

Pan-Africanism has been organizationally expressed through a variety of 20th-century conferences, organizations, and unions between African nations. Early organization expression can be charted back to the Chicago Congress of Africa (1893) and the African Associa-

tion (1897). The first of seven Pan-African Congresses, organized by Henry Sylvester Williams of Trinidad, was held in London in 1900. It was followed by four congresses organized by U.S. born scholar-activist W. E. B. DuBois held in 1919 (Paris), 1921 (London and Brussels), 1923, and 1927 (New York). The most influential congress was held in Manchester, England, in 1945. This conference had the largest attendance of African-born delegates, placed greater emphasis on the creation of a movement to achieve Pan-Africanist objectives, and adopted resolutions that condemned colonialism and promoted African independence.

The majority of the delegates to the early Pan-African meetings and organizations were colonially educated and relatively privileged African men from all over the world, including Henry Sylvester Williams of Trinidad, W. E. B. DuBois from the United States, Jomo Kenyatta of Kenya, Kwame Nkrumah of Ghana, and George Padmore from Trinidad. Many of these Pan-Africanists would go on to lead independence struggles in their respective African or African diasporan nations.

Organizations associated with the Pan-African movement include the African Association (1897), Pan-African Association (PAA), United Negro Improvement Association (1914), Société Africaine de Culture (1950), the Organization of African Unity (1963), and the All-African People's Revolutionary Party (1972).

**PANAMANIAN NATIONALISM**    From the Spanish-American War to the secession of Panama, there is a direct line of American interventions. Theodore Roosevelt claimed for the United States the right to police the entire hemisphere. Panamanian nationalism is a unique case in Latin American affairs, since the Republic of Panama came into existence with the encouragement and aid of the United States. Yet today the United States is the prime target of Panamanian nationalism.

Inhabitants of the republic began to display a nationalistic attitude during the same period that Mexican nationalism reacted against American superiority, National Socialism appeared in Germany, and fascism triumphed in Italy. Panama protested and at times revolted against an international status that closely resembled the structure of a protectorate directed by the United States.

In 1903, the United States had obtained by treaty a de facto sovereignty over the land strip through which the canal was to flow; it had been assigned to the United States in perpetuity. Thus Panama became an independent nation through an event which, from the start, deprived it of jurisdiction over its territory.

The canal had made Panama's existence possible, but

had at the same time poisoned it with hatred of the great power in whose shadow it now lived. A political life of sorts had developed, but parties were mostly personal factions, and the leaders belonged to the small clique able to trace their ancestors back to colonial times. Under Article 136 of the Constitution the government could ask the United States to supervise elections or to keep order. It was a provision that served only to confirm the status of protectorate, and when used it was a source of popular anger.

A revision of the treaty of 1903 was undertaken under President Franklin D. Roosevelt. The convention of friendship and cooperation of 1936 ruled that the United States must relinquish the right of intervention in the domestic affairs of the republic. In return Panama promised to collaborate in the defense of the canal. The republic continued to be divided into the Canal Zone and the territory of the republic proper. There was and still is a vast difference in wages, living standards, and general outlook on life between the citizens of the United States, who often display an ardent and sometimes imprudent nationalism, the Panamanians who work in the Canal Zone for the Americans, and finally the Panamanians who share the general poverty and misery that Latin Americans have been heir to. It was only to be expected that certain Panamanian politicians should fall under the spell of the German National Socialist movement, and that, in consequence, the republic was looked on as a potential danger spot in hemispheric defense. Nationalism centered on the question of control of the canal as well as on such subjects as national symbols (e.g., the display of the flag). In the 1930s Panamanian nationalism was easily controlled or at least appeased by concessions from its U.S. populations.

The Panama Canal Treaty of 1978 consummated negotiations that had been carried on between the United States and Panama for almost fourteen years. Long pent-up frustrations and a rising tide of Panamanian nationalism combined to produce major rioting along the Canal Zone border area in 1964, with many casualties. The Panamanian chief of government, General Omar Torrijos, obtained ratification support through a national plebiscite, and President Jimmy Carter succeeded in winning a two-thirds vote in the U.S. Senate in support of the treaty ratification. The treaty has helped to answer charges of colonialism and has changed the focus of U.S. interest in the canal from one of ownership to one of use. The treaty, together with the Neutrality Treaty of 1977, is based on the two nationalistic definitions of their national interests and is consistent with their respective national values.

The United States transferred the canal, along with the rest of the 360,240-acre Canal Zone, to Panamanian jurisdiction on December 31, 1999, in accordance with 1977 and 1978 treaties.

**PAN-AMERICANISM** Term that first appeared in the New York City press in the period immediately preceding the 1889–1890 Inter-American Conference held in Washington, D.C. According to Joseph B. Lockey, a leading historian of the movement, Pan-Americanism from that time forward could be described as the cooperative relationship of the sovereign states of the Western hemisphere, a relationship based on the principles of law, nonintervention, and equality. Lockey's assessment, of course, represents the Pan-American ideal. Efforts on the part of the American states to achieve these goals in the wake of the Washington conference were not always successful.

The period from 1810 to the late 1880s, depicted in most studies as the golden Pan-Americanism era, witnessed a series of conferences involving a number of Spanish American nations. Inspired by a fear of foreign aggression, the main objective of these conferences was mutual security.

With the convening of the 1889–1890 Washington conference a second phase of Pan-Americanism began that would last until the early 1930s. The emergence of the United States as a major power provided the opportunity for that country to sponsor this phase of the movement. The agendas for the conferences during this period were carefully orchestrated by North American policy makers. The United States preferred to deal with economic, scientific, and cultural topics that did not lend themselves to confrontation and polemics. Latin American nations preferred to use the Pan-American conferences as vehicles for promoting the concepts of equality, respect for the rule of international law, and adherence to the principles of sovereignty and absolute nonintervention.

As the United States became more imperialistic and more menacing at the end of the century, the Latin Americans, especially their writers and poets, became ever more alarmed, finally coming out openly in their opposition to the growing influence of an alien civilization. The Generación of 1898 in Spain found its counterpart in South America. Pan-Hispanism became its watchword. The writer who articulated this new awareness was the Uruguayan José Enrique Rodó in his famous essay "Ariel" written in 1899.

Ironically, in the years following World War I, when the United States enjoyed seemingly uncontested domination in the Americas, Latin Americans obtained their greatest success in forcing discussion, if not resolution, of political issues at Inter-Americans meetings. Proposals at Santiago in 1923 for an American League of Nations, an Inter-American court with mandatory arbitration, and the restructuring of the Pan-American Union, combined with the call at Havana in 1928 for the acceptance of the principle of nonintervention, demonstrated the persistence of Latin Americans to develop an Inter-American system governed by the rule of law and bound by the principle of international equality.

A new phase of the Pan-American movement started after the Montevideo conference (1933). After years of passionate, yet in the final analysis fruitless, advocacy of a wide range of political issues, the Latin Americans were at last able to witness the U.S. government public adherence to most of these very same principles—the most important, of course, being the principle of nonintervention. The lessening of tensions within the hemispheric community led in turn to the development of solidarity both before and during World War II. The postwar era has formed the latest phase of Pan-Americanism, dating effectively from the signing of the 1947 Rio Treaty and the subsequent 1948 Bogotá conference. The establishment of the Organization of American States at Bogotá laid the groundwork for the development of the current Inter-American system.

**PAN-ARABISM** In the twilight of the Ottoman Empire, which collapsed after World War I, the Turkish sultans promoted Pan-Islamism as a vehicle for holding together their disparate subjects throughout the Middle East and insulating the empire against revolution. After Istanbul's hold on the Arab states had been broken, a notion of Pan-Arabism emerged that underscored the idea that there is such a thing as an Arab nation, speaking a common language, sharing a common culture and history, and encompassing the peoples of many Arab states. However, no consensus developed concerning exactly what it is: an expression of anticolonial resistance against France and Britain, opposition to the new semicolonial governments in the mandates that followed the collapse of the Ottoman Empire, some kind of renewed Pan-Islamism, or something else.

Most defintions of Pan-Arabism included the ultimate political objective of Arab unity. To the Ba'thi, who later ruled in both Iraq and Syria, it meant the creation of a single independent Arab state encompassing the entire Arab nation. Another interpretation associated with Egypt's revolutionary leader, Gamal Abdel Nasser, was that Pan-Arabism should involve solidarity among Arab governments. They should cooperate in opposing outside efforts to influence events in the Arab world. Both of these interpretations, while not denying an Islamic dimension, emphasize the secular character of Pan-Arabism.

The objective of creating a single unifying state was never achieved. Experiments in combining states mostly failed, the most dramatic example being that of Syria and Egypt, who created a short-lived "United Arab Republic." Solidarity was weak and ineffective during the June 1967 war against Israel, which resulted in "occupied territories," some of which are still in Israeli hands. This humiliation diminished faith in the already fading prestige and luster of Pan-Arabism as an important force in the Arab world. It was relegated to the sidelines of Middle Eastern politics, as political Islam became more appealing and powerful.

**PAN-GERMAN LEAGUE** In the age of nationalism in the latter half of the 19th and early part of the 20th centuries, there were many expansionist "Pan" movements bearing names like Pan-American, Pan-Slav, or Pan-German. The latter took the form of an energetic political party, the Pan-German League, founded in 1891, which put heavy pressure on the German government to pursue a more aggressive foreign policy aiming to make Germany a "world power." It favored an activist colonial policy and a blue-water battle fleet to protect those colonies, as well as to challenge the naval preeminence of Great Britain. Its proclaimed goal was to "consolidate all Germans around the world," and it was vociferous in defending the interests of German ethnic minorities outside Germany's borders. It was the most aggressive and radical of a number of patriotic societies during the era of the German Empire, and it supported and helped finance such organizations as the German Colonial Society and German Army League. Under the long-time leadership of Heinrich Class, the league regarded anti-Semitism as an important basis for German assertiveness around the world. During most of its existence the Pan-German League opposed the German governments of the day, scorning them as too soft. In despair, Chancellor Bethmann Hollweg declared in 1912: "Politics cannot be made with these idiots!"

During World War I the Pan-German League became a persistent advocate of widespread annexations that would ultimately constitute a German-dominated *Mitteleuropa* (Central Europe). It enjoyed the apogee of its influence during the final two years of the war, when Marshall Paul von Hindenburg and General Erich Ludendorff were largely in control of Germany. Although they shared many goals, Class and Adolf Hitler did not get along, and the league sank into insignificance after

Hitler came to power in 1933. It disbanded in 1939, its objectives having been taken over and radicalized even further by the Nazis.

## PAN-IBERIANISM

**PAN-IBERIANISM** Political doctrine that favors the union of the nations of the Iberian peninsula. It appeared at the end of the 18th century, and soon took on a republican, federal, and progressive character. Pan-Iberianism was popular among Spanish thinkers in the 19th century, but in Portugal, though supported by important intellectual figures such as Teófilo Braga and Antero de Quental, it remained very unpopular. In contrast, Pan-Iberianism hit a chord with Catalan and Galician nationalists, who saw in it an ideal way out of Castilian dominance.

The minority Spanish Democratic Party, founded in 1849, reflected the paniberianist platform of some elite political and literary circles. A Hispano-lusitan League was formed in Madrid in 1854. Later, Pan-Iberianism was a political platform solely of the republican federal party, except for a short revolutionary period between October 1868 and April 1869 when General Prim tried to convince King Ferdinand of Portugal to accept a unified peninsular throne.

Pan-Iberianism evolved later as a premise, rather than an explicit political doctrine, for certain left-wing social and political positions. This became clear at the proclamation of the Portuguese republic in 1910, and in the ideologies of anarchist groups both in Spain and Portugal.

Pan-Iberianism can be viewed as a form of centripetal nationalism such as the German or Italian unification movements, aimed at reversing the economic and political decadence of both Spain and Portugal. When it tried to avoid frontal collision with Portuguese nationalism, Pan-Iberianism took many forms, from just cultural and economic, to the proposal of a very loose republican federation or a mere dynastic union, so Castile would not dominate Portugal. Precisely, this doctrine's greatest obstacle has been the incompatibility of national interests among its inspirers.

As a result of the French political model, in the mid-1850s, even among defenders of an Iberian federation, state and cultural unity tended to be identified. At the end of the century, the distinction between state and nation allowed Pan-Iberianism a second wind, because political union was no longer equivalent to cultural and national subordination. In 1897, the Catalan nationalist leader and theoretician Enric Prat de la Riba proposed a new kind of Pan-Iberianism according to a national division of the Iberian peninsula, which in his view was traditionally composed of Portugal, Castile, and Catalonia. He later extended the scope of a hypothetical Iberia from Lisbon to the Rhône river. Pan-Iberianism combined for Catalan nationalists the orderly fulfillment of their self-rule desires with an equal standing with Portugal, which Catalonia still envied for her success in breaking away from Castile's grip in 1640.

Since 1986, the participation of Spain and Portugal in the European integration process has swallowed Pan-Iberianism by consolidating the peninsula in a single market and a partial political unity, albeit with a faraway capital in Brussels.

## PAN-ISLAMISM

**PAN-ISLAMISM** A transethnic and transnational political movement that started in the 19th century. Its aim was to raise the political consciousness of Muslims to create a unified front and protect the interest of Muslim communities against colonialism. This movement does not negate the idea of nationalism or ethnicity but rather seeks to consolidate them. Even though Islamic solidarity is based on religious affinities among Muslims, Pan-Islamism evolved in reaction to the penetration of European capitalism and Russian expansion into the less developed Muslim countries in the 19th century. Muslim *ulema* consistently called for cooperation and unity among Muslims irrespective of their race, language, and ethnicity. The concept of *umma*, the ecumenical Islamic community, has become the main religious source of this political movement.

When Pan-Islam emerged as a religious-political program of the Ottoman state in the mid-19th century, Pan-Islamism was an intellectual and popular phenomenon to which Muslim merchants and politicians subscribed to protect and further their interests against European economic, technological, and missionary activities. The Ottoman intellectuals had been appropriating religious ideas for political purposes since 1860 to protect the empire against European colonial powers. Pan-Islamism in the Ottoman Empire had domestic and international dimensions. In response to the 1878 Turko-Russian War, in which the Ottoman state was forced to give up Bosnia-Herzegovina and the large territory in the eastern Anatolian frontiers, the Ottoman state formulated Pan-Islamic foreign policy.

Pan-Islamism was inherently a defensive ideology against the penetration of European colonialism. After the occupation by various colonial powers of Cyprus and Bosnia (1878), Tunisia (1881), and Egypt (1882) and the Central Asian khanates, the Ottoman intellectuals formulated Pan-Islamism as a countercolonial ideology against colonial expansion into their everyday life. Pan-Islamism was articulated by Jamal al-Din al-Afghani (d. 1897), Namık Kemal (1840–1888), Ali Suavi (1838–1878), and other Ottoman scholars, and concretized by the Ottoman bureaucracy. Pan-Islamism functioned and evolved as nationalism by endowing it with nationalistic significance.

Pan-Islamism (*Ittihad-i Islam*) in the Ottoman context transformed the Muslim sense of communal-religious identity into a political identity. Abdülhamid II utilized Islamic political consciousness for domestic and international political purposes, the most important of which was the protection of the state. The domestic goal of Pan-Islamism promoted by Abdülhamid II aimed to capture the loyalty of the masses during profound social transformation. Abdülhamid II needed the allegiance of the masses to centralize the state, whereas the masses needed the sultan's commitment to Islamic values to overcome their alienation from the political spehre and exclusion from the economic domain. As a result of Pan-Islamism, the Muslims of the Ottoman Empire believed that the state was their own and that the rulers were concerned for their well-being. Pan-Islamism was a protonationalist movement to create a modern nation-state by fusing culture with politics. Islamic political consciousness, for the Muslims of the 19th century, provided a surrogate political identity for Muslims in the Balkans, Central Asia, and the Ottoman territories.

Pan-Islamic activities politicized the concept of *umma* and *caliphate* without promising redemption or exile (*hijra*) but rather a political program to protect the Muslim land against colonialism. In this period, Muslim intellectuals in tsarist Russia played a formative role in blending Islam with nationalism. Ismail Gaspıralı of Crimea redefined the concept of territory as a signifier of an Islamic space in which freedom could be actualized. To politicize the concept of homeland, the Crimean newspaper *Tercüman* (Interpreter) adapted an invented hadith: *hub al-watan min al-iman* (the love of homeland stems from the love of faith). In practice, Pan-Islamism became a powerful vehicle for secularization and internalization of the modern concepts of homeland (*watan*) and nationalism. The Muslim communities were divided in their reaction to Abdulhamid's message of Pan-Islamism. The fascinating and rich spectrum of responses to the policies of Pan-Islamism indicated that it became the precursor for more narrow territorial and state-centric nationalism. It politicized the Muslim consciousness and paved the way for ethnonationalism. The relationship between Islam and nationalism is more symbiotic than antagonistic. Nationalism in Turkey and other Muslim countries emerged from and was internalized in Islamic idioms and concepts. Print technology, newspapers, and communication channels facilitated the formation of Islamic and national communities.

During World War I, the ruling Committee of Union and Progress did not hesitate to evoke Islamic concepts, and the declaration of war was justified in Islamic terms. Even though these religious calls for a holy war (jihad) did not prevent the dismemberment of the Ottoman state, Pan-Islamic organizations in India evolved to defend the rigths of Muslims and ultimately formed modern Pakistan. With the abolition of the caliphate, the Pan-Islamic movements lost their center of gravity and the age of Pan-Islamic congresses started. There were at least five major Pan-Islamic congresses: Mecca, 1924; Cairo, 1926; Mecca, 1926; Jerusalem, 1931; and Geneva, 1935. In reaction to the Palestinian–Israeli conflict, the Muslim states formed the Organization of Islamic Conference in 1969 to protect the interest of Muslim states. This modern incarnation of the Pan-Islamic organization has been active in promoting political and economic cooperation among Muslim governments. Transnational Islamic solidarity has been articulated and turned into a policy during the Bosnian crisis (1991–1996).

The major work on Pan-Islamism is Jacob M. Landau's *The Politics of Pan-Islam: Ideology and Organization* (Oxford University Press, 1990). See also M. Hakan Yavuz, "The Patterns of Political Islamic Identity: Dynamics of National and Transnational Loyalties and Identities," in *Central Asian Survey* 14(3) (1995), pp. 341–372.

## PAN-OTTOMANISM

The year 1839 marked the declaration of *Hatti Sherif of Gulhane* by the Ottoman state. This abolished religious and other types of discrimination and granted all subjects of the empire equality of rights. From then until the mid-1910s, the theme of Ottomanism became a central focus in the internal politics of the Ottoman Empire. The initial declaration met the strong resistance of conservative provincial élites, the clergy, and the Muslim people who considered the non-Muslims, derogatively referred to as the "infidels" (*giaur*) to be nothing less than second-class citizens.

After the conclusion of the Crimean War (1853–1856), reform efforts gained strength with the *Hatti Humayun*, which reiterated key promises of equality. From then until 1876, the Ottoman policy, led by a succession of reformer *Grand Vezirs* (prime ministers), aimed to implement the equality of citizens in the empire. It was a very difficult task because the tiny minority of reformers did not have a mass following among the Muslims. Many of their efforts remained on paper only, with very few of them succeeding.

The government had also to contend with a group of Muslim liberal dissidents, who became known as the "Young Ottomans." The group was formed in 1865 with the goal of furthering the reform efforts, which they deemed too slow. A central concern of all these efforts was the attempt to develop an Ottoman civic identity that would relate to the whole population of the Ottoman state. The key to the success of such an agenda was to attract the following of the non-Muslim population. This was difficult because of the long-standing tradition of communal association among this population and because of the failure to promote tangible meritocracy irrespective of religious and other particularistic criteria. Moreover, some of the non-Muslim communities, most notably the Greek Orthodox, were urban and better educated than the Muslims. The growing incorporation of the Ottoman state into the world economy, and its dependency on the world market, benefited at least a part of this group, whose financial prosperity was viewed with great resentment by the Muslims.

The principles of liberalism found support among the rich Greek Orthodox banking elite of Constantinople, and in conjunction with members of the Ottoman reform circles a conspiracy was set up, leading in 1876 to the deposition of the sultan and the rise to the throne of Murad V. The plan, orchestrated in Masonic lodges, proved successful for a while, but Murad turned out to be mentally unstable. He was deposed and Abdul Hamid II rose to the throne. The reformers called in Parliament and succeeded in getting a constitution approved by the new sultan. Soon, however, the events of the Eastern Crisis (1875–1878) overwhelmed these efforts. When Russia and the Ottoman Empire went to war, the sultan suspended the Parliament and, in effect, he ruled as a personal monarch from that point on (1878–1908). Reformers were silenced or killed, or fled abroad, and strict censorship was imposed.

Among the dissidents who fled to Paris and elsewhere in Europe were those who formed the Young Turk movement. This movement preserved ties with the non-Muslims and cooperated with them. The two main wings of the movement included the liberals and the more nationalistic fraction. The liberals were supported by the non-Muslims. In the aftermath of the Young Turk revolution (1908), these groups became important players in Ottoman politics.

During this period, there was a second effort to secure a Greek-Ottoman alliance. This was led by Ion Dragoumis and Athanasios Souliotis. Both were ardent Greek nationalists who had been involved in organizing the Greek paramiliatry offensive in Macedonia (1904–1908). However, they came to the conclusion that the only meaningful solution for the peoples of the Ottoman Empire was to resolve their differences peacefully. Their efforts to create a pro-Ottoman group of representatives in the post-1908 Ottoman parliaments failed, however, as the majority of deputies sided with the Greek nationalists. Following the Ottoman defeat in the Balkan wars of 1912–1913, and the loss of the majority of the empire's European possessions, support for Ottomanism weakened. Gradually, out of the critique of Ottomanism by Muslim intellectuals (such as Yusuf Akcura), the Young Turk intelligentsia begun to articulate the notion of a Turkish identity. This was the effective end to all prospects of Muslim–Christian cooperation, which had dominated the agenda since the mid-19th century.

For a discussion of different aspects of this movement, see Dimitrios Kitsikis, *Comparative History of Greek and Turkey in the Twentieth Century* (in Greek; Athens: Hestia, 1978); S. M. Hanioglou, *The Young Turks in Opposition* (New York: Oxford University Press, 1995); and Victor Roudometof, "Nationalism and Statecraft in Southeastern Europe 1750–1923" (unpublished doctoral dissertation, University of Pittsburgh, 1996), Chapter 6, for further bibliography.

**PAN-SCANDINAVIANISM**    Refers to the belief in a common Scandinavian cultural heritage based on the medieval literature of sagas and Eddic poetry and a belief in "common societies, common languages, common faith." The study of this medieval literature began in Denmark and Sweden in the 17th and 18th centuries, with Olof Rudbeck and Thomas Bartholin. These scholars and others produced enormous tomes establishing the North as the symbolic genesis of Western culture. For example, it was argued that Greek and Roman heroes like Hercules could be shown to have Swedish antecedents and that the cult of Apollo was actually a variant of the worship of the Norse god Baldr. Pan-Scandinavian unions among the kingdoms, considered many times by Danish and Swedish monarchs but never achieved after the Kalmar Union in 1397, were generally based on these notions of a common Scandinavian culture.

Nationalists often opposed this view of a general Scandinavian cultural heritage because it blocked their attempts to use the literature as evidence of their national uniqueness. Icelandic nationalists, for instance, argued that the medieval sagas represented the cultural heritage of Iceland alone and did not want to share this literature with Danes or Swedes. Danish scholars also opposed Swedish interpretations that held that sagas located in Sweden were the most historically reliable. British saga scholars also had political motivations for opposing Pan-Scandinavianism because they preferred to think of the Icelandic sagas as being the cultural precursors of Britain and as culturally distinct from Denmark, particularly after Anglo-Danish hostilities during the Napoleonic wars. Sometimes, however, the interests of nationalism and Pan-Scandinavianism met: In their fear of German encroachments, Danish nationalists also became Scandinavist, and the Norwegian-Swedish help in the war of 1848–1857 against the German states is still celebrated in Denmark.

Today, Pan-Scandinavianism refers to a general belief in a common Scandinavian culture or in joint cultural endeavors among the nations through the Nordic Union. The concept is sometimes revived, however, by the opponents to Swedish and Danish membership in the European Union, who favor a unity within Scandinavia instead. One example of such unity is the cooperation of Norway, Sweden, and Denmark in SAS, the Scandinavian Airlines System.

## PAN-SLAVISM

The oldest and most well-known macro-nationalist identity is that of Pan-Slavism. The assumptions of its initial adherents in the 19th century were that those who spoke Slavic languages had a common early history as well as common moral and spiritual qualities, and that this could be projected forward into a common destiny to ensure their survival and to promote their shared political, economic, and cultural interests. The goals of the Pan-Slavists were a strengthening of the position of the Western, Eastern, and Southern Slavs; a democratization of the empires in which they found themselves; autonomy in some form; followed by a process of Slavic reunion. Although essentially unsuccessful in its early period, elements of its philosophy have remained visible to this day.

Although later expropriated by Russia and the Russians to a large degree, it was not by origin a product of the Eastern Slavs. Rather it developed in Austro-Hungary among the Western Slavs—peoples seeking strength in numbers in their challenges to existing states of oppression by Germans and Magyars. The idea of a single people artificially divided by others into tribes speaking different dialects became part of the sustaining legend. Many of the themes of this early Pan-Slavism derived from the idealization of the Slavs, their heroic history, their rural culture, and their bright future by the German Johann von Herder (1744–1803). These were soon echoed by Slav historians and linguists who, in their writings, began to separate out their own peoples from the eponymous nationality of the empire in which they lived and to attempt a standardization of their languages, as well as to seek an all-around improvement in their status. The Czech historian František Palacký (1798–1876) was at the forefront of seeking to document a specifically Czech history and to synthesize post-French revolutionary ideas of freedom with the meritorious features of Slav character in order to strengthen their position within Austria-Hungary by way of getting a federation of Slavs there. Another Czech, Jan Kollar, called for a range of immediate measures such as the creation of a Slav periodical, a library, an academy, and local organizations.

With her failure in the Crimean War against the West Europeans, the development of German unification, and the problems the Austro-Hungarian Slavs encountered in making progress, the epicenter of Pan-Slavism passed to Moscow and the Russians in the 1860s, complementing the existing vogue of Slavophilism. Among the leading articulators of the Russian version were the historian Mikhail P. Pogodin (1800–1875); the publicist Nikolai Ya. Danilevskiy (1828–1885), with his vehement opposition to the divisive anarchy of conflicting ideas in the West and his sense of Russia's destiny to lead; the poet and diplomat Fyodor I. Tyutchev (1803–1873); and the conservative publicist Mikhail N. Katkov (1818–1897). Under their influence, in Russia Pan-Slavism took on a more militant and expansionist aspect, akin to her old policy of unifying all the Russias and in line with her more contemporary aspirations as a great power which could protect and promote more general Slav interests. It also took on a more overtly religious element. These various new features came to have an impact on numerous others in Russia, including the writer and former radical rebel Fyodor M. Dostoyevsky (1822–1881), who came to perceive the Russian mission vis-à-vis her fellow Slavs as a necessity for the very progress of civilization. Official government support was, however, limited and its impetus was lost by the end of the 1880s.

Pan-Slavism was to be revived from time to time with congresses in the first decade of the 20th century and, more particularly, with Hitler's assault on Eastern Europe. Stalin the pragmatist resorted to appeals to Slavic unity to aid the war effort, and the advent of the satellite states after World War II seemed to offer new opportunities for the realization of goals. Further echoes of Pan-Slavism could be found in the writings of a number of dissenters in the 1960s to 1980s (including Aleksandr Solzhenitsyn and Viktor Chalmayev), the creation of the Commonwealth of Independent States (CIS) in the 1990s, in Russian policy in Bosnia and Kosovo in the mid- to late 1990s in support of the Serbs, and in the agreements for a union of Belarus, Russia, and subsequently the state of Yugoslavia in the late 1990s.

In practice, little real progress was achieved by the movement. It was repeatedly undermined by the very nationalism it sought to tap. Its ideals were confused, being both conservative and revolutionary; it relied on a largely legendary past; it lacked a convincing relationship with present reality; and its supposed supporters sought contradictory goals from the outset. The Slavs had long been split and differentiated by particular identities—more so than the Germans or Italians of the 19th century. Different traditions and religions had taken root among them. They revolted against rule of one group by another (Poland in 1861, West Ukrainians in the 1940s, and Yugoslavia in 1948); they fought each other in wars great and small (the Balkan wars and World Wars I and II); and they clashed with each other within Slavic states (in Poland and Yugoslavia). Lacking much actual or natural unity, the Slavic states and their elites came to resent Russia's insistence on leadership; her playing the dominating role model; her attempts at Russifying the language of any union; and her making of Orthodoxy (and later her version of Communism) the essence of the moral and spiritual code, with Moscow as the Third Rome. Today there is similar resentment within the CIS and a steady falling away of support.

Among the best full-length and short studies of Pan-Slavism are M. B. Petrovich's *The Emergence of Russian Pan-Slavism 1856–1870* (Columbia University Press, 1956), H. Kohn's *Panslavism—Its History and Ideology* (Notre Dame University Press, 1960), and L. L. Snyder's *Macro-Nationalisms* (Greenwood Press, 1984).

**PAN-TURANISM** The Turkic peoples are associated with a number of macronationalisms such as Pan-Islamism, Pan-Turkism, and Pan-Ottomanism, all of them connected with schemes for national regeneration. Perhaps the best known of these is that of Pan-Turanism. Many of the macronationalisms suffered because of the breadth and remoteness of the level of identification required of the adherents, and this is no more so than in the case of Pan-Turanism. Pan-Turkism was, by contrast, relatively intelligible, with its concepts a shared early history, a common core language, and a widespread religious affinity among Turkic peoples currently finding themselves in a fragmented diaspora. Pan-Turanism, however, went well beyond that into the realms of mythology and fantasizing with its perception of a community of interests and a shared destiny for all the peoples of the Turan basin of Central Asia, with its eastern perimeter being the mountain bowl along the old Russo-Chinese frontier and its western border the Caspian Sea. While identification with a geographic entity has been a basis for a number of modern nationalisms (in contrast with the cultural/ethnic/linguistic nationalisms), this case required identification with a somewhat nebulous geographic unit at an inexplicit period of history. In terms of ethno-cultural factors it was, in addition, an area that could not be shown to have had a unified linguistic/cultural group as its inhabitants at any prior point in time. The advocates sought to embrace Turkic, Mongol, Iranian, and Finno-Ugrian peoples into their fold as inhabitants of the supposed former homeland of Turan, described in Persian

epic poetry. From these various sources, the so-called Turanian culture had been spread in diverse tongues by writers, scientists, and leaders of ostensibly different backgrounds, ranging from Attila the Hun through Chinghis Khan to Tamerlane.

This conceptual framework emerged from the work of the journalist and philosopher Mehmad Ziya (1876–1924) under the pseudonym of Ziya Gokalp. Exponents in the early 20th century sought to divest Ottoman Turkey of its non-Turanian peoples, to return to pristine forms prior to the fragmentation, and to evoke a pan-national pride as against the ostensible internationalism of Islam. The latter would, however, retain a role in spiritual and moral guidance in Turan.

While the ideas served to reinforce Pan-Turkism in general, Pan-Turanism in practice ran up against the political realities of existing multilinguistic territorial units dividing up the Turks and others in the Turan basin; against the vested interests of the leaderships of these territories; and against other types of division as between those on the left and those on the right of the political spectrum. To the pre-World War I Turkish government it was a propaganda tool against Russian imperial control over part of Turan and numerous other Turkic peoples, but the idea of a republic of Turan was to founder thereafter. Elements of the ideas could still be detected in some of the Pan-Turkic, antifragmentation views that reemerged in the Soviet Union in the 1920s, when Sultan Galiev conceived a socialist version of it, governed by its own centralized, monolithic, and yet autonomous Communist Party, serving as a launch pad for attracting other eastern Moslems to the Communist cause. Galiev, and his ideas, quickly ran up against the more centralizing schemes of Stalinism. With the collapse of the USSR, opportunities arose again, but Turkey was able only to offer limited support to what quickly emerged as newly autonomous territories in the Turanian area, all with their own elites bent on self-preservation.

Gokalp's major work was edited by N. Berkes as *Turkish Nationalism and Western Civilisation* (republished by Greenwood Press, 1981). A sound commentary on the ideas is presented in L. L. Snyder in *Macro-nationalisms* (Greenwood Press, 1984). See also M. Czaplicka, *The Turks of Central Asia* (Clarendon Press, 1918).

**PAN-TURKISM** Refers to a similar sentiment expressed by national groups except that the desire is to achieve a political arrangement that encompasses all peoples of Turkic origin rather than one particular national group. Turkic nationalism is thus a supranational movement that seeks to form a political unit based on the cultural affinities of peoples of Turkic origin. The popularity of this movement has ebbed and flowed throughout contemporary history, but has generally gained most support during and after the collapse of empires within the region concerned, most noticeably during the decline of the Ottoman and Soviet Empires.

One of the first writers on the subject to suggest the possibility of a Turkic national movement was the orientalist Arminius Vambery who started writing on the subject in the 1860s. However, the most famous advocate of Turkic nationalism was the Crimean Ismail Bey Gasprinsky (1851–1914) who, among other things, called for the union of the Turkic peoples of Russia and set up the magazine *Tercüman* (Interpreter) in which a simplified version of Osmanli Turkish was used. Gasprinsky envisaged that in creating a language that could be understood "by the boatman of the Bosphorus as easily as by the cameleer of Kashgar" a cohesive Pan-Turkic and Pan-Islamic community would eventually be formed. Gasprinsky was acutely aware of the potential influence that the print media could have on populations and set about increasing the circulation of his newspaper with the objective of establishing greater unity between the various Turkic groups via the establishment of a common language.

At the turn of the century, the promotion of Gasprinsky's common Turkic language (*tawhid-I lisan* or *lisan-I umumi,* unified language or common language) was supported by the Islamic reformist movement, the *Jadids.* However, this support was not uniform and dissent was apparent with certain ethnic groups, such as the Kazakhs, who preferred to develop a distinctive Kazakh language. These divisions within the movement were reflected in the All-Muslim Congress of 1917 during the period of provisional government in Russia. The congress supported the use of Gasprinsky's common Turkic language as the medium of instruction in the upper schools. However, in primary and secondary schools the national language of the region was to be the main language; the common Turkic language was relegated to the status of a secondary compulsory subject. During the political upheaval of 1917 a unified Turkic national movement failed to materialize; instead, most political activity centered on each of the individual national groups or, alternatively, on the preexisting political entities such as Bukhara and Khiva.

The aspirations of Turkic nationalism gained renewed political salience during the collapse of the Soviet Union in 1991; the disintegration of the federation generated new hope for a Pan-Turkic federation. Although within Central Asia certain political movements, such as the Kazakh party *Alash* and the Uzbek party *Birlik,* seek to promote greater Turkic unity, such pronouncements are treated skeptically by other na-

tional groups within the region, such as the Turkmen and the Kirghiz, who are wary that it may be a vehicle of dominance by the larger national groups. However, a looser federation may be more practicable, and many of the states of the region took steps toward this end in 1993 when they agreed to swap the Cyrillic alphabet for the Roman script, while Turkey added five letters to its alphabet that represent sounds in the Central Asian languages.

**PARAGUAYAN NATIONALISM** In the case of Paraguay, the tools that facilitated military victory in the Chaco warfare did not guarantee domestic order. Rafael Franco, a war hero, saw this clearly and, as he had in 1928, set out to galvanize the Paraguayan republic and institute modern Paraguayan nationalism.

In February 1936 ex-army officers associated with Franco overthrew the Ayala regime. They set out to forge a revolutionary process for the country that went far beyond the modest programs of reforms. To this end they developed a radical doctrine, Febrerismo, which drew inspiration from an odd combination of corporatist ideologies, and they rejected representative democracy as an American imperialist charade.

The Febreristas failed to deliver their promised reforms. They did introduce some important labor legislation, but only managed superficial changes in terms of agrarian reform. The Paraguayan population, at this time, was mostly rural. In the end, the Febreristas were not in power long enough to pursue their innovations. On August 13, 1937, a military coup finished with Franco's regime and shortly thereafter the liberals were restored to power.

In spite of their ejection of Franco, the liberals could not disregard the well-built nationalist attitude that his movement had inaugurated in Paraguay. The Liberal Party now ruled only in partnership with charismatic nationalist army officers. For the liberals, the only answer was to find a strong, influential military leader who was also one of their own. Estigarribia, who was then minister to Washington and a war hero, seemed the best alternative. He was elected to the presidency in absentia in 1939.

The Febreristas' short period of rule served as a populist call. Now the young people of Paraguay—the veterans, some of the radical student and trade union groups, and the intellectuals—concentrated their fervor on Estigarribia. He, in turn, used their support to evade his liberal sponsors and create an authoritarian state.

The device for this change was the Constitution of 1940. Although the drafting of this document was entrusted to Cecilio Báez, a conservative, in fact it turned out to be thoroughly corporatist in character. It featured a unicameral legislature, a nonelected council of state, and broad powers for the presidency. Armed with these powers, which resemble those granted to Getulio Vargas in Brazil under the Estado Novo, Estigarribia started to neutralize his own political movement. He was well on his way to achieving this goal when he died in an airplane crash on September 5, 1940. After this circumstance, the corporatist state of Estigarribia was transformed into a dictatorship. A year later the Liberal Party was outlawed.

The Allied victory in Europe in 1945 pointed out the time for change in Paraguay. Now, under pressure from the civil society, the government opened the political system widely, legalizing the Liberal, Febrerista, and even the Communist Parties. The abrupt liberalization set the scenario for civil warfare. In January 1947 a military putsch ended the blooming Febrerista influence and handed over power exclusively to the right-wing faction of the tradition Colorado Party.

On March 7, 1947, an insurrectional movement started. Febrerista militants assaulted the central police barracks in Asunción, capital city of Paraguay. The following day junior officers in the northern town of Concepción moved against the pro-Colorado regime. They were almost immediately joined by armed Febreristas, Communists, and some liberals. Hundreds of people were killed and tortured during the next five months. The Colorados formed a compulsory peasant militia, which was forced to develop a bloody campaign alongside the army. Together they had crushed the rebel army by mid-August; they then went on to wreak a terrible revenge on all their political opponents.

In May 1954, another revolt broke out, led by Colorado patrician Epifanio Méndez Fleitas and General Alfredo Stroessner. In July Stroessner was elected president. No one at the time could have guessed that this was the beginning of a thirty-four-year dictatorship, unchallenged in the country from the late 1950s to the early 1980s. This consolidated the conservative, oligarchic, and anticommunist Colorado hegemony in Paraguayan politics, which still prevailed in the mid-1990s.

**PARIZEAU, JACQUES** 1930–. Within the constantly shifting sands of Quebec separatist politics, Jacques Parizeau has fostered an image of being one of only a handful of solid rocks. Born in 1930 to a wealthy, decidedly upper-class family, the eldest of three boys had the best private school education that money could buy. Yet, instead of pursuing a career in one of the liberal professions (i.e., law, medicine), as many of his francophone classmates did at the time, the young Parizeau enrolled in l'École des Hautes Études Commerciales

(HEC) in Montreal, and received his undergraduate degree in economics and commerce. After two years of postgraduate work at l'Institut des sciences politiques in Paris, he traveled to London to complete his doctoral studies in economics at the London School of Economics, working with Nobel Prize winner (1977) James Meade. Immediately afterwards, in 1956, Parizeau returned to Quebec to take up a teaching post at the HEC, his alma mater.

Parizeau's introduction to Quebec politics came shortly thereafter by way of entry into the growing state bureaucracy of Quebec's Quiet Revolution of the early 1960s. Part of the young technocratic class of professors with social science degrees from foreign universities, Parizeau proved indispensable to liberal leader Jean Lesage's plans for an enlarged role for the Quebec state. At the time, much of Quebec's economy and wealth was controlled by a small group of Canadian and American anglophones, and it was the responsibility of individuals like Parizeau to develop economic strategies to wrestle back some of that control and place it in the hands of members of Quebec's majority francophone population. This Parizeau did diligently until 1966, when Lesage's liberals were defeated by Daniel Johnson's Union Nationale.

Still, Parizeau decided to continue working in his capacity as economic adviser within the Quebec bureaucracy, seemingly uninterested in the vagaries of party politics. That changed in a sudden moment of inspiration in 1967 while on his way to a conference in Banff, Alberta, on the economic and constitutional future of Canada: "When boarding the train at Windsor station [in Montreal] I was a federalist," proclaimed Parizeau, "when getting off the train in Banff, I was a separatist." Shortly afterwards, Parizeau officially moved into political life by joining René Lévesque's newly formed Parti Quebecois (PQ). At the time Parizeau publicly stated that the only reason he had entered politics was to push for the sovereignty of Quebec, and that the best way to attain such a goal was to join a political party devoted almost entirely to that end.

During the early 1970s Parizeau and Lévesque worked to build the PQ into a respectable political party. However, they failed to take power in both the 1970 and 1973 provincial elections. Parizeau began to lose interest in politics, and during the 1974 and 1975 school years returned to teaching at the HEC's Institut d'economie. He returned to campaign in the 1976 election, which saw the PQ, and Parizeau, catapulted into power. Parizeau asked for, and was given, the portfolio of ministry of finance, a position he felt most competent to fill. There he spent four years, through the active use of state intervention, on building a strong Quebec economy.

Committed to holding a referendum on "sovereignty-association" (Lévesque's term for a new political partnership with Canada) the PQ formulated a question that asked the population for a mandate to negotiate a new constitutional deal with Canada in 1980. Parizeau was enraged by the very formulation of what he took to be a soft question, demonstrating for the first time his hard-line approach to Quebec's independence by insisting that it should be a question about outright independence, and not simply a mandate to negotiate. The *oui* side lost the referendum 40.4 to 59.6 percent, which was followed by several years of stagnation and loss of direction for the party.

In 1984 Parizeau finally broke with the PQ and returned to full-time teaching and consulting. Three years later Lévesque left as leader of the PQ, and was succeeded by Pierre-Marc Johnson. Soon Johnson quit, and calls rang out for Parizeau to take the helm, in the hope that he would rejuvenate the beleaguered party. Parizeau accepted and in 1988 became leader of the PQ and leader of the opposition in Quebec's National Assembly. Often siding with the hard-liners of the party, Parizeau put the PQ back on track toward the goal of independence, and was rewarded for his efforts with a PQ victory in the 1994 election.

True to their word, the PQ held a referendum on sovereignty in the fall of 1995. Again Parizeau took a hard line on the issue of sovereignty: There was to be no partnership with Canada, it was full independence or nothing. The *non* side won by a slim margin: 50.6 to 49.4 percent. In a speech following the announcement of the results, a bitter and angry Parizeau blamed "l'argent et le vote ethnique" for the loss. The next day he resigned from politics and began his retirement.

Laurence Richard has written a biography of Parizeau, *Jacques Parizeau: Un bâtisseur* (Les Éditions de L'Homme, 1992). As well, Parizeau himself has a book, *Pour un Québec souverain* (vlb éditeur, 1997), which is a collection of his speeches and writings.

**PARK, CHUNG HEE** 1917–1979, Chung Hee Park ruled South Korea for eighteen years (1961–1979) during the time of rapid economic development known as the economic miracle. The characterization of his power has continued to fuel debates until even recent years. Since the state under his presidency is credited with leading Korea's successful economic planning and implementation, the assessment of his authoritarian rule inevitably intersects with his role in Korea's economic development. For instance, although Koreans see

their democratization since the late 1980s as an irreversible turn in their history, some Koreans, as the result of the financial crisis of the 1990s, expressed a certain grave nostalgia for a strong state, similar to that of Chung Hee Park, which could rescue Korea from the crisis and lead another economic miracle.

The strong executive power of Park's regime, which subordinated the legislature and judiciary system, was sustained by the military power and the economic program that brought the regime a great deal of legitimacy. But another key cornerstone of his draconian power was the version of nationalism with which both his political power and the economic policy were implicated. Park's version of nationalism was wrapped in heated appositional rhetoric against North Korea and Communism. Park's successful coup d'état in 1961 pledged an uncompromising opposition to Communism and its realization through liberal economic development with strong leadership. With the well-known motto "Steel equals national power," Park maintained that the purpose of the economic reforms was to hasten the day of peaceful unification of Korea and to ensure national prosperity by solidifying national strength. In other words, according to his argument, the national strength of a country hinges on its economic capability. The increase of exports, a prime policy, was essential to attaining national regeneration and prosperity. The stated purpose of the economic development program was to strengthen the nation and its ability to defeat North Korea, as much as to enhance the welfare of citizens. Anti-North Korean nationalism served as the ideological glue that held together the Korean state and society. The characteristics of Park's rule cannot be fully understood without recognizing this characteristic of nationalism under the national division of Korea in which the existence of South Korea has been defined by its opposition to North Korea.

There are two opposite assessments of Park's regime and the political and economic development of South Korea. Some argue that the strong state ensured the absolute autonomy of the economic planning board, which then applied the principle of rationality and efficiency in recruiting well-trained economists and policy makers and in devising timely industrial planning. Compared to a putative characteristic of Latin American development in which the state and the local capital tended to be subordinated to foreign capital, the South Korean state under Park was nationalist enough to guard the domestic market from the direct investment of foreign capital and even to begin to develop nuclear weapons, though that decision ran the risk of increasing tensions with the United States. Seen from this perspective, Park's regime was rational and nationalist. Furthermore, this nationalist economic program under the state's leadership created the middle class, a critical agent of democratization. In other words, Park's draconian rule was a necessity if Korean democratization were to succeed.

In contrast, others contend that this perspective obscures the fact that Korea's economic development excluded significant groups and regions from sharing in the benefits of expanding the state bureaucracy and of increasing the number of factories and jobs. Furthermore, Park's dictatorship under the auspices of the United States derailed Korea's historical trajectory from other developmental models such as the socialist path that appeared immediately after the independence of Korea from the Japanese rule in 1945. Instead, Park's political and economic power was based on a dependency on America and its imposition of a capitalist economy on Korea. In this perspective, Park's regime was anything but rational and nationalist.

## PARNELL, CHARLES STEWART    1846–1891, Born into a prominent land-owning Anglo-Irish Protestant family in Avondale, County Wicklow, Ireland, Parnell was an unlikely candidate to be the Irish nationalist leader he became. Educated in three English boarding schools and at Cambridge, where he was suspended in 1869 for a disciplinary infraction, he returned to an Irish political cauldron. He was elected to the British Parliament in 1875. Utilizing his good looks, commanding presence, popularity in Ireland, and mastery of parliamentary tactics, he was able to obstruct legislation in order to publicize his demands for home rule in Ireland and fairer and more sensitive treatment of the impoverished Irish. In 1877, at the age of thirty-one, he was elected president of the Home Rule Confederation of Great Britain, making him Ireland's most visible politician.

In 1879 he became the first president of the Irish Land League (later renamed the Irish National League), which opposed eviction and heavy-handed landlordism. This added a dimension of agrarian agitation to his other tactics designed to bring self-rule to Ireland. A year later he was elected chairman of the home rule group in Parliament. So obstructionist were their methods that thirty-six Irish members of parliament were suspended. His aggressive activities landed him in Dublin's Kilmainham jail in 1881. This only increased his popularity in Ireland. He negotiated his release less than a year later by agreeing to use all his influence to diminish agitation in return for considerable concessions to Irish land tenants.

His political career was abruptly ended in 1889–1890 by a husband's suit publicizing his long-standing adulterous relationship with Mrs. Katherine O'Shea. The court found him and his lover guilty. Given the strong public moral indignation this scandal created in Britain, he was expelled from the Irish parliamentary party. His marriage to Katherine in June 1891 was severely criticized in Catholic Ireland and cost him even further support and popularity. He died in Katherine's Brighton home in October 1891. Nevertheless, Irish nationalism owes him a large debt for the pioneering and courageous work he had done in its behalf.

## PAŠIĆ, NIKOLA    1845–1926, Serb politician, leader of the National Radical Party (*Narodna radikalna stranka,* or NRS), and several times prime minister of Serbia and Yugoslavia. Pašić, who had studied engineering in Zurich, became a leading figure in the NRS, which had been founded in 1880. His political activities brought Pašić into frequent conflict with the Obrenović dynasty in Serbia.

The NRS sought to maintain the Serbian state and to expand it to include all other Serbs. Although the NRS had its origins as an agrarian party, under Pašić's leadership, it became a party for the new Serb bourgeoisie. In 1883, Pašić was sentenced to death for participation in the Timok uprising, but the sentence was commuted. Pašić spent the years from 1883 to 1889 in exile.

The NRS won all of the seats in the Serb parliament in the 1888 elections and they quickly embarked on constitutional reform. A year later, the radicals forced Milan Obrenović to resign as ruler of Serbia, and Pašić was amnestied. However, several years later, in 1899, Pašić confessed and was sentenced for treason, but the government awarded him immediate amnesty. Due to his confession, many political allies and enemies alike regarded Pašić as a political opportunist.

The NRS controlled the government in Serbia from 1903 until World War I. In World War I, Pašić's government was forced to retreat from Serbia to Greece along with the Serb army. On September 4, 1914, Pašić announced that Serbia would seek to establish a South Slavic state. Negotiations toward this goal, which lasted several years, produced significant disagreement on the structure of the future state. Whereas Pašić and his government clearly viewed Serbia as the Piedmont of a Serb-led and centralist kingdom of the South Slavs, the Croats and Slovenes favored either a state of the Habsburg South Slavs or a South Slavic state along confederal or federal lines. On July 20, 1917, Pašić reached a compromise with representatives of the Croats and Slovenes. The Corfu Declaration called for the establishment of a constitutional monarchy of the South Slavs, which would be led by the Serb Karađorđević dynasty.

After World War I, Pašić and the NRS viewed Yugoslavia primarily as an enlargement of the prewar Serbian state. Pašić's understanding of the principle of national unity (*narodno jedinstvo*) made it logical that the Serb nation would lead the new Yugoslav state. He regarded the Croats and Slovenes as distinct groups, albeit related to the Serbs.

In December 1920, Pašić became prime minister again, a post that he held almost continuously until April 1926. During the first six months of 1921, Pašić succeeded in pushing through a centralist constitution. It was ratified on June 28, 1921, St. Vitus Day (*Vidovdan*). The constitution was opposed by the Croats and by a substantial portion of other parties. Although the radicals emerged victorious in both the 1923 and the 1925 elections, Pašić's abrasive and autocratic style of governance led to a perceptible sharpening of tensions between the country's main national groups. In particular, Croat Peasant Party leader Stjepan Radić continued to receive the full support of the Croat population in his struggle against Pašić's centralism. However, in November 1925, after a shift by the Croat Peasant Party toward the radical position, Radić entered the Pašić government. Faced with a corruption scandal affecting his family, Pašić resigned from the government in April 1926. Pašić remained a proponent of strong centralist rule, a position that earned him many enemies among the non-Serb politicians of Yugoslavia. During the course of the 1920s, Pašić also encountered increasing criticism from the Serbs of the former Habsburg Empire (*prečanski Srbi*), who resented that the government favored Serbs from Serbia (*Srbijanci*). Pašić died in December 1926 before he could reenter government. After his death, the NRS was substantially weakened.

**PATRIOTISM**    Patriotism originally refers to the love of *patria,* which in turn derives its meaning from the Latin *pater,* that is, "father." The *patria* is thus the fatherland, the soil where our ancestors were buried and where we were born, a soil characterized by a community of memory. During classical antiquity, in the work of Cicero, for example, *patria* became associated with *respublica* (the "public thing") and with its emphasis on common liberty and common good. Henceforth, patriotism is equated with love of the republic, as found, for example, in the work of Machiavelli. This love relies on civic virtue. It is based on the assumption that being a citizen of a free republic implies the obligation to sustain its political institutions and to defend the common liberty of the people against corruption and tyranny.

The supreme object of love is not the state nor the land but the freedom guaranteed by the republic. If the latter slides into tyranny, the citizen is no longer obliged to abide by its laws.

Nevertheless, one should not conclude that republican patriotism relies on abstract universal principles. The love of common liberty is embodied in the love of a particular republic and in the culture and history arising out of the common practice of citizenship. Patriots do not defend liberty as such, but rather the liberty of the republic in which they live. It is this particular embodiment of liberty that enables the republic to obtain the commitment it needs from its citizens. But one has to bear in mind that the primary object of loyalty remains the *free* republic and not so much the country as such. In this sense, republican patriotism has to be distinguished from a nationalism defending the cultural unity and particularity of a people. In fact, it is often argued that patriotism is similar to *civic* nationalism as found, for example, in England, France, or the United States, where the defenders of the political principles of the nation call themselves "patriots" rather than "nationalists."

This being said, the embodiment of liberty in the political institutions of the republic also implies that citizens ahve a priority over noncitizens. In this sense, it implies an act of exclusion. Although it is not inevitable, this priority can be pursued to the extent that the liberty of the republic, or at least its security, may be ensured only at the expense of others, that is, noncitizens. Thus, despite its celebration of the love of common liberty and its emphasis on compassion and solidarity, patriotism may sometimes appear as an essentially egoistic endeavor that legitimizes the indifference of citizens toward "aliens" within the republic and foreign issues.

This possible ambiguity has been reinforced by the expansion of ethnic nationalism in the 19th century and its use of patriotism to legitimize the defense of cultural homogeneity and traditions. The *patria* was then equated with the cultural nation, thereby challenging republicans on their own ground. In France, far-right ethnic nationalists such as Cahrles Maurras would go as far as presenting the fight against the republic as the duty of French patriots. Similarly, German patriotism was based upon *Kulturnation* and *Volksgeist* and celebrated the superiority, uniqueness, and purity of Germany. Thus understood, patriotism literally meant love of the fatherland, not of liberty or republic. Nonetheless, since World War II there has been a revival of republican patriotism and of the will to distinguish it from nationalism as bespeak, in different ways, the works of Simone Weil, Quentin Skinner, Maurizio Viroli, Michael Walzer, and Jürgen Habermas, to name only a few.

## PÄTS, KONSTANTIN

1874–1956, First Estonian president after the country won its independence from Russia in 1920. In 1940 Päts was confronted with the most agonizing dilemma that a patriotic leader could face: Should he resist by force the mighty Soviet Union's moves to occupy and annex the country in 1940, thereby risking not only defeat but as many as 25,000 countrymen's deaths, as had Finland in 1939? He sought another solution in an attempt to save his nation from devastation. Believing he could temporarily stave off disaster for the Estonian nation until the frightening political situation improved, President Päts signed a document accepting Stalin's demands. He and most other Estonian leaders were then deported to the Soviet Union. He died in a mental asylum in Russia, and his remains were later returned to his native Estonia. The new Moscow-controlled government, aided by local Estonian Communists (numbering only 133 in the entire country) staged elections to Parliament, during which no mention of any impending annexation by the Soviet Union was made. Only Communist-dominated organizations were allowed to nominate candidates. Deputies obedient to the Communists won 92.8 percent of the votes. The new Parliament formally asked to join the Soviet Union on July 22, 1940, and was accepted on August 6, 1940. The other Baltic states were led through the same procedure and met the same fate in August 1940. Russia continued into the 21st century to insist that all three Baltic states had voluntarily joined the USSR.

## PAVELIĆ, ANTE

1889–1959, Founder of the Croatian extreme nationalist *Ustaša* movement and leader of the wartime Axis puppet "Independent State of Croatia" (1941–1945). Born in 1889 in the village of Bradina in central Bosnia, Pavelić became an early believer in Ante Starčević's integral nationalist ideas as interpreted by Josip Frank's virulently anti-Serbian Pure Party of Right. In 1927 he was elected to the Yugoslav Parliament as a deputy from Zagreb for the nationalist Croatian bloc, a party that received only 40,000 votes in all of Croatia. On January 7, 1929, the day after King Alexander proclaimed Yugoslavia a royal dictatorship, Pavelić founded the "*Ustaša* Croatian Revolutionary Organization" dedicated to the establishment, by any means necessary, of an ethnically pure independent Croatian state. He subsequently fled the country.

In November 1929, a Belgrade court sentenced him to death in absentia for publicly advocating the over-throw of the Yugoslav state while visiting Bulgaria, where Pavelić had gone to forge links with the Internal Macedonian Revolutionary Organization (VMRO). He later set up headquarters under Mussolini's protection in fascist Italy. Following the *Ustaša*-sponsored and VMRO-executed assassination of Yugoslavia's King Alexander in 1934, he was placed by Mussolini under house arrest in Siena. Pavelić returned to Zagreb on April 15, 1941, and assumed the title of *Poglavnik* (chief) of the *Ustaša*-run but Axis-controlled "Independent State of Croatia" (*Nezavisna Država Hrvatska, or NDH*), which Hitler's armies had carved out of a defeated and dismembered Yugoslavia a few days earlier.

Once in power, Pavelić and his cohorts set about the task of the state's ethnic purification. Serbs, who accounted for nearly a third of the NDH's population of 6.3 million, bore the brunt of the onslaught. All in all, more than 300,000 Serbs perished in Pavelić's Croatia, along with 80 percent of the NDH's 37,000 Jews. The death camp in the town of Jasenovac accounted for the lion's share of these murders.

Pavelić met on four occasions with Hitler, whose support the former sought in containing Rome's territorial ambitions in Croatia. In May 1941 the *Poglavnik* had already been compelled to repay his Italian benefactor by ceding to Mussolini Istria, Rijeka, Dalmatia from Zadar to Split, and the Adriatic islands. Delighted by Italy's collapse in September 1943, Pavelić hurried to declare Dalmatia united with the rest of the homeland. Yet, the main beneficiary of Italy's surrender was not Pavelić, whom Dalmatians resented for having earlier abandoned them, but Tito and his Communist partisans, whom locals admired for their uncompromising anti-Axis stance.

Paranoid and fearful of being poisoned, Pavelić rarely ventured outside the Croatian capital during his reign, and neither ate nor drank whenever he did do so. On May 8, 1945, with Germany's unconditional surrender imminent, Pavelić fled the country and escaped to Italy and then Argentina. There he founded in 1956 the Croatian Liberation Movement (*Hrvatski Oslobodilački Pokret*) as a successor to the old *Ustaša* organization. Pavelić survived several assassination attempts by agents of Yugoslavia's postwar Communist regime before dying in Madrid, Spain, in 1959.

## PAZ, OCTAVIO

1914– , Mexican poet and essayist, recipient of the Nobel Prize for literature in 1990 and one of the leading Mexican poets and intellectuals of the 20th century. In the 20th century, Paz was the leader of the generation that, toward the end of the 1930s, was largely responsible for establishing the outlines of contemporary Mexican literary criticism and cultural thought.

Paz was born and raised in Mixcoac, now part of Mexico City. His father, Octavio Paz Solórzano, was a columnist who wrote a biography of Emiliano Zapata and helped found agrarian reform. Paz attended French and English language schools and read widely in the library of his grandfather, the novelist Ireneo Paz, before transferring to public schools, and ultimately the National Preparatory School, where he studied law. He founded the magazine *Barandal* in 1931–1932, followed by *Cuadernos del Valle de Mexico* in 1933–1934. Paz abandoned his legal studies in 1937 to visit Yucatán, where he helped establish a progressive school for workers and discovered Mexico's pre-Columbian past. That same year he went to republican Spain to attend the Second International Congress of Anti-fascist Writers.

In 1938 Paz returned to Mexico and helped found the journal *Taller* to explore his new ideas. In 1943 he helped to found *El Hijo Prodigo,* a periodical representing the Mexican vanguard, poets who believed that writing had a special mission. In 1945 he joined the Mexican diplomatic service and went to Paris, where he was strongly influenced by the surrealist movement. In 1952 he served as Mexican ambassador in India and Japan, extending his interests in Eastern art and architecture and in the classics of Buddhism and Taoism. He returned to Mexico in 1953.

Paz's work reached maturity in the late 1940s. Appearing in 1949 was his Libertad bajo palabra, championing the Latin American critical avant-garde. In 1950 he published a classic analysis of the Mexican people, "El laberinto de la soledad." He published poetry and essays, lectured on and presented new poets and painters, founded journals and a theatrical group, translated ancient and modern poetry, and participated in literary and political polemics. In 1956 he published "El arco y la lira," an important work examining the function of poetry itself. Paz returned to Paris in 1959 and was renamed ambassador to India in 1962, a post he resigned in 1968 in protest over the massacre of students in Tlatelolco Square.

During the 1970s he founded two significant magazines, *Plural* in 1971 and *Vuelta* in 1977, which he continued to edit in the 1990s, demonstrating his anticipation of the postmodern. Paz has also written unpublished short stories and a play. His published works in Spanish include nearly thirty volumes of poetry, over thirty volumes of essays, numerous anthologies of poetry in Spanish, as well as anthologies of poetry in translation from the French, English, Portuguese, Swedish,

Chinese, and Japanese. His own poetry and essays have been translated into numerous languages.

Paz has taught at major universities in the United States and Europe. He is a member of the Colegio Nacional of Mexico and the Consejo Superior de Cooperación Iberoamericana, and has won the International Prize for Poetry (1963), the Cervantes Prize (1981), the International Prize for Literature (1982), and the Menéndez Pelayo Prize (1987).

**PAZNYAK, ZYANON** 1944– , Belarusian nationalist leader, anti-Communist disident, art historian and archaeologist, chairman of the Belarusian Popular Front, deputy of the Supreme Council of Belarus SSR, later Republic of Belarus, who was the first political refugee from the CIS to ask for political asylum in the United States after the breakdown of the Soviet Union; born in Iuje, Belarus.

Paznyak belonged to that strata of the Soviet population that Communist ideologists called a *creative inteligentsia* in opposition to the technical one. The class of white-collar workers was a hotbed either for servile heralds of the regime or for its ardent critics. Paznyak belonged to the latter.

His grandfather, Jan Paznyak (1897–1939), was a prominent figure among the prewar Belarusian nationalists based in Vilnius, now the capital of Lithuania, then controlled by Poland. He was a cofounder of the Belarusian Catholic Democrat Union set up in 1917 in St. Petersburg. Jan Paznyak supported the idea of an independent Belarus republic organized along national grounds with the capital in Vilnius. He spoke out in favor of Belarusian as a language of instruction at schools and a language of sermons in Catholic churches. In 1939 Paznyak was shot dead by Soviet security.

Zyanon Paznyak inherited his grandfather's attitudes. In 1967 he graduated in arts from the Belarusian Institute of Arts and Drama Studies. Yet at the university he was suspected of nationalism for he openly spoke in Belarusian. The use of Belarusian in a public life has been regarded as a kind of nationalism.

In 1976 Paznyak switched his activities from contemporary drama studies toward the distant past of the country. He was employed as an historian and archaeologist at the Institute of History of the Belarusian Academy of Sciences. In 1988 Paznyak carried out excavations in the Kurapaty Forest on the northern outskirts of Mensk that showed that during the years 1937–1941 up to 200,000 civilians were executed there. Later Paznyak founded the academic society *Martyroloh Belarus* ("A Martyrology of Belarus") to commemorate victims of the Stalinist terror in Belarus.

In October 1988 at the Second Congress of the *Martyroloh Belarus* the Belarusian Popular Front (BPF) *Adradzhennie* ("The Renewal") was founded along the lines of similar civil partisan organizations set up earlier that year in the three Baltic republics and Ukraine. Paznyak was elected president of the BNF. Soon the BNF became the only real opposition to the Communist authorities of Belarus. In 1990 Paznyak was elected to the Supreme Council of the Belarusian SSR.

After the failed coup d'état in Moscow in August 1991, the BNF led by Paznyak succeeded in pursuing a declaration of independence for the Republic of Belarus. Thanks to Belarusian nationalists, Belarus adopted a new national symbol, flag, and anthem, the same that had been used by the Belarus National Republic, a formerly independent Belarusian state proclaimed under German patronage at the end of World War I.

Paznyak, as well as his grandfather, claimed that the Grand Duchy of Lithuania (formally dismantled in 1795) was in fact a Belarusian state. Paznyak sought to reclaim *iskonnyje zemli* ("ancient territories") inhabited by indigenous Belarusian populations, including the Lithuanian capital of Vilnius, the Polish town of Bialystock, and a significant part of Russia encompassing towns of Smolensk, Briansk, Nevel, Sebez, Novozybkov, and Drogobuz. In 1990 a parliamentary faction of the BNF even led unofficial talks with a group of Russian deputies about handing the Smolensk District over to Belarus.

Paznyak also came out with the idea of confining Belarusian citizenship only to the indigenous population. According to him, so-called indigenous or native peoples in Belarus are the only Belarusians; others belong to the category of national minorities.

The power struggle led by Paznyak with the Communists reached its peak in 1994 when Paznyak decided to run for the presidency. In the presidential elections he ended up in third place out of six candidates after Lukashenka and the prime minister Viacheslau Kebich. Paznyak desperately tried to oppose the authoritarian practices of President Lukashenka.

In April 1995 he held a hunger strike staged by members of Parliament in the Parliament building in order to protest against the referendum on integration with Russia. The strike was crushed by the Special Task Unit. Being under permanent threat of political repression Paznyak opted for emigration.

In 1996 Zyanon Paznyak, along with his colleague Siarhej Naumchuk, applied for political asylum in the United States. He now lives in Brooklyn, New York.

## PERÓN, EVA 1919–1952, The wife of Argentine President Juan D. Perón and, according to many, a political leader in her own right. Born the illegitimate daughter of Juan Duarte and Juana Ibarguren in the small town of Los Toldos (a province outside of Buenos Aires), at the age of fifteen, Evita moved to the rapidly expanding capital where she began a career as a radio, theater, and film actress. She married General Juan D. Perón in 1945 (Perón was president of the republic between 1946 and 1955, and 1973 and 1974), becoming his second wife. She was regarded by members of Perón's party as well as his enemies (mostly from the upper middle class and the oligarchy) as the president's right hand, although the extent to which Eva Duarte was responsible for Perón's rise to power is still a much contested issue in Argentine political history.

Before her death from cancer at the age of thirty-three, Eva Perón (popularly known by her diminutive, Evita) had worked in a variety of capacities to forward the cause of Perónism, a populist political movement centered largely around the personality cult of General Perón, which had widespread support among the lower classes and labor unions, with an economic vision rooted in the national appropriation of (largely British-owned) public works and resources. Evita was first given her own office in the Department of Posts shortly after Perón became president. Soon after she began to work for the Perónist Party in an unofficial and quite controversial position in the Ministry of Labor. In 1947, Evita became the owner of a relatively unimportant newspaper, *Democracia*, whose sales subsequently skyrocketed when photos of Evita and articles on Perónism began to appear regularly.

In June 1947, in her role as the first lady of Argentina, Evita made a lavish three-month goodwill tour of Europe where she met with General Franco and the Pope, among other important figures. The *New York Times* deemed this widely criticized trip "the most original diplomatic mission in recent times." Although it was panned by the European left as an unnecessary display of wealth given the impoverished state of postwar Europe, it was looked on favorably by many Argentineans. After her European trip, Evita began to take on a more overt political role in the country.

Despite many failed attempts since 1911, in 1947 the right to vote was won for Argentinean women, an achievement that many attribute to Evita. In July 1947, Evita became the head of the Perónist Women's Party, which by 1952 had 500,000 members and 3600 offices. In 1948, the Maria Eva Duarte de Perón Foundation was created; Evita later renamed it the Eva Perón Foundation. The foundation provided monetary and other types of assistance to persons who lacked resources. Evita exercised sole responsibility over this organization, which employed thousands of permanent employees and construction workers. Shortly before her death, Evita stood before thousands of people in the Plaza de Mayo of Buenos Aires and refused a popular call for her vice presidency.

The story of the life of Eva Perón has been immortalized in a wide variety of genres from theatrical musical (Andrew Lloyd Webber and Tim Rice's *Evita*), to popular film (Alan Parker's *Evita*, 1996), to autobiography (*La razón de mi vida*) to fictional biography (Tomás Eloy Martinez' *Santa Evita: Novela* [Planeta, 1995]). There are a number of biographies about Evita including Nicholas Fraser and Marysa Navarro's *Eva Perón* (W. W. Norton & Co., 1985), J. M. Taylor's *Eva Perón: The Myths of a Woman* (University of Chicago Press, 1979), Alicia Dujovne Ortiz's *Eva Perón* (St. Martin's Press, 1996), and Otelo Borrani and Roberto Vacca's *Eva Perón* (Centro Editor de America Latina, 1970).

**PERÓN, JUAN** 1895–1974, Born in Lobos, Buenos Aires province, Juan Domingo Perón was the son of an indigent peasant of Italian background and a Spanish Creole mother. Perón grew up in lower middle class social and financial insecurity, steeped in gaucho lore of freedom. He entered the Colegio Militar in 1911 and was deeply interested in Argentine and military history. In 1930, he entered public life, taking part in General José E. Uriburu's takeover of Yrigoyen's government to establish a military dictatorship. During 1939–1940 he traveled in Europe and was military attaché to Mussolini's Italy. He returned to Argentina by way of Spain, scarred from civil war.

Back in Argentina, Perón became a member of the secret military society GOU (Grupo de Oficiales Unidos) and took part in its coup of June 4, 1943, overthrowing the government of Ramón S. Castillo and forestalling the probable succession to the presidency of conservative Robustiano Patrón Costas. Dissatisfied with the increasingly conservative orientation of the military government, Perón organized a colonels' military clique and placed General Edelmiro J. Farrel in the presidency (February 24, 1944) and himself in active roles. As minister of war, he refurbished the army; as secretary of labor, he protected workers and increased their salaries; and as vice president he attempted to shore up public opinion in favor of a new Argentina. Ousted and sent to Martín Garcia Island by his opponents, he was triumphantly brought back to Buenos Aires on October 17, 1945, by the workers, supported by the Campo de Mayo army and some police units.

Having established a strong political base from an alliance of his military following with that of the loyal workers, Perón became a candidate for the presidency; he was determined to find a new middle way for Argentina, deeply rooted in its own historical past, avoiding the extremes of fascism on the right (although his enemies accused him of being fascist) and that of Communism on the left; to restore the constitution and to make it work; to incorporate all elements of society into participation in the public political and economic life, too long controlled by the land-holding oligarchy; and to make Argentina genuinely free from foreign controls, both economic and political (i.e., to resist what he and many other Argentines believed to be U.S. attempts at hegemony of the Western hemisphere). On February 24, 1946, he was elected president in a free election, largely by lower and middle classes, but also supported by those who resented what they considered to be U.S. attempts to influence the election.

As president, Perón sought to centralize power in the presidency and to establish control over every phase of public life—military, political, judicial, labor, economic, moral, and ideological—depending preferably on constitutional means and popular support. His administration falls into three periods:

1. 1946–1949, was the high point of Perón's success. Argentina was riding a crest of post-World War II prosperity. Large accumulation of capital was on hand and the nation was proud to be under a constitutional government again. Perón was conciliatory and slow in establishing controls, but quick to move toward his goals: He established IAPI (Argentine Institute for the Promotion of Trade) in 1946; increased power, prestige, fringe benefits, and gave higher wages to labor; Eva Perón distributed social welfare benefits; he announced the Five-Year Plan (Plan Quinquenal) and began its implementation—especially for the nationalization of the economy by purchase of foreign-owned railways, river steamship companies, and public utilities; acceleration and diversification of industrialization; and use of Argentine wealth, not only for domestic development of Argentina, but also to increase the nation's international power and prestige, thereby claiming for Argentina a "Third Position" of positive neutrality in the Cold War developing between Western powers and the Soviet Union.

Perón established his power politically by organizing the Perónist Party (1949) and by bringing Congress under his control. Acting on his belief that social justice was more important than the letter of the law, he purged those judges who differed, and established courts sympathetic to his views. Women received the right to vote in 1947, and when the constitution was amended in 1949 to give the president more power and to permit his reelection, women were also given the right to hold office. Political support from the Church strengthened by law made religious instruction in schools compulsory. After 1947 university rectors were appointed by the president, and all university fees were waived in 1949. The size of the military expanded, as well as its budget; salaries of officers were raised and living conditions improved. A name, "Justicialismo," was given to the whole.

2. 1949–1952, a decreasing rate of progress reached a point of decline. Perón was still popular with masses, but tensions were increasing; the economy, particularly in rural areas where the agricultural industries had supported Argentina for decades, showed decline, due in part to bad weather but attributed primarily to government neglect and discrimination.

3. The period 1952–1955 saw the decline and ebb of Perón and his regime. The year 1952 saw the reelection of Perón and also the death of his wife and political colleague, Eva Perón. This was the end of the period of strong expansion. Fatigue, both personal in Perón's case (accentuated by grief over the loss of his wife) and throughout the administration, became increasingly evident. Financial scandals reduced government prestige, nationalists resented invitations to increase foreign capital, and labor contacts deteriorated with Eva gone. His acts further alienated his long-standing enemies among the intellectuals (from Communists to fascists) and members of the oligarchic group; the Church turned from supporter to powerful foe due to a series of attacks—perhaps because the Church approved the formation of a Christian Democratic Party, perhaps in retaliation for the Church's reproach of Perón's insistence on teaching of Justicialismo, perhaps even because of the Church's stand regarding the popular demand for canonization of Evita. Difficulties increased within the government, growing out of the diverse interests of the groups within it, as well as the problems involved in changing the old into something new by constitutional, not revolutionary means. Powerful leadership, which Perón was unable to provide at the moment, was essential; he was overthrown by the military on September 19, 1955, and Perón went into exile, leaving a nation that found it almost as difficult to live without him as with him.

In November 1972, Perón returned to Buenos Aires for a brief visit during which he refused to accept the nomination for president by the Justicialist (formerly Perónist) Party, selecting Hector J. Cámpora in his stead; he then returned to Spain.

Cámpora was elected president on April 15, 1973. Perón returned to Argentina, and after the resignation of Cámpora in June 1973 became a nominee for president. Elected in September with 62 percent of the votes, he became president for the third time in October 1973; his wife, María Estela Martinez de Perón, became the vice president. Perón died of a heart attack on July 1, 1974, and María Estela Martinez de Perón assumed the presidency from 1974–1976.

**PÉTAIN, HENRI** 1856–1951, In World War I, Pétain commanded the French forces that stopped the Germans at the Battle of Verdun. He became commander in chief in 1917 and marshal in 1918. After the war he commanded a joint French-Spanish force in 1926 that defeated Abd-el-Krim in Morocco. In 1939 he was named as France's ambassador to Spain, ruled by a new Spanish dictator, Francisco Franco, who had served under him in Morocco.

On May 10, 1940, Hitler unleashed his armies against France. Invading the Netherlands and Belgium (thereby avoiding the face of the Maginot Line that was unprotected from the rear) German forces used lightning warfare (*Blitzkrieg*) tactics against a French army that was poorly and lethargically led and in some respects technologically outdated. Pétain was recalled from Spain and named vice premier in order to strengthen the nation's morale. Instead, he advocated an armistice. The French government was forced to abandon Paris within one month.

Britain pleaded urgently that France both honor its earlier agreement not to seek a separate peace and even consider a political union of the two countries. The latter proposal was understandably unwelcome in a country that had spent centuries ridding itself of English domination and influence. British Prime Minister Winston S. Churchill testified that French soldiers had fought valiantly, but their political and military leaders had been so quickly seized by defeatism that the French cabinet could not muster the tenacity or eagerness to persist after the shock of initial defeats.

A demoralized French cabinet, under the influence of the aging marshal, chose to surrender on June 22, 1940, barely forty days after the German attack. The terms were very harsh. The northern half of France, including Paris, and the whole of the Atlantic coast to the Spanish border were to be occupied by German troops at French expense. The rest of France was to be ruled by a French government, led by Pétain and friendly to Germany. This government was to supply its conquerors with food and raw materials needed for the German war effort. The French army was to be disbanded.

Its navy was confined to ports under the control of the Germans and the Italians. The fate of the French navy especially distressed the British. They were unaware that the French naval commander in chief, Admiral Darlan, had secretly ordered his fleet commanders to scuttle his ships if the Germans or Italians tried to seize them by force. When the British tried to take control of the French Atlantic squadron in Mers-el-Kebir in Algeria, the French commander resisted. The British destroyed the squadron, an action that caused a wave of anti-British feeling in France.

This sentiment played into the hands of the cunning Premier Pierre Laval and the eighty-year-old Pétain, who had long opposed the Third Republic as a decadent, inefficient regime. They quickly abolished the Third Republic and established a repressive Vichy Republic (named after the spa in France where the new government established its seat of power). Without prompting by the Germans, they denied Jews and Freemasons the protection of the law. In all, 75,000 Jews were, with the help of the French police, deported from France during Vichy rule, and only 2600 returned. Foreigners who had come to France to escape Hitler's persecution were placed in French concentration camps. Unless they were able to escape, they were later returned to Germany where an uncertain, usually fatal, future awaited them.

Many French were relieved to have achieved a peace at any price. Nevertheless, many felt numbing humiliation and were aware that a tragic debacle had befallen the French nation. What followed was as much a French civil war as a war against the Germans. For the next four years there were two Frances, one fighting against the Germans and one trying to ignore the conflict and minimize damage to the French population. The French individual could find sound patriotic reasons for supporting each. It was up to the individual to decide which France was his. France still has not fully recovered psychologically from the terrible tension of the Vichy years. A poll in 1992 showed that 82 percent of the French people considered the Vichy government to be guilty of "crimes against humanity," and 90 percent thought that their country should admit it.

Local resistance forces and delegates from General Charles de Gaulle's headquarters in London assumed political control in liberated France, arresting or executing Vichy officials. On August 19, 1944, resistance fighters rose up in Paris against the German occupiers. Six days later, Free French units commanded by General Philippe Leclerc took control of the city, which a disobedient German commander had saved from senseless destruction by refusing to burn and destroy as ordered by Hitler. De Gaulle arrived with the French troops, and the following day he led a triumphant march down the broad Champs-Élysées.

The Vichy government, including Pétain, fled to Germany. For the next year and a half, de Gaulle's provisional government exercised unchallenged authority in liberated France. Pétain voluntarily returned to France to face charges of treason. He was tried in July and August 1945, found guilty, and sentenced to death. Because of Pétain's advanced age, de Gaulle commuted the mashal's sentence to life in prison. He died on the island of Yeu in 1951. The resistance movement had brought together persons from all backgrounds and political convictions. De Gaulle announced during the war that "while the French people are uniting for victory they are assembling for a revolution." He hoped that this predominantly young, patriotic, idealistic, but at the same time practical core of French people would provide the spark for national revival and change.

**PETLIURA, SYMON** 1879–1926, Ukrainian activist who became supreme commander of the army of the Ukrainian People's Republic (UNR) and president of the Directory of the UNR. Born in Poltava, Petliura attended the Poltava Theological Seminary until being expelled in 1901 for membership in a Ukrainian political cell. From 1900, he was active in the Revolutionary Ukrainian Party (RUP, later the Ukrainian Social-Democratic Labor Party). To avoid arrest he moved to the Russian Kuban in 1902 where he worked as a schoolteacher and with the local RUP branch. He was arrested in December 1903 and released four months later, at which time he moved to L'viv to work with the RUP there. During the next several years he continued his political work in St. Petersburg, in Kyiv, and in Moscow, where he also worked as a bookkeeper.

As a leader of the Social-Democratic Party, Petliura helped to create the Central Rada (Council) of Ukraine. After the February 1917 Russian Revolution, Petliura was elected as head of the Ukrainian Military Committee of the Western Front. In June he became general secretary of military affairs for the Central Rada, charged with organizing and building a Ukrainian army, which he later led in battle against the Bolsheviks. After resigning from this position due to disagreements with others in the Central Rada (Petliura wanted to focus on building a Ukrainian nation-state and its institutions, while his long-time Social-Democratic colleague Volodymyr Vynnychenko wanted to concentrate on building Ukrainian socialism, a disagreement that weakened the Central Rada), he formed the Haidamaka Battalion of Slobidska Ukraina (The Steppe-Fighter Battalion of Eastern Ukraine) which helped defend Kyiv against the Bolsheviks in 1918.

When the pro-German Hetmanate government was

formed in April 1918, Petliura was arrested. Released four months later, he went to Bila Tserkva where he helped lead (with Vynnychenko and Evhen Konovalets) the uprising against the Hetmanate. Taking Kyiv in December 1918, this group formed the Directory government of the revived UNR with Vynnychenko as president and Petliura as otaman (Ukrainian cossack term for leader) of the UNR army.

The Directory was a weak government with an inadequate military. In 1919 there were six competing armies in Ukraine (Directory, Bolshevik, White/Tsarist, Entente, Polish, anarchist) and Kyiv changed hands five times. The Ukrainian state needed help to survive. Petliura turned to the Whites for aid, but was rejected as a separatist against the Russian Empire. To gain French assistance (France had 60,000 troops in Odessa), the socialist Vynnychenko was replaced by Petliura as president of the Directory, but this move also failed since the French wanted a unified Russia and gave their support to the Whites. By December 1919 Petliura and the UNR army had been driven out of Kyiv and into Poland by the Bolsheviks.

In 1920 Petliura made a deal with Poland. In exchange for recognizing the Polish annexation of Galicia and Volhynia, which alienated western Ukrainian nationalists such as Konovalets, the Polish army would help retake Kyiv. Invading Soviet-controlled Ukraine in April 1920, the combined Polish-UNR army took Kyiv in May. The Bolsheviks counterattacked and drove the Poles back to Warsaw, where they were narrowly stopped. This led to peace between Poland and Bolshevik Russia. Petliura and the UNR army were disbanded and interred in Poland, ending Ukrainian independence for seventy years.

Petliura set up the UNR government-in-exile in Tarnow, Poland, before it was dispersed about Europe. In 1924 Petliura moved to Paris where he attempted to continue the government in exile, and where he edited and published many articles on Ukrainian national liberation. He was assassinated by a Bessarabian Jew in 1926 who claimed vengeance for Petliura's role in anti-Jewish pogroms in 1918–1920. Tens of thousands of Jews were killed in Ukraine during this period, most by White forces but many by Directory troops. As commander in chief of the Directory army, Petliura was blamed. In fact, Petliura had tried to prevent such acts and to build relations with Ukrainian Jews, but his attempts failed. After his death, the Petliura Ukrainian Library was founded in Paris as a depository of documents from this period. Petliura has had lasting impact as the personification of Ukrainian independence from 1917 to 1920.

**PIEDMONT NATIONALISM**    Piedmont, located in the northwest corner of modern Italy, was the birthplace of Italian unification. In 1831 a young Genoan political thinker, Giuseppe Mazzini, founded the "Young Italy" movement. He remained the intellectual head and prophet of the unification drive for a free, independent, and republican Italy until his death in 1872.

In 1848, uprisings occurred throughout Italy, and the Pope was even temporarily driven out of Rome. But with the aid of French troops, the rebellion was quelled. With its failure, nationalists' eyes turned increasingly toward the Kingdom of Piedmont-Savoy, whose capital was Turin and which was ruled by one of the oldest ruling families in Europe, the house of Savoy. It had been the only regime in Italy that had fought hard for freedom from Austria.

Piedmont's King Victor Emmanuel, who was to become the first king of a united Italy, became a popular focus on attention for those who wanted change. A politically shrewd man, he appointed as Piedmontese prime minister Conte Camillo di Cavour, not a brilliant man, but a pragmatist who knew that Italy could never become independent as a result of spontaneous mass uprisings of idealists. The political hold of Austria had to be broken, and he knew that Italians would need the help of a foreign power to do this. Therefore, he turned to the new French emperor, Napoleon III. The French leader agreed to support Piedmont in any war against Austria under the condition that in the event of victory, France be rewarded with Nice and Savoy. The deal was sealed by the marriage of Victor Emmanuel's fifteen-year-old daughter, Clotilde, to Napoleon's cousin, Jerome. With such a commitment tucked away in his breastpocket, Cavour sought a way to bring about war with Austria. Two blunders by the latter country played directly into his hands. One was Austria's decision to impose military conscription on its dominions of Lombardy and Venetia, a move that drove many draft dodgers into Piedmont. The tension that arose as a result of Piedmont's refusal to turn these young men over to the Austrian authorities gave Cavour the excuse he needed to begin military preparations.

The second blunder was committed just when the French emperor was beginning to have second thoughts about the promises he had made earlier to Piedmont. In the spring of 1859 Austria issued an ultimatum to Piedmont, demanding that it either disarm itself or go to war. Cavour, of course, chose the latter. With Napoleon's assistance Piedmont faced the powerful but indecisive Austrian army and defeated it at Magenta on June 4 and at Solferino on June 24. It conquered all Lombardy and Milan.

After these important victories, Napoleon grew weary of the war and concluded an armistice with the Austrians at Villafranca on July 11. Cavour was understandably furious at the French, but the movement toward Italian unity had gained such momentum that it could no longer be stopped. Revolutionary assemblies in Tuscany, Modena, Parma, and Romagna voted in August 1859 to unite with Piedmont. France and Britain spoke out against any foreign (i.e., Austrian) intervention to foil these popular decisions. In March 1860, plebiscites in the four areas confirmed the steps taken by the assemblies. True to his earlier promise, Cavour delivered Savoy and Nice to the French. He ordered Piedmontese troops to march southward into the papal states. On September 18 they crushed the Pope's forces at Castelfidardo and then defeated a remaining Neapolitan army at Capua. These successes prompted the Piedmontese parliament to annex southern Italy. In October plebiscites in Naples, Sicily, the Marches, and Umbria revealed overwhelming popular support for union with Piedmont. In February 1861 Victor Emmanuel II was proclaimed king of Italy.

## PINOCHET UGARTE, AUGUSTO

PINOCHET UGARTE, AUGUSTO   1915–, Chilean army officer and dictator, 1973–1989. Pinochet was born in Valparaiso. At the age of seventeen he entered the Escuela Militar, graduated in 1936, and was promoted to second lieutenant in 1938. He and his wife, Lucía Hiriart, had three daughters and two sons.

In his professional career Pinochet was prompted to specialist in military geography and geopolitics. His 1968 book *Geopolitica* went through several editions. He held several staff and command posts and was a member of the Chilean military mission in Washington, D.C., in 1956. He taught at the Escuela Militar, at the Academia de Guerra, and at Ecuador's national war college in the 1950s and 1960s. By 1970, Pinochet had risen to the rank of division general, and the next year he became commandant of the Santiago garrison, the most sensitive and influential of Chilean army assignments. By this time, Pinochet had become very critical of politics in general and Marxism specifically. As Santiago garrison commandant he was an eyewitness to the social, economic, and political turbulence accompanying the administration of Socialist Salvador Allende Gossens. This led Pinochet at first to remain loyal to Allende in a premature coup d'état and later as commander in chief, to be a member of a military junta, aided by training and financing from the U.S. Central Intelligence Agency, that staged a successful one. In the following months after the takeover of the country, 4000 suspected opponents of the coup were either killed or disappeared and tens of thousands more tortured. The end of the 1970s seemed to bring a lessening of repression: the dissolution of DINA in 1977, the end of disappearances, return of some of the expropriated land. Much of the repression, however, was redirected to new opposition groups, such as union organizers. Pinochet went on to become the president de facto of the dictatorship for the remaining seventeen years. His regime drafted a new constitution for Chile. It placed Pinochet in office until 1989 or possibly 1997 and provided for the gradual return to civilian rule, restoring a limited, appointed, National Congress in 1990 and an elected president in 1997. It also established a new status for ex-presidents who had served more than six years—"senator for life."

One of Patricio Aylwin's first acts as president was the creation of the National Truth and Reconciliation Commission on April 25, 1990. The eight-member commission headed by attorney Raul Rettig was mandated "to clarify the whole truth on the most serious violations of human rights" during the military rule. The commission collected more than 3400 cases to investigate and produced a three-volume, 2000-page document known as the Rettig Report. Initially silent, the armed forces responded with its own four-volume report. In 1992, the National Corporation for Reconciliation and Reparation continued the work of the Rettig commission. It reported in 1996 that 3197 people died or went missing between September 1973 and March 1990 as a result of human rights violations at the hands of state agents. Of these, 1102 were classified as "disappeared" and 2095 as deaths.

Pinochet was detained in London on October 16, 1998, on an extradition warrant from the Spanish judiciary. The warrant sought to bring charges against Pinochet for the murder or "disappearance" of more than 3100 Chilean and foreigners during the general's military coup in 1973 and the subsequent seventeen years of dictatorship. After being detained in Britain for nearly seventeen months, Pinochet was not extradited, but was released to Chile in March 2000.

## POLISH NATIONALISM

POLISH NATIONALISM   The Republic of Poland, once the largest state in Europe (in the mid-1500s), has had shifting borders over the centuries and remains situated at the boundaries between Eastern and Western Europe.

Modern Poland has often been in conflict with Russia, long before the Soviet Empire brought it into the Communist fold, and much of Polish nationalism has been forged out of the effort to maintain autonomy from its giant neighbor to the east. In the 1860s, for example,

Poland was partitioned, resulting in one portion of the realm becoming little more than a Russian province.

Caught between the Russians on the one side and the Germans and Austrians on the other, Polish desires for independence seemed somewhat bleak until Wilson's Fourteen Points, issued on January 8, 1918, called for the creation of an independent Polish state (point 13). The Inter-Allied Conference of June 1918 endorsed Polish independence and the Poland that emerged between the wars was the sixth largest country in Europe.

Its troubles were far from over, however, because the Second Republic faced serious economic and political problems, including conflicts among ethnic groups. Polish nationalism sometimes collided with the aspirations of the large Ukrainian population living in the republic's borders (about 16 percent of the nation's population), Jews (ca. 10 percent), Belarusians (ca. 6 percent), and Germans (ca. 3 percent).

All of those difficulties paled, however, with the onslaught of World War II. Despite a nonaggression pact with Soviet Russia (1932) and a declaration of nonaggression with Nazi Germany (1934), Poland became a battleground. The Red Army invaded Poland from the east on September 17, 1939, and on the 28th Hitler and Stalin agreed on a partition. In the Soviet sectors the upper classes were attacked; in Nazi-occupied Poland three million Polish Jews were forced into ghettos and exterminated.

Polish independence after the war became a secondary issue for British Prime Minister Winston Churchill and U.S. President Franklin D. Roosevelt, both of whom were primarily concerned with their country's relationships with the Soviet Union. The postwar republic, renamed the Polish People's Republic in 1952, was comprised almost entirely of Poles, with the expulsion of Germans and the mass relocation of Ukrainians. The new Poland was subjected to Sovietization, including the nationalization of industry, the expropriation of large blocks of land, and ultimately a series of political repressions especially until the death of Stalin in 1953.

Although Polish nationalism persisted through Soviet rule, as it had in previous centuries, it was not until the 1980s that the movement gathered enough momentum to bring about serious change. The growth of Solidarity, a trade union opposition movement, and such cultural dissidence as the Polish Student Theatre movement in the 1970s helped to create the stage for the triumphant arrival of Polish Pope John Paul II in Warsaw in 1979.

One year after the Pope's visit, workers went on strike in the Lenin Shipyards in Gdansk, led by an electrician named Lech Walesa. In 1981 General Wojciech Jaruzelski declared martial law and arrested Solidarity leaders and the movement seemed doomed. Solidarity supporters held large demonstrations, however, protesting the martial law and a year later Walesa was released and martial law suspended.

Meanwhile the Polish opposition to Soviet rule mushroomed. The underground press rivaled the official press in its publications; people met in churches to plan opposition activities and Father Jerzy Popieluszko began a monthly "Mass for the Fatherland." When state security officers killed him, thousands of mourners occupied his church for ten days.

Workers struck again in April and May of 1988 and in February 6, 1989, "Round Table Talks" opened between the Polish United Workers' Party, Solidarity, and other parties and civic organizations. These negotiations led to constitutional changes and a coalition government. In December 1990 Lech Walesa was elected president.

**POLITICAL THEOLOGY**    The idea of political theology comes from Carl Schmitt (1888–1985), a widely read and influential German theorist infamous for his affiliation with the Nazi Party. Schmitt's ideas proved decisive in shaping larger currents of ultraconservative thought during the Weimar era and following the Nazi seizure of power. Even though "political theology" is typically associated with Schmitt, in reality, it is more of a collaborative affair involving a constellation of different ideologies and philosophies. Currently, political theology has attracted a new generation of subscribers in Europe, Russia, and the United States. Those drawn to this ideology are typically hostile to, as they see it, the degradation of national sovereignty, the paralysis associated with liberal politics, and the cultural malaise brought on by globalization and geopolitcal destabilization.

Beginning with the premise that modern political concepts are rooted in theological precursors, Schmitt subjected bourgeois liberalism and parliamentary democracy to a reactionary and nationalist critique. The relationship between theological notions and their political relatives was formulated such that the experiences of the Weimar Republic were made comprehensible through the historical ascendancy of deism and liberalism. As Schmitt stated, "The idea of the modern constitutional state triumphed together with deism, a theology and metaphysics that banished the miracle from the world. This theology and metaphysics rejected not only the transgression of the laws of nature through an exception brought about by direct intervention, as is found in the idea of a miracle, but also the sovereign's direct intervention in a valid legal order." Western liberalism, then, marked the intrusion of an alien socio-political complex into the life of the German nation and the demise of that state's natural mode of political practice.

Moreover, Schmitt and other kindred spirits like Ernst Jünger and Oswald Spengler, to name only two, rejected liberalism on the grounds that the structure of parliamentary democracy resulted in a negative dissipation of power among competing interests and a situation in which proceduralism and impersonal rules were allowed to negate the substantively rational needs of the nation. In short, Wilsonianism and the reorganization of the German state after World War I created a political process prone to "everlasting discussion" and passivity when confronting periods of crisis. These crises, according to Schmitt, were *exceptional* moments and, as states of the exception, immune from normative resolution or rule under constitutionally mandated law.

Essentially, the exception implicitly represented the miracle moment in the life of the German people: authentic existence and a community of blood achieved through conflict with the enemy. What the state and nation required was strong leadership invested with unlimited power to suspend the normal operation of society. Hence, the sovereign (i.e., the dictatorial state) required unencumbered room to navigate domestically and exert its will on neighboring people. Schmitt concocted, consequently, the idea of the *Großraum*: a space or national territory in which the essential character and lifestyle of the Germanic people could flourish. The nationalism contained in political theology, then, is a means of social, political, cultural, and economic regeneration. If the democratic state has elevated secular adventurers to the status of law makers, the political sphere will be returned to the realm of the sacred in which leadership is invested with a divine, rather than popular, authority. If utilitarianism has reduced national culture to a monochromatic wasteland, it will be redeemed through *Volk*, blood, and soil. And if the material underpinnings of society have been weakened by greed and finance, the domination of money will be abrogated by the domination of sovereignty.

Further investigations of this subject should begin with the works of Carl Schmitt, especially his *Political Theology* (The MIT Press, 1985). Jeffrey Herf's *Reactionary Modernism* (Cambridge, 1984) offers an excellent analysis of prewar conservatism and guide to further reading, while Franz Neumann's classic *Behemoth* (Oxford, 1944) remains authoritative.

## PORTUGUESE COLONIES AND NATIONALISM Portugal was formerly a mighty colonial power that spread its language and culture to Brazil, Africa, and Asia. This empire was many times larger in size and population than the mother country. The Portuguese still possess islands in the Atlantic Ocean that are important links between the Western and Eastern hemispheres: the Azores (west of Portugal) and Madeira (north of the Spanish-owned Canary Islands off northwest Africa). Its valuable strategic positions always enabled Portugal to escape prolonged international isolation and to regain a status of relative respectability after 1945. This was true despite the fact that until 1974 it, like Spain, had an authoritarian political system that was repugnant to most persons in democratic countries. The process of decolonization ultimately brought Portugal's fascist regime to its knees in 1974.

As a country facing the sea, Portuguese sights were always directed outward, and the bulk of the population was attracted to the coast because of this maritime and external commercial orientation. By 1337 their mariners had already landed on the Canary Islands. Overseas exploration was particularly encouraged by Prince Henry the Navigator (1394–1460), a far-sighted and imaginative man who established a maritime school to assemble and extend his country's knowledge of the sea. Portuguese mariners explored the African coast, and in 1488 Bartolemeu Dias rounded the Cape of Good Hope and reached East Africa. In 1497 Vasco da Gama set sail for India. He returned to describe the land to a receptive and curious Europe.

To minimize a potentially dangerous rivalry between Spain and Portugal in the wake of Columbus's discovery of the New World, the sovereigns of the two countries agreed to the Treaty of Tordesillas in 1494. It divided the world in such a way that Spain would receive the Philippines (named after the Spanish king) and most of the Western hemisphere (including large chunks of the contemporary United States, such as California, the Southwest, and Florida). Portugal received what is now Brazil and parts of Africa and Asia. Both countries continued generally to observe this agreement, which had the Pope's approval. But to their consternation, other European powers, especially Britain, France, and the Netherlands, did not. Pedro Alvares Cabral landed in Brazil in 1500 and claimed it for Lisbon. Revenue from Brazilian sugar, coffee, diamonds, and other minerals became important to the Portuguese economy.

Such activity stimulated important advances in cartography and astronomy and also helped redirect the attention of Europe outward toward the larger world. It enabled Portugal to build a massive empire that included Mozambique, Angola, and Guinea-Bissau in Africa, East Timor, Macao (which the Chinese gave to

Portugal in 1557 as a reward for its fight against pirates and which the Portuguese gave back on December 19, 1999), and Portuguese India (with its capital of Goa, conquered in 1510). Portuguese naval squadrons were stationed permanently in strongholds in or around the Atlantic and Indian Oceans. The Portuguese also sent settlers to some of these imperial holdings, especially to the Azores, Madeira, and Brazil.

These colonial activities were advantageous to Portugal. It acquired gold and other precious stones, silks, and spices, which were treasured in Europe at that time, and needed foodstuffs, especially wheat. It also provided an occupation for those portions of the feudal nobility that could no longer be supported by domestic agricultural production. Settlement in the colonies offered many Portuguese the hope for a better life. Finally, the desire to convert the peoples of the world to Roman Catholicism furnished the entire enterprise with a spirit of crusade and gave it a religious and spiritual justification.

Portugal faced the post-Napoleonic era with a restored monarchy but with the liberal ideas of the French Revolution in the heads of many of its citizens. These new notions, combined with the long rupture in reliable communication with their American colony, spelled the end of its empire in the Western hemisphere. The Portuguese had fought heroically for their national independence. Brazilians decided to do the same, and they succeeded.

It is a country now almost entirely stripped of its colonial empire, but it is much healthier and stronger as a result. The last straw was the seemingly endless wars in Portugal's African colonies, which the Portuguese called *Ultramar* (overseas territories). Portuguese settlers had always mingled more easily with nonwhite native populations than did the British, French, and Belgian colonizers. One still sees the results of this in Brazil, where blacks and whites live together relatively harmoniously (albeit under a predominantly white élite). Also, nothing resembling an *apartheid* ("separateness") policy ever developed, such as in South Africa.

Portugal hung onto its empire long after the other European nations had decided to relinquish theirs. That stemmed from a conviction that Portuguese rule was both good and tolerable for the subject peoples. Also important were the economic benefits for Portugal and the fact that there were over a million Portuguese living in the colonies. Foreign Minister Franco Nogueira wrote in 1967 that the Portuguese considered themselves "to be an African nation." However, the bulk of the native populations in the colonies did not consider themselves to be Portuguese. Since 1913 the Portu-

guese had had to quell occasional native uprisings in Africa. In 1961 these uprisings reerupted, first in Angola around such groups as the Popular Movement for the Liberation of Angola (MPLA), the Angolan National Liberation Front (FNLA), and the National Union for Total Angolan Independence (UNITA). Then they occurred in 1963 in Mozambique (led by the Front for the Liberation of Mozambique) and in Guinea-Bissau. The Portuguese government decided to hold onto the African colonies at all costs, fearing that their loss would spell the doom of the Portuguese state. In fact, it was this decision more than any other that led to the ultimate downfall of the Portuguese fascist regime.

By 1974 there were 170,000 men in the Portuguese army, 135,000 stationed in Africa. The lion's share of these troops was four-year conscripts, who increasingly resented their role in quelling native rebellions against a regime that fewer and fewer Portuguese wished to preserve. The need to expand the size of the army to cope with the African wars brought many young men from the lower classes and the universities into the officers' corps. These groups had earlier been largely excluded from the officers' ranks and were more inclined to sympathize with the rebels' aims. These young officers gradually lost faith in the kinds of arguments that had long been used to justify the protracted colonial struggle. Many became inspired by the revolutionary ideas espoused by their African adversaries. They grew to dislike their more traditional military superiors. These radicalized lower ranking officers formed the illegal Movement of the Armed Forces (MFA), which became the core of opposition to the regime.

Their convictions and confidence were enormously strengthened by the appearance in February 1974 of a book, *Portugal and the Future*, written by the monacled General Antonio de Spinola, former commander in Guinea-Bissau, whose legendary bravery in battle had won him the admiration of the lower ranks. Spinola advocated a political solution to the colonial question and the establishment of a sort of Portuguese commonwealth of nations, similar to that of the British. It is not surprising that Portugal's leader, Dr. Marcelo Caetano, reportedly could not sleep the night after he had read the book. His regime was overthrown in the "Carnation Revolution" on April 24–25, 1974. Rarely in history has such a fundamental political change occurred with so little loss of life.

In 1961 India had simply invaded and annexed the mini-territories of Goa, Damão and Diu. That is the year that Portugal's army became bogged down in colonial wars. Between September 1974 and November 1975 Portugal's millstones were cast off one by one: first Portuguese Guinea (now Guinea-Bissau), then Mozambique, Angola, the Cape Verde Islands, São Tomé and Príncipe. The plotters formed a "Junta of National Salvation," which announced that the colonies would be granted the right of self-determination and that political exiles would be permitted to return to Portugal. The new leaders were in such a hurry to cut their former colonies totally loose that they made little effort to try at least to introduce a stable transfer of power to groups that might have been willing to legitimize their rule through democratic elections. The MFA's strong Marxist bias inclined it to hand over power in the colonies to like-minded revolutionaries.

The rapid Portuguese withdrawal from the African territories and East Timor in the Far East reduced overnight most of Portugal's land area and its worldwide population by 65 percent. This created a particularly great refugee problem for the home country. Between 1974 and 1976 at least a half million refugees poured into Portugal, mainly from Angola. In March 1977 the new Marxist leader in Angola ordered the expulsion of all persons holding Portuguese passports, so a new wave a expellees began to pour in. The United States helped pay for the airlift of the *retornados* and gave Portugal more than $1 billion over five years to help cope with the financial crisis. The returnees arrived in a chaotic Portugal with few possessions and with worthless currencies. Many were convinced that their home government had sold out to revolutionary terrorists and were therefore deeply embittered and inclined toward active, anti-Communist and conservative politics.

Reconciliation with its former colonies was made politically easier since Portugal supported the Black African position toward South Africa. One-seventh of the white South Africans is of Portuguese origin. In 1991 Portugal mediated the Estoril Accord, ending Angola's 16-year civil war. It participated, along with American, Russian, and Angolan observers, in the political-military commission to supervise the truce and prepare for elections. It also sent peacekeeping forces to Mozambique in the early 1990s. Emotional ties with Africa are still strong, but economic links have become much weaker. In the 1990s only about 1 percent of Portugal's foreign trade was with Angola and Mozambique.

In 1996 Portugal and its six former colonies, including Brazil, fulfilled a long-held ambition by uniting their 200 million people (of whom 162 million are Brazilians) in the Community of Portuguese-Speaking Countries (CPLP). Its task is to protect their common language and promote cooperation. The post of secretary general is rotated alphabetically every two years.

The only actual colony that remained until the end of the century was Macao, a tiny (six square miles) outpost on the southern coast of the People's Republic of China, forty miles (sixty-four kilometers) across the Canton River Estuary from Hong Kong. Only about 10,000 of the estimated 427,000 are Portuguese, although 110,000 hold Portuguese passports and can therefore live and work anywhere in the EU if they choose. Few of the Chinese who live there speak Portuguese. In fact, English is used far more than Portuguese. After the 1974 revolution, Lisbon wanted to give up the colony, which is an important trade outlet and source of foreign capital for Beijing. In 1979 officials from both countries met secretly in Paris, where the Portuguese acknowledged Chinese sovereignty over the territory and agreed to administer it until China wanted it back. China assumed full control on December 19, 1999, after 442 years of Portuguese rule. The Chinese promised to respect Macao's Western, capitalist society and economy until at least 2050 and allow considerable autonomy in local affairs.

Technically speaking, Portugal still had another colony, namely Portuguese (East) Timor. Portugal and the United Nations never officially recognized Indonesia's annexation of the eastern half of the Timor Island on July 17, 1976. Almost half of East Timor's population was killed, and a native independence movement continued to resist Indonesian authority.

In 1996 the Nobel Peace Prize was awarded to José Ramos-Horta, a U.S.-educated human rights activist whose leftist Portuguese father had been deported to East Timor, and to Roman Catholic Bishop Carlos Filipe Ximenes Belo, a native of Timor, who had studied in missionary schools in Portugal and Rome. Portuguese President Jorge Sampaio, whose country had provided refuge for many East Timorese dissidents, called the award "a wonderful surprise."

The situation changed dramatically in 1998 when the Indonesian government of long-time ruler Suharto was overthrown, and the new leader offered the 800,000 East Timorese the opportunity to choose autonomy or independence. In May 1999, following more than fifteen years of UN-sponsored negotiations in which the Portuguese were more closely involved than any other nation, Portugal signed an agreement with Indonesia calling for a referendum in August 1999. Despite an overwhelming vote in favor of independence, pro-Indonesian militias, supported by elements of the Indonesian army, murdered thousands of East Timorese who had supported independence and drove many more out of East Timor. After several weeks of butchery, a UN peacekeeping force led by Australia restored order and paved the way toward self-rule.

**PORTUGUESE NATIONALISM** The Portuguese sense of distinct nationhood was decisively shaped by the struggle to free Portugal from Spain's domination. Its national identity still defines itself most clearly in terms of its distinctiveness from the Spanish nation. The 16th century had been Portugal's "Golden Age." Spain claimed the Portuguese throne on the grounds that the mother of King Philip II of Spain was descended from Portuguese nobility. In 1580 the two countries were united in a dual monarchy. This was supposed to leave the Portuguese with domestic autonomy. In fact, Spaniards were appointed to Portuguese offices.

Portugal was compelled to participate in and to help finance through heavy taxes a costly and protracted war against England. This not only cost Portugal most of its lucrative markets in the Orient, but the bulk of its fleet as well. Disillusioned about Spanish rule, and taking advantage of a revolt in Catalonia, the Portuguese also revolted. French support helped the rebellion to succeed in 1640, when the House of Bragança was established as the Portuguese ruling family (which it remained until the monarchy fell in 1910). The Spanish did not accept Portuguese independence without a fight, though. Until 1668 it struggled unsuccessfully to win back the country. To guarantee that it would never again fall under Spanish domination, Portugal entered into an alliance with the sea power, Britain, which always had a sharp strategic eye for coastal countries that could be useful allies. This partnership lasted into the 20th century.

The Portuguese are a highly individualistic people. At the same time they are tolerant, friendly, polite, and patient, and they form a relatively cohesive society. Without these qualities, the Portuguese would not have survived the radical changes that have occurred in the country since 1974. The population is largely homogeneous. But there are about 100,000 blacks from the former African colonies; 10 percent of Lisbon's population is black, some of whom have been the targets of racist attacks. There are also about 90,000 Gypsies, who have not integrated as well in Portugal as they have in Spain.

Few European countries have such a large portion of its population living abroad as does Portugal. Since the 15th century the Portuguese have emigrated in large numbers, first to Brazil, and then after Brazilian independence, to such destinations as North America, Venezuela, Angola, and Mozambique. However, after 1955 the greatest number of Portuguese emigrants, two-thirds of whom left agricultural areas in Portugal, went to industrialized Western European countries, especially France and Germany, in order to find employment. From 1960 until 1972 a million and a half Portuguese left the country, mainly in the direction of other West European nations.

The United States and Venezuela have become the favorite destination for Portuguese. The United States accepts the greatest annual number of Portuguese emigrants. More than a million Portuguese live there, over 600,000 of whom are from the Azores. By 1987 the total number of Portuguese living abroad was more than four million—roughly 40 percent of the country's total population. They send back more than $2 billion in remittances every year, which in 1986 accounted for 13 percent of Portugal's GDP. With the Portuguese economy thriving in the European Union (EU), from 30,000 to 40,000 are returning home every year.

Portugal is a nation whose cultural influence extends far beyond its own borders. Today nearly 200 million people speak Portuguese. Its outward-looking orientation was beautifully reflected by its greatest literary figure, Luiz de Camões (1524–80), who wrote poetry and dramatic comedies. In 1572 he published perhaps the greatest piece of Portuguese literature, *Os Lusíadas* (The Lusitanians), a long epic poem celebrating Portuguese history and heroes. His story is linked with that of Vasco da Gama's voyage to India and is infused with much Greek mythology.

Portuguese culture has also been enriched by experiences and influences from abroad. For instance, the novelist John Dos Passos and the undisputed king of march music John Philip Sousa were both sons of Portuguese emigrants and received their artistic inspiration in the United States. In 1998 a Portuguese writer won the Nobel Prize for literature for the first time. Jose Samarago was born into a home with no books, grew up in poverty, never went to the university, and toiled as a metalworker until the fall of dictator Antonio Salazar enabled him, an active Communist, to publish his first novel in 1974. The best known of his imaginative novels are *Baltasar and Blimunda* and *The Year of the Death of Ricardo Reis*. He expressed his hope on receiving the honor that "Portuguese will become more visible and more audible." Earlier in the century Egas Moniz had won the Nobel Prize for medicine.

The greatest foreign cultural influence comes from Brazil. For years after 1974 one of the most popular television serials in Portugal was a sort of soap opera from Brazil called "Gabriela." Set in Rio de Janeiro and using an all-Brazilian cast, this *telenovela* (TV serial) filled Portugal's air waves with Brazilian slang, songs, accents, and dress. Many other such series have subsequently been brought in from Brazil.

Chiefly because of its small size and high degree of

centralization, there are few different dialects spoken within Portugal, except in Miranda do Douro in the northeast. But of the 150 million persons in the world who speak Portuguese as a native language, only 10 million live in the mother country. It is not surprising that the language spoken in this small country is being changed by the Portuguese spoken outside, especially in Brazil. Oral expression is being strongly penetrated by Brazilian words and idiomatic phrases. Most magazines on Portugal's newsstands are from Brazil. The economic prowess of Brazil has meant that the Portuguese being learned by foreigners abroad is now primarily Brazilian.

A passionate debate began in 1986 over whether Portugal should simply recognize this fact and negotiate a linguistic agreement with Brazil and other former colonies. Proponents argue that a common structure of the language must be preserved and that the constant evolution of the language should be incorporated in the mother country. Critics decry the "crime against the patrimony of the Portuguese language" and "a disgusting resignation to Brazil's economic interests." No effort to erect a barrier against the flood of foreign cultural influences could succeed in a country like Portugal, which is adapting itself so quickly to the changing world it faces. Millions of Portuguese want no such barrier anyway. Nevertheless, the government established tough requirements that as of 1995 40 percent of all TV shows had to be in Portuguese, three-fourths of which must be produced in Portugal.

Portugal has undergone a dramatic transformation since joining the EU in 1986. The economy experienced an unprecedented boom and has been modernized and liberalized. In 1998 there were two showcases of the country's economic development. The world exposition in Lisbon commemorated the 500th anniversary of Vasco da Gama's first voyage to Brazil and drew millions of visitors. Also the eleven-mile Vasco da Gama Bridge spanning the Tagus River opened. In April 1994 they celebrated the 20th anniversary of the "Carnation Revolution." They can look with satisfaction on the legacies of that revolution: a stable parliamentary democracy, membership in the EU, and sustained economic growth that has raised living standards. Portugal's democratic constitution has been reformed and strengthened, and Portuguese have rediscovered a sense of national pride.

**POWELL, ENOCH** 1912–1998, Born in Birmingham, England, Powell received a degree in classics from Cambridge, was a professor of Greek at the University of Sydney in Australia, and rose from the rank of private to brigadier during the war, becoming a member of the general staff. He entered the House of Commons in 1950 as a member of the Conservative Party, from which he resigned in 1974 in disagreement over his party's support of the United Kingdom's entry into the European Common Market. Subsequently elected to Parliament in the same year as a member of the Ulster Unionist Party of Northern Ireland, Powell continued to serve in Parliament until 1987.

Powell is perhaps best known for his polarizing "rivers of blood" speech on April 20, 1968, to an annual meeting of Conservative Party members in Birmingham, during which he spoke out against nonwhite immigration and hinted at widespread civil unrest. He was dismissed from his position of shadow minister of health in Edward Heath's shadow cabinet because of the perceived racist overtones of his speech, but his appeal to British nationalism resounded with a public feeling threatened by an apparent "flood" of nonwhite immigrants. Subsequent public opinion polls and voting patterns seemed to certify the claims that Powell had merely articulated what many had been thinking anyway. Although he continued as a controversial symbol of British nationalism and xenophobia, and although race relations in the United Kingdom remained problematic, Powell's political influence waned. Suffering from Parkinson's disease, Enoch Powell died in London on February 8, 1998.

A critical look at Powell is provided by Paul Foot, *The Rise of Enoch Powell: An Examination of Enoch Powell's Attitude to Immigration and Race* (Penguin, 1969) and B. Smithies and P. Fiddick, *Enoch Powell and Immigration* (Sphere Books, 1969). A partial biography and generally favorable attempt to assess Powell's significance is T. E. Utley, *Enoch Powell: The Man and His Thinking* (Kimber, 1968). Also informative are Enoch Powell, *Freedom and Reality* (Paperfront, 1969) and *A Nation or No Nation?* (Batsford, 1978).

Adapted from Grieves, Forest, *Conflict and Order: An Introduction to International Relations*. © 1977 by Houghton Mifflin Company. Used with permission.

**PRIMO DE RIVERA, MIGUEL** 1870–1930, Spain managed to remain neutral in World War I, but in 1921 Moorish forces humiliated it so severely in a battle at Anual in North Africa that public pressure forced the government to conduct an investigation of the army, which had never contented itself with merely military matters. Before the inquiry could be completed, the military's rage at such "impudence" boiled over. The army seized power in September 1923 and formed a government under General Miguel Primo de Rivera, the captain general of Catalonia. He had established a dazzling military record in Cuba, the Philippines, and Morocco before becoming governor of Cadiz and captain general of Valencia and Madrid. With the backing of King Alfonso XIII, Primo de Rivera's government banned all opposition parties, dissolved the Cortes (Parliament), slapped severe controls on the press and the universities, and established a military Directory. He openly expressed great admiration for the kind of fascist political order Mussolini was establishing in Italy. In 1925 a civilian dictatorship under Primo de Rivera replaced the military one.

The new Spanish leader launched extensive public works and economic and administrative modernization programs. With the help of the French, he ended the war in Morocco in 1926. But without the support of the masses, the youth, or the intelligentsia, Primo de Rivera's authoritarian government could not survive the jolt the worldwide depression gave to Spain and most other European countries at the end of the 1920s. He therefore resigned in January 1930 and died in Parisian exile. Demonstrations in favor of a republic became so intense that King Alfonso XIII was forced to flee the country on April 13, 1931. The almost immediate proclamation of the Second Republic (the first being in the early 1870s) unleashed such enthusiasm from its supporters that 200 churches were burned to the ground.

Primo de Rivera's son, José Antonio, founded the Falange (Fascist Party) in 1933. In the first year of the civil war (1936–1939), he was captured and executed by loyalists to the republic. This made him a martyr for the fascists and later for dictator Francisco Franco.

## PRIMORDIALISM

Primordialism refers to a conception of ethnicity and nationality that stresses the objective, enduring, and fundamental character of these group identities. The primordial attachments of a group, such as language, race ("blood"), kinship, religion, territory, and custom, are viewed as basic and psychologically overpowering; they may even be coercive in terms of the instinctive loyalties they engender within members of the group. As the term also implies, primordial characteristics are stable, elemental, and basic to the very existence of the group, present from the time the group first formed or came into being. A primordialist perspective conceives of ethnicities and nationalities as real, invariant, often biologically rooted phenomena or crystallized essences that can be objectively defined and studied, and/or subjected to legal and political forces. For example, Stalin's famous definition (in *Marxism and the National and Colonial Question*, originally written

in 1912) of a nation as "a historically evolved, stable community of language, territory, economic life and psychological make-up manifested in a community of culture" is a primordialist one and it laid the theoretical basis for the construction of the multiethnic and multinational Soviet state. Primordialist conceptions, of course, still dominate many popular considerations of ethnicity or nationality and may be unquestioningly believed in by members of a group; their strongly held attachments to what they perceive as uniquely and distinctively theirs often motivates members of a group to collective action, including violence, against other groups similarly perceived as primordially real.

Most scholars of ethnicity and nationality today are critical of this primordialist perspective and emphasize the subjectively constructed character of these group identities. Ethnicities and nationalities are real only in the sociological sense of being continuously constructed by members of the group, and the ethnicity or nationality in question is not permanently enduring but constantly changing as it interacts with other groups and is subjected to broader historical processes. Thus, B. Anderson's (*Imagined Communities: Reflections on the Origin and Spread of Nationalism*, Verso, 1991) pithy definition of a nation "as an imagined political community" starkly contrasts with Stalin's primordialist conception and epitomizes the opposite constructivist perspective in which the self-ascription or categorization of the group is its most, and sometimes only, distinguishing characteristic.

A basic discussion of primordialism in relation to new nations is provided by C. Geertz in his essay "The Integrative Revolution: Primordial Sentiments and Civil Politics in the New States" which appears as Chapter 10 in *The Interpretation of Cultures* (Basic Books, 1973). A nice consideration of more modern, nonprimordialist approaches to ethnicity and nationalism appears in T. H. Eriksen's *Ethnicity and Nationalism: Anthropological Perspectives* (Pluto Press, 1993). For a sophisticated critique of the persistence of primordialist approaches and their dangers in Russia, see V. Tishkov's *Ethnicity, Nationalism and Conflict In and After the Soviet Union: The Mind Aflame* (Sage, 1997).

## PRINCIP, GAVRILO

1894–1918, Bosnian Serb nationalist, born in Bosansko Grahovo. He began his high school studies in Tuzla and Sarajevo, Bosnia, at the time part of the Austro-Hungarian Monarchy, but in 1912 moved to Belgrade, Serbia. On the eve of the first Balkan war (1912), Princip volunteered for the Serbian military but was rejected for medical reasons. For the next two years he studied in Belgrade, where he completed his studies in 1914, while at the same time following political developments in Bosnia.

In 1913 Princip joined the "Union or Death" organization, better known as the Black Hand, which had been formed in 1911. It consisted primarily of Serb nationalists and was committed to the liberation of the monarchy's South Slavic lands, and their unification with Serbia. The students believed that political violence, particularly assassinations of prominent Austrian officials, was the only effective way of achieving their goal.

While in Belgrade in early 1914, Princip learned that Archduke Franz Ferdinand, the heir to the Habsburg throne, was supposed to visit the Bosnian capital of Sarajevo in June 1914. Princip and two accomplices went to Sarajevo, where they worked with other students to prepare the assassination of the archduke. The fact that the archduke planned to visit Sarajevo on St. Vitus Day (Vidovdan, 28 June), a Serb national holiday, was taken by the students as an intentional insult by the Austrian authorities against the Serbs. That same day, June 28, Princip carried out the assassination of the archduke and archduchess while they made their way through the streets of Sarajevo.

In October 1914 Princip was tried by a military court in Sarajevo, and sentenced to twenty years hard labor. He served his prison sentence in Terezín, Bohemia, where he died in April 1918 from tuberculosis. In 1921 his remains were transferred to Sarajevo by the Yugoslav government. He has been hailed as a national hero and martyr in Serb nationalist circles ever since.

## PROKOFIEV, SERGEY

1891–1953, Russian Soviet composer. Of all the Russian composers of the twentieth century, Prokofiev seems to be the most direct successor to the nationalist patriotic tradition of the group *Moguchaia kuchka,* especially of Borodin. Even in the former Soviet Union, the music of Prokofiev was considered as genuinely national, despite its strong component of innovation and modernism that was unacceptable to Stalin and his ideologists.

Prokofiev's early masterpiece, *Scythian Suite* (1916), assembled from the music of an unstaged ballet *Ala and Lolly,* was based on the myths of pre-Slavic nomadic tribes of Scythians who inhabited the steppes near the Black Sea until 400 B.C. and then vanished. Prokofiev's composition, "a slap in the public's face" (Alexander Siloti), provoked a scandal in its St. Petersburg premiere, stunning the audience with specially designed "barbaric" dissonances and rhythms, "archaic" melodies, and vio-

lent dynamics. An obvious "neoprimitivist" counterpart to Stravinsky's *The Rite of Spring,* Prokofiev's *Scythian Suite* appeared at the climax of an enchantment with an elemental power of pre-Slavic barbarians, which inspired the Slavophilian faction of Russian literature and visual art of the period (Valery Briusov, Nikolai Gumilev, Nikolai Roerich).

Nevertheless, the ballet *Ala and Lolly* has been rejected by Diaghilev because "its music does not seek out for Russianism." Wishing to improve the situation, Prokofiev undertook a search of his "national" style in his next ballet for Diaghilev. The ballet, *Skazka o shute semerykh shutov pereshutivshem (The Story of a Buffoon Who Tricked Seven Others,* also known as *Chout,* and as *The Buffoon,* 1915–1916), was a setting of several satiric folktales from the Afanasiev collection. The protagonist, the Buffoon, plays a series of violent tricks, provoking other buffoons to kill their wives and promising to revive them with the aid of a magic whip. Intending to supply Russian tales with "national music," Prokofiev studied folk songs, writing in a letter to Stravinsky, that "turning the pages of a song anthology opened for me plenty of interesting possibilities." The brilliantly orchestrated music of the ballet is infused with witty quotations and idioms of Russian village dance and game songs. Distorting diatonic system of folk songs with chromaticism, Prokofiev found striking effects and grotesque shifting. Such a stylization was close to the neonationalist manner of Stravinsky and artists of the group *Mir Iskusstva.*

After *The Buffoon,* Prokofiev's style changed, indicating his move to a deeper approach to Russian melodicism. This tendency formed during Prokofiev's middle, so-called "Western" period (the composer left Russia in 1918), in various compositions, such as a constructivist ballet *Stal'noi skok (The Steel Trot,* 1926), a ballet *Bludnyi syn (The Prodigal Son,* 1929), and an opera *Ognennyi angel (The Fiery Angel,* 1919–1928), where "Russian" tendency revealed itself within Valery Briusov's setting of a German Middle Ages plot.

Prokofiev's "national" style reached its zenith after his repatriation to the Soviet Union in 1934, in compositions developing patriotic concepts. The best known of them are the films *Alexander Nevsky* (1938; its music was reworked as a cantata in 1939) and *Ivan Groznyi (Ivan the Terrible,* 1942–1946), both written by Prokofiev in collaboration with the prominent film director Sergei Eisenstein. These films appeared in prewar and war time, when Stalin's ideological propaganda called artists to bring to public attention heroic events and figures of old Russian history, emphasizing parallels with the present moment. Glorifying the 13th-century Russian prince

Alexander Nevsky, who saved Rus' by defeating the Teutonic Knights in the famous Battle on the Ice of Chudskoe Lake, Eisenstein and Prokofiev drew an obvious parallel between Nevsky and Stalin. The same process was carried out in the second film, although the analogy between Ivan Groznyi and Stalin brought the artists into a difficult position, since they needed to glorify the 16th-century Russian ruler not only for his unification of the nation and strengthening of the state, but also for his catastrophic internal repressions, which set a historical precedent to Stalin's purges. In the opera *Voina i mir* (*War and Peace,* 1941–1952), based on the famous Tolstoy novel, parallels were drawn between the two pairs of confronting political figures, Napoleon–Kutuzov and Hitler–Stalin. Remarkably, Prokofiev's highly effective patriotic music failed to satisfy the official Soviet concept of patriotic nationalism; while the first part of the opera, "Peace," was approved and successfully staged, the second part, "War," was not staged until after the composer's death. The reason was that Stalin and his ideologists did not approve of Prokofiev's portrait of "the people" (*narod*), who, in accordance with a classical nationalist tradition established by the composers of *Moguchaia kuchka,* was presented in the opera as the main protagonist.

The melodic style that Prokofiev developed in his "Russian" period is distinguishably national, revealing its close relationship with the principles of melodic style of Russian folk songs. "Liberalizing folk melodic elements and dispersing them out of their context, to the author's original music thematicism" (Izaly Zemtsovsky), Prokofiev employed them in his symphonies and other works not connected with a nationalist theme. However, in his patriotic compositions, Prokofiev created a number of themes that sounded stunningly close to the folk sources, and at the same time bore a distinguishing mark of Prokofiev's individuality. Some of these themes, such as "Arise, Ye, Russian People" from *Alexander Nevsky,* and Kutuzov's aria from *War and Peace,* glorifying Moscow, "the mother of Russian cities," composed with the intention of instilling in the audience a strong patriotic feeling, became enormously popular and important in war time and postwar Russia.

The important primary source is Sergei Prokofiev's *Autobiography, Articles and Reminiscences,* compiled and edited by S. Shlifshtein, translated by Rose Prokofieva (Moscow: Foreign Languages Publishing House, 1960; rev. 1968). The most complete biography is Harlow Robinson's *Sergei Prokofiev* (New York: Viking, 1987). Relevant discussions are Malcolm Hamrick Brown's "Stravinsky and Prokofiev: Sizing Up the Competition" in *Confronting Stravinsky: Man, Musician and Modernist,*

Jann Pasler, ed. (Berkley: University of California Press, 1986); and Richard Taruskin's "Art and Politics in Prokofiev" in *Society* **29** (1) (November–December 1991), pp. 60–64.

**PROPAGANDA** One of the most serious and least understood problems of social control is above the national level, at the level of the world social system. At the world level there is an extremely dangerous lack of means of restraining or counteracting propaganda that fans the flames of international, interracial, and interreligious wars. At present, every national regime asserts that its national sovereignty gives it the right to circulate any propaganda it cares to, however untrue such propaganda may be and however contradictory to the requirements of the world system. The most inflammatory of such propaganda usually takes the form of statements by prominent national leaders, often sensationalized and amplified by their own international broadcasts and sensationalized and amplified still further by media in the receiving countries.

Propaganda must be based on current beliefs and symbols to reach people. On the other hand, propaganda must also follow the general direction of evolution, which includes the belief in progress. A normal, spontaneous evolution is more or less expected, even if people are completely unaware of it, and in order to succeed, propaganda must move in the track of that evolution.

All propaganda must play on the fact that the nation will be industrialized, more will be produced, greater progress is imminent, and so on. No propaganda can succeed if it defends outdated production methods or obsolete social or administrative institutions. Though occasionally advertising may profitably evoke the good old days, political propaganda may not. Rather, it must evoke the future, the tomorrows that beckon, precisely because such visions impel the individual to act. But in this straining toward the future the propagandist must always beware of making precise promises, assurances, and compromises. Goebbels constantly protested the affirmations of victory emanating from the Führer's headquarters. The pull toward the future should refer to general currents of society rather than to precise events. Nevertheless, the promise made by Khrushchev that Communism would be achieved by 1980 leaves enough margin; for though the desired effect was obtained in 1961, the promise will be forgotten in 1980 if it has not been fulfilled.

The explosions of nationalism in Cameroon, Algeria, Indochina, and so on cannot be explained except as results of reaction against colonialism. The colonial society saw in nationalism the image, the grandeur, the effectiveness of its dreams of freedom, and adopted its form and passion to become victors over colonial powers. But this reasoning on the part of some intellectuals had no reality, no force, no efficacy until that nationalist passion inflamed hearts, until there was the systematic creation of a national exaltation with regard to a nation that did not exist. This was propaganda.

The 19th century was a great breeding ground of ideology, and propaganda needed an ideological setting to develop. During the 20th century propaganda was used on an infinitely greater scale than ever before, and this was made possible by the technical development of the means of mass communications.

Propaganda, as the establishment envisioned it, consisted of making a few points exclusively for mass consumption and then endlessly repeating them. According to this reactionary vision, the masses reacted only to the constant repetition of the simplest ideas, motivated by emotion rather than by reason. There was no room for nuance or interpretation: Propaganda had to be positive or negative, based on love or hatred. There could only be right or wrong; and so the ability to see two sides of a question was the very antithesis of propaganda.

The new concept of propaganda is based on the exploitation of modern technological and social trends. Combined with the decline of public interest in politics as well as the personalization of political issues, propaganda makes possible the creation of the illusion of a "participatory democracy," a euphemism for the manipulation of people unhappy with the political system's performance. These changes are not only tactical; rather, they reflect deeper changes in world culture and politics.

**PRUSSIAN NATIONALISM**    Perhaps more than any other European state, Prussia did not evolve, but was made by the human hand. A series of extraordinarily able rulers in the 17th and 18th centuries enabled Prussia to rise like a meteor to the ranks of the major European powers. The Elector Principality of Brandenburg was an area in the German East that had resisted domination by the Poles, a relatively insignificant, poor, and backward territory on the periphery of the decentralized German Empire ruled by a dynasty from southern Germany, the Hohenzollerns. Brandenburg and East Prussia had become linked in 1525. Taking advantage of the severe turmoil causd by the Reformation, the last Supreme Master of the German Order, Albrecht von Brandenburg-Ansbach from the family of Hohenzollern, simply assumed in 1525 the earthly title of "Duke of Prussia." In 1660 the last ties that bound East Prussia to Poland were severed. The Hohenzollern Dynasty was

able to gain control of West Prussia, Pomerania, and Silesia. Ultimately it acquired huge chunks of territory in the Rhineland and Westphalia as well. From a poor land known derisively as "the sandbox of the empire" with no raw materials and a population of little over a million persons grew a huge and powerful kingdom ultimately embracing about two-thirds of all Germans and serving as the foundation for the first truly unified German Empire in 1871.

From 1640 to 1688, Friedrich Wilhelm, "the Great Elector," laid the cornerstone for a powerful Prussia. He had spent three years in the Netherlands during his youth, and there he had been deeply influenced by the Calvinist dynamism and sense of obligation. From the Thirty Years War he had drawn the lesson that his state needed to enhance its military prowess. He said: "Alliances are good, but one's own power is even better; one can more safely depend on that." He therefore enlarged the Prussian army from 3000 to 30,000 soldiers.

He also established an oft-forgotten Prussian humanitarian tradition that lasted for a century and a half and that strengthened Prussia. When the French king invalidated the Edict of Nantes in 1685, which had granted considerable religious and civil liberty to the Huguenots (French Protestants), Friedrich Wilhelm responded with the Edict of Potsdam opening the Prussian gates to the religiously persecuted. More than 20,000 French Huguenots, most of them skilled craftsmen and businessmen, poured into Prussia, and by the year 1700 one out of three residents of Berlin was French. Far from attempting to Germanize these newcomers, newcomers were permitted to retain their own language and customs. The Huguenots built their own schools and churches and powerfully contributed to the arts and to the vibrant economic life of Prussia. More than 20,000 Protestants from Salzburg fled the counter-reformation, and in the course of the 18th century there was a steady stream of emigrants and religious refugees to Prussia: Mennonites, Scottish Presbyterians, Jews, and sometimes Catholics. In some ways, Prussia in the 18th century was to the persecuted of Europe what America was in the 19th century: a religiously tolerant land that erected no exclusive nationalist impediments and that offered opportunities to talented and hard-working peoples.

Friedrich I ascended the throne in 1688. He was a well-educated and cultured man who maintained a glittering, but excessively extravagant court. He established another Prussian tradition that is also frequently overlooked today: He turned Prussia, especially Berlin, into a leading home for science and the arts. He founded the Academies of Art and Science. He ordered the building of many edifices, such as the Charlottenburg Palace, which changed the face of Berlin from that of a provincial town to one of the most dignified cities in Europe. Through patient and skillful diplomacy he also achieved an important political goal: In 1701 he won the German emperor's approval for the Prussian elector to bear the title of "king." This considerably boosted the prestige of a poor country on the outskirts of the German Empire.

When Friedrich Wilhelm I (so named because his father had not been a king) was crowned in 1713, Prussia gained a ruler who was capable, but greatly different from his predecessor. What one now most often associates with Prussia was largely due to his influence: the spirit of Spartan simplicity and the conscientious fulfillment of one's obligations to the state, which was to be ruled by the king alone, but for the good of the subjects. As he told his son, "The dear Lord placed you on the throne, not in order to be lazy, but in order to work and to rule his lands well." He discarded the luxurious court life his father had conducted to compete with the glittering courts of France and Austria. He created a first-rate civil service staffed by duty-conscious, highly respected, but poorly paid officials. His popular name, "the Soldier King," revealed his priority. Although during his entire reign he led his country into only one short war, he poured four-fifths of all state income into the army, whose size he doubled to 70,000 men. The stunningly rapid growth of the Prussian army in size and importance prompted the Frenchman Mirabeau to remark shortly after the death of Friedrich Wilhelm I: "Other states possess an army; Prussia is an army which possesses a state!"

Prussia was located in the middle of Europe with a conglomeration of often unconnected territories, no natural frontiers, a relatively small population, and no concept of "nation" to hold it together and give it purpose. Prussia had to have a strong army to maintain itself in the prevailing international setting. One could argue the Prussian army was disproportionately large in relation to the country's population and financial strength. But the new army was still considerably smaller than those of Austria, France, and Russia, and "militarism" was by no means restricted to Prussia during this "Age of Absolutism." Further, the Prussian army never "possessed" the state. It was the most disciplined army in the world and never made the slightest attempt to rule the state. The army was, without a doubt, first rate. Carlyle once wrote that Prussia had a shorter sword than Austria, France, and Russia, but it could draw it out of the sheath much more swiftly. The Prussian army was open to the newest military technology. Also, it increasingly

became a citizens' army and less a mercenary force. Prussia was one of the first countries in the world to learn that its own citizens serve better than the troops of a foreign country. Its discipline and well-planned supply system was also a blessing for the civilian population in those areas where the army operated. In an age of undisciplined armies that "lived off the land," the civilian population was constantly subjected to plunder, murder, and rape. Civilians seldom needed to fear such horrors from the new Prussian army.

Friedrich Wilhelm I was interested solely in establishing the best organized, most modern and efficient state and military in the world. Unlike his father and his son, who in 1740 became King Friedrich II, he was utterly disinterested in art and education. Friedrich II was called "the Great" during his own lifetime. This was not only because of his wars and his successful, but sometimes morally questionable foreign policy, but also because of his reforms, his intellectual and cultural achievements as a young man, and the kind of state he helped to create. The Prussian state was feared by its neighbors because of its military strength and qualities as a state. It had an uncorrupted administration, an independent judiciary, and a state of law (*Rechtsstaat*) in which there was more legal equality for all citizens than could be found in most other European states at the time. By the standards of the 18th century, which should be used to judge the state ruled by Friedrich, Prussia was a modern and enlightened state. It was not regarded as a nation, a concept that did not enter most German minds until French troops brought it into the politically fragmented center of Europe we now call Germany a few years after Friedrich II's death in 1786. Nor was it a democracy. But enlightenment in politics at first meant basing the affairs of state on reason. This manifested itself in Europe initially in the form of absolutism. France under Cardinal Richelieu was an early model. Not until the French Revolution, when a brand of enlightenment that stressed popular sovereignty and "liberty, equality, and fraternity" emerged, was Prussia challenged by a state and by ideas that were clearly more modern than its own.

**PSYCHOLOGY OF NATIONALISM**   The formation of a national identity is a process by which salient identity symbols become the means of a person's and subsequently the primary in-group's notion of distinctiveness and well-being. Salient primeval symbols among social and political groups play a meaningful role in determining intergroup categorization and consciousness by accentuating the similarities among group members while highlighting the differences of nongroup members. When groups endeavor to maintain and protect their identity, then they are engaged in a process of national formation that is psychological and physiological. For a group to actually become a nation, they must incorporate within themselves the symbols of a nation and seek either to enhance or protect their identity community.

William Bloom argued that the process of identification is based on the need to survive, starting initially with one's parents then other significant figures, while censoring behavior that does not conform to group norms. This is followed by incorporating social roles in order to function within society. The incorporation of social mores and roles contribute to the individual's and subsequently to the group's common psychological bonds and the ability to act in cohesive fashion.

See William Bloom, *Personal Identity, National Identity and International Relations* (Cambridge University Press, 1990).

## PUERTO RICAN NATIONALISM

A sense of Puerto Ricanness as a sign of attachment to two civil societies, from which the identities are constructed (national and diasporic). In the context of today's Puerto Ricans a profound split between "cultural nationalism" and "political nationalism" corresponds to the dynamics of a historical process where national "identity" and "new culture" are redefined.

For nearly thirty years, since 1837, Puerto Ricans had been waiting uncomplainingly for autonomy promised by the "Leyes especiales." Finally, on November 25, 1865, Antonio Cánovas del Castillo, the overseas minister, invited representatives of Puerto Rico and Cuba to Madrid to propose extraordinary laws governing the composition and extent of local administration.

Demands for reform in the Spanish Antilles were coming from a number of sources, metropolitan and colonial. Despite the limitations of the declaration, Puerto Rican liberals welcomed the opportunity to press their demands. Most conservatives, however, were against the decree, although a select elite favored some moderate reforms. Even the separatists gave their support to the quest for reform. But the promise was not to be kept.

The separatists, disillusioned with Spain, become convinced that revolution was the only remedy. In less than a month, between September and October 1868, three unconnected revolutionary movements shook the Spanish world both in the peninsula and in its Antillean colonies. The third revolution was the "Grito de Yara" in Cuba, which signaled the beginning of the Ten Year War (1868–1878).

By the mid-19th century, Ramón Emeterio Betances and Ruiz Belvis, leaders of the separatist faction, were expelled from the island. Betances and Ruiz Belvis went to New York to begin a pilgrimage to encourage Puerto Rican independence. Ruiz Belvis went on to Chile, where he soon died, while Betances settled for a while in Santo Domingo and began to set up a revolutionary movement to free the island, organizing the Puerto Rican Revolutionary Committee.

The exciting years following the Spanish revolution witnessed the creation of Puerto Rico's first political parties, which had not existed before 1870. The first party was the liberal Partido Liberal Reformista. A few months later, the conservatives formed the Partido Liberal Conservador. From then on, the two parties competed for an electorate of approximately 20,000. The liberal party favored reforms and political integration, while the conservatives, who later were called "Unconditionals," defended the establishment values.

On February 11, 1891, Luis Muñoz Rivera, the editor of *la Democracia*, began to publish a series of articles in which he proposed a pact between the autonomistas and the Spanish Liberal Fusionist Party of Práxedes Mateo Sagasta. This alliance, he argued, would increase the Partido Autonomista's chances of becoming the government party in the island, thus improving the outlook for autonomous rule for Puerto Rico.

Conditions on the island were to be overtaken by a series of international actions. On February 24, 1895, the Cubans, tired of waiting for promised reforms, rebelled once more and began the fighting that eventually led to the Spanish-American War and Cuban Independence. The harsh warfare that followed affected Puerto Rico in many ways. The island's separatists in exile, led by the venerable Dr. Ramón Emeterio Betances, joined the Cubans and organized a Puerto Rican Section of the Cuban Revolutionary Party.

On November 9, 1897, Governor Sabás Marín was informed of three decrees establishing an autonomous regime in Puerto Rico. These acts provided the framework for the autonomic government soon to be established.

On May 12, 1898, Puerto Rico had its first taste of the war that on April 19 had broken out between the United States and Spain. The climax came two and a half months later. On July 25, the *U.S.S. Gloucester* sailed fearlessly into the bay of Guánica and landed a few troops who symbolically raised the Stars and Stripes for the first time on Puerto Rican soil. The invasion of Puerto Rico had started, and with it an American experiment in colonialism.

Between October 1898, when the American flag was raised at "La Fortaleza" and November 1948, when the

Puerto Ricans chose their first elective governor, a full half century was to pass by. During this period, colonial tutelage was put to the examination. The system called for the executive power to be controlled by Washington, especially in such key areas as justice, education, and security. Washington also controlled the legal system through presidential appointments to the Puerto Rican Supreme Court and the role of the United States. The substance of colonialism was preserved, although the semantics changed. Puerto Rico was not called a "colony," but a "dependency" or "possession," juridically defined as an "unincorporated territory."

From the social perspective, Puerto Ricans (as other diasporas) function within multiple and ambiguous registers of nationalism. These new "imagined communities" (U.S. Puerto Ricans) maintain both an affiliation and loyalty to their mainland at the same time that they claim and fight for their own place in America. This tendency increasingly points toward a situation of double citizenships.

The implosion of the fragments does not erase the nation but advances its claims as a dominant discourse of identity. Despite this, the island-city as both a mythical land and as a colonized territory, still occupies a symbolically central place as the "real" and ultimate "mainland."

In this cultural context, nationalism becomes political rhetoric with multiple meanings. The ethnic and cultural identities accomplish greater importance in present-day political movements; cultural nationalism comes to the vanguard of contemporary social analysis.

Yet cultural nationalism, which emphasizes the cultural rather than the politically defined boundaries of a nation, constitutes one of the less understood forms of nationalism. It is frequently seen as a transient ideology, as a "superficial" kind of nationalism, or as a strategy designed by state bureaucrats and intellectuals. What remains constant in the analysis of cultural nationalism is the recognition that the forging of a cultural identity from an historical past or from recent inventions is an effective basis for political mobilization. This is manifest in the case of Puerto Rico. This idea points to the processes through which nations are modeled, imagined, and communicated through state institutions, cultural policies, or official versions of history, and to the ways in which "nationals" receive and manipulate official constructions of nationhood.

In Puerto Rico views of national identity had been disseminated in the nationalistic literature since the late 19th century, but it was in the 1950s that an official view of Puerto Rican national culture became popular. After the establishment of the Commonwealth in 1952,

which gave the island autonomy over local affairs, the government initiated a demagogic discourse about cultural nationalism while also maintaining the political and economic dependency on the United States.

The present moment of interdependence, in which the world becomes a universe with an increasing condition of mutuality, paradoxically affirms the power of the United States as a relatively uncontested supranational power. The dislocation of the nation (the relative liberation of the nation from the state), the increasing nomadism of material and emotional insecurity, and the proliferation of global migrations account for the creation of diasporas, border and traveling cultures, that in turn deterritorialize and displace the spaces of the nation.

**PUJOL, JORDI** 1930 –, Catalan nationalist leader and ideologue; president of the *Generalitat,* or Catalan government, since 1980. He started to be active in Catholic and Catalan nationalist youth groups in 1946, under the dictatorship in Spain of Francisco Franco. In May 1960, he was detained by the police for his "separatist" activities and put in jail until 1962, when he was condemned to confinement in the city of Girona for one more year.

In the politically repressed atmosphere of the 1960s, Pujol, although a physician by education, focused on launching and inspiring institutional projects for Catalonia, such as an autochtnonous private bank and the first encyclopedia in Catalan, *Enciclopèdia Catalana.* Later, as the change of regime neared, Pujol entered politics by founding in 1974 the moderate nationalist party *Convergència Democràtica de Catalunya* (CDC, Democratic Convergence of Catalonia) of which he has been the uncontested leader. It was a *convergence* of an ideologically diverse prodemocracy group that shared Catalan nationalism. At the beginning, the party mostly reflected Pujol's inkling for the Swedish social-democratic model and a strong pro-European Community stance. CDC's official line mimicked its founder's ideological evolution toward a right-of-center, probusiness, pragmatic liberalism, still solidly in favor of European integration.

In 1977, Pujol was elected a member of the Spanish Parliament in the first free legislative elections after the civil war. Once the Constitution of 1978 and the Catalan Statute of Autonomy of 1979 were approved and ratified by popular referendum, Pujol devoted himself to Catalan politics. He won by a relative majority in the reestablished Catalan autonomous elections of 1980. Jordi Pujol became the 116th president of the *Generalitat,* and was reelected by an absolute majority in 1984,

1988, 1992, and 1995. He won for a sixth time in 1999. Since 1979, CDC, a member of the Liberal International, has maintained a permanent—if sometimes uneasy—electoral coalition with the smaller but older Christian Democrat party, *Unió Democràtica de Catalunya*, creating *Convergència i Unió* (CiU).

At the forefront of the recuperated Catalan government, Pujol's priorities have been to restore the vitality of the Catalan language and culture after four decades of attempted obliteration; the transfer of competencies from Madrid's central government; the consolidation of self-rule; and the socioeconomic development of Catalonia to bring it up to northern European standards. Pujol has pursued the maximum degree of autonomy, falling short of advocating independence from Spain. In the late 1990s, this position is labeled "shared sovereignty."

Pujol's political formula has been widely imitated among Spain's seventeen autonomous communities, which nonetheless have difficulty matching the historical relevance of Catalonia and the Basque Country. Since 1993, Pujol's coalition has acted as a kingmaker in a Spanish Parliament with relative majorities. In 1993–1996, CiU supported a minority socialist government; from 1996, a conservative one. Outside Catalonia, Pujol is an unpopular figure, due to the traditional Spanish anti-Catalan sentiment and to the popular perception that, behind his ambiguity, what he seeks is independence.

Jordi Pujol has tried to promote abroad a distinct Catalan identity within Spain. He is a leader of the European regional movement, having presided over the Assembly of European Regions, a powerful interest group, in 1992–1996.

His critics accuse Pujol of messianism, with a tendency to confuse himself with Catalonia. His iron-fisted control of his party and, by extension, of Catalan mainstream nationalism, is legendary. CDC is an archetypal example of transition parties in Spain: nearly all dominated by charismatic anti-Francoist activists but with insufficient internal democracy. As the country's system of liberties has matured, and other parties have changed leaders and evolved, Pujol's patriarchal style seems increasingly anachronistic. Pujol's lengthy, uninterrupted rule has experienced charges of nepotism and of slow responsiveness regarding corruption cases.

Jordi Pujol is already considered a towering figure of Catalan nationalism. He has presided over the longest, fullest, and most peaceful period of self-rule since the Principality of Catalonia lost its liberties in 1716. After centuries of official preeminence of the Spanish language, Catalan is increasingly present in public life and the mood of the population regarding the nation's future—cultural and otherwise—tends to be optimistic.

Apart from speech collections, Jordi Pujol is the author of, notably, *Fer Poble, fer Catalunya* (*Making the People, Making Catalonia*, 1965); *Una política per Catalunya, avui* (*A Policy for Catalonia, Today*, 1976); *Des dels turons a l'altra banda del riu* (*Escrits de presó*) (*From the Hills Beyond the River* (*Writings from Jail*, 1978); and *Construir Catalunya* (*To Build Catalonia*, 1979).

## PUSHKIN, ALEXSANDR

1799–1837, Russian poet and writer, whose brilliant literary works conceived a completely new epoch in Russia that can be compared to the Italian Renaissance. Pushkin was born in Moscow on June 6, 1799. He started writing his first lyrical poems in 1812 in the Tsarskoselskii Lyceum, which became famous for the dissemination of revolutionary and patriotic ideas. After graduation Pushkin returned to St. Petersburg and actively participated in a secret political society. The political activity of young Pushkin was reflected in his new poems penetrated with stinging and witty political thoughts. The tsar's disfavor with Pushkin's radical writing resulted in the poet's exile.

The literary heritage of Pushkin was greatly influenced by Russian folklore. Various folklore characters had been reborn in his poems (*Ruslan and Lyudmila*, 1820). His enchantment with romanticism produced *The Demon* (1824) and *The Gypsies* (1824). Deeply interested in the history of Russia, he wrote a historical drama *Boris Godunov* (1825). All of Pushkin's talent as a national Russian poet is revealed fully in a work on which he spent seven years. His magnum opus, *Eugene Onegin* (*Evgenii Onegin*, 1830), is honored by every Russian as an encyclopedia of Russian life. This novel in verses realistically portrays the social and intellectual life of Russians of the 19th century. It laid the foundation for other classical Russian novels.

Pushkin is honored by the Russians as a man of letters, whose brilliant works include various literary genres from romantic and realistic poems, novels and plays, to stories and dramas. His language intertwined standard bookish expressions with live colloquial phrases that were rich in style and in the expressions and flexibility of the new Russian language. In the society where the rich spoke French and the poor used the old Church Slavic language, the works of Pushkin revitalized and boosted the development of the Russian language.

The name of Pushkin symbolizes Russia for every Russian because his works embodied the Russian national spirit, realistically depicting the Russian life, the Russian revolutionary thoughts, Russia itself. Pushkin's works were and still are a source of inspiration for

Russian composers, ballet choreographers, and movie producers. Slavophils also extensively used the creative writing of Pushkin as the symbol of Russian spirituality. After a duel with Baron George d'Anthes, who allegedly had an affair with the poet's wife, Pushkin died on February 8, 1837.

For further reading, see A. Pushkin, *The Bronze Horseman: Selected Poems of Alezxandr Pushkin,* translated by D. M. Thomas (Penguin, 1982); A. Pushkin, *Complete Prose Fiction,* Translated and edited by Paul Debreczeny (Stanford University Press, 1983). These two books present collections of some of his best writings translated into English. These two books are literary criticisms of his poetry: A. Briggs, *Alexandr Pushkin* (Barnes and Noble, 1983), and B. Brasol, *The Mighty Three: Poushkin, Gogol, Dostoevsky: A Critical Trilogy* (Willaim Farquhar Payson, 1934).

# Q

**QADDAFI, MUAMMAR AL-** 1942–, This controversial leader was born in the coastal city of Misratah, not far from Tripoli, Libya's capital, in an environment of egalitarian simplicity and tribal integrity. Qaddafi, a colonel in the signal corps, led a group of young army officers in a bloodless coup on September 1, 1969, that overthrew the Sannusi Kingdom and introduced a republican order. Immediately after assuming power, Qaddafi disclosed his ideological orientation, a blend of revolutionary Pan-Arabism and popular Islam. From the beginning of his regime, Qaddafi manifested apprehension about the big colonial powers who, in his own assessment, adamantly opposed seeing the rebirth of the Arab nation. He sought to merge Libya with Egypt and Syria in an Arab Federation, although he achieved few tangible results. He supported Egypt in its confrontation with Israel during the 1973 war, but expressed dismay over Egyptian President Anwar al-Sadat's predisposition to peace with the Jewish state. Disillusionment with his ability to play a significant role in Arab affairs soured his relations with several Arab states, and triggered a brief punitive war by Egypt in the summer of 1976.

Shifting his attention to domestic concerns, Qaddafi seemed intent on transforming Libya's traditional society. A poor, illiterate, and unhealthy society prompted the Libyan leader to define his immediate challenge in terms of eradicating his countrymen's poverty. To this end, he aspired to train his people to assume authority, in preparation for empowering them in a political system resting on popular organization. Apparently influenced by the structure of the Communist Party of the Soviet Union, Qaddafi established people's committees at the levels of governorates, municipalities, and zones. Direct elections occurred at the zone level (the lowest), whereas seats at the two higher levels were filled by appointment. Qaddafi's Green Book did away with the Revolutionary Command Council that had governed

Libya since the coup, instituting the General People's Congress instead. Qaddafi announced in 1977 the establishment of the people's authority, ushering in the Socialist People's Libyan Arab Jamahiriyya.

Qaddafi toyed with several approaches for modernizing Libya; finally he seems to have realized the difficulty of achieving real modernization for his country. Plummeting revenues from oil and threat from Libya's militant Islamic oppositon, charges about association with international terrorism, and accusations of involvement in the Lockerbie affair appear to have swayed Qaddafi to shift his policy objectives from grandiose developmental theories to sheer political survival. In 1996 he released a book entitled *Tahya Dawlat al-Huqara'* (*Long-Live the State of the Contemptibles*), in which his previous ambitions for Libya have retreated to the status of a dream concerning the founding a state run by ordinary people. Qaddafi insists that the arrival of this state requires a long time; the process demands that people's marginalization and meaninglessness reach an unprecedented level before the eruption of the revolution that ultimately empowers them. Qaddafi seems to have concluded that the modernization of Libya, if it were to come true, will not happen during his lifetime.

**QUEBEC NATIONALISM** Quebecois resolutely resist assimilation and assert their right to manage most of their own affairs and determine their own destiny. Most regard themselves as a nation, even though they are Canadian citizens. Quebec nationalism never dies although it sometimes dies down temporarily.

In 1760 Britain conquered New France. The memory of the *Conquête* still nourishes Quebec nationalism. Lord Durham found in 1838 "two nations warring within the bosom of a single state." In 1867 Quebec became a founding member of the Canadian Confederation, which Quebecois consider to be a "union of two peoples" (anglophones and Quebecois), rather than of many provinces, of which Quebec is only one. They retained French civil law and authority over education and religion.

Quebec leaders insisted that their sons should not be called on to die for Britain in faraway wars. Henri Bourassa declared in 1907: "There is Ontario patriotism, Quebec patriotism or western patriotism, but there is no Canadian patriotism." Nor did Quebecois feel loyalty and emotional attachment toward France, which was no longer the France of their ancestors. Most were repelled by the French Revolution, which attacked the royal family and Catholic Church. French social experimentation shocked many Quebecers, who until the 1960s were socially conservative. The introduction of conscription in both world wars ignited intense emotions, and many Quebecers openly protested or went into hiding to avoid recruiters.

For more than two centuries, many anglophones fostered illusions that the Quebecois would become absorbed into the Anglo-Saxon mainstream. They often viewed Quebecois as a priest-ridden, traditional-bound, backward, clannish, and riotous people. Quebecers resented the arrogant sense of superiority on the part of anglophones, who dominated much of Quebec's economy, and who, in the opinion of many Quebecois, sought to destroy their culture. The Quebec nation has always been held together by a common memory of Quebecers' past and a separate language and culture. On their license plates are the words, *Je me souviens* ("I remember"), which underscores the importance of Quebec's past for the present values and feeling of community. After World War II, Quebec adopted a new flag that underscores the province's French character: the white *fleur-de-lis* in each quadrant. It is far more visible throughout the province than the Canadian maple leaf flag, which had been adopted in the 1960s to placate Quebec sensitivities by purging all traces of the British heritage.

The 1960s ushered in a reform wave that unalterably changed the province and the attitudes of its people. People spoke of a "Quiet Revolution." The most fundamental assumptions and beliefs of Quebecers about politics, religion, economics, and society were scrutinized and, to a large extent, discarded. Rather than viewing technology, business, industrialization, and urbanization as threats to their unique culture, Quebecois now regarded them as instruments for improvement. Instead of turning to the Catholic Church to protect them from the modern world, they became more secular in their outlook and took a more positive view of the

state as a tool to help Quebec develop itself and catch up with the rest of Canada. They gained self-confidence that they could modernize while still being completely French in outlook, institutions, and language. They developed the courage, not only fundamentally to challenge Canadian federalism, but even to challenge the very existence of Canada as a unified country.

The secularization of the province's schools produced a new kind of graduate: one with less knowledge of philosophy, French poets, and Catholic scholasticism, but with more technical and business training. It created a larger middle class, with the kinds of technical skills that would enable young Quebecois to operate in the province's business élite and to enter the civil service. They sought control of the province's economy. Their rationale was that if Quebecers were to be "masters in their own house," they would have to have more influence within the economy, which was largely controlled by anglophone Canadians and Americans.

Quebecers drew a much sharper boundary around their conception of the Quebec nation to fit the geographical boundaries of Quebec province. Although they were to remain sensitive to the treatment of francophones in other parts of Canada, Quebecers no longer felt a national link with them; the term "French Canadian" fell into disfavor.

The 1967 Montreal Expo became a source of pride for Quebecers, one-third of whom live in Montreal. It attracted the world's attention to the accomplishments and the aspirations of a much-changed province and to a festering wound in the heart of Canada. French President Charles de Gualle visited the Expo and exclaimed: *"Vive le Quebec libre!"* The Canadian government indignantly called such language "unacceptable" and ordered him to leave within hours. His words became a rallying cry for those who wanted a totally independent Quebec.

The stakes were raised in 1970, when the Front for the Liberation of Quebec (FLQ) resorted to terrorism to achieve separation. The Quebec government requested troops to quell the violence, and Prime Minister Pierre Elliott Trudeau, himself from Quebec, complied.

Many Quebecois remained frustrated, and political forces were emerging within Quebec that steered toward Quebec independence. In the 1960s a heterogeneous coalition of Quebecers took shape that wanted to push the Quiet Revolution further. This diversity was never easy to manage, but for two decades it was held together by the only Quebecer who possessed the necessary charisma, political skill, and patience to be its leader: René Lévesque.

Lévesque's Parti Quebecois (PQ) government, which

ruled Quebec from 1976 to 1985, introduced Bill 101. This requires that all public signs (including road signs) and every form of commercial advertising be exclusively in French. It restricts access to English-language schools to children with at least one parent who had been educated in English in Quebec. That means that not only immigrant children, but the offspring of anglophones from other Canadian provinces are required to attend French-language schools. It went beyond Bill 22, which declared that French alone is the province's "official language," by requiring that French alone be used for provincial legislation, public administration, the judicial system, most public institutions. It must be used as the working language in all businesses within the province. Employers are required to write all communications to their employees in French, and they cannot dismiss or demote an employee simply because he speaks no English. A watch-dog Office of the French Language was set up to settle disputes arising from this law. Bill 101 created new opportunities for francophones, who constitute 82 percent of Quebec's population, and forced the anglophone minority, not the francophone majority, to pay the economic price for unilingualism.

Reforms in Canada weakened the PQ's argument that Quebec should be independent and helped produce a narrow defeat in its 1980 referendum. Because of the Official Languages Act of 1969, the use of French has been expanded throughout Canada, and the number of bilingual Canadians has greatly increased. More and more anglophones in Quebec have accepted the necessity of speaking French. In other provinces, such as New Brunswick, both French and English are used in public life, and everywhere in Canada a francophone can deal with the federal government in French. In the federal capital of Ottawa, both languages are used on the street and in Parliament. Every prime minister, governor general, speaker of the House of Commons, and mid- to high-ranking military officer, as well as at least three of nine Supreme Court justices, must speak both languages, and parliamentary debates are conducted in both.

The federal government produced a new constitution in 1982 that spells out provincial rights more accurately than did the British North America Act (BNA). It contains a bill of rights that can be invoked by those who perceive language discrimination anywhere in Canada. It took audacious steps in 1987 to secure language harmony and finally win Quebec endorsement of the 1982 Constitution. It reached a ground-breaking "Meech Lake Accord" with the ten provincial premiers. This

would have made Quebec "a distinct society," explicitly recognized the coexistence of French and English language groups as "a fundamental characteristic of Canada," and given Parliament and the provincial legislatures the role of preserving—but not promoting—the francophone and anglophone character of Canada. Quebec was the first province to ratify the accord.

Anglophone Canadians reacted angrily in 1988 when Quebec prohibited the use of English on outdoor commercial signs, an action that seemed to violate the rights of Quebec's anglophones. This struck critics as a foretaste of how Quebec might use the powers implied by the "distinct society" clause in the accord. It provoked a backlash and made bilingualism harder to sell in the rest of Canada. In 1989 separatism roared back on the political agenda when the PQ, led by Jacques Parizeau and running again on an independence platform, regained power in the provincial elections. By June 1990, Meech was dead. Many Quebecers interpreted its downfall as a rejection of them by the rest of Canada.

The outcome ignited a new wave of Quebec nationalism, which in turn stirred up even more anti-Quebecois resentment in anglophone Canada. It left a legacy of polarization and volatility and brought to the surface stresses and strains in the very fabric of Canadian society. It put wind in the sails of a new separatist party in the House of Commons, the Bloc Quebecois, and a rising Reform Party in the West.

Prime Minister Brian Mulroney, himself from Quebec, promised that his government would present its own proposals to build "a new and stronger Canada." His problem was to devise constitutional reforms more comprehensive than the Meech Lake Accord that would satisfy both Quebec and all the other groups clamoring for greater autonomy from the central government. The government organized hearings throughout the land to hear the complaints and suggestions of hundreds of thousands of Canadians. The goal was to turn around Westerners' and other anglophones' anti-Quebec sentiment and get them to accept a constitutional plan that would also be compatible with Quebec's demands for recognition as a "distinct society." Quebec had to be offered a palatable alternative to sovereignty.

A "Charlottetown Accord" emerged in August 1992. Quebec would be recognized as a "distinct society," characterized by its language, culture, and civil law tradition. At the same time, it offered protection to anglophone communities in Quebec and francophone communities elsewhere. Every mainstream political party and institution supported the package except the Reform Party and the PQ. But in an October 26, 1992, referendum it was rejected. For Quebec separatists, the no-vote confirmed that Canada would never recognize Quebec's special character.

Parizeau ordered a referendum in Quebec on October 30, 1995, to clear the way for independence. This time, the separatists came closer to victory than ever before, wining 49.4 percent of the votes in a huge 94 percent turnout. This was a gain of ten percentage points since 1980; 60 percent of Quebec's francophones voted "oui," while nearly all anglophones and immigrants voted "non." Never had Quebecers displayed such deep dissatisfaction with the status quo. Parizeau, who resigned as premier after the disappointing defeat, was correct in saying that for many Canadians "this Quebec problem is like a never-ending visit to the dentist." Regarding the outcome as a moral victory, Quebec's new leader, Lucien Bouchard, proclaimed: "Let us keep the faith. The next time will be the right one."

Parizeau admitted in his memoirs that he had been prepared to declare Quebec's independence immediately after a yes vote in 1995, not after negotiations with Ottawa. This reminded Canadians that those who support Quebec sovereignty, although divided among themselves on tactics and on the definition of the term, are dead serious about Quebec independence. One who tries to bind Canada together faces a dilemma: Any solution acceptable to Quebec is unacceptable to anglophone Canada and vice versa.

See Dominique Clift, *Quebec Nationalism in Crisis* (McGill-Queen's University, 1980); William D. Coleman, *The Independence Movement in Quebec 1945–1980* (University of Toronto, 1984); Jacques Parizeau, *For a Sovereign Quebec* (1997); John Saywell, *The Rise of the Parti Québécois 1967–1976* (University of Toronto, 1977).

**QUTB, SAYYID** 1906–1965, The official abrogation of the Ottoman Empire by Kemal Atatürk in 1924 rendered Muslims without a caliph for the first time in about 1300 years. Four years later Hasan al-Banna, a schoolteacher, founded al-Ikhwan al-Muslimun (Muslim Brethren movement) in Egypt, with the declared objective of reinstating the Islamic state. Sayyid Qutb, born in the village of Musha in central Egypt to a family of erudition, studied under al-Banna, joined the Muslim Brethren movement, and eventually became its leader following the death of his mentor. Earlier, he enlisted in the Wafd, the main Egyptian nationalist party, but quit in 1942 in protest against its cooperation with the Brit-

ish. His subsequent membership in the Sa'dist party did not last long, because he resigned from it in protest against sequestering some of his journal articles.

Qutb had a difficulty maintaining friendships and associations. He vehemently attacked the corruption of the Egyptian government and openly called for its replacement. He underwent a metamorphosis from a believer in social liberalism and political socialism into an Islamic activist believing in the need for reactivating pristine Islam. During his early years of intellectual development he was heavily influenced by the writings of mainstream Egyptian writers such as Taha Husayn and 'Abbas Mahmud al-'Aqqad. In his ardent liberalism, Qutb went in his novel *Ashwak* (*Thorns*) to the extent of sanctioning nudity.

The drastic change in Qutb's ideological orientation came about as a result of his extended U.S. visit, which he documented in a book entitled *Amrika allati Ra'aytuha* (*The America that I Saw*). He condemned the American society on grounds of its racism, materialism, and sexual permissiveness. Even though he expressed appreciation for American and other Western contributions to science and knowledge, he felt that they were deficient in morality and brotherhood. Upon return to Egypt he extended support to the military officers who overthrew the monarchy in a 1952 coup, assuming that they would transform Egypt into an Islamic society governed in accordance with shari'a. When Qutb's wishes did not materialize, he withheld his support for the new regime. The Egyptian authorities charged the Muslim Brethren of conspiring to assassinate President Gamal Abdel Nasser in 1954, unleashing a massive wave of repression against the Brethren that took them underground. Qutb spent several years in prison; on release he resumed his antigovernmental campaign. Finally, he was arrested in 1965 on charges of scheming to overthrow Nasser. He was executed shortly afterwards, despite international pleas to spare his life.

Qutb is best remembered for his ideological discourse, appearing in his well-known book *Ma'alim 'ala al-Tariq* (*Signposts on the Road*), which he wrote during imprisonment. He saw a dichotomous world, one characterized by *jahiliyyah* (ignorance) and another by *hakimiyyah* (God's sovereignty). Arguing in favor of a universalistic Islamic conception of life guided by divine sovereignty, Qutb identified seven conceptual characteristics pertaining to the oneness of God, divinity, fixity, comprehensiveness, equilibrium, positiveness, and realism.

# R

RACISM   Though racism has been around in one form or another since the beginning of mankind, with the term *race* dating back to the 13th century, it was constructed as a more or less coherent ideology only at the end of the 18th century. In 19th-century Western Europe the belief that mankind is divided into different races gained influence within both political and academic circles. A race was defined as a subspecies of man; each race being genetically different from the other and, hence, race mixing was considered degenerating to one's own race. Within the different races a clear hierarchy was established: the white or Caucasian race was considered to be the most developed race, whereas the black or Negro race was seen as underdeveloped and slavish. Anti-Semitism was also given a racist interpretation with the Jews being described as a "bastard race." Though racism originated within the white West, it is not by definition restricted to it. Through time various black, Asian, and Jewish racist ideologies and ideologues have existed.

Racism became mixed with ethnic nationalism at the beginning of the 19th century. Particularly in France, racist "philosophers" like de Gobineau and de Maistre laid the foundation for prefascist organizations such as the *Action Française,* which combined French nationalism with classic racism. However, most fascists in South Europe rejected racism and, though to a lesser extent, anti-Semitism. It was instead in Central and Eastern Europe that ethnic nationalism came to be fully intermingled with racism. The most destructive mix, of course, was Hitler's National Socialism, which combined loyalty to the German(ic) nation and the Aryan race. In postwar Europe the Holocaust is generally considered as the inevitable result of racism and, as a consequence, racism has become synonymous with evil.

In the United States and South Africa, racism developed in separate directions. In the South of the United States racism became part of "national" culture and, to some extent, was institutionalized through the legal system of slavery. Even after the abolition of slavery, as a result of the Confederate's defeat in the American Civil War, racism and race have remained influential within (Southern) American politics until this date. Racism is even more important within the American radical right than nationalism (in contrast to Europe). Some racist or "white supremacist" organizations combine classic racism and traditional Southern racism (e.g., the Ku Klux Klan), while others adhere strictly to the Nazi myth of the superior Aryan race (e.g., the Aryan Nations). In South Africa, on the other hand, racism became the legal basis of the political system of apartheid, which included the strict separation of races, the superiority of the white race, but, unlike the South of the United States, did not include pure slavery.

In the 1980s various types of racism have been introduced in the academic literature. The belief in different races placed in a strict hierarchy is now often referred to as "classic racism." In contrast, "new racism" has been introduced to describe ideologies that distinguish between different (rigid) cultures, which are equal but different; that is, they have the same rights, but should be kept strictly separated. This term was introduced in reaction to a noted development within the, again initially French, extreme right, which developed this ideology of "equal but different," which it labeled "ethno-pluralism." In some ways, ethno-pluralism or new racism is a crossover of nationalism and racism. In addition, the term "everyday racism" has come into vogue, particularly among antiracists and minority advocates, referring to a more subjective form of racism; that is, when a member of a minority feels discriminated against, she or he *is* the victim of racism.

Among the classic studies on the concept and history of racism are Pierre L. van den Berghe, *Race and Racism*

(John Wiley, 1967); Imanuel Geiss, *Geschichte des Rassismus* (Suhrkamp, 1988); and Robert Miles, *Racism* (Routledge, 1989).

## RADIĆ, STJEPAN

**RADIĆ, STJEPAN**    1871–1928, Croat politician, born in Trebarjevo Desno, Croatia. Educated in Croatia and France, Radić emerged as an important Croat student activist in the 1890s and the leader of a group known as the Progressive Youth. In 1904 Radić founded the Croat People's Peasant Party (HPSS), which he led until his death. He was the first politician in Croatia to direct his activities explicitly and exclusively at the country's peasant majority. In 1910 he was elected to the Croatian *Sabor* (Diet) and served in that institution until 1918, when it was abolished.

Radić's political activity may be divided into two periods: the Austro-Hungarian (1904–1918) and the Yugoslav (1918–1928). In the first period, he and his brother Antun (1867–1919) developed an agrarian ideology that articulated the peasantry's right to a leading role in Croatian society, and addressed the peasants' social and economic problems. More importantly, as a Croat nationalist, his party played an active and crucial role in mobilizing the peasantry behind the Croat national cause by linking peasant socioeconomic emancipation to Croat national liberation.

After the creation of the Kingdom of Serbs, Croats, and Slovenes ("Yugoslavia") in December 1918 and the introduction of universal manhood suffrage, Radić's party emerged as the only significant political party in Croatia and, by 1923, the second largest in Yugoslavia. He opposed Yugoslav unification because he feared that Croatia would be dominated by the numerically stronger Serbs. He was able to transform his hitherto small HPSS into a national movement by linking peasant social liberation to Croat nationalism and the cause of an independent Croatian state. To challenge the new Yugoslav monarchy, in December 1920 Radić renamed his party the Croat Republican Peasant Party (HRSS).

In 1923–1924 Radić traveled first to Britain and then the Soviet Union to gain international support for his Croat national movement, but failed. Returning to Yugoslavia in August 1924, he was arrested by the authorities in January 1925 for joining the Soviet-sponsored Peasant International. He was released only in July 1925, after agreeing to recognize the Yugoslav monarchy and entering a government coalition with the National Radical Party (NRS) of Nikola Pašić, the main Serbian political party. Radić's party, now known as the Croat Peasant Party (HSS), remained in government from July 1925 to January 1927, and Radić served briefly as minister of education from November 1925 to April 1926.

When Radić left government in 1927, he attempted to link forces with Yugoslavia's other reform-minded opposition parties. In November 1927 he formed an alliance with Svetozar Pribićević's Independent Democratic Party (SDS), which was known as the Peasant Democratic Coalition. This coalition, which drew its support from Yugoslavia's Croat and Croatian Serb populations, led a campaign to introduce major political reform in the country. Above all, this meant local self-government, the elimination of corruption in government, and an end to what Radić perceived to be Serbia's economic exploitation of the other parts of the country. On June 20, 1928, Radić and four of his party colleagues were shot by a Montenegrin Serb deputy during a session of the National Parliament in Belgrade. Two died instantly, and Radić died on August 8, 1928. The Peasant Democratic Coalition withdrew from Belgrade and demanded sweeping political reform, including a new constitution and the country's federalization.

Radić's significance for Croatian nationalism lies in the fact that his party became a national mass movement in the 1920s, which gradually encompassed Croatia's peasants, intellectuals, and middle classes under one political banner.

## RASPUTIN, VALENTIN

**RASPUTIN, VALENTIN**    1937–, One of the leading Russian writers, born in the Siberian village of Ust-Uda in the Irkutsk region. Rasputin is a representative of a movement called "Village Prose" and member of the Soviet and Russian Writers' Union (1975–1981).

Rasputin graduated from Irkutsk University and started his career as a journalist. He published several collections of short stories in 1960s that were not noticed by the wider public and by critics at the very beginning. In 1967 he published a story, *Money for Maria*, followed by *The Last Term* (1970), *Live and Remember* (1975), and *Farewell to Matyora* (1976), which made Rasputin famous in the Soviet Union.

From the very beginning Rasputin portrayed nostalgic pictures of quiet rural life and described strong Russian characters with high moral standards in exceptional life situations. In *Money for Maria* he depicts the conflict of individual altruism and egoism of simple Siberian people in the Soviet village. In *The Last Term* Rasputin tells a story of the last days of an old woman called Anna and depicts the behavior of grown-up sons and daughters and old friends. The overall atmosphere of the everyday life of dying Anna is rather alert and full of restless expectations, even some kind of mystification. *Live and Remember* is a tragic story about a Russian woman, Nastya, who decides to hide her husband from Soviet authorities during World War II. *Farewell to Matyora* is a poetic story about an island by the Siberian river Angara and a village that is to be replaced by an artificial sea. Matyora is a symbolic island of intact individuals—old, simple Russian women living in their memories of the past and busy with the everyday uncertainties. Those stories made Rasputin one of the most well-known Soviet-Russian writers of the time. Most of his works of the period paint vivid psychological episodes of the rural (village) life of ordinary but colorful Soviet, Russian people with high moral values who are in situations of conflict.

At the beginning of the 1980s, Rasputin survived a murder attempt, but it took several years to restore his writing abilities. In 1985 he published a new story entitled *Fire* in which he discussed the loss of moral principles in the Soviet society.

During 1990–1997 Rasputin was a publicist and wrote a series of articles in the Russian periodicals. He called for a spiritual revival of Russia, closely connected with the Orthodox Church. Rasputin also sharply criticized the handling of environmental problems in Russia.

Some of Rasputin's short stories include *French Lessons, Vassily and Vassilissa,* and *Rudolfio.*

## REAGAN, RONALD

1911–, Born into a lower middle class family in Tampico, Illinois, Reagan received an undergraduate degree in economics at Eureka College, where he was a varsity football player. He embarked on a career in sportscasting and acting, activities that helped him utilize his natural charisma and develop the considerable oratorical skills that always served him well as a politician. He also was introduced to confrontational politics as a six-term president of the Screen Actors Guild. During World War II, he served as a captain in the air corps and was involved in making training films for the military. Not until he ran for governor of California at age fifty-five in 1967 did he devote full time to public service. After two unsuccessful attempts to achieve the Republican Party nomination for president, he won a landslide victory over Jimmy Carter in 1980.

He had intended to devote the first of his two presidential terms primarily to domestic policy and the introduction of supply-side, monetarist economic policy. Nevertheless, he was an irrepressibly fervent and proud American patriot, who was a total anticommunist. He steered through Congress a massive arms budget that

could contain the Soviet Union, to which he referred in 1983 as the "evil empire." He enunciated the "Reagan Doctrine" in his 1985 State of the Union speech, which promised to aid all anticommunist insurgencies. This doctrine justified U.S. assistance to guerrillas in Afghanistan, Angola, and Nicaragua. In the latter case, however, such assistance had been forbidden by Congress and led to the biggest crisis of his presidency, the Iran-Contra scandal. Members of his administration had illegally sold weapons to Iran and diverted the profits surreptitiously to Nicaraguan Contras.

In 1983 he launched the search for a workable missile defense through the Strategic Defense Initiative (SDI). He also withstood enormous protest in Europe and approved the deployment of American intermediate nuclear forces (INF) on European soil in 1983 to counter the earlier Soviet deployment of SS-20 missiles, which could reach targets in all European NATO countries.

The second term was one of dramatic foreign policy moves. When Mikhail Gorbachev came to power in March 1985, he and Reagan established a close and constructive personal relationship. The two approved of dramatic arms control breakthroughs. For instance, in 1987 they agreed to destroy *all* INF weapons. They also agreed to massive reductions of intercontinental nuclear weapons. When he left the presidency in January 1989, he enjoyed a 68 percent overall job approval rating, and 71 percent approval for his handling of foreign affairs. Some admirers credit him for "winning the Cold War," while others would simply argue that he had been a staunch defender of American security and interests and reaped the foreign political praise he deserved.

## RECOGNITION, CONCEPT OF

Although the longing for recognition has always existed, it became more difficult to satisfy after the collapse of rigid social hierarchies and of the aristocratic honor system because identity was no longer stable and dependent on traditional institutional roles. Similarly, the new egalitarian and universal notion of dignity and the development of social mobility entailed growing expectations of equal recognition. Moreover, at the end of the 18th century, inspired by Rousseau and von Herder, romanticism put forward the ideas of originality and authenticity. All individuals were endowed with a unique way of being human that they had to discover within themselves. Being original meant being authentic, that is, true to oneself. Henceforth, one had to be recognized not only as an equal human being but also as a unique individual. The same logic applied at the collective level: Nations and cultures had to be recognized as equally valuable and unique. Denying that recognition to a cultural group was seen as being harmful to all the members constituting it.

Thus, the concept of recognition refers to an aspiration and a need to see one's existence socially confirmed and valued. It arises when one considers that one is being ignored as a unique and entitled individual worthy of respect. In this sense, it is essentially a reaction to an unsatisfactory status. There are no objective criteria for assessing recognition. It is a fundamentally subjective issue, because it refers to the *feeling* of being valued or not regardless of one's legal rights. The look others direct toward us is a crucial part of the social construction of our self-understanding and self-definition, hence, recognition is closely related to identity. When people claim to be *mis*recognized, they usually mean that an identity which is not representative of who they *really* are—that is, of how they think they should be seen—is being imposed on them. The desire for recognition is thus a desire for understanding, empathy, and deeper respect. And since a systematic lack of respect can be seen as a form of oppression, or at least as a harmful condition, recognition can possibly be described as a step toward emancipation. Similarly, the recognition of a group can be experienced by its members as a precondition for their own recognition and autonomy. Along these lines, couching the demand for recognition in ethnic terms is particularly attractive because it allows people to accede to a certain status and sense of dignity without having to prove anything—such as virtue or certain aptitudes—but the mere existence of descent or blood ties.

However, the outcome of collective recognition is not necessarily individual emancipation. As Isaiah Berlin has pointed out, the craving for status can be so strong that people may be willing to jeopardize their own personal autonomy in order to fulfill it. They may prefer being misgoverned by insiders who nevertheless treat them as equals, rather than being properly ruled by outsiders who do not recognize them for that which they believe they should be recognized. Thence, the longing for recognition is often one of the driving forces behind nationalist movements as well as minority claims, since both feed on people's dissatisfaction with their status.

**REGIONALISM** Stated broadly, regionalism is belief in the distinctiveness of a region: consciousness of distinguishing conditions and traits that characterize the region and its inhabitants, as well as identification of self with these regional particularities. The idea of regionalism arose in Europe at the close of the 19th century, and it remains an important organizing principle in fields as diverse as politics, sociology, history, and the arts.

A region is generally defined as an area that appears cohesive and homogeneous based on certain criteria having to do with way of life; these criteria may include culture, language or dialect, race or ethnicity, climate and topography, history and tradition, and economic system or stage of development. Regions may be identifiable within a nation (New England, the Ruhr Valley), or may reach across national borders (Tex-Mex borderlands, the Middle East). Either way, lack of a one-to-one correspondence with a sovereign political state is the primary feature that differentiates the concept of region from that of nation.

Because regions and nations share so many definitional characteristics, the question of their relationship is often begged. On the one hand, because a region exists without the coercion or government of a corresponding state, regional affinities may be seen as more natural or genuine than national ones. On the other hand, because a region is not legitimized by a corresponding state, regionalism may be interpreted as spurious identification or misplaced loyalty. Because individuals may simultaneously identify themselves with a region and a nation, regionalism sometimes is seen as challenging or competing with nationalism; when the programs and priorities of regionalism seriously conflict with those of nationalism, regionalism may be considered a separatist subnationalism.

Regionalism was established as a modern category of analysis first in the field of geography. Indeed, the rise of geography as a modern discipline was tied closely to the work of scholars who developed the first definitions and theories of region, especially Paul Vidal de La Blanche of France. The concept became significant in the United States following World War I, as regionalist artistic movements in painting and literature flourished throughout the nation in the 1920s and 1930s, and "scientific regionalism" became an organizing principle of federal public policy during the New Deal.

In recent decades, the concept of regionalism has been taken up by economists and other social scientists studying the phenomenon of globalization. As nations become less significant players in the world economy, analysts have turned their attention to regional trade blocs and alliances.

**RENAISSANCE** In the Northern city-states of Italy, notably Florence, Padua, and Venice, the Renaissance, literally meaning "rebirth," was born. The term *Renais-*

sance or *del Rinascimento* in its Italian usage denoted *trecento, quattrecento,* and *cinquecento* or three hundred, four hundred, and five hundred, respectively. These numerical designations signified the periods of cultural transformation and nascent national consciousness that followed 13th-, 14th-, and 15th-century Europe.

To be sure, from the city-state to world empire, the static and orderly medieval universe of Europe underwent gradual degeneration. And in the centuries that followed the 13th, the Renaissance lent itself to a complex, yet novel, regeneration in almost every mode of existence. In the words of the late encyclopedist B. Groethuysen of Berlin University, "No historical epoch has been so difficult to characterize or has given rise to such extensive controversy as the Renaissance. Vassari in the 16th century referred to *renascita* of art, but it was not until the 19th century, especially in the writings of Stendhal and Michelet," that Renaissance was considered "as a distinct cultural epoch." Accordingly, for Burckhardt, the Renaissance represented a sense of liberation from the stifling yoke of Middle Ages and certainly a manifestation of individualism as its indelible mark. Other writers, including Emile Gebhart, Henry Thode, Paul Sabatier, Louis Courajod, and Carl Neuman, also reflected on the causes and effects of Renaissance and each attached particular significance to its origin, development, and expansion (*Encyclopaedia of the Social Sciences* 1949, 278–279).

In essence, the ascendancy of both commerce and national monarchies in Europe followed the disintegration of the feudal system in its midst. These changes became more evident in England, France, Germany, Italy, and Spain. Scholasticism and asceticism, once integral aspects of medievalism, lost their intrinsic *raison d'etre* and appeal in favor of individual consciousness and modernity. In large measure, the Renaissance period inaugurated a most sublime cultural phenomena in human aspirations. In politics, economics, arts, literature, and architecture, the Renaissance, which lasted from the 13th to the 17th century, embraced a new conception of humanity in general and those of the state, religion, and society in particular. These developments reached their maturation during the Enlightenment period of the 18th century. Above all, the Renaissance represented a synthesis of classical humanism, and it gradually rendered the universalism of medieval christendom obsolete.

As time passed, the Renaissance period rekindled the Greco-Roman universalism of human values. It reasserted the merits of optimism, liberty, and individualism as manifestations of a new existence. In arts, in politics, and in other facets of social life, patronage by

patricians and clergy opened the Renaissance vistas of good citizenship, civic responsibility, and ultimately patriotism to all. Among the pioneers of the Renaissance period, Francesco Petrarca or Petrarch (1304–1374), often considered the father of humanism and the Italian patriotism, equated the "public good" with knowledge, education, and adherence to moral philosophy. He also pondered the secular and universal values of antiquity and sought to regenerate the classical roots of Italian language and rhetoric. Ciceronian in admiration, Petrarch revived the educational ideals implicit in the works of the Roman orator Cicero. Erasmus (1466–1536) upheld the humanism of toleration and rationality in religious thoughts and Niccolò Machiavelli (1469–1527), as statesman-philosopher, in *The Prince,* considered the ethics of politics, limited government, and its universality. Francois Rabelais (1495–1553), as a monk in *Gargantua* and *Pantagruel,* satirically pondered superstition, repression, and naturalism in France. Further, Sir Thomas More (1478–1535), as a lawyer in *Utopia,* expounded the virtues of good society and the evils of bad, and William Shakespeare (1564–1616), as the most acclaimed dramatist and poet of monumental works, left his indelible literary imprint on the world scene. If nationalism is to be considered a manifestation of particularism, then the pioneers of the Renaissance period were the most ardent nationalists. They personified the most exalted attributes of their roots, and national identity for sublimation.

During the Renaissance, nationalism and consciousness in one's fatherland represented the fusion of old and new. After all, in the Renaissance period "the literati rediscovered the Greco-Roman patriotism, but this new attitude never penetrated the masses, and its secularism was soon swept away by the retheologization of Europe through Reformation and Counter Reformation. But the Reformation, especially in the Calvinistic form, revived the nationalism of the Old Testament" (Kohn, 1944, 19). Above all, the Greco-Roman past was a prologue to the future and nationalism was a resounding venue to consolidate the human yearnings for national legitimation and loyalty. Again, in the words of Kohn, the nationalism of the Renaissance era "merely outlined the possibilities of future developments." The identification of Renaissance with antiquity and that which was once Greek *polis* and the Roman *partia* gave the secularist and the nationalist individual a patriotic devotion to one's land, origin, identity, and feelings (Kohn, *The Idea of Nationalism,* 121–123).

The maturation of "national consciousness" and its transformation into national state during the 17th and 18th centuries was quite evident. As Carlton Hayes observes: "By the seventeenth century, in Western Europe, the states of Sweden, Denmark, Holland, France, Spain Portugal and England, were really national." These states included "a definite geographical area inhabited by populations that were marked off from their neighbours by a difference of speech; each possessed an independent political organisation and pursued an independent economic policy; and the citizens of each cherished peculiar customs and traditions" (Hayes, 1933, *Essays on Nationalism,* 40). In essence, the emergence of nationalism, which the Renaissance set into motion, was in part the product of "the Protestant Revolution and the Catholic Reformation." These two events, envisaged by Luther and Calvin, "were landmarks in the development of national patriotism" (Hayes, 1933, 38).

If the nascent nationalism of the Renaissance era was the exclusive lot of the privileged few and the elite, it became an integral part of the greater whole and masses later. In its most triumphant state of maturation, the national feelings of the earlier times were reincarnate in the liberal nationalism of the English, American, and French Revolutions.

For additional sources on Renaissance see Liah Greenfield, *Nationalism: Five Roads to Modernity* (Cambridge, Mass.: Harvard University Press, 1992); B. Groethuysen, "Renaissance" in the *Encyclopedia of the Social Sciences,* Vol. XIII (New York: Macmillan, 1949); Otto Benesch, *The Arts of the Renaissance in Northern Europe* (Cambridge, Mass., 1945); K. Burdach, *Reformation, Renaissance, Humanismus* (Berlin, 1926); D. Bush, *The Renaissance and English Humanism* (Toronto: The University of Toronto Press, 1939); Denys Hay, *The Renaissance Debate* (New York: European Problem Series, 1965) and *The Italian Renaissance in Historical Background* (New York: 1961); J. H. Hayes Carlton, *Essays on Nationalism* (New York: Macmillan, 1933); John Earnst Knapton, *Europe 1450–1815,* Vols. 1 and 11 (New York: Charles Scribner's Sons, 1961); Hans Kohn, *The Idea of Nationalism: A Study in Its Origins and Background* (New York: Macmillan, 1944); and Hans Kohn, *Prelude to Nation-States: The French and German Experience, 1789–1815* (Princeton, N.J.: D. Van Nostrand Company, 1967).

**RENAN, ERNEST** 1823–1892, French philosopher, politician, and historian of Christianity issues; born in Tréguier, Brittany. Educated in the priesthood, Renan is best known for his views on religion, although he renounced the Roman Catholic Church in the middle of his life. For Renan, politics and religion were intimately linked. He claimed, for example, that Second Empire materialism could only be countered by intellectualism and spiritualism. He progressively moved from liberal political to more authoritarian views, favoring constitutional monarchy early in his career, then later rejecting the idea of democracy in favor of a clerical monarchy.

Renan is the author of numerous essays on religion such as "La Vie de Jésus" (1863), and on political issues, among which is his famous speech "Qu'est-ce qu'une nation?" (What is a nation?), given at the Sorbonne on March 11, 1882. The speech lays out important questions about what constitutes legitimate nationhood. It is still a landmark for 20th-century theoreticians of nationhood, and appears in countless critical volumes on the nation, although it has recently been used primarily as a contrasting point of departure for less circumstantial analyses. The essay questions national belonging in what appears to be global, almost timeless discourse. However, put back into its political context, it was a resounding call to claim Alsace, which had been annexed by Germany in 1871, as part of France. Based on historical observations ranging from the Roman Empire to the first days of the French Republic, Renan's analysis examines nationhood in terms of territorial size; racial, linguistic, and religious affiliations; and common history. Renan's basic argument is that the desire of a specific group to belong to a nation should supercede racial, linguistic, and religious considerations in determining national affiliation. He also affirms that nations are often built on historical errors that ignore the actual past. The underlining aim of "Qu'est-ce qu'une nation?" is that, in spite of Alsacian closeness to Germanic culture and language, the common past of the region with France and the consent of the overwhelming majority of its population to be reattached to France were unquestionable arguments to reclaim the region as French. Renan's plea that the desire of local populations be respected was, however, only valid to defend French interests. It does not, for example, take into account French colonial rule in many parts of the world.

In spite of the contradictory views he expressed during his life, Renan's political writings influenced French leaders of different political colors: nationalists like Maurice Barrès and Charles Maurras, and more liberal republicans like Georges Clémenceau.

**RHODES, CECIL** 1853–1902, Mining magnate who was instrumental in the spread of British imperialism in southern Africa. In 1871 health problems brought him to Natal where his eldest brother was already established as a cotton farmer. Once there he became involved in the mining of diamond and gold and was instrumental in the formation of the DeBeers Company. Rhodes firmly believed that economic power was critical to the project of British imperialism. It was under his influence that the British incorporated three and a half million square miles of territory into its empire between 1884 and 1900. The scope of Rhodes's imperialism included the British colonization of Africa, the Near East, South America, and the islands and coasts of the Pacific.

Rhodes was a committed agent of British imperial expansion and he was, above all, committed to the idea of Anglo-American unity. He is said to have gained lifelong inspiration from two sources: the first from Ruskin's famous inaugural lecture at Oxford in which he appealed to his young listeners to rise to the greatness of England's worldwide destiny as an expanding and colonizing power; the second from his belief in the idea of "greater Britain" first propounded by Charles Dilke, which proposed the unity and superiority of the Anglo-Saxon race. It is said that Rhodes was the first British statesman whose imperialism was motivated both by the desire for economic gain and by the desire to advance the worldwide hegemony of white English-speaking people.

The Rhodes scholarship at Oxford was set up with the deliberate purpose of advancing the idea of creating a union of the English-speaking peoples throughout the world, including the United States of America. The scholarship established enduring ties among the white Commonwealth, the English-speaking world, and Germany. The scholarship stipulated that there would always be two Rhodes scholars from each state in the American Union. Rhodes's aim in setting aside such a large portion of the scholarship to the Americans stemmed from his belief in the importance of the United States to furthering the cause of Anglo-Saxon global supremacy.

A thorough and current biography of Rhodes is *Rhodes: The Race for Africa,* by Anthony Thomas ( Jonathan Ball, 1996).

## RIEFENSTAHL, LENI

1902–, Born in Berlin of middle-class parents, this controversial filmmaker and photographer studied art, danced with the Russian Ballet, and acted in several German films before opening her own production company in 1931. She filmed, directed, and edited five propaganda films for Hitler. All elevate the German community over the individual and suggest the superiority of the Aryan race. She was best known for *Triumph of the Will,* filmed at the 1934 Nazi Party rally in Nuremberg. It opens with the words "Germany Awakes" and attempts to portray the tight bond between Hitler and the wildly enthusiastic German nation. Her film *Olympia* about the 1936 Berlin Olympics not only provides a record of the games' highlights, but it attempts to make a connection between many of the athletes' well-developed bodies and the evolution of the Aryan race.

After World War II, she was blacklisted until 1952, when she returned to film work. Since then she has won recognition for her still photography of the Nuba tribe in the Sudan as well as her underwater photography. In her memoirs, published in 1987, she still denied that her films were Nazi propaganda and nationalist glorification.

## RIGHT-WING EXTREMISM

The origin of the concept and study of right-wing extremism is found in the study of historic fascism. Initially, ultranationalist organizations and ideas in postwar Western Europe were labeled neofascist, neo-Nazi, and later right-wing radical or radical right. In the mid-1970s right-wing extremism (or extreme right) came into vogue as a collective noun within the social sciences, and most notably within political science. Since the beginning of the 1980s, a broad consensus regarding the use of the term *right-wing extremism* has existed in Western Europe. Particularly since the fall of the Berlin Wall, the concept of right-wing extremism has been expanded to include similar phenomena outside of its traditional borders, in particular Eastern Europe, but also former parts of the British Empire (Australia, New Zealand, and even India). In recent years, various forms of populism (neo-, national, right-wing) have been gaining ground as complementary or even alternative terms to right-wing extremism.

Today, despite the lack of a generally accepted definition, most definitions of right-wing extremism are still very similar to the main definitions of fascism and National Socialism. Right-wing extremism is generally defined as a political ideology that is constituted of a combination of nationalism, racism, xenophobia, antidemocracy, and the strong state (or authoritarianism). Though most authors fail to specify what combination of features is necessary to constitute right-wing extremism, three different approaches can be distinguished: the quantitative, in which all features are equal and only the number of features is decisive; the qualitative, in which one (or more) feature is "more equal" than others; and the mixed approach, in which both a certain number of and certain features have to be present. Most of the authors that do specify the necessary combination of features work within the qualitative (or mixed approach), notably, the extremism-theoretical school, which follows the official definition of the German state, in which at least the feature of antidemocracy has to be present to speak of extremism.

Research on right-wing extremism has so far focused primarily on political parties in Western Europe. Various "waves" of right-wing extremism have been proclaimed on the basis of the electoral successes of (alleged) extreme right parties in postwar Western Europe and its individual countries. Though it has not always been clear which political parties are part of "the extreme right party family," there is little doubt that "the" extreme right has been on the rise since the mid-1980s. The prototype of the contemporary extreme right party is the Front National, which is supported by some 15 percent of the French electorate. As with all extreme right parties, it combines a general nationalist and xenophobic agenda with welfare chauvinism (the defense of the welfare state for "the own people"), staunch law and order policies, and populist antiparty sentiments. Its electorate is increasingly constituted by lower educated, male blue-collar workers—the stereotypical right-wing extremist.

The relationship between right-wing extremism and nationalism is rather diffuse because the terms are sometimes clearly distinguished and sometimes used interchangeably. Nevertheless, subtle differences between nationalism and right-wing extremism remain. First, right-wing extremism is used in a more narrow way than nationalism. In "neutral" terms, it refers to an extreme form of nationalism (e.g., ultranationalism). In normative terms, it refers to "bad" nationalism (e.g., intolerant nationalism or exaggerated nationalism). Second, right-wing extremism is used mainly with reference to concrete organizations, most notably political parties, rather than to more general "moods" or national characters. Third, several nationalist organizations that started out with a left-wing (Communist) ideology or rhetoric, such as the IRA or ETA, are generally not defined as right-wing extremist, despite the large degree of ideological similarity.

On the definition and ideology of the extreme right, see Cas Mudde, *Neither Right-wing, Nor Extremist. Xenophobic Nationalist Parties in Europe* (Manchester: Manchester University Press, 2000). Despite the confusing terminology, the best study of the contemporary extreme right is by Hans-Georg Betz, *Radical Right-Wing Populism in Western Europe* (Macmillan/St. Martin's Press, 1994). Valuable edited volumes on the topic include Peter H. Merkl and Leonard Weinberg, eds., *The Revival of Right-Wing Extremism in the Nineties* (Frank Cass, 1998) and Paul Hainsworth, ed., *The Politics of the Extreme Right. From the Margins to the Mainstream* (Cassell Publishers, 1999).

**RIGHT-WING RADICALISM** The term *right-wing radicalism*, or *radical right*, was integrated into social science in the 1960s, influenced by Daniel Bell's 1964 edited volume of the same name. It soon made inroads into the Germanic language countries (*Rechtsradikalismus*), in large part through the behavioralist Cologne-Michigan school. As a consequence of the strong tradition of liberal radicalism in Latin countries, the term *right-wing radicalism* never gained much ground in the south of Europe. Moreover, in the mid-1970s the term increasingly lost ground to the new term *right-wing extremism*, or *extreme right*, even within Northern Europe. In most recent European studies, the term *right-wing radicalism* is used at best interchangeably with the term *right-wing extremism*. In Northern America, however, the term *radical right* has kept its dominance.

Two different traditions and meanings of the term *right-wing radicalism* can be broadly distinguished: the German and the American. In the German tradition the term *radicalism* (and *extremism*) is used to describe a certain view vis-à-vis democracy, both containing a left-wing and right-wing variant. This tradition is strongly based on the official definition of the German state, which explicitly defines the "fundamental principles of the free democratic order" and, since 1973, the distinction between radicalism and extremism. Simply stated, the difference between radicalism and extremism is that the former is *verfassungswidrig* (opposed to the constitution), whereas the latter is *verfassungsfeindlich* (hostile toward the constitution). This difference is of the utmost practical importance for the political parties involved because extremist parties are extensively watched by the (federal and state) *Verfassungsschutz* and can even be banned, whereas radical parties are free from this control.

In the American tradition, the term *radical right* is still commonly used, yet has a broader and even somewhat different meaning than in the European literature. Authors working within the American tradition use the term *radical right* to denote a wide range of groups and small political parties, which share some of the following, often particularly American, ideological features: nativism, populism, hostility to central government, nationalism, anticommunism, Christian fundamentalism, militarism, and xenophobia. As a consequence of the broad definition of radical right in the American context, in part a consequence of political struggle, the term has been applied to a broad and eclectic variety of political organizations, ranging from the very pro-Israel Christian Right to the rabid anti-Semite Aryan Nations; from the unorganized skinheads to the right-wing of the Republican Party (e.g., Pat Buchanan); from the white supremacists to the (black) Nation of Islam; and from the militias to the neoconservatives.

The first major work on the (American) radical right is Bell's *The Radical Right* (Anchor Books, 1964). An encyclopedia of radical right (broadly defined) groups in the world is provided by Ciarán Ó Maoláin, *The Radical Right. A World Directory* (ABC-Clio, 1987). An excellent discussion of the German tradition of radicalism/extremism is Uwe Backes, *Politischer Extremismus in demokratischen Verfassungsstaaten. Elemente einer normativen Rahmentheorie* (Westdeutscher Verlag, 1989).

## RIMSKY-KORSAKOV, NIKOLAY   1844–1908, Russian composer. The youngest and, by self-definition, "the convinced" member of the Balakirev Circle, Rimsky-Korsakov developed a musical aesthetic that in many regards differed from Stasov's theory. Interested neither in social-historical themes, nor in the portrayal of the suffering of lower class people, Rimsky-Korsakov turned in his operas to folk poetic models such as Russian fairy tales, heroic poems (*byliny*), spirituals verses (*dukhovnye stikhi*), and Slavic pagan and Christian myths. Rimsky-Korsakov used their content for the embodiment of ethical concepts in the spirit of several modern philosophical ideas developed by Vladimir Soloviev and Dostoyevsky. The influence of Dostoyevsky's idea that "beauty will save the world" can be found in many of Rimsky-Korsakov's operas, from *Snegurochka* (*Snow Maiden,* 1881) to *Legend of the Invisible City of Kitezh and Maiden Fevroniya* (1903–1905). In the former, a beautiful Snow Maiden, whose birth enraged the Slavonic God of Sun, Yarilo, saves the people by means of her death, returning Sun's warmth back to the Earth. In the latter work, the Maiden Fevroniya miraculously saves Kitezh from the Tatar invasion by means of a spiritual feat, praying for her city to become invisible for enemies.

The opposition of "real" and "fantastic" worlds in Rimsky-Korsakov's universe is represented by a stratification of musical language: Personages of the "real" world are portrayed with folk songs and idioms. For the "fantastic" world and characters, in contrast, Rimsky-Korsakov developed special means, inventing artificial scales and "supernatural" harmonic progressions. The choral scenes in Rimsky-Korsakov's operas opened a new direction in the development of Russian nationalist musical tradition, depicting various ancient Slavonic rituals, such as Shrove-tide (*Maslenitsa*) or Midsummer Night (*Noch' na Ivana Kupalu*).

The symphonic works of Rimsky-Korsakov represent both Russian and Oriental trends developed by "The Mighty Handful." His First Symphony (1861–1865), written by the young and inexperienced composer under the guidance of Balakirev, was celebrated by his contemporaries as "the first Russian symphony," reflecting a strong need for a national symphony in the post-

reform Russian society. However, at the beginning of the 1860s, the concept of a national symphony was not yet fully developed in the Balakirev Circle; only the second movement of Rimsky-Korsakov's First Symphony, variations on the folk song "On the Tatar Captivity" (*Pro tatarsky polon*), can be claimed as "Russian." Otherwise, the symphony follows the Western European model of the symphony. The real "first Russian symphonies" appeared several years later. In the opinion of Russian and Soviet critics, this honor belongs to Chaikovsky's and Borodin's First Symphonies, written in 1866 and 1867, respectively.

Rimsky-Korsakov's best orchestral works belong to program music. His *Svetlyi Prazdnik* (Russian Easter Overture, 1888) is written on the themes of traditional church chants (*obykhod*) interwoven with ancient Russian dance tunes. Rimsky-Korsakov considered the combination of Christian and pagan elements to be typical for Russian religious consciousness. In accord with the aesthetic of the composers of "The Mighty Five" who made a bell ringing the distinguished idiom of Russian music, Rimsky-Korsakov introduced in his overture the Easter ringing of the church bells.

Rimsky-Korsakov's symphonic suite *Sheherazade* (after the Arabian "A Thousand and One Nights"; 1888), presenting a colorful imaginative world of oriental fairy tales and erotic sensuousness, is the *locus classicus* of the "Russian Orient." Together with Borodin's Polovetsian Dances from *Prince Igor* and Stravinsky's *Firebird,* *Sheherezada* contributed to the enormous success of Diagilev's "Russian Seasons" in Paris (1909–1910), which made Russian music a source of long-lasting influence on Europe. Paradoxically, the French audience, unfamiliar with Russian music, perceived Russian exoticism as a genuine characteristic of national Russianness.

Rimsky-Korsakov was the only composer of the Balakirev Circle who broke with its tradition of conscious dilettantism. In 1871, after accepting an invitation to join the St. Petersburg Conservatory as professor of composition and orchestration, he undertook rigorous self-studies in counterpoint and harmony, and achieved a superlative academic technique, which he transmitted to his numerous pupils, Russian composers of the next two generations, including Lyadov, Glazunov, Prokofiev, and Stravinsky. In the early 1880s, Rimsky-Korsakov became the leader of a new school of composers, known as *Beliaevskii kruzhok* (the Beliaev Circle). In this school, the aspiration for Russian nationalism that had been crucial for "The Mighty Handful" receded to a new orientation on the German model of instrumental music. This musical style, known as *Russian academism*, strove for the technical perfectionism that was also alien for the composers of the Balakirev Circle.

In Russia, the zenith of public celebration and appreciation of Rimsky-Korsakov occurred at the end of the 1890s, at the turning point of social history, when the national ideals of "kuchkizm" and "peredvizhnichestvo" ceased to be considered as relevant to the new time. The stylizing methods of Rimsky-Korsakov, who worked with ancient models of Russian folklore, came into perfect accord with the aesthetics of the "Russian Modern" (also known as "New Russian Style," or neonationalism). Reviving traditional details of Russian wooden architecture and elements of folk art, adherents of this movement strived "to tie the broken threads between the artist and the nation" (Vasnetsov). The fairytale operas of Rimsky-Korsakov (*Snegurochka, Sadko, Kashchey the Deathless, Tsar Saltan,* and *The Golden Cockerel*), especially his fantastic characters, inspired nearly all artists of this movement, including Vasnetsov, Vrubel', Serov, Bilibin, Golovin, Rerikh, Bakst, Benois, and Goncharova.

The primary sources are Rimsky-Korsakoff's *My Musical Life,* translated by Judah A. Joffe, with an introduction by Carl Van Vechten (New York: Alfred A. Knopf, 1923), and Vasily Yastrebtsev's *Reminiscences of Rimsky-Korsakov,* edited and translated by Florence Jonas, with an introduction by Gerald Abraham (New York: Columbia University Press, 1985). Gerald Abraham's *Rimsky-Korsakov* (London: Duckworth, 1945; rev. 1949), the only biographical source available in English, is obsolete in its critical part. A revised Western concept of Rimsky-Korsakov is presented in the chapter "Safe Harbors" in Richard Taruskin's *Defining Russia Musically* (Princeton, N.J.: Princeton University Press, 1997). Contemporary Russian essays on Rimsky-Korsakov are collected in the special issue of "Musikal'naia Akademiia" (Moscow, 1994, No.2), devoted to the 150th anniversary of the composer's birthday.

**RIVERA, DIEGO**  1886–1957, Artist, born in Guanajuato, Mexico. Rivera was both the most well-known and the most controversial artist to come out of Mexico. His works decorate major museums and public buildings worldwide, but the overt Communist themes contained in many of them inspired protest and condemnation when they were first exhibited.

Although Rivera painted numerous canvasses, it is his murals for which he is best known. Traveling through Italy in 1920–1921, Rivera was struck by the power of the mosaics and frescoes; in them he saw a form of popular art capable of reaching the masses. By this time he had developed a revolutionary zeal and hoped that his murals could bring this message to the people, much as Renaissance painters had brought the message of the church.

As a young man, Rivera studied with the great Mexican folk artist and engraver José Guadalupe Posada, a man he later referred to as the "most important" of his teachers. From Posada he developed a respect and appreciation for the beauty of the land, the history, and the common people of Mexico, themes often brought out in his art.

Rivera was also inspired by the rich artistic legacy of pre-Columbian Mexico. He suggested that, rather than looking to Europe for inspiration, artists in the New World should look closer to home. The "classic art of America [was] to be found between the Tropic of Cancer and the Tropic of Capricorn." This love of indigenous art and his hostility toward the Spanish conquistadors comes forth in much of Rivera's work. For example, his mural at Mexico's National Palace contains images of a preconquest "Golden Age." In the middle of an idyllic landscape, priests in ceremonial garments perform sacred rituals surrounded by men and women engaging in their daily activities; the mood is joyous and peaceful. This may be compared with images of the conquistadors from the same mural. Led by a misshapen and grotesque Cortés, the Spanish have enslaved the native people; the mood has become harsh and forbidding.

In addition, the struggles of the peasants and the Mexican revolution left a deep impression on Rivera; he sided quite strongly with the populist aims of Emiliano Zapata and the *agraristas.* So resolute was Rivera's commitment that the most frequently repeated figure in all of his murals is that of Zapata. A section of his fresco at the Palace of Cortés in Cuernavaca, later reproduced by the artist in a lithograph, shows the revolutionary leader, machete in hand and white horse at his side, standing over the body of a soldier.

Rivera's work has been criticized by his detractors as Communistic, primitive, ugly, and degrading to Mexico because he portrayed the "dregs of society." To his supporters, on the other hand, his work embodies the heart and soul of the Mexican people, celebrates a glorious past, and promotes pride in Mexico's heritage. Regardless of one's opinion of his art, it is difficult to deny Rivera's love for his subject matter.

A comprehensive biography of the artist is Bertram Wolfe's *The Fabulous Life of Diego Rivera* (Scarborough House, 1990). *My Art, My Life* (Dover Publications, 1991) is an account in Rivera's own words.

**RODÓ, JOSÉ ENRIQUE**  1871–1917, Uruguayan intellectual, philosopher, essayist, and one of the most widely recognized Latin American thinkers. At the age of twenty-nine he wrote his most famous work, *Ariel* (1900), in which he proposed that Latin American nations should turn away from the utilitarianism of the United States and look back to their roots in ancient Greece and Rome in order to develop a distinctly "Latin" identity. Born into a middle-class family in Montevideo, Rodó grew up reading European and Latin American authors from his father's extensive library. He began his literary career as the editor for the *Revista Nacional de Literatura y Ciencias Sociales* (*The National Review of Literature and the Social Sciences,* 1895). Rodó considered journalism, and writing in general, to be an integral part of the pursuit of nation building and intellectual debate.

*Ariel* was published at the turn of the century, and is seen today as embodying the height of Latin American modernist prose. Appearing just two years after the Spanish-American War (1898), *Ariel* can be seen as a warning for Latin American nations about U.S. expansionism. In this essay, Rodó assumes the position of an elder who wants to guide the youth of America, which he saw as Latin America's repository of force for cultural progress. He saw North American utilitarianism and the dispersion of democratic ideas as potentially destructive forces for the Americas. He proposed instead a socially stratified regime based on a form of humanism influenced by neoclassicism. Rodó has been criticized for cultural elitism (specifically, eurocentrism) and for the erasure of contributions made by Amerindians to the cultural development of the Americas, but today, *Ariel* is still perceived as one of the canonical works of a Latin American philosophical tradition. His other famous works include *Motivos de Proteo* (*Proteus' Motives,* 1909) and *El Mirador de Próspero* (*The Mirror of Prospero,* 1913).

In the political realm Rodó served twice as deputy in the Parliament. He died in Palermo, Italy, in 1917. Three years later, his remains were brought back to Uruguay and buried in the National Pantheon in front of the remains of Uruguayan Independence leader José Artigas (1764–1850). This symbolic gesture demonstrated how important a figure Rodó had become for Uruguayan intellectual and national identity.

A recent translation of *Ariel* is Margaret Sayers Peden (1998), with a prologue by Carlos Fuentes. For a critical work, see Mario Benedetti's *Genio y figura de José Enrique Rodó* (Buenos Aires: Editorial Universitaria de Buenos Aires, 1966).

## RODRIGUEZ DE FRANCIA, GASPAR 1766–1840, Political leader of Paraguay from 1814 to 1840. One of

three major 19th-century rulers of Paraguay, Francia was viewed by his elite contemporaries and traditional historians as a ruthless tyrant who isolated Paraguay and whose iron rule obliterated all who opposed him—foreigners, intellectuals, and the Paraguayan elite. Revisionist historians perceive him as an honest, populist ruler who promoted an autonomous, social revolution within Paraguay and encouraged the economic development of the country.

Born in Asunción to a Brazilian military officer and his elite Paraguayan wife, Francia earned a doctorate in theology in 1785 at the University of Cordoba, Argentina. He then taught theology at Asunción Real Colegio y Seminario de San Carlos. Upon his dismissal for his liberal ideas on religion and politics, he turned to law. He never married and did not use his political opportunities to amass wealth. He gained political experience by serving on the municipal council of Asunción from 1807 to 1809 and won enough respect for his legal and administrative knowledge to be given the responsibility of defining the qualifications for participation in the revolutionary junta. Eventually commanding the junta, he advocated Paraguayan independence from both Spanish and Argentine domination and wrote the first constitution of Paraguay, which the Congress adopted in October 1813. The National Congress of 1814 elected him supreme dictator. Even though there were periods of shared power as well as self-imposed exile between 1811 and June 5, 1816, when the Popular Congress elected him perpetual autocrat, Francia was the most powerful and popular politician for the first twenty-nine years of Paraguayan independence.

To promote the nation's self-sufficiency, Francia encouraged greater utilization of state lands through government enterprises and low rents for small farmers who produced food for local consumption. He promoted internal trade, controlled external commerce and immigration, increased industrial production in both the private and public sectors, improved communications and transportation, and reduced taxes. To limit government costs, he maintained only a small bureaucracy. The state helped pay soldiers' debts, provided food for destitute inmates, and aided foreign exiles.

At his death Paraguay possessed a prosperous, independent national economy and a centralized political system. His economic and political power and willingness to use force created critics among the elite and laid the basis for autocratic rule in Paraguay. Even though military officers and civilians maneuvered for power after his death, the peaceful transfer of power that occurred testifies to the strength of his administration. A dedicated nationalist, popular with the masses, Francia was a dictator whose paternalistic policies benefited a large majority of Paraguayans.

**ROMAN EMPIRE**  A single city arose to become the ruler of the entire Mediterranean world and much of Europe. Since the concept of "the nation" was unknown in the ancient world, its preeminence cannot be considered to have been the result of nationalistic conquest. The history of ancient Rome is long and exceedingly complicated, and it is punctuated with magnificent victories and achievements, as well as ignoble failures, corruption, and civil war. That history can be divided roughly into three periods: It was ruled by kings from about 753 B.C. (according to Roman legend) until 509 B.C., when a revolt led to the establishment of a republic, governed by elected consuls. The Roman Republic lasted until 45 B.C., when Julius Caesar established an empire subsequently ruled by emperors. In 185 A.D. this mighty empire was divided into a Western Empire, led from Rome, Milan, and Trier in present-day Germany, and an Eastern Empire, ruled from Constantinople (now Istanbul) in Turkey. The former empire finally collapsed in 476 A.D., whereas the Eastern one continued to exist for another thousand years.

According to their own legend, the Romans were descendants of a group of Greeks who had accompanied Aeneas, one of the sons of the Trojan King Priam. Aeneas had escaped from the burning city of Troy and had sailed across the Mediterranean Sea before being blown ashore at the mouth of the Tiber River. There he allegedly founded a city called Lavinium. In fact, Italy was settled around 1200 by Indo-European tribes that moved into the area from the West. Since the Trojans were Indo-Europeans themselves, there might have been some truth in the Roman belief that they were descended from the Greeks.

Two important preconditions for the rise of Rome were the decline of Etruscan rule over northern and central Italy in the 5th and 4th centuries B.C., as well as the Roman domination of various tribes in Italy and the Greek cities in the south. Rome had been constantly threatened by those tribes within Italy and by Gauls who poured into the peninsula from the north. Once it was even captured and burned. The city was saved several times by such heroes as Cincinnatus and Camillus.

One Greek city in southern Italy, Tarentum, sent for the help of Pyrrhus, king of Epirus in northern Greece, who arrived in 280 B.C. with a huge fleet carrying a herd of elephants and 25,000 troops. This army clashed with the Romans outside of Heraclea in 280 B.C. The Romans fought extremely well, but when Pyrrhus sent his elephants roaring and screaming against the enemy troops,

who had never seen such beasts before, the soldiers panicked and retreated. Though he won the battle, Pyrrhus had lost far more soldiers than had the Romans, and his weakened troops therefore were eventually beaten at Benventum. Today, the words "pyrrhic victory" refer to any success that is achieved at too high a price.

The victory over Pyrrhus, along with other swift and successful campaigns, established Roman domination over the Italian peninsula in the first part of the 3rd century B.C. and permitted the Romans for the first time to cast their sights farther. Rome challenged the major naval power in the western Mediterranean at the time: the Phoenician metropolis of Carthage (located a few miles outside the present city of Tunis in North Africa). Carthage had numerous colonies extending all along the coasts of North Africa and Spain, and it dominated Sardinia and the western part of Sicily. In the first Carthaginian (Punic) War (264–241 B.C.) between the land power Rome and the sea power Carthage, Rome demonstrated its unusual adaptability by skillfully utilizing its allies in order to acquire sea power of its own and by gaining the three large islands, Sicily, Sardinia, and Corsica. After the Romans had finally expelled the Gauls from the mainland peninsula, Carthage, which had been provoked by Roman meddling in Spain, sought revenge in a second round of battles known as the Second Punic War lasting from 218 to 202.

The Carthaginians, led by a brilliant young general named Hannibal, threatened the very heart of Rome's Italian domain. In 218 B.C. he moved an army of 100,000 foot soldiers, 1300 cavalry, and forty elephants from Spain over the Pyrenees and Alps right into Italy. But it was too cold in the mountains, and he lost all his elephants and many of his troops during this journey. Nevertheless, he was able to assemble an army on Italian soil in 218 B.C. Although the Romans tried to avoid open battle, except at Cannae, Hannibal's forces succeeded through skillful maneuvering in destroying several Roman armies. But Hannibal was never able to take Rome. He remained until 203 B.C. when he received word of an end run that the Romans were planning on Carthage itself. He departed hastily to his city's rescue, but to no avail. Roman troops had captured the city and destroyed it, salting the soil in the hope that nothing would ever grow again. From this harshness came the expression "a Carthaginian peace." At last, Rome was unchallenged master of the western Mediterranean.

Rome could now direct its sights eastward toward Greece. Between 198 and 190 B.C., Rome won victories in Greece. This not only opened the Roman door wide to Greek cultural influence, but it also gave the Romans a firm foothold in Asia Minor. Punitive expeditions against disloyal allies and the destruction of cities like Carthage and Corinth in 115 B.C. revealed the foreign political pattern for the conquest of the eastern Mediterranean area. By 63 B.C. nearly all the countries in the Mediterranean region were paying tribute to Rome. The burden of constant war and of administering the enormous empire overextended the resources of a small state that had transformed itself into a large and powerful metropolis.

The Romans' encounter with Greece during the conquest of the eastern Mediterranean area influenced Roman life and thought in such a way that the Roman poet Horace could write that the "conquered Greeks conquered their victors." Greek slaves taught the children of the wealthy in the Roman Empire. The Greek language assumed a role during the republic that in some ways corresponded to that of the French language in the 17th and 18th centuries. On the other hand, the Romans clung to their traditional political and cultural norms and deeply mistrusted foreign influences. They were willing to adopt those technical and institutional achievements of other peoples whom the Romans considered worthy of emulating. For instance, many weapons systems were patterned after those of the conquered peoples. The critical examination and adoption of whatever was considered better, combined with the steadfastness of a self-reliant identity, gave Roman policies their dynamism and flexibility.

After many years the Republican constitution became increasingly incapable of solving the many social problems of such a large realm. The defense of the vast empire, with its many administrative requirements, called for an effective central bureaucracy. But the Old Republic did not have such an institution and was therefore unable to perform many essential functions. Numerous military campaigns claimed thousands of casualties and therefore left large tracts of land either to fall fallow or into the hands of the large landowners. Following the campaigns, many unemployed soldiers drifted into Rome, thereby adding to the city's mounting problems.

In earlier times no one was permitted to enter the city of Rome with weapons. Standing armies with nothing to do and former peasants who had lost their land to large landowners broke down the old customs that had integrated the army with the society and the state. At this point, the earlier observation of the Greek philosopher, Aristotle, applied to Rome: Masters of weapons are also masters of the state.

The emperors considered their main task to be the security of the empire's extensive borders. However, as the threat of invasion became greater and greater after the beginning of the 3rd century A.D., the Roman world was unable to withstand the mounted attacks of Germans, Slavs, Huns, Persians, Turks, Mongolians, Berbers, and, later, of Arabs.

In 284 A.D. Diocletian, the son of a freed slave from Illyria, became emperor. He realized that the Roman Empire had grown too large to be governed by one man, so in 285 A.D. he divided it into an eastern and a western part. He assumed rule over the eastern portion, with its seat in Nicomedia in Asia Minor. The subsequent Western emperors held court at Milan and Trier. Emperor Constantine, who became sole emperor of Rome in 324 A.D., continued the reorganization of the Empire. He built a new city on the site of the former Byzantium, a strategically important crossroad between Asia and Europe, and named it after himself: Constantinople. From then on, the Roman Empire was administered from that city, and Rome lost much of its significance. There, Roman civilization mingled with that of Greece and of Asia.

Disciples of and converts to Christianity had been circulating in most parts of the empire since the 1st century A.D., converting many to their belief in a single, almighty God. Gradually Christianity penetrated Roman society, and Constantine decided to convert and make it the empire's official religion. After his death in 337 A.D. there was less and less cooperation and coordination between the eastern and western parts of the empire. While Constantinople was a safe distance from the marauding tribes of Europe, the western part became the object of sustained attacks by Goths, Visigoths, and Vandals. Rome was temporarily captured and sacked in 410 A.D. In 476 the East Gothic chief, Odoacer, marched his troops into the city and deposed the last western Roman emperor, Romulus Augustulus. Thereafter, sheep grazed on the overgrown ruins of the Forum, once the scene of the power behind the heart of the empire.

The destruction of Rome was without precedent. But many aspects of this great empire have been salvaged for posterity, including its literature and philosophy, which were protected in the Christian cloisters. Further testimonies to the splendor of the Roman past are the unique accomplishments in architecture, such as domes, columns, and basilicas, and in engineering, such as bridges, aqueducts, and highways. Most of the important European roads today follow the same routes established by the Romans. Its legal thinking was groundbreaking, including the *Pax Romana,* which was the first step toward international law. Therefore, Italy's ancient past is significant not only to Italians, but to all persons touched by Western civilization.

**ROMANTICISM** The meaning of romanticism is highly contested. Aside from German, English, and French manifestations, to say nothing of a multitude of other national species of romantic thought, analytical problems are compounded by psychological, sociological, political, historical, literary, theological, and aesthetic concerns. Many argue that romanticism is a historically bounded movement confined to the late 18th and early 19th centuries, the so-called Romantic Age, while a compelling counterargument can be made that romanticism consists of an enduring response toward the potentialities and recurring crises of modernity. Of the varieties of romanticism found during the Romantic Age, the Germans most decisively cultivated an explicit and self-conscious nationalistic discourse.

In its initial phase, German romanticism is nearly synonymous with the poets, theologians, and philosophers oriented around Berlin and Jena from the end of the 18th to the first years of the 19th centuries. The decisive figures were, *inter alia,* Friedrich and August Wilhelm Schlegel, Ludwig Tieck, Friedrich von Hardenberg (Novalis), Wilhelm Heinrich Wackenroder, Ernst Schleiermacher, and Friedrich W. J. Schelling. In contrast to the classical tradition, the romantics were imbued with a spirit of immediacy, mystery, individuality, and doubt rather than mediation, objectivity, institutions, and certainty. The romantics also championed sensations, feelings, and the miracle of nature over the lifeless abstraction of rationalism and science: Faust's soliloquy in his "book-lined tomb" is characteristic of the romantic frustration with abstraction and pedantry.

The first German romantics were generally cosmopolitan in character. Their ethos of individuality was not incompatible with an ideology of totality and the "Absolute." As such, the nationalist and political strains evident in the successive romantic period were greatly diminished. The element that propelled romanticism toward social critique and nationalism was Napoleon's wars of conquest. Dissatisfied with the substance of his previous work, Friedrich Schlegel guided or was dragged along by a new generation of writers beyond the fluffy prose and politically detached romanticism of the previous years. This sentiment was expressed well by Wilhelm Schlegel who, in 1806, declared that what Germany needed was "direct, energetic, and particularly, patriotic" forms of poetry. The new romantics wasted little time in confronting the particularity and, as they saw it, the cultural superiority of the German nation.

The education and development of the individual, an early romantic concern, gave way in the new phase to the cultivation of the *Volk.* Napoleon was seen as an aesthetic and political alien and the spirit of cosmopolitanism was abandoned in favor of a new organic nationalism and a conception of society that might best be described as mechanical and medieval. The new nationalistic romanticism was propelled by Arnim, Eichendorff, Fichte, Fouqué, Max von Schenkendorf, and Uhland among others. These writers imagined the ascendancy and preservation of German culture as being dependent on the formation of a unified German nation. This was the basis of Fichte's 1808 *Address to the German Nation.* Here, Fichte summoned Germany to the task of spiritual and political leadership.

Another view of romanticism is represented by those who see the phenomena not limited to any "Romantic Age" but as a durable and perennial response to modernity. Here, romanticism becomes a critique of capitalist labor processes, class inequalities, colonialism, paternalism, the internationalization and homogenization of culture, fragmentation and instability, and alienation of the self. From this perspective, romanticism spreads itself out to include right and left, reactionary and progressive, authoritarian and democratic, or nationalistic and antinationalistic varieties. Taking this route, thinkers as diverse as Hegel, Karl Marx, and Walt Whitman can reasonably be portrayed as antinationalist or progressive romantics of sorts. Conversely, fascism, anti-Semitism, political theology, and some contemporary nationalist political movements like Buchananism in the United States might be viewed, at least partially, as expressions of "right-wing" romanticism.

Further inquiry might begin with M. H. Abrams, *Natural Supernaturalism* (Norton, 1971) and J. L. Talmon, *Romanticism and Revolt* (Harcourt, Brace, and World, 1967).

**ROOSEVELT, FRANKLIN D.** 1933–1945, 32nd President of the United States; profoundly shaped the nature of American life, leading the country out of the Great Depression and through World War II. F.D.R., as he was affectionately known, initiated a series of New Deal reforms and rode a wave of popularity to become the only U.S. president to serve four terms in office.

Roosevelt was, as historian Arthur Schlesinger, Jr., puts it, "the best loved and the most hated American President of the 20th Century." He was loved for his personal charm and able leadership, and hated by those who disliked the dramatic changes that he brought about, primarily in terms of his New Deal reforms that mobilized the resources of the federal government on behalf of the less fortunate.

When he took office in 1933, the United States was

in the throes of the Great Depression; not only was the economy in a shambles, but widespread unemployment and economic deprivation had demoralized much of the country. Raised in an unpretentious but wealthy family he was taught from an early age to express concern toward the less fortunate. This education, along with his training at Groton School, lay the groundwork for Roosevelt's New Deal policies of increased government involvement in the economic problems of the nation's citizenry. Although not lacking opposition, Roosevelt's policies became a fundamental part of both the national identity and public policy in the United States through the remainder of the century. His marriage to Theodore Roosevelt's niece Eleanor Roosevelt furthered his sensitivity to the plight of the underprivileged. At the time of their marriage in 1905 she was involved in settlement work in the slums of New York City.

The crisis of the Great Depression in the 1930s raised questions about the very ability of the American system to thrive economically and, for some, confirmed the critiques of American democracy offered by both Communism and fascism. A fourth of the labor force lost their jobs and the gross national product was cut in half. Against this bleak economic picture and its ensuing pessimism in the national political culture, F.D.R.'s energetic and buoyant personality inspired new confidence.

Roosevelt moved quickly to provide a protective floor under the ailing economy and its workers with a system of social security, and federal involvement in the economy with large-scale public works, unemployment compensation, minimum wage laws, and guarantees for collective bargaining. The Works Projects Administration (WPA) hired the unemployed to build the infrastructure of the nation, from post offices and bridges to schools and parks.

Laissez-faire economists and much of the business elite were critical of his policies but his policies were widely popular and he was swept into office time and again. The economy was stimulated not only by public service projects, of course, but also by large expenditures by the War Department at the outset of World War II, the second major milestone of Roosevelt's presidency.

As commander in chief of U.S. forces, Roosevelt was given credit by many for saving his country from war as well as economic deprivation. He not only mobilized the military but also the civilian sectors of the country with rousing nationalist rhetoric that attacked the evils of fascism and Hitler. After overseeing the end of the war and attending the Yalta Conference, laying the groundwork for American involvement in the postwar world order, Roosevelt died on April 12, 1945.

## ROOSEVELT, THEODORE

**ROOSEVELT, THEODORE** 1858–1919, Roosevelt, who had served as assistant secretary of the navy from 1897 to 1898, was placed on William McKinley's ticket as vice president because of his reputation as an enthusiastic imperialist who vigorously defended America's present and future national interests. He embodied the vitality and dynamism of an America that had come of age and had decided to wield greater influence in the world. He was the very symbol of American nationalism.

While still involved with the navy, he ordered the Pacific fleet to Philippine waters in order to be able to claim the islands if hostilities broke out, which they did. America took charge of the Philippines in 1898. He organized, equipped, and paid for a unit of "Rough Riders" to fight in Cuba for independence from Spain in 1898. He became immortalized by leading a much publicized charge up San Juan hill.

When McKinley was assassinated in 1901, Roosevelt became president until 1909. Although he was, in fact, hesitant to employ American military force in Latin America and was inclined to employ force only when it was absolutely necessary, his slogan was to "speak softly and carry a big stick." He combined both methods in fomenting revolution in Colombia in order to build a canal across the newly created country of Panama. He won a Nobel Prize in 1906 for successfully mediating the Treaty of Portsmouth, an achievement that turned the international spotlight on America.

Out of power, Roosevelt advocated an early entry into the war against Germany in 1914. He also opposed President Woodrow Wilson's call for a "peace without victors," a call that was ultimately rejected by America's allies at the Versailles Conference in 1919. Roosevelt wanted the Central Powers to be occupied after the war. He died in 1919 before the consequences of the postwar peace settlement could be seen.

## ROUSSEAU, JEAN-JACQUES

**ROUSSEAU, JEAN-JACQUES** 1712–1778, Moralist, essayist, political philosopher, born in Geneva. One of the most eloquent and engaging philosophers of all time, Rousseau was also an influential novelist, educational theorist, and composer. Generally regarded as a profound but mercurial political thinker, Rousseau's occasional writings on nationalism are surprisingly straightforward and consistent. While not particularly extensive, these passages complement the more developed accounts of romanticism and democratic citizenship for which he is best known.

A man who, in his own life, wandered unhappily from country to country, Rousseau's nationalist sentiments are often interpreted in highly personal terms.

The view that Rousseau's nationalist writings are in some respects "self-critical" has been fed by the fact that he authored no fewer than three harshly critical autobiographies: *The Confessions, Rousseau in Judgment of Jean-Jacques,* and *Dreams of a Solitary Walker.* Of more enduring significance, however, is that Rousseau's nationalist ideas constitute an early and influential challenge to the rational cosmopolitanism of the French Enlightenment.

In his *Discourse on the Origin of Inequality* Rousseau hypothesizes that nations are prepolitical communities that originate in a state of nature. He develops this argument at length in his *Essay on the Origin of Languages,* in which he suggests that different "passions," "needs," and "climates" give rise to different languages, nations, and governments. Rousseau often uses the term *nation* to refer to communities much smaller than the nation-states of today, and he returns to the examples of Geneva and Corsica throughout many of his works. In his *Political Economy* and *Considerations on the Government of Poland,* however, Rousseau extends his account of nationalism to larger national states.

Specifically, Rousseau advocates what one might today call policies of nation building in the political, economic, and cultural spheres. In the political realm, he recommends mass democratic deliberation as a means to national cohesion as well as an end in itself. While the details of how this "popular sovereignty" is meant to operate are complex, it is often noted that Rousseau's famous concept of the "general will" is more or less analogous to the "national interest"—provided, of course, that this interest is democratically determined.

In the economic sphere, Rousseau advocates redistribution of wealth and a communal right to property. He argues that this will bring men closer to a state of "natural equality," a state in which he suggests people may have lived prior to the development of agriculture and, in turn, private possession of land. Beyond these more abstract declarations, however, Rousseau's *Political Economy* emphasizes the practical strengths of what we might today call a "middle-class" nation (wherein no citizen is too rich or poor to offer his services to the republic).

It is, however, with his advocacy of cultural nation building that Rousseau is at his most controversial. Echoing Machiavelli, the *Social Contract* recommends the adoption of a "civil religion" through which people will be inculcated with a love of their homeland. Nor are other cultural institutions to be left to chance: In a brilliant defense of cultural isolationism, Rousseau's *Letter to D'Alembert* advocates the protection of Geneva's "virtuous" native customs against the "corrupting" cosmopolitan theater.

Rousseau frequently mentions hatreds *among* nations as a regrettable side effect of these policies promoting national identity and domestic social justice. He devotes one of his more extensive, most poetic, and yet least read essays, *A Lasting Peace,* to a balanced commentary on the Abbé de Ste. Pierre's proposal for a federation of Europe. Employing typically wistful prose, Rousseau concludes that the project must ultimately fail, "not because it is utopian, [but] because men are crazy, and because to be sane in a world of madmen is in itself a kind of madness." Instead, Rousseau suggests that nations should attempt to live in peaceful isolation yet be ready to vigorously defend their borders.

Rousseau's political writings have been extremely influential. Whether based on an accurate reading or not, they inspired both Robespierre and other more moderate leaders of the French and American Revolutions. Rousseau's romantic nationalism is likewise a precursor to the thought of von Herder and the German romantics. In recent times, various social democratic thinkers have made much of Rousseau's view that strong national patriotism is a prerequisite of social justice. (This view is in sharp contrast to that of Marx, who argues that national identities impede justice by dividing the workers of the world against themselves.) If not a cause for unambiguous celebration then, the sheer vastness of interpretation of Rousseau's work is a tribute to the author's enduring ability to inspire.

Rousseau's work can be appreciated with little introduction. Luckily, however, the most widely available English translations of his texts boast essays by leading interpreters. For a reasonably extensive collection of his political writings, see *The Discourses and Other Early Political Writings* and *The Social Contract and Other Later Political Writings,* V. Gourevitch, ed. (Cambridge: Cambridge University Press, 1997). English translations of relevant writings not in these collections are difficult, but not impossible, to find. The standard edition of Rousseau's works in French is the five-volume *Oeuvres-Complètes,* B. Gagnebin and M. Raymond, eds. (Paris: Plèiade, 1959–1995).

For those who desire a detailed account of Rousseau's life and work, Maurice Cranston's recently completed three-volume series, *Jean Jacques, The Noble Savage,* and *The Solitary Self* (Chicago: Chicago University Press, 1982; 1991; 1997) is likely to become definitive. For an introduction to Rousseau's political writings viewed through the lens of his *Emile,* see Roger D. Masters, *The Political Philosophy of Rousseau* (Princeton, N.J.: Princeton University Press, 1968). Last but not least, Anne M. Cohler's *Rousseau and Nationalism* (New York: Basic Books, 1970) is of obvious substantive interest.

**RUSSIAN NATIONALISM** Russian nationalism is complex because there are two ways to understand the term that translates into English as "Russian." The Russian language makes a crucial distinction between *russkii* and *rossiiskii*. *Russkii* has an ethnic connotation and refers to those who are ethnically Russian, that is, through blood. *Rossiiskii*, on the other hand, is connected to the multiethnic empire of the tsars and has a state or civic connotation. Although ethnic Russians played a large role in the Russian Empire, loyalty to the tsar, rather than ethnicity, was the most important aspect of identity during much of the imperial period. The expansion of the empire from the mid-16th century to the late 19th century incorporated a large non-Russian and non-Orthodox population into the empire and many native élites were co-opted into the imperial regime. This bifurcation of Russian identity hampered the development of a coherent Russian nationalism. The near simultaneous creation of the Russian state and empire meant that Russian identity was closely tied to the empire and its institutions, rather than to the Russian people themselves. At the same time, the identity and legitimacy of the empire rested on the claim that it was the successor to Byzantium (and through Byzantium, to Rome itself), Kyivan Rus (the center of the first eastern Slavic state and the foundation of Russian Orthodox religion), and the steppe empires of the east (especially the Golden Horde). While the emphasis placed by the regime on any specific claim was fitted to circumstances, this three bases of legitimacy provided different and sometimes contradictory conceptions of Russian identity, beyond the *russkii/rossiiskii* divide.

A consistent element of Russian nationalism has been the belief that Russia has a universal mission to fulfill. In the first half of the 16th century, the notion of Russia as the "Third Rome" developed (Rome and Constantinople being the first two). According to this belief, Russia had a mission to redeem humanity because it was the only truly Christian empire. Later messianic doctrines included the Slavophiles, Westernizers, and Marxist-Leninists. These ideologies had the effect of subsuming Russian nationalism into universalist concepts, at the expense of an ethnic Russian identity.

The reforms of Tsar Peter the Great (1682–1725) touched all parts of the Russian state and society. Peter was able to impose Western forms on the nobility, including manners, dress, language, and, most notably, shaving the traditional Russian beard. The introduction of an alien culture to the Russian upper classes sharpened and solidified preexisting divisions between the élites and the masses. In essence, these two groups lived in completely separate worlds with two separate cultures and identities. The nobles centered around the increasingly Europeanized imperial court, military, and the bureaucracy, while the rest based their culture on the atomized peasant villages. A unified national identity, often seen as a necessary component of nationalist development, was absent throughout most of Russia's history.

The invasion of Russia by the armies of Napoleonic France sparked the Patriotic War of 1812. The myth of a Russia united against the French invaders quickly gave way to the fears of the nobility. Importing liberal nationalist ideology, with its egalitarian implications, could destroy the status and power of the upper classes. As a result, the regime of Tsar Nicholas I (1825–1855) searched for an alternative ideology and basis of legitimacy. Responsibility for this task fell to Count S. S. Uvarov, who developed the tripartite notion of orthodoxy, autocracy, and nationality. Two of the three, however, were unacceptable. The Orthodox Church was fully subordinated to the state, impoverished, and intellectually regressive. The Church's ties to the regime had delegitimized it in the eyes of many Russians. Nationality was far more problematic. Given the multinational nature of the empire, making ethnic Russians the principal people of the empire, as the concept of "nationality" implied, was a recipe for revolts by the vast non-Russian population. In addition, if the Russian Empire was based on the Russian people, the tsar would be reduced to an agent of the latter. This was obviously distressing to Nicholas I. Autocracy, referring to the power of the tsar and his army, became the defining feature of imperial identity.

While the military capacity of many European states was bolstered by the influx of nationalist ideology, as the early successes of the Napoleonic Empire illustrated, Russia's lack of a coherent national identity meant that it fell behind the industrialized nation-states of Europe. This was most evident in the outcome of the Crimean War (1853–1856). Although Tsar Alexander II (1855–1881) initially promoted a version of civic nationalism to correct for Russia's weaknesses, this was largely abandoned in the wake of the 1863–1864 Polish rebellion. His successors, Alexander III (1881–1894) and Nicholas II (1894–1917), embarked on a program of "Russification" in which a sense of ethnic Russian solidarity was promoted and forcible assimilation of non-Russians was attempted. This policy was a failure. First, it was applied inconsistently and haltingly. Second, non-Russians responded with nationalist movements of their own. Finally, it was too little, too late. The factors working against the development of a coherent Russian nationalism were not fully overcome by the time of the Bolshevik Revolution in 1917.

The leadership of the Soviet Union took a protean

approach to Russian nationalism. The early regime attempted to crush expressions of nationalism in favor of the supremacy of the internationalist class struggle. However, Joseph Stalin's rise to power and his slogan of "Socialism in One Country" ushered in a revival of Russian nationalist symbols and a closer identification of Russia with the Bolshevik Revolution and the USSR. When Nazi Germany invaded the Soviet Union in June 1941, Stalin made explicit use of Russian nationalism in a desperate attempt to rally Russians to fight "the Great Patriotic War" and defend "Mother Russia." Consequently, in the minds of many Russians, Russia came to be closely identified with the Soviet Union. Stalin's successors were inconsistent in their toleration and use of Russian nationalism.

The collapse of the Soviet Union in December 1991 was largely due to the rise of nationalist movements throughout the USSR. Boris Yeltsin, elected president of the Russian Soviet Federated Socialist Republic (RSFSR) in June 1991, promoted the rights of the RSFSR in opposition to the Soviet center and was instrumental in the defeat of the August coup by hard-line Communists. The emergence of the Russian Federation represented yet another opportunity for the Russian state and people to define what is Russia and who is Russian.

For further reading, see Geoffrey Hosking, *Russia: People and Empire* (Harvard University Press, 1997), and John Dunlop, *The Rise of Russia and the Fall of the Soviet Empire* (Princeton University Press, 1993).

## RUSSIAN NATIONALISM (POST-SOVIET)
Mikhail Gorbachev's policy of *perestroika* unleashed a wave of anti-Soviet sentiment and nationalist mobilization throughout the former Soviet Union. Although Russian and Soviet interests were considered nearly coterminous throughout most of the Communist era, by 1989 there was an observable split between them. Critics charged the central government with transferring Russia's wealth of the poorer non-Russian republics; sparking russophobia throughout the country; polluting Russia's natural resources; and degrading Russian culture through its sovietization program. Leading this charge were nationalist writer Valentin Rasputin and former Communist Party member Boris Yeltsin. Yeltsin rose from disgraced politburo member to president of Russia through an alliance with the liberal-democratic opposition and a populist campaign in defense of Russia's rights and interests as distinct from the Soviet Union. Yeltsin's heroic actions in defense of democracy and republic sovereignty during the failed coup by communist hard-liners on August 19–21, 1991, destroyed the le-

gitimacy of the Communist order and the Soviet state. In early December the presidents of Ukraine, Belarus, and Russia met to dissolve the Soviet Union. The emergence of an independent Russia on December 25, 1991 led one Russian writer to ask: "How will we live when the USSR has disintegrated and Russia is left alone with itself?"

Few had given much thought to what a post-Soviet Russia would look like. Russian politicians, commentators, and ordinary citizens were suddenly forced to consider some fundamental questions about their future as a people and a state. Defining the new Russian state has been largely a process of defining the Russian nation, and vice versa. Four general conceptions of post-Soviet Russian nationalism have emerged: liberal-democratic; Russkii; imperialist; and neo-Slavophile. Although there are differences of opinion between individuals, with some holding inconsistent and contradictory views, most fall into one of these categories.

The liberal-democratic faction, best represented by former Foreign Minister Andrei Kozyrev and Valery Tishkov, former minister of nationalities, looked primarily to the cosmopolitan West for their vision of a democratic, peaceable, and multiethnic Russia. They accepted the borders of the Russian Federation and promoted the concept of a civic Russian national identity within those borders. The basis of their conception of Russian nationalism rests on the distinction between *russkii* and *rossiiskii*, both of which translate into English as "Russian" but have very different meanings in the Russian language; the former is ethnic in nature and the latter has a civic connotation. The liberal-democrats were very influential in the early days of post-Soviet Russia and were instrumental in shaping the Constitution of the Russian Federation (December 1993), which uses the nonethnic, inclusive, and civic *rossiiskii* instead of the ethnic *russkii*.

Directly opposed to the liberal-democrats are those who reject the civic design of the Russian state and support, instead, the transformation of Russia into a nation-state for the ethnic Russians (i.e., a *russkii* conception). Members of this "Russkii bloc," including political scientist Ksenia Myalo and Dimitrii Rogozin, founder of the Congress of Russian Communities, have argued that the physical survival and spiritual revival of the Russian nation is only possible if the Russian people have a state of their own. The Russian Federation (which they would like to see renamed to reflect their ethnic sentiments) should be owned by the ethnic Russians and governed by them; non-Russians should be treated as minorities and not allowed to set up autonomous political entities. While the Russian Federation, for all its outwardly civic characteristics, is dominated by ethnic Russians, the extreme Russkii view is in the small minority.

Far more popular are the imperialists (often called the Red-Brown coalition), who serve as the main political opponent of the liberal-democrats. This bloc is by far the most heterogeneous and includes such groups as neofascists, monarchists, former and current Communists, neo-Stalinists, and Russian nationalists. However, they have a common theme: Russian national identity is inherently tied to imperial structures and Russia cannot survive without some kind of empire. They argue that the Eurasian empire, in either its tsarist or Soviet forms, constituted an organic cultural entity that developed naturally, inevitably, and for the good of the people it ruled (even if they do not perceive it as such now). For them, the breakup of the USSR was a tragedy and the Russian Federation is an incomplete and unnatural aberration. They urge for the reconstruction of some type of union throughout most of the former USSR. In addition, the imperialists seem obsessed with military power, the great power status of Russia/USSR, and the dangers of Westernization. Vladimir Zhirinovsky (leader of the ironically named Liberal Democratic Party) and Gennady Zyuganov (head of the Communist Party) are prime examples of this faction. The imperialist position began to lose some of its steam by 1994–1995 once the Commonwealth of Independent States (CIS) had clearly failed to be a vehicle for the reintegration of the former USSR. Many Imperialists consequently turned toward the neo-Slavophiles.

The final grouping has been called neo-Slavophile. Although they share the imperialists' resistance to Westernization, the neo-Slavophiles' opposition to empire fundamentally divides the two camps. Emerging out of the nationalist writings of such authors as Aleksandr Solzhenitsyn and Valentin Rasputin, the neo-Slavophiles urged Russia to cast off its imperial burden and promoted an inward-looking ideology that focused on healing the Russian soul and rebuilding Russia's spiritual life. They see Russia's place in a larger Slavic civilization and support a peaceful unification with the other eastern Slavic states (Ukraine and Belarus). Recent moves by Russia to form a union with Belarus, and the possibility that Ukraine may join, are indicative of this conception of Russian identity.

At present, Russian nationalism and national identity lack coherence. No bloc has emerged to authoritatively define the Russian nation. A centrist position seems to be coalescing that draws from all sides, but predictions are both impossible and unwise in the turbulent post-Soviet period.

For further reading, see Ilya Prizel, *National Identity and Foreign Policy* (Cambridge University Press, 1998); Gennady Zyuganov, *My Russia* (M. E. Sharpe, 1997); Aleksandr Solzhenitsyn, *Rebuilding Russia* (Farrar, Straus, and Giroux, 1991); Vera Tolz, "Conflicting 'Homeland Myths' and Nation-State Building in Postcommunist Russia," *Slavic Review* 57(2) (Summer 1998), pp. 267–294.

## RWANDAN NATIONALISM

Rwanda is one of the most troubled African countries today; it is wracked by devastating ethnic civil wars that seem to never end. Some scholars have attributed the incessant ethnic civil strife to issues of resource scarcity and high population densities. Population pressures in Rwanda are nothing new. In the midst of resource scarcity, one sector of its society, the Tutsi ethnic group, evolved a highly intricate feudal society based on livestock. The population of Rwanda is divided into three distinct ethnic groups sharing a common language. The pygmoid Twa constitute less than 1 percent of the population and are rarely seen, being hunters and forest dwellers. The Bantu Hutu represent 85 percent of the population. They were the first to inhabit Rwanda and have always been agriculturalists with a loose political structure, preferring to govern themselves in small units centered around clan chiefs, which made them very vulnerable to outside invasion.

Some four centuries ago a tall, slender, and aristocratic people known as the Tutsi conquered Rwanda. Although they never constituted more than 15 percent of the population, their hierarchical organization, built around a king known as the mwami, their development of specialized warrior castes, and above all their possession of cattle enabled them to dominate the Hutu. The Tutsi are purported to have been a group of pastoralists that originated from Ethiopia or the Nile valley. By the late 18th century, a single Tutsi-ruled state, headed by a mwami or king, occupied much of Rwanda and dominated the Hutu, the vast majority of the population in feudal arrangement centered around the rearing of cattle. After the Berlin Conference of 1884, Rwanda came under German colonial rule and became part of German East Africa. By the end of World War I, the country was occupied by Belgium soldiers. Rwanda came under a League of Nations mandate and became part of what was then known as the Belgian mandate of Ruanda-Urundi. In 1946 it became a UN trust territory under the control of Belgium. Under German and Belgian rule, the Hutu had been marginalized while the Tutsi had been favored by the colonial masters as administrators and tax collectors. The already fragile association between the Hutu and Tutsi erupted in 1959 after the Hutu had demanded a greater voice in the country's affairs. On July 24, 1959, Mwami Rudahigwa died suddenly under mysterious circumstances without having designated his successor. This proved the occasion for the decisive clash between the Tutsi and the embryonic Parmehutu, the political organization of the Hutu, led by Gregoire Kayibanda. While the Tutsis quickly installed the mwami's nephew as the new king and prepared a terrorist campaign against leading Hutu politicians, the Hutu masses staged an uprising under Parmehutu direction. The mwami was deposed and fled the country along with thousands of other Tutsi refugees, and a provisional Hutu government was installed.

In 1961 a UN-supervised referendum resulted in an 80 percent victory for the Parmehutu Party and the decisive rejection of the monarchy. Periodic fighting between Hutus and Tutsis continued, and additional thousands of refugees fled the country. Rwanda became independent in 1962 with Hutu majority rule. More than 100,000 Tutsi fled to neighboring Burundi, which continued to be dominated by the minority Tutsi. Tutsis in exile formed a guerilla movement dedicated to the overthrow of the Rwandan government and the restoration of the monarch. In 1973 a coup installed Major General Juvénal Habyarimana as head of a military regime. The military coup was part in response to the policies of the Kayibanda government that advocated austerity measures and the continuation of stringent soil conservation policies imposed during Belgian colonial rule. Civilian rule was restored under a new constitution that established in 1978 a one-party state with Habyarimana remaining in power as president.

In 1990 Rwanda was invaded by forces composed largely of Tutsi exiles. Intermittent warfare continued into 1993, when a peace accord was signed, but the accord's implementation stalled. When Habyarimana and Burundi's president were killed in a suspicious plane crash in 1994, civil strife erupted. Rwandan soldiers and Hutu gangs are reported to have killed as many as 1 million Tutsis and Twas during this upheaval. The Tutsi rebel forces resumed fighting and won control of the country. Pasteur Bizimungu, a Hutu, was named president. Perhaps as many as 2 million Rwandans, mainly Hutus, fled the country, crowding into camps in Zaire and other neighboring countries, where disease claimed tens of thousands of lives. In 1994, more than a million Hutu refugees fled Rwanda in a panicked mass migration afraid of reprisals from the new Tutsi-dominated government. In 1996, 500,000 of those refugees returned to Rwanda to escape fighting in Zaire. In short, Rwanda has never been able to sort its nationalism in a peaceful manner. Throughout history, Rwanda's story has been one of tension and warfare between the Hutus and the Tutsis.

For further reading see Gérard Prunier, *The Rwanda Crisis: History of a Genocide* (London: C. Hurst, 1998); "The Atlantic Report: Rwanda," in *The Atlantic Monthly* (June 1964); "Violence and Unrest in Central Africa," in *The Atlantic Monthly* (November 22, 1996); and Christopher C. Taylor, *Sacrifice as Terror: The Rwandan Genocide of 1994* (Oxford: Berg, 1999).

# S

**SADAT, ANWAR AL-** 1918–1981, Soldier, politician, and president of Egypt. Sadat was born in the Delta village of Mit Abu al-Kum on December 25, 1918. In 1925 his family moved to Cairo, where he received his primary and secondary education. He entered the Royal Military Academy in 1936 and was commissioned in 1938. Sadat was cashiered from the army and jailed during World War II because of contacts with German agents; he similarly was imprisoned after the war for involvement in assassination attempts on pro-British Egyptian politicians. Readmitted to the military in 1949, he soon became part of the Free Officers group, the secret organization within the army that seized power in July 1952. Under the new regime dominated by Gamal Abdel Nasser, Sadat held various posts: minister of state, editor of the government newspaper *al-Jumhuriyya*, chair of the National Assembly, and vice-president of Egypt in the 1960s. He succeeded Nasser as president of Egypt on the latter's death in September 1970.

Although coming to power as Nasser's chosen successor, during his tenure as president, Sadat in effect reversed many of Nasser's policies. His domestic program is known as "The Opening," an attempt to open the state-dominated economy created by Nasser to domestic private enterprise and more importantly to attract Western and oil-state investment to Egypt. Part of The Opening was a break with Egypt's previous main external source of economic and military aid, the Soviet Union, and a rapprochement with the United States. Most dramatic was his position toward Israel. In October 1973 Egypt combined with Syria to mount an offensive aimed at dislodging Israel from the Egyptian and Syrian territory it had occupied in 1967. The war of October 1973 failed to do this directly; but Egypt's better performance in the war provided Sadat with the legitimacy that subsequently allowed him to enter into the U.S.-mediated "peace process" of the mid- and late

1970s. By 1977 Egypt had entered into direct negotiations with Israel; by 1979 formal peace between the two countries was realized, Egypt in the process obtaining the return of the Sinai Peninsula. Peace with Israel, along with his generally pro-Western orientation, were central factors in Sadat's assassination by Islamic militants in October 1981.

Sadat also had a different nationalist emphasis from Nasser. Where the former saw Egypt as part and parcel of a larger Arab nation and promoted Egyptian leadership of Arab nationalism, Sadat's emphasis—as his memoirs vividly illustrate—was on the land of Egypt and Egypt as a distinct national community. By 1971 the name "United Arab Republic" had been abandoned and replaced by the "Arab Republic of Egypt." The 1973 alliance with Syria notwithstanding, Egypt's closest allies in the Arab world in the 1970s were conservative monarchies such as Saudi Arabia. Sadat's placement of Egyptian national interest above Arab solidarity appeared most obviously in his policy toward Israel, where he was willing to break Arab ranks by entering into bilateral peace negotiations, and where the peace arrangement eventually concluded in effect took Egypt out of the Arab camp confronting Israel. Sadat's shift away from Arab nationalism toward Egyptian territorial nationalism was both a return to the territorial nationalist orientation that had prevailed in Egypt prior to the Nasser period, and a prominent example of the drift toward narrower state nationalism in place of a wider Arab affiliation that has occurred in the Arab world since the 1970s.

Sadat's own narrative of his life and career is presented in *In Search of Identity: An Autobiography* (1978). A critical biography is David Hirst and Irene Beeson, *Sadat* (1981). A more sympathetic account can be found in Joseph Finklestone, *Anwar Sadat: Visionary Who Dared* (1996).

# SALAZAR, ANTÓNIO

1889–1970, To attack the financial problems, especially inflation, which years of chaos had exacerbated, Portugal's ruling generals, who had seized power in a coup d'état in 1926, named an economics professor from the University of Coimbra, Dr. António de Oliveira Salazar, as finance minister with full powers in 1928. He created the first financial stability his country had known in the 20th century. In 1932 he became both leader of the only legal party and prime minister, the post that until 1974 remained the heart of political power in Portugal. He established a fascist state, called the *Estado Novo* ("New State"), which he guided until his incapacitation in 1968. In 1933 a Constitution was promulgated that had a few trappings of parliamentary government, such as a unicameral National Assembly and a directly elected president. However, its essence was an authoritarian, corporative state. All opposition was silenced.

The corporatist character of the new Constitution was embodied in an advisory organ called the Corporative Chamber. This allegedly united all classes by bringing together representatives of diverse economic and professional groups to evaluate all legislation. Over the years other organizations were established to encompass workers, employers, craftsmen, landowners, rural laborers, fishermen, women, and youth. Their purpose was to lock all citizens tightly into a bundle of groups, all directed from the top by Salazar. There was only one legal political party, the Unión Nacional ("National Union"), which never played a central role in Portugal, as did the Nazi or Fascist Parties in Germany and Italy.

The Portuguese political system was complicated in theory, but it was rather simple in practice. Salazar, with the advice of trusted cronies from industry, the military, and the Church, made all crucial political decisions. Freedom of press and assembly were curtailed, and all written and electronic communications were censored. Critical professors were dismissed, and strikes were outlawed. As every Portuguese knew, the secret police (PIDE) was omnipresent. It is estimated that 1 in 400 Portuguese was a paid informant.

When the Spanish civil war broke out in 1936, Salazar ordered the creation of a "Portuguese Legion" to fight on Gen. Francisco Franco's side, and about 6000 Portuguese fought against the Spanish Republic. Portugal also tolerated the transport of munitions from France across its territory until mid-1937, when the British, Portugal's closest ally for three centuries, pressured Salazar into closing its borders to such war material. On March 17, 1939, Franco and Salazar signed a nonaggression and friendship pact. It was amended on July 29, 1940, to obligate both governments to discuss their mutual security interests with one another whenever the "independence or security" of one of the countries is endangered. That pact still remains valid. Portugal, like Spain, did not become linked militarily and diplomatically with Germany and Italy before and during World War II. Portugal even profited from its neutrality by becoming one of Europe's major centers for spies from all belligerent countries. It allowed the Allied powers to use the Azores for military purposes. However, Salazar's sympathies were revealed when he ordered a day of national mourning after Germany's Hitler had committed suicide.

Portugal's valuable strategic position and long-standing relationship with Britain enabled it to become a founding member of NATO. In 1955 Portugal was admitted to the United Nations. However, Portugal remained in an economic, social, and political condition of stagnation and immobility, ruled and administered by an aging dictator and a tight clique of generals, admirals, and bureaucrats, who, through a swarm of spies, rendered the population submissive, but increasingly dissatisfied and restless. The country's seemingly interminable colonial wars in Africa sapped its strength and resources.

After Salazar suffered a debilitating stroke in 1968, a law professor, Dr. Marcelo Caetano, assumed leadership over a regime that was in the process of rapid decay. He hoped to reform and liberalize the authoritarian system his predecessor had created, but it had become far too late for that. Portugal had just about reached the exploding point, and all that was needed was a spark. That spark came in 1974 from the same institution that had stepped into the Portuguese political sphere many times before and had established the half-century dictatorship in the first place—the military.

# SAN MARTÍN, JOSÉ DE

1778–1850, A major force in breaking the Spanish yoke in South America. His tactical brilliance brought him success that made him a national hero in several South American countries, especially in his native Argentina.

In 1812, upon returning home from a twenty-year career in Europe as a soldier in the Spanish army, San Martín joined the rebel Buenos Aires government. As a general for the forces seeking liberation, he won several key battles against the Spanish.

San Martín then turned his attention to freeing Peru. He crossed the Andes—an action that has drawn comparison to Hannibal's traversal of the Alps—and quickly drove the Spanish out of Chile. A brilliant sea attack devised by San Martín surprised the Spanish, and he conquered Lima in July 1821.

After his success against the Spanish, San Martín contributed to the development of nationalism more by what he did not do rather than by what he did: He refused to take power in Peru. Lacking the political ambition that so many nationalist visionaries possessed, San Martín wanted to avoid a struggle among independence leaders. He met with Simón Bolívar in 1822, and resigned his protectorship of Peru shortly thereafter. San Martín's gentlemanly departure from Peru allowed the independence movement to flourish.

Once he returned to Argentina, San Martín became disillusioned by the internal strife within the nationalist government. He left his homeland for Europe and died in Bologne-sur-Mer, France.

Authoritative works include John C. Medford's *San Martín: The Liberator* (Greenwood, 1950; 1971) and Ricardo Rojas's *San Martín, Knight of the Andes* (Cooper Square, 1945).

## SANDINO, AUGUSTO CÉSAR

1895–1934, Nicaraguan patriot, anti-imperialist, and guerrilla leader, born in Niquinohomo, Nicaragua. Sandino waged a guerrilla war from 1926 to 1933 against U.S. marines who were occupying Nicaragua. U.S. forces first entered Nicaragua in 1912 and were withdrawn in 1925. At that time Sandino joined an armed revolt by the Liberal Party against Nicaragua's pro-American Conservative government. This revolt prompted the United States to deploy marines in Nicaragua once again, but Sandino, alone among the liberal commanders, refused to negotiate or lay down his arms until the United States withdrew. After suffering losses in pitched battles, Sandino and his followers waged a guerrilla war against the marines from a remote border area near Honduras, where they established a type of agricultural commune. Sandino's actions were informed by a mélange of nationalist, "spiritualist," anarchist, and Communist ideas that he had picked up while working for U.S. corporations in Costa Rica and Mexico.

The U.S. counterinsurgency campaign against Sandino involved aerial bombardments and forced relocation of villagers, but the marines were unable to capture Sandino, due in part to the intelligence provided by local sympathizers. The American journalist Carleton Beals, however, was able to conduct several interviews with Sandino, which first appeared in *The Nation* and were subsequently published worldwide. A small anti-war movement developed in the United States, and Congress eventually cut off funding for the occupation. U.S. marines were finally withdrawn from Nicaragua by President Herbert Hoover in early 1933.

After the marine withdrawal, Sandino entered into negotiations with the Nicaraguan government, but he was arrested and executed in February 1934 on the orders of General Anastasio Somoza García, the commander of the U.S.-created National Guard. Somoza later established a dynastic dictatorship in Nicaragua.

After his death Sandino became a symbol of anti-imperialism not only in Nicaragua, but throughout much of Latin America. Radical opponents of the Somoza dictatorship later named their movement after Sandino; the Sandinista National Liberation Front (FSLN), formed in 1961, led a successful insurrection against the dictatorship of Somoza García's son, Anastasio Somoza Debayle, in 1978–1979. During the decade of Sandinista rule in Nicaragua (1979–1990), Sandino's image became nearly ubiquitous. Black-and-white images of Sandino's gaunt, impassive visage, peering out from under his cowboy hat, greeted one at virtually every turn.

Gregorio Selser's *Sandino* (Monthly Review, 1981) is a standard biography. The history of Sandino's movement is recounted in Neill Macaulay's *The Sandino Affair* (Duke, 1985). Donald C. Hodges has explored Sandino's thought in two works: *Intellectual Foundations of the Nicaraguan Revolution* (Texas, 1986) and *Sandino's Communism* (Texas, 1992).

## SARMIENTO, DOMINGO

1811–1888, Argentine writer, educator, politician, and ambassador to the United States (1864), born in the province of San Juan. Prior to his presidency (1868–1874), Sarmiento moved in and out of exile in Chile where he wrote some of his most prominent works: impassioned political pamphlets aimed at overturning existing Argentine political regimes, the most famous being the government of Juan Manuel de Rosas.

As president of Argentina, Sarmiento embarked on a national "civilization" campaign that promoted a massive wave of immigration from Europe and the institution of national programs for education. Perhaps due to his extensive travels in the United States, Europe, and colonized African nations, about which he wrote extensively, he has been referred to as the father of sociology in Argentina. Sarmiento is also considered to have been the first large-scale urban planner in South America.

His best known work, *Facundo: civilización y barbarie* (*Life in the Argentine Republic in the Days of the Tyrants*, 1845), is a political pamphlet that has been interpreted broadly as both fiction and nonfiction and narrates the life of prominent "caudillo" (chief from the provinces) Juan Facundo Quiroga (1790–1835). Sarmiento depicts Facundo as a ruthless, free-spirited warlord who epitomizes what Sarmiento saw as the current state of barbarism in the Argentine nation. *Facundo* also represented an attack on the political ideology of Juan Manuel de Rosas (in power between 1829 and 1851), whom Sarmiento saw as a national threat due to his protectionist national policies.

Sarmiento saw the vast expanse of unpopulated Argentine land (which he referred to as "the desert") as a hindrance to the cultural and economic development of his nation. *Facundo* became Sarmiento's philosophical and theoretical basis for a multitude of future written treatises and projects dealing with education and public works, immigration, cartography, and legal reform. Sarmiento envisioned the prospect of Euroean immigration as the most promising civilizing force for the Argentine nation. Along with Juan Bautista Alberdi (1810–1884), he is regarded by historians as responsible for the massive waves of immigration to Argentina from Italy, Spain, and Eastern Europe roughly between 1860 and 1930. During these years, as Sarmiento had foreseen, "the city" (Buenos Aires) became the center of cultural production. Contemporary critics of Sarmiento faulted him for what they saw as his uncritical admiration for the United States (he wrote works on the lives of educator Horace Mann and Abraham Lincoln).

Although he agreed with Sarmiento on a variety of theoretical points, Alberdi disagreed with what he saw as Sarmiento's simplistic dichotomy between civilization and barbarism, and his view of unpopulated Argentine land as a source of barbarism and a detriment to the national project. Like Sarmiento, Alberdi was a proponent of large-scale European immigration to Argentina, evidenced by the emphasis on Argentina's "open-door" policy in the Constitution of 1853 of which he is thought to be the primary author. Alberdi thought that Argentina should prepare for European immigration by eliminating protective tariffs, readying the country for foreign investment, large loans, and business opportunities. He is said to have called Sarmiento a caudillo of the pen and to have accused him of the murder of a caudillo from the province of La Rioja during his governorship of his home province, San Juan. Alberdi saw Sarmiento as embodying the same forces of barbarism that he had vowed to eradicate from Argentina.

A recent critical work on Sarmiento's *Facundo* and the Argentine nation is Diana Sorensen Goodrich's *Facundo and the Construction of Argentine Culture* (University of Texas Press, 1996). Other biographical sources include *The Life of Sarmiento* by Allison Williams Bunkley (Princeton University Press, 1952) and Roberto Tamagno's *Sarmiento, los liberales y el imperialismo inglés* (Buenos Aires: Pena Lillo, 1963).

**SARO-WIWA, KENULE** 1941–1995, Saro-Wiwa is proof that political environments compel people to engage in nationalist activities. The Ogoni ethnic group, estimated population 500,000, to which Saro-Wiwa belongs is one of the several ethno-national groups who inhabit Nigeria's Niger Delta. On account of their smaller populations, all the groups who inhabit the Niger Delta are designated as minorities. This is in contrast to the other larger Nigerian ethnic groups. Paradoxically, while the delta is the source of almost all hydrocarbon exports whose proceeds sustain the Nigerian state, the region is also the most impoverished in Nigeria. The environmental degradation that results from reckless hydrocarbon extraction in the area is all that the inhabitants receive in contrast to the wealth that accrues to the Nigerian state from that resource.

Saro-Wiwa used his writing talents to force the Ogoni quest for justice on the Nigerian state, Shell, and other oil companies who operate in the delta. His books, *On a Darkling Plain: An Account of the Nigerian Civil War* (1989) and *Genocide in Nigeria: The Ogoni Tragedy* (1992), say volumes about that quest.

The late 1980s marked the advent of open demands by the delta groups for their fair share from the wealth that accrued from the exploitation of the resources in their land and a stop to the environmental degradation of their fragile ecosystem. Saro-Wiwa was the architect of the struggle that entailed those demands. Saro-Wiwa's political growth and maturity are both functions of his quest for the rights of his Ogoni people.

The events of Nigeria's immediate postindependence years when much of the Niger Delta was within the Igbo-dominated Eastern Region offered Saro-Wiwa the chance to realize that the nature of the Nigerian state makes it virtually impossible for minority groups like the Ogoni to get their fair share of their entitlements in Nigeria. Saro-Wiwa's personal conviction that Biafra would be unfavorably disposed to the rights of minority groups made him decide to side with federal Nigeria against Biafra in their three-year war from 1967 to 1970.

Saro-Wiwa's hope that minority rights might fare better in a federal Nigeria was dashed even with the creation of the Rivers State in 1967. Saro-Wiwa's mobilization of the Ogoni began with the formation of the Ogoni Central Union (OCU) in 1990. It was on the auspices of the OCU that he authored the Ogoni Bill of Rights, a political and contentious frame document that framed age-old Ogoni demands and grievances as "a separate and distinct ethnic nationality within the Federal Republic of Nigeria." The Bill of Rights justified the Ogoni struggle for economic and political equity in Nigeria at the same time as it dignified and animated it.

The immediate and logical outcome of the Bill of Rights was the formation of the Movement for the Survival of Ogoni People (MOSOP). MOSOP became the vehicle that conveyed Saro-Wiwa and the Ogoni struggle to the rest of the world. MOSOP was the platform on which Saro-Wiwa and the Ogoni beckoned to the world community of environmental activists to adopt the Ogoni cause as part of their overall agenda.

Saro-Wiwa and eight other Ogoni activists were arrested in May 1994 by the Nigerian military authorities and charged with the murder of four Ogoni men who were killed in the course of a political rally that turned riotous. Found guilty after what was termed a show trial Saro-Wiwa and his eight codefendants were sentenced to death by hanging. Their sentence was carried out on November 10, 1995, despite huge "international publicity and outcries."

*A Month and a Day: A Detention Diary* (Penguin, 1995) is Saro-Wiwa's eloquent account of his first prolonged detention in 1994.

## SAUD, IBN

1880–1953, ʿAbd al-ʿAziz ibn ʿAbd al-Rahman Al Faysal Al Saʿud, founder of the modern Kingdom of Saudi Arabia, was born in Riyadh and died in Taʾif. Ibn Saud was born to the most influential family in Najd, the central plateau of the Arabian peninsula. The Saudis had ruled much of the peninsula under a series of monarchical regimes in the 18th and 19th centuries, although each of the kingdoms had come to a violent end. While Ibn Saud was still a young child, Riyadh was captured by a rival notable family of Najd, the Rashidis of Haʾil, and thus his formative years were spent in exile in Kuwait. It was Ibn Saud's remarkable achievement not just to resurrect Saudi control over Riyadh, but also to extend it from there, and to establish a stable government, throughout the territory of modern Saudi Arabia.

Earlier Saudi leaders had conquered territory in Arabia by harnessing the religious zeal of bedouin tribes that belonged to the strict Islamic reformist movement popularly known as Wahhabism. Those gains were lost because the Wahhabis refused to compromise with such powerful regional leaders as Muhammad Ali of Egypt and his suzerain, the Ottoman sultan. Ibn Saud learned from his predecessors' mistakes and was always careful not to provoke retaliation from powerful neighbors, especially Britain. Thus he maintained cordial relations with the British during World War I, accepting protection and a subsidy from them, but did little to aid their war effort materially, lest he suffer retribution should Ottoman control over Arabia be reestablished after the war. He waited patiently for an opportunity to conquer the Hijaz, including the holy cities of Mecca and Madina, because Sharif Hussein of Mecca enjoyed British favor. Ibn Saud seized the province in 1925, after Britain's support for Sharif Hussein ended. When the religiously motivated tribal forces, the Ikhwan, who had played very important roles in Ibn Saud's conquests, began raiding British-protected Iraq and Transjordan against his wishes, he broke their power in a series of clashes in 1929–1930.

Bringing Arabia's unruly tribes under his control was but one of the elements of Ibn Saud's attempts to construct a relatively stable state. He maintained influence among the tribes, and indeed all of his nascent country's important social groups, by a long succession of marriages, rumored to number from several dozen to several hundred. He established a rudimentary administrative system by dividing the country into provinces, each of which was governed by a member of his family. Ibn Saud retained close personal control over national governmental affairs until the last years of his life, creating a council of ministers only in 1953, shortly before his death. Ibn Saud's prestige and personality were vital to holding together both state and society, and his death thus could have caused a crisis in the kingdom. His longevity helped to prevent the crisis from erupting, however. He had named his son Saʿud as crown prince in 1932, and the long-set succession proceeded smoothly.

Ibn Saud's stamp is still easily seen on Saudi Arabia today. Every one of its kings since 1953 has been a son of the monarchy's founder, and the state remains under the control of the Saudi family, which is thought to number at least 20,000 people. This familial dominance in some ways still resembles that of shaykhly families in 19th-century Arabian tribes, but Ibn Saud deserves recognition for the notable changes he wrought in creating the modern Saudi state and society.

A popular biography of Ibn Saud is David Howarth's *The Desert King* (1964). H. St. John Philby knew Ibn Saud and recorded his impressions of the man in *Arabian Jubilee*. Joseph Kostiner has published very good work on the development of Saudi Arabia under Ibn Saud, most notably in his *The Making of Saudi Arabia* (Oxford University Press, 1993).

## SAUDI NATIONALISM

King ʿAbd al-ʿAziz's establishment of the Kingdom of Saudi Arabia in 1932 gradually gave rise to a unique version of nationalism in this predominantly tribal state. The foundations of Saudi nationalism rest on two sources of allegiance, one segmentary and another inclusive. Loyalty to one's tribe and unwavering acceptance of the political supremacy of al-Saud complement each other. Saudi traditional nationalism expresses itself in the trilogy of God, the king, and the homeland. This entailed al-Saud's adoption of the Wahabi interpretation of Islam, and recognition of the tribe as a viable form of social identification, in exchange for legitimizing their political control. The Saudi people are regionally conscious people. The domineering role of Najd (located in central Arab) in running the affairs of the kingdom its reticently resented by the inhabitants of Hijaz and the Shi'is in the eastern province.

Apart from the resoluteness of King 'Abd al-'Aziz and the commitment of his successors, the development of Saudi nationalism owes much to the kingdom's tremendous oil wealth. Among the vast majority of Saudis, the oil boom in the 1970s cultivated a strong sense of territorial national pride. Saudi royals began to think of their country as a regional political power and as a world economic force. To ensure the continuation of widespread public support, the ruling élite have transformed Saudi Arabia into an allocation state. They resorted to borrowing and eschewed taxation in order to shore up the population against untoward oil price fluctuations, probably to prevent the possibility of popular disaffection with the regime.

Saudi nationalism confronts serious challenges in the years ahead. These include resolving the impending succession question, rationalizing spending, stimulating production, coping with public attitudinal change in this age of informational revolution, and laying more modern institutional grounds for the eventuality of rising public demands for political participation.

## SAVISAAR, EDGAR

**SAVISAAR, EDGAR** 1950 –, Estonian politician; born in Harju region, Estonia. In 1973 he finished Tartu University with a specialty in history. In 1980 – 1988 he worked at the Estonian Planning Committee as the head of a department. Since the *perestroika* years, he became actively involved in local politics. In 1988 Savisaar became the founder of the Estonian Popular Front — the movement of nationally minded Estonians which gathered as the Estonian Communists and intellectuals and the wider masses of people in support of Gorbachev's reforms. The movement became a model for popular organizations in the Soviet Union, although they were not always nationally minded. The popular fronts were established in the other Baltic republics, in Caucasus, and in Russia. However, the Estonian Popular Front remained one of the most influential reformist movements in Estonia and thus in the whole USSR during Gorbachev's rule.

In 1989 – 1990 Savisaar was chairman of the Planning Committee and minister of economics. He was a dele-

gate to the Estonian Supreme Soviet (Parliament) and People's Deputies' Congress of the USSR in Moscow. In 1990 Savisaar was appointed the prime minister of Estonia while it was still within the USSR. He maintained the same official position of prime minister after the establishment of reindependence in Estonia on August 24, 1991, which followed the failure of Putch in Moscow. The same year he founded a new party — the Central Party — and became its chairman. In 1992 – 1995 he was the deputy speaker at the Estonian parliament, Riigikogu; in 1995, minister of interior; and in 1996 – 1999, chairman of the Tallinn City Council; since 1999, chairman of the Central Party Faction in the Parliament. Savisaar's Central Party won parliamentary and local government elections in 1999. However, he and his party were unable to form a coalition with other parties because they refused to cooperate with Savisaar. He has been considered to be too authoritarian and a schemer. For that reason his own party split in 1997.

Savisaar has promoted central leftist, social democratic ideas in Estonia: progressive income taxation, interethnic integration, and cultural autonomy for the non-Estonians. He has strongly supported the aspirations of the non-Estonians and, thus, his electorate has consisted of, besides the Estonians, also Russian-speaking voters, the number of which has been the biggest in comparison with the other Estonian-dominated (Estonian-based) parties. During the parliamentary elections in 1995 the party advocated the need to sign agreements on minority rights' protection with the countries of the CIS. Although representing an ethnocentrist party, Savisaar has also been an advocate of the Russian speakers representative organizations in Estonia, the cultural autonomy of the Russian-speaking people.

See E. Savisaar, *I Believe In Estonia* (Tallinn: TEA Publishers, 1999)(in Estonian).

## SCHILLER, FRIEDRICH

**SCHILLER, FRIEDRICH** 1759 – 1805, Born the son of an army captain in Marbach in the southwest German region of Wuerttemberg, Schiller attended the military academy, Karlsschule. He became a military surgeon, a profession he loathed. At age twenty-two, he wrote *The Robbers*, which was a scathing attack on political tyranny. When it was staged in Mannheim in 1782, it was a public sensation, but the duke of Württemberg was so infuriated by it that Schiller was forced to flee. Considered the finest German dramatist of his time as well as the most popular poet of the middle class, Schiller's career spans the emotional Storm and Stress to the sober, rational classicism. His play, *Don Carlos*, best marks this transition. Schiller spent his last ten years in

Weimar where his writing was enriched by his friendship with Goethe, which was also marked with rivalry.

A prolific writer, his works not only dealt with psychological and philosophical themes, but he was intensely interested in politics and history. Many of his most famous works are tragedies or epics set in a political and historical background and advocating freedom and nobility of spirit. Schiller wrote works about such political themes as the Thirty Years War (1618–1648), which he followed with a dramatic trilogy, *Wallenstein* (1798–1799), Scotland (*Mary Stuart,* 1800), France (*The Virgin of Orleans,* 1801), and Switzerland (*William Tell,* 1804). Because of his 1788 history of the Netherlands' revolt against Spain, he was awarded a chair in history at the University of Jena. He died of tuberculosis at the age of forty-five, too early to have become well acquainted with the sentiment of German nationalism, which was given wings by the French occupation of Germany until 1813.

## SCHÖNHUBER, FRANZ 1923–, Personification of the German extreme right in the 1980s and 1990s. Born in 1923 in a small rural village in Upper Bavaria, Schönhuber joined the NSDAP (Nazi Party) at the age of eighteen and the Waffen-SS a year later. During the war he served most of the time as instructor in the French Charlemagne division. After the war he became a journalist for various newspapers before moving to the *Bayerischer Rundfunk* (BR). In the 1970s he became a famous personality in Bavaria as presenter of the popular program *Jetzt red i* (*Now I Speak*).

In 1981 Shönhuber published an autobiography of his wartime experiences entitled *Ich war dabei* (*I was there*), which led to a storm of negative publicity. Schönhuber was accused of trivializing the crimes of the Waffen-SS and the Nazi regime. As a consequence, he was fired by the BR in April 1982; it was this experience that led him to cofound *Die Republikaner* (The Republicans, REP). After a short struggle with his cofounders, Schönhuber took control of the party. Under his leadership the REP transformed from a national conservative into an extreme right party. Schönhuber's personal hobbyhorses were German nationalism (including unification of Germany into the 1937 borders), *Vergangenheitsbewältigung* (the way in which the German state dealt with the Nazi past), and the decay of morality. In the 1989 European elections the REP gained its biggest electoral success, gaining 7.1 percent of the German vote, which brought Schönhuber together with five party members into the European Parliament.

Schönhuber has always been a very controversial person, being both admired and despised by people inside and outside his party. As a former journalist, he was able to create a remarkably positive image of himself and his party within the (South) German media, which strengthened his leadership within the party. However, his extravagant and authoritarian behavior also led to much criticism and in 1994 he was (for the second time) ousted as party leader. He left the REP to become an independent author within extreme right circles (among others, for the infamous journal *Nation und Europa*), before an unsuccessful return on the electoral list of the *Deutsche Volksunion* (DVU) in the 1998 parliamentary and the 1999 European elections.

Schönhuber wrote half a dozen books, the most interesting being the autobiographic *Ich war dabei* (Müller Verlag, 1981). More than 130,000 copies have been sold in eleven editions. The most authoritative biography on Schönhuber is by Kurt Hirsch and Hans Sarkowicz, *Schönhuber: Der Politiker und seine Kreise* (Eichborn Verlag, 1989).

## SCHOPENHAUER, ARTHUR 1788–1860, In the early 19th century Friedrich Hegel had developed a popular dialectic theory that predicted inevitable progress and the emergence of ever-clearer reason in human affairs. He believed that no state had ascended farther on this course than Prussia. Schopenhauer rejected the optimism of idealists like Hegel and elaborated a pessimistic philosophy. It is said that he scheduled his lectures at the University of Berlin at the same time as Hegel's in order to force students to choose between the two opposing views. The main inspiration for him was Kant's analysis of the role of will. He accepted the notion that in both man and the universe will is the "thing-in-itself," a view that he explained in his classic 1819 study, *The World as Will and Idea.* The will can objectify itself in phenomena, and the universe is idea. Since no one person can comprehend the entire "world will," an individual considers the world to be his own idea. Schopenhauer does not argue that the will is rational. Looking at nature and life, he saw no evidence that there was a rational process at work. Instead, he saw life as a blind purposeless impulse, as confusion rather than order. People like Hegel, who saw underlying rationality in the universe, were victims of wishful thinking. Life is desire that can never be satisfied; its essence is restlessness and movement.

Any thinking man will be pessimistic because he will never find satisfaction in life. Although one can never totally escape from this pessimism, there are three places to turn for temporary solace. One is art and music, in which both eternal ideas and the restless movement of life can be combined; but one cannot live every moment of his life in artistic ecstasy. A second is sympathy, which subordinates individualism, minimizes conflict, creates a degree of unity among men, and forms the basis for ethics. The third is to renounce the very will to live. This does not mean suicide, which results from dissatisfaction with present conditions, but a complete indifference to living. None of these are final solutions because any solace they provide will be dashed again, and man will be cast back into pessimism. There is little room in Schopenhauer's thought for devotion to the nation.

## SCHUMACHER, KURT

1895–1952, Never in the history of the Social Democratic Party of Germany (SPD) did one person so dominate the party as did Kurt Schumacher. He opposed all forms of totalitarianism as inherently evil, asserting that "every kind of reservation vis-à-vis the idea of democracy means the greatest imaginable danger for the German future" and that "democracy is the state, and the state which can live in Europe is democracy, and we reject every other form." In his commitment to democracy, he was entirely oriented toward the political values of the Western Allies and of the smaller democratic nations in Western Europe. Very early he had cast off any thoughts of Germany playing a politically neutral, intermediary role between East and West. He maintained publicly that "the whole German people in thought and deed belong to the West." This democratic commitment, along with his charisma and determination, is an important reason why such diverse personalities as Willy Brandt, Carlo Schmid, Helmut Schmidt, and Herbert Wehner, who would not have been prototypical social democrats before 1933, were drawn to the SPD after 1945.

Because of his aim to establish a democratic order, he opened the SPD's doors to young ex-Nazis, especially from the Hitler Youth and the Waffen-SS. Schumacher saw great dangers for German democracy if such persons, who had been too young to form independent opinions during the Third Reich, were not persuaded of the necessity and desirability of Western liberal democracy and were not brought into the democratic movement. Schumacher had seen a democracy collapse in the 1920s and 1930s partly because the youth had not been persuaded to support it. At the same time, Schumacher was utterly convinced that those who had suffered most in their opposition to Nazi terror had now come to the SPD, which therefore had the sole moral right and obligation to take complete political command of the new Germany. This conviction strengthened his obstinate refusal to share power with any other party, even though some SPD leaders at the state level had taken a more independent course and had entered governing coalitions with other parties. An SPD that could not rule the new Germany alone would remain in unyielding opposition to the government.

Schumacher's commitment to democracy and individual rights and his determination for the SPD to rule the new Germany made a clean break with the Communists necessary. He stuck to his principle stated on May 6, 1945: there could be no cooperation with the Communist Party of Germany (KPD) because of the latter's entirely different way of viewing ideas and the political world and because of its close attachment to the Soviet Union; the SPD must refuse to become the "autocratically manipulated instrument of any foreign, imperial interest." He was able to point to developments in the Soviet zone to strengthen his point. In January 1946, he stated: "If that which we are experiencing in the Eastern zone were actually socialism, then European humanists could pronounce the death sentence of socialism." Only truly independent parties could join forces, but German Communists had become "Russian patriots," for whom Germany and socialism had become secondary matters. Because they used brute force to suppress democracy, Schumacher called them "nothing but twin copies of National Socialists varnished with red."

Schumacher's economic thinking and interpretation of that setting had been shaped by Marxism. He assumed that Germans had become such an impoverished people that most had sunk into a proletarian mass that hated capitalism. He thought that there was a "latent proletarian revolution" present in Germany and that a class struggle was forming in which the enlarged working class would emerge victorious. He called for widespread nationalization of banks, insurance companies, and heavy industry. These calls found much support among the German population, the French and British governments, who were in the process of nationalizing much of their own industry and banks, and American authorities.

Under Schumacher foreign policy occupied an important place in SPD politics for the first time. He was an emphatic patriot. He always insisted that since the SPD encompassed the "other Germany" which had opposed Hitler and had suffered greatly as a result, Germany under its leadership had a right to determine its own fate and to take its place as an equal member in the community of nations. "We [Social Democrats] fought the Nazis . . . before anyone else in the world bothered about them," and later "we opposed the Nazis at great cost when it was still fashionable for the rest of the world to vie for their goodwill."

His highest goal was the reunification of Germany within its 1937 borders on the basis of self-determination. This meant that his party rejected both the Oder-Neisse line as the permanent border between Germany and Poland and France's claims to the Saar area. The SPD also demanded that Berlin remain the capital of Germany. His party's insistence on reunification prompted it to oppose German rearmament and partial integration into a united Europe. He branded Konrad Adenauer "Chancellor of the Allies" for accepting these policies. The SPD's fixation on national unity lasted throughout the 1950s.

In general, Schumacher's foreign policy objectives could not be achieved under the conditions that prevailed in Europe during his lifetime. He could not communicate effectively with the occupying powers and put himself in their shoes. Therefore, he could never understand their attitudes or behavior. His economic objectives were, in some important ways, unrealistic and increasingly out of step with the aspirations of his own countrymen. The stubborn pursuit of his economic goals also contributed to the widespread impression in West Germany that the social democrats were not qualified to rule in Bonn and to the party's disheartening electoral setbacks. Under Schumacher, the SPD's domestic and foreign policies were inflexible and out of touch.

See David Childs, *From Schumacher to Brandt* (Pergamon, 1966), Lewis Edinger, *Kurt Schumacher* (Stanford, 1965), Heinrich G. Ritzel, *Kurt Schumacher in Selbstzeugnissen and Bilddokumenten* (Rowohlt, 1972), and Wayne C. Thompson, *The Political Odyssey of Herbert Wehner* (Westview, 1993).

## SCOTT, SIR WALTER

1771–1832, Poet, novelist, and historian; born in Edinburgh, Scotland. Scott started his literary career writing poetry, but his medium later became the historic novel (of which he is considered the inventor). He was fascinated by the early romantic literature that was being produced at his time, and later received much of his inspiration from the German romanticists—not least from the romantic notion of the nation that was part of the *Nationalromantik*.

Scott was also strongly influenced by the poetry of his countryman Robert Burns. Burns has been referred to as both the first Scottish romanticist and the first Scottish nationalist. Scott would, in his own work, express similar predilections. As had Burns, Scott would celebrate in his writing, the mythic, glorious Scottish past, and a strong sense of love for Scotland pervades most of his work.

Characteristic of Scott, however, was an ambivalent national identity. While celebrating the history of the Independence Wars, the Jacobite rebellions of the 18th century, and the uniqueness of Scottish culture, Scott also throughout his life remained an ardent supporter of the political union between Scotland, England, and Wales in 1707, which had established the United Kingdom of Great Britain.

There was little doubt in his mind that the Union of 1707 was of great benefit to his beloved Scotland. These benefits, he thought, Scotland could not afford to jeopardize by mimicking the development of nationalist movements in other European countries during this period. It has thus been argued that Sir Walter exercised a kind of "unionist nationalism" or cultural nationalism, which celebrated Scottish culture and history while at the same time quite happily and pragmatically embracing the political and economic benefits of being part of the British Empire.

In his own time, and especially after 1832 (the year Scott died and the year radical constitutional reform was introduced in the United Kingdom), Scott's apolitical celebration of Scottishness found favor among the new powerful Scottish bourgeoisie, and eventually came to characterize the development of Scottish nationalism until the latter half of the 20th century.

Conflict between Scottish and English ways of life is a recurring theme in Scott's literature. He was preoccupied with the clash of the two national cultures, expressed as the struggle between passion and practicality, the past and the present, the archaic and the advanced—or as he would phrase it: the struggle between the "heart" and the "head." This struggle is nowhere better portrayed than in his first novel, *Waverley: Or 'Tis Sixty Years Since* (1814). In this novel the focus is on the difficult relationships between reason and passion, between modernism and loyalty to the old ways, between the cultures of England/Lowland Scotland and Highland Scotland.

Of all of Walter Scott's different roles, the one he was most proud of was probably that of reconciliator. All his life Scott strove to find a middle way that would incorporate both a strong love for the Scottish nation and a loyalty to the British Empire. And he largely succeeded in doing so. For example, in 1822 Walter Scott, the self-proclaimed Jacobite, was made a baronet by his personal friend King George IV of Britain. For his visit to Edinburgh, Scott persuaded the king to wear a Highland costume, thus uniting all the previously conflicting symbols in a peaceful, cooperative manner.

Scott's reconciliatory and pragmatic attitude was appreciated not only in his own time but by many generations of Scots to come. Until the 1960s, when political nationalism for the first time gained a foothold in Scotland, Scott's formula of unionist nationalism was the one generally adhered to.

For further reading, see James Kerr, *Fiction Against History: Scott as Storyteller* (Cambridge: Cambridge University Press, 1989); Moray McLaren, *Sir Walter Scott: The Man and Patriot* (London: Heinemann, 1970); Paul H. Scott, *Walter Scott and Scotland* (Edinburgh: W. Blackwood, 1981); Hesketh Pearson, *Walter Scott: His Life and Personality* (London: Hamish Hamilton, 1987; 1954); J. H. Alexander and David Hewitt, eds., *Scott and His Influence* (Aberdeen, Association for Scottish Literary Studies, 1983); and Ian Dennis, *Nationalism and Desire in Early Historical Fiction* (Houndmills: MacMillan Press Ltd., 1997).

## SCOTTISH NATIONALISM

Because of its belatedness and the special form it has taken, Scottish nationalism is usually regarded as a "freak of history." Although Scotland has a long history of nationhood, its history of politically expressed demands for radical constitutional change is very short.

In 1707, the Scottish Parliament voted in favor of relinquishing Scotland's status as an independent nation-state and making the country part of the United Kingdom of Great Britain—now to be ruled from Westminster. It was an unpopular decision with the majority of the Scots, and Scottish nationalists have since been arguing along with the national poet, Robert Burns, that the Scots were "bought and sold for English gold." Thus, the foundations for contemporary Scottish nationalism can be seen as having been laid around this time.

Early Scottish nationalism has sometimes been associated with the Jacobite Rebellions in the first half of the 18th century. The extent of the nationalist element in Jacobitism has been much debated. However, the myths surrounding the fruitless Jacobite struggle have taken up a prominent position in modern Scottish national identity, mainly as a consequence of Robert Burns' celebratory poetry (late 18th century) and Walter Scott's romantic reinvention of that particular part of Scottish history (early 19th century).

Walter Scott is probably the single most important figure in the reinvention of Scottish national identity in the 19th century. Almost single-handedly he created the enduring image of Bonnie Scotland of the Highland clans now recognized throughout the world, as well as Scottish cultural unionist nationalism. This curious construct contained both a patriotic pride in Scottish history and culture, and an ardent support for the Union of 1707. For several reasons, mainly to do with economic well-being and social position, this apparently paradoxical type of nationalism appealed to changing Scottish elites throughout the 19th century. They had little incentive to challenge cultural unionist nationalism and, like the great thinkers of the Scottish Enlightenment before them, were quite content with their status as "North Britons." The British Empire provided the Scottish elites with great opportunities for careers and for climbing the social ladder, and to allow political nationalism to develop in Scotland would have been to jeopardize these benefits.

Still, some voices of discontent were heard around the turn of the 19th century when the Scottish Home Rule Association (SHRA) advocated an increased Scottish involvement in Scottish affairs. The SHRA, however, were liberal decentralists rather than political nationalists, and World War I prevented any serious steps from being taken in regard to increased autonomy for Scotland. In the 1920s a literary group known as the Scottish Literary Renaissance, led by Hugh MacDiarmid, argued strongly in favor of Scottish independence. The movement nevertheless remained an elitist phenomenon with little popular support.

The same can be said for the first political parties established in the late 1920s and early 1930s with increased Scottish autonomy or independence as their main goal. The Scottish Party and the National Party of Scotland merged in 1934 to form the Scottish National Party, but support for the nationalist cause in Scotland remained low. The lack of support for political nationalism in general, and for the SNP in particular, may be explained largely by two facts: For the first few years of its existence there was considerable internal strife within the party caused by disagreement about the end goals of political nationalism and the position of the party on the left-right political scale, and World War II created a sense of British patriotism and a temporary boom in Scottish economy.

The latter parameter also explains why, little more than twenty years later, Scottish political nationalism was seemingly unstoppably on the rise. By then, Great Britain had been through severe recessions, and the Scots now witnessed the welfare state being cut while experiencing social and economic decline. As the benefits of union gradually waned, so did support for it. By the end of the 1960s a new confidence in Scotland's ability to make it without the United Kingdom arrived with the discovery of North Sea oil off the coast of Scotland. The SNP gradually started building up considerable support, arguing for a larger Scottish share of oil revenues. In the 1974 general election this stand, expressed in the hugely successful SNP slogan "It's Scotland's Oil!", provided the SNP with its largest share of seats at Westminster, eleven, and the support of more than a third of the Scottish voters. Since World War II, the Labour Party had always been able to rely on the return of approximately half of the seventy-two Scottish MPs, and after this severe setback the British Labour Party reintroduced Scottish (and Welsh) home rule in the party manifestos. Political nationalism had placed itself firmly on the agenda in Scotland.

The year 1979 saw a temporary culmination of political nationalism in Scotland. This was the year when, in a referendum, the Scots were asked their opinion about the possible establishment of a separate Scottish Assembly with devolved powers. With the exception of the Conservative Unionist party and some Labour Party dissenters, all Scottish parties supported the establishment of a Scottish Assembly. So did the media, and so did the major part of Scottish academia. The result of the referendum was a major disappointment for those favoring Scottish home rule. Two-thirds of eligible voters turned out, and of those 52 percent said "yes." Because a limit (40 percent of all eligible voters) was insisted on by opponents of devolution, this was not enough to establish the assembly. In the following general election, support for the SNP dwindled, and as Margaret Thatcher's conservatives took over the government of Britain, Scottish political nationalism entered a decade of crisis.

Through the 1980s and 1990s, as Margaret Thatcher's and John Major's conservative governments grew increasingly unpopular, political nationalism slowly regathered momentum. Representatives of the Labour Party, the liberal democrats, and most of civic society in Scotland now joined hands to form the Scottish Constitutional Convention to try to bring about some kind of devolution of powers from Westminster. What had previously been fierce battles about the nature and the role of Scottish national identity now changed tone into a more confident and pragmatic debate about the possible uses of Scottish culture in the nationalist project.

In 1997 New Labour swept to power in a landslide general election in which Scotland did not return a single conservative unionist MP. As promised during the election campaign, within a year the New Labour government scheduled a referendum on the devolution of powers from Westminster to a reestablished Scottish parliament. This time the result was a resounding "yes": of the 60 percent of Scots who turned out to vote, 74 percent voted in favor of the reestablishment of the Scottish Parliament.

There is still a great debate about the nature of Scottish nationalism. Some argue that Scottish nationalism

is entirely exclusive and ethnic, but most Scots prefer to think of it as overwhelmingly civic with some ethnic/cultural elements. Whereas the SNP used to be divided over the question of end goals, today there is largely a consensus in support for the idea of integrating a future independent Scotland into the European Union, rather than claiming a fully sovereign nation-state. However, Scottish nationalists could face an uphill battle just keeping these issues on the agenda: The low turnout in 1999 for the first Scottish Parliament elections in 292 years, and the general apathy toward the working of that Parliament, could be an indication that political nationalism in Scotland has yet again entered a stage of lethargy.

For further reading, see T. M. Devine and R. J. Finlay, eds., *Scotland in the 20th Century* (Edinburgh: Edinburgh University Press, 1996); Gordon Donaldson, *Scotland, the Shaping of a Nation*, 3rd ed. (Nairn: David St. John Thomas Publishers, 1993); Christopher Harvie, *Scotland and Nationalism, Scottish Society and Politics 1707–1994*, 2nd ed. (London: Routledge, 1994); Michael Lynch, *Scotland—a New History* (London: Pimlico, 1992); Andrew Marr, *The Battle for Scotland* (London: Penguin, 1992); David McCrone, *Understanding Scotland. The Sociology of a Stateless Nation* (London: Routledge, 1992); David McCrone, Alice Brown, and Lindsay Paterson, *Politics and Society in Scotland,* 2nd ed. (Houndsmills and London: Macmillan Press Ltd., 1998); and Tom Nairn, *The Break-Up of Britain: Crisis and Neo-Nationalism* (London: New Left Books, 1977).

## SECESSION

**SECESSION** The act of formal withdrawal from an alliance, federation, or association. Due to the manner in which nation-states came about, national boundaries often include several ethnic groups. In countries that have not been colonized by Europeans, such as those of Western and Eastern Europe, the majority ethnic group usually controls the politics and economy, leaving the minorities with little representation or means of acquiring equality. Minority groups are often forced to live, study, and work in the language and culture of the dominant group. Under these circumstances, minority groups occasionally rebel and demand to have their own separate states. Such acts are often described as declarations of independence if successful, and attempts at secession when they fail.

Secession does not require a difference between ethnic groups. When several groups with differing viewpoints exist within one nation, a secession attempt might come about when those opinions become so contrary that people holding them cannot coexist.

Secession often results in civil war, because the dominant forces in a country do not want to lose land, tax revenues, and political control. In the case of an ethnically based secession, the majority might also fear for the safety and autonomy of members of the majority who live in the area that is seceding.

Famous secessions include that of the Southern states of the United States, leading to the American Civil War; that of Croatia, leading to the Bosnian war; and that of Muslims from India, forming Pakistan and Bangladesh.

The breakup of the Soviet Union came about as different republics seceded and declared their independence. Fifteen new states emerged without a war. However, within several republics, small groups attempted to secede, causing bloody repressions. The secession of ethnic Russians in the Trans-Dniester region of Moldova led to war and then a peace treaty granting special status to the region within the republic of Moldova. The secession of Armenians in Nagorno-Karabakh, a region inside Azerbaijan, has costs thousands of lives, and remains to be satisfactorily settled.

## SELF-DETERMINATION

In 1960 the United Nations passed a general resolution entitled the "Declaration on the Granting of Independence to Colonial Countries and Peoples" by a vote of eighty-nine to zero with abstentions from the United States, Great Britain, France, and the other leading colonial powers. This declaration addressed a contradiction of the original 1945 Charter, which in the first two articles had recognized the right of both the state to sovereignty and the nation to self-determination. The struggle in the immediate aftermath of World War II for self-determination, spearheaded by colonial people against imperial control, soon revealed this contradiction. Rather than allowing the "nation" to supersede the state, the negotiated 1960 Declaration specified that only colonial victims of European imperialism were entitled to self-determination. However, there is no clear or objective basis for determining if a people are the victims of colonization or merely a national minority. Compounded by the indiscriminate use of the term *national self-determination*, this ambiguity has consistently undermined a unified international response to ethnic crisis, and may have even encouraged the secessionist movements that broke up the Soviet Union and Yugoslavia at tremendous cost to human life.

The first international recognition of national self-determination was no less problematic. Following World War I, national self-determination was favored as a tool for encouraging the internal breakup of the defeated imperial powers. While indeed this principle proved expedient for the breakup of the defeated powers, it was less effective as a basis for reconstituting a new stable political order. The advocates of national self-determination overlooked the fact that the nation, as a territorially bounded and homogeneous entity, is neither universal nor primordial. The result of this failure was not only perpetual political instability in the new states constituted from the former Austro-Hungarian and Ottoman Empires, but a new legal principle that would be used against the victorious states twenty years later by Nazi Germany at Munich.

Despite its dismal failure as a principle of international law, self-determination has not been resolutely rejected. Arguably, the ambiguity in the law works to the benefit of UN members by providing an interpretive space to support flexible response or lack thereof to crises on a case-by-case basis. Furthermore, as most of these leading powers are democracies and subject to electoral sanction, advocating a brute *Realpolitik* that unconditionally favors state sovereignty over the nation's self-determination is not always possible. Most of these states were themselves constituted from the struggle by a people against a sovereign governing body, a fact that remains at the core of the democratic electorate's conception of the political.

In fact, it is in this very struggle that the concept of self-determination first found political expression as one of the potential bases of sovereignty. Generally associated with the American and French democratic revolutions, self-determination of a people has long emerged within the discourse on sovereignty, though the term itself only came into use in the 19th century. For example, already in 1324 Marsillius of Padua, in his *Defensor Pacis*, argued that power must be concentrated and should be derived from the people, or more specifically—their "greater and healthier part," and cannot be limited by natural law since that is created by the people themselves. However, it would take quite some time for his ideas to find full political expression. In the 16th and 17th century, the horrors of the religious wars prompted a number of scholars, including Jean Bodin (1588–1679) and Thomas Hobbes (1588–1679), to advocate strong centralized government in the principle of state sovereignty. For both of these scholars, centralization of power was essentially to ward off the evils of anarchy, and neither could conceive of a way to reconcile centralized authority with popular self-determination.

With absolutism came a new era of stability and economic development. By the 18th century philosophers were again finding an audience for the idea of popular sovereignty, this time not as a means of escaping anarchy and feudalism, but as a challenge to absolutism. But fear of anarchy, prompted by the upheaval of the 17th-century English revolution and anticipated by Aristotle, encouraged some, including Rousseau, to offer a more precise definition of the people. Rousseau advocated the aggregation of people through culture for fear that a democratic society would otherwise degenerate into anarchy. The people once reconstituted in "the nation" would have not only a strong and stable government, but would also have a just government that served their interests as individuals. In 1795, the French Declaration of the Rights of Man proclaimed: "Each people is independent and sovereign, whatever the number of individuals who compose it and the extent of the territory it occupies. This sovereignty is inalienable."

With the American and French Revolutions, popular self-determination leapt from a political and moral theory to a blueprint for political action, carrying with it the new concept of the nation as a moral agent. In fact, by the mid-19th century the nation would break away from its original form as a necessary component of stable democracy, and would become an end unto itself, at the expense of both the individual and democracy. Nevertheless, in 1918 Wilson gave legitimacy to the principle of national self-determination, a principle that largely served the immediate interests of restoring political stability to Europe. The consequence, while certainly unintended, was to facilitate a reactivation of world war twenty years later. Despite the obvious vulnerability of self-determination to interpretive abuse, it survived World War II to became the basis for the creation of a host of new states.

With the 1975 Conference on Security and Cooperation in Europe, the Helsinki Accord clearly rejected any violation of the territorial status quo in Europe. Nevertheless, in 1991 Germany backed the secessions of Slovenia and Croatia, and the United States supported Bosnia's in March 1992. War would erupt only in the aftermath of the Western declarations in support of the breakup of Yugoslavia. The Western decision to hold national self-determination over the integrity of the Yugoslav state was certainly motivated by the fear that Serbian influence would otherwise go unchecked. However, it had the unintended consequence of devolving power into the hands of those willing to embrace ethnic cleansing as a means to national self-determination.

**SELF-GOVERNANCE, NATIVE AMERICAN** Authorized on October 5, 1988, when Congress passed Public Law 100-472, the Indian Self-Determination Amendments of 1987 and cited as the Indian Self-Determination and Education Assistance Act Amend-

ments of 1988. The act offered a major change in the relationship between tribal governments and the federal government in Section 209 entitled Tribal Self-Governance Demonstration Project. The self-governance project, as it became known, allowed the secretary of interior for five years to conduct "a research and demonstration project" in order to "authorize the tribe to plan, conduct, consolidate, and administer programs, services and functions authorized under the Act of April 16, 1934" (IRA). The self-government demonstration project was designed to strengthen tribal sovereignty by utilizing self-governance compacts and annual funding agreements to give back authority and control to the tribes. The self-governance compacts and annual funding agreements were designed to provide tribal governments with control and decision-making authority over the federal financial resources provided for the benefit of tribal members and to reduce the size of the federal bureaucracies that previously supervised such programming and funding, namely, the Bureau of Indian Affairs and Indian Health Service.

The specific goals of the self-governance act written into the self-governance act and the compacts were (1) formalize relations between the United States and Indian tribes on a government-to-government basis as provided for in the U.S. Constitution; (2) downsize the Bureau of Indian Affairs and Indian Health Service to be compatible with their new roles; (3) recognize American Indian tribes' right to determine internal priorities, redesign and create new tribal programs, and reallocate financial resources to more effectively and efficiently meet the needs of their tribal communities; (4) promote greater social, economic, political, and cultural stability and self-sufficiency among Indian tribes by better using the resources obligated in treaties, executive orders, and acts of Congress; (5) establish better fiscal accountability through expanded tribal government decision-making authority; (6) institute administrative cost efficiencies between tribal governments and the United States through reduced bureaucratic burdens and streamlined decision-making processes; and (7) change the role of the federal departments and agencies serving Indian tribes by shifting their responsibilities from day-to-day management of tribal affairs to that of protectors of and advocates for tribal interests.

A major dilemma occurred in the first years of the self-governance project in that the federal agencies who were supposed to turn over both funding and control of programming to tribal governments did not do so willingly. The late Art Gahbow, chair of the Mille Lacs Band of Ojibwe, offered the following testimony to Congress in regards to this problem. "The self-governance project allowed for the first time since the treaty days for tribal governments to develop, administer and basically run every program on their reservations without direct supervision of such programs by the BIA, HUD, IHS or any of the other federal agencies that had so dominated their lives previously. Federal agency control was diminished but it did not disappear all together, even though initial evaluations identify that the programs administered by these tribes have been far more effective and efficient than previous federally administrated programs. . . . Due to the BIA's complete lack of cooperation at all administrative levels, our budgetary analysis of BIA expenditures for the benefit of the Mille Lacs Band took several different turns before it stopped in a dead-end. The BIA simply would not give us *any* budgetary information regarding non-banded funds for the Mille Lacs Band. . . . We strongly doubt that the BIA has the capacity to negotiate and transfer Federal funds to our Tribe under a Self-Governance funding agreement. Without the continued active support of Congress, the entire Tribal Self-Governance Demonstration Project will simply be thrown into the historical archives of a bloated bureaucracy that miserably and tragically failed to fulfill its essential mission."

There were other concerns that the federal government's motive behind Public Law 100-472 was to reinstate the "termination" policies of the 1950s by sending all federal programs to the tribes in order to end the trust responsibility of the federal government for such programs. The trust responsibility is protected in the Self-Governance Demonstration Act and the Tribal Self-Governance Act of 1994. Specific language is included in these acts that "nothing in this Act shall be construed to diminish the federal trust responsibility to Indian tribes, individual Indians, or Indians with trust allotments."

The verdict is still out on the effectiveness of the Native American self-governance act. Thirty-some tribes are presently self-governance tribes and each has developed self-governance offices that negotiate tribal compacts and annual funding agreements with the Bureau of Indian Affairs. These tribes report better service to tribe members at reduced costs and African and European nations have shown some interest in the self-governance program as a possible alternative to their homeland and refuge policies.

A thorough text on Native American self-governance is *American Indian Policy: Self-Governance and Economic Development* (Greenwood Press, 1994), edited by Lyman H. Legters and Fremont J. Lyden.

## SENECA FALLS CONVENTION   The first women's rights convention in the United States was held on July 19–20, 1848, in Seneca Falls, New York. This moment marks the beginning of the primarily white women's suffrage movement that would finally culminate in the Nineteenth Amendment to the Constitution in 1921. Developing out of the antislavery movement, women argued that all people had a right to equality. Feminist activists, such as Elizabeth Cady Stanton and Lucretia Mott, with the support of abolitionist Frederick Douglass, called the convention to consider "the social, civil and religious conditions and rights of women." Assembled at the convention were roughly 100 to 300 women and men. The focus of the convention was the adoption of the Declaration of Sentiments and Resolutions. The Declaration of Sentiments and Resolutions was intentionally modeled after the American Declaration of Independence to highlight the limited scope of the revolutionary vision.

The women at the convention stated clearly that the cause of women's grievances was the tyranny of men. Both the historical gathering of women and their declaration challenged the patriarchal foundations of the U.S. nation. In the declaration women argued that the government wrongly denied women their inalienable rights to life, liberty, and happiness and therefore they refused allegiance and insisted on change. The declaration demanded individual rights for women, full legal equality, full rights to education and commercial opportunity, and to collect wages. The most radical and difficult resolution, narrowly passed, was the call for women's suffrage. The convention was consciously intended to ignite a larger women's emancipation movement. Although the convention was publicly ridiculed and criticized, it was an important event in the history of America.

For more information, see Stanton, Elizabeth Cady, Susan B. Anthony, and M. J. Gage, eds., *The History of Woman Suffrage*, 6 vols. (New York: National American Woman Suffrage Association, 1888–1922) and Ellen Carol DuBois' *Feminism and Suffrage: The Emergence of an Independent Women's Movement In America* (Cornell University Press, 1978).

## SENEGALESE NATIONALISM   Senegal was the oldest French colony in continental Africa. Its quest for national identity was eminently affected by the French colonial rule in this part of Africa's political landscape.

Historically, the early European explorers in search of gold and other precious metals utilized Senegal as a point of entry into other parts of Africa. The French settlement in Senegal began in the coastal town of St. Louis, named after the patron saint of King Louis XIV in 1658. It inaugurated an important historical period in France's West African, three-pronged colonization in general and of Senegal in particular. The French consolidation of the vast lands through pincers operations began from the Maghrib in the North, the Congo Brazzaville in the South, and the Senegal River in the West. Subsequently, Dakar became the capital of the French West African colonial empire, which consisted of some eight other colonial holdings.

Further francophone attempts at colonization in Senegal, however, did not begin until the middle of the 17th century. In fact, it was in 1792, when the Peace of Paris established its colonial status quo ante in Senegal. In 1817, St. Louis was restored as part of the first permanent occupation of African territories by the French. The British also occupied Senegal in 1816. They did so only as a military ploy to penetrate Fouta Jalon. Their expedition, however, essentially remained devoid of any significant attempt to impose British civil, administrative, and colonial rule, as Great Britain had done in other parts of Africa. The French, therefore, found the designated territory and protectorate of the Senegal open to colonial experimentation in military affairs, trade, agricultural activities, and settlement.

To be sure, the earliest indigenous opposition to the French rule in Senegal, as a form of nascent nationalism, was short lived. Opposition was met headlong through France's military operations. The tactics included the suppression of internal revolt and, later, diplomacy and the treaties of friendship with the local chiefs, which the French did not have difficulty ratifying. Among challenges to French rule in Senegal were those by Trarza and the Brakna Arab Muslims in the 19th century. They asserted their "suzerainty" over Oualo. Their anti-French drives, however, were unsuccessful and they were crushed by France's military forces. The nominal recognition of the Arab suzerainty in Oualo, which ended between 1855 and 1857, did not end the Senegalese-Arab insurrection. Mahmadu Lamine led a yearlong revolt against the French. He declared himself as the Islamic mahdi or messiah and engaged in battle with the local king in Bondou, assassinating him in the process. Immediately, thereafter, Lamine died of wounds inflicted by the French in battle.

Among French rulers in Senegal, Faidherbe played a decisive role in bringing the colonial outpost closer to its dominating objectives. As its governor general, Faidherbe established the territory's civil administrative, educational, and banking systems. During the subsequent centuries, the French influence in Senegalese social existence became more entrenched. Gradually, French presence in Senegal altered the setting's traditional mode of existence and left an indelible mark on its cultural, social, and political organizations prior and following independence.

Notwithstanding Senegal's affinity and assimilationist approach toward French culture, factors of religion and ethnicity also played decisive roles in the country's nationalistic postures. In retrospect, both Islam and Christianity penetrated Senegal, gradually replacing its indigenous belief system. The earliest missionaries of French Capuchins in Senegal under Peres Alexis and Bernardin who visited Senegal in 1635 did not accomplish their ideal objectives. Thereafter, no systematic attempt was made to establish the Christian missions in this land, until the 19th century. In the centuries that followed the 16th, however, Christianity did not attract followers as Islam did. Senegal's adherence to Islam began in the 12th century and ever since it has defined its predominant religious identity.

In essence, Senegal's over three-century-long relations with France, and the extension of French citizenship to the inhabitants of its major cities until 1916, rendered the country unique in the continent. In fact, during the First French Republic in 1794, the decree of sixteen *Pluviose* and the Royal Ordinance of 1833 extended French citizenship and political rights to the inhabitants of the colony, which included Saint Louis and Goree, just off Cape Verde Island. Again the revised French Constitution of 1946 introduced broad changes in Senegal's relations with its colonial power. It redefined the perquisites of the French citizenship for educated Senegalese adult males. Later in 1872, these political rights were granted to the people of Lebu. Moreover, close cooperation among various ethnic groups, namely, the Serer, Wolof, and Tokolor and their favorable outlook toward France's assimilationist politics and culture, moved the country in a less radical and more moderate nationalistic direction by its pre- and postindependence leaders.

The representation of Senegal in the French Parliament in 1848 changed in 1957, when it attained a semi-self-governing status under France's *Loi Cadre* provisions. In 1958, Senegal became a member of President de Gaulle's French *communaute* and in 1958, together with French Soudan, formed the Mali Federation. The dissolution of the Mali Federation in 1960 brought about changes in both Senegal and Mali political status as independent states.

Among Senegal's nationalist leaders, Leopold Sedar Senghor, the former French-educated president of both the Mali Federation and Senegal, played a decisive role in reinvigorating the country's national sentiments. As a former professor of philosophy in the French Lycee Marcellin-Berthelot, Senghor's treatise on negritude, African personality, and Pan-Africanism redefined the concept of nationalism in Africa in general and of Senegal in particular.

In 1948, Senghor established the *Bloc Démocratique Senegalas*. As its founder, Senghor sought to bring about greater autonomy for the party. The party eventually defeated SFIO and gained seats in the French National Assembly. Senghor, together with the Caribbean intellectuals, notably Aime Cesaire, expounded on Africa's heritage and culture. In his treatise on negritude, which he depicted as "antiracial racialism" reflection, he delved into philosophical discussion on the positive and negative attributes of the French "civilizing mission" in Africa and on African assimilation to its culture. He also pondered the differences between the universal civilization and the "civilization of the universal," which he aspired to embrace humanity. Senghor was a cultural nationalist, who also analyzed the problems of governance in Senegal. Earlier in 1945, Lamine Gueye was the leader of the Senegalese faction of the *Section Francaise de l'International Ouvriere*. A politician of Wolof ethnic background, Gueye attempted also to bring about changes in France's colonial policies in Senegal. In short, Senegal's ethnic cohesion has had a moderating influence on its nationalistic aims and has rendered the country less vulnerable to the vicissitudes of the nationalistic fervor evident in Africa and elsewhere in the world.

For additional sources see Philip Curtin, Steven Feierman, Leonard Thompson, and Jan Vansina, *African History* (Madison, Wisc.: University of Wisconsin Press, 1978); J. D. Fage, *An Introduction to the History of West Africa* (Cambridge, 1961); William Foltz, *From French West Africa to the Mali Federation,* (New Haven, Conn.: Yale University Press, 1965); Baron William M. Hailey, *An African Survey* (New York, 1956); Leopold Sedar Senghor, "On Negritude: The Psychology of the African Negro," in *Diogene* 37 (1962); Leopold Sedar Senghor, "l'Espirit de la civilisation ou le lois de la culture negro-africaine," in *Presence Africaine* (Paris, 1967); and Paul Sigmund, *The Ideologies of the Developing Nations* (New York: Praeger, 1967).

## SERBIAN NATIONALISM

Beginning in 1804, a series of uprisings against Ottoman rule led to the emergence of an independent Serbian state, which was established in 1878. However, the exact definition of Serb identity was vague and subject to constant dispute throughout the 19th and 20th centuries.

Vuk Stefanović Karadžić, the 19th-century linguistic reformer of the Serbian language, was in many respects the father of Serbian nationalism. Karadžić adopted a linguistic definition of the Serbs, including all speakers of the Štokavian dialect, regardless of religious affiliation or geographic location, as Serbs. However, Karadžić acknowledged the right of some Štokavian-speaking peoples to call themselves names other than Serbs. Karadžić's ideas were subsequently given additional political meaning by Ilija Garašanin, who sought to extend the borders of the Serbian state to include all Serbs. As expressed in Garašanin's 1844 *Načertanije* (*Proposal*), this demand assumed a central position in Serbian nationalism. Garašanin's ideas formed a political program for the expansion of the Serbian state at the expense of the Ottoman and the Habsburg empires. This program was also reflected in the desire to avenge the loss of the medieval Serbian state of the Nemanjić dynasty to the Ottoman Empire. The Battle of Kosovo on *Vidovdan* (St. Vitus Day), June 28, 1389, became the symbol of this loss, although most historians agree that the battle was not as decisive as portrayed by Serbian historiography. As can be seen below, *Vidovdan* acquired a number of salient meanings for Serbian nationalism.

The main body of Serbian nationalism developed along lines similar to those followed by other nationalisms in Eastern Europe. The primary objectives of early Serb nationalists were liberation from Ottoman rule and the establishment of a Serbian nation-state. Due to the fact that Serbs resided in areas far outside the boundaries of the medieval Nemanjić state and the Ottoman Empire, Serbian nationalism necessarily preoccupied itself increasingly with the fate of Serbs outside of Serbia proper and their non-Serb neighbors. As the realization of a Serbian nation-state drew closer, the relationship between Serbs and other South Slavs therefore grew in salience. It was in this context that the notion of the Serbian state of 1878 as the Piedmont for a South Slavic Risorgimento emerged. The Serbian statesman Nikola Pašić played a crucial and long-term role in positioning Serbia as a South Slavic Piedmont.

Serbia achieved international recognition as an independent state at the Congress of Berlin in 1878. However, the government of Serbia regarded its borders as truncated, and therefore sought ties to Serbs and other South Slavs in the Habsburg Empire. This produced considerable antagonism between Austria-Hungary and Serbia in the decades before World War I. After the violent 1903 ouster of the Obrenović dynasty by the Karadordević dynasty, the Austro-Serbian antipathy only worsened. This period also witnessed a growing tension between the civilian rulers of Serbia and the Serb military. The former wished to maintain rule in the hands of civilians. The latter, as typified by the nationalist conspiratorial organization *Ujedinjenje ili smrt* (Union or Death, also known as *Crna ruka,* or the Black Hand), idolized the Prussian military and its strong role as a unifier and maintainer of the German state.

On June 28, 1914, the Austrian Archduke Franz Ferdinand was assassinated by a Bosnian Serb nationalist in Sarajevo, an act that set into motion the events that would lead to World War I. World War I had catastrophic consequences for the Serb population. Historians continue to debate the role of *Crna ruka* in aiding the assassin. After initial and surprising victories against the forces of Austria-Hungary, the Serb army was forced to retreat to the island of Corfu. During the march to the Adriatic, the Serbs sustained catastrophic, decimating losses from combat, disease, and famine. Serb nationalists subsequently depicted the calamity in religious-mythical terms as the "Golgotha and resurrection" of the Serb nation.

Serbia emerged traumatized but victorious from World War I. Already in 1915, the Serbian government had declared its intent to establish a state including the Serbs, Croats, and Slovenes. However, the political leadership of Serbia, led by Prime Minister Nikola Pašić, regarded the new Yugoslav state as an expansion of the pre-1914 state. Pašić and his colleagues believed that the Serb should play a special and leading role in Yugoslavia because they alone of the South Slavs had managed to win their own independence in the 19th century. This view, considerable already before 1914, received substantial impetus from the dramatic role of the Serb nation in World War I. This attitude led to significant disagreements with the political representatives of the non-Serb peoples of Yugoslavia, who generally desired a looser federal or confederal state structure instead of a centralist regime based in Belgrade.

The St. Vitus Day Constitution of June 28, 1920, in effect signified the victory of the Serbian centralist state view over the confederal or federal plans of the non-Serbs. During the next ten years, Serb nationalist politicians and their Croat and Slovene nationalist counterparts proved unable to craft a durable and stable compromise for governance of the state known as the Kingdom of Serbs, Croats, and Slovenes. In the late 1920s, the deterioration of parliamentary democracy culminated in the assassination in 1928 of Stjepan Radić and several other deputies of the Croat Peasant Party on the floor of Parliament.

On January 6, 1929, King Aleksandar Karađorđević discarded the St. Vitus Day Constitution and proclaimed a royal dictatorship. As part of the dictatorship, "tribal" identities would be abandoned in favor of a single and modern Yugoslav nationalism. Aleksandar also formally changed the name of the country to the Kingdom of Yugoslavia. This produced dissatisfaction among Serb nationalists, who saw Yugoslav nationalism as a disavowal of Serbian nationalism. It also failed to

win many converts among the non-Serbs who viewed the unitarist course as de facto Serbian nationalism. In 1939, Serb and Croat political leaders signed a compromise agreement giving Croatia virtual autonomy within Yugoslavia. A group of Serb nationalists led by Slobodan Jovanović and Dragiša Vasić established the *Srpski kulturni klub* (Serb Cultural Club) in 1937, protested the *Sporazum*, and attacked Yugoslav nationalism under the banner of "strong Serbdom, strong Yugoslavia." Other Serb nationalists withdrew into mystical and messianic notions of Serbian nationalist identity. This trend was exemplified by Miloš Crnjanski and Justin Popović.

World War II proved just as traumatic to Serbian nationalism as World War I. Serbia was occupied by Germany, and the attempts of the Serbian puppet regime to portray itself as the legitimate representative of the Serb nation failed. Serb nationalism found more effective representation by the *Četnik* royalist forces of Dragoljub (Draža) Mihailović, who fought guerrilla warfare in Yugoslavia. Massacres perpetrated by Mihailović's forces in Bosnia-Herzegovina, in particular, the royalists' extreme anti-Muslim variant of Serbian nationalism, alienated large portions of the population. However, by the end of World War II, the Communist Partisan movement of Josip Broz Tito emerged as the dominant force in Yugoslavia.

During Communist Yugoslavia, Tito's administration took care to prevent the dominance of any single nationality over the other nationalities in Yugoslavia. In 1966, Tito expelled the Yugoslav interior minister, Aleksandar Ranković, a Serb, from the League of Communists of Yugoslavia. This was widely perceived as an attack on Serb nationalists.

From the early 1960s, Serb intellectuals led by Dobrica Ćosić began to challenge publicly the official ideology of Yugoslavism and its slogan of *bratstvo i jedinstvo* (brotherhood and unity). Increasingly after the purge of Ranković, Serb nationalist intellectuals perceived Yugoslavia as a detrimental experience for the Serb nation.

In the late 1980s Serbian nationalism reemerged prominently on both the political and the intellectual stage. In 1986, the Serbian Academy of Arts and Sciences composed a salient memorandum. This draft document was the most inclusive expression of the Serb nationalist sentiment that postwar Yugoslavia and Yugoslavism had produced negative political, cultural, and economic consequences for the Serb nation. In particular, the memorandum directed its anger at the loose federal constitutional structure of Yugoslavia and at the existence of two autonomous republics, Kosovo and Vojvodina, within Serbia. The memorandum accused Kosovo

Albanians in particular of trying to destroy the Serb population there through biological reproduction. In sum, the memorandum argued that what Serbia and the Serbs had won in battle during the war, they had lost in peacetime.

In politics, Slobodan Milošević, a Communist, adopted nationalism as a tool to gain popular support. As part of a self-proclaimed "antibureaucratic revolution," Milošević withdrew the autonomy of Kosovo and Vojvodina in 1989 and installed a subordinate leadership in Montenegro as well. Meanwhile, nationalist politicians emerged in Croatia and Bosnia-Herzegovina who demanded that the Serbs in those territories be allowed to join Serbia. Croatia, Slovenia, and Bosnia-Herzegovina viewed this as a substantial threat to the security of Yugoslavia and their respective republics. Non-Serb politicians in these republics began to voice their own demands for independence.

In 1991, Yugoslavia collapsed as Slovenia and Croatia declared their independence. In April 1992, armed hostilities began in Bosnia-Herzegovina. Serb nationalists in Bosnia-Herzegovina and Croatia, with assistance from the Serbian government, initiated a process of "ethnic cleansing," the forced removal of non-Serbs from territory considered to be Serbian. Although numerous atrocities were committed, the campaign did not completely succeed, and the war ended in November 1995. Since the end of the war in Bosnia-Herzegovina, tensions between Serbs and ethnic Albanians in Kosovo have been the main focal point of Serbian nationalism.

**SEXUALITY AND NATIONALISM** Nationalist boundaries are also sexual boundaries—erotic intersections where people make intimate connections across ethnic, racial, and national borders. The borderlands that lie at the intersections of ethnic and national boundaries are "ethno-sexual frontiers" that are surveilled and supervised, patrolled and policed, regulated and restricted, but which are constantly penetrated by individuals forging sexual links with ethnic and national "others." Some of this sexual contact is by "ethno-sexual settlers" who establish long-term liaisons, join and/or form families, and become members of ethno-national communities "on the other side." Some of this sexual contact is by "ethno-sexual sojourners" who stay for a brief or extended visit, enter into sexual liaisons, but eventually return to home communities. Some of this sexual contact is by "ethno-sexual adventurers" who undertake expeditions across ethno-national boundaries for recreational, casual, or "exotic" sexual encounters, often more than once, but who return to their sexual home bases after each excursion. Some of this sexual contact is by "ethno-sexual invaders" who launch sexual assaults across ethno-national boundaries, inside alien territory, seducing, raping, and sexually enslaving racial, ethnic, or national "others" as a means of sexual domination and colonization.

It is the sexualized nature of things ethnic, racial, and national that heats up discourse on the values, attributes, and moral worth of "us" and "them," that arouses passions when there are violations of sexual contact rules, that raises doubts about loyalty and respectability when breaches of sexual demeanor occur, that stirs reactions when questions of sexual purity and propriety arise, and that sparks retaliations when threats to sexual boundaries are perceived or detected.

There is, of course, more than one kind of sexual boundary inside and between ethnic, racial, or national communities. It is the issue of multiple sexualities in ethno-sexual contact that brings most clearly to light contradictory tensions in the relationship between nationalism and sexuality. Across cultures, "appropriate" enactments of heterosexuality are perhaps the most regulated and enforced norms in societies. In particular, "correct" heterosexual masculine and feminine behavior constitutes gender regimes that often lie at the core of nationalist culture. "Our" women (virgins, mothers, pure) versus "their" women (sluts, whores, unclean). "Our" men (virile, strong, brave) versus "their" men (degenerate, weak, cowardly). These heteronormative ethno-sexual stereotypes are nearly universal depictions of "self" and "other" as one gazes across nationalist time and space. Because of the common importance of proper gender role and sexual behavior to ethnic community honor, a great deal of attention is paid to sexual demeanor in both formal and informal rules of conduct.

For instance, in many cultures men's power and strength translate into sexual potency and virility, whereas women might be more likely defined as steadfast and loyal, traits that imply sexual restraint and purity. There are certainly many cultural variations in the ways in which evaluations of male and female sexual behavior are distinguished by different gender roles. Nonetheless, women and men are often tied together by notions of honor; where women's sexual demeanor can be seen to reflect on male relatives' honor—an impure woman can dishonor her male relatives in ways that often do not seem to work in reverse, where women kin are not seen to be dishonored by men's sexual impurity.

Nationalist ideology, movements, and conflicts tend to be sexualized in several ways. First, nationalist ideologies often reflect conservative, traditional views of the nation, which place the heterosexual family at the center of national values and processes, with women as reproducers of the nation and vessels of nationalist culture, and with men as defenders of home and nation and as heads of the kin and national "family." Second, nationalist movements are routinely militarized movements that stress masculine cultural traits such as power, strength, and honor—traits that are often imbued with sexual meanings that translate into male (but not female) sexual potency and virility, and which often value and enforce female (but not male) sexual purity. Third, nationalist conflicts, like many military conflicts, frequently include sexual strategies or aspects that can take several forms: rape, sexual "collaboration," or sexual slavery. Fourth, nonheterosexualities (homosexuality, bisexuality, transgendered identities and behaviors) tend not to be integrated into nationalist ideologies and imaginings of the nation, but rather are likely to be defined as characteristics of marginal, alien "others," haunting the edges of the nation, and seen as potential threats to national solidarity.

Recent, groundbreaking works revealing the links between sexuality and nationalism include George Mosse's *Nationalism and Sexuality: Middle-Class Morality and Sexual Norms in Modern Europe* (University of Wisconsin Press, 1985); A. Parker, M. Russo, D. Sommer, and P. Yaeger, eds., *Nationalisms and Sexualities* (Routledge, 1991); and Anne McClintock's *Imperial Leather: Race, Gender and Sexuality in the Colonial Context* (Routledge, 1995).

## SHAH OF IRAN (MOHAMMAD REZA PAHLAVI)

1919–1980, Last ruler of the Pahlavi Dynasty in Iran prior to the establishment of the Islamic Republic of Iran in 1979, born in Tehran and died in exile in Cairo. The last shah of Iran was both a quintessential and paradoxical nationalist figure who embarked on numerous modernization and development programs for Iran— collectively referred to as the White Revolution (1963–1975). He staged elaborate spectacles that glorified Iranian history and consciously strove to strengthen Iranian national identity; and yet twice he was forced into involuntary exile from Iran due to forces in the country which could also be considered nationalist. The shah's advent to power symbolized these contradictions. He assumed the throne in 1941 when his father, Reza Shah the Great, who had founded the Pahlavi Dynasty in 1925, was forced into exile by the British and Soviet forces who then occupied Iran and feared possible collaboration between Reza Shah and the Nazis. From 1951 to 1953 the shah was involved in a power struggle with Mohammad Mossaddeq, an Iranian nationalist leader who had attempted to seize state control over the vast British petroleum interests in Iran, and in August 1953 the shah was forced to leave Iran by Mossaddeq supporters. First permitted to rule by external forces, the shah then was restored to power in a successful counter-coup against

Mossaddeq, which had been covertly supported and engineered by the United States' Central Intelligence Agency. The events of 1978–1979, which culminated in the Islamic Revolution against his reign, proved fatal; no foreign power could rescue him that time.

The shah deliberately strove to modernize and industrialize Iran and believed that Iran would become a regional, then world power—if not during his lifetime, then during that of his son, Crown Prince Reza. Development—from land reform to electrification, from the construction of dams and a network of paved roads to the establishment of modern armed services equipped with the most advanced weaponry Iranian oil earnings could buy—unquestionably occurred during the quarter century (1953–1978) of the shah's uninterrupted rule, but this modernization came at a tremendous social price. Numerous peasants did not benefit from the shah's widely proclaimed land reform program; if anything, their situation deteriorated, as they were evicted from traditional land-working arrangements and migrated for seasonal or permanent labor in large numbers to the cities, particularly Tehran, the population of which mushroomed. All the shah's programs were dependent on oil revenues, and Iran, unlike Arab states in the Gulf or even Iraq, had a very large population (ca. 40 million by the late 1970s) over which these earnings somehow had to be distributed.

Iranians correctly perceived that the shah's various programs were dependent on the Westerners who directed them, particularly Americans who numbered in the tens of thousands and lived comfortably and visibly as expatriates. The shah's lifestyle and those of the extended royal family were ostentatious, consciously secular, and Western in a country that was traditionally conservative and deeply Islamic. Even the shah's attempts to glorify Iranian culture were misplaced, honoring Iran's pre-Islamic history at the expense of its Islamic heritage. Thus, most spectacularly in fall 1971 he staged at considerable expense an elaborate ceremony celebrating 2500 years of Persian culture and dynastic rule on the plains of Persepolis, the ceremonial capital of the Persian Achaemenid Empire founded by Cyrus the Great in the 6th century B.C.; attended by numerous heads of state and delegations from throughout the world, the ceremony extolled the glories of ancient Iranian history and was meant to symbolize the security and stability of the shah's rule, a reign that ignominiously unraveled seven years later.

Nationalism typically is associated with modernization, industrialization, and secularism—all programs the shah vigorously promoted. The Iranian Revolution confounded theorists precisely because it heralded a traditional religious nationalism, a phenomenon that today is increasingly familiar; it is seen from India and the rise of the ruling Hindu party to the civil war in Algeria.

While self-serving, the shah's own accounts of his rule are worth reading: *Mission for My Country* (McGraw-Hill, 1961) and *Answer to History* (Stein and Day, 1980). Less partial, informative accounts are provided by M. Zonis's *Majestic Failure: The Fall of the Shah* (University of Chicago Press, 1991) and F. Halliday's *Iran: Dictatorship and Development* (Penguin, 1979). For a detailed study of the failure of the shah's land reform program and the White Revolution, see E. J. Hooglund's *Land and Revolution in Iran 1960–1980* (University of Texas Press, 1982).

**SHAMIL** 1797–1871, Russian republic of Dagestan's (located in the northeastern Caucasus) most famous son. For decades this Islamic leader led the mountain people of Dagestan and Chechnya in a bloody struggle against the invading armies of Russia and his name is still revered as a nationalist icon in the region today. Shamil was born in the village of Gimry in Daghestan in 1797 and belonged to the largest Daghestani nationality, the Avars. As a youth Shamil joined the religious *sufi* (mystical) brotherhood of the *Naqshbandiyya* order and loyally followed his leader, the Imam (Chosen One) Ghazi Muhammad, in fighting against the Russians, who had gained nominal control of Daghestan in 1813. Shamil earned great respect as a warrior and, at the last stand of Ghazi Muhammad (whose anti-Russian forces had been surrounded by Russian troops), Shamil was one of only two survivors. As legends around him grew, Shamil quickly rose through the ranks of *murids* (holy warriors) fighting against the Russian infidels. After Ghazi Muhammad's death in 1832 at the hands of the Russians, he was eventually succeeded by Shamil who commenced a *jihad* against the invading Russians.

Contemporaries describe Shamil as a charismatic leader who was able to unify the tribes and peoples of multiethnic Daghestan and Chechnya as never before. By 1834 Shamil had organized an independent Islamic state in Daghestan and led his followers in a series of well-executed raids against Russia. On one occasion Shamil was surrounded at the city of Ahulgo, a mountain stronghold, but was able to once again escape his enemies. Prior to his escape, Shamil was forced to hand over his eldest son Jalal-al Din to the Russians as a hostage to ensure his good faith, and this appears to have only increased the Imam's hatred of the Russians.

When not fighting with the Russians, Shamil spent his time organizing a state based on the tenants of the *Shariah* (Islamic law). As *amir al-mu'minin* (commander of the faithful), it was Shamil's duty to enforce the fundamentalist brand of Islam practiced by the *Naqshbandiyya* religious order. Smoking, drinking, and immodest dress were forbidden in Shamil's theocracy and laws were enacted according to the scriptures of the Koran. Although Shamil sought the assistance of the recognized leader of the Sunni Muslim world, the Ottoman sultan, Shamil's efforts to unite with fellow Muslims and expand his fundamentalist version of Islam were limited to the northeastern Caucasus.

Although he launched almost three decades of war against Russia, time was not on Shamil's side in his uneven struggle with the transcontinental Russian Imperium. Tsar Alexander II was determined to conquer the north Caucasus flank and, after the Crimean War of 1853–1856, two large, well-equipped armies were sent to suppress Shamil's forces. After several costly defeats that drained the Imam's resources in both logistic and human terms, Shamil and his diminished followers retreated to the mountain fortress of Gunib. Here the redoubtable leader was finally run to the ground by three Russian armies. Shamil was initially determined to fight to the death but on September 6, 1859, he surrendered to the Russians to prevent the death of his family and loyal followers.

Shamil was subsequently taken to Russia where he was cordially received by Tsar Alexander II who appears to have respected the Imam as a worthy opponent. Shamil was then exiled to the city of Kaluga, 150 miles southwest of Moscow. In 1870 Shamil was permitted to partake in a pilgrimage to Mecca where he subsequently died in the year 1871.

After the collapse of Shamil's struggle, resistance against Russia in the northern Caucasus came to an end. The Russian army used burnt earth tactics to defeat the last Muslim holdouts in Chechnya and the neighboring lands of the Circassian highlanders. The Chechens and other Muslim mountaineers who followed Shamil, however, continue to cherish the great Imam as a source of inspiration in their struggles with the Russians. During the Russian-Chechen War of 1994–1996, Chechen nationalists, such as Djokhar Dudayev, often compared their struggle to that of Shamil and used this historical figure as a rallying point for Chechen patriotism. In the neighboring multiethnic republic of Daghestan the Avars still have a certain national prestige that comes from being the people who produced the Caucasus's greatest hero.

For a history of Shamil's struggle see Moshe Gammer, *Muslim Resistance to the Tsar. Shamil and the Conquest of Chechnia and Daghestan* (London: Frank Cass, 1994); J. Milton Mackie, *The Life of Schamyl* (Boston:

John Jewett and Co., 1856); and M. H. Chichagova, *Shamil na Kavkaze i v Rossii* (St. Petersburg: S. Muller, 1889). For a description of the contemporary importance of Shamil, see Sebastian Smith, *Allah's Mountains. Politics and War in the Russian Caucasus* (London: I. B. Tauris and Co., 1998).

**SHAMIR, YITZHAK** 1915–, A one-time wanted terrorist and Mossad spy, Yitzhak Shamir served for fifteen years in leadership positions in the Likud Party and the Knesset, rising from immigration director to speaker, foreign minister, and three-time prime minister. Born Yitzhak Yezernitsky in the small shtetl town of Ruzinoy, Eastern Poland, in 1915, Shamir attended Hebrew school and in youth was an active member of the Zionist Betar movement formed by Jabotnsky. He attended law school in Warsaw and, in 1935, moved to Palestine and entered Hebrew University in Jerusalem.

Soon after, he joined the nationalist military organization "Etzel," and in 1940 followed Avraham Stern into the extremist splinter group "Lechi" (Freedom Fighters of Israel). A paramilitary group, Lechi was devoted to driving the British out of Palestine and counted terrorist attacks and planned assassination among its tactics. Wanted as a member of Lechi, Shamir was arrested and jailed by the British police in late 1941, but escaped to rejoin his Lechi unit nine months later. By 1942, Shamir rose to a leadership position in Lechi, rejecting Menachem Begin's offer to rejoin Etzel. Shamir served as Lechi's principal director of operations until 1946 when he was again arrested and sent to a prison camp in Africa. The following year he escaped again, digging a tunnel out of the camp and hiding for a week inside a petrol tanker. Five days after Israel's declaration of independence in 1948, Shamir returned and resumed his command of Lechi, where he oversaw one of the organization's most notorious and widely condemned attacks, the September 1948 assassination of the UN mediator, Count Folke Bernadotte. After Lechi's was outlawed and disbanded, Shamir attempted a political career as a pro-Soviet nationalist, but turned to the private sector soon after.

In 1955 Shamir was recruited as an agent for Mossad (the Israeli Intelligence Agency), where he rose rapidly and was known for his distrust of the Americans and British, and his attempts to forge new relationships with the KGB and the Soviet Union. In 1964 he was forced out of Mossad and was offered the position of immigration director in Begin's Heirut Party. He was elected to the Knesset in 1973 as a member of the Likud Party, becoming chairman in 1975. After Likud's surprising victory in 1977, Shamir became the speaker of the Knesset, in Israel's first right-wing dominated government. Following Moshe Dayan's resignation from the foreign minister's post, Shamir joined the Begin cabinet as foreign minister, a position he retained after the 1981 election. In that capacity, he negotiated the terms of the normalization of relations with Egypt and worked to open relations with the Soviet Union and China.

Likud's second term proved more controversial. Elected with a smaller majority, Begin proved less popular with the public, especially as Arab disturbances in the occupied territories grew more severe, and the 1982 invasion into Lebanon—planned as a brief, defensive campaign—appeared to drag on, incurring casualties and international disapproval. Public approval further dropped as inflation rose and Israel seemed to plunge into a moral and economic crisis. Begin resigned in late August 1983 and his party elected Shamir to replace him. After the close results of the 1984 general election, in which Labor won by a slim margin, Shamir formed a joint unity party with Labor and its leader Shimon Peres, serving as deputy prime minister and minister of foreign affairs between 1984 and 1986 and as prime minister from 1986 to 1988. In 1988 he won the elections and again formed a national unity government but maintained sole premièreship. Like Begin, Shamir regarded the occupied territories not only as necessary for security, but as ideologically and indisputably part of the "whole Israel." While he proposed direct peace negotiations between Israel, Egypt, the United States, and a joint Jordanian-Palestinian representation, and led the Israeli delegation in the Madrid peace talk of 1991, Shamir steadfastly resisted any land-for-peace deals. It was this conviction and continued support of Israeli settlements in the West Bank that most sharply divided Shamir and Peres during the unity government period and put significant strain on American-Israeli relations in the late 1980s.

In 1990, after a protracted disagreement over peace negotiations, Peres and his Labor Party withdrew from the coalition, effectively collapsing Shamir's government. However, with a slim coalition majority, Shamir managed to survive and remained at his post for two more years. He led his party again in the 1992 elections but was defeated and stepped down from his role in the Likud leadership. He retired from government altogether in 1996.

**SHEVARDNADZE, EDUARD** 1928–, Georgian leader. His association with nationalism was to come late in life following his return as leader of his native Georgia in 1992, and has to be set against a long career more associated with internationalism. Born in Mamati, Western

Georgia, his very upbringing was internationalist, his father being both a teacher of Russian and a Communist. Shevardnadze's own education was initially confined to a state secondary school, before he joined the Communist Party in 1948, whereupon he trained in a party school. Only subsequently, at age thirty-one, was he to gain a correspondence degree in history.

His choice of career and career path was also that of a conformist with the prevailing official internationalist outlook. First an instructor with the Young Communist League under Stalin, he rose through the ranks of that organization in Georgia to become its first secretary from 1957 to 1961; he moved on in the full party organization to become its leader in the republic from 1972 to 1985. Equally, following drafting into the MVD, he also rose up the ladder of local government before focusing on republican central government and the law and order field. Successively, between 1964 and 1972 he was first deputy minister and minister in charge of the police. Higher postings followed in both the party and state structures, culminating in appointment as USSR minister of foreign affairs in 1985. The rise was to end in December 1990 with his resignation and criticism of Gorbachev's "creeping dictatorship." Following his resignation from the Communist Party in August 1991, he served again briefly as foreign minister under Yeltsin, as the Soviet Union collapsed, from November to December 1991.

Despite being an outsider with a distinct Georgian accent, during all this time there were few signs of active concern specifically for Georgia as opposed to the international USSR. He was widely perceived as a Russifier, particularly for the part he played in 1978 when the new Georgian Constitution omitted Georgian as an official language of the republic. Even the modified version, after protests he tried to defuse, only gave it equality with Russian, and evoked further criticism from the intelligentsia. His claim, at the Georgian Party Central Committee meeting before the Twenty-Fifth Congress of the Communist Party in 1976, that "for us Georgians, the sun does not rise in the East, but in the North, in Russia—the sun of Lenin's ideas" was forever to be held against him by many as his lifelong true credo. He himself has sought to defend some of his role in this period, declaring that the violent suppression of demonstrators in Tbilisi in 1956 and Khrushchev's subsequent comments about Georgians "dealt a painful blow to my national pride." The killing of nineteen Georgian demonstrators in April 1989 was similarly a factor turning him against central government's attempt to retain control of its empire.

It was in his post-Soviet career in Georgia (to which he returned in March 1992 to be elevated by the paramilitaries to the chairmanship of the State Council af-

ter the overthrow of his overtly nationalist predecessor Zviad Gamsakhurdia) that we see the emergence of a more nationalistic Shevardnadze. Much was the result of necessity in the face of the precarious task of building a new state, and of protecting and promoting the interests of what he now stressed was his homeland. Among the issues shaping this new turn of speech and action were Georgia's continued struggle with her breakaway provinces of Ossetia and Abkhazia, with their resultant problems of Georgian refugees; Russia's involvement in support of the Abkhazians; Russia's pressure to get Georgia to join the Commonwealth of Independent States; the continued presence of Russian troops and bases in Georgia; unwillingness to accept further military and economic integration within the CIS; assassination attempts against him by Georgians who gained refuge in Russia; and continued problems with other ethnic minorities within Georgia. Shevardnadze's nationalist reactions included a growing hostility toward Russia, the pursuit of closer relations with NATO for purposes of defense, and his own baptism into the Georgian Orthodox Church on November 23, 1992.

Shevardnadze's main statement of his more recent views is in *The Future Belongs to Freedom* (Free Press, 1991). For an account of recent influences on his changing views, see *The Wars of Eduard Shevardnadze* by C. M. Ekedahl and M. A. Goodman (Hurst and Co., 1997).

## SHINTOISM

SHINTOISM   The Shinto tradition is indigenous to Japan and its practice is rarely found elsewhere. Its evolution is closely linked to interpretations of the uniqueness of the Japanese people that lay at the heart of Shintoism as a state ideology in the late 19th and 20th centuries.

Until the Japanese came into contact with Chinese civilization in the 6th and 7th centuries, they assumed that the natural world as they knew it was the sacred, original world. The traditional lineage groups, or *uji*, centered around a world of *kami* (sacred spirits or epiphanies). After contact with China, Japanese rulers paid tribute to Chinese courts, from which in turn they received kingly titles. Gradually those responsible for the religious ceremonies of the lineage groups became recognized as political rulers.

As Japanese leaders sought to emulate China through political unification and the systemization of the old belief systems, the Sinicized term "Shinto" was adopted to signify "the way of the kami." The sovereign ruler's claims to legitimacy were anchored both in his inheritance of the ancient way of the kami and also monarchical systems of rule found in Chinese philosophies of governing. Japanese rulers were simultaneously the supreme political authority of the nation, the supreme priest, and the living or manifest kami, a genealogical descendant of their uji ancestor, Amaterasu Omikami (the Sun Goddess). This is the origin of what later was referred to outside of Japan as the "myth" of the "divine emperor" and the source of "emperor worship" as it was known from the late 1860s to the mid-1940s.

The belief in the uniqueness of Japan's imperial genealogy was reinforced by the comparative geographical isolation of the country. Myths of divine protection linked isolation with a presumption of Japanese invulnerability from outside powers. In the 13th century, for example, the Mongols attempted two invasions of Japan, with the second one amassing about 140,000 men. The invaders were held at bay for almost two months until a typhoon struck, destroying much of the invading fleet. Japanese success was attributed to the *kamikaze* ("divine wind") that helped destroy the enemy. The kamikaze was seen as intervention by the kami of Ise Shrine, one of Japan's most important Shinto centers, and thus reinforced the Japanese belief that their land was protected by the kami. It was thus no historical accident that, during World War II, pilots who flew suicide missions against Allied ships were called kamikaze.

During the 18th century, the Japanese developed a political theory in which religious, familistic, and political ideas merged. This theory, known as *kokutai* (translated variously as "national polity," "national essence," or "essence of the state"), conceptualized the state as a large family, with the emperor at the head. The relationship between the emperor and his subjects was like that between a father and his children; and the obligations of loyalty and service to the emperor took precedence over all other obligations. This family concept of the state rested in turn on the belief in the direct descent of the imperial line from Amaterasu Omikami, the Sun Goddess. The ideas that characterized *kokutai* were part of a reaction against foreign influence, and it is perhaps not surprising that a century later these ideas were revived when Japanese rulers sought first to unify the country after the civil conflicts of the late feudal period and then to assert Japanese national supremacy in Asia.

The politicized form of Shinto that was linked to the concept of imperial divinity is commonly referred to as State Shinto, and should not be confused with the daily Shinto rituals commonly performed by the Japanese people at thousands of shrines around the country. State Shinto dates from the Meiji period (1868–1912) and was a self-conscious government appropriation of traditional religious beliefs and rituals to build national identity and unity. Emphasizing devotion to the emperor, State Shinto inculcated belief in the uniqueness and inherent superiority of the Japanese people. During the period of State Shinto, which lasted until the end of World War II, Shinto was technically not a religion but a government institution whose priests were government officials.

Buttressing State Shinto was the hierarchical ordering of Japanese society, which had been reinforced by Confucian norms imported from China over the centuries. In the last decade of the 19th century, Shinto and Confucian political values were legitimized in two documents that signaled the beginning of the strident nationalism marking Japan's entry into the 20th century. One was the Meiji Constitution of 1889, which, despite a number of provisions that resembled Western European constitutions of the era, proclaimed the authority of the emperor to be "sacred and inviolable." The Constitution, in fact, was presented to the people as a gift of the emperor.

The following year saw the proclamation of the Imperial Rescript on Education, which became a critical source of political indoctrination until the end of World War II. The rescript called on imperial subjects to demonstrate loyalty and filial piety, to offer themselves to the state in the event of emergency, and to thus "guard and maintain the prosperity of Our Imperial Throne coeval with heaven and earth." Copies of the Imperial Rescript on Education were distributed to every school in Japan and all students were required to memorize the text as part of their moral education. Ceremonial readings of the rescript developed into elaborate rituals, and Shinto priests were mobilized to distribute the document. In turn, they standardized the rites conducted around it. This intertwining of public education and Shinto ritual helps to explain the importance of State Shinto during the formative period of modern Japanese nationalism. Shinto shrines and priests transmitted the "Imperial Way" and invoked loyalty to state and emperor alike. In this way, the rites of the shrines helped popularize the doctrine of kokutai, and contributed to Japanese expansion and aggression in the late 19th and 20th centuries, beginning with the Sino-Japanese War in 1894–1895.

By the 1930s, State Shinto was fused with militarism, and political and intellectual voices opposed to the nationalist line were largely silenced. State ideology criticized the assumptions of imported Western ideologies that were antithetical to Japanese history, which (according to the official interpretation) was grounded in the lineage connecting Amaterasu Omikami and the emperor.

One of the chief goals of the post-World War II occupation was the disestablishment of State Shinto, accompanied by the emperor's renunciation of any divinity. With these changes and the introduction of the democratic constitution of 1947, the period of State

Shinto ended. The residue of State Shinto, however, may be seen in occasional controversies over situations that appear to violate the constitutional stipulation of separation of state and religion. The role of Shinto ritual connected with the Imperial House has provoked criticism, for example, in the funeral rites for the former Emperor Hirohito, which some leftist politicians boycotted. In other cases, government ministers have been criticized for attending ceremonies at Yasukuni, a Shinto shrine in Tokyo dedicated since 1945 to the apotheosis of Japan's war dead. Although some rightist politicians continue to assert Shinto as symbolic of Japanese national identity, the increasing political pluralism of the country makes it unlikely that there will be any resurgence of State Shinto as it existed in the prewar period.

The best scholarly treatment of the role of Shinto in Japanese nationalism is Helen Hardacre's *Shinto and the State, 1868–1988* (Princeton, 1989).

## SHOLOKHOV, MIKHAIL

1905–1984, Russian-Soviet writer, Noble Prize winner (1965), born in Veshenskaya, Russia, a village on the Don River. He participated in the civil war (1918–1922) and later depicted the experiences of the war in his short stories and novels.

Sholokhov's first short stories were published in 1923. In the collection *The Stories of the Don* (1926) Sholokhov portrayed the life of the cossacks whose activities and everyday life became his main topic afterward.

Sholokhov's greatest and most important work is the novel *The Silent Don* (4 vols., 1928–1940; two volumes in English as *And Quiet Flows the Don*, 1934, and *The Don Flows Home to the Sea*, 1940) in which he analyzes the complex situation after the revolution in rural Russia: the tragedy of the Bolshevik Revolution and the civic war. With more than 600 characters, the novel is an epic narrative of the great social clashes in rural Russia on the Don River. It also represents a saga about the division of the local people into the new classes of Bolsheviks and Kulaks, about the individual and social psychology of the Russian people during the years of the Bolshevik's seizure of power. *The Silent Don* is a dramatic story about cossack character, traditions, different individualities, domestic life, habits, and so on. From one side it is a narrative about the simple people of Russia, about the masses, about the ideology and class struggle; from the other side, it is a story of psychological and individual collisions in Russia at the beginning of 1920s. In later years the authorship of *The Silent Don* by Sholokhov was questioned. International experts, however, concluded the authenticity of the Sholokhov writings at the beginning of the 1990s.

In 1941, during World War II Sholokhov became a war correspondent. His wartime experience inspired various stories of which one of the most notable is his last short story, *The Fate of the Man*. In this short tale, Sholokhov writes of the tragic personal happenings of a simple, ordinary Russian man during the war and his spiritual strength that led to eventual optimism.

*Virgin Soil Upturned* (1933–1960; also published in English as *Seeds of Tomorrow*) is another big novel about collectivization in the Soviet Union. It presents a picture of the class struggle in rural Russia during the formation of the collective farms (*kolkhozes*). In 1931 Sholokhov sent chapters of his new novel called *With Blood and Sweat* to the literary magazine *Novy Mir* (*New World*). The publisher, however, changed the title to *Virgin Soil Upturned*. The author's attitude toward the new name of the novel was rather hostile. The main characters of the novel are the peasant masses during the years of the formation of collective farms in the USSR. With the peasant people for background, the moral principles of certain tragic individuals are portrayed, their inner fight between political beliefs, their understanding of the world, and real life; the philosophical conflict between constructiveness and destructiveness is examined.

In his short stories and novels, Sholokhov uses Russian folklore. He received the Stalin Prize in 1941, the order of Lenin in 1955, and the Lenin Prize in 1960. In 1965 he was awarded the Nobel Prize in literature.

Kholokov's works include *The Silent Don* (1928–1940), *Virgin Soil Upturned* (1932–1960), *The Fate of the Man*, and *They Fought for Their Country* (1942).

## SHUKHEVYCH, ROMAN

1907–1950, Little known outside Ukraine and its diaspora, and unable to enjoy the fruits of success as a partisan commander, Roman Shukhevych was the dominant Ukrainian national activist of the late 1940s—the era of guerilla conflict against the Soviet state with the aim of establishing an independent Ukraine.

He was born in 1907, the son of a judge married to the daughter of a clerical family, in the West Ukrainian settlement of Krakovets (then in Austria-Hungary), and brought up as a religious believer. After secondary schooling and technical college in L'viv, he completed his studies in Danzig as a civil engineer. During these formative years of education he joined the Ukrainian Military Organization (UVO), later to become a leading figure in it. In 1930, following the creation of the Organization of Ukrainian Nationalists (OUN) the previous year, he became commander of the Fighting Division of its National Executive in West Ukraine, and in 1938–1939 was involved in establishing Brotherhood of Ukrainian Nationalist militia units of the so-called Ukrainian Carpathian Sich in Carpatho-Ukraine, then part of a Czechoslovak state undergoing dismemberment by Hungary and Germany. This background of experience in the western/non-Soviet territories of Ukrainian population was later to be of value in extending his military campaigns against the Red Army into its Czech and Polish satellites.

As in the case of so many Ukrainians, the eastward expansion of the Nazi regime brought Shukhevych into contact with the Germans. The degree and the nature of these contacts has always been a contentious issue, particularly the question of who was using whom and to what ends. Shukhevych certainly shared the German war aims of destroying Stalinist/Soviet rule in Ukraine, but his end goal was almost certainly not that of subordinating Ukraine to German rule. Indeed he is said to have protested German attempts to have his units swear loyalty to Hitler. Subsequently he acted as an unofficial commander when these units were reorganized in Poland as the German-commanded Nachtigall battalion of about 1000 Ukrainians. In late June 1941, in Wehrmacht uniforms, this unit entered L'viv (as the Germans invaded the USSR), where some may have participated in reprisals against Jews and collaborators with the recently installed and repressive Soviet regime there. An independent Ukrainian state was declared there on June 30 under the Bandera group of the OUN, without consultation with the Germans, and Shukhevych became a member of this short-lived administration as deputy defense minister. It was quickly dissolved by the Germans and the leaders imprisoned, again apparently evoking a protest from Shukhevych. He survived, though Nachtigall, which by August had reached Vinnitsa in Ukraine, was returned to Germany, before being sent east again in April 1942 against Soviet partisans in Belarus. Complaints about insubordination, and a refusal to renew the agreement to fight for the Germans, led to the arrest of the unit's officers and its disbandment, but Shukhevych escaped the purge to join the Ukrainian underground in the L'viv area in the spring of 1943.

Meanwhile, in 1942, a number of independent Ukrainian nationalist militia units fused to form the Ukrainian Insurgent Army (UPA) and, following the deaths of its initial leaders, Shukhevych became commander in chief in 1943, under the nom de guerre Taras Chuprynka, the surname referring to the forelock worn by Ukrainian cossacks. The UPA, under Shukhevych, did not hinder, but being illegal, did not actively help the German's creation of the Ukrainian Halychyna division of the Waffen-SS, in the hope of tapping some of these well-trained soldiers for its own ranks.

At the Third Congress of the OUN in 1943, Shukhevych was elected head, and in November of that year he called together and addressed a conference in the forests of Zhytomyr where he asked representatives of thirteen anti-Soviet opposition groups to organize a common front. Also toward the end of that year, the UPA set up a commission to convene a Supreme Liberation Council (UHVR)—a would-be parliament in waiting. This held its first meeting in July 1944, just before Soviet reoccupation of Western Ukraine and Shukhevych became chairman of its General Secretariat (equivalent to prime minister) and supreme commander of the Military Department of OUNB under the UHVR. In July 1944 he was involved in secret negotiations to avoid conflicts of interest with the Halychyna Division, now part of the retreating German forces.

With the return of the Soviets and the reincorporation of West Ukraine into the USSR, Shukevych's parents and his wife, Natalia Shukhevych-Berezyns'ka, were deported to Siberia. His son Yuriy was arrested at age thirteen in the fall of 1947 and sentenced in the spring of 1948 to ten years for being Shukhevych's progeny. Subsequent refusals to denounce his father led him to spend almost forty years in prison and exile before his return to L'viv in October 1989.

Availing itself of captured weapons, Shukhevych's UPA attacked administrative centers and Communist officials, opposed the collectivization of West Ukraine and the appropriation of grain, and resisted the forced deportations from there, which went on into 1947. Fighting was extensive, particularly in the Carpathians, and involved thousands on both sides, with UPA raiding parties going into both Slovakia and southeast Poland. By these methods, Shukhevych sought to bolster the morale of his people, to gain support among other oppressed ethnic groups in the USSR, and to terrorize the terrorizers into a greater sensitivity, while bringing the issue of Ukrainian independence to the attention of the outside world.

On March 5, 1950, Shukhevych was killed in a Soviet MVD attack on his base in the village of Bilohorshcha near L'viv. His son was taken from prison to identify the body, though news of his death was withheld until October 21.

Although unsuccessful in attaining his primary goal of independence, his methods of insurgency survived the onslaught of Soviet forces for a surprising amount of time, and he is now publicly honored in a Ukraine that eventually achieved independence by more peaceful means.

The only biography of Shukevych remains that of P. Mirchuk, *Roman Shukevych (Gen. Taras Chuprynka)—komandyr armii Bezsmertnykh* (Society of Veterans of the UPA, 1970). For aspects of his career from largely sympathetic sources, see L. Shankovsky's *Ukrainska povstancha armiia,* in *Istoriia ukrainskoho viiska* (1953) and M. Kalba's *Nakhtigal (kurin DUN) u svitli faktiv i dokumentiv* (Ukrapress, 1984). Contemporary documentary sources on the UPA are to be found in I. Shtendera and P. Potichny, *Litopys Ukrainskoi povstanskoi armii* (Vyd-vo Litopys UPA, 1976).

## SHUSHKEVICH, STANISLAU

**SHUSHKEVICH, STANISLAU** 1934–, Professor, Belarusian nationalist leader, nuclear physicist, chairman of the Belarusian Social Democrat Party, former vicerector of Belarus University in Minsk, chairman of the Supreme Council of the Belarusian SSR, later the Republic of Belarus, born in Minsk, Belarus.

Shushkevich's biography symbolizes the puzzled past of the Belarusian nation. His mother had been born into a rigorous Catholic family, whereas his father was brought up in Orthodox traditions. Shushkevich himself used to speak with his Russian Ukrainian-born wife in Russian, but communicated with his father in Belarusian. Although he had been a member of the Communist Party of the Soviet Union since 1967, he did not belong to the nomenklatura. Nationalists claimed that Shushkevich turned his back on his father, a renowned Belarusian nationalist writer who had spent seventeen years in concentration camps in Siberia during the Stalin era. It is interesting to point out that Shushkevich was Lee Harvey Oswald's Russian language teacher during his time in Minsk in the early 1960s. This means that he had the confidence of Soviet authorities at that time.

Shushkevich stepped into politics after the Chernobyl accident in 1986, when the nuclear power plant on the Belarusian-Ukrainian border exploded. The Soviet authorities attempted to keep information on the impact of the disaster away from the Belarusian population. In 1989 Shushkevich disclosed classified materials on the accident that showed that at least onefifth of Belarusian territory was seriously contaminated with radioactive fallout. Shushkevich regarded the Chernobyl accident as genocide of the Belarusian nation. Tackling the ecological issues, Shushkevich also became aware of other issues of national importance such as preserving the Belarusian language and culture.

In 1989–1990 Shushkevich was elected to the Supreme Council of the USSR and the Supreme Council of the Belarusian SSR. Still being a member of the CP of the Soviet Union, Shushkevich soon entered into contact with nationalists. After the failed coup in Moscow in August 1991, chairman of the Supreme Council of the Belarusian SSR, Mikalaj Dzemianciej, who had supported the coup stepped down and Shushkevich became the new chairman.

In December 1991 Shushkevich along with Russian President Boris Yeltsin and Ukrainian President Leonid Kravchuk signed the Belovezhskaya Accords, which formally put an end to the Soviet Union. Shushkevich was asked by the other signatories to deliver the news to president of the USSR, Mikhail Gorbachev. Shushkevich was not happy with the outcome of the proceedings, because he preferred Gorbachev's plan to federalize the USSR more to that of dismantling the Union.

Being the head of a newly independent state, Shushkevich expressed support of Belarusian nationalists, particularly their nationalist interpretation of the past. On his first visit to the United Nations in New York, Shushkevich even brought a copy of the statute of the Grand Duchy of Lithuania (1529) as a gift for the secretary-general to stress that the medieval legislature in the ancient Lithuanian state should be regarded as Belarusian. Shushkevich also became the first Belarusian senior official to use Belarusian in his speeches. Before that, only deputies of the Belarusian Popular Front spoke Belarusian during parliamentary proceedings.

Once answering a question about Belarusian nationalism, Shushkevich said that nationalism is a positive phenomenon if its aim leads to establishing a Belarusian language. According to him, only a sovereign Belarusian state could provide such an opportunity. Shushkevich claimed that there were only slight differences between the Russian and Belarusian mentality and he acknowledged that Russian culture positively influenced Belarusian culture and vice versa. In high politics Shushkevich took a moderate stance. Though he opposed Russian interference in the internal affairs of Belarus, he did argue that the two countries should remain together.

In July 1993 a no-confidence vote against Shushkevich failed, but on January 1994, only a few days after U.S. President Bill Clinton had visited Belarus, the Parliament, controlled by the Communists, voted him out of the office. Shushkevich was accused of dissolving the Soviet Union. Later that year Shushkevich made an attempt to return to power during the presidential elections, but ended up third after Lukashenka and Paznyak. In 1996 after the November Referendum changed the 1994 Constitution, Lukashenka dissolved the Supreme Council and Shushkevich found himself on the margins of politics. In 1998 he founded the Belarusian Social Democrat Party *Hramada* ("The Union").

**SIBELIUS, JEAN** 1865–1957, Born in Hämeenlinna in southern Finland, he is considered to be more than a national composer for Finland. He is seen as a national hero, and a symbol of what a small nation can achieve. He was born at a time of national awakening, and he composed music fitting to the awakening and its demands for independence, but which was well received outside of Finland also. This is a crucial fact to his continuing fame nationally and internationally.

Finnish national awakening started in the 1840s in literary circles. The movement involved intellectuals in many fields, all calling for a national culture that would be based on Finnish heritage, as distinct from Swedish, Western, or Russian influences. Sibelius was inspired by the early figures of the awakening, such as poet Runeberg, statesman Snellman, and educator Lönnrot. Like them, he spoke Swedish as his mother tongue. He was born into the middle class, but pretended to be an aristocrat. He went to a Finnish-speaking secondary school, and therefore became fluent in Finnish, an important fact for his national popularity. He studied music in Helsinki, Berlin, and Vienna, and became well known internationally.

*Kullervo* (1892) was his first important composition riding high on the wave of Finnish nationalism. It was based on *Kalevala,* the epic of Finland. Sibelius utilized *Kalevala* considerably in his later work also. His key composition regarding nationalism is *Finlandia* (1899), which has been seen as a response to the February Manifesto of 1899, with which the Russian Empire strengthened its resolve to Russify Finland, an autonomous part of the empire. Nationalistic lyrics were later added to *Finlandia,* and it very nearly became Finland's national anthem after the nation gained independence in 1917. Sibelius's last great composition, *Tapiola* (1926), was, again, based on *Kalevala.*

Sibelius's music was innovative and spoke for an international audience. It was also well received outside of Finland. That his compositions were based on nationalist themes created international interest in Finnish culture and nation. His unique position in Finland's cultural life was the greatest guarantee of his continuing popularity there. *Finlandia* is still played on occasions of nationalism, such as national holidays.

For further reading, see Lisa DeGorog, *From Sibelius to Sallinen: Finnish Nationalism and the Music of Finland* (New York: Greenwood Press, 1989); Harold Johnson, *Jean Sibelius* (New York: Knopf, 1959); and Erik Tawastsjerna, *Sibelius,* 2 vols. (Berkeley: University of California Press, 1976).

**SIKH NATIONALISM** Sikhs trace the origins of their religion to the teachings of Nanak (1469–1539), who preached a monotheistic theology that incorporated principles and rituals from Hinduism and Islam, and professed to transcend both. Nanak, generally referred to as Guru Nanak (for "teacher" or "preceptor"), was born in the Punjab region, which in 1947 was divided between India and Pakistan. The highest concentration of Sikhs, whose name derives from *sishya* (pupil or disciple) is in the Punjab, and the contemporary northwest Indian state of that name is the focus of Sikh nationalism, although loyalty to Sikhism as a community is found among Sikhs elsewhere in India, as well as in Europe and North America. A history of persecution and common religious tenets, including the central role of scripture, the *Adi Granth,* help establish the sense of identity undergirding Sikh nationalism.

Increased persecution of the Sikhs under the Mughal Empire in the 17th and 18th centuries contributed to the transformation of the Sikhs into a warrior community. The adoption of many of the external symbols of Sikhism was fostered particularly by the 10th Guru, Gobind Singh (1666–1708): the taking of the surname Singh (lion) by Sikh males and Kaur (lioness or princess) by females; the wearing of steel bracelets and daggers; and unshorn hair. To this day, Sikh men around the world are typically identified by their turbans and uncut beards.

The Sikhs were successful in establishing an independent state during the first half of the 19th century—up to the British conquest and annexation of Punjab in 1849. Statehood contributed both to a general sense of Punjabi identity and to the more specific sense of Sikh accomplishment that became part of the complicated politics of the region in the 20th century.

Modern Sikh nationalism traces its organizational roots to the formation in 1920 of the Akali Dal ("army of the faithful") by a paramilitary group of Sikh volunteers. The original goal of the Akali Dal was to unify and control the management of all Sikh shrines, but by the 1930s, it had become a political party. It helped to politicize the Sikh peasantry in the Punjab, contested elections, and increasingly agitated for a Sikh homeland. After Indian independence and the partition of the Punjab region in 1947, the Akali Dal led the campaign for redrawing India's internal state boundaries in order to create a "Punjabi Suba," a state in which Punjabi would be the dominant language. This effort was designed to appeal primarily to Sikhs, although Hindus in the state also spoke Punjabi. The position of the central government, however, precluded reorganization of state boundaries to satisfy the claims of religious communities due to fears of religious conflict and potential secessionist movements. Although the post-1947 Punjab state was further divided in 1966 into the two new states of Punjab, where Sikhs were in the bare majority, and the predominantly Hindu state of Haryana, those who sought a specifically Sikh state continued to be dissatisfied.

After the 1966 division, the primary goal of the Akali Dal became electoral supremacy in the new state of Punjab, but this goal was frustrated by political divisions among Sikhs (not all of whom supported the Akali Dal), as well as by competition from the center-dominated Congress Party. To enhance its following, the Akali Dali pointed to numerous grievances against the central government, such as disputes over the status of Chandigarh, built as the postwar capital of Punjab, and over the disposition of river waters to neighboring states. On balance, however, most of these grievances were less relevant to the rise of militant Sikh nationalism in the late 1970s and early 1980s than other factors. The most important of these factors was the transformation of the long-standing Sikh communal identity by an unusual combination of political competition and intrigue born out of the specific context of Punjab's state politics.

Ironically, it was Congress's political machinations that led to the rise of a more extremist version of Sikh nationalism and ultimately to the assassination of Prime Minister Indira Gandhi. To encourage divisions within the Akali Dal and thus ensure Congress political pre-eminence in Punjab, Congress politicians encouraged Sikh religious leaders as a way of undermining Akali Dal support in the rural areas. The most important of these leaders was Sant ("holy man") Jarnail Singh Bhindranwale, whose name subsequently became synonymous with the demands for an independent Sikh state of Khalistan.

Interpretations vary as to the weight of Bhindranwale's contributions to the increasing political turmoil and violence in Punjab during the early 1980s, but as a Sikh revivalist and proselytizer, his popular appeal—particularly to young men disadvantaged by changing economic and social conditions in Punjab—drew him to the center of public and media attention as the most visible representative of extremist Sikh nationalism of the period. The central government increasingly attacked real and perceived terrorists and took over direct rule of the state in 1983. Bhindranwale and his closest followers set up their armed headquarters in the Golden Temple, the symbolic center of the Sikh religion in the Punjabi city of Amritsar. In June 1984, when Prime Minister Indira Gandhi ordered the Indian army to force them out in "Operation Bluestar," Bhindranwale was killed, along with hundreds of his supporters and hundreds of Indian troops. Even among those Sikhs

who had never supported the extremists' cause, Operation Bluestar was interpreted as an assault on the heart of the Sikh community. Five months later, Mrs. Gandhi was assassinated by two of her Sikh bodyguards, an act that in turn led to the massacre of thousands of Sikhs by mobs in New Delhi and elsewhere.

The events of 1984 left a sordid legacy in Indian politics and reinforced the sense of persecution already inherent in Sikh nationalism. Sikhs outside of Punjab contributed financial and political support to mainstream as well as illegal Sikh organizations. Although the situation within Punjab appeared to stabilize by the early 1990s, in September 1995, Sikh terrorists assassinated the chief minister of Punjab and the potential for long-term political accommodation in the state was again placed in doubt. Extremists in general and terrorists in particular represent the fringes of Sikh nationalism, and the majority of Sikhs living in India have accommodated themselves to the dominant political arrangements. The violent legacy of the 1980s, however, makes it unlikely that nationalist sentiments among Sikhs will disappear in the near future.

There is an extensive academic literature on the history and politics of Punjab that provides insight into the development of Sikh nationalism. Particularly useful is the work of Paul R. Brass, including his *Ethnicity and Nationalism: Theory and Comparison* (Sage, 1991), and Joyce J. M. Pettigrew's *The Sikhs of the Punjab: Unheard Voices of State and Guerrilla Violence* (Zed, 1995).

## SIMONSEN, ROBERTO

1889–1948, Brazilian economist and industrialist. Raised in the port city of Santos, Simonsen studied engineering at São Paulo's Escola Politécnica. He graduated in 1909. In the 1910s, as director of a construction company in Santos, Simonsen experimented with methods of scientific management as well as with new forms of labor negotiation.

In the 1920s and 1930s, Simonsen became Brazil's most distinguished advocate of industrialization, and emerged as the leading spokesman for São Paulo's powerful industrialist federation. In 1933 he founded the Escola Livre de Sociologia e Política; his appointment as professor of economic history at this institution for advanced study in the social sciences led him to compose his most famous work, *História economica do Brasil, 1500–1820* (1937).

By the late 1930s Simonsen had become a staunch supporter of the regime of Getúlio Vargas, participating in several national economic commissions in which he called for protective tariffs, state intervention, and economic planning to promote industrial development. Simonsen eagerly defended this position at the end of

World War II, when Brazil faced intensified foreign competition and U.S. pressure for a return to liberal trade policies.

With the transition to democracy, Simonsen successfully ran for the federal senate in 1947. After winning his senatorial bid he continued to promote the interests of industry, calling for the suppression of the newly legalized Communist Party, which he considered the principal threat to "social peace." Simonsen died while delivering an address to the Brazilian Academy of Letters, to which he had been elected in 1946.

## SITTING BULL  1831–1890, Perhaps the most well-known Native American leader of his time. His fame has endured time, and he remains perhaps the most famous American Indian ever known internationally. Much of this legacy is due to Hollywood myths and his one-year participation in Buffalo Bill Cody's Wild West Show in 1885. Sitting Bull, however, was an ardent nationalist for whom the reservation was a horror and American civilization a threat.

Sitting Bull was born to a Hunkpapa Lakota (Sioux) band at the Grand River in what is today South Dakota. His Hunkpapa name was Tatanka Yotanka. He grew up at a time when his people dominated the plains. He attained leadership early, in the 1860s, determined to resist white encroachments on traditional Lakota territories and to preserve the Hunkpapas' culture with its communal ethic. He rejected virtually everything that the dominant culture deemed of value. He was a strong spiritual leader, a courageous warrior, and a charismatic orator, all qualities that helped him to gain tribal respect as a leader. The Lakota society favored decentralized leadership, however, and many other leaders, such as Red Cloud, were attracted to relatively easy life in reservations with a guaranteed food source. Therefore Sitting Bull's leadership was incomplete, and Lakota factionalism intense, leading to the end of Lakota sovereignty by 1876. Sitting Bull remained loyal to his dream of a Lakota nation, but eventually acknowledged what could not change.

Sitting Bull did not participate in the treaty conference of 1868, which resulted in the Lakotas signing off much of their homeland for reservation annuities. Additional U.S. encroachment on the Black Hills of South Dakota, sacred land for the Sioux, led to a confrontation as the Sioux defended their homeland. The Sioux forces led by Sitting Bull, Gall, and Crazy Horse defeated Colonel Custer in the battle at the Little Bighorn River in June 1876. The U.S. army hunted the Sioux bands relentlessly after this, forcing Crazy Horse to surrender in 1877, while Sitting Bull escaped to Canada, where he stayed until 1881.

After his return from Canada, Sitting Bull surrendered, and took to living in the Standing Rock Reservation. He had lost much of his influence, and reservation agents undermined his leadership. Sitting Bull was critical of Christianity, and favored a religious revivalism called the Ghost Dance. This advocated the disappearance of the whites and the return of the buffalo. The reservation agent feared Sitting Bull's participation in this religion because of his potential leadership and wanted him arrested. The old leader resisted, and the reservation police killed him in December 1890, just before the Wounded Knee massacre, when the dream of Lakota sovereignty died.

Sitting Bull's life and death signifies the determination of a capable leader to lead his people in their quest for independence, but not all Lakotas shared his views. Sitting Bull is seen as one of the most important Native American leaders as he defended the right of his people to their homeland against the push of white settlement.

The best biographies of Sitting Bull are Gary Clayton Anderson, *Sitting Bull and the Paradox of Lakota Nationhood* (New York: HarperCollins, 1996); Robert Utley, *The Lance and the Shield: The Life and Times of Sitting Bull* (New York: Henry Holt, 1993); and Stanley Vestal, *Sitting Bull, Champion of the Sioux: A Biography* (Boston: Houghton Mifflin, 1932).

## SKRYPNYK, MYKOLA  1872–1933, Prominent Ukrainian Bolshevik and leader of the first Soviet Ukrainian government, renowned for his support of Ukrainian culture and language. Born in Yasynuvata (now in Donetsk Oblast), Skrypnyk was a student at the St. Petersburg Technical Institute when he was arrested in 1901. After his arrest he quit school and became a Marxist revolutionary. In November 1917, after he had been arrested fifteen times and internally exiled on seven occasions for opposition to the Russian monarchy, he was a member of the Bolshevik Supreme Command of the Military-Revolutionary Committee. In December he was elected to the People's Secretariat—the first Soviet government in Ukraine—and was appointed its chairman by Vladimir Lenin in March 1918.

Skrypnyk was a prominent Bolshevik, but also believed in the equality of Soviet Russia and Soviet Ukraine. At Tahanrih in April 1918, he led the movement for the creation of an independent Ukrainian Communist Party. This position was voted down at the Moscow Congress in July 1918 when the Communist Party (Bolshevik) of Ukraine, CP(B)U and later the CPU, was officially formed as a branch of the Russian party. Yet Skrypnyk still gave the keynote address at the founding of the CP(B)U. Skrypnyk held many important posts in the Bolshevik leadership: He was an intelligence officer (*chekist*) and a Bolshevik commissar against counterrevolutionaries; a member of the politburo of the CPU from 1925 to 1933, an all-union Communist Party Central Committee member from 1927 to 1933, member of the executive committee and head of the Ukrainian delegation to the Communist International; chair of the nationalities question for the All-Ukrainian Commission for the History of the October Revolution and CPU, 1926–1931; and he headed the Commissariat of Education from 1927 to 1933 and presided over the Ukrainian Society of Marxist Historians, 1928–1933. In practical terms, these positions meant that Skrypnyk was in the ideal position to advocate a policy of Ukrainianization.

Skrypnyk was a staunch believer in Marxism, and he felt that the best way to strengthen Communism was to present it in a way that was understandable to the people. In Ukraine, this meant using the Ukrainian language, literature, art, and culture to spread Communism. Skrypnyk led a program of Ukrainianization in the 1920s. This included attempting to recruit Ukrainians to the Communist Party and giving them important positions within the party, making Ukrainian the official language of government, education, and the press, and promoting Ukrainian culture. His program had considerable success; by 1932, 88 percent of all schoolchildren were being educated in Ukrainian, and 80 percent of all books and 90 percent of all newspapers were published in Ukrainian. This led to a strong Ukrainian cultural and literary revival in the 1920s.

Skrypnyk was also active in fighting what he saw as Russian chauvinism, and in promoting Ukrainian political and economic autonomy. In 1922 Joseph Stalin, as general secretary of the Communist Party, wanted to integrate the entire Soviet territory into a unified Russian Soviet state. Skrypnyk and others (particularly in Georgia and Central Asia) saw this as Russian imperialism, and protested. Lenin agreed with them and proposed a federal system of national republics. Skrypnyk accepted this, and the Ukrainian Soviet Socialist Republic was created in December 1922. Skrypnyk also saw the Soviet Red Army as an agent of Russification, so he founded Ukrainian-language officer schools and reserve units.

Despite his support of Ukrainianization, Skrypnyk was a firm Leninist and opposed Ukrainian nationalism and an independent Ukrainian nation as being dangerous to Communism. Skrypnyk personally played a role in purging many Ukrainian nationalists and intellectuals in this period. Stalin shared this opposition to nationalism and began to purge Ukrainian nationalists from the party in 1928. In the 1930s Ukraine's cultural revival was abruptly halted with the arrest of many cultural figures. Skrypnyk himself was soon targeted because Ukrainianization was seen as a threat to collectivization (collectivization in Ukraine led to the Great Famine in which 5 to 7 million peasants died). In February 1933 he was accused of causing Ukraine's economic problems and was removed as commissar of education. In June he was charged with counterrevolutionary nationalism. Rather than recant his support for Ukrainianization, Skrypnyk killed himself in July.

Many consider Skrypnyk to have been the ultimate authority on Ukrainian culture and politics from the Soviet era. His reputation was rehabilitated in the late 1950s during Nikita Khrushchev's political thaw. Skrypnyk was also considered to be one of the original national Communists (Communists who also support Ukrainian national growth) and provided inspiration for the national Communists of the late 1980s and 1990s—it was national Communists like Leonid Kravchuk who provided the necessary support for Ukraine's declaration of independence from the Soviet Union in 1991.

## SLAVERY

Slavery—the practice of holding humans in bondage—has had a strong connection to nationalist movements. Slavery and nationalism have been intertwined since slavery itself was known to begin in Sumer during the fourth millenium B.C. The relationship of nationalism and slavery is two faceted: On one hand, slavery was often established as a result of nationalist fervor within a government; on the other hand, slaves themselves fostered nationalism as a product of their resistance or rebellion.

Countless governments throughout world history established slavery as the result of wars with other nations or as a means of controlling specific ethnic groups. The most recent example is Germany's Nazi government of the 20th century. Adolf Hitler and his government enslaved millions of Jews, Gypsies, and prisoners of war in order to replace the 13 million German workers who were drafted. Fierce nationalism by the Nazis also contributed to the enslavement of non-Aryan peoples.

On the other hand, slaves themselves developed nationalism. Typically, nationalist sentiments among slaves evolved from slave resistance, which ranged from simple refusal to perform expected tasks to establishing their own republics. The first notable slave revolt with nationalist fervor was led by Spartacus, who began a successful military campaign against the Roman Republic in 73 B.C. In 869, in present-day southern Iraq, the

East African Zanj rebelled against their masters and formed an independent government. During the 13th century, military slaves in Egypt rebelled and formed the Mamluk slave dynasty.

The best example of former slaves' nationalism is the slave revolts in Saint Domingue from 1791 to 1803. Led by Toussaint L'Overture and inspired by the French Revolution of 1789, Saint Domingue slaves fought for their freedom against the possible reinstitution of slavery by Napoleon Bonaparte. In 1804, Haiti declared its independence, becoming the Western hemisphere's first republic of former slaves and second oldest free nation.

The apex of slave resistance and subsequent nationalism began in the Americas two centuries before the Haitian Revolution. Indian slaves in Brazil rebelled against their owners to gain their freedom and to preserve their cultural heritage. Slaves of African descent throughout the Caribbean and Latin America fostered nationalism by establishing maroon societies, which were enclaves of former slaves with their own systems of government. Several semi-independent maroon societies survive today in Belize, Colombia, French Guiana, Jamaica, and Suriname.

An important study is *A Historical Guide to World Slavery*, edited by Seymour Drescher and Stanley Engerman (Oxford, 1998).

## SLAVOPHILE MOVEMENT  Slavophilism was a body of intellectual thought that arose during the 1840s, following Russia's successful wars with Persia and Turkey and the suppression of the revolt in Poland, and stood in contrast to the Westernized strand of Russian political and religious philosophy. That said, a number of individual writers did move from one position to the other in the course of their lives. In general, the debate between the two groups was over the national essence and virtues of Russia meriting future development, and over the degree to which the Russian/Slavic nature, experience, and needs were on the one hand unique in their historic path and present development or, on the other hand, universal and likely to benefit from borrowings from the West. Among the Slavophiles there was a marked degree of veneration for the patriarchal traditionalism of the pre-Petrine Muscovite past and the integral Orthodox Christian faith and civilization of that past. Theirs was a belief in an organic togetherness within a preeminently peasant culture, wherein the individual submerged himself within the village commune to achieve a true individuality as part of the greater whole. Such a society should be fostered and form the essence of Russia's future reforms. This was not just a society more suited to the Russian/Slavic

soul, it was morally superior to anything the West had to offer—a form of messianic nationalism. Peter the Great, in his borrowings from the West, had erred in taking not merely scientific and technological elements but also ideological and ethical concepts and institutions that placed a bureaucracy between the tsar and his people. Further Napoleonic era attempted impositions had also left little or no trust in the West among the Slavophiles. They believed that, for Russian society, the further development of contradictory, abstract, rationalist ideas, and a bourgeois-capitalist, laissez-faire phase of corruption through materialism and individualism would be anathema, however approriate in the barbaric West. Ideas of popular sovereignty and external political rights endangered freedom of the inner spirit and the pursuit of spiritual truth and freedom. The tsar should continue his act of self-sacrificing government of the people, preserving their inner freedoms. Secular Western forms of government overemphasized the role of reason and experience in human affairs, as against the power of emotion and faith, and created instead a spiritual bondage. It was Russia's mission indeed to share its revelation of real justice with others and to act as guardians of the true faith rather than vice versa.

Among the chief articulators of Slavopile ideas were Ivan V. Kireyevskiy (1806–1856), a former Westernizer often, though questionably, called the father of Slavophilism; Aleksey S. Khomyakov (1804–1860), another founding figure who regarded the West as rotten and inferior compared to the Russian autocracy; Ivan S. Aksakov (1823–1886), a journalist and later Pan-Slavic nationalist; his brother Konstantin S. Aksakov (1817–1860), a venerator of the peasantry whom he believed had best preserved the national principles against alien, impersonal, even tyrranical, impositions; and Yuriy F. Samarin (1819–1876), an active advocate of peasant emancipation and the village commune, both for its economic and moral virtues. Besides their internal inconsistencies, not all of these and other writers thought exactly alike. There were differences of emphasis over the religious dimension and over which borrowings from abroad were legitimate. Some, like Kireyevskiy, were more conservative than others, for example, Khomyakov.

Nineteenth-century Russian officialdom regarded the Slavophiles with suspicion and, from the 1860s, they largely merged with the more externally oriented Pan-Slavists. The Soviet successor regime neglected the movement and its influence almost entirely. Despite this, a number of the ideas have continued to have resonance to this day. Soviet officials offered critiques of non-nationalist dissenters in the 1960s and 1970s involving the rejection of alien ideas such as bourgeois democracy; Aleksandr Solzhenitsyn and other nationalists such as Vadim Soloukhin took up various themes of nostalgia for aspects of the past and critiques of the West; and the anti-Yeltsinites of the 1990s again railed against ideological, economic, and religious innovations all too obviously borrowed from the West—borrowings once again seen by many as destined to undermine the true Russia.

A well-established study of the movement is found in N. V. Riasanovskiy's *Russia and the West in the Teachings of the Slavophiles* (Cambridge, 1952). An impressive series of studies of individual Slavophiles is provided by P. K. Christoff in *An Introduction to Nineteenth Century Russian Slavophilism*, Vols. 1–4 (Mouton and Princeton, 1961–1991). More general accounts can be found in E. C. Thaden's *Conservative Nationalism in Nineteenth Century Russia* (Washington University Press, 1964) and A. Walicki's *The Slavophile Controversy* (Notre Dame University Press, 1989).

**SLOVAK NATIONALISM** Traditional histories of the Slovak people have sought to excavate a teleology for the very new Slovak nation based on its alleged 1000-year struggle against Hungarians and then Czechs. While the materials for the Slovak nation can be found in both its people's history *and* myths, an account of Slovak nationalism must necessarily separate the materials employed by nationalists from the actual processes of nation formation by contextualizing these phenomena in the broader political and cultural history of the Central Europe.

Written in broad outline, histories of the Slovak nation begin with the Christianizing 9th-century Great Moravian Kingdom, even though it lasted only approximately sixty years and, as its name suggests, was not exclusively a Slovak affair. The year 907 is often said to mark the beginning of the 1000-year interruption in the national development of the Slovak people. Hungarian tribes did in fact overrun the great Moravian Empire in the early 10th century, eventually taking possession of the area that is today's Slovakia, but which they called "Northern Hungary." They incorporated their conquered people into a multiethnic political territory under the control of the *natio Hungarica*, a corps of nobleman preserved not so much by a common culture as a legal and institutional framework. It took nearly 1000 years for this Magyar nobility to embrace a Hungarian national identity and reject Latin in favor of Hungarian as the official language of state. Unlike the Magyar nobility, the largely Slavic peasantry of Northern Hungary was denied any opportunity for national development through political and or cultural centralization. Latin and German provided the common languages of law and commerce, obviating any structural force that might have facilitated the rise of Slovak from the fragmented Slavic vernaculars of Northern Hungary.

Magyar political influence on the Slavs of Northern Hungary mounted with the 16th-century breakup of Hungary—the result of the dual pressures from the expansionist Turks and Habsburgs. Northern Hungary, a region loosely approximating today's Slovakia, became the political core of the Habsburg-dominated Hungary. Nominal stability afforded by Habsburg rule, along with the influx of Germans and Hungarians, augmented the already existent assimilationist pressures on those Slavs capable of rising out of serfdom. Nevertheless, complete assimilation of Northern Hungary's Slavs was staved off by economic backwardness, oppressive serfdom, and geographic isolation.

The modern origins of a national culture for the Slavs of Northern Hungary have usually been associated with the 17th-century influx of Czech Protestants in Northern Hungary. Their arrival, in the aftermath of the subjugation of Protestant Bohemia to Catholic Habsburg rule, offered to the Slavs of Northern Hungary Biblical Czech as a literary language similar to the local vernacular. This was especially important for Slovak Protestants who sought to distance themselves as much as possible from Rome. However, it was Rome, acting through the hand of the Catholic priest Antonin Bernolák (1752–1813), that created the first distinct "Slovak" literary language in 1787.

Conflict between Slovak Protestants and Catholics over the national language and then the contours of national identity was begun in earnest by the celebrated Slav poet and Lutheran Jan Kollár (1793–1852) and the equally well-known author and Lutheran, Jozef Šafárik (1795–1861). In defense of a Czechoslovak literary language, they mounted an early challenge to Bernolák's codification, believing that only through the already well-established Czech language could Slovaks realize cultural greatness. While their proposal to merge Czech and Slovak proved unappealing to important factions of Slovaks and Czechs, political conditions would eventually favor such a model of national expression, albeit in principle more than in practice.

With hindsight, the decisive figure in the "rediscovery" of the Slovak language and nation was certainly the Protestant and Slovak nationalist L'udovit Štúr (1815–1856). Rebuffed by the leading figure behind the Czech linguistic revival, Josef Jungmann, Štúr abandoned his own project to synthesize a Czechoslovak language. Instead he resolved to elevate a central Slovak vernacular that would prove resistant to Czech linguistic assimilation, be distinct from Bernolák's Catholic Western Slovak, and be closer to the dialects spoken in Eastern Slovakia. His hope was to integrate the three ostensibly divisible regions of Slavic Northern Hungary into a single Slovak nation. Štúr's vision for the Slovak nation would eventually provide the basic contours for Slovakia's national development. However, it would be several decades before the political winds could give loft to his vision.

The poverty of most of Northern Hungary's Slavs, and the opportunities afforded by assimilation into the increasingly dominant Hungarian cultures, undermined the impact of the above-mentioned Czechoslovak and Slovak models. If political salvation was the key to national self-development, the Romanovs gave first hope to Slovakia through the Pan-Slav movement, especially in the aftermath of Russia's intervention to suppress the Hungarian national uprising. However, the continuing struggle between the Habsburgs and the Hungarians afforded a few small opportunities for the Czechoslovak and Slovak nationalists in whom the Habsburgs found a political tool for stunting Hungary's national development. However, following the recognition of Hungarian autonomy in 1867, the mere survival of these competing Slovak national identities was challenged by the new vigorous official policy of Hungarian cultural assimilation.

In 1918, the Allied effort to contain Hungarian and Austrian influence led to the recognition of a new state in Central Europe, spearheaded by Czech politicians T. G. Masaryk and Edvard Beneš. Fearing the obstructionist potential of the three million ethnic Germans in Bohemia, Masaryk strongly advocated the Czechoslovak national idea, secure in the belief that the Slovaks would prove unconditional allies and that a Czechoslovak national identity could easily be promoted now that any hope of nationalist Pan-Slavism had been eliminated with the fall of Imperial Russia. In fact, the only threat that most Czechs could find in the new region of Slovakia was from Hungary and the Hungarians. The Czechs took advantage of an initial post-World War I Hungarian military defense of its northern province to implement an aggressive policy of de-Magyarization. To absorb Slovakia into the fold of the new state, the idea of a Czechoslovak language and nationality was promoted as a legal recognition of both Czech and Slovak as equal and yet potentially distinct manifestations of a single nationality and language. The Czechs either assumed or hoped that under such a rubric, Slovaks would become assimilated into the now well-established Czech national culture. Most nationally conscious Slovaks, while enjoying privileged status as members of the "state-forming" nation, feared assimilation and thus objected to the idea of the "Czechoslovak" nation. Nevertheless, virtually all recognized the importance of supporting a new Czechoslovak Constitution, though only those with already well-established ties to Prague, largely Protestants, were given a hand in the drafting.

However, placing the Slovak people on a path of national self-discovery marked only by a policy of de-Magyarization failed to guarantee the Czechs a domestic political ally. Certainly most Slovak nationalists would come to support inclusion in a greater Czechoslovakia, fearing that continued inclusion in Hungary might bring about a return to the earlier process of assimilation. Nevertheless, Slovak national liberation came at a high price in the economic realm. Once the industrial center of a largely agricultural economy, Slovakia now found itself dwarfed by the extraordinary might of Bohemia's industrial economy. Severed from its critical intellectual, economic, and investment ties to Budapest, Slovakia found itself poorly equipped to compete on what was ostensibly a level domestic playing field. Despite modest investment from Prague, Slovak industry contracted during what was for the rest of Czechoslovakia an important time of growth. Unfortunately, Prague's emphasis on culture and education rather than economics allowed the central government to overlook this important source of social discontent, and left open to both the Slovak nationalists and the communists an important source of social discontent.

However, it must be said that after the Hungarians, the second most significant and immediate victim of the new government's policies in Slovakia was the venerated Catholic Church. Indeed Czech nationalism did revile the Church as an oppressive force tied to Habsburg tyranny and the historical injustices committed first against Huss and then the Bohemian nobility. Furthermore, Prague's attempts to fully secularize Czechoslovakia threatened age-old Church privileges. Under the leadership of Monsignor Andrej Hlinka (1864–1938), Slovak Catholics were quick to react to alleged injustices by using the Church's organizational resources in Slovakia to lay the groundwork for what was to become a new and distinctly Catholic Slovak nationalism: a nationalism with an antimodern, antiprogressive, antisecular, antisocialist, and even antidemocratic hue. Although indeed the Catholic Church in Slovakia could not claim a monopoly on Slovak nationalism, it did provide an essential institutional framework for nearly all the leading Slovak nationalist movements. Furthermore, priests assumed leadership roles in these many factions. Hence, for the duration of the Czechoslovak First Republic (1918–1938), Hlinka and his allies were able to mobilize growing numbers of the discontented to the Slovak nationalist cause, even after having won concessions from Prague for the Church.

Economic depression in the 1930s offered a major boost to the anti-Czechoslovak causes. The first generation of new Slovaks was quick to view the now well-established Czech administrators and teachers, originally sent to help Slovakia on its feet, as obstacles to social and economic advancement. Slovak nationalists, those from the Church, the more fascist minded and a few well-placed figures backed by irredentist Hungary, turned this resentment to their political advantage by eventually securing the largest electoral mandate in Slovakia for the Hlinka's Slovak People's Party. Nevertheless, the majority of Slovaks consistently cast their lot with the "cross-national" Czechoslovak parties.

The same economic crisis that left the Slovaks unemployed afflicted Czechoslovakia's other minorities, especially the Germans from the heavily industrial Sudetenland. The government in Prague, under mounting pressure from a host of opposition movements, and trying to form grand coalition governments whenever possible, turned to the obstructionist Slovak nationalists on more than one occasion, in exchange for important and ostensibly divisive concessions. However, the Slovak nationalists only agreed to participate in government from 1927 to 1929, preferring otherwise an oppositional status and occasional support to the government on specific legislative issues. To compound the government's problems, a belligerent Nazi Germany saw in Czechoslovakia, and the plight of the Sudeten Germans, an opportunity for substantial political expansion. While the Czechoslovak government had secured for itself one of the most powerful militaries in Europe, its domestic political institutions proved ill equipped to handle the Nazi threat. The Nazi's easily capitalized on, and intervened in, Czechoslovakia's domestic politics by forging alliances with and making promises to not only the Sudeten Germans, but the Slovak nationalists as well. Following the Munich crisis, the Slovak nationalists, armed with Hitler's promises and the fear of falling back into the arms of Hungary, abandoned Czechoslovakia and those Slovaks who favored the Czechoslovak cause. In 1939, the priest Dr. Josef Tiso (1887–1947) replaced Hlinka, pushing the Slovak people at Hitler's behest into their own nation-state.

For further reading on Slovakia, consult James Felak's *At the Price of the Republic. Hlinka's Slovak People's Party, 1929–1938*, published in 1994 by University of Pittsburgh Press, and Carol Skalnik Leff's *The Czech and Slo-*vak Republics: Nation versus State* issued by Westview Press in 1996.

## SLOVAK NATIONALISM, POST-1939

On New Year's Day 1993, Slovakia became an independent state with a new opportunity to define and codify its national identity, no easy task for a nation that bears a heavy historical burden as progeny of the leading antidemocratic political mobilizations of the 20th century. Under the democratic Czechoslovak First Republic (1918–1938), Slovak nationalism first took coherent form under the tutelage of the Catholic Church, which sought to defend its interests against the perceived excesses of Czech progressivism in the interwar years. In fascism and Nazi Germany, Slovak nationalism found a new patron that would grant it not mere autonomy from Prague, but outright sovereignty (1939–1945) "at the price of the Republic." Forcibly reunited with the Czechs after the war, Slovakia realized nominal political autonomy only in the aftermath of the Soviet repression of the Prague Spring. While indeed the events of the First Republic were significant for mobilizing Slovak nationalism as a political force, they in no way determined the fate of the Slovak nation. Five years of national sovereignty would leave a far more lasting legacy.

From 1939 to 1945, the Slovak state expunged Czech and foreign influences to the best of its abilities, imposing a new vision of national culture on the Slovak people. Major policies included the appropriation of Jewish property and resources, the deportation of virtually all Slovak Jews, and an attempted implementation of a Catholic corporatist state model according to the antidemocratic principles embodied in the Catholic doctrines of Pius XI's *Quadragesimo Anno.*

As an ally of Nazi Germany, the Catholic priest, Dr. Tiso, and his government avoided the labor quotas demanded by the Reich, offering Slovak Jews instead of "real" Slovak workers. Furthermore, rather than support the dependents of the young Jewish men sent off as slave labor, Slovakia paid the Nazis to dispose of the Jewish women and children as they saw fit. Fully integrated into the Nazi economy, the Slovak people tasted prosperity as never before.

There has been some controversy regarding the extent of Slovakia's sovereignty during the war. Elements of the official ideology of the Slovak state had been articulated and promoted by its leadership well before their alliance with Hitler and their defection from Czechoslovakia, suggesting at least a harmony of interests between Nazi Germany and Slovakia. While indeed clergy in the Slovak state sought to protect those Jews who had converted to Catholicism, they otherwise did little to temper anti-Semitic zeal, which proved greater in Slovakia than in Germany. This harmony, and Slovak ready compliance with the Reich's general demands, permitted Slovakia a fair amount of autonomy in domestic affairs and very much minimized the Germany military presence. Indeed, the shortage of German troops in Slovakia was a deciding factor in the allied decision of 1944 to mount a partisan uprising against the fascist Slovak government.

However, while the Slovak state participated in the crackdown against this partisan movement, Germany from this point forward intervened far more directly in Slovak domestic affairs. The impact of the uprising was to be largely felt after the war when it was used to exaggerate the strength of Slovak resistance to fascism. However, the leaders of the Slovak state were unable to find absolution in the claim that their hands had been tied by Nazi Germany.

Following the war, Slovakia was reintegrated into Czechoslovakia. Opposed to both Czech leftist tendencies and integration into a centralist Czechoslovakia, Slovakia was nevertheless forced to resume its position as junior partner under the Czechs, of whom many considered Slovaks guilty of national betrayal. But Slovak nationalists could at least find consolation in the expulsion of much of Slovakia's Hungarian minority. In 1948 Czechoslovakia fell under the Soviet realm of influence.

Under the Communist Party, Prague rejected Masaryk's cultural process of assimilation as inadequate, implementing a new project of economic integration. Slovakia experienced industrialization on the Soviet model, which meant the erection of huge ungainly inflexible factories according to the logic of the planned economy. However, economic development did not weaken the will for self-rule, which expressed itself during the de-Stalinization of the Soviet bloc in the 1960s. Whereas the Czechs protested on behalf of freedom of self-expression and "democracy with a human face," the Slovaks called for autonomy within a Czechoslovak federation. Their demands, unlike those of the Czechs, were not interrupted by the Warsaw Pact invasion on August 20, 1968. The ensuing decentralization of Czechoslovak politics did little to promote the cause of Czechoslovak nation building, as some had hoped, and would prove one of the major causes of the definitive breakup of the renaissant democratic Czechoslovakia. As under the First Republic, the institutional arrangements had the unintended consequence of creating forums through which political elites could mobilize and articulate regional and particularistic grievances, but offered no mechanism through which these grievances could then be remedied.

The fall of the Czechoslovakia Communist regime in November 1989 created a new opportunity for political competition over alternative national visions. The principal forum for the debate over the future Slovakia was the regional Slovak National Council—granted institutional authority during Czechoslovakia's 1968 federation—where Vladimir Mečíar quickly assumed a leadership role following the 1990 elections. While elected as a member of the Slovak equivalent of Havel's Civic Forum, he quickly abandoned the progressive platform of his party for a specifically nationalist and anti-Czech framework.

Mečíar's major critique of the Prague government, a reminder of earlier tensions, centered on the alleged unsuitability of Václav Klaus's Czechoslovak free-market economic reforms to Slovakia. Furthermore, the Czechs, and the economist Klaus in particular, favored the centralization of economic policy in Prague, while the Slovaks, including Mečíar, wanted Bratislava to determine the direction of Slovakia's economy. While at the outset of the debate neither side advocated the actual complete separation of their two nations, their inability to come to a mutually agreeable institutional arrangement for the new Czechoslovakia drove both sides to consider going it alone. One of the most reliable public polls, conducted in August 1991, revealed that of Czechs, only 8 percent favored a split, and of the Slovaks, 16 percent. Nevertheless, a political stalemate convened the leading Czech and Slovak representatives in Brno on August 26, 1992, to draft the dissolution of Czechoslovakia set for New Year's Day 1993.

Vladimir Mečíar, one of the instruments in the breakup of Czechoslovakia, has maintained a dominant position in the new Slovakia. His leadership has done little to promote Slovakia's reputation in the eyes of the European Union and NATO. The government has made little effort to condemn the atrocities of the fascist Slovak Republic. The government policy toward the Hungarian minority reveals none of the empathy that might be expected from a people who have built their national identity around a history of oppression at the hands of allegedly intolerant majorities. Furthermore, Mečíar's reluctance to work within the spirit of democracy, manifested in his belligerent treatment of the presidency and his attempt to restructure the electoral institutions to ensure a permanent majority for his party, has been repeatedly cited by international observers as examples of potentially serious undemocratic tendencies in Slovakia. In international affairs, the mismanagement of the conflict with Hungary over the Danubian hydroelectric dam has only further discredited Slovakia. This record suggests that as long as the Slovak people continue to tolerate Mečíar's nationalism and bully tactics, it will lag behind the Czech Republic, Poland, and Hungary.

For further reading on Slovakia, consult James Felak's *At the Price of the Republic, Hlinka's Slovak People's Party, 1929–1938*, published in 1994 by University of Pittsburgh Press, and Carol Skalnik Leff's *The Czech and Slovak Republics: Nation versus State* issued by Westview Press in 1996.

**SLOVENE NATIONALISM**    The Slovenes are a South Slavic nation who settled in Southeastern Europe in the 7th century. They originally occupied an area about twice the size of present-day Slovenia. Over the centuries, however, Slovene national frontiers have been substantially reduced. By the mid-8th century the Slovenes were subjected first to Bavarian and then Frankish domination. In the 960s the Slovene lands were incorporated into the Holy Roman Empire, and from that point to 1918 the Slovenes would remain closely bound to their German-speaking neighbors in Carinthia, Styria and Carniola, mainly as part of the Habsburg Austrian (later Austro-Hungarian) Empire.

Since its emergence in the mid-19th century, Slovene nationalism has been shaped primarily by the struggle for Slovene cultural, socioeconomic, and political emancipation from the Austrian Germans. The local nobility was German, and the towns of Slovenia had a predominantly German character.

The Slovene national movement took shape in the first half of the 19th century. It was led by a small group of intellectuals, many of whom were initially drawn from the ranks of the Slovene Catholic clergy. The first stage in the development of Slovene nationalism was the cultural and literary revival. Of great importance was the work of the Slovene linguist Jernej Kopitar, who published a Slovene grammar in 1808. Slovene nationalism thereafter championed the cause of the Slovenian language.

Slovene nationalism became overtly political during the 1848 revolutions, when demands were raised for a unified Slovenia within a restructured Austrian empire. This autonomous Slovenia would use the Slovene language in administration and education. The Slovenes, like the monarchy's other nationalities, were greatly disappointed by the Habsburg counterrevolution. After 1848 a policy of centralization and Germanization was introduced from Vienna. Nevertheless, in 1864 a group of Slovene nationalists founded the *Slovenska matica* (Slovene Foundation) in Ljubljana, which acted as an important cultural and literary society. Its task was to publish literary and scholarly works in the Slovenian language.

After the Austro-Hungarian *Ausgleich* (1867), the Austrian half of the monarchy, which included the Slovene lands, experienced gradual democratization and economic modernization. In 1906 universal manhood suffrage was introduced in the Austrian half for the central parliament in Vienna. By the 1890s the Slovenes began forming political parties. The most important for Slovene nationalism was the Slovene People's Party (SLS), formed in 1905 by the merger of several Catholic clericalist parties in the Slovene lands. The SLS became the most important Slovene voice in the Vienna parliament, under the leadership of Janez Krek, Ivan Šušteršič, and Anton Korošec (1872–1940). Under the auspices of the SLS, numerous banks, economic cooperatives, and unions were formed. The SLS evolved into a broadly based Slovene national movement, designed above all to defend Slovene interests against the dominant Germans in the Austrian half of the monarchy.

The formation of the Kingdom of Serbs, Croats and Slovenes ("Yugoslavia") in December 1918 and the peace settlement were mixed blessings for Slovene nationalism. On the one hand, Slovene territory was partitioned. Most Slovenes ended up in the new Yugoslav state, but southern Carinthia went to Austria and the western Slovene lands to Italy; about one-third of all Slovenes lived outside of Yugoslavia. On the other hand, despite the imposition of a centralized state system ruled from Belgrade, the Slovenes received many administrative posts in Slovenia, given their high rate of literacy. What is more, important new cultural and educational institutions were formed: the University of Ljubljana in 1919, and the Slovene Academy of Sciences in 1938.

In the interwar period, the SLS was the only significant Slovene party on the Yugoslav political stage. It was led by Korošec to his death in 1940. The SLS stood for Slovene political and cultural autonomy, but Slovene fear of Italian, German, and Hungarian expansionism meant that Slovene nationalism was tempered, and not directed against Belgrade. In 1927–1928 the SLS participated in the Yugoslav government, and Korošec even served as Yugoslav premier from July to December 1928.

With the imposition of the royal dictatorship in January 1929, the SLS was forced temporarily into opposition. But in 1935 the SLS joined Milan Stojadinović's Yugoslav Radical Union (JRZ), which also included some Serbian Radicals and Bosnian Muslims. Korošec again served as a cabinet minister. The SLS's close cooperation with Belgrade cost the Slovenes dearly during World War II. When the Axis invaded and partitioned Yugoslavia in April 1941, Slovenia was divided between Nazi Germany and fascist Italy, and all manifestations of Slovene nationalism were eradicated.

The end of World War II, like the end of the first, brought mixed blessings to Slovene nationalism. With the creation of Josip Broz Tito's Communist Yugoslavia, Slovenia became one of the country's six constituent federal republics. Slovenia was also larger in 1945 than before the war, since most of the formerly Italian-held Slovene lands were incorporated into Yugoslavia. However, the introduction of Communism and the concomitant eradication of political pluralism and all manifestations of Slovene nationalism tempered the initial enthusiasm most Slovenes may have felt for the gains they made in 1945.

In the years following Tito's death (1980), Slovene nationalism slowly reemerged. The most salient feature of Slovene nationalism since the mid-1980s has been its demand for the devolution of political power from Belgrade to the Yugoslav federal republics. When this failed, Slovenia seceded from the Yugoslav federation in 1991. Independent Slovenia, which is almost purely Slovene in national composition, has created a democratic political system and appears to be heading for membership in the European Union. The main aims of Slovene nationalism seem to have been achieved.

## SMETANA, BEDŘICH

**SMETANA, BEDŘICH** 1824–1884, Czech composer, born in Litomyšl, the Czech Republic (then the Habsburg Monarchy). Smetana is best known for the composition of a patriotic symphonic poem, *Ma Vlast* (My Homeland), and for his operas inspired by Czech folktales and mythology. He is recognized as the composer whose work brought international recognition to Czech music and culture.

Smetana's work and life were to a large degree shaped by the 19th-century Czech national revival, and by an array of personal tragedies. During the 1848 revolution he composed his first symphonic song with a Czech libretto, *Valka* (The War). Yet, the promising career of the young composer was hampered by the deaths of three out of his four children, and later of his wife, Kateřina Kolařova. Smetana's work gained recognition only in the 1860s, after the premiere of a patriotic opera, *Braniboři v Čechach* (The Brandenburgers in Bohemia). This was followed by his most popular work, *Prodana Nevěsta* (The Bartered Bride), which introduced a new genre in the field, comedy. In 1869 and 1867 Smetana composed two operas, *Dalibor* and *Libuše*. The lat-

ter had its premiere at the opening night of the Czech National Theater in 1881.

In 1874 Smetana lost his hearing. In spite of this tragic event, however, he composed two of his greatest works, *Ma Vlast* and *Z meho života* (From My Life). Deaf and impoverished, Smetana died in 1884 in an institution for mentally disturbed, yet his operas and symphonies remain the most popular works of Czech classical music recognized at home and abroad. The tunes of Smetana's *Ma Vlast* were played during the Nazi occupation every time the BBC broadcast the Czech Language News, and the Czech currency bears his portrait. The most extensive biography of the composer was assembled during a 1994 conference and is entitled *Bedřich Smetana in 1824–1884: Report of the International Musicology Conference,* May 24–25, 1994 (Praha: Muzeum Bedřicha Smetany, 1995).

## SMETONA, ANTANAS

**SMETONA, ANTANAS** 1874–1944, Lithuanian nationalist leader, lawyer, chairman of the Lithuanian Council, chairman of the Presidium of the State Council, twice president of the Republic of Lithuania, chairman of the Lithuanian Nationalist Union, one of the first European leaders who introduced an authoritarian regime after World War I; born in Uzulenis, Lithuania.

It is significant that the very first president of Lithuania had peasant roots, an academic education, and a Polish wife with pedigree. All of these facts found their reflection in his politics: Antanas Smetona was populist in his speeches, moderate in political writings, and conservative in his deeds. At the turn of the century, Antanas Smetona studied at a number of gymnasiums in Lithuania, Latvia, and Russia and in 1902 he graduated from the Faculty of Law, St. Petersburg University. He followed the advice of his high school teacher Jonas Jablonskis, the author of the first grammar of modern Lithuanian, who recommended to young Lithuanians that they study either law or medicine, because, according to him, only these two professions could ensure them the considerable income necessary that would allow them to become full-time nationalist activists.

After graduation, Antanas Smetona returned to Lithuania and settled down in Vilnius, the historical capital of the Grand Duchy of Lithuania, where he got a job at a bank. In Vilnius, Smetona joined the ranks of the local Lithuanian intellectuals, who pursued the idea of national autonomy within the Russian Empire. In 1903, he became a cofounder of the Lithuanian Democratic Party, the first Lithuanian liberal party. The Democrats declared as their short-term goal the achievement of a broader autonomy of Lithuania as a federal state within

Russia. However their long-term goal was restoration of complete Lithuanian independence.

Smetona was not as radical as his party fellows, who urged prompt solutions. During the 1905 revolution, Smetona advocated the idea of the evolutionary restructuring of the Lithuanian nation and did not support the idea of military action against the Russian authorities. In 1907, he left the liberals and along with the nationalist Catholic priest Juozas Tumas launched a newspaper *Viltis* ("The Hope"), which represented the moderate wing of the Lithuanian Nationalists. In 1914, in an attempt to establish himself in the emerging Lithuanian political scene, Smetona once against changed his political preferences. He abandoned the Catholics and embarked on a more determined way symbolized by the title of the new political magazine *Vairas* ("The Steer") that he had started to published.

During the German occupation in 1915, Antanas Smetona stood out from other Vilnius-based Lithuanian nationalists as a prominent political thinker. He was elected chairman of the Lithuanian Aid Society for War Refugees. Together with other members of his nonpartisan organization, Smetona became part of the emerging Lithuanian political elite.

In September 1917, the German authorities granted the Lithuanians official permission to convene a conference of Lithuanian nationalist activists in Vilnius. The conference, attended by about 200 delegates, mostly priests and teachers, from all over Lithuania, elected the Lithuanian Council, the supreme representative body of the Lithuanian nation. Antanas Smetona was elected chairman of the council. The Germans regarded the council as an advisory body to the ruling authorities, while the Lithuanians viewed the council as a future body of Lithuanian legislation in its embryonic stage.

In December 1917, the Lithuanian Council led by Smetona signed a document that declared independence of Lithuania, though bound through common foreign and economical policy to the German Reich. The text of declaration with references to German protection was repeated on February 16, 1918 and was regarded as the founding document of modern Lithuanian statehood. In autumn of 1917 plans were made to establish the Kingdom of Lithuania within the German Reich and Smetona strongly advocated the idea of the monarchy. On July 11, 1918, the Lithuanian Council, absent of its left-wing members, voted for Duke of Wurtemberg von Urach to become king of Lithuania under the name of Mindaugas II. (The first and only Lithuanian king, Mindaugas I, ruled for a decade in the middle of the 13th century.)

Toying with the idea of monarchy undermined Smetona's authority within and outside the country. He became associated with reactionary conservative forces. April 1919 witnessed Smetona's political comeback when the Lithuanian State Council almost unanimously elected him first president of Lithuania. However, the following year a new president was elected—Alexandras Stulginskis, a candidate of the Christian democrats. Smetona's own party, the Lithuanian National Progress Party (LNNP), did not get a single mandate in the Seimas (Parliament). In 1924, the LNPP was transformed into the Lithuanian Nationalist Union (LNU). Two years later Smetona together with two other members of the LNU entered Parliament.

During his absence from high politics between 1920 and 1926, Smetona edited a number of nationalist magazines. On several occasions he emphasized that Lithuanians lacked maturity for active political involvement and that Lithuanian political parties did not meet the needs of the nation, because they actually were just mere imitations of the Western patterns that were not suitable for the Lithuanian nation.

At the end of 1926, in cooperation with the Christian democrats and the army, Antanas Smetona carried out a coup. The lawful President Kazys Grinius was forced to step down and Smetona became president for the second time. His title was *Tautos Vadas* ("The Chief of the Nation").

In 1927 in Dimitravas a concentration camp was opened, and during its five-year existence almost 1000 opposers of the regime had been imprisoned there. In the early 1930s Smetona embarked on less authoritarian practices after he expelled from the post of premier minister his long-lived party fellow, hard-liner nationalist Augustinas Voldemaras.

Although all political parties with the exception of the Lithuanian Nationalist Union were banned in 1936, Smetona ruled more like an autocratic strongman than a fascist dictator. Smetona's "mild dictatorship" was based on nationalist as well as political grounds, therefore he was more tolerant to national minorities than Communists. The fact that he was married to Polish-born Lithuanian noble Zofija Chodakowska was not without importance.

After the occupation of Lithuania by the Soviet Union in June 1940 Smetona fled the country. In 1941 he emigrated to the United States where he died under mysterious circumstances in a fire at his home in Cleveland, Ohio, in 1944.

**SMUTS, JAN** 1870–1950, South African statesman, politician, military leader, and lawyer, who played major roles in South African politics, in British military successes in two world wars, and in the formation of the League of Nations and the United Nations. A native of Capetown, South Africa, and scion of an established Dutch family, he studied law at Cambridge University and returned home to practice at the bar in the Transvaal Republic, later becoming state attorney in that government. At the outbreak of the Boer War in 1899, he accepted a military command in the Boer army and quickly rose to the rank of general. Although an Afrikaner, he became a fervent supporter of British efforts toward unification of its South African territories as part of the British Empire. That came to pass in 1910 with the creation of the Union of South Africa. Smuts became minister of the interior in the first union government, and later accepted appointments as minister of defense, minister of finance, and minister of justice. He served Great Britain in both world wars, first as a member of the World War I war cabinet, a time in which he helped organize the Royal Air Force, and again in World War II as a British field marshal.

At the end of World War I at the Paris Peace Conference, he emerged as an influential founder of the League of Nations, coauthored the covenant of the league, and helped fashion the mandate system, which set up great power trusteeships over the former German colonies. He became prime minister of the Union of South Africa in 1919. Although he suffered political defeat in 1924, he returned to national government in 1933, and again served as prime minister in 1939 on the eve of war with Nazi Germany.

A long-time internationalist, in 1945 in San Francisco he became a founding member of the United Nations, and was chiefly responsible for drafting the preamble to the United Nations Charter. With the Nationalist Party parliamentary victory in the 1948 elections he resigned his position, when the new South African government formally legalized the apartheid system that segregated white and nonwhite ethnic groups for the next forty-five years. In September 1950 he died outside Pretoria, South Africa.

## SNEGUR, MIRCEA

**1940–**, Snegur rose through the ranks of the Moldavian Communist Party apparatus until he reached the top in 1989, just as the Soviet order was collapsing. He began his career as an agronomist and manager of state farms. From 1971 to 1978 he worked in the ministry of agriculture. He then became director general of the research production association Selektsiya Chisinau, where he served until 1981. In 1981, Snegur became secretary of the Communist Party Committee of Yedinetskyi District. In 1985, he moved into a national position, as a secretary in the Central Committee of the Communist Party of Moldavia. In 1989, as Moldavia renamed itself Moldova and moved toward independence from Russia, Snegur became chairman of the Presidium of the Supreme Soviet of Moldova. When Moldova declared independence, Snegur was voted president of the new republic. He served in this capacity until 1996. A charismatic leader and willing to follow the will of the people, Snegur made effective use of political developments to bolster his career.

In the late 1980s, when the Popular Front of Moldavia formed and gained popularity, Snegur, although a Communist, used much of the same rhetoric. The front's primary goal was union with Romania, and Snegur spoke of breaking away from the Soviet Union and rejoining with this ancient partner. In 1990, the legislature, under the leadership of Snegur, adopted a declaration of republic sovereignty and changed the name of the republic to Moldova. In 1991, as the Soviet Union collapsed, Snegur refused to recognize a coup similar to the one in Moscow, aimed at keeping the Soviet Union together. He called on the people of Moldova to support independence, and succeeded in persuading more than 100,000 people to demonstrate in the capital.

Shortly after this, the area of Trans-Dniester, which had been calling for independence since 1989, formally broke away. The Moldovan government tried to regain control, and violence ensued. However, the situation calmed after President Snegur threatened to resign if the Supreme Soviet insisted on using force to control the situation. Since talks began only after the Supreme Soviet also repudiated the idea of immediate union with Romania, Snegur openly broke with the leadership of the Popular Front and declared that union with "another state" was out of the question.

Snegur ran unopposed in elections in December 1991. Eighty-three percent of registered voters voted, and Snegur won 98 percent of the vote despite a call by the Popular Front of Moldova to boycott elections. During his five years as president, the biggest issue facing Snegur was that of Trans-Dniester. War broke out between the two sides in 1992, and peace talks were held on and off for the next few years. The two sides reached a tentative settlement in 1995, and in September of that year, Snegur met with the president of the breakaway republic. These talks failed and negotiations were suspended, but Snegur then met with President Yeltsin of Russia and President Kuchma of Ukraine, and they were able to settle on the wording of a memorandum aimed at reaching a political settlement.

In November 1996, new presidential elections were held in Moldova. Several candidates opposed Snegur, and since no candidate won a majority of votes, a run-off was held between Snegur and Petru Lucinschi, the chairman of the Parliament. Lucinschi won with 53 percent of the vote. Political analysts believe Snegur did not lose because of his political views, as Lucinschi's did not differ markedly, but rather because he had begun to blame the Parliament on the prime minister for all of the republic's problems, and had accused the government of incompetence and involvement in corruption.

## SNIEČKUS, ANTANAS

**SNIEČKUS, ANTANAS** 1903–1974, Lithuanian national Communist leader, a Comintern activist, secretary of the Lithuanian Communist Party, director of the State Security Department, long-lived first secretary of the Central Committee of the Lithuanian Communist Party, called "The Master" by the local Communists in the Lithuanian Soviet Socialist Republic, born in Kudirkos Naumiestis, Lithuania.

Sniečkus began to lead the CC of LCP in 1941 and did not let it loose until his death in 1974. Sniečkus was appointed head of the Lithuanian Communists after his successful performance as chief of state security of the Lithuanian SSR (1940–1941) in the wake of the occupation of Lithuania by Soviet troops in June 1940. During a short period in office Sniečkus succeeded in putting in jail and deporting to Soviet imprisonment camps up to 30,000 people charged with nationalism and anticommunist activities. The unleashed terror soon earned him the name "Butcher of the Nation." After World War II Sniečkus's own family took refuge in the United States. In the 1970s his adopted son Aleksandras Stromas voted the same way and sought political asylum in the United States as well. Recently declassified archival documents in Vilnius showed that in the 1960s and the 1970s Sniečkus was a keen reader of Lithuanian émigré publications supplied by the KGB. A positive shift toward national issues after Stalin's death is one of the main features that distinguishes Sniečkus from Communist leaders of other Soviet republics.

In his very early years Sniečkus had been fascinated by radical anticlerical leftist ideas radiating from revolutionary Russia. He had rejected the traditional way his Catholic family of farmers lived. The 1917 revolution found him in Russian hinterlands where his gymnasium had been relocated from Vilnius occupied by the German army. In Russia fourteen-year-old Sniečkus wanted to enlist in the Red Guards but was rejected due to his young age.

After the armistices in 1918 Sniečkus returned to Lithuania as a convinced professional revolutionary committed to a vision of the world revolution of proletariat. Nevertheless his attempts to spark a revolution in southern Lithuania failed and he turned to underground activities.

Since 1925 Sniečkus had been active as an agent of the Comintern seeking to undermine Lithuanian independence in favor of the Soviet Union. Twice imprisoned in Kaunas he was finally released in 1933 according to the agreement between Lithuania and the USSR.

After the occupation of Lithuania in 1940 Sniečkus was made director of the State Security Department to launch political repressions against his former persecutors and ideological enemies of the cultural and political establishment of the Lithuanian Republic. The next year his loyalty was awarded with the top post of first secretary of the CC of the LCP.

According to accounts of Sniečkus's relatives, Stalin happened to tell Sniečkus that they both were the only real revolutionaries throughout the Soviet Union. During the Stalinist era Sniečkus was a marionette of Moscow. He was in charge of mass deportations of the Lithuanian population to Siberia. However, at the same time he managed to get out of Soviet concentration camps some prominent figures of Lithuanian cultural life. After Stalin's death, Sniečkus embarked on a more independent type of politics mostly thanks to Stalin's successor Beria, who successfully used the nationalist card in his power game.

Beria came up with the idea that each Soviet Republic should be ruled by a domestic national-born administration. In 1953–1956, thousands of Russian-speaking white-collar workers were being recalled from Lithuania as well as from other non-Russian republics. Sniečkus did not miss the opportunity to replace Russian-speaking Communists with Lithuanian cadre who soon became the backbone of an emerging Lithuanian nomenklatura. Sniečkus despised Khrushchev because of his simple-mindedness and rude behavior.

Sniečkus's changed attitudes toward the national aspect of Lithuanian society are documented by his sport preferences. During the Stalin era at international sport tournaments Sniečkus urged his party comrades to show their support for Russian teams, since he assumed that it could help to increase feelings of internationalism. In the late 1950s Sniečkus became a fan of Vilnius's soccer team "Zalgiris" (formerly "Spartak") named after the glorious medieval battle won by Lithuanians and Polish against the German Knights in 1410. Moreover, as of the middle of the 1950s in his official addresses Sniečkus had switched from Russian to Lithuanian.

During the Khrushchev period Sniečkus became even more aware of Lithuanian national issues and paid more attention to the glorious moments of Lithuania past. In the 1960s he decided to rebuild a number of

Lithuanian castles, first of all, Trakai castle, the ancient seat of the grand duke of the Grand Duchy of Lithuania.

Hard-liners accused him of nationalism but Sniečkus survived all attempts to topple him despite the fact that there had been open hostility between Sniečkus and Khrushchev. There is evidence that during the coup against Khrushchev Sniečkus sided with Brezhnev. Sniečkus was a close ally of Kosygin, a secretary for ideology, Brezhnev's friend and aide, for whom he built a summer residence in Palanga, a famous Lithuanian resort on the Baltic Sea. His alliance with Brezhnev secured him unrestrained control over Lithuanian internal affairs. Even the autodaphe of Romas Kalanta and the following mass demonstration in Kaunas in 1971 did not hamper his position. During this final years in power Sniečkus led more or less independent cultural politics. Sniečkus enabled broad cultural contacts between the Soviet Lithuania and the Lithuanian emigration, which contributed to development of a Lithuanian national identity on both sides of the Iron Curtain. The number of Lithuanian books significantly increased, Lithuanian folklore was introduced into the official culture of Soviet Lithuania, and the Lithuanian language (in addition to Russian) became the language of administration. Nevertheless despite his countless efforts Sniečkus failed to retain full control over national industry, which in the 1960s and the 1970s became the domain of central administration in Moscow due to centralization of the Soviet economy.

Biographers are divided about his personality. Some argue that Sniečkus preferred Lithuania over the Soviet Union but was a captive of his time, while others claim that he was no more than an obedient servant of Moscow. Nevertheless both sides agree that Sniečkus made a big contribution to the modernization of the country, reducing at the same time the extent of possible Russification to a minimum and fostering national life.

## SOCIAL DARWINISM

Social Darwinism is a conservative social theory that applies biological conceptions, particularly the concept of natural selection, to human society, often in ways inconsistent with Charles Darwin's theory of evolution and his own moral sentiments. Generally, social Darwinism is opposed to welfare programs, social reform efforts, and government intervention in the lives of individuals.

The main claim of social Darwinism is that human beings living in society, like plants and animals living in nature, are affected by the law of natural selection, so that more fit organisms tend to survive, flourish, and reproduce, while less fit organisms tend to decline and disappear. Although it is ostensibly a secular theory, so-cial Darwinism nevertheless tends to associate fitness (or strength) with social virtues such as thrift, sobriety, and hard work, and unfitness (or weakness) with vices such as intemperance, idleness, and indolence. Social Darwinism also tends to defend laissez-faire capitalism, for only in the absence of government interference can nature properly reward the virtuous and punish the degenerate. Therefore, efforts to assist the poor, provide for public education, or regulate housing, work conditions, banking, or trade are at best pointless attempts to thwart nature's plan and are at worst pernicious attempts to help the less fit dominate the more fit.

Popularized by social theorists such as Herbert Spencer, Walter Bagehot, and William Graham Sumner, social Darwinism enjoyed considerable vogue in both America and Europe during the last three decades of the 19th century and the first decade of the 20th century.

Considered by many to be the apostle of social Darwinism, Spencer was not the first to apply the theory of evolution to the development of human society. However, he did so with such power and clarity that he influenced an entire generation of social scientists, on both sides of the Atlantic Ocean. Spencer's version of social evolutionism is reassuringly optimistic. In his principal works, including *Social Statics* (1851), *First Principles* (1862), *The Man Versus the State* (1884), and the multivolume *Synthetic Philosophy* (completed in 1896), Spencer argues that the evolution of human society is tending toward a condition of justice and peace, in which individuals will be able to enjoy their natural rights—including the right to fail—without hindrance or interference. He also envisions a world in which government itself will become increasingly unnecessary. According to Spencer, this idyllic condition will not be achieved through the efforts of reformers or revolutionaries. Rather, competition and conflict will force human society to evolve until a perfect society is reached. Even so, Spencer, who coined the phrase "survival of the fittest," concedes that in the meantime human life will be brutal and harsh. Spencer writes, "If they are sufficiently complete to live, they do live, and it is well they should live. If they are not sufficiently complete to live, they die, and it is best they should die." It is notable that Spencer developed many of the key elements of his theory of social evolution before Darwin published *The Origin of Species* (1859), although he later incorporated Darwin's more sophisticated theory of natural selection into his own work.

Walter Bagehot, an English economist and journalist, applied the theory of natural selection to the development and competition between entire nations and societies. In *Physics and Politics* (1872), Bagehot argued that national characters are themselves more or less fit for the purpose of survival, with progressive and forward-looking nations having a definite advantage over more hidebound societies. Whereas early societies needed a certain amount of homogeneity in order to survive, modern societies progress only when they are open to variation and change. Hence, he concluded, more backward or traditional nations are doomed to be dominated by more modern and adaptable societies, which promote rather than punish variation and innovation. This conclusion was seen by many as a justification for national imperialism.

The leading proponent of social Darwinism in the United States was William Graham Sumner, a Yale University economist and sociologist. Sumner borrowed from Spencer an aversion to reformism and a commitment to a kind of social determinism. According to Sumner, every society is encumbered by evils, some which are natural and others which are created by human beings themselves. There is nothing that can be done about the natural evils which, in any event, affect all individuals equally. As for the social evils, such as poverty, only individuals themselves can solve them, through personal virtues such as industriousness, sobriety, and thrift. Sumner's hero, in *What Social Classes Owe to Each Other* (1883) and other writings, is the "forgotten man," who is neither a social reformer nor a willing benefactor of other classes. Instead, he works hard, takes care of his family responsibilities, and pays (unwillingly and unnecessarily) for the idleness of others.

Social Darwinism was well fitted to the entrepreneurial spirit and ethos of rugged individualism that characterized America's Gilded Age and, as such, was embraced by captains of industry such as Andrew Carnegie and John D. Rockefeller. However, social Darwinism was not merely an individualistic creed. It also fit well with the popular nationalist, imperialist, militarist, and racist ideologies of the late 19th century. Although some prominent social Darwinists (including Sumner himself) were outspoken anti-imperialists, Theodore Roosevelt captured the prevailing sentiment: "In this world the nation that has trained itself to a career of unwarlike and isolated ease is bound, in the end, to go down before other nations which have not lost the manly and adventurous qualities." Social Darwinist ideas also were incorporated into the program of the American and British eugenics movements, which aimed at improving and preserving Anglo-Saxon racial stock and eliminating hereditary defects through the control of human procreation.

The broad popularity of social Darwinism declined precipitously after World War I, due to the blistering criticism of progressives, growing dissatisfaction with militarism and national imperialism, and advances in hereditary science. However, aspects of social Darwinism were given new life a few decades later, with the emergence of National Socialism in Germany during the 1930s. Nazi policies of military expansion, racial purification, and genocide depended on a social Darwinist world view and aimed at the creation of an Aryan, Nordic, or Germanic racial utopia. After World War II, social Darwinism once again declined in popularity, mainly due to its association with Nazism. However, with the development of the discipline of sociobiology, some basic presuppositions of social Darwinism have regained respectability.

The classic work on Social Darwinism in the United States is Richard Hofstadter, *Social Darwinism in American Thought*, rev. ed. (Beacon, 1955). For a discussion of Social Darwinism in Europe and the United States, see Mike Hawkins, *Social Darwinism in European and American Thought, 1860–1945* (Cambridge University Press, 1997).

## SOCIOBIOLOGY

Sociobiology is an area of study that falls between biology and sociology. It assumes that "the organism is only DNA's way of making more DNA." On the biological side, Edward O. Wilson is the founder; Wilson first became famous for his studies of social insects. Altruism among ants, bees, wasps, termites, and so on is his focus for analysis. Altruism is behavior that benefits the fitness (the reproductive success) of others at the cost of reducing the fitness or even life of the altruist. For example, some animals under some conditions will emit alarm calls to warn others, or to mimic injuries to distract predators. The challenge is then how to reconcile this altruism with the selfishness of natural selection. Richard Dawkins (1976) argued that the ultimate unit of replication is the gene, not the organism. Thus, seeming selflessness is, in fact, the ultimate in genetic selfishness. To extend this argument, if the cost–benefit ratio of the transaction is smaller than the coefficient of relatedness between the beneficiary and altruist, we can expect an altruistic transaction.

Pierre L. Van Den Berghe applied this theory to his work *The Ethnic Phenomenon* (1987). He argued that ethnicity, racism, and sometimes nationalism have their origin in the gene and are shaped and reshaped by cultures. Human beings do share some basic biological characteristics with other animals. And, again, ethnicity is the extension of kinship.

An understanding of many fundamental features of human behavior will continue to elude us unless we compare our behavior with that of other species. Human behavior reveals three distinct but interrelated levels: (1) genetic, (2) ecological, and (3) cultural. Human sociality is a special case of animal socialty in general. In human society, genes enable organisms to successfully compete against, and thereby hinder reproduction of, organisms that carry alternative alleles of the genes in question, and successfully cooperate with organisms that share the same alleles of the genes. In ethnic racial theories this is called *primordialism*.

This line of deterministic arguments implies that nationalism, racially and ethnically motivated, is determined by the gene and thus is incurable. It lies somewhere between nature and nurture.

**SOLIDARITY MOVEMENT**   Poland's Solidarity movement played a central role in bringing an end to the Soviet domination of Eastern Europe, and to the Soviet Union itself. *Solidarność* was created out of a lengthy period of struggle, the initial intent of which was to reform the Soviet-style system in Poland, and only later did it become an effort to alter that system in fundamental ways. In 1968 and 1970, students and workers endured repression in response to their demonstrations and, in the case of the workers, deadly force. In 1970, the official toll was some forty-three people dead; unofficially, the estimates are vastly greater. This experience terrified the dissidents, who kept their heads low. The result was that reform died as an option. Then, in 1976, Gomulka's successor, Edward Gierek, who had sworn he would never allow deadly force to be used against the workers again, was confronted with worker riots; his word was good. The result was that the fear lifted. Within a short time, an open opposition of intellectuals appeared, while undergrounds that had been quietly developing among workers continued to spread, and to become more open, and the two connected somewhat with each other.

The Polish Pope's visit in 1979 was a galvanizing event that brought out millions of people. The sight of masses of people stretched out as far as anyone could see made a powerful impression that went beyond the spiritual. Solidarity spokesman Janusz Onyszkiewicz said: "Before the Pope's visit, people used to talk all the time in terms of 'we' and 'they.' Everybody knew what 'they' was: the ruling group, the Party, the whole establishment. 'We' was not so clear. People felt fairly atomized and somehow 'we' was practically family. With the pope's visit, people saw themselves, and they realized that 'we' was not just myself, my family and my five friends, but millions—basically the nation. And 'they' were a very tiny, isolated group. So we really felt that

we had power." Staszek Handzlik, a future leader of Solidarity recalled: "What I remember most clearly is that people concentrated on one issue: their feeling that the days of Gierek, and maybe of the whole Communist system in Poland, were almost over."

The next year, workers in the shipyards struck against price increases; they were actively supported by farmers, students, and intellectuals. For the first time, the authorities agreed to negotiate with strikers. But time dragged and there was little movement toward agreement, as the party leadership feared angering the Soviets. Workers all over the country feared that the strikers would face a repeat of the killings of 1970 unless others did something. Finally, almost two weeks after the shipyard workers went out, they were joined by steelworkers and miners, whose added strength precluded the possibility that the government could decide to crush the shipyard workers alone. Within days, the right of the workers to form a union and to strike was acknowledged.

This victory did not end the conflict; it was only the beginning, as the authorities sought continually to undermine Solidarity and to take back its gains, and the workers broadened the rights they had won. The sixteen months of legal Solidarity were a period of intense conflict: between Solidarity and the party leadership; within Solidarity, as militants demanded firmer action against the moderate leadership; and within the party as the party leadership was besieged by Solidarity supporters, who constituted a good third of the party. The period ended only when Prime Minister Wojciech Jaruzelski, in December 1981, organized a coup d'état and arrested some 10,000 Solidarity leaders, activists, and supporters.

But this effort to return to the status quo ante was doomed from the start, because people refused to accept it. The government was never able to recapture its lost authority. With the murder of the popular priest Popieluszko in 1984, the government was put on the defensive and the opposition blossomed and was soon operating in the open once again. It became evident that the government would never be able to carry through on its plans for economic reform unless it granted the Polish population the political democratization it was demanding. Strikes at the beginning and the end of the summer of 1988 lay the basis for the negotiations that ultimately dismantled the Communist state in Poland and removed most of the basis of Soviet domination.

Before the year was out, the Soviet Empire had fallen apart. Two years later, the Soviet Union itself lay dead. There is little doubt that the Solidarity movement was a catalyst for all of this change. Mieczyslaw Rakowski, the last Communist prime minister and the last general secretary of the party in Poland, said of Gorbachev that "After some years, he told Jaruzelski and me that Poland in very many points had influenced him in his particular approach in the situation in the Soviet Union. And in the end of the '80s he asked us for material about our reforms, our concept, and we sent it to him."

Two good books with differing points of view on Solidarity are *Breaking the Barrier* by Lawrence Goodwyn (Oxford University, 1991) and *The Polish Revolution* by Timothy Garton Ash (Vintage Books, 1985).

**SOLZHENITSYN, ALEKSANDR** 1918–, Russian writer and Nobel Prize winner. Solzhenitsyn was born in Kislovodsk, Russia. He studied mathematics at the University of Rostov and took correspondence courses on literature in Moscow. In 1941–1945 he served in the Soviet army. As a perfectionist and idealist he was searching for better political solutions for the Soviet Union and criticized Stalin in one of his letters at the end of World War II. But during the Stalin years any critical remarks about Marxism-Leninism-Stalinism were punished and in the spring of 1945 Solzhenitsyn was arrested. He was sentenced to eight years of imprisonment. He spent the first years of his imprisonment in Moscow, but he was later sent to Siberia. In the middle of the 1950s Solzhenitsyn was exiled to Central Asia and Central Russia where he worked as a teacher and began to write stories. His first short story, *One Day in the Life of Ivan Denisovitch,* was published in one of the leading Soviet literary periodicals *Novy Mir (New World)* in 1963. All of a sudden, Solzhenitsyn became a celebrity. The story, from one side, is based on the author's forced-labor camp experiences expressed through the eyes of a simple Russian man; from the other side, it is a generalization of Russian imprisonment as a whole. Solzhenitsyn portrays just one day, every minute of an ordinary Russian in the Soviet jail, his big-small events, contacts with other prisoners of various nationalities, guards, outside life reflections, and memories. In the story he accuses the Soviet Union of totalitarianism since its first days of existence and that fact contrasted Solzhenitsyn with other critics, who criticized just Stalin's "cult of personality" during Khrushchev's thaw period.

In 1963 Solzhenitsyn published a book entitled *Two Stories.* In 1964 Nikita Khrushchev was removed from power and ideological control was tightened by the Soviet authorities. The following two novels, *The First Circle* (1968) and *Cancer Ward* (1963–1966), were therefore published as samizdat ("self-published," unofficial, illegal publications) in the USSR and were printed and translated abroad.

In 1969 Solzhenitsyn was expelled from the Soviet Writers' Union for criticizing Soviet authorities about censoring some of his books. In 1970 he received the Nobel Prize in literature. In 1973 parts of his famous *Gulag Archipelago* were published in Paris and he was immediately attacked by some critics, which ended in 1974 with Solzhenitsyn being stripped of Soviet citizenship. He was officially accused of treason and deported to West Germany. Later the writer moved to the United States where he finished some earlier works he had started in the USSR and also wrote and published new books.

In the 1960s and 1980s Solzhenitsyn was considered by the Soviet intellectuals as the conscience of the nation. The publications of *The Gulag Archipelago* ["gulag" is an acronym from the Soviet state camp system], were not just camp experiences of the author but elaborate and extensive exposes of the Soviet system as a tremendous assembly of prisons, terrorism, and secret police in various periods of its existence. The works displayed the history of the 20th century USSR as a whole. He portrays a dual picture of the reality: the hell of the camps opposed by freedom for purification, sacrifice, and renascence. Faith is one of the basic elements of his religious philosophy.

In emigration he rewrote *August 1914,* published as *The Red Wheel,* a study on Russian national character that led to the tragedy of totalitarianism, and biographical prose. Living in the United States, Solzhenitsyn, however, rejected the Western model of democracy and individual freedom, instead favoring an authoritarian regime based on traditional Christian values.

In 1990 Solzhenitsyn proposed the idea of establishing a Slavic state on the territories of Russia, Ukraine, Belarus, and northern Kazakhstan, for which he was widely criticized as a Russian chauvinist.

In 1991 the Soviet authorities dropped treason charges against Solzhenitsyn and the writer returned to live in Russia in 1994. The next year he published *Invisible Allies,* a tribute to those people who helped to smuggle his works out of the USSR. At the same time Solzhenitsyn has maintained his critical attitude toward modern Russia.

In one of his latest books, *Russia in Downfall* (1998), Solzhenitsyn analyzes the Russian character. Historically it has been religious-peasant integrity characterized by simplicity of behavior, humility, compassion, repentance, openness, humor, and magnanimity.

All Solzhenitsyn's works are the result of detailed scientific research and didactic technique. They express the moral values of the Russian Orthodox Church and the author's belief in the progress of Russian historical achievements.

## SOUTH AFRICAN HOMELANDS, NATIONALISM IN

Unknown to most nonspecialists, South Africa's "national states," also referred to as bantustans, homelands, cultural groups, and so on, were stillborn in the heyday of Afrikaner rule. Among harsh critics of white South Africa's apartheid political base, these units were a bad conceptual idea made worse in practice. South Africa's far right wing argued favorably about the merit of the policy's aspiration but they argued that it was never implemented. The right wing charged that the scheme was undermined by the very government that had introduced this arrangement as the solution to an otherwise inevitable black–white violent confrontation. Whereas in the rest of Africa some independent states have to contend with 300 to 400 tribal/linguistic groups within their borders, South Africa contained a mere 10 distinguishable black tribal groupings—in addition to distinct fragments within the white, coloured, and Asian/Indian communities.

Domestic socially fragmented societies are virtually a universal phenomenon and, indeed, before and after the termination of the Cold War, we witnessed the particularly violent fractionating of Yugoslavia, Somalia, and Rwanda, as well as the ongoing ethnic-originated nationalist fragmentations in Sudan, Senegal, Angola, Ethiopia, Liberia, Sri Lanka, Kashmir, Indonesia, Russia, Turkey, Iraq, Lebanon, and so on. However, South Africa's national states, by contrast to numerous other domestically troubled states throughout the world, were avidly encouraged by the white ruling regime to formally break off from South Africa and pursue the mythical glories of independence. For these homelands they would have been few. Most had only skimpy assets; very poorly developed human and economic infrastructures; and in the end they functioned mostly as poverty-struck bedrooms for distant daily commuters to the industries located within adjacent white South Africa. Those without formal jobs in South Africa were to pursue the advantages of national self-determination in their national states, which were very bleak economic entities.

The world responded to the claims of the "independent" homelands' nationalism by totally ignoring them. Only South Africa claimed to enjoy reciprocal diplomatic recognition and relations with the four that had attained "independent status." Several of the projected ten homelands experienced greatly fractured geographies—resembling on a map a battered slice of Swiss cheese. Ideally, the homelands were to contain all blacks, about 70 percent of South Africa's total population, but they would officially comprise only about 15 percent of the lands, which within the homelands'

borders produced under 2 percent of the combined homelands and South Africa's wealth. Their elite, of course, did profit handsomely from this nationalistic arrangement. What money did circulate in the homelands was mostly derived from South Africa's "temporary" subsidies, and not an inconsiderable amount from easily available, internationally dubious sources.

The four independent (though not recognized as such by the international community) national states were to demonstrate to the rest of the world the advantages of separating ethnic-based sociopolitical entities. These were the states named Transkei, Bophuthatswana, Ciskei, and Venda. Indeed, four decades after the independence of many other African countries, ethnic-based antagonism within half of them has produced devastating casualty statistics emanating from their internal and external wars. Military coups and rule have hardly stabilized those countries and several are now termed "collapsed states." In purely measurable data terms, at least two of these "national states," Transkei and Bophuthatswana, enjoyed greater size, populations, and some economic and welfare advantages over some dozen African states whose independence was not contested. However, the position of South Africa's African National Congress, the victorious party of President Nelson Mandela, adamantly opposed such schemes and even refused the installation of a federal structure that might have been a half-measure in favor of continued national identification. The new, majority-based black-dominated government easily reincorporated these four national entities into South Africa and held that no longer would they have to face the future without sharing in the wealth that the whites had been engineering to their own greatly disproportionate advantage. The separate identities of these "national" entities have today been completely eradicated.

## SOUTH AFRICAN NATIONALISM

The Republic of South Africa, the country at the southernmost tip of the African continent, has had two modern nationalist struggles, one essentially by white settlers against the European colonialists, and the second by black South Africans against the white minority's apartheid system.

The South African War (1899–1902) pitted the English-speaking Boers, with support of the Afrikaner population, against the British colonial forces. Although in principle a war between white settlers and the white colonial power, both sides used black Africans extensively in their campaigns. In addition to those killed in battle, an estimated 25,000 Afrikaner and 14,000 black African women and children succumbed to malnutrition and disease in the racially segregated concentration camps to which they were driven by British forces. The liberal leader in Britain accused the government of using "methods of barbarism."

The rebellion against the colonial administration was unsuccessful and the British reorganized the country for a more efficient administration during a period of postwar "reconstruction." The police and tax systems were made more effective and colonial control over gold mining was ensured. White settler minorities were given clear power over the black majority, which was effectively barred, from political power and influence. The so-called "native question" was solved by systematic segregation of the races according to a plan developed by the South African Native Affairs Commission (SANAC).

On May 31, 1910, the Union of South Africa was created by an act of the British Parliament and a South African Constitutional Convention. The Constitution created a new nation that resembled other constitutional democracies except for its exclusion participation by the majority population, the black Africans. The rights of Afrikaans- and English-speaking whites were protected and efforts were under way to unite the two white populations of the new nation (although they were never fully successful in doing so).

The other major nationalist movement in South Africa was among the nonwhite populations, the various native African peoples and Indians ("Coloureds") inspired in part by Mohandas K. Gandhi and the Indian Freedom movement. It was in fact in South Africa that Gandhi developed his methods of nonviolent resistance, Satyagraha, in the late 19th and early 20th centuries.

On January 8, 1912, the nonwhite nationalist movement founded the South African Native National Congress, later the African National Congress (ANC), which became the focal point of opposition to white minority dominance. During its early years the ANC relied primarily on legal means to advocate reform; in the early 1950s it turned toward Gandhian style nonviolent direct action as did its rival Pan Africanist Congress (PAC) founded in 1959. In the wake of the Sharpeville massacre in 1960 both groups, frustrated with their lack of progress, used various forms of violent resistance until the ANC returned to nonviolent action in the early 1990s.

The use of armed struggle, for example, the bombing campaign by ANC's Umkhonto We Sizwe (Spear of the Nation), may have been counterproductive. Acts of terrorism alienated many black and white supporters alike and the South African government merely escalated its militarization of the country. The townships where the black population was segregated were designed to be easily controlled by the government's military and difficult for guerrillas. In the early 1980s the ANC began to question whether armed struggle could ever be successful. Key leaders like antiapartheid Archbishop Desmond Tutu called on the ANC to suspend its armed struggle in 1988 (although he did not oppose the prospect of returning to it if nonviolence proved unsuccessful).

Campaigns of civil resistance were organized throughout the country, as was worldwide support for the antiapartheid struggle. A mass democratic movement emerged including the informal alliance of several groups calling for a nonracial democratic government under the leadership of the ANC. By the late 1980s the defiance of the opposition had become so powerful that the government had lost control, especially in the townships. The use of boycotts, mass demonstrations, strikes, civil disobedience, hunger strikes, and other tactics of nonviolent resistance resulted in the collapse of the apartheid system in the 1990s. Nelson Mandela, leader of African National Congress, was released from jail and was shortly thereafter elected president of the new Republic of South Africa.

**SOVEREIGNTY AND NATIONALISM** An international legal concept that, when applied to a group or state, indicates an exercise of supreme political control over a given territory. Note that there is also the concept and reality of limited internal sovereignty within a state. Sovereignty thus has both external or international implications in state-to-state relations as well as having internal or domestic implications through its dealings with its citizens. Sovereignty consists of, but is not limited to, the ability to make laws, execute and enforce them, pursue a policy of peace or war, and engage in commerce.

Historically, nationalism was based on two tenets. First the principle of freedom and sovereignty and, second, that nations should constitute sovereign states. Indeed, many wars of liberation and nationalist struggles have been waged in a quest for sovereignty as sovereignty entitles the nation to exercise control over itself.

The modern legitimate sovereign state obtains its authority from the people with consent as a recognized basis for public authority. The French Declaration on the Rights and Duties of Man and Citizen echoes this when it states: "the source of all sovereignty resides essentially in the nation, no group, no individual may exercise authority not emanating expressly therefrom." On this point Goethe said: "Nothing is good for a nation but that which arises from its own core and its own general wants, without apish imitation of another."

The ability of a nation-state to exercise sovereignty both internally and within the international community serves several purposes. First, a sovereign state is recognized as an international subject with all the rights and responsibilities as such. All states may not recognize a new state immediately or even in the short term. Thus the way a nation chooses to strive for sovereignty bears greatly on who will recognize it as sovereign and when it will be so recognized. Nations who choose a peaceful path instead of one of either insurgency or warfare will generally more quickly obtain legitimacy in the international community. Second the nation itself, as such, gains legitimacy when recognized as sovereign.

Third, the nation that becomes a sovereign state wields power in the international community that it probably did not have as a group within a state or states. However, the amount of power will of course depend on a variety of factors such as resources, economic policy, political structure, and, to some extent, geography.

Books on sovereignty and autonomy include *Sovereignty through Interdependence*, by Henry Gelber, and *Autonomy: Applications and Implications*, edited by Markku Suksi.

**SOVIET NATIONALISM** The Bolshevik Revolution of 1917 was a watershed in the history of the Russian people. Based on Marxist-Leninist ideology, it contained an internationalist and universal mission of sparking proletariat revolutions throughout Europe, which would ultimately lead to the destruction of the capitalist system in the industrialized West. Marxism is generally antinational, because it sees nationalism as a bourgeois creation designed to distract the proletariat from the class struggle and divide the working class along ethnic lines. Expressions of nationalism were perceived as reactionary and contrary to the interests of the revolution. However, the Bolsheviks were quite willing to utilize nationalist sentiments and promises of self-determination to aid in their struggle to secure political power. It was believed that with the establishment of true socialism, the various nations would be drawn together by their common class interests and national differences would become politically irrelevant.

The early Leninist government aimed at marking a sharp break with the socioeconomic system and nationalities policies of the imperial regime. The first order of business was to combat "Great Russian Chauvinism" and equalize relations between the states's many ethnic groups. This was done in a number of ways. Ethnically defined administrative entities (republics and other sub-republic units) were established ostensibly to provide non-Russian ethnic groups with autonomy and protection from Russian domination. Non-Russian languages, cultures, and traditions were encouraged (within limits). Symbols of Russian culture (especially the Orthodox Church) were assailed. Finally, the regime embarked on a policy of "indigenization," designed to promote non-Russian cadres in order to balance the overwhelming numbers of Russians in the Communist Party. Nevertheless, the party, in defense of the USSR in its earliest years, used Russian nationalism to rally the population against the Western powers—a fact not lost to those on the Soviet borderlands who often equated Communism with continued domination by Russians.

The internationalist slogans of the early Bolshevik period, which subsumed Russian identity into a universalistic ideology, soon gave way to more particularist and nationalist tendencies once it became clear that the Russian Revolution would not spread throughout Europe. The victory of Joseph Stalin and his notion of "Socialism in One Country" in the mid-1920s over Leon Trotsky's internationalist "Permanent Revolution" meant that Soviet state interests were elevated above an interest in world revolution. This ushered in a revival of Russian nationalist symbols and the closer identification of "Russia" with the Bolshevik Revolution and the USSR. In addition, the state embarked on a policy of Russification of non-Russian populations and promoted the notion that the Russians were the "elder brothers" of the Soviet people. This shift was called the "Nationalization of October" and drew the tacit support of nationalist emigre groups. Stalin, however, was not a nationalist, but rather a "Red patriot" who used nationalist sentiments to defend and further the socialist revolution.

Soviet and Russian nationalism merged after Nazi Germany's invasion of the USSR on June 22, 1941. The "Great Patriotic War," as it was called, was seen less as a conflict between capitalists (fascism was seen as its most extreme form) and socialists, and more as a struggle for national survival because, it was argued, the interests of the Soviet Union and the Russian nation were essentially the same. As a result, Stalin's regime embraced Russia's historic heroes and symbols, and established a de facto alliance with the Russian Orthodox Church. Once the war was over, however, use of Russian nationalism dramatically decreased and an emphasis was once again placed on Marxist-Leninist ideology.

The post-Stalinist era was marked by a constantly shifting relationship between the regime and Russian nationalism with the Khrushchev government moving away from Stalin's reliance on Russian nationalism as a major pillar of Soviet nationalism. At the same time, the notion that the people of the Soviet Union were moving toward a supranational "Soviet People" became official state policy after the 22nd Party Congress in 1961. This did not mean that the individual ethnic groups would lose their separate identities and assimilate into one Soviet "nation." Instead, this "brotherly alliance" of nations intended to make ethnic differences politically irrelevant. Although this notion was overly optimistic, the regime emphasized an "internationalist" education and encouraged numerous Soviet cultural rituals in order to establish a collective Soviet memory (especially important was the history of World War II). Furthermore, the Soviet Union as a whole, rather than the eponymous republics, was promoted as the homeland of the Soviet peoples.

Many non-Russians perceived the Sovietization of the USSR as merely a cover for a new round of Russification. Mandatory education in the Russian language for all Soviet citizens was revived after a hiatus during the 1960s. Ethnic Russians were encouraged to move outside of the Russian Soviet Federated Socialist Republic (RSFSR) by state policies that offered Russian-language schools, newspapers, and other cultural establishments; non-Russians outside of their republic were given nothing of the sort. Many Russians bypassed republic institutions and relied on all-union organizations to fulfill their daily needs. Russians were rarely classified as a minority population, regardless of where they resided in the Soviet Union. Survey data indicate that an overwhelming percentage of Russians considered the USSR, as a whole, their homeland. By contrast, most non-Russians named their eponymous republics as their homeland.

Severe economic problems during the late 1970s and 1980s generated a wave of anti-Soviet sentiment among non-Russians and Russians alike. Mikhail Gorbachev's attempts to reform the Soviet socioeconomic and political structures furthered, rather than restrained, the growing nationalist unrest plaguing the country. Gorbachev considered himself primarily a Soviet patriot and was often accused of not understanding either the seriousness of the USSR's nationalities problems or how little Sovietization was internalized by the non-Russian peoples. More importantly, however, the ties between Soviet and Russian interests frayed. Nationalist writers such as Valentin Rasputin and Aleksandr Solzhenitsyn had long argued that Russia's interests were distinct from those of the Soviet Union. This assumed political expression with the rise of Boris Yeltsin as the champion of the Russian people in opposition to the policies of the Soviet center. The attempted coup in August 1991 by Communist hard-liners delegitimized the Soviet system and led to its collapse in December 1991. While some remain nostalgic for the Soviet Union, the experiment of Soviet nationalism was a failure.

For further reading, see Walker Connor, *The National Question in Marxist-Leninist Theory and Strategy* (Princeton University Press, 1984); E. H. Carr, *Socialism in One Country* (Macmillan Co., 1958); John Dunlop, *The Faces of Contemporary Russian Nationalism* (Princeton University Press, 1983); *Ethnic Russia in the USSR*, Edward Allworth, ed. (Pergamon Press, 1980); and *The Nationalities Question in the Soviet Union*, Graham Smith, ed. (Longman, 1990).

**SOVIET UNION AND NATIONALISM**  The Soviet Union's approach to nationalism was divided into two distinct spheres: nationalism in the USSR and nationalism outside its borders. With regard to nationalism outside the borders of the USSR, Moscow tended to view it overall as a force laden with potential to advance "progressive" goals and other Soviet interests, such as decolonization and nationalization of means of production. Especially in the post-World War II period, the Soviet Union regarded nationalism as a force that could advance its aims and was a very prominent feature of its policy in the Third World.

In the internal domain, Soviet regard for nationalism often fluctuated depending on changes in leadership and state interests, and as a product of both ideological and practical considerations it was beset with innate contradictions. Constant tension existed between the Soviet Union's declared ideology on self-determination and its state interest in preservation of its territorial integrity. Moreover, the ideological inheritance that the Soviet Union received from Marx and Lenin on nationalism was teeming with intrinsic disparities. Both Marx and Lenin saw nationalism as a bourgeoisie ideology that was part of the superstructure that would ultimately disappear with the end of capitalism. Lenin especially viewed nationalism as a product of imperialist exploitation. However, both Lenin and Marx saw the revolutionary potential inherent in nationalism to advance revolution, and thus at times advocated support for the principle of self-determination and some national movements. In addition, Lenin feared potential Russian chauvinism and maintained that an adoption by Russian Communists of an accommodating stance toward the national sentiments and political wills of the non-Russian peoples of the former Russian Empire would foster attraction for the new Soviet state among them and peoples in Asia and Africa and thus be conducive to advancing Communism. In an attempt to contrast with the capitalist states, the new Soviet state wanted to present itself as nonimperialist and a country in which minority groups have equal rights. Thus, in its first years of existence the Soviet Union was formally tolerant of the desire for self-determination on the part of many former subject peoples of the empire.

Despite the fact that by 1922, the Soviet Union had reincorporated, in many cases by force, most of the former peoples of the Russian Empire, in its rhetoric the Soviet Union adopted the principle of self-determination of nations, and this was enshrined in the nominal federal structure of the Soviet Union and all three of the Soviet constitutions, which formally declared the right of the component states to secede from the union. The pseudo-federal structure was further institutionalized with the creation of a number of autonomous units within the member republics, and the establishment of a house of the Soviet legislature, the Soviet of the Nationalities, composed of delegates elected from the various republics and autonomies.

Lenin and Stalin had advocated an approach to the national question based on the principle of "nationalist in form, socialist in content." Communist ideology could be communicated to the masses in their native language by co-ethnic elites. In its early years, Moscow adopted a policy of institutionalizing the use of the languages of many of the peoples of the USSR. Most of the non-Russian languages were officially recognized and the development of their literatures was encouraged, albeit within the limitations of official ideology. Cultural elites in the republics were allowed to write in their "national languages" and to publish classical "national" literary pieces as long as they included revolutionary and pro-proletarian messages. In the 1920s, the Soviet Union implemented a policy of *korenizatsiia* (indigenization) of the political elites in the local republics. In later years, Moscow generally appointed a member of the main indigenous ethnic group to head a republic's Communist Party, along with a Slavic deputy. The leaders of the republics generally possessed local power bases and were versed in the culture and ways of the republic's titular ethnic group. They routinely appointed associates who were close to them, often from their own ethnic and even regional or clan grouping.

In official ideology, the Soviets, based on Lenin's precepts, believed that in a Communist society nations would voluntarily choose to blend into one culture, and create a new supra-ethnic identity, which in the case of the Soviet Union came to be known as the "Soviet man." Under the guise of an attempt to accelerate the formation of the new supra-ethnic identity, and the materialization of Lenin's postulate of the *sblizhenie* (blending) and eventual *sliianie* (merging) of nations, Moscow

implemented policies that promoted Russian language and culture. The Cyrillic alphabet, for example, was imposed on most of the languages of the Soviet peoples, and from the 1930s, Moscow implemented a policy of Russification among the Soviet peoples. Instead of placing formal limitations on the use of non-Russian languages, positive incentives for Russification were created: Greater resources were given to the Russian-language schools in the republics, lessons at the top universities across the USSR were conducted in Russian, and access to positions of power in the center mandated full command of Russian. Members of the non-Russian groups had to learn Russian in order to attain major positions of power in their own republics and in the center, whereas Russian residents of non-Russian republics were not forced to learn the local languages, not even when they filled important positions in those republics. As a result of this policy by 1979, 62.2 percent of the non-Russians considered themselves fluent in Russian.

National groups whose collective loyalties were claimed to be doubted by the regime were often persecuted and some were exiled from their traditionally claimed lands, such as the Chechens, Crimean Tatars, and the Volga Germans who were exiled within the USSR during World War II.

The inherent contradictions within the Soviet policy on nationalism was a significant factor contributing to its downfall in 1991. In general, Moscow stressed both ethnic and territorial-based identity and this created a situation of inherent tensions. The Soviet Union termed as nations many of the larger ethnic groups in the country, and granted them territorial units. The political borders and the ethnic borders in the USSR were rarely congruent. Thus, many Soviet citizens lived in national units belonging to ethnic groups other than their own. This also produced an additional element of built-in tension due to the problematic relationship between the republics and their co-ethnics beyond their borders in other Soviet republics, and between members of different ethnic minorities within the republics. This became evident in many of the conflicts that erupted under Gorbachev and in the post-Soviet period, such as over Karabagh.

In addition, the USSR institutionalized and essentially reinforced the ethnic identity of its citizens: in internal passports, most other identifying documents, as well as many official administrative forms, the ethnic identity of the citizens was noted. Paradoxically, in the Soviet state, which attempted to promote a supra-ethnic state identity, ethnicity was an issue during almost every encounter a citizen had with the state bureaucracy.

This process strengthened the ethnic awareness of each citizen. Children automatically received the ethnic identity of their parents, and if they were born to parents of two different ethnic groups, at age sixteen they could choose the ethnic identity of one of their parents, but they could not freely select their self-identification. Thus, paradoxically the Soviet system prevented the assimilation of ethnic groups into larger units, despite its Russification policy. In addition, Russian society rarely allowed full assimilation of many of the non-Russians, especially the Muslim minorities; thus, on the individual level full assimilation was hardly possible in the Soviet Union, despite ideological rhetoric.

In many component republics of the Soviet Union, especially in Central Asia and the Caucasus, Moscow left many of the traditional power structures intact, as long as the prevailing local elites were willing to maintain stability and the flow of resources to the center. The continued existence of these traditional elites assisted the growth of nationalism in these republics.

For further reading, see Rogers Brubaker, *Nationalism Reframed: Nationhood and the National Question in the New Europe* (Cambridge: Cambridge University Press, 1996); Walker Connor, *The National Question in Marxist-Leninist Theory and Strategy* (Princeton, N.J.: Princeton University Press, 1984); Ronald Grigor Suny, *The Revenge of the Past: Nationalism, Revolution, and the Collapse of the Soviet Union* (Stanford, Calif.: Stanford University Press, 1993); and Yuri Slezkine, "The USSR as a Communal Apartment, or How a Socialist State Promoted Ethnic Particularism," in Geoff Eley and Ronald G. Suny, eds., *Becoming National* (New York: Oxford University Press, 1996).

**SOYINKA, WOLE** 1934–, Nigerian playwright, poet, novelist who won the Nobel Prize for literature in 1986. Akinwande Oluwole ('wole) Soyinka is widely seen as Africa's most accomplished playwright as well as one of the significant figures in contemporary world literature. Soyinka's acknowledgment as a pioneer of modern African drama written in the English language is responsible for the fondness with which some critics and admirers of his work call him "Our own W. S." Soyinka is a writer who has erased the imaginary boundary between creative activity and commitment to social justice and human liberty in his country of Nigeria, in Africa, and in the world at large.

Such intermingling of the personal with the political in his life earned Soyinka the wrath of Nigerian state authorities at various times including two years of detention without trial (1968–1969) by Gen. Yakubu Gowon's military government during the Nigeria-Biafra war. Indeed, Soyinka's work and life cannot be separated, for the former derives considerably from his passionate concern for his society. One of Soyinka's acts of political bravado occurred in the 1960s when he was alleged to have compelled a continuity announcer at the Western Nigerian Broadcasting Corporation Station at gunpoint to switch tapes in favor of Chief Obafemi Awolowo's Action Group. For that he was tried but was discharged and acquitted on technical grounds.

In spite of his refusal to identify himself with any particular political ideology, Soyinka has on several occasions proclaimed his implicit belief in "what goes under the broad umbrella of socialist ideology" for the reason that for Africa, "there is no route outside of socialism, in terms of harnessing our energies, our resources, and catching up with modern society." Soyinka distanced himself from negritude, an Africanist cultural movement propagated by people like Leopold Sedar Senghor (who later became president of Senegal) and the black Matinican poet and political activist Aime Cesaire for the exotic, narcissistic, and idealized irrational manner in which its proponents portrayed Africanness. Soyinka's foray into political activism and publicist controversy predated his actual attempt to join a political party (People's Redemption Party) in 1979 during Nigeria's four-year Second Republic.

To most Nigerians, Soyinka is a courageous, selfless, and uncompromising crusader and advocate for social justice and individual freedom. During Nigeria's latest ordeal under the repressive military dictatorship of the late Gen. Sani Abacha, Soyinka was forced into self-exile in the United States from where he joined hands with other Nigerians to campaign for the termination of military rule. Soyinka was one of the brains behind *Radio Kudirat: The Voice of Democracy*. Named for the assassinated wife of M. K. O. Abiola, the presumed winner of the June 12 presidential election, *Radio Kudirat* broadcast daily into Nigeria for much of the life of the Abacha regime as the voice of Nigerian opponents of military rule.

Soyinka's autobiography appears in a trilogy: *Ake: The Childhood Years* (London: Collings 1981), *Isara: A Voyage around Essay* (New York: Random House 1989), and *Ibadan: The Penkelemes Years: A Memoir: 1946–1965* (London: Methuen 1995).

**SPANISH COLONIES AND NATIONALISM** Spain possesses islands in the Atlantic Ocean that are important links between the Western and Eastern Hemispheres. According to the 1479 Treaty of Alcacovas, the Canary Islands (off the northwest coast of Africa) are Spanish, and the Azores (west of Portugal) and Madeira (north of the Canaries) are Portuguese. The Spanish have the Balearic Islands in the Mediterranean, the largest of which is the tourist mecca of Majorca. Spain also owns a few islands off the Moroccan coast and the cities of Ceuta and Melilla on the northern coast of Morocco. These holdings are a miniscule reminder of the great colonial power Spain once was. It spread its language and culture to colonies in Latin America, Africa, and Asia that were many times greater in size and population than the mother country.

Spanish attention had remained largely focused on Iberia until 1492. In that year the Spanish captured Granada, the last Moslem foothold on Spanish soil. The triumphant entry into that city of Ferdinand and Isabella, whose marriage had sealed the unity of Aragon and Castile, signified the end of the seven and one-half century reconquest of the Iberian peninsula. Spain took shape as a unified kingdom over an ethnically diverse area. The reconquest sparked a flourish of Spanish literature and artistic achievement that lasted at least two centuries. It also allowed Spaniards to concentrate their energy on overseas expansion and exploration.

As every American schoolchild knows, the year 1492 was significant for another event: Christopher Columbus, a native of Genoa (Italy) working for the Spanish, sailed west in search of India. Instead he bumped into the island of Santo Domingo in the Caribbean. His discovery opened European eyes to an entirely new part of their world and launched an era of Spanish colonialism that spread Hispanic culture and languages to dozens of modern-day countries.

To minimize a potentially dangerous rivalry between Spain and Portugal in the wake of Columbus's discovery, the sovereigns of the two countries agreed to the Treaty of Tordesillas in 1494. It divided the world in such a way that Spain would receive the Philippines (named after the Spanish king) and most of the Western hemisphere (including large chunks of the contemporary United States, such as California, the Southwest, and Florida). Portugal received what is now Brazil and parts of Africa and Asia. Both countries continued generally to observe this agreement, which had the Pope's approval. But to their consternation, other European powers, especially Britain, France, and the Netherlands, did not.

Spain had several motives for establishing and maintaining an empire. In contrast with other European colonial powers except Portugal, Dominican and Franciscan friars were always close on the heels of the *conquistadores* in order to convert, educate, and sometimes protect the native populations. The 1542 *Leyes Nuevas* (New Laws of the Indies) offered some protection to Indians and were based on considerations of the legal and moral problems of conquest and rule. Although they were often ignored, they were unique in European colonies of the time. Also, the *conquistadores*, the royal court, and the private companies that stood behind them clearly sought wealth, status, and power. The Spanish kings insisted that all trade with the colonies be conducted through Seville and be reserved for Castile. Actually, most of the trade was organized by Genoese and southern German merchants.

The Spanish kings also claimed one-fifth of all precious metals imported from the New World. Such metals greatly enriched the Spanish treasury, but they also created inflation within Spain and serious economic distortions. This wealth was used to add glitter to the royal and noble courts, to finance massive Spanish imports, and also to finance Spanish armies and navies. These military forces were constantly embroiled abroad maintaining an empire that encompassed the present-day Benelux countries, Italy and, through the Habsburg throne, all of the Austrian Empire. Throughout the 17th century Spanish money and troops also supported the Catholic struggle against Protestantism. Since almost none of its wealth was invested in productive facilities within the home country itself, Spain remained poor despite its temporary wealth.

Any chance of Spain's restoring its former imperial grandeur and power was undercut by that social and political convulsion that changed Europe irrevocably—the French Revolution and the accompanying French military conquest of most of Europe. Spain faced the post-Napoleonic era with a restored monarchy but with the liberal ideas of the French Revolution in the heads of many of its citizens. These ideas would not permit a quiet return to the authoritarian government of earlier years. Also, these new notions, combined with the long rupture in reliable communication with their American colonies, spelled the end of their empires in the Western hemisphere.

The Spanish had fought heroically for their national independence. Now their American colonies decided to do the same. Spain's isolation from its American colonies during the Napoleonic wars had loosened its grip and given Latin American leaders a taste of local rule, which they liked. They therefore revolted. Again, the Spanish treasury was drained by protracted war far from its own shores. After the disastrous Spanish defeat at the battle of Ayacucho in 1825, the vast and mighty Spanish Empire had been reduced to the islands of Cuba, Puerto Rico, Guam, and the Philippines.

Spain was badly shaken in 1898 by its war against the United States. This conflict was sparked by an explosion of dubious origin on a U.S. vessel, the *Maine*, which was anchored in Havana harbor. American soldiers, including those led by Theodore Roosevelt's "Rough Riders," entered the battlefield with the cry "Remember the *Maine!*" The war left Spain with 200,000 dead in Cuba, a sorely humiliated officer corps, an empty treasury, and a denuded empire. The United States took Cuba, Puerto Rico, Guam, and the Philippines. Spain retained only a smattering of holdings in West Africa and Morocco.

In February 1976, four months after Francisco Franco's death, Spain relinquished Spanish Sahara, with its rich phosphate deposits, to Morocco and Mauritania. It hoped that the inhabitants could determine their own future. Algeria greatly resented this solution, and a bloody struggle occurred over control of this colony. Morocco simply annexed it. It showed Spain little gratitude.

With the backing of over a dozen Arab states, Morocco revived its claims to Ceuta (where 15,000 out of a total population of 70,000 are Muslims, and which is located only 14 kilometers from the Spanish mainland) and Melilla (where 27,000 Moroccans and 45,000 Spaniards, including 15,000 soldiers, live). These are the remnants of a string of fortresses Spain built in North Africa after Andalusia was reconquered. There is tension there between Arab residents (many of whom are illegal) and Spaniards, who show no signs of wanting to be ruled by Morocco. In 1997 Spain fenced off the enclaves to prevent illegal immigrants from using them to gain access to Europe. However, these 2.5-meter-high barriers are easy to breach and have not prevented the enclaves from becoming centers for illegal immigration to southern Europe. Arabs there do not have rights as Spanish citizens. Muslim leaders negotiated with local Spanish officials to improve their social and political conditions, but resistance to their demands remains strong within the Spanish majority.

The major change in Spain's foreign policy is that it has turned its primary attention toward Europe. Spain's entry into Western Europe (through the EU and NATO) signaled certain other foreign policy changes. Franco had established a special relationship with Latin America, where there were many authoritarian regimes similar to his own. After Franco, Spaniards openly condemned most Latin American dictatorships. Nevertheless, the king left no doubt when he was awarded a prize in Germany for his work toward European unity that although Spain is rooted in Europe, it is also part of the Hispanic world. This was underscored during the Falkland Islands conflict, when it refused to support the British war effort.

Despite the importance Spain places on *Hispanidad,* its growing European focus weakens its ties with Latin America. Historical links with its colonies were severed much earlier than were those of Britain and France. Unlike France, Spain is not the senior member of a currency zone. Its trade with Latin America is insignificant. In 1992 Spain had hoped to celebrate in grand style the 500th anniversary of Columbus's voyage. But it found at a meeting in Madrid of nineteen presidential guests from Latin America and Portugal that the New World had developed mixed feelings about that explorer who had sailed under the Spanish flag.

**SPANISH NATIONALISM**   (In Spanish, *españolismo.*) Political doctrine that defends the Spanish nation. It is most commonly identified with administrative and political centralism, militant Catholicism, and a unified, Castilian-based culture. Other expressions of Spanish nationalism are Pan-Iberianism and Pan-Hispanism. Foreign invasions and great quests have also spurred the emergence of patriotic sentiment, such as the reconquest from Islamic occupation, which culminated in 1492 with the Catholic kings' victory in Granada against the Moors. In the early 19th century, Napoleon's invasion of the Iberian peninsula, and subsequent enthronement of his brother Joseph Bonaparte as Spanish king provoked a rebellion to oust the French ruler. The War of Independence in 1808–1814 is both effect and cause of a movement with many of the characteristics of modern nationalism.

The development of Spanish nationalism is tied to the state-building process by the monarchy dominated by Castile. In the 17th century, King Philip II's pro-Castile, pro-Catholic stance encouraged the imperial possessions in the Netherlands to revolt against Spanish rule. With the arrival of the French dynasty of the bourbons to the throne in 1714, Spain adopted the French model of political centralization. The new King Philip V signaled the new regime by abolishing the liberties of the Catalonia-Aragon Kingdom as retaliation for their support for his Habsburg adversary, Charles, in the War of Succession.

The Spanish liberal Constitution adopted by the *Cortes* (Parliament) of Cádiz in 1812 follows the ideological assumption of national sovereignty and sets out to abolish the *fueros*, or local and regional customary law and privileges from the feudal era that regulated the relations of the Basque provinces with the monarchy. The 1812 Constitution was nullified by the enthronement of the absolutist King Ferdinand VII in 1814 and the *fueros* were reestablished, but the historical process of modernization through unification was under way, so the Basques fought a losing battle against Spain's homogenization forces all along the 19th century. Two Carlist wars (from Charles of Austria, the absolutist contender to the monarchy in the early 18th century who would have, unlike the Bourbons, respected the *fueros*), fought between 1833–1839 and 1872–1876, ended in the monarchy's triumph and the abolitionist laws of 1841 and 1876 that completed the homogeneity in public law of all Spanish territory.

The loss of the last major colonies in 1898 signified the definitive end of the once-enormous Spanish Empire and prompted a very pessimistic national mood. The feeling of decadence and international humiliation and irrelevance had the effect among some sectors of society and the military of fostering a nostalgia for an idealized, glorious national past. In the decades following what is called the "Disaster of 1898," this translated into the extreme right, involutionist positions that defined the nationalist coup of 1936 that caused the civil war. Until his death in 1975, General Francisco Franco implemented a nationalist and religious agenda also known as "national Catholicism."

Still, the long-term goal of Spanish nationalism, to assimilate the peninsular languages and cultures into the Castilian one—as other old nation-states such as France and Great Britain have—has not been achieved. At present, Spain is a quasi-federal state where Spanish (Castilian) is the official language, but Catalan, Basque, and Galician are also official in different regions. The greatest historical failure of Castilian-centered nationalism is that a weaker peninsular nation, Portugal, has remained an independent country. Furthermore, the emergence of peripheral nationalist movements within Spain is directly related to the pursuit of political and cultural homogeneity by the center.

## SPENCER, HERBERT

1820–1903, British social philosopher and scholar, born in Derby, England. Although Spencer's ideas have now fallen out of favor, during his lifetime he was an enormously popular writer; his books had sold over 100,000 copies before the turn of the century and industrialist Andrew Carnegie praised him as the greatest thinker of the time. Much of his education was relatively informal and focused on the natural sciences, an emphasis that informs much of his work. Born prior to the strict compartmentalization of disciplines, Spencer attempted to construct a global theory of the social and physical world. His multivolume work *Synthetic Philosophy* endeavors to apply universal evolutionary and organizational principles to such varied fields as biology, psychology, and sociology.

When he was growing up, Spencer was immersed in a sociopolitical milieu of middle-class radicalism that promoted individualism, free trade, and limited government. He later advocated such laissez-faire ideas in his books *Social Statics* and *The Man Versus the State,* suggesting that the tasks of government should be simply to protect the rights of individuals and to defend the nation. It was Spencer, not Charles Darwin, who coined the phrase "survival of the fittest." In his view, open and unfettered competition would lead to adaptation and the eventual betterment of individuals, societies, and "races." These ideas later found popularity in the doctrine of "social Darwinism."

For Spencer, "superorganic" bodies such as societies evolved in much the same ways as did biological organisms. As this occurred, populations became more specialized, moving from relatively simple and homogeneous structures toward differentiated and complex communities: a process he referred to as "speciation." Thus, variations in norms, traditions, and culture could all be explained as evolutionary adaptations to disparate environmental conditions.

According to Spencer, societies are in a constant cyclical process of movement between "militant" (centralized, coercive, and regulated) and "industrial" (decentralized, cooperative, and politically free) phases. External threats or the need to integrate diverse populations spur a move toward militarism. Once threats have been mitigated and/or dissimilar populations assimilated, social pressures move societies toward an industrial period. As Spencer noted, civilizations are never completely militant nor exclusively industrial. His typology presents two polar types of organization; actual societies display elements of both in varying amounts.

Spencer saw hostility between populations as a natural element in the course of societal evolution; it operated as a trigger for movement between militant and industrial phases. Conflict compelled a society to develop greater regulation, expansion, and coordination of systems for the production and distribution of goods and services. This expansion, however, created tension and led to campaigns for greater autonomy. Despite his view of conflict as a causal agent of change, Spencer had a utopian vision of an industrial capitalist society in which individual freedoms abounded and the need for war and government regulation was obsolete.

Examples of Herbert Spencer's ideas can be found in *First Principles* (P. F. Collier and Son, 1902), *Social Statics* (Robert Schalkenbach Foundation, 1954), and *The Man Versus the State* (Liberty Classics, 1981). For a biography of Spencer, see *Herbert Spencer, the Evolution of a Sociologist* by J. D. Y. Peel (Basic Books, 1971).

**SPENGLER, OSWALD** 1880–1936, Spengler's book *The Decline of the West,* published in 1918, was a best-selling revolutionary book of "German philosophy" rich in cultural and historical pessimism and laced with documentation and mystical ideas about such things as "race beauty," "voice of the blood," and "cosmic force." He discussed eight cultures in world history, each of which is followed by a "civilization" phase that represents decline and decay.

Throughout the 1920s he published a string of political books and pamphlets, bearing such titles as *The New Reich* (1924) and *The Hour of Decision* (1933). He remained one of the most widely read German historians, despite the fact that he was not a recognized scholar with a university chair. Many Germans found his insights applicable to the unloved, conflict-laden Weimar Republic. He rejected democracy, liberalism, and the West, which he regarded as decadent, and his attacks helped weaken the struggling republic and prepare the path for the National Socialists. Although he disagreed with some of the Nazis' race theories and publicly criticized them (and was ultimately dismissed by them), they and other antidemocrats used his ideas as evidence of the bankruptcy of the old world and the need to create a new one by heroic means. After Germany's ruination in 1945, some Germans saw his predictions of decline and fall as having been proven true.

**SPORTS AND NATIONALISM** The study of sports and nationalism is still in its infancy, but it is a significant growth area. Several works are scheduled for publication, such as Mayall and Cronin's *Sporting Nationalisms* and many have been recently published, such as Mangan's *Tribal Identities: Nationalism, Europe, Sport* and Mangan, Holt, and Lanfranchi, eds., *European Heroes: Myth, Identity, Sport.* As the field of sports sociology widens, with the publication of journals such as *Soccer and Society,* so the works on the sport/nation nexus proliferate, though the impetus for these innovations has come from outside the usual parameters of the study of nationalism.

The study of sport and nationalism has three main aspects. First, there is the analysis of sport as a mechanism of national solidarity, which promotes common identity and unity. As such, there are many works on sport and colonialism, particularly concentrating on the ways in which sports were forced on colonial peoples as a means of social segregation but were also utilized by indigenous nationalists to forge national unity and pride. This brings us into the role of sport in the nation-building processes of the 19th century. There has been much work on Victorian sport in England and France, but little on the use of sport in later nation-building

movements in Eastern Europe, though the colonial experience, particularly southern Africa, has been dealt with to a greater extent. Another issue here is the nexus of sport and the military. This was most apparent with the fascist projects in Italy and Germany, where sports (particularly athletics and gymnastics) were promoted as a way of engendering and facilitating the production of the perfect national body, the physical Aryan. Elsewhere, sports, nationalism, and militarism have gone hand in hand in constructing the national individual strong enough to defend the nation.

A second aspect of the sport/nationalism nexus is the role of sport as an instrument of confrontation between nations, stimulating aggression, producing stereotypes, and creating hierarchies of superiority and inferiority. Sometimes, sports can be used as a vehicle short of war for the creation of national antagonisms. Simon Kupers work on footballing enmities gives ample illustration of this by considering the Celtic-Rangers division in Glasgow and the ways in which historical national enmities between the Netherlands and Germany are reproduced in the proximity of the football pitch. On other occasions, sports provide a forum for the airing of national antagonisms, which lead to further violence away from the arena. Here, one thinks of the so-called "football war" between El Salvador and Peru and the first acts of aggression in the Serb-Croatian war, which occurred when Serb police began beating Croatian supporters who were joined by the subsequent captain of the Croatian national football team, Zvonimir Boban. The most famous example of sports being used to promote national superiority was the 1936 Berlin Olympics, which were used as a showcase for Aryan man.

The third aspect of sports and nationalism is the role of sport as a cultural bond linking nations across national boundaries and generating a common enthusiasm. Within the field of sports studies several volumes have been written on the importance of sports in the Soviet Union. In this context sports fulfilled three objectives, all designed to overcome national differences and project the image of a transcendent Communist being. First, sports were used to project a positive image of the Soviet Union outward, thus bringing different nationalities together into a unified projection and actively promoting the achievements of Communism. Second, sports offered a non-national form of association. Most sporting institutions were tied to organizations that were non-national in outlook such as the army or other aspects of the bureaucracy. Finally, sports were used as a means of internally projecting an affiliation to the state that would come to constitute something akin to Soviet nationalism.

With increasing trends toward globalization, sports

are increasingly becoming a mechanism for the subversion of national or state boundaries, in many ways. The free flow of information around the world means that diasporic national groupings can become more closely integrated, such as the Bad Blue Boys (Dinamo Zagreb supporters) in Zagreb and Sydney. Globalization may also operate to diminish national boundaries. As sporting teams become increasingly international, and regional competition between teams rather than nations becomes more important, some suggest that sport will become less nationalized. For example, it is estimated that more than 98 percent of Manchester United soccer supporters reside outside the United Kingdom.

As sports become more economically important and the mass media continues to convey more information about them (the Manchester United team has its own cable TV channel), their significance with regards to nationalism will also increase. Whereas, in earlier years, sports were about the physical manifestation of the nation in the form of the body, they are increasingly becoming about the image of the nation and its projection both outwardly and inwardly.

For more on sports and nationalism, see S. Kuper, *Football Against the Enemy* (London, 1993); J. A. Mangen, *The Game Ethic and Imperialism* (London, 1985); J. A. Mangen, *Tribal Identities: Nationalism, Europe, Sport* (London, 1996); J. A. Mangen, R. Holt, and P. Lanfranchi, eds., *European Heroes: Myth, Identity, Sport* (London, 1996); and D. Mayal and M. Cronin, eds., *Sporting Nationalisms: Identity, Immigration and Assimilation* (London, 1998).

**STALIN, JOSEPH** 1879–1953, General secretary of the Communist Party of the Soviet Union from 1922 until 1953. Within a few years of obtaining this post his accumulation of power and the centralized nature of command within the Soviet Union meant that Stalin was the effective head of state for three decades. Stalin was born in Gori, Georgia, entering into life in fairly humble surroundings; his father was a cobbler and his mother the daughter of peasants. His original name was Joseph (Yossif) Vissarionovich Djugashvili but he assumed various aliases during his revolutionary days as an opponent to the tsarist regime. Initially, after assuming several names, Djugashvili adopted the pseudonym Koba meaning "the indomitable" but in 1913 he adopted the pseudonym Stalin ("man of steel") and this is the name that he finally became known by throughout the world.

In 1899 Stalin began working for the Russian Social Democratic Labor Party and sided with Lenin's Bolsheviks after the fateful second congress where the party split into the so-called "majority" group (the Bolshe-

viks) and the "minority" group (the Mensheviks). In 1913, Lenin set Stalin the task of writing a theoretical article on the nationalities problem. It was largely as a result of this that Stalin, in the first government after the Soviet revolution of 1917, was given the post of commissar (minister) of nationalities. However, it was his promotion to the post of general secretary of the party's Central Committee that proved to be a watershed in his political career. The post was felt by many of the other more central figures of the party to be dull and monotonous, yet it allowed Stalin to accumulate a formidable degree of power, information, and influence. This he used to full effect after the death of Lenin in January 1924, purging the party of his political rivals by first siding with the right wing of the Communist Party against his leftist rivals (Trotsky, Zinoviev, Kamenev) and then taking on many of the leftist programs and attacking the "Right Opposition" (such as Bukharin). With the Communist Party purged of those who may have mounted a challenge to his authority, Stalin proceeded to consolidate his control of the party machinery and became the unassailable leader of the Soviet Union until his death in March 1953.

Stalin's major theoretical contribution to the debate on the national question was written in 1913 in reply to the Austrian socialists Karl Renner and Otto Bauer who had put forward the view that the triumph of socialism would result in an increasing differentiation of nations rather than a merging of nations. To harness this tendency they suggested the principle of extraterritorial autonomy whereby each nation would be "treated not as a territorial corporation, but as a union of individuals." In reaction to this unique and challenging view, Lenin appointed Stalin the job of producing a critique of the Austrians' theory and a comprehensive counterproposal. The outcome of Stalin's research was his well-known essay "Marxism and the National Question," which defined the nation as a "historically evolved, stable community arising on the foundation of a common language, territory, economic life, and psychological make-up, manifested in a community of culture." The essay argued that Bauer had confused the concept of the nation with that of an ethnic group and the main outcome of Stalin's writings was therefore the reassertion of the principle of the territoriality of the nation. This principle of the "territoriality of ethnicity" proposed by Stalin was taken up by the party and was reflected in the form of federation that was later adopted.

After the revolution of 1917 demands from the various nationalities of the Soviet Union came to the fore, thus presenting a challenge to the Bolshevik's assumption that the unity of the workers would prevail over the particularism of nationalism. The question thus arose as to whether under certain circumstances particular national demands and interests could override the common interests of the proletariat. Stalin's approach was unconditional; the interests of the proletariat must always come first even if this meant that a nation's right to decide its own fate was sacrificed. As early as the 12th congress of the Russian Communist Party in April 1923 he outlined his position: "It should be borne in mind that besides the right of nations to self-determination there is also the right of the working class to consolidate its power, and to this latter right the right of self-determination is subordinate. There are occasions when the right of self-determination conflicts with the other, the higher right—the right of a working class that has assumed power to consolidate its power. In such cases—this must be said bluntly—the right to self-determination cannot and must not serve as an obstacle to the exercise by the working class of its right to dictatorship."

In practice, Stalin's policies toward the various nationalities of the Soviet Union entailed the Russification of the population, "Great Russian Chauvinism," and the forced expulsion of nations from their homelands. Stalin oversaw a languages program that led to statewide teaching of Russian as the second language. This had begun in the early 1930s and was finally made compulsory by a decree in 1938, despite the fact that Lenin had advocated that a compulsory official language should be abolished. During World War II it became increasingly apparent that the Russian nation was to be treated as the leading nation among all the nationalities of the federation. This chauvinism was to take the form of the "elder brother" syndrome in the closing stages of World War II. The Russian nation was said to have lent the greatest support in the war and was therefore to be viewed as the leading nation within the Soviet Union. At a banquet for Red Army commanders in 1945 Stalin stated that "I drink above all to the health of the Russian people, because it is the most outstanding nation of all nations. I propose a toast to the health of the Russian people because it earned in this war general recognition as the guiding force of the Soviet Union among all the peoples of our country." At approximately the same time (1941–1944) certain nations were viewed as a threat to the security of the Soviet Union and were therefore deported from their homelands. Eight nations in all were moved, an estimated total of 1.5 million, under conditions that resulted in thousands of deaths.

**STANDING BEAR (CHIEF)** 1829–1908, Clanhead or chief of the Ponca Indians, born near the Niobrara river in northeast Nebraska. In the spring and summer of 1877, Standing Bear and the Ponca people were forcibly removed by the U.S. army from their Nebraska homelands to Oklahoma under a federal policy to consolidate as many tribes as possible in Indian Territory in Oklahoma. Nearly one-third of the Ponca died either on the trip to Oklahoma or from sicknesses after reaching Oklahoma. Standing Bear had lost his daughter to disease on the trip to Oklahoma and the death of his son in Indian Territory set into motion events that were to bring a measure of justice and worldwide fame to this leader of the Ponca people.

After much hardship in Oklahoma and unwilling to bury his son in the strange country, Standing Bear gathered thirty some members of his band and on January 11, 1879, left for Nebraska, leaving behind the rest of the Ponca people. Because Indians were not to leave their reservation without the permission of the Indian agent, Standing Bear had violated federal law and he and his followers became federal fugitives. Many of those who remained behind feared reprisals on themselves for his leaving. Standing Bear and his followers traveled over 500 miles, mostly on foot, hiding from the U.S. Army and others who were sent out to find them and bring them back to Oklahoma. After a month of traveling, Standing Bear's group reached the Omaha tribe, relatives of the Ponca, but still eighty miles from their home.

Standing Bear and his small band were arrested by Brigadier General George Crook on the Omaha reservation and transported to Omaha, Nebraska, where they were held in jail for transportation back to Oklahoma. General Crook, who later became famous for the capture of Apache Chief Geronimo, is theorized to have been sympathetic to Standing Bear's plight, and that he contacted *Omaha Daily Herald* newspaper editor Thomas Tibbles with regards to Standing Bear and his peoples' situation. Tibbles recruited two prominent Omaha attorneys, Andrew J. Poppleton and John L. Webster, who filed a writ of *habeas corpus* against General Crook in the federal district court of Judge Elmer S. Dundy. The federal government disputed the right of Standing Bear to obtain a writ of *habeas corpus* on the grounds that an Indian was not a "person" nor a citizen so couldn't bring suit against the government. Judge Dundy had to rule on whether a Native American was a human being and an American citizen with the same rights guaranteed by the Constitution as other Americans.

On May 12, 1879, Judge Dundy filed in favor of Standing Bear. The government appealed Dundy's decision, but on June 5, 1880, the U.S. Supreme Court of the United States dismissed the case, leaving Standing

Bear and his small band of Poncas free and clear in the eyes of the law to return to their homelands. The government had taken over or sold all of the Ponca land in Nebraska, so Standing Bear and his followers were free but had no home to return to, other than Oklahoma, which they refused to do.

Standing Bear with the aid of Tibbles and Susette (Bright Eyes) LaFlesche traveled throughout the eastern United States speaking on Native American rights and the plight of the homeless Ponca. Standing Bear won the support of Henry Wadsworth Longfellow, Helen Hunt Jackson, many clergy, and other prominent people. Much like Martin Luther King, nearly a century later, Standing Bear called for peaceful civil disobedience and legal action in securing that all Americans could enjoy the civil liberties and rights guaranteed to them by the U.S. Constitution.

Due to Standing Bear's oratory efforts, President Rutherford B. Hayes appointed a government commission that investigated and found the Ponca situation to be unjust. In August 1881, 26,236 acres of the old reservation were returned to the Ponca by the government and nearly 300 Poncas returned to Nebraska to join Standing Bear on their ancestral lands next to the Niobrara River. The majority of the tribe, including some of Standing Bear's own relatives, chose to stay in Oklahoma. Thus, Standing Bear's actions were not popular among many of his own people and definitely not with the U.S. government. But he felt that what he had to do was morally right to ensure that "there should be laws to govern the Indians the same as the whites."

Standing Bear's fight for equal justice is chronicled in *Standing Bear and the Ponca Chiefs* (University of Nebraska Press, 1995), by Thomas Henry Tibbles, and in Dee Brown's *Bury My Heart at Wounded Knee* (Holt, Rhinehart & Winston, 1970). Other books on the cultural and political struggles of the Ponca are *The Ponca Tribe* (University of Nebraska Press, 1995), by James H. Howard, and *An Unspeakable Sadness: The Dispossession of the Nebraska Indians* (University of Nebraska Press, 1997) by David J. Wishart.

**STARČEVIĆ, ANTE**  1823–1896, Croatian nationalist ideologue born on May 23, 1823, in the village of Žitnik in the Lika region of Croatia. In 1848 Starčević earned a doctorate in philosophy from the university in Pest. Initially sympathetic to the Illyrian movement, which stressed South Slavic cultural and linguistic unity, in 1852 he broke with Illyrianism and began publishing articles promoting independent statehood for Croatia based on the principle of Croatian "state right." According to this doctrine, Croatians had possessed their own

state ever since their arrival on the shores of the Adriatic Sea in the 7th century. To Starčević and his close associate, Eugen Kvaternik, Croatia's incorporation into the Hungarian Kingdom dating back to 1102 had been the result of the Croatian nobility willingly choosing as its leader the same person who happened to be the ruler of Hungary. Croatia's links to Hungary and subsequently with the Habsburg Empire were thus of a strictly personal nature and, argued Starčević, should be dissolved so that full Croatian statehood may be restored.

This independent Croatian state, Starčević believed, was to include all territory from Albania to the Danube River and from the Slovenian Alps all the way to Bulgaria, since, in his opinion, the Croats (mostly Catholic) and Bulgarians (mostly Orthodox) were the only two South Slavic peoples. Slovenes were deemed by Starčević to be "Mountain Croats," while Serbs, who in the late 19th century accounted for some 25 percent of the population in the Croatian lands, were "Orthodox Croats." The Serbs' allegedly separate identity was the fabrication of Russian propaganda, and the name "Serb," wrote Starčević in an 1868 polemic, was probably derived from the Latin *servus,* meaning slave. Combined with the idea that only Croats could inhabit the Croatian state, these claims added up to a Croatian integral nationalism that altogether denied the existence of a Serbian nation.

In 1861, Starčević and Kvaternik founded the Croatian Party of Right (as in state right). In elections held that same year, Starčević won a seat in the parliament in Zagreb, the Croatian capital. There, his denunciations of Habsburg rule over Croatia and his avowed refusal to trust anyone but "God and the Croatians" earned him a brief prison sentence (in 1863) as well as lasting popularity, especially among young intellectuals and students. Starčević opposed the 1868 Croatian-Hungarian *Nagodba* (Agreement), which confirmed Croatia's subordinate status within Hungary, and in the late 1870s he began viewing Orthodox Russia as a likely Croatian ally against the Habsburg Empire.

His new pro-Russian orientation caused Starčević to moderate his hostility toward the "Orthodox Croats." By 1883, although still considering Serbs to be simply a religious minority within Croatia, he accepted their right to identify themselves as Serb if they remained loyal to the Croatian state. In June 1893, Starčević held an unprecedented meeting of reconciliation with Bishop Josip Juraj Strossmayer, whose plans to unite the Serbian and Croatian nations in a common South Slav (i.e., Yugoslav) polity had earlier rendered the two men bitter political and ideological rivals.

In 1895, the year before Starčević's death, the Party of Right split into a staunchly anti-Serbian Pure Party of Right led by Josip Frank, a Jewish convert to Catholicism, and a more moderate faction favoring increased cooperation with the Serbs. The latter eventually merged with Strossmayer's Yugoslav-minded followers, while descendants of the former established in 1929 the fascist *Ustaša* movement.

**STASOV, VLADIMIR**  1824–1906, Russian critic, publicist and historian of music and arts; ethnographer and archeologist; head of the Department of Arts in the St. Petersburg Imperial Public Library; born in St. Petersburg. Stasov was the main ideologist and advocate of nationalism and "Russianness" in Russian music of the 19th century and was active as a critic for more than fifty years, from 1848 to 1906.

Influenced by the aesthetic theories of Vissarion Belinsky and Nikolai Chernyshevsky, which were applied mainly to Russian literature, Stasov searched for national identity and the national element (*narodnost*) in art. His doctrine, finally shaped by the 1860s, was summarized in three major essays: "Twenty Five Years of Russian Art" (1882–1883), "The Impediments to New Russian Art" (1885), and "Arts of the Nineteenth Century" (1901). Stasov believed that the national element could be best expressed in a work if the artist drew themes from the everyday life of contemporary Russia, or from Russia's past or folklore. The aim of artworks on historical themes should be a "projecting of the past into the present." Having access to rare historical documents in the St. Petersburg Public Library, Stasov was a great help to composers who created Russian historical operas. (In particular, the librettos of Mussorgsky's *Khovanshchina* and Borodin's *Prince Igor* were written together with Stasov.) Stasov also advised Russian artists, such as Repin, Antokolsky, and Kramskoi, who were interested in themes from Russian history. In addition, Stasov assisted Russian composers with topics from Western history and literature. (To name just a few, he wrote a program for Tchaikovsky's symphonic poem *Manfred*, and provided original English tunes for Balakirev's incidental music to Shakespeare's *King Lear*.)

Striving and struggling for "artistic truth" (*khudozhestvennaia pravda*), that is, for a realistic portrayal of the people's life in the works of art, Stasov considered realism to be inseparable from the national element. From this perspective, he argued the superiority of opera as the most realistic musical genre. Accordingly, he extolled the predilection of Russian composers for program music, which, thanks to its tight connection with literature, brings music closer to life and, therefore, produces a greater effect on the listener than an "abstract" symphony.

To be national, Stasov declared, composers have to use folk melodies. For him, folklorism did not mean a simple quotation or imitation, rather, Stasov calls on the composers to study folk songs creatively, searching for ways to absorb the melodic and harmonic peculiarities of Russian songs into their individual compositional styles.

Stasov considered the oriental element to be the crucial characteristic of the Russian national style: As a historian, he believed that all aspects of Russian culture and civilization are of Asian heritage and, therefore, strongly influenced by the Orient. In Stasov's view, Russian composers, expressing their oriental impressions "vividly and strikingly," shared a general Russian sympathy with everything Oriental.

A friend and passionate adherent of Glinka and Dargomyzhsky, the founders of New Russian Music School, Stasov became an inspirer, aesthetic adviser, and powerful advocate for the young composers of the next generation who united around Balakirev in the early 1860s, and became known in the West as "The Mighty Five." The Russian title of the group, *moguchaia kuchka* ("The Mighty Handful"), was coined by Stasov, who became the first biographer of Mussorgsky, Rimsky-Korsakov, and their predecessor Glinka.

Advocating for Russian music, Stasov sometimes came to chauvinist conclusions, depreciating the achievements of Western composers who did not fit his theory of musical realism. For example, he disliked Brahms for his predilection for "absolute music," considering him to be a musical formalist who composed symphonies "for the sake of art." Rejecting the European academic system of conservatory training for its "useless, routine and pedanticism," Stasov praised the absence of such training in Russia as a highly positive factor, one that helped Russian music to preserve its freshness and originality. Therefore, on this point Stasov supported the position of Balakirev and the Slavophiles, who opposed Anton Rubinstein's party of Germanophiles. A pronounced Russian nationalist, nevertheless, Stasov expressed the opinion that Western Europe should be a model for Russian development. In this issue he was in accord with the so-called "Westernizers."

Stasov's aesthetic theory was revived in the Soviet Union starting in 1927, because major Stasov's points fitted well with the doctrine of the social realism developed by Stalin and Zhdanov. Demanding from socialist art that it be "national in form and socialist in content," Soviet ideologists adopted Stasov's requirements, such as musical realism, cultivation of the national element, obligatory folklorism, promotion of opera as a superior musical genre, and opposition to formalism. Many of Stasov's ideas were misunderstood, misrepresented, or driven to absurdity. In the new context, Stasov's theory, progressive for the time when the Russian Music School was in its formative period, turned out to be a reactionary tool in the hands of Soviet nationalist politicians.

In English, Stasov's critical writing can be found in *Stasov. Selected Essays on Music*, translated by Florence Jonas, with an introduction by Gerald Abrahams (London: Barrie & Rockliff, 1968). A comprehensive biography of Stasov and discussion of his aesthetic theory is Yury Olkhovsky's *Vladimir Stasov and Russian National Culture* (Ann Arbor, Mich.: UMI Research Press, 1983).

## STATE, CONCEPT OF

The emergence of the modern state is linked to the Thirty Years War (1618–1648) and the crumbling of the Holy Roman Empire. Terms such as *state, nation,* and *nation-state* often appear in popular usage to be interchangeable, but in fact they denote different concepts. *Nation* is really a cultural term referring to a body of people united by a common sense of identity and shared values vis-à-vis "outsiders." This unity is usually based on such cultural factors as shared group history, language, religion, ethnic homogeneity and common customs. *State*, on the other hand, refers to both a political idea and a composite legal entity that exists under international law. A *nation-state* suggests a congruency between cultural and political-legal boundaries, a condition not often found in modern international relations where states are often either multinational or nationality groups straddle international boundaries. Nonetheless, the state provides a powerful organizing force and instrument of expression for nationalism.

Niccolò Machiavelli (1469–1527) was probably the first political theorist to describe the essence of the modern state in *The Prince*, which offered advice to Italian rulers on how to establish and maintain a state. Legal recognition of the state emerged with the Peace of Westphalia (1648), which ended the Thirty Years War and replaced notions of any hierarchial international authority of Pope and emperor with a recognized system of states managing their own affairs.

Under modern international law, the legal basis of the state rests on the following four elements: (1) a more or less permanent population, (2) a defined territory, (3) an organized government, and (4) sovereignty. A fifth important political element is recognition of statehood by other established states. Sovereignty, a concept articulated by Jean Bodin in his *Les Six Livres de la République* (1576) as the supreme decision-making authority within a state, poses important dilemmas for international relations. The supreme power of each state over its populace and territory, independent of any external authority, lays the groundwork for conflict in a world of competing sovereign states.

For a legal discussion of the state, see William Slomanson, *Fundamental Perspectives on International Law*, Chapter 2 (West, 1995). Richard Cox's *The State in International Relations* is a collection of historical excerpts on views of the state and its attributes. A good examination of the phenomenon of the state is Robert Jackson and Alan James, eds., *States in a Changing World: A Contemporary Analysis* (Clarendon Press, 1993). For a thorough geographical discussion, with extensive bibliography, see Martin Ira Glassner, *Political Geography* (John Wiley & Sons, 1996).

Adapted from Grieves, Forest, *Conflict and Order: An Introduction to International Relations*. © 1977 by Houghton Mifflin Company. Used with permission.

## STEREOTYPES, NATIONAL

Exaggerated and inaccurate generalizations about a national group that are resistant to change even in the face of contradictory evidence are national stereotypes. They are usually part of an ideology that justifies and rationalizes institutionalized inequality on the basis of national origin, race, and/or ethnicity.

Stereotypes about national groups are usually negative and are transmitted through social interaction with primary groups (i.e., family, friends, and peers) and secondary socializing agents (i.e., the media, educational system, religious instruction). They can be categorized in two types: (1) those that assert the inferiority of a national group and (2) those that negatively assess the progress of a group. These notions also serve to unify the dominant group through the creation of ingroup solidarity in relation to an outgroup and justify dominant group control and privilege.

The nature of national stereotypes is dependent on the particular conditions and context. They are also subject to change over time in accordance with alterations in intergroup relations. Efforts aimed at reducing the impact of stereotypes has been the goal of multicultural education.

## STRAUSS, RICHARD

1864–1949, Strauss was a distinguished conductor and considered one of the best romantic opera composers of the early 20th century. He wrote music for the orchestra. His illustrative orchestral works were intended to convey visual and literary impressions. Among his most famous works is *Der*

*Rosenkavalier,* a comedy that premiered in 1911. As conductor of the Berlin Philharmonic concerts from 1894–1895, he composed *Thus Spake Zarathustra,* based on Friedrich Nietzsche's popular iconoclastic philosophy. This and other works, such as *Don Quixote* (1898), were considered at the time to epitomize musical modernism. From 1919 to 1924 he served as codirector of the Vienna State Opera. After the Nazis seized power, he functioned briefly as the president of the Reich Music Chamber, but he was officially exonerated in 1948 from any charges of collaboration. Many consider his last major works, *Metamorphoses* (1946), *Three Songs* and *Abendrot (Evening Red),* both composed in 1948, to be the swan songs of the expiring German romanticism.

## STRAVINSKY, IGOR   1882–1971, Russian composer.

A student of Rimsky-Korsakov, Stravinsky inherited his teacher's nationalist musical style, but radically transformed it. His contemporaries considered him a first composer who "successfully having his 'Russian style' rid of covertly European features, brought Russian music at the very helm of world music, turning it into a thing of capital universal significance" (Arthur Lourie).

A climax of Stravinsky's nationalism is his first, so-called "Russian" period (approximately until 1923), although the national element persisted through his "neo-classical" and "serial" periods. Stravinsky's first ballet, *Zhar-ptitsa (The Firebird,* 1909–1910), is a product of the 19th-century Russian aesthetic tradition, in particular, developing Rimsky-Korsakov's method of combining Russian and Western European fairytale sources in the libretto, and inserting Russian folk songs into the texture of refined contemporary European musical style (with a noticeable tribute to French impressionism, especially Debussy). Stravinsky's most revolutionary works are written on subjects found and revived from the archaic folk traditions. Thus, *Vesna sviashchennaia (The Rite of Spring,* 1911–1913) embodies a pagan agrarian rite, *Svadebka (Les Noces,* or *The Wedding,* 1914–1923) presents village customs of a Christian and pre-Christian Russian wedding ceremony, *Petrushka* (1910–1911) is based on traditions of the Russian Shrove-tide fair theater, and *Baika pro Lisu, Petukha, Kota da Barana (Renard,* 1917) is a modernist revival of a grotesque show of Russian wandering minstrels-cum-clowns *(skomorokhi),* performing a folktale. *Skazka o beglom soldate i chorte (Histoir de Soldat,* 1918), written in the traditions of the folk theater, is the synthesis of a Russian peasant tale from Alexander Afanasiev's collection, and a distorted German legend on Faust, anachronistically mixed with attributes of modern life, such as the stock exchange, tango, and ragtime.

After *The Firebird,* Stravinsky rejected both ethnographical and Westernized approaches to Russian folk songs developed by the composers of the Balakirev Circle and Tchaikovsky. *Petrushka* amazed a contemporary Russian audience with its "tasteless use of rotten trash" (Prokofiev) such as vernacular urban tunes, street vendors' cries, and barrel-organ ditties. In *The Rite of Spring,* Stravinsky utilized Slavic and non-Slavic (Lithuanian) folk material, distorting it in the manner that Simon Karlinsky terms "cubist." Liberating folk idioms from their context, Stravinsky turned them into morphemes of his compositional language. This method corresponded to the contemporary Russian experiments in poetry (Velemir Khlebnikov, Marina Tsvetaeva), and in the visual arts (such as neonationalist artists of the group *Mir Iskusstva,* in particular, Mikhail Larionov and Natalia Goncharova). In *Svadebka,* which audiences perceived as a strikingly authentic folklore composition, the folk material is not genuine: Stravinsky invented it himself, operating with archaic tetrachords and providing them with dissonant harmonization divorced from European modal structures and tonal centricity. Stylized in this way, the folk-like wedding laments and songs seem to be a genuine artifact of a primitive society.

Both *The Rite of Spring* and *Les Noces* present the primeval Russian/Slavonic rituals that ended with a sacrifice of a virgin. (In the first work it is a real assassination of the Chosen Victim to propitiate Nature; in the second, a metaphorical sacrifice of the Bride to benefit a kin.) Stravinsky chose a strictly impersonal method of depicting the ritual: His heroine-victims, deprived of face and individuality, are shown as submissive members of the community, who express no protest and do not call for an audience's compassion. Such a discourse of Stravinsky, who was mainly interested in the archetypal essence of a ritual, not in emotions of its participants, inspired or troubled many of his contemporaries. The Russian (both Soviet and post-Soviet) point of view is that Stravinsky's neoprimitivist concepts do not bear a social or political agenda, exemplifying "a desire to present an unbiased view of the customs of the societies based on mythological consciousness" (Dmitry Pokrovsky). By contrast, an American scholar, Taruskin, argues that Stravinsky's presentation of the darkest aspects of a primitive society—such as forced sacrifice, compulsion of the individual to the community, and acceptance of authority—coincided with many ideas and values of the fascist national-socialist theory. At the same time, Taruskin brings to light that the concepts of *The Rite of Spring* and *Les Noces* influenced the Russian ultranationalist movement, Eurasianism, whose ideologists believed that the social and ideological structure of the archaic society might serve as a model for a "Slavic United States," a perfect state of the future. Eurasianists, who kept the faith in the Messianic mission of Russia, hoped that such a state would save the world from the disasters brought by the Western civilization.

An important primary source is *Dialogues and a Diary* by Igor Stravinsky and Robert Craft (Garden City, N.Y.: Doubleday, 1963). Influential Russian monographs include Boris Asaf'ev's *A Book about Stravinsky,* translated by Richard F. French, with an introduction by Robert Craft (Ann Arbor, Mich.: University of Michigan Press, 1982), and Mikhail Druskin's *Igor Stravinsky: His Life, Works and Views,* translated by Martin Cooper (Cambridge, England: Cambridge University Press, 1983). Contemporary American scholarship is represented in *Confronting Stravinsky: Man, Musician and Modernist,* Jann Pasler, ed. (Berkeley: University of California Press, 1986). The most developed concept of Stravinsky's nationalism is Richard Taruskin's essay "Stravinsky and the Subhuman" in his *Defining Russia Musically* (Princeton, N.J.: Princeton University Press, 1997) and his substantial two-volume work *Stravinsky and the Russian Tradition: A Biography of the Works Through 'Mavra'* (Berkeley: University of California Press, 1996.)

**STREICHER, JULIUS** 1885–1946, National Socialist politician, publisher, and propagandist, born in Fleinhausen, Bavaria. Commonly known outside Germany as "World Jew-baiter No. 1," Streicher was probably the most single-minded anti-Semite in a political movement notorious for its biological nationalism.

A schoolteacher by profession and a decorated veteran of World War I, Streicher acquired his anti-Semitic outlook in the aftermath of German defeat. In 1920 he joined the fledgling Nuremberg chapter of the right-wing German Socialist Party and became founder, owner, and publisher of its newspaper, *Deutscher Sozialist,* a forerunner of *Der Stürmer.* Two years later he switched allegiance to Adolf Hitler and the National Socialist German Workers Party, and in 1925 he was appointed its *Gauleiter* (district leader) for Franconia. In January 1933 he won a seat in the Reichstag.

A poor administrator but skillful agitator, Streicher used his party position and considerable ability as a public speaker to incite hatred of Jews and political enemies. During the years following Hitler's accession to power, he advocated various anti-Jewish measures, such as the destruction of synagogues and a prohibition on Jews using public transportation, that were later widely adopted in Germany. At Hitler's behest, he directed the nationwide anti-Jewish boycott of April 1, 1933, and he was widely credited with inspiring the so-called Nuremberg laws of September 15, 1935, which deprived Jews of German citizenship.

Streicher was best known, however, as the scandalmongering publisher of *Der Stürmer,* an anti-Semitic weekly newspaper founded in 1923. With a circulation peaking at nearly half a million by the mid-1930s, it preached an especially virulent form of racism and gave the crudest possible expression to nationalistic neo-Darwinism. One scholar has described the paper as "the Nuremberg equivalent to an American boy's clandestine copy of *Playboy*," and certainly part of its appeal was pornographic. A typical issue might feature a story on a young Aryan girl raped by a Jew, as well as cartoons with grotesque caricatures of Jews and lead articles depicting them as "deadly vermin" or bacteria. A popular "pillory" column introduced in 1933 printed the names and addresses of German women alleged to have had sexual intercourse with Jewish men. The paper's general message was simple and repetitive: Jews without individual exception were a morally degenerate and satanic race; they bore responsibility for the punitive Treaty of Versailles; they aspired to rule the world and pollute the blood of the German *Volk* by ruining its women; and an awakened German nation must combat the menace. Streicher himself sometimes proposed deportation as a solution to "the Jewish problem," but more typical in later years was his statement in 1941: "The causes of the world's misfortunes will be forever removed only when Jewry in its entirety is annihilated."

Contentious and much-disliked within the Nazi hierarchy, Streicher fell from grace after a secret party tribunal in 1940 heard evidence of sexual misconduct, sadistic treatment of political prisoners, and corrupt financial dealings. In quietly banning Streicher from Nuremberg, however, Hitler permitted him to continue publishing *Der Stürmer,* the one paper the Nazi leader professed to read with relish from first page to last. Hitler, who once remarked that he needed a "tangible enemy" in order to stir up mass fanaticism, recognized the propaganda value of *Der Stürmer's* persistent demonization of Jews. Indeed, there can be little doubt that Streicher helped to create a climate of opinion favorable, or at any rate indifferent, to their extermination. Consequently, the International Military Tribunal at Nuremberg found him guilty of crimes against humanity, charging in its indictment that Streicher had created "a legacy of almost a whole people poisoned with hate, sadism, and murder." He was hanged on October 16, 1946.

The definitive biography of Streicher has yet to be

written; surely its author will need to combine intricate knowledge of German politics with expertise in psychopathology. The best available biography in English is Randall L. Bytwerk's useful but far from complete *Julius Streicher* (Dorset Press, 1988), which includes appendices with full translations of three *Der Stürmer* articles and two stories from *The Poisonous Mushroom,* an illustrated children's book produced by Streicher's publishing firm. Two informative essays on Streicher's career are Robin Lenman's "Julius Streicher and the Origins of the NSDAP in Nuremberg, 1918–1933," in *German Social Democracy and the Triumph of Hitler,* edited by Anthony Nicholls and Erich Mattias (George Allen and Unwin, 1971), and Chapter 4 of Edward N. Peterson's *The Limits of Hitler's Power* (Princeton University Press, 1969). G. M. Gilbert's *Nuremberg Diary* (Farrar, Straus and Co., 1947) contains a fascinating account of the author's interview with Streicher shortly before his execution.

## STROESSNER, ALFREDO   1912–, President of Paraguay (1954–1989). Alfredo Stroessner ruled Paraguay for thirty-five years, thus becoming the most longlasting dictator in Latin America's history. He was born in Encarnación, a southern border town on the Paraná River, to a German immigrant father and Paraguayan mother. In 1929, at the age of sixteen he entered the Military Academy in Asunción. Three years later the Chaco war broke out and, even though his studies were not completed, Stroessner was sent to the front. Decorated for bravery at the battle of Boquerón (1932), he was awarded his commission as a second lieutenant and given an artillery command. He won a second medal after the battle of El Carmen (1934). By the end of the war (1935) he was a first lieutenant.

At war's end Stroessner continued to receive favorable notice from his commanding officers, rising to captain in 1936 and major in 1940. In October 1940 he was selected as one of a group of junior officers to go to Brazil for special artillery training. After returning to Paraguay, Stroessner continued to rise in the military hierarchy. President Higínio Morínigo rewarded him for staying loyal during an unsuccessful coup in 1943 by sending him to the Superior War School; after graduating he was appointed commander of Paraguay's main artillery unit. In 1946 Stroessner was assigned to the army's general staff headquarters.

The civil war of 1947 brought Stroessner to real prominence because he was one of the few officers who remained loyal to the government. Morínigo ordered him to use his artillery to smash a revolt by the navy, which had taken over the Asunción shipyards in the name of the rebel cause. Next, Stroessner took command of the southern front and successfully prevented two heavily armed rebel gunboats from ascending the Paraguay River to bombard the capital. When the rebels were finally defeated, in August 1947, he was one of a handful of officers heading a purged and reorganized army.

Post-civil war Paraguay was dominated by the Colorado Party, one of Paraguay's two traditional parties, which had provided mass support for Morínigo. With their rivals eliminated, the Colorados had decisive political power, which they took advantage of by removing Morínigo in 1948 and seizing power for themselves. From the culmination of the civil war until May 1954, Paraguay had five different presidents. Stroessner was deeply involved in all the plotting. On October 25, 1948, he backed the wrong side in a coup and had to flee the country hidden in the trunk of a car; three months later he slithered back into Paraguay and rallied his artillery regiment to support the winning side in a new coup. After that he rose rapidly to the top, becoming army commander in chief in April 1951. In May 1954 he ousted the Colorados' Federico Chaves, who still headed a faction-ridden administration, and seized the presidency for himself.

Stroessner based his government on two pillars: the army and the Colorado Party. As a much-decorated veteran of two wars he enjoyed great prestige among the soldiers. The few officers who opposed him were soon eliminated, with major purges taking place in February 1955 and June 1959. Those coincided with upheavals inside the Colorado Party, for Stroessner encouraged party bickering that allowed him to play the factions off against each other. By mid-1959 factional purges had eliminated all independent spirits among the Colorados, leaving Stroessner with a harmless organization that he could dominate.

The control of a political party with a mass following made Stroessner's right-wing military dictatorship unique. By manipulating party symbols and patronage he was able to generate mass demonstrations in support of his policies. Businessmen, professionals, youth, women, veterans, and peasants were tied to the regime through the Colorados' ancillary divisions, which reached into every village and every city block. Though his economic policies tended to favor large landowners and foreign investors, Stroessner was able to reward his followers through public works projects that generated jobs and contracts. Up to about 1981 steady economic growth and material improvements made the regime popular. Those who refused to conform, however, such as the opposition Liberal and Febrerista Parties and the Catholic Church, were ruthlessly persecuted.

Stroessner's regime began to crumble during the

1980s. Inflation became unmanageable, capital dried up for new public works projects, and the emergence of a new middle class plotted to remove General Andrés Rodríguez as army commander; the latter struck first. During the night of February 2, 1989, Rodríguez's tanks forced Stroessner to abandon power and leave the country for Brazilian exile.

## SUDANESE NATIONALISM

Sudan, Africa's largest country, is composed of many ethnic groups. North Sudan is predominantly inhabited by Arabs who practice Islam. In the south, African tribes that practice Christian and animist beliefs are dominant. The relationship between the North and South has often been volatile.

Egyptian society has long influenced the region. During the 6th century, Christian kingdoms—the Nubia, Makuria, and Alodia—were influenced by Egypt and the Aksum (Ethiopia). After the 7th century, Islam was spread to North Sudan by nomadic Arab tribes.

During the 16th century, the Funj Kingdom united various Islamic tribes and emerged as a powerful regional force. The Funj governance was a loose confederation of past Sudanese power centers that pledged allegiance to the kingdom to ensure trade and stability. An Islamic spiritual revival in the 18th century established religious orders based on the philosophy of Ahmed Ibn Idris Al Fasi. The two dominant orders were the Sammaniya and Khatmiya. Infighting among the Funj tribes made Sudanese vulnerable to Egyptian intrigue. In 1820 an Egyptian army invaded Sudan and the region was brought into the Egyptian-Ottoman system as a province. The Khatmiya orders were favored during this period. Some material advances were made in the region, but a vigorous slave trade continued to operate in the South.

British influence in Egypt and Sudan increased throughout the 19th century. Most modern nationalist movements in Sudan have their origins as movements against both Egyptian and British authority. General Charles Gordon administered the Egyptian Sudan between 1874 and 1880 and attempted to suppress the trade of African slaves (from the South) by Arabs.

In 1881 Muhammad Ahmed, a leader in the Sammaniya order, developed a following among the Muslim tribes and proclaimed himself "the Mahdi." The mahdi, in Islamic tradition, will appear during chaos and establish an ideal Islamic order. Muhammad Ahmed fused this idea with the goal of expelling the Egyptians and British. His movement appealed to the Sammaniya who had experienced diminished authority under Egyptian and British governance.

In 1882 the British government established virtual control over Egypt after it suppressed an Egyptian army revolt. Meanwhile, the mahdi's followers won a series of battles against the Egyptians and British in Sudan and each victory enhanced the reputation of Muhammad Ahmed. The mahdi's army killed General Gordon, in charge of the Egyptian troops in Khartoum, on January 26, 1885, but Muhammad Ahmed died six months following this assault. Abdullah Taaisha assumed control of the movement, which caused dissension among some tribes, but he did increase control over the South and attempted to invade Egypt in 1896.

In 1898 British officers and Egyptian troops reconquered Sudan and defeated the Mahdists at Omdurman. General Kichener subsequently destroyed the tomb of the mahdi. The British also established authority in the South to limit French influence in the region. In 1899 both Egypt and Britain formally governed Sudan, but Britain exercised the real authority over both Egypt and Sudan. A serious nationalist revolt occurred in Khartoum throughout 1923–1924. Once defeated, Egyptian troops—who had participated in the 1923–1924 revolt—were ordered by the British to leave Sudan. Some Egyptian officials were allowed to return after the Anglo-Egyptian Treaty (1936).

Throughout this period a nationalist movement in North Sudan was established. Many groups had an anti-Egyptian perspective, particularly after the Anglo-Egyptian Treaty was negotiated without Sudanese input. Nationalists often funneled their activities through the "Graduates' General Congress," which began as an alumni association for Gordon College. Newspapers, *Al Hadara, Al Sudan,* and *Al Fagr,* debated conceptions of an independent Sudan. In 1931 students and teachers led a strike in Khartoum supporting Sudanese nationalists goals.

There was continued ablation of the mahdi and this support coalesced around the mahdi's son, Sayed Abdel Rahman al-Mahdi. He often cooperated with the British. He also established a network that collected the traditional zakat (religious tax) throughout Islamic Sudan. Following World War II, Sayed Abdel Rahman al-Mahdi openly led the Ummah Party. A moderate nationalist party, it opposed Egyptian influence and worked within the British mandate toward an independent Sudan.

A coalition of Unionist parties also agitated for independence. This party, the Nationalist Union Party (NUP), had its origins in the Graduates Assembly and the backing of the Khatmiya. They were more aligned with Egyptian nationalists and opposed to the traditional authority of the Ummah Party.

Following World War II, against the wishes of Egyptian authorities, the British followed a policy designed to make Sudan an independent state. In July 1952 nationalist military officers in Egypt deposed King Faruk and they agreed that Sudan could be established as an independent state. In 1953 parliamentary elections were held for a transitional authority meant to prepare Sudan for full independence. The pro-Egyptian NUP won a majority, but as they began to assume power, southern Sudanese factions became increasingly discontent with their lack of representation in the new state. Nonetheless, an independent Sudanese nation was established on January 1, 1956.

Since independence there have been periods of parliamentary government (1956–1958, 1965–1969, 1986–1989) interrupted by military intervention that occurred due to the inability of civilian administrations to establish arrangements that satisfied the African South and factions in the North. In the first elections following formal independence (1956) the Ummah won a majority and formed a new government. The NUP and the Peoples' Democratic Party opposed them. A coup, led by General Ibrahim Abboud, ended Sudan's first experiment with representative governance. During Abboud's rule (1958–1964) discontent southerners began a civil war (1963 to 1971).

The well-organized National Islamic Front (NIF) did run candidates in the 1965 elections. This party has traditional ties to the Egyptian Muslim Brotherhood. It has never won a majority but exercised influence in Sudan after these elections.

Gafaar Muhammad al-Nimeri, a military officer who led a coup in 1969, allowed the South greater autonomy as a means of ending the civil war, but had to appease— or jail—various factions (the military, the National Islamic Front, the Ummah, the Communists, Southerners, and students) throughout his rule. In April 1983, Nimeri instituted Sharia law (Islamic law), which was unacceptable to groups in the South. Soon the Sudanese Peoples Liberation Army (SPLA), led by former Sudanese army Colonel John Garang, began military operations against government forces in the south.

Nimeri's government was deposed by the military in 1985. In elections the following year, Saddiq al-Mahdi—head of the Ummah Party and grandson of the mahdi—was elected president. The Southern region did not participate in the election. General Omar Bashir deposed Saddiq al-Mahdi's government in 1989.

Hasan Turabi, leader of the NIF, exercises considerable authority in the new government although he has no formal position. Sudan, now considered an Islamic republic, established closer relations with Iran and supported Iraq in the Gulf War, but became isolated from its immediate neighbors. The current governance of Sudan regards the Sharia as the primary authority within the state and has renewed military actions against the SPLA. The SPLA has split into groups based on tribal affiliation and traditional regional authority. Groups led by Riak Macher and Kurbino Kwaynan (SSIM) appear to be aiding the government forces against the SPLA. Ongoing famine, exacerbated by the civil conflicts in Sudan and neighboring regions, has caused catastrophic human suffering in the South. Estimates are generally in the range of two million dead as a result of these conflicts.

There have been accusations that Sudan supports terrorism (in particular, that it backed an assassination attempt on Egyptian President Hosni Mubarak) which have isolated the country diplomatically and economically. The United States destroyed a facility in Sudan that it claimed could produce nerve gas, but recent investigations by the United Nations and other agencies have found no evidence to indicate this information was accurate. Despite these events, there is some evidence that Hasan Turabi will allow for the reestablishment of political parties, and that Omar Bashir will attempt to normalize relations with regional countries and the West. The separatist movements in the South, while suffering tremendous losses, show no signs of abatement in the long term.

## SULEYMENOV, OLZHAS

1936–, Kazakh writer and politician. Born in May 1936 in Alma-Ata, then the capital of the Kazakh Soviet Republic. Suleymenov, after completing his schooling in 1954, joined the geological faculty of the Kazakh State University, graduating in 1959. While a student he began to write poetry. In 1958, he also attended the Gorky Literary Institute (Moscow). In 1959 he published his first set of poems in Moscow. In 1961–1975 he worked variously as a journalist, an editor of the literature journal *Prostor*, an editor in the film studio *Kazakh-film*, and in the administration of the Kazakh Union of Writers. His poem "Zemlia poklonis cheloveku" (1961) brought him wide recognition.

In 1975 Suleymenov published his book 'Az-I-ia', which was a historical-philosophical essay on Turkic historical destiny, in which he explored the history of interaction between nomads (Turks) and settlers (Slavs) and the place of the Kazakhs in the historical development in Eurasia. The publication was condemned by Moscow policy makers as "nationalistic." The book was confiscated and banned until 1989. Suleymenov became one of the most prominent Kazakhi dissidents of the 1970s and only personal protection from the Kazakh first secretary D. Kunaev saved the writer from imprisonment. 'Az-I-ia' won him nationwide recognition in Kazakhstan and a reputation as the "opener of the difficult issues in the national history." After political rehabilitation, he worked in various positions with the Union of Writers. He became one of the most influential writers in Kazakhstan in the 1980s. With the introduction of Gorbachev's policy of *glasnost*, Suleymenov became increasingly active in political life. After the *Alma-Ata* students' uprising in December 1986 (Soviet leaders condemned the uprising as a "nationalist" plot), he sharply criticized Moscow policy makers for the "mistakes of their policies in Kazakhstan." This won him a reputation as the "voice of the Kazakh intelligentsia."

In February 1989 Olzhas Suleymenov, on the wave of growing criticism of nuclear testing in Semipalatinsk, founded one of the first political movements in Kazakhstan, *Nevada-Semipalatinsk*. The movement became one of the most active and influential during 1989–1991 and exacerbated the rise of national parties and organizations. In 1991, he founded the People's Congress of Kazakhstan.

Suleymenov remains one of the most popular writers and politicians in post-Soviet Kazakhstan. He has supported moderate nationalism, liberal reforms, and a balanced approach to the Law on Languages. He and his supporters' political stands have made the mainstream Kazakh nationalism more liberal and compromising.

Suleymenov has published sixteen books (mainly in Russian) and written screenplays for four movies. He is a member of the Issyk-Kyl Forum and a member of the Presidential Council for the president of Kazakhstan.

For further reading, see O. Suleymenov, *Zemlia, poklonis cheloveku!* (Moscow, 1961); O. Suleymenov, *As-I-ia'* (Alma-Ata, 1989); and M. Olcott, *Central Asia's New States: Independence, Foreign Policy and Regional Security* (Washington, D.C., 1995).

## SUN LANGUAGE THEORY

In the Turkish Republic in the 1920s and 1930s, the state wished to formulate a nationalism that fulfilled a series of often conflicting goals and assumptions. Based on European models of nationalism then current, the state assumed that national identity was ethnically and linguistically based. At the same time, it wished to reinforce Turkish claims to Anatolia by appropriating ancient Anatolian cultures into a single Turkish history. There was also a need to formulate a vision of Turkish nationalism that would include minority groups living in the Turkish Republic, especially the large Kurdish minority in the East. Finally, the Turkish state needed to formulate a relationship between Turkey and Europe that would allow Turkey to adopt Western technology and specialized

vocabulary without these innovations threatening the state's status as protector of indigenous culture.

One attempt at satisfying these varied needs in the 1930's was the Sun Language Theory (*Güneş Dil Teorisi*), which claimed to prove that Turkish was the first human language and that Turks were the first nation. Through this "theory," Turks were able to appropriate *all* languages and cultures and thus could equally claim inheritance of French vocabulary and a Hittite legacy in Anatolia. After a short period of official support, the excesses of the Sun Language Theory seem to have been rejected. Without the support of the state, this vision of the Turkish nation (which no doubt was very foreign to the average Turkish citizen of the time) quickly faded from the literature. It has no adherents today and is mostly remembered as a colorful footnote in the history of Turkish nationalism.

## SUN YATSEN

1866–1925, Known as the father of the Republic of China and the founder of the Nationalist Party or Kuomintang (KMT) as well as one of the most famous advocates of Chinese nationalism, Sun was born in 1866 in Kuangtung Province fifteen miles from Macao and not far from Hong Kong. At the age of thirteen, Sun went to Hawaii, where he attended middle school, high school, and college. He subsequently returned to China and to Hong Kong, where he graduated from Hong Kong Medical College in 1892. However, he soon gave up medicine to devote his time and energy to propagating Chinese nationalism and overthrow of the Manchu government in China.

Sun championed revolution in contrast to most Chinese intellectuals and reformists of the time who advocated political and social change while retaining Chinese culture and the Chinese political system. During Sun's early career as a revolutionary, he spent much of his time abroad founding revolutionary organizations and seeking help, including monetary support, for the cause of ending what he termed "foreign rule" (Manchus or Manchurians) of China while his followers in China sought actively and aggressively to foment revolution.

In 1894, in Hawaii, Sun created the Hsing Chung Hui (Revive China Society), the first of a number of nationalistic, revolutionary organizations he founded or led. In 1905, while in Japan, he formed the Tung Meng Hui (Revolutionary Alliance), a group with the stated objective of overthrowing the "foreign" Manchu or Ch'ing Dynasty. Sun's various organizations had ties with secret societies in China with which Sun was connected and helped advertise the cause of revolution. On October 10, 1911, Sun's supporters in China, after a number of failed attempts, succeeded in starting a revolt that set off a chain reaction and brought down the Manchus.

Sun became the provisional president of the Republic of China established on January 11, 1912. However, he abdicated almost immediately in order to avoid a civil war in China. (Yuan Shih-kai in the meantime had consolidated power in Beijing and had won the alliance and support of the Western powers.) Subsequently Sun, notwithstanding his Western education and his respect for Western learning, U.S. constitutionalism, and America's political system, because of disappointment with the West owing to their support of Yuan, invited Soviet representatives to China who advised him on party organization and other matters.

This accounts for the fact that the Nationalist Party has a Leninist organizational structure. It also explains some of Sun's views propounded at the time, including his view of nationalism, which emphasizes Chinese traditionalism to a large extent. In the early 1920s, after Yuan died and various warlords ruled the country causing chaos and widespread dissatisfaction, Sun made several other attempts to establish a democratic government in China, but failed. Sun died in 1925.

During his lifetime Sun wrote about politics, political philosophy, and political development. He was a prodigious thinker and a prolific writer and speaker. Unfortunately his manuscripts were burned in 1922 in a fire that was deliberately set and many of his writings were permanently lost. Sun intended to collect his ideas into a "great treatise" but died before he could accomplish that task.

Sun's political ideals or philosophy are summarized in his most famous work entitled *San Min Chu I* (*Three Principles of the People*). Sun's first principle and his most important was nationalism. In fact, it seems accurate to say that nationalism provided the basis or foundation for Sun's other principles and nearly everything Sun taught and stood for. Sun observed that China had fallen under the influence of cosmopolitanism and thus Chinese lacked an ability to distinguish between themselves and outsiders, causing them to fall victim to Manchu rule in the same way that Korea had succumbed to Japanese colonialism and much of the world was under European control. If China were to survive, Sun contended, it must adopt and cultivate nationalism.

The term nationalism or *min zu* (which can also be translated as race) clearly had racial or ethnic overtones. To Sun it meant instilling consciousness into the Chinese people or "race." Sun observed that the population of white countries had increased by as much as tenfold in the 18th century, while China's population was static. He said also that China was oppressed ethnically, politically, and economically. It was being humiliated. Its territory was being taken. It was being drained economically because of a trade deficit. China, in short, said Sun, was engaged in a struggle of a different kind than it had ever experienced before. Chinese must thus, he argued, become "race conscious" or develop a sense of nationalism (one and the same to Sun). Otherwise China would not survive and would devolve into several European colonies.

However, nationalism, or Chinese "race consciousness" was propounded by Sun not as a racial theory but rather for the purpose of nation building. Sun believed, and taught, that China's survival and it becoming strong and important once again, as well as democratic, depended on nurturing a spirit of nationalism. Sun's second and third principles depended on the success of creating nationalism and in so doing building the Chinese nation.

Democracy (Sun's second principle) was applicable to China, he argued, but could not be defined as it was in the West. To Sun, China had limited government and egalitarianism already. Also personal liberties were widely practiced. What China needed was freedom from imperialism. China also needed democracy to unleash the energy of the Chinese people, give them confidence, and prevent personal goals from causing corruption. Democracy, Sun realized, could not be implanted in China quickly. It had to be realized in stages: military control, followed by a period of "tutelage" and finally real democracy.

People's livelihood, Sun's third principle, has been called socialism, though Sun thought of it more as an enriching of China. He did not think China had as rich a class as in the West and did not talk about an exploiting class or classes or about class struggle. He did think that tax policies were needed to prevent people from having unearned incomes.

Sun's teachings, according to Western scholars, do not constitute an ideology because they were too simple. His critics say that they are shallow, contradictory, and more. On the other hand, Sun contended that he wrote and spoke so that people could understand and did not need an interpreter. Another explanation is that during his life he was constantly on the move and sought to wrest political control from leaders in Beijing.

Chiang Kaishek implemented and propagated Sun's teachings when he unified China and subsequently as president of the Republic of China. Sun's "principles" also became the ideological foundation of the Nationalist Party and the government of the Republic of China when it ruled China and later after it moved to Taiwan.

Sun's critics say that his view that democracy must be attained in stages rationalized Chiang's dictatorship. Others say that Taiwan was very fortunate because it did not try to democratize too quickly, observing many nations that did and failed.

In Taiwan, Sun is regarded with special respect and his teachings are widely read, though not sanctified the way Mao's works were in China. In recent years, Sun is given credit for making a connection between political modernization and economic modernization, a link that explains both the Taiwan economic and political miracles.

Sun was viewed by Communist leaders in China, including Mao, as an important revolutionary, but one who did not go far enough. In more recent years, Sun has become even more respected in China.

Details on Sun's life and ideas can be found in C. Martin Wilbur, *Sun Yat-sen: Frustrated Patriot* (New York: Columbia University Press, 1976).

## SWEDISH NATIONALISM

Sweden is a constitutional monarchy whose kingdom included Finland until 1809. The country was unified with the other Scandinavian monarchies under the Kalmar Union in 1397. The efforts of Erik of Pomerania to enforce absolutist rule led to several revolts by Swedish nobles and peasantry. After Erik was deposed in 1439, the council seized power under Karl Knutsson Bonde. Out of these revolts, the peasantry gained some voice in the government, and the Swedish Parliament, with its four estates of nobles, clergy, burgers, and peasants, came into being. In 1523, following a massacre of Swedish nobles ordered by Christian II, Sweden, under the leadership of the nobleman Gustaf Vasa, broke with the union completely. Under the domination of absolutist, unifying monarchs such as Gustavus II Adolphus and Charles XII, Sweden and Denmark fought for control of the Scandinavian region. Eight major wars were fought between 1563 and 1721, resulting in Sweden gaining Scania (Skåne—the southern portion of Sweden) in 1658. Under the reign of Gustavus II Adolphus (1611–1632), Sweden became the dominant power in the area. Wars with Poland and Russia also gave Sweden a considerable Baltic Empire, including Estonia, Latvia, and Livonia.

The 17th and 18th centuries were idealized as the "golden period" of Swedish greatness, when Sweden ruled over a large empire and enjoyed independence and prosperity. Artists expressed the cultural prestige of Sweden through metaphors of the classical age. The Swedish admiration of French and Italian culture, strengthened when the French nobleman Bernadotte (1763–1844) became King Charles XIV John, served to connect the country to larger traditions of classicalism. In the 17th century, Olof Rudbeck and other scholars wrote lengthy treatises proving that the Goths were Swedish and that the Swedes were the rightful heirs of the civilizations of Greece and Rome. These scholars also looked back to the medieval sagas and Eddic poems as evidence of their high levels of cultural sophistication, particularly to the *fornaldarsögur,* a group of stories of highly fantastic events, many of which are situated in Sweden. Despite their legendary qualities, these sagas were nevertheless accepted uncritically by many as historically accurate.

During the 19th century, Swedish nationalists broke away from their engagement with French and Italian culture and consciously sought a more "Swedish" style. An example of this is the "Opponents," a group of late 19th-century artists who studied in France but opposed aspects of the Paris Academy impressionists. They exhibited their art independently and formed an artists' association in 1886. Scenes from Swedish pastoral life were a favorite subject of these artists, the most prominent of whom was probably Anders Zorn (1860–1920). Other writers and artists also idealized the landscape of the Swedish countryside, whose qualities were seen as particularly exemplified by the Dalarna region in central eastern Sweden. In Sweden, however, national romanticism was not entirely backward looking, as it was in most other European countries. Along with a cultural conservatism, its exponents advocated a political liberalism that sought the breakdown of class barriers.

Sweden also expressed its sense of cultural hegemony in its assimilationist policy toward Finns and Lapps. During Swedish rue, Finnish language and customs were discouraged. When Sweden lost Finland and its Baltic possessions to Russia in the 19th century, it began to decline as a European power. Norway was also in union with Sweden between 1814 and 1905, but they had their own constitution, parliament, and taxation system, and Sweden did not seriously attempt to direct Norwegian internal affairs. Today, Sweden remains on cooperative terms with the other Scandinavian countries through the Nordic Union, and Swedish nationalism is not a particularly prominent feature of Swedish political life, although the romantization of Swedish culture continues. Sweden joined the European Union in 1995.

## SWISS NATIONALISM

Because Switzerland is a heterogeneous multilingual country, with the bulk of its citizens speaking German, French, or Italian, expressions of nationalism are subdued or directed against other groups within the country. Although only a minority of Swiss is fully multilingual, the fact that the language groups are separated and largely concentrated in single-language, autonomous cantons prevents the lingual diversity from being a major problem for unity, as in Belgium. While French- and Italian-speaking Swiss somewhat resent the dominance of German in the federal institutions in the capital, Bern, most Swiss share pride in their country's stability and prosperity.

During the great depression of the 1930s, Switzerland was able to preserve its democratic order at a time when most of the democracies in Europe collapsed. It also managed to remain neutral during World War II. It declared its determination to fight to the last man if it were invaded. This threat, backed by the Swiss military reputation and determination, helped to dissuade Hitler and Mussolini from attacking.

Switzerland did not remain free as a result of military deterrence alone. Faced with the prospect that it could share the fate of other occupied countries, it made compromises with Nazi Germany in the name of "neutrality" that now make it seem to many Swiss and non-Swiss that the country may have bought its freedom at a very high moral price. It continued to trade with Germany and Italy, and some of the products that it sold were obviously used for armaments. Further, thousands of Jews and political refugees were denied entry into Switzerland and therefore ended up in prisons or extermination camps. An agreement with Germany in 1938 required Jews to obtain visas and have a special stamp (a "J") in their passports.

Recently declassified Allied intelligence documents reveal the extent to which the Swiss reaped handsome profits by serving as bankers both for the Nazis and their Jewish victims. Prominent Nazis were steady customers of Swiss banks: Hitler reportedly deposited royalties from *Mein Kampf,* and Hermann Goering made regular trips to Zurich to deposit art masterpieces stolen from museums in occupied countries. The banks purchased from the Nazis hundreds of millions of dollars of looted gold, and other stolen funds were invested in Swiss enterprises. Bank secrecy was introduced in 1934 to accommodate Jews who wanted to deposit their assets quietly outside of Germany, and then those same secrecy laws were used to prevent the heirs from claiming those assets after the war.

The Swiss refusal to discuss or deal with these problems cracked in 1996 under intense pressure from Jewish organizations and foreign governments. Attempting to contain this gigantic public relations disaster, the Swiss government took steps to investigate the extent and fate of Jewish wealth and Nazi loot sent to neutral Switzerland during the war, find dormant accounts left by Jews, and use the funds to help survivors.

While few Swiss are proud today of such past policies, Swiss national survival seemed to require them at the time. On the positive side, Switzerland was a base during the war for Allied spies, such as Allen Dulles, as well as for international Jewish agencies operating in Europe. It also offered protection to thousands of refugees who would otherwise have joined the many victims of fascism.

The large number of foreigners working in Switzerland (about a sixth of total residents) elicits some nationalist reactions, especially from the "Swiss Democrats," formerly called the National Action for People and Homeland (NA). It aims its arrows toward what it sees as a threatening perversion of the Swiss character caused by foreign workers and rapid urbanization. This openly patriotic and nationalist party reached its zenith in 1970 when a majority of Swiss voters was almost persuaded in a referendum to limit the numbers of foreign workers. In the 1990s the less democratic, neo-Nazi Patriotic Front, entered the anti-immigrant scene.

In their opposition to foreign workers these parties touch a very sensitive nerve. The country has traditionally been very hospitable to political exiles; for example, it took in 16,000 Hungarians after 1956 and 14,000 Czechoslovaks after 1968. Swiss industry learned very early that high levels of production could be achieved only by attracting foreign workers. No one doubts that the hotel and restaurant industries would never be able to survive without foreign workers. About half of these workers are Italians, followed by Germans and Spaniards.

Many Swiss are nevertheless uneasy about their very visible presence. This visibility has been especially enhanced by a wave of arrivals: Sri Lankan Tamils, Kurds, Pakistanis, and Congolese. In a 1987 referendum, voters accepted by a two-to-one margin a new law tightening rules regarding immigration and political asylum. It extended to peacetime the government's emergency powers to close the border to all refugees. The Swiss government also maintains a fund to send asylum seekers arriving by air back to their homelands on the next flight. As classrooms in Swiss schools sometimes swell with foreign children and as rundown areas with predominantly foreign residents begin to appear in some cities, cultural clashes are inevitable.

Not wishing to tarnish Switzerland's image as a land of refuge or to harm its economy, Swiss voters rejected by a two-to-one margin proposed laws to limit the percentage of foreigners; in 1994 a majority accepted a government ban on all forms of racism, including a belittling of the Holocaust, and 53.6 percent rejected in 1996 a proposal to tighten regulations over asylum seekers from Africa and Asia. Nevertheless, the Swiss government has been very attuned to the discontent and has quietly reduced the percentage of foreigners in Switzerland to 17 percent of the total population. It can do this because, although foreign workers enjoy many rights and social benefits while in the country, many must renew their work permits every year.

Over a fourth of the workforce is foreign; those with permanent work permits, with the same employment rights as Swiss nationals, slightly outnumber those with limited rights. By carefully restricting the number of renewals, the government can slowly reduce the foreign population. Further, foreign workers must live in the country four years before they are permitted to bring their families. This policy is not always appreciated by the countries from which the guest workers come; they often accuse Switzerland of "egotism" and of "exporting unemployment." But this policy enables Switzerland both to control its own employment and to pacify Swiss fears of an excessive foreign presence.

In general, Switzerland avoids any alliances or actions that might involve it in any kind of political, economic, or military action against other states. The Swiss are armed to the teeth in order to demonstrate their determination to defend their neutrality and in order to dissuade any belligerent in a European war from viewing Swiss territory as a military vacuum and thereby inviting invasion.

Switzerland is not in NATO. Its and Austria's neutrality separates NATO's northern and southern halves. But Swiss neutrality is defined much more narrowly than merely refusing to join a military alliance such as NATO. Earlier, its political leaders never publicly commented on foreign political events, such as elections or coups d'état, or on foreign military actions, such as the Soviet Union's invasions of Czechoslovakia in 1968 or of Afghanistan in 1979. This changed in August 1990, when for the first time Switzerland applied sanctions against Iraq, which had invaded Kuwait.

Although the Swiss conception of neutrality has also prevented the country from joining the United Nations, Switzerland has joined many of its specialized organizations, and it pays more than half a billion Swiss francs (more than 72 Swiss francs per inhabitant). Geneva is the seat of the United Nation's European headquarters. It has held that the United Nation's provision for sanctions against member states is incompatible with Swiss neutrality. The Swiss Federal Council and Parliament gradually reached the conclusion that Switzerland could no longer remain outside the United Nations, which

they believed would officially take note of Swiss neutrality. They are supported by most university educated Swiss and by the country's most prestigious newspapers. Nevertheless, three out of four Swiss citizens still oppose entry. In a 1986 referendum, Swiss voters overruled their government and all main parties by three to one on this issue. The magnitude of the no vote has discouraged the government from submitting it to another vote.

Switzerland now participates in and helps finance UN peacekeeping operations. In 1989 it took the bold step of actually sending unarmed but uniformed medical personnel, administrators, and observers to Namibia, and later to Western Sahara. This was the first deployment of Swiss troops abroad since the Battle of Marignano in 1515. Switzerland also sends officers and aircraft to assist the United Nations in the Middle East. In 1996 it broke with its tradition by allowing NATO troops to pass through its territory on their way to implement the peace in Bosnia. By giving sanctuary to 400,000 refugees from the former Yugoslavia, it also turned its back on its refugee policy before and during World War II. The growing internationalism is strongest in the French- and Italian-speaking parts of the country.

In 1991 Switzerland celebrated the 700th anniversary of its birth. Instead of patting themselves on the back for the peace and prosperity they have enjoyed, the Swiss are ruminating about their role in the modern world. This reexamination has dramatically been extended to the country's wartime dealings with Nazi Germany and the possible misuse of bank secrecy laws to prevent the return of Jewish assets to Holocaust victims. The debate continues about whether Switzerland had paid too high a moral price to remain neutral.

See Rolf Kieser and Kurt Spillman, eds., *The New Switzerland* (SPROSS, 1996), and J. Steinberg, *Why Switzerland?* (Cambridge University, 1996).

## SYRIAN NATIONALISM

In 1932 Antun Sa'ade founded the Syrian Social Nationalist Party (SSNP), which proposed that the Syrians form a complete nation. Witnessing the catastrophic conditions that befell the populations of Greater Syria during World War I heavily influenced Sa'ade in formulating the tenets of Syrian nationalism. He was tormented by the particularism of the Syrians and their loss of identity beyond the veneer of religion. Sa'ade argued that the people of Syria failed to see themselves as belonging to a nation-state, did not exhibit appreciation for orderly work, lacked the will to pursue long-term objectives, and did not manifest high moral principles. Sa'ade announced that digging into history led to his retrieval of the lost Syrian identity. Influenced by the discourses of Communism and fascism—then in vogue—Sa'ade employed scientific national philosophy to legitimize Syrian nationalism, which embraced the populations of Syria, Lebanon, Jordan, Iraq, and parts of Palestine.

The three basic principles of Syrian nationalism stress that Syria is for the Syrians, that the Syrian nation consists of a nuclear social structure, and that its interests rise above all other interests. Teachings on Syrian nationalism call for the creation of a society of social and economic abundance in which citizens learn to become self-respectful and self-confident and appreciate the importance of order and hard work. These qualities, Sa'ade insisted, were prerequisites for the pursuit of happiness and achievement of national sovereignty.

Syrian nationalism has been on the retreat since the independence of Syria and Lebanon in 1943. First, it was discarded by most Christians following the withdrawal of the French from Syria and Lebanon in 1946. Second, the advocacy of Arab nationalism by Gamal Abdel al-Nasser in Egypt, and the Ba'th Party in Syria in the mid-1950s had an overwhelming swaying impact on Muslims in Greater Syria. The inherent secular, almost antireligious orientation of Syrian nationalism has not been particularly appealing either to traditional or to activist Muslims whose numbers are noticeably increasing in the region.

**SZÁLASI, FERENC** 1897–1946, The figurehead leader of Hungary's National Socialist far right, Szálasi can best be described as an enigmatic, racist, confused populist. Hitler's forces brought Szálasi to power on October 16, 1944, after a botched attempt by Hungary's regent, Miklós Horthy, to withdraw Hungary from the war the previous day. Szálasi was sentenced to death by a Hungarian war crimes tribunal and executed in 1946.

Szálasi's far-right movement, manifested first in his army officer-based Party of National Will and eventually in his larger fusion Arrow Cross Party (*Nyilaskeresztes Párt*), evolved from a political nuisance in 1935–1936 to a political force that won nearly one-third of the popular vote in the 1939 elections. During the late 1930s and early 1940s, Horthy's government developed a love–hate relationship with the far right and its leaders. Szálasi himself was repeatedly jailed and released, his parties banned and then reconstituted several times.

Szálasi's plans for the Hungarian nation and state have been described as quixotic, abstract, and even downright inane. A former general staff officer in the Hungarian army, Szálasi's motto was "God, peasant, citizen, and soldier" and he foresaw a utopian Hungary led by a paternalistic elite of army officers. The spiritual fundament of Szálasi's "Hungarism," his national philosophy, was a Christian belief in God and a church that the state could mobilize for political means. He believed the Hungarian or, as he described it, the Turanian race had a God-given obligation to rule much of southcentral Europe, vaguely defined by the former borders of the Greater Hungarian Kingdom. True nationalism, according to Szálasi's modified social Darwinist concepts, must be exclusivist and imperialist; otherwise, it could not be vital and worthy of survival. In practical terms, Szálasi's nationalism meant annulment of the Treaty of Trianon, the 1920 peace agreement that had decreased Hungary's size and population by more than 65 percent, and expansion beyond Hungary's previous borders, creating a "Great Carpathian-Danube Fatherland."

The core of Szálasi's "Hungarist" state was to be an industrial peasant economy of agriculturally based small industry rather than manufacturing. He was vehemently anti-Bolshevik, yet his brand of national socialism favored the small peasant and worker; he supported social welfare programs designed to provide jobs and housing; he talked abstractly of state-led corporate capitalism; and he preached of the coming of a future "classless" Hungarian society. This prevented the landowning far right from coming to terms with his movement.

In his writing and speeches, Szálasi was an ardent anti-Semite. In his opinion, Jews were responsible for the evils of liberal individualism and unbridled capitalism, on the one hand, and collectivism, embodied in Marxism and Bolshevism, on the other. He proclaimed that the Jewish credit economy would have to be replaced by a "Hungarian" one. Szálasi wrote that until the end of the war, the Jews of Hungary should perform service for the nation, their status regulated by law. After the conclusion of the war, all Hungarian Jews would be expelled to a land to be determined by international agreement, and banned from ever returning to Hungary. Although he was not as pathologically committed to the "solving of the Jewish question" as his Nazi counterparts, under his rule, Arrow Cross thugs murdered thousands of Jews and Szálasi himself consented to the deportation of Jewish labor groups to Germany culminating in the infamous forced marches to Hegyeshalom.

While Szálasi and his cohorts had enjoyed close connections with Nazi Germany, including financial support, Hitler mistrusted Szálasi, preferring the more stable Horthy regime until Hungary's doomed attempt to withdraw from the war. Szálasi came to power only as a last resort and surprised his Nazi benefactors by attempting to carve out significant sovereignty during his short reign. He also fully mobilized Hungary for a last-gasp failed effort to thwart the advancing Red Army and oversaw a political terror that resulted in the deaths of tens of thousands of Hungarians, the majority of whom were Jews and political opponents of the Arrow Cross.

The best and most accessible English language texts on Szálasi are István Deák's chapter "Hungary" in Hans Rogger and Eugen Webber's *The European Right: A Historical Profile*, published by the University of California Press in 1966, and Miklós Lackó's *Arrow Cross Men, National Socialists 1935–44*, published by Akadémiai Kiadó in 1969. Margit Szőllősi-Janze's *Die Pfeilkreuzlerbewegung in Ungarn*, published in Oldenbourg in 1989, is the most comprehensive study of Hungary's Arrow Cross movement.

## SZÉCHENYI, ISTVÁN

1791–1860, Count Széchenyi, a member of one of Hungary's most important great landowning families, played a key role in the reform movement in Hungary in the early to mid-1800s, earning him the moniker "the Great Reformer." His father, Count Ferenc Széchenyi, founded Hungary's National Museum and National Library, and his mother was the daughter of Count György Festetics, who built Hungary's first center for agricultural study, the Georgikon. Largely self-educated, István soon developed an interest in the cultural and economic modernization of Hungary. Experiences abroad as a soldier in the Napoleonic wars; as a favorite of diplomats, soldiers, and countesses alike; and as a world traveler from 1815 to 1817 exposed him to alternatives and persuaded him that Hungary's aristocrats must reform if Hungary wished to retain any influential role in Europe.

Unlike his fellow reformer and nemesis, Lajos Kossuth, who gave highest priority to Hungary's political and administrative independence, Széchenyi believed that Hungary was not yet ready for separation from Austria. Rather, Hungary's modernization was a long-term project inextricably linked with Austria. Hungary must first build the economic, political, and cultural institutions necessary to support a state and a national culture. In the course of his life, he embarked on countless projects designed to create this infrastructure for Hungary.

It was in economics and political economy that Széchenyi made his most exceptional contributions to Hungary. In 1827 he created the National Casino to promote business contacts, although throughout his life he adamantly refused to admit Jews or women into this select club. In 1830 Széchenyi wrote his most important book, *Credit (Hitel)*. *Credit* was an attempt to convince Hungary's noble elite of the need to adopt a monetary, rather than exchange/barter-based economic system, and to eliminate the manorial system. In *Light (Világ)*, the count further denounced feudalism as the primary restraint preventing Hungary's advance. He blamed his Hungarian brethren, not Vienna, for Hungary's backwardness, and challenged his fellow nobles to reform.

Széchenyi backed his words with actions. He established shipbuilding and manufacturing ventures in Buda-Pest and other Hungarian cities, as well as establishing Hungary's first commercial bank. Some of the count's other projects included building the Lánchid (Chain Bridge), the first permanent bridge over the Danube linking Buda and Pest; regulating the Danube's water flow; and founding the first steamship company on the Balaton. To promote Hungarian culture, he led a group of aristocrats who established the Hungarian National Academy in 1825 and played a key role in the construction of the National Theater, Hungary's preeminent Hungarian-language theater. He was the first to address the Hungarian Diet in Hungarian and his books were purposely published in Hungarian to popularize the language. He understood the link between culture, economics, and politics, but most of his cohorts did not. Not a compelling speaker, disliked by Hungary's conservative nobles who deemed him too radical, distrusted by the more radical reformers because of his magnate background and his lack of sympathy for democratic ideas, Széchenyi never developed a substantial following.

In the early 1840s, the battle between the reformer Széchenyi and the rising, more radical Kossuth heated up. Széchenyi, in part jealous of Kossuth's popularity, believed that Kossuth's diatribes would split Hungary between rich and poor. His feud with Kossuth and the liberals eventually led to his joining a Habsburg-appointed conservative administration in 1844. He oversaw a highly successful project which made the Tisza, Hungary's second largest river, navigable.

During the first phase of the 1848–1849 revolution when Vienna accepted the Hungarian demands for autonomy, emancipation of the serfs, and legalization of civil rights, Széchenyi and Kossuth temporarily put aside their dispute. Széchenyi joined the Batthyány government as minister of public works and transport. With great vigor he set out to draft legislation and initiate massive building projects. Yet, as relations with Vienna deteriorated, Széchenyi became convinced that the Hungarians must seek reconciliation. When a Habsburg victory in Italy was assured and war with Hungary appeared imminent, Széchenyi's fragile psyche gave way. Transported to a mental asylum outside Vienna, "the Greatest Hungarian" retreated into isolation. Thereafter, he wrote a number of political works, but his remaining life was tormented, marked by several unsuccessful sui-cide attempts. Despairing and insane, the count succeeded in taking his own life on April 8, 1860.

The authoritative study of Széchenyi is still George Bárány's *Stephen Széchenyi and the Awakening of Hungarian Nationalism, 1791–1841*, published by Princeton University Press in 1968. Several of Széchenyi's own writings, such as *Credit (Hitel)* and *Light (Vilag)*, have been translated into English.

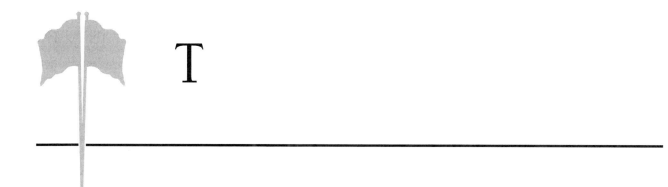

# T

**TAIWANESE NATIONALISM**   The term *Taiwanese nationalism* may have several meanings and is thus somewhat confusing and difficult to define. That difficulty in part stems from problems in defining who is "Taiwanese" among the populace of the island of Taiwan. The term most often refers to the Chinese population of the island that migrated there before the end of World War II. This, however, means that the natives, or the aborigines (somewhat less than 2 percent of the population), are not considered Taiwanese. There is also disagreement, because Taiwanese are frequently said to be those who speak Taiwanese, a dialect of Chinese that originates from southern Fujian Province or the Amoy dialect. Defining Taiwanese this way, the Hakka, who comprise from 10 to 15 percent of the population, are not necessarily Taiwanese, since some of them do not speak Taiwanese, or speak Hakka as their native tongue, even though they are pre-World War II immigrants. The term *Taiwanese* has also been used to define the current population of the island, being all inclusive, to mean anyone who is a citizen of the Republic of China.

Assuming for the moment that the original definition, "pre-World War II Chinese migrants (including the Hakka)," is correct, Taiwanese nationalism probably finds its origins in the Japanese period, or the time when Taiwan was a colony of Japan (1895–1945). However, some have argued that it preceded that and began when Taiwan was a colony of Holland for a generation in the 17th century, or was self-governing for a subsequent generation, or was ruled by China for more than two centuries after that. The problem with the latter argument is that there were no national institutions of any kind on the island before the Japanese colonized Taiwan, and the Chinese communities on the island were isolated (though not from trade and contacts with other places in East Asia) from each other and no serious attempts were made to change this.

Soon after Japan was granted jurisdiction over Taiwan in the Treaty of Shimonoseki that ended the Sino-Japanese War (1894–1895), Chinese on the island at the time, or Taiwanese, announced the formation of the Republic of Taiwan. This effort was not well planned and did not have the support of many Chinese on the island because of family rivalries, fear of warlordism, and other reasons. The effort thus failed after a few days. However, it seemed to have been an expression of Taiwanese nationalism.

Taiwanese subsequently began to develop an identity under the Japanese in some part because Tokyo rejected a policy of assimilation and treated Taiwanese as inferiors for what may be called ethnic or racial reasons. This sense of identity evolved into demands for self-rule. This, however, did not go very far both due to Japanese suppression of democratic tendencies and the fact that most Taiwanese were satisfied with the stability and economic advances Japanese control brought.

During the Japanese period, some Taiwanese maintained their "Chineseness" and remained loyal to China, but most did not—seeing Japan as more progressive and viewing China as having abandoned them. Taiwanese nationalism, however, was also diluted by loyalty to Japan, which was fairly strong. More than 200,000 Taiwanese were conscripted into the Japanese military during World War II and more than 30,000 died. A considerable number fought in China, some in regiments that committed atrocities against Chinese in Nanking and elsewhere. Recognizing the allegiance of Taiwanese to Japan, the United States abandoned a plan to invade Taiwan toward the end of the war, assuming that the local Chinese would fight with the Japanese island to protect the island. Thus, some scholars argue that Taiwanese nationalism did not really develop until after the Japanese period.

Following World War II, through agreements made at Cairo and Postsdam during the war, Taiwan was returned to China. Chiang Kaishek thus administered the Japanese surrender and evacuation of the island in 1945. Chiang, however, was engaged in a civil war with the Communists on the mainland at the time and ignored social and economic problems that soon began to fester in Taiwan. He also made a poor choice when he appointed Chen Yi as governor. Chen ruled the island in a very undemocratic fashion and treated the Taiwanese as traitors who had been "Japanized."

Alienated Taiwanese took to the streets in 1947 in what became known as the February 28 "uprising" or "revolution" for the date it began. Taiwanese beat and killed many mainland Chinese (Chinese who came to Taiwan after the war) and expressed their displeasure with the government. Chiang Kaishek responded and sent troops to restore order. Nationalist Chinese soldiers slaughtered more than 10,000 Taiwanese in the process.

Taiwanese nationalism after this incident took on a decidedly anti-nationalist Chinese sentiment. It could not develop very well, however, because the government was controlled by mainland Chinese, or recent immigrants, who possessed the means to instill in the people a sense of Chinese nationalism. Given their control of the media, the educational system, and more, and their subsequent success in engineering miraculous economic growth, they succeeded at least superficially.

However, owing to the fact that Taiwanese were the majority of the population (85 percent) and democratization was proceeding apace, Taiwanese nationalism evolved rather strongly in the 1970s and 1980s. It reflected latent anti-mainland Chinese and anti-Nationalist Party sentiments. However, it was also energized by fear of the People's Republic of China and Beijing's predatory intentions and the fact that Taiwan and China had in many ways grown permanently separate as a product of the Cold War and as a result of time.

As the Cold War drew to a close and finally ended, further democratization in Taiwan presented an even more formidable barrier between Taiwan and China. In 1986, an opposition political party, the Democratic Progressive Party, formed that was predominantly Taiwanese and claimed to represent Taiwanese interests. It put a provision supporting Taiwan's independence in its platform and leaders of the party called for a new constitution and some for the formation of a "Republic of Taiwan." Taiwanese also began demanding greater use of the Taiwanese dialect on television and radio and more political power at this time, which they attained.

In 1988, when Chiang Chingkuo, Chiang Kaishek's son who was president of the Republic of China, died and Lee Teng-hui (a Taiwanese, though Hakka) became president, many saw the main objective of Taiwanese nationalism, Taiwanese rule, as having been fulfilled. Lee, however, kept Chiang Chingkuo's policies of not separating Taiwan formally or legally from China by continuing to espouse a one-China policy. Yet conflicts with Beijing and the fact of democracy fomenting different ideas while allowing the expression of Taiwanese nationalist sentiments weakened the one-China idea and caused many to think that Lee had in fact abandoned it. Meanwhile, many mainland Chinese had long since forsaken any hope of returning to China and began to think of Taiwan as home and of themselves as Taiwanese. (Chiang Chingkuo even referred to himself as Taiwanese in the mid-1980s.)

Reversing to some degree the growth of a unique Taiwanese nationalism, one separate from Chinese nationalism, during the late 1980s and 1990s, with links, especially economic ones (through trade and investment ties) proliferating with China and citizens from Taiwan visiting China in large numbers, many of them seeing relatives, a Chinese identity began to grow again in Taiwan. Many Taiwanese in fact, as had been true for a long time, felt themselves caught in a dilemma between identifying as Chinese or Taiwanese (when, in fact, they were both).

At this juncture, it is difficult to predict the future of Taiwanese nationalism. Clearly it has, and will continue, to be encouraged by democracy. It has also benefited from various global trends. But it is also subject to countervailing pressures and influence from threats by the People's Republic of China against Taiwan and by the United States' one-China policy.

**TANZANIAN NATIONALISM**    The coastal area of Tanzania first felt the impact of foreign influence as early as the 8th century, when Arab traders arrived. By the 12th century, traders and immigrants came from as far away as Persia (now Iran) and India. They built a series of highly developed city-states and trading states along the coast, the principal one being Kilwa, a settlement of Persian origin that held ascendancy until the Portuguese destroyed it in the early 1500s.

The Portuguese navigator Vasco da Gama explored the East African coast in 1498 on his voyage to India. By 1506, the Portuguese claimed control over the entire coast. This control was nominal, however, because the Portuguese did not colonize the area or explore the interior. Assisted by Omani Arabs, the indigenous coastal dwellers succeeded in driving the Portuguese from the area north of the Ruvuma River by the early 18th century. Claiming the coastal strip, Omani Sultan Seyyid Said (1804–1856) moved his capital to Zanzibar in 1841.

European exploration of the interior began in the mid-19th century. Two German missionaries reached Mt. Kilimanjaro in the 1840s. British explorers Richard Burton and John Speke crossed the interior to Lake Tanganyika in 1857. David Livingstone, the Scottish missionary-explorer who crusaded against the slave trade, established his last mission at Ujiji, where he was "found" by Henry Morton Stanley, an American journalist-explorer, who had been commissioned by the *New York Herald* to locate him.

German colonial interests were first advanced in 1884. Karl Peters, who formed the Society for German Colonization, concluded a series of treaties by which tribal chiefs in the interior accepted German "protection." Prince Otto von Bismarck's government backed Peters in the subsequent establishment of the German East Africa Company.

In 1886 and 1890, Anglo-German agreements were negotiated that delineated the British and German spheres of influence in the interior of East Africa and along the coastal strip previously claimed by the Omani sultan of Zanzibar. In 1891, the German government took over direct administration of the territory from the German East Africa Company and appointed a governor with headquarters at Dar es Salaam.

Although the German colonial administration brought cash crops, railroads, and roads to Tanganyika, European rule provoked African resistance, culminating in the Maji Maji rebellion of 1905–1907. This rebellion temporarily united a number of southern tribes and ended only after an estimated 120,000 Africans had died from fighting or starvation. It is considered by most Tanzanians to have been one of the first stirrings of nationalism.

German colonial domination of Tanganyika ended after World War I when control of most of the territory passed to the United Kingdom under a League of Nations mandate. After World War II, Tanganyika became a UN trust territory under British control. Subsequent years witnessed Tanganyika moving gradually toward self-government and independence.

Britain was, at the time, concerned with the islands of Zanzibar and Pemba, which were declared a British protectorate in 1890. In 1919, the League of Nations gave Britain a mandate to administer part of German East Africa, now known as Tanganyika. (Belgium, with a similar mandate, took over the administration of Ruanda and Urundi, i.e., Rwanda and Burundi.) In 1946 Tanganyika became a UN trust territory.

A legislative council was set up in 1926. It was enlarged in 1945, and restructured in 1955 to give equal representation to Africans, Asians, and Europeans, sitting as thirty "unofficials" with the thirty-one "officials."

In 1954, a schoolteacher, Julius Nyerere, founded the Tanganyika African National Union (TANU), which promoted African nationalism and won a large public following. The colonial authorities responded with constitutional changes increasing the voice of the African population while reserving seats for minority communities.

Elections were held in 1958–1959 and again in 1960. The result was overwhelming victory for TANU, which was by this period campaigning for independence as well as majority rule. The new government and the British government agreed at a constitutional conference in London to full independence for Tanganyika in December 1961. Zanzibar achieved independence in 1963 as a separate and sovereign country, under the al-Busaidy sultan.

Tanganyika became a republic in December 1962, one year after achieving independence, and the direct presidential election brought TANU's leader, Julius Nyerere, to the presidency. In 1965 the Constitution was changed to establish a one-party system. Meanwhile, in Zanzibar, a revolution had overthrown the Arab sultan on January 12, 1964, one month since independence; the Constitution was abrogated; Abedi Amani Karume was declared the first African president of the People's, Republic of Zanzibar; and the country became a one-party state under the Afro-Shirazi Party. On April 26, 1964, Tanganyika and Zanzibar united as the United Republic of Tanzania, with Julius Nyerere as president and the head of state, and Karume as his vice president, retaining at the same time the presidency of Zanzibar. In 1971 Karume was assassinated in Zanzibar and Aboud Jumbe succeeded him as president of Zanzibar and vice president of Tanzania. In 1977, the two ruling parties, TANU and the Afro Shirazi Party, merged to form the Chama Cha Mapinduzi (CCM). In 1984 Jumbe resigned his posts and Ali Hassan Mwinyi was elected to replace him in Zanzibar.

In 1985 Nyerere stepped down voluntarily as head of state and Ali Hassan Mwinyi succeeded him as head of state; Idriss Abdul Wakil replaced Mwinyi in Zanzibar. Presidential elections, for the Union, were held every five years from 1965 with, under the one-party system, the electorate voting yes or no to a single presidential candidate. In general elections (held at the same time as the presidential elections) the choice was between two candidates put forward by the CCM. Pressure for reform grew within Tanzania and among international donors. The government of Ali Hassan Mwinyi responded with constitutional changes that permitted opposition parties from 1992 and so brought in a multiparty system under which parliamentary and presidential elections were held in October 1995 and contested by thirteen political patties. In 1990, Abdul Wakil, having completed one term in office, declined to stand for a second term in office in Zanzibar and Salmin Amour replaced him and was elected a few months later as president of Zanzibar and second vice president of the union. Mwinyi stepped down in 1995, having completed constitutionally two terms in office and Benjamin William Mkapa of CCM was elected as head of state of Tanzania.

For further reading, see: Coulson, Andrew. 1982. *Tanzania: A Political Economy*. London: Clarendon Press; Kaniki, M. H. Y. 1979. *Tanzania Under Colonial Rule*. London: Longman; Kimambo, I. N. and Temu, A. J. 1969. *A History of Tanzania*. Evanston: University of Northwestern Press, Published for the Historical Association of Tanzania; McHenry, Dean E. Jr. 1994. *Limited Choices: The Political Struggle for Socialism in Tanzania*. Boulder: Lynne Rienner Publishers; Pratt, Cranford. 1976. *The Critical Phase in Tanzania 1945–68*. Cambridge: Cambridge University Press; Yeager, Rodger. 1989. *Tanzania: An African Experiment*. Boulder: Westview Press.

**TATAR NATIONALISM** Although the Tatars from south Siberia played a major part in the Mongol conquest of Russia in the 13th century and subsequently fought long against Russian counter-thrusts in the 16th century, their national awareness of themselves as a people, in need of a settled territory of their own, was to be a much more recent phenomenon. Indeed, by the time of its emergence in the 19th century, Tatars had, for two centuries, been split apart into different groups in widely dispersed parts of Russia, including the Crimean Tatars by the Black Sea, the Tatars of the Volga and Siberia, and the Nogai Tatars of the north Caucasus. Indeed, they were frequently perceived by Russians and even themselves as but divorced elements within an even larger community of Turkic/Moslem peoples embracing much of Central Asia and south Siberia. The development of a coherent Tatar nationalism and a claim to territory was thus made all the more difficult, even though they persistently managed to resist full assimilation by the Russians, convert en masse to Islam, and actually to embrace some of the neighboring East Finns of the Volga region.

It was the Crimean Ismail Gasprali (1851–1914) who first sought to set aside the alleged decline and decadence of the Tatar/Turkic community and find a new basis for their future survival by taking up a common language reform, modernization of Islamic theology and education, and the creation of a shared identity among the Moslem/Turkic peoples. His was initially more a concept of cultural and spiritual rather than political unity however. Tatar nationalism before 1917 was a macro-national identity among Turkic groups with varying measures of hostility toward their Russian conquerors. For the time being, this unity largely overrode any differences between the coreligionists. By the time of the Russian Moslem Congress of May 1917 there was some division between those who wanted all Moslem/Tatars to be administered as one and those who backed the idea of one Moslem people divided into several state units. Volga Tatars, among the most developed of the Moslem peoples, were at the forefront in this movement and the debates within it, as well as playing a significant part in the new Russian Parliament from its inception in 1906.

After the revolutions of 1917 they were also to play a major part in the quest by Sultan Galiev and others in the 1920s to provide an alternative focus to Moscow for Moslems of the east, from which a Communist model could be spread.

It was the Soviet creation of a specifically Tatar autonomous republic on May 27, 1920, that produced a more active, but also more restricted, form of Tatar nationalism, even though it left 75 percent of narrowly defined Tatars beyond its borders. For Soviet Russia this offered the possibility of more fully dividing the Turkic peoples from each other (for example, the Tatars so-called from the Chuvash and Bashkirs of the Volga) while providing a facade of federalism behind which to continue ruling them from Moscow or through the agency of the Russian population in the area where they had already become a majority by the end of the 18th century. For the Tatars themselves, although Pan-Turkic aspirations continued to exist, the idea of a potentially more autonomous republic could also begin to take root now that they at least had a defined territory. Any Tatar optimism about genuine internationalism being fostered within the new regime was however steadily to be crushed by continued Russification and immigration. Nonetheless, some of the Tatar intelligentsia remained wedded to a rehabilitation of their history, literature, and identity and, by the end of the Soviet regime, a drive for greater real autonomy was present in the Tatar autonomous republic just as it was in places like Chechnya.

This more militant nationalism emerged particularly in the shape of a popular front umbrella organization, the Tatar Public Center (TOTS), founded in 1989. Its manifesto called for an upgrading of the territory to full union republic status, on a par with the likes of Estonia; a more genuinely federal structure, with real sovereignty for the constituent parts in economic affairs, education, law, and purely internal matters such as social provision and culture; more democratic elections and pluralism; equality for minorities; full consultation on further immigration, encouragement of economic development, and on budgetary contributions to the center; closer links with the Tatar diaspora; and full reinstatement of Tatar as the state language alongside Russian. Others complemented this with calls for a Latin script for all the Turkic languages, in place of the Cyrillic imposed by Stalin.

Although not in the ranks of the full republics most likely to gain independence in the short term, the Tatar parliament made a declaration of sovereignty on August 30, 1990, with the territory now to be called Tatarstan. With the fall of the USSR, and the failure to gain the full independence, army, and currency sought by groups like TOTS and the more radical integralist Ittifak (Unity) Party, nationalist efforts, including those of the new style national Communists in the leadership, were now directed at the government of the Russian Federation, of which Tatarstan remained a part. The other issues raised in the TOTS manifesto were all pressed home, undeterred by Yeltsin's resistance to any post-1991 loss of more territory but encouraged by the successes of fellow Moslems in Chechnya.

Among the nationalist advances of the new era, pushed through by overtly nationalist pressure and the government of nationalistically oriented Communists, were the March 1992 referendum supporting an upgraded form of sovereignty against central government wishes; the refusal to sign Russia's new federation treaty, also in March 1992; the inclusion of the declaration of sovereignty in Tatarstan's new constitution of November 1992 and the passage of laws contradicting federal legislation; and the attainment of a power-sharing treaty with Moscow in February 1994, going well beyond the devolution of power contained in the Russian republic constitution. Tatar nationalism was also successful in gaining support for the change of alphabet; in halting the adoption of new Russian internal passports in 1997 (documents in Russian with the Russian two-headed eagle on the cover and no mention of nationality or dual citizenship with Russia and Tatarstan); in opposing the setting up in 1997 of a regional branch of the federal treasury; in adopting protectionist economic measures and import quotas in 1998; and in gaining acceptance of special coins for utility payments and coupons for designated shops as a possible precursor to a separate currency. Tatars have regularly pointed out that Estonia gained its independence with a far smaller population, while Palau's mere 16,000 has not prevented it from membership in the United Nations. Tatarstan is also a relatively well-endowed country, with a skilled labor force and calm ethnic relations, despite the rise of these demands.

Presently blocking the attainment of Tatar nationalist goals is the fact that the entire area is surrounded by Russian territory; the presence of almost as many Russians as Tatars in the republic (as well as other minorities, making 51 percent of the population non-Tatar); dependence on Russia for a number of key resources; division between outright national secessionist groups and the ruling national Communists; the bilateral agreement providing some satisfaction to Russians and Tatars alike; and the caution of the ruling élite.

The best informed works on the Tatars are A. Rorlich's *The Volga Tatars—The Profile of a People in National Resilience* (Hoover Institution, 1986) and "One or more Tatar nations?" in Edward Allworth's *Muslim Communities Reemerge* (Duke University Press, 1994). See also Marie Bennigsen Broxup's "Tatarstan and the Tatars," in G. Smith, ed., *The Nationalities Question in the Post-Soviet States* (Longman, 1996).

## TCHAIKOVSKY, PYOTR ILYICH  1840–1893, Russian composer. A graduate of the newly founded St. Petersburg Conservatory and pupil of the "Westernizer" Anton Rubinstein, Tchaikovsky, who traveled over the world more than any of his contemporaries, positioned his distinctively Russian music within the context of European culture and civilization. From Rubinstein, Tchaikovsky inherited a predilection for the "German" genre of "absolute" music (symphony), and a strong interest in Western literature. His orchestral music was inspired by great works by Shakespeare, Dante, and Byron (the program overtures to *Romeo and Juliet*, *The Tempest*, and *Hamlet*, fantasia *Francesca da Rimini*, and a symphonic poem *Manfred*) and "freed, Tchaikovsky's emotional power to a degree which he would not achieve with the material of Russian plays" (Asafiev). The hero of Tchaikovsky's nonprogrammatic symphonies, a Russian intellect, a Tchaikovsky contemporary, inherited Dostoyevskian suffering and Byronic solitude.

Tchaikovsky was the first Russian composer to put the human life and the human soul in the center of his symphonic concepts, whereas his contemporaries, the composers of the Balakirev Circle, "were tossing between a fervent Romanticism and a populism with its complex of guilt toward the oppressed 'younger brothers'" (Klimovitsky). Quoting Russian folk songs, Tchaikovsky was the first to use them for representation not only of subjects and objects of folk origin, but as a dimension for a musical characterization of the romantic hero alienated from the crowd. His method, leading to "distancing" folk songs from their context, was opposite to the "stylistically pure" folk canon developed by "The Mighty Five."

A distinguished symphonist, Tchaikovsky nevertheless experienced a strong aspiration for opera, stating that "opera and only opera brings you close to people . . . makes you the property not merely of separate little circles but—with luck—of whole nations." Of his nine operas, Tchaikovsky's highest achievements are *Evgeniy Onegin* (1877–1878) and *Pikovaia Dama* (*The Queen of Spades*, 1890), both based on celebrated works by Pushkin. Pushkin's novel *Evgeniy Onegin*, considered by its contemporaries to be "an encyclopedia of Russian life," inspired Tchaikovsky to create the work praised by Sergei Prokofiev as "the most intrinsically Russian opera, in which every role corresponded completely to the Russian character, each in its own way." Tchaikovsky essentially sentimentalized Pushkin's novel, being influenced by another famous Russian literary work, the story *Bednaia Liza* (*Poor Liza*) by Nikolai Karamzin. Tchaikovsky's "Karamzianism" reveals itself, primarily, in the shift of the main protagonist from the ironic and cold-minded hero (Onegin) to the romantic and sentimental heroine (Tatiana) who, by an association with Karamzin's Liza, was perceived by the sympathetic Russian audience as "Poor Tania." The musical language of Tchaikovsky's *Evgeniy Onegin*, based mainly on the idioms of Russian contemporary urban art song (*bytovoi romans*), which were extremely popular in the second part of the 19th century, was perceived in Russia as genuinely national. Paradoxically, in the West, Tchaikovsky's musical style was perceived as universally European, since the relatively new genre of *bytovoi romans* remained practically unknown abroad.

In contrast to *Evgeniy Onegin*, Pushkin's *Pikovaia Dama* presents just a small fragment of Russian life shown through the prism of a "gambling story." Again, as in the case of the libretto of *Evgeniy Onegin*, Tchaikovsky introduces Karamzinian accents into Pushkin's concept. Emphasizing a sentimental plot line, Tchaikovsky changes Pushkin's portrait of German: a primary motivation of German's crime became neither his gambling passion, nor his striving for money, but his true love to Liza. Against Pushkin, but in accord with Karamzin, Tchaikovsky ends his opera with the suicide of a heroine: Tchaikovsky's Liza, like Poor Liza of Karamzin, drowns herself. Moreover, Tchaikovsky adds the suicide of a hero as well: German stabs himself. Another source of Tchaikovsky's inspiration came from the literary works of Dostoyevsky. Describing the process of darkening of German's consciousness by musical means, Tchaikovsky undoubtedly took into considera-

tion the psychoanalytical findings of Dostoyevsky. Russian audiences of the 1890s celebrated *Pikovaia Dama* for truthful emotional portraits of contemporary characters, and for distinctively Russian musical discourse originating as in the *Evgeniy Onegin*, from the genre of urban *bytovoi romans*. Some dimensions of *Pikovaia Dama* turned out to be prophetic for Russian art of the 20th century. For example, Tchaikovsky's musical stylization of the 18th century Russian Baroque influenced the artists of the group *Mir Iskusstva*; Tchaikovsky's image of St. Petersburg was of a city inhabited by mysteries and phantasmas, inspired young poets of the Russian Silver Age.

In Russia, Tchaikovsky's *Evgeniy Onegin* and *Pikovaia Dama* "achieved the status of art works congenial to Pushkin, constituting the pride of Russian national poetry" (Dmitry Shostakovich). Trying to define the Rusianness of Tchaikovsky's music, Hermann Laroche opined that "Tchaikovsky combined in a very complicated way a cosmopolitan responsiveness and ability to absorb everything with a strong national Russian underpinning." Reflecting on the national character of his music, Tchaikovsky wrote: "It seems to me that I am truly gifted with the ability to express truthfully, sincerely, and simply the feelings, moods, and images suggested by a text. In this sense I am a realist and fundamentally a Russian."

The important primary source is *"To My Best Friend." Correspondence between Tchaikovsky and Nadezhda von Meck, 1876–1878*, translated by Galina von Meck (Oxford: Clarendon Press, 1993). The best biography is Alexander Poznansky's *Tchaikovsky: The Quest for the Inner Man* (New York: Schirmer Books, 1991). The influential work of Russian criticism is Boris Asafiev's *O muzyke Chaikovskogo* (Leningrad: Muzyka, 1972). David Brown's four-volume monograph *Tchaikovsky* (New York: Norton, 1978–1992) presents traditional Western criticism. A contemporary criticism is Richard Taruskin's "P.I. Tchaikovsky and the Ghetto" and "Tchaikovsky and the Human: A Centennial Essay" in his *Defining Russia Musically* (Princeton, N.J.: Princeton University Press, 1997). A recent Russian contribution is Arkady Klimovitsky's essays "Otzvuki russkogo sentimentalizmav pushkinskikh operakh Chaikovskogo" (*Muzykal'naia Akademia*, 1995, No. 1), and "Chaikovskij and das russishe 'Silberne Zeitalter'" in *Caikovskij-Studien, Band 1*, Thomas Kohlhase, ed. (Mainz: Schott, 1995).

**TER-PETROSSIAN, LEVON** 1945–, President of the Republic of Armenia from 1991 to 1998. Ter-Petrossian's political career was launched in 1988, when he joined a political movement demanding the administrative transfer of an Amernian-populated region called Nagorno-Karabakh from Azerbaijani to Armenian jurisdiction. Ter-Petrossian quickly emerged as the leader of what was first called the Karabakh movement, and later became known as the Armenian National Movement (ANM). He played an extremely important role in shaping the agenda and the philosophy of the ANM, which soon expanded to encompass other issues in addition to the Karabakh problem. Most importantly, the movement embraced the idea of independence from the Soviet Union, which was more controversial for Armenia than for a number of other Soviet republics demanding secession from the Soviet Union. For Armenia the idea of secession was especially controversial due to the long-standing perception among Armenian political élites that Armenia could not survive as an independent state either politically or economically. According to this view Armenia's problematic history with its neighbors, and Turkey in particular, as well as the fact that it was landlocked and poor in natural resources made the idea of independence untenable.

Under Ter-Petrossian's leadership, the ANM challenged this approach, and asserted that independence was the best policy to secure Armenia's survival and prosperity. Ter-Petrossian understood, however, that independence required establishing nonantagonistic relations with all of Armenia's neighbors, including Turkey and Azerbaijan. Ter-Petrossian and the ANM maintained that conflicts should be settled through direct negotiation and mutual compromise, and Armenia should jettison unrealistic aspirations, which inevitably lead to reliance, and therefore dependence, on third countries. The ANM won the parliamentary elections in 1990, and Ter-Petrossian became chairman of the Supreme Soviet of Armenian SSR. Soon thereafter a referendum on independence was conducted, and on September 23, 1991, Armenia declared independence. A month later Ter-Petrossian was elected the first president of the new Republic of Armenia.

The first term of his presidency was marked by the war in Nagorno-Karabakh, which gradually escalated after the Soviet Union collapsed. Efforts to control the escalation and find a negotiated solution failed. Armenia also went through a dramatic economic decline due to the war, the resulting economic blockade by Azerbaijan and Turkey, and the restructuring of its Soviet-style economy. The Armenian side did prevail on the battlefield, nonetheless, and in 1994 a cease-fire agreement was reached with Azerbaijan. Ter-Petrossian's government also succeeded in arresting the economic decline in 1994 and registering limited economic growth. The

catastrophic decline in living standards, however, had eroded Ter-Petrossian's popularity. He won the elections for a second term in 1996 with a very narrow margin, and the election results were contested by the opposition.

In 1998, two years into his second term, Ter-Petrossian endorsed a draft agreement proposed by the OSCE to settle the Karabakh conflict. A set of powerful members of his own government, including the prime minister, the minister of interior and security, and the defense minister, came out against the agreement, and a large group of Parliament members defected to the opposition, which turned Ter-Petrossian's support base in the legislature into a minority. After dominating Armenian politics for ten years, he resigned in February 1998.

**TERRITORIAL IMPERATIVE**  By its very nature, the study of nationalism is interdisciplinary. A significant contribution from the fields of biology, anthropology, and zoology is the concept of the *territorial imperative*. In essence, this theory maintains that human beings are merely advanced animals, driven at a base level by instinct and unconscious impulses. Like animals that strive to stake out and defend territory for themselves or their kin group, human beings establish certain areas as private property, mark it, and attack those who trespass. Nationalism is merely the open manifestation of this phenomenon. Land ownership and private property are not human constructions, but rather natural and inherent characteristics of human existence.

Although there is little formal unity to this theoretical framework, its proponents trace its roots to the works of zoologist Konrad Lorenz, biologist Robert Ardrey, and the anthropologist Desmond Morris, collectively known as the LAM group. Lorenz argued that human beings were driven by many of the same instincts as the "lower" animals; in particular, aggression. While humans can sometimes mitigate against aggressive impulses, the potential for aggressive actions, especially against outsiders, always remains. Ardrey expanded on Lorenz's findings in his seminal work, *The Territorial Imperative*, in which he argued in favor of man's "innate territorial nature," deemed to be one of the basic and most important principles of human evolution. The defense of territory draws individuals together and serves as the catalyst for the human qualities of self-sacrifice, altruism, sympathy, and trust. Xenophobia is seen as the flip-side of the territorial imperative. Although Morris rejected the notion of man's inherent aggressiveness, he argued that man, little more than a naked ape, was driven to aggressive actions by genetically determined responses to certain environmental conditions and signals sent to us by others. This more interactive account of the territorial imperative does not detract from its place in the LAM paradigm.

The territorial imperative theory sparked significant debate and, as Louis Snyder observed, it "fell into the whirlpool of the old hereditary-environment clash." The strongest criticism of the LAM paradigm was that it oversimplified human existence and the causes of aggressive behavior by improperly taking animal behavior and making an analogy to human beings. The work was deemed ambiguous, impressionistic, distorted, and, in some cases, simply erroneous. On the other hand, the LAM paradigm had a number of defenders who focused on the growing body of research on social-psychology. While admitting that its early proponents may have oversimplified their findings, some contend that more experimentation needs to be done before it can be discarded out of hand. The debate between the instinctivists, like the LAM group, and the neobehaviorists, who argue that human actions are a reflection of one's environment and social conditioning, continues.

For further reading, see Konrad Lorenz, *On Aggression*; Robert Ardrey, *The Territorial Imperative*; Desmond Morris, *The Naked Ape; Man and Aggression*, Ashley Montagu, ed. (Oxford University Press, 1973); and Louis L. Snyder, "Nationalism and the Territorial Imperative," in *Canadian Review of Studies in Nationalism* 3 (Autumn 1975), pp. 1–21.

**TERRORISM**  Terrorism is illegitimate violence used to try to affect change, often for political or ideological purposes. Groups, states, and individuals can engage in acts of terrorism. Targets of terrorism may be either civilians or military personnel. The moral, legal, and political implications of the application of the term to an act have spawned the phrase "One man's terrorist is another man's freedom fighter."

Terrorism as a subject of discourse has become quite prominent. One reason for the increased attention it has drawn is the growth of modern technology. Communication, and access to it, has spread so that those seeking to affect political change, whether they be in a small European village or a large city in Africa, have a means to publicize their justifications and their actions. Groups labeled as "terrorist" regularly issue press releases, invite interviews, and maintain web pages.

Alternately the growth and power of the media and attention it has paid to terrorism has been a factor. Stories about terrorist groups the world over regularly merit television and print headlines. Yet another reason for the popularization of the discussion around terrorism is changes in the nature of warfare. Although terrorists are not necessarily at war with another individual, group, or state, their ability to engage in violence has changed with technological advances in the fields of weaponry and military strategy.

The vulnerability of the United States to terrorism has also been a factor leading to increased discussion and activity around the prevention of terrorism and states policy toward perceived terrorists. With the bombing of the World Trade Center, an act of international terrorism, and the bomb that destroyed the federal building in Oklahoma City, an act of domestic terrorism, the United States has viewed it to its advantage to raise the level and volume of discussion.

The United Nations through the actions of member states has been an active participant in the efforts to define and prevent terrorism. Numerous resolutions, recommendations, and studies have been produced by the General Assembly, Special Rapporteurs, and others within the UN structure. A defining purpose of the United Nations, as stated in its charter, is to maintain international peace and security. Terrorism, particularly that carried out on an international scale, threatens international peace and security, so it is no wonder why this international organization has been active on the issue.

Groups and individuals, whether ethnic or religious, trying to affect political change are often accused of engaging in terrorism or are labeled as terrorists. These groups often define themselves and are perceived by their supporters as national liberation movements, thus the connection with nationalism. Modern examples include but are certainly not limited to the Irish Republican Army (IRA), the ETA (the Basque movement), the Palestine Liberation Organization (PLO; prior to their establishing the Palestinian National Authority), and the African National Congress (ANC; prior to their becoming an accepted political party in power). Although all of these groups have espoused a kind of nationalism particular to their situation, all have also been labeled terrorists at one stage of their existence or another.

Some so-called terrorist groups in an effort to further their nationalist aspirations do engage in the bombing of buildings and cars, the murder of individuals, and the hijacking of airplanes. Numerous international legal mechanisms exist to deal with these acts. They include treaties and conventions relating to offenses committed on board aircraft, the taking of hostages, and crimes against internationally protected persons. Despite these legal proscriptions against some of the deeds of terrorists there is a lack of international consensus on whom may be designated a terrorist.

One international legal scholar, Roslyn Higgins, has stated that terrorism cannot be defined solely by the acts committed or targets chosen. Another international legal scholar, Richard Falk, has defined the "good terrorist" as one for whom political violence is a last resort and is used to prevent the occurrence of greater evils. Falk acknowledges the contradictions of the good terrorist as one who ultimately renounces violence and terrorism.

The transition from illegitimate liberation movement or terrorist organization to legitimate political actor exemplifies the pragmatism of the international community. While some certainly continue to label the Palestinian National Authority as terrorists they are now nonetheless an internationally accepted player on the international political stage. The need to find a solution to the problems in the Middle East has necessitated an acceptance and facilitation, albeit limited, of the nationalist goals of the former PLO. Whether these needs are based on economics, political expediency, humanitarian necessity, or a changing of the political guard they occur around the world and bring certain nationalist aspirations out of the demonized realm of terrorism and onto the platform of discussion of self-determination and sovereignty.

## THATCHER, MARGARET

1925–, In the literature on Margaret Thatcher's rule, no word appears with greater frequency than *revolution*. Her leadership dealt with change, not with mere stewardship. Many viewed that change as "radical" and "nationalist." Her message of radical conservationism bore her name: "Thatcherism." No other British prime minister has had the suffix "ism" attached to his name. The first woman to lead a British political party or a major Western nation, Thatcher had the determination of a visionary and the ruthlessness of an outsider. She did not come from the establishment and never owed her success to it. She was ready to admit that modern Britain was a failure, and she could not understand why its leaders were so content with themselves while the country performed so poorly. To her, they seemed interested only in managing Britain's decline.

In the 1980s Thatcher dominated her country and party like no leader since Winston Churchill. Her kind of leadership involved leading people where they initially did not want to go. Former Tory cabinet member Norman Tebbit said that "she has changed not only her own party but her country and has compelled the others to adjust themselves to that agenda." She did so by the sheer force of her personality and the rock-hard conviction of her ideas. She was a "conviction politi-

cian," a term which she herself coined. In a speech given shortly after her election in 1979, she asserted that "in politics it is the half-hearted who lose. It is those with conviction who carry the day." She rejected the cozy politics of compromise and repudiated the very foundation of politics in Britain: the consensus under which it had been governed since the 1950s. She once said that "I am in politics because of the conflict between good and evil, and I believe that in the end good will triumph." The fervor of her conviction paralyzed those who wavered. Her biographer, Hugo Young, called her greatest gift her "inspirational certainty."

Thatcher was always a populist, who had an uncanny knack for capturing the public mood, whether the issue was nuclear weapons or South Africa. Nevertheless, she was the ultimate example that a political leader need not be popular. She was charismatic and successful, but she was autocratic, unbending, and unloved. By the end of 1981 she was the most unpopular prime minister since polling had begun. But she declared: "I will not change just to court popularity."

For her, fear and respect were far more important in politics than love and affection. She had authority and respect because of her courage and what she accomplished and represented. She strode resolutely forward to remake her country in her own self-image: brisk, hard-working, frugal, and self-sufficient. She combined some of the best 19th-century values with 20th-century energy. She rejected the spirit of failure. She was a strong leader who entered office with a sense of mission: to make Britain great again or, as she noted, to put the "Great" back into Britain. "I came to office with one deliberate intent: to change Britain from a dependent to a self-reliant society—from a give-it-to-me to a do-it-yourself nation; to a get-up-and-go, instead of a sit-back-and-wait-for-it Britain."

Thatcher won respect because of her combination of decisiveness and luck. Napoleon's standard question about his generals, "Has he luck?", could also be applied to her. She had luck! It has been said that the world stands aside for a "man" who knows where he is going. When she moved into the prime minister's office, she promised "three years of unparalleled austerity," and for three years the pain of Thatcherism was far more evident than the benefits. Nevertheless, she held firm to her monetarist policies, vowing that "I will not stagger from expedient to expedient." She declared that the voters did not want "a government to be so flexible that it became invertebrate. You don't want a government of flexi-toys."

By 1982 her party was well behind in the polls, and she seemed to be heading for sure defeat in the next elections. Then the unexpected occurred. The Argentines gave her the chance to reassert herself and soar in the polls. Their troops invaded a small group of offshore islands that had long been settled and ruled by the British. Until then Thatcher had neglected this festering problem and was unprepared to deal with it. Nevertheless, she responded quickly and galvanized the nation with her firmness and resolution in organizing the recapture of the Falkland Islands. The British basked again briefly in imperial glory, and she became an international figure who startled a world that had become almost supine in the face of naked aggression. An overwhelming majority of them applauded their leader for her ability to handle the crisis. Her wartime leadership greatly improved her electoral prospects. In December 1981 her approval rating had stood at 25 percent, making her the least popular prime minister since World War II; six months later her popularity had doubled.

In foreign affairs, she was the first British prime minister since Harold Macmillan to have real influence over both superpowers. She came to office with no clear set of foreign policy priorities, and her moral approach to politics was less suited to this complicated arena than to domestic politics. Nevertheless, she set a bold example of resolution, as she strode the world stage commanding respect and exercising influence out of all proportion to the United Kingdom's power and size. Her frank, personal diplomacy enhanced her and her country's influence.

Anticommunism had strongly shaped her opinions since the war, and these sentiments were strengthened in the mid-1970s by Aleksandr Solzhenitsyn's attacks on Marxism-Leninism. During her first term, she continually criticized Moscow's leaders for their blustering, menacing behavior, and human rights violations. But after her 1983 victory, she became convinced that Western nations should encourage change in the Soviet Union in a more constructive way. Her government began advocating an opening to the East and a search for practical forms of cooperation. She recognized Mikhail Gorbachev as a different kind of Soviet leader. She invited him to visit London in December 1984, four months before he became leader of the Soviet Communist Party. He impressed everyone with his candid and independent thinking. At the conclusion of his visit, she told the BBC that "I like Mr. Gorbachev; we can can do business together." She called for a realistic, assessment of the USSR and warned against "starry-eyed thinking that one day Communism will collapse like a pack of cards, because it will not." She assumed a role as interlocutor between the superpowers and convinced President Ronald Reagan that he too could get along with the

new Soviet leader. She thus played a significant part in winning the Cold War. Because she was the West's most forceful spokesperson for individual rights, democracy, and the virtues of capitalism, she was greatly respected in the ex-Communist world.

She was implacably hostile to the IRA, but she signed the 1985 Anglo-Irish declaration that, for the first time, accepted the Irish Republic's claim to have a say in Northern Irish affairs. She was respected in the British Commonwealth. However, Britain's relations with many of its partners deteriorated because of her opposition to economic sanctions against South Africa.

She was admired abroad, especially in America, more than she was at home. Her political instincts had been shaped when Britain's allies were across the Atlantic and the enemy in Europe. At a time when most of Britain's foreign policy and business elite had long accepted that the United Kingdom's relations with Europe were at least important as its Atlantic ties, she gave absolute priority to the alliance with the United States. "No one of my generation can forget that America has been the principal architect of a peace in Europe which has lasted forty years." The Americans appreciated her unflagging support, but the "special relationship" was not what it once was. Washington relied on Thatcher to block the threat of a closed "fortress Europe," which, it was feared, could be created by the EC's move toward a single market in 1992. But her obstreperousness toward her European counterparts risked driving Britain toward the periphery, not the heart of Europe, where it could have real influence. Also, the end of the Cold War somewhat diminished America's need for a trusty British ally in Europe. Increasingly important for the United States were relations with the EC itself and with such new powers as Germany, whose unification in 1990 Thatcher had opposed.

Her image in the EC suffered because of her battles to change the Common Agricultural Program (CAP), to reduce the United Kingdom's budget bill to Brussels, and to oppose the transfer of power to community institutions. She was in favor of European economic and political cooperation, and she never contemplated taking the United Kingdom out of the EC. As a member of Heath's cabinet, she had been bound by collective responsibility and had therefore supported British entry in the 1972 referendum. But she insisted that "we must look after British interests," and she was sensitive about grants of British sovereignty to bureaucrats in Brussels. "I do not believe in a federal Europe, and I think to ever compare it with the United States of America is absolutely ridiculous." Always the consummate populist, she was also well aware that her critical stance toward the EC was popular with British voters. This domestic political bonus helped inspire her to take an uncompromising stance toward her EC counterparts. Roy Jenkins said in 1985, while he was president of the European Commission, that "as a proponent of the British case, she does have the advantage of being almost totally impervious to how much she offends other people. . . . I have seen her when she was a new prime minister surrounded by others who were against her and being unmoved by this in a way that many other people would find difficult to withstand."

Her objections to European unification did not endear her in European capitals. Piet Dankaert, president of the European Parliament from 1982 to 1984, described her as "the witch in the European fairy tale—always clearly recognizable and always the person liable to turn everything upside down." She had no sympathy for her continental colleagues, as she made clear in 1984: "There are nine of them being tiresome, and only one of me. I can cope with the nine of them, so they ought to be able to stand one of me." Even at home she was never able to persuade all her cabinet to embrace her views on Britain's role in the EC. Her deputy prime minister, Sir Geoffrey Howe, who launched her downfall because of unbridgeable differences on European policy, accused her of seeing a continent "positively teeming with ill-intentioned people scheming, in her words, to extinguish democracy."

## THOREAU, HENRY DAVID  1817-1862, American essayist, moral philosopher, poet, and naturalist; born Concord, Massachusetts. Admired by Mohandas Ghandi for his contribution to the theory of civil disobedience (even though Thoreau was not committed to nonviolence) and by essayist Ralph Waldo Emerson for his personification of the American spirit, Thoreau was a prominent member of the American transcendentalists, a defender of individualism and nonconformity, and an active participant in the American antislavery movement.

In his principal writings, including his essay "On the Duty of Civil Disobedience" (1849), *Walden* (1854), and later lectures and addresses on slavery, Thoreau is concerned with the tendency of government to interfere with the independence of individuals, as well as with the eagerness of many individuals to place their consciences in the unworthy keeping of the state. Thoreau wrote, "Must the citizen ever for a moment, or in the least degree, resign his conscience to the legislator? Why has every man a conscience, then?"

Thoreau's life was punctuated by two famous symbolic acts. In 1845, at the suggestion of Ellery Chan-

ning, Thoreau built a crude hut on land owned by Emerson near Walden Pond, about two miles away from the center of Concord. He moved in to his cabin—appropriately—on July 4, 1845, Independence Day, and remained there for two years, living on the very edge of society, but not beyond it. Thoreau conceived of his Walden sojourn as an experiment in living, writing, "I went to the woods because I wished to live deliberately, to front only the essential facts of life, and see if I could not learn what it had to teach, and not, when I came to die, discover that I had not lived."

In 1846, Thoreau was arrested for failure to pay his poll tax, which he argued helped sanction and practically sustain the institution of slavery, as well as an unjust war against Mexico. For this early refusal, Thoreau spent a single night in the county lockup, before the tax was paid, probably by his Aunt Maria. Thoreau explained his defiance of the law: "It is not a man's duty, as a matter of course, to devote himself to the eradication of any, even the most enormous wrong; he may still properly have other concerns to engage him; but it is his duty, at least, to wash his hands of it, and if he gives it no thought longer, not to give it practically his support."

In general, Thoreau preferred individual expressions of conscientious disobedience to the work of organizations and committees. Even so, Thoreau worked as a conductor on the Underground Railroad, during the 1840s and 1850s, harboring fugitive slaves on their way to the safety of Canada. He also spoke out against the institution of slavery in public lectures and addresses. In his 1854 address, "Slavery in Massachusetts," Thoreau's venom was directed not toward the southern, slave-holding states but, rather, toward citizens of the northern, free states, who remained complicit in the peculiar institution through their submission to the Fugitive Slave Law, which required them to participate in the capture of runaway slaves. Thoreau also defended the radical abolitionist John Brown, after his failed raid on the federal armory at Harpers Ferry, Virginia, praising Brown, in an 1859 address, for having "the courage to face his country herself when she was wrong."

In his own time, Thoreau was generally regarded as a failure. He never had a regular career and, after a brief stint as a teacher and another in his family's pencil business, he earned a meager living by working sporadically as a land surveyor, woodsman, boat builder, house builder, and carpenter. His books, which are now universally recognized as classics in American literature, sold poorly. Even *Walden* sold only about 2000 copies in Thoreau's lifetime

Nonetheless, Thoreau has become something of a

cultural icon, inspiring and energizing subsequent generations of political activists, radicals, and nonconformists. And, among the American transcendentalists, Thoreau has endured best, in part because of the clarity of his commitments and his willingness to translate his ideals into personal action.

A fine general biography of Thoreau is Walter Harding, *The Days of Henry Thoreau,* 2nd ed. (Princeton, 1992). An excellent intellectual biography is Robert D. Richardson, *Henry Thoreau: A Life of the Mind* (University of California Press, 1986).

## TIBETAN NATIONALISM

**TIBETAN NATIONALISM**  Tibet, often called the "roof of the world" because of its location on a high plateau in the Himalayan mountains in South Asia, no longer exists as an independent republic because of a Chinese takeover in 1949–1950. Tibetan nationalism persists as a movement, however, perpetuated by a well-organized government-in-exile hosted by India and the charismatic leadership of Tenzen Gyatso, the Fourteenth Dalai Lama.

The Tibetan struggle for autonomy far outdates the modern notion of nationalism, and Tibetan history is full of stories about efforts to develop an independent Tibetan culture. Since the 16th century the Tibetan people have been held together to varying degrees by the institution of the Dalai Lama, a title ironically conferred by the powerful Tumed Mongol leader Altan Khan. The Dalai Lama is regarded as the incarnation of a *bodhisattva* Avalokiteshvara, a mythic monkey believed to be the progenitor of the Tibetans and a figure of great compassion.

After the death of each Dalai Lama the search begins for the child into whose body the soul of the deceased has entered. In 1642 the Dalai Lamas became not only the spiritual but also the political rulers of the Tibetan peoples and, in fact at the time, most of the Mongols became Tibetan Buddhists as well.

In modern times the Tibetans first faced domination by the British colonialists who considered Tibet as a trade route to China and a buffer zone between Russia and British India. At the turn of the century the Indians entered Tibet, allegedly on a political mission; they were met with Tibetan resistance that was suppressed by violence. The Dalai Lama fled to China. Three years later the British granted the Chinese suzerainty over Tibet (without consulting the Tibetans). The Chinese chose to take over direct control of Tibet militarily in 1910 for the first time in ten centuries; the Dalai Lama fled to India.

After the Chinese Revolution in 1911–1912 the Tibetans expelled the Chinese and declared their independence. In 1949 the new Chinese Communist government "liberated" Tibet. After an outbreak of violence following a popular uprising in Lhasa in 1959, the Dalai Lama once again fled to India as did many of his followers.

The Dalai Lama set up a government-in-exile in Dharamsala, India, and appealed to the world community to take up their cause. The Tibetans formed a network of communities in exile, a system of public schools, a health care system, and a process for resettling refugees in new homes in various countries while at the same time retaining their connection to the broader Tibetan community. The parallels between the exiled Tibetans and the Jewish diaspora has not escaped the Dalai Lama's attention and he has consulted with rabbinical leaders for advice on how to maintain a religious community among a people who are scattered across the face of the earth.

A believer in the Buddhist ancient concept of ahimsa (nonharmfulness) and a follower of Gandhi, the Dalai Lama has followed a strictly nonviolent strategy in his construction of a Tibetan nationalist movement. As he travels around the world heralding the Tibetan independence cause, he also speaks to people about how to live more satisfying lives filled with inner peace and to apply nonviolence to large-scale social problems.

Not only did he receive the Nobel Peace Prize for his efforts, he has also endeared himself to many people around the world and become an outspoken advocate of nonviolence in human affairs.

## TILAK, B. G.

**TILAK, B. G.**  1856–1920, One of the most influential predecessors of a specifically Hindu form of Indian nationalism, Bal Gangadhar Tilak was born to a high caste (Brahman) family in the west Indian state of Maharashtra. Like many young, educated men of his generation, Tilak studied law; but unlike many of his peers, he chose not to enter government service, putting his energy instead into journalism.

Tilak combined social conservatism and political extremism, using his Marathi-language publications to arouse public support for traditional Hindu values and to oppose British rule. He promoted the celebration of annual festivals dedicated to the Hindu god Ganesh and to the 17th-century Maratha hero, Shivaji, as ways of concretizing national sentiment in the people. In recent years, popular commemorations of Shivaji, a warrior who challenged Mogul (Muslim) rule in Maharashtra, have been associated with a politicized Hinduism and the rise of the Hindu nationalist Bharatiya Janata (Indian People's) Party (BJP) and the Shiv Sena in Maharashtra.

As the Indian nationalist movement gathered strength in the late 19th and early 20th centuries, two currents—known as moderate and extremist—emerged. While the moderates shared many values of English liberalism and anticipated the gradual evolution of India toward self-government, extremists like Tilak rejected both British rule and much of Western culture, particularly the secular view of politics held by most moderates. Tilak was an early advocate of *swaraj* (self-rule) and *swadeshi* (economic self-reliance), both precursors to Gandhi's noncooperation and civil disobedience movements. Although he never personally used violent methods, Tilak was twice arrested by the British for encouraging violence. The first detention was relatively short, but the second arrest, in 1908, resulted in six years of confinement in Burma.

Tilak's assertion of the authority and superiority of traditional Hindu culture was the subject of his three books, one of which was a lengthy social commentary on the *Bhagavad Gita*, the ancient sacred poem of Hinduism. Rejecting the moderates' position of reforming Hindu customs, Tilak subscribed to an organic theory of society and supported the organization of Indian society along caste lines, the maintenance of the privileged position of the upper castes, and the seclusion of women. His positions alienated many Muslims from the nationalist movement and also contributed to the 1907 schism of the Indian National Congress, the chief nationalist organization opposing British rule.

After his return from imprisonment in 1914, Tilak moderated his nationalism to the extent that he supported mainstream Congress positions such as contesting elections that were part of the British reform effort and signing a pact with the All-India Muslim League to pursue mutual nationalist goals. By the time of his death in 1920, the earlier Moderate–extremist split had been replaced by unity behind the new leadership of Mohandas K. Gandhi. Tilak is remembered through the title Lokamanya ("Honored by the People") and his commitment to building popular nationalist support through vernacular media and assertive Hinduism. His legacy of cultural nationalism has endured in the persistent appeal of militant Hindu organizations, such as the BJP and the paramilitary Rashtriya Swayamsevak Sangh.

## TISZA, KÁLMÁN  1830–1902, A Calvinist politician from the northeastern section of Hungary, Count Tisza came to prominence in 1859 with his opposition to the Protestant Patent, a legislative effort to limit the autonomy of Hungary's Protestant churches. In 1861, he became the first leader of the *Határozati Párt* (Resolution Faction) in the Hungarian Parliament and, with

Kálmán Ghyczy, he formed the core of the leadership of the independence-oriented (left-center) parliamentary block. He was Parliament's leading anti-Habsburg spokesman, regularly and resolutely denouncing Vienna for violating the Hungarian nation's ancient political rights. He fiercely opposed the Compromise of 1867, which legally transformed Austria-Hungary into a dual empire. In 1875 he reversed his course, arguing that opposition to the agreement might now lead to Hungary's demise or annihilation. He abandoned his former stance and joined forces with Ferenc Deák's Liberal Party, which cooperated with Vienna. This change of heart apparently impressed Emperor Franz Joseph, who appointed Tisza minister of the interior for the Hungarian half of the Austro-Hungarian Empire in 1875. Later that same year, the emperor named Tisza prime minister of Hungary, a post he held continually until 1890.

Tisza's real support came from the gentry and his variant of Hungarian nationalism was typically chauvinistic and paternalistic. His concept of the nation was one of a noble *natio*, in which the civil rights and democratic privileges extended only to the ancient Hungarian nobility, which did include nonethnic Hungarians. Though he professed to agree with the idea of universal suffrage in principle, he backtracked by arguing that conditions in Hungary were not suitable for its implementation. Using corrupt parliamentary practices, Tisza consistently beat back all measures he perceived as threats to the political supremacy of the Hungarian nobility, such as expanded suffrage, or to Hungarian cultural supremacy, such as educational and language rights for Hungary's ethnic minorities.

Under Kálmán Tisza's leadership, Hungary's political system devolved into a patronage system in which advance depended less on talent than connections and slavish party loyalty. Tisza's Liberal Party, which was liberal only to the extent that supported constitutionalism and religious toleration, consolidated its power but was unable to develop any true governing principle. On the other hand, his half-measures and patchwork solutions, general commitment to free trade, and defense of the political relationship with Vienna provided Hungary with the stability it needed to further the process of economic modernization begun in the Reform Era and the post-1848 Bach period.

Presently, no biography of Kálmán Tisza exists. However, his politics and rule are mentioned extensively in András Gerö's *The Hungarian Parliament (1867–1918)*. *A Mirage of Power*, published in 1997 as part of Columbia's Social Science Monograph series and in Gábor Vermes' biography of Kálmán's son István, *István Tisza*,

*The Liberal Vision and Conservative Statecraft of a Magyar Nationalist,* published in 1985. Additionally, numerous well-known histories of the Habsburg Empire, such as C. A. Macartney's *The Habsburg Empire 1790–1918* and Robert Kann's *A History of the Habsburg Empire 1526–1918,* cover aspects of Tisza's career.

**TITO, JOSIP BROZ.** 1892-1980, Politician and Communist leader. Born in Kumrovec, Croatia, which was then part of the Austro-Hungarian monarchy, Tito was of mixed Croat-Slovene parentage. In January 1915, during World War I, he was mobilized and served in the Austro-Hungarian army on the Russian front. Captured that spring, he spent the rest of the war as a prisoner in Russia. Released after the February 1917 revolution in Russia, he eventually served with the Bolsheviks during the Russian civil war.

In 1920 Tito returned to what was then the Kingdom of the Serbs, Croats and Slovenes, commonly referred to as Yugoslavia. He found employment as a metal worker in Zagreb and soon joined the Communist Party of Yugoslavia (KPJ). By 1927 he was an important activist in the party's Zagreb (Croatia) section, and was imprisoned the following year. Upon his release Tito went to the Soviet Union. In December 1934, while in Moscow, he was elected to the politburo of the KPJ's Central Committee. In Moscow Tito served in the Yugoslav Section of the Communist International's (Comintern) Balkan Secretariat. At the Comintern's Seventh Congress (1935) he served as a member of the Yugoslav delegation. He returned to Yugoslavia in 1936, and the following year, after the Comintern dismissed the entire leadership of the KPJ, he was made general secretary of the KPJ.

Before World War II, the KPJ was a relatively small and factionalized party, weakened even further by government persecution. But during the war Tito led the partisan movement, known formally as the National Liberation Army, against the Axis occupiers and their native collaborators, as well as to the Chetnik forces that fought to restore the royalist Yugoslav government-in-exile. In November 1942, during the partisan occupation of the Bosnian town Bihać, Tito formed a political wing known as the Anti-Fascist Council for the National Liberation of Yugoslavia (AVNOJ). In November 1943, Tito's partisans held the second session of AVNOJ in Jajce (Bosnia). There they formed a temporary government, the National Committee for the Liberation of Yugoslavia, and announced their intention to create a federal republic after the war. Tito was named leader of this republic and marshal of Yugoslavia. By that point, the Western Allies, realizing that the partisans were offering stiffer resistance against the Axis than the Chetniks, shifted their support to Tito.

In November 1945 Tito was formally elected prime minister of the Federal People's Republic of Yugoslavia, which was renamed the Federal Socialist Republic of Yugoslavia in 1948. In 1953 Tito became president, and in 1974 was named president for life. Of all the new Communist states of East Central Europe, only Tito's Yugoslavia had managed to achieve power without the assistance of the Soviet Red Army. As such, Tito's Yugoslavia demonstrated greater independence than the other Communist regimes. This was at the root of split between Tito and the Soviet leader Joseph Stalin in 1948, when Yugoslavia was expelled from the Soviet-backed Communist Information Bureau (Cominform). After the break, the KPJ was renamed the League of Communists of Yugoslavia (SKJ) and communist Yugoslavia charted an independent course both domestically and abroad.

To promote a socialist Yugoslav identity and nationalism, Tito introduced a federal system that formally provided for equality between the country's six federal republics. In foreign policy, Tito became a leading proponent of the Nonaligned movement, which sought to pursue a middle course between the Soviet Union and United States during the Cold War.

**TOJO, HIDEKI** 1884–1948, Born in Tokyo and became lieutenant general when Japan was following a path to fascism. Hideki Tojo was a member of the Tosei faction, which criticized the cabinet for being responsible for the economic depression that had beset the country since 1929. The Tosei faction and other members of the right wing launched a coup d'état in 1936, killing the cabinet members and police officers. The military officials, led by Tojo, literally seized control of Japanese politics for ten years from the mid-1930's.

Tojo played an important role in the army, promoting military expansion in the neighboring countries and the declaration of war against England and America in the early 1940s. He became prime minister in October 1941, then declared the war against America and England, attacking Pearl Harbor in December. Although Germany and Italy joined Japan to fight against the former Soviet Union, these two countries surrendered before the war ended. Due to the aggravation of the war and a lack of subsistence in Japan, Tojo received criticism from his followers and the Japanese people as well. He finally resigned from the cabinet in 1944.

The war ended with Japan's acceptance of the Potsdam declaration in 1945. The Allied Force General Headquarters was established in Tokyo, demilitarizing

Japanese fascism and promoting democracy in politics. In the same year, the Tokyo Trial (Far East International Military Tribunal) was held to try as war criminals those who had initiated and promoted the war. Hideki Tojo was tried along with twenty-seven officials; they were recognized as class A war criminals. Tojo and six other war criminals were sentenced to death by hanging in 1948.

## TONE, THEOBALD WOLFE   1763–1798, Founder of the Society of United Irishmen, a Protestant born in Dublin, Ireland. He struggled for an Ireland independent of English rule. Tone drafted and published a pamphlet titled "An Argument on Behalf of the Catholics in Ireland." He was appointed to the leadership body of the Catholic Committee, to serve as Secretary, by John Keogh in 1792. He is revered as a leader worth emulating by many modern-day Irish Republicans and nationalists in the struggle for national sovereignty for Northern Ireland.

"An Argument on Behalf of the Catholics in Ireland," his most famous publication, sought to convince the Dissenters, a primarily Protestant political group, that they and the Catholics had a mutual interest in an Ireland independent of England. The pamphlet resulted in widespread notoriety for Tone. Tone identified the key problem for the Irish nation as the lack of a national government and its provincial status.

Trained as a barrister in England, the French Revolution was the formative event spurring Tone's interest in politics. Tone saw independence of Ireland as the primary objective. He was strictly nonsectarian in his approach to Irish politics and wanted to substitute the term "Irishman" for Protestants, Catholics, and Dissenters.

Tone, upon his request, received a commission in the French army in 1796. During his time with the French army, France was at war with England. Tone convinced members of the French army that their liberation of Ireland from English rule would aid in their own battle against England. Tone then took part in two attempted French landings on Ireland. Tone was arrested on board ship in October 1798. Due to inclement weather he was held there for three weeks. Upon landing in Ireland Tone made a plea to be treated as a prisoner of war, a plea that was rejected. He was tried by court-martial and sentenced to death. While in prison awaiting execution, guards found him with a cut throat, an injury that eventually killed him before the hangman's noose.

Tone holds a place of high regard within the anals of Irish Republican history. Homage was paid in the naming of the *Wolfe Tone Weekly,* a republican newspaper

that ran from 1937 until 1939 and the *Wolfe Tone Annual,* which was a digest of articles on separatist history. Tone's legacy survives in the form of the Wolfe Tone Society, a literary and debating group that draws much of its support from the Irish Republican community and in the musical group, the Wolfe Tones, which are famous for their renditions of Irish rebel songs.

For unparalleld insight into the revolutionary, there is Tone's self-titled authobiography. Additionally useful are Sean Cronin's *For Whom the Hangmen's Rope Was Spun: Wolfe Tone and the United Irishmen* and *Freedom the Wolfe Tone Way* by Sean Cronin and Richare Roche.

## TOTALITARIANISM   Few social science concepts have sparked more discussion and controversy than that of totalitarianism, in part because of its partisan use by a great variety of persons. These range from Italian opponents of Benito Mussolini's fascist regime, who coined the adjective *totalitarian* to describe it, to Cold War critics of the Soviet Union who justified American containment policy by portraying a totalitarian enemy demonically bent on destroying democracy and individual freedom. The confusion fostered by polemics is compounded by scholarly disagreement over which political systems, if any, should fall under the rubric totalitarian. Although a few social philosophers loosely apply it to modern technological and consumerist societies, most scholars believe that Nazi Germany, Stalinist Russia, Maoist China, and perhaps fascist Italy best exemplify the totalitarian state. They also generally agree that the rise of these regimes is somehow connected with the social, economic, and political catastrophes of the early 20th century, most notably the spread of virulent forms of nationalism.

For many investigators of the phenomenon, totalitarianism denotes a highly centralized political system exhibiting a "syndrome" or cluster of characteristics that sets it apart from classical tyranny and authoritarianism. These characteristics include rule by a single mass-based party headed by an all-powerful, charismatic dictator; an all-encompassing ideology, often with fiercely nationalistic components, that legitimizes the ruling elite and enables it to mobilize the populace in support of the regime's policies and projects; a centrally directed economy; and an effective monopoly on the means of mass communication and coercion, including a vast propaganda apparatus and a system of police terror.

Proponents of this totalitarian "model" draw a sharp distinction between regimes like Hitler's or Stalin's and more traditional types of despotism, such as the dynastic monarchies of the Persian Gulf or the military juntas of Latin America. In traditional autocracies, the argument runs, rulers generally content themselves with outward obedience and acquiescence from their subjects; they suppress civil liberties but refrain from systematic efforts to control thought or to transform society and human nature. By contrast, totalitarian dictatorships, driven by ideological imperatives and an unlimited claim to allegiance, intrude into the very souls of citizens, attempting to fashion a "New Soviet Man," a "Maoist Man," or a "Nordic Man." To accomplish their aims, they rely on organized mass enthusiasm, thoroughgoing indoctrination, and calculated terror, all of which contribute to isolate the individual by undermining the network of private associations—and potential sources of opposition to the regime—that makes up civil society.

Scholars who subscribe to the theory of totalitarianism contend that this type of system, so dependent on 20th-century technology for its operation, has no historical antecedents. Moreover, they concur in assigning partial blame for its emergence to the chaotic aftermath of World War I. Beyond this broad agreement, however, opinions vary widely. Some writers, such as J. L. Talmon, trace the intellectual origins of totalitarianism to Jean-Jacques Rousseau's doctrine of the general will, while others fault Hegel or Marx or the various 19th-century advocates of racist ideology. Still others, such as the psychoanalyst Erich Fromm, believe the cause of totalitarianism lies less in the influence of ideas than in the psyche of modern man, ostensibly uprooted, "morally alone," insecure, and masochistically inclined to escape the burdens of freedom by submitting to dictatorial authority. Hannah Arendt, on the other hand, emphasized the decline of the liberal nation-state, with its constitutional protections and championing of abstract and universal human rights, and its replacement by a tribal nationalism that knows only the right of the *Volk* or favored race.

Nationalism, indeed, may be an essential link between regimes as apparently unlike as fascist Italy and the Soviet Union. Noting "analogous origins and converging lines of development," Raymond Aron observed that fascist states "move from an exacerbated nationalism to a kind of socialism," while Communist states, "starting from revolt and in the name of freedom, have resulted in a regime of authoritarian government and patriotic exaltation." In an important refinement of this interpretation, A. James Gregor propounded a theory of "developmental fascism," holding that Benito Mussolini's regime presented a form of dictatorship "appropriate to partially developed or underdeveloped, and consequently status deprived, national communities in a period of intense international competition for place and status." In this view, the belligerently nationalist

ideology and the highly centralized authority of Mussolini's totalitarian state permitted it more efficiently to harness resources and mobilize the masses on behalf of modernization and economic development. In pursuit of similar goals, Joeseph Stalin forsook the internationalism of classical Marxist theory for a more nation-centered approach—hence the doctrine of "socialism in one country" and Stalin's often strident appeals to Russian nationalism during the industrialization drive of the 1930s and the Great Patriotic War of 1941–1945.

The totalitarian model probably found widest acceptance during the 1950s with the appearance of such now-classic works as Arendt's *The Origins of Totalitarianism* and Friedrich and Brzezinski's *Totalitarian Dictatorship and Autocracy*. By the late 1960s, however, an increasing number of scholars in comparative political studies were raising questions about the model's usefulness. Among other criticisms, they pointed out that it understates differences between the Nazi and Soviet regimes; that totalitarian parties, whatever their aspirations may be, have never achieved the monolithic control over state and society suggested by the model; and that totalitarianism has antecedents in governments such as Calvin's Consistorium in Geneva or the Ch'ing-Dynasty in China and consequently is not unique to the 20th century.

Whatever the validity of these academic criticisms, the concept of totalitarianism acquired new life in the political arena when East European dissidents revived it with considerable effect in the years following the Soviet invasion of Czechoslovakia in 1968. Intellectuals like Václav Havel and Leszek Kolakowski regarded the Soviet and East European governments as totalitarian, often comparing them to Nazi Germany and employing the term *posttotalitarianism* to signify Communist regimes in an advanced state of atrophy. As Kolakowski explained it, the decay of belief in Marxism-Leninism led Soviet leaders to rely increasingly on an implicit appeal to Russian-Soviet nationalism and pride in the USSR's Superpower status in order to maintain their legitimacy. At the same time, the domination of Eastern Europe that this status entailed threatened the survival of national cultures in the region and had to be counteracted by a campaign of persistent moral pressure on the "bureaucratic tyranny" of the satellite governments. Under the right circumstances, such pressure would lead to reform and national liberation. Viewed from this perspective, the collapse of Communism in Europe seems in part the outcome of a struggle between an imperialist-totalitarian "integral nationalism" and a more humanitarian and liberal nationalism in the Enlightenment tradition.

Leonard Schapiro's *Totalitarianism* (Praeger Publishers, 1972) offers a brief and admirably lucid introduction to the subject. Abbott Gleason's *Totalitarianism: The Inner History of the Cold War* (Oxford University Press, 1995) surveys the literature and recounts the history of the concept from its origin in fascist Italy to its adoption by Russian scholars near the end of the Gorbachev era. Perhaps the best known studies are Hannah Arendt's *The Origins of Totalitarianism* (World, Meridian Books, 1958) and Carl J. Friedrich and Zbigniew K. Brzezinski's *Totalitarian Dictatorship and Autocracy* (Harvard University Press, 1956). The discussion in Carl J. Friedrich, Michael Curtis, and Benjamin J. Barber's *Totalitarianism in Perspective: Three Views* (Praeger Publishers, 1969) highlights the inadequacies of totalitarianism as a descriptive model. Two influential novels that brilliantly portray the inner workings of totalitarian societies are George Orwell's *Nineteen-Eighty-Four* (Harcourt, Brace and World, 1949) and Arthur Koestler's *Darkness at Noon* (Bantam Books, 1968).

## TOURÉ, SEKOU

1922–1984, Sekou Touré, descendent of Almamy Samory Touré who resisted French colonialism in the late 1800s, was a revolutionary Pan-Africanist leader and first president of independent Guinea in 1958. He was an active trade unionist and founded the first trade union in Africa. He was also a strong proponent of African independence, Pan-Africanism, and noncapitalist social development.

Sekou Touré attended the French technical school in Conakry, the capital of Guinea, but was expelled for leading a food strike. His organizing efforts continued and in 1952 he became secretary general of the People's Democratic Party of Guinea (PDG) and a leader in the national liberation movement. In 1958, Guinea became the one colony of France to reject the proposal of a Franco-American community and opt for complete and immediate independence. As a result, France cut all ties with the independent state and pulled out all resources. Under Touré's leadership, Guinea pursued a noncapitalist path of development and encouraged the assertion of the "African personality."

Guinea was recognized and supported by the socialist world and pursued a noncapitalist program of development. In 1958, Touré signed the Conakry declaration of Ghana-Guinea unity with President Kwame Nkrumah of Ghana. In 1960, these nations were joined by Mali when they declared a Ghana-Guinea-Mali union through the signing of a declaration with Modibo Keita of Mali. These were steps taken toward the ultimate Pan-African objective of political unity among African nations. In 1966, after Ghanian President Kwame Nkrumah was overthrown by a coup d'état, Sekou Touré offered him the post of co-president, which he held until

his death in 1972. Touré remained president of Guinea until his death in 1984.

Sekou Touré authored *Strategies and Tactics of the Revolution* (1977) and *Africa on the Move* (1977).

## TOUSSAINT L'OUVERTURE, FRANÇOIS

ca. 1743–1803, A military and political leader central to the Haitian revolution, Toussaint was the patriarch of Haitian nationalism.

Born a slave on the Breda plantation in Saint Domingue, Toussaint was the son of African natives. Although Toussaint's knowledge of European culture and his devout Roman Catholicism distanced him from his African roots, they were important to his success as a nationalist visionary. Toussaint's creolization made him an ideal leader of French Creole rebels.

Timely switches of loyalty also contributed to Toussaint's success. In the slave rebellions of the early 1790s, Toussaint was allied with the Spanish and the French royalty. In control of the eastern two-thirds of the island, the Spanish were attempting to conquer French Saint Domingue, which was the most coveted colony of the European powers. Blacks supported the Spanish and the French crown because they believed that these two powers—not the French revolutionaries—offered the best opportunity for emancipation. In 1794, however, after France's National Convention outlawed slavery in the colony, Toussaint switched his support to the French. His quick rout of the Spanish earned him the rank of general.

Toussaint parlayed his military success into personal control of the colony. After driving out the Spanish and English from the island, he laid the foundation for Haitian independence by giving only nominal allegiance to France. He secured the stability of his fledgling charge by winning control of eastern Hispaniola from the Spanish in 1800.

Toussaint coalesced Haitian nationalism not only from his military exploits but from his years as political administrator of the colony. Once he had earned the title of lieutenant governor of St. Domingue in 1796, Toussaint worked to establish a Haitian nationalist government. The most important step to that end was Toussaint's efforts in reuniting the mulatto-held southern region with the black-dominated northern region.

In 1801, Toussaint controlled all of Hispianola and assumed the title of governor for life. His limited deference to France drew the ire of Napoleon Bonaparte, who recently had been emboldened to squash colonial insurgence by the Treaty of Amiens. Given a respite from European entanglements, Bonaparte sent his brother-in-law, General Charles Leclerc, and 20,000 troops to St. Domingue in January 1802. Toussaint, whose power had been weakened by internal strife, was also rendered ineffectual by the international ambivalence toward helping a republic of former slaves. He surrendered to Leclerc, was deported, and jailed in France. Toussaint L'Ouverture died at Fort de Joux on April 7, 1803.

Despite Toussaint's arrest and subsequent efforts by the French to subdue the remaining revolutionary leaders, another former slave, Jean Jacques Dessalines, declared Haiti's independence on January 1, 1804. In large part because of Toussaint's foundational efforts, Haiti is the Western hemisphere's second oldest free nation.

Important biographies include C. L. R. James's *The Black Jacobins* (Allison and Busby, 1963) and Percy Waxman's *The Black Napoleon* (Harcourt and Brace, 1931).

## TRANSNATIONALISM

Transnationalism involves a variety of multifaceted social relations that are both embedded in and transcend two or more nation-states: relations that cross-cut sociopolitical, political, territorial, and cultural borders. The globalization of society plays an important role in its emergence and maintenance. The ever-increasing flow of people, goods, ideas, and images between various parts of the world enhances the blending of cultures and a "hyphenation of identity."

Transnationalism should not be seen as static, but as a constantly evolving process. Among other things, it affects and is affected by economic and political power relations, social organization and structure, and cultural practices and beliefs. Likewise, transnationalism should not be seen as simply a global phenomenon that eradicates local identifications and systems of meaning. On the contrary, these are essential for the maintenance of transnational ties.

A key factor in transnationalism is transmigration. Transmigration refers to a situation in which international migrants maintain ties to their homeland. Individuals are thus simultaneously connected to two or more nations. These kinship and friendship networks, in turn, facilitate the movement of people back and forth between their host country and their country of origin. For example, a Senegalese immigrant to Canada may make regular return visits to Senegal to visit relatives. These trips help to sustain cross-national ties. Of course, circumstances may not allow all individuals the luxury of such visits. In such cases, the flow of things may be important. Letters, videotapes, or specialty products such as food or clothing from "home" might foster transnational identities. Likewise, an established transnational community may serve as a magnet for future migrants. A Turkish worker may move to Germany because a preexisting Turkish population makes the transition easier by providing social and economic contacts.

The effect of the expansion of transnationalism is the subject of much debate. Some scholars propose that the cultural hybridization resulting from international migration is a liberating and antihegemonic course. Rather than one homogeneous set of relatively well-defined cultural standards, individuals are confronted with a "choice" of multiple, competing identities. Further, the rising influence of global media and multinational corporations leads to a decline in the power of national political systems. This in turn leads to greater independence of individuals from state control. The result may be a weakening of nationalism.

Others dispute this view, suggesting that transnationalism may actually increase nationalism. In an attempt to promote loyalty and maintain a desired influx of capital and goods, countries of origin may promote an ideal of cultural or ethnic unity among the emigrants. This may make assimilation in the receiving country more difficult and could provoke nationalistic disturbances as various groups attempt to "defend" an idealized national identity of the host nation against alien "invaders." An example of this type of upheaval would be the attacks on foreign guest workers by right-wing youths in Germany.

Transnational sociopolitical processes are likely to take on even more importance in the future. Technological advancements in communication and transportation make the creation and maintenance of transnational networks easier than ever, and global political and economic restructuring have the potential to reduce the role of the state as a central organizing principle.

Numerous recent volumes deal with various issues of transnationalism, including *Transnationalism from Below*, edited by Michael P. Smith and Luis E. Guarnizo (Transaction Publishers, 1998), and *Nations Unbound: Transnational Projects, Postcolonial Predicaments and Deterritorialized Nation-States*, edited by Linda Basch, Nina Glick Schiller, and Cristina Szanton Blanc (Gordon and Breach Publishers, 1994).

## TRIBALISM

The term *tribalism* refers to the process of belonging to a tribe as an identity community through a blood connection via patrilineal descent. In general, those who belong to a tribe are expected to support their fellow tribal members against outsiders and defend their honor. This bond and commitment to kinship has been used by state elites in the Arabian peninsula such as Saudi Arabia, Kuwait, Qatar, and Oman to consolidate loyalty to the state. In other Arab and African states, tribal loyalty has been used as a tool by ruling elites to recruit troops and government officials for sensitive posts to help staff agencies. In Iraq, the regime of Saddam Hussein relies heavily on tribal identity from the town of Tikrit, Saddam's birth place, to recruit for the Republican Guard and other security services. Tribal kinship ties are also important in African states, where similar processes of recruitment have taken place in such countries as Uganda and Nigeria. In the post-Cold War era, tribalism has taken on greater significance since the term has been used to refer to the rise of ethnic conflict in the Balkans and Central Asia. In the Balkans, the Kosovo Albanians have used their kinship solidarity to challenge Serbian rule in the province.

For an excellent discussion on this concept, see Dale F. Eickelman, *The Middle East and Central Asia: An Anthropological Approach,* 3rd ed. (Upper Saddle River, N.J.: Prentice Hall, 1998) especially chapter 6 "What Is a Tribe." Also consider Philip Khoury and Joseph Kostiner, *Tribes and State Formation in the Middle East* (Berkeley, Calif.: University of California Press, 1990).

## TRIBAL TERMINATION, POLICY OF

During the 1950s and early 1960s, the U.S. Congress enacted legislation that led to the termination of the federally recognized governmental status of over 110 Native American tribes. Resolution 108, known as the Termination Act of 1953, allowed federally recognized tribal governments to seek termination of their federal recognition status, which was initially derived through treaties between the U.S. government and individual Native American nations. The Bureau of Indian Affairs carried out the act through financial payments to individual members of tribes who agreed to be terminated and through programs that fostered assimilation into mainstream American society. One such program, the Urban Relocation Program, paid Native American individuals and families to leave their tribal homelands (reservations) and relocate to urban areas such as Chicago, San Francisco, and Denver. Terminated tribal lands and assets were then sold by the Bureau of Indian Affairs and the federal trust responsibility over tribal property and assets ended. The federal government was no longer responsible to terminated Native Americans for medical service at Indian Health Service facilities, education and job training programs from the Bureau of Indian Affairs, or any other tribally based programs. Thousands of members of terminated tribes were thrown into poverty either in urban ghettos or rural communities near their old homeland. Most experienced the same discrimination that plagued other minority groups in America during this time period. Tribal cultures and languages also vanished among several of the terminated tribes as their members assimilated into American society.

In the 1980s, during President Reagan's administration, the termination policy was exposed as a failure and nearly all of the terminated tribes were restored to federally recognized status by 1995. The federal government today classifies tribes in three categories: (1) federally recognized, (2) state recognized, and (3) unrecognized tribes. The federal government is obligated to the first group to protect tribal lands and resources and to provide them with health care, education, and economic development assistance.

Native Americans found that the loss of even subnational sovereignty can have a devastating impact on the people who previously enjoyed such status. The termination of sovereignty does not temper the nationalist ideals of a people, ideals that may lead to the restoration of sovereignty. In this case sovereign restoration was through nonviolent means, but oftentimes nationalistic movements utilize terrorism and warfare to regain their sovereign status.

For a more in-depth explanation of the complexity of Native American tribal government and federal Indian policy, see *American Indian Tribal Governments* (University of Oklahoma Press, 1989) by Sharon O'Brien.

## TROTSKY, LEON

1879–1940, An inspiring orator, brilliant theoretician, skilled organizer, and dedicated Communist revolutionary who provided crucial support to the Bolshevik Revolution in 1917 and to its preservation afterward. He lined up behind Lenin in 1902 although he did not join the Bolshevik Party until 1917. He founded the St. Petersburg Soviet during the failed 1905 revolution. In 1917 he presided over the Petrograd Soviet and helped engineer Lenin's takeover of power. After Lenin pulled Russia out of World War I, Trotsky negotiated the Brest-Litovsk Treaty ceding thousands of square miles of occupied territory to Germany but establishing a cease-fire. In the civil war that followed from 1918 to 1920 Trotsky organized the Red Army and ruthlessly led it to victory against Lenin's enemies.

Trotsky developed an international perspective on how to defend the Bolshevik Revolution, which stood alone in the world. The infant Soviet Union could be saved by revolutions in the capitalist countries that now encircled the new state. The Soviet Union should help foment such revolutions and bring about a socialist "United States of Europe" that would be a prelude to world revolution and eliminate nations and nationalism from the earth. He relied on his theory of "permanent revolution" elaborated in 1906. The new government would immediately introduce socialist reforms and repudiate foreign debts, thereby precipitating a financial crisis in the capitalist countries. At home he supported Lenin's New Economic Policy (NEP) and advocated a policy of Soviet reintegration into the world economy in order to eliminate the shortages of food and goods.

After Lenin's death in January 1924, Trotsky clashed head-on with Stalin, who was establishing the groundwork for his own takeover of power in 1929, when he maneuvered Trotsky out of power and forced him into exile. Trotsky opposed Stalin's idea of "socialism in one country," by which the new regime would concentrate on building socialism in the Soviet Union and hope that other countries would follow suit sometime in the future. Trotsky also opposed Stalin's heavy concentration of power in his own hands and found the dictator's system unstable in that such extreme bureaucratization could ultimately spark another revolution or lay the foundation for the capitalists' return to power. Echoing some later ideas of Mikhail Gorbachev, he advocated a form of market socialism that could eliminate the black market, as well as some political democracy in the planning process. Thus, multiparty politics, prices determined by markets, and free-trade unions were necessary.

In Mexican exile, he founded the Fourth International in 1938 to oppose Stalin. Branding Trotsky as a dangerous traitor, Stalin sent an assassin to murder him with an icepick while he sat in a barber's chair.

**TRUDEAU, PIERRE** 1919–, Born into a prominent and wealthy Montreal family of a Scottish mother, from whom he learned to speak perfect English, and a Quebecois father, Trudeau was educated at the Jesuits' College Jean de Brebeuf in Montreal, the University of Montreal law school, the Sorbonne, the London School of Economics, and Harvard University. Like many Quebecois, he deftly eluded the recruiters during World War II, and, instead, spent an enviable youth reading philosophy and traveling both to Europe and to exotic places, such as the Holy Land, China, and Tibet. Always an eccentric person with a "swinging" image, he often wore gaudy and intentionally inappropriate clothing, and he drove his sports car to the site of the 1949 asbestos strike, to show his support for the strikers. Nevertheless, he always had at his disposal one of the most powerful minds ever produced in Canada.

In his many articles in the journal *Cité Libre* (*Free City*), he used his powerful logic and language to attack his fellow Quebecois' notions of authority. He called for the use of political power as a positive instrument of the people's will to bring about social and economic progress. He advocated a kind of social democracy, free

from the church and centered in the city, rather than in the villages and farms. He and, increasingly, other Quebec intellectuals wanted a modern, forward-looking Quebec, in step with the times, while retaining its French character.

Trudeau is often incorrectly credited with having ushered in the changes in Canada designed to undercut the separatist movement in Quebec. He was later to lend his prestige and intellect to bridging the huge gulf that had developed between Quebec and the rest of Canada. He was a law professor at the University of Montreal who had not yet joined the Liberal Party in 1963 when the new liberal government of Lester Pearson appointed a Royal Commission on Bilingualism and Biculturalism to find and document the causes of the crisis and to propose ways of dealing with the serious frictions that existed between "the two founding races." The commission's first report in 1965 left no doubt that francophones were severely handicapped in their efforts to advance economically and to preserve their language and culture. It documented the fact that these two aspirations were linked. The conclusion was that "Canada, without being fully conscious of the fact, is passing through the greatest crisis of its history." Many of the reforms that followed were based on this groundbreaking report.

Pearson found an undeniably competent and effective lieutenant and ultimate successor in Trudeau, who joined the party in 1965 and was elected to the House of Commons that same year. Trudeau wanted to demonstrate that the aspirations of francophone Canada could be furthered in Ottawa, as well as in Quebec City. He feared that the kind of Quebec nationalism that was emerging would not only destroy Canada, but would drive Quebec into isolation. Only a tolerant federalism could remedy the situation.

In 1966 he was appointed justice minister, and he lent his support to enlarging what was called "cooperative federalism." This meant in practice that all ten provinces would be granted their full powers under the British North America Act (BNA, Canada's constitution until 1982) and that Ottawa would return to the provinces all the powers that it had assumed during the 1950s. It also instituted periodic meetings and consultations between the governments in Ottawa and the ten provincial capitals, so that provincial concerns could be aired and influence on federal policy strengthened. These meetings are still a part of routine Canadian political practice. After bitter and prolonged debate, the liberal government decided to remove a symbol from the country's flag that many francophones found to be insulting: the Union Jack, a reminder of Canada's British imperial heritage. The present flag, with a single red maple leaf on a white field, was adopted.

Perhaps the most important measure the Trudeau government took to quell the fears of francophones was to create a bilingual Canada, in which francophones would feel equal and at home everywhere. In 1969 the Official Languages Act made Canada a bilingual country. The brunt of this new law was felt most immediately in the federal civil service, where more and more jobs were reserved for bilingual Canadians. In coming years this law was to have increasing impact on many dimensions of Canadian life. This was not universally greeted. Many anglophones, particularly in the West, found it an unnecessary and unjustified imposition, and many Quebecois found that it did not go far enough in protecting French language rights.

The policies of the Pearson and Trudeau governments were in the long run very important for the salvation of Canada as a unified country. But in the 1960s and 1970s they were unable to satisfy the ardor of Quebec nationalism. No Canadian needed a reminder in the 1970s that his country was in danger of ripping apart. If a peaceful solution were not found, Canada would be buffeted by something rare in the Canadian experience: violence. In the early 1960s a rough separatist group led by the young socialist firebrand, Pierre Bourgault, emerged. Bombs exploded in Montreal in 1963, and riots accompanied the British Queen's visit to Quebec City to commemorate the 1864 Confederation Conference. In 1970 Trudeau sent troops to Montreal to quell murderous terrorist acts by the Front for the Liberation of Quebec (FLQ).

The Trudeau government embarked on a nationalist campaign to increase the Canadian hold over the country's own economy and energy resources. The very joints of the Canadian state began to creak under the weight of competing visions of federalism, nationalism, and regionalism. Canada was in crisis, so its political and legal minds set out to find a constitutional solution that could save the country from tearing apart.

The Trudeau government, voted back into power after a nine-month breather in 1980, fought a successful battle against the Partí Québécois's (PQ) effort to win a provincial referendum in May 1980 that could have paved the way to separatism. To undercut the PQ's appeals, Trudeau promised a new federal arrangement. This culminated in the Constitution Act of 1982.

After leaving power in 1984, Trudeau became the most noted critic of efforts, such as the Meech Lake (1987) and Charlottetown (1992) Accords, to grant Quebec special privileges within the confederation. He feared a dangerous weakening of Ottawa's power:

"Those Canadians who fought for a single Canada, bilingual and multicultural, can say goodbye to their dream."

See Richard Gwyn, *The Northern Magnus. Pierre Trudeau and Canadians* (Paper Jacks, 1981), Thad McIlroy, ed., *A Rose Is a Rose: A Tribute to Pierre Elliott Trudeau in Cartoons and Quotes* (Doubleday, 1984), and George Radwanski, *Trudeau* (Signet, 1978).

**TRUMAN, HARRY S.**  1884–1972, Born of humble circumstances in Lamar, Missouri, and too poor to attend college, Truman lived the "American Dream" by rising to the nation's highest office. After earning a living in farming and small business, he was elected to the U.S. Senate in 1935 as a supporter of the New Deal. Because he could get along well with a broad spectrum of democrats and because of unacceptable opposition to Vice President Henry A. Wallace, Truman was added to President Franklin D. Roosevelt's ticket in 1944. When the president died on April 12, 1945, Truman became president. He had met Roosevelt only a couple of times and had not even been informed about the Manhattan Project to develop a nuclear bomb. He was thrust into America's international responsibilities where decisions had to be made at the top that would greatly influence the subsequent peace and the postwar international order that had to protect American interests and values. He saw himself as the nation's chief decision maker and relished this job, popularizing the slogan that "the buck stops here!"

The range of difficult issues with which he had to deal was staggering. He made the morally difficult decision to have two atomic bombs dropped on Japan in order to bring the war to an end. Together with Stalin and Churchill/Atlee at the Potsdam Conference, he helped determine Allied policy toward a defeated Germany. It was on his watch that the United Nations was created and a UN Human Rights Charter adopted, which he strongly supported and which is increasingly relevant in the world. He ordered that aid be sent to Greece and Turkey to help them defend themselves against Communism. In 1947 this offer was enshrined and broadened in the "Truman Doctrine," which promised American aid to all "free peoples who are resisting attempted subjugation by armed minorities or by outside powers." It provided the rationale for "containment," justifying later policies to limit the spread of Communism by the Soviet Union and the People's Republic of China (PRC), which was established in 1949.

The effort to stem Communism was also a rationale for his administration's Marshall Plan (named after his secretary of state, General George C. Marshall). This called for material assistance to European countries, including Germany, and for the kind of European cooperation that would create favorable circumstances for European integration. When the wartime alliance broke down and the Soviet Union came to be perceived as a threat, he ordered an airlift to break the Soviet siege of West Berlin in 1948–1949. He also approved of American participation in NATO, which constituted a historic break with the American tradition of avoiding long-term peacetime alliances. America's vital interests were now seen to be at stake in Europe. In 1950 he ordered U.S. military intervention in Korea to stop Communist aggression on that peninsula. However, when his popular commander on the ground, General Douglas McArthur, insisted on widening the war into China, Truman removed him for insubordination.

Truman never enjoyed popularity at home and barely won reelection in 1948, against all predictions. He initially fueled the flames of McCarthyism by introducing a loyalty program and permitting the Justice Department to prosecute U.S. Communist leaders. But when Senator Joseph McCarthy elevated the "Red Scare" to a truly scary level, Truman did what he could to contain it by vetoing bills that seemed to promote it.

President Truman enlarged the powers of the office by increasing the number of advisers, making plentiful use of his veto power, sending troops to Europe and Korea on his own authority, and underscoring the president's role as commander in chief by removing a general who had questioned it. He also demonstrated that being an effective president was more important than being popular at the moment. When he left office in January 1953, his approval rating stood at only 31 percent. Not until after his death in 1972 did historians and politicians begin to consider him one of America's truly great leaders.

## TUDJMAN, FRANJO

**TUDJMAN, FRANJO** 1922–1999, Nationalist president of Croatia, initially elected in 1990, reelected in 1992 and 1997. Born on May 14, 1922, in the village of Veliko Trgovişće north of Zagreb, Tudjman joined Tito's Communist partisans in 1941. After the war he held various posts at the Federal Defense Ministry and army headquarters in Belgrade. There he became disillusioned with the tendency to exaggerate the number of Serbs killed by Croatia's wartime fascist *Ustaša* regime, which Tudjman believed was being used to silence any discussion of Croatia's status within Yugoslavia.

He achieved the rank of major general in the Yugoslav army in December 1960, after completing his training at the Higher Military Academy in Belgrade in 1957. In 1961 Tudjman left active military service to head

the Institute for the History of the Workers' Movement in Zagreb, which he directed until 1967. In 1965 he obtained a doctorate in history from the University of Zagreb. His written works dealt mostly with Yugoslavia's pre-1945 political and military history, with an emphasis on interwar discrimination against Croatia by the Serbian-led government in Belgrade. Regarding World War II, Tudjman endeavored to show that the total number of victims of the *Ustaša* regime was a low 60,000 (including Serbs, Jews, leftist Croats, and others), rather than the 700,000 Serbs officially claimed. In 1967 he was expelled from the Communist Party and removed from his university teaching post.

As a member of Croatia's chief cultural organization, *Matica Hrvatska*, Tudjman was an active participant in the 1971 Croatian Spring, during which nationalist intellectuals and students sought to loosen the Socialist Republic of Croatia's ties with the Yugoslav federation. For this Tudjman was sentenced to two years' imprisonment in October 1972 (later reduced to nine months). In February 1981 Tudjman was again sentenced to three years in prison, this time on charges of spreading propaganda hostile to the Yugoslav state during interviews with foreign journalists. In November 1984 he was released on condition that he not make any public speeches for five years. In February 1989 he violated this ban by speaking at the founding meeting of the Croatian Democratic Union (*Hrvatska Demokratska Zajednica*, HDZ).

With Communist regimes collapsing all over Eastern Europe and an increasingly nationalist leadership in Belgrade seeking to recentralize Yugoslavia under Serbian control, the HDZ won the April 1990 elections in Croatia on a platform of confederation or independence. Parliament subsequently elected Tudjman president on May 30, 1990.

When confederation talks failed, Croatia declared itself independent on June 25, 1991. A war ensued between Croatia and Belgrade-backed Croatian Serb rebels based in the town of Knin. More than 10,000 Croats were killed, some 300,000 were forced to flee their homes, and Croatia lost nearly a quarter of its territory to the rebel Serbs by the time a lasting cease-fire was signed in early January 1992. That same month Croatia was recognized as an independent state, an achievement for which Tudjman was rewarded with victory in the direct presidential elections of November 1992.

In the 1992–1995 Bosnian war, Tudjman first allied himself and the Bosnian Croats with the Bosnian Muslims against the Serbs. He then orchestrated a Croat-Muslim war (May 1993–March 1994), before agreeing, under intense international pressure, to the creation of a Croat-Muslim federation linked to Croatia.

In August 1995, after years of building up the Croatian army, Tudjman presided over the successful liberation of most Serb-held Croatian territory. Despite clear autocratic tendencies, such as his government's persecution of the independent press and his own repeated refusal to acknowledge the opposition's success in Zagreb after the October 1995 municipal elections, Tudjman was once again reelected president in 1997.

## TUNISIAN NATIONALISM

Tunisia historically served as a meeting place between northern and southern Africa, and between sea and desert. Its political heritage dates back to the ancient civilization of Carthage. The arrival of conquering Arab tribes and Islam in the 8th century integrated the area into the Muslim-Arab world. Several local dynasties ruled over Tunisia until the Ottoman Empire took control in the early 16th century. Ottoman rule was generally indirect, as local governors (known as *Bey*) established hereditary dynasties that dominated local politics.

As in other parts of the Ottoman Empire, the involvement and interest of European powers in Tunisia increased during the 19th century. Following its 1830 occupation of Algeria, France was intent on securing its new colony by gaining control of neighboring Tunisia as well. The Ottoman Empire's weakened position offered Tunisia's local governors an even greater degree of political freedom, and the possibility of exploring new political and legal frameworks. Fearing a European invasion and recognizing the country's militarily and technologically unfavorable situation, several Tunisian officials sought to reform the army and government bureaucracy. Another important measure undertaken was the 1861 Constitution, which included plans for a parliamentary political system of sorts. These measures could not curb external intrigues that led to the French takeover of the country in 1881 and the establishment of a protectorate, replacing Ottoman rule. The position of the local *Bey* was retained, but the French resident-general became the significant political power in Tunisia.

In spite of the French contribution to Tunisia's economy and infrastructure, many Tunisians resented the foreign rule imposed on them, and sought to revive their own political and cultural identity as a first step in regaining independence. Several prominent religious and intellectual figures began to ponder issues that laid the theoretical foundation of Tunisian nationalism.

Tunisia's early nationalists wrestled not only with political questions, but also confronted cultural dilemmas, such as their attitude toward Western culture. A number of Tunisian thinkers advocated the acceptance of Western culture as part of efforts to revive the country, while others equated Western civilization with French rule and called for a return to Islam as the only solution to the country's weakened position. As a growing number of Tunisians attended French universities and became appreciative of Western culture, the former group had a greater impact on the development of Tunisian nationalism. The calls for independence, together with the desire to absorb many western ideas into Tunisian society, were the main features of the Tunisian nationalist movement. Many nationalist leaders had reservations about the role of Islam and religion in their movement and later in an independent state, but recognized Islam's importance in Tunisia's traditional society. They later sought to incorporate Islamic features into the ranks of their movement.

In 1908 a small group known as the "Young Tunisians" was formed. A more significant organization was the *Destour* (Arabic for "Constitution") Party, established after World War I. The party was inspired by the Constitution of 1861, and pursued a moderate policy toward France, arguing that France should cooperate with Tunisia but not play a dominant role in the country's politics and society. The protectorate authorities banned the Destour Party in 1933. A new and more radical nationalist party, the *Neo-Destour* Party (led by Habib Bourguiba), emerged the following year. The Neo-Destour demanded Tunisia's independence, but reflecting many of its leader's positive attitudes toward French and Western culture, also called for securing close links with France, once independence would be achieved. Although its leaders were frequently arrested and exiled by French authorities, the nationalist movement resisted German pressure during World War II to denounce France, and remained supportive of the Allies. This position, however, did not help the nationalist cause after the war, as France sought to maintain its rule over the country. Tunisia's struggle for independence became increasingly violent, as the nationalists gained popularity among the Tunisian public. By 1955, France had agreed to wide reforms in Tunisia, which amounted to independence, officially proclaimed the following year. With the final departure of French troops from the Bizerte military base in 1963, complete independence was achieved. The other central component of Tunisian nationalism, promoting a pro-Western political and social agenda, is an important feature of Tunisia today, and an ideological heir to a movement and ideology that had a major impact on Tunisia during the 20th century.

**TÜRKEŞ, ALPARSLAN** 1917–1996, Turkish politician long synonymous with extreme rightist politics in republican Turkey. Alparslan Türkeş was born in Nicosia, Cyprus, but moved to the Turkish Republic at the age of fifteen. In Turkey, he became a military officer but, by his late twenties, was already deeply involved in right-wing political activities. He was briefly detained in a crackdown of Pan-Turkists at the end of World War II. In 1960, he played a prominent role in a military coup against the Menderes government and was considered a radical on the military council (the National Unity Committee or NUC) that ruled the country after the coup. He and his supporters were, however, soon purged and Türkeş was quietly posted as a military attaché in New Delhi as moderates on the NUC maneuvered the country back toward democracy. In 1963, Türkeş returned to Turkey, gave up his commission, and entered politics. By 1965, he was the head of the Republican Peasants and Nation Party (after 1969, the Nationalist Action Party) and remained a prominent political figure in Turkish life until his death, holding cabinet posts in a number of coalition governments.

During his political life, Türkeş served as the voice for an extremist and often racist version of Turkish nationalism. In the 1940s he was accused of sympathizing with the Nazis and there is certainly a quality reminiscent of far-right movements of the 1930s in the stylings of Türkeş and his followers: hand salutes, youth groups, and a propensity toward street violence as a means of political change. Notable in Türkeş's vision of the Turkish identity has been an emphasis on pre-Islamic symbols: the informal name for his followers, the *Bozkurts*, or Grey Wolves, was meant to recall ancient steppe traditions as was his title, *Başbuğ*, or leader. Türkeş's vision of Turkish identity stressed the racial bonds between all Turkic peoples and called on the Turkish Republic to take greater responsibility for Turkic peoples living beyond its borders. At times, he carried this belief further, calling for the eventual creation of a Greater Turkey that would encompass all Turkic peoples of the world. Domestically, his politics were marked by virulent anticommunism and support for hard-line opposition to Kurdish identity politics. In the 1990s Türkeş's politics became somewhat more mainstream and his rhetoric became less violent. In the years directly before his death, he began to take on something of the role of elder statesman in Turkish politics though many in Turkey, particularly on the left, never lost their distrust for him.

**TURKISH NATIONALISM** The Republic of Turkey (Türkiye Cumhuriyeti) was founded in 1923 in the wake of the disintegration of the Ottoman Empire and the struggle against efforts by other foreign powers to control this region that bridges Europe and Asia after World War II.

Mustafa Kemal Atatürk, the "father of the Turks," led the uprising against Allied military efforts to claim the former Ottoman territory as early as December 1918. Allied troops occupied portions of Istanbul and set up a military administration there. French General Franchet d'Esperey, in a bold symbolic gesture reminiscent of Mehmed the Conqueror's entrance into Istanbul in 1453, rode into the city on a white horse. The Allies, along with French, Greek, and Italian troops, all began to lay claim to portions of what became the Republic of Turkey, some of them leaving a path of death and destruction in their wake.

Mustafa Kemal (not yet proclaimed Atatürk) joined with other Turkish nationalists to prevent external control of their homeland and came into conflict with the sultan and other religious authorities, who had thrown in their lot with the Allies. Mustafa Kemal created a provisional government in Ankara, 300 miles from Istanbul, and the Allies and the sultan's government began to move against it. They arrested key nationalist sympathizers in Istanbul on March 16, 1920, and declared that Mustafa Kemal and his coconspirators were infidels who should be shot on sight.

On April 23, 1920, a nationalist parliament called the Grand National Assembly met in Ankara and elected Mustafa Kemal as its president. The following June the Allies countered by offering the Treaty of Sevres to the sultan, which he signed two months later, agreeing to a greatly reduced state that gave much of the Ottoman territory to Greece and established an independent Armenia. Mustafa Kemal repudiated the treaty and began the struggle against both Greek and Armenian forces that eventually resulted in a nationalist victory.

The Turks defeated the Greeks in 1921 and 1922 and on November 1, 1922, the Grand National Assembly abolished the sultanate. Sultan Mehmed VI fled into exile shortly thereafter and the Allies negotiated the Treaty of Lausanne with Mustafa Kemal's government; it was signed on July 24, 1923. The following October the nationalists gained control of Istanbul. On October 29 the Republic of Turkey was established with Ankara as its capital.

In contrast to the Kemalist nationalism of the new republic, a parallel movement of Pan-Turkish nationalism continued to thrive in some sectors of the population. Pan-Turkism advocated the political unification of all Turkish-speaking peoples and became popular around the time of the disillusion of the Ottoman Empire. Similarly, Pan-Turanianism advocated a union of peoples who, according to a widely disputed 19th-century theory, had a common heritage: Turkish, Mongol, Tungus, Finnish, Hungarian, and other related languages.

## TURKMENISTANI NATIONALISM

Turkmenistan is a small nation of 3.7 million that achieved independence after the Soviet disintegration in 1991. This event allowed Turkmen people to establish their own nation-state for the first time in their history. The rise of Turkmenistani nationalism can be traced in three stages. During the first stage from medieval time to the 19th century, the Turkmen tribes populated vast areas to the east of the Caspian Sea and formed their distinct language, culture, and identities. Throughout this period, these Turkic-speaking nomads interacted with their Persian-speaking neighbors and gradually embraced Islam, although they preserved some features of their shamanic past and were strongly influenced by Sufi mysticism. An oral tradition of literature and poetry, which featured use of the traditional musical instrument the *dutar* helped them to preserve their distinct national culture through numerous wars and interventions.

The second stage is associated with Russia/Soviet dominance in Central Asia. This stage began at the end of the 19th century with the incorporation of most of the Turkmen tribes into the Russian Empire (although many Turkmen were left in the neighboring Afghanistan and Iran, totaling almost 2.5 million in 1994). The turning point of this period was the devastating defeat of the Turkmens by the Russian army in 1881 at Geok-Tepe, where the Turkmen losses exceeded 150,000 lives. The incorporation of the Turkmenistani territory into the Russian Empire brought a number of changes, including modernization of the economy, education, and political systems. After the Russian Revolution of 1917, it took several years for the Bolsheviks to establish firm control over the territory of the present Turkmenistan and to quell local resistance (also known as the *Basmachi* movement). In 1924 the Turkmen Soviet Socialist Republic was created. The Soviet regime introduced secularism, persecuted Islamic clergy, and closed mosques. The Soviets also introduced the Latin and later the Cyrillic alphabet, raised literacy levels, and brought modern industries to the area. However, the Soviet modernization came at the severe price of thou-sands who perished during Stalin's purges. Gradually, with the emergence of mass literacy and the new intelligentsia, and a relaxation of the repression, modern Turkmenistani nationalism began to emerge.

The third stage began after the Soviet disintegration in 1991. Unlike the Baltic republics or Azerbaijan, Gorbachev's policy of *perestroika* did not induce a national liberation movement or mass political participation in Turkmenistan. The road to Turkmenistani independence in 1991 was without large-scale national-liberation wars and conflicts; it was instead a quite peaceful process with the exception of small-scale inter-ethnic conflicts in 1990. In 1990, the Turkmen language replaced Russian as the official language, and in 1993 a Latin-based script replaced the Cyrillic alphabet. The republic did not experience any large-scale inter-ethnic conflicts or mass emigration of people, probably because of the relatively homogeneous ethnic structure (Turkmens represent 77 percent of the total population). The Turkmenistani leader Saparmurad Niyazov turned to the revival of the traditional values of Turkmen society to realize his version of Turkmenistani nationalism by trying to bring cohesion to the nation in which tribal-clan relations still play an important role. Niyazov's national policy is represented by the slogan *"Khalq, Vatan, Turkmenbashy!"* (People, Fatherland, Turkmenbashy), which combines the extreme forms of etatism, egalitarianism, and authoritarianism. He has presented himself as the core of the society, as the leader who unites all Turkmen tribes and all ethnic groups living in the republic. The cornerstones of national unity are the ideas of the national liberation struggle against Russian colonialism, the moral power of Islam, and Niyazov's personality.

For further reading, see J. Anderson, "Authoritarian Political Development in Central Asia: The Case of Turkmenistan," in *Central Asian Survey* (Abingdon, UK) **14**(4) (1995), pp. 509–528; S. Akbarzadeh, "National Identity and Political Legitimacy in Turkmenistan," *Nationalities Papers*, **27**(2) (1999) assesses some features of the post-Soviet national development; R. Kaiser, *The Geography of Nationalism in Russia and the USSR* (Princeton, N.J.: Princeton University Press, 1994); and S. Turkmenbashy, *Independence, Democracy, Prosperity* (Alma-Ata; New York: Noy Publications, 1994) gives the official overview of Turkmenstani politics.

# U

UGANDAN NATIONALISM   The formation of kingdoms in present-day Uganda can be traced back to the 15th century when Luo peoples began to occupy the territory. Among the most powerful of these kingdoms were the kingdoms of Bunyoro, Buganda, and Ankole in modern-day Uganda and the Karagwe kingdom in northwest Tanzania. Bunyoro grew to be the largest and most influential of these kingdoms until the end of the 17th century. It enjoyed a vibrant economy, a loose political structure, and a dominant trade position due to its exclusive control of the region's salt mines. Prior to 1650, Buganda had been a small kingdom ruled by a kabaka. But with the decline in influence of the Bunyoro kingdom, the kingdom of Buganda grew immeasurably and dominated the region. It had extensive military might, which allowed it to impose its will over other lesser kingdoms and to demand tribute from them. European influence came with the arrival of British explorers such as Sir Burton and Henry Stanley in the 1860s and 1870s. In 1888 Britain assigned political and economic power over the region to the British East Africa Company by royal charter. The company's control over the area was consolidated in 1891 when a treaty was signed with the Kingdom of Buganda, the leading kingdom in the area. In 1894 the British government took control of the Baganda Kingdom and declared it a protectorate. By the turn of the 20th century, the protectorate had been expanded to include other lesser kingdoms such as Bunyoro, Toro, Ankole, and Bugosa.

The imposition of colonial rule brought with it a new master whose intent was to exploit Uganda's resources. Like elsewhere in Africa the British imposed taxes and forced the local people to engage in the growing of new crops such as coffee and cotton for export to Britain. Although the authority of the chiefs, particularly that of the Baganda king (the kabaka), was preserved during colonial rule, most of the land was ceded to Britain as "Crown Land." Through a system of indirect rule, the Baganda were co-opted into the British colonial system as administrators over their less powerful neighbors. Baganda agents served as local tax collectors and labor organizers in areas in other parts of the country. Wherever they went, the Baganda insisted on the dominance of their language, Luganda, and imposed their culture on unwilling groups, which included food habits, traditional dress, and their newly adopted religion of Christianity and in some instances Islam. Other ethnic groups, particularly the Bunyoro, who had lost some of their lands to the Baganda and had previously fought both the Baganda and the British, greatly resented this dominance.

In 1907 the Banyoro rose in a rebellion called *nyangire,* or "refusing," which led to the withdrawal of Baganda subimperial agents. However, the arrival of the railway and the introduction of cotton around Lake Victoria, the heartland of the Buganda Kingdom, put the Baganda peoples in an advantageous position over the rest of Uganda. The Baganda people benefited materially and educationally from the sale of cotton as they were able to send their children to mission schools. However, in spite of the prosperity that the Buganda enjoyed from the sale of cash crops, three issues continued to cause grievance through the 1930s and 1940s. The strict regulation by the colonial government of the trade in cash crops, the setting of prices, and the use of Asians as intermediaries were greatly resented by the Baganda. Because of these unfair colonial practices, the Baganda rioted in 1949, burning down the houses of progovernment chiefs. The rioters had three demands: the right to bypass government price controls on the export sales of cotton, the removal of the Asian monopoly over cotton ginning, and the right to representation in local government in place of the chiefs appointed by the British.

They also criticized the youong kabaka, Frederick Wal-ugembe Mutesa II, for his neglect of the needs of his people.

The events in India in 1947, in which the British had backed down and given independence to India, encouraged the peoples of Uganda that they too could obtain independence. They began to form political pressure groups such as the Uganda African Farmers Union founded in 1947 and the Uganda National Congress founded in 1952. The British government soon began to prepare for the inevitable independence of Uganda. The colonial government removed restrictions on African cotton ginning, rescinded price controls on African-grown coffee, encouraged cooperatives, and established the Uganda Development Corporation to promote and finance new projects. Elected African representatives were allowed in the Legislative Council, which had heavily favored the European community. In 1961 it was announced by the colonial govenment that elections for "responsible government" would be held in March 1961 and would lead to eventual independence. These elections were boycotted by the Baganda who wanted to secede from the rest of Uganda and form their own country. However, after discussion with the British, the Baganda king agreed to take the largely cere-monial position of Uganda's head of state, which the Ba-ganda considered of great symbolic importance. The Uganda People's Congress (UPC) won the majority of seats in the elections and would control the government while the Baganda king who had boycotted the elections would symbolically be the head of state. In the aftermath of the April 1962 election leading up to independence, Uganda's national parliament consisted of forty-three UPC delegates, twenty-four Kabaka Yeka (KY, the kabaka's party) delegates, and twenty-four Democratic Party (DP) delegates. The new UPC-KY coalition led Uganda into independence in October 1962, with Milton Obote as prime minister and the kabaka as head of state.

After independence, the other kingdoms resented the special status accorded to the Kabaka Party and pressured Obote to drop the kabaka. In April 1966, Obote suspended the Constitution and declared himself executive president. The Buganda declared Obote's actions null and void, passing a resolution demanding the withdrawal of the central government from Buganda soil by March 30, 1966. On May 24 government troops stormed the kabaka's palace, seizing it after a day's fighting. Mutesa II consequently fled to Britain, where he died three years later. To consolidate his power, Obote introduced a republican constitution that abolished the four kingdoms and made Uganda a uni-tary state. In 1969 he introduced the "Common Man's Charter," which was designed to transform Uganda into a socialist state. Opponents of these measures believed that Obote was trying to turn Uganda into a Communist state. On January 25, 1971, when Obote was attending the Commonwealth Conference in Singapore, Major-General Idi Amin seized power with considerable internal and external support. With two years, Amin had imposed one of the severest dictatorships in Africa. Throughout 1971 he systematically eliminated soldiers suspected of remaining loyal to Obote. After an abortive invasion of Uganda by Obote's supporters in September 1972, Amin began to murder civilians in large numbers. Uganda went through years of civil war until the arrival of Museveni and his National Resistance Army (NRA) in 1986. The NRA quickly established a new government with Museveni as president. Although Museveni put national reconciliation at the top of his government's priorities, various groups opposed his takeover, in some cases forcefully. Thus the government was engaged in various types of military and security operations against dissident groups from 1987 through 1991. Museveni justified his continued reign without democratic reforms by noting that the nation needed time to recover from dictatorship and war before democratic elections could be held. The first presidential elections under Museveni's rule were held in May 1996 with Paul Ssemogerere running as the main candidate opposing President Museveni. Museveni was elected with a comfortable majority, winning 74.2 percent of the six million votes cast. He continues to revive the Ugandan economy and to politically stabilize the country.

For further reading, see Tony Avirgan and Martha Honey, *War in Uganda: The Legacy of Idi Amin* (Westport, Conn.: Hill, 1982); G. S. K. Ibingira, *The Forging of an African Nation: The Political and Constitutional Evolution of Uganda from Colonial Rule to Independence, 1894–1962* (New York: Viking Press, 1979); Kenneth Ingham, *The Making of Modern Uganda* (Westport, Conn.: Greenwood Press, 1983); Jan Jelmert Jorgensen, *Uganda: A Modern History* (New York: St. Martin's Press, 1981); Samwiri Rubaraza Karugire, *A Political History of Uganda* (Exeter, N.H.: Heinemann Educational Books, 1980); and Bob Measures and Tony Walker, *Amin's Uganda* (London: Minerva, 1998).

## UKRAINIAN NATIONALISM

Ukraine is an independent nation-state, formerly the second largest republic of the Soviet Union. It became independent in 1991 after a two-year period of political mobilization led by Rukh, a coalition of associations initially founded to support *perestroika*.

From the late 18th century until the Russian Revolution, what is now Ukraine was divided between the Russian and Austrian Empires. Ukrainian nationalism arose as an organized movement in the mid-19th century Russian Empire's western borderlands. Since then, however, it has had weak support in this region (currently, Eastern Ukraine), and strong support from its more nationally conscious western areas, formerly ruled by the Austrian Empire. Frequently, scholars have attributed such uneven patterns of national mobilization to social structural differentiation—in particular, differences in market penetration. But Ukrainians occupied similar socioeconomic positions in both these regions. Instead, the origins of Ukraine's uneven pattern of national mobilization are a result of the very different administrative structures the two empires developed for governing their national peripheries.

The tsarist government pursued a pattern of highly centralized rule in what later became Eastern Ukraine. Indeed, it developed a variety of legal and administrative obstacles specifically designed to consolidate central state power and prevent Ukrainian political activists from forging sustained political ties to the wider peasant population (most notably, it banned the use of the Ukrainian language in popular publications and jailed national activists). However, explicit Russification (manifested, for example, in state restrictions on cultural activities) might not have prevented national mobilization. More fundamentally, eastern Ukrainians lacked political opportunities to mobilize national consciousness due to the closed nature of the tsarist political system. The state prevented most forms of local political mobilization prior to the 1905 revolution, and thus it created obstacles for Ukrainian national mobilization, as well. Consequently, until the time of the 1917 revolution, Ukrainian nationalism was limited to small-scale cultural activities and semisecret political societies that the government quickly and easily repressed.

The course of national mobilization was very different in the Austrian-ruled territories that now constitute Western Ukraine. In marked contrast to the Romanov empire, the Habsburg state was a highly decentralized federation. As a counterbalance to restive Hungarian and Polish elites, Austrian government officials encouraged local political activity as well as various forms of ethnic mobilization. Organized political activities were further facilitated by the Austrian Constitution of 1867, which guaranteed individual liberties, and freedom of the press, speech, and assembly, as well as protecting (and perhaps, promoting) the rights of individual nationalities. Consequently, by the time the Austrian Empire collapsed, Western Ukrainians were politically experienced and organizationally consolidated. For example, Ukrainians in Galicia were represented by six legal political parties, and had achieved a high degree of political organization through a growing network of Ukrainian schools, voluntary associations, and periodicals. Thus, while the Ukrainian national movement in the Russian Empire was small and politically inconsequential, in Galicia it had won important concessions from local state elites who formerly wielded power unchallenged.

By the time these two empires collapsed following World War I, they had created remarkably different political opportunities for subsequent Ukrainian nationalism. Galicia soon came to be considered the core of the Ukrainian national independence movement. By contrast, only a small minority of the local Eastern Ukrainian elite joined the Ukrainian independence movement. Local peasants identified primarily with locale and religion, developing little political solidarity not only with the Ukrainian national movement, but also with other political causes. As a result of these regional differences, the Pan-Ukrainian national independence movement that formed in 1917 remained a small and fragile coalition, easily split by outsiders. In 1918, Western and Eastern Ukraine were united, and the resultant Ukrainian National Republic declared independence. With little difficulty, however, the Soviet state used military force to annex first Eastern Ukraine (ca. 1919) and then Western Ukraine (ca. 1939).

Ukrainian nationalism as an organized social movement declined during the Soviet period. But state building and federalist structures together with rapid urbanization encouraged the establishment of a variety of institutions that provided new foundations for Ukrainian national awareness in Eastern Ukraine. Ukrainian-language cultural institutions were created throughout Ukrainian cities during the first decades of Soviet rule and created the technical infrastructure for transforming cities that had long been islands of Russian culture into Ukrainian cultural zones. Hence, even though the Soviet state is largely viewed as having suppressed Ukrainian culture, Soviet state-supported universities, theaters, operas, ballet troupes and other institutions of high culture in fact together created an important institutional basis for the consolidation of a nationally conscious urban elite and provided the resources for disseminating beliefs in common national destiny, culture, and language among Ukraine's population.

Soviet nationality policies shifted during the Brezhnev era—in large part because of the real threats increasingly nationally conscious and assertive non-Russian elites posed to central rule. This shift led to widespread changes in Soviet institutions: Ukrainian language schools, universities, and theaters became Russian or bilingual, and many books, journals, and newspapers that had previously been published in the Ukrainian language began to come out in Russian. With time, the Ukrainian language gradually lost its status relative to the Russian language, particularly in Eastern Ukraine. Soviet Ukrainian elites who did not show full support for these changes were demoted or removed from positions of authority in the republic. A small circle of dissidents who protested the restrictions placed on the Ukrainian language were arrested and sentenced to prison terms for anti-Soviet activities. Others were forced to emigrate. As a result, millions of Ukrainians ceased speaking Ukrainian because, as they put it, this language "had no future." In Western Ukraine, where national consciousness remained relatively high, these policy changes provoked growing resentment.

The state of the Ukrainian language was a central focus of protest for Ukrainian intellectuals and more broadly for Western Ukrainians almost from the moment that Gorbachev introduced his policy of *glasnost* or "openness." Tiny Galicia was at first far more politically mobilized than any other Ukrainian region. A full year before independence, its population had voted the Communist Party out of office. Eastern Ukrainians were slow to join this pro-reform association, and chapters of Rukh organized in Eastern Ukrainian cities frequently splintered into Ukrainian-speaking and Russian-speaking factions. As a result, with the exception of the capital, Kyiv, Eastern Ukraine remained politically controlled by the Communist Party until the Soviet state collapsed. Nevertheless, when given the choice, Ukrainians voted in overwhelming numbers for independence after the Soviet Union's dissolution, and polls now indicate that national consciousness is growing steadily among Eastern Ukrainians.

Two broad surveys offer slightly different perspectives on Ukrainian national mobilization, Paul Magocsi's *A History of Ukraine* (Seattle: University of Washington Press, 1996) and Orest Subtelny's *Ukraine* (University of Toronto Press, 1988). For a discussion of the national movement during World War II, see John Armstrong's *Ukrainian Nationalism* (Columbia University Press, 1963). Taras Kuzio and Andrew Wilson's *Ukraine: From Perestroika to Independence* (St. Martin's Press, 1994) and Andrew Wilson's *Ukrainian Nationalism in the 1990s* (Cambridge University Press, 1997) give a detailed account of the independence movement before and after the Soviet Union's collapse.

**UNITED ARAB REPUBLIC** 1958–1961, Political entity created by the union of Egypt and Syria. It was viewed at the time as a major step in the direction of comprehensive Arab unity. In retrospect, save for the union of Yemen and South Yemen in 1990, it has proved to be the only voluntary merger of separate Arab states in the modern era.

The UAR was created in the 1950s, when many of the new political units of the Arabic-speaking world were perceived as artificial and illegitimate creations by their peoples. Its immediate catalysts were the growth of Pan-Arabist political sentiment in the Arab East, particularly in Syria, and the popularity of Egypt's President Gamal Abdel Nasser after his assumption of a position of Arab leadership in the struggle against imperialism in the mid-1950s. Syrian politicians had floated various suggestions for an Egyptian-Syrian federation between 1955 and 1957. As political factionalism within Syria threatened political stability, in January 1958 a delegation of Syrian army officers flew to Egypt and importuned Nasser for immediate union. Initially reluctant to take the plunge, Nasser accepted only after obtaining Syrian agreement to a complete merger of the two countries under his leadership. Syria's civilian politicians acceded to his terms with varying degrees of enthusiasm. The creation of the UAR was declared on February 1, 1958; referenda in Egypt and Syria in the same month overwhelmingly endorsed the union and ratified Nasser's selection as president.

The government of the UAR was dominated by Nasser and Egypt. Nasser stood at the pinnacle of his popularity as an Arab nationalist leader in the late 1950s. In addition, by acquiescing to Nasser's terms for union including the abolition of political parties, Syria's political leadership in effect surrendered their fate to Nasser. Although Syrians participated in UAR cabinets, and local administration in Syria remained largely in Syrian hands, national and international policy was determined by Nasser in Cairo.

Only a limited degree of genuine integration between the "northern region" and the "southern region" of the UAR was achieved in the three-and-a-half year history of the union. Until the eve of the dissolution of the union the economies of the two regions remained distinct, with separate currencies, foreign trade regimes, and relatively little interregional exchange of goods or labor. Ultimately the most serious failure of integration was in the military sphere, where the armies of the two regions remained largely intact under an Egyptian-officered high command.

Syrian discontent with the Egyptian-dominated UAR accumulated over time. Nasser's natural allies on the Syrian left, the Ba'th Party, were alienated by their marginalization in the union government and resigned their posts by the end of 1959. In the later years of the union,

Nasser controlled Syria through an Egyptian "viceroy," Marshall ʿAbd al-Hakim ʿAmir, supported by Nasserist enthusiasts in the security services. It was central government efforts at greater integration in 1961 that sparked the demise of the UAR. In July new economic decrees moving in the direction of a socialized economy would have seriously affected private enterprise in Syria. In August measures increasing administrative centralization disrupted the existing security apparatus and increased Syrian disaffection. On September 28 military units in Damascus seized control of the city; Syrian units elsewhere gradually came out in support of the uprising. Nasser at first considered repression of the rebellion. By September 29, when it became clear that most of the Syrian military had risen, he grudgingly accepted Syria's secession from the UAR. Now shorn of its northern region, Egypt continued to call itself the United Arab Republic until 1971.

Even after its collapse, the UAR remained a potent reference point and symbol of what might have been for Arab nationalists. Unsuccessful attempts to forge similar constitutional unity among Arab nationalist regimes continued through the 1960s and into the 1970s. The meaningfulness of the UAR as a symbol of Arab nationalism seems to have diminished with the passage of time, as Pan-Arabism fades with the consolidation of the legitimacy of existing states.

The UAR has yet to find its historian. The circumstances leading to its creation are analyzed in Patrick Seale, *The Struggle for Syria* (1965). A good brief account of the experiment in unity is available in Malcolm Kerr, *The Arab Cold War: Gamal ʿAbd al-Nasir and His Rivals, 1958–1970* (3rd ed., 1971). Egyptian-oriented accounts of its internal politics are given by Anthony Nutting (*Nasser*, 1972) and Robert Stephens (*Nasser: A Political Biography*, 1971). The Syrian side of the story is presented in Tabitha Petran's *Syria* (1972).

**UNITED NATIONS** In 1945 the world emerged out of the destruction, devastation, and misery caused by two successive world wars to enter a new stage in its organic evolution threatened more than ever by nuclear annihilation and innumerable internal conflicts. International cooperation has occurred on a variety of levels for countless centuries, but not until 1945 did the world witness so many independent nations collectively take the extra step at cooperation for the greater good. Preceded by the League of Nations, the victors of World War II rallied together in an attempt to form "an organization of peace loving states" to maintain international peace and security and to cooperate for social progress. The United Nations came into being on October 24, 1945, after fifty-one sovereign nations rati-

fied and unanimously adopted the charter signed four months earlier in San Francisco. The preamble to the charter made it clear what the founders had in mind. They set out four primary goals: "to save succeeding generations from the scourge of war, which twice in our lifetime has brought untold sorrow to mankind . . . , to reaffirm faith in fundamental human rights . . . , to establish conditions under which justice and respect for the obligations arising from treaties and other sources of international law can be maintained; and to promote social progress and better standards of life in larger freedom."

This international organization is significant to the analysis of nationalism for several reasons. First, it is the most daring and enduring step ever taken by such a large number of independent nations to give up elements of their sovereignty for collective security. Second, since its formation over fifty years ago, the world has undergone dramatic social, political, economic, technological, and geographic change. With increased cooperation, interdependence, and contact, nationalistic movements have witnessed a resurgence in recent years. Democracy has been the battle cry for a growing number of nations throughout the world. With the end of the Cold War and such advances in communications technologies, falling trade barriers, and a growing international financial system, diverse nations and peoples are being pulled together more than ever before. On the one hand, these developments have resulted in a number of positive outcomes for many people around the world. One such outcome has been the evolution of the role of the United Nations in world affairs. Yet, on the other hand it is these same developments that have resulted in a resurgence of nationalism in many countries around the globe that have threatened the initiatives and fundamental purpose of the United Nations, namely, to promote peace and cooperation among nations.

As we enter the 21st century, the United Nations is faced with the challenge of addressing internal conflicts arising out of numerous nationalistic movements. From Burundi to Kosovo and from East Timor to Northern Ireland, the question arises: Where does the domain of the United Naitons begin and to what extent can this body address issues that are internal to a sovereign nation? On October 3, 1993, the killing of eighteen American peacekeepers in Somalia and the dragging of one marine through the streets of Mogadishu marked a turning point in attitudes among many U.S. lawmakers. Peacekeeping among warring factions is a laudable enterprise, but at what risk? As the United Nations celebrated its fifty-year anniversary in 1995, this was the question that weighed heavy on many people's minds. The problem at that time was the continuing war in

Bosnia-Herzegovina. Four years later it is Kosovo and the conflict between the Serbs and the ethnic Albanians that lingers. As the United Nations enters the new millennium, the questions remain. Are internal conflicts between groups simply an internal matter of a sovereign nation or does the United Nations have a mandate to intervene?

According to one scholar, "for the first 45 years of its existence, the U.N.'s operational responsibilities were very much limited by the confrontation of the two superpowers . . . . Then overnight, it was asked to become operational in a wide variety of situations around the world, becoming a kind of worldwide 911 emergency number, and it was simply not geared up for that kind of activity either in terms of resources or in terms of mindset. Those growing pains are still evident." Since the end of the Cold War, the world is no longer divided into two blocs, and conflicts are threatening stability throughout the world. It is often nationalist conflicts with deep cleavages along ethnic and religious lines that make these so volatile. Whether it is Bosnia, Rwanda, Somalia, Sudan, or Afghanistan, ethnic conflicts have caused great misery for many people around the world. These problems are directed at the heart of a larger question about national sovereignty versus individual liberty and human rights. In its next fifty years, the United Naitons will have to address this question and in doing so redefine its purpose and mission as a global body for peace and human welfare.

Some bibliographic references include Wendell Gordon's *The United Nations at the Cross-Roads of Reform* (M. E. Sharpe, 1994), Rosemary Righter's *Utopia Lost: The United Nations and World Order* (Twentieth Century Fund Press, 1995), and Stanley Meisler's *United Nations: The First Fifty Years* (Grove/Atlantic, 1995).

## U.S. NATIONALISM, POST-1914

American nationalism since World War I has been marked by a return to the civic nationalist tradition first developed by the country's founders. This resurgence has been led by women, minorities, and their advocates. By many measures of institutionalized political power, women and minorities were excluded categorically from full membership in the American nation prior to 1914. This gradually ceased to be the case as the level of organization increased among these excluded groups and they became aligned in broad coalitions united by the goal of securing civil rights for all American adults. The resultant movements gradually developed protest tactics that posed serious challenges to the "patriotic" organizations that had so effectively denied much of the population political rights after the Civil War. This wave of protest culminated in the civil rights movement and the passage of the Civil Rights Act of 1964—an event that signaled an end to the long-standing hegemony of American ethnic nationalist movements and a return to the civic nationalist tradition enshrined in the American Constitution.

Civic nationalist movements only gradually developed the organizational power to challenge the powerful grassroots ethnic nationalist movements that proliferated in the United States at the turn of the century. Grassroots American nationalism was led during the 19th century by native-born whites who strove to place limits on federal power from below, and to restrict the rights of excluded groups (minorities in particular) that had successfully won federal recognition from above. During the first decades of the 20th century, this countermovement grew even more politically powerful throughout the United States. Grassroots ethnic nationalism's successful exclusion of African Americans from power is perhaps its best known achievement, but immigration restriction in the 1920s is a less known case that proves just how pervasive and well-organized ethnic nationalist movements became at the federal level during this period.

Advocates of restrictive immigration policy aroused massive public protest following World War I with arguments that southeastern Europeans had brought diseases, prejudices, and economic problems to the United States, and filled public institutions with the feeble-minded, insane, epileptics, and paupers: that these immigrants had lowered the country's standard of living, depressed American wages, and created slums, and that their allegiance to foreign powers (e.g., the Pope) led them to spread ideas opposed to private property, free speech, and the separation of church and state. The argument that evoked the strongest public response was racial: Nationalist groups contended that southern and eastern Europeans were racially incompatible with "old stock" Americans, and their arrival had diluted the country's "racial stock" and would cause "race suicide." Only the exclusion of these "lower races" would avert the country's certain collapse. In response to public opinion, members of Congress who had been opposed to national origins quotas prior to 1917 abruptly altered their positions on immigration policy. After making long speeches ensuring the public that this legislation would protect the country's racial foundations and ensure the numerical predominance of the Celtic, Teutonic, and Anglo-Saxon races in the population, a landslide of votes passed the 1924 Immigration Act, which effectively put a stop to legal immigration and instituted a national origins quota system intended to maintain the 1890 ethnic composition of the white American population. It was only with the passage of the 1965 Amendments to the Immigration and Nationality Act that the national origins quota system was abolished and replaced with an ethnic-blind preference system. The amendments took effect in 1968, at which point a rapid shift of immigrant's ethnic origins occurred away from Europe to Asia and countries of the Western hemisphere like Mexico, the Dominican Republic, Jamaica, Haiti, and Colombia.

The overturning of the national origins restriction system came as the culmination of an unprecedented wave of public protest led by the civil rights movement. Called by some the "Second American Revolution," this movement triumphed over ethnic nationalist movements and reaffirmed the country's commitment to the civic nationalist traditions of its founders. From the 1950s to the middle of the 1960s, mass protests challenged and overturned many of the legal barriers that excluded southern African Americans from full citizenship. Activists from this movement reinvigorated other causes—women's rights, environmentalism, the war on poverty—and fueled an ethnic revival among racial and ethnic minorities and indigenous peoples. The resurgence of civic nationalism in the United States has promoted a form of pluralist "multiculturalism" that celebrates the triumph of ethnic and racial diversity over the forces of assimilation, although the broad-based coalitions that conquered the older ethnic nationalists have long since collapsed under disintegrative pressures. A "new" ethnic nationalism exemplified by black power movements, as well as new transnational social movements of human rights, radical feminism, gay pride, and lesbian rights, continue to fight for inclusion and broader political support for the rights of marginal groups. Such efforts have experienced a fair degree of success. They have also spurred countermovements such as the pro-life movement, as well as a resurgence of white supremacist and anti-immigrant movements that seek to place limits on further inclusion. Nonetheless, these changes have been unable to erode the legal and organizational structures that were successfully established by the civil rights movement, and that provide firmer foundations for American civic nationalism. Although grassroots opposition continues to the civic nationalist tradition enshrined in the American constitution, the threats such countermovements pose have diminished over the course of the 20th century as a consequence of the increasing organizational power and sophistication of advocates that defend the civil rights of minorities, women, immigrants, as well as other groups that have tended to be the target of ethnic nationalists.

Hence, the Ku Klux Klan's membership has declined from a peak of four million members in the 1920s to a few thousand today, and efforts to deny recent immigrants access to social services have been declared unconstitutional.

The civil rights movement is examined in Morris's *Origins of the Civil Rights Movement* (Free Press, 1984). The women's movement is the subject of Freeman's *The Politics of Women's Liberation* (McKay, 1975). Twentieth-century debates on American national identity are analyzed from a variety of perspectives in Sollors's *Theories of Ethnicity* (New York University Press, 1996), which also includes a useful bibliographic essay by the editor on theories of American ethnicity.

**USTAŠA MOVEMENT** 1929–1945, Axis-sponsored extreme nationalist movement that ruled Croatia during World War II. A violent fascist, anti-Serbian, anticommunist, and anti-Semitic group descended from Josip Frank's Pure Party of Right, itself formed in 1895 as an offshoot of Ante Starcevic's Party of Right (as in Croatian "state right").

Founded on January 7, 1929, by Ante Pavelić, the *Ustaša* Croatian Revolutionary Organization (*ustaša* meaning one who takes part in an *ustanak,* or uprising) was dedicated to bringing about an ethnically pure independent Croatian state by any means necessary. Sentenced to death in absentia for advocating the overthrow of the Yugoslav state in late 1929, Pavelić subsequently took refuge in fascist Italy. Throughout the 1930s a few hundred fanatical Pavelić loyalists trained at bases in Italy and Hungary, while sympathizers back home engaged in random terrorism, such as the 1932 so-called "Lika Uprising," which amounted to little more than an attack on an isolated police station in the Velebit mountains.

Following the *Ustaša*-sponsored assassination of Yugoslavia's King Alexander in 1934, Mussolini imprisoned its roughly 700 Italian-based members on the island of Lipari. On April 15, 1941, they returned to Zagreb, where Pavelić assumed the title of *Poglavnik* (chief) of the *Ustaša*-run but Axis-controlled Independent State of Croatia (*Nezavisna Drzava Hrvatska*, NDH).

Despite its name, the new state was independent only on paper. Ultimate authority resided with the occupying powers of Germany and Italy, among whom the country was divided for military purposes. Agreements signed in Rome in May 1941 rendered the new Croatia a de facto Italian protectorate. Furthermore, the NDH was deprived of several traditional Croatian areas, namely, the Dalmatian coastline from Zadar to Split, most Adriatic islands, Istria, and the port of Rijeka, all of which were ceded to Italy. The NDH was compensated for these territorial losses with control over all of Bosnia-Herzegovina, however.

Throughout its four-year reign, the *Ustaša* regime relentlessly attempted to render the NDH an ethnically pure state. Viewing the Muslims (12 percent of the NDH's population of 6.3 million) mostly as ethnic Croats of the Islamic faith to be flattered and welcomed back into the Croatian fold, the regime focused on the Serbs, who accounted for roughly a third of the NDH's population. According to a notorious statement by Mile Budak, NDH minister of education, one-third of them were to be deported, one-third exterminated, and the remaining third were to be converted to Catholicism.

The enthusiasm with which the regime's henchmen massacred Serbs sometimes shocked even German SS officers. The mass killings which took place at the camp of Jasenovac alone leave no doubt as to the genocidal nature of the *Ustaša* government's intentions toward the Serbian minority. The extent of Serbian losses at Jasenovac and in the NDH as a whole remains a highly controversial topic to this day. Serbian nationalists claim that 700,000 Serbs were killed there, while Croatian nationalists, including the country's first post-Communist President, Franjo Tudjman, maintain that number is closer to 60,000. Over 300,000 Serbs perished in the NDH (more than 100,000 in Croatia and some 200,000 in Bosnia), or roughly one-sixth of the state's ethnic Serbs. Eighty percent of Bosnia and Croatia's approximately 37,000 Jews were also liquidated.

In early May 1945 the *Ustaša* regime crumbled as Germany unconditionally surrendered to the Allies. Pavelić fled the country and died in Spain in 1959.

## UZBEK NATIONALISM

**UZBEK NATIONALISM** The Uzbek people, essentially an amalgamation of Turkic tribes, came to dominate the Transoxiana region of Central Asia in the 15th century, but rarely controlled their own fate and, even when they did, they were rarely united. Thus, they were initially led by Mongols and later dominated by Moghuls, Persians, and Russians, while the 16th century saw the emergence of the three distinct though mainly Uzbek khanates/emirates of Bokhara, Khiva, and Khokand. Initially taken into the Russian Empire as protectorates in the mid- to late 19th century, the Uzbeks were to play only a limited role in the phase of unifying nationalist movements of the early 20th century, retaining their separate princely families (except in Khokand) until 1920. While there were uprisings against the Russian and Soviet systems by opponents of the draft in 1916 and by the Basmachi movement in the 1920s, the Uzbek element was still largely subsumed by a broader Islamic and Pan-Turkic identity among the rebels.

The new Soviet regime, although briefly allowing a measure of national Communism among the ethnic minorities in the 1920s, was itself fundamentally committed to a longer term program of internationalism—one even broader than Pan-Turkism. However, its policies of unifying peoples of a common language, creating literary language-based identities, establishing divisive and somewhat artificial territories in 1924–1925, and its imposition of a quasi-federal system actually served to reinforce a more specifically Uzbek national identity in the longer run, without ever fully eradicating the earlier clan-based Turkic/Islamic identity, and before any alternative Soviet identity could emerge.

While in the Soviet era Uzbek nationalism did not rise to the heights of activism achieved in Ukraine or the Baltic republics, there remained an underlying hostility toward rule by the alien pagans from Moscow, even on those rare occasions when Uzbeks themselves were to be found in prominent positions in the central leadership. The late 1960s and 1970s were witnesses to a number of documented instances of self-assertive pride in, and glorification of, a superior past prior to the era of Russian domination, in both literature and history writing among Uzbeks, as well as instances of favoritism in the advancement of fellow Uzbeks to positions of some power in the Uzbek republic hierarchy. Attention was drawn by both cultural and political figures to the principle of self-determination and the right to secession proclaimed in the Soviet Constitution. In the late 1980s and early 1990s, a broader discontent manifested itself, particularly through the umbrella movement Birlik (Unity), formed in November 1988. From its earliest mass demonstrations in March and April 1989, it took an ostensibly internationalist line toward all inhabitants of the Uzbek Republic, but firmly sought greater protection for the economic, political, and cultural interests of that republic as against those of Moscow and the USSR. The movement, however, was soon weakened by internal divisions and by governmental adoption of some of its popular proposals. Indeed, on June 20, 1990, the Uzbek Parliament adopted a declaration of sovereignty over a range of internal affairs. Despite Birlik and this declaration, Uzbekistan largely gained independence in late 1991 by default—by the collapse of the will and ability of the federal center to maintain its hold.

Uzbek identity and self-awareness were further developed in the era of independence. The need to forge a clear identity for the new state prompted even some of its carryover Communist leaders to take positions less internationalist than in the past, and yet equally not as locally clan based as previously. This was motivated by both internal and external factors. Among the latter was the danger of spillover from Moslem fundamentalism in the south in Afghanistan and in the east from the civil conflict in Tajikistan. Attempts at distancing itself from Moscow and Russia had the same effect. Indeed, she not only sought to protect her own interests but also to project herself as the prime regional power in place of Russia by, for example, blocking Russian military equipment from passing through her territory en route to Tajikistan. This nationalist mood, as evidenced by foreign policy, has also been reflected in her pride in not having any Russian troops on her territory and her halfhearted, even truculent, membership of the Russian-sponsored Commonwealth of Independent States. By joining the G.U.A.M. group of states in 1998 she has further emphasized her separation from Russia. More locally she displayed some concern for the situation of the Uzbek diaspora in Tajikistan and Kazakhstan and came into conflict with Kyrgyzstan over water supplies that threatened her very existence.

Internally, the nationalism involved a rediscovery of a separate past and rehabilitation of figures such as Tamerlane on the 660th anniversary of his birth in 1996—the tyrant of Soviet historiography now becoming a benificent and wise father to his alleged people. Governmental propagation of national unity has openly opposed "divisive" and "destabilizing" political forces, including ethnic minority-oriented parties and publications. About 30 percent of her population consists of non-Uzbek peoples, even by official reckoning. The Tajik cultural group Samarkand was harassed and accused of political aspirations, irredentism, and separatist tendencies, especially in 1992–1993, and Uzbek has been increasingly biased against multilingualism in education and the media.

Among the most useful of the steadily growing literature on Uzbekistan are James Critchlow's *Nationalism in Uzbekistan* (Westview, 1991); Gregory Gleason's "Uzbekistan—From Statehood to Nationhood," in I. Bremmer and R. Taras, eds., *Nation and Politics in the Soviet Successor States* (Cambridge, 1993); and I. A. Karimov's *Uzbekistan on the Threshold of the 21st Century* (St. Martin's Press, 1998).

# V

**VARGAS, GETÚLIO** 1883–1954, President of Brazil (1930–1945 and 1951–1954). Vargas's personal and political prowess stemmed largely from his family heritage and his experience in the authoritarian political system in the border state of Rio Grande do Sul. The third of five sons of a regionally prominent family, Vargas was born at São Borja, a small town in western Rio Grande do Sul on Brazil's frontier with Argentina. His parents, General Manoel do Nascimento Vargas and Candida Dornelles Vargas, were from rival groups that regularly took opposite sides in armed political contests. Initially intent on pursuing a military career, he resigned from the army after five years to study law in Porto Alegre.

Vargas first plunged into the political system as a law student, campaigning for the gubernatorial candidate of the Republican Party. He graduated in 1907 and was appointed to the district attorney's office in Porto Alegre. Two years later he then returned to São Borja to practice law and to run successfully for a seat in the state legislature. Membership in the legislature, however, assured the political future of those who demonstrated unquestioning support of the Republican governor. The perennial governor, Borges de Medeiros, ruled by de facto in all matters except finance, placed maintaining a balanced budget and treasury surplus above building public works and providing social services, and insisted on personal loyalty from all party officials. In 1912, Vargas learned that even mild criticism of Borges's rule was unacceptable. For such a mistake he was removed from the state legislature and barred from reelection for five years. When he later became the head of the nation, Vargas was never to demand such obedience from his followers, but he would share Borges's ideas about keeping the reins of power in his own hands.

Vargas soared to the national spotlight in the 1920s, a decade of dissent and revolts by young military officers (tenentes) and disgruntled civilians against corrupt rule by professional politicians in the service of the rural oligarchy. The tenentes were eventually defeated—killed,

jailed, or exiled by the government—but they remained heroes to much of the press and the urban population. In 1922 Vargas traveled to Rio de Janeiro as a newly elected congressman and head of his state's congressional delegation. Four years later he was elevated to the cabinet as finance minister of President Washington Luís Pereira de Sousa, and in 1928, following an uncontested election, Vargas replaced Borges de Medeiros as governor of Rio Grande do Sul. Vargas would move on to accept the nomination of the reformist Liberal Alliance, a coalition formed from Republican Party regimes in three states and opposition parties elsewhere. The Vargas campaign was also supported by the tenentes and their civilian followers, who were clamoring for political and social change. Despite his popularity in the cities, he was badly defeated by the entrenched rural-based political machines in seventeen of the twenty states.

While Vargas appeared to accept defeat gracefully, he patiently waited for the advantageous moment to launch a decisive onslaught on the federal government. That moment came on October 3, 1930, when the revolution broke out simultaneously in Rio Grande do Sul, Minas Gerais, and Paraíba, the states that had backed his presidential campaign. After three weeks, by which time the rebels were controlling most of the coastal states, the army high command in Rio de Janeiro staged a coup d'état to halt the intraservice war. The military junta exiled President Washington Luís, and agreed to transfer power to Vargas when he arrived in the capital. On November 3 Getúlio Vargas was installed as sole chief of the provisional government for an indefinite term.

Moving quickly to consolidate his position, Vargas suspended the 1891 Constitution. In response to widespread expectations for social reform, he created new cabinet ministries for labor and education. With regard to the armed forces, Vargas granted amnesty to the military rebels of the 1920s. He was now undisputed dictator of Brazil.

The Constitutionalist Revolution of 1932, which

raged for three months before collapsing, was far costlier in lives and treasure than the Revolution of 1930. It was limited chiefly to the state of São Paulo, because elsewhere all interventionists and the armed forces remained loyal to the dictatorship. Although Vargas's national popularity remained high, the São Paulo rebels claimed a moral victory, for within a year elections were held for the constituent assembly that wrote the Constitution of 1934. This charter incorporated all reforms enacted by the provisional government, restored full civil rights, and provided for the election of a new congress as well as elected state governors and legislatures. On July 17, 1934, the constituent assembly elected Vargas president of Brazil for a four-year term.

Vargas was no believer of any ideology: he was motivated by love of power and what he saw as Brazil's national interests. Following the abortive Communist-led revolt in November 1935, Vargas relied on his congressional majority to suspend civil rights and balloon police authority. A spurious Communist threat was the avowed justification for the coup d'état of November 10, 1937, which Vargas and the armed forces staged to create the allegedly totalitarian Estado Novo (New State).

Deeply patterned on the European fascist dictatorships, the Estado Novo lacked the usual political party, militia, and national police loyal to the dictator. His domestic policies continued as before to focus chiefly on the urban population and on the need to strengthen the material and human bases for industrialization. The major social reforms under the Estado Novo were enactment of a minimum wage law and codification of all labor legislation enacted since 1930, which had the effect of bringing urban workers into the political arena as staunch supporters of Vargas. Nevertheless, political parties and elections were outlawed.

Despite his apparent identification with fascism and the pro-German bias of some Brazilian military commanders, Vargas finally decided that Brazil's interests would best be served by supporting the United States. In 1942 Brazil entered World War II as one of the Allied powers, and in 1944 Brazil sent a substantial expeditionary force to fight in the Italian campaign.

The incongruity of waging war against dictatorships in Europe while living under a dictator at home was not lost on the Brazilian people, who pressed for an early return to democracy. During 1945 Vargas abolished censorship, released political prisoners, issued a new electoral law authorizing political parties, and called for the election of a new government in December. Fearing that he was planning another coup d'état, the army, led by officers recently returned from Italy, overthrew Vargas on October 29, 1945, installing an interim civilian regime to preside over the December elections.

He returned to politics as the candidate of his Brazilian Labor Party in the 1950 presidential elections. He waged a vociferously populist campaign and won overwhelmingly. He took office on January 31, 1951. However, as a democratically elected president obliged to share power with a divided Congress, Vargas proved unable to cope with the soaring inflation that eroded his labor following, or with the widespread ultranationalism to which his past policies had contributed. When the military withdrew its support and demanded his resignation, he complied on August 24, 1954; later that day he committed suicide. Vargas left a political testament in which he presented his death as a sacrifice on behalf of Brazilian workers.

**VASIĆ, DRAGIŠA** 1885–1945, Serb lawyer and intellectual, vice president of Serb Cultural Club, 1937–1941. Vasić grew up in a conservative Serb family. One of his relatives, Major Ljubomir Vulović, was executed in 1917 for participating in the Black Hand secret society. The harsh manner in which the Serb radicals had conducted the trial provoked a strong antipathy for the party in Vasić. In 1919, Vasić published his first book, *Karakter i mentalitet jednog pokoljenja (Character and Mentality of One Generation)*. This book, and his further publications in the 1920s, expressed his fundamental dissatisfaction with the new Yugoslav state. During this decade, Vasić pursued an avid interest in Russian literature and flirted briefly with Communism.

In 1937, Vasić cofounded and became the vice president of the Serb Cultural Club (*Srpski kulturni klub*, or SKK). In 1939, Vasić, Slobodan Jovanović, and other Serb nationalist intellectuals rejected the compromise agreement (*Sporazum*) signed by Prime Minister Cvetković and Croat Peasant Party leader Vladko Maček. Vasić and his colleagues on the Serb political right viewed the agreement, which provided for the creation of a separate administrative unit for a large proportion of the Croats, as an act of treason against the Serb nation. Vasić edited the SKK's main organ, *Srpski glas (Serbian Voice)*, which was published from November 1939 until the Yugoslav government banned it in June 1940. Vasić and the SKK continued to support the existence of a Yugoslav state, but only one in which the Serb nation would clearly play the predominant role. They rejected the unitarist policies of the 1921 Yugoslav constitution and the 1929 dictatorship, viewing them as a dangerous deviation from a pure Serbian path. Any concessions to the non-Serbs in Yugoslavia were portrayed as automatically detrimental to the Serb nation. The SKK claimed to want an agreement with the Croats, yet their writings made it clear that such an agreement could be only obtained if the borders of the Croatian unit ran along the borders of Serb settlement in Croatia. This condition was unacceptable to Croat politicians. While maintaining a strong stance against Croats and Slovenes, the writings of the SKK increasingly portrayed elements of the Serb nation as internal enemies. After the invasion of Yugoslavia by Germany, Vasić joined the *Četnik* forces, serving as an ideological advisor to their leader, Dragoljub Mihajlović. In 1945, Vasić was killed by rival members of the *Četnik* forces.

## VENEZUELAN NATIONALISM

Venezuela's revolutionary and modernizing nationalism has been fermenting for a long time. Like so many of her fellow Spanish American countries, Venezuela fell into a long period of domestic strife following her liberation. Much of the 19th century was marked by contention between liberals and conservatives ceaselessly struggling for political power.

Venezuela's modern problems are usually traced to Cipriano Castro, who ruled from 1899 to 1908. He was noted for his personal vices and misrule as well as for his cavalier attitude toward international obligations. In 1902 Venezuela was blockaded and bombarded by warships of Great Britain, Germany, and Italy because he refused to pay debts claimed by them on various grounds. Castro finally paid, and later traveled to Germany for his health. While he was there, in 1907, Vice President Juan Vicente Gómez took over the government and ruled Venezuela with an iron hand until his death in 1935.

Although Castro had discouraged foreign investors, Gómez invited them in to develop the country's resources, not so much on principle as from lack of it. A genuine opposition to Gómez's political rule and economic policies quickly developed. A group of intellectuals, centered among the students, were inspired in their opposition by the writings of the Venezuelan novelist Rómulo Gallegos. Known as the Generation of 1928, they raised the banner of social justice, economic nationalism, and democracy. They were particularly bitter over the foreign control of Venezuelan economy.

Late in 1947 presidential elections were held, and the AD's (Acción Democrática) candidate, Rómulo Gallegos, was victorious. One of the first tasks the Gallegos government undertook was to gain a higher percentage of the oil companies' profits. It also set up plans for a state-owned oil company to exploit Venezuela's reserve fields, and launched a broad-based attack on the conditions in housing, education, and agriculture. The most important issue facing the AD government was that of land reform. In 1948 this reform regime was ousted by the same young officers who had brought it to power in 1945; it was too reformist and civilian to suit them.

One officer, Marcos Pérez Jiménez, was a member of the military triumvirate that ruled until 1950, when he became sole dictator. During his rule, Pérez Jiménez violated many of the nationalist principles of Venezuela's reform parties. He failed to check the penetration of the foreign oil companies into new oil-producing lands.

Most of Venezuela's nationalist energies are directed toward internal problems. The important exception has been the increasing hostility against Castro's Cuba. The orientation of AD's traditional national values is both domestic and foreign, as indicated by its official goal of bringing to Venezuela a democratic revolution, nationalist, anti-imperialist, and antifeudal. Venezuela had been the paradise of military caudillos. Until 1958 there had been a long and inglorious line of this type of ruler, rarely interrupted by any attempt to give the country some semblance of constitutional government. But Venezuela had also become one of the foremost producers of oil, and by the time the tyrant of the Andes, Juan Vicente Gómez, had died in 1935, the petroleum industry was firmly entrenched in the country, providing it with its main source of income. Inevitably, oil became the principal issue in the revolutionary propaganda that came to the fore in 1945.

Hugo Chávez, a forty-five-year-old former army colonel who was jailed after leading an unsuccessful coup attempt in 1992, won the December 1999 presidential elections comfortably on a platform for radical change, along the lines of nationalism and the leftist movement, beginning with the revision of the constitution and the election of a new parliament. His platform called for junking the 1961 Constitution, which he dismissed as an anachronism and replacing it with a new charter that he said would eliminate corruption and strengthen democracy by weakening the forty-year stranglehold on power of the country's two traditional political parties (COPEI, Christian Democratic party, formally organized in 1946 and AD, Democratic Action Party). Until 1999, Venezuela had been ruled by liberals and conservatives for forty years, with widespread corruption, leaving an estimated 80 percent of people below the poverty line, despite its multibillion dollar oil industry.

## VENIZÉLOS, ELEUTHÉRIOS

1864–1936, Born in 1864 in western Crete. In 1866, after the failure of the Cretan revolt, Venizélos's family fled to Greece, but returned in 1872, to the city of Hania. After studying law in Athens, Venizélos was elected as deputy to the Cretan parliament. His advocacy of morality in political life, coupled with his brilliance as a lawyer, meant that his reputation soon spread to Athens and abroad. Greek Cretans revolted in 1895, but Venizélos was against it, realizing that Greece, having gone bankrupt in 1893, would be unable to help the islanders. By 1897, he finally assumed the leadership of the revolutionaries. Following the revolution, the Great Powers granted Crete its autonomy, and Venizélos became the organizational mastermind of the local government. His quarrel with the governor, Prince George of Greece, led to Venizélos assuming the leadership of the opposition (1901). The conflict brought the administration to a halt, until 1905 when Venizélos led another revolution, with the islanders once again proclaiming their union with Greece. From then on, Venizélos and his compatriots repeatedly pressed this demand.

The turning point for Venizélos came in 1910. The military officers who had instigated the 1909 coup called on him to go to Athens to form a government. Venizélos formed the Liberal Party, and won a massive majority, which allowed him to carry out an ambitious program of national reorganization, including constitutional reform, organizing the bureaucracy and the army, a new cabinet structure, and progressive labor and agricultural legislation. In the Balkan wars of 1912–1913, Greece, in coalition with Serbia, Montenegro, and Bulgaria, defeated the Ottoman forces and occupied Epirus and a large portion of Macedonia, including Thessaloniki. This time, Crete finally won union with Greece.

The outbreak of World War I led to the most important political conflict in modern Greek history: the "national schism." On one side, with King Constantine, were the old class of patron politicians whom Venizélos had displaced, along with their clients, the elite of the pre-1912 kingdom of Greece, and the yeomen and peasants of the "Old Greece" (pre-1881). This group looked on Germany as their patron. On the other side, with Venizélos, were Cretans, Epirotes, and (Greek) Macedonians, the landless peasants of Thessaly, and a coalition of Hellenic diaspora capitalists. This group supported Great Britain, because Venizélos had reached an understanding with the British that would serve both British and Greek interests. In 1914–1915, successive government crises took place, leading to extreme polarization between the two camps. In 1916, the royalist government concluded an agreement with Bulgaria, surrendering Greek fortifications to the Central Powers. Bulgarian forces moved in to occupy eastern Macedonia. In August 1916, military officers allied with Venizélos staged a coup in Thessaloniki and were soon joined there by Venizélos. The national schism became territorial: Greece now had two states, one in Thessaloniki, and one in Athens.

In 1917, after Allied intervention, King Constantine left Greece, and Venizélos assumed leadership. He led Greece into World War I and Greek and Allied forces pressed the Bulgarian forces in Macedonia, leading to the collapse of the front and to Bulgaria's surrender. Domestically, Venizélos's second administration failed to unite Greeks, and anti-Venizélists continued to resist his authority, both peacefully and militarily. Venizélos took advantage of the fortuitous conclusion of World War I to sign two key treaties: the Neuilly Treaty with Bulgaria (1919), which gave Greece most of her claims in the North, and the Sèvres Treaty with the Ottomans (1920), which gave Greece a portion of Asia Minor. The latter represents a high point of Greek nationalist aspirations; it created the "Greece of the two continents and the five seas" and was the closest the Greek nation-state ever came to a fulfillment of the "Great Idea." Yet, only days after its signing, there was an attempt on Venizélos's life. On November 1, Venizélos lost the elections, and promptly resigned from politics. The anti-Venizélists who assumed government went on to promote the Greek expedition into Asia Minor, which led to the Asia Minor debacle of 1922.

In 1923 Venizélos again became a principal negotiator for Greece, signing the Lausanne Treaty with the newly formed Turkish Republic. He attempted to coordinate Greek political forces once again, but, confronted with the stubborn attitudes of the Greek democrats, decided to stay out of politics. In 1924 Greece became a republic, but Venizélos's evaluation of the situation proved to be correct: successive coups d'état and government crises made Greece practically ungovernable. When an exhausted and frustrated public called on him once again, Venizélos reentered politics and swept to victory to form a second administration (1928–1932), which introduced a plethora of reforms and institution building. In foreign policy, Venizélos reached an understanding with the Turkish Republic, thus becoming the founder of "Greek-Turkish friendship." His administration fell prey to the 1929 depression; and it suffered another defeat in 1933. Military officers allied with him in another coup in 1935, but this was an ill-fated movement and Venizélos (and many of his followers) had to flee from Greece. He died a year later in Paris.

Venizélos has been called the "father of modern Greece" and rightly so, as his work practically defined the fate of the Greek nation-state for the 20th century. Politicians of both the left and the right are still eager to proclaim themselves his successors. There is a large body of literature on Venizélos; Mark Mazaower's article, "The Messiah and the Bourgeoisie: Venizelos and Politics in Greece, 1909–1912," in *Historical Journal* 35(4) (1992), pp. 885–904, contains references to almost all the important publications and is a valuable bibliographical guide.

**VERNACULAR LANGUAGES** The term *vernacular language* refers to a language that is considered indigenous to a region and its population. It is often opposed by scholars to official "national" languages that serve an entire country. Nationalists, however, frequently assume that each vernacular language deserves its own nation-state. This assumption is based on their belief that local populations have historically spoken a unique vernacular language and that this "natural" first language is the defining characteristic of a person's national identity.

Nationalist writings imply that vernacular languages preceded—and in some important sense provided the impetus for—contemporary nationalism. However, studies show that the relationship between vernacular languages and nationalism is far from easy. Today, much of the world speaks a first language whose origins are not local and instead can be traced to the emergence of modern states and the spread of Protestantism, democracy, and capitalism from Western Europe across the globe. The resultant political, religious, and economic transformations dramatically changed the functions language was expected to serve, and created powerful pressures for members of local speech communities to reject the use of older vernaculars.

Under what circumstances have linguistic minorities responded to these assimilative pressures by reasserting political loyalty to a local vernacular? There have been many attempts to theorize the conditions under which vernacular nationalist movements arise. One that is particularly noteworthy is Ernest Gellner's *Nations and Nationalism*.

Gellner defines nationalism as the belief that every culture deserves its own political roof. It is impossible prior to industrialization because in agrarian societies differences of speech and culture are condoned by custom and arouse little enmity. While a profound cultural and often linguistic barrier separates rural and urban populations, linguistic minorities in an agrarian society have neither the interest nor the ability to extend the reach of their particular language. The vernaculars that rural populations speak rarely possess the formal qualities that would allow them to expand their functions to government and other institutions necessary to nation building. Most communication in such societies is oral. Written communication is customarily reserved for specific uses, most often of a religious nature. Taboos prohibit such sacred languages from serving profane political or economic purposes.

Gellner contends that vernacular nationalism first becomes possible during the early stages of industrialization. A modern economy necessitates frequent, precise, and exact communication across territories. This type of communication requires literacy in a standardized, written language. As subsistence economies are replaced by markets, rural laborers are displaced from their former livelihoods and drawn into uncertain urban labor markets where their old skills are rarely needed and their access to formal education is limited. Rising expectations, mass migration from rural to urban regions, and limited access to education together create considerable conflict between the literate minority and the illiterate majority during the early stages of industrialization, and promote a new consciousness of cultural differences. However, the friction of early modernization itself is insufficient to sustain nationalism. Vernacular nationalism occurs in the relatively few cases where "proto-national" rural groups begin industrialization equipped with what Gellner refers to as "size, historicity, reasonably compact territory and a capable and energetic intelligentsia." In other words, the author contends, vernacular nationalism will occur among rural populations that are reasonably large and possess a well-codified history, an identifiable homeland, and a literate elite able to transform local vernaculars into the sort of medium that is necessary for success in industrial society. Speech communities that have a strong association with a world religion tend to possess these resources.

Gellner predicts that linguistic minorities must already possess many of the attributes of nationhood at the onset of industrialization if they are to successfully break off from established states. This explains some cases better than others. The Austro-Hungarian Empire indeed ceased to exist as the result of vernacular nationalist movements led by Hungarians and Poles (nationalities that clearly possessed "size, historicity, reasonably compact territory and a capable and energetic intelligentsia") during the early stages of industrialization, when a majority of these ethnic groups was still engaged in agriculture. But these conditions did not hold in the case of the nationalist movements that led to the dissolution of the Soviet Union and Yugoslavia. These two state socialist countries survived early periods of ethnic disunity, industrialized successfully, achieved universal literacy and relatively high living standards, as well as relative interethnic harmony, and then collapsed suddenly under surprisingly powerful independence movements initiated by their most economically advanced nationalities. Why, then, did these movements occur? Arguably, decades of highly decentralized socialist state building promoted vernacular nationalism by creating a variety of cultural institutions that made up for earlier deficits in "size, historicity, reasonably compact territory and a capable and energetic intelligentsia." These latter two cases suggest that vernacular nationalism is not simply a function of the ano-mie and rootlessness of industrialization, but rather, may occur later in response to political arrangements and institutions that gradually weaken the ability of the central state to maintain order over peripheral elites.

Ernest Gellner's *Nations and Nationalism* provides the fullest account of his theory of the relationship be-tween language, industrialization, and nationalism. The relationship between vernacular languages and nation-alism is examined in the Austro-Hungarian case in Hans Kohn's *The Habsburg Empire, 1804–1918* (Van Nos-trand, 1961), in the Soviet case in Michael Smith's *Lan-guage and Power in the Creation of the USSR, 1917–1953* (Mouton de Gruyter, 1998), and in the Yugoslav case in Ivo Banac's *The National Question in Yugoslavia* (Cornell University Press, 1984).

## VERSAILLES, TREATY OF

**VERSAILLES, TREATY OF**   By the fall of 1918 a mil-lion fresh American troops in France tipped the balance in World War I, and on November 11, 1918, the ex-hausted and starving Germans saw no alternative to ca-pitulation. France and Britain had technically been vic-torious, but they were left breathless and demoralized. It has often been said that Britain lost an entire genera-tion. About 1.3 million Frenchmen had been killed and more than a million crippled. Northeastern France, the country's most prosperous industrial and agricultural sector, was largely devastated. Europe's winning na-tions had suffered enormous human and material losses in order to obtain victory. This inclined their leaders to demand a heavy price from Germany in the Treaty of Versailles. The settlement is a glaring example of the fact that policies which may be righteous are not al-ways wise.

The first major problem with the Versailles treaty was the manner in which it was written. In contrast to all previous peace settlements in Europe, the van-quished (in this case, the Germans) were not included in the negotiations. If the Germans had been included, perhaps they would have felt some responsibility for the treaty, but as it was, it represented a dictated peace and thus the Germans never felt any moral obligation to subscribe to its terms. The settlement had a strong whiff of "victor's justice."

Prior to American entry into the conflict, President Woodrow Wilson had proposed a "peace without vic-tory" and later issued a written document containing fourteen points as a basis for European peace that con-tained very lofty language. The Germans later accepted the text, but it faded into the background at Versailles as French Prime Minister Georges Clemenceau ("the old ti-ger") virtually dictated the terms of what turned out to be

an attempt at revenge. Little did he know that he was helping to sow the seeds of disaster, particularly in the mind of a wounded Austrian corporal, Adolf Hitler.

When the terms were forwarded to Berlin in mid-May 1919, with the warning that nonacceptance would result in an immediate resumption of hostilities, the Germans could hardly believe their eyes. They had ex-pected to lose all territory conquered during the war, as well as Alsace-Lorraine to France, but they also lost a tenth of their prewar population and an eighth of their territory. Danzig was made a free city and the province of Posen was ceded to Poland, and a narrow corridor was cut right through West Prussia to connect these areas with Poland. Worse, the coal-rich Saar region was placed under League of Nations and French control for fifteen years. France stationed its troops in Germany west of the Rhine and obtained mandates in the former German colonies of Togo and Cameroons, and in Syria and Lebanon as well.

The territorial losses, combined with the loss of practically all its merchant marine fleet, made it far more difficult for Germany to pay the shockingly high reparations demanded of it. The Rhineland was occu-pied by Allied soldiers and was to be demilitarized per-manently. Germany's high seas fleet was to be turned over to the Allies, a requirement that prompted the Ger-mans to scuttle all their naval ships, which had been interned at Scapa Flow in the Orkney Islands north of Scotland in mid-1919. The future German army was to be restricted to 100,000 career officers and men with no military aircraft, tanks, or other offensive weapons.

Perhaps worst of all, Article 231 of the treaty placed sole responsibility for the outbreak of the war and therefore all its destruction on the shoulders of Ger-many and its allies. This article had been written by a young American diplomat, John Foster Dulles, as a compromise to the French, who had wanted to annex the Rhineland and to have even higher reparation pay-ments from Germany. But Dulles had to admit later that "it was the revulsion of the German people from this article of the Treaty which, above all else, laid the foun-dation for the Germany of Hitler." At the time of the Treaty, Adolf Hitler was only beginning to emerge from the political shadows. He was a fiery speaker, capable of stirring his listeners with haranguing, emotional tira-des. For the next quarter of a century he never ceased to rail against the weak Weimar Republic and the wick-edness of the Versailles treaty.

The document made a mockery of many of Wood-row Wilson's fourteen points, such as "open covenants openly arrived at," freedom of the seas, the "impartial adjustment of all colonial claims," and, of course, the self-determination of nations. Borders were drawn by the Great Powers that left a fourth of all inhabitants in Central Europe outside of the countries to which they would have belonged ethnically. This helped plant the seeds for the nationalist unrest and tension in that region during the interwar years and after the end of the Cold War. The victors permitted the right of self-determination only where people wanted to detach themselves from Germany, such as in northern Schleswig and part of Upper Silesia. Wherever an area's population clearly wanted to join Germany, such as Austria or northern Bohemia, no referendum was permitted. Such hypocrisy stimulated within Germany cynicism toward both the treaty and any German government that would sign it. Of course, Germany's harsh policy toward a collapsing Russia at Brest-Litovsk had provided a disastrous precedent. Nevertheless, Germany's short-sightedness in 1918 could not reasonably be invoked to justify an equally short-sighted Allied policy a year later.

As Chancellor Philipp Scheidemann said to the National Assembly in 1919, "Which hand would not wither up which put itself and us into these bonds?" The treaty was a millstone around the neck of the new Weimar Republic. It was unfortunate that national humiliation coincided with the birth of the first democracy in Germany. When at last it had adopted the political organization extolled by the victorious Allies, it had become an international outcast. It not only helped create a deep division in German society, but it seriously hampered the normalization of Germany's relations with the outside world. It could only be maintained by force, but the United States quickly withdrew from Europe's military affairs, and Britain and France gradually lost the will to enforce it energetically. One day a spellbinding demagogue would be able to untie the "fetters of Versailles" right before the eyes of a weary and lethargic Europe and reap much applause within Germany for this.

**VICHY GOVERNMENT** Name given to the French government led by the Maréchal Philippe Pétain, a military hero of World War I who requested an armistice after the defeat of French troops by the German army in 1940. France was first divided into two zones, one occupied by the Germans and the other unoccupied. The government, including Pétain's prime minister Laval, moved from Paris to the town of Vichy, a spa south of the Jura mountains that offered convenient space to organize the new regime administration. The Vichy government consisted of individuals from numerous political groups, ranging from pro-German fascists to more liberal leaders who saw the occupation of France by a foreign power as the possibility for deep social changes.

In spite of its internal competing forces, the government generally sought collaboration with the German occupying forces. It also supported the *Révolution Nationale* (National Revolution), a political and social program established to counter what the majority of Vichy leaders considered the decadence of the 1930s, which, according to many, caused the disastrous French military defeat. The program, a Vichy not a German creation, demanded a return to absolute morality and discipline, in opposition to the Third Republic's alleged weakness. Consequently, the National Revolution emphasized Catholic and traditional values such as the merits of peasant life and regional traditions, a centralized government, and censorship and propaganda in the media. In spite of its authoritative nature, the regime sought, and at first received, popular support among the French population. Pétain was often portrayed as the strict but well-intended father of the nation, a father that demanded temporary sacrifice from his "children" in view of brighter tomorrows and of peace. The implementation of the National Revolution included the recruiting of children and youth that were seen, as they were in Nazi Germany, as the future power of the country. Its motto became *travail, famille, patrie* (work, family, nation). The term *République française* was replaced by *État français* (republic by state) to strengthen its power. The Vichy government forcefully condemned Communism, which it depicted as the real enemy of France. It became responsible for a number of anti-Masonic and anti-Jewish laws that supported Nazi anti-Semitism and subsequently led to the transfer of hundreds of thousands of individuals to German concentration camps and gas chambers.

Although the National Revolution was an ideological program, its application justified the economical strain imposed on France by the German demands for goods and money, while ensuring security for the German troops located on the French territory. After 1942, it became obvious that the Vichy government was not accomplishing much in France, and that the economical weight of the occupation was actually increasing. The French population was suffering more and more in spite of the government's collaboration and in the fall of 1942, Germany occupied the whole French territory. The Vichy government consequently lost all support among the population and the Résistance started to get organized. In 1943, almost two years before the liberation, an unofficial *tribunal d'épuration* (purification tribunal) announced that the collaborators would be punished after the war. Immediately following the liberation, this tribunal organized the trials of the most prominent collaborators, including Pétain's. Under de

Gaulle's guidance, the Fourth Republic applied a policy of silence on Vichy in an attempt to promote the orderly reconstruction of the country and to appease political conflicts and rancor. Resentment however has not died as indicated by the recent trial of Maurice Papon, a police official during the occupation who actively collaborated with the Germans in locating Jews, but escaped trial in 1945.

In many respects, the Vichy government and the National Revolution exemplify antirevolutionary and antirepublican sentiments typical of a fraction of the French population that gave rise to the current extreme right party, *Le Front National.*

For further reading, see Robert O. Paxton, *Vichy France. Old Guard, New Order, 1940–1944* (1972) and Henry Rousso, *Le Syndrome de Vichy 1944 à nos jours,* 2nd ed. (Paris: Seuil, 1990).

## VICTOR EMMANUEL (KING)

In the aftermath of the 1848 uprisings throughout Italy, Italian nationalists turned to the Kingdom of Piedmont, whose capital was Turin, to act as the motor for Italian unification. It was ruled by one of the oldest ruling families in Europe, the house of Savoy. It was the only regime in Italy that fought hard for freedom from Austria.

The Piedmont king, Victor Emmanuel II, was a man of rough manners and visible virility. He became a popular focus of attention for those who wanted change. But he was also a politically shrewd man. This was revealed by his appointment as Piedmontese prime minister of a man whom he personally detested: Conte Camillo di Cavour, not a brilliant man, but a pragmatist who was well aware that Italy could never become independent as a result of spontaneous mass uprisings of idealists. The political hold of Austria had to be broken and he knew that Italians would need the help of a foreign power to do this. Therefore, he turned to the new French emperor, Napoleon III. Victor Emmanuel approved, claiming to have heard *"il grido di dolore"* ("the cry of woe") from all over Italy against Austrian repression. In February 1861 Victor Emmanuel II was proclaimed king of Italy.

On October 22, 1922, a later king, Victor Emmanuel III, made a fateful decision for Italy. Benito Mussolini had mobilized his Black Shirts for a march on Rome. Mussolini showed that he had not been entirely confident that such a seizure of power would succeed by remaining close to the Swiss border in order to be able to escape into exile in case it failed. King Victor Emmanuel III rejected the prime minister's appeal to sign a declaration of martial law in order to prevent the marchers from entering the Eternal City. He allowed the marching throng into Rome and then appointed Mussolini

prime minister. Rome fell to the fascists without a shot being fired.

More than two decades later, another force was at Rome's doorstep. After capturing Sicily in mid-1943, the Allied powers began bombing Rome on July 19. The sober reality of war right in the city of Rome brought Mussolini's downfall. The Fascist Grand Council, formerly a malleable tool in Mussolini's hands that had not met since 1939, demanded his resignation, which King Victor Emmanuel III ordered the next day. Mussolini was arrested as he left the royal palace although he was not killed by an enraged Italian mob until almost two years later. A majority of Italian voters in a national referendum held in June 1946 chose to abolish the monarchy and to establish a democratic republic.

## VIENNA, CONGRESS OF

Austrian foreign minister, Prince Klemens von Metternich, was a Rhinelander who led Austria from collaboration with Napoleon to an alliance with his enemies and therefore ensured victory. He was able in 1814 to assemble six emperors and kings, eleven princes, and ninety accredited envoys at the Congress of Vienna for eight months in order to reconstruct Europe after the fall of Napoleon. The flood of political figures and their entourages provided many Viennese the splendid opportunity to rent out their houses at exorbitant prices and to escape to the countryside to count their windfall profits.

Those foreign notables who could not afford the high prices either slept in the city's beautiful parks or in or under their carriages. Most envoys spent their time in cafes, at balls, at receptions, or at tournaments trying to amuse themselves while the major powers, Britain, Austria, Prussia, Russia and, surprisingly, the loser—France—were deciding Europe's fate behind closed doors. In the final settlement, Austria's hold over peoples in Eastern and Southern Europe was recognized. The Austrian monarch thus continued to rule over a multinational empire led by Germans and composed of Czechs, Slovaks, Poles, Hungarians, Italians, Croatians, Slovenes, Serbs, and others.

The statesmen at the Congress of Vienna were tired of revolution and were interested in restoring much of which had existed a quarter of a century earlier. None wanted a unified Germany and none wanted the dissolution of his own state. Their chief objective was to protect Europe from a renewal of the kinds of shocks and challenges that had come out of France. None talked of popular sovereignty, but all spoke of legitimate monarchy. In the end, Prussia gave up some land to a newly created kingdom of Poland, but received the northern part of Saxony, Swedish Pomerania, and the island of Rugen, as well as territory in the Rhineland and Westphalia. These new territories were separated from the rest of Prussia by Hanover, Brunswick, and Hesse-Cassel, but they placed it along a common border with France. Its job was one that was earlier performed by Austria: Prevent France, whose 1789 borders remained practically unchanged, from threatening Central Europe. As a result of the settlement, Prussia grew into Germany, while Austria grew out of Germany toward Northern Italy and the Balkans. The mineral resources in upper Silesia and the Rhineland provided Prussia with the potential to become the greatest industrial power in Germany and ultimately in Europe.

The Congress of Vienna had no interest in a unified Germany, but it did create a German Confederation to replace the old empire that had died a quiet death almost a decade earlier. The confederation was a loose association of thirty-five sovereign German principalities (including the five kingdoms of Prussia, Hanover, Bavaria, Württemberg, and Saxony) and four free cities. Its sole institution was a Federal Parliament (Bundestag) in Frankfurt, whose chairman was always an Austrian and whose delegates were not elected, but were appointed by the member states. In other words, it was a diplomatic organization, not a real parliament. It was dominated by Austria and Prussia, whose main goal by now was to prevent all change. They were not alone.

Austria's attention now more than ever had to be directed away from the German world. Still, it was determined to compete with Prussia for dominance within Germany. Prussia had been granted German lands in the Rhine and Palatinate areas in order to help keep a potentially revengeful France from springing beyond its borders. This arrangement, which led Prussia into the heart of Germany and Austria out of it, ultimately helped Prussia to defeat Austria in the struggle for control of Germany.

The violent events that had shaken Europe in the past quarter century had left many Germans and non-Germans alike longing for peace, order, and authority. All members of the confederation pledged, however, to introduce constitutions, which, if they were observed, would always place limits on rulers. Such constitutions never saw the light of day in most German states until more than three decades later. This included Prussia and Austria, where absolutism was quickly restored and which joined with Russia in a "Holy Alliance" in 1815 to suppress signs of revolution anywhere in Europe. Only in southern Germany were constitutions introduced that established monarchies and brought more citizens into political life. The most shining example was Baden where the first signs of parliamentary democracy in Germany became visible. After 1815 there was an ultraconservative reaction led by the govern-

ments of Prussia and Austria. Britain left this pact almost as soon as it had been created, but Russia, Austria, and Prussia remained. All three ultimately paid very dearly for their determination to dig in their heels and to ignore the signs of the times.

For a full century after the Congress of Vienna, Europe did manage to avoid the kind of continent-wide conflagration that had occurred earlier and that would recur in 1914 and again in 1939. However, it is no longer possible for the great powers to mandate national boundaries without consideration for the nationalist aspirations of the subject peoples. The events of recent years have demonstrated this, with the disintegration of the artificially constructed nation of Yugoslavia being the most obvious case in point.

**VIETNAMESE NATIONALISM** Although the concept of nationalism is often described as a Western concept, the product of rising ethnic and cultural consciousness in late 18th- and 19th-century Europe, a strong case can be made for the contention that the Vietnamese people have had a sense of national identity for nearly 2000 years, as a consequence of their historic struggle to protect their independence against the efforts of their powerful northern neighbor to assimilate them into the Chinese empire. Conquered by the Han dynasty in the 2nd century B.C.E., the Vietnamese people—then inhabiting the Red River Valley in what is today known as North Vietnam—were ruled by China for 1000 years. Chinese institutions and values were introduced, and the ruling élite was heavily indoctrinated with the ideology of state Confucianism. Consciousness of the country's separate identity never entirely disappeared, however, and rebellions periodically broke out against Chinese rule. In 939 C.E., rebel forces took advantage of the collapse of the Tang Dynasty and restored Vietnamese independence. During the next several centuries, Vietnam (then known as Dai Viet, or Great Viet) expanded southward along the coast of the South China Sea to the Gulf of Thailand, eventually becoming one of the most dynamic states in mainland Southeast Asia.

Expansion, however, had its price, for settlers in the frontier atmosphere of the southern territories chafed under northern rule, and for 200 years after 1600 the country was essentially divided into two separate de facto states. Although the country was reunified under the new name Viet Nam by the Nguyen Dynasty in 1802, regional differences persisted, facilitating French conquest during the final decades of the century. Taking advantage of regional tensions, the French colonial regime divided the country into three separate territories, with the colony of Cochin China in the south, and the protectorates of Annam and Tonkin in the center and the north. Cochin China, an area that for centuries had been actively engaged in commercial activities throughout the region, was exposed to a heavy dose of Western capitalism, while the remaining parts of the country remained under the influence of traditional values.

The first stage of resistance to French rule had been led by Confucian elites, who sought to restore the traditional monarchical system. By the early years of the 20th century, however, a new generation of young Vietnamese emerged who were familiar with the Western concept of nationalism and determined to build an independent state, with modern Western institutions, in Vietnam. Several political parties emerged during the 1920s, but they were badly divided by differences over tactics and final objectives, while their urban leadership failed to comprehend the aspirations of the peasantry, who composed the vast majority of the population, and they were thus unable to generate a mass following.

In 1930, the young revolutionary Ho Chi Minh (then known as Nguyen Ai Quoc, or Nguyen the Patriot) founded the Indochinese Communist Party (ICP). Born in 1890, Ho had been inspired by the desire to restore national independence since his adolescence, and in 1919, while living in Paris, he had addressed a public appeal to the victorious Allied leaders gathered at Versailles to grant self-determination to all the peoples of French Indochina, and throughout the colonial world. When his appeal was ignored, he turned to Communism, where he was electrified by the promise of the Bolshevik leader Vladimir Lenin to promote the destruction of the entire system of world imperialism and the creation of a future Communist utopia.

As the founder and leader of the ICP, Ho Chi Minh artfully combined the appeal of patriotism with that of social justice and political equality into a program that appealed to millions of his compatriots. In so doing, he frequently encountered suspicion from Soviet officials in Moscow, who sometimes doubted his credentials as an orthodox Marxist. By the same token, many non-Communists suspected that under the exterior pose of a fervent patriot seeking only the liberation of his people from colonial rule, Ho was a veteran Communist who sought to impose an alien system designed in Moscow or Beijing.

Although the debate over Ho Chi Minh's ultimate goals has never been resolved, it cannot be denied that it was his party, and his program, that was able to mobilize the support of millions of Vietnamese to bring about the eviction of the French and the restoration of national independence—although the country was temporarily divided into two zones—in 1954. During the next two decades, Ho and his colleagues in the North resumed their efforts to reunite the country under the party's authority. While many non-Communist nationalists in the south possessed a fervent sense of national pride equal to that of their rivals, they lacked the sense of discipline and cohesion that Ho Chi Minh had implanted in the ICP, and in 1975 Communist forces completed their conquest of the south. The country was reunified a year later.

Today, a united Vietnam is ruled by Ho Chi Minh's successors in the Communist Party (now renamed the Vietnamese Communist Party, or VCP). But the legacy of the past looms over the present, as national unity is undermined by regional differences between north and south that have deep roots in Vietnamese history. While many northerners continue to reflect the values of an ancient agrarian society, many southerners see a role for the future Vietnam in the international marketplace. In that struggle for the soul of Vietnam, the future of the country's national identity is at stake.

**VILLA, PANCHO**    1878–1923, Mexican revolutionary leader, born Doroteo Arango in San Juan del Río, Durango, Mexico. He adopted the name Pancho Villa as a young man after allegedly wounding a landowner in defense of his sister and fleeing from the authorities. (He was soon caught, but escaped from jail.) Villa then spent many years as a soldier, bandit, butcher, cattle rustler, and mule driver, mainly in the northern state of Chihuahua. He is said to have murdered several people and committed countless robberies and acts of arson before joining, in 1910, Francisco Madero's successful revolt against the dictatorship of Porfirio Díaz.

Villa was recruited to the revolution by a deputy of Madero, who allegedly promised him amnesty for his crimes if Madero triumphed. Villa joined the federal army after Madero's victory, but General Victoriano Huerta imprisoned, and very nearly executed, Villa for insubordination. Villa escaped to El Paso, Texas, and, following Huerta's coup against Madero in 1913, which resulted in Madero's assassination, promptly took up arms against Huerta back in Chihuahua. Villa joined the Constitutionalist movement led by Venustiano Carranza, and proceeded to organize what has been called the largest revolutionary army in Latin American history. Villa's División del Norte (Northern Division) gradually grew to include as many as 100,000 troops, mainly peasants, miners, and cowboys.

In his campaign against Huerta, Villa seized large estates in Chihuahua and handed them over to his officers; free medical care was established; dozens of schools were built; and generous benefits were extended to war widows and orphans. Villa helped drive Huerta from power in 1914 and briefly occupied Mexico City with Emiliano Zapata, the leader of a radical peasant movement centered in Morelos and adjacent states south of Mexico City. Neither Villa nor Zapata, however, aspired to wield state power; their perspectives were basically provincial, and they quickly returned to Chihuahua and Morelos, respectively.

After 1914 Carranza, with the backing of the United States, attempted to subdue Villa and Zapata, return lands to estate owners, and reconsolidate state power. Villa suffered a series of defeats at the hands of the Constitutionalist General Alvaro Obregón, including an ambush in the border town of Agua Prieta, which was made possible when the U.S. government allowed Constitutionalist troops to maneuver within U.S. territory. A furious Villa, intent upon provoking a U.S. invasion of Mexico that would swing Mexican nationalist sentiments behind him, invaded Columbus, New Mexico, in March 1916, killing sixteen Americans. This was the first foreign invasion of the United States since the War of 1812, and General John J. Pershing was sent into Mexico with 5000 troops to capture Villa. Pershing's year-long "Punitive Expedition" failed to capture Villa, but neither did it inflame Mexican nationalism in the way Villa expected. Villa, who was forced to adopt guerrilla warfare, could not prevent Carranza's forces from occupying Chihuahua, ending his reforms, and largely restoring the landed elite. Villa's army slowly disintegrated after 1916.

Villa and the last of his followers finally surrendered in 1920, following the murder of Carranza, and Villa was rewarded with a huge estate in Canutillo, Durango, and a large sum of U.S. money. He was ambushed and killed in July 1923, presumably by agents of Obregón, who feared his popular influence. Following his death Villa, like Zapata (who was assassinated by Carranza's troops in 1919), was rhetorically incorporated by the postrevolutionary state into Mexico's quasi-official pantheon of nationalist heroes. The heirs of Villa's assassins, ironically, would ritualistically invoke his image and ideals many decades after his murder.

The definitive study of Villa and his movement is Friedrich Katz's monumental *The Life and Times of Pancho Villa* (Stanford, 1998).

## VIOLENCE

When we turn on the television or pick up a newspaper we are regularly inundated with visions of a world in disarray. Images of "ethnic cleansing" in Kosovo, wholesale killing in Rwanda, clashes between Protestants and Catholics in Northern Ireland, the beating of Turkish workers by neo-Nazi youth in Germany, and many other examples fill the airwaves. Even a relatively brief encounter with the mass media can produce numerous examples of violence in the service of nationalism.

Defining violence is a difficult task; the term is packed with ambiguities and charged with political implications. When we speak of violence we may be referring to acts that range from the killing of large groups of people through the destruction of property to symbolic displays of power. Which categories of action we include in the definition likely reflects our views of the appropriate uses of power and authority.

Narrow definitions of violence, popular on the right, may restrict usage to illegal or "illegitimate" acts of coercion, thus excluding from consideration state-sanctioned deeds such as those of the police or military. Broad definitions, popular on the left, extend beyond physical action to include the systematic deprivation of individual choice, thereby including a large number of social injustices under the rubric of "structural violence." In between are a range of more or less restricted definitions that typically concentrate the infliction of physical injury regardless of the actors. Our "ordinary" understanding of the term would likely fall into this last category.

Violence should be recognized as a separate form, rather than simply a degree, of conflict. Although conflict may take the form of violence, it is not an inevitable endpoint. Neither is a higher level of conflict necessarily associated with a higher level of violence. Substantial conflict may exist for long periods without ever taking a violent turn.

Scholars have proposed a number of causes of nationalist and ethnic violence. One of the most popular is competition for scarce resources. In this view economic deprivation becomes linked with ethno-nationalist tension. As they compete, groups develop negative attitudes toward one another; each is seen as the cause of the other's difficulties. This in turn leads to resentment, which can manifest itself in violent episodes.

Others have suggested that the size of minority populations is a factor in precipitating violence. According to this perspective, small numbers of "foreigners" are not problematic, however, when their populations rise beyond a certain threshold, cultural clashes may cause hostilities to erupt. In some instances the newcomers may be seen as a danger to traditional values or ways of life. In others, particular groups may be seen as harboring criminal tendencies that represent a threat to law and order or public safety. Notions of the "dangerous" nature of African American males plays into this class of concerns and is used to justify repression. Finally, memories of past actions may magnify present-day fears. Recollection of the savage World War II *Ustaša* regime has had a substantial impact on modern Serb beliefs about the bloodthirsty nature of Croats.

Another explanation concentrates on the nature of

identity formation. One of the fundamental procedures in forming collective identities is the construction of boundaries dividing ingroup from outgroup. As part of this process, confrontations with outsiders may be deliberately staged as a mechanism of boundary solidification. Likewise, two organizations competing for the support of the same ethnic group may have an incentive to outdo one another in nationalistic fervor. Failure to do so may open a party to charges that it is "soft" on ethnic issues.

Some scholars suggest that violence arises only when other forms of protest begin to wane. Research indicates that violence tends to occur late in mobilization cycles. As participation in protest begins to drop off, more extreme elements may become frustrated and turn to violent activity as the only available means of disruption.

A quality overview of a variety of perspectives on violence is *Violence and Its Alternatives*, edited by Manfred Steger and Nancy Lind (St. Martin's Press, 1999). Readers looking for volumes that concentrate on the relation of violence to nationalism are advised to pick up *Racist Violence in Europe*, edited by Tore Björgo and Rob Witte (St. Martin's Press, 1993) or *Nationalism and Violence*, edited by Christopher Dandeker (Transaction Publishers, 1998).

## VYNNYCHENKO, VOLODYMYR 1880–1951, Modernist playwright. Vynnychenko headed the governing council of Ukraine's first independent government, the short-lived Central Rada (1917–1918), and was later considered by the Soviet government to be one of the chief ideologues of "Ukrainian bourgeois nationalism."

Vynnychenko first became active in the Ukrainian national movement while a student at Kyiv University, where in 1902 he joined to the Revolutionary Ukrainian Party, later renamed the Ukrainian Social Democratic Workers Party. From 1907, he served on this organization's central committee and edited its journal *Struggle* (*Borot'ba*). After a year in prison for his political activities, he lived in exile until 1917.

Upon his return to Ukraine, Vynnychenko became a prominent leader in the national independence movement. He joined the Central Rada in 1917 as vice president, was the first president of the general secretariat, and then headed the oppositional Ukrainian National Union and the Directorate of the Ukrainian National Republic before the independence movement was crushed by Soviet forces. In 1920, while once again in exile, Vynnychenko organized the Ukrainian Communist Party

and began to negotiate with Lenin and other Soviet leaders for the independence of a Ukrainian socialist state. Although he was offered a number of high positions in the Soviet Ukrainian government, including a seat in the politburo of the Central Committee of the Communist Party (Bolshevik) of Ukraine, his efforts ended in defeat and he returned to exile. Vynnychenko devoted the remainder of his life to literary and artistic activity.

Vynnychenko was a prolific writer who produced twenty plays, fourteen novels, and two memoirs over the course of his life. His collected works were published in the 1920s in Soviet Ukraine in a twenty-four-volume edition, but most were later banned until the Soviet Union's collapse. In his novels and plays, Vynnychenko rejected the populism characteristic of many of his contemporaries and predecessors, concentrating instead on the psychological and moral problems of the Ukrainian intelligentsia. Not surprisingly, his works were criticized harshly by Gorky, Lenin, and other Soviet leaders for their individualism. Nevertheless, his plays enjoyed considerable popularity in Ukrainian and Russian theaters prior to the imposition of socialist realism. They later once again became important during the *glasnost* period, when they were successfully revived by prominent theater companies in Kyiv and L'viv. Since independence, Vynnychenko's writings have been republished in Ukraine and have been reintroduced to the school curriculum. Today, Vynnychenko is recognized for his dramatic works, which remain highly influential, and for his three-volume memoir, *Rebirth of a Nation*, in which he vividly depicts the Ukrainian socialists' struggle to gain national recognition from the various forces occupying Ukraine during the 1917–1919 period.

An English-language translation of Vynnychenko's writings, entitled *Selected Short Stories* (Longwood Academic, 1991) has appeared, although much of his work remains untranslated or out of print. Vadym Stelmashenko's annotated bibliography, *Volodymyr Vynnychenko: Anotovana bibliografiia* (Canadian Institute of Ukrainian Studies, 1989), represents the most comprehensive guide to his work and scholarly analyses. Hryhory Kostiuk's biography, *Volodymyr Vynnychenko to ioho doba* (New York, 1980), is available only in Ukrainian.

# W

**WAFD PARTY** Egypt's leading nationalist party under the parliamentary monarchy (1922–1952). On November 13, 1918, a group of Egyptian notables led by Saʿd Zaghlul approached the British authorities in Egypt to request permission to send a delegation (*wafd*) to the Paris Peace Conference. When the British questioned their credentials to speak on behalf of Egypt the group circulated petitions seeking popular endorsement, in the process creating an organized nationalist movement subsequently known as the Wafd. The exile of Wafdist leaders in March 1919 sparked the Egyptian "Revolution" of 1919, a nationalist uprising which began three years of protest and noncooperation with the British in Egypt and which ultimately resulted in Great Britain giving Egypt formal independence in February 1922. Much of the protest of 1919–1922 was directed by the Wafd, which at that time regarded itself not as a political party but as the organized expression of the will of the Egyptian nation.

The dynamics of Egyptian politics under the parliamentary monarchy have been described as a triangular contest between the king seeking to extend his personal authority, the British seeking to protect their strategic and economic position in Egypt, and the Wafd opposing both in the name of democracy and nationalism. The Wafd won parliamentary majorities in Egypt's few relatively free elections under the monarchy, but held ministerial office only in 1924, for a few months in 1928, again briefly in 1930, in 1936–1937, in 1942–1944 (in that instance installed by the British), and in 1950–1952. The party's nationalist sheen of the 1920s gradually faded in the 1930s and 1940s, partially because of internal corruption under Zaghlul's successor Mustafa al-Nahhas and partially because of its wartime collaboration with the British occupier. The Wafd ceased to operate in January 1953, when the new military regime dissolved all political parties.

The Wafd has experienced a revival of sorts since the mid-1970s, when President Sadat's economic and political opening of Egypt allowed the reemergence of formal political parties. Led by the old Wafdist Fuʿad Serag al-Din the party had periodically contested Egyptian legislative elections, obtaining a minority opposition voice in the National Assembly but never denting the overall political control of the legislature by the government party.

Both under the monarchy and in its recent reincarnation, the Wafd has been the organized voice of Egyptian liberal nationalism. Secular in its internal organization (Egyptian Christians and Jews holding prominent positions in the party), relatively democratic in ethos (opposed to both royal autocracy and British interference), and laissez-faire in economic outlook, the Wafd has reflected and articulated the liberal worldview that took hold among Western-influenced Egyptians in the early 20th century. Its nationalist vision has been primarily territorial nationalist, seeing Egypt as a distinct nation with its own destiny rather than as part of a larger Arab nation or Muslim community.

The history of the Wafd under the monarchy is explicated in Janice Terry, *The Wafd 1919–1952* (1982). Its relationship with other political forces during the interwar period is analyzed in Marius Deeb, *Party Politics in Egypt: The Wafd and Its Rivals, 1919–1939* (1979).

**WAGNER, RICHARD** 1813–1883, Born in Leipzig, Wagner is considered one of the geniuses of German culture. However, his career as a romantic composer is not without controversy. He was a revolutionary, liberal, art theorist, conductor, poet, anti-Semite, and chauvinist. His political involvement forced him to spend many years abroad (in such places as Riga, Paris, and especially Switzerland, in addition to a variety of German states). Several of his most famous operas were written while he was in exile. He became involved in the Revolution of 1848 and was compelled to flee Dresden.

King Ludwig II of Bavaria invited him to Munich in 1866 and built him an opera house (Festspielhaus) in Bayreuth where his works were performed. The *Flying Dutchman, Tristan and Isolde, The Ring of the Nibelung, Lohengrin,* and *Parzival* are among his most famous works. Many of his operas glorify the German Middle Ages, their legends and mysticism, and thus endeared his works to Hitler. The same can be said about his political writings, bearing such titles as *Art and Revolution* (1849), *Artwork of the Future* (1849), and *Judaism in Music* (1850). His exuberance for German national and cultural identity was exploited by German nationalists and the Nazis, who paid ostentatious homage to Wagner during the Third Reich.

**WALESA, LECH** 1943–, Born in Popowo, Poland. Walesa rose to world prominence in August 1980 as the leader of a strike at the Lenin Shipyard in Gdansk, where he had worked as an electrician, that sparked the creation of the trade union Solidarity. Poland's Communist regime granted legal recognition to the union at the end of that month. Although Walesa and his top advisers strove to pursue a so-called "self-limiting revolution" that would not directly challenge the regime's political monopoly, Communist leader General Wojciech Jaruzelski declared martial law and moved to break up the movement in December 1981.

Walesa spent a year in jail but was awarded the Nobel Peace Prize in 1983. Faced with a deteriorating economy and renewed wave of strikes in 1988, Jaruzelski sought out Walesa as a partner who could restore stability in return for lifting the ban on Solidarity and negotiations on political and economic reform. The so-called "Roundtable Talks" paved the way for semi-free elections and a non-Communist government in the summer of 1989 while allowing Jaruzelski to assume the new post of president.

Walesa initially chose to remain chairman of Solidarity rather than accept a position in Parliament or the cabinet. However, in 1990 Walesa began demanding early, direct elections for a new president. Though Jaruzelski resigned and Walesa handily won the race to succeed him that fall, the campaign exposed and widened fractures within Solidarity. In particular, the more nationalist, religious, and conservative elements of the movement (which tended to support Walesa) divided against the more cosmopolitan "European," secular, and liberal elements (which tended to support the candidacy of Prime Minister Tadeusz Mazowiecki). While many credit Walesa for using his popularity and ability to communicate with ordinary Poles to lend crucial support for reform as president, others accuse him of irresponsibly seeking to expand his office's powers and destabilizing the political environment with occasional hints of staging a coup such as that his political hero, Józef Piłsudski (leader of the movement for national independence during World War I), had carried out in 1926. Walesa's bid for a second five-year term was narrowly defeated by Aleksander Kwasniewski, the former Communist leader of the Democratic Left Alliance, in December 1995.

An excellent account of the Solidarity movement and Walesa's role within it is found in David Ost's *Solidarity and the Politics of Anti-Politics: Opposition and Reform in Poland since 1968* (Temple, 1990). Krzysztof Jasiewicz presents a balanced assessment of Walesa's presidential term in his chapter "Poland: Walesa's Legacy to the Presidency," in Ray Taras, ed., *Postcommunist Presidents* (Cambridge, 1997), pp. 130–167.

**WALKER, DAVID** 1785–1830, Born of a free mother and a slave father, Walker left his native North Carolina while in his teens, and settled in Boston where he earned a living as a dealer in old clothes. He is best known for a small but explosive pamphlet that circulated clandestinely through the antebellum South and "rumored" slave uprisings as the only possible solution to the black problem. The full title of Walker's work is "Walker's Appeal in Four Articles Together With a Preamble to the Colored Citizens of the World, But in Particular and Very Expressly to Those of the United States" (1829).

Commonly known as "Walker's Appeal" it laid down cardinal precepts such as there should be no effective defense of the country until the country is willing to recognize the manhood of blacks, and no real love of country until respect is extended to those who suffer at the hands of white America. Walker went on to insist that before peace and happiness among whites and blacks can be established "that Americans must make a national acknowledgment to us (blacks) for the wrong they have inflicted on us." Walker's pride in blackness, his respect for the achievements of blacks in the ancient world, and his belief in African moral character and the need for African autonomy provided elements for a cultural nationalism. Although falling short of a theory of culture, Walker began a theory of class, the inspiration coming partly from Christianity and partly from a reading of history. He was one of the foremost spokesmen of his time to speak out about a growing dissatisfaction of the passing of laws concerning Africans in America, which he expressed in his appeal, calling on his people through the world to resist oppression.

Walker helped establish the rationale for Pan-

Africanism, a position eventually held with such conviction and at such length that total African liberation has achieved enduring value as an ideology among other black nationalists.

**WALLOON NATIONALISM** Wallonia contains about 33 percent of Belgium's population, and about 44 percent of Belgians consider French their native language. Walloon nationalism emerged as a reaction to economic stagnation (after a long period of regional domination) and the growing prosperity and political might of Flanders. In the 19th and early 20th centuries, Wallonia benefited from the economic and political exploitation of Flanders, as well as linguistic policies that led to the creation of a privileged, French-speaking elite in Belgium. Wallonia had a flourishing commercial and industrial (coal and steel) economy, whereas the Flemish economy consisted primarily of farming and textiles. However, in the early 20th century, Flanders began to prosper. By the 1960s, Wallonia had exhausted its supplies of coal and the Flemish economy began to surpass that of Wallonia. Conflict increased between Flemings and Walloons in the 1960s and 1970s. In 1980, Belgium instituted reforms that led to regional governments in 1992 for Flanders, Brussels, and Wallonia. Belgium still has a national parliament, but because Flemings are the national majority and have more seats in parliament, they hold a measure of political control that Walloons fear may be used against them.

The 1960s saw the first Walloon national movement, the Popular Walloon movement (*Mouvement Populaire Wallon*). Most subsequent movements were short lived or co-opted. The most successful Walloon nationalist movement has been the Walloon Rally (*Rassemblement Wallon*). The 1990s have seen the Agir and Front National (FN) parties. In 1994, the FN sent one representative to the European Parliament and elected twenty-six members in the cantonal elections. The FN has been successful in both Brussels and Wallonia, but it gets its highest scores in the poor southern Hainaut district, with 8 percent of the vote in the 1991 legislative elections. In 1995, Agir and the FN worked together in Wallonia and gained 6.3 percent of the vote, while the FN alone in Brussels got 7.6 percent. The FN and Agir's nationalism is principally racist and xenophobic, a strong reaction to the presence of immigrants in Wallonia and especially Brussels. The FN suffers from poor organization and an unfocused political program, outside of its virulent anti-immigrant stance. In comparison to Flemish nationalism, Walloon nationalism has been rather unsuccessful in gaining power through elections.

See Gwenael Brees, *L'Affront national: le nouveau visage de l'extrême droite en Belgique* (Brussels: EPO, 1991); Jo Gerard, *L'épopée des Wallonnes et des Wallons* (Braine-l'Alleud: J.-M. Collet, 1997); Marc Swyngedouw, "The Extreme Right in Belgium: Of a Non-existent Front National and an Omnipresent Vlaams Blok," in Hans-Georg Betz and Stefan Immerfall, eds., *The New Politics of the Right: Neo-Populist Parties and Movements in Established Democracies* (New York: St. Martin's Press, 1998); and Lode Wils, *Histoire des nations belges. Belgique, Flandre, Wallonie: quinze siècles de passé commun*, translated by Chantal Kesteloot (Ottignies: Quorum, 1996).

**WAR AND NATIONALISM** *War* is a term for armed conflict. It can occur intrastate, and thus be termed a civil war, or it can occur between two or more states or national groups transcending state boundaries. However, it is noteworthy that for some states to be officially at war, regardless of the existence of an armed conflict, there must be a formal declaration of war.

One state with such a declaration requirement is the United States. The U.S. Constitution, as part of its separation of powers provisions, mandates that only Congress can declare war. This provision is found in Article I, §8.11. So, even though the United States has been involved in numerous armed conflicts, there have been relatively few declarations of war. Examples are the Korean War, the Vietnam War, and the Gulf War. This involvement in armed conflict without a formal declaration is not restricted to the international practice of the United States as many other states similarly engage in armed conflict.

International legal scholars and social scientists have pondered the reasoning and consequences behind war and the prevalence of armed conflict. The body of international law that governs war is known as humanitarian law. Humanitarian law covers both internal and international conflicts. Two contemporary examples of the application of humanitarian law can be found in the International Criminal Tribunal for Yugoslavia (ICTY) and the International Criminal Tribunal for Rwanda (ICTR). While the latter tribunal was necessitated by a civil conflict between tribes, the former, the tribunal on Yugoslavia, is the result of a war between competing ethnic groups. The wars in the former Yugoslavia have been commonly characterized as ethnic conflicts.

Ethnic conflict and wars of national liberation are junctures where nationalism and war meet. Ethnic groups in conflict with each other may war over competing nationalist aspirations and claims. Additionally, nationalist groups who allege state repression, whether real or perceived, may wage wars of national liberation to free themselves from the shackles of the controlling government. Moreover, when efforts to achieve sovereignty, autonomy, or a form of self-determination through political channels have failed, war may become a viable option. War is thus not seen as a goal of a nation, but rather a means to an end.

Many contemporary conflicts have been cited as ethnic conflicts, the result of nationalist sentiment gone amok. International society, as a result of the war in Bosnia, has gone so far as to create the phrase "ethnic cleansing" to describe a policy or result of removing those not of a particular ethnicity from a given area. While this is clearly not the exclusive domain of nationalism, as racism and xenophobia can also be implicated, nationalist sentiment can be called on to carry out the task of ethnic cleansing.

Nationalism has also had a historically significant role in the popularization and mobilization of the "average citizen" around the issue of war. Furthermore, war was a necessary catalyst in the shaping of the modern nation-state as a determinant of boundaries. Michael Howard has written: "From the very beginning the principle of nationalism was almost indissolubly linked, both in theory and practice, with the idea of war."

World Wars I and II are rife with examples of efforts by leaders to rally the masses around war efforts by hearkening to latent or manifest nationalist sentiments. World War I has its causal factor, albeit the subject of scholarly debate, in Balkan nationalism. World War II had the Nazi appeal to both nationalist and racist sentiments as well as the resistance movements mobilized against the expansion of empires.

A rather grim but commonly cited statistic relating to war is that between the period of 3600 B.C. and the year 1960 humankind has only known 292 years of universal peace. Moreover in the other 5268 years over 14,000 wars have been waged taking 1240 million lives.

## WASHINGTON, BOOKER T.
1858–1915, Founded the Tuskegee Institute in 1881 in Alabama and devoted his life to the education of blacks. Washington, who was considered more of an accommodationist than a nationalist, felt that blacks during Reconstruction should, for the moment at least, abandon political agitation and seek to "get along" with whites, while concentrating on improving their economic lot. This, of course, made Washington popular among whites. They welcomed the idea that blacks should settle down and accept their status of second-class citizenship and at the same time train themselves in exploitable laboring skills. Washington emerged as a national spokesman for blacks when he delivered a speech at the Cotton States and International Exposition in Atlanta in September 1895. Whites hailed the Atlanta Exposition speech as an end to black agitation for equality in return for a chance to gather economic scraps from the booming industrial table while educator W. E. B. DuBois mocked it as the "The Atlanta Compromise." Washington's attempts at other endeavors such as his establishment of the Negro Business League in 1900 made few gains except in fields where blacks did not have to fight white businesses, such as banking and insurance, neither of which attracted white competition for black clientele.

Washington's strongest critic was activist DuBois whose "youth prepared him to champion an ideal" while Washington's youth "prepared him for a life defined by the reality of oppression," as stated by author Arnold Rampersad. This can be seen as the major difference in their nationalist vision for blacks. DuBois' whole orientation, his intellectual references, and historical models were far removed from those of Washington, who admired capitalists and hated unions. As he would make increasingly clear with time, DuBois was struck by the essential vulgarity of such whites as Andrew Carnegie who financially supported Washington, and was opposed to any alliance of black workers with a system responsible for the enslavement of their forefathers. But during Reconstruction and beyond, militant voices, such as DuBois and poet Paul Laurence Dunbar, did not resound among whites now deafened by the rising storm of imperialist propaganda, nor did they appeal to most blacks, who were beginning to think of their position as all but hopeless. The way of accommodation and acceptance as seen by Washington seemed to many to be the only way for the present. Carnegie donated $600,000 to the Tuskegee Institute; Washington was consulted on various appointments to military posts, and was considered by whites to be an "ambassador." However, later on DuBois, with such tactics as the establishment of the Niagara Movement and the NAACP, was to successfully wrest the leadership of the black masses from Washington's hand.

## WASHINGTON, GEORGE
1732–1799, Known as the father of his country, the first president of the United States (1789–1797) established his reputation as commander in chief of the colonial armies in the American Revolutionary War (1775–1783) and subsequently became a symbol of American virtues and a premier hero of American nationalism.

The 1865 painting of Washington on the ceiling of the U.S. capitol rotunda symbolizes the esteem in which he was held as a founder of the nation, espouser of democratic values, and adept statesman. In that painting he is seen in celestial glory, surrounded by classic personifications of liberty and freedom, and nearly deified as he was in the years following his death at the close of the 18th century.

Despite his minimal military training, he provided decisive leadership facilitating the Continental army's successful routing of the superior British military and the eventual independence of its American colonies. His military leadership thrust him into the presidency of the Constitutional Conventional of the new republic where he played a formative role in fashioning the U.S. Constitution. Washington helped to create the federal system of government that balances states rights with the national government and at the national level a tripartite division of power among the executive, legislative, and judicial branches.

Washington resisted a move to make him king of the new republic, choosing instead to become its first president and reinforcing the idea of representative democracy that was a hallmark of early American nationalism. Throughout the nation's history he served as a model to schoolchildren of American virtues of honesty and democracy.

More difficult for later generations of Americans was the fact that the first president was a substantial slaveowner, a fact that for most people at the time was not problematic. At the age of eleven he inherited 10 slaves from his father and at the time of his own death in 1799, 316 slaves sustained Washington's 8000-acre Mount Vernon estate.

Because his presidency occurred in the formative years of the United States, he was involved in building the foundation of the new nation. He oversaw the creation of the Bill of Rights (1791) and the establishment of a mint for U.S. currency and the First Bank of the United States (1791).

Washington's Proclamation of Neutrality in 1793 prevented the involvement of the new nation in military attacks by England, Spain, Austria, and Prussia on the new French republic. His isolationism with regard to extended foreign entanglements can be seen in his farewell address, in which he warned the American people against alliances that would result in involvement in disputes in which it had no interest. Closer to home, however, he did not hesitate to send troops into battle. He ordered military action against the Iroquois and facilitated the movement of settlers in Ohio and elsewhere. He also sent troops against farmers in Western Pennsylvania who refused to pay a whiskey tax (1794), thus demonstrating the authority of the new state to govern the territory within its boundaries.

After his death the nation mourned the loss of its founding father and the U.S. Congress declared, in the words penned by Henry Lee, that Washington was "first in war, first in peace, and first in the hearts of his countrymen."

**WEBER, MAX** 1864–1920, Weber, the highly influential pioneer of "interpretive sociology," discusses "the Nation" under two different headings in *Economy and Society* (University of California Press, 1978), his encyclopedic, though unfinished, "outline of interpretive sociology." Part of Weber's analysis is located in his chapter on "Ethnic Groups" (Part Two, Chapter V), while part is located in his chapter on "Political Communities" (Part Two, Chapter IX). This organizational bifurcation reflects a deep, conceptual ambivalence. On the one hand, Weber conceives of nations as groups united by a common subjective belief in a "blood" relationship; on the other hand, he conceives of them as groups united in a common program of social action, oriented to political autonomy. Oscillating between these two conceptual poles, Weber could never decide which was more important for defining "the Nation," ethnicity or politics. This ambivalence has its source in a perennial problem, namely, the troubling relationship between "nation" and "state."

Weber's approach to sociology calls for the explanation of "social action" in terms of its "subjective meaning" for the acting individuals. In some cases, as with "the Nation," this requires analysis of the relationship between the subjective meanings of social action and such objective characteristics of actors as "race" or native language.

Thus, in Part Two, Chapter V, of *Economy and Society* Weber distinguishes three concepts—"race," "ethnicity," and "nationality"—which are linked by the common idea of "blood," that is, common biological descent.

Weber uses the term "race" to refer to objective genetic relationships, hence, to "common inherited and inheritable traits that actually derive from common descent." Such traits include, of course, skin color, eye color, hair color and texture, and many other objective physical characteristics. Weber insists, however, in the strongest possible terms, that there is no scientific evidence that action orientations are in this sense racial; that one racial group is more emotional, another more inclined to instrumental rationality, because of biological inheritance.

In contrast, Weber uses "ethnic" and "ethnicity" to refer to a subjective belief in common descent, whether objectively justified or not, the latter frequently being the case. Such a belief can arise from common "racial" (i.e., biological) characteristics, such as skin color, but also from the most diverse customs and cultural practices, such as styles of hair and beard, of dress, of eating, of sexual relations, and so on, *ad infinitum*. Put the other way round, Weber saw an extraordinarily strong tendency for people to interpret common and distinguishing characteristics—whether biological or cultural in origin—in terms of common descent.

The problem with this subjective belief, for Weber's type of sociology, is that it leads to the most diverse types of social action, or to none at all. Weber concludes that "the collective term 'ethnic' would [have to] be abandoned, for it is unsuitable for a really rigorous analysis," because it "dissolves if we define our terms exactly."

Weber's analysis of "the Nation" and "nationality" overlaps his analysis of "ethnic group" and "ethnicity" as regards people's subjective interpretation of their own and others' objective racial and cultural characteristics—both point to "the vague connotation that whatever is felt to be distinctively common must derive from common descent." But the two diverge as regards the patterns of social action that result from this type of subjective belief, for "nation" and "nationality" point to "[a] specific objective of . . . social action," namely, "the *autonomous polity*."

In short, Weber's first approach to "nation" and "nationality" suggests that they be defined as subtypes of the (amorphous) categories "ethnic group" and "ethnicity," subtypes defined in terms of a specific pattern of political action. Here Weber's ambivalence emerges. His analysis of "nation" and "nationality" emerges from the idea of "ethnicity," but it is pulled—strongly—toward the idea of autonomous political action: "the concept ['nation'] seems to refer—if it refers at all to a uniform phenomenon—to a specific kind of pathos which is linked to the idea of a powerful political community . . . ; such a state may already exist or it may be desired. The more power is emphasized, the closer appears to be the link between nation and state (398)." The implication is that political action should be the defining characteristic of "nation" and "nationality." And, yet, as much as Weber seems drawn toward this conclusion, he pulls away from it, for there are political communities "for which the term nationality does not seem quite fitting." The Swiss are a classic case: "they have a strong sense of community," but this identity is not "ethnic." For this reason Weber hesitates to give them the name "nation," even though "the pride of the Swiss in their own distinctiveness, and their willingness to defend it vigorously, is neither qualitatively different nor less widespread than the same attitudes in any 'great' and powerful 'nation.'"

But, then, what is the political significance of "ethnicity?" It is one possible basis of "political community," but according to Weber's analysis, "ethnicity" is neither necessary or sufficient to cause social action oriented to political autonomy; it does not even seem to make any difference to its course.

Weber died before he could complete his analysis of this subject. However, the work that he did complete points toward a shift of focus, from the category "nation," to that of "political community." If nations are the subset of ethnic groups oriented to political autonomy, then they are equally the subset of groups oriented to political autonomy that are based on ethnicity. What remains to be worked out are the various possible bases of political community, the relations among them, and the relations of each to the possible forms of "the state."

**WEBSTER, DANIEL** 1782–1852, American attorney, orator, and politician, born Salisbury, New Hampshire. Webster may be best known for his critical role in the passage of the Compromise of 1850, which came in the twilight of a long and impressive political career dedicated to the principles of conservative nationalism.

First as a member of the Federalist Party, and then as a member of the Whig Party, Webster held several elected and appointed offices, serving in the House of Representatives (1813–1817, 1823–1827), the United States Senate (1827–1841, 1845–1850), and as secretary of state (1841–1843, 1850–1852) under the administrations of William Henry Harrison, John Tyler, and Millard Fillmore. Although he harbored strong presidential ambitions, Webster was never nominated by a national party, but did run unsuccessfully in 1836 as a favorite son candidate from Massachusetts.

Early in his career, which spanned five eventful decades, Webster established his reputation as a nationalist by arguing, and winning, several important cases before the U.S. Supreme Court, including three cases that either weakened the authority of the states or expanded the authority of the federal government. In *Dartmouth College v. Woodward* (1819), Webster argued that charters granted by states are, in effect, binding contracts which the states cannot violate or unilaterally amend. In *McCulloch v. Maryland* (1819), Webster argued that no state government had the power to tax an agency of the federal government. Finally, in *Gibbons v. Ogden* (1824), a case involving the right of the state of New York to confer a steamboat monopoly, Webster defended the federal government's exclusive authority to regulate interstate commerce.

In 1832, while serving in the U.S. Senate, Webster denounced John C. Calhoun's doctrine of nullification, which asserted that state governments had the authority to override federal laws perceived to be unconstitutional or oppressive, as well as the right to secede from the Union as a last resort. Webster also spoke unsuccessfully on behalf of rechartering the Bank of the United States, in spite of the protests of President Andrew Jackson, who believed the bank to represent a dangerous, undemocratic, and unconstitutional expansion of federal power. Webster's stance on this issue was unpopular, and may have contributed to his defeat in the 1836 presidential election.

Later, as the danger of Southern secession grew more serious, Webster would find himself in an unlikely alliance with an ailing Henry Clay and a desperately ill (but unreconstructed) Calhoun, the other two members of the so-called Great Triumverate, in support of the Compromise of 1850. The compromise, which included both pro- and antislavery provisions, was designed to impede the movement toward disunion, rather than resolve the slavery issue once and for all. On the antislavery side, it abolished the slave trade in Washington, D.C., and admitted California into the Union as a free state. On the proslavery side, it established territorial governments for Utah and New Mexico without explicit mention of slavery (thereby endorsing the doctrine of popular sovereignty) and strengthened the existing Fugitive Slave Law. The compromise also adjusted the boundary of Texas in favor of New Mexico, compensating Texas for the loss through debt relief. Although Webster was not the principal architect of this compromise, his impassioned and moving speech of March 7, 1850, was believed to be critical to its passage in the Senate.

The Compromise of 1850 may have helped to postpone the outbreak of the Civil War by a few years, but it cost Webster the support of many of his Massachusetts constituents, including essayist Ralph Waldo Emerson, who wrote in 1851, "The history of this country has given a disastrous importance to the defects of this great man's mind." It was the modification of the Fugitive Slave Law that proved most offensive to the North, for this provision required citizens of free states to participate actively in recapturing runaway slaves. As a result of the outcry against him, Webster once again found his presidential ambitions thwarted.

Few figures in American history have had as large an impact on the fate of the nation. Honored by his many admirers as a courageous patriot who always placed the welfare of his country ahead of his own political ambitions, Webster also is sometimes condemned as a treacherous compromiser without firm moral convictions, and as the eager stooge of banking, shipping, and manufacturing interests.

An outstanding biography of Webster is Robert V. Remini, *Daniel Webster: The Man and His Time* (W. W. Norton & Company, 1997). For portraits of Webster as a nationalist, see Richard Current, *Daniel Webster and the Rise of National Conservatism* (Little, Brown, 1955); and Robert Dalzell, Jr., *Daniel Webster and the Trial of American Nationalism, 1843–1852* (Houghton Mifflin, 1973).

**WEBSTER, NOAH** 1758–1843, U.S. lexicographer, born in West Hartford, Connecticut. Webster is best remembered for his role as the first standardizer of American English. In 1782, the year after Lord Cornwallis's surrender at Yorktown effectively ended the American Revolution, Webster became an elementary schoolteacher. He quickly discovered that the only spelling and reading primers were written in the King's English; these books contained only British words and usages and were completely devoid of any forms that were peculiarly American. Convinced that U.S. political independence meant little unless accompanied by cultural independence, he set out to develop textbooks that would provide American schoolchildren with the building blocks for an American language.

In 1783 Webster produced *The American Spelling Book*, the first such work published in the United States and one that put an indelible stamp on American English. This work demonstrates Webster's preference for American yeoman simplicity over British affectation by eliminating unnecessary letters (such as the "k" in "topick" and the "u" in "flavour"), substituting "z" for "s" in words such as "organisation," and reversing "e" and "r" in words such as "theatre." It also provided standardized spellings for a number of non-British words popular in the United States such as "antelope," "boss," and "cookie." "The Blue-Backed Speller," as it was popularly called, was enthusiastically received at a time when spelling in the United States was a creative art; it was used in schools for over 100 years and eventually sold more copies than any book in U.S. publishing history except the Holy Bible.

In 1784 Webster came out with *The American Grammar*. Based on the theory that grammar should reflect popular usage and not some artificial standard of speaking and writing, this work legitimized American forms and usages that were generally simpler than those allowed by British conventions. In 1785 he developed *The American Reader*. This work eventually replaced the *New England Primer* (ca. 1690) and its emphasis on religion by dealing instead with patriotism, particularly the lives of revolutionary heroes. Although not as enduring as his speller, this work enjoyed widespread use in schools until the 1830s.

Webster supported the idea of a national government at the time of the Articles of Confederation and later backed President George Washington's administration. In 1828 he made his last contribution to the development of U.S. cultural nationalism in the form of the two-volume *An American Dictionary of the English Language*. In keeping with the same theory that informed his *Grammar,* "Webster's Dictionary," as it was popularly called, defined words as they were used by the general public as well as by the well-educated elite, and set a national standard for words and usages. Although it was not as successful as his other works, mostly because of its size and price, it set the standard for future dictionaries of American English, thus making the name "Webster" a household word.

Webster contributed immeasurably to the development of cultural nationalism in the United States. Before the publication of his four works, regional differences in the spelling, usage, and meaning of American English abounded. Webster, perhaps more than any other single individual, helped to make American English a uniform language and a unifying instrument.

Webster's autobiography is Richard M. Rollins, ed., *The Autobiographies of Noah Webster: From the Letters and Essays, Memoir, and Diary* (1989). A biography is John S. Morgan, *Noah Webster* (1975). Luisanna Fodde, *Noah Webster: National Language and Cultural History in the United States of America, 1758–1843* (1994); Benjamin T. Spencer, *The Quest for Nationality* (1957); and Kenneth Silverman, *A Cultural History of the American Revolution* (1976) discuss Webster's contributions to U.S. cultural nationalism.

## WEIZMANN, CHAIM

1874–1952, Leader in the creation of the modern state of Israel and generally regarded as the leading figure in the Zionist movement after its founder Theodor Herzl. Weizmann served as head of the World Zionist Organization for virtually all of the crucial period from the end of World War I to the founding of Israel in 1948.

Weizmann was born in Russia and eventually settled in England where he became a prominent chemist at the University of Manchester. He led the Jewish delegation to the Paris Peace Conference held in the aftermath of World War I. There he lobbied successfully for the assignment of the area of Palestine (formerly part of the defeated Ottoman Empire) as a territory under the mandate of Great Britain. This followed on the heels of his having taken a leading role in the negotiations leading up to the British government's issuance in 1917 of the Balfour Declaration, which "view(ed) with favour the establishment in Palestine of a national home for the Jewish people."

As Arab–Jewish conflict in Palestine worsened in the 1920s, Weizmann faced opposition from within the Zi-

onist Organization from critics who charged he was too conciliatory toward the Arabs and too accommodating of British interests in the region. This criticism came to a head in the late 1930s after Weizmann agreed to support the British policy of dividing Palestine into Jewish and Arab sectors. He ultimately lost the Zionist leadership after criticizing the anti-British violence of Jewish militia groups such as the Irgun Zvai Leumi.

Despite having no official position, Weizmann was chosen by the Zionist leadership to deal with U.S. President Harry Truman in 1948. Weizmann's skills as a negotiator once again came into play with the result that the United States recognized the fledgling state of Israel and provided it with a large loan. He then served as the first president of Israel from 1949 until his death in 1952.

## WELSH NATIONALISM

Wales is an integral part of the United Kingdom of Great Britain and Northern Ireland. The region retains some historical traditions that distinguish it from England, as well as a persistent sense of cultural identity associated notably with the Welsh language, and also has a small nationalist party.

Celtic tribes settled in Wales around 1000 B.C.E. Modern Welsh trace their language and some aspects of their culture to the Celtic Age, which lasted until the beginning of the Roman Era in the late 1st century. The patron saint of Wales, David (*Dewi* in Welsh), was born in the 5th century in Pembrokeshire, southwest Wales, and his monastery was located not far from the present site of the lovely St. David's Cathedral, long an important pilgrimage destination.

For most of the period from the end of the Roman period (5th century) to the English conquest, Wales was divided into self-governing principalities. Despite several attempts at unity, decentralized authority facilitated the imposition of nominal English control over the Welsh princes. William of Normandy's victory in 1066, however, marked the beginning of the outright military conquest of the Welsh territories. The conquest period (11th through 15th centuries) gave rise to legends associated with Welsh resistance to the English and contributed to an early, proto-nationalist sentiment of Wales as a victim of English expansion. Llywelyn the Great's (Llywelyn ap Gruffydd) refusal to pay tribute to King Edward I of England led to the king's invasion of Wales in 1277, and his construction of the massive castles that mark the north of Wales—Conwy, Beaumaris, and Caernarfon. Llywelyn was captured and killed, and to legitimize his conquest, Edward's first son (who, according to tradition, was conceived at Caernarfon Castle) was proclaimed Prince of Wales in 1301. That title has descended to the modern era, when it was last bestowed on the current Prince of Wales, Charles, at Caernarfon Castle in 1969.

After Edward's conquest, successive revolts were quashed by the English. The last major rebellion came in the early 15th century, when Owain Glyndwr rallied the Welsh who, suffering from famine and plague, bitterly resented their English overlords. His brief military successes were accompanied by plans for Welsh autonomy, including parliaments, but his revolt was crushed in 1408. The formal political integration of Wales and England took place under Henry VIII, whose Acts of Union between 1536 and 1543 introduced a uniform political and judicial system throughout England and Wales (but not Scotland). The Welsh language was excluded from official channels, which further contributed to the gulf between the Anglicized gentry and professional classes, and the Welsh-speaking, predominantly rural, classes.

From the perspective of Welsh nationalists, the social and economic history of Wales from the 16th to the 20th centuries was a form of internal colonialism. English political and military control brought cultural domination and as England rose to international preeminence in the 18th and 19th centuries, Wales was consigned to a largely peripheral role in British economic development. The region became the source of raw materials such as wool, oak (for the ships of the British navy), slate from the quarries of northeast Wales, and coal from the southern valleys.

The coal mines contributed to the development of an Anglicized industrial belt in south Wales. At the same time, the mining towns contributed to the richness of the Welsh musical tradition, as men's choirs formed among working-class communities. These choirs continue to be a distinctive element of Welsh culture, as does the custom of singing as a prelude to sporting events. The *eisteddfod,* a musical and literary gathering first recorded in the 12th century, is perhaps an even better known Welsh tradition. In recent years, both the National Eisteddfod and a multitude of local *eisteddfodau* have become popular contests and fairs for musicians, poets, and other artists. The eisteddfod is considered by the Welsh to be a showcase for Welsh culture, and thus has taken on political as well as artistic connotations.

Religious nonconformism, principally Methodism, is another feature of Welsh social and economic development. The refusal to conform to Anglicanism received fervent support in Wales beginning in the 18th century, and by the late 19th century, the Anglican church was largely alien to the religious life of most of the Welsh population. Formal disestablishment of the church in Wales, including the end of forced payment of tithes to the church, and disendowment of Church properties, was concluded in 1920.

Resentment of the privileged position of the established church was part of a nascent Welsh nationalism that began in the late 19th century, primarily as a defense of the Welsh language, which as a Celtic language is closer to Breton than Gaelic. Despite a now-infamous Welsh Not campaign in the 19th century to punish the use of Welsh in the classroom, there were still after World War I an estimated one million Welsh speakers (about 39 percent of the population). However, the numbers dropped dramatically thereafter, and by the 1990s less than 5 percent of the population was monolingual in Welsh.

Plaid Cymru, the Welsh Nationalist Party, was founded in 1925 by a group of writers and scholars, and its primary objective has long been the preservation of the Welsh language and culture. Nationalist sentiment in Wales, as elsewhere in Europe, flowered in the 1960s and early 1970s, and in 1966, Plaid Cymru elected its first member of parliament. Although it received 12 percent of the popular vote in the 1970 general election, by the 1980s and 1990s, it was averaging under 10 percent. Its primary challenge by the late 1990s was to expand its electoral support beyond Welsh speakers in preparation for elections to a new Welsh assembly. Although the assembly was only narrowly approved by Welsh voters in a 1997 referendum, Plaid Cymru saw it as laying the foundation for Welsh autonomy in a broader European Union of regions.

The long-term prospects of Welsh nationalism are uncertain. Twentieth-century secularism has undermined religious nonconformity as the center of Welsh communal life. Regions near the English border continue to be strongly Anglicized, and even those areas with a long history of resentment against English economic exploitation, such as southern Wales, are tightly integrated into the national political system through the Labour Party. Labour has dominated Welsh politics since the ex-miner and leading cabinet minister of the post-World War II Labour government, Aneurin Bevan, was first sent to the House of Commons in 1929. Like his liberal predecessor, David Lloyd George, who was prime minister during World War I, Bevan is regarded as a "famous son" of Wales, but neither he nor George was a nationalist in the contemporary sense. Similarly, Dylan Thomas, one of the most famous 20th-century Welshmen, wrote only in English, as has poet R. S. Thomas (no relation), a passionate defender of the Welsh way of life.

Despite the long history of political and economic integration of Wales with England, there are nonetheless signs that Welsh nationalism may be more significant than the proliferation of Welsh symbols such as the red dragon, leeks, and daffodils (worn prominently on St. David's Day, March 1). Since the Welsh Language Act of 1967, there has been a steady expansion in the use of Welsh, alongside English, for official purposes. Welsh is mandatory in most primary and secondary schools, almost 20 percent of the population claims to be bilingual in Welsh and English, and Welsh-language media—radio and TV channels and newspapers—were common by the 1990s. For Welsh nationalists, the process of devolution in the United Kingdom and the start-up of a regional assembly in the capital city of Cardiff are the beginning of a hoped-for process of reversing the long tradition of English domination of Welsh social, economic, political, and cultural life.

Particularly useful references for the history of Welsh nationalism are Kenneth O. Morgan's *Rebirth of a Nation: Wales 1880–1980* (Oxford, 1981) and Charlotte Aull Davies, *Welsh Nationalism in the Twentieth Century* (Praeger, 1989). See also the web site maintained by Plaid Cymru.

## WESTPHALIA, PEACE OF

The Peace of Augsburg (1555) had recognized that the new Protestant faith had an equal status with the Catholic and that each territorial prince and free city would decide which faith should be practiced by all residents under their control. *Cuius regio, eius religio* ("whoever rules chooses the religion") was the formula for a kind of religious freedom that was restricted to the rulers. However, this did not permanently settle the religious question in Germany. A Catholic counter-reformation, set in motion in Rome and supported by the Habsburg emperors, heated tensions between German Protestants and Catholics, who formed a Protestant Union and Catholic League in 1608 and 1609, respectively. All that was needed was a spark in Bohemia to ignite the almost indescribably destructive Thirty Years War on German soil that ravaged this weak and divided land from 1618 until 1648.

Germany was crisscrossed by marauding foreign armies that lived off the land in a manner summarized by Wallenstein: "The war must feed the war." No door, wall, or fortress could protect the civilian population from the armies that cut wide swaths through the countryside and cities, followed by hordes of often disease-ridden camp followers, and leaving a trail of wreckage, ashes, and corpses behind them. Germany was left breathless, devastated, and demoralized from the plunder and destruction. In some areas such as Wurttemberg, the Palatinate, Thuringia, and Mecklenburg, two-thirds of the inhabitants had been eradicated, and overall losses in Germany ranged from a third to a half

of the total population. The total population dropped from about 20 million to 10 to 14 million. Thus, Germany, which at the beginning of the 17th century had the largest number of inhabitants in all of Europe, fell behind that of France for the next century and a half and behind that of Russia to the present day. It was more than a century before it reached its pre-1618 level. In addition to human deaths, 1600 cities and 18,000 villages had been totally demolished, and livestock, farmland, and the rest of the economic infrastructure had been left in shambles. In comparative terms, the destruction to Germany was far greater in 1648 than in 1945. Only an atomic war could produce comparable damage today.

Who won this thirty-year nightmare? The Peace of Westphalia in 1648 provides the answer. Sweden took control of the city of Wismar, the Dukedom of Bremen-Verden (except the city of Bremen), the islands of Rügen, Usedom, and Wollin, and part of Pomerania, thereby depriving Germany of the outlets to the sea via the Elbe, Weser, and Oder Rivers. France got most of Alsace, the cities of Metz, Toul, Verdun, Breisach, and the Rhine, and achieved protector status over ten German imperial cities. Germany's western border, which had existed since the 9th century, was thus fundamentally altered. Switzerland and the Netherlands were granted full independence from Germany.

The German princes' official right to determine the religious beliefs of all their subjects was withdrawn, at least in theory. Most important for subsequent international law, the German princes were granted full sovereignty within their own territories, including the right to make treaties with foreign powers. The proviso that these treaties could not be directed against the emperor or the empire remained valid only on paper. It is the treaty's recognition of the nation-state's sovereignty that is most frequently cited today in international law and politics and in discussions about whether and what limits should be placed on such sovereignty. Germany was left with almost 2000 sovereign states ranging from the large territories of Brandenburg, Austria, Saxony, and Bavaria, to eighty-three free and imperial cities (including Hamburg and Frankfurt am Main), and countless ecclesiastical and other small units, some of which included as few as about 2000 inhabitants. At a time when centralizing, centripetal forces were at work in England and France, centrifugal forces prevailed in Germany, throwing it farther and farther away from national unity, which was not achieved until 1871.

## WHEATLEY, PHILLIS

1753–1784, African American poet. Wheatley was born in Senegal, West Africa, captured, and sold, at eight years of age, as a slave to John Wheatley, the owner of a shipping company in Boston. The Wheatleys granted her a privilege unusual for a slave, allowing her to learn to read and write. Phillis Wheatley published her first and only collection of poems in 1773, at age eighteen, entitled "Poems on Various Subjects, Religious and Moral," sealing her place in history as the progenitor of the African American literary tradition.

Unable to find an American publisher, her mistress Susannah Wheatley succeeded in finding a publisher in England who delighted in Phillis's piety. Her collection of poetry was a compilation of Biblical and mythological references, elegies, and dedications to historical figures. However, Phillis edited or omitted some poems from the collection she thought were too revolutionary for her British audience, particularly those which documented major incidents in the American struggle for independence. "On the Death of Mr. Snider Murder'd by Richardson" (1770) told of young Christopher Snider, who Phillis called "the first martyr for the common good," who was killed on February 22, 1770, when Ebenezer Richardson, a British informer, fired indiscriminately at an angry mob of colonial sympathizers surrounding his home. Poems such as "To the King's Most Excellent Majesty on His Repealing the American Stamp Act" (1768); "America" (1768), in which she accused Britannia of laying "some taxes on her darling son"; and "To the Right Honourable William, Earl of Dartmouth," in which she condemned tyranny, rejoiced in the American struggle for emancipation and displayed her burgeoning sense of nationalism.

Soon after the publication of her poetry, Susannah Wheatley died and Phillis was set free. Her collection gained recognition from such notable Bostonians as Thomas Hutchinson, then governor of Massachusetts Bay; James Bowdoin, later a founder of Bowdoin College; and John Hancock, signer of the Declaration of Independence. As a result, she had the honor of meeting then General George Washington who had asked to meet the slave poet who had written "To His Excellency General Washington" (1775), which praised his valor and predicted his ascendancy to a seat of higher power.

In her elegy "On the Death of General Wooster" (1778), in the voice of the dying David Wooster, she poignantly declared, But how, presumptuous shall we hope to find / Divine acceptance with th'Almighty mind— / While yet (O deed Ungenerous!) They disgrace / And hold in bondage Afric's blameless race? / Be victory our's, and generous freedom theirs. In these lines, she boldly exposed the cruel irony of the American fight to break England's shackles while Africans suffered in manacles bound to their American masters. This poem revealed her longing for the emancipation of the colonies from England, her own freedom, and that of other slaves, truly freedom for all. This desire was most evident in her letter of February 11, 1774, to the Reverend Samson Occum, "in every human breast, God has implanted a Principle, which we call Love of Freedom; it is impatient of Oppression, and pants for Deliverance."

For further reading, see *The Collected Works of Phillis Wheatley,* John Shields, ed. (New York: Oxford University Press, 1988); *The Norton Anthology of African American Literature,* Henry Louis Gates and Nellie Y. McKay, eds. (New York: W. W. Norton, 1991), pp. 164–176; and *Crossing the Danger Water: Three Hundred Years of African-American Writing,* Deirdre Mullane, ed. (New York: Doubleday, 1993), pp. 39–46.

**WHITMAN, WALT**   1819–1892, American poet, critic, and journalist; born in Long Island, New York. Best known as the author of *Leaves of Grass,* a bold experiment in the creation of a uniquely American literature, Whitman also explored themes of democratic culture and democratic individuality in later prose works such as *Democratic Vistas* (1871) and *Specimen Days* (1882). In spite of his well-known love affair with America and all things American, Whitman never stoops to national chauvinism. Instead, his nationalism celebrates the plurality, multiplicity, and diversity that characterizes both his perception of the American nation and his vision of the democratic individual.

Whitman spent his early career working as a reporter and editor for newspapers and magazines in New York and Louisiana. Although ostensibly a member of the Democratic Party, he dabbled in Free Soil politics, which in 1848 cost him a prestigious job as editor of the Brooklyn *Daily Eagle.* Later that year, Whitman would campaign actively for Martin Van Buren's Free Soil ticket, which ran reluctantly on an antislavery platform. He also edited a Free Soil newspaper called the *Freeman.*

In 1855, Whitman published the first edition of *Leaves of Grass.* Undeterred by the disinterest of publishers, Whitman released the thin volume anonymously and at his own expense. Subsequent editions—Whitman would publish a total of nine between 1855 and his death in 1892—revised and rearranged the original poems, and added new ones, including "Crossing Brooklyn Ferry," "Passage to India," "Starting from Paumanok," and "Chants Democratic." Whitman's poems were both fiercely patriotic, touching on themes such as territorial expansion, liberty, individualism, and democracy, and deeply personal, dealing frankly with erotic issues and Whitman's own sexual confusion.

Initially, Whitman had few admirers. However, Ralph Waldo Emerson, the Sage of Concord, quickly came to Whitman's defense, characterizing *Leaves of Grass* as "the most extraordinary piece of wit and wisdom that America has yet contributed" and "American to the bone." Similarly, Henry David Thoreau, who traveled to Brooklyn in order to meet Whitman in 1855, proclaimed the poet to be "apparently the greatest democrat the world has ever seen." Even so, many early readers found the blatant sexuality of *Leaves of Grass* shocking and Whitman's apparent (but often misunderstood) taste for self-dramatization crude and tiresome.

During the Civil War, Whitman worked as a war correspondent and as a government clerk, first in the Department of the Interior, and then (after he was dismissed on charges of indecency) in the office of the attorney general. He also spent considerable time in military hospitals in and around Washington, D.C., where he helped care for both Union and Confederate wounded. Some of Whitman's most well-known poems emerged from the Civil War era and are contained in *Drum Taps*, originally published in 1865, and in *Memories of President Lincoln*, both incorporated into later editions of *Leaves of Grass*.

Whitman's literary talent was not limited to poetry. His later essay *Democratic Vistas* represents for some critics a major achievement in the study of the culture of democracy, and his other major later prose work, *Specimen Days*, has been admired for its subtle exploration of representative images of 19th-century American life.

Whitman came to regard himself as the democratic poet *par excellence*, and posterity has, to some extent, come to share this view. However, for most of the 20th century, Whitman has been read, primarily, for his artistic achievements, rather than for his moral, social, and political ideas. This is ironic, for Whitman himself deplored art for art's sake. European readers have always regarded Whitman as an evocative symbol of American democracy. But only recently have American critics appreciated Whitman as a poet of a democratic culture that is, if not uniquely American, at least characteristically so.

An excellent introduction to Whitman is James E. Miller, Jr., *Walt Whitman*, updated ed. (Twayne, 1990). An illuminating account of Whitman's perspective on democratic culture is George Kateb, "Whitman and the Culture of Democracy," in *The Inner Ocean* (Cornell University Press, 1992). For a discussion of Whitman's

writing in historical political context, see Betsy Erkkila, *Whitman the Political Poet* (Oxford University Press, 1989).

**WILHELM II** 1859–1941, In the exuberance following German unification in 1871, the young, inexperienced, and impetuous Wilhelm II became kaiser in 1888. The new ruler hoped to become popular in Germany by canceling the Anti-Socialist Law, introducing some domestic reforms, and conducting an energetic German foreign and colonial policy. Noting that Bismarck had wholly different ideas, he fired the "Iron Chancellor" in 1890. He was then free to take the lead over a people optimistic about the prospects for Germany's future.

Biographer Lamar Cecil described the German state Wilhelm ruled as "a bizarre juxtaposition of modernity and reactionism . . . enchained in a political system that was manifestly anachronistic." The last kaiser's failure was not because he was a "quantité négligeable," Wilhelm's favorite term for describing others. An accomplished charmer, he had an effervescent manner, a swift comprehension of issues, resoluteness in action, and undeniable courage under fire. He aspired to be a "peace kaiser," despite his bluster, bravado, and closets full of uniforms. But he had a complicated, troubled personality and rocky relations with other German and European nobility. His quick judgment was often the result of impetuosity and a short attention span. He generally lacked dignity, tact, and seriousness of purpose. Chancellors, whom he alone appointed until he abdicated in 1918, survived by their skill in flattering him. Favoritism, not talent, was the primary quality for any office. Advice, no matter how deftly proffered, annoyed him, and he detested being lectured to, as Bismarck had done. He accepted only sugar-coated information and ignored warnings of possible dangers in his chosen courses of action. At the same time, he was easily manipulated, and he reduced everything to prejudice (with which he was richly endowed) and personality.

Wilhelm frittered away his domestic support and international standing through blabbering, boasting, and bad judgment. He was wearisome to other monarchs and government leaders, who mistakenly took him at his word that he alone was the one who made German policy. He fancied himself as a "master diplomat" and never relinquished his ultimate decision-making authority, no matter how many mistakes he made.

Although at times the assertive kaiser was sidelined or marginalized during World War I, he continued to have considerable power. For a while during the war he protected Chancellor Bethmann Hollweg and General Erich von Falkenhayn from the intrigues of Field Marshall Paul von Hindenburg and General Erich Ludendorff. In 1917–1918 he resisted the latters' pressure to appoint a military man as chancellor. He succeeded in postponing unrestricted submarine warfare until 1917, sensing that it would have disastrous consequences for Germany by bringing the Americans into the war. The kaiser seldom intervened in military operations. But he rejected, on grounds of magnanimity, a bombing raid on an Allied conference in northeastern France on March 26, 1918, that had been convened to coordinate the final war effort against the Germans.

Wilhelm was boastful about Germany's power. He had a way, as one of his biographers noted, of approaching every issue with an open mouth. Although in actual crises the young kaiser tended to be cautious, he seemed to many non-Germans to represent a restless country with more power than it could use well. His expression of nationalism became identified with aggressive saber-rattling, bluster, and military challenges to other countries' vital interests. This convinced some people that nationalism itself was wrong and a threat to peace and stability. One cannot escape the conclusion that Germany might have evolved differently if Wilhelm II had not ruled it for three decades. He abdicated at the end of World War I and lived out the rest of his life in Holland.

## WILSON, WOODROW

1856–1924, 28th president of the United States (1913–1921). Wilson somewhat reluctantly led the United States into war and tried to establish peace, promoting a just and rational international order and providing key leadership for the creation of the League of Nations at the Paris Peace Conference in 1919.

Profoundly affected by the horrors of the Civil War and its aftermath as a young man growing up in the South, Wilson devoted much of his energy to promoting peace and received the 1919 Nobel Prize for Peace. During his presidency he tried to curb nationalistic expansionism of the great powers and advocated respect for the rights of weaker countries. He advocated preparing Filipinos for self-government and opposed a U.S. exemption from Panama Canal tolls. Although he authorized a small expedition under Gen. John Pershing after Pancho Villa executed sixteen American citizens in 1916, Wilson opposed formal military intervention in Mexico even when its instability and attitude toward the United States appeared threatening to many American officials.

Not surprisingly, many of Wilson's efforts to mitigate expansionist nationalism and preserve the peace met with disappointment, including his failure to sustain American neutrality during World War I and to engage in secret peace negotiations and mediate the conflict. Even after the sinking of the British liner *Lusitania* by the Germans, he strove to avoid war and persuade the Germans to abide by the rules of war.

Perhaps Wilson's most enduring legacy was his role in the founding of the League of Nations, precursor to the United Nations, and his proclamation of fourteen points for international relations at the end of the War enunciated in an address to the U.S. Congress on January 8, 1918. Wilson strongly encouraged the creation of the League of Nations armaments by the Allies at the Paris Peace Conference following the end of World War I. Its purpose was to promote international cooperation, the arbitration of international conflicts, and the reduction of armaments.

Wilson's fourteen points embodied the principles that Wilson had advocated generally, applying them to a proposed postwar geopolitical environment. Wilson called for an international association of nations to provide guarantees of "political independence and territorial integrity to great and small states alike." He advocated safeguards for the peoples of various countries (Russia, Belgium, France, Austria-Hungary, Romania, Serbia, Montenegro, Poland, and Turkey) and the creation of open covenants of peace and international relations in which "diplomacy shall proceed always frankly and in the public view." Wilson called for the "Absolute freedom of navigation upon the seas, outside territorial waters," and "The removal, so far as possible, of all economic barriers and the establishment of an equality of trade conditions among all the nations."

Prince Maximilian of Baden, the German imperial chancellor, sent a note to President Wilson on October 3–4, 1918, proposing an immediate armistice and subsequent peace negotiations based on the fourteen points.

High-minded and principled, Wilson was sometimes inflexible and intolerant of others. When unsuccessfully soliciting American public support for the Treaty of Versailles, Wilson had a nervous collapse and a stroke of paralysis.

## WORLD WAR I

There was general shock and indignation in all of Europe when Archduke Franz Ferdinand's assassination was announced. On July 5 and 6, 1914, Germany granted its ally, Austria-Hungary, a free hand to deal with the matter, and Russia (and indirectly

France) gave the Serbians a similarly free hand. Only in the final days of the crisis did the German chancellor desperately try to regain control of the situation. Subsequent events revealed that German interests would have been better served by a tighter German rein on Austrian policy. However, in the eyes of German leaders, there appeared to be no alternative to their policy of allowing Austria to deal harshly with Serbia at this time.

On July 28, Austria-Hungary declared war on Serbia, and two days later Russia made the critical decision to order general mobilization, thus indicating its unwillingness to allow the Austrian-Serbian war to remain localized. German leaders had for a long time made it clear that they perceived a Russian general mobilization to be a threat to Germany itself. When Russia refused to withdraw its call to arms, Germany sent a last warning to both Russia and France. When the German note remained unanswered by August 1, Germany declared war on Russia. It did not immediately declare war on France, but France mobilized its army on August 1. With Russia, Germany, and France carrying out general military buildups, a European war had become unavoidable. When Germany violated Belgian territory in order to gain easier access to France, Britain also entered the war, thereby transforming the European war, which Germany probably would have won, into a world war.

All the European powers shared responsibility for the outbreak of World War I. Some, such as Austria-Hungary and Serbia, bore the greatest responsibility. Germany, Russia, and France must be blamed for not having sufficiently restrained their respective allies and thereby having allowed a local Balkan squabble (where there had already been two wars in 1912 and 1913) to ignite a world war. Britain bears the least responsibility for the war that came. Nevertheless, crowds of people in all belligerent countries greeted the outbreak of war with a gaiety that is usually reserved for carnival time. Two million German, more than a million French, a million British, a million Austrian, a half million Italian, and countless Russian soldiers perished in the four-year bloodletting which followed. The war also destroyed the old Europe, and what could be pieced back together collapsed a mere two decades later.

Almost immediately after the start of hostilities, German troops knifed through Belgium and into France according to a carefully laid "Schlieffen Plan," but by mid-September at the Battle of the Marne, they were stopped in their tracks before reaching Paris. For four years two opposing armies faced each other in trenches stretching from the English Channel to the Swiss border and pro-

tected by mazes of barbed wire, machine gun nests, mortar, and heavy artillery batteries. Chemical warfare (gas) was also introduced during the grisly conflict. Occasionally massive attacks were launched against the opposing trenches that sometimes brought infinitesimal gains and always huge human losses. For instance, in the inconclusive Battle of the Somme in 1916, the Germans lost 650,000 men and the Allies 614,000.

It was a different story in the east, where warfare was highly mobile and brought huge gains and losses of territory. After an initial Russian advance into East Prussia, German forces scored stunning victories against the Russians at Tannenberg and the Masurian Lakes. Out of these victories was born the legend of military genius and invincibility that surrounded the victorious Generals Paul von Hindenburg and Erich Ludendorff for the remainder of the war. By 1916 their authority over military and political questions alike exceeded even that of the kaiser and the chancellor.

The German successes in the east enabled their armies to march right into the heart of Russia. Still, the badly shaken tsarist empire managed to put up stiff resistance. It became clear to the Germans that the two-front war was a vice that could eventually crush Germany. This became especially apparent when the United States entered the war on the Allied side in the spring of 1917. President Woodrow Wilson had been determined to keep the Americans out of the war, but the Germans made several blunders that drew the United States into the conflict. A high official in the German Foreign Office, Arthur Zimmermann, sent a telegram to the Mexican government promising territorial rewards north of the Mexican border if it would support Germany in the war. This telegram was intercepted by the Americans and understandably antagonized American leaders and public opinion.

The most serious German mistakes involved naval warfare against neutral shipping. By the spring of 1915, German surface ships had been swept from all the major seas except the North and Baltic Seas. Because of the ever-tightening British blockade of the North Sea and English Channel outlets, the bulk of the German navy, which had been built up with so much fanfare and political sacrifice, remained bottled up in Germany's northern ports. This blockade also brought increasing hunger and deprivation to the German population and gradually led German leaders to use submarines to strike at Allied shipping. Submarines were regarded as a particularly hideous weapon at the time since they torpedoed ships without warning and without any capacity to help survivors. A particular outcry had gone up in the United States when a large passenger liner, the

*Lusitania,* was torpedoed off the coast of Ireland in mid-1915, with a loss of 1198 lives, including 139 Americans. The indignation in America was such that the Germans promised not to repeat such attacks.

For a while German submarine activity died down, but by early 1917 Generals Hindenburg and Ludendorff, backed by their immense popularity, forced the adoption of unrestricted submarine warfare on the unwilling chancellor. The head of the German Admiralty misjudged the ultimate effect of America's entry into the war to be "exactly zero"; in any case, it was widely believed that Britain would be forced to its knees before Americans would arrive. Although the first American divisions did not arrive in France until almost a year later, the immediate boost to Allied morale and the military contribution made by American soldiers in the final months of the war were decisive in the defeat of Germany.

**WORLD WAR II** By the spring of 1939, Britain and France had already allowed Germany to become the dominant power in Europe. Hitler's greatest mistake was that he cast this enormous accomplishment away by leading Germany into war. After 1938 he had no further diplomatic victories. From 1939 to 1941 he led Germany to dazzling successes, but all were of a military nature. With relative ease his newly created army (*Wehrmacht*) overran part of Poland, Denmark, Norway, Holland, Belgium, Luxembourg, Yugoslavia, and Greece. The most miraculous victory was the victory over France. Most German generals shuddered at the thought of attacking France, remembering the failure of the 1914 advance and the four-year war of attrition that had sapped Germany's strength and will. But Hitler had great faith in the tank warfare tactics developed by General Heinz Guderian and in the brilliant strategic plan devised by General Friedrich Erich von Manstein. He also recognized the most important factor: France was unwilling to fight a sustained war. In six weeks, Germany had rolled into France via a flank attack around its famed Maginot Line of supposedly impregnable fortresses.

By the summer of 1940, Germany controlled Europe from the Arctic Circle to the Pyrenees and from the Atlantic Ocean to the Soviet Union. If Hitler had made a generous peace offer to France, he might have destroyed Britain's and other countries' will to resist, but Hitler never thought of such a possibility. He could not grant a magnanimous peace because, as he himself later wrote, the victory of the stronger always involved "the destruction of the weaker or his unconditional subservience." He had a knack for seeing the weakness in his enemies, but he was unable to build anything lasting. Also, because he considered himself to be infallible and irreplaceable, he insisted on doing everything quickly; he could not plant anything that required time to grow. Based on his writings and actions, one can say with reasonable certainty that Hitler sought to establish German hegemony in Europe and direct domination over the Soviet Union, which along with the older European powers' overseas colonies, would occupy the bottom of Hitler's power pyramid. Above them would be the rest of the European countries, divided into Germanic lands bordering on Germany, servant peoples, such as the Poles, and satellites and quasi-independent states. On top would be an all-powerful Germany. This German-dominated order would place Hitler in a good position later to struggle against America and Japan for world domination. That he did not accomplish this ambitious goal was due in large measure to serious mistakes that he himself made after such stunning successes.

In 1940, he launched an aerial attack against Britain which left rubble piles throughout the country, but which also inspired heroic action in what Prime Minister Winston Churchill called Britain's "finest hour." While still involved in this furious struggle, violating the treaty whereby Germany and Russia had split up Poland between them, Hitler unleashed his armies against the Soviet Union in mid-1941. This was against the advice of his generals and created another two-front war, the first of which had been such a nightmare for Germany during World War I. The attack was launched too late, so in a repeat of Napoleon's humiliation, "General Winter" saved the weaker Russians. Cold weather and snow closed in on the German troops, many of whom had not been issued proper winter equipment. After initial victories against an enemy that Hitler had grossly underestimated, the German advance ground to a stop. Hitler saw his dreams of grandeur buried under Russian snow and ice.

In the midst of this truly desperate situation, Hitler compounded his difficulties even further. On December 7, 1941, Japan attacked the U.S. fleet at Pearl Harbor in Hawaii, and the United States responded by declaring war on Japan, but not on Germany. Germany had no treaty obligation with Japan, but inexplicably and without conferring with anyone, Hitler declared war against the United States. Germany had no military means for conducting military operations against the Americans, but this step decisively tipped the scales in favor of his opponents and ultimately sealed Germany's defeat. Thereafter, he had no idea how to extricate Germany from ruin. For example, he could not follow up on General Erwin Rommel's victories in North Africa in the summer of 1942, and, of course, he excluded the very idea of a political settlement. His only order was "Hold at all costs!" In 1942, Germany began losing territory in the east, especially after a disastrous defeat at Stalingrad in early 1943.

By the fall of 1944, enemy armies were advancing on Germany from the east and west. More and more Germans saw the hopelessness of the situation and began to regard conquest by the Western Allies as liberation. But Hitler did not share this secret war aim of many ordinary people. He personally assumed command of the German forces. Then he unleashed a torrent of powerful rockets on London and its suburbs using technology only recently developed. These attacks by what he called his "wonder weapons" merely served to harden even more the determination of the British and their American ally. Disregarding warnings from military advisers that the Red Army was poised for a massive strike from the east, Hitler ordered his last military offensive against the Western Allies in the Belgian Ardennes Forest in late 1944. The element of surprise and extremely bad weather which kept Allied aircraft grounded for a few days helped the Germans gain initial success and stop the Western powers' advance on Germany. However, once American and British air power could be brought into action, the German offensive was halted, and by the first week of January the German forces were being decimated or rolled back. As some of Hitler's generals had warned, the Red Army crashed through the German line in the East, and in one violent movement pushed from the Vistula to the Oder Rivers. Because Hitler had squandered his last reserves in the Ardennes offensive, he had nothing left to stop the Russian advance.

Hitler's decisions that led to a slowdown of the Western Allied advance and favored a rapid Russian advance into the heart of Germany had unfortunate consequences for postwar Germany. In the first half of February 1945, President Roosevelt, Prime Minister Churchill, and General Secretary Stalin met in Yalta in the Crimea to discuss the postwar control of Germany and to divide Germany into zones of occupation. The lines they drew were heavily influenced by the calculations of where exactly the Allied armies would be in Germany at the end of the war. At the time, it appeared that Russian troops would be somewhat farther within Germany than was actually the case when hostilities ceased. However, based on the decisions made at Yalta, U.S. troops had later to be pulled back from Saxony and Thuringia, which were within the designated Soviet zone. Also, the collapse of cooperation among the four Allies after the war left the temporary line drawn between the Soviet zone of occupation and the zones of the Western Allies as the line of division between East and West Germany until 1990.

Seeing enemy armies advancing within his own country's territory and with no hope of stopping them, any rational and responsible leader with a concern for his own citizens would have done anything to salvage whatever would be necessary for their survival. Hitler was not such a leader. In late 1941, he had made a chilling statement to the Danish and Croatian foreign ministers: "If ever the German people is no longer sufficiently strong and willing to sacrifice its own blood for its existence, then it should fade away and be destroyed by another, stronger power. . . . In that situation, I will lose no tears for the German people." On March 18 and 19, 1945, he gave two orders which demonstrated that he had not changed his mind and that he now thought it was time to carry through with the end of Germany. He ordered all Germans in areas threatened by the invasion forces in the west to leave their homes and set out on what could only have been a death march eastward. The following day he gave the so-called "Nero order": "to destroy all military, transport, communications, industrial and supply facilities as well as anything of value within the Reich which could be used by the enemy for continuing his struggle either immediately or in the foreseeable time." When Albert Speer, his trusted confidant and munitions minister, objected to this policy, which would have completely eliminated the Germans' ability to survive after defeat, Hitler answered "ice-coldly": "If the war is lost, then the people will be lost also. . . . In that case the people will have shown itself as the weaker, and the future would belong solely to the strengthened Eastern people. Whoever survives this struggle would be the inferior ones anyway since the superior ones have already fallen."

Hitler himself chose not to be among the survivors. On April 30, 1945, a few hours before his underground bunker in Berlin was captured by Soviet troops, he stuck a pistol in his mouth and pulled the trigger. Speer and others did their best to prevent Hitler's orders from being carried out. But their effect was that most Germans, at least in the western part of Germany, did view the enemy occupation of Germany as a liberation. While the occupation forces expected to find a nation of fanatic Nazis on their hands, they found instead a shell-shocked, seriously disillusioned people who had been far more thoroughly "de-Nazified" by Hitler's treatment of Germany in the closing months of the war than the carefully planned De-Nazification and reeducation program would otherwise ever have been able to accomplish. The occupation powers interpreted the

Germans' passivity and willingness to cooperate as typical German servility, but it was rather a reflection of the extent to which Germans felt themselves to have been deceived and betrayed by Hitler.

**WYSZYNSKI, STEFAN CARDINAL** 1901–1981, Named Poland's primate in 1952 and played a leading role in the country until his death in 1981. By the time Wyszynski took office, the church and state had developed quite hostile relations. In 1949, the Vatican mandated that all party members and sympathizers be excommunicated. The government responded by arresting priests and seizing all church properties, except for the churches and churchyards themselves. Wyszynski himself was arrested and placed in an isolated monastery in 1953; he was only released after a workers' upheaval brought Wladyslaw Gomulka to power, and with him some changes in policy.

A combination of the church's political strength and the regime's relative tolerance allowed the church considerably more influence in Poland than it enjoyed in other Soviet bloc states. Under Wyszynski, the church ran an independent university; it gave shelter to the *Catholic Weekly,* an independent paper; it won the right in 1956 to organize the Clubs of the Catholic Intelligentsia as independent discussion clubs; and from 1956, it sponsored a group of five deputies to the parliament—until, in 1968, they opposed repressing student demonstrations, and were soon removed. All of these institutions were without parallel in the Soviet bloc.

Under Wyszynski's leadership, the church sent a letter of forgiveness for the horrors Germany had inflicted on Poland during World War II. In the letter, the church hierarchy used the phrase: *"We forgive and ask for forgiveness."* This statement angered many Poles, who felt they had done nothing that required forgiveness, while they had been brutally attacked and assaulted by the Germans. The government bitterly attacked the church for taking this position, but it was unable to reap much political benefit from the incident.

Wyszynski was cautious about his approach to the government. He consistently pushed for more rights for the church: to build more churches, to allow the right to travel for the clergy; to broadcast mass on the media; to restore religious education in the schools. He was more guarded about broadening democratic rights generally. But, as an opposition emerged, he did meet with its activists at times and he verbally encouraged them.

Upon hearing of the strikes that the Solidarity union began, Wyszynski urged the workers to return to work; later, in a sermon that was broadcast on television, he suggested that there were faults on both sides and that the strikes were a threat to the nation. He was saved from the consequences of this action because the government broadcast had excised some portions of the sermon, and the church could claim that in doing so it had distorted the meaning of his words. In the ensuing months, Wyszynski's representative worked closely with Lech Walesa, leader of Solidarity. Wyszynski died in May 1981, at a time when the conflict between the party and Solidarity was intensifying.

Two good books with differing points of view on Solidarity are *Breaking the Barrier,* by Lawrence Goodwyn (Oxford University, 1991), and *The Polish Revolution,* by Timothy Garton Ash (Vintage Book, 1985).

# X

**XENOPHOBIA**  An unreasonable fear or hatred of foreigners or strangers, or of that which is foreign or strange.

Xenophobia is often a driving force and rallying cry behind nationalism. Hatred and fear of those of a different nationality can lead to fighting, either political or military, for one's own nationality. On the other hand, nationalists attempting to gain power or to drum up support may use xenophobic rhetoric, or attempt to fan the flames of existing fears and hatred. Xenophobia is found throughout the world, from the Americas to Europe, from Asia to Africa.

Asian xenophobia is illustrated by Japanese nationalism. The Japanese trace their roots back to their gods, and contend that their blood is pure, that they do not share ancestry with other peoples of Asia or elsewhere. The Japanese generally distrust all other nationalities, especially other "inferior" Asian people. During World War II, the Japanese killed Chinese, Koreans, and Southeast Asians. Many Korean women were forced into sexual slavery by Japanese soldiers, and Korean men and women were brought to Japan as laborers. The descendants of these laborers, who have been in Japan for two or three generations and speak Japanese as their first language, are still considered outsiders; they are required to carry alien resident registration cards and are fingerprinted every few years.

African xenophobia has roots in racial, religious, and class differences. The genocide and subsequent war in Rwanda in the early 1990s reflect this. Hutu and Tutsi, which are historic class designations but are now seen as racially different, coexisted uneasily in Rwanda. Political unease set off a few days of atrocious murders, which have been followed by years of retributions. Both sides have been fueled by nationalistic and xenophobic rhetoric.

In the United States, political dialogue in the 1990s has played on the xenophobia of the people. Politicians have used this tool to call for massive welfare reform, the end of affirmative action, the removal of social benefits from legal immigrants, and legislation to make English the official language, and therefore the only one used by the government.

In Europe, xenophobia can be seen today, from the rise of the right in France and Germany, which blames most of Europe's problems on the large influx of immigrants from Northern Africa and the Middle East, to Slovakia, which has moved to marginalize its minorities, especially the Roma and Hungarians, by declaring Slovakian the national language and redrawing voting districts. The rise of the Nazis, a highly nationalistic party, in Germany in the 1930s was also fueled by xenophobia, as Germans felt the whole world was against them, and saw successful Jewish- and foreign-owned businesses flourishing as their own spending power melted away.

# Y

**YELTSIN, BORIS** 1931–, Russian president 1991–1999, born in the village Butka of Sverdlovsk oblast. In 1955 he graduated as a construction engineer from the Polytechnic Institute in Urals. Yeltsin became a Communist Party member in 1961. In 1955–1968 he worked as master, engineer, and head of construction enterprises in Sverdlovsk. In 1968 Yeltsin started his party career, first as the CPSU Sverdlovsk oblast party secretary, and in 1985–1987 as the first secretary of the Moscow City Party Committee. Being rather forthright he gained enemies. As a result of conflict with the hardline Moscow city party members he was dismissed during the Plenum of the Central Committee of the CPSU in October 1987. During 1987–1989 Yeltsin worked as a deputy chairman of the State Committee of Construction. In 1989 he was elected as a deputy to the People's Deputies Congress and to the Supreme Soviet (Parliament) of the Russian Federation. In July 1990 Yeltsin quit the Communist Party.

On June 12, 1991 (currently a national holiday in Russia), Yeltsin was elected the first president of Russia by popular vote. While president of Russia within the USSR, he promoted Russian national values, independent institutions lacking in the Soviet system (academy of sciences, party organization), and the ideas of sovereign existence with the other republics in his speeches all over the Soviet Union and in the Russian Federation.

In August 1991, during the coup d'état against the political reforms in Moscow, Yeltsin led the resistance fight against the hard-liners. He subsequently aimed at the formation of a loose confederation of Commonwealth of Independent States (CIS) as a replacement for the USSR. In December 1991 he favored the signing of the agreement in Belarus, which actually served as the beginning of the CIS.

The Yeltsin term can be divided into four stages. The first stage occurred in the reform year of 1992. He used his powers to initiate a program of radical economic reforms to transform centralized Russia into a reform democratic state starting with the liberalization of prices and privatization under acting Prime Minister Yegor Gaidar. He also appointed his own representatives to the regions to bypass the local legislatures dominated by Communists, and he banned the CPSU. Russia replaced the position of the USSR in many international organizations, including the United Nations where Russia took over the USSR seat as a permanent member of the Security Council. In the international arena, however, the Russian position was weakening in comparison with the late Soviet Union. The reformist economic policy, direct regional control, and international Western-oriented policy of Russia were opposed by the Communists who dominated in the Supreme Soviet (Parliament) of Russia in 1991–1993. According to the Russian Federation Constitution (adopted in 1979 and amended in later years, which resulted in a mixture of the Soviet and the new Russian clauses) authority in Russia overlapped between the president and the parliament. Various presidential decrees were thus overruled (nullified) by the Supreme Soviet.

In 1993 the conflict progressed rapidly and corresponded to the beginning of the second stage of Yeltsin's power. To save his policy and to gain popular approval for his reforms, Yeltsin announced a referendum. In April 1993, according to the results of the referendum, the people of Russia supported Yeltsin; however, the power struggle in Moscow did not end. In September of the same year Yeltsin decided to break the power deadlock and asked one of his toughest opponents, Vice President Aleksandr Rutskoy, to resign. Instead, Rutskoy refused and was backed by the members of the Supreme Soviet. At the end of September Vice President Rutskoy, Chairman of the Parliament Khazbulatov, legislators, and anti-Yeltsin demonstrators occupied the parliamentary building. They were mainly hard-line Communists and Russian nationalists. The conflict ended with the military takeover of the Parliament building by Yeltsin supporters. The leaders of the violent opposition were arrested but in February 1994 they were granted amnesty.

In December 1993 a new Constitution was popularly approved and a new lower chamber of the Parliament—the State Duma—was elected. The Communists won most of the seats in the State Duma. During the next elections in 1995 they gained fewer seats, but dominated in the following parliamentary elections.

The third stage of Yeltsin's rule is connected with the war in Chechnya in 1994–1996. In 1990 Yeltsin had toured Russia and promised to its political constituents as much independence as they could sustain. Subsequently two regions of Russia, rich in raw materials—Yakutia and Tatarstan—discussed the possibilities of independence. Chechnya, an economically rather poor region but having experienced the Stalin deportation policy, however, was the only one to resolutely declare itself independent in 1991, which caused fighting between the Russian army and the Chechen military groupings in the region. During the war thousands of military personnel and civilians were killed. The war ended in 1996 with the signing of an agreement according to which the final political status over the Northern Caucasus region of Chechnya was to be determined in 2001.

The fourth period of Yeltsin's rule began in 1996 when he decided to run for reelection as president despite his extremely low popular support. However, Yeltsin was successful. Yeltsin's continuing weak physical condition (heart problems and other constant illnesses) barred him from an active role in leading the country. In 1998 the country survived a severe financial crises; in 1999 Russian business and political leaders were accused of corruption and money laundering in the West. President Yeltsin, however, seemed to focus on personnel problems in leadership and changed prime ministers five times during 1998 and 1999. Another chechen war broke out. The Russian troops again entered Chechnya in the name of dissolving the Islamist terrorist, bandit groups. Yeltsin resigned on December 31, 1991; he appointed his prime minister, Vladimir Putin as acting president.

Further reading: Leon Aron, *Yeltsin: A Revolutionary Life* (HarperCollins, 2000); Jonathan Steele, *Eternal Russia: Yeltsin, Gorbachev, and the Mirage of Democracy* (Harvard University Press, 1995).

**YOUNG TURKS** European term for the Committee of Union and Progress (CUP), at a first a secret society and then, after 1908, a political party in the Ottoman Empire. The CUP dominated the political life of the Ottoman Empire for a decade from the constitutional revolution of 1908 to the defeat of the empire in World War I. The party's prominence during this eventful period gave it the rare distinction of having played an important role in the development of up to four nationalisms: Turkish, Armenian, Arab, and Albanian.

The CUP started life as an association of reform-minded men who wished to strengthen the empire by curtailing the autocratic powers of Sultan Abdülhamid II and restoring the Ottoman parliamentary Constitution, which had been suspended in 1878. When unrest fomented by the Young Turks in Macedonia led to restoration of the Constitution in 1908, the CUP seemed to have achieved its goals. It suffered internal dissension and lost much of its initial, massive public support, however, because the idea of reform meant different things to different people. Many Arabs and Albanians, for example, expected liberal constitutionalism to promote decentralization and greater local autonomy. The group that came to dominate the CUP, in contrast, saw centralization as the best means of marshaling the resources needed to defend the empire from external and internal threats. The eventual supremacy of this viewpoint was aided by a series of international crises, which increased pressure on the CUP to defend Ottoman interests. These crises started almost immediately in 1908, when nominally Ottoman Bulgaria declared independence and Austria-Hungary annexed Bosnia. War came when Italy invaded Tripolitania in 1911, followed by the first Balkan war in 1912. The Ottomans appeared almost powerless in each of these crises. A group of CUP military officers carried out a coup in 1913, which brought to power the men who would involve the empire in World War I. The most important of them were Enver, Cemal, and Talat Pashas. Enver Paşa in particular has long been thought to have favored Turkish nationalism.

Yet the reputation of the Young Turks as nationalists has undergone thorough scrutiny in recent years. The charge that they tried to "Turkify" the multiethnic empire seems now much more open to debate. Turkish cultural awareness—a forerunner of the Turkish nationalism of the Mustafa Kemal Atatürk period—grew in this period but had little effect on government policies, at least until the later stages of World War I. The government could ill afford to adopt a revolutionary new attitude that would likely alienate a large part of the Ottoman population without promising any clear advantage. Although most CUP leaders spoke Turkish as their first language, their policies continued to stress Ottomanism and, after 1913, Islam. It was their government's centralization program which caused protests from many members of the notable class in the provinces, who had enjoyed a fair degree of local autonomy during the reign of Abdülhamid II. This prepared the ground for revolts in Albania in 1910–1912 and the Hijaz in 1916. Albanians and Arabs later looked to these revolts as important milestones in the development of their nationalist movements.

The CUP played a much larger role in the history of Armenian nationalism. During World War I practically all Armenians of eastern Anatolia fled to Russia, were deported to the south and west, or were killed. Beyond that elementary fact there is practically no point of agreement. At one extreme the wartime Young Turk regime is accused of orchestrating a genocidal campaign that murdered well over one million Armenians. At the other extreme, the charge of genocide is rejected: Although several hundred thousand Armenians may have died in eastern Anatolia, their deaths were the result of the chaos and brutality of the Ottoman-Russian war front, which also saw the deaths of many more Muslims. Wherever the truth may lie, the Armenian community clearly suffered an awful catastrophe that continues to affect Armenian nationalism today.

Numerous studies of the CUP are readily available. An early work is Feroz Ahmad's *The Young Turks* (Oxford University Press, 1969). Şükrü Hanioğlu's *The Young Turks in Opposition* (Oxford University Press, 1995) is a thorough study of them in the pre-1908 period. Hasan Kayalı's *Arabs and Young Turks* (University of California Press, 1997) is an excellent study of the CUP and nationalism.

**YUGOSLAV NATIONALISM** Yugoslav nationalism has from the beginning been characterized by confusion over the relationship between a Yugoslav nation and individual, previously existing South Slavic nations. Within Yugoslavia, Yugoslav nationalism suffered from the constant suspicion of Croats, Slovenes, and Macedonians, who viewed it as a veiled form of Serbian nationalism.

Yugoslav nationalism emerged in the 19th century from a complex mixture of Illyrianism and the nationalisms of Slovenes, Croats, Serbs, and Montenegrins. The Illyrian movement of the 19th century, led by the Croat Ljudevit Gaj, proposed the establishment of a single nation for South Slavs. Gaj's program sought to build an Illyrianist conscious through a common language, but the patchwork of dialects of the South Slavic lands frustrated his search for this base. By 1836, however, Gaj settled on the Štokavian dialect, the same dialect chosen by the Serb language reformer Vuk Karad-

žić. In addition to facing opposition from those Serbs who still favored Old Church Slavonic, the Illyrianist movement thus also encountered conflict with those who, like Karadžić, saw Štokavian as the basis of the Serb nation. Meanwhile, the Slovenes, who had begun to modernize their own distinct language, also viewed the Illyrianist effort with considerable suspicion. In Croatia, the Illyrianist movement was eclipsed by the Croatian integral nationalism of Ante Starčević and Eugen Kvaternik, who viewed all South Slavs, except for the Bulgars, as Croats.

With the Illyrianist movement marginalized, the Croats Bishop Josip Juraj Strossmayer and Franjo Rački emerged as the leading advocates of South Slav unity. They saw the South Slav, or Yugoslav, cause as the appropriate answer to the efforts of German and Hungarian nationalists in the Austro-Hungarian Empire. Their program therefore remained focused on those South Slavs living within the borders of the empire.

The efforts of Strossmayer were viewed with suspicion by Ilija Garašanin, who had emerged in the meantime as the leader of the Serbian nationalist movement. Garašanin's Serb integral nationalism was diametrically opposed to the Croatian integral nationalism of Starčević. The antipathy between the emergent nationalisms of the Croats and the Serbs was strengthened by Josip Frank, a follower of Starčević. Unlike Starčević, Frank adopted a pro-Austrian version of Croatian nationalism, and increased agitation against Serbs residing in Croatia.

However, in 1905, under the leadership of Frano Supilo and Ante Trumbić, a Croato-Serb Coalition (*Hrvatsko-srpska koalicija*) emerged which called for the unification of the South Slavs in the face of the threat of German nationalism. The coalition sought cooperation between the South Slavs of the Austro-Hungarian Empire and the Serbian state. The political program quickly gained popularity and was adopted by many political leaders, including Stjepan Radić, the leader of the Croat Peasant Party.

During the first year of World War I, the leadership of Serbia proclaimed its intent to form a state of the Serbs, Croats, and Slovenes. After lengthy negotiation, the Kingdom of the Serbs, Croats, and Slovenes was proclaimed on December 1, 1918. However, the establishment of this state, which formally became known as Yugoslavia in 1929, was accompanied by severe disagreement between the main constituent groups. In particular, it became clear that the Serb political leadership viewed Yugoslavia as an extension of the Serbian state rather than as a truly unitarist, or Yugoslav state. Throughout the 1920s, the non-Serbs in Yugoslavia complained that their concerns went unheeded and that the centralist governmental, social, and economic structures of the pre-1914 Serbian state had been imposed on them without their consent.

In January 1929, after a period of parliamentary unrest and the assassination of Stjepan Radić, King Aleksandar of Yugoslavia proclaimed a royal dictatorship. All parties carrying "tribal," that is, national names other than "Yugoslav" were banned. Advocates of Yugoslav unity argued that, in order to survive external threats from neighboring nations, the South Slavs should abandon the "tribal" (plemenski) identities that were in fact retarding their political and economic development. Aleksandar stated that a real effort could be made to create a strong and unitarist Yugoslav nation. However, the non-Serb groups viewed the unitarist ideology as de facto Serbian nationalism, and few non-Serbs supported the regime, which consisted overwhelmingly of Serb politicians. The ideological shift required of Croats and Slovenes to Yugoslav nationalism was viewed as much greater than the shift required of Serbs. In particular, the Croats grew increasingly dissatisfied with the royal dictatorship, even though it was relaxed slightly in 1931. In October 1934, Croat and Macedonian terrorists assassinated King Aleksandar.

After the assassination, the Yugoslav government increased its efforts to reach a compromise with the Croat political leadership. In August 1939, shortly before the beginning of World War II, a compromise (Sporazum) was finally signed, granting Croatia wide autonomy in its own administrative district. Yet ideological radicalization continued to increase on both the Croat and the Serb political right until the Nazi invasion of Yugoslavia in April 1941.

World War II witnessed the establishment of a fascist puppet dictatorship in Croatia and large-scale massacres in Croatia, Serbia, and Bosnia-Herzegovina. The Communist partisans, led by Josip Broz Tito, emerged as the only truly Yugoslav movement during the war.

After World War II, the partisans formed a state based on Yugoslav and Communist ideology. Yugoslav nationalism was strengthened by the desire to forget the trauma of World War II. It also emerged strengthened from the Tito-Stalin split of 1948. Reconciliation between the divergent groups in Yugoslavia was promoted under the banner of bratstvo i jedinstvo (brotherhood and unity). However, by the 1950s, Tito abandoned all formal and centralized attempts to create a single Yugoslav identity out of the many cultures of Yugoslavia. Only a small minority of the citizens of Yugoslavia identified themselves as Yugoslavs in censuses.

Communist Yugoslavia retained a federal constitutional system of six republics (Slovenia, Croatia, Bosnia-Herzegovina, Serbia, and Macedonia) and two autonomous regions (Kosovo and Vojvodina). This system allowed for extensive maneuvering and shifting alliance formation based on republican interests and identities, especially after the constitutional revisions of 1963.

In the late 1960s and early 1970s, Yugoslav nationalism was challenged by resurgent Croatian nationalism in a period known as the "Croatian Spring." Tito's regime carried out purges in order to crack down on Croatian nationalism, thus sending a signal that there were limits to "particularist" expressions of republican nationalism. These purges claimed many liberal reformers, thus leading to the rise of bureaucratic Communists who assumed the leadership of the republics in the 1980s. Moreover, the 1974 Yugoslav Constitution included the devolution of considerable power to the individual republics within Yugoslavia. After Tito's death in 1980, the rotating federal presidency accentuated the balancing act between the republics.

In the late 1980s, the leadership of the Republic of Serbia sought to end the autonomy of Kosovo and Vojvodina. This move was viewed by the other republics as a threat to the stability of Yugoslavia and as indicative of renascent Serbian nationalism. Nationalist movements in Croatia and Slovenia emerged victorious in the 1990 elections on a platform of independence. In June 1991, Croatia and Slovenia proclaimed their independence, initiating the collapse of the Yugoslav state.

# Z

**ZAGHLUL, SA'D** 1857–1927, Egyptian lawyer, nationalist leader, prime minister of Egypt in 1924. Son of a landed Delta family, Zaghlul received part of his education at the religious university al-Azhar. Progressing from government clerk to lawyer to judge, by the early 20th century he held the posts of minister of education and of justice. On the eve of World War I Zaghlul was vice president of the Egyptian Legislative Assembly.

He became the Egyptian nationalist leader immediately after World War I. In November 1918 Zaghlul and other Egyptian notables requested British permission to form a delegation (*wafd*) that would attend the Paris Peace Conference and present the case for Egyptian independence. When their request was denied, the Wafd was organized as a nationalist movement. It was the exile (to Malta) of Zaghlul and other Wafdist leaders that served as the spark for the Egyptian "Revolution" of 1919, an outbreak of anti-British demonstrations and violence. Three years of continuing nationalist protest within Egypt, much of it inspired and directed by Zaghlul and the Wafd, eventually forced the British to grant Egypt formal independence (February 1922).

When parliamentary institutions were established in 1922–1923, the Wafd became a political party. It won 90 percent of the seats in Egypt's first parliamentary elections in January 1924; Zaghlul became the first prime minister of independent Egypt. His efforts to exert ministerial control over the administration engendered royal and British hostility. The assassination of a British official in the Sudan provided the occasion for a British ultimatum, which produced the resignation of Zaghlul and his ministry. He died in August 1927.

Zaghlul was the embodiment of Egyptian opposition to British occupation in the early 20th century. His vision of Egyptian nationalism was a predominantly territorial one conceiving of Egypt as a distinct national community separate from the Arab and Muslim worlds.

He continues to be a symbol of fervent Egyptian patriotism and of Egyptian territorial nationalism.

There is no English-language biography of Zaghlul. A brief account emphasizing his early career is available in the *Encyclopedia of Islam*. His post-World War I career is discussed in Elie Kedourie, "Sa'd Zaghlul and the British," in his *The Chatham House Version and other Middle-Eastern Studies* (1970), pp. 82–159; Marius Deeb, *Party Politics in Egypt: the Wafd and Its Rivals, 1919–1939* (1979); and Afaf Lutfi al-Sayyid Marsot, *Egypt's Liberal Experiment, 1922–1936* (1977).

**ZAIRE, NATIONALISM IN** Present-day Zaire, which was known as the Belgian Congo during the colonial era, was settled by Bantu peoples originating from the Cameroun and the central African region. By the 15th century a series of kingdoms based on long-distance trade developed in the region. By the 15th century when Portuguese explorers arrived in the area, they found much of Zaire and Angola under the control of the Bantu Bakongo kingdom. In 1879, Henry Stanley was sent by the king of Belgium, King Leopold II, to claim the Congo for the king through treaties with local chiefs. The Berlin Conference of 1884–1885 gave the Congo to King Leopold II as his own personal estate to do with as he wished. Under King Leopold II, the peoples of the Congo suffered greatly from harsh exploitation. Widespread atrocities practiced by concessionary companies on rubber plantations aroused international protests. In 1908, the control of the Congo moved from the hands of King Leopold II to the Belgian government through the granting of a proper colonial status to the Belgian Congo.

After many years of colonial rule, nationalist parties began to demand independence, which was given in 1960 with Patrice Lumumba as first prime minister. However, soon after independence, a major political crisis broke out. On July 5, the army mutinied and mineral rich Katanga (later known as Shaba) seceded under the leadership of Moise Tshombe. During the upheaval some Europeans were killed and many fled the country. In September 1960, Colonel Joseph Desire Mobutu, the army's twenty-nine-year-old chief of staff, interceded militarily in a power struggle between President Joseph Kasavubu and Prime Minister Patrice Lumumba. He arrested Lumumba and handed him over to Katanga rebels who soon murdered him. Mobutu then returned power to Kasavubu in 1961. The government called on the United Nations to send peacekeeping troops to maintain order, particularly in Shaba province. The UN forces departed in 1964. Soon after the departure of UN forces, leftist rebels established a "People's Republic" in Stanleyville. The rebels clashed with foreign mercenaries and members of the Congolese army. Thousands of people died in the skirmishes. Belgian soldiers were then brought in to intervene. The country was renamed the Democratic Republic of the Congo in 1964. In 1965, with CIA backing, General Joseph Mobutu staged a second coup and seized power. He named himself president for five years and canceled elections scheduled for 1966.

In the 1970s Mobutu established his Popular Movement of the Revolution (MPR) as the only political party allowed to function in the country. Under an Africanization policy, Mobutu changed the country's name to the Republic of Zaire. He also changed his name to Mobutu Sese Seko. Zairians were also ordered to Africanize their names and adopt African dress. His government, under what he termed "Zairianization" policy, seized 2000 foreign-owned businesses. Most of the nationalized companies were distributed among Mobutu and his associates. Many of these businesses collapsed because of the new owners' inexperience. As the Zairian economy continued to crumble, Mobutu and his circle grew richer by skimming the profits generated by exports of the country's mineral wealth and by pocketing foreign aid.

Opposition to Mobutu's excesses began to emerge in the late 1970s. Former Katangan secessionists invaded in 1977 from Angola, where they had been living in exile. Mobutu was able to suppress the rebellion with the help of troops from Morocco and military assistance from his Western allies, including the United States and France. French and Belgian troops helped put down a second Shaba invasion the following year. From then on, opposition was dealt with ruthlessly. For example, opponents of Mobutu's one-party rule who had formed the Union Democracy and Social Progress (UDPS) in

1982 were constantly harassed and its leaders imprisoned throughout the 1980s.

By 1990 Mobutu came under intense pressure from the opposition forcing him to announce the creation of a multiparty democratic system. However he stalled the implementation of the reforms by suspending a national multiparty conference set up to draft a new constitution. At the same time international pressure came from the U.S. Congress, which in 1990 cut direct military and economic aid because of alleged corruption and human rights abuses by Mobutu's regime. Since the ascendancy to power of Mobutu in 1965 and the subsequent Cold War years, the United States had supplied hundreds of millions of dollars in aid to Mobutu.

Due to intense internal and external pressure, Mobutu agreed in 1991 to form a government with UDPS leader Etienne Tshisekedi as prime minister. But Tshisekedi was fired before the end of the year. In 1992, the multiparty conference resumed amid continuing riots. The conference elected Tshisekedi as prime minister to head a transitional government. The conference also adopted a draft constitution that advocated a bicameral parliament and a system of universal suffrage to select the president, who would hold a largely ceremonial post. Tshisekedi was able to cling to the post of prime minister until 1994 when elections were delayed due to disagreements between Mobutu and the opposition.

In 1994 events in Rwanda spilled over into eastern Zaire with a domino effect that spelled trouble for Mobutu's regime. About 1.3 million ethnic Hutus left Rwanda, fleeing Rwanda's civil war and settled in camps in eastern Zaire. Among them were many of the Hutu militants responsible for the genocidal killings of Rwanda's Tutsi. Two years later in 1996, ethnic Tutsis in eastern Zaire revolted when threatened with expulsion. Led by veteran guerrilla fighter Laurent Kabila and supported by several neighboring countries, the uprising grew into an anti-Mobutu rebellion. Hundreds of thousands of Hutu refugees were forced to return to Rwanda by the brewing upheaval in eastern Zaire. Mobutu, frail with prostate cancer, tried to make last minute political maneuvers by replacing Prime Minister Tshisekedi with General Likulia Bolongo.

In May 1997, with Kabila's rebels poised to take Kinshasa, Mobutu relinquished power and left the country into exile in Morocco where he died of prostate cancer a year later. Kabila immediately declared himself head of state and quickly changed the country's name back to the Democratic Republic of the Congo. However, other Tutsi rebel factions who were not happy with Kabila's seizure of power continued to fight Kabila's army with the support of countries such as Rwanda, now under Tutsi control, and Uganda. The civil war in Zaire that was intended to remove Mobutu's regime soon threatened to engulf the entire Central and Southern African subcontinent. Several southern African countries led by Zimbabwe joined the war in support of Kabila. By 1999 the fight had reached stalemate and the integrity of Zaire as well as the future of Zairian nationalism became uncertain.

Further reading: G. Nzongola-Ntalaja, *The Crisis in Zaire: Myths and Realities* (Trenton, N.J.: Africa World Press, 1986); Jacques Depelchin *From the Congo Free State to Zaire: How Belgium Privatized the Economy: A History of Belgian Stock Companies in Congo-Zaïre from 1885 to 1974* (Oxford: Codesria Book Series, 1992); Astri Suhrke and Howard Adelman, *The Path of a Genocide: The Rwanda Crisis from Uganda to Zaire* (London: Global, 1999); Gerard Prunier, *Rwanda in Zaire: From Genocide to Continental War* (London: C. Hurst, 1999); Georges Nzongola-Ntalaja, *From Zaire to the Democratic Republic of the Congo* (Uppsala: Nordiska Afrikainstitutet, 1998); and Suleyman Ali Baldo and Peter Rosenblum, *Zaire: Transition, War, and Human Rights* (New York: Human Rights Watch, 1997).

**ZAPATA, EMILIANO** 1879–1919, Leader of a radical peasant movement during the Mexican Revolution; born in Anenecuilco, Morelos, Mexico. Zapata was born to a relatively prosperous landowning family, served in the army, worked as a stable hand and sharecropper, and became a skilled horseman. He was elected mayor of Anenecuilco in 1909, during a time when the large sugar estates of Morelos, south of Mexico City, had begun encroaching on adjacent community lands. Zapata was a champion of traditional community rights and an implacable foe of the sugar barons, who were mainly absentee landlords. In late 1910 Zapata joined Francisco Madero's successful revolt against the long-standing dictatorship of Porfirio Díaz, mobilizing a large peasant army in the southern states of Morelos, Guerrero, Tlaxcala, and adjacent areas.

Zapata broke with the conservative Madero in 1911, after the latter refused to return lands to local communities. With the help of a handful of radical intellectuals, Zapata issued his "Plan of Ayala" in late 1911, which disavowed Madero and called for the return of community lands and political autonomy for Mexico's villages. Madero responded by suspending constitutional rights in areas where Zapata was strong. After General Victoriano Huerta and the military removed and murdered Madero in 1913, Zapata joined forces with the "Con-

stitutionalist" movement led by Venustiano Carranza. Huerta fell in 1914, and Zapata briefly held Mexico City with Pancho Villa, a constitutionalist general from the northern state of Chihuahua. But neither Zapata nor Villa was interested in wielding state power; their perspectives were provincial, and their movements were rooted in the distinctive popular concerns of Mexico's southern and northern regions, respectively.

After 1914 Carranza, with the help of the United States, attempted to subdue Zapata and Villa, reconsolidate the central state, and return lands to big estates. Villa was largely defeated by 1916, and Zapata was forced to lead a guerrilla struggle against the new regime in his home state of Morelos. Land reform was a central component of the new Mexican Constitution of 1917, due in large part to Zapata's movement, but it remained little more than a promise. Zapata was ambushed and murdered by Carranza's forces in 1919.

Following his death, Zapata became an important image and symbol in Mexico's nationalist iconography and political struggles. The image of Zapata with his cowboy boots, chaps, handlebar mustache, large sombrero, and impassive countenance is a potent symbol of the Mexican Revolution and of a certain Mexican national character, stoic and dignified in the face of adversity, an image instantly recognizable to subsequent generations of Mexicans. The postrevolutionary political elite, the heirs of Zapata's assassins, repeatedly invoked Zapata's legacy and ideals, none more successfully than President Lázaro Cárdenas, who enacted a substantial land reform during the 1930s. Zapata (and Villa) were rhetorically incorporated by the regime into Mexico's pantheon of great patriotic heroes. At the same time, Zapata remained a potent symbol for opponents of the postrevolutionary state, especially peasants and workers who felt betrayed by the regime's empty promises and subservience to economic elites. Armed rebels who rose up against the regime in the southern state of Chiapas in 1994 called themselves the Zapatista Army of National Liberation.

The definitive study of Zapata and the movement he led is John Womack, Jr.'s *Zapata and the Mexican Revolution* (Vintage, 1968). Arturo Warman's *"We Come to Object": The Peasants of Morelos and the National State* (Johns Hopkins, 1980) examines the postrevolutionary period in Zapata's stronghold.

**ZHOU, ENLAI** 1898–1976, World-class politician and a leader of the Chinese Communist movement. Born in Huian, Jiangsu, China, Zhou lived in a most turbulent era of Chinese history. Determined to save China from the savage of Western imperialism, Zhou joined the Communist movement while studying in Paris, France, and quickly became one of the most influential leaders in China on his return from Europe. After the founding of the People's Republic of China, Zhou served as premier from 1949 to 1976, and was best known for his political skills mediating among various factions within the Communist Party, and his diplomatic skills to end PRC's international isolation.

Zhou's career as a professional revolutionary began in 1919 when he returned from Japan where he studied briefly, and joined the student patriotic movement in Tianjing. From 1920 to 1924, Zhou studied in France, and became a leader of an overseas Chinese Communist Party organization. When Sun Yatsen established the Huangpu Military Academy in Guangzhou in 1924, Zhou was invited to become the director of its powerful Department of Political Affairs. Sun died in 1925 while his revolution to end military rule of the warlord was failing. His successor, General Chiang Kaishek, broke the alliance Sun had established with the Chinese Communist Party (CCP). Zhou and several communist leaders organized an unsuccessful military uprising in 1927, and then went underground in Shanghai, operating the headquarters of the CCP from there. In 1931, Zhou joined Mao Zedong in Jiangxi, and became the general political commissioner of the Red Army. At a critical meeting in Zunyi during the Long March, held after the defeat of the Red Army by the nationalist government, Zhou sided with Mao Zedong, thus ending the rule of the leftist party leaders who were trained in the Soviet Union. Mao subsequently became the leader of the Chinese Communist movement.

In December 1936, a nationalist general, Zhang Xueliang, kidnapped Chiang Kaishek. Zhou flew to Xian and negotiated a peaceful settlement of the crisis in which Chiang agreed to form the second United Front with the CCP to resist the Japanese aggression that had already resulted in the occupation of China's Manchuria at the time. Zhou served as the representative of the CCP in Chongqing, the wartime capital of the nationalist government in World War II. When civil war broke out in 1946, Zhou returned to Yan'an and became the deputy chief of staff of the People's Liberation Army.

In 1949, Zhou was appointed prime minister, a position he held for twenty-six years until his death in 1976. He vastly increased China's international standing by winning the support of the Third World countries, and by his skillful handling of relations with major powers. He played a major role in the normalization of Sino-U.S. relations in 1972. In the endless political campaigns Mao had launched since 1949, Zhou survived

by showing his absolute loyalty to Mao, which in turn made him somewhat controversial. Zhou was supportive of all the campaigns, including the cultural Revolution, which resulted in the widespread persecution of millions of innocent people. At the same time he was also known for attempting to minimize all the damages whenever his power permitted, and for extending protection to many who would have been persecuted otherwise.

His dedication to his work and affection for the people won him a reputation as the "People's Premier." At his death, Zhou himself became a victim of an increasingly intense power struggle between the reformers led by Deng Xiaoping and the "Gang of Four" led by Jiang Qing, Mao's wife. People turned out spontaneously in Tiananmen Square in Beijing to mourn their beloved premier. The events ended in a violent crackdown of the radicals on April 5, 1976, and the second downfall of Deng Xiaoping. Having devoted his whole life to his country, Zhou still left behind the unfulfilled dream of turning China into a modernized nation.

Zhou's writing is compiled into a single volume *Selected Works of Zhou Enlai* (Beijing: Foreign Language Press, 1981). The official biography is *Biography of Zhou Enlai* (Beijing: Central Documentary Publisher, 1998). Other biographies include *Zhou Enlai: A Biography*, by Dick Wilson (Viking, 1984), and *Eldest Son: Zhou Enlai and the Making of Modern China, 1898–1976*, by Han Suyin (London: Cape, 1994).

**ZIMBABWEAN NATIONALISM** Zimbabwe was colonized by Great Britain starting from the 1890s. For ninety years Zimbabweans struggled under the yoke of colonial rule. During these ninety years of colonial rule African nationalism developed from low-key resistance to a revolutionary form of struggle that eventually led to Zimbabwe attaining its independence in 1980. Throughout Zimbabwe's colonial interlude, political activity among the African population has always been present in one form or another. Initially nationalism manifested itself in less aggressive forms, which formed the foundation for the final violent liberation struggle in the 1970s.

Lured by promises of rich mineral resources, British business tycoon Cecil Rhodes sent a column of white settlers from South Africa to present-day Zimbabwe in 1890. On their arrival, the settlers and Cecil Rhodes's British South Africa Company (BSAC) began to alienate African land and invaded Matabeleland, the seat of Lobengula's Ndebele kingdom. This led to the first show of resistance against colonialism in 1893. Rather than surrender to the superior European fire power Lobengula and a few of his people fled north. Many of Lobengula's people were forced into reserves of marginal quality and their cattle were confiscated by the settlers. The BSAC introduced many regulations intended to impose hardship and suffering on the local Africans. Men were forced to work on settler farms and mines, taxes such as a hut tax and a poll tax were exacted on the Africans, forcing many to look for employment on white-owned farms. These hardships galvanized the Africans who rose against the settlers in what is known as the First Chimurenga, which translates into the "First War of Liberation or Resistance" in Shona.

The First Chimurenga was fought fiercely on two fronts between 1896 and 1898; in the south by the Ndebele and in the north by the Shona peoples. In both cases, the struggle was organized by indigenous religious figures (spirit mediums) and traditional authorities. Initially, the white settlers were taken by surprise with Ndebele and Shona soldiers scoring victories and killing hundreds of whites. The British government sent in reinforcements from South Africa and repelled the Ndebele attacks around Bulawayo. The suppression of the First Chimurenga was ruthless. As reinforcements arrived from England and South Africa, Africans developed a system of hiding in caves. The whites used dynamite to force them out, and in this way the populations of whole villages died in caves. Many of those who came out of the caves alive were immediately executed.

After the First Chimurenga, political activity tended to be low key until the 1920s when African political pressure groups began to mushroom throughout Zimbabwe (then called Southern Rhodesia). Notable political pressure groups included the Rhodesian Bantu Voters Association (BANVA), which was founded in 1923. The leaders of this association believed that the vote should replace the spear in deciding political issues. However, the organization failed to galvanize mass support as its membership consisted mainly of teachers, clerks, and nurses. Several other protest movements such as the Industrial Commercial Workers Union (ICU), Gwelo Native Welfare Association, and the Matebele Home Society rose to politely challenge racist colonial policies. In 1934 the Southern Rhodesian African National Congress (SRANC) was formed under the leadership of the Reverend Thompson Samkange. This party tried to persuade the government to introduce political and social reforms but its demands went unheeded.

During the 1940s a new militant organization, the African Voice Association, was founded. Led by Benjamin Burombo, often referred to as the father of African nationalism because his organization was proletarian in character, the association demanded improved wages and working conditions, representation in Parliament, and better educational opportunities for the Africans. The organization also led the opposition to the government's land policies under the Land Apportionment Act in which Africans were being evicted from alienated land and their cattle numbers reduced. Burombo became the principal exponent of the peasants' resistance to this and other schemes such as the Native Land Husbandry Bill, which further eroded peasants' rights. The cumulative effect of the association's efforts was that it drew attention to the grievances of both rural and urban Africans and gave organizational form to African resistance against minority rule.

Burombo's bold activities paved the way to mass nationalism. The mass political activity in Zimbabwe, Zambia, and Malawi rose to a new level in opposition to the proposed formation of the Federation of Rhodesia and Nyasaland. Africans in the three territories formed the All-African Convention which energetically lobbied against the federation and sent delegates to the first Federal Conference in London in 1952. In spite of this opposition, however, the Federation of Rhodesia and Nyasaland was established on September 4, 1953. The African National Youth League (ANYL) led by young and energetic leaders such as James Chikerema, George Nyandoro, and Edison Sithole was formed in 1955 to oppose the continued alienation of African lands. With its newspaper, Chapupu, it galvanized support, especially among the young, for the nationalist cause. In 1957 ANYL and the SRANC merged to form the African National Congress with Joshua Nkomo as president. The organization quickly gained mass support as its message clearly articulated the major grievances of land, wages, and racial discrimination. It was banned in 1959 following the declaration of a state of emergency and many of its leaders, including Joshua Nkomo, were arrested.

Emboldened by events taking place elsewhere in Africa such as the granting of independence to Ghana and seventeen other African countries by 1960, the protest leadership in Zimbabwe formed new parties such as the National Democratic Party (NDP), the Zimbabwe African Peoples Union (ZAPU), and the Zimbabwe African National Union (ZANU), which adopted a more militant approach than the SRANC. New leaders in these organizations included the likes of Ndabaningi Sithole, Robert Mugabe, Leopold Takawira, Enos Nkala, and Manrice Nyagumbo, whose shared belief that Africans must be their own liberators led to the next phase in the development of nationalism in Zimbabwe, the phase of revolutionary nationalism.

It soon became apparent that the white minority government was not about to transfer power to the African majority. The ascendancy to power of the more right-wing Ian Smith in April 1964 added impetus to the nationalist cause. The signal to proceeed with the struggle came in November 1965, with the Unilateral Declaration of Independence by Smith's government. ZAPU led by Joshua Nkomo set up camp in Zambia and ZANU led by Mugabe set up camp in Tanzania and prepared to fight the minority white government for independence. The Second Chimurenga began in earnest on April 28, 1966, when seven guerrillas of the Zimbabwe African National Liberation Army (ZANLA), the military wing of ZANU, were killed in what has become known as the Battle of Chinhoyi. During the 1970s, ZANLA and the Zimbabwe People's Revolutionary Army (ZIPRA), the military wing of ZAPU, fought fiercely against the well-equipped Rhodesian forces. However, the politicization of the masses about their plight, particularly the land question, resulted in extensive support for the "freedom fighters" from the peasants and urban dwellers. Internationally support for the struggle came from many countries in the form of training and weapons, including Tanzania, Mozambique, Angola, Zambia, Ethiopia, Algeria, Romania, Bulgaria, Yugoslavia, China, North Korea, and the former Soviet Union.

By 1979 the white renegade minority government of Ian Smith had been brought to its knees and began to seek a way out through a negotiated settlement. This move culminated in the signing of the Lancaster House Agreement in London in December 1979, the movement of the freedom fighters into Assembly Points in early 1980, the general election in February 1980 in which ZANU (Patriotic Front), under the leadership of Robert Mugabe, was victorious, and the subsequent achievement of independence on April 18, 1980. Although at the time of independence the two major nationalist factions of Joshua Nkomo and Robert Mugabe threatened to plunge the new independent nation into the abyss of civil war, the spirit of national unity defused the tensions. The new leadership embarked on a path to transform Zimbabwe into a modern and peaceful nation.

Further reading: Ibbo Mandaza, *Race, Colour and Class in Southern Africa: A Study of the Coloured Question in the Context of an Analysis of the Colonial and White Settler Racial Ideology, and African Nationalism in Twentieth Century Zimbabwe, Zambia, and Malawi.* (Harare: SAPES Books, 1997); Sam Moyo, *Economic Nationalism and Land Reform in Zimbabwe* (Harare: SAPES Books, 1994); Stanlake John Thompson Samkange, *The Origin of African Nationalism in Zimbabwe* (Harare, Zimbabwe: Harare Pub. House, 1985); and Wellington W. Nyangoni, *African Nationalism in Zimbabwe (Rhodesia)* (Washington, D.C.: University Press of America, 1978).

**ZIONISM** Nationalist movement promoting the creation of a Jewish national state in Palestine called *Eretz Israel* ("Land of Israel"). The modern movement originated in Eastern and Central Europe during the latter part of the 19th century, but claims ancient roots and is named after one of the hills of ancient Jerusalem, Zion.

The Jewish diaspora gave rise to several "messiahs" urging Jews to return to their homeland in the 16th and 17th centuries, as opposed to the assimilationist message of some movements like the *Haskala* ("Enlightenment") movement of the late 18th century. In 1897 Austrian journalist Theodor Herzl convened the first Zionist Congress in Basel, Switzerland, contending that although assimilation was desirable it was impossible to achieve in anti-Semitic European societies. Jews must return to their homeland, he argued, to escape persecution. His argument resonated with the experience of much of the Jewish diaspora, many of whom had faced anti-Semitism in a myriad of forms.

Herzl established a weekly Zionist publication in Vienna, *Die Welt* ("The World") and the Zionist congresses continued to meet, first annually and then every two years. Although the Ottomans did not respond favorably to the Zionists plea for a Palestinian homeland, their British successors did. In 1903 the British government suggested that a homeland be established in Uganda, however, rather than the traditional Holy Land, an idea soundly rejected by the Zionists.

Although early Zionism never mobilized the grassroots Jewish community it was a powerful force that inspired a Jewish cultural renaissance, published its own newspapers, and stimulated the development of modern Hebrew. A series of pogroms and repressions in Russia following the 1905 revolution created a wave of Jewish emigrants who went to Palestine and the Zionist movement gained momentum.

The Balfour Declaration in 1917, written by Arthur James Balfour, the British foreign secretary, committed Great Britain to the creation of a Jewish state in Palestine. In the years following World War I the Zionists promoted Jewish settlements in both rural and urban Palestine and cultivated the development of autonomous institutions in the region. Estimated at 108,000 in 1925, the Jewish population of Palestine more than doubled by 1933. Many Palestinian Arabs saw their interests as directly threatened by Zionism from its early days and vowed to suppress it, thus provoking the creation of a secret Jewish army called *Haganah* ("The Defense") in 1920.

The Holocaust in Nazi Germany did much, of course, to encourage Jews to seek refuge in Palestine and eventually led to widespread public sympathy for a Jewish homeland. The creation of the state of Israel on May 14, 1948, resulted in the displacement of native Arab Palestinians and acutely heightened tensions between Arabs and Zionists. The homeland sought by Zionist nationalists was achieved, but at a great price; the new Israelis found themselves surrounded by hostile Arab neighbors.

Zionism itself thus became a litmus test for many in terms of their loyalties. Zionist organizations and many Jewish congregations worldwide, on the one hand, encouraged Jews to immigrate to Israel and raised financial support for the effort. On the other hand, the Palestinian Arabs, large numbers of them forced into refugee camps, developed their own nationalist movement that until negotiations leading to peace accords of 1993 vowed to destroy the state of Israel.

## ZOLA, ÉMILE

1840–1902, French novelist, journalist, and essayist. Spearheading the literary school known as naturalism, Zola obtained great popular and critical success as a novelist during the 1870s and 1880s for his multivolume saga about the Rougon-Macquart family. His style and subject matter, considered obscene by parts of the upper class and the Catholic press, however, prevented him from achieving widespread social recognition. He was never elected to the French Academy, for instance, despite nineteen nominations. This ambivalent position as both a public figure and an outsider to the conservative elite in part explains his role in the Dreyfus affair during the late 1890s.

Alfred Dreyfus, a French military officer of Jewish background, was falsely accused of selling artillery secrets to Germany, court-martialed, and convicted of treason in 1894. Émile Zola was at the forefront of the struggle that eventually freed Dreyfus and exposed the anti-Semitism that pervaded French nationalist circles. Zola's most famous contribution to this campaign was his open letter to the president of France, which, on January 13, 1898, filled the front pages of 300,000 copies of the newspaper *L'Aurore* under the headline "J'Accuse." The title was taken from the letter's dramatic climax in which Zola detailed the conspiracy against Dreyfus and the subsequent cover-up by prominent generals and the War Ministry.

The letter caused an immediate scandal, and signaled the explosion of the Dreyfus affair, until then a low-level quixotic feud between the small, relatively ineffectual group denouncing injustice and most of the rest of France, including politicians and newspapers, preferring to believe in the guilt of a single Jewish officer than to question the honor of the French army. The sudden publicity of the affair led to street demonstrations and the formation of two opposing factions pitting truth and justice against the preservation of national cohesion and the integrity of the French state and its institutions.

Zola's position on the Dreyfus affair was potentially damaging and even dangerous, and indeed he was accused of libel, found guilty in a court of law, and forced into exile for a year. Much of France had accepted the guilty verdict and its underlying assumption of the treasonous nature of the Jewish population. But Zola's highly publicized intervention and trial led to the reopening of the Dreyfus case, and his eventual release.

The affair, and Zola's role in it, were a defining moment in the evolution of French nationalism. First, it marked the emergence of intellectuals as a political force. The term *intellectual* itself was popularized during the affair, originally to describe and castigate the defenders of Dreyfus. Petitions and articles backing Zola, signed by some of the great scholars and authors of the time, like Marcel Proust, were circulating after the publication of "J'Accuse." This mobilization later precipitated the rise of a countervailing intellectualized right-wing nationalism propagated by writers like Maurice Barrès and Charles Maurras. It is no coincidence for instance that Maurras's journal *L'Action française* was founded in 1899.

Second, it forced a direct assessment of the nature of the French nation. The confrontation between the universalist ideals of the revolution and a more narrow, particularist, anti-individualist, and antiparliamentarian conception of French national character had marked much of the 19th century. To Zola the affair was clearly a test of the practical application of these conflicting views and of the strength of France's first stable republic. The increasing militarism of the time, caused in large part by heightened geopolitical competition within Europe, and in particular with recently victorious Germany, threatened hard-won republican values.

Last, Zola played an important role in the history and mythologizing of French republicanism. The 100th anniversary of the Dreyfus affair was for instance celebrated at the highest levels of government, in newspapers and other media, and at public ceremonies and demonstrations.

ISBN 0-12-227232-3

90018